A-Z LONDON

D0259915

CONTENTS

REFERENCE

Motorway	M1
A Road	A2
Under Construction	
Proposed	
B Road	B408
Dual Carriageway	
One-way — Traffic flow on A Roads is indicated by a heavy line on the driver's left.	→
Junction Name	MARBLE ARCH
Restricted Access	
Pedestrianized Road	
Track & Footpath	
Residential Walkway	
Railway	Tunnel / Level Crossing
Stations:	
National Rail Network	⇌
Docklands Light Railway	DLR
Underground Station ⊖ is the registered trade mark of Transport for London	
Croydon Tramlink — The boarding of Tramlink trams at stops may be limited to a single direction, indicated by the arrow.	Tunnel / Stop

Map Continuation	62	Large Scale Map Pages 160
Built-Up Area	BANK / STREET
House Numbers A & B Roads only	51 19 / 22 48
Car Park Selected	P
Church or Chapel	†
Fire Station	■
Hospital	H
Information Centre	i
National Grid Reference	530
Police Station	▲
Post Office	★
Toilet	▽
with facilities for the Disabled	▽
Educational Establishment	
Hospital or Hospice	
Industrial Building	
Leisure or Recreational Facility	
Place of Interest	
Public Building	
Shopping Centre or Market	
Other Selected Buildings	

SCALE

Pages 4-156
2.88 inches to 1 Mile

0 ¼ ½ ¾ Mile
0 250 500 750 Metres 1 Kilometre

1:22,000
7.31cm to 1 mile
4.55cm to 1 km

Copyright of Geographers' A-Z Map Company Limited

Head Office : Fairfield Road, Borough Green, Sevenoaks, Kent TN15 8PP Tel: 01732 781000 (General Enquires & Trade Sales)

Showrooms : 44 Gray's Inn Road, London WC1X 8HX   Tel: 020 7440 9500 (Retail Sales)   www.a-zmaps.co.uk

Ordnance Survey® This product includes mapping data licensed from Ordnance Survey with the permission of the Controller of Her Majesty's Stationery Office.

© Crown Copyright 2003 Licence number 100017302

Copyright © Geographers' A-Z Map Co. Ltd. 2004
Edition 5 2001   Edition 5B 2004

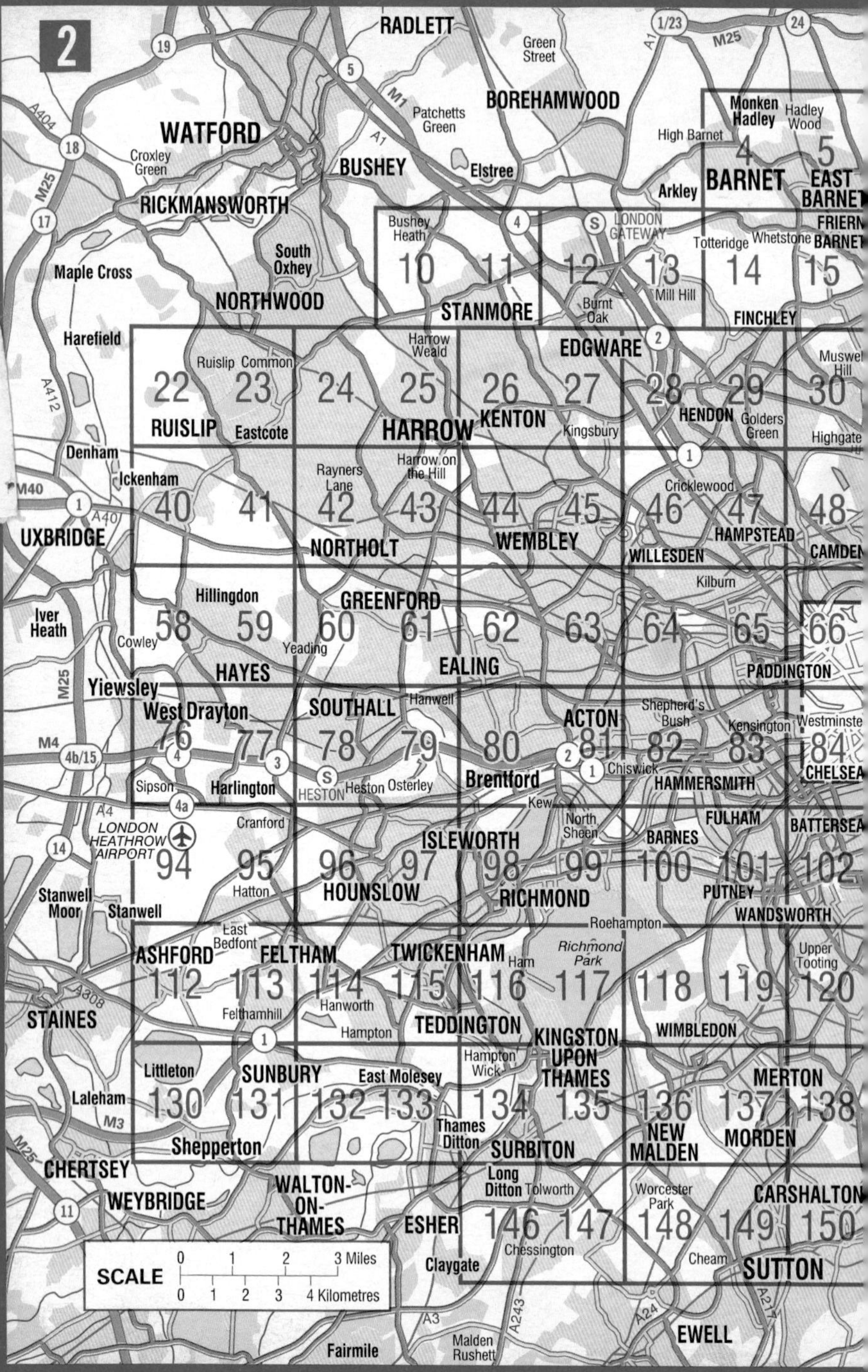

2

RADLETT

Green Street

1/23 M25 24

BOREHAMWOOD

Patchetts Green

Monken Hadley Hadley Wood

High Barnet **4** **5** EAST BARNET

WATFORD Croxley Green BUSHEY Elstree Arkley **BARNET** FRIERN BARNET

RICKMANSWORTH Bushey Heath LONDON GATEWAY Totteridge Whetstone

Maple Cross South Oxhey **10** **11** **12** **13** **14** **15**

NORTHWOOD **STANMORE** Burnt Oak Mill Hill FINCHLEY

Harefield Harrow Weald **EDGWARE** **2** Muswell Hill

22 Ruislip Common **23** **24** **25** **26** **27** **28** **29** **30**

RUISLIP Eastcote **HARROW** **KENTON** Kingsbury HENDON Golders Green Highgate

Denham Ickenham Rayners Lane Harrow on the Hill Cricklewood **1**

40 **41** **42** **43** **44** **45** **46** **47** **48**

UXBRIDGE **NORTHOLT** **WEMBLEY** WILLESDEN HAMPSTEAD CAMDEN

Iver Heath Hillingdon **GREENFORD** Kilburn PADDINGTON

Cowley **58** **59** **60** **61** **62** **63** **64** **65** **66**

Yiewsley HAYES Yeading **EALING**

West Drayton **SOUTHALL** Hanwell **ACTON** Shepherd's Bush Kensington Westminster

76 **77** **78** **79** **80** **81** **82** **83** **84**

Sipson Harlington HESTON Heston Osterley Brentford Chiswick HAMMERSMITH CHELSEA

Kew FULHAM

LONDON HEATHROW AIRPORT Cranford North Sheen BARNES BATTERSEA

94 **95** **96** **97** **98** **99** **100** **101** **102**

Stanwell Moor Stanwell Hatton **HOUNSLOW** **ISLEWORTH** **RICHMOND** PUTNEY WANDSWORTH

Roehampton

East Bedfont Richmond Park Upper Tooting

ASHFORD FELTHAM TWICKENHAM Ham

112 **113** **114** **115** **116** **117** **118** **119** **120**

STAINES Felthamhill Hanworth **TEDDINGTON** WIMBLEDON

Hampton Hampton Wick **KINGSTON UPON THAMES**

Littleton **SUNBURY** East Molesey **MERTON**

Laleham **130** **131** **132** **133** **134** **135** **136** **137** **138**

Shepperton Thames Ditton **SURBITON** **NEW MALDEN** **MORDEN**

CHERTSEY WALTON-ON-THAMES Long Ditton Tolworth Worcester Park **CARSHALTON**

WEYBRIDGE ESHER **146** **147** **148** **149** **150**

Claygate Chessington Cheam **SUTTON**

Fairmile Malden Rushett EWELL

SCALE 0 1 2 3 Miles 0 1 2 3 4 Kilometres

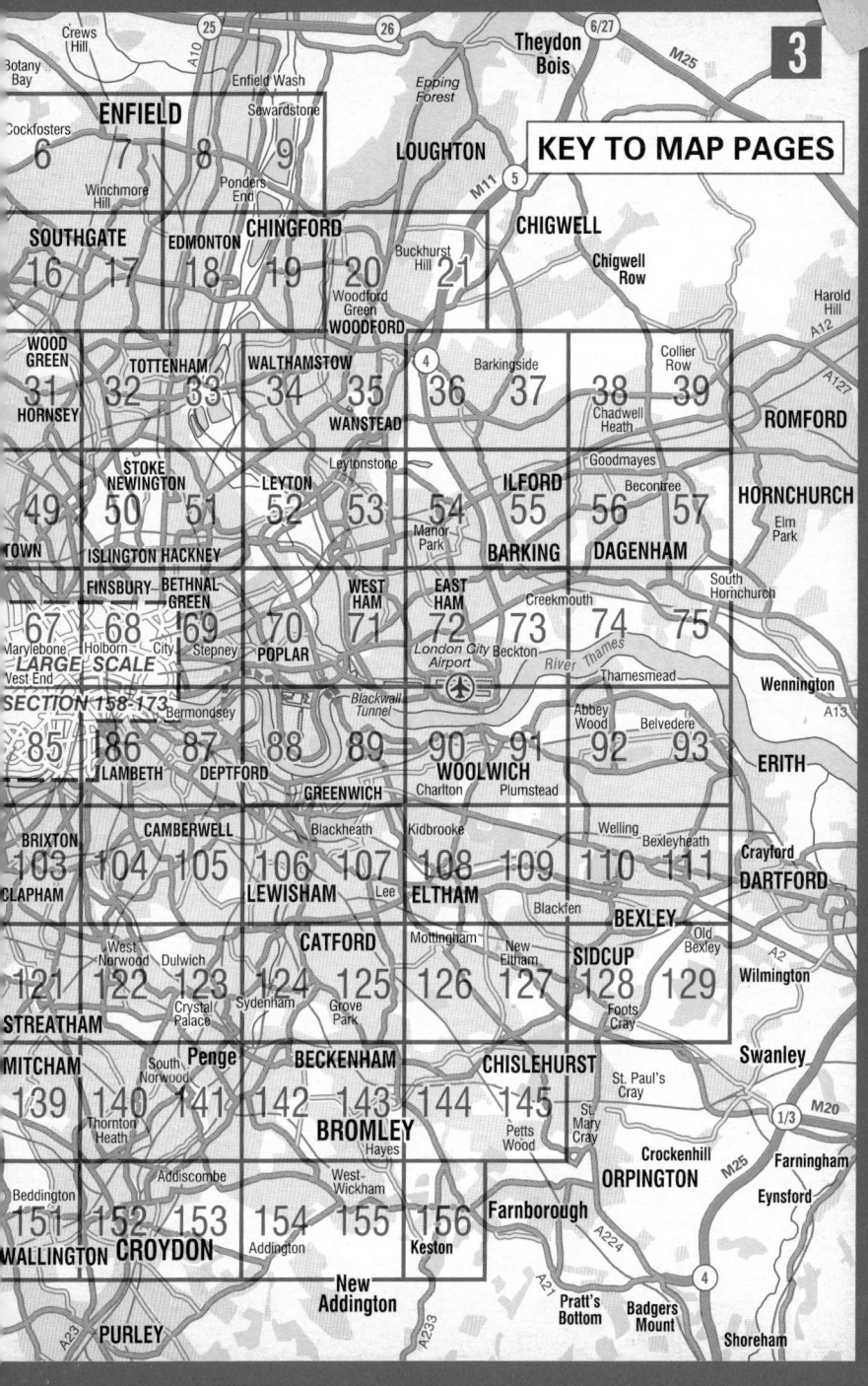

KEY TO MAP PAGES

3

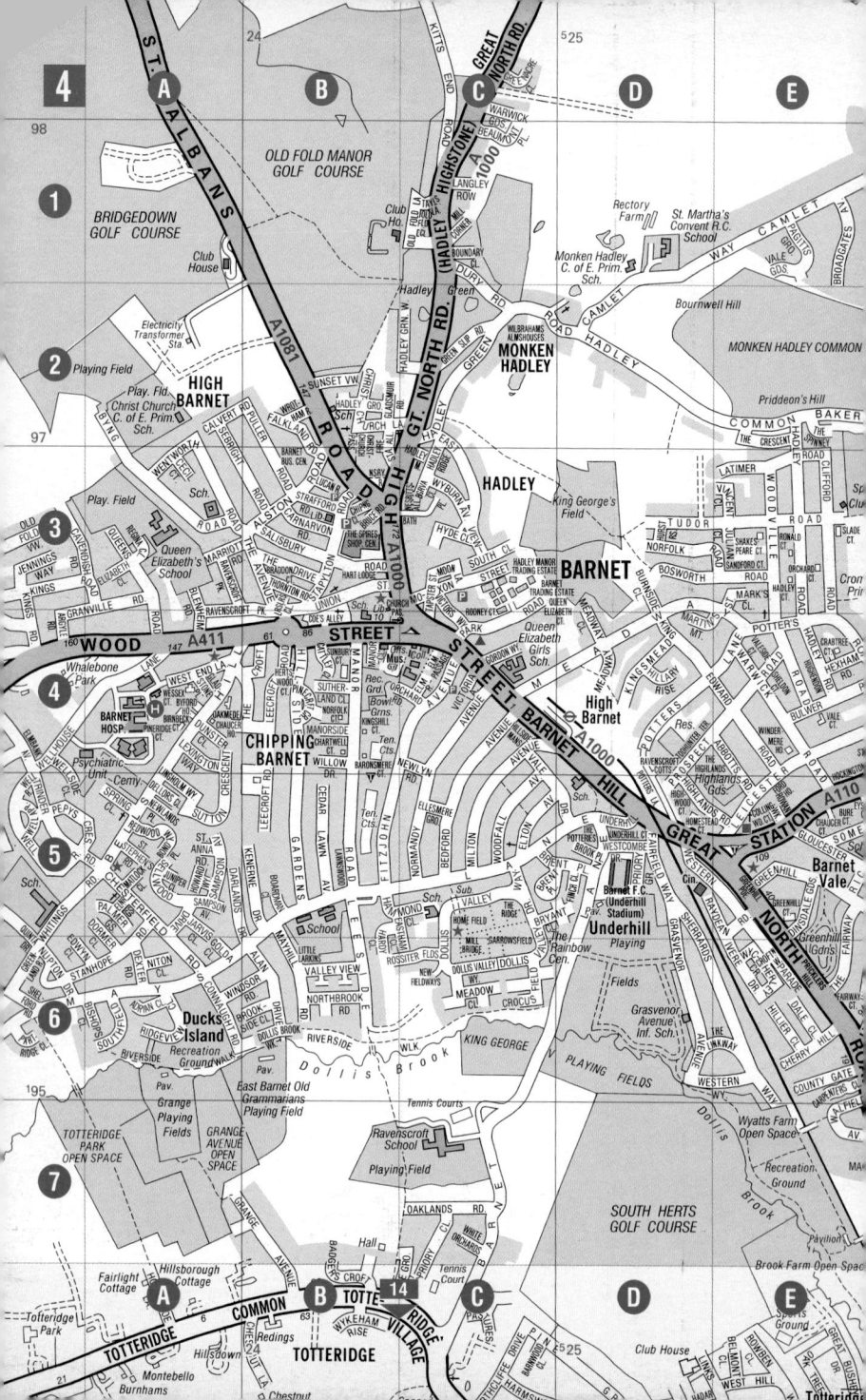

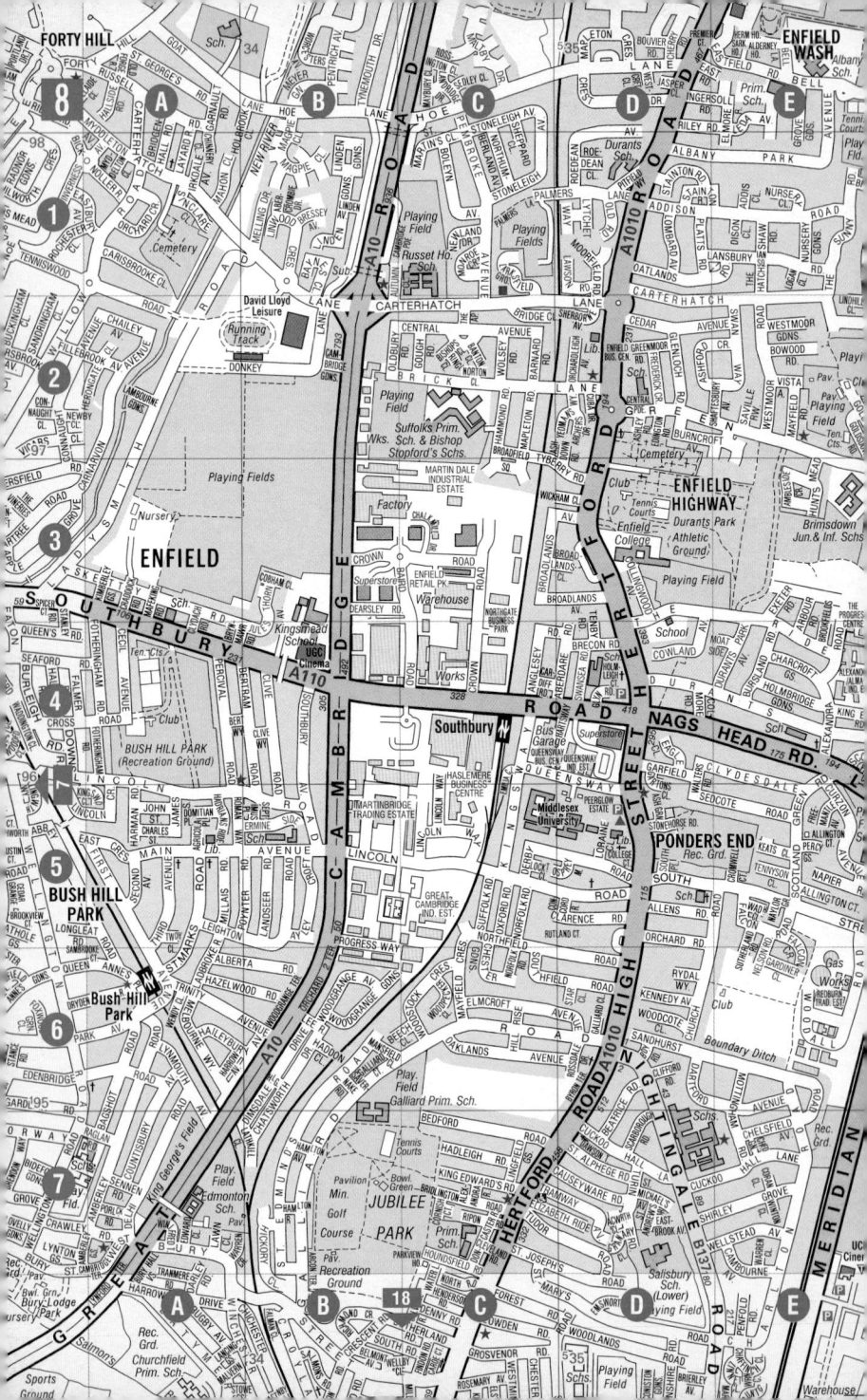

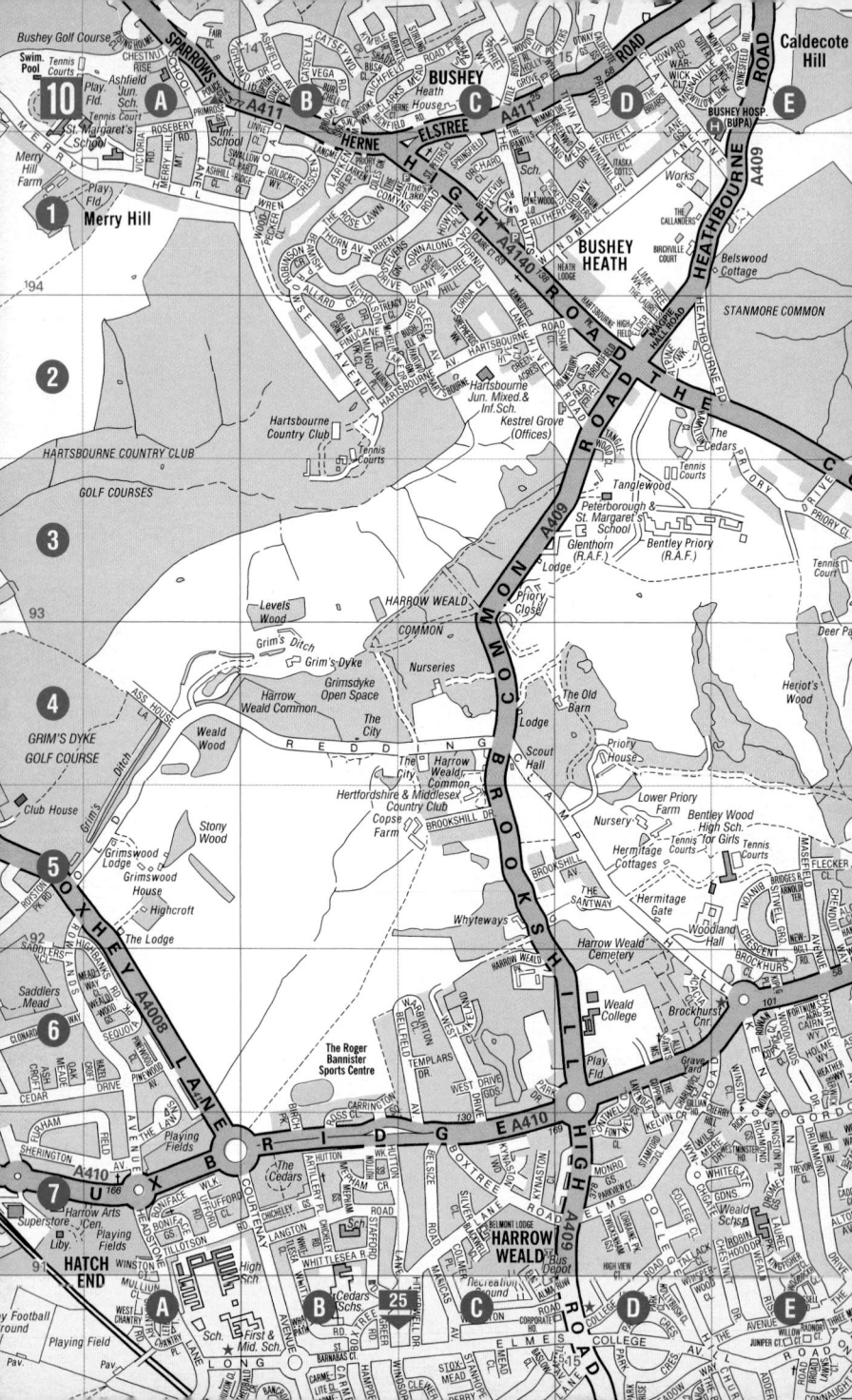

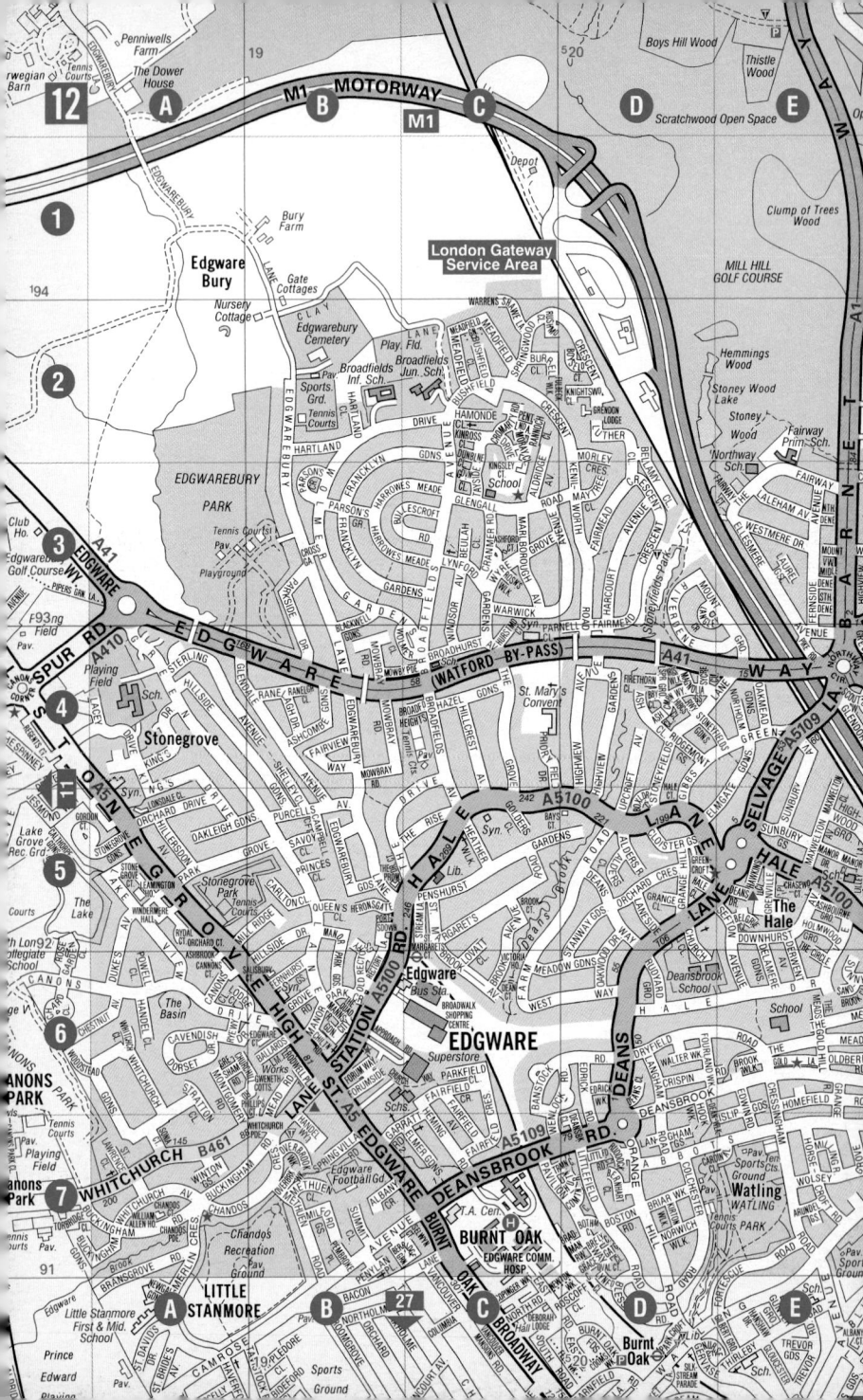

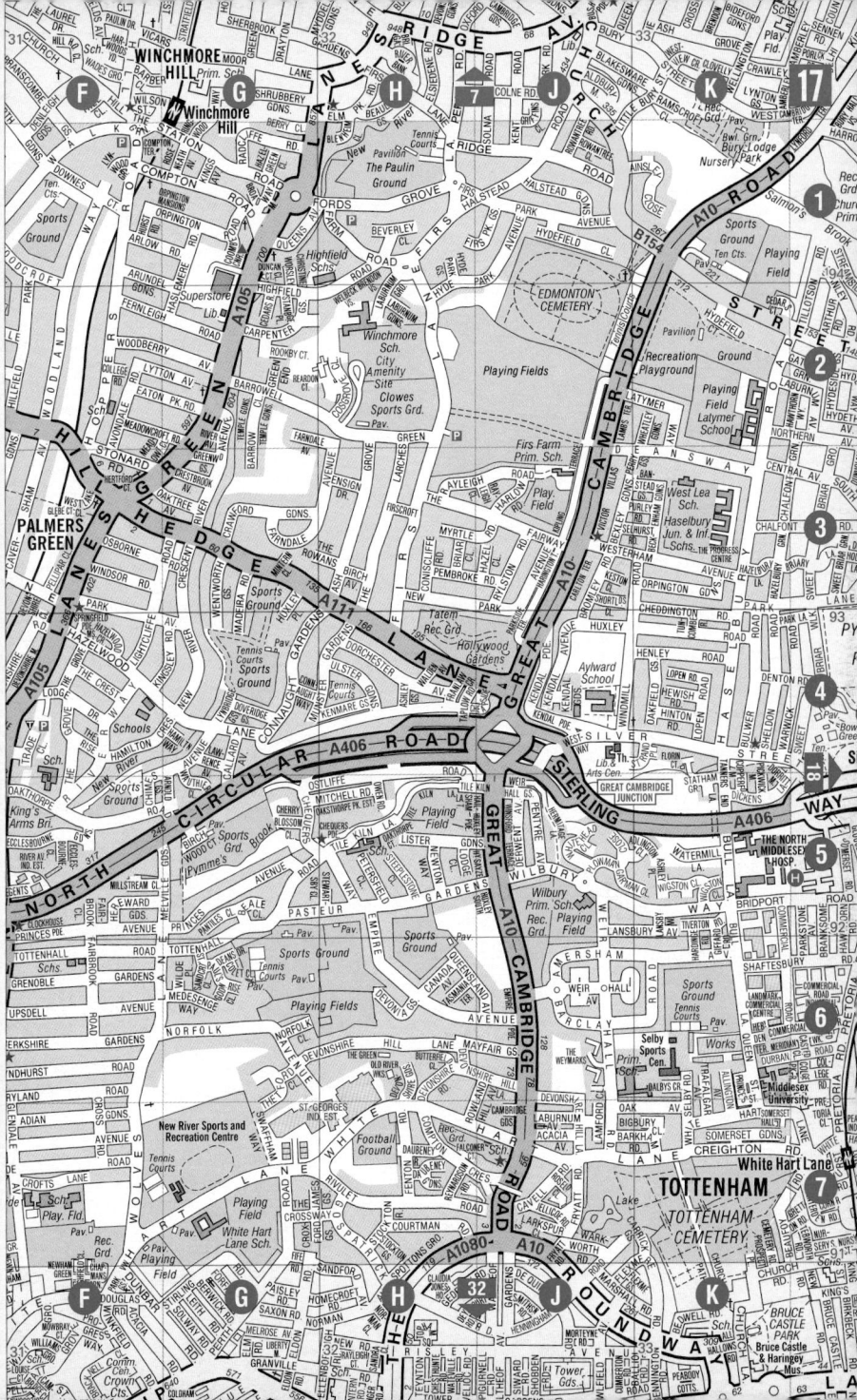

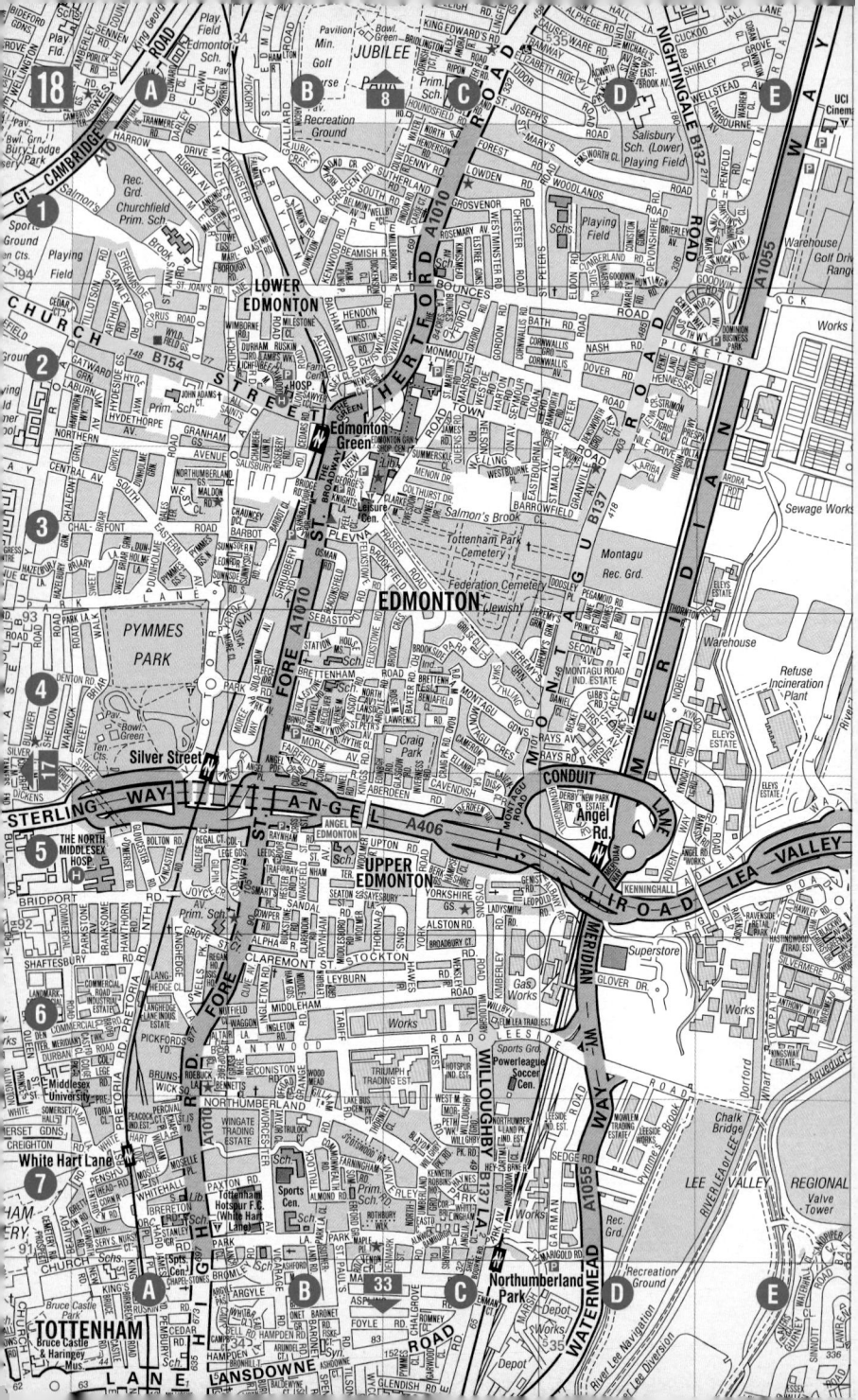

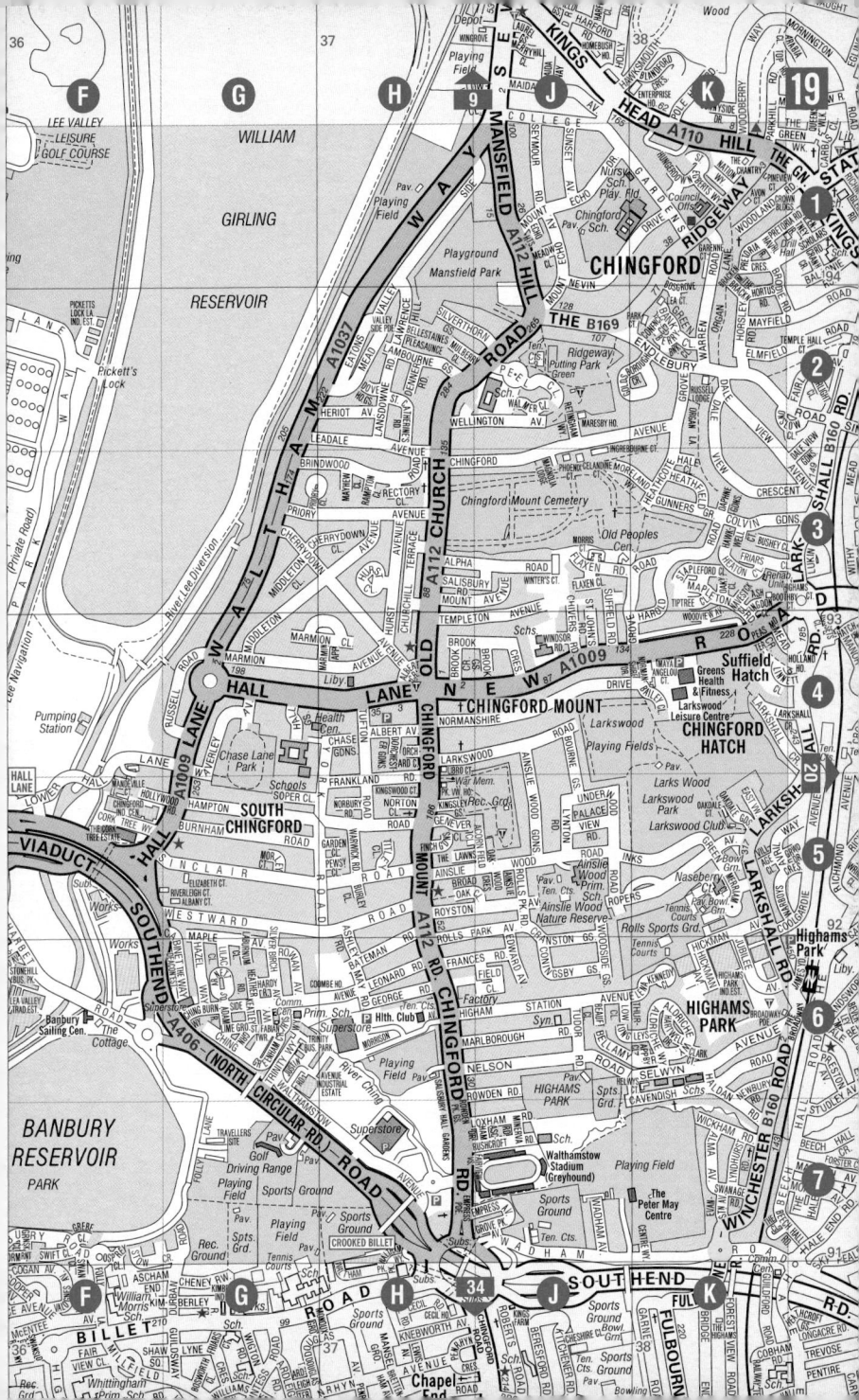

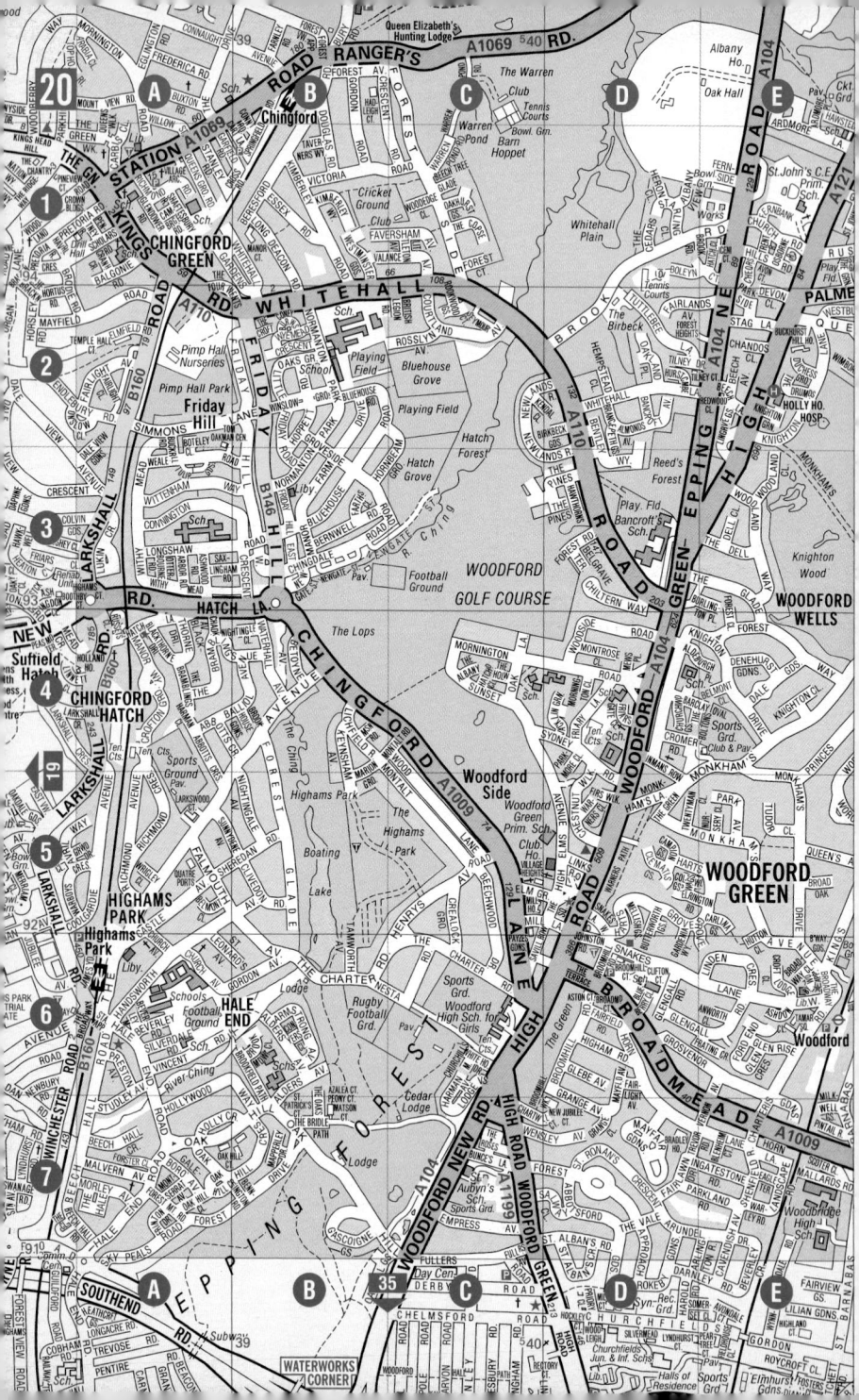

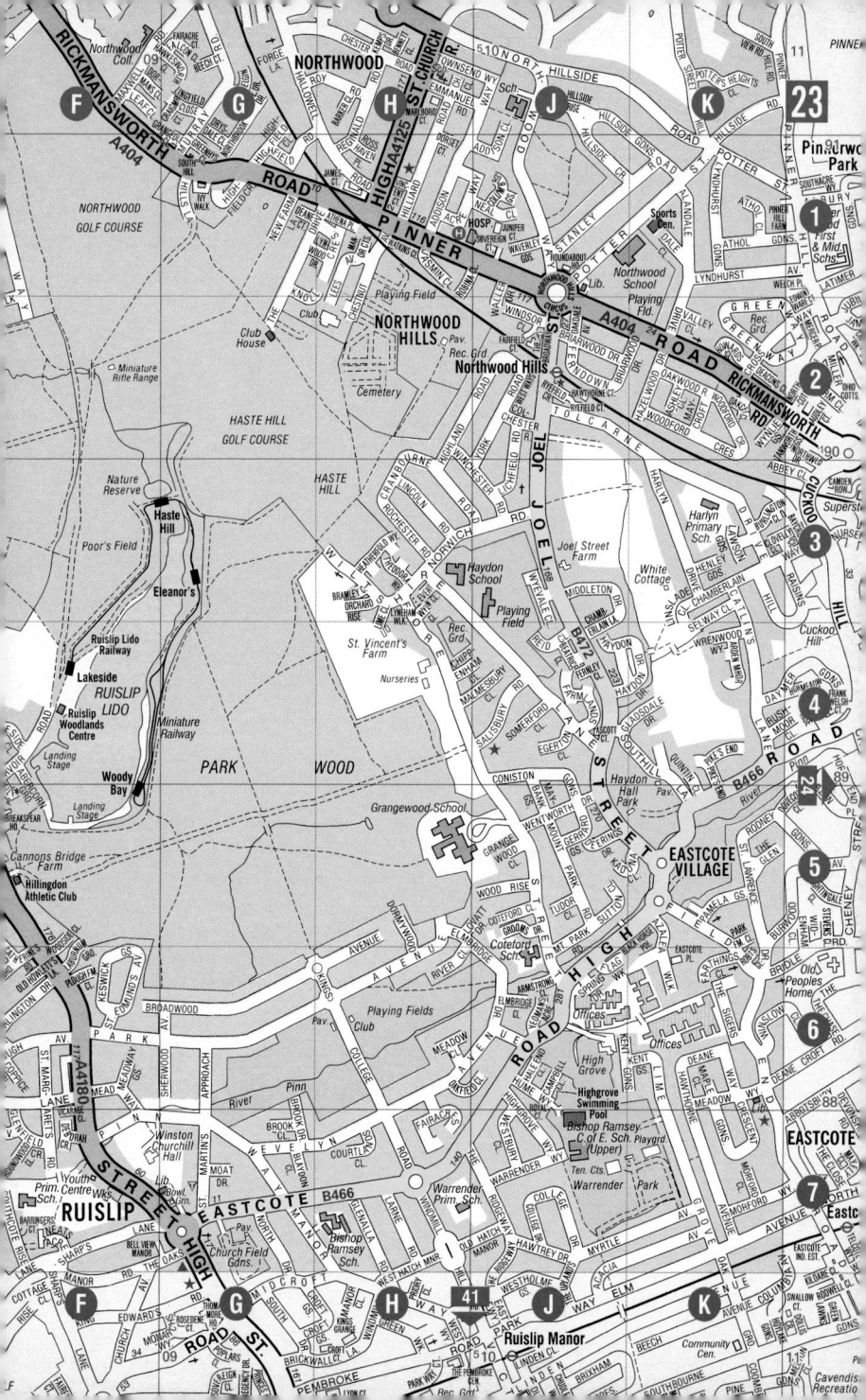

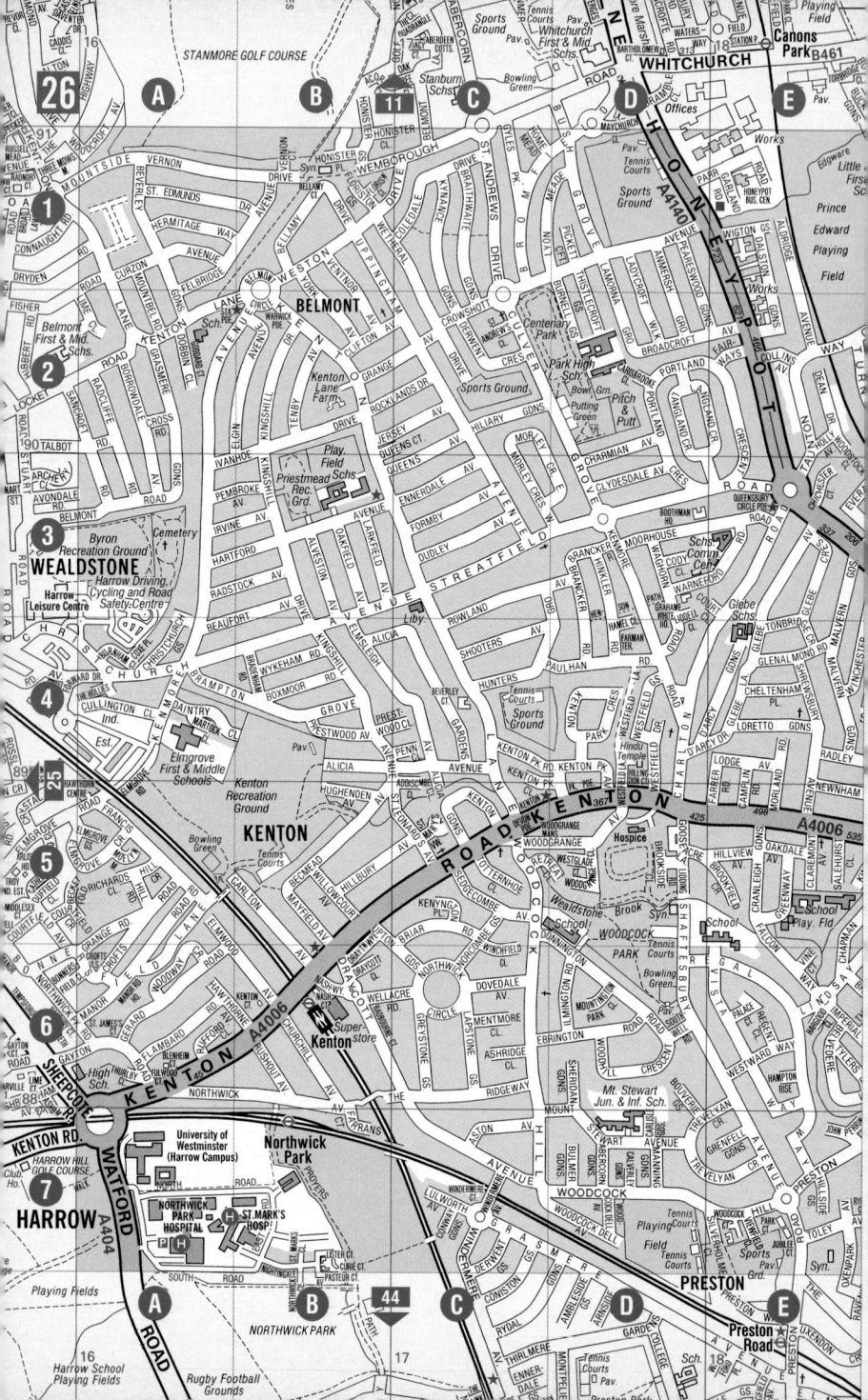

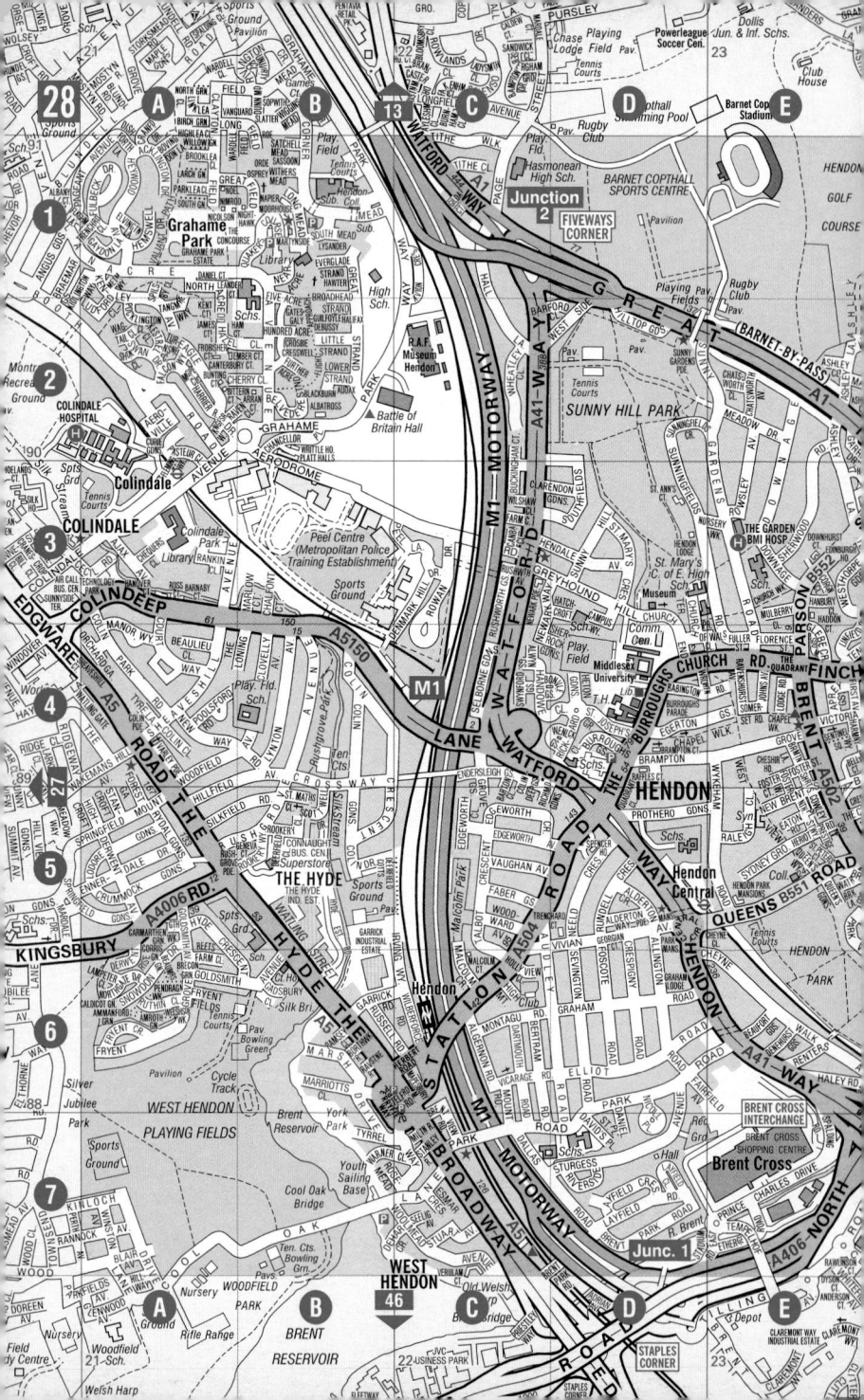

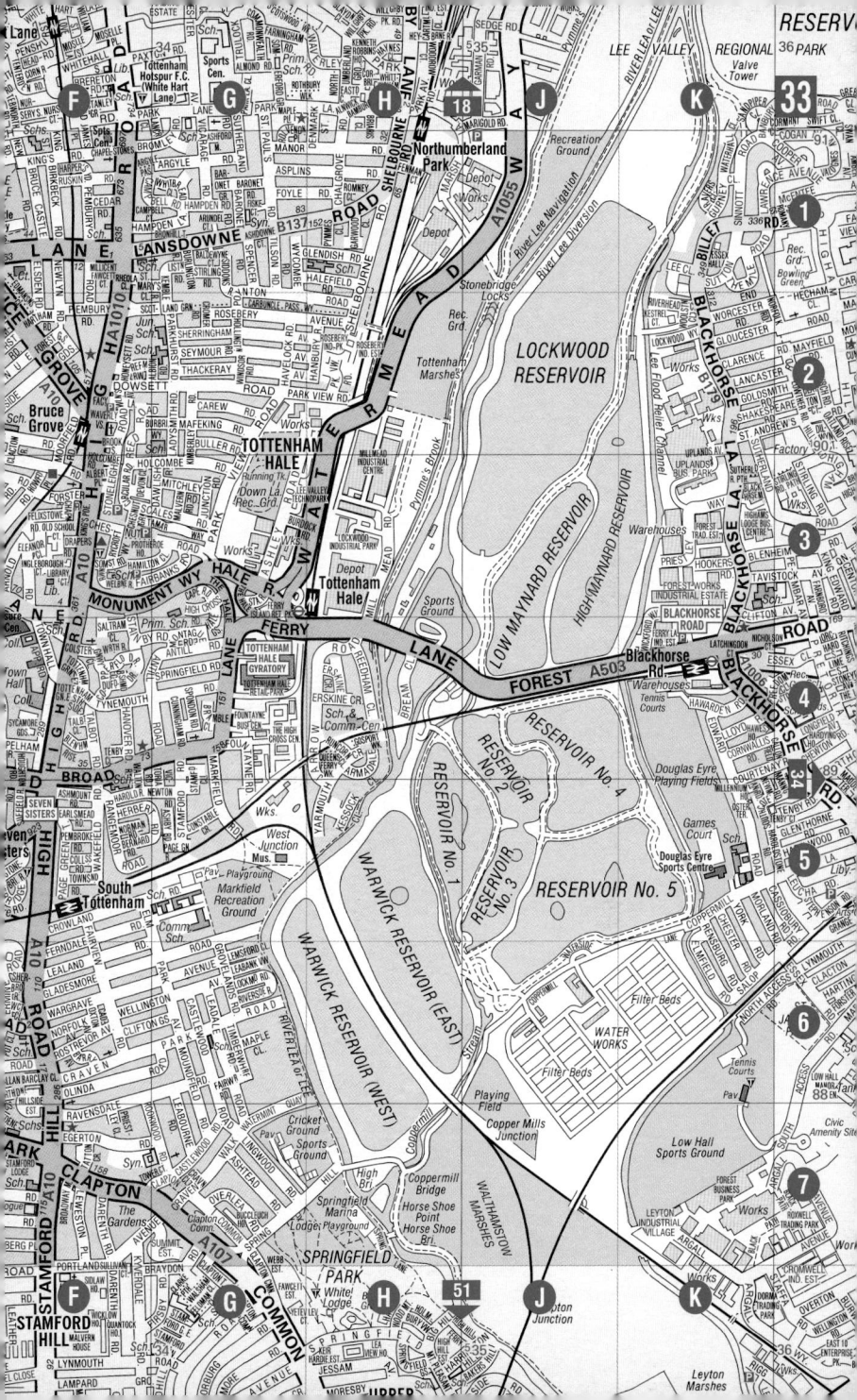

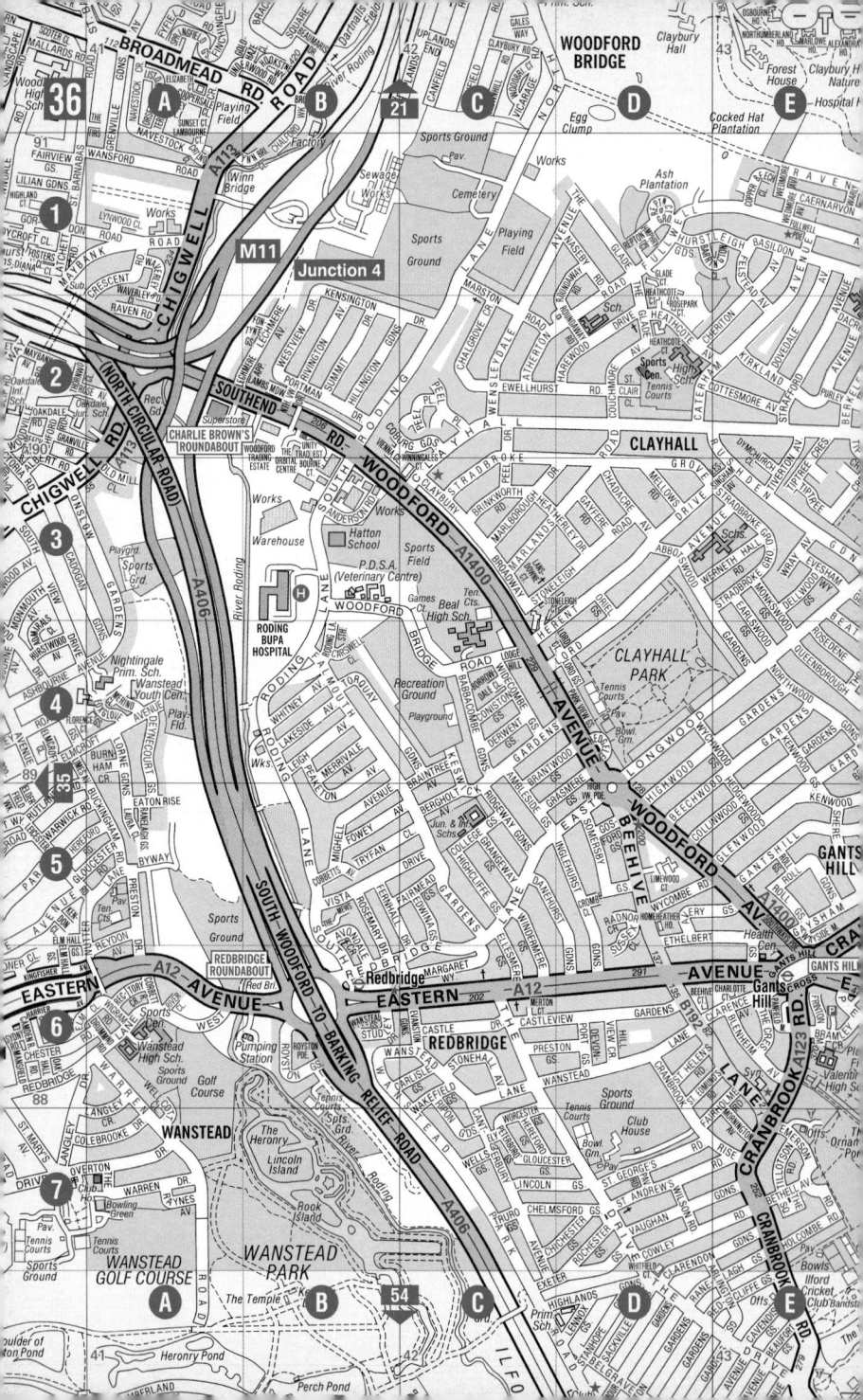

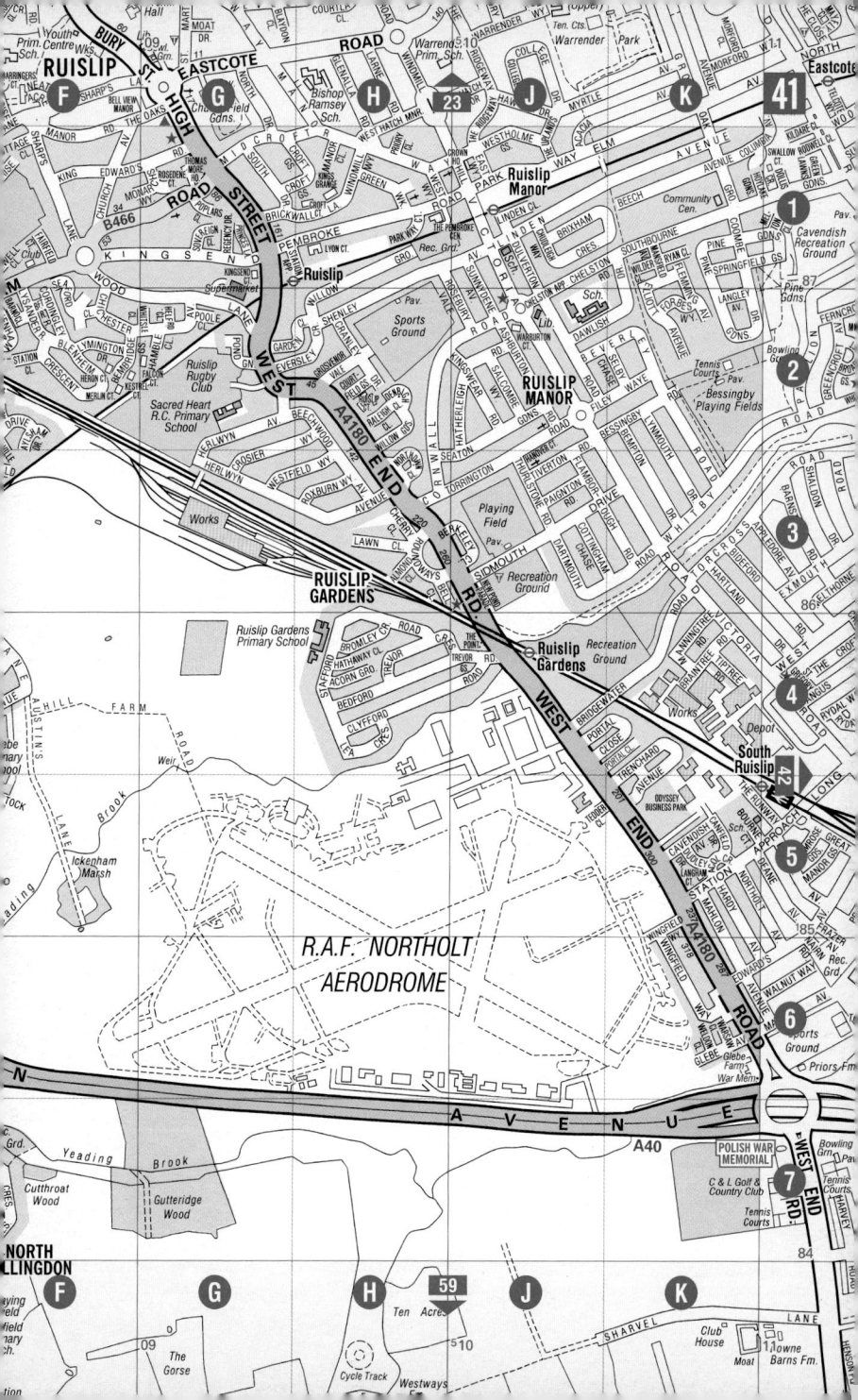

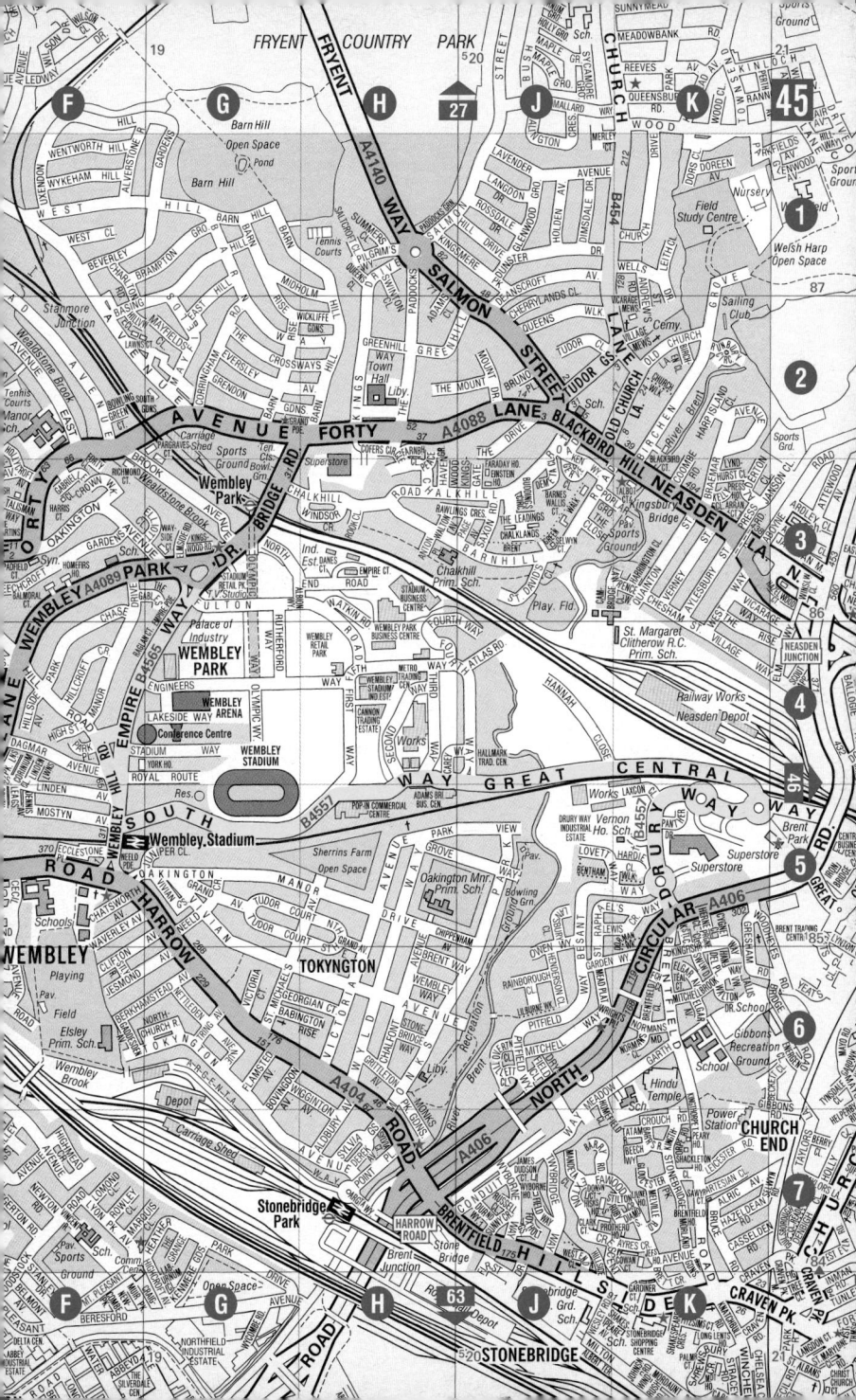

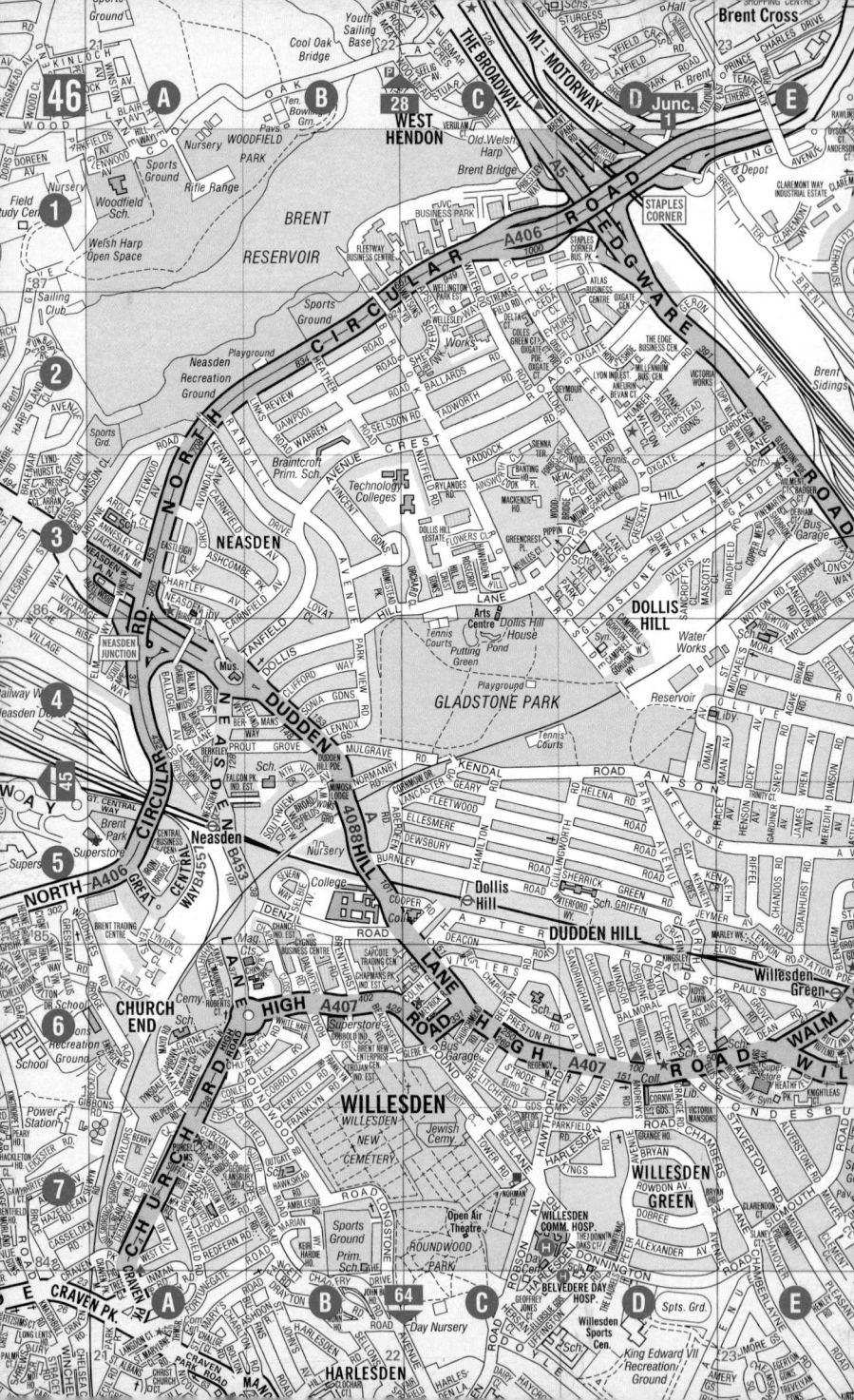

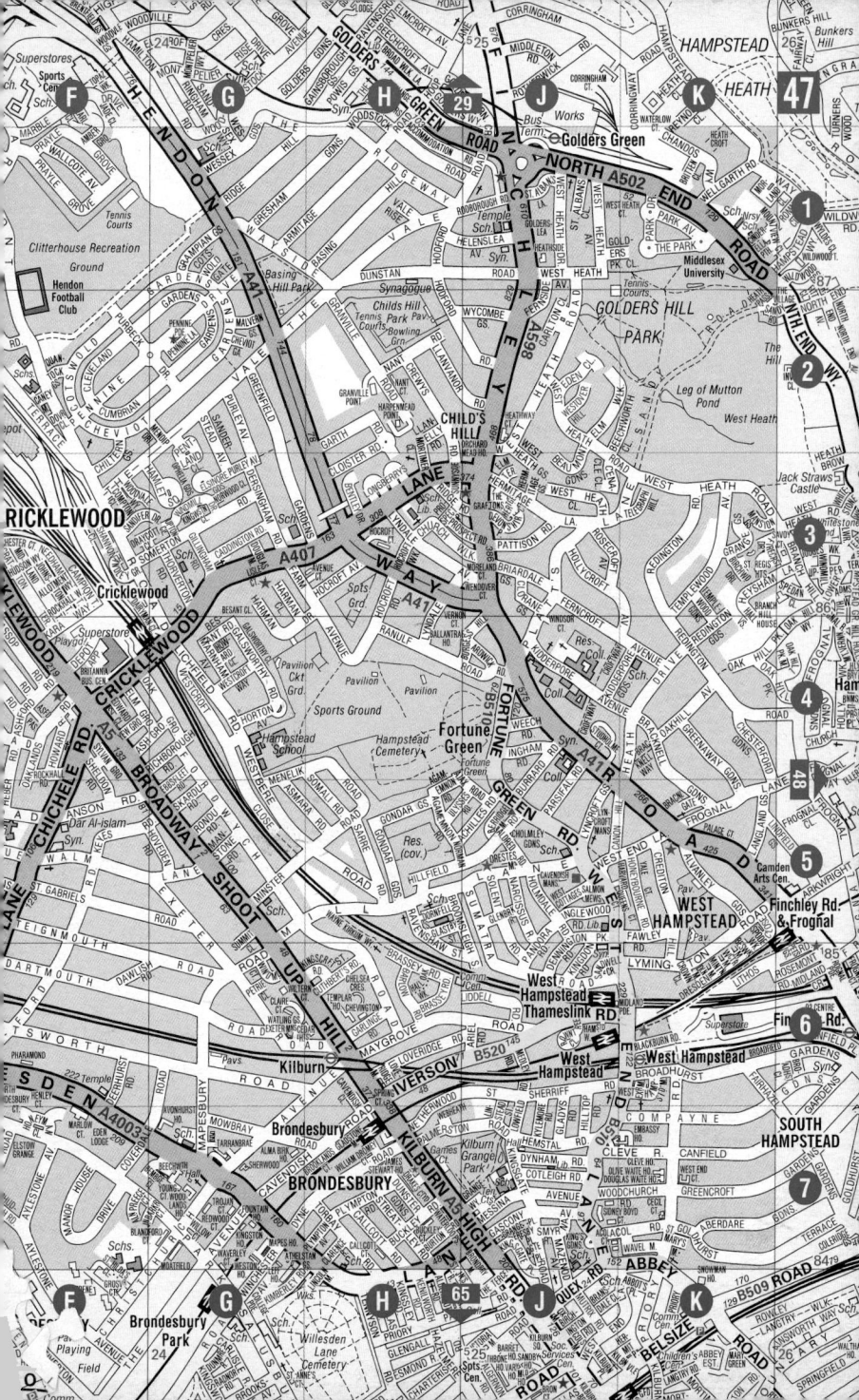

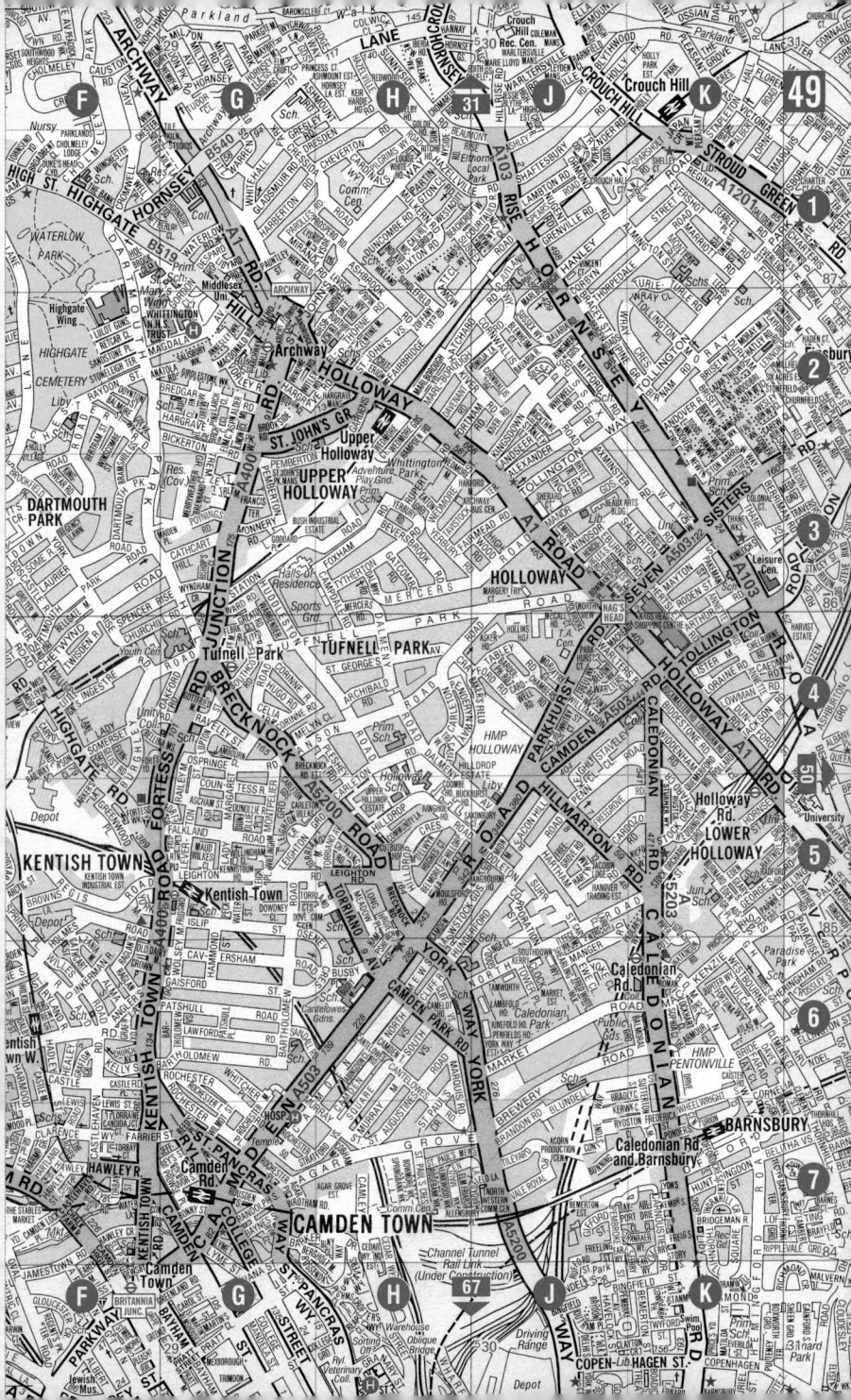

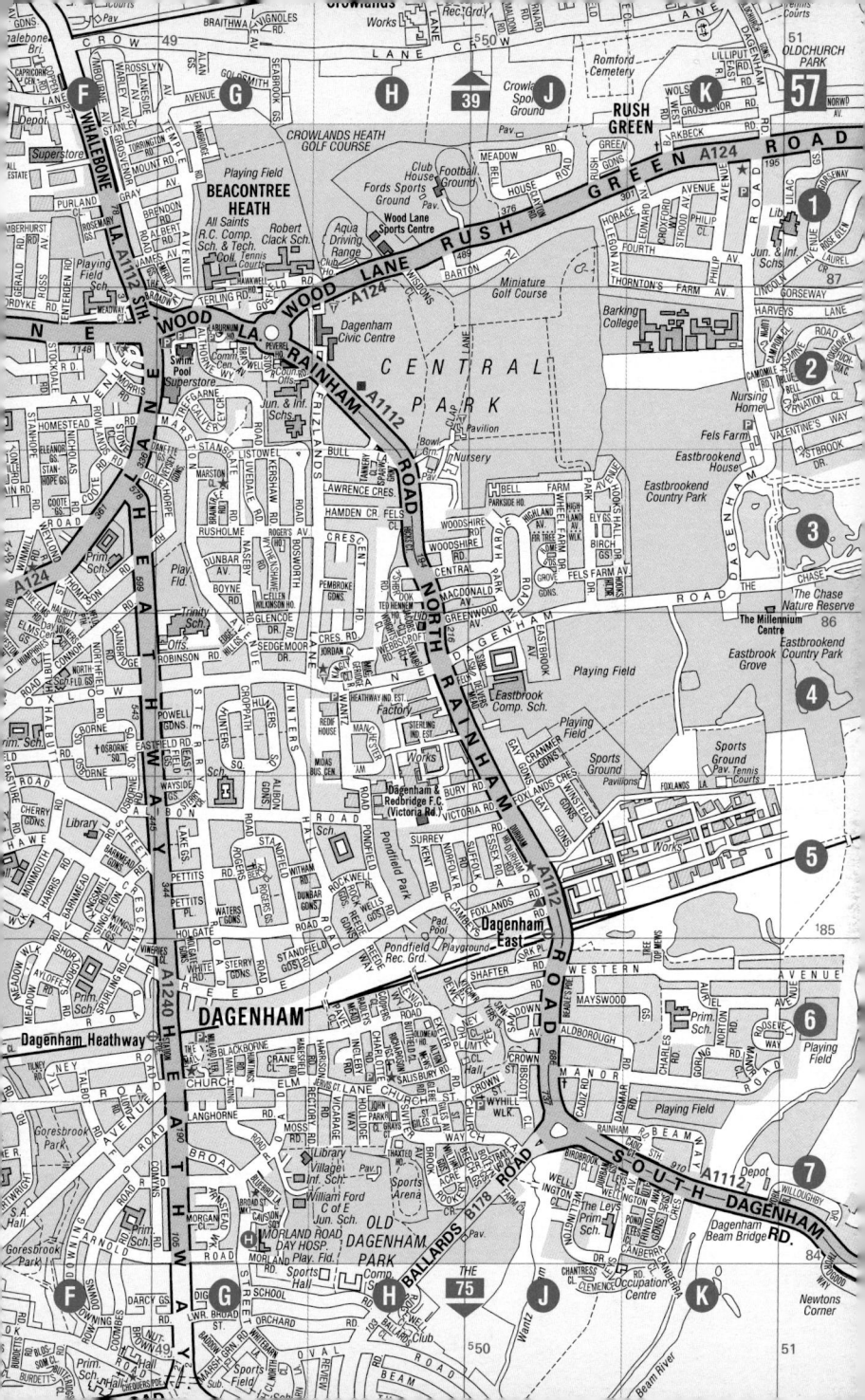

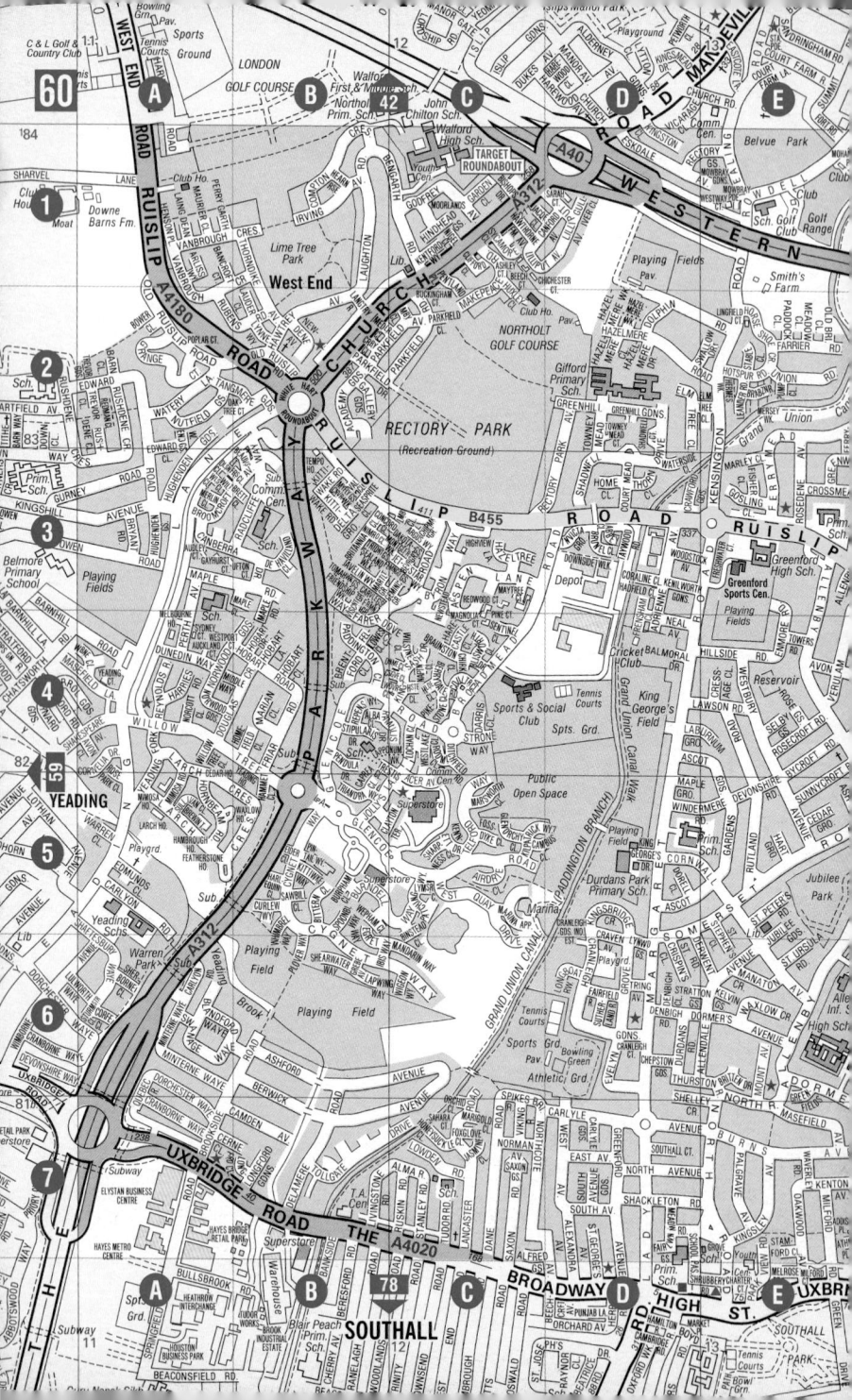

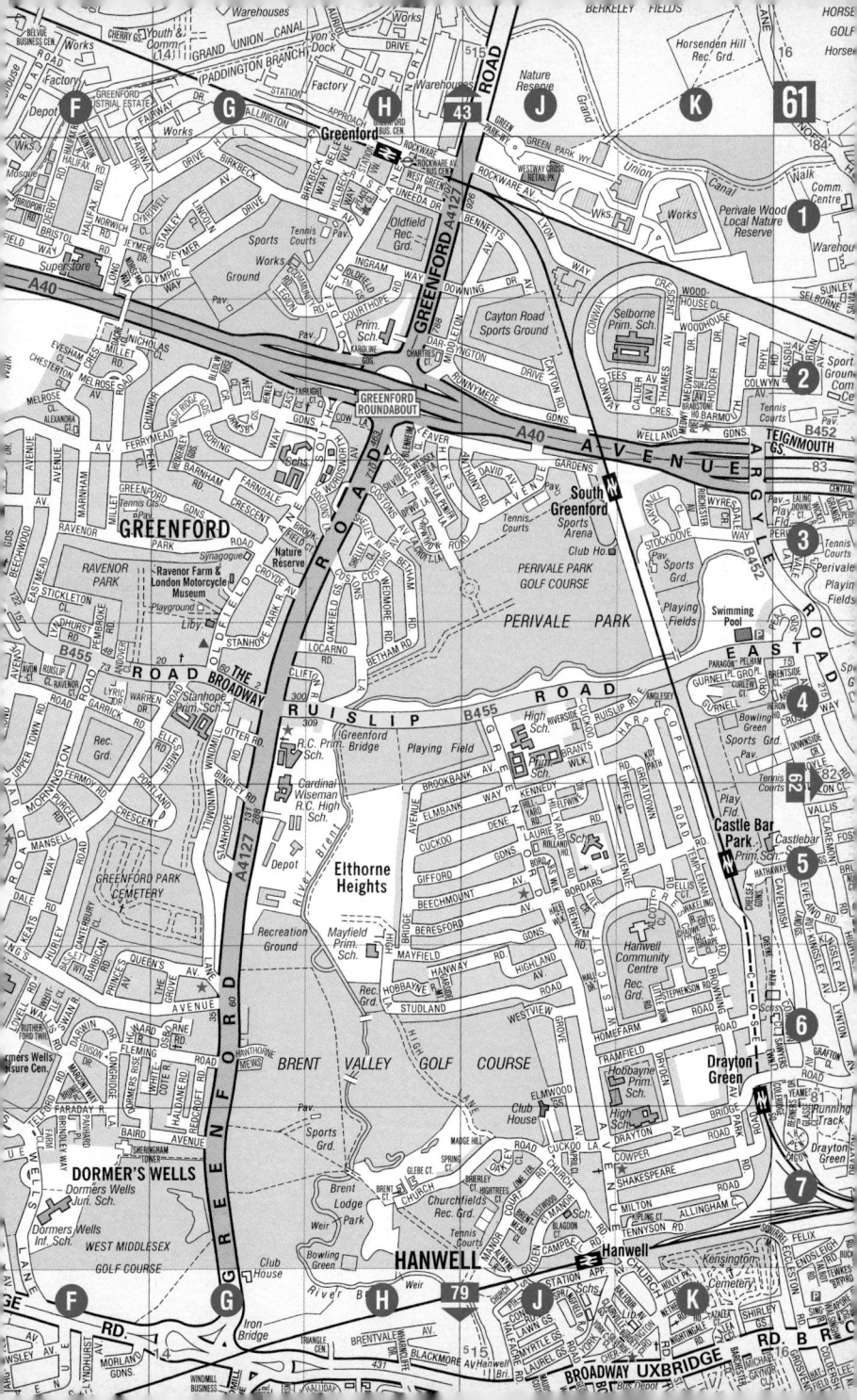

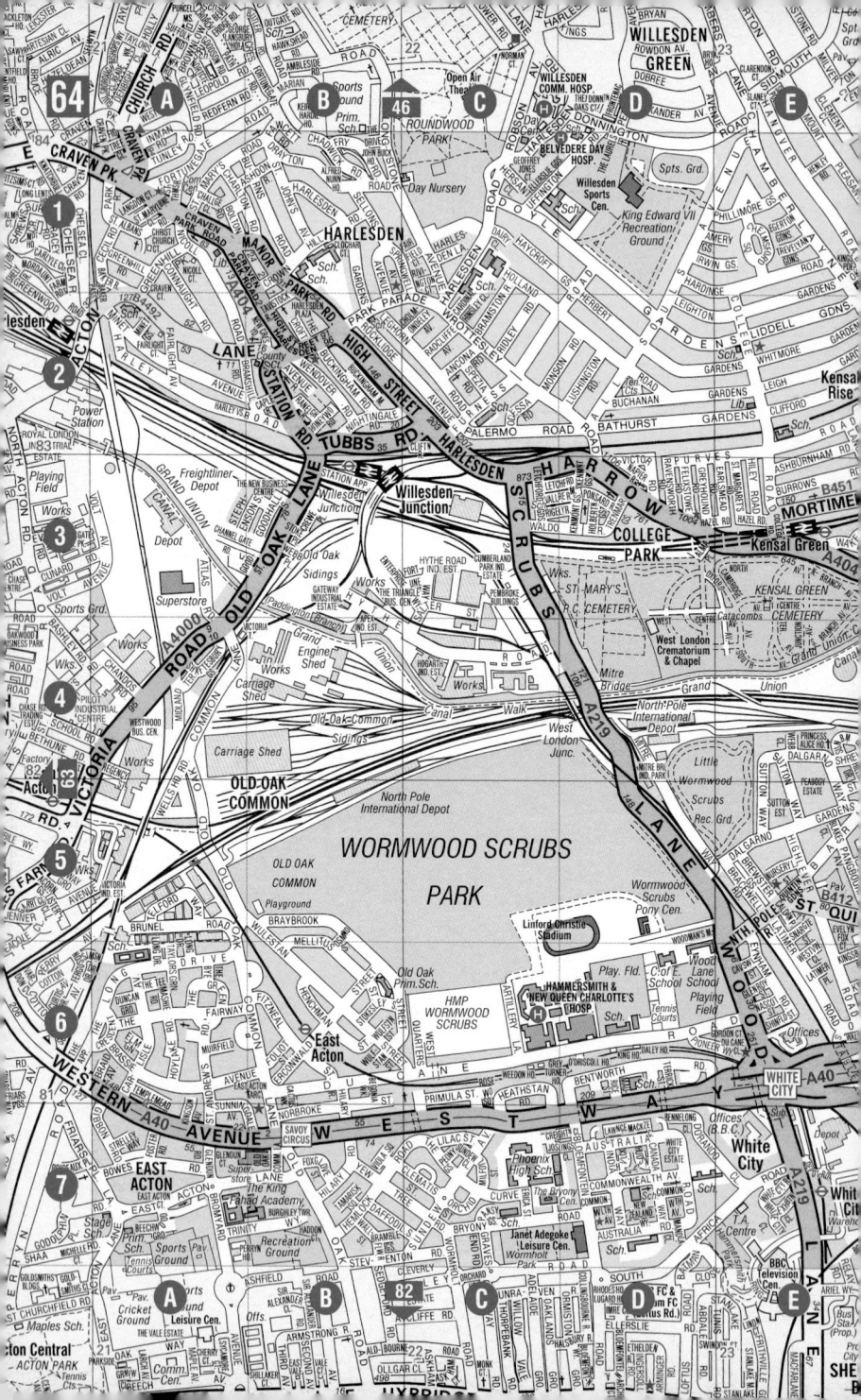

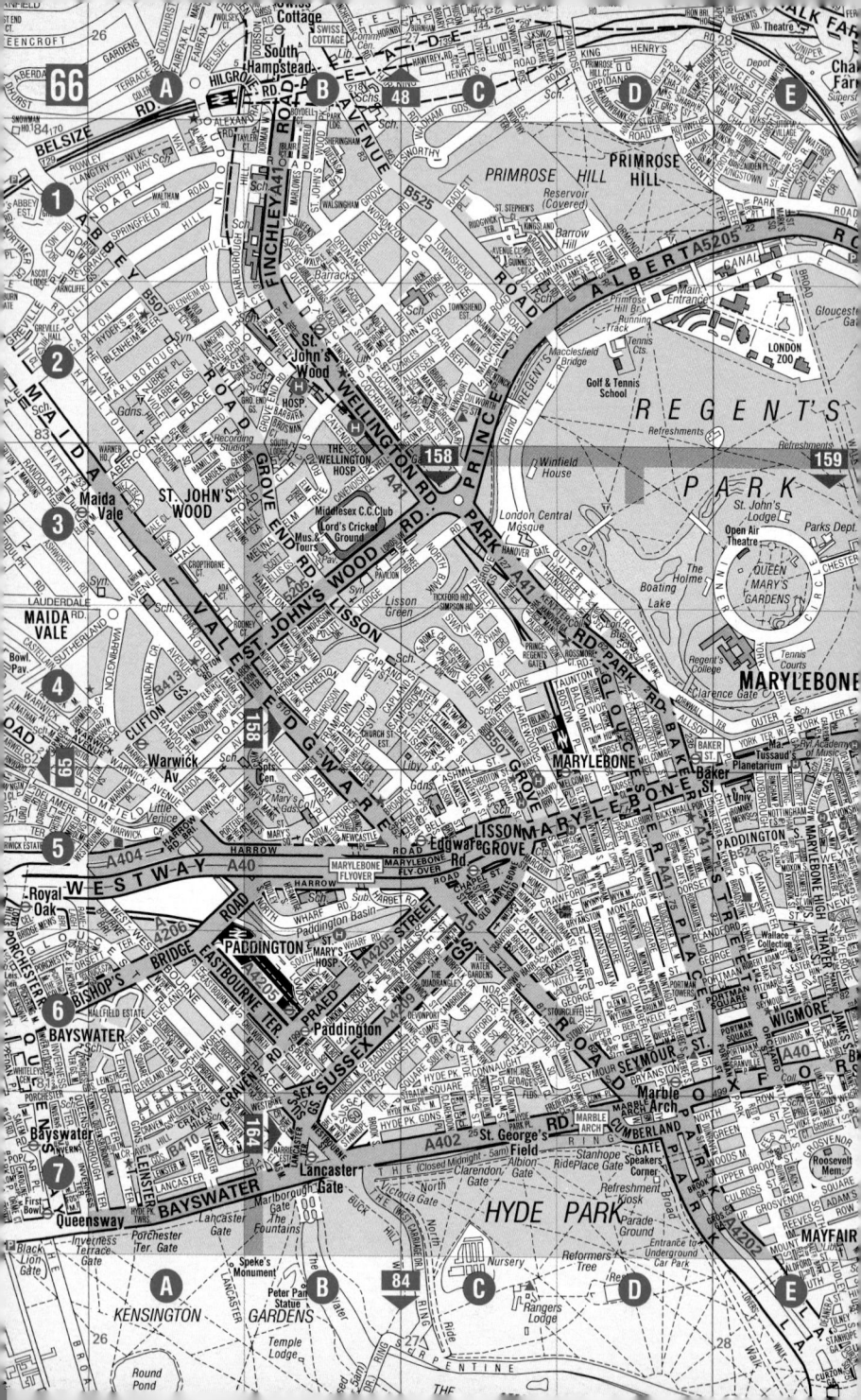

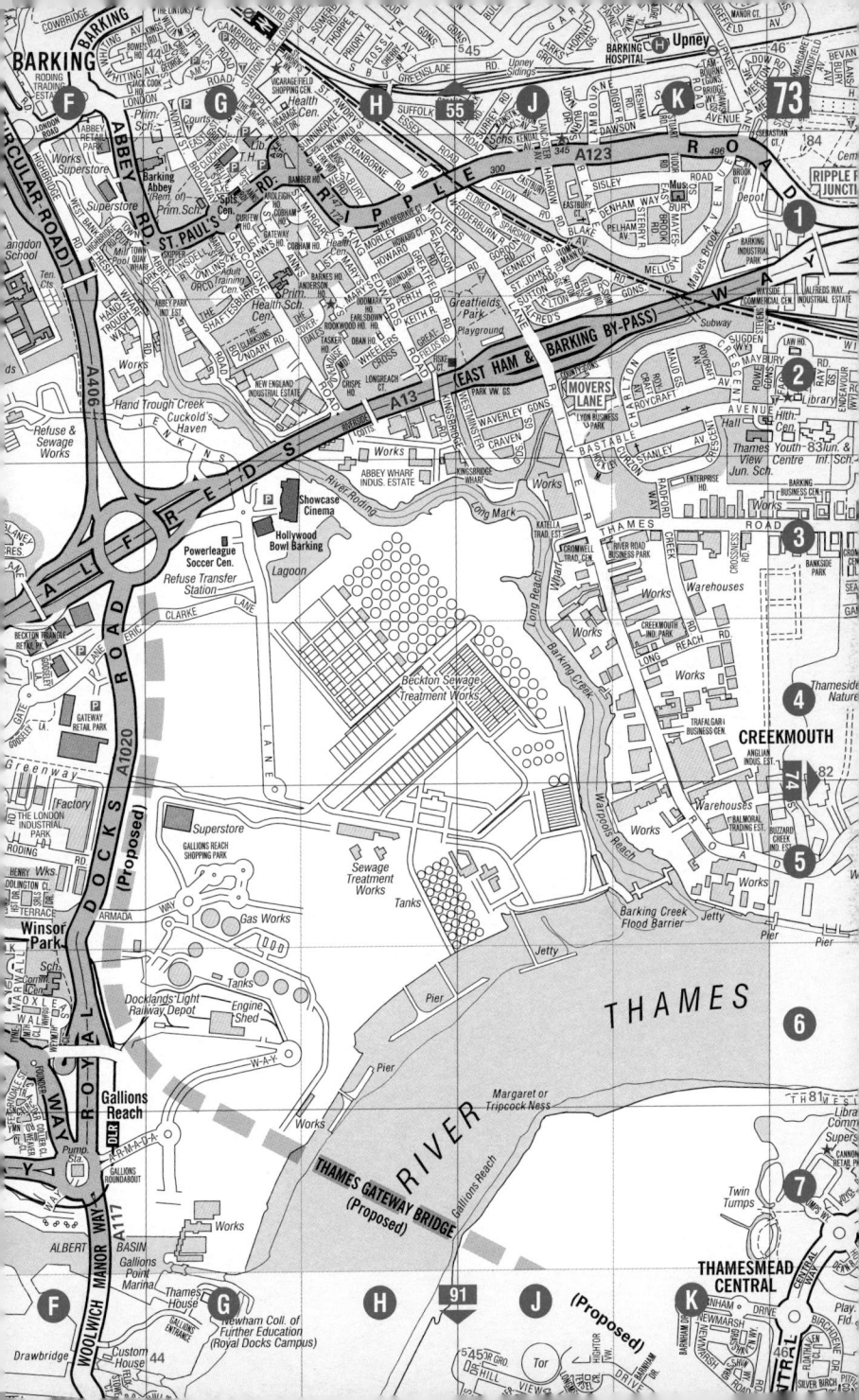

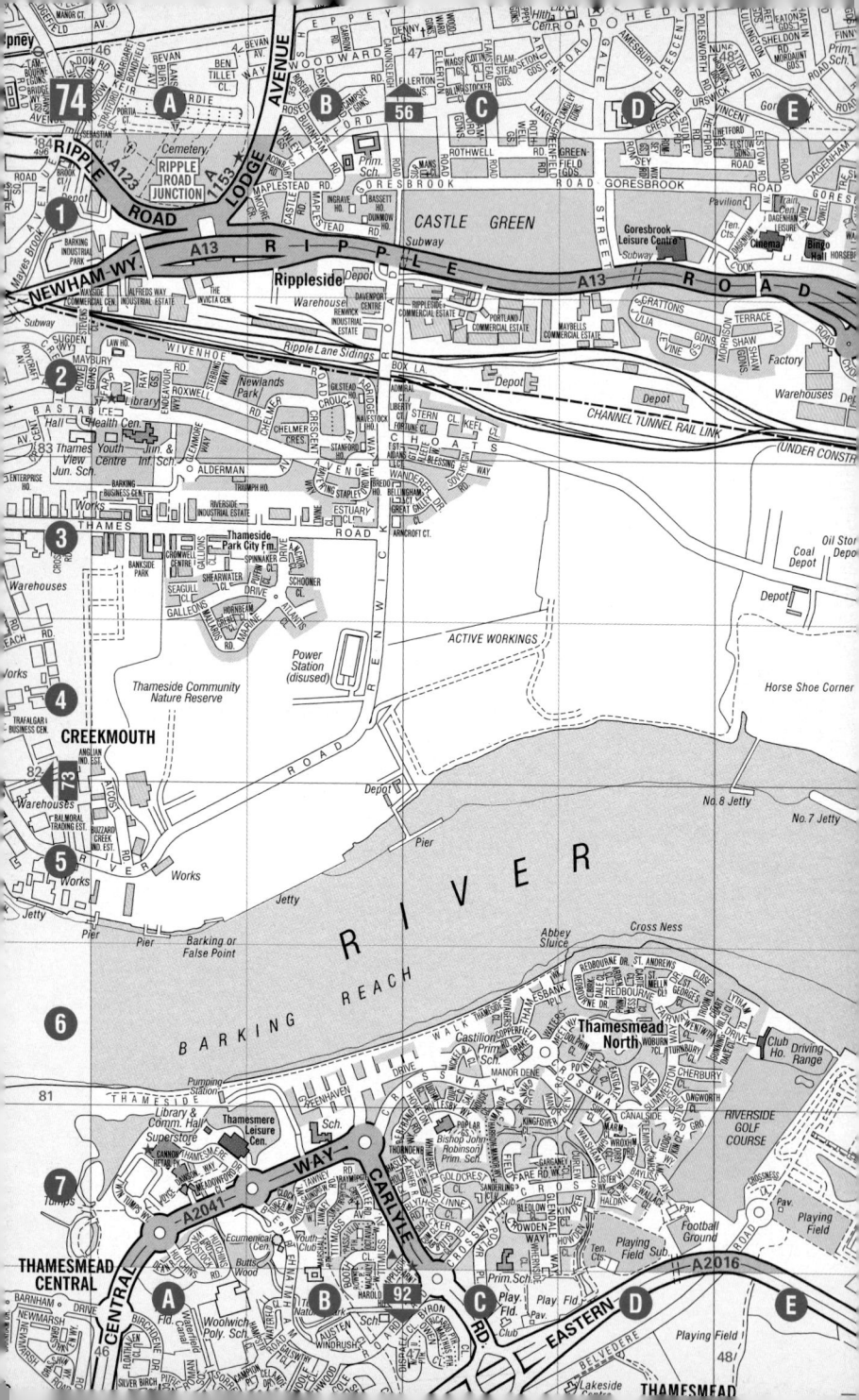

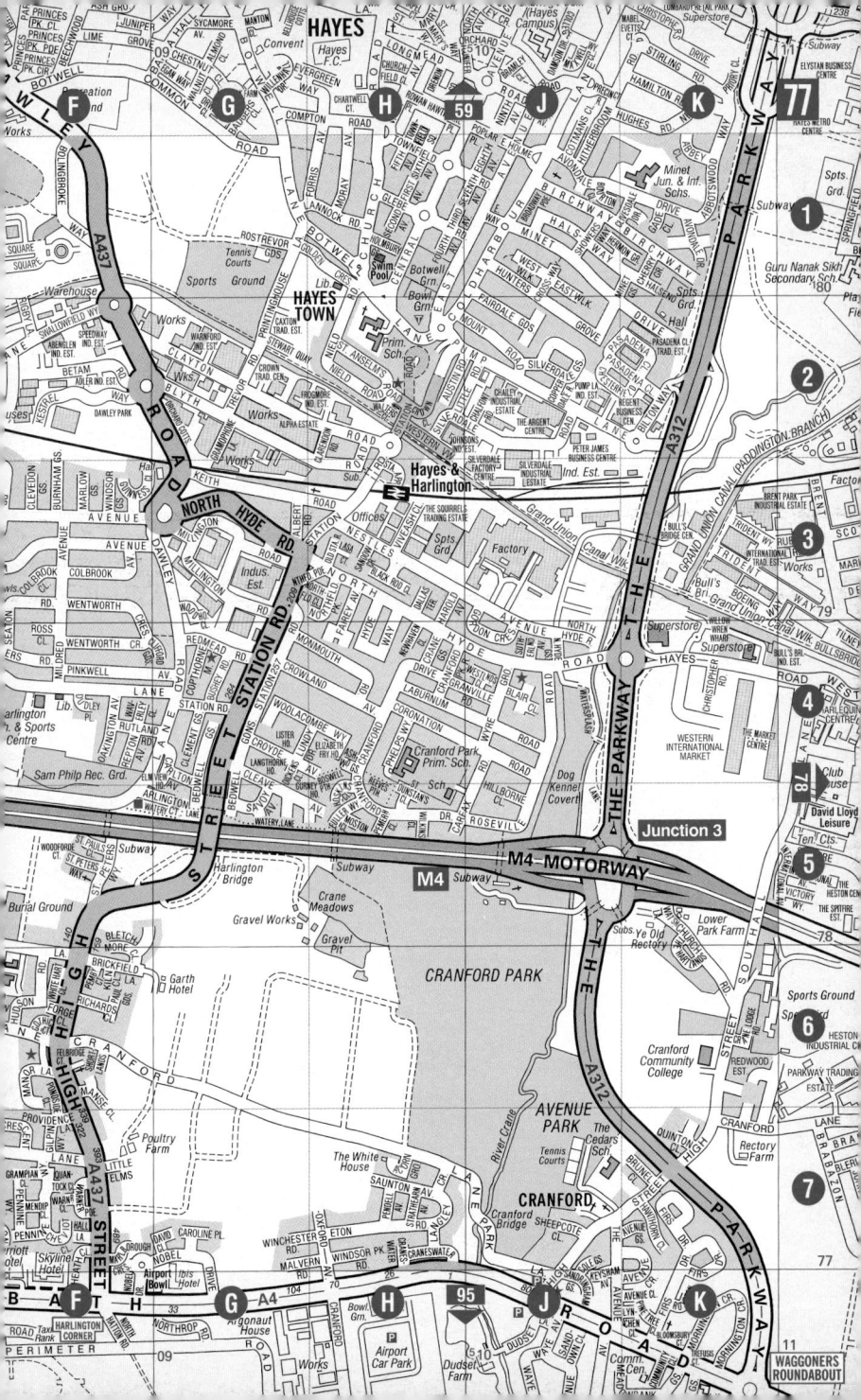

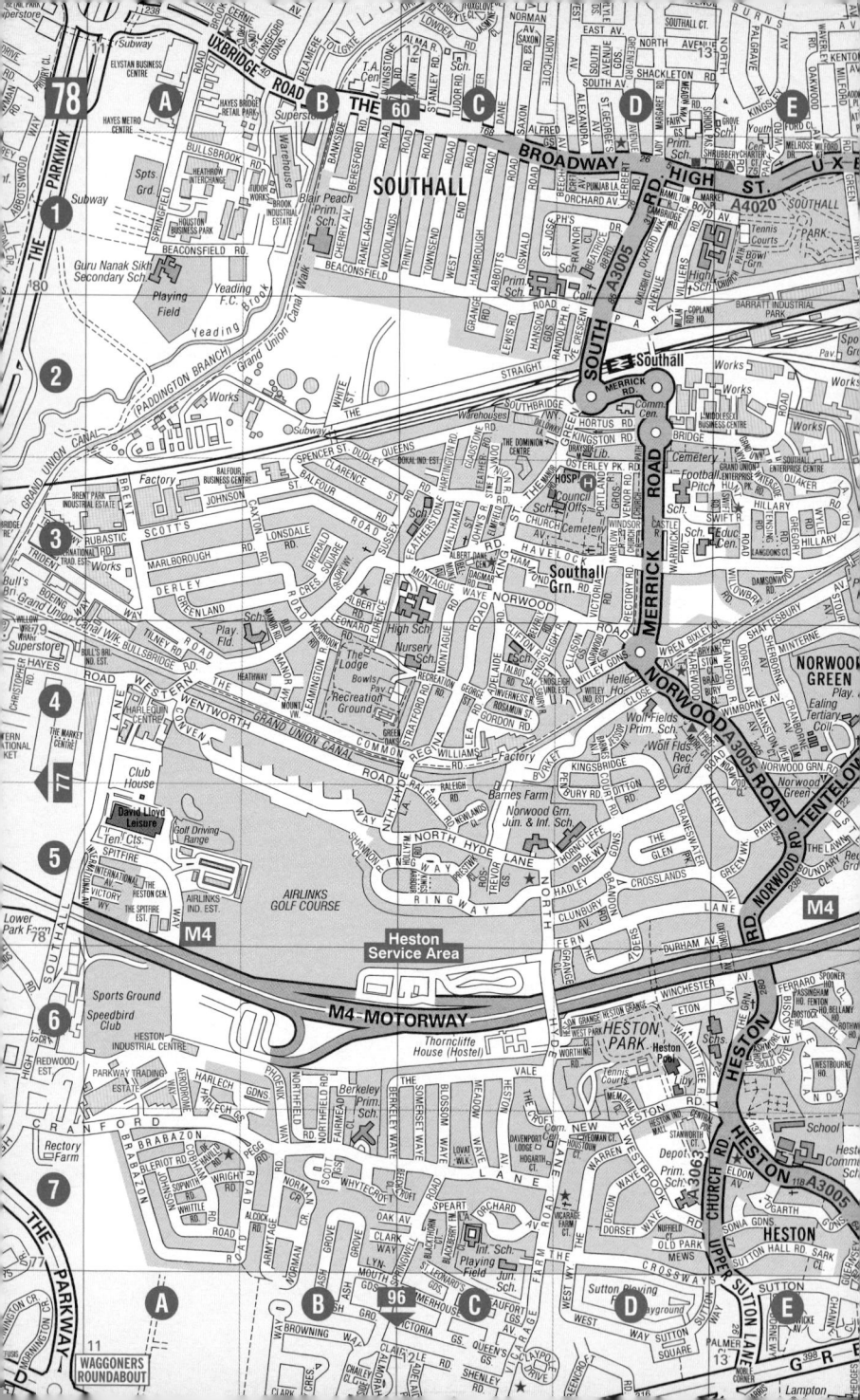

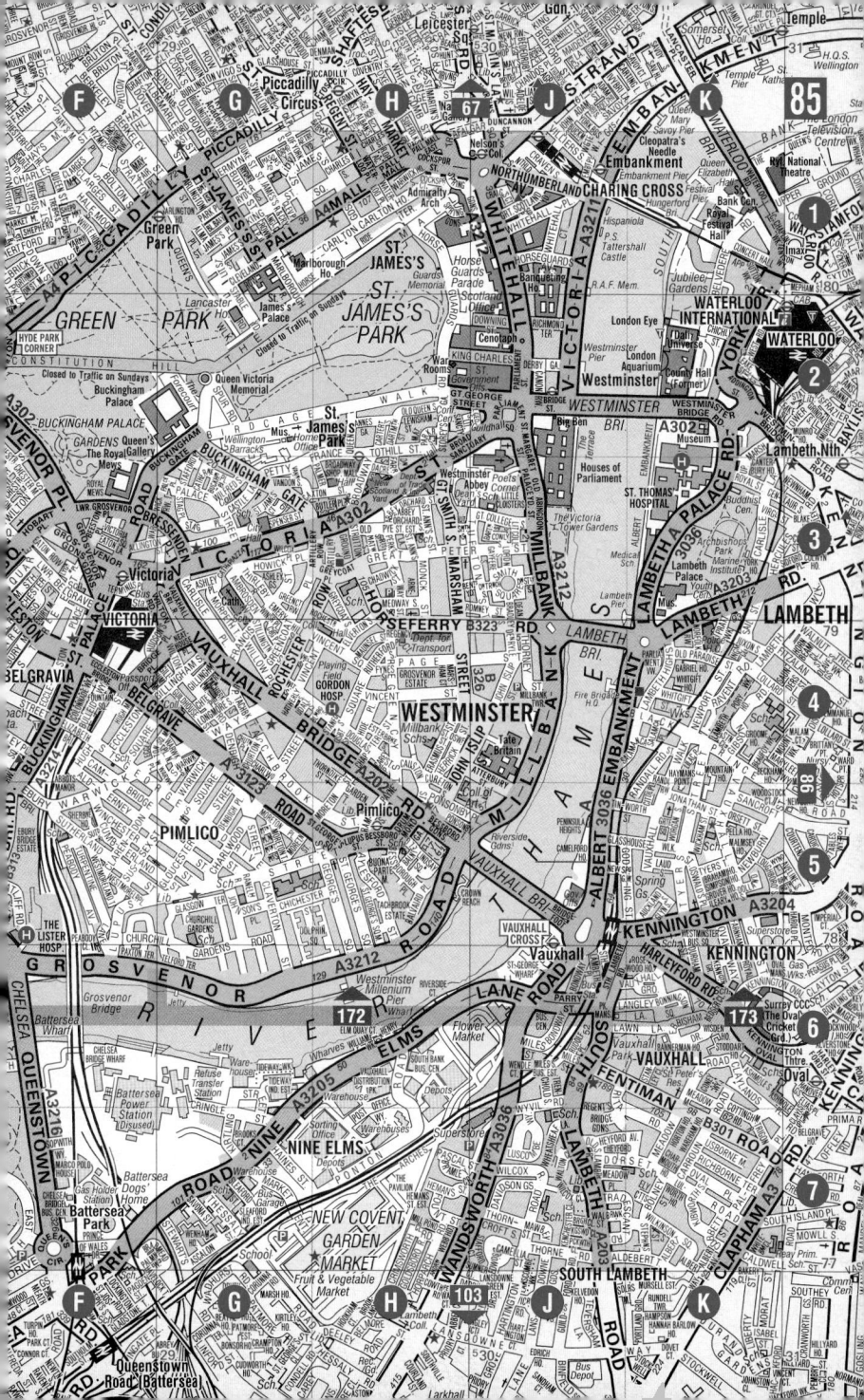

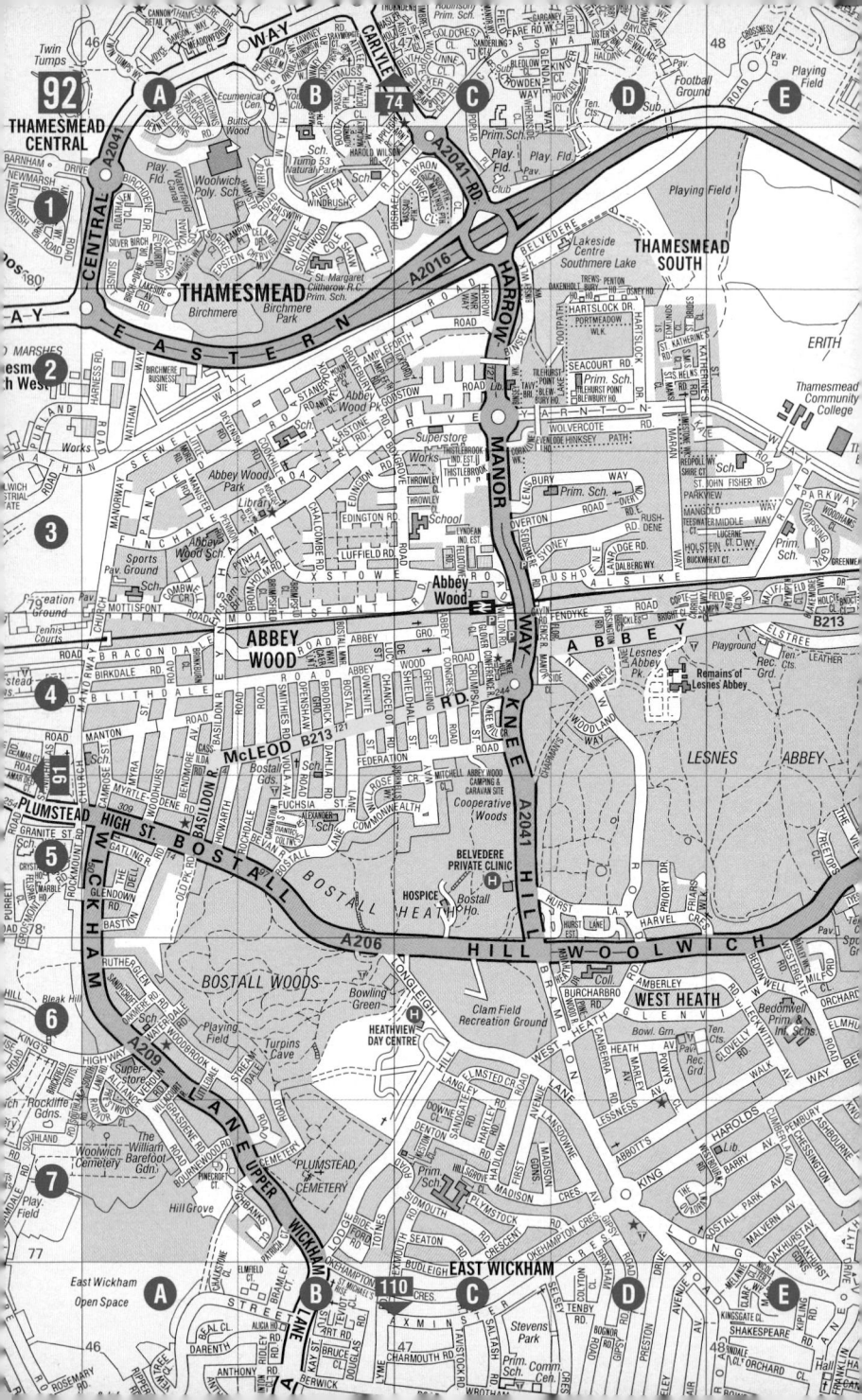

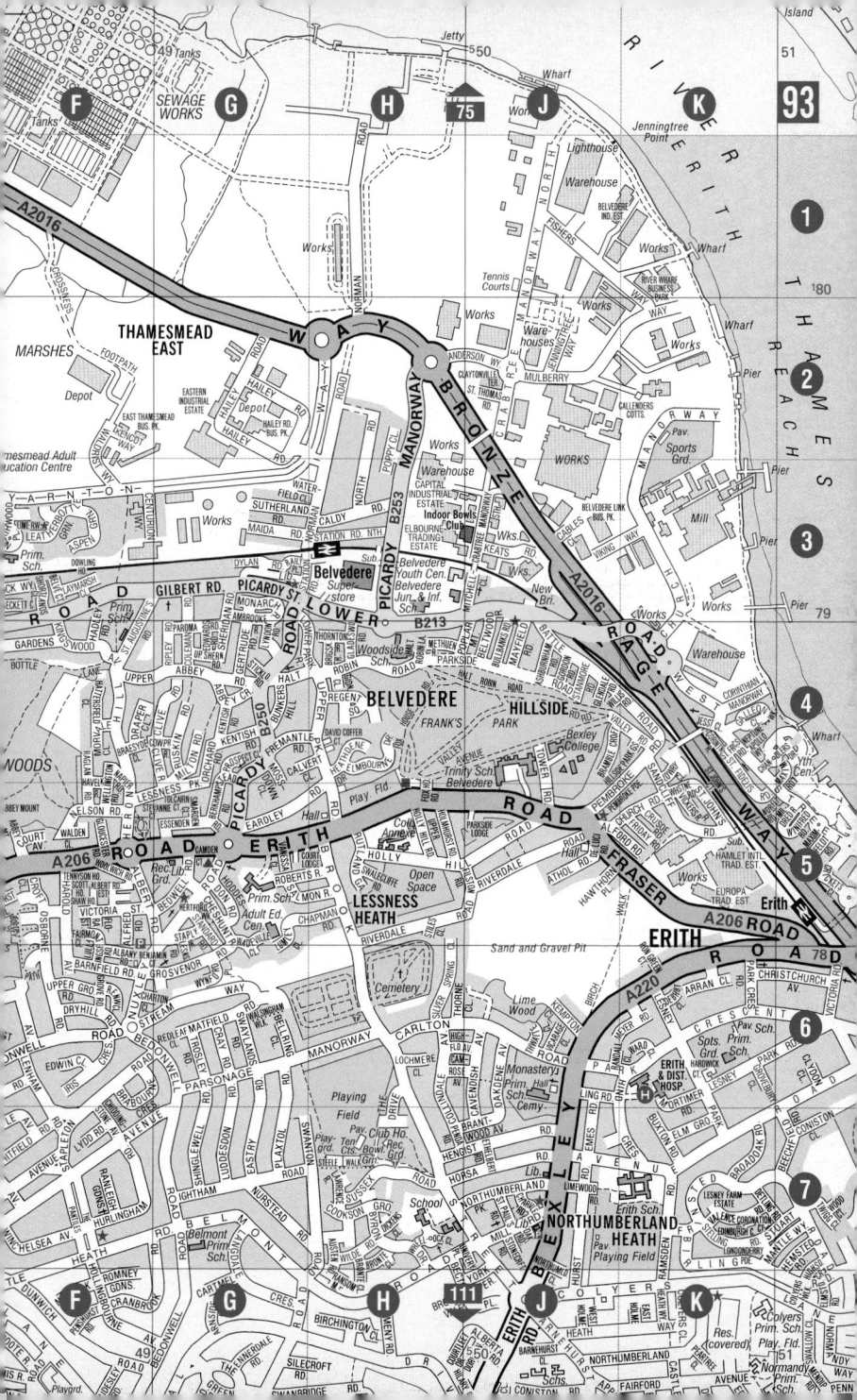

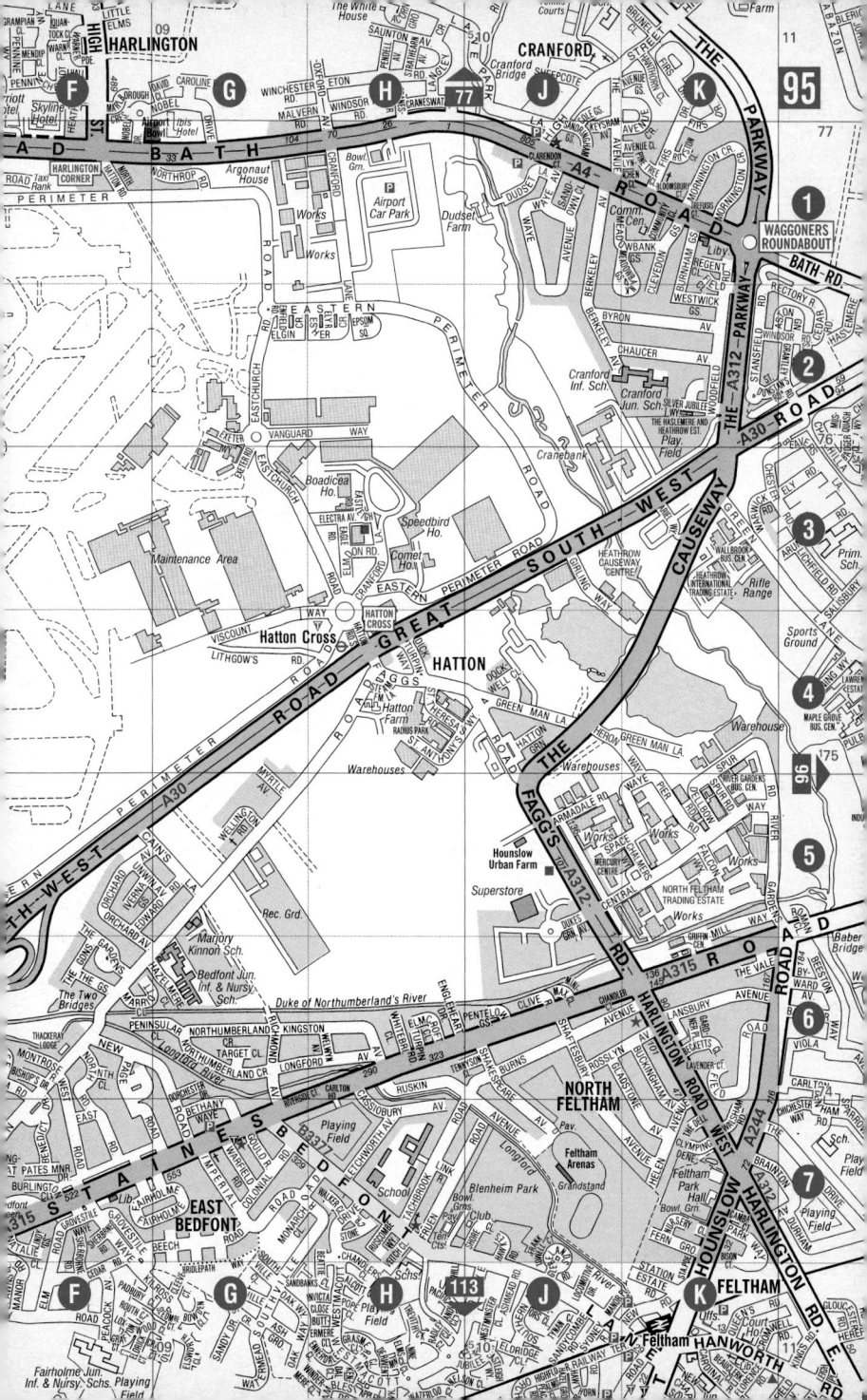

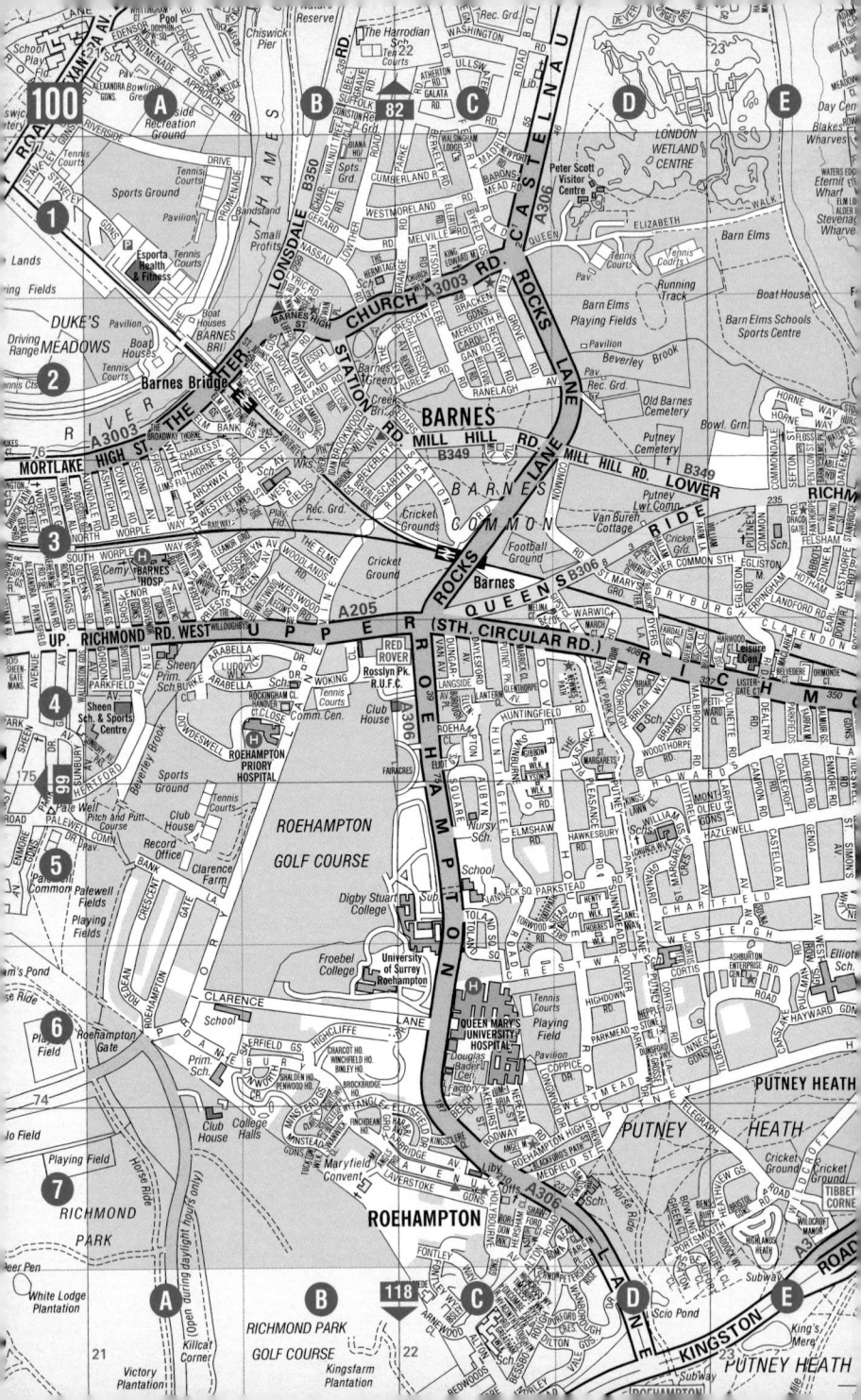

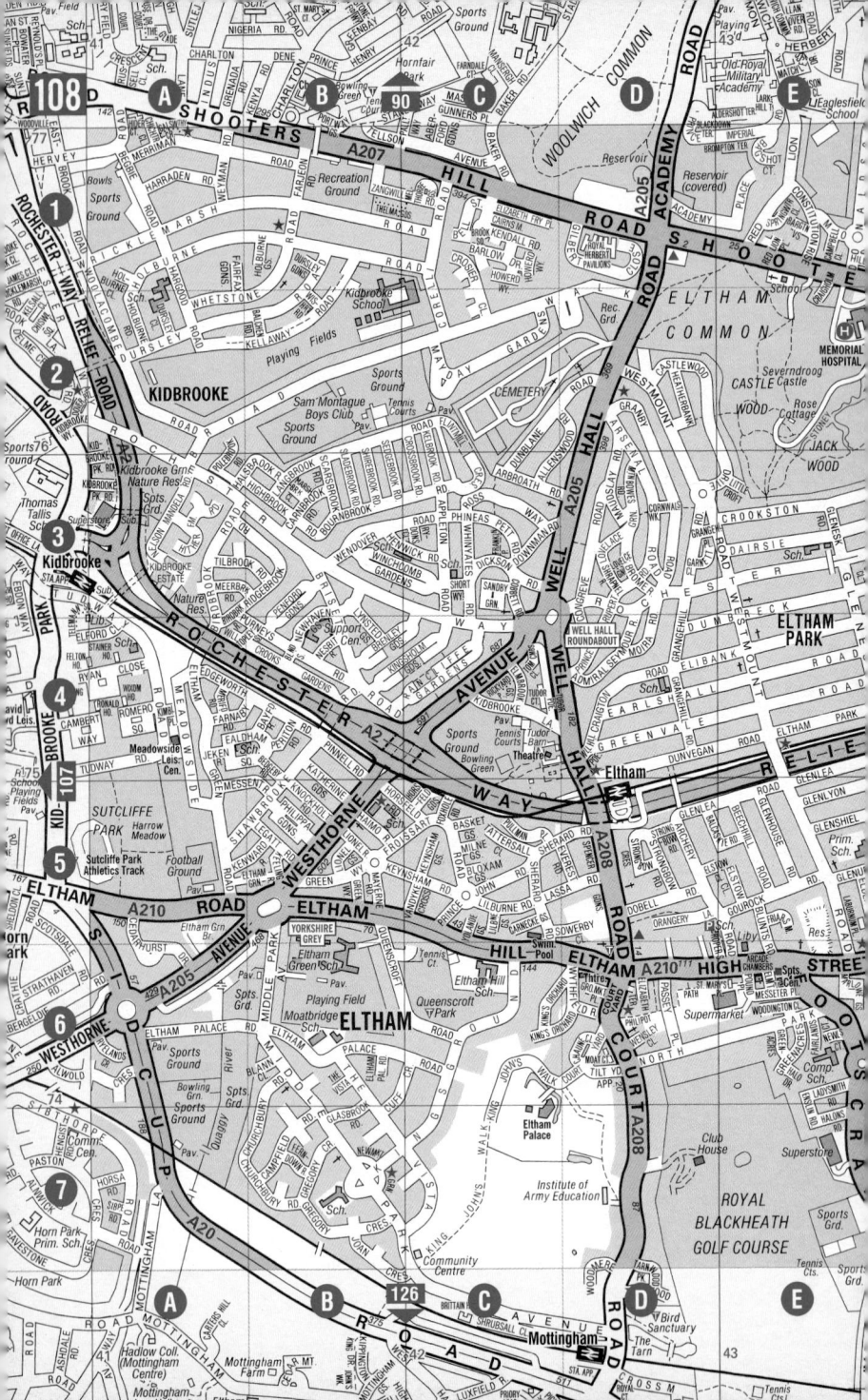

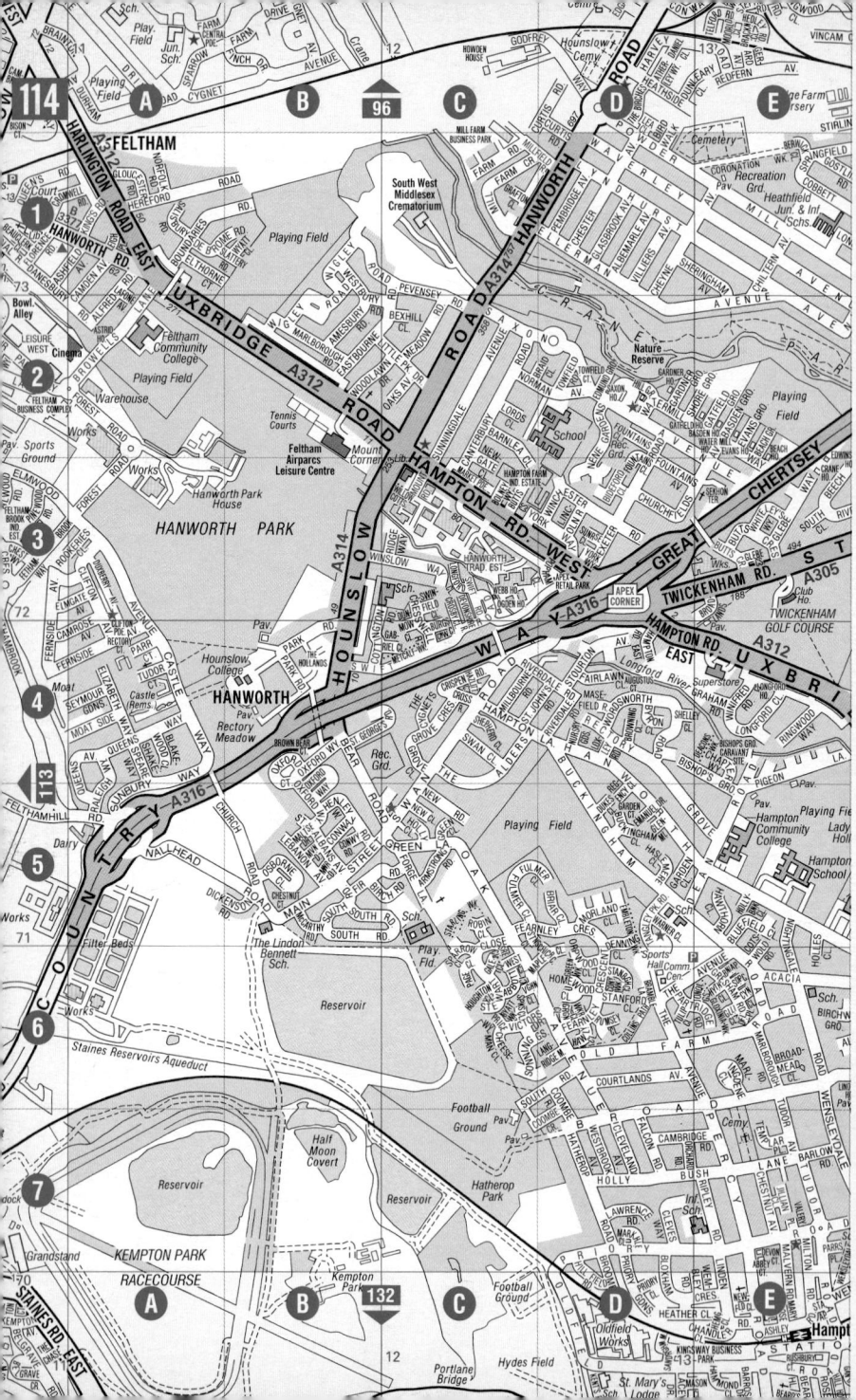

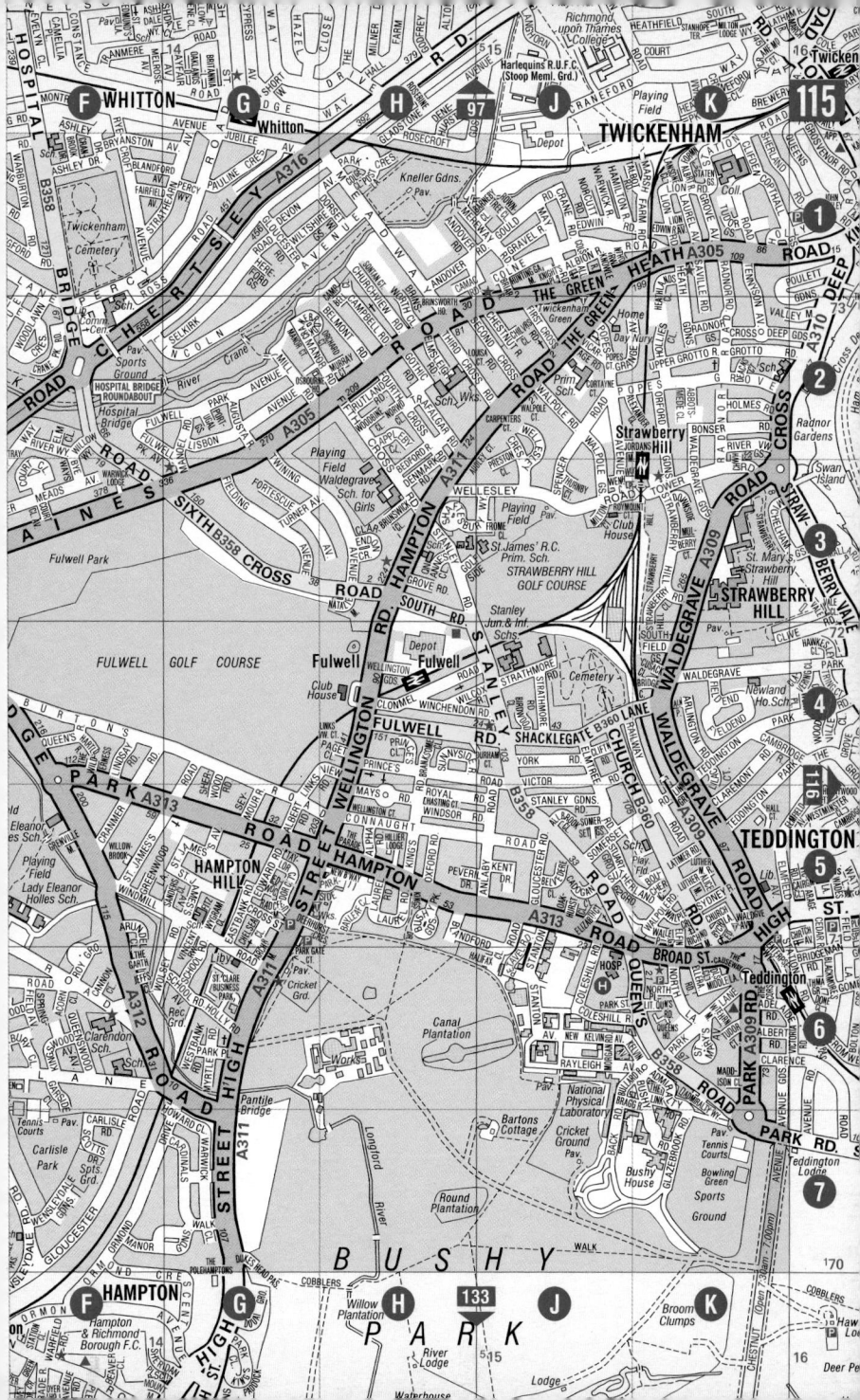

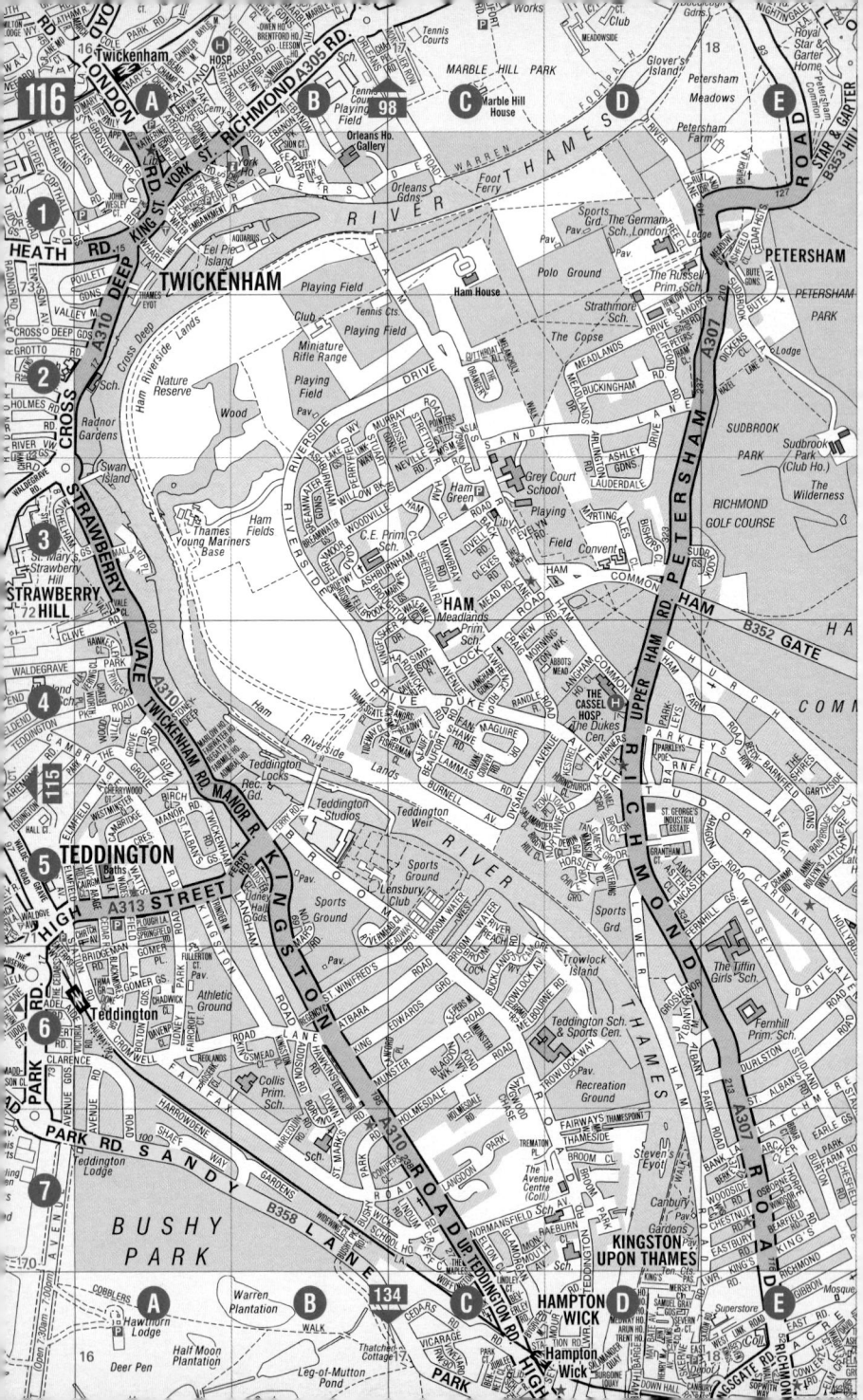

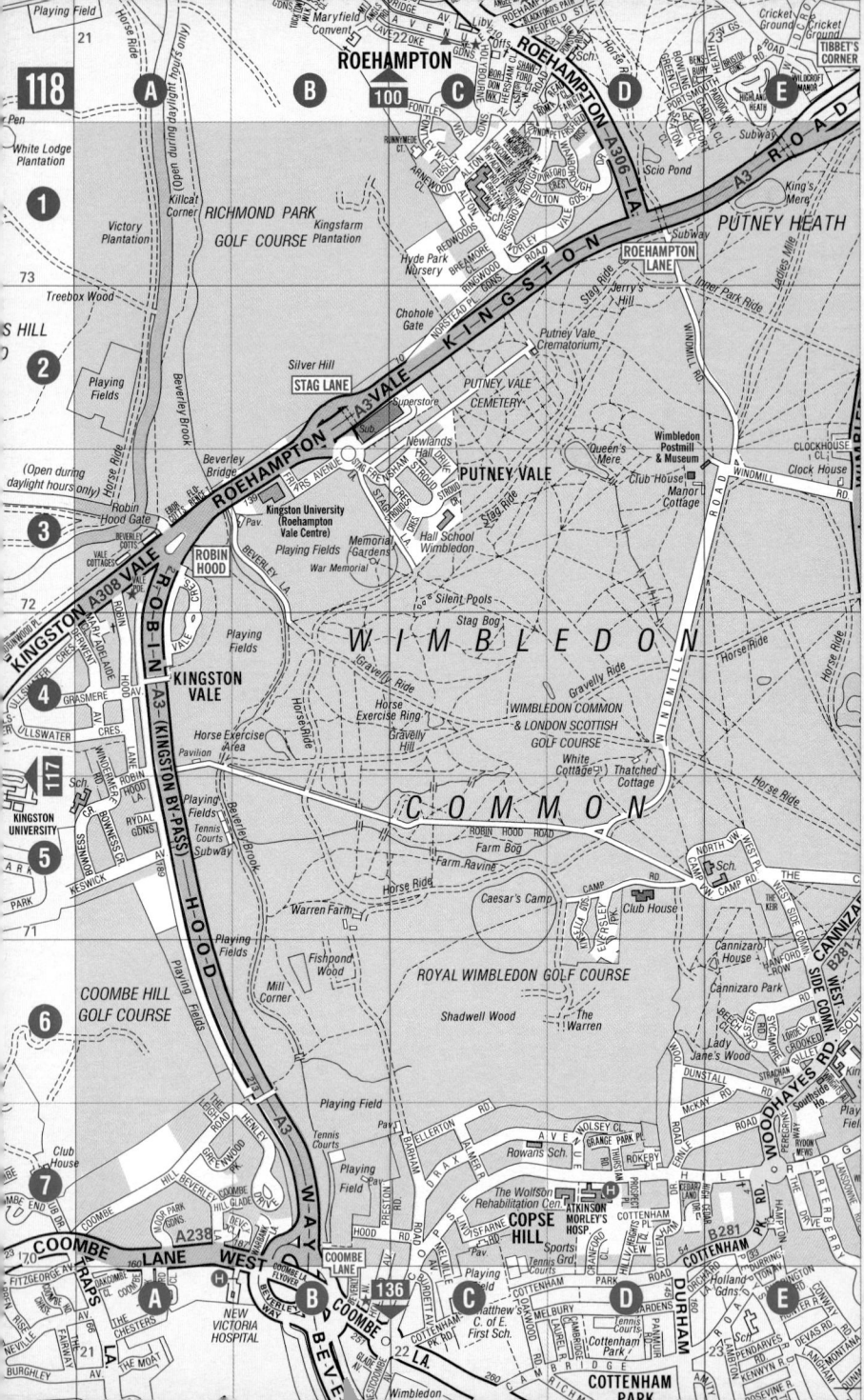

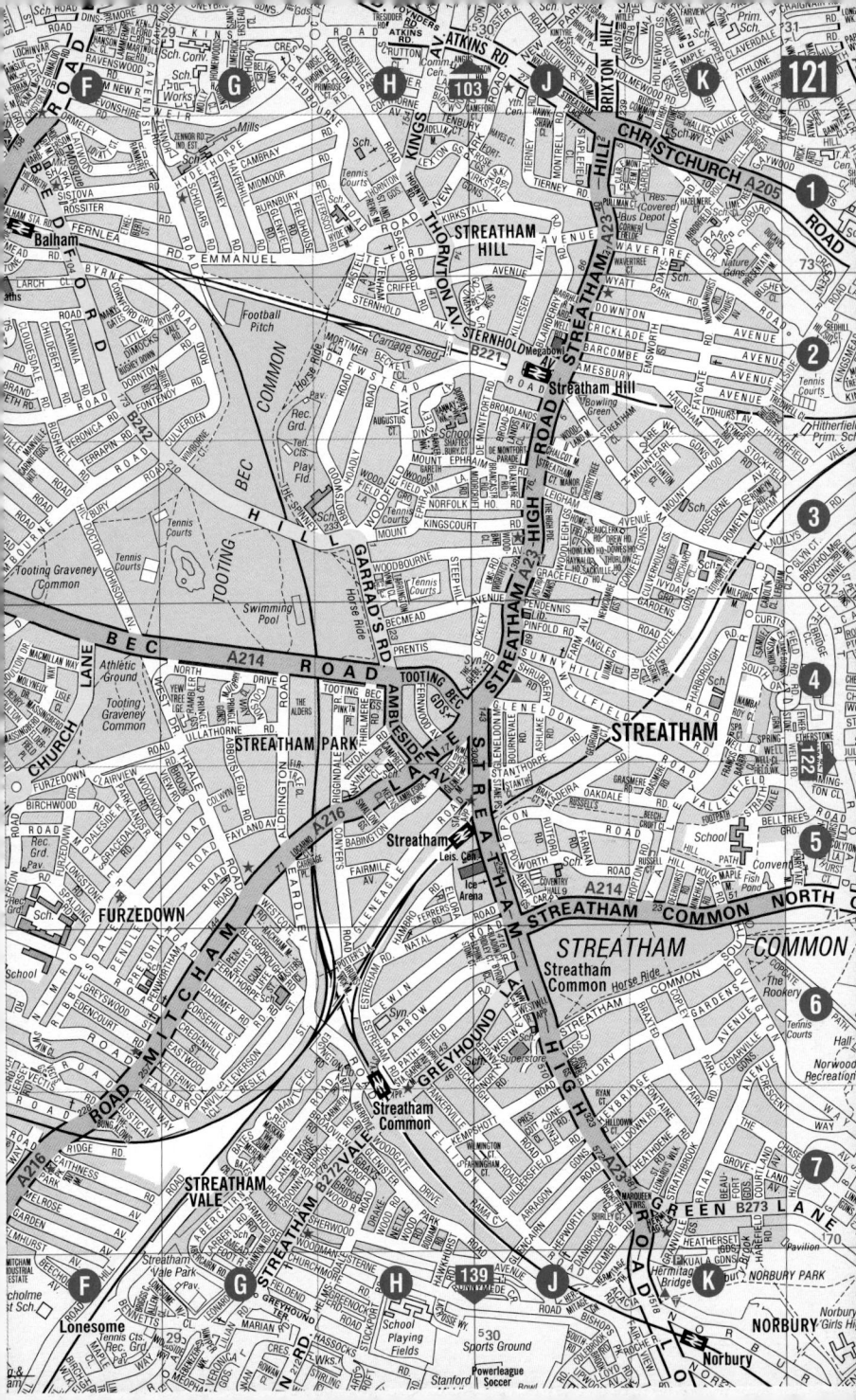

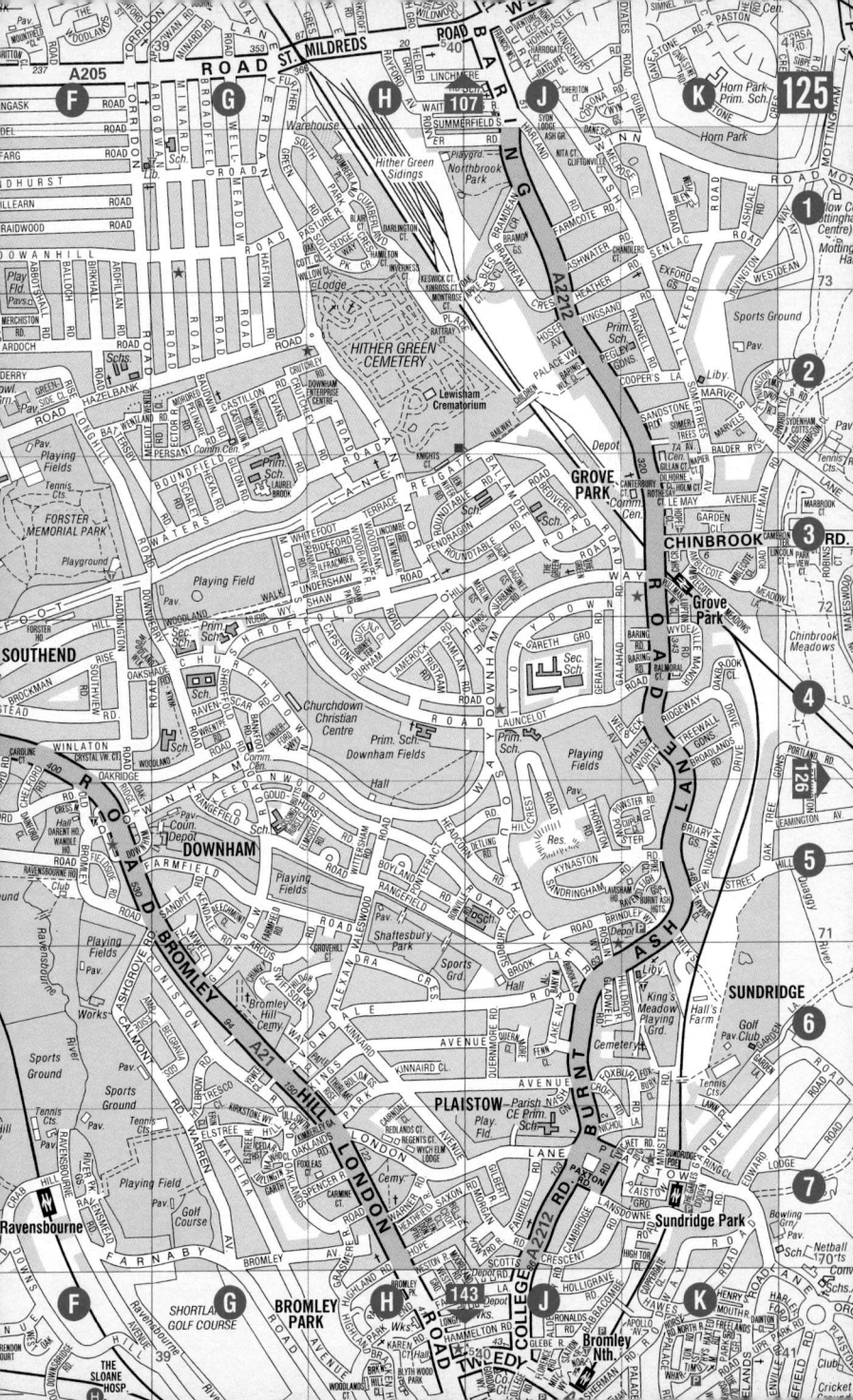

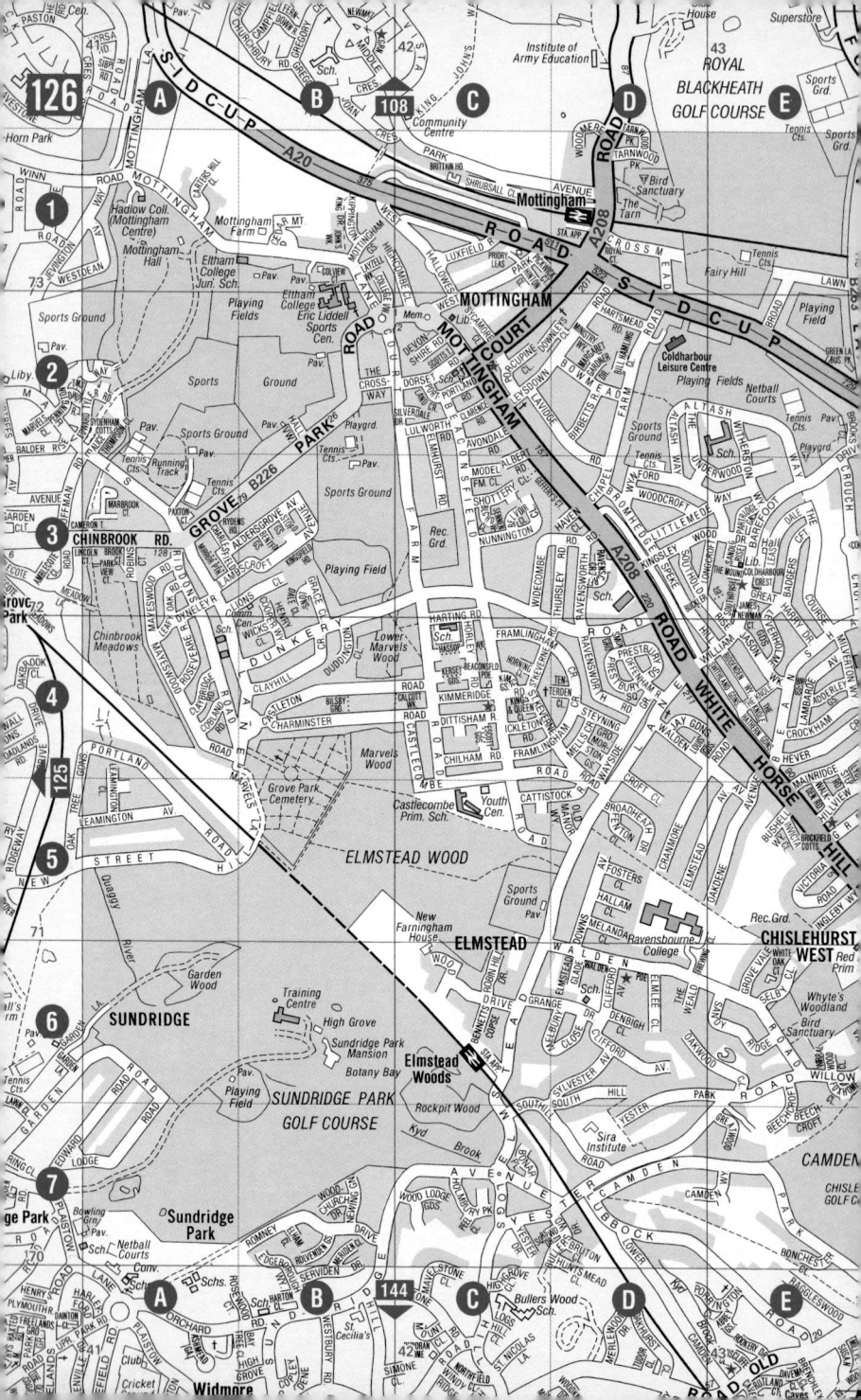

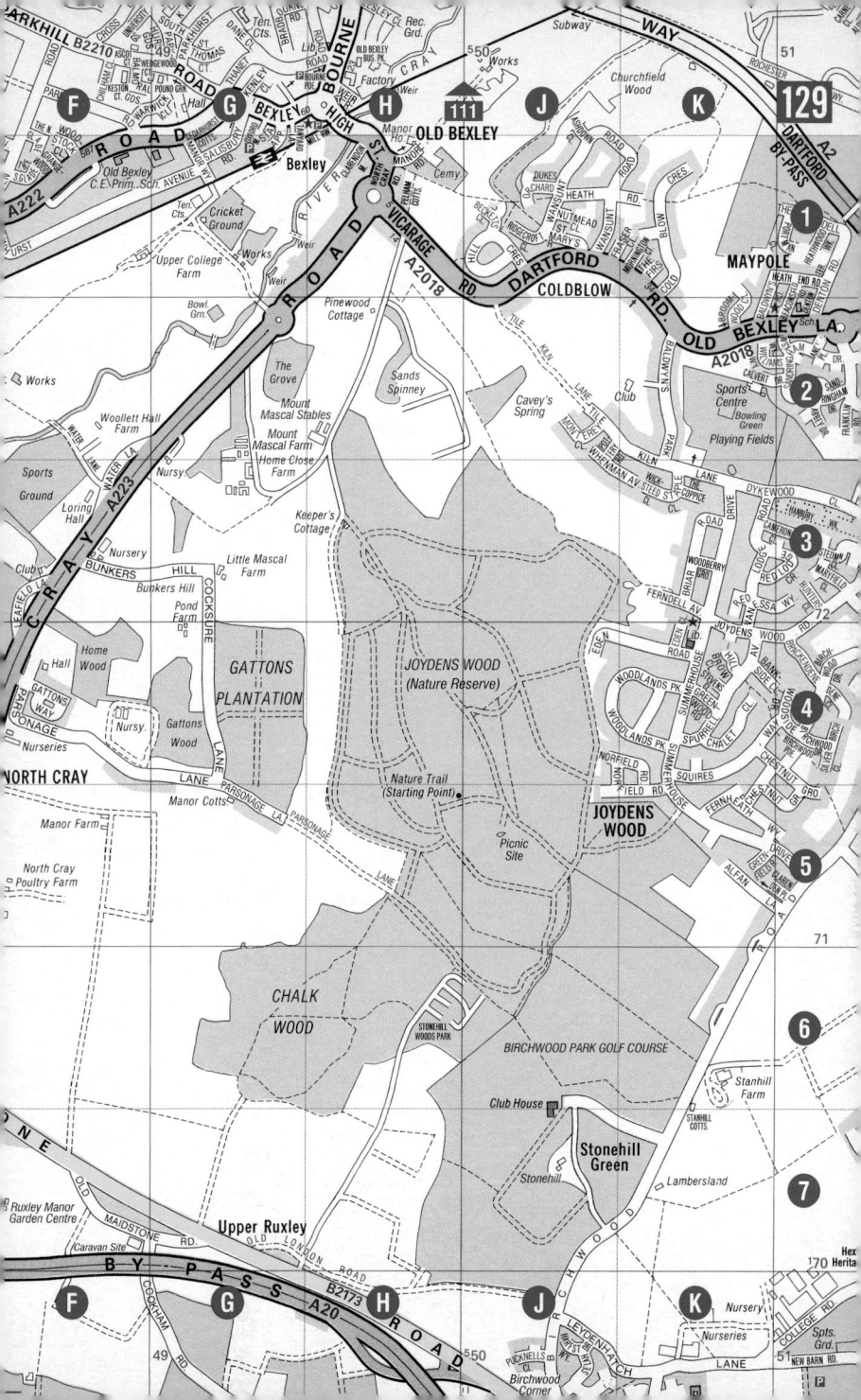

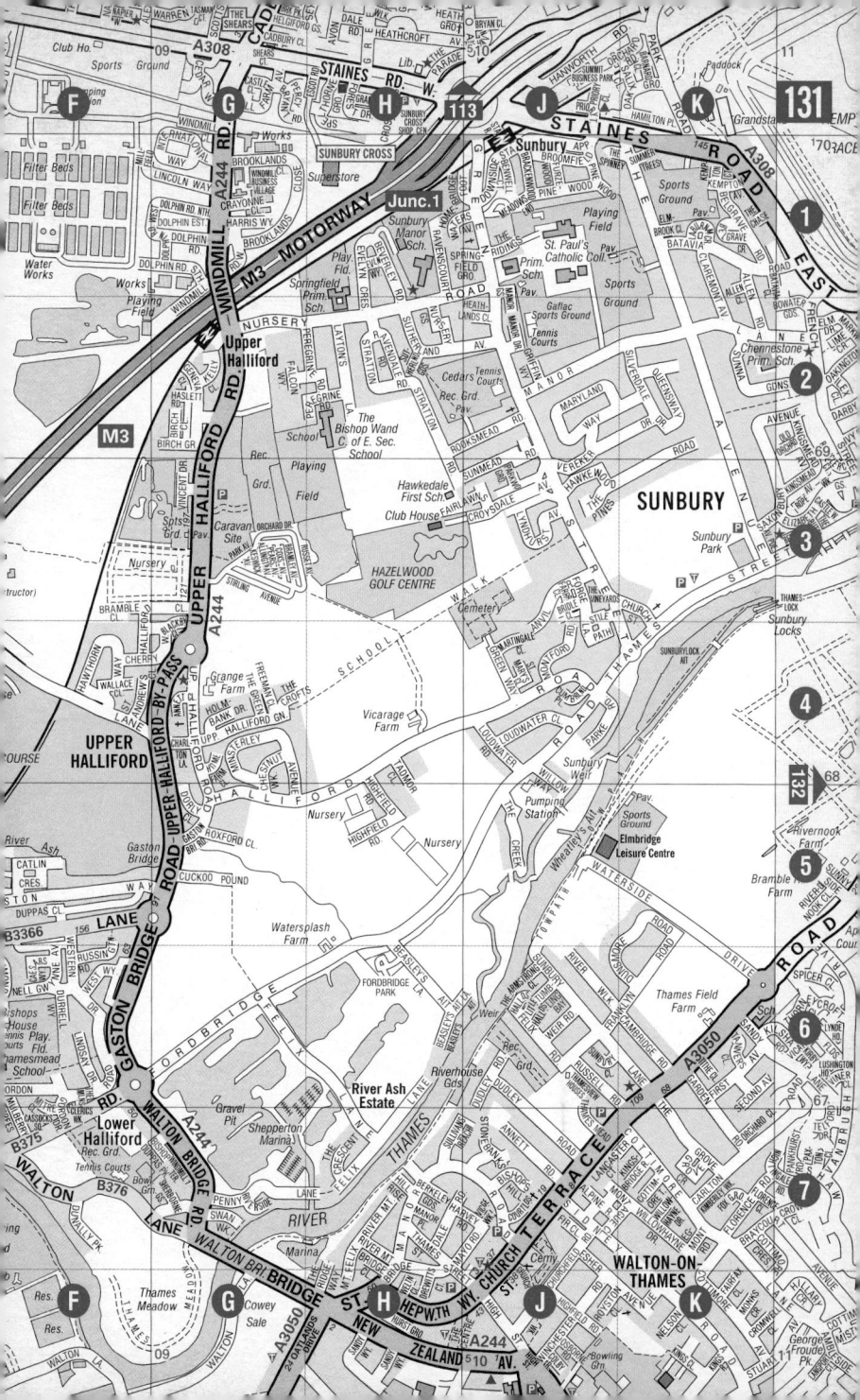

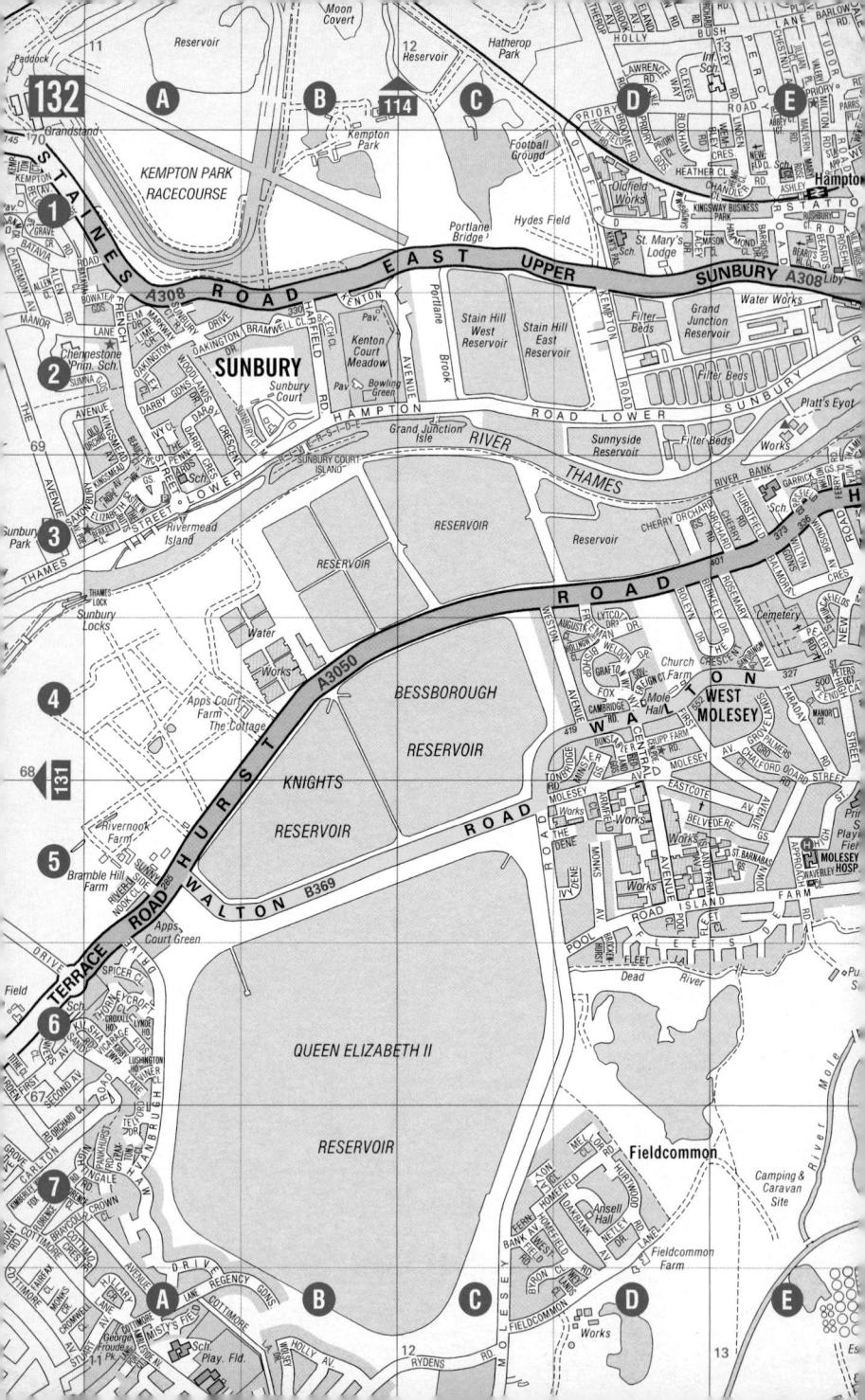

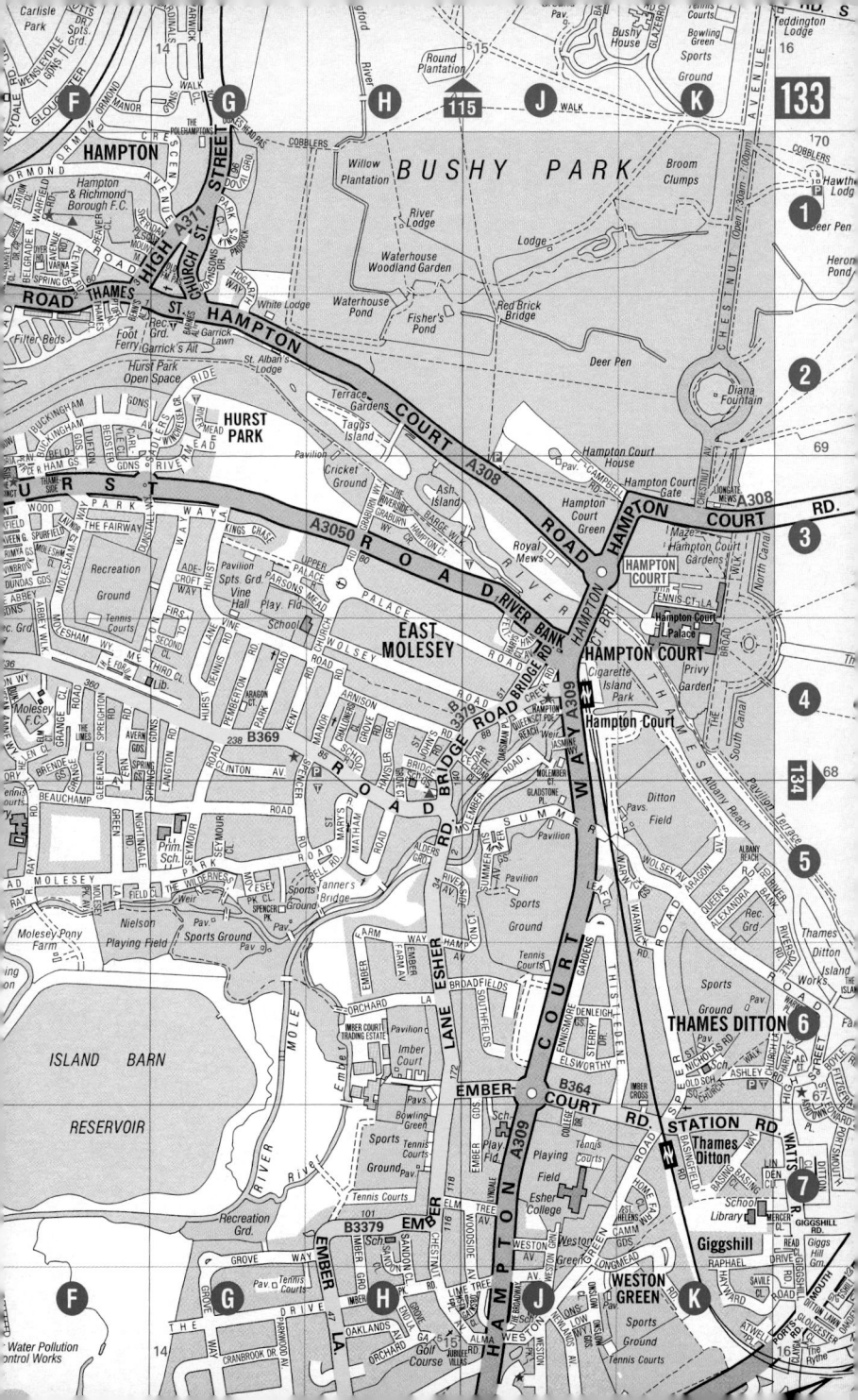

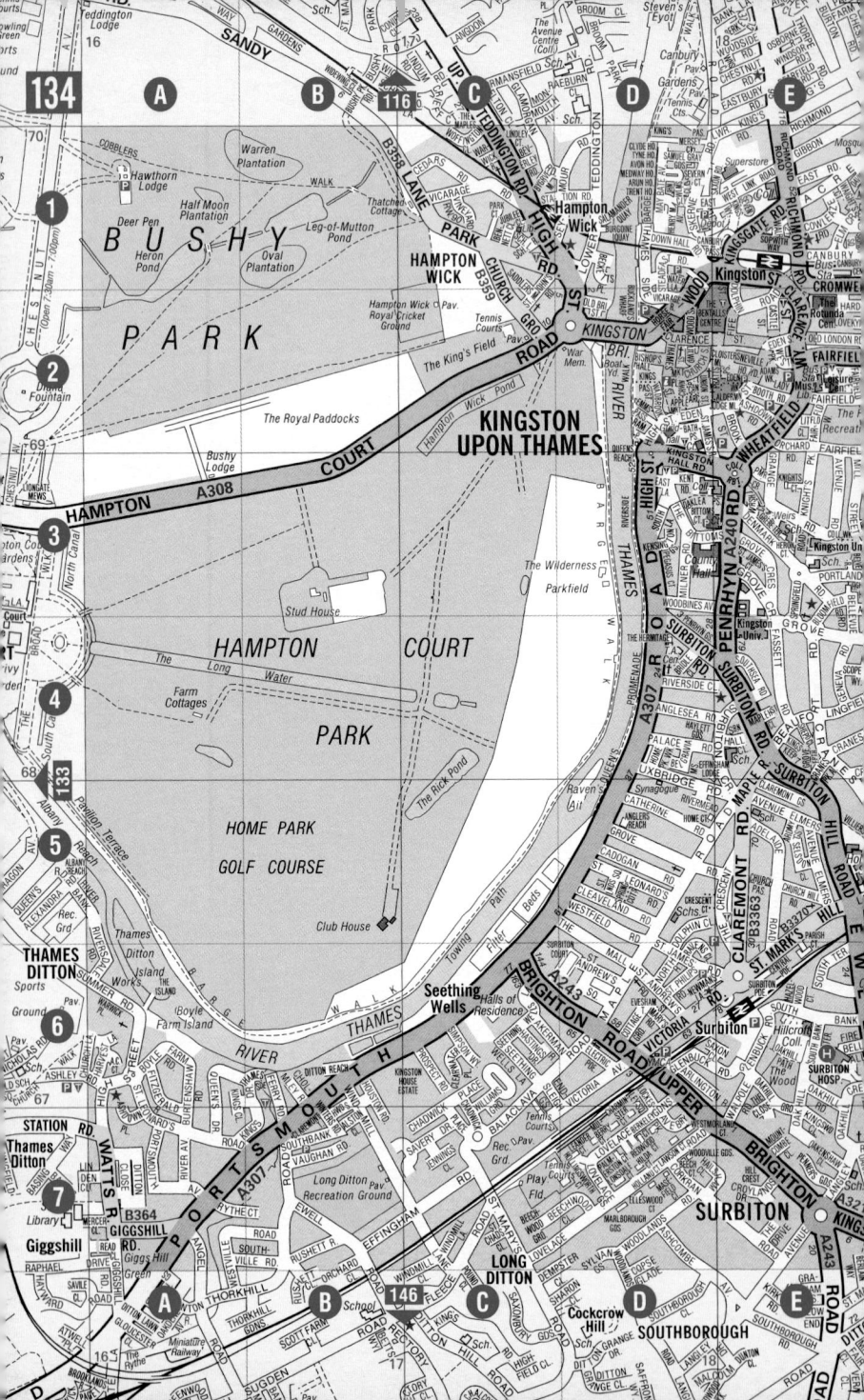

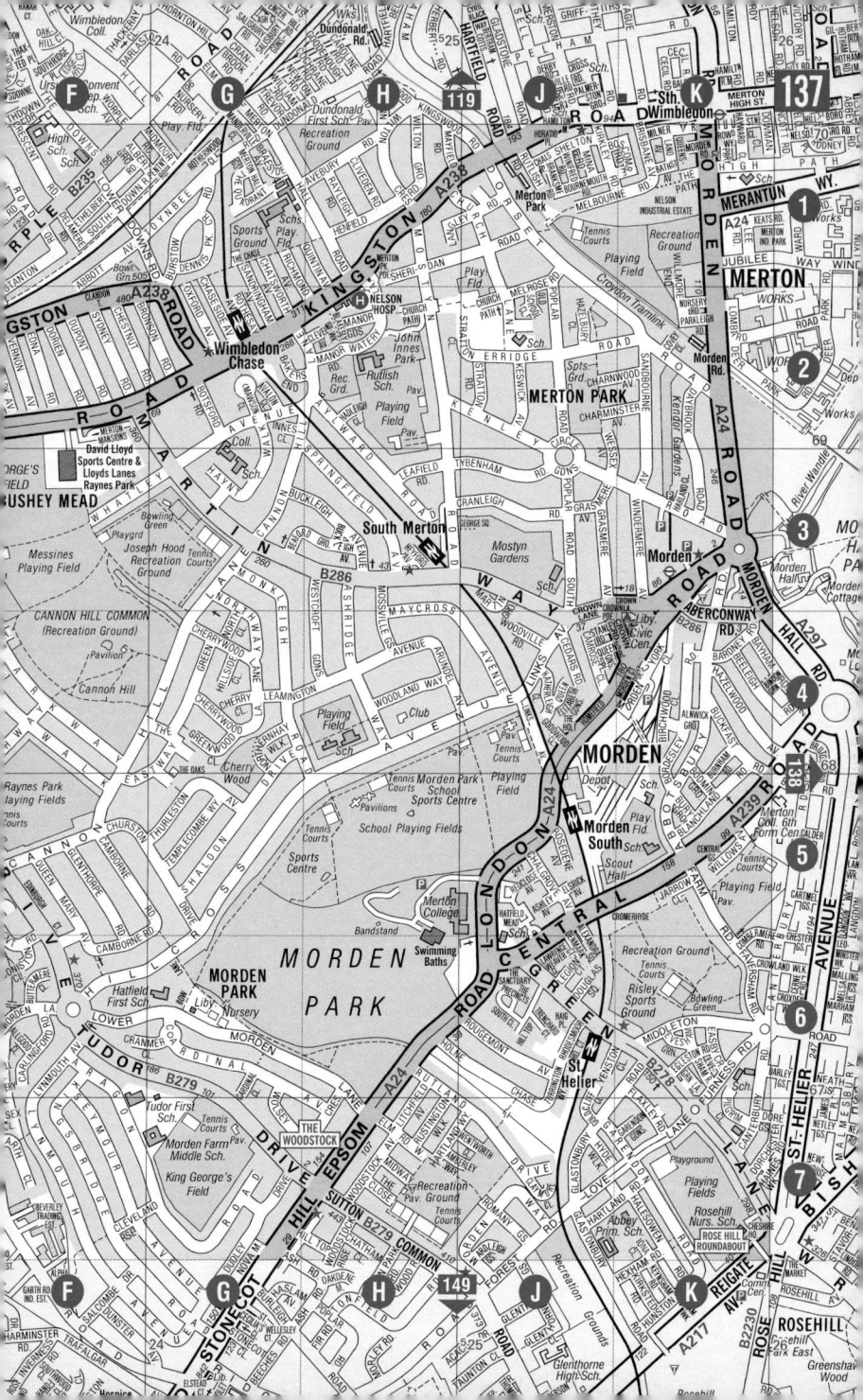

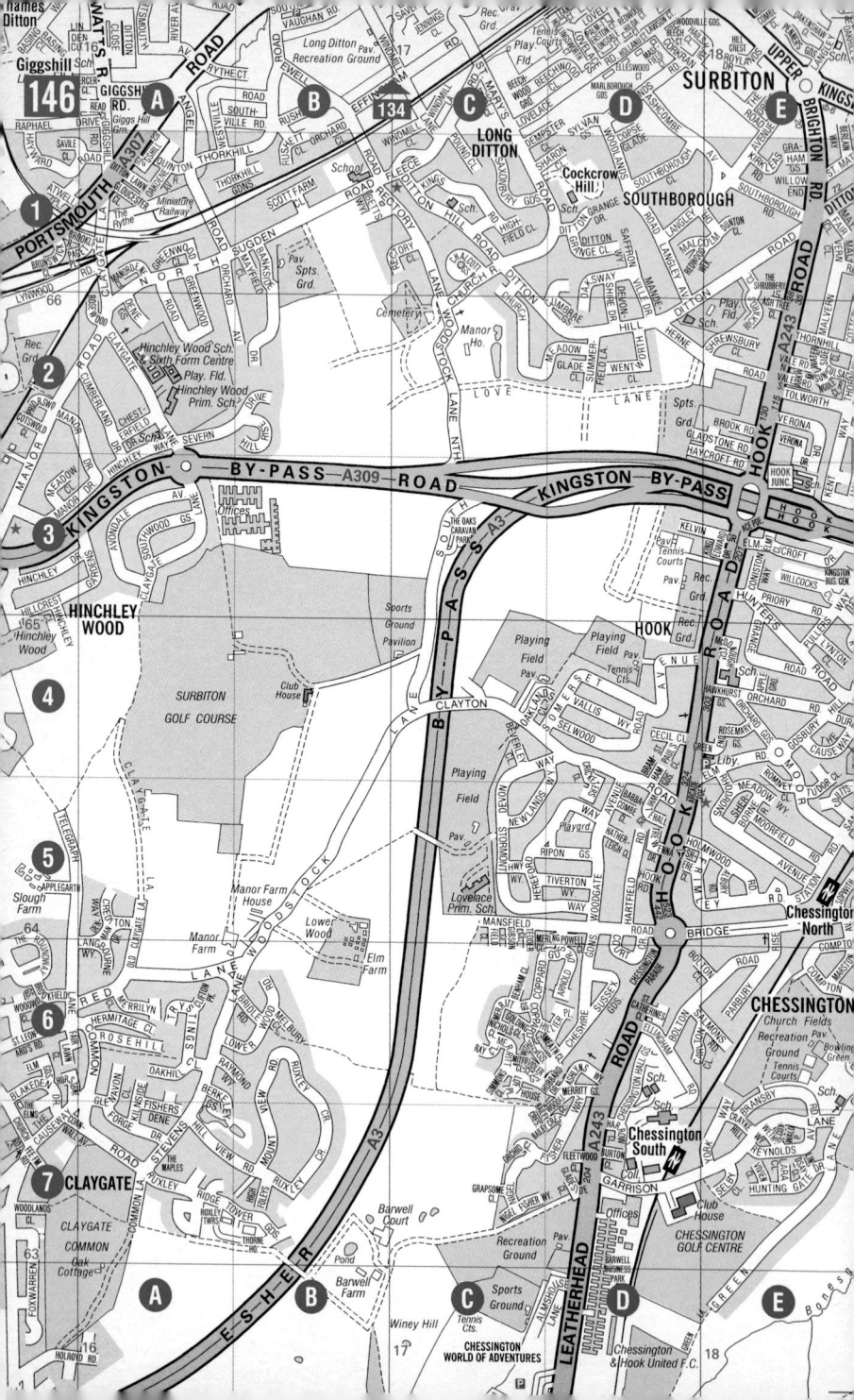

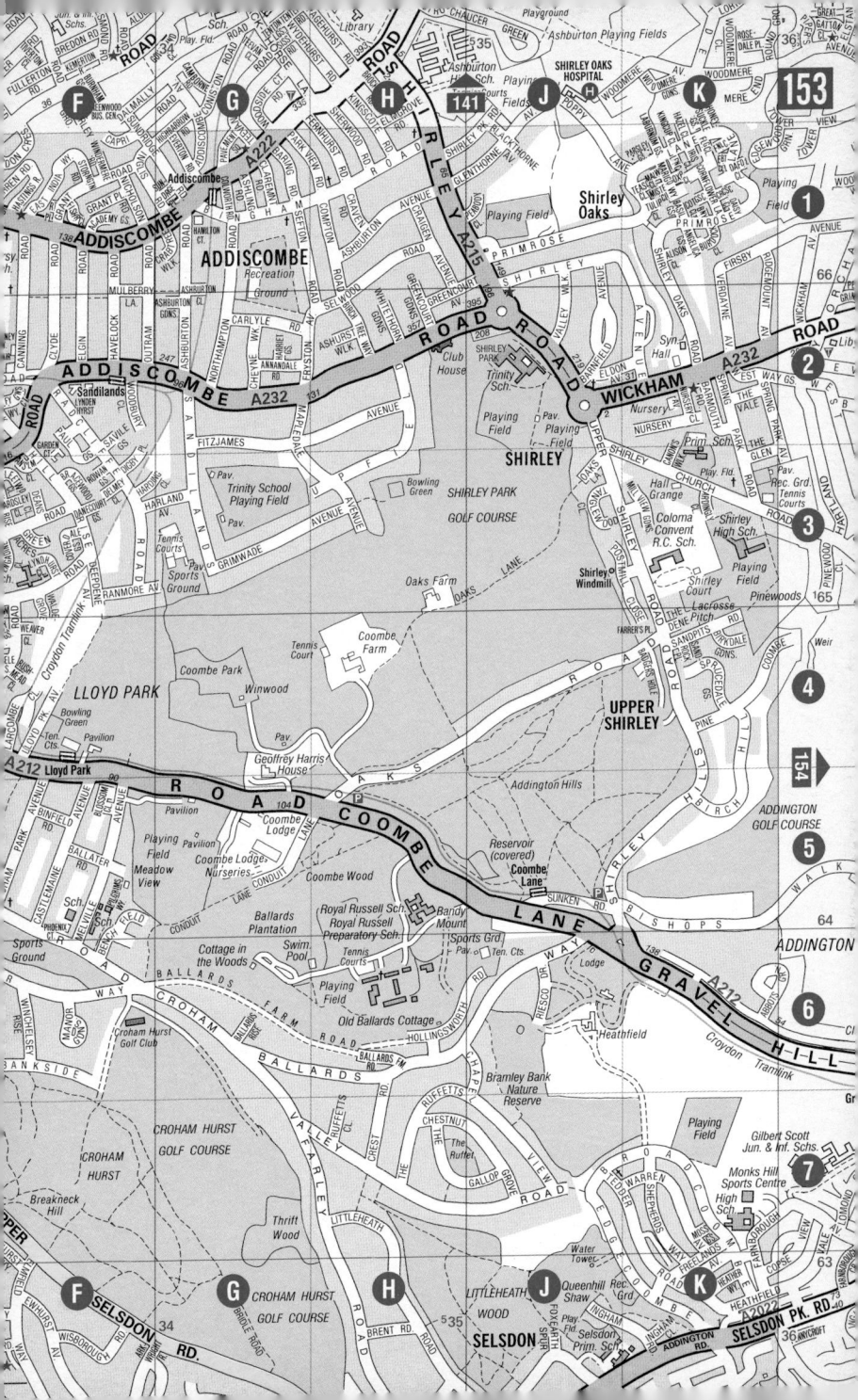

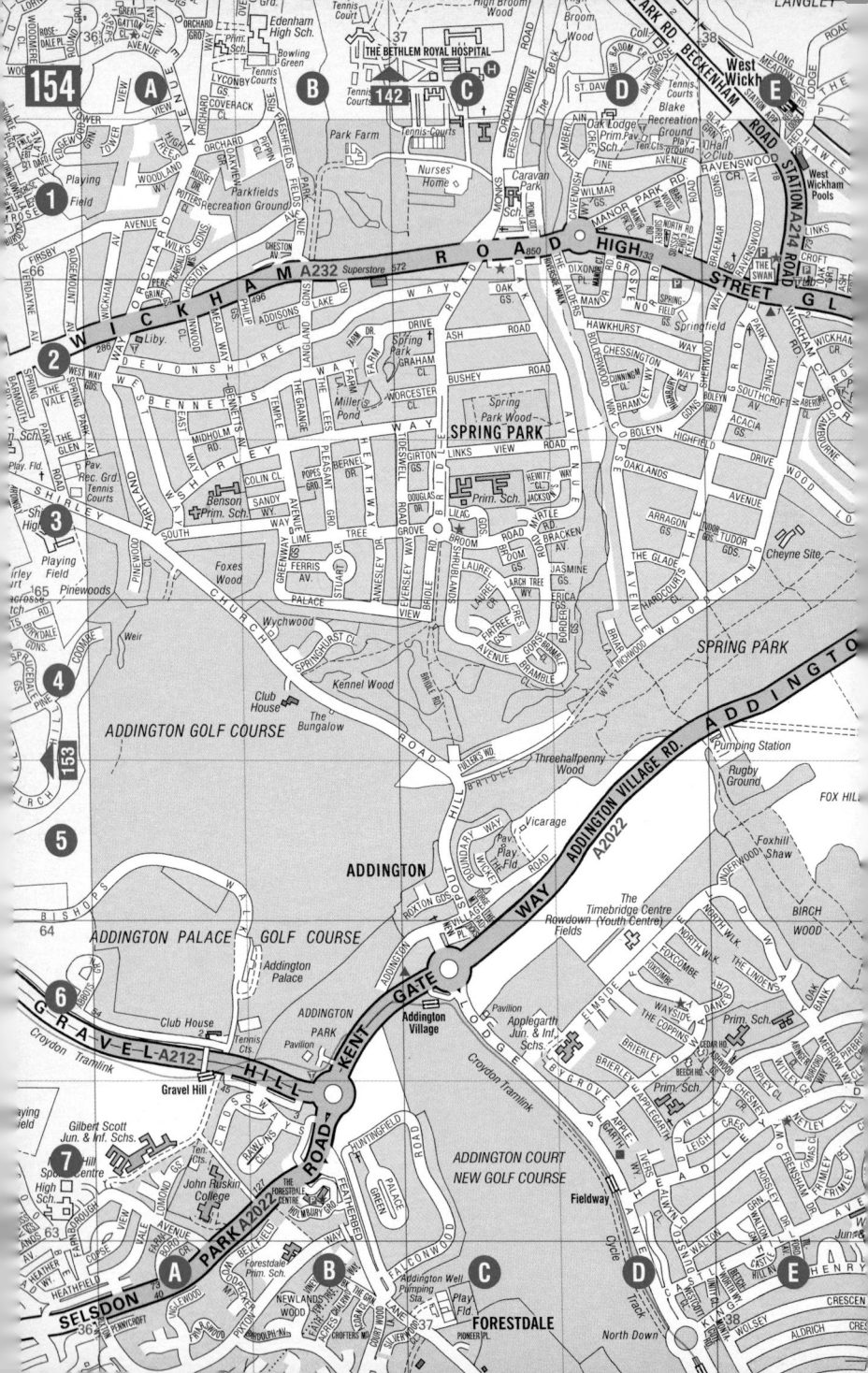

SUPER SCALE SECTION

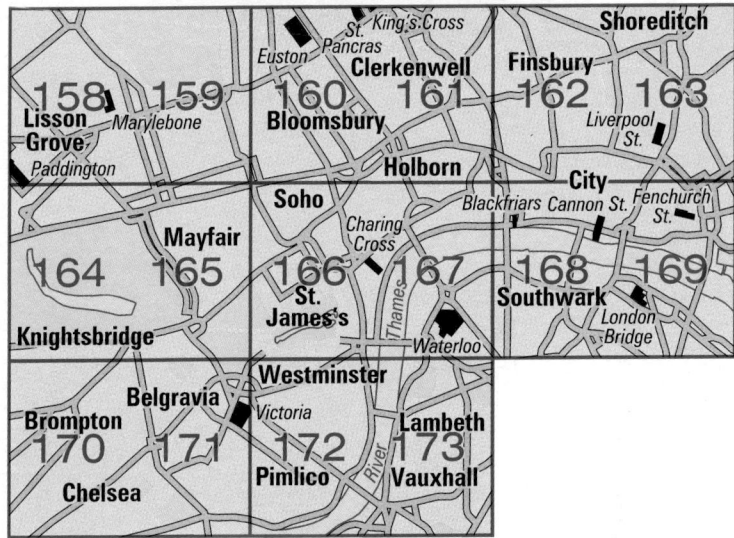

REFERENCE

A Road	A41
B Road	B524
Dual Carriageway	
One Way Street Traffic flow on A Roads is indicated by a heavy line on the drivers' left.	→
B' road / Minor road	→
House Numbers A & B Roads only	37 20 3 14
Restricted Access	
Pedestrianized Road	
Footpath	
Residential Walkway	
Congestion Charging Zone	● ● ●
National Rail Network	⇌
Docklands Light Railway	DLR
Underground Station	⊖ is the registered trade mark of Transport for London

Page Continuation	Large Scale Map Pages 166 66
Car Park Selected	P
Church or Chapel	†
Fire Station	■
Information Centre	🅸
National Grid Reference	527
Police Station	▲
Post Office	★
Toilet	▽
with facilities for the Disabled	▽
Educational Establishment	
Hospital or Hospice	
Industrial Building	
Leisure or Recreational Facility	
Place of Interest Open to the Public	
Public Building	
Shopping Centre or Market	
Other Selected Building	

SCALE

5¾ inches to 1 mile   **1:11000**   **9.1cm to 1km**

0 50 100 200 300 Yards ¼   ½ Mile

0 50 100 200 300 400 500   750 Metres   1 Kilometre

158

ST. JOHN'S WOOD

A · **B** · 66 · **C** · **D** · **E**

NEVILLE CT.
HOSPICE
BARBARA BROSNAN CT.
CONVENT
ABBEY RD.
GROVE END RD.
CAVENDISH AV.
WELLINGTON RD.
DOCK CLINE
COCHRANE ST.
PRINCE ALBERT ROAD (Regent's Canal)
Sch.
ST. JOHN'S WD. HIGH
NEW ST.
GREENBERRY ST.
NORTH GATE

ABBEY HO.
183

1
HAMILTON GDNS.
HALL RD.
GROVE END RD.
SOUTH LODGE
ST. JOHN'S WOOD
CIRCUS RD.
CIRCUS LODGE
ELM TREE RD.
ELM TREE CT.
GROVE CT.
ELM TREE RD.
ADDISON CT.
CAVENDISH CL.
WELLINGTON AV.
A41
The Wellington Hospital
ST. JOHN'S WOOD CHURCH GARDENS
St. John's Wood Church Gardens
Media Centre
Winfield House

GROVE END RD.
HALL RD.
HAMILTON HO.
M.C.C. Cricket Mus. & Tours
Middlesex C.C.C. & Marylebone C.C. (Lord's)
WOOD ROAD
PARK
London Central Mosque
Playground

2
ASCOT CT.
MELINA CT.
SCOTT ELLIS GDNS.
GROVE END HO.
STOREY CT.
TEMPLAR CT.
HAMILTON TERRACE
A5205
PAVILION
LORDS VW.
OAK TREE RD.
BLAZER CT.
LORDS
42
NORTH BANK
REGENT CT.
GROVE GDNS.
113
LORNE CT.
HANOVER GATE
ABBEY LODGE
HANOVER TER.
KENT TER.
Children's Boating Pond

3
ADA CT.
RODNEY CT.
NORTHWICK CT.
ST. JOHN'S
PINNER CT.
NORTH WICK CL.
CUNNINGHAM PL.
HENDERSON DR.
POLLITT DR.
CAPLAND STREET
VICTORIA-PAS
Grand Union
TICKFORD HO.
SIMPSON HO.
HUGHENDEN HO.
COTTESLOE HO.
VERNEY HO.
SWAIN ST.
FROME CT.
MISSENDEN
GRENDON HO.
CHETWODE HO.
BERNHARD CRES.
BERNARD HO.
RESHAM CRES.
PAVELEY STREET
ALPHA CT.
PALGRAVE GDS.
PRINCE REGENTS GATE
ROSSMORE CT.
Royal Coll. of Obstetricians & Gynaecologists
ROSSMORE ROAD
London Business Sch

CLIFTON RD.
BROWNING CL.
CLARENDON
BLOMFIELD RD.
MAIDA
CLIFTON CT.
ABERDEEN PL.
LYONS PL.
FISHERTON ST.
RICHARDSON ST.
EDGWARE
ORCHARDSON ST.
PENFOLD ST.
FRAMPTON ST.
HATTON ST.
TADEMA HO.
EASTLAKE HO.
DICKENS HO.
GIBBON HO.
JORDANS ST.
CAPLAND ST.
SAMFORD ST.
Coll.
GATEFORTH ST.
CHERWELL HO.
SALISBURY
MILNE ST.
WHITEHAM ST.
PLYMPTON
ASHBRIDGE
ALPHA HO.
KIMBLE HO.
BROADLEY ST.
HAREWOOD
ORCHAM GATE
SCH. & CYT.
HAYES
MORDEN HO.
LASCELLES HO.
FARNHAM HO.
BLAND FORD SQ.
IVOR
SCH.
TAUNTON
BALCOMBE
LINHOPE ST.
BOSTON PL.
DORSET
TAUNTON PL.
MELCOMBE
BALCOMBE ST.
CENTRAL

4
PARSONS HO.
COMPTON HA.
HETHPOOL HO.
CITHARA ST.
BOSCOBEL
ROSENDALE'S
CHURCH STREET ESTATE
LISSON GROVE
BROADLEY GDNS.
ASHMILL ST.
SHROTON ST.
DAVENTRY ST.
BENDALL ST.
HARROWS
SCH.
HIGHWORTH
MAY CL.
SHERINGHAM ST.
MARYLEBONE
Hosp.
HARWOOD ROW
HARWOOD Hosp.
WALMER
WYNDHAM
KNOX ST.
YORK ST.
CRANFIELD PL.

5
PARK PL.
HOW-LEY PL.
JOHN AIRD CT.
ST. MARY'S MANS.
ST. MARY'S GDNS.
Sports Cen.
City of Westminster College
BRAITHWAITE HALL TWR.
HALL TWR.
FLEMING CT.
ST. MARY'S SQ.
PADDINGTON GN.
NEWCASTLE PL.
EDGWARE RD.
BOURNE
LISSON
ARANSON ST.
PENFOLD ST.
B507
SCH.
CHAPEL ST.
HOMER ST.
SEPT. ST.
HARCOURT ST.
LIBERT
VIRGIL PL.
MELCOMBE
WALMER
WYNDHAM
YORK ST.

6
BISHOP'S BRI. RD.
HERMITAGE ST.
DUDLEY ST.
SCH.
NORTH WHARF
HARROW ROAD
WESTWAY A40 MARYLEBONE FLY-OVER A501 MARYLEBONE RD.
HARROW ROAD
Sub.
HARBET
PADDINGTON BASIN
STREET
CHAPEL ST.
HOMER RW.
CRAWFORD
WATSON'S
SHOULDHAM
BELL ST.
246
CRAWFORD ST.
Seymour Leisure Cen.
BRYANSTON
WYNDHAM PL.

7
PADDINGTON
EASTBOURNE T.
CHILWORTH ST.
PRAED STREET
SOUTH WHARF ROAD
St. Mary's Hosp.
Med. Sch.
Mus.
WINSLAND ST.
LONDON ST.
NORFOLK SQUARE
A4205 PRAED ST.
ST. MICHAEL'S
STAR ST.
SOUTHWICK ST.
A4209 SUSSEX GARDENS
ST. MICHAEL'S
BANKSIDE CALL
THE QUADRANGLE
SOUTHWICK
NORFOLK CRES.
NORFOLK PL.
THE WATER GARDENS
CAMBRIDGE SQUARE
BURWOOD PL.
PARK WEST
PARK WEST PL.
CATO ST.
BRENDON ST.
HARROWBY
NUTFORD PL.
EASTLEIGH PL.
FURSECROFT
CUMBERLAND MANSIONS
MOLYNEUX ST.
BROWN ST.
BRYANSTON
GLEN-STON M.

A · **B** · 164 · **C** · **D** · **E**

SUSSEX
CHILWORTH ST.
GLOUCESTER
CONDUIT
SPRING ST.
TALBOT SQ.
RADNOR M.
137
327
SUSSEX SQUARE
DEVONPORT
SOME
OXFORD SQ.
STOURCLIFFE CL.
HYDE PK. CRES.
SWICK PL.
HYDE PK. GDNS.
KENDAL ST.
NORTH RISE
ARCH
CONNAUGHT ST.
ST GEORGE'S FLDS.
SEY-MOUR ST.
Syn.
BRYANSTON
SQUARE

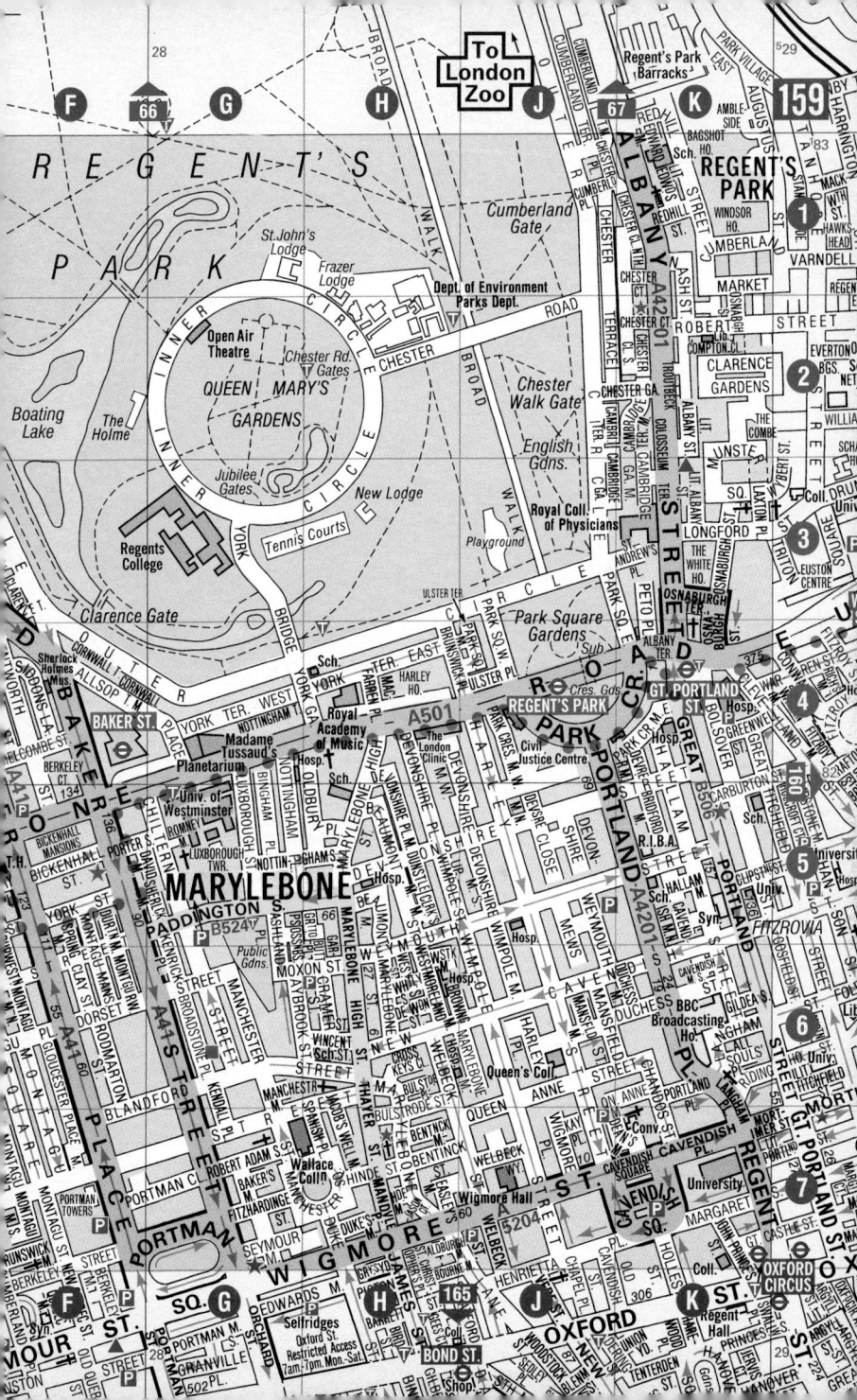

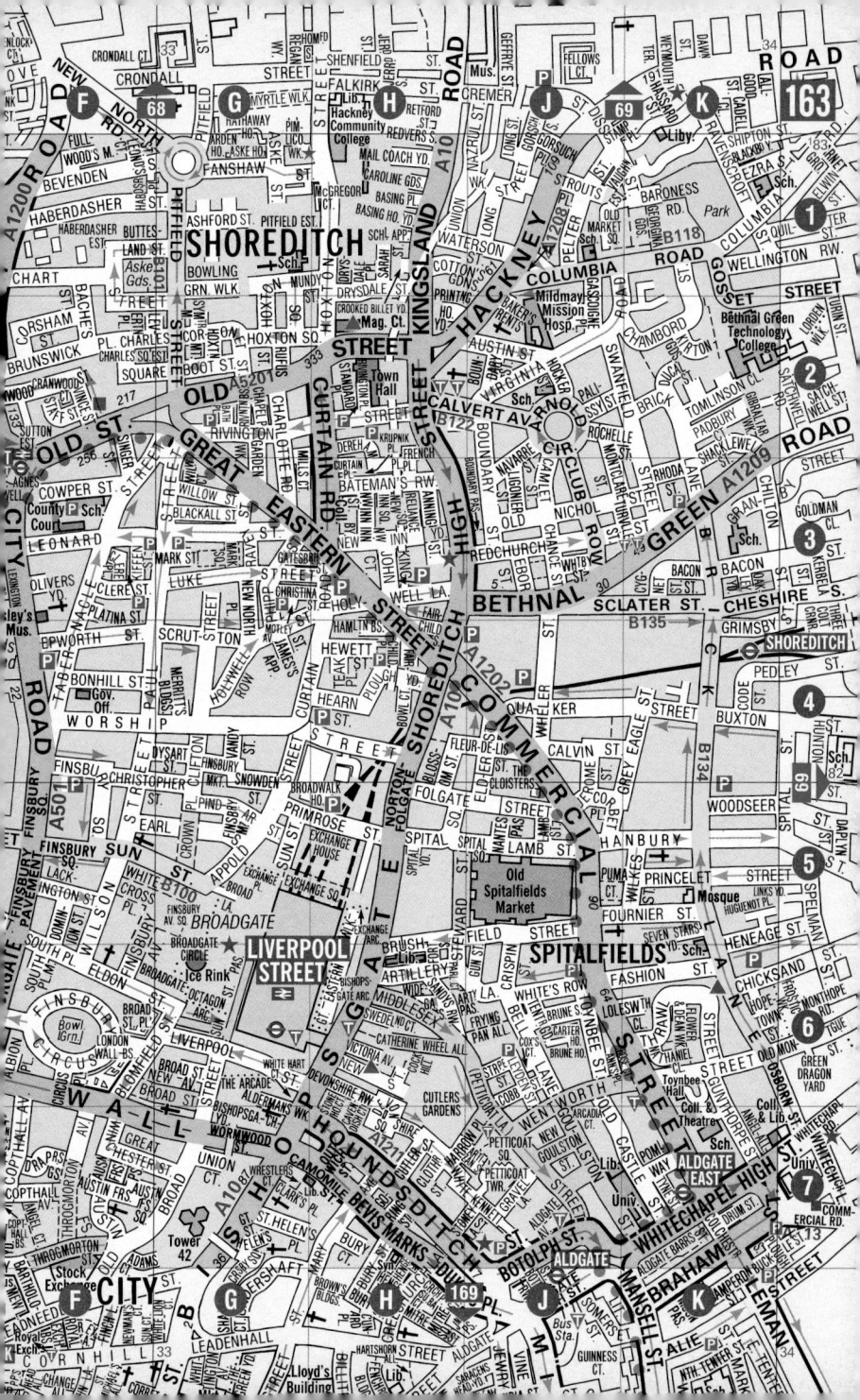

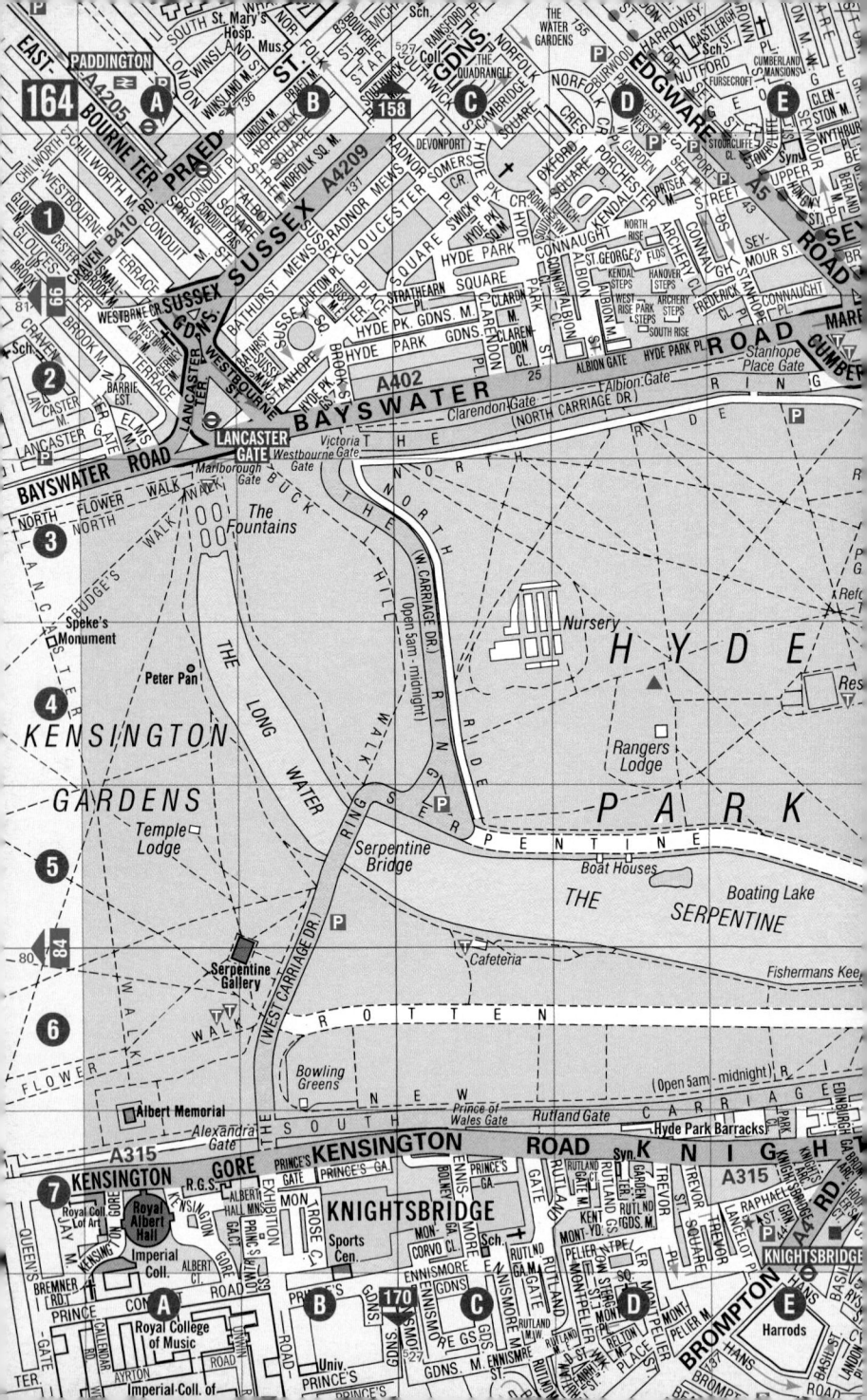

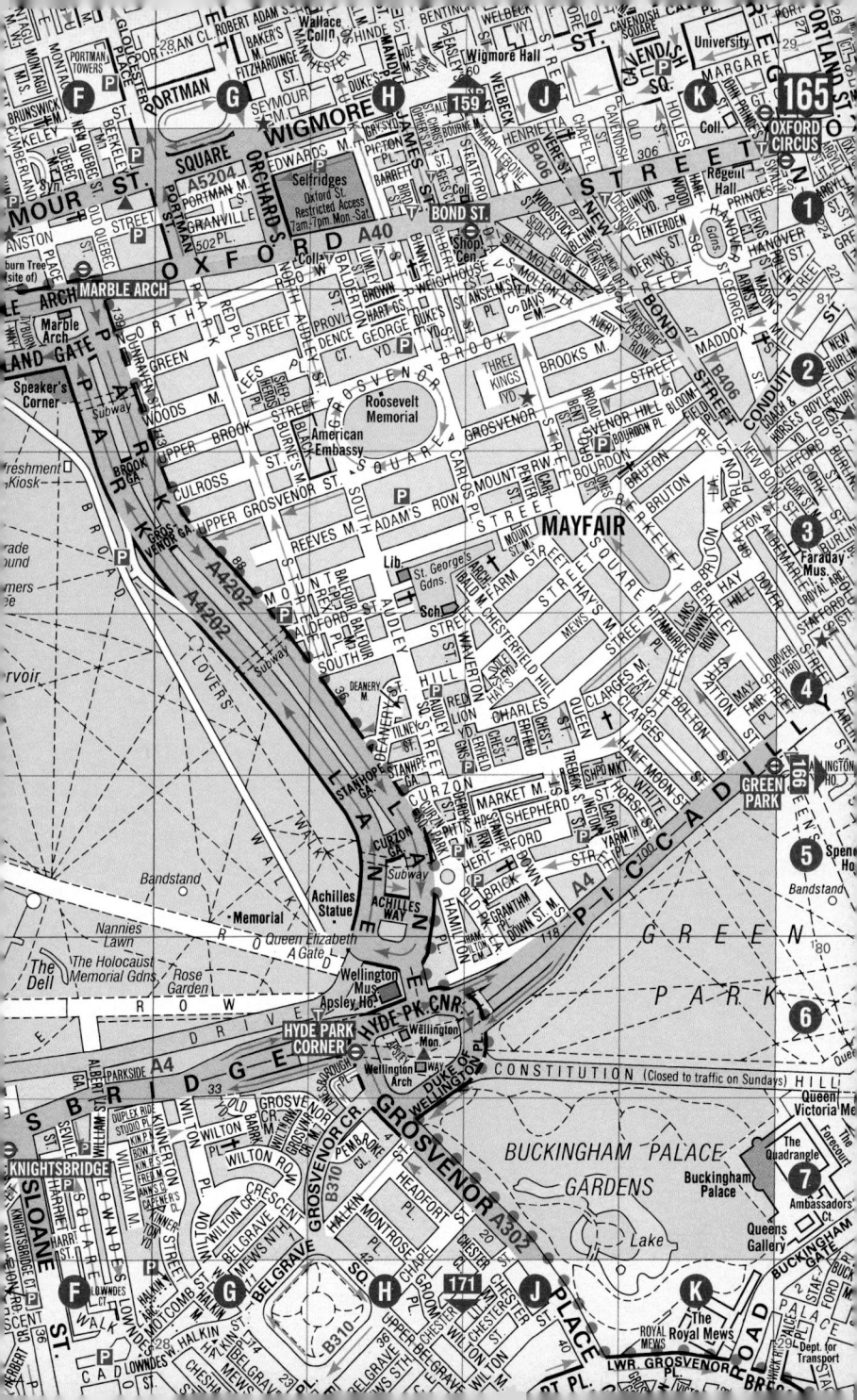

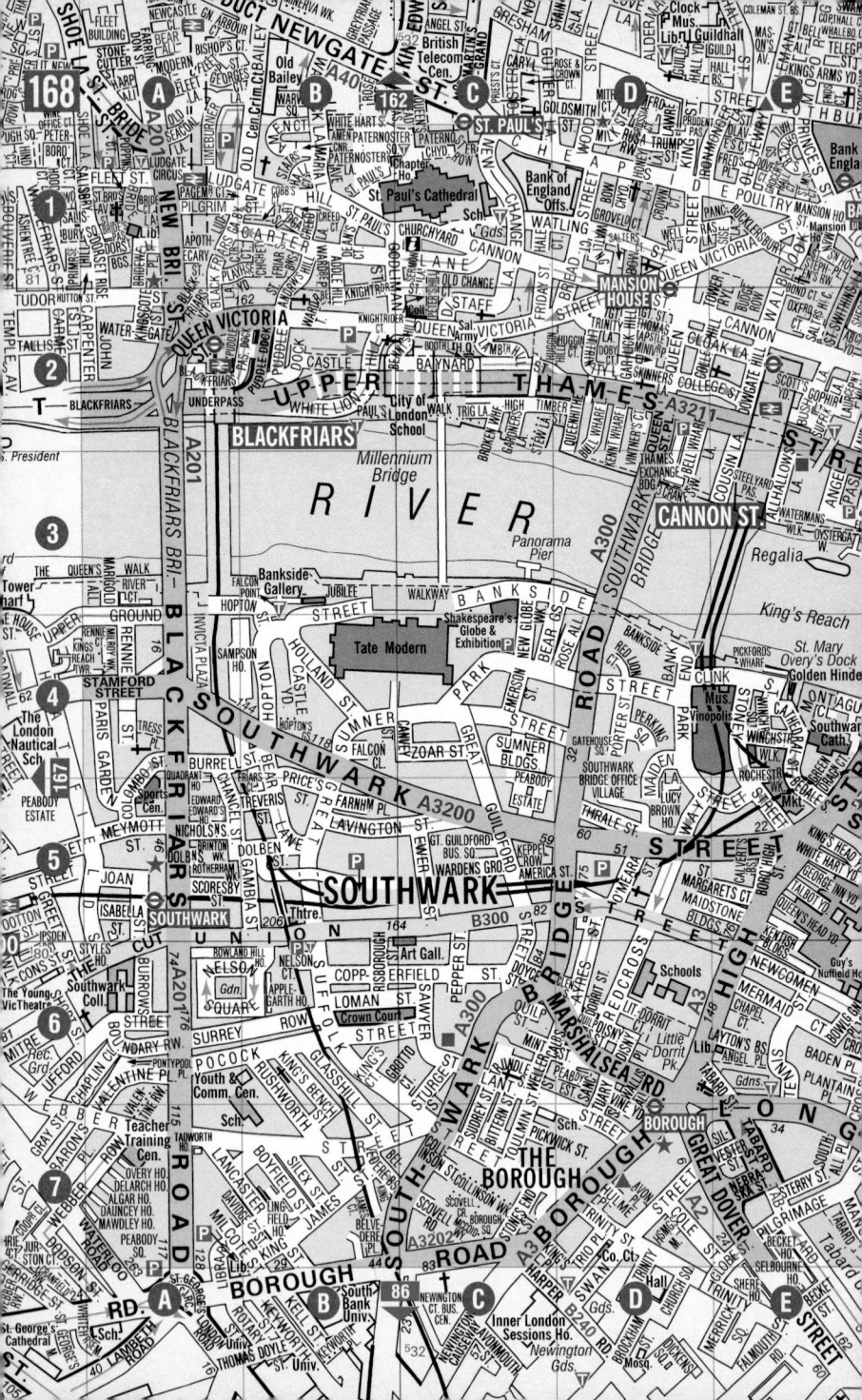

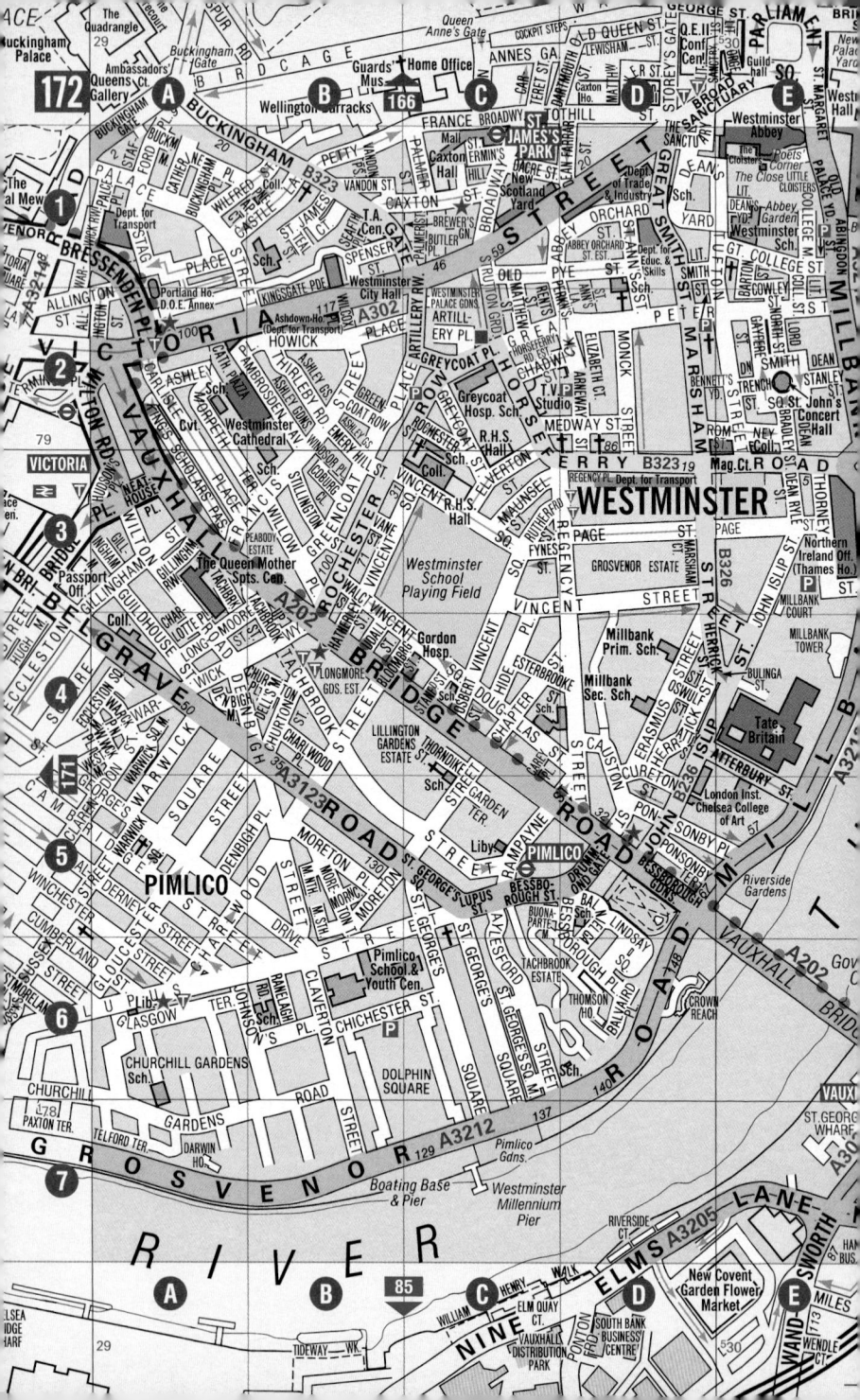

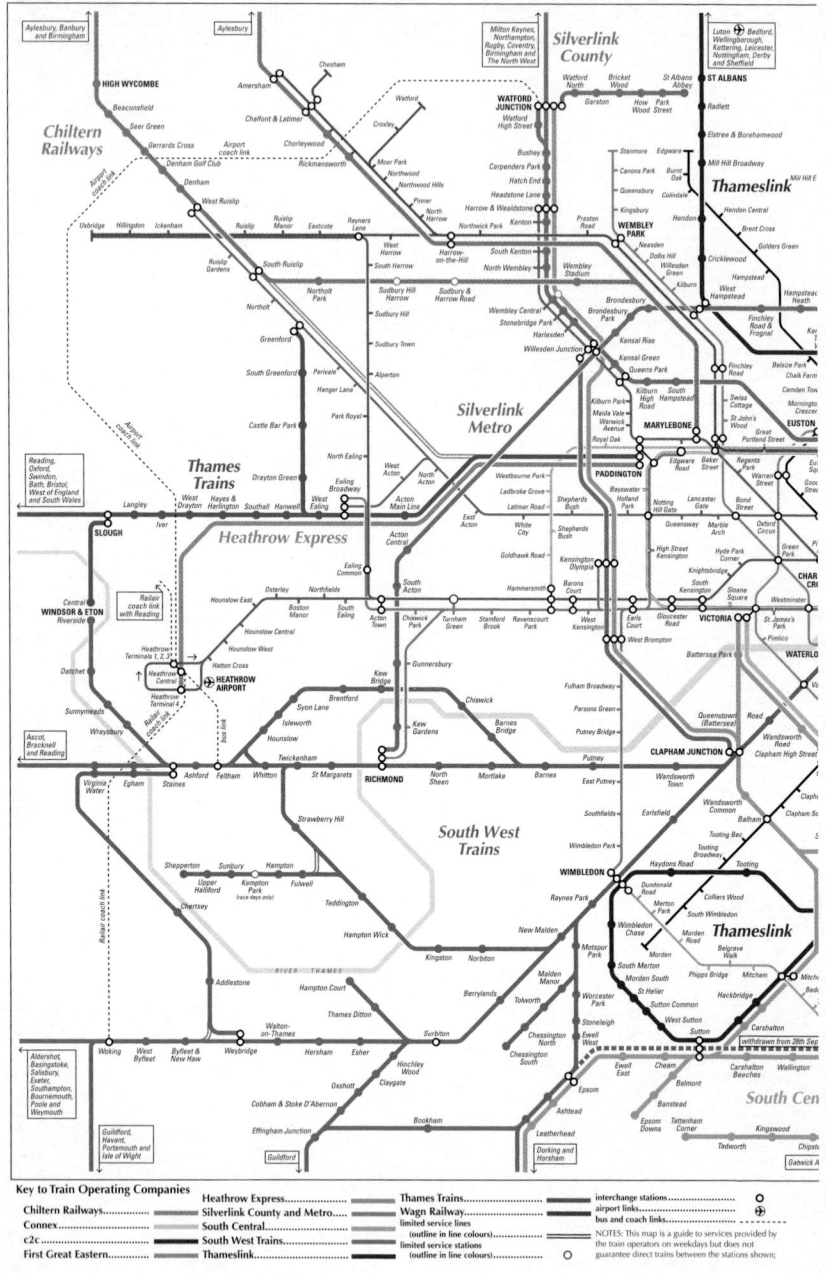

Key to Train Operating Companies

Chiltern Railways..............	Heathrow Express................
Connex............................	Silverlink County and Metro....
c2c................................	South Central...................
First Great Eastern.............	South West Trains...............
	Thameslink......................

Thames Trains..................	
Wagn Railway..................	
limited service lines	
(outline in line colours)	
limited service stations	
(outline in line colours)	

interchange stations...................... ○
airport links.............................. ✈
bus and coach links........................

NOTES: This map is a guide to services provided by
the train operators on weekdays but does not
guarantee direct trains between the stations shown;

174

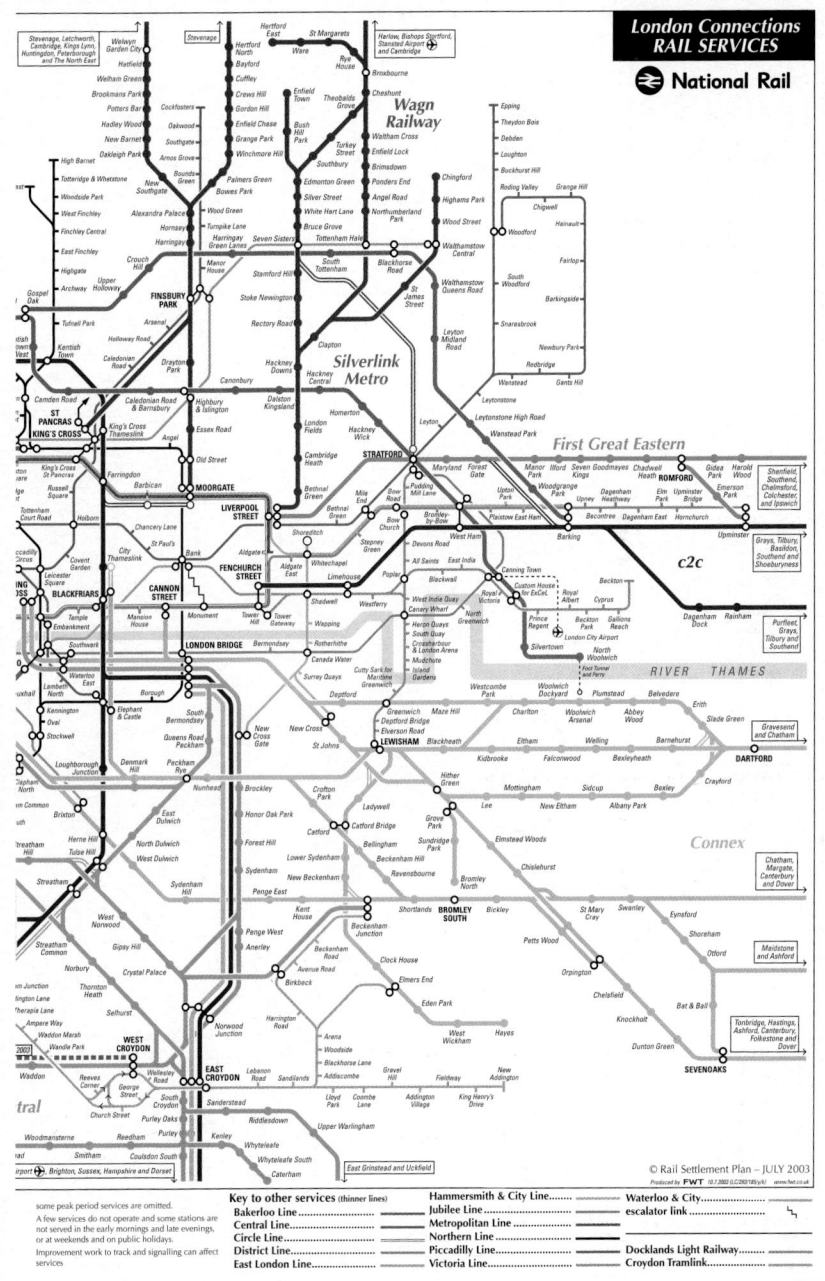

London Connections
RAIL SERVICES

National Rail

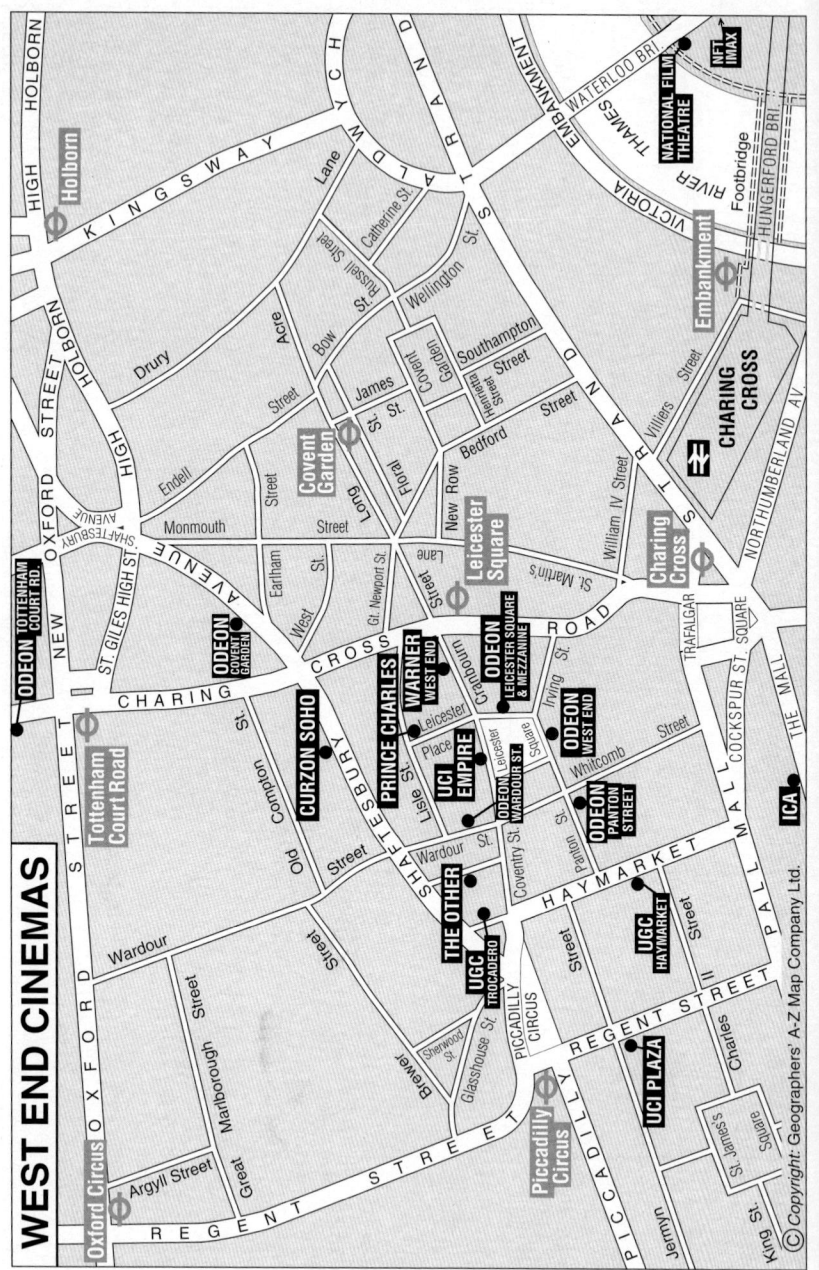

WEST END CINEMAS

Ⓟ Oxford Circus

Ⓟ Holborn

Ⓟ Tottenham Court Road

ⓅTottenham Court Rd.

ODEON TOTTENHAM COURT RD.

ODEON COVENT GARDEN

Ⓟ Covent Garden

CURZON SOHO

PRINCE CHARLES

WARNER WEST END

UCI EMPIRE

ODEON LEICESTER SQUARE & MEZZANINE

Leicester Square

ODEON Leicester Square WARDOUR ST.

ODEON WEST END

Ⓟ Charing Cross

≋ CHARING CROSS

Embankment

Ⓟ Embankment

NFT IMAX

NATIONAL FILM THEATRE

THE OTHER

UGC TROCADERO

ODEON PANTON STREET

UGC HAYMARKET

ICA

Ⓟ Piccadilly Circus

UCI PLAZA

© Copyright: Geographers' A-Z Map Company Ltd.

176

WEST END THEATRES

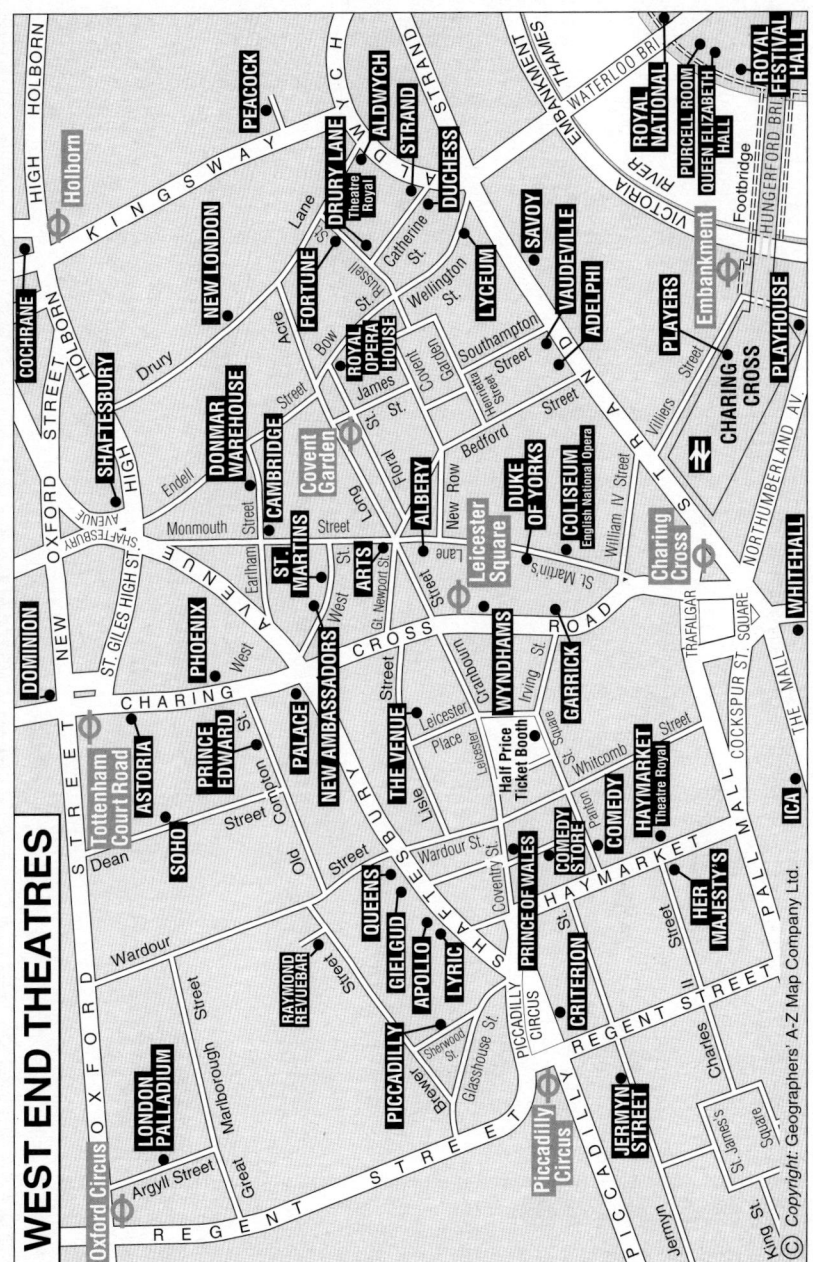

INDEX

Including Streets, Places & Areas, Industrial Estates, Selected Flats & Walkways,
Junction Names and Selected Places of Interest.

HOW TO USE THIS INDEX

1. Each street name is followed by its Postcode District (or, if outside the London Postcodes, by its Locality Abbreviation(s)) and then by its map reference;
e.g. **Aaron Hill Rd.** E6 . . . .5E **72** is in the E6 Postcode District and is to be found in square 5E on page **72**. The page number is shown in bold type.

2. A strict alphabetical order is followed in which Av., Rd., St., etc. (though abbreviated) are read in full and as part of the street name; e.g. **Abbots Grn.** appears after **Abbotsford Rd.** but before **Abbotshade Rd.**

3. Streets and a selection of flats and walkways too small to be shown on the maps, appear in the index with the thoroughfare to which it is connected shown in brackets;
e.g. **Abady Ho.** SW1 . . . .3D **172** (off Page St.)

4. Addresses that are in more than one part are referred to as not continuous.

5. Places and areas are shown in the index in **BOLD TYPE** and the map reference is to the actual map square in which the town centre or area is located and not to the place name shown on the map; e.g. **ABBEY WOOD** 4C **92**

6. An example of a selected place of interest is *Ainslie Wood Nature Reserve. . . .5J **19***

7. Junction names are shown in the index in Bold Type; e.g. Angel 2B **68**

8. Map references shown in brackets; e.g. **Abbey Orchard St.** SW1 . . . .3H **85** (1C **172**) refer to entries that also appear on the large scale pages **158-173**.

GENERAL ABBREVIATIONS

All. : Alley	**Cl.** : Close	**Gdns.** : Gardens	**Mdw.** : Meadow
App. : Approach	**Coll.** : College	**Gth.** : Garth	**Mdws.** : Meadows
Arc. : Arcade	**Comn.** : Common	**Ga.** : Gate	**M.** : Mews
Av. : Avenue	**Cnr.** : Corner	**Gt.** : Great	**Mt.** : Mount
Bk. : Back	**Cott.** : Cottage	**Grn.** : Green	**Mus.** : Museum
Blvd. : Boulevard	**Cotts.** : Cottages	**Gro.** : Grove	**Nth.** : North
Bri. : Bridge	**Ct.** : Court	**Hgts.** : Heights	**No.** : Number
B'way. : Broadway	**Cres.** : Crescent	**Ho.** : House	**Pal.** : Palace
Bldg. : Building	**Cft.** : Croft	**Ho's** : Houses	**Pde.** : Parade
Bldgs. : Buildings	**Dpt.** : Depot	**Ind.** : Industrial	**Pk.** : Park
Bungs. : Bungalows	**Dr.** : Drive	**Info.** : Information	**Pas.** : Passage
Bus. : Business	**E.** : East	**Intl.** : International	**Pav.** : Pavilion
Cvn. : Caravan	**Emb.** : Embankment	**Junc.** : Junction	**Pl.** : Place
C'way. : Causeway	**Ent.** : Enterprise	**La.** : Lane	**Pct.** : Precinct
Cen. : Centre	**Est.** : Estate	**Lit.** : Little	**Prom.** : Promenade
Chu. : Church	**Ests.** : Estates	**Lwr.** : Lower	**Quad.** : Quadrant
Chyd. : Church Yard	**Fld.** : Field	**Mnr.** : Manor	**Res.** : Residential
Circ. : Circle	**Flds.** : Fields	**Mans.** : Mansions	**Ri.** : Rise
Cir. : Circus	**Gdn.** : Garden	**Mkt.** : Market	**Rd.** : Road

Rdbt. : Roundabout
Shop. : Shopping
Sth. : South
Sq. : Square
Sta. : Station
St. : Street
Ter. : Terrace
Twr. : Tower
Trad. : Trading
Up. : Upper
Va. : Vale
Vw. : View
Vs. : Villas
Vis. : Visitors
Wlk. : Walk
W. : West
Yd. : Yard

LOCALITY ABBREVIATIONS

Ashf : **Ashford**	Chig : **Chigwell**	Hayes : **Hayes**	Rich : **Richmond**	Thor H : **Thornton Heath**
Avel : **Aveley**	Chst : **Chislehurst**	Houn : **Hounslow**	Rom : **Romford**	Twick : **Twickenham**
Bark : **Barking**	Col R : **Collier Row**	Ilf : **Ilford**	Ruis : **Ruislip**	Uxb : **Uxbridge**
Barn : **Barnet**	Cray : **Crayford**	Isle : **Isleworth**	Rush G : **Rush Green**	Wall : **Wallington**
Beck : **Beckenham**	Croy : **Croydon**	Kes : **Keston**	Shep : **Shepperton**	Walt A : **Waltham Abbey**
Belv : **Belvedere**	Dag : **Dagenham**	King T : **Kingston Upon Thames**	Short : **Shortlands**	Walt C : **Waltham Cross**
Bexl : **Bexley**	Dart : **Dartford**	Lon : **London**	Sidc : **Sidcup**	Walt T : **Walton-on-Thames**
Bex : **Bexleyheath**	E Mos : **East Molesey**	Lough : **Loughton**	S'hall : **Southall**	Well : **Welling**
Bore : **Borehamwood**	Edg : **Edgware**	Mawney : **Mawney**	S Croy : **South Croydon**	Wemb : **Wembley**
Bford : **Brentford**	Enf : **Enfield**	Mitc : **Mitcham**	Staines : **Staines**	Wenn : **Wennington**
Brom : **Bromley**	Eps : **Epsom**	Mord : **Morden**	Stan : **Stanmore**	W Dray : **West Drayton**
Buck H : **Buckhurst Hill**	Erith : **Erith**	N Mald : **New Malden**	Sun T : **Sunbury-on-Thames**	W Mole : **West Molesey**
Bush : **Bushey**	Esh : **Esher**	N'olt : **Northolt**	Surb : **Surbiton**	W W'ck : **West Wickham**
Cars : **Carshalton**	Felt : **Feltham**	Nwood : **Northwood**	Sutt : **Sutton**	Weyb : **Weybridge**
Chad H : **Chadwell Heath**	G'frd : **Greenford**	Orp : **Orpington**	Swan : **Swanley**	Wfd G : **Woodford Green**
Chert : **Chertsey**	Hamp : **Hampton**	Pinn : **Pinner**	Tedd : **Teddington**	Wor Pk : **Worcester Park**
Chess : **Chessington**	Harr : **Harrow**	Rain : **Rainham**	T Ditt : **Thames Ditton**	

A

Q2 Centre NW3 . . . . .6A **48**
101 Bus. Units SW11 . . . .3D **102**
198 Gallery 6B **104**
. . . . *(off Railton Rd.)*

Aaron Hill Rd. E6 . . . . .5E **72**
Abady Ho. SW1 . . . . .3D **172**
. . . . *(off Page St.)*
Abberley M. SW4 . . . . .3F **103**

Abbess Cl. E6 . . . . .5C **72**
. . . . SW2 . . . . .1B **122**
Abbeville M. SW4 . . . . . .4H **103**
Abbeville Rd. N8 . . . . .4H **31**
. . . . SW4 . . . . .6G **103**
Abbey Av. HA0: Wemb 2E **62**
Abbey Bus. Cen. SW8 . . . . .1G **103**

Abbey Cl. E5 . . . . .4G **51**
. . . . HA5: Pinn 3K **23**
. . . . SW8 . . . . .1H **103**
. . . . UB3: Hayes 1K **77**
. . . . UB5: N'olt 3D **60**
Abbey Ct. NW8 . . . . .2A **66**
. . . . *(off Abbey Rd.)*

Abbey Ct. SE17 . . . . .5C **86**
. . . . *(off Macleod St.)*
. . . . TW12: Hamp 7E **114**
Abbey Cres. DA17: Belv 4G **93**
Abbeydale Ct. E17 . . . . .3F **35**
. . . . UB1: S'hall 6F **61**
. . . . *(off Dormers Ri.)*

Adam Rd.—Albany Rd.

Adam Rd. E4 6G 19
Adams Bri. Bus. Cen.
HA9: Wemb 5H 45
Adams Cl. KT5: Surb 6F 135
NW9 2H 45
Adams Ct. E17 6A 34
EC2 6E 68 (7F 163)
Adams Gdns. Est. SE16 2J 87
Adams Ho. *E14* *6F 71*
(off Aberfeldy St.)
Adams M. N22 7E 16
Adamson Rd. E16 6J 71
NW3 7B 48
Adamson Way
BR3: Beck 5E 142
Adams Pl. *E14* *1D 88*
(off Nth. Colonnade, The)
N7 5K 49
Adamsrill Cl. EN1: Enf 6J 7
Adamsrill Rd. SE26 4K 123
Adams Rd. BR3: Beck 5A 142
N17 2D 32
Adam's Row
W1 7E 66 (3H 165)
Adams Sq. DA6: Bex 3E 110
Adam St. WC2 7J 67 (4K 159)
Adams Wlk. KT1: King T 2E 134
Adams Way CR0: Croy 6F 141
Adam Wlk. SW6 7E 82
Ada Pl. E2 1G 69
Adare Wlk. SW16 3K 121
Ada Rd. HA0: Wemb 3D 44
SE5 7E 86
Adastral Ho. *WC1* *5G 161*
(off New North St.)
Ada St. E8 1H 69
Ada Workshops E8 1H 69
Adderley Gdns. SE9 4E 126
Adderley Gro. SW11 5E 102
Adderley Rd.
HA3: Harr 1K 25
Adderley St. E14 6E 70
Addey Ho. SE8 7B 88
ADDINGTON 5C 154
Addington Ct. SW14 3K 99
Addington Gro. SE26 4A 124
Addington Ho. *SW9* *2K 103*
(off Stockwell Rd.)
Addington Rd.
BR4: W W'ck 4E 154
CR0: Croy 1A 152
CR2: S Croy 7K 153
E3 3C 70
E16 4G 71
N4 6A 32
Addington Sq. SE5 6D 86
(not continuous)
Addington St.
SE1 2K 85 (7H 167)
Addington Village Rd.
CR0: Croy 6B 154
(not continuous)
Addis Cl. EN3: Enf 1E 8
ADDISCOMBE 1G 153
Addiscombe Av.
CR0: Croy 1G 153
Addiscombe Cl.
HA3: Harr 5C 26
Addiscombe Ct. Rd.
CR0: Croy 1E 152
Addiscombe Gro.
CR0: Croy 2E 152
Addiscombe Rd.
CR0: Croy 2E 152
Addis Ho. *E1* *5J 69*
(off Lindley St.)
Addisland Ct. *W14* *2G 83*
(off Holland Vs. Rd.)
Addison Av. N14 6A 6
TW3: Houn 1G 97
W11 1G 83
Addison Bri. Pl. W14 4H 83
Addison Cl. BR5: Orp 6G 145
HA6: Nwood 1J 23
Addison Cres. W14 3G 83
Addison Dr. SE12 5K 107
Addison Gdns. KT5: Surb 4F 135
W14 3F 83
Addison Gro. W4 3A 82
Addison Ho. NW8 1A 158
Addison Pk. Mans. *W14* *3F 83*
(off Richmond Way)
Addison Pl. SE25 4G 141
UB1: S'hall 7E 60
W11 1G 83
Addison Rd. BR2: Short 5A 144
E11 6J 35
E17 5D 34
EN3: Enf 1D 8
IG6: Ilf 1G 37
Addison Rd. SE25 4G 141
TW11: Tedd 6B 116
W14 2G 83
Addisons Cl. CR0: Croy 2B 154
Addison Ter. *W4* *4J 81*
(off Chiswick Rd.)
Addison Way HA6: Nwood 1H 23
UB3: Hayes 6J 59
Addle Hill EC4 6B 68 (1B 168)
Addlestone Ho. *W10* *5E 64*
(off Sutton Way)
Addle St. EC2 6C 68 (7D 162)
Addy Ho. SE16 4J 87
Adecroft Way
KT8: W Mole 3G 133
Adela Av. KT3: N Mald 5D 136
Adela Ho. *W6* *5E 82*
(off Queen Caroline St.)
Adelaide Av. SE4 4B 106
Adelaide Cl. EN1: Enf 1K 7
HA7: Stan 4F 11
SW9 4A 104
Adelaide Ct. BR3: Beck 7B 124
NW8 *2A 66*
(off Abbey Rd.)
W7 2K 79
Adelaide Gdns.
RM6: Chad H 5E 38
Adelaide Gro. W12 1C 82
Adelaide Ho. E15 2H 71
E17 2B 34
SE5 2E 104
W11 *6H 65*
(off Portobello Rd.)
Adelaide Rd. BR7: Chst 5F 127
E10 3D 52
IG1: Ilf 2F 55
KT6: Surb 5E 134
NW3 7B 48
SW18 5J 101
TW5: Houn 1C 96
TW9: Rich 4F 99
TW11: Tedd 6K 115
TW15: Ashf 5A 112
UB2: S'hall 4C 78
W13 1A 80
Adelaide St.
WC2 7J 67 (3E 166)
Adelaide Ter. TW8: Bford 5D 80
Adela St. W10 4G 65
Adelina Gro. E1 5J 69
Adelina M. SW12 1H 121
Adeline Pl. WC1 5H 67 (6D 160)
Adeliza Cl. IG11: Bark 7G 55
Adelphi Ct. *E8* *7F 51*
(off Celandine Dr.)
SE16 *2K 87*
(off Garter Way)
W4 6K 81
Adelphi Cres. UB4: Hayes 3G 59
Adelphi Ter. WC2 7J 67 (3F 167)
Adelphi Theatre *3F 167*
(off Strand)
Adelphi Way UB4: Hayes 3H 59
Adeney Cl. W6 6F 83
Aden Gro. N16 4D 50
Aden Ho. *E1* *5K 69*
(off Duckett St.)
Adenmore Rd. SE6 7C 106
Aden Rd. EN3: Enf 4F 9
IG1: Ilf 7G 37
Aden Ter. N16 4D 50
Adeyfield Ho. *EC1* *2F 163*
(off Cranwood St.)
Adie Rd. W6 3E 82
Adine Rd. E13 4K 71
Adler Ind. Est. UB3: Hayes 2F 77
Adler St. E1 6G 69
Adley St. E5 5A 52
Adlington Cl. N18 5K 17
Admaston Rd. SE18 7G 91
Admiral Ct. IG11: Bark 2B 74
SM5: Cars 1C 150
SW10 *1A 102*
(off Admiral Sq.)
W1 *6G 159*
(off Blandford St.)
Admiral Ho. *SW1* *3B 172*
(off Willow Pl.)
TW11: Tedd 4A 116
Admiral Hyson Ind. Est.
SE16 5H 87
Admiral M. W10 4F 65
Admiral Pl. SE16 1A 88
Admirals Cl. E18 4K 35
Admirals Ct. *E6* *6F 73*
(off Trader Rd.)
SE1 *5J 169*
(off Horselydown La.)
Admiral Seymour Rd.
SE9 4D 108
Admiral's Ga. SE10 1D 106
Admiral Sq. SW10 1A 102
Admiral St. SE8 2C 106
Admirals Wlk. NW3 3A 48
Admirals Way E14 2C 88
Admiralty Arch *1H 85 (4D 166)*
Admiralty Cl. SE8 7C 88
Admiralty Rd.
TW11: Tedd 6K 115
Admiralty Way
TW11: Tedd 6K 115
Admiral Wlk. W9 5J 65
Adolf St. SE6 4D 124
Adolphus Rd. N4 2B 50
Adolphus St. SE8 7B 88
Adomar Rd. RM8: Dag 3D 56
Adpar St. W2 5B 66 (5A 158)
Adrian Boult Ho. *E2* *3H 69*
(off Mansford St.)
Adrian Ho. *N1* *1K 67*
(off Barnsbury Est.)
SW8 *7J 85*
(off Wyvil Rd.)
Adrian M. SW10 6K 83
Adriatic Bldg. *E14* *7A 70*
(off Horseferry Rd.)
Adriatic Ho. *E1* *4K 69*
(off Ernest St.)
Adrienne Av. UB1: S'hall 4D 60
Adron Ho. *SE16* *4J 87*
(off Millender Wlk.)
Adstock Ho. *N1* *7B 50*
(off Sutton Est., The)
Advance Rd. SE27 4C 122
Adventurers Ct. *E14* *7F 71*
(off Newport Av.)
Advent Way N18 5D 18
Adys Lawn NW2 6D 46
Ady's Rd. SE15 3F 105
Aegon Ho. *E14* *3D 88*
(off Lanark Sq.)
Aerodrome Way
TW5: Houn 6A 78
Affleck St. N1 2K 67 (1G 161)
Afghan Rd. SW11 2C 102
Afsil Ho. *EC1* *6K 161*
(off Viaduct Bldgs.)
Agamemnon Rd. NW6 4H 47
Agar Cl. KT6: Surb 2F 147
Agar Gro. NW1 7G 49
Agar Gro. Est. NW1 7H 49
Agar Ho. *KT1: King T* *3E 134*
(off Denmark Rd.)
Agar Pl. NW1 7G 49
Agar St. WC2 7J 67 (3E 166)
Agate Cl. E16 6B 72
Agate Rd. W6 3E 82
Agatha Cl. E1 1H 87
Agaton Rd. SE9 2G 127
Agave Rd. NW2 4E 46
Agdon St. EC1 4B 68 (3A 162)
Agincourt Rd. NW3 4D 48
Agnes Av. IG1: Ilf 4E 54
Agnes Cl. E6 7E 72
Agnes Gdns. RM8: Dag 4D 56
Agnes Ho. *W11* *7F 65*
(off St Ann's Rd.)
Agnes Rd. W3 1B 82
Agnes St. E14 6B 70
Agnew Rd. SE23 7K 105
Agricola Pl. EN1: Enf 5A 8
Aidan Cl. RM8: Dag 4E 56
Aigburth Mans. *SW9* *7A 86*
(off Mowll St.)
Aileen Wlk. E15 7H 53
Ailsa Av. TW1: Twick 5A 98
Ailsa Ho. *E16* *7E 72*
(off University Way)
Ailsa Rd. TW1: Twick 5B 98
Ailsa St. E14 5E 70
Ainger M. *NW3* *7D 48*
(off Ainger Rd., not continuous)
Ainger Rd. NW3 7D 48
Ainsdale *NW1* *1A 160*
(off Harrington St.)
Ainsdale Cl. BR6: Orp 7H 145
Ainsdale Cres.
HA5: Pinn 3E 24
Ainsdale Dr. SE1 5G 87
Ainsdale Rd. W5 4D 62
Ainsley Av. RM7: Rom 6H 39
Ainsley Cl. N9 1K 17
Ainsley St. E2 3H 69
Ainslie Ct. HA0: Wemb 2E 62
Ainslie Wlk. SW12 7F 103
Ainslie Wood Cres. E4 5J 19
Ainslie Wood Gdns. E4 4J 19
Ainslie Wood Nature Reserve
5J 19
Ainslie Wood Rd. E4 5H 19
Ainsty Est. SE16 2K 87
Ainsty St. SE16 2J 87
Ainsworth Cl. NW2 3C 46
SE15 2E 104
Ainsworth Ho. *NW8* *1K 65*
(off Ainsworth Way)
Ainsworth Rd. CR0: Croy 1B 152
E9 7J 51
Ainsworth Way NW8 1A 66
Aintree Av. E6 1C 72
Aintree Cl. UB8: Uxb 6D 58
Aintree Cres. IG6: Ilf 2G 37
Aintree Est. *SW6* *7G 83*
(off Aintree St.)
Aintree Rd. UB6: G'frd 2B 62
Aintree St. SW6 7G 83
Airbourne Ho.
SM6: Wall *4G 151*
(off Maldon Rd.)
Aird Ho. *SE1* *3C 86*
(off Rockingham St.)
Airdrie Cl. N1 7K 49
UB4: Hayes 5C 60
Airedale Av. W4 4B 82
Airedale Av. Sth. W4 5B 82
Airedale Rd. SW12 7D 102
W5 3C 80
Airlie Gdns. IG1: Ilf 1F 55
W8 1J 83
Airlinks Ind. Est.
TW5: Houn 5A 78
Air Pk. Way TW13: Felt 2K 113
Airport Ga. UB7: W Dray 1B 94
Air St. W1 7G 67 (3B 166)
Airthrie Rd. IG3: Ilf 2B 56
Aisgill Av. W14 5H 83
(not continuous)
Aisher Rd. SE28 7C 74
Aislibie Rd. SE12 4G 107
Aiten Pl. W6 4C 82
Aithan Ho. *E14* *6B 70*
(off Copenhagen Pl.)
Aitken Cl. CR4: Mitc 7D 138
E8 1G 69
Aitken Rd. SE6 2D 124
Ajax Ho. *E2* *2H 69*
(off Old Bethnal Grn. Rd.)
Ajax Rd. NW6 4H 47
Akabusi Cl. CR0: Croy 6G 141
Akbar Ho. *E14* *4D 88*
(off Cahir St.)
Akehurst St. SW15 6C 100
Akenside Rd. NW3 5B 48
Akerman Rd. KT6: Surb 6C 134
SW9 2B 104
Akintaro Ho. *SE8* *6B 88*
(off Alverton St.)
Alabama St. SE18 7H 91
Alacross Rd. W5 2C 80
Alamaro Lodge SE10 3H 89
Alandale Dr. HA5: Pinn 1K 23
Aland Ct. SE16 3A 88
Alander M. E17 4E 34
Alan Gdns. RM7: Rush G 7G 39
Alan Hocken Way E15 2G 71
Alan Preece Ct. NW6 7F 47
Alan Rd. SW19 5G 119
Alanthus Cl. SE12 6J 107
Alaska Bldgs. SE1 3E 86
Alaska St. SE1 1A 86 (5J 167)
Alastor Ho. *E14* *3E 88*
(off Strattondale Ho.)
Alba Cl. UB4: Hayes 4B 60
Albacore Cres. SE13 6D 106
Albain Cres. TW15: Ashf 2A 112
Alba M. SW19 2J 119
Alban Highwalk EC2 7D 162
(not continuous)
Albany W1 7G 67 (3A 166)
Albany Cl. DA5: Bexl 7C 110
N15 4B 32
SW14 4H 99
UB10: Uxb 5C 40
Albany Ct. E4 5G 19
E10 7C 34
NW8 *1A 158*
(off Abbey Rd.)
NW10 *3D 64*
(off Trenmar Gdns.)
Albany Courtyard
W1 7G 67 (3B 166)
Albany Cres. HA8: Edg 7B 12
Albany Mans. SW11 7C 84
Albany M. BR1: Brom 6J 125
KT2: King T 6D 116
N1 7A 50
SE5 6C 86
SM1: Sutt 5K 149
Albany Pde. TW8: Bford 6E 80
Albany Pk. Av. EN3: Enf 1D 8
Albany Pk. Rd.
KT2: King T 6D 116
Albany Pas. TW10: Rich 5E 98
Albany Pl. N7 4A 50
Albany Reach
KT7: T Ditt 5K 133
Albany Rd. BR7: Chst 5F 127
DA5: Bexl 7C 110
DA17: Belv 6F 93

Albany Rd.—Alexander Rd.

Albany Rd. E10 ... 7C 34
E12 ... 4B 54
E17 ... 6A 34
KT3: N Mald ... 4K 135
N4 ... 6A 32
N18 ... 5D 18
RM6: Chad H ... 6F 39
SE5 ... 6D 86
SW19 ... 5K 119
TW8: Bford ... 6D 80
TW10: Rich ... 5F 99
W13 ... 7B 62
Albany St. NW1 ... 2F 67 (1K 159)
Albany Ter. NW1 ... 4K 159
TW10: Rich ... 5F 99
(off Albany Pas.)
Albany, The IG8: Wfd G ... 4C 20
Albany Vw. IG9: Buck H ... 1D 20
Alba Pl. W11 ... 6H 65
Albatross St. SE18 ... 7J 91
Albatross Way SE16 ... 2K 87
Albemarle SW19 ... 2F 119
Albemarle App. IG2: Ilf ... 6F 37
Albemarle Av.
TW2: Twick ... 1D 114
Albemarle Gdns. IG2: Ilf ... 6F 37
KT3: N Mald ... 4K 135
Albemarle Ho. SE8 ... 4B 88
(off Foreshore)
SW9 ... 3A 104
Albemarle Pk. BR3: Beck ... 1D 142
HA7: Stan ... 5H 11
Albemarle Rd.
BR3: Beck ... 1D 142
Albemarle St.
W1 ... 7F 67 (3K 165)
Albemarle Way
EC1 ... 4B 68 (4A 162)
Alberta Av. SM1: Sutt ... 4G 149
Alberta Est. SE17 ... 5B 86
(off Alberta St.)
Alberta Ho. E14 ... 1E 88
(off Gaselee St.)
Alberta Rd. DA8: Erith ... 1J 111
EN1: Enf ... 6A 8
Alberta St. SE17 ... 5B 86
Albert Av. E4 ... 4H 19
SW8 ... 7K 85
Albert Barnes Ho. SE1 ... 3C 86
(off New Kent Rd.)
Albert Bigg Point E15 ... 2E 70
(off Godfrey St.)
Albert Bri. SW3 ... 6C 84 (7D 170)
SW11 ... 6C 84
Albert Bri. Rd. SW11 ... 7C 84
Albert Carr Gdns.
SW16 ... 5J 121
Albert Cl. E9 ... 1H 69
N22 ... 1H 31
Albert Cotts. E1 ... 5G 69
(off Deal St.)
Albert Ct. E7 ... 4J 53
SW7 ... 3B 84 (7A 164)
Albert Ct. Ga. SW7 ... 7E 164
(off Knightsbridge)
Albert Cres. E4 ... 4H 19
Albert Dane Cen.
UB2: S'hall ... 3C 78
Albert Dr. SW19 ... 2G 119
Albert Emb. SE1 ... 3K 85
(Lambeth Pal. Rd.)
SE1 ... 5J 85 (6F 173)
(Vauxhall Bri.)
Albert Gdns. E1 ... 6K 69
Albert Ga.
SW1 ... 2D 84 (6F 165)
Albert Gray Ho. SW10 ... 7B 84
(off Worlds End Est.)
Albert Gro. SW20 ... 1F 137
Albert Hall Mans.
SW7 ... 2B 84 (7A 164)
(not continuous)
Albert Ho. E18 ... 3K 35
(off Albert Rd.)
SE28 ... 2G 91
(off Erebus Dr.)
Albert Mans. CR0: Croy ... 1D 152
(off Lansdowne Rd.)
Albert Memorial ... 2B 84 (7A 164)
Albert M. E14 ... 7A 70
(off Northey St.)
N4 ... 1K 49
SE4 ... 4A 106
W8 ... 3A 84
Albert Pal. Mans. SW11 ... 1F 103
(off Lurline Gdns.)
Albert Pl. N17 ... 3F 33
W8 ... 3K 83
Albert Rd. BR2: Short ... 5B 144
CR4: Mitc ... 3D 138
DA5: Bexl ... 6G 111
DA17: Belv ... 5F 93
E10 ... 2E 52
E16 ... 1C 90
E17 ... 5C 34
E18 ... 3K 35
HA2: Harr ... 3G 25
IG1: Ilf ... 3F 55
IG9: Buck H ... 2G 21
KT1: King T ... 2F 135
KT3: N Mald ... 4B 136
N4 ... 1K 49
N15 ... 6E 32
N22 ... 1G 31
NW6 ... 2H 65
RM8: Dag ... 1G 57
SE9 ... 3C 126
SE20 ... 6K 123
SE25 ... 4G 141
SM1: Sutt ... 5B 150
TW1: Twick ... 1K 115
TW3: Houn ... 4E 96
TW10: Rich ... 5E 98
TW11: Tedd ... 6K 115
TW12: Hamp ... 5G 115
TW15: Ashf ... 5B 112
UB2: S'hall ... 3B 78
UB3: Hayes ... 3G 77
UB7: W Dray ... 1A 76
W5 ... 4B 62
Albert Rd. Est. DA17: Belv ... 5F 93
Albert Sq. E15 ... 5G 53
SW8 ... 7K 85
Albert Starr Ho. SE8 ... 4K 87
(off Bush Rd.)
Albert St. NW1 ... 1F 67
Albert Studios SW11 ... 1D 102
Albert Ter. IG9: Buck H ... 2H 21
NW1 ... 1E 66
NW10 ... 1J 63
W5 ... 4B 62
Albert Ter. M. NW1 ... 1E 66
Albert Victoria Ho. N22 ... 1A 32
(off Pellatt Gro.)
Albert Wlk. E16 ... 2E 90
Albert Way SE15 ... 7H 87
Albert Westcott Ho.
SE17 ... 5B 86
Albert Whicher Ho. E17 ... 4E 34
Albert Yd. SE19 ... 6E 122
Albery Ct. E8 ... 7F 51
(off Middleton Rd.)
Albery Theatre ... 2E 166
(off St Martin's La.)
Albion Av. SW8 ... 2H 103
Albion Cl. RM7: Rom ... 6K 39
W2 ... 7C 66 (2D 164)
Albion Ct. W6 ... 4D 82
(off Albion Pl.)
Albion Dr. E8 ... 7F 51
Albion Est. SE16 ... 2K 87
Albion Gdns. W6 ... 4D 82
Albion Ga. W2 ... 2D 164
(not continuous)
Albion Gro. N16 ... 4E 50
Albion Ho. E16 ... 1F 91
(off Church St.)
SE8 ... 7C 88
(off Watsons St.)
Albion M. N1 ... 1A 68
W2 ... 7C 66 (2D 164)
W6 ... 4D 82
Albion Pl. EC1 ... 5B 68 (5A 162)
EC2 ... 5D 68 (6F 163)
SE25 ... 3G 141
W6 ... 4D 82
Albion Rd. DA6: Bex ... 4F 111
E17 ... 3E 34
KT2: King T ... 1J 135
N16 ... 4D 50
N17 ... 2G 33
SM2: Sutt ... 6B 150
TW2: Twick ... 1J 115
TW3: Houn ... 4E 96
UB3: Hayes ... 6G 59
Albion Sq. E8 ... 7F 51
(not continuous)
Albion St. CR0: Croy ... 1B 152
SE16 ... 2J 87
W2 ... 6C 66 (1D 164)
Albion Ter. E4 ... 4J 9
E8 ... 7F 51
Albion Vs. Rd. SE26 ... 3J 123
Albion Way
EC1 ... 5C 68 (6C 162)
HA9: Wemb ... 3G 45
SE13 ... 4E 106
Albion Wharf SW11 ... 7C 84
Albion Yd. N1 ... 2J 67
Albrighton Rd. SE22 ... 3E 104
Albuhera Cl. EN2: Enf ... 1F 7
Albury Av. DA7: Bex ... 2E 110
TW7: Isle ... 7K 79
Albury Cl. TW12: Hamp ... 6F 115
Albury Ct. CR2: S Croy ... 4C 152
(off Tanfield Rd.)
CR4: Mitc ... 2B 138
SM1: Sutt ... 4A 150
UB5: N'olt ... 3A 60
(off Canberra Dr.)
Albury Dr. HA5: Pinn ... 1A 24
Albury Ho. SE1 ... 7B 168
(off Boyfield St.)
Albury M. E12 ... 2A 54
Albury Rd. KT9: Chess ... 5E 146
Albury St. SE8 ... 6C 88
Albyfield BR1: Brom ... 4D 144
Albyn Rd. SE8 ... 1C 106
Alcester Cres. E5 ... 2H 51
Alcester Rd. SM6: Wall ... 4F 151
Alcock Cl. SM6: Wall ... 7H 151
Alcock Rd. TW5: Houn ... 7B 78
Alconbury DA6: Bex ... 5H 111
Alconbury Rd. E5 ... 2G 51
Alcorn Cl. SM3: Sutt ... 2J 149
Alcott Cl. TW14: Felt ... 1H 113
W7 ... 5K 61
Alcuin Ct. HA7: Stan ... 7H 11
Aldam Pl. N16 ... 2F 51
Aldborough Ct. IG2: Ilf ... 5K 37
(off Aldborough Rd. Nth.)
ALDBOROUGH HATCH ... 4K 37
Aldborough Rd.
RM10: Dag ... 6J 57
Aldborough Rd. Nth.
IG2: Ilf ... 5K 37
Aldborough Rd. Sth.
IG3: Ilf ... 1J 55
Aldbourne Rd. W12 ... 1B 82
(not continuous)
Aldbridge St. SE17 ... 5E 86
Aldburgh M. W1 ... 6E 66 (7H 159)
(not continuous)
Aldbury Av. HA9: Wemb ... 7H 45
Aldbury Ho. SW3 ... 5C 170
(off Marlborough St.)
Aldbury M. N9 ... 7J 7
Aldebert Ter. SW8 ... 7J 85
Aldeburgh Cl. E5 ... 2H 51
Aldeburgh Pl. IG8: Wfd G ... 4D 20
Aldeburgh St. SE10 ... 5J 89
Alden Av. E15 ... 3H 71
Alden Ct. CR0: Croy ... 3E 152
Aldenham Dr. UB8: Uxb ... 4D 58
Aldenham Ho. NW1 ... 1B 160
(off Aldenham St.)
Aldenham St.
NW1 ... 2G 67 (1C 160)
Alden Ho. E8 ... 1H 69
(off Duncan Rd.)
Aldensley Rd. W6 ... 3D 82
Alderbrook Rd. SW12 ... 6F 103
Alderbury Rd. SW13 ... 6C 82
Alder Cl. SE15 ... 6F 87
Alder Gro. NW2 ... 2C 46
Aldergrove Gdns.
TW4: Houn ... 2C 96
Alder Ho. NW3 ... 6D 48
SE4 ... 3C 106
SE15 ... 6F 87
(off Cator St.)
Alder Lodge SW6 ... 1E 100
Alderman Av. IG11: Bark ... 3A 74
Aldermanbury
EC2 ... 6C 68 (7D 162)
Aldermanbury Sq.
EC2 ... 5C 68 (6D 162)
Alderman Judge Mall
KT1: King T ... 2E 134
Aldermans Hill N13 ... 4D 16
Aldermans Wlk.
EC2 ... 5E 68 (6G 163)
Aldermary Rd.
BR1: Brom ... 1J 143
Alder M. N19 ... 2G 49
Aldermoor Rd. SE6 ... 3B 124
Alderney Av. TW5: Houn ... 7F 79
Alderney Gdns. UB5: N'olt ... 7D 42
Alderney Ho. EN3: Enf ... 1E 8
N1 ... 6C 50
(off Arran Wlk.)
Alderney Rd. E1 ... 4K 69
Alderney St.
SW1 ... 4F 85 (4K 171)
Alder Rd. DA14: Sidc ... 3K 127
SW14 ... 3K 99
Alders Av. IG8: Wfd G ... 6B 20
ALDERSBROOK ... 2K 53
Aldersbrook Av. EN1: Enf ... 2K 7
Aldersbrook Dr.
KT2: King T ... 6F 117
Aldersbrook La. E12 ... 3D 54
Aldersbrook Rd. E11 ... 2K 53
E12 ... 2K 53
Alders Cl. E11 ... 2K 53
W5 ... 3D 80
Aldersey Gdns. IG11: Bark ... 6H 55
Aldersford Cl. SE4 ... 5K 105
Aldersgate St.
EC1 ... 5C 68 (5C 162)
Alders Gro. KT8: E Mos ... 5H 133
Aldersgrove Av. SE9 ... 3B 126
Aldershot Rd. NW6 ... 1H 65
Aldershot Ter. SE18 ... 7E 90
Aldersmead Av.
CR0: Croy ... 6K 141
Aldersmead Rd.
BR3: Beck ... 7A 124
Alderson Pl. UB2: S'hall ... 1G 79
Alderson St. W10 ... 4G 65
Alders, The BR4: W W'ck ... 1D 154
N21 ... 6F 7
SW16 ... 4G 121
TW5: Houn ... 6D 78
TW13: Felt ... 4C 114
Alderton Cl. NW10 ... 3K 45
Alderton Rd. CR0: Croy ... 7F 141
SE24 ... 3C 104
Alderville Rd. SW6 ... 2H 101
Alder Wlk. IG1: Ilf ... 5G 55
Alderwick Ct. N7 ... 6K 49
(off Cornelia St.)
Alderwick Dr.
TW3: Houn ... 3H 97
Alderwood M. EN4: Barn ... 1F 5
Alderwood Rd. SE9 ... 6H 109
Aldford Ho. W1 ... 4G 165
(off Park St.)
Aldford St. W1 ... 1E 84 (4H 165)
Aldgate E1 ... 7J 163
(off Whitechapel High St.)
EC3 ... 6E 68 (1H 169)
Aldgate Av. E1 ... 6F 69 (7J 163)
Aldgate Barrs E1 ... 7K 163
Aldgate High St.
EC3 ... 6F 69 (1J 169)
Aldgate Triangle E1 ... 6G 69
(off Coke St.)
Aldham Ho. SE4 ... 2B 106
(off Malpas Rd.)
Aldine Ct. W12 ... 2E 82
(off Aldine St.)
Aldine Pl. W12 ... 2E 82
Aldine St. W12 ... 2E 82
Aldington Cl. RM8: Dag ... 1C 56
Aldington Ct. E8 ... 7G 51
(off London Flds. W. Side)
Aldington Rd. SE18 ... 3B 90
Aldis M. SW17 ... 5C 120
Aldis St. SW17 ... 5C 120
Aldred Rd. NW6 ... 5J 47
Aldren Rd. SW17 ... 3A 120
Aldrich Cres. CR0: Croy ... 7E 154
Aldriche Way E4 ... 6K 19
Aldrich Gdns. SM3: Sutt ... 3H 149
Aldrich Ter. SW18 ... 2A 120
Aldrick Ho. N1 ... 1K 67
(off Barnsbury Est.)
Aldridge Av. HA4: Ruis ... 2A 42
HA7: Stan ... 1E 26
Aldridge Ri. KT3: N Mald ... 7A 136
Aldridge Rd. Vs. W11 ... 5H 65
Aldridge Wlk. N14 ... 7D 6
Aldrington Rd. SW16 ... 5G 121
Aldsworth Cl. W9 ... 4K 65
Aldwick Cl. SE9 ... 3H 127
Aldwick Rd. CR0: Croy ... 3K 151
Aldworth Gro. SE13 ... 6E 106
Aldworth Rd. E15 ... 7G 53
Aldwych WC2 ... 6K 67 (2G 167)
Aldwych Av. IG6: Ilf ... 4G 37
Aldwych Ct. E8 ... 7F 51
(off Middleton Rd.)
Aldwych Theatre ... 1G 167
(off Aldwych)
Aldwyn Ho. SW8 ... 7J 85
(off Davidson Gdns.)
Alers Rd. DA6: Bex ... 5D 110
Alesia Cl. N22 ... 7D 16
Alestan Beck Rd. E16 ... 6B 72
Alexa Ct. SM2: Sutt ... 6J 149
W8 ... 4J 83
Alexander Av. NW10 ... 7D 46
Alexander Cl. BR2: Short ... 1J 155
DA15: Sidc ... 5J 109
TW2: Twick ... 2J 115
UB2: S'hall ... 1G 79
Alexander Ct. BR3: Beck ... 1F 143
HA7: Stan ... 3F 27
Alexander Evans M.
SE23 ... 2K 123
Alexander Fleming Mus. ... 7B 158
Alexander Ho. E14 ... 3C 88
(off Tiller Rd.)
Alexander M. W2 ... 6K 65
Alexander Pl.
SW7 ... 4C 84 (3C 170)
Alexander Rd. BR7: Chst ... 6F 127
DA7: Bex ... 2D 110
N19 ... 3J 49

A-Z London 181

Alexander Sq.—Altham Rd.

Alexander Sq.
SW3 4C **84** (3C **170**)
Alexander St. W2 6J **65**
Alexander Studios *SW11* *4B* ***102***
(off Haydon Way)
Alexander Ter. SE2 5B **92**
Alexandra Av. HA2: Harr 1D **42**
N22 1H **31**
SM1: Sutt 3J **149**
SW11 1E **102**
UB1: S'hall 7D **60**
W4 7K **81**
Alexandra Cl. HA2: Harr 3E **42**
SE8 6B **88**
TW15: Ashf 7F **113**
Alexandra Cotts. SE14 1B **106**
Alexandra Ct. N14 5B **6**
SW7 1A **170**
TW3: Houn 2F **97**
TW15: Ashf 6F **113**
UB6: G'frd 2F **61**
W2 *7K* ***65***
(off Moscow Rd.)
W9 *4A* ***66***
(off Maida Va.)
Alexandra Cres.
BR1: Brom 6H **125**
Alexandra Dr. KT5: Surb 7G **135**
SE19 5E **122**
Alexandra Gdns. N10 4F **31**
SM5: Cars 7E **150**
TW3: Houn 2F **97**
W4 7A **82**
Alexandra Gro. N4 1B **50**
Alexandra Ho. *E16* *7K* ***71***
(off Wesley Av.)
IG8: Ilf 7K **21**
W6 *5E* ***82***
(off Queen Caroline St.)
Alexandra Mans. *SW3* *7A* ***170***
(off King's Rd.)
Alexandra M. N2 3D **30**
SW19 6H **119**
Alexandra Palace ***2H 31***
Alexandra Pal. Way N22 4G **31**
Alexandra Pde. HA2: Harr 4F **43**
Alexandra Pk. Rd. N10 2F **31**
N22 1G **31**
Alexandra Pl. CR0: Croy 1E **152**
NW8 1A **66**
SE25 5D **140**
Alexandra Rd. CR0: Croy 1E **152**
CR4: Mitc 7C **120**
E6 3E **72**
E10 3E **52**
E17 6B **34**
E18 3K **35**
EN3: Enf 4E **8**
KT2: King T 7G **117**
KT7: T Ditt 5K **133**
N8 3A **32**
N9 7C **8**
N15 5D **32**
NW8 1A **66**
RM6: Chad H 6E **38**
SE26 6K **123**
SW14 3K **99**
SW19 6H **119**
TW1: Twick 6C **98**
TW3: Houn 2F **97**
TW8: Bford 6D **80**
TW9: Rich 2F **99**
TW15: Ashf 7F **113**
W4 2K **81**
Alexandra Rd. Ind. Est.
EN3: Enf 4E **8**
Alexandra Sq.
SM4: Mord 5J **137**
Alexandra St. E16 5J **71**
SE14 7A **88**
Alexandra Ter. *E14* *5D* ***88***
(off Westferry Rd.)
Alexandra Wlk. SE19 5E **122**
Alexandra Yd. E9 1K **69**
Alexandria Rd. W13 7A **62**
Alexis St. SE16 4G **87**
Alfan La. DA2: Dart 5K **129**
Alfearn Rd. E5 4J **51**
Alford Ct. *N1* *1D* ***162***
(off Shepherdess Wlk.)
Alford Grn. CR0: Croy 6F **155**
Alford Ho. N6 6G **31**
Alford Pl. N1 2C **68** (1D **162**)
(not continuous)
Alford Rd. DA8: Erith 5J **93**
Alfoxton Av. N15 4B **32**
Alfreda St. SW11 1F **103**
Alfred Cl. W4 4K **81**
Alfred Finlay Ho. N22 2B **32**
Alfred Gdns. UB1: S'hall 7C **60**
Alfred Ho. *E9* *5A* ***52***
(off Homerton Rd.)
E12 *7C* ***54***
(off Tennyson Av.)
Alfred M. W1 5H **67** (5C **160**)
Alfred Nunn Ho. NW10 1B **64**
Alfred Pl. WC1 5H **67** (5C **160**)
Alfred Prior Ho. E12 4E **54**
Alfred Rd. DA17: Belv 5F **93**
E15 5H **53**
IG9: Buck H 2G **21**
KT1: King T 3E **134**
SE25 5G **141**
SM1: Sutt 5A **150**
TW13: Felt 2A **114**
W2 5J **65**
W3 1J **81**
Alfred's Gdns. IG11: Bark 2J **73**
Alfred St. E3 3B **70**
Alfreds Way IG11: Bark 3F **73**
Alfreds Way Ind. Est.
IG11: Bark 1A **74**
Alfreton Cl. SW19 3F **119**
Alfriston KT5: Surb 6F **135**
Alfriston Av. CR0: Croy 7J **139**
HA2: Harr 6E **24**
Alfriston Cl. KT6: Surb 5F **135**
Alfriston Rd. SW11 5D **102**
Algar Cl. HA7: Stan 5E **10**
TW7: Isle 3A **98**
Algar Ho. SE1 7A **168**
Algar Rd. TW7: Isle 3A **98**
Algarve Rd. SW18 1K **119**
Algernon Rd. NW6 1J **65**
SE13 4D **106**
Algiers Rd. SE13 4C **106**
Alibon Gdns. RM10: Dag 5G **57**
Alibon Rd. RM9: Dag 5F **57**
RM10: Dag 5F **57**
Alice Gilliatt Ct. *W14* *6H* ***83***
(off Star Rd.)
Alice La. E3 1B **70**
Alice M. TW11: Tedd 5K **115**
Alice Owen Technology Cen.
EC1 *1A* ***162***
(off Goswell Rd.)
Alice Shepherd Ho. *E14* *2E* ***88***
(off Manchester Rd.)
Alice St. SE1 3E **86**
(not continuous)
Alice Thompson Cl.
SE12 2A **126**
Alice Walker Cl. SE24 4B **104**
Alice Way TW3: Houn 4F **97**
Alicia Av. HA3: Harr 4B **26**
Alicia Cl. HA3: Harr 5C **26**
Alicia Gdns. HA3: Harr 4B **26**
Alicia Ho. DA16: Well 1B **110**
Alie St. E1 6F **69** (1K **169**)
Alington Cres. NW9 7J **27**
Alington Gro. SM6: Wall 7G **151**
Alison Cl. CR0: Croy 1K **153**
E6 6E **72**
Alison Ct. SE1 5G **87**
Aliwal Rd. SW11 4C **102**
Alkerden Rd. W4 5A **82**
Alkham Rd. N16 2F **51**
Allan Barclay Cl. N15 6F **33**
Allan Cl. KT3: N Mald 5K **135**
Allanson Ct. *E10* *2C* ***52***
(off Leyton Grange Est.)
Allan Way W3 5J **63**
Allard Cres.
WD23: Bush 1B **10**
Allard Gdns. SW4 5H **103**
Allardyce St. SW4 4K **103**
Allbrook Cl. TW11: Tedd 5J **115**
Allcott Ho. *W12* *6D* ***64***
(off Du Cane Rd.)
Allcroft Rd. NW5 5E **48**
Allder Way CR2: S Croy 7B **152**
Allenby Cl. UB6: G'frd 3E **60**
Allenby Rd. SE23 3A **124**
UB1: S'hall 3E **60**
Allen Cl. CR4: Mitc 1F **139**
TW16: Sun T 1K **131**
Allen Ct. *E17* *6C* ***34***
(off Yunus Khan Cl.)
UB6: G'frd 5K **43**
Allendale Av. UB1: S'hall 6E **60**
Allendale Cl. SE5 2D **104**
SE26 5K **123**
Allendale Rd. UB6: G'frd 6B **44**
Allen Edwards Dr. SW8 1J **103**
Allenford Ho. *SW15* *6B* ***100***
(off Tunworth Cres.)
Allen Rd. BR3: Beck 2K **141**
CR0: Croy 1A **152**
E3 2B **70**
N16 4E **50**
TW16: Sun T 1K **131**
Allensbury Pl. NW1 7H **49**
Allens Rd. EN3: Enf 5D **8**
Allen St. W8 3J **83**
Allenswood Rd. SE9 3C **108**
Allerford Ct. HA2: Harr 5G **25**
Allerford Rd. SE6 3D **124**
Allerton Ho. *N1* *1E* ***162***
(off Fairbank Est.)
Allerton Rd. N16 2C **50**
Allerton St. N1 3D **68** (1E **162**)
Allerton Wlk. N7 2K **49**
Allestree Rd. SW6 7G **83**
Alleyn Cres. SE21 2D **122**
Alleyndale Rd. RM8: Dag 2C **56**
Alleyn Ho. *SE1* *3D* ***86***
(off Burbage Cl.)
Alleyn Pk. SE21 2D **122**
UB2: S'hall 5E **78**
Alleyn Rd. SE21 3D **122**
Alley Way UB8: Uxb 7A **40**
Allfarthing La. SW18 6K **101**
Allgood Cl. SM4: Mord 6F **137**
Allgood St. E2 2F **69** (1K **163**)
Allhallows La.
EC4 7D **68** (3E **168**)
All Hallows Rd. N17 1E **32**
Allhallows Rd. E6 5C **72**
Alliance Cl. HA0: Wemb 4D **44**
Alliance Ct. W3 5H **63**
Alliance Rd. E13 5A **72**
SE18 6A **92**
W3 4H **63**
Allied Ind. Est. W3 2A **82**
Allied Way W3 2A **82**
Allingham Cl. W7 7K **61**
Allingham St. N1 2C **68**
Allington Av. N17 6K **17**
TW17: Shep 3G **131**
Allington Cl. SW19 5F **119**
UB6: G'frd 7G **43**
Allington Ct. EN3: Enf 5E **8**
(not continuous)
SW1 *2K* ***171***
(off Allington St.)
SW8 2G **103**
Allington Rd. BR6: Orp 7J **145**
HA2: Harr 5G **25**
W10 3G **65**
Allington St.
SW1 3F **85** (2K **171**)
Allison Cl. SE10 1E **106**
Allison Gro. SE21 1E **122**
Allison Rd. N8 5A **32**
W3 6J **63**
Alliston Ho. *E2* *2K* ***163***
(off Gibraltar Wlk.)
Allitsen Rd. NW8 2C **66**
(not continuous)
Allnutt Way SW4 5H **103**
Alloa Rd. IG3: Ilf 2A **56**
SE8 5K **87**
Allom Ho. *W11* *7G* ***65***
(off Clarendon Rd.)
Allonby Dr. HA4: Ruis 7D **22**
Allonby Gdns. HA9: Wemb 1C **44**
Allonby Ho. *E14* *5A* ***70***
(off Aston St.)
Alloway Rd. E3 3A **70**
Allport Ho. *SE5* *3D* ***104***
(off Denmark Hill)
All Saints Cl. N9 2B **18**
All Saints Ct. *E1* *7J* ***69***
(off Johnson St.)
SW8 *7F* ***85***
(off Prince of Wales Dr.)
TW5: Houn *1B* ***96***
(off Springwell Rd.)
All Saints Dr. SE3 2G **107**
(not continuous)
All Saints Ho. *W11* *5H* ***65***
(off All Saints Rd.)
All Saints M. HA3: Harr 6D **10**
All Saints Pas. SW18 5J **101**
All Saints Rd. SM1: Sutt 3K **149**
SW19 7A **120**
(not continuous)
W3 3J **81**
W11 5H **65**
All Saints St. N1 2K **67**
All Saints Twr. E10 7D **34**
Allsop Pl. NW1 4D **66** (4F **159**)
All Souls Av. NW10 2D **64**
All Souls' Pl. W1 5F **67** (6K **159**)
Allwood Cl. SE26 4K **123**
Alma Av. E4 7K **19**
Alma Birk Ho. NW6 7G **47**
Almack Rd. E5 4J **51**
Alma Ct. HA2: Harr 2H **43**
Alma Cres. SM1: Sutt 5G **149**
Alma Gro. SE1 4F **87**
Alma Ho. TW8: Bford 6E **80**
Alma Pl. CR7: Thor H 5A **140**
NW10 3D **64**
SE19 7F **123**
Alma Rd. DA14: Sidc 3A **128**
EN3: Enf 5F **9**
KT10: Esh 7J **133**
SM5: Cars 5C **150**
SW18 4A **102**
UB1: S'hall 7C **60**
Alma Rd. Ind. Est. EN3: Enf 4E **8**
Alma Row HA3: Harr 1H **25**
Alma Sq. NW8 2A **66**
Alma St. E15 6F **53**
NW5 6F **49**
Alma Ter. SW18 7B **102**
W8 3J **83**
Almeida St. N1 1B **68**
Almeida Theatre ***1B 68***
(off Almeida St.)
Almeric Rd. SW11 4D **102**
Almer Rd. SW20 7C **118**
Almington St. N4 1K **49**
Almond Av. SM5: Cars 2D **150**
UB7: W Dray 3C **76**
UB10: Uxb 3D **40**
W5 3D **80**
Almond Cl. BR2: Short 7E **144**
HA4: Ruis 3H **41**
SE15 2G **105**
TW13: Felt 1J **113**
TW17: Shep 2E **130**
UB3: Hayes 7G **59**
Almond Gro. TW8: Bford 7B **80**
Almond Rd. N17 7B **18**
SE16 4H **87**
Almonds Av. IG9: Buck H 2D **20**
Almond Way BR2: Short 7E **144**
CR4: Mitc 5H **139**
HA2: Harr 2F **25**
Almorah Rd. N1 7D **50**
TW5: Houn 1B **96**
Almshouse La.
KT9: Chess 7C **146**
Alnmouth Ct. *UB1: S'hall* *6G* ***61***
(off Fleming Rd.)
Alnwick N17 7C **18**
Alnwick Gro. SM4: Mord 4K **137**
Alnwick Rd. E16 6A **72**
SE12 6K **107**
ALPERTON **2E 62**
Alperton La. HA0: Wemb 3C **62**
UB6: G'frd 3C **62**
Alperton St. W10 4H **65**
Alphabet Gdns.
SM5: Cars 6B **138**
Alphabet Sq. E3 5C **70**
Alpha Bus. Cen. E17 5B **34**
Alpha Cl. NW1 4C **66** (3D **158**)
Alpha Est. UB3: Hayes 2G **77**
Alpha Gro. E14 2C **88**
Alpha Ho. NW1 4C **158**
NW6 2J **65**
SW9 4K **103**
Alpha Pl. NW6 2J **65**
SM4: Mord 1F **149**
SW3 6C **84** (7D **170**)
Alpha Rd. CR0: Croy 1E **152**
E4 3H **19**
EN3: Enf 4F **9**
KT5: Surb 6F **135**
N18 6B **18**
SE14 1B **106**
TW11: Tedd 5H **115**
UB10: Uxb 4D **58**
Alpha St. SE15 2G **105**
Alphea Cl. SW19 7C **120**
Alpine Av. KT5: Surb 2J **147**
Alpine Bus. Cen. E6 5E **72**
Alpine Cl. CR0: Croy 3E **152**
Alpine Copse BR1: Brom 2E **144**
Alpine Gro. E9 7J **51**
Alpine Rd. E10 2D **52**
KT12: Walt T 7J **131**
SE16 4J **87**
(not continuous)
Alpine Vw. SM5: Cars 5C **150**
Alpine Wlk. HA7: Stan 2D **10**
Alpine Way E6 5E **72**
Alric Av. KT3: N Mald 3A **136**
NW10 7K **45**
Alroy Rd. N4 7A **32**
Alsace Rd. SE17 5E **86**
Alscot Rd. SE1 4F **87**
(not continuous)
Alscot Rd. Ind. Est. SE1 3F **87**
Alscot Way SE1 4F **87**
Alsike Rd. SE2 3D **92**
Alsom Av. KT4: Wor Pk 4C **148**
Alston Cl. KT6: Surb 7B **134**
Alston Rd. N18 5C **18**
SW17 4B **120**
Altair Cl. N17 6A **18**
Altash Way SE9 2D **126**
Altenburg Av. W13 3B **80**
Altenburg Gdns. SW11 4D **102**
Alt Gro. SW19 7H **119**
Altham Ct. HA2: Harr 1F **25**
Altham Rd. HA5: Pinn 1C **24**

Angle Cl.—Arches, The

Angle Cl. UB10: Uxb 1C 58
Angle Grn. RM8: Dag 1C 56
Anglers Cl. TW10: Rich 4C 116
Angler's La. NW5 .... 6F 49
Anglers Reach KT6: Surb 5D 134
Anglers, The KT1: King T 3D 134
(off High St.)
Anglesea Av. SE18 .... 4F 91
Anglesea Ho.
KT1: King T 4D 134
(off Anglesea Rd.)
Anglesea M. SE18 .... 4F 91
Anglesea Rd.
KT1: King T 4D 134
SE18 .... 4F 91
Anglesey Cl. TW15: Ashf 3C 112
Anglesey Ct. W7 .... 4K 61
Anglesey Ct. Rd.
SM5: Cars 6E 150
Anglesey Gdns.
SM5: Cars 6E 150
Anglesey Ho. E14 .... 6C 70
(off Lindfield St.)
Anglesey Rd. EN3: Enf 4C 8
Anglesmede Cres.
HA5: Pinn 3E 24
Anglesmede Way
HA5: Pinn 3E 24
Angles Rd. SW16 .... 4J 121
Anglia Cl. N17 .... 7C 18
Anglia Ct. RM8: Dag 1D 56
(off Spring Cl.)
Anglia Ho. E14 .... 6A 70
(off Salmon La.)
Anglian Ind. Est.
IG11: Bark 4K 73
Anglian Rd. E11 .... 3F 53
Anglia Wlk. E6 .... 1E 72
(off Napier Rd.)
Anglo Rd. E3 .... 2B 70
Angrave Ct. E8 .... 1F 69
(off Scriven St.)
Angrave Pas. E8 .... 1F 69
Angus Cl. KT9: Chess 5G 147
Angus Dr. HA4: Ruis 4A 42
Angus Gdns. NW9 .... 1K 27
Angus Ho. SW2 .... 7H 103
Angus Rd. E13 .... 3A 72
Angus St. SE14 .... 7A 88
Anhalt Rd. SW11 .... 7C 84
Ankerdine Cres. SE18 .... 7F 91
Anlaby Rd. TW11: Tedd 5J 115
Anley Rd. W14 .... 2F 83
Anmersh Gro. HA7: Stan 1D 26
Annabel Cl. E14 .... 6D 70
Anna Cl. E8 .... 1F 69
Annandale Gro.
UB10: Uxb 3E 40
Annandale Rd.
CR0: Croy 2G 153
DA15: Sidc 7J 109
SE10 .... 6H 89
W4 .... 5A 82
Anna Neagle Cl. E7 .... 4J 53
Annan Way RM1: Rom 1K 39
Anne Boleyn Ct. SE9 .... 6G 109
Anne Boleyn's Wlk.
KT2: King T 5E 116
SM3: Sutt 7F 149
Anne Case M.
KT3: N Mald 3K 135
Anne Compton M. SE12 .... 7H 107
Anne Goodman Ho. E1 .... 6J 69
(off Jubilee St.)
Anne of Cleeves Ct.
SE9 .... 6H 109
Annesley Av. NW9 .... 3K 27
Annesley Cl. NW10 .... 3A 46
Annesley Dr. CR0: Croy 3B 154
Annesley Ho. SW9 .... 1A 104
Annesley Rd. SE3 .... 1K 107
Annesley Wlk. N19 .... 2G 49
Anne St. E13 .... 4J 71
Anne Sutherland Ho.
BR3: Beck 7A 124
Annett Cl. TW17: Shep 4G 131
Annette Cl. HA3: Harr 2J 25
Annette Rd. N7 .... 3K 49
(not continuous)
Annett Rd. KT12: Walt T 7J 131
Annetts Cres. N1 .... 7C 50
Anne Way
KT8: W Mole 4F 133
Annie Besant Cl. E3 .... 1B 70
Annie Taylor Ho. E12 .... 4E 54
(off Walton Rd.)
Anning St.
EC2 .... 4E 68 (3H 163)
Annington Rd. N2 .... 3D 30
Annis Rd. E9 .... 6A 52
Ann La. SW10 .... 6B 84
Ann Moss Way SE16 .... 3J 87
Ann's Cl. SW1 .... 7F 165
Ann's Pl. E1 .... 6J 163
Ann St. SE18 .... 5G 91
(not continuous)
Ann Stroud Ct. SE12 .... 5J 107
Annsworthy Av.
CR7: Thor H 3D 140
Annsworthy Cres. SE25 .... 2D 140
Ansar Gdns. E17 .... 5B 34
Ansdell Rd. SE15 .... 2J 105
Ansdell St. W8 .... 3K 83
Ansdell Ter. W8 .... 3K 83
Ansell Gro. SM5: Cars 1E 150
Ansell Ho. E1 .... 5J 69
(off Mile End Rd.)
Ansell Rd. SW17 .... 3C 120
Anselm Cl. CR0: Croy 3F 153
Anselm Rd. HA5: Pinn 1D 24
SW6 .... 6J 83
Ansford Rd. BR1: Brom 5E 124
Ansleigh Pl. W11 .... 7F 65
Anson Cl.
RM7: Mawney 2H 39
Anson Ho. E1 .... 4A 70
(off Shandy St.)
SW1 .... 7A 172
(off Churchill Gdns.)
Anson Pl. SE28 .... 2H 91
Anson Rd. N7 .... 4G 49
NW2 .... 4D 46
Anson Ter. UB5: N'olt 6F 43
Anstey Ct. W3 .... 2H 81
Anstey Ho. E9 .... 1J 69
(off Templecombe Rd.)
Anstey Rd. SE15 .... 3G 105
Anstey Wlk. N15 .... 4B 32
Anstice Cl. W4 .... 7A 82
Anstridge Path SE9 .... 6H 109
Anstridge Rd. SE9 .... 6H 109
Antelope Rd. SE18 .... 3D 90
Antenor Ho. E2 .... 2H 69
(off Old Bethnal Grn. Rd.)
Anthony Cl. NW7 .... 4F 13
Anthony Cope Ct. N1 .... 1F 163
(off Chart St.)
Anthony Ho. NW1 .... 4C 158
(off Ashbridge St.)
Anthony Rd. DA16: Well 1A 110
SE25 .... 6G 141
UB6: G'frd 3J 61
Anthony St. E1 .... 6H 69
Anthony Way N18 .... 6E 18
Antigua Wlk. SE19 .... 5D 122
Antilles Bay E14 .... 2E 88
Antill Rd. E3 .... 3A 70
N15 .... 4G 33
Antill Ter. E1 .... 6K 69
Antlers Hill E4 .... 5J 9
Anton Cres. SM1: Sutt 3J 149
Antoneys Cl. HA5: Pinn 2B 24
Anton Pl. HA9: Wemb 3H 45
Anton St. E8 .... 5G 51
Antony Ho. SE14 .... 7K 87
(off Barlborough St.)
SE16 .... 4J 87
(off Raymouth Rd.)
Antrim Gro. NW3 .... 6D 48
Antrim Ho. E3 .... 1B 70
(off Birdsfield La.)
Antrim Rd. NW3 .... 6D 48
Antrobus Cl. SM1: Sutt 5H 149
Antrobus Rd. W4 .... 4J 81
Anvil Cl. SW16 .... 7G 121
Anvil Rd. TW16: Sun T 3J 131
Anworth Cl. IG8: Wfd G 6E 20
Apeldoorn Dr. SM6: Wall 7J 151
Apex Cl. BR3: Beck 1D 142
Apex Corner
Feltham 3D 114
Mill Hill 4F 13
Apex Ct. W13 .... 7A 62
Apex Ind. Est. NW10 .... 4B 64
Apex Pde. NW7 .... 4E 12
(off Selvage La.)
Apex Retail Pk.
TW13: Felt 3D 114
Aphrodite Ct. E14 .... 4C 88
(off Homer Dr.)
Aplin Way TW7: Isle 1J 97
Apollo Av. BR1: Brom 1K 143
Apollo Bldg. E14 .... 4C 88
Apollo Bus. Cen. SE8 .... 5K 87
Apollo Ct. E1 .... 7G 69
(off Thomas More St.)
SW9 .... 1A 104
(off Southey Rd.)
Apollo Ho. E2 .... 2H 69
(off St Jude's Rd.)
N6 .... 7D 30
SW10 .... 7B 84
(off Milman's St.)
Apollo Pl. E11 .... 3G 53
SW10 .... 7B 84
Apollo Theatre 2C 166
(off Shaftesbury Av.)
Apollo Victoria Theatre 2A 172
(off Wilton Rd.)
Apollo Way DA8: Erith 4K 93
SE28 .... 3H 91
Apostle Way CR7: Thor H 2B 140
Apothecary St.
EC4 .... 6B 68 (1A 168)
Appach Rd. SW2 .... 5A 104
Apple Blossom Ct. SW8 .... 7H 85
(off Pascal St.)
Appleby Cl. E4 .... 6K 19
N15 .... 5D 32
TW2: Twick 2H 115
Appleby Gdns.
TW14: Felt 1H 113
Appleby Rd. E8 .... 7G 51
E16 .... 6H 71
Appleby St. E2 .... 2F 69
Appledore Av. DA7: Bex 1J 111
HA4: Ruis 3K 41
Appledore Cl. BR2: Short 5H 143
HA8: Edg 1G 27
SW17 .... 2D 120
Appledore Cres.
DA14: Sidc 3J 127
Appledore Way NW7 .... 7A 14
Appleford Ho. W10 .... 4G 65
(off Bosworth Rd.)
Appleford Rd. W10 .... 4G 65
Apple Gth. TW8: Bford 4D 80
Applegarth CR0: Croy 7D 154
(not continuous)
KT10: Esh 5A 146
Applegarth Dr. IG2: Ilf 4K 37
Applegarth Ho. SE1 .... 6B 168
SE15 .... 7G 87
(off Bird in Bush Rd.)
Applegarth Rd. SE28 .... 1B 92
W14 .... 3F 83
Apple Gro. EN1: Enf 3K 7
KT9: Chess 4E 146
Apple Mkt. KT1: King T 2D 134
Apple Rd. E11 .... 3G 53
Appleshaw Ho. SE5 .... 3E 104
Appleton Cl. DA7: Bex 2J 111
Appleton Gdns.
KT3: N Mald 6C 136
Appleton Rd. SE3 .... 3C 108
SE9 .... 3C 108
Appleton Sq. CR4: Mitc 1C 138
Apple Tree Av. UB8: Uxb 5B 58
Appletree Cl. SE20 .... 1H 141
Appletree Gdns.
EN4: Barn 4H 5
Apple Tree Yd.
SW1 .... 1G 85 (4B 166)
Applewood Cl. N20 .... 1H 15
(not continuous)
NW2 .... 3D 46
UB10: Uxb 4A 40
Applewood Dr. E13 .... 4K 71
Appold St. EC2 .... 5E 68 (5G 163)
Apprentice Way E5 .... 4H 51
Approach Cl. N16 .... 4E 50
Approach Rd. E2 .... 2J 69
EN4: Barn 4G 5
HA8: Edg 6B 12
KT8: W Mole 5E 132
SW20 .... 2E 136
TW15: Ashf 6E 112
Approach, The EN1: Enf 2C 8
NW4 .... 5F 29
W3 .... 6K 63
Aprey Gdns. NW4 .... 4E 28
April Cl. TW13: Felt 3J 113
W7 .... 7J 61
April Ct. E2 .... 2G 69
(off Teale St.)
April Glen SE23 .... 3K 123
April St. E8 .... 4F 51
Apsley Cl. HA2: Harr 5G 25
Apsley House 2E 84 (6H 165)
Apsley Ho. E1 .... 5J 69
(off Stepney Way)
NW8 .... 2B 66
(off Finchley Rd.)
TW4: Houn 4D 96
Apsley Rd. KT3: N Mald 3J 135
SE25 .... 4H 141
Apsley Way NW2 .... 2C 46
W1 .... 2E 84 (6H 165)
(not continuous)
Aquarius TW1: Twick 1B 116
Aquarius Bus. Pk. NW2 .... 1C 46
(off Priestley Way)
Aquila St. NW8 .... 2B 66
Aquinas St.
SE1 .... 1A 86 (5K 167)
Arabella Dr. SW15 .... 4A 100
Arabia Cl. E4 .... 7K 9
Arabian Ho. E1 .... 4A 70
(off Ernest St.)
Arabin Rd. SE4 .... 4A 106
Aragon Av. KT7: T Ditt 5K 133
Aragon Cl. BR2: Short 1D 156
EN2: Enf 1E 6
TW16: Sun T 6H 113
Aragon Ct. KT8: E Mos 4G 133
Aragon Dr. HA4: Ruis 1B 42
Aragon Ho. E16 .... 7J 71
(off Capulet M.)
Aragon Rd. KT2: King T 5E 116
SM4: Mord 6F 137
Aragon Twr. SE8 .... 4B 88
Aral Ho. E1 .... 4K 69
(off Ernest St.)
Arandora Cres.
RM6: Chad H 7B 38
Aran Dr. HA7: Stan 4H 11
Arapiles Ho. E14 .... 6F 71
(off Blair St.)
Arbery Rd. E3 .... 3A 70
Arbon Ct. N1 .... 1C 68
(off Linton St.)
Arbor Cl. BR3: Beck 2D 142
Arbor Ct. N16 .... 2D 50
Arboretum Ct. N1 .... 6D 50
(off Dove Rd.)
Arborfield Cl. SW2 .... 1K 121
Arborfield Ho. E14 .... 7C 70
(off E. India Dock Rd.)
Arbor Rd. E4 .... 3A 20
Arbour Ho. E1 .... 6K 69
(off Arbour Sq.)
Arbour Rd. EN3: Enf 3E 8
Arbour Sq. E1 .... 6K 69
Arbroath Rd. SE9 .... 3C 108
Arbury Ct. SE20 .... 1H 141
Arbury Ter. SE26 .... 3G 123
Arbuthnot La.
DA5: Bexl 6E 110
Arbuthnot Rd. SE14 .... 2K 105
Arbutus St. E8 .... 1F 69
Arcade CR0: Croy 2C 152
Arcade Chambers SE9 .... 6E 108
Arcade Pde. KT9: Chess 5D 146
Arcade, The CR0: Croy 3C 152
(off High St.)
E14 .... 6D 70
E17 .... 4C 34
EC2 .... 6G 163
IG11: Bark 7G 55
SE9 .... 6E 108
(off High St.)
Arcadia Av. N3 .... 2J 29
Arcadia Cen., The W5 .... 7D 62
Arcadia Cl. SM5: Cars 4E 150
Arcadia Ct. E1 .... 7J 163
Arcadian Av. DA5: Bexl 6E 110
Arcadian Cl. DA5: Bexl 6E 110
Arcadian Gdns. N22 .... 7E 16
Arcadian Rd. DA5: Bexl 6E 110
Arcadia St. E14 .... 6C 70
Archangel St. SE16 .... 2K 87
Archbishop's Pl. SW2 .... 7K 103
Archdale Bus. Cen.
HA2: Harr 2G 43
Archdale Ct. W12 .... 1D 82
Archdale Ho. SE1 .... 7G 169
(off Long La.)
Archdale Pl. KT1: King T 3H 135
Archdale Rd. SE22 .... 5F 105
Archel Rd. W14 .... 6H 83
Archer Cl. KT2: King T 7E 116
Archer Ho. SE14 .... 1A 106
SW11 .... 1B 102
W11 .... 7H 65
(off Westbourne Gro.)
W13 .... 1B 80
(off Sherwood Cl.)
Archer M. TW12: Hamp 6G 115
Archer Rd. BR5: Orp 5K 145
SE25 .... 4H 141
Archers Ct. BR2: Short 4K 143
CR2: S Croy 5C 152
(off Nottingham Rd.)
Archers Dr. EN3: Enf 2D 8
Archers Lodge SE16 .... 5G 87
(off Culloden Cl.)
Archer Sq. SE14 .... 6A 88
Archer St. W1 .... 7H 67 (2C 166)
Archer Ter. UB7: W Dray 7A 58
Archery Cl. HA3: Harr 3K 25
W2 .... 6C 66 (1D 164)
Archery Rd. SE9 .... 5D 108
Archery Steps W2 .... 2D 164
Arches Bus. Cen., The
UB2: S'hall 2D 78
(off Merrick Rd.)
Arches Leisure Cen. 6G 89
Arches, The HA2: Harr 2F 43
NW1 .... 7F 49
SW8 .... 7H 85

Arches, The—Arundel Ct.

Arches, The *WC2* *4F 167*
(off Villiers St.)
Archgate Bus. Cen. N12 .....5F 15
Archibald M. W1 ...7E 66 (3J 165)
Archibald Rd. N7 ....4H 49
Archibald St. E3 ....3C 70
Archie Cl. UB7: W Dray 2C 76
Arch St. SE1 ....3C 86
ARCHWAY 2G 49
Archway Bus. Cen. N19 .....3H 49
Archway Cl. N19 ....2G 49
SM6: Wall 3H 151
SW19 ....3K 119
W10 ....5F 65
Archway Mall N19 ....2G 49
Archway M. *SW15* *4G 101*
(off Putney Bri. Rd.)
Archway Rd. N6 ....6E 30
Archway St. SW13 ......3A 100
Arcola St. E8 ....5F 51
Arcon Ter. N9 ....7B 8
Arctic St. NW5 ....5F 49
Arcus Rd. BR1: Brom 6G 125
Ardbeg Rd. SE24 ....5D 104
Arden Cl. HA1: Harr 3H 43
SE28 ....6D 74
WD23: Bush 1E 10
Arden Ct. Gdns. N2 ....6B 30
Arden Cres. E14 ....4C 88
RM9: Dag 7C 56
Arden Est. N1 ....2E 68
Arden Grange N12 ....4F 15
Arden Ho. N1 ....1G 163
SE11 ....4G 173
SW9 ....*2J 103*
(off Grantham Rd.)
Arden M. E17 ....5D 34
Arden Mhor HA5: Pinn 4K 23
Arden Rd. N3 ....3H 29
W13 ....7C 62
Ardent Cl. SE25 ....3E 140
Ardent Ho. *E3* *2A 70*
(off Roman Rd.)
Ardfern Av. SW16 ....3A 140
Ardfillan Rd. SE6 ....1F 125
Ardgowan Rd. SE6 ....7G 107
Ardilaun Rd. N5 ....4C 50
Ardingly Cl. CR0: Croy 3K 153
Ardleigh Gdns. SM3: Sutt ...7J 137
Ardleigh Ho. IG11: Bark 1G 73
Ardleigh M. IG1: Ilf 3F 55
Ardleigh Rd. E17 ....1B 34
N1 ....6E 50
Ardleigh Ter. E17 ....1B 34
Ardley Cl. HA4: Ruis 7E 22
NW10 ....3A 46
SE6 ....3A 124
Ardlui Rd. SE27 ....2C 122
Ardmay Gdns. KT6: Surb ...5E 134
Ardmere Rd. SE13 ....6F 107
Ardmore La. IG9: Buck H 1E 20
Ardmore Pl. IG9: Buck H 1E 20
Ardoch Rd. SE6 ....2F 125
Ardra Rd. N9 ....3E 18
Ardrossan Gdns.
KT4: Wor Pk 3C 148
Ardshiel Cl. SW15 ....3F 101
Ardwell Av. IG6: Ilf 5G 37
Ardwell Rd. SW2 ....2J 121
Ardwick Rd. NW2 ....4J 47
Arena Bus. Cen. N4 ....6C 32
Arena Est. N4 ....6B 32
Arena, The EN3: Enf 1G 9
Ares Ct. *E14* *4C 88*
(off Homer Dr.)
Arethusa Ho. *E14* *4C 88*
(off Cahir St.)
Argali Ho. *DA18: Erith* *3E 92*
(off Kale Rd.)
Argall Av. E10 ....7K 33
E17 ....7A 34
Argall Way E10 ....1K 51
Argenta Way HA9: Wemb 6G 45
NW10 ....7H 45
Argent Cen., The
UB3: Hayes 2J 77
Argent Ct. KT9: Chess 3G 147
Argon M. SW6 ....7J 83
Argon Rd. N18 ....5E 18
Argos Ct. *SW9* *1A 104*
(off Caldwell St.)
Argos Ho. *E2* *2H 69*
(off Old Bethnal Grn. Rd.)
Argosy Ho. SE8 ....4A 88
Argosy La. TW19: Staines ...7A 94
Argus Cl. RM7: Mawney 1H 39
Argus Way UB5: N'olt 3C 60
Argyle Av. TW3: Houn 6E 96
(not continuous)
Argyle Cl. W13 ....4A 62
Argyle Ho. E14 ....3E 88
Argyle Pas. N17 ....1F 33
Argyle Pl. W6 ....4D 82
Argyle Rd. E1 ....4K 69
EN5: Barn 4A 4
E15 ....4G 53
E16 ....6K 71
HA2: Harr 6F 25
IG1: Ilf 2E 54
N12 ....5E 14
N17 ....1G 33
N18 ....4B 18
TW3: Houn 5F 97
UB6: G'frd 3K 61
W13 ....5A 62
Argyle Sq. WC1 ....3J 67 (1F 161)
Argyle St. WC1 ....3J 67 (1E 160)
Argyle Wlk. WC1 ....3J 67
Argyle Way SE16 ....5G 87
Argyll Av. UB1: S'hall 1F 79
Argyll Cl. SW9 ....3K 103
Argyll Gdns. HA8: Edg 2H 27
Argyll Mans.
SW3 ....6B 84 (7B 170)
W14 ....*4G 83*
(off Hammersmith Rd.)
Argyll Rd. SE18 ....3G 91
W8 ....2J 83
Argyll St. W1 ......6G 67 (1A 166)
Arica Ho. *SE16* *3H 87*
(off Slippers Pl.)
Arica Rd. SE4 ....4A 106
Ariel Ct. SE11 .....4B 86 (4K 173)
Ariel Rd. NW6 ....6J 47
Ariel Way TW4: Houn 3K 95
W12 ....1E 82
Aristotle Rd. SW4 ....3H 103
Arkell Gro. SE19 ....7B 122
Arkindale Rd. SE6 ....3E 124
Arklay Cl. UB8: Uxb 4B 58
Arkley Cres. E17 ....5B 34
Arkley Rd. E17 ....5B 34
Arklow Ho. *SE5* *6D 86*
(off Albany Rd.)
Arklow M. KT6: Surb 2E 146
Arklow Rd. SE14 ....6B 88
Arklow Rd. Trad. Est.
SE14 ....6A 88
Ark, The *W6* *5F 83*
(off Talgarth Rd.)
Arkwright Ho. *SW2* *7J 103*
(off Streatham Pl.)
Arkwright Rd.
CR2: S Croy 7F 153
NW3 ....5A 48
Arlesey Cl. SW15 ....5G 101
Arlesford Rd. SW9 ....3J 103
Arlingford Rd. SW2 ....5A 104
Arlington N12 ....3D 14
Arlington Av. N1 ....1C 68
(not continuous)
Arlington Cl. DA15: Sidc 7J 109
SE13 ....5F 107
SM1: Sutt 2J 149
Arlington Cl. TW1: Twick 6C 98
Arlington Ct. UB3: Hayes 5G 77
W3 ....*2H 81*
(off Mill Hill Rd.)
Arlington Dr. HA4: Ruis 6F 23
SM5: Cars 2D 150
Arlington Gdns. IG1: Ilf 1E 54
W4 ....5J 81
Arlington Ho. *EC1* *1K 161*
(off Arlington Way)
SE8 ....*6B 88*
(off Evelyn St.)
SW1 ....1G 85 (4A 166)
W12 ....*1D 82*
(off Tunis Rd.)
Arlington Lodge SW2 ......4K 103
Arlington M. TW1: Twick 6B 98
Arlington Pk. Mans. *W4* *5J 81*
(off Sutton La. Nth.)
Arlington Pas.
TW11: Tedd 4K 115
Arlington Pl. SE10 ....7E 88
Arlington Rd. IG8: Wfd G 1J 35
KT6: Surb 6D 134
N14 ....2A 16
NW1 ....1F 67
TW1: Twick 6C 98
TW10: Rich 2D 116
TW11: Tedd 4K 115
TW15: Ashf 5B 112
W13 ....6B 62
Arlington Sq. N1 ....1C 68
Arlington St. W1 ...1G 85 (4A 166)
Arlington Way
EC1 ....3A 68 (1K 161)
Arliss Ho. HA1: Harr 5K 25
Arliss Way UB5: N'olt 1A 60
Arlow Rd. N21 ....1F 17
Armada Ct. SE8 ....6C 88
Armadale Cl. N17 ....4H 33
Armadale Rd. SW6 ....7J 83
TW14: Felt 5J 95
Armada St. *SE8* *6C 88*
(off McMillan St.)
Armada Way E6 ....5F 73
(Gallions Reach Shop. Pk.)
E6 ....7F 73
(Woolwich Mnr. Way)
Armagh Rd. E3 ....1B 70
Armfield Cl.
KT8: W Mole 5D 132
Armfield Cres.
CR4: Mitc 2D 138
Armfield Rd. EN2: Enf 1J 7
Arminger Rd. W12 ....1D 82
Armistice Gdns. SE25 .....3G 141
Armitage Rd. NW11 ....1G 47
SE10 ....5H 89
Armour Cl. N7 ....6K 49
Armoury Rd. SE8 ....2D 106
SE13 ....2D 106
Armoury Way SW18 ....5J 101
Armsby Ho. *E1* *5J 69*
(off Stepney Way)
Armstead Wlk.
RM10: Dag 7G 57
Armstrong Av. IG8: Wfd G 6B 20
Armstrong Cl. BR1: Brom ...3C 144
E6 ....6D 72
HA5: Pinn 6J 23
KT12: Walt T 6J 131
RM8: Dag 7D 38
Armstrong Cres. EN4: Barn ...3G 5
Armstrong Rd. SE18 ....3G 91
SW7 ....3B 84 (2A 170)
TW13: Felt 5C 114
W3 ....1B 82
Armstrong Way
UB2: S'hall 2F 79
Armytage Rd. TW5: Houn ...7B 78
Arnal Cres. SW18 ....7G 101
Arncliffe NW6 ....2K 65
Arncliffe Cl. N11 ....6K 15
Arncroft Ct. IG11: Bark 3B 74
Arndale Wlk. SW18 ....5K 101
Arne Ho. SE11 ....5G 173
Arne St. WC2 ......6J 67 (1F 167)
Arnett Sq. E4 ....6G 19
Arne Wlk. SE3 ....4H 107
Arneways Av.
RM6: Chad H 3D 38
Arneway St.
SW1 ....3H 85 (2D 172)
Arnewood Cl. SW15 ....1C 118
Arneys La. CR4: Mitc 6E 138
Arngask Rd. SE6 ....7F 107
Arnhem Pl. E14 ....3C 88
Arnhem Way SE22 ....5E 104
Arnhem Wharf E14 ....3B 88
Arnison Rd.
KT8: E Mos 4H 133
Arnold Cir. E2 ......3F 69 (2J 163)
Arnold Cl. HA3: Harr 7F 27
Arnold Ct. N22 ....7D 16
Arnold Cres. TW7: Isle 5H 97
Arnold Dr. KT9: Chess 6D 146
Arnold Est. SE1 ....2F 87 (7K 169)
(not continuous)
Arnold Gdns. N13 ....5G 17
Arnold Ho. *SE3* *7A 90*
(off Shooters Hill Rd.)
SE17 ....*5B 86*
(off Doddington Gro.)
Arnold Mans. *W14* *6H 83*
(off Queen's Club Gdns.)
Arnold Rd. E3 ....3C 70
N15 ....3F 33
RM9: Dag 7F 57
SW17 ....7D 120
UB5: N'olt 6C 42
Arnold Ter. HA7: Stan 5E 10
Arnos Gro. N14 ....4C 16
Arnos Gro. Ct. *N11* *5B 16*
(off Palmer's Rd.)
Arnos Rd. N11 ....4B 16
Arnot Ho. *SE5* *7C 86*
(off Comber Gro.)
Arnott Cl. SE28 ....1C 92
W4 ....4K 81
Arnould Av. SE5 ....4D 104
Arnsberg Way DA7: Bex 4F 111
Arnside Gdns.
HA9: Wemb 1D 44
Arnside Rd. DA7: Bex 1G 111
Arnside St. SE17 ....6D 86
Arnulf St. SE6 ....4D 124
Arnulls Rd. SW16 ....6B 122
Arodene Rd. SW2 ....6K 103
Arosa Rd. TW1: Twick 6D 98
(not continuous)
Arpley Sq. *SE20* *7J 123*
(off High St.)
Arragon Gdns.
BR4: W W'ck 3D 154
SW16 ....7J 121
Arragon Rd. E6 ....1B 72
SW18 ....1J 119
TW1: Twick 7A 98
Arran Cl. DA8: Erith 6K 93
SM6: Wall 4F 151
Arran Ct. NW9 ....2B 28
NW10 ....3K 45
Arrandene Open Space ***6H 13***
Arran Dr. E12 ....1B 54
Arran Ho. *E14* *1E 88*
(off Raleana Rd.)
Arran M. W5 ....1F 81
Arran Rd. SE6 ....2D 124
Arran Wlk. N1 ....7C 50
Arras Av. SM4: Mord 5A 138
Arrol Ho. SE1 ....3C 86
Arrol Rd. BR3: Beck 3J 141
Arrow Ct. *SW5* *4J 83*
(off W. Cromwell Rd.)
Arrowhead Ct. E11 ....6F 35
Arrow Rd. E3 ....3D 70
Arrowscout Wlk.
UB5: N'olt 3C 60
Arrows Ho. *SE14* *7J 87*
(off Clifton Way)
Arrowsmith Ho. SE11 ......5G 173
Arsenal F.C. (Highbury)
................***3B 50***
Arsenal Rd. SE9 ....2D 108
Arsenal Way SE18 ....3G 91
Artemis Ct. *E14* *4C 88*
(off Homer Dr.)
Arterberry Rd. SW20 ......7E 118
Artesian Cl. NW10 ....7K 45
Artesian Gro. EN5: Barn 4F 5
Artesian Rd. W2 ....6J 65
Artesian Wlk. E11 ....3G 53
Arthingworth St. E15 ....1G 71
Arthur Ct. *CR0: Croy* *3E 152*
(off Fairfield Path)
SW11 ....1E 102
W2 ....*6K 65*
(off Queensway)
W10 ....*6F 65*
(off Silchester Rd.)
Arthur Deakin Ho. *E1* *5K 163*
(off Hunton St.)
Arthurdon Rd. SE4 ....5C 106
Arthur Gro. SE18 ....4G 91
Arthur Henderson Ho.
SW6 ....*2H 101*
(off Fulham Rd.)
Arthur Horsley Wlk. *E7* *5H 53*
(off Twr. Hamlets Rd.)
Arthur Rd. E6 ....2D 72
KT2: King T 7G 117
KT3: N Mald 5D 136
N7 ....4K 49
N9 ....2A 18
RM6: Chad H 6C 38
SW19 ....5H 119
Arthur St. EC4 .....7D 68 (2F 169)
Artichoke Hill E1 ....7H 69
Artichoke M. *SE5* *1D 104*
(off Artichoke Pl.)
Artichoke Pl. SE5 ....1D 104
Artillery Cl. IG2: Ilf 6G 37
Artillery Ho. E15 ....6G 53
SE18 ....*5E 90*
(off Connaught M.)
Artillery La. E1 ....5E 68 (6H 163)
W12 ....6C 64
Artillery Pas. E1 ....6J 163
Artillery Pl. HA3: Harr 7B 10
SE18 ....5D 90
SW1 ....3H 85 (2C 172)
Artillery Row
SW1 ....3G 85 (2C 172)
Artisan Cl. E6 ....6F 73
Artizan St. E1 ....7J 163
Arts Theatre ***2E 166***
(off St Martin's St.)
Arun Ct. SE25 ....5G 141
Arundale *KT1: King T* *4D 134*
(off Anglesea Rd.)
Arundel Av. SM4: Mord 4H 137
Arundel Bldgs. *SE1* *3E 86*
(off Swan Mead)
Arundel Cl. CR0: Croy 3B 152
DA6: Bex 6F 111
E15 ....4G 53
SW11 ....5C 102
TW12: Hamp 5F 115
Arundel Ct. BR2: Short 2G 143
HA2: Harr 4E 42
N12 ....6H 15
N17 ....1G 33
SE16 ....*5H 87*
(off Varcoe Rd.)
SW3 ....*5D 170*
(off Jubilee Pl.)

Ashurst Cl.—Avenons Rd.

Ashurst Cl. SE20 1H 141
Ashurst Dr. IG2: Ilf 6F 37
IG6: Ilf 5G 37 (Hamilton Av.)
IG6: Ilf 4G 37 (Horns Rd.)
TW17: Shep 5A 130
Ashurst Gdns. SW2 1A 122
Ashurst Rd. EN4: Barn 5J 5
N12 5H 15
Ashurst Wlk. CR0: Croy 2H 153
Ashvale Rd. SW17 5D 120
Ash Vw. Cl. TW15: Ashf 6A 112
Ash Vw. Gdns. TW15: Ashf 5A 112
Ashville Rd. E11 2F 53
Ash Wlk. HA0: Wemb 3C 44
Ashwater Rd. SE12 1J 125
Ashway Cen., The KT2: King T 1E 134
Ashwell Cl. E6 6C 72
Ashwin St. E8 6F 51
Ashwood Av. UB8: Uxb 6C 58
Ashwood Gdns. CR0: Croy 6D 154
UB3: Hayes 4H 77
Ashwood Rd. E4 3A 20
Ashworth Cl. SE5 2D 104
Ashworth Est. CR0: Croy 1J 151
Ashworth Mans. *W9* *3K 65* *(off Elgin Av.)*
Ashworth Rd. W9 3K 65
Aske Ho. N1 1G 163 (not continuous)
Asker Ho. N7 4J 49
Askern Cl. DA6: Bex 4D 110
Aske St. N1 3E 68 (1G 163)
Askew Cres. W12 2B 82
Askew Est. *W12* *1B 82* *(off Uxbridge Rd.)*
Askew Rd. W12 2B 82
Askham Ct. W12 1C 82
Askham Rd. W12 1C 82
Askill Dr. SW15 5G 101
Askwith Rd. RM13: Rain 3K 75
Asland Rd. E15 1G 71
Aslett St. SW18 7K 101
Asmara Rd. NW2 5G 47
Asmuns Hill NW11 5J 29
Asmuns Pl. NW11 5H 29
Asolando Dr. SE17 4C 86
Aspen Cl. N19 2G 49
UB7: W Dray 1B 76
W5 2F 81
Aspen Copse BR1: Brom 2D 144
Aspen Dr. HA0: Wemb 3A 44
Aspen Gdns. CR4: Mitc 5E 138
TW15: Ashf 5E 112
W6 5D 82
Aspen Grn. DA18: Erith 3F 93
Aspen Ho. DA15: Sidc 3A 128
SE15 *6J 87* *(off Sharratt St.)*
Aspen La. UB5: N'olt 3C 60
Aspenlea Rd. W6 6F 83
Aspen Lodge *W8* *3K 83* *(off Abbots Wlk.)*
Aspen Way E14 7D 70
TW13: Felt 3K 113
Aspern Gro. NW3 5C 48
Aspinall Rd. SE4 3K 105 (not continuous)
Aspinden Rd. SE16 4H 87
Aspley Rd. SW18 5K 101
Asplins Rd. N17 1G 33
Asprey Pl. BR1: Brom 2C 144
Asquith Cl. RM8: Dag 1C 56
Assam St. E1 6G 69
Assata M. N1 6B 50
Assembly Pas. E1 5J 69
Assembly Wlk. SM5: Cars 7C 138
Ass Ho. La. HA3: Harr 4A 10
Association Gallery *3G 163* *(off Leonard St.)*
Astall Cl. HA3: Harr 1J 25
Astbury Bus. Pk. SE15 1J 105
Astbury Ho. SE11 2J 173
Astbury Rd. SE15 1J 105
Astell St. SW3 5C 84 (5D 170)
Aste St. E14 2E 88
Astey's Row N1 7C 50
Asthall Gdns. IG6: Ilf 4G 37
Astins Ho. E17 4D 34
Astleham Rd. TW17: Shep 3A 130
Astle St. SW11 2E 102
Astley Av. NW2 5E 46
Astley Ho. *SE1* *5F 87* *(off Rowcross St.)*
SW13 *6D 82* *(off Wyatt Dr.)*
Aston Av. HA3: Harr 7C 26
Aston Cl. DA14: Sidc 3A 128
Aston Ct. IG8: Wfd G 6D 20
Aston Grn. TW4: Houn 2A 96
Aston Ho. SW8 1H 103
W11 *7H 65* *(off Westbourne Gro.)*
Aston M. RM6: Chad H 7C 38
Aston Pl. SW16 6B 122
Aston Rd. SW20 2E 136
W5 6D 62
Aston St. E14 5A 70
Aston Ter. SW12 6F 103
Astonville St. SW18 1J 119
Astor Av. RM7: Rom 6J 39
Astor Cl. KT2: King T 6H 117
Astor Ct. *E16* *6A 72* *(off Ripley Rd.)*
SW6 *7A 84* *(off Maynard Cl.)*
Astoria Mans. SW16 3J 121
Astoria Wlk. SW9 3A 104
Astra Ho. *SE14* *6B 88* *(off Arklow Rd.)*
Astrid Ho. TW13: Felt 2A 114
Astrop M. W6 3E 82
Astrop Ter. W6 2E 82
Astwood M. SW7 4A 84
Asylum Rd. SE15 7H 87
Atalanta St. SW6 7F 83
Atbara Rd. TW11: Tedd 6B 116
Atcham Rd. TW3: Houn 4G 97
Atcost Rd. IG11: Bark 5A 74
Atcraft Cen. HA0: Wemb 1E 62
Atheldene Rd. SW18 1K 119
Athelney St. SE6 3C 124
Athelstane Gro. E3 2B 70
Athelstane M. N4 1A 50
Athelstan Gdns. NW6 7G 47
Athelstan Ho. *KT1: King T* *4F 135* *(off Athelstan Rd.)*
Athelstan Rd. KT1: King T 4F 135
Athelstone Rd. HA3: Harr 2H 25
Athena Cl. HA2: Harr 2H 43
KT1: King T 3F 135
Athenaeum Ct. N5 4C 50
Athenaeum Pl. N10 3F 31
Athenaeum Rd. N20 1F 15
Athena Pl. HA6: Nwood 1H 23
Athenia Ho. *E14* *6F 71* *(off Blair St.)*
Athenlay Rd. SE15 5K 105
Athens Gdns. *W9* *4J 65* *(off Harrow Rd.)*
Atherden Rd. E5 4J 51
Atherfold Rd. SW9 3J 103
Atherley Way TW4: Houn 7D 96
Atherstone Ct. *W2* *5K 65* *(off Delamere Ter.)*
Atherstone M. SW7 4A 84
Atherton Dr. SW19 4F 119
Atherton Hgts. HA0: Wemb 6C 44
Atherton M. E7 6H 53
Atherton Pl. HA2: Harr 3H 25
UB1: S'hall 7E 60
Atherton Rd. E7 6H 53
IG5: Ilf 2C 36
SW13 7C 82
Atherton St. SW11 2C 102
Athlone Cl. E5 5H 51
Athlone Ct. E17 3F 35
Athlone Ho. *E1* *6J 69* *(off Sidney St.)*
Athlone Rd. SW2 7K 103
Athlone St. NW5 6E 48
Athlon Ind. Est. HA0: Wemb 1D 62
Athlon Rd. HA0: Wemb 2D 62
Athol Cl. HA5: Pinn 1K 23
Athole Gdns. EN1: Enf 5K 7
Athol Gdns. HA5: Pinn 1K 23
Atholl Ho. *W9* *3A 66* *(off Maida Va.)*
Atholl Rd. IG3: Ilf 7A 38
Athol Rd. DA8: Erith 5J 93
Athol Sq. E14 6E 70
Athol Way UB10: Uxb 3C 58
Atkin Bldg. *WC1* *5H 161* *(off Raymond Bldgs.)*
Atkins Dr. BR4: W W'ck 2F 155
Atkinson Ct. *E10* *7D 34* *(off Kings Cl.)*
Atkinson Ho. *E2* *2G 69* *(off Pritchards Rd.)*
E13 *4H 71* *(off Sutton Rd.)*
SE17 *4D 86* *(off Catesby St.)*
Atkinson Rd. E16 5A 72
Atkins Rd. E10 6D 34
SW12 7G 103
Atlanta Ho. *SE16* *3A 88* *(off Brunswick Quay)*
Atlantic Ct. *E14* *7F 71* *(off Jamestown Way)*
Atlantic Ho. *E1* *5A 70* *(off Harford St.)*
Atlantic Rd. SW9 4A 104
Atlantic Wharf *E1* *7K 69* *(off Jardine Rd.)*
Atlantis Cl. IG11: Bark 3B 74
Atlas Bus. Cen. NW2 1D 46
Atlas Gdns. SE7 4A 90
Atlas M. E8 6F 51
N7 6K 49
Atlas Rd. E13 2J 71
HA9: Wemb 4J 45
N11 7K 15
NW10 3A 64
Atlas Wharf E9 6C 52
Atley Rd. E3 1C 70
Atlip Rd. HA0: Wemb 1E 62
Atney Rd. SW15 4G 101
Atterbury Rd. N4 6A 32
Atterbury St. SW1 4J 85 (4D 172)
Attewood Av. NW10 3A 46
Attewood Rd. UB5: N'olt 6C 42
Attfield Cl. N20 2G 15
Attfield Ct. *KT1: King T* *2F 135* *(off Albert Rd.)*
Attilburgh Ho. *SE1* *7J 169* *(off Abbey St.)*
Attleborough Ct. SE26 2G 123
Attle Cl. UB10: Uxb 2C 58
Attlee Cl. CR7: Thor H 5C 140
UB4: Hayes 3K 59
Attlee Rd. SE28 7B 74
UB4: Hayes 3J 59
Attlee Ter. E17 4D 34
Attneave St. WC1 3A 68 (2J 161)
Atwater Cl. SW2 1A 122
Atwell Cl. E10 6D 34
Atwell Pl. KT7: T Ditt 7K 133
Atwell Rd. SE15 2G 105
Atwood Av. TW9: Rich 2G 99
Atwood Ho. *W14* *4H 83* *(off Beckford Cl.)*
Atwood Rd. W6 4D 82
Atwoods All. TW9: Rich 1G 99
Aubert Ct. N5 4B 50
Aubert Pk. N5 4B 50
Aubert Rd. N5 4B 50
Aubrey Beardsley Ho. *SW1* *4B 172* *(off Vauxhall Bri. Rd.)*
Aubrey Mans. *NW1* *5C 158* *(off Lisson St.)*
Aubrey Moore Point *E15* *2E 70* *(off Abbey La.)*
Aubrey Pl. NW8 2A 66
Aubrey Rd. E17 3C 34
N8 5J 31
W8 1H 83
Aubrey Wlk. W8 1H 83
Auburn Cl. SE14 7A 88
Aubyn Hill SE27 4C 122
Aubyn Sq. SW15 5C 100
Auckland Cl. SE19 1F 141
Auckland Ct. UB4: Hayes 4A 60
Auckland Gdns. SE19 1E 140
Auckland Hill SE27 4C 122
Auckland Ho. *W12* *7D 64* *(off White City Est.)*
Auckland Ri. SE19 1E 140
Auckland Rd. E10 3D 52
IG1: Ilf 1F 55
KT1: King T 4F 135
SE19 1F 141
SW11 4C 102
Auckland St. SE11 5K 85 (6G 173)
Audax NW9 2B 28
Auden Pl. NW1 1E 66 (not continuous)
SM3: Sutt 4E 148
Audleigh Pl. IG7: Chig 6K 21
Audley Cl. N10 7A 16
SW11 3E 102
Audley Ct. E18 4H 35
HA5: Pinn 2A 24
TW2: Twick 3H 115
UB5: N'olt 3A 60
Audley Dr. E16 1K 89
Audley Gdns. IG3: Ilf 2K 55
Audley Pl. SM2: Sutt 7K 149
Audley Rd. EN2: Enf 2G 7
NW4 5C 28
TW10: Rich 5F 99
W5 5F 63
Audley Sq. W1 1E 84 (4H 165)
Audrey Cl. BR3: Beck 6D 142
Audrey Gdns. HA0: Wemb 2B 44
Audrey Rd. IG1: Ilf 3F 55
Audrey St. E2 2G 69
Audric Cl. KT2: King T 1G 135
Augurs La. E13 3K 71
Augusta Cl. KT8: W Mole 4D 132
Augusta Rd. TW2: Twick 2G 115
Augusta St. E14 6D 70
Augustine Rd. HA3: Harr 1F 25
W14 3F 83
Augustus Cl. TW8: Bford 7C 80
W12 2D 82
Augustus Ct. SW16 2H 121
TW13: Felt 4D 114
Augustus Ho. *NW1* *1A 160* *(off Augustus St.)*
Augustus Rd. SW19 1F 119
Augustus St. NW1 2F 67 (1K 159)
Aultone Way SM1: Sutt 2K 149
SM5: Cars 3D 150
Aulton Pl. SE11 5A 86 (6K 173)
Aurelia Gdns. CR0: Croy 5K 139
Aurelia Rd. CR0: Croy 6J 139
Auriel Av. RM10: Dag 6K 57
Auriga M. N1 5D 50
Auriol Cl. KT4: Wor Pk 3A 148
Auriol Dr. UB6: G'frd 7H 43
UB10: Uxb 6C 40
Auriol Ho. *W12* *1D 82* *(off Ellerslie Rd.)*
Auriol Pk. Rd. KT4: Wor Pk 3A 148
Auriol Rd. W14 4G 83
Aurora Ho. *E14* *6D 70* *(off Kerbey St.)*
Austell Gdns. NW7 3F 13
Austell Hgts. *NW7* *3F 13* *(off Austell Gdns.)*
Austen Cl. SE28 1B 92
Austen Ho. *NW6* *3J 65* *(off Cambridge Rd.)*
Austen Rd. DA8: Erith 7H 93
HA2: Harr 2F 43
Austin Av. BR2: Short 5C 144
Austin Cl. SE23 7A 106
TW1: Twick 5C 98
Austin Ct. E6 1A 72
EN1: Enf 5K 7
SE15 *3G 105* *(off Philip Wlk.)*
Austin Friars EC2 6D 68 (7F 163) (not continuous)
Austin Friars Pas. EC2 7F 163
Austin Friars Sq. EC2 7F 163
Austin Ho. *SE14* *7B 88* *(off Achilles St.)*
Austin Rd. SW11 1E 102
UB3: Hayes 2H 77
Austin's La. HA4: Ruis 4F 41
UB10: Ruis, Uxb 3E 40 (not continuous)
Austin St. E2 3F 69 (2J 163)
Austin Ter. *SE1* *1K 173* *(off Morley St.)*
Austral Cl. DA15: Sidc 3K 127
Australia Rd. W12 7D 64
Austral St. SE11 4B 86 (3K 173)
Austyn Gdns. KT5: Surb 1H 147
Autumn Cl. EN1: Enf 1B 8
SW19 6A 120
Autumn Lodge *CR0: Croy* *4E 152* *(off South Pk. Hill Rd.)*
Autumn St. E3 1C 70
Avalon Cl. EN2: Enf 2F 7
SW20 2G 137
W13 5A 62
Avalon Rd. SW6 1K 101
W13 4A 62
Avarn Rd. SW17 6D 120
Avebury Ct. *N1* *1D 68* *(off Imber St.)*
Avebury Pk. KT6: Surb 7D 134
Avebury Rd. E11 1F 53
SW19 1H 137
Avebury St. N1 1D 68
Aveley Mans. *IG11: Bark* *7F 55* *(off Whiting Av.)*
Aveley Rd. RM1: Rom 4K 39
Aveline St. SE11 5A 86 (5H 173)
Aveling Pk. Rd. E17 2C 34
Ave Maria La. EC4 6B 68 (1B 168)
Avenell Rd. N5 3B 50
Avenfield Ho. *W1* *2F 165* *(off Park La.)*
Avening Rd. SW18 7J 101
Avening Ter. SW18 7J 101
Avenons Rd. E13 4J 71

B

Baker Beal Ct.—Barfleur Ho.

Baker Beal Ct. DA7: Bex ... 3H 111
Baker Ho. W7 ... 1K 79
WC1 ... 4F 161
(off Colonnade)
Baker La. CR4: Mitc ... 2E 138
Baker Pas. NW10 ... 1A 64
Baker Rd. NW10 ... 1A 64
SE18 ... 7C 90
Bakers Av. E17 ... 6D 34
Bakers Ct. SE25 ... 3E 140
Bakers End SW20 ... 2G 137
Baker's Fld. N7 ... 4J 49
Bakers Gdns. SM5: Cars ... 2C 150
Bakers Hall Ct. EC3 ... 3G 169
Bakers Hill E5 ... 1J 51
EN5: Barn ... 2E 4
Bakers Ho. W5 ... 7D 62
(off Grove, The)
Bakers La. N6 ... 6D 30
Bakers M. W1 ... 6E 66 (7G 159)
Bakers Pas. NW3 ... 4A 48
(off Heath St.)
Baker's Rents E2 ... 3F 69 (2J 163)
Baker's Row E15 ... 2G 71
EC1 ... 4A 68 (4J 161)
BAKER STREET ... 4D 66 (4F 159)
Baker St. EN1: Enf ... 3J 7
NW1 ... 4D 66 (4F 159)
W1 ... 5D 66 (4F 159)
Bakers Yd. EC1 ... 4J 161
Bakery Cl. SW9 ... 7K 85
Bakery M. KT6: Surb ... 1G 147
Bakery Path HA8: Edg ... 6C 12
(off St Margaret's Rd.)
Bakery Pl. SW11 ... 4D 102
Bakewell Way
KT3: N Mald ... 2A 136
Balaam Ho. SM1: Sutt ... 4J 149
Balaams La. N14 ... 2C 16
Balaam St. E13 ... 4J 71
Balaclava Rd. KT6: Surb ... 7C 134
SE1 ... 4F 87
Bala Grn. NW9 ... 6A 28
(off Ruthin Cl.)
Balcaskie Rd. SE9 ... 5D 108
Balchen Rd. SE3 ... 2B 108
Balchier Rd. SE22 ... 6H 105
Balcombe Cl. DA6: Bex ... 4D 110
Balcombe Ho. NW1 ... 3E 158
(off Taunton Pl.)
Balcombe St.
NW1 ... 4D 66 (3E 158)
Balcon Ct. W5 ... 6F 63
Balcorne St. E9 ... 7J 51
Balder Ri. SE12 ... 2K 125
Balderton Flats W1 ... 1H 165
(off Balderton St.)
Balderton St. W1 ... 6E 66 (1H 165)
Baldewyne Ct. N17 ... 1G 33
Baldock St. E3 ... 2D 70
Baldrey Ho. SE10 ... 5H 89
(off Blackwall La.)
Baldry Gdns. SW16 ... 6J 121
Baldwin Cres. SE5 ... 1C 104
Baldwin Gdns. TW3: Houn ... 1G 97
Baldwin Ho. SW2 ... 1A 122
Baldwins Gdns.
EC1 ... 5A 68 (5J 161)
Baldwin St. EC1 ... 3D 68 (2E 162)
Baldwin Ter. N1 ... 2C 68
Baldwyn Gdns. W3 ... 7K 63
Baldwyn's Pk. DA5: Bexl ... 2K 129
Baldwyn's Rd. DA5: Bexl ... 2K 129
Bale Rd. E1 ... 5A 70
Bales Ter. N9 ... 3A 18
Balfern Gro. W4 ... 5A 82
Balfern St. SW11 ... 2C 102
Balfe St. N1 ... 2J 67
Balfour Av. W7 ... 1K 79
Balfour Bus. Cen.
UB2: S'hall ... 3A 78
Balfour Gro. N20 ... 3J 15
Balfour Ho. W10 ... 5F 65
(off St Charles Sq.)
Balfour M. N9 ... 3B 18
W1 ... 1E 84 (4H 165)
Balfour Pl. SW15 ... 4D 100
W1 ... 7E 66 (3H 165)
Balfour Rd. BR2: Short ... 5B 144
HA1: Harr ... 5H 25
IG1: Ilf ... 2F 55
N5 ... 4C 50
SE25 ... 5G 141
SM5: Cars ... 7D 150
SW19 ... 7K 119
TW3: Houn ... 3F 97
UB2: S'hall ... 3B 78
W3 ... 5J 63
W13 ... 2A 80
Balfour St. SE17 ... 4D 86
Balfour Ter. N3 ... 2K 29
Balfron Twr. E14 ... 6E 70
Balgonie Rd. E4 ... 1A 20
Balgowan Cl.
KT3: N Mald ... 5A 136
Balgowan Rd. BR3: Beck ... 3A 142
Balgowan St. SE18 ... 4K 91
BALHAM ... 1E 120
Balham Continental Mkt.
SW12 ... 1F 121
(off Shipka Rd.)
Balham Gro. SW12 ... 7E 102
Balham High Rd. SW12 ... 3E 120
SW17 ... 3E 120
Balham Hill SW12 ... 7F 103
Balham New Rd. SW12 ... 7F 103
Balham Pk. Rd. SW12 ... 1D 120
Balham Rd. N9 ... 2B 18
Balham Sta. Rd. SW12 ... 1F 121
Balin Ho. SE1 ... 6E 168
(off Long La.)
Balkan Wlk. E1 ... 7H 69
Balladier Wlk. E14 ... 5D 70
Ballamore Rd.
BR1: Brom ... 3J 125
Ballance Rd. E9 ... 6K 51
Ballantine St. SW18 ... 4A 102
Ballantrae Ho. NW2 ... 4H 47
Ballard Cl. KT2: King T ... 7K 117
Ballard Ho. SE10 ... 6D 88
(off Thames St.)
Ballards Cl. RM10: Dag ... 1H 75
Ballards Farm Rd.
CR2: Croy, S Croy ... 6G 153
Ballards La. N3 ... 1J 29
N12 ... 7D 14
Ballards M. HA8: Edg ... 6B 12
Ballards Ri.
CR2: S Croy ... 6G 153
Ballards Rd. NW2 ... 2C 46
RM10: Dag ... 2H 75
Ballards Way
CR2: S Croy ... 6G 153
Ballast Quay SE10 ... 5F 89
Ballater Rd.
CR2: S Croy ... 5F 153
SW2 ... 4J 103
Ball Ct. EC3 ... 1F 169
(off Cornhill)
Ballina St. SE23 ... 7K 105
Ballin Ct. E14 ... 2E 88
(off Stewart St.)
Ballingdon Rd. SW11 ... 6E 102
Balliol Av. E4 ... 4B 20
Balliol Rd. DA16: Well ... 2B 110
N17 ... 1E 32
W10 ... 6E 64
Balloch Rd. SE6 ... 1F 125
Ballogie Av. NW10 ... 4A 46
Ballow Cl. SE5 ... 7E 86
Ball's Pond Pl. N1 ... 6D 50
Balls Pond Rd. N1 ... 6D 50
Balmain Cl. W5 ... 1D 80
Balmain Ct. TW3: Houn ... 1F 97
Balmain Lodge
KT5: Surb ... 4E 134
(off Cranes Pk. Av.)
Balman Ho. SE16 ... 4K 87
(off Rotherhithe New Rd.)
Balmer Rd. E3 ... 2B 70
Balmes Rd. N1 ... 1D 68
Balmoral Av. BR3: Beck ... 4A 142
N11 ... 6K 15
Balmoral Cl. SW15 ... 6F 101
Balmoral Ct. BR3: Beck ... 1E 142
(off Avenue, The)
HA9: Wemb ... 3F 45
KT4: Wor Pk ... 2D 148
SE12 ... 4K 125
SE16 ... 1K 87
(off King & Queen Wharf)
SE27 ... 4C 122
SM2: Sutt ... 7J 149
Balmoral Cres.
KT8: W Mole ... 3E 132
Balmoral Dr. UB1: S'hall ... 4D 60
UB4: Hayes ... 4G 59
Balmoral Gdns.
DA5: Bexl ... 7F 111
IG3: Ilf ... 1K 55
W13 ... 3A 80
Balmoral Gro. N7 ... 6K 49
Balmoral Ho. E14 ... 3D 88
(off Lanark Sq.)
E16 ... 7K 71
(off Keats Av.)
W14 ... 4G 83
(off Windsor Way)
Balmoral M. W12 ... 3B 82
Balmoral Rd. E7 ... 4A 54
E10 ... 2D 52
HA2: Harr ... 4E 42
KT1: King T ... 4F 135
KT4: Wor Pk ... 3D 148
NW2 ... 6D 46
Balmoral Trad. Est.
IG11: Bark ... 5K 73
Balmore Cres. EN4: Barn ... 5K 5
Balmore St. N19 ... 2F 49
Balmuir Gdns. SW15 ... 4E 100
Balnacraig Av. NW10 ... 4A 46
Balniel Ga. SW1 ... 5H 85 (5D 172)
Balsam Ho. E14 ... 7D 70
(off E. India Dock Rd.)
Baltic Cen., The
TW8: Bford ... 5D 80
Baltic Cl. SW19 ... 7B 120
Baltic Ct. SE16 ... 2K 87
Baltic Ho. SE5 ... 2C 104
Baltic Pl. N1 ... 1E 68
Baltic St. E. EC1 ... 4C 68 (4C 162)
Baltic St. W. EC1 ... 4C 68 (4C 162)
Baltimore Ho. SE11 ... 5J 173
Baltimore Pl. DA16: Well ... 2K 109
Balvaird Pl.
SW1 ... 5H 85 (6D 172)
Balvernie Gro. SW18 ... 7H 101
Balvernie M. SW18 ... 7J 101
Bamber Ho. IG11: Bark ... 1H 73
Bamber Rd. SE15 ... 1F 105
Bamborough Gdns. W12 ... 2E 82
Bamburgh N17 ... 7C 18
Bamford Av. HA0: Wemb ... 1F 63
Bamford Ct. E15 ... 5D 52
(off Clays La.)
Bamford Rd. BR1: Brom ... 5E 124
IG11: Bark ... 6G 55
Bampfylde Cl. SM6: Wall ... 3G 151
Bampton Ct. W5 ... 6D 62
Bampton Dr. NW7 ... 7H 13
Bampton Rd. SE23 ... 3K 123
Banavie Gdns. BR3: Beck ... 1E 142
Banbury Cl. EN2: Enf ... 1G 7
Banbury Ct. SM2: Sutt ... 7J 149
WC2 ... 2E 166
Banbury Ho. E9 ... 7K 51
Banbury Rd. E9 ... 7K 51
E17 ... 7E 18
Banbury St. SW11 ... 2C 102
Banbury Wlk. UB5: N'olt ... 2E 60
(off Brabazon Rd.)
Banchory Rd. SE3 ... 7K 89
Bancroft Av. IG9: Buck H ... 2D 20
N2 ... 5C 30
Bancroft Cl. TW15: Ashf ... 5C 112
Bancroft Ct. SW8 ... 7J 85
(off Allen Edwards Dr.)
UB5: N'olt ... 1A 60
Bancroft Gdns. BR6: Orp ... 7K 145
HA3: Harr ... 1G 25
Bancroft Ho. E1 ... 4J 69
(off Cephas St.)
Bancroft Rd. E1 ... 3J 69
HA3: Harr ... 2G 25
Bandon Cl. UB10: Uxb ... 2B 58
BANDONHILL ... 5H 151
Bandon Ri. SM6: Wall ... 5H 151
Banfield Rd. SE15 ... 3H 105
Bangalore St. SW15 ... 3E 100
Bangor Cl. UB5: N'olt ... 5F 43
Banim St. W6 ... 4D 82
Banister Ho. E9 ... 5K 51
SW8 ... 1G 103
(off Wadhurst Rd.)
W10 ... 3G 65
(off Bruckner St.)
Banister Rd. W10 ... 3F 65
Bank Av. CR4: Mitc ... 2B 138
Bank Bldgs. E4 ... 6A 20
(off Avenue, The)
E17 ... 3K 33
Bank End SE1 ... 1C 86 (4D 168)
Bankfoot Rd. BR1: Brom ... 4G 125
Bankhurst Rd. SE6 ... 7B 106
Bank La. KT2: King T ... 7E 116
SW15 ... 5A 100
Bank M. SM1: Sutt ... 6A 150
Bank of England ... 6D 68 (1E 168)
Bank of England Mus. ... 1F 169
Bank of England Offices
EC4 ... 1C 168
Banks Ho. SE1 ... 3C 86
(off Rockingham St.)
Banksian Wlk. TW7: Isle ... 1J 97
Banksia Rd. N18 ... 5E 18
Bankside CR2: S Croy ... 6F 153
EN2: Enf ... 1G 7
SE1 ... 7C 68 (3C 168)
(not continuous)
UB1: S'hall ... 1B 78
Bankside Art Gallery
... 7B 68 (3B 168)
Bankside Av. UB5: N'olt ... 2J 59
Bankside Cl. DA5: Bexl ... 4K 129
SM5: Cars ... 6C 150
TW7: Isle ... 4K 97
Bankside Dr. KT7: T Ditt ... 1B 146
Bankside Pk. IG11: Bark ... 3A 74
Bankside Rd. IG1: Ilf ... 5G 55
Bankside Way SE19 ... 6E 122
Banks La. DA6: Bex ... 4F 111
Banks Way E12 ... 4E 54
Bank, The N6 ... 1F 49
Bankton Rd. SW2 ... 4A 104
Bankwell Rd. SE13 ... 4G 107
Bannerman Ho.
SW8 ... 6K 85 (7G 173)
Banner St. EC1 ... 4C 68 (4D 162)
Banning St. SE10 ... 5G 89
Bannister Cl. SW2 ... 1A 122
UB6: G'frd ... 5H 43
Bannister Ho. SE14 ... 6K 87
(off John Williams Cl.)
Bannockburn Rd. SE18 ... 4J 91
Banqueting House
... 1J 85 (5E 166)
Banstead Gdns. N9 ... 3K 17
Banstead Rd. SM5: Cars ... 7B 150
Banstead Rd. Sth.
SM2: Sutt ... 7B 150
Banstead St. SE15 ... 3J 105
Banstead Way SM6: Wall ... 5J 151
Banstock Rd. HA8: Edg ... 6C 12
Banting Dr. N21 ... 5E 6
Banting Ho. NW2 ... 3C 46
Bantock Ho. W10 ... 3G 65
(off Third Av.)
Banton Cl. EN1: Enf ... 2C 8
Bantry Ho. E1 ... 4K 69
(off Ernest St.)
Bantry St. SE5 ... 7D 86
Banwell Rd. DA5: Bexl ... 6D 110
Banyard Rd. SE16 ... 3H 87
Baptist Gdns. NW5 ... 6E 48
Barandon Rd. W11 ... 7F 65
Barandon Wlk. W11 ... 7F 65
Barbanel Ho. E1 ... 4J 69
(off Cephas St.)
Barbara Brosnan Ct.
NW8 ... 2B 66 (1A 158)
Barbara Cl. TW17: Shep ... 5D 130
Barbara Hucklesby Cl.
N22 ... 2B 32
Barbauld Rd. N16 ... 3E 50
Barber Beaumont Ho. E1 ... 3K 69
(off Bancroft Rd.)
Barber Cl. N21 ... 7F 7
Barbers All. E13 ... 3K 71
Barbers Rd. E15 ... 2D 70
Barbican Arts Cen.
... 5C 68 (5D 162)
Barbican Rd. UB6: G'frd ... 6F 61
Barbican Theatre ... 5D 162
(off Silk St.)
Barb M. W6 ... 3E 82
Barbon Cl. WC1 ... 5K 67 (5F 161)
Barbot Cl. N9 ... 3B 18
Barchard St. SW18 ... 5K 101
Barchester Cl. W7 ... 1K 79
Barchester Rd. HA3: Harr ... 2H 25
Barchester St. E14 ... 5D 70
Barclay Cl. SW6 ... 7J 83
Barclay Ho. E9 ... 7J 51
(off Well St.)
Barclay Oval IG8: Wfd G ... 4D 20
Barclay Path E17 ... 5E 34
Barclay Rd. CR0: Croy ... 3D 152
E11 ... 1H 53
(not continuous)
E13 ... 4A 72
E17 ... 5E 34
N18 ... 6J 17
SW6 ... 7J 83
Barcombe Av. SW2 ... 2J 121
Barcombe Cl. BR5: Orp ... 3K 145
Bardell Ho. SE16 ... 7K 169
(off Parkers Row)
Barden St. SE18 ... 7J 91
Bardfield Av.
RM6: Chad H ... 3D 38
Bardney Rd. SM4: Mord ... 4K 137
Bardolph Av. CR0: Croy ... 7B 154
Bardolph Rd. N7 ... 4J 49
TW9: Rich ... 3F 99
Bard Rd. W10 ... 7F 65
Bardsey Pl. E1 ... 4J 69
(off Mile End Rd.)
Bardsey Wlk. N1 ... 6C 50
(off Douglas Rd. Nth.)
Bardsley Cl. CR0: Croy ... 3F 153
Bardsley Ho. SE10 ... 6E 88
(off Bardsley La.)
Bardsley La. SE10 ... 6E 88
Barents Ho. E1 ... 4K 69
(off White Horse La.)
Barfett St. W10 ... 4H 65
Barfield Av. N20 ... 2J 15
Barfield Rd. BR1: Brom ... 3E 144
E11 ... 1H 53
Barfleur Ho. SE8 ... 5B 88

Barford Cl. NW4 . . . 2C **28**
Barford St. N1 . . . 1A **68**
Barforth Rd. SE15 . . . 3H **105**
Barfreston Way SE20 . . . 1H **141**
Bargate Cl. KT3: N Mald . . . 7C **136**
SE18 . . . 5K **91**
Barge Ho. Rd. E16 . . . 2F **91**
Barge Ho. St.
SE1 . . . 1A **86** (4K **167**)
Bargery Rd. SE6 . . . 1D **124**
Barge Wlk. KT1: King T . . . 3D **134**
KT8: E Mos . . . 3H **133**
Bargrove Cl. SE20 . . . 7G **123**
Bargrove Cres. SE6 . . . 2B **124**
Barham Cl. BR2: Short . . . 1C **156**
BR7: Chst . . . 5F **127**
HA0: Wemb . . . 6B **44**
RM7: Mawney . . . 2H **39**
Barham Ct.
CR2: S Croy . . . 4C ***152***
(off Barham Rd.)
Barham Ho. *SE17 . . . 5E* ***86***
(off Kinglake St.)
Barham Rd. BR7: Chst . . . 5F **127**
CR2: S Croy . . . 4C **152**
SW20 . . . 7C **118**
Baring Cl. SE12 . . . 2J **125**
Baring Ho. *E14 . . . 6C* ***70***
(off Canton St.)
Baring Rd. CR0: Croy . . . 1G **153**
EN4: Barn . . . 4G **5**
SE12 . . . 7J **107**
Baring St. N1 . . . 1D **68**
Barker Cl. HA6: Nwood . . . 1H **23**
KT3: N Mald . . . 4H **135**
Barker Dr. NW1 . . . 7G **49**
Barker M. SW4 . . . 4F **103**
Barkers Arc. W8 . . . 2K **83**
Barker St. SW10 . . . 6A **84**
Barker Wlk. SW16 . . . 3H **121**
Barkham Rd. N17 . . . 7J **17**
Barkham Ter. SE1 . . . 1K **173**
BARKING . . . **7G 55**
Barking Abbey . . . 1G 73
Barking Bus. Cen.
IG11: Bark . . . 3A **74**
Barking Ind. Pk.
IG11: Bark . . . 1K **73**
Barking Northern Relief Rd.
IG11: Bark . . . 7F **55**
Barking Rd E6 . . . 5H **71**
Barking Rd. E13 . . . 2A **72**
E16 . . . 5H **71**
(not continuous)
BARKINGSIDE . . . **3G 37**
Bark Pl. W2 . . . 7K **65**
Barkston Gdns. SW5 . . . 4K **83**
Barkway Ct. N4 . . . 2C **50**
Barkwith Ho. *SE14 . . . 6K* ***87***
(off Cold Blow La.)
Barkwood Cl. RM7: Rom . . . 5J **39**
Barkworth Rd. SE16 . . . 5H **87**
Barlborough St. SE14 . . . 7K **87**
Barlby Gdns. W10 . . . 4F **65**
Barlby Rd. W10 . . . 5E **64**
Barleycorn Way E14 . . . 7B **70**
Barleyfields Cl.
RM6: Chad H . . . 6B **38**
Barley La. IG3: Ilf . . . 7A **38**
RM6: Chad H . . . 7A **38**
Barley Mow Pas. EC1 . . . 5B **162**
W4 . . . 5K **81**
Barleymow Way
TW17: Shep . . . 4C **130**
Barley Shotts Bus. Pk.
W10 . . . 5H **65**
Barling *NW1 . . . 6F* ***49***
(off Castlehaven Rd.)
Barlings Ho. *SE4 . . . 4K* ***105***
(off Frendsbury Rd.)
Barlow Cl. SM6: Wall . . . 6J **151**
Barlow Dr. SE18 . . . 1C **108**
Barlow Ho. *N1 . . . 1E* ***162***
(off Fairbank Est.)
SE16 . . . 4H ***87***
(off Rennie Est.)
W11 . . . 7G ***65***
(off Walmer Rd.)
Barlow Pl. W1 . . . 7F **67** (3K **165**)
Barlow Rd. NW6 . . . 6H **47**
TW12: Hamp . . . 7E **114**
W3 . . . 1H **81**
Barlow St. SE17 . . . 4D **86**
Barlow Way RM13: Rain . . . 5K **75**
Barmeston Rd. SE6 . . . 2D **124**
Barmor Cl. HA2: Harr . . . 2F **25**
Barmouth Av. UB6: G'frd . . . 2K **61**
Barmouth Rd.
CR0: Croy . . . 2K **153**
SW18 . . . 6A **102**
Barnabas Ct. N21 . . . 4F **7**
Barnabas Rd. E9 . . . 5K **51**
Barnaby Cl. HA2: Harr . . . 2G **43**
Barnaby Ct. NW9 . . . 3A **28**
SE16 . . . 2G ***87***
(off Scott Lidgett Cres.)
Barnaby Pl. SW7 . . . 4A **170**
Barnaby Way IG7: Chig . . . 3K **21**
Barnard Cl. BR7: Chst . . . 1H **145**
SE18 . . . 4E **90**
SM6: Wall . . . 7H **151**
TW16: Sun T . . . 7K **113**
Barnard Gdns.
KT3: N Mald . . . 4C **136**
UB4: Hayes . . . 4K **59**
Barnard Gro. E15 . . . 7H **53**
Barnard Hill N10 . . . 1F **31**
Barnard Ho. *E2 . . . 3H* ***69***
(off Ellsworth St.)
Barnard Lodge EN5: Barn . . . 4F **5**
W9 . . . 5J ***65***
(off Admiral Wlk.)
Barnard M. SW11 . . . 4C **102**
Barnardo Dr. IG6: Ilf . . . 4G **37**
Barnardo Gdns. E1 . . . 7K **69**
Barnardo St. E1 . . . 6K **69**
Barnardos Village
IG6: Ilf . . . 3G **37**
Barnard Rd. CR4: Mitc . . . 3E **138**
EN1: Enf . . . 2C **8**
SW11 . . . 4C **102**
Barnards Ho. *SE16 . . . 2B* ***88***
(off Wyatt Cl.)
Barnard's Inn EC4 . . . 6J **161**
(not continuous)
Barnbrough *NW1 . . . 1G* ***67***
(off Camden St.)
Barnby Sq. E15 . . . 1G **71**
Barnby St. E15 . . . 1G **71**
NW1 . . . 2G **67** (1B **160**)
Barn Cl. *NW5 . . . 5H* ***49***
(off Torriano Av.)
TW15: Ashf . . . 5D **112**
UB5: N'olt . . . 2A **60**
Barn Cres. HA7: Stan . . . 6H **11**
Barncroft Cl. UB8: Uxb . . . 5D **58**
Barneby Cl. TW2: Twick . . . 1J **115**
BARNEHURST . . . **3J 111**
Barnehurst Av. DA7: Bex . . . 1J **111**
DA8: Bex, Erith . . . 1J **111**
Barnehurst Cl. DA8: Erith . . . 1J **111**
Barnehurst Rd. DA7: Bex . . . 2J **111**
Barn Elms Pk. SW15 . . . 3E **100**
BARNES . . . **2B 100**
Barnes All.
TW12: Hamp . . . 2G **133**
Barnes Av. SW13 . . . 7C **82**
UB2: S'hall . . . 4D **78**
Barnes Cl. E12 . . . 4B **54**
Barnes Ct. E16 . . . 5A **72**
IG8: Buck H, Wfd G . . . 5G **21**
N1 . . . 7A **50**
Barnes End KT3: N Mald . . . 5C **136**
Barnes High St. SW13 . . . 2B **100**
Barnes Ho. IG11: Bark . . . 1H **73**
SE14 . . . 6K ***87***
(off John Williams Cl.)
Barnes Pikle W5 . . . 7D **62**
Barnes Rd. IG1: Ilf . . . 5G **55**
N18 . . . 4D **18**
Barnes St. E14 . . . 6A **70**
Barnes Ter. SE8 . . . 5B **88**
Barnes Wallis Ct.
HA9: Wemb . . . 3J **45**
BARNET . . . **3B 4**
Barnet Bus. Cen. EN5: Barn . . . 3B **4**
Barnet By-Pass NW4 . . . 2E **28**
NW7 . . . 6G **13**
Barnet Dr. BR2: Short . . . 2C **156**
Barnet F.C. (Underhill Stadium)
. . . 5D 4
Barnet Ga. La. EN5: Barn . . . 1H **13**
Barnet Gro. E2 . . . 3G **69** (1K **163**)
Barnet Hill EN5: Barn . . . 4C **4**
Barnet Ho. N20 . . . 2F **15**
Barnet La. EN5: Barn . . . 7C **4**
N20 . . . 1C **14**
Barnet Mus. . . . 4B 4
Barnet Trad. Est. EN5: Barn . . . 3C **4**
Barnetts Ct. HA2: Harr . . . 3F **43**
Barnett St. E1 . . . 6H **69**
BARNET VALE . . . **5E 4**
Barnet Way NW7: Bore . . . 3E **12**
Barnet Wood Rd.
BR2: Short . . . 2A **156**
Barney Cl. SE7 . . . 5A **90**
Barn Fld. NW3 . . . 5D **48**
Barnfield KT3: N Mald . . . 6A **136**
Barnfield Av. CR0: Croy . . . 2J **153**
CR4: Mitc . . . 4F **139**
KT2: King T . . . 4D **116**
Barnfield Cl. N4 . . . 7J **31**
SW17 . . . 3B **120**
Barnfield Gdns.
KT2: King T . . . 4E **116**
SE18 . . . 6F **91**
Barnfield Pl. E14 . . . 4C **88**
Barnfield Rd.
CR2: S Croy . . . 7E **152**
DA17: Belv . . . 6F **93**
HA8: Edg . . . 1J **27**
SE18 . . . 6F **91**
(not continuous)
W5 . . . 4C **62**
Barnfield Wood Cl.
BR3: Beck . . . 6F **143**
Barnfield Wood Rd.
BR3: Beck . . . 6F **143**
Barnham Dr. SE28 . . . 1K **91**
(not continuous)
Barnham Rd. UB6: G'frd . . . 3G **61**
Barnham St. SE1 . . . 2E **86** (6H **169**)
Barn Hill HA9: Wemb . . . 1G **45**
Barnhill HA5: Pinn . . . 5A **24**
Barnhill Av. BR2: Short . . . 5H **143**
Barnhill La. UB4: Hayes . . . 3K **59**
Barnhill Rd. HA9: Wemb . . . 3J **45**
UB4: Hayes . . . 3K **59**
Barningham Way NW9 . . . 6K **27**
Barnlea Cl. TW13: Felt . . . 2C **114**
Barnmead Gdns.
RM9: Dag . . . 5F **57**
Barnmead Rd. BR3: Beck . . . 1K **141**
RM9: Dag . . . 5F **57**
Barn M. HA2: Harr . . . 3E **42**
Barn Ri. HA9: Wemb . . . 1G **45**
BARNSBURY . . . **7K 49**
Barnsbury Cl.
KT3: N Mald . . . 4J **135**
Barnsbury Cres.
KT5: Surb . . . 1J **147**
Barnsbury Est. N1 . . . 1K **67**
(not continuous)
Barnsbury Gro. N7 . . . 7K **49**
Barnsbury Ho. SW4 . . . 6H **103**
Barnsbury La. KT5: Surb . . . 2H **147**
Barnsbury Pk. N1 . . . 7A **50**
Barnsbury Rd. N1 . . . 2A **68**
Barnsbury Sq. N1 . . . 7A **50**
Barnsbury St. N1 . . . 7A **50**
Barnsbury Ter. N1 . . . 7K **49**
Barnscroft SW20 . . . 3D **136**
Barnsdale Av. E14 . . . 4D **88**
Barnsdale Rd. W9 . . . 4H **65**
Barnsley St. E1 . . . 4H **69**
Barnstable La. SE13 . . . 4E **106**
Barnstaple Ho. *SE10 . . . 7D* ***88***
(off Devonshire Dr.)
SE12 . . . 5H ***107***
(off Taunton Rd.)
Barnstaple Rd. HA4: Ruis . . . 3A **42**
Barnston Wlk. *N1 . . . 1C* ***68***
(off Popham St.)
Barn St. N16 . . . 2E **50**
Barn Theatre, The . . . 1A 128
Barn Way HA9: Wemb . . . 1G **45**
Barnwell Ho. *SE5 . . . 1E* ***104***
(off St Giles Rd.)
Barnwell Rd. SW2 . . . 5A **104**
Barnwood Cl. HA4: Ruis . . . 2F **41**
N20 . . . 1C **14**
W9 . . . 4K **65**
Baron Cl. N11 . . . 5K **15**
Baroness Rd. E2 . . . 3F **69** (1K **163**)
Baronet Gro. N17 . . . 1G **33**
Baronet Rd. N17 . . . 1G **33**
Baron Gdns. IG6: Ilf . . . 3G **37**
Baron Gro. CR4: Mitc . . . 4C **138**
Baron Rd. RM8: Dag . . . 1D **56**
Baronsclere Ct. N6 . . . 7G **31**
BARONS COURT . . . **5G 83**
Barons Ct. IG1: Ilf . . . 2H **55**
SM6: Wall . . . 3H **151**
Baron's Ct. Rd. W14 . . . 5G **83**
Barons Court Theatre . . . 5G 83
(off Comeragh Rd.)
Baronsfield Rd.
TW1: Twick . . . 6B **98**
Barons Ga. EN4: Barn . . . 6H **5**
W4 . . . 3J **81**
Barons Keep W14 . . . 5G **83**
Barons Mead HA1: Harr . . . 4J **25**
Baronsmead Rd. SW13 . . . 1C **100**
Baronsmede W5 . . . 2F **81**
Baronsmere Ct. EN5: Barn . . . 4B **4**
Baronsmere Rd. N2 . . . 4C **30**
Baron's Pl. SE1 . . . 2A **86** (7K **167**)
Barons, The TW1: Twick . . . 6B **98**
Baron St. N1 . . . 2A **68**
Baron's Wlk. CR0: Croy . . . 6A **142**
Baron Wlk. CR4: Mitc . . . 4C **138**
E16 . . . 5H **71**
Barque M. SE8 . . . 6C **88**
Barrack Rd. TW4: Houn . . . 4B **96**
Barra Hall Cir. UB3: Hayes . . . 7G **59**
Barra Hall Rd. UB3: Hayes . . . 7G **59**
Barratt Av. N22 . . . 2K **31**
Barratt Ho. *N1 . . . 7B* ***50***
(off Sable St.)
Barratt Ind. Pk. E3 . . . 4E **70**
UB1: S'hall . . . 2E **78**
Barratt Way HA3: Harr . . . 2H **25**
Barrenger Rd. N10 . . . 1D **30**
Barret Ho. NW6 . . . 1J **65**
SW9 . . . 3K ***103***
(off Benedict Rd.)
Barrett Ho. *SE17 . . . 5C* ***86***
(off Browning St.)
Barrett Rd. E17 . . . 4E **34**
Barrett's Grn. Rd.
NW10 . . . 3J **63**
Barrett's Gro. N16 . . . 5E **50**
Barrett St. W1 . . . 6E **66** (1H **165**)
Barrhill Rd. SW2 . . . 2J **121**
Barrie Ct. *EN5: Barn . . . 5F* ***5***
(off Lyonsdown Rd.)
Barriedale SE14 . . . 2A **106**
Barrie Est. W2 . . . 7B **66** (2A **164**)
Barrie Ho. *W2 . . . 7A* ***66***
(off Lancaster Ga.)
Barrier App. SE7 . . . 3B **90**
Barrier Point Rd. E16 . . . 1A **90**
Barringers Ct. HA4: Ruis . . . 7F **23**
Barringer Sq. SW17 . . . 4E **120**
Barrington Cl. IG5: Ilf . . . 1D **36**
NW5 . . . 5E **48**
Barrington Ct. NW5 . . . 5E **48**
SW4 . . . 2J **103**
W3 . . . 2H ***81***
(off Cheltenham Pl.)
Barrington Rd. DA7: Bex . . . 2D **110**
E12 . . . 6E **54**
N8 . . . 5H **31**
SM3: Sutt . . . 2J **149**
SW9 . . . 3B **104**
Barrington Vs. SE18 . . . 1E **108**
Barrington Wlk. SE19 . . . 6E **122**
Barrosa Dr. TW12: Hamp . . . 1E **132**
Barrow Av. SM5: Cars . . . 7D **150**
Barrow Cl. N21 . . . 3G **17**
Barrow Ct. *SE6 . . . 1H* ***125***
(off Cumberland Pl.)
Barrowdene Cl. HA5: Pinn . . . 2C **24**
Barrowell Grn. N21 . . . 2G **17**
Barrowfield Cl. N9 . . . 3C **18**
Barrowgate Rd. W4 . . . 5J **81**
Barrow Hedges Cl.
SM5: Cars . . . 7C **150**
Barrow Hedges Way
SM5: Cars . . . 7C **150**
Barrowhill KT4: Wor Pk . . . 2A **148**
Barrowhill Cl.
KT4: Wor Pk . . . 2A **148**
Barrow Hill Est. *NW8 . . . 2C* ***66***
(off Barrow Hill Rd.)
Barrow Hill Rd.
NW8 . . . 2C **66** (1C **158**)
Barrow Point Av.
HA5: Pinn . . . 2C **24**
Barrow Point La.
HA5: Pinn . . . 2C **24**
Barrow Rd. CR0: Croy . . . 5A **152**
SW16 . . . 6H **121**
Barrow Wlk. TW8: Bford . . . 6C **80**
Barrs Rd. NW10 . . . 7K **45**
Barry Av. DA7: Bex . . . 7E **92**
N15 . . . 6F **33**
Barrydene N20 . . . 1G **15**
Barry Ho. *SE16 . . . 4H* ***87***
(off Rennie Est.)
Barry Rd. E6 . . . 6C **72**
NW10 . . . 7J **45**
SE22 . . . 6G **105**
Barset Rd. SE15 . . . 3J **105**
(not continuous)
Barson Cl. SE20 . . . 7J **123**
Barston Rd. SE27 . . . 3C **122**
Barstow Cres. SW2 . . . 1K **121**
Barter St. WC1 . . . 5J **67** (6F **161**)
Barters Wlk. HA5: Pinn . . . 3C **24**
Bartholomew Cl.
EC1 . . . 5C **68** (6B **162**)
(not continuous)
SW18 . . . 4A **102**
Bartholomew Ct. *E14 . . . 7F* ***71***
(off Newport Av.)
EC1 . . . 3D ***162***
(off Old St.)
HA7: Stan . . . 7J **11**
Bartholomew Ho. IG8: Ilf . . . 7K **21**
Bartholomew La.
EC2 . . . 6D **68** (1F **169**)
Bartholomew Pl. EC1 . . . 6C **162**
Bartholomew Rd. NW5 . . . 6G **49**
Bartholomew Sq. E1 . . . 4H **69**
EC1 . . . 4C **68** (3D **162**)
Bartholomew St. SE1 . . . 3D **86**
Bartholomew Vs. NW5 . . . 6G **49**
Barth Rd. SE18 . . . 4J **91**
(not continuous)

Bartle Av. E6 2C **72**
Bartle Rd. W11 6G **65**
Bartlett Cl. E14 6C **70**
Bartlett Ct. EC4 6A **68** (7K **161**)
Bartlett Ho's. *RM10: Dag 7H* ***57***
(off Vicarage Rd.)
Bartletts Pas. *EC4 7K* ***161***
(off Fetter La.)
Bartlett St. CR2: S Croy 5D **152**
Bartlow Gdns. RM5: Col R 1K **39**
Barton Av. RM7: Rush G 1H **57**
Barton Cl. DA6: Bex 5E **110**
E6 6D **72**
E9 5J **51**
NW4 5C **28**
SE15 3H **105**
TW17: Shep 6D **130**
Barton Ct. *W14 5G* ***83***
(off Baron's Ct. Rd.)
Barton Grn. KT3: N Mald 2K **135**
Barton Ho. *N1 7B* ***50***
(off Sable St.)
SW6 3K ***101***
(off Wandsworth Bri. Rd.)
Barton Mdws. IG6: Ilf 4F **37**
Barton Rd. DA14: Sidc 6E **128**
W14 5G **83**
Barton St. SW1 3J **85** (1E **172**)
Bartonway *NW8 1B* ***66***
(off Queen's Ter.)
Bartram Cl. UB8: Uxb 4D **58**
Bartram Rd. SE4 5A **106**
Bartrams La. EN4: Barn 1F **5**
Bartrip St. E9 6B **52**
Barts Cl. BR3: Beck 5C **142**
Barville Cl. SE4 4A **106**
Barwell Bus Pk.
KT9: Chess 7D **146**
Barwell Ho. *E2 4G* ***69***
(off Menotti St.)
Barwick Dr. UB8: Uxb 5D **58**
Barwick Ho. *W3 2J* ***81***
(off Strafford Rd.)
Barwick Rd. E7 4K **53**
Barwood Av.
BR4: W W'ck 1D **154**
Bascombe Gro.
DA1: Bexl, Cray 7K **111**
Bascombe St. SW2 6A **104**
Basden Gro. TW13: Felt 2E **114**
Basden Ho. TW13: Felt 2E **114**
Basedale Rd. RM9: Dag 7B **56**
Baseing Cl. E6 7E **72**
Basevi Way SE8 6C **88**
Bashley Rd. NW10 4K **63**
Basil Av. E6 3C **72**
Basildene Rd. TW4: Houn 3B **96**
Basildon Av. IG5: Ilf 1E **36**
Basildon Cl. SM2: Sutt 7K **149**
Basildon Ct. *W1 5H* ***159***
(off Devonshire Rd.)
Basildon Rd. SE2 5A **92**
Basil Gdns. CR0: Croy 1K **153**
SE27 5C **122**
Basil Ho. *SW8 7J* ***85***
(off Wyvil Rd.)
Basilon Rd. DA7: Bex 2E **110**
Basil Spence Ho. N22 1K **31**
Basil St. SW3 3D **84** (1E **170**)
Basin App. E14 6A **70**
Basing Cl. KT7: T Ditt 7K **133**
Basing Ct. SE15 1F **105**
Basingdon Way SE5 4D **104**
Basing Dr. DA5: Bexl 6F **111**
Basingfield Rd.
KT7: T Ditt 7K **133**
Basinghall Av.
EC2 6D **68** (7E **162**)
Basinghall Gdns.
SM2: Sutt 7K **149**
Basinghall St.
EC2 6D **68** (7E **162**)

Basing Hill HA9: Wemb 2F **45**
NW11 1H **47**
Basing Ho. *IG11: Bark 1H* ***73***
(off St Margarets)
Basing Ho. Yd.
E2 3E **68** (1H **163**)
Basing Pl. E2 3E **68** (1H **163**)
Basing St. W11 6H **65**
Basing Way KT7: T Ditt 7K **133**
N3 3J **29**
Basire St. N1 1C **68**
Baskerville Gdns. NW10 4A **46**
Baskerville Rd. SW18 7C **102**
Basket Gdns. SE9 5C **108**
Baslow Cl. HA3: Harr 1H **25**
Baslow Wlk. E5 4K **51**
Basnett Rd. SW11 3E **102**
Basque Ct. *SE16 2K* ***87***
(off Garter Way)
Bassano St. SE22 5F **105**
Bassant Rd. SE18 6K **91**
Bassein Pk. Rd. W12 2B **82**
Bassett Gdns. TW7: Isle 7G **79**
Bassett Ho. RM9: Dag 1B **74**
Bassett Rd. E7 4B **54**
W10 6F **65**
Bassett St. NW5 6E **48**
Bassett Way UB6: G'frd 6F **61**
Bassingbourn Ho. *N1 7A* ***50***
(off Sutton Est., The)
Bassingham Rd.
HA0: Wemb 6D **44**
SW18 7A **102**
Bassishaw Highwalk
EC2 6D **162**
Basswood Cl. SE15 3H **105**
Bastable Av. IG11: Bark 2J **73**
Basterfield Ho. *EC1 4C* ***162***
(off Golden La. Est.)
Bastion Highwalk EC2 6C **162**
Bastion Ho. *EC2 6D* ***162***
(off London Wall)
Bastion Rd. SE2 5A **92**
Baston Mnr. Rd.
BR2: Kes, Short 3K **155**
Baston Rd. BR2: Short 1K **155**
Bastwick St. EC1 4C **68** (3C **162**)
Basuto Rd. SW6 1J **101**
Batavia Cl. TW16: Sun T 1K **131**
Batavia Ho. *SE14 7A* ***88***
(off Batavia Rd.)
Batavia M. SE14 7A **88**
Batavia Rd. SE14 7A **88**
TW16: Sun T 1K **131**
Batchelor St. N1 1A **68**
Bateman Cl. IG11: Bark 6G **55**
Bateman Ho. *SE11 6B* ***86***
(off Otto St.)
Bateman Rd. E4 6H **19**
Bateman's Bldgs. W1 1C **166**
Bateman's Row
EC2 4E **68** (3H **163**)
Bateman St. W1 6H **67** (1C **166**)
Bates Cres. CR0: Croy 5A **152**
SW16 7G **121**
Bateson St. SE18 4J **91**
Bates Point *E13 1J* ***71***
(off Pelly Rd.)
Bate St. E14 7B **70**
Bath Cl. SE15 7H **87**
Bath Ct. EC1 4J **161**
SE26 3G ***123***
(off Droitwich Cl.)
Bathgate Rd. SW19 3F **119**
Bath Gro. *E2 2G* ***69***
(off Horatio St.)
Bath Ho. *E2 4G* ***69***
(off Ramsey St.)
SE1 3C ***86***
(off Bath Ter.)
Bath Ho. Rd. CR0: Croy 1J **151**
Bath Pas. KT1: King T 2D **134**

Bath Pl. EC2 3E **68** (2G **163**)
EN5: Barn 3C **4**
W6 5E ***82***
(off Peabody Est.)
Bath Rd. E7 6B **54**
N9 2C **18**
RM6: Chad H 6E **38**
TW5: Houn 1A **96**
TW6: Houn 1A **94**
UB3: Hayes 1A **94**
UB7: Hayes, Houn, W Dray
1A **94**
W4 4A **82**
Baths App. SW6 7H **83**
Baths Rd. BR2: Short 4B **144**
Bath St. EC1 3C **68** (2D **162**)
Bath Ter. SE1 3C **86**
Bathurst Av. SW19 1K **137**
Bathurst Gdns. NW10 2D **64**
Bathurst Ho. *W12 7D* ***64***
(off White City Est.)
Bathurst M. W2 6B **66** (2B **164**)
Bathurst Rd. IG1: Ilf 1F **55**
Bathurst St. W2 7B **66** (2B **164**)
Bathway SE18 4E **90**
Batley Cl. CR4: Mitc 7D **138**
Batley Pl. N16 3F **51**
Batley Rd. EN2: Enf 1H **7**
N16 3F **51**
Batman Cl. W12 1D **82**
Batoum Gdns. W6 3E **82**
Batson Ho. *E1 6G* ***69***
(off Fairclough St.)
Batson St. W12 2C **82**
Batsworth Rd.
CR4: Mitc 3B **138**
Battenberg Wlk. SE19 6E **122**
Batten Cl. E6 6D **72**
Batten Ho. SW4 5G **103**
W10 3G ***65***
(off Third Av.)
Batten St. SW11 3C **102**
Battersby Rd. SE6 2F **125**
BATTERSEA **1E 102**
Battersea Bri. SW3 7B **84**
SW11 7B **84**
Battersea Bri. Rd. SW11 7C **84**
Battersea Bus. Cen.
SW11 3E **102**
Battersea Chu. Rd.
SW11 1B **102**
Battersea Dogs' Home 7F 85
Battersea High St.
SW11 1B **102**
(not continuous)
Battersea Pk. 7D 84
Battersea Pk. Children's Zoo
7E 84
Battersea Pk. Rd. SW8 2C **102**
SW11 2C **102**
Battersea Ri. SW11 5C **102**
Battersea Sq. SW11 1B **102**
Battery Rd. SE28 2J **91**
Battishill St. N1 7B **50**
Battlebridge Ct. *N1 2J* ***67***
(off Wharfdale Rd.)
Battle Bri. La.
SE1 1E **86** (5G **169**)
Battle Bri. Rd. NW1 2J **67**
Battle Cl. SW19 6A **120**
Battledean Rd. N5 5B **50**
Battle Ho. *SE15 6G* ***87***
(off Haymerle Rd.)
Battle Rd. DA8: Erith 4J **93**
DA17: Belv, Erith 4J **93**
Batty St. E1 6G **69**
Baudene M. *NW4 4D* ***28***
(off Burroughs, The)
Baudwin Rd. SE6 2G **125**
Baugh Rd. DA14: Sidc 5C **128**
Baulk, The SW18 7J **101**
Bavant Rd. SW16 2J **139**

Bavaria Rd. N19 2J **49**
(not continuous)
Bavent Rd. SE5 2C **104**
Bawdale Rd. SE22 5F **105**
Bawdsey Av. IG2: Ilf 4K **37**
Bawtree Rd. SE14 7A **88**
Bawtry Rd. N20 3J **15**
Baxendale N20 2F **15**
Baxendale St. E2 3G **69**
Baxter Cl. UB2: S'hall 3F **79**
UB10: Uxb 3D **58**
Baxter Rd. E16 6A **72**
IG1: Ilf 5F **55**
N1 6D **50**
N18 4C **18**
Bayard Ct. DA6: Bex 4H **111**
Bay Ct. *E1 4K* ***69***
(off Frimley Way)
W5 3E **80**
Baycroft Cl. HA5: Pinn 3A **24**
Baydon Ct. BR2: Short 3H **143**
Bayer Ho. *EC1 4C* ***162***
(off Golden La. Est.)
Bayes Ct. *NW3 7D* ***48***
(off Primrose Hill Rd.)
Bayfield Ho. *SE4 4K* ***105***
(off Coston Wlk.)
Bayfield Rd. SE9 4B **108**
Bayford M. *E8 7H* ***51***
(off Bayford St.)
Bayford Rd. NW10 3F **65**
Bayford St. E8 7H **51**
Bayford St. Bus. Cen.
E8 7H ***51***
(off Sidworth St.)
Baygrove M. KT1: King T 1C **134**
Bayham Pl. NW1 1G **67**
Bayham Rd. SM4: Mord 4K **137**
W4 3K **81**
W13 7B **62**
Bayham St. NW1 1G **67**
Bayhurst Wood Country Pk.
5B 22
Bayleaf Cl.
TW12: Hamp 5H **115**
Bayley St. WC1 5H **67** (6C **160**)
Bayley Wlk. SE2 6E **92**
Baylis M. TW1: Twick 7A **98**
Baylis Rd. SE1 2A **86** (7J **167**)
Bayliss Av. SE28 7D **74**
Bayliss Cl. N21 5D **6**
Bayne Cl. E6 6D **72**
Baynes Cl. EN1: Enf 1B **8**
Baynes M. NW3 6B **48**
Baynes St. NW1 7G **49**
Baynham Cl. DA5: Bexl 6F **111**
Bayonne Rd. W6 6G **83**
Bays Cl. SE26 5J **123**
Bays Ct. HA8: Edg 5C **12**
Bayshill Ri. UB5: N'olt 6F **43**
Bayston Rd. N16 3F **51**
BAYSWATER **7A 66**
Bayswater Rd.
W2 7K **65** (3A **164**)
Baythorne St. E3 5B **70**
Bayton Ct. *E8 7G* ***51***
(off Lansdowne Dr.)
Bay Tree Cl. BR1: Brom 1B **144**
Baytree Cl. DA15: Sidc 1K **127**
Baytree Ct. SW2 4K **103**
Baytree Ho. E4 7J **9**
Baytree Rd. SW2 4K **103**
Bazalgette Cl.
KT3: N Mald 5K **135**
Bazalgette Gdns.
KT3: N Mald 5K **135**
Bazalgette Ho. *NW8 3B* ***158***
(off Orchardson St.)
Bazeley Ho. *SE1 7A* ***168***
(off Library St.)
Bazely St. E14 7E **70**
Bazile Rd. N21 6F **7**

BBC Broadcasting House
5F 67 (6K 159)
Beacham Cl. SE7 5B **90**
Beachborough Rd.
BR1: Brom 4E **124**
Beachcroft Rd. E11 3G **53**
Beachcroft Way N19 1H **49**
Beach Gro. TW13: Felt 2E **114**
Beach Ho. *SW5 5J* ***83***
(off Philbeach Gdns.)
TW13: Felt 2E **114**
Beachy Rd. E3 7C **52**
Beacon Cl. UB8: Uxb 5A **40**
Beacon Ga. SE14 3K **105**
Beacon Gro. SM5: Cars 4E **150**
Beacon Hill N7 5J **49**
Beacon Ho. *E14 5D* ***88***
(off Burrells Wharf Sq.)
SE5 7E ***86***
(off Southampton Way)
Beacon Pl. CR0: Croy 3J **151**
Beacon Rd. SE13 6F **107**
TW6: Houn 6C **94**
Beacons Cl. E6 5C **72**
Beaconsfield Cl. N11 5K **15**
SE3 6J **89**
W4 5J **81**
Beaconsfield Pde. SE9 4C **126**
Beaconsfield Rd.
BR1: Brom 3B **144**
CR0: Croy 6D **140**
DA5: Bexl 2K **129**
E10 2E **52**
E16 4H **71**
E17 6B **34**
KT3: N Mald 2K **135**
KT5: Surb 7F **135**
N9 3B **18**
N11 3K **15**
N15 4E **32**
NW10 6B **46**
SE3 7H **89**
SE9 2C **126**
SE17 5D **86**
TW1: Twick 6B **98**
UB1: S'hall 1B **78**
UB4: Hayes 1A **78**
W4 3K **81**
W5 2C **80**
Beaconsfield Ter.
RM6: Chad H 6D **38**
Beaconsfield Ter. Rd.
W14 3G **83**
Beaconsfield Wlk. E6 6E **72**
SW6 1H **101**
Beacontree Av. E17 1F **35**
BEACONTREE HEATH **1G 57**
Beacontree Rd. E11 1H **53**
Beadle's Pde. RM10: Dag 6J **57**
Beadlow Cl. SM5: Cars 6B **138**
Beadman St. SE27 4B **122**
Beadnell Rd. SE23 1K **123**
Beadon Rd. BR2: Short 4J **143**
W6 4E **82**
Beaford Gro. SW20 3G **137**
Beagle Cl. TW13: Felt 4K **113**
Beak St. W1 7G **67** (2B **166**)
Beal Cl. DA16: Well 1A **110**
Beale Cl. N13 5G **17**
Beale Pl. E3 2B **70**
Beale Rd. E3 1B **70**
Beal Rd. IG1: Ilf 2E **54**
Beam Av. RM10: Dag 1H **75**
Beaminster Gdns. IG6: Ilf 2F **37**
Beaminster Ho. *SW8 7K* ***85***
(off Dorset Rd.)
Beamish Dr. WD23: Bush 1B **10**
Beamish Ho. *SE16 4H* ***87***
(off Rennie Est.)
Beamish Rd. N9 1B **18**
Beam Vs. RM9: Dag 2J **75**
Beamway RM10: Dag 7K **57**

Beanacre Cl.—Bedgebury Rd.

Beanacre Cl. E9 6B 52
Bean Rd. DA6: Bex 4D 110
Beanshaw SE9: Chst 4E 126
Beansland Gro.
RM6: Chad H 2E 38
Bear All. EC4 6B 68 (7A 162)
Bear Cl. RM7: Rom 6H 39
Beardell St. SE19 6F 123
Beardow Gro. N14 6B 6
Beard Rd. KT2: King T 5F 117
Beardsfield E13 2J 71
Beard's Hill TW12: Hamp 1E 132
Beard's Hill Cl.
TW12: Hamp 1E 132
Beardsley Ter. RM8: Dag 5B 56
(off Fitzstephen Rd.)
Beardsley Way W3 2K 81
Beard's Rd. TW15: Ashf 6G 113
Bearfield Rd. KT2: King T 7E 116
Bear Gdns. SE1 1C 86 (4C 168)
Bear La. SE1 1B 86 (4B 168)
Bear Rd. TW13: Felt 4B 114
Bearsted Ri. SE4 5B 106
Bearsted Ter. BR3: Beck 1C 142
Bear St. WC2 7H 67 (2D 166)
Beasley's Ait
TW16: Sun T 6H 131
Beasley's Ait La.
TW16: Sun T 6H 131
Beaton Cl. SE15 1F 105
Beatrice Av. HA9: Wemb 5E 44
SW16 3K 139
Beatrice Cl. E13 4J 71
HA5: Pinn 4J 23
Beatrice Ct. IG9: Buck H 2G 21
Beatrice Ho. W6 5E 82
(off Queen Caroline St.)
Beatrice Pl. W8 3K 83
Beatrice Rd. E17 5C 34
N4 7A 32
N9 7D 8
Beatrice Rd. SE1 4G 87
TW10: Rich 5F 99
UB1: S'hall 1D 78
Beatrix Ho. SW5 5K 83
(off Old Brompton Rd.)
Beatson Wlk. SE16 1A 88
(not continuous)
Beattie Cl. TW14: Felt 7H 95
Beattie Ho. SW8 1G 103
Beattock Ri. N10 4F 31
Beatty Ho. E14 2C 88
(off Admirals Way)
NW1 4G 67
SW1 6B 172
(off Dolphin Sq.)
Beatty Rd. HA7: Stan 6H 11
N16 4E 50
Beatty St. NW1 2G 67
Beattyville Gdns. IG6: Ilf 4E 36
Beauchamp Cl. W4 3J 81
Beauchamp Ct. HA7: Stan 5H 11
Beauchamp Pl.
SW3 3C 84 (1D 170)
Beauchamp Rd. E7 7K 53
KT8: E Mos 5F 133
KT8: E Mos, W Mole
 5F 133
SE19 1D 140
SM1: Sutt 4J 149
SW11 4C 102
TW1: Twick 7A 98
Beauchamp St.
EC1 5A 68 (6J 161)
Beauchamp Ter. SW15 3D 100
Beauclerc Ct.
TW16: Sun T 2A 132
Beauclerc Rd. W6 3D 82
Beauclerk Cl. TW13: Felt 1K 113
Beauclerk Ho. SW16 3J 121
Beaudesert M.
UB7: W Dray 2A 76
Beaufort Av. HA3: Harr 4A 26
Beaufort Cl. E4 6J 19
RM7: Mawney 4J 39
SW15 7D 100
W5 5F 63
Beaufort Ct. E14 2C 88
(off Admirals Way)
EN5: Barn 5F 5
N11 5A 16
(off Limes Av., The)
TW10: Rich 4C 116
Beaufort Dr. E6 5E 72
NW11 4J 29
Beaufort Gdns. IG1: Ilf 1E 54
NW4 6E 28
SW3 3C 84 (1D 170)
SW16 7K 121
TW5: Houn 1C 96
Beaufort Ho. E16 7K 71
(off Fairfax M.)
SW1 6C 172
(off Aylesford St.)
Beaufort M. SW6 6H 83
Beaufort Pk. NW11 4J 29
Beaufort Rd. HA4: Ruis 2F 41
KT1: King T 4E 134
TW1: Twick 7C 98
TW10: Rich 4C 116
W5 5F 63
Beaufort St.
SW3 6B 84 (7A 170)
Beaufort Ter. E14 5E 88
(off Ferry St.)
Beaufort Way KT17: Eps 7C 148
Beaufoy Ho. SE27 3B 122
SW8 7K 85
(off Rita Rd.)
Beaufoy Rd. N17 7K 17
Beaufoy Wlk.
SE11 4K 85 (4H 173)
Beaulieu Av. E16 1K 89
SE26 4H 123
Beaulieu Cl. CR4: Mitc 1E 138
NW9 4A 28
SE5 3D 104
TW1: Twick 6D 98
TW4: Houn 5D 96
Beaulieu Ct. W5 5E 62
Beaulieu Dr. HA5: Pinn 6B 24
Beaulieu Gdns. N21 7H 7
Beaulieu Lodge E14 3F 89
(off Schooner Cl.)
Beaulieu Pl. W4 3J 81
Beaumanor Gdns. SE9 4E 126
Beaumaris Dr.
IG8: Wfd G 7G 21
Beaumaris Grn. NW9 6A 28
Beaumaris Twr. W3 2H 81
(off Park Rd. Nth.)
Beaumont W14 4H 83
(off Kensington Village)
Beaumont Av.
HA0: Wemb 5C 44
HA2: Harr 6F 25
TW9: Rich 3F 99
W14 5H 83
Beaumont Bldgs. WC2 1F 167
(off Martlett Ct.)
Beaumont Cl.
KT2: King T 7G 117
Beaumont Ct. E5 3H 51
HA0: Wemb 5C 44
NW9 2B 28
(off Cherry Cl.)
W1 5H 159
(off Beaumont St.)
W4 5J 81
Beaumont Cres. W14 5H 83
Beaumont Dr.
TW15: Ashf 5F 113
Beaumont Gdns. NW3 3J 47
Beaumont Gro. E1 4K 69
Beaumont Ho. E10 7D 34
E15 1H 71
(off John St.)
Beaumont Lodge E8 6G 51
(off Greenwood Rd.)
Beaumont M. HA5: Pinn 3C 24
W1 5E 66 (5H 159)
Beaumont Pl. EN5: Barn 1C 4
TW7: Isle 5K 97
W1 4G 67 (3B 160)
Beaumont Ri. N19 1H 49
Beaumont Rd. BR5: Orp 6H 145
E10 7D 34
(not continuous)
E13 3K 71
SE19 6C 122
SW19 7G 101
W4 3J 81
Beaumont Sq. E1 5K 69
Beaumont St.
W1 5E 66 (5H 159)
Beaumont Ter. SE13 7G 107
(off Wellmeadow Rd.)
Beaumont Wlk. NW3 7D 48
Beauvais Ter. UB5: N'olt 3B 60
Beauvale NW1 7E 48
(off Ferdinand St.)
Beauval Rd. SE22 6F 105
Beaux Arts Building 3J 49
Beaverbank Rd. SE9 1H 127
Beaver Cl. SE20 7G 123
TW12: Hamp 1F 133
Beaver Ct. BR3: Beck 7D 124
Beaver Gro. UB5: N'olt 3C 60
Beavers Cres. TW4: Houn 4A 96
Beavers La. TW4: Houn 2A 96
Beavers Lodge
DA14: Sidc 4K 127
Beaverwood Rd.
BR7: Chst 6J 127
Beavor Gro. W6 5C 82
(off Beavor La.)
Beavor La. W6 5C 82
Bebbington Rd. SE18 4J 91
Beccles Dr. IG11: Bark 6J 55
Beccles St. E14 6B 70
Bec Cl. HA4: Ruis 3B 42
Bechervaise Ct. E10 1D 52
(off Leyton Grange Est.)
Bechtel Ho. W6 4F 83
(off Hammersmith Rd.)
Beck Cl. SE13 1D 106
Beck Ct. BR3: Beck 3K 141
BECKENHAM 1C 142
Beckenham Bus. Cen.
BR3: Beck 6A 124
Beckenham Crematorium
BR3: Beck 3J 141
Beckenham Gdns. N9 3K 17
Beckenham Gro.
BR2: Short 2F 143
Beckenham Hill Est.
BR3: Beck 5D 124
Beckenham Hill Rd.
BR3: Beck 6D 124
SE6 6D 124
Beckenham La.
BR2: Short 2G 143
Beckenham Pl. Pk.
BR3: Beck 7D 124
Beckenham Rd.
BR3: Beck 1K 141
BR4: W W'ck 7D 142
Beckers, The N16 4G 51
Becket Av. E6 3E 72
Becket Cl. SE25 6G 141
SW19 7K 119
(off High Path)
Becket Fold HA1: Harr 5K 25
Becket Ho. E16 7K 71
(off Constable Av.)
SE1 7E 168
Becket Rd. N18 4D 18
Becket St. SE1 3D 86 (7E 168)
Beckett Cl. DA17: Belv 3F 93
NW10 6A 46
SW16 2H 121
Beckett Ho. E1 5J 69
(off Jubilee St.)
SW9 2J 103
Becketts Cl. DA5: Bexl 1J 129
TW14: Felt 6K 95
Becketts Ho. IG1: Ilf 3E 54
Becketts Pl. KT1: King T 1D 134
Beckett Wlk. BR3: Beck 6A 124
Beckfoot NW1 1B 160
(off Ampthill Est.)
Beckford Cl. W14 4H 83
Beckford Dr. BR5: Orp 7H 145
Beckford Ho. N16 5E 50
Beckford Pl. SE17 5C 86
Beckford Rd. CR0: Croy 6F 141
Beckham Ho.
SE11 4K 85 (4H 173)
Beck La. BR3: Beck 3K 141
Becklow Gdns. W12 2C 82
(off Becklow Rd.)
Becklow M. W12 2C 82
(off Becklow Rd.)
Becklow Rd. W12 2B 82
(not continuous)
Beck River Pk.
BR3: Beck 1C 142
Beck Rd. E8 1H 69
Becks Rd. DA14: Sidc 3A 128
Beck Theatre, The
 6H 59
BECKTON 5E 72
BECKTON PARK 6D 72
Beckton Retail Pk. E6 5E 72
Beckton Rd. E16 5H 71
Beckton Triangle Retail Pk.
E6 4F 73
Beck Way BR3: Beck 3B 142
Beckway Rd. SW16 2H 139
Beckway St. SE17 4E 86
(not continuous)
Beckwith Rd. SE24 5D 104
Beclands Rd. SW17 6E 120
Becmead Av. HA3: Harr 5B 26
SW16 4H 121
Becondale Rd. SE19 5E 122
BECONTREE 4D 56
Becontree Av. RM8: Dag 4B 56
Becquerel Ct. SE10 3H 89
Bective Pl. SW15 4H 101
Bective Rd. E7 4J 53
SW15 4H 101
Becton Pl. DA8: Erith 7H 93
Bedale Rd. EN2: Enf 1H 7
Bedale St. SE1 1D 86 (5E 168)
Beddalls Farm Ct. E6 5B 72
BEDDINGTON 4J 151
BEDDINGTON CORNER 7E 138
Beddington Farm Rd.
CR0: Croy 7J 139
Beddington Gdns.
SM5: Cars 6E 150
(not continuous)
Beddington Grn.
BR5: Orp 1K 145
Beddington Gro.
SM6: Wall 5H 151
Beddington La.
CR0: Croy 5G 139
Beddington Pk. Cotts.
SM6: Wall 3H 151
Beddington Path
BR5: Orp 1K 145
Beddington Rd.
BR5: Orp 1J 145
IG3: Ilf 7K 37
Beddington Ter.
CR0: Croy 7K 139
Beddington Trad. Est.
CR0: Croy 1J 151
Bede Cl. HA5: Pinn 1B 24
Bedefield WC1 3J 67 (2F 161)
Bede Ho. SE4 1B 106
(off Clare Rd.)
Bedens Rd. DA14: Sidc 6E 128
Bede Rd. RM6: Chad H 6C 38
Bedfont Cl. CR4: Mitc 2E 138
TW14: Felt 6E 94
Bedfont Grn. Cl.
TW14: Felt 1E 112
Bedfont Ind. Pk.
TW15: Ashf 3E 112
Bedfont Lakes Country Pk.
 2E 112
Bedfont Lakes Vis. Cen.
 3D 112
Bedfont La. TW13: Felt 7H 95
TW14: Felt 7H 95
Bedfont Pk. Ind. Est.
TW15: Ashf 3E 112
Bedfont Rd. TW13: Felt 1E 112
TW14: Felt 1E 112
TW19: Staines 6A 94
Bedford Av. EN5: Barn 5C 4
UB4: Hayes 6K 59
WC1 5H 67 (6D 160)
Bedfordbury WC2 7J 67 (2E 166)
Bedford Cl. N10 7K 15
W4 6A 82
Bedford Cnr. W4 4A 82
(off South Pde.)
Bedford Ct. CR0: Croy 1C 152
(off Tavistock Rd.)
WC2 7J 67 (3E 166)
(not continuous)
Bedford Ct. Mans. WC1 6D 160
Bedford Gdns. W8 1J 83
Bedford Hill SW12 1F 121
SW16 1F 121
Bedford Ho. SW4 4J 103
(off Solon New Rd. Est.)
Bedford M. N2 3C 30
SE6 2D 124
BEDFORD PARK 3A 82
Bedford Pk. CR0: Croy 1C 152
Bedford Pk. Cnr. W4 4A 82
Bedford Pk. Mans. W4 4K 81
Bedford Pas. SW6 7G 83
(off Dawes Rd.)
W1 5G 67 (5B 160)
Bedford Pl. CR0: Croy 1D 152
WC1 5J 67 (5E 160)
Bedford Rd. DA15: Sidc 3J 127
E6 1E 72
E17 2C 34
E18 2J 35
HA1: Harr 6G 25
HA4: Ruis 4H 41
IG1: Ilf 3F 55
KT4: Wor Pk 2E 148
N2 3C 30
N8 6H 31
N9 7C 8
N15 4E 32
N22 1J 31
NW7 2F 13
SW4 4J 103
TW2: Twick 3H 115
W4 3K 81
W13 7B 62
Bedford Row
WC1 5K 67 (5H 161)
Bedford Sq.
WC1 5H 67 (6D 160)
Bedford St. WC2 7J 67 (2E 166)
Bedford Ter. SW4 5J 103
Bedford Way
WC1 4H 67 (4D 160)
Bedgebury Gdns. SW19 2G 119
Bedgebury Rd. SE9 4B 108

Bedivere Rd.—Bellwood Rd.

Bedivere Rd. BR1: Brom ...3J 125
Bedlam M. SE11 ...3J 173
Bedlow Way CR0: Croy ...4K 151
Bedmond Ho. SW3 ...5C 170
(off Ixworth Pl.)
Bedonwell Rd.
DA7: Belv, Bex, Erith. ..6E 92
SE2 ...6E 92
Bedser Cl. CR7: Thor H ...3C 140
SE11 ...6K 85 (7H 173)
Bedser Dr. UB6: G'frd ...5H 43
Bedster Gdns.
KT8: W Mole ...2F 133
Bedwardine Rd. SE19 ...7E 122
Bedwell Ct.
RM6: Chad H ...7D 38
(off Broomfield Rd.)
Bedwell Gdns.
UB3: Hayes ...5G 77
(not continuous)
Bedwell Ho. SW9 ...2A 104
Bedwell Rd. DA17: Belv ...5G 93
N17 ...1E 32
Beeby Rd. E16 ...5K 71
Beech Av. DA15: Sidc ...7A 110
HA4: Ruis ...1K 41
IG9: Buck H ...2E 20
N20 ...1H 15
TW8: Bford ...7B 80
W3 ...1A 82
Beech Cl. N9 ...6B 8
SE8 ...6C 88
SM5: Cars ...2D 150
SW15 ...7C 100
SW19 ...6E 118
TW15: Ashf ...5F 113
TW16: Sun T ...2B 132
UB7: W Dray ...3C 76
Beech Copse BR1: Brom ...1D 144
CR2: S Croy ...5E 152
Beech Ct. BR1: Brom ...1H 143
(off Blyth Rd.)
BR3: Beck ...7B 124
HA6: Nwood ...1G 23
IG1: Ilf ...3E 54
(off Riverdene Rd.)
KT6: Surb ...7D 134
UB5: N'olt ...1C 60
W9 ...5J 65
(off Elmfield Way)
Beech Cres. Ct. N5 ...4B 50
Beechcroft BR7: Chst ...7E 126
Beechcroft Av. DA7: Bex ...1K 111
HA2: Harr ...7E 24
KT3: N Mald ...1J 135
NW11 ...7H 29
UB1: S'hall ...1D 78
Beechcroft Cl. SW16 ...5K 121
TW5: Houn ...7C 78
Beechcroft Ct. NW11 ...7H 29
(off Beechcroft Av.)
SM2: Sutt ...7A 150
Beechcroft Gdns.
HA9: Wemb ...3F 45
Beechcroft Ho. W5 ...5E 62
Beechcroft Rd. E18 ...2K 35
KT9: Chess ...3F 147
SW14 ...3J 99
SW17 ...2C 120
Beechdale N21 ...2E 16
Beechdale Rd. SW2 ...6K 103
Beech Dell BR2: Kes ...4D 156
Beechdene SE15 ...1H 105
(off Carlton Gro.)
Beech Dr. N2 ...2D 30
Beechen Cliff Way
TW7: Isle ...2K 97
Beechen Gro. HA5: Pinn ...3D 24
Beechen Pl. SE23 ...2K 123
Beeches Av.
SM5: Cars ...7C 150
Beeches Cl. SE20 ...1J 141
Beeches Rd. SM3: Sutt ...1G 149
SW17 ...3C 120
Beeches, The
CR2: S Croy ...5D 152
(off Blunt Rd.)
E12 ...7C 54
TW3: Houn ...1F 97
Beeches Wlk.
SM5: Cars ...7B 150
Beechey Ho. E1 ...1H 87
(off Watts St.)
Beechfield Cotts.
BR1: Brom ...1A 144
Beechfield Ct.
CR2: S Croy ...4C 152
(off Bramley Hill)
Beechfield Gdns.
RM7: Rush G ...7J 39
Beechfield Rd.
BR1: Brom ...2A 144
DA8: Erith ...7K 93
N4 ...6C 32
SE6 ...1B 124
Beech Gdns. EC2 ...5C 162
(off Beech St.)
RM10: Dag ...7J 57
W5 ...2E 80
Beech Gro. CR4: Mitc ...5H 139
(not continuous)
KT3: N Mald ...3K 135
Beech Hall Cres. E4 ...7A 20
Beech Hall Rd. E4 ...7K 19
Beech Haven Ct.
DA1: Cray ...5K 111
(off London Rd.)
Beech Hill EN4: Barn ...1G 5
Beech Hill Av. EN4: Barn ...1F 5
Beech Ho. E17 ...3F 35
SE16 ...2J 87
(off Ainsty Est.)
Beech Ho. Rd. CR0: Croy ...3D 152
Beechill Rd. SE9 ...5E 108
Beech La. IG9: Buck H ...2E 20
Beech Lawns N12 ...5G 15
Beechmont Cl.
BR1: Brom ...5G 125
Beechmore Gdns.
SM3: Sutt ...2F 149
Beechmore Rd. SW11 ...1D 102
Beechmount Av. W7 ...5H 61
Beecholme N12 ...5E 14
Beecholme Av.
CR4: Mitc ...1F 139
Beecholme Est. E5 ...3H 51
Beech Rd. N11 ...6D 16
SW16 ...2J 139
TW14: Felt ...7G 95
Beechrow TW10: Rich ...4E 116
Beech St. EC2 ...5C 68 (5C 162)
RM7: Rom ...4J 39
Beech Tree Cl. HA7: Stan ...5H 11
N1 ...7A 50
Beech Tree Glade E4 ...1C 20
Beech Tree Pl.
SM1: Sutt ...5K 149
Beechvale Cl. N12 ...5H 15
Beech Wlk. NW7 ...6F 13
Beech Way NW10 ...7K 45
TW2: Twick ...3E 114
Beechway DA5: Bexl ...6D 110
Beechwood Av.
CR7: Thor H ...4B 140
HA2: Harr ...3F 43
HA4: Ruis ...2H 41
N3 ...3H 29
TW9: Rich ...1G 99
TW16: Sun T ...6J 113
UB3: Hayes ...7F 59
UB6: G'frd ...3F 61
UB8: Uxb ...6C 58
Beechwood Circ.
HA2: Harr ...3F 43
Beechwood Cl.
KT6: Surb ...7C 134
N2 ...4D 30
(off Western Rd.)
NW7 ...5F 13
Beechwood Ct.
SM5: Cars ...4D 150
TW16: Sun T ...6J 113
W4 ...6K 81
Beechwood Cres.
DA7: Bex ...3D 110
Beechwood Dr. BR2: Kes ...4B 156
IG8: Wfd G ...5C 20
Beechwood Gdns.
HA2: Harr ...3F 43
IG5: Ilf ...5D 36
NW10 ...3F 63
Beechwood Gro.
KT6: Surb ...7C 134
W3 ...7A 64
Beechwood Hall N3 ...3H 29
Beechwood Ho. E2 ...2G 69
(off Teale St.)
Beechwood M. N9 ...2B 18
Beechwood Pk. E18 ...3J 35
Beechwood Ri. BR7: Chst ...4F 127
Beechwood Rd.
CR2: S Croy ...7E 152
E8 ...6F 51
N8 ...4H 31
Beechwoods Ct. SE19 ...5F 123
Beechworth NW6 ...7G 47
Beechworth Cl. NW3 ...2J 47
Beecroft La. SE4 ...5A 106
Beecroft M. SE4 ...5A 106
Beecroft Rd. SE4 ...5A 106
Beehive Cl. E8 ...7F 51
UB10: Uxb ...7B 40
Beehive Ct. IG2: Ilf ...6D 36
Beehive La. IG4: Ilf ...5D 36
Beehive Pl. SW9 ...3A 104
Beeleigh Rd.
SM4: Mord ...4K 137
Beemans Row SW18 ...2A 120
Bee Pas. EC3 ...1G 169
(off Lime St.)
Beeston Cl. E8 ...5G 51
Beeston Ho. SE1 ...3D 86
(off Burbage Cl.)
Beeston Pl. SW1 ...3F 85 (1K 171)
Beeston Rd. EN4: Barn ...6G 5
Beeston Way TW14: Felt ...6A 96
Beethoven St. W10 ...3G 65
Beeton Cl. HA5: Pinn ...1E 24
Begbie Rd. SE3 ...1A 108
BEGGAR'S HILL ...6B 148
Beggar's Hill KT17: Eps ...7B 148
Beggars Roost La.
SM1: Sutt ...6J 149
Begonia Cl. E6 ...5D 72
Begonia Pl.
TW12: Hamp ...6E 114
Begonia Wlk. W12 ...6B 64
Beira St. SW12 ...7F 103
Bekesbourne St. E14 ...6A 70
Belcroft Cl. BR1: Brom ...7H 125
Beldanes Lodge NW10 ...7C 46
Beldham Gdns.
KT8: W Mole ...2F 133
Belfairs Dr. RM6: Chad H ...7C 38
Belfast Rd. N16 ...2F 51
SE25 ...4H 141
Belfield Rd. KT19: Eps ...7K 147
Belfont Wlk. N7 ...4J 49
(not continuous)
Belford Gro. SE18 ...4E 90
Belford Ho. E8 ...1F 69
Belfort Rd. SE15 ...2J 105
Belfry Cl. SE16 ...5H 87
Belfry Rd. E12 ...2B 54
Belgrade Rd. N16 ...4E 50
TW12: Hamp ...1F 133
Belgrave Cl. N14 ...5B 6
NW7 ...5E 12
W3 ...2H 81
Belgrave Ct. E13 ...4A 72
E14 ...7B 70
(off Westferry Cir.)
SW8 ...7G 85
(off Ascalon St.)
W4 ...5J 81
Belgrave Cres.
TW16: Sun T ...1K 131
Belgrave Gdns. HA7: Stan ...5H 11
N14 ...4C 6
NW8 ...1K 65
Belgrave Hgts. E11 ...1J 53
Belgrave Ho. SW9 ...7A 86
Belgrave M. Nth.
SW1 ...2E 84 (7G 165)
Belgrave M. Sth.
SW1 ...3E 84 (1H 171)
Belgrave M. W.
SW1 ...3E 84 (1G 171)
Belgrave Pl.
SW1 ...3E 84 (1H 171)
Belgrave Rd. CR4: Mitc ...3B 138
E10 ...1E 52
E11 ...2J 53
E13 ...4A 72
E17 ...5C 34
IG1: Ilf ...1D 54
SE25 ...4F 141
SW1 ...4F 85 (4K 171)
SW13 ...7B 82
TW4: Houn ...3D 96
TW16: Sun T ...1K 131
Belgrave Sq.
SW1 ...3E 84 (1G 171)
Belgrave St. E1 ...5K 69
Belgrave Ter. IG8: Wfd G ...3D 20
Belgrave Wlk. CR4: Mitc ...3B 138
Belgrave Yd. SW1 ...2J 171
BELGRAVIA ...3E 84 (2H 171)
Belgravia Cl. EN5: Barn ...3C 4
Belgravia Ct. SW1 ...2J 171
Belgravia Gdns.
BR1: Brom ...6G 125
Belgravia Ho. SW1 ...1G 171
(off Halkin Pl.)
SW4 ...6H 103
Belgravia M. KT1: King T ...4D 134
Belgravia Workshops N19 ...2J 49
(off Marlborough Rd.)
Belgrove St.
NW1 ...3J 67 (1F 161)
Belham Wlk. SE5 ...1D 104
Belinda Rd. SW9 ...3B 104
Belitha Vs. N1 ...7K 49
Bellamy Cl. E14 ...2C 88
HA8: Edg ...2D 12
UB10: Uxb ...3C 40
W14 ...5H 83
Bellamy Ct. HA7: Stan ...1B 26
Bellamy Dr. HA7: Stan ...1B 26
Bellamy Ho. TW5: Houn ...6E 78
Bellamy Rd. E4 ...6J 19
EN2: Enf ...2J 7
Bellamy's Ct. SE16 ...1K 87
(off Abbotshade Rd.)
Bellamy St. SW12 ...7F 103
Bellasis Av. SW2 ...2J 121
Bell Av. UB7: W Dray ...4B 76
Bell Cl. HA4: Ruis ...3H 41
HA5: Pinn ...2A 24
Bellclose Rd.
UB7: W Dray ...2A 76
Bell Ct. NW4 ...4E 28
Bell Dr. SW18 ...7G 101
Bellefields Rd. SW9 ...3K 103
Bellegrove Cl.
DA16: Well ...2K 109
Bellegrove Pde.
DA16: Well ...3K 109
Bellegrove Rd.
DA16: Well ...2H 109
Bellenden Rd. SE15 ...1F 105
Bellermine Cl. SE28 ...1K 91
Bellestaines Pleasaunce
E4 ...2H 19
Belleville Rd. SW11 ...5C 102
Belle Vue UB6: G'frd ...1H 61
Belle Vue Est. NW4 ...4F 29
Bellevue La.
WD23: Bush ...1C 10
Bellevue M. N11 ...5K 15
Bellevue Pk.
CR7: Thor H ...3C 140
Bellevue Pl. E1 ...4J 69
Belle Vue Rd. E17 ...2F 35
NW4 ...4F 29
Bellevue Rd. DA6: Bex ...5F 111
KT1: King T ...3E 134
(not continuous)
N11 ...4K 15
SW13 ...2C 100
SW17 ...1C 120
W13 ...4B 62
Bellew St. SW17 ...3A 120
Bell Farm Av. RM10: Dag ...3J 57
Bellfield CR0: Croy ...7A 154
Bellfield Av. HA3: Harr ...6C 10
Bellflower Cl. E6 ...5C 72
Bell Gdns. E10 ...1C 52
(off Church Rd.)
Bellgate M. NW5 ...4F 49
BELL GREEN ...4A 124
Bell Grn. SE26 ...4B 124
Bell Grn. La. SE26 ...5B 124
Bell Hill CR0: Croy ...2C 152
Bell Ho. SE10 ...6E 88
(off Haddo St.)
Bellhouse Cotts.
UB3: Hayes ...7G 59
Bell Ho. Rd. RM7: Rush G ...1J 57
Bellina M. NW5 ...4F 49
Bell Ind. Est. W4 ...4J 81
BELLINGHAM ...3C 124
Bellingham N17 ...7C 18
(off Park La.)
Bellingham Ct. IG11: Bark ...3B 74
Bellingham Grn. SE6 ...3C 124
Bellingham Rd. SE6 ...3D 124
Bellingham Trad. Est.
SE6 ...3D 124
Bell Inn Yd. EC3 ...6D 68 (1F 169)
Bell Junc. TW3: Houn ...3F 97
Bell La. E1 ...5F 69 (6J 163)
E16 ...1H 89
EN3: Enf ...1E 8
HA9: Wemb ...3D 44
NW4 ...4F 29
TW1: Twick ...1A 116
Bellmaker Ct. E3 ...5C 70
Bell Mdw. SE19 ...5E 122
Bell Moor NW3 ...3A 48
(off E. Heath Rd.)
Bello Cl. SE24 ...7B 104
Bellot Gdns. SE10 ...5G 89
(off Bellot St.)
Bellot St. SE10 ...5G 89
Bellring Cl. DA17: Belv ...6G 93
Bell Rd. EN1: Enf ...1J 7
KT8: E Mos ...5H 133
TW3: Houn ...3F 97
Bells All. SW6 ...2J 101
Bells Hill EN5: Barn ...5A 4
Bell St. NW1 ...5C 66 (5C 158)
SE18 ...1C 108
BELL, THE ...3C 34
Belltrees Gro. SW16 ...5K 121
Bell Vw. Mnr. HA4: Ruis ...7F 23
Bell Water Ga. SE18 ...3E 90
Bell Wharf La.
EC4 ...7C 68 (3D 168)
Bellwood Rd. SE15 ...4K 105

A-Z London 193

Bell Yd. WC2 ......6A 68 (1J 167)
Belmarsh Rd. SE28 ......2J 91
BELMONT 2A 26
Belmont Av. DA16: Well ...2J 109
　EN4: Barn 5J 5
　HA0: Wemb 1F 63
　KT3: N Mald 5C 136
　N9 ....1B 18
　N13 ....5E 16
　N17 ....3C 32
　UB2: S'hall 3C 78
Belmont Circ. HA3: Harr ...1B 26
Belmont Cl. E4 ....5A 20
　EN4: Barn 4J 5
　IG8: Wfd G 4E 20
　N20 ....1E 14
　SW4 ....3G 103
　UB8: Uxb 6A 40
Belmont Ct. N5 ....4C 50
　NW11 ....5H 29
Belmont Gro. SE13 .....3F 107
　W4 ....4K 81
Belmont Hall Ct. SE13 ...3F 107
Belmont Hill SE13 .....3E 106
Belmont La. BR7: Chst ...5F 127
　(not continuous)
　HA7: Stan 1C 26
Belmont Lodge HA3: Harr ...7C 10
Belmont M. SW19 .....2F 119
Belmont Pde. BR7: Chst ...5G 127
　NW11 ....5H 29
Belmont Pk. SE13 .....4F 107
Belmont Pk. Cl. SE13 ...4G 107
Belmont Pk. Rd. E10 ...6D 34
Belmont Ri. SM2: Sutt ...6H 149
Belmont Rd. BR3: Beck ...2A 142
　BR7: Chst 5F 127
　DA8: Erith 7G 93
　HA3: Harr 3K 25
　IG1: Ilf 3G 55
　N15 ....4C 32
　SE25 ....5H 141
　SM6: Wall 5F 151
　SW4 ....3G 103
　TW2: Twick 2H 115
　UB8: Uxb 7A 40
　W4 ....4K 81
Belmont St. NW1 .....7E 48
Belmont Ter. W4 .....4K 81
Belmore Av. UB4: Hayes ...6J 59
Belmore St. SW8 ....1H 103
Beloe Cl. SW15 .....4C 100
Belsham St. E9 .....6J 51
Belsize Av. N13 .....6E 16
　NW3 ....6B 48
　W13 ....3B 80
Belsize Ct. NW3 .....5B 48
Belsize Ct. Garages NW3 ...5B 48
　(off Belsize La.)
Belsize Cres. NW3 ....5B 48
Belsize Gdns. SM1: Sutt ...4K 149
Belsize Gro. NW3 ....6C 48
Belsize La. NW3 .....6B 48
Belsize M. NW3 .....6B 48
Belsize Pk. NW3 .....6B 48
Belsize Pk. Gdns. NW3 ...6B 48
Belsize Pk. M. NW3 ...6B 48
Belsize Pl. NW3 .....5B 48
Belsize Rd. HA3: Harr ...7C 10
　NW6 ....1K 65
Belsize Sq. NW3 .....6B 48
Belsize Ter. NW3 .....6B 48
Belson Rd. SE18 .....4D 90
Beltane Dr. SW19 .....3F 119
Belthorn Cres. SW12 ...7G 103
Belton Rd. DA14: Sidc ...4A 128
　E7 ....7K 53
　E11 ....4G 53
　N17 ....3E 32
　NW2 ....6C 46
Belton Way E3 .....5C 70

Beltran Rd. SW6 .....2K 101
Beltwood Rd. DA17: Belv ...4J 93
BELVEDERE 3G 93
Belvedere Av. IG5: Ilf ...2F 37
　SW19 ....5G 119
Belvedere Bldgs.
　SE1 ......2B 86 (7B 168)
Belvedere Cl.
　TW11: Tedd 5J 115
Belvedere Ct. DA17: Belv ...3F 93
　NW2 ....6F 47
　(off Willesden La.)
　SW15 ....4E 100
Belvedere Dr. SW19 ...5G 119
Belvedere Gdns.
　KT8: W Mole 5D 132
Belvedere Gro. SW19 ...5G 119
Belvedere Ind. Est.
　DA17: Belv 1J 93
Belvedere Link Bus. Pk.
　DA8: Erith 3J 93
Belvedere M. SE3 .....7H 89
　SE15 ....3J 105
Belvedere Pl.
　SE1 ......2B 86 (7B 168)
　SW2 ....4K 103
Belvedere Rd. DA7: Bex ...3F 111
　E10 ....1A 52
　SE1 ......1H 85 (6H 167)
　SE2 ....1C 92
　SE19 ....7F 123
　W7 ....3K 79
Belvedere Sq. SW19 ...5G 119
Belvedere Strand NW9 ...2B 28
Belvedere, The SW10 ...1A 102
　(off Chelsea Harbour)
Belvedere Way HA3: Harr ...6E 26
Belvoir Cl. SE9 .....3C 126
Belvoir Rd. SE22 .....7G 105
Belvue Bus. Cen.
　UB5: N'olt 7F 43
Belvue Cl. UB5: N'olt ...7E 42
Belvue Rd. UB5: N'olt ...7E 42
Bembridge Cl. NW6 ...7G 47
Bembridge Gdns.
　HA4: Ruis 2F 41
Bembridge Ho. SE8 ...4B 88
　(off Longshore)
Bemersyde Point E13 ...3K 71
　(off Dongola Rd. W.)
Bemerton Est. N1 ....7J 49
Bemerton St. N1 ....1K 67
Bemish Rd. SW15 ....3F 101
Bempton Dr. HA4: Ruis ...2K 41
Bemsted Rd. E17 ....3B 34
Benares Rd. SE18 ....4K 91
Benbow Cl. W6 ......3E 82
　(off Benbow Rd.)
Benbow Ho. SE8 .....6C 88
　(off Benbow St.)
Benbow Rd. W6 .....3D 82
Benbow St. SE8 .....6C 88
Benbury Cl. BR1: Brom ...5E 124
Bence Ho. SE8 .....4A 88
　(off Rainsborough Av.)
Bench Fld. CR2: S Croy ...6F 153
Bench, The TW10: Rich ...3C 116
Bencroft Rd. SW16 ...7G 121
Bencurtis Pk.
　BR4: W W'ck 3F 155
Bendall M. NW1 ....5D 158
Bendemeer Rd. SW15 ...3F 101
Benden Ho. SE13 ....5E 106
　(off Monument Gdns.)
Bendish Point SE28 ...2G 91
　(off Erebus Dr.)
Bendish Rd. E6 .....7C 54
Bendmore Av. SE2 ...5A 92
Bendon Valley SW18 ...7K 101
Benedict Cl. DA17: Belv ...3E 92
Benedict Ct. RM6: Chad H ...6F 39
Benedict Dr. TW14: Felt ...7F 95

Benedict Rd. CR4: Mitc ...3B 138
　SW9 ....3K 103
Benedict Way N2 ....3A 30
Benedict Wharf
　CR4: Mitc 3B 138
Benenden Grn.
　BR2: Short 5J 143
Benedict Gdns. SW16 ...2J 139
Ben Ezra Cl. SE17 ...4C 86
　(off Asolando Dr.)
Benfleet Cl. SM1: Sutt ...3A 150
Benfleet Ct. E8 ......1F 69
Benfleet Way N11 ...2K 15
Bengal Ct. EC3 .....1F 169
　(off Birchin La.)
Bengal Ho. E1 .....5K 69
　(off Duckett St.)
Bengal Rd. IG1: Ilf ...4F 55
Bengarth Dr. HA3: Harr ...2H 25
Bengarth Rd. UB5: N'olt ...1C 60
Bengeo Gdns.
　RM6: Chad H 6C 38
Bengeworth Rd.
　HA1: Harr 2A 44
　SE5 ....3C 104
Ben Hale Cl. HA7: Stan ...5G 11
Benham Cl. KT9: Chess ...6C 146
　SW11 ....3B 102
Benham Gdns. TW4: Houn ...5D 96
Benham Rd. W7 .....5J 61
Benham's Pl. NW3 ...4A 48
Benhill Av. SM1: Sutt ...4K 149
Benhill Rd. SE5 .....7D 86
　SM1: Sutt 3A 150
Benhill Wood Rd.
　SM1: Sutt 3A 150
BENHILTON 2K 149
Benhilton Gdns.
　SM1: Sutt 3K 149
Benin St. SE13 .....7F 107
Benjafield Cl. N18 ...4C 18
Benjamin Cl. E8 .....1G 69

Benjamin Franklin House
　................4E 166
　(off Craven St.)

Benjamin St.
　EC1 ......5B 68 (5A 162)
Ben Jonson Cl. N1 ...2E 68
Ben Jonson Ho. EC2 ...5D 162
Ben Jonson Pl. EC2 ...5D 162
Ben Jonson Rd. E1 ...5K 69
Benledi St. E14 .....6H 71
Bennelong Cl. W12 ...7D 64
Bennerley Rd. SW11 ...5C 102
Bennets Fld. Rd.
　UB11: Uxb 1D 76
Bennet's Hill
　EC4 ......7C 68 (2B 168)
Bennet Cl. SW1 ...1G 85 (4A 166)
Bennett Cl. DA16: Well ...2A 110
　HA6: Nwood 1H 23
　KT1: King T 1C 134
Bennett Ct. N7 .....3K 49
Bennett Gro. SE13 ...1D 106
Bennett Ho. SW1 ...3D 172
　(off Page St.)
Bennett Pk. SE3 .....3H 107
Bennett Rd. E13 ....4A 72
　N16 ....4E 50
　RM6: Chad H 6E 38
Bennetts Av. CR0: Croy ...2A 154
　UB6: G'frd 1J 61
Bennett's Castle La.
　RM8: Dag 2C 56
Bennetts Cl. CR4: Mitc ...1F 139
　N17 ....6A 18
Bennetts Copse
　BR7: Chst 6C 126
Bennett St. W4 .....6A 82

Bennetts Way
　CR0: Croy 2A 154
Bennett's Yd.
　SW1 ......3H 85 (2D 172)
Benningholme Rd.
　HA8: Edg 6F 13
Bennington Rd.
　IG8: Wfd G 7B 20
　N17 ....1E 32
Benn's All. TW12: Hamp ...2F 133
Benn St. E9 ....6A 52
Benns Wlk. TW9: Rich ...4E 98
　(off Michelsdale Dr.)
Benrek Cl. IG6: Ilf ...1G 37
Bensbury Cl. SW15 ...7D 100
Bensham Cl.
　CR7: Thor H 4C 140
Bensham Gro.
　CR7: Thor H 2C 140
Bensham La. CR0: Croy ...7B 140
　CR7: Thor H 5B 140
Bensham Mnr. Rd.
　CR7: Thor H 4C 140
Ben Smith Way SE16 ...3G 87
Benson Av. E6 .....2A 72
Benson Ct. TW3: Houn ...4E 96
　UB8: Uxb 5A 58
Benson Ho. E2 .....2J 163
　(off Ligonier St.)
　SE1 ....5K 167
　(off Hatfields)
Benson Quay E1 ....7J 69
Benson Rd. CR0: Croy ...3A 152
　SE23 ....1J 123
Bentalls Cen., The
　KT1: King T 2D 134
Bentfield Gdns. SE9 ...3B 126
Benthal Rd. N16 ....2G 51
Bentham Ct. N1 .....7C 50
　(off Ecclesbourne Rd.)
　SE1 ....3D 86
　(off Falmouth Rd.)
Bentham Rd. E9 ....6K 51
　SE28 ....7B 74
Bentham Wlk. NW10 ...5J 45
Ben Tillet Cl. E16 ...1D 90
Ben Tillet Ho. N15 ...3B 32
Bentinck Cl. NW8 ...2C 66
Bentinck Ho. W12 ...7D 64
　(off White City Est.)
Bentinck M. W1 ...6E 66 (7H 159)
Bentinck Rd. UB7: W Dray ...1A 76
Bentinck St. W1 ...6E 66 (7H 159)
Bentley Dr. IG2: Ilf ...6G 37
　NW2 ....3H 47
Bentley Ho. SE5 .....1E 104
　(off Peckham Rd.)
Bentley Rd. N1 .....6E 50
Bentley Way HA7: Stan ...5F 11
　IG8: Buck H, Wfd G ...2D 20
Benton Rd. IG1: Ilf ...1H 55
Bentons La. SE27 ...4C 122
Benton's Ri. SE27 ...5D 122
Bentry Cl. RM8: Dag ...2E 56
Bentry Rd. RM8: Dag ...2E 56
Bentworth Ct. W12 ...6D 64
Bentworth Ct. E2 ...3K 163
　(off Granby St.)
Bentworth Rd. W12 ...6D 64
Benville Ho. SW8 ...7K 85
　(off Oval Pl.)
Benwell Ct.
　TW16: Sun T 1J 131
Benwell Rd. N7 .....4A 50
Benwick Cl. SE16 ...4H 87
Benwood Ct. SM1: Sutt ...3A 150
Benworth St. E3 ...3B 70
Benyon Ho. N1 .....1E 68
　(off De Beauvoir Est.)

Benyon Ho. EC1 .....1K 161
　(off Myddelton Pas.)
Benyon Rd. N1 .....1D 68
Berberis Cl. IG1: Ilf ...6F 55
Berberis Ho. E3 .....5C 70
　(off Gale St.)
Berberis Wlk.
　UB7: W Dray 4A 76
Berber Pl. E14 .....7C 70
Berber Rd. SW11 ...5D 102
Berberry Cl. HA8: Edg ...4D 12
Bercta Rd. SE9 .....2G 127
Berenger Twr. SW10 ...7B 84
　(off Worlds End Est.)
Berenger Wlk. SW10 ...7B 84
　(off Worlds End Est.)
Berens Ct. DA14: Sidc ...4K 127
Berens Rd. NW10 ...3F 65
Berens Way BR7: Chst ...3K 145
Beresford Av.
　HA0: Wemb 1F 63
　KT5: Surb 1H 147
　N20 ....2J 15
　TW1: Twick 6C 98
　W7 ....5H 61
Beresford Dr. BR1: Brom ...3C 144
　IG8: Wfd G 4F 21
Beresford Gdns. EN1: Enf ...4K 7
　RM6: Chad H 5E 38
　TW4: Houn 5D 96
Beresford Rd. E4 ...1B 20
　E17 ....1D 34
　HA1: Harr 5H 25
　KT2: King T 1F 135
　KT3: N Mald 4J 135
　N2 ....3C 30
　N5 ....5D 50
　N8 ....5A 32
　SM2: Sutt 7H 149
　UB1: S'hall 1B 78
Beresford Sq. SE18 ...4F 91
Beresford St. SE18 ...3F 91
Beresford Ter. N5 ...5C 50
Berestede Rd. W6 ...5B 82
Bere St. E1 ....7K 69
Bergen Ho. SE5 .....2C 104
　(off Carew St.)
Bergen Sq. SE16 ...3A 88
Berger Cl. BR5: Orp ...6H 145
Berger Rd. E9 .....6K 51
Berghem M. W14 ...3F 83
Bergholt Av. IG4: Ilf ...5C 36
Bergholt Cres. N16 ...7E 32
Bergholt M. NW1 ...7G 49
Berglen Ct. E14 ...6A 70
Bering Sq. E14 ....5C 88
Bering Wlk. E16 ...6B 72
Berisford M. SW18 ...6A 102
Berkeley Av. DA7: Bex ...1D 110
　IG5: Ilf 2E 36
　RM5: Col R 1J 39
　TW4: Houn 1J 95
　UB6: G'frd 6J 43
Berkeley Cl. BR5: Orp ...7J 145
　HA4: Ruis 3J 41
　KT2: King T 7E 116
　TW2: Twick 3J 115
　(off Wellesley Rd.)
　TW8: Bford 6A 80
Berkeley Ct. CR0: Croy ...4D 152
　(off Coombe Rd.)
　KT6: Surb 7D 134
　N3 ....1K 29
　N14 ....6B 6
　NW1 ....4F 159
　NW10 ....4A 46
　NW11 ....7H 29
　(off Ravenscroft Av.)
　SM6: Wall 3G 151
　W5 ....7C 62
　(off Gordon Rd.)
Berkeley Cres. EN4: Barn ...5G 5

Berkeley Dr.
KT8: W Mole 3D 132
Berkeley Gdns.
KT10: Esh 6A 146
KT12: Walt T 7H 131
N21 ....7J 7
W8 ....1J 83
Berkeley Ho. SE8 ....5B 88
(off Grove Ct.)
TW8: Bford 6D 80
(off Albany Rd.)
Berkeley M. W1 ...6D 66 (1F 165)
Berkeley Pl. SW19 ......6F 119
Berkeley Rd. E12 ....5C 54
N8 ....5H 31
N15 ....6D 32
NW9 ....4G 27
SW13 ....1C 100
UB10: Uxb 7E 40
Berkeley Sq. W1 ...7F 67 (3K 165)
Berkeley St. W1 ...7F 67 (3K 165)
Berkeley Twr. E14 ....1B 88
(off Westferry Cir.)
Berkeley Wlk. N7 ....2C 49
(off Durham Rd.)
Berkeley Waye
TW5: Houn 6B 78
Berkely Cl.
TW16: Sun T 3A 132
Berkhampstead Rd.
DA17: Belv 5G 93
Berkhamsted Av.
HA9: Wemb 6F 45
Berkley Gro. NW1 ....7E 48
Berkley Rd. NW1 ....7D 48
Berkshire Cl. W7 ....4K 61
(off Copley Cl.)
Berkshire Gdns. N13 .....6F 17
N18 ....5C 18
Berkshire Ho. SE6 ......4C 124
Berkshire Rd. E9 ....6B 52
Berkshire Sq. CR4: Mitc ...4J 139
Berkshire Way CR4: Mitc ...4J 139
Bermans Way NW10 ....4A 46
BERMONDSEY 2G 87 (7K 169)
Bermondsey Sq.
SE1 ....3E 86 (7H 169)
Bermondsey St.
SE1 ....1E 86 (5G 169)
Bermondsey Trad. Est.
SE16 ....5J 87
Bermondsey Wall E. SE16 ..2G 87
Bermondsey Wall W.
SE16 ....2G 87 (6K 169)
Bernal Cl. SE28 ....7D 74
Bernard Angell Ho. SE10 ...6F 89
(off Trafalgar Rd.)
Bernard Ashley Dr. SE7 ...5K 89
Bernard Av. W13 ....3B 80
Bernard Ho. SW16 ....3J 121
Bernard Cassidy St. E16 ...5H 71
Bernard Gdns. SW19 .....5H 119
Bernard Mans. WC1 ......4E 160
(off Bernard St.)
Bernard Rd. N15 ....5F 33
RM7: Rush G 7J 39
SM6: Wall 4F 151
Bernard Shaw Ct. NW1 ...7G 49
(off St Pancras Way)
Bernard St. WC1 ...4J 67 (4E 160)
Bernard Sunley Ho. SW9 ...7A 86
(off Sth. Island Pl.)
Bernays Cl. HA7: Stan 6H 11
Bernays Gro. SW9 ......4K 103
Bernel Dr. CR0: Croy 3B 154
Berne Rd. CR7: Thor H ...5C 140
Berners Dr. W13 ....7A 62
Berners Ho. N1 ....2A 68
(off Barnsbury Est.)
Berners M. W1 ...5G 67 (6B 160)
Berners Pl. W1 ...6G 67 (7B 160)
Berners Rd. N1 ....1B 68
N22 ....1A 32

Berners St. W1 ...5G 67 (6B 160)
Berner Ter. E1 ....6G 69
(off Fairclough St.)
Berney Ho. BR3: Beck 5A 142
Berney Rd. CR0: Croy ...7D 140
Bernhardt Cres.
NW8 ....4C 66 (3C 158)
Bernhart Cl. HA8: Edg ...7D 12
Bernville Way HA3: Harr ...5F 27
Bernwell Rd. E4 ....3B 20
Berridge Grn. HA8: Edg ...7B 12
Berridge M. NW6 ....5J 47
Berridge Rd. SE19 ......5D 122
Berriman Rd. N7 ....3K 49
Berriton Rd. HA2: Harr ...1D 42
Berrybank Cl. E4 ....2K 19
Berry Cl. N21 ....1G 17
NW10 ....7A 46
RM10: Dag 5G 57
Berry Ct. TW4: Houn 5D 96
Berrydale Rd.
UB4: Hayes 4C 60
Berryfield Cl. BR1: Brom ...1C 144
E17 ....4D 34
Berryfield Rd. SE17 ......5B 86
Berry Hill HA7: Stan 4J 11
Berryhill SE9 ....4F 109
Berryhill Gdns. SE9 .....4F 109
Berry Ho. E1 ....4H 69
(off Headlam St.)
BERRYLANDS 6G 135
Berrylands KT5: Surb 6F 135
SW20 ....3E 136
Berrylands Rd. KT5: Surb ...6F 135
Berry La. SE21 ....4D 122
Berryman Cl. RM8: Dag ...3C 56
Berryman's La. SE26 .....4K 123
Berrymead Gdns. W3 .....1J 81
Berrymede Rd. W4 ....3K 81
Berry Pl. EC1 ...3B 68 (2B 162)
Berry St. EC1 ...4B 68 (3B 162)
Berry Way W5 ....3E 80
Bertal Rd. SW17 ....4B 120
Bertha Hollamby Ct.
DA14: Sidc 5C 128
(off Sidcup Hill)
Bertha James Ct.
BR2: Short 4K 143
Berthons Gdns. E17 ....5F 35
(off Wood St.)
Berthon St. SE8 ....7C 88
Bertie Ho. NW10 ....4C 46
SE26 ....6K 123
Bertram Cotts. SW19 ....7J 119
Bertram Rd. EN1: Enf 4B 8
KT2: King T 7G 117
NW4 ....6C 28
Bertram St. N19 ....2F 49
Bertrand Ho. SW16 ....3J 121
(off Leigham Av.)
Bertrand St. SE13 ......3D 106
Bertrand Way SE28 ......7B 74
Bert Rd. CR7: Thor H 5C 140
Bert Way EN1: Enf 4A 8
Berwick Av. UB4: Hayes ...6B 60
Berwick Cl. HA7: Stan 6E 10
TW2: Twick 1E 114
Berwick Cres. DA15: Sidc ...7J 109
Berwick Ho. N2 ....2B 30
Berwick Rd. DA16: Well ...1B 110
E16 ....6K 71
N22 ....1B 32
Berwick St. W1 ...6G 67 (7B 160)
Berwyn Av. TW3: Houn ...1F 97
Berwyn Rd. SE24 ....1B 122
TW10: Rich 4H 99
Beryl Av. E6 ....5C 72
Beryl Ho. SE18 ....5K 91
(off Spinel Cl.)
Beryl Rd. W6 ....5F 83
Berystede KT2: King T ...7H 117
Besant Cl. NW2 ....3G 47

Besant Ct. N1 ....5D 50
SE28 ....1B 92
(off Titmuss Av.)
Besant Ho. NW8 ....1A 66
(off Boundary Rd.)
Besant Pl. SE15 ....4F 105
Besant Rd. NW2 ....4G 47
Besant Wlk. N7 ....2K 49
Besant Way NW10 ....5J 45
Besford Ho. E2 ....2G 69
(off Pritchard's Rd.)
Besley St. SW16 ....6G 121
Bessant Dr. TW9: Rich ...1G 99
Bessborough Gdns.
SW1 ....5H 85 (5D 172)
Bessborough Pl.
SW1 ....5H 85 (5D 172)
Bessborough Rd.
HA1: Harr 1H 43
SW15 ....1C 118
Bessborough St.
SW1 ....5H 85 (5C 172)
Bessemer Ct. NW1 ....7G 49
(off Rochester Sq.)
Bessemer Rd. SE5 ....2C 104
Bessie Lansbury Cl. E6 ...6E 72
Bessingby Rd. HA4: Ruis ...2K 41
Bessingham Wlk. SE4 ....4K 105
(off Aldersford Cl.)
Besson St. SE14 ....1J 105
Bessy St. E2 ....3J 69
Bestwood St. SE8 ....4K 87
Beswick M. NW6 ....6K 47
Beta Pl. SW9 ....4K 103
Betchworth Cl. SM1: Sutt ...5B 150
Betchworth Rd. IG3: Ilf ...2J 55
Betchworth Way
CR0: Croy 7E 154
Bethal St. SE1 ....5H 169
Betham Rd. UB6: G'frd ...3H 61
Bethecar Rd. HA1: Harr ...5J 25
Bethell Av. E16 ....4H 71
IG1: Ilf 7E 36
Bethel Rd. DA16: Well ...3C 110
Bethersden Cl.
BR3: Beck 7B 124
Bethersden Ho. SE17 .....5E 86
(off Kinglake St.)
Bethlehem Ho. E14 ....7B 70
(off Limehouse C'way.)
BETHNAL GREEN 3H 69
Bethnal Green Mus. of Childhood
.......................3J 69
Bethnal Grn. Rd.
E1 ....4F 69 (3J 163)
E2 ....4F 69 (3J 163)
Bethune Av. N11 ....4J 15
Bethune Cl. N16 ....1E 50
Bethune Ho. N16 ....7D 32
NW10 ....4K 63
Bethune Rd. N16 ....7D 32
NW10 ....4K 63
Bethwin Rd. SE5 ....7B 86
Betjeman Cl. HA5: Pinn ...4E 24
Betjeman Cl. UB7: W Dray ...1A 76
Betony Cl. CR0: Croy ...1K 153
Betoyne Av. E4 ....4B 20
Betsham Ho. SE1 ....6E 168
(off Newcomen St.)
Betstyle Cir. N11 ....4A 16
Betstyle Ho. N10 ....7K 15
Betstyle Rd. N11 ....4A 16
Betterton Dr. DA14: Sidc ...2E 128
Betterton Ho. WC2 ......1F 167
(off Betterton St.)
Betterton Rd.
RM13: Rain 3K 75
Betterton St.
WC2 ....6J 67 (1E 166)
Bettons Pk. E15 ....1G 71
Bettridge Rd. SW6 ......2H 101
Betts Cl. BR3: Beck 2A 142

Betts Ho. E1 ....7H 69
(off Betts St.)
Betts M. E17 ....6B 34
Betts Rd. E16 ....7K 71
Betts St. E1 ....7H 69
Betts Way KT6: Surb ...1B 146
SE20 ....1H 141
Betty Brooks Ho. E11 ....3F 53
Betty May Gray Ho. E14 ...4E 88
(off Pier St.)
Beulah Av. CR7: Thor H ...2C 140
Beulah Cl. HA8: Edg 3C 12
Beulah Cres.
CR7: Thor H 2C 140
Beulah Gro. CR0: Croy ...6C 140
Beulah Hill SE19 ....6B 122
Beulah Path E17 ....5E 34
Beulah Rd. CR7: Thor H ...3C 140
E17 ....5D 34
SM1: Sutt 4J 149
SW19 ....7H 119
Bevan Av. IG11: Bark 7A 56
Bevan Ct. CR0: Croy 5A 152
Bevan Ho. TW1: Twick ...6D 98
(off Boswell St.)
Bevan Rd. EN4: Barn 4J 5
SE2 ....5B 92
Bevan St. N1 ....1C 68
Bev Callender Cl. SW8 ...3F 103
Bevenden St. N1 ...3D 68 (1F 163)
Bevercote Wlk.
DA17: Belv 6F 93
(off Osborne Rd.)
Beveridge Ct. SE28 ....7B 74
(off Saunders Way)
Beveridge Rd. NW10 .....7A 46
Beverley Av. DA15: Sidc ...7K 109
SW20 ....1B 136
TW4: Houn 4D 96
Beverley Cl. EN1: Enf 4K 7
KT9: Chess 4C 146
N21 ....1H 17
SW11 ....4B 102
SW13 ....2C 100
Beverley Cotts. SW15 ....3A 118
Beverley Ct. HA2: Harr ...3H 25
HA3: Harr 4C 26
N2 ....4D 30
(off Western Rd.)
N14 ....7B 6
SE4 ....1B 106
(not continuous)
TW3: Houn 4E 96
W4 ....5J 81
Beverley Cres. IG8: Wfd G ...1K 35
Beverley Dr. HA8: Edg ...3G 27
Beverley Gdns. HA7: Stan ...1A 26
HA9: Wemb 1F 45
KT4: Wor Pk 1C 148
NW11 ....7G 29
SW13 ....3B 100
Beverley Ho. BR1: Brom ...5F 125
(off Brangbourne Rd.)
Beverley La. KT2: King T ...7A 118
SW15 ....3B 118
Beverley M. E4 ....6A 20
Beverley Path SW13 ....3B 100
Beverley Rd. BR2: Short ...2C 156
CR4: Mitc 4H 139
DA7: Bex 2J 111
E4 ....6A 20
E6 ....3B 72
HA4: Ruis 2J 41
KT1: King T 1C 134
KT3: N Mald 4C 136
KT4: Wor Pk 2E 148
RM9: Dag 4E 56
SE20 ....2H 141
SW13 ....3B 100
TW16: Sun T 1H 131
UB2: S'hall 4C 78

Beverley Rd. W4 ....5B 82
Beverley Trad. Est.
SM4: Mord 7F 137
Beverley Way SW20 ....1B 136
Beversbrook Rd. N19 ....3H 49
Beverstone Rd.
CR7: Thor H 4A 140
SW2 ....5K 103
Beverston M. NW1 ......6E 158
Bevill Allen Cl. SW17 ...5D 120
Bevill Cl. SE25 ....3G 141
Bevin Cl. SE16 ....1A 88
Bevin Ct. WC1 ....3K 67 (1H 161)
Bevington Path SE1 .....7J 169
Bevington Rd. BR3: Beck ...2D 142
W10 ....5G 65
Bevington St. SE16 ......2G 87
Bevin Ho. E2 ....3J 69
(off Butler St.)
Bevin Rd. UB4: Hayes ...3J 59
Bevin Sq. SW17 ....3D 120
Bevin Way WC1 ....2A 68 (1J 161)
Bevis Marks EC3 ...6E 68 (7H 163)
Bewcastle Gdns. EN2: Enf ...4D 6
Bew Ct. SE22 ....7G 105
Bewdley St. N1 ....7A 50
Bewick M. SE15 ....7H 87
Bewick St. SW8 ....2F 103
Bewley Ho. E1 ....7H 69
(off Bewley St.)
Bewley St. E1 ....7J 69
SW19 ....6A 120
Bewlys Rd. SE27 ....5B 122
Bexhill Cl. TW13: Felt 2C 114
Bexhill Rd. N11 ....5C 16
SE4 ....6B 106
SW14 ....3J 99
Bexhill Wlk. E15 ....1G 71
BEXLEY 7H 111
Bexley Gdns. N9 ....3J 17
RM6: Chad H 5B 38
BEXLEYHEATH 4F 111
Bexley High St.
DA5: Bexl 7G 111
Bexley Ho. SE4 ....4A 106
Bexley La. DA1: Cray 5K 111
DA14: Sidc 4C 128
Bexley Mus. 6J 111
Bexley Rd. DA8: Erith ...7J 93
SE9 ....5F 109
Beynon Rd. SM5: Cars ...5D 150
Bianca Rd. SE15 ....6G 87
Bibsworth Rd. N3 ....2H 29
Bibury Cl. SE15 ....6E 86
(not continuous)
Bicester Rd. TW9: Rich ...3G 99
Bickenhall Mans. NW1 ...5F 159
(not continuous)
Bickenhall St.
W1 ....5D 66 (5F 159)
Bickersteth Rd. SW17 ...6D 120
Bickerton Rd. N19 ....2G 49
BICKLEY 3C 144
Bickley Cres.
BR1: Brom 4C 144
Bickley Pk. Rd.
BR1: Brom 3C 144
E10 ....7D 34
Bickley St. SW17 ....5C 120
Bicknell Ho. E1 ....6G 69
(off Ellen St.)
Bicknell Rd. SE5 ....3C 104
Bicknoller Rd. EN1: Enf ...1K 7
Bicknor Rd. BR6: Orp ...7J 145
Bidborough Cl.
BR2: Short 5H 143
Bidborough St.
WC1 ....3J 67 (2E 160)
Biddenham Ho. SE9 ....4E 125
Biddenham Ho. SE16 .....4K 87
(off Plough Way)

Bidder St. E16 ....4G 71
  (not continuous)
Biddesden Ho. SW3 ....4E 170
  (off Cadogan St.)
Biddestone Rd. N7 ....4K 49
Biddulph Ho. SE18 ....4D 90
Biddulph Mans. W9 ....3K 65
  (off Elgin Av.)
Biddulph Rd. W9 ....3K 65
Bideford Av. UB6: G'frd 2B 62
Bideford Cl. HA8: Edg 1G 27
  TW13: Felt 3D 114
Bideford Gdns. EN1: Enf 7K 7
Bideford Rd. BR1: Brom ...3H 125
  DA16: Well 7B 92
  EN3: Enf 1G 9
  HA4: Ruis 3K 41
Bidwell Gdns. N11 ....7B 16
Bidwell St. SE15 ....1H 105
Big Ben 2J 85 (7F 167)
Bigbury Cl. N17 ....7J 17
Biggerstaff Rd. E15 ......1E 70
Biggerstaff St. N4 ....2A 50
Biggin Av. CR4: Mitc 1D 138
Biggin Hill SE19 ....1B 140
Biggin Hill Cl.
  KT2: King T 5C 116
Biggin Way SE19 ....7B 122
Bigginwood Rd. SW16 .....7B 122
Biggs Row SW15 ....3F 101
Big Hill E5 ....1H 51
Bigland St. E1 ....6H 69
Bignell Rd. SE18 ....5F 91
Bignold Rd. E7 ....4J 53
Bigwood Ct. NW11 ....5K 29
Bigwood Rd. NW11 ....5K 29
Bilberry Ho. E3 ....5C 70
  (off Watts Gro.)
Billet Cl. RM6: Chad H 3D 38
Billet Rd. E17 ....1K 33
  RM6: Chad H 3B 38
Billets Hart Cl. W7 ....2J 79
Bill Hamling Cl. SE9 .....2D 126
Billing Cl. RM9: Dag 7C 56
Billingford Cl. SE4 ......4K 105
Billing Ho. E1 ....6K 69
  (off Bower St.)
Billingley NW1 ....1G 67
  (off Pratt St.)
Billing Pl. SW10 ....7K 83
Billing Rd. SW10 ....7K 83
Billing St. SW6 ....7K 83
Billington M. W3 ....1H 81
  (off High St.)
Billington Rd. SE14 ......7K 87
Billinton Hill CR0: Croy ...2D 152
Billiter Sq. EC3 ....1H 169
Billiter St. EC3 ......6E 68 (1H 169)
Bill Nicholson Way N17 ....7A 18
  (off High Rd.)
Billockby Cl. KT9: Chess ...6F 147
Billson St. E14 ....4E 88
Bilsby Gro. SE9 ....4B 126
Bilsby Lodge HA9: Wemb ...3J 45
  (off Chalklands)
Bilton Cen., The
  UB6: G'frd 1B 62
Bilton Rd. UB6: G'frd 1A 62
Bilton Towers W1 ....1F 165
  (off Gt. Cumberland Pl.)
Bilton Way EN3: Enf 1F 9
  UB3: Hayes 2K 77
Bina Gdns. SW5 ....4A 84
Binbrook Ho. W10 ....5E 64
  (off Sutton Way)
Bincote Rd. EN2: Enf 3E 6
Binden Rd. W12 ....3B 82
Bindon Grn. SM4: Mord ...4K 137
Binfield Rd.
  CR2: S Croy 5F 153
  SW4 ....1J 103
  SW8 ....1J 103

Bingfield St. N1 ....1J 67
  (not continuous)
Bingham Ct. N1 ....7B 50
  (off Halton Rd.)
Bingham Pl. W1 .....5E 66 (5G 159)
Bingham Rd. CR0: Croy ...1G 153
Bingham St. N1 ....6D 50
Bingley Rd. E16 ....6A 72
  TW16: Sun T 7J 113
  UB6: G'frd 4G 61
Binley Ho. SW15 ....6B 100
Binney St. W1 .....6E 66 (1H 165)
Binnie Cl. SE10 ....7D 88
  (off Greenwich High Rd.)
Binnie Ho. SE1 ....3C 86
  (off Bath Ter.)
Binnington Twr.
  BR2: Short 6C 144
Binns Rd. W4 ....5A 82
Binns Ter. W4 ....5A 82
Binsey Wlk. SE2 ....2C 92
Binstead Cl. UB4: Hayes ...5C 60
Binyon Cres. HA7: Stan 5E 10
Birbetts Rd. SE9 ....2D 126
Bircham Path SE4 ....4K 105
  (off Aldersford Cl.)
Birchanger Rd. SE25 .....5G 141
Birch Av. N13 ....3H 17
  UB7: W Dray 6B 58
Birch Cl. E16 ....5G 71
  IG9: Buck H 3G 21
  N19 ....2G 49
  RM7: Mawney 3H 39
  SE15 ....2G 105
  (off Bournemouth Cl.)
  TW3: Houn 2H 97
  TW8: Bford 7B 80
  TW11: Tedd 5A 116
  TW17: Shep 2G 131
Birch Ct. RM6: Chad H 6C 38
  SM6: Wall 4F 151
Birch Cres. UB10: Uxb 1B 58
Birchdale Gdns.
  RM6: Chad H 7D 38
Birchdale Rd. E7 ....5A 54
Birchdene Dr. SE28 ......1A 92
Birchen Cl. NW9 ....2K 45
Birchend Cl. CR2: S Croy ..6D 152
Birchen Gro. NW9 ....2K 45
Birches Cl. CR4: Mitc 3D 138
  HA5: Pinn 5C 24
Birches, The BR2: Short ...4H 143
  (off Durham Av.)
  BR6: Orp 4E 156
  E12 ....4C 54
  N21 ....6E 6
  SE7 ....6K 89
  TW4: Houn 7D 96
Birchfield Ho. E14 ....7C 70
  (off Birchfield St.)
Birchfield St. E14 ....7C 70
Birch Gdns. RM10: Dag 3J 57
Birch Grn. NW9 ....7F 13
Birch Gro. DA16: Well 4A 110
  E11 ....4G 53
  SE12 ....7H 107
  TW17: Shep 2G 131
  W3 ....1G 81
Birch Hill CR0: Croy 5K 153
Birch Ho. N22 ....1A 32
  (off Acacia Rd.)
  SE14 ....1B 106
  SW2 ....6A 104
  (off Tulse Hill)
  W10 ....4G 65
  (off Droop St.)
Birchington Cl.
  DA7: Bex 1H 111
Birchington Ho. E5 ......5H 51

Birchington Rd.
  KT5: Surb 7F 135
  N8 ....6H 31
  NW6 ....1J 65
Birchin La. EC3 ....6D 68 (1F 169)
Birchlands Av. SW12 .....7D 102
Birchmead BR6: Orp 2E 156
Birchmead Av. HA5: Pinn ...4A 24
Birchmere Bus. Site
  SE28 ....3H 92
Birchmere Lodge SE16 ....5H 87
  (off Sherwood Gdns.)
Birchmere Row SE3 ......2H 107
Birchmore Hall N5 ....3C 50
Birchmore Wlk. N5 ....3C 50
Birch Pk. HA3: Harr 7B 10
Birch Rd. RM7: Mawney ...3H 39
  TW13: Felt 5B 114
Birch Row BR2: Short 7E 144
Birch Tree Av.
  BR4: W W'ck 5H 155
Birch Tree Way
  CR0: Croy 2H 153
Birch Va. Ct. NW8 ....3B 158
  (off Pollitt Dr.)
Birchville Ct. WD23: Bush ..1D 10
Birch Wlk. CR4: Mitc 1F 139
  DA8: Erith 6J 93
Birchway UB3: Hayes 1J 77
Birchwood Av.
  BR3: Beck 4B 142
  DA14: Sidc 2B 128
  N10 ....3E 30
  SM6: Wall 3E 150
Birchwood Cl.
  SM4: Mord 4K 137
Birchwood Ct. HA8: Edg ...2J 27
  N13 ....5G 17
Birchwood Dr. DA2: Dart ..4K 129
  NW3 ....3K 47
Birchwood Gro.
  TW12: Hamp 6E 114
Birchwood Pde.
  DA2: Dart 4K 129
Birchwood Rd. BR5: Orp ...4H 145
  BR8: Swan 7J 129
  DA2: Dart 7J 129
  SW17 ....5F 121
Birdbrook Cl. RM10: Dag ...7J 57
Birdbrook Ho. N1 ....7C 50
  (off Popham Rd.)
Birdbrook Rd. SE3 ....3A 108
Birdcage Wlk.
  SW1 ....2G 85 (7A 166)
Birdham Cl. BR1: Brom ...5C 144
Birdhurst Av.
  CR2: S Croy 4D 152
Birdhurst Gdns.
  CR2: S Croy 4D 152
Birdhurst Ri. CR2: S Croy ..5E 152
Birdhurst Rd.
  CR2: S Croy 5E 152
  SW18 ....5A 102
  SW19 ....6C 120
Bird in Bush Rd. SE15 ....7G 87
Bird in Hand La.
  BR1: Brom 2B 144
Bird-in-Hand Pas. SE23 ...2J 123
Bird in Hand Yd. NW3 ....4A 48
  (off Holly Bush Va.)
  NW3 ....4A 48
  (Perrin's Ct.)
Birdlip Cl. SE15 ....6E 86
Birdsall Ho. SE5 ....3E 104
Birds Farm Av.
  RM5: Col R 1H 39
Birdsfield La. E3 ....1B 70
Bird St. W1 .....6E 66 (1H 165)
Birds Wlk. TW2: Twick 1D 114
Birdwood Cl. TW11: Tedd ..4J 115
Birkbeck Av. UB6: G'frd ...1G 61
  W3 ....7J 63

Birkbeck College
  ....5H 67 (5D 160)
Birkbeck Ct. W3 ....1K 81
Birkbeck Gdns.
  IG8: Wfd G 2D 20
Birkbeck Gro. W3 ....2K 81
Birkbeck Hill SE21 ......1B 122
Birkbeck M. E8 ....5F 51
  W3 ....1K 81
Birkbeck Pl. SE21 ....2C 122
Birkbeck Rd. BR3: Beck ...2J 141
  DA14: Sidc 3A 128
  E8 ....5F 51
  EN2: Enf 1J 7
  IG2: Ilf 5H 37
  N8 ....4J 31
  N12 ....5F 16
  N17 ....1F 33
  NW7 ....5G 13
  RM7: Rush G 1K 57
  SW19 ....5K 119
  W3 ....1K 81
  W5 ....4C 80
Birkbeck St. E2 ....3H 69
Birkbeck Way UB6: G'frd ..1H 61
Birkdale Av. HA5: Pinn 3E 24
Birkdale Cl. BR6: Orp 7H 145
  SE16 ....5H 87
Birkdale Ct. UB1: S'hall ...6G 61
  (off Redcroft Rd.)
Birkdale Gdns.
  CR0: Croy 4K 153
Birkdale Rd. SE2 ....4A 92
  W5 ....4E 62
Birkenhead Av.
  KT2: King T 2F 135
Birkenhead St.
  WC1 ....3J 67 (1F 161)
Birkhall Rd. SE6 ....1F 125
Birkwood Cl. SW12 ......7H 103
Birley Lodge NW8 ....2B 66
  (off Acacia Rd.)
Birley Rd. N20 ....2F 15
Birley St. SW11 ....2E 102
Birling Rd. DA8: Erith 7K 93
Birnam Rd. N4 ....2K 49
Birnbeck Ct. EN5: Barn ...4A 4
  NW11 ....5H 29
Birrell Ho. SW9 ....2K 103
  (off Stockwell Rd.)
Birse Cres. NW10 ....3A 46
Birstall Rd. N15 ....5E 32
Biscay Ho. E1 ....4K 69
  (off Mile End Rd.)
Biscay Rd. W6 ....5F 83
Biscoe Cl. TW5: Houn 6E 78
Biscoe Way SE13 ....3F 107
Biscott Ho. E3 ....4D 70
Bisenden Rd. CR0: Croy ..2E 152
Bisham Cl. SM5: Cars 1D 150
Bisham Gdns. N6 ....1E 48
Bishop Cl. N12 ....4E 14
  TW9: Rich 3E 98
Bishop Duppas Pk.
  TW17: Shep 7G 131
Bishop Fox Way
  KT8: W Mole 4D 132
Bishop Ken Rd. HA3: Harr ..2K 25
Bishop King's Rd. W14 ....4G 83
Bishop Rd. N14 ....7A 6
Bishops Av. BR1: Brom ...2A 144
Bishops Av. E13 ....1K 71
  RM6: Chad H 6C 38
  SW6 ....2F 101
Bishops Av., The N2 .....6B 30
  W2 ....6K 65 (6A 158)
Bishops Cl. E17 ....4D 34
  EN1: Enf 2C 8
  EN5: Barn 6A 4
  N19 ....3G 49

Bishops Cl. SE9 ....2G 127
  SM1: Sutt 3J 149
  TW10: Rich 3D 116
  UB10: Uxb 2C 58
  W4 ....5J 81
Bishops Ct. EC4 ....7A 162
  HA0: Wemb 4B 44
  W2 ....6H 65
  (off Bishop's Bri. Rd.)
  WC2 ....7J 161
Bishopsdale Ho. NW6 ....1J 65
  (off Kilburn Va.)
Bishops Dr. TW14: Felt ...6F 95
  UB5: N'olt 1C 60
Bishopsford Rd.
  SM4: Mord 7A 138
Bishopsgate EC2 ...6E 68 (1G 169)
Bishopsgate Arc. EC2 ...6H 163
Bishopsgate Chyd.
  EC2 ....5E 68 (7G 163)
Bishopsgate Institute & Libraries
  ....6H 163
  (off Bishopsgate)
Bishops Grn. BR1: Brom ..1K 143
  (off Up. Park Rd.)
Bishops Gro. N2 ....6C 30
  TW12: Hamp 4D 114
Bishops Gro. Cvn. Site
  TW12: Hamp 4E 114
Bishop's Hall
  KT1: King T 2D 134
Bishops Hill KT12: Walt T ..7J 131
Bishops Ho. SW8 ....7J 85
  (off Sth. Lambeth Rd.)
Bishops Mead SE5 ......7C 86
  (off Camberwell Rd.)
Bishops Pk. Rd. SW6 ....2F 101
  SW16 ....1J 139
Bishops Rd. CR0: Croy ...7B 140
  N6 ....6E 30
  SW6 ....1G 101
  SW11 ....7C 84
  UB3: Hayes 6E 58
  W7 ....2J 79
Bishop's Ter.
  SE11 ....4A 86 (3K 173)
Bishopsthorpe Rd. SE26 ..4K 123
Bishop St. N1 ....1C 68
Bishops Vw. Ct. N10 .....4F 31
Bishops Wlk. BR7: Chst ...1G 145
  CR0: Croy 5K 153
  HA5: Pinn 3C 24
Bishop's Way E2 ....2H 69
Bishopswood Rd. N6 .....7D 30
Bishop Way NW10 ......7A 46
Bishop Wilfred Wood Cl.
  SE15 ....2G 105
Bishop Wilfred Wood Ct.
  E13 ....2A 72
  (off Pragel St.)
Bisley Cl. KT4: Wor Pk ...1E 148
Bison Cl. TW14: Felt 7K 95
Bispham Rd. NW10 .....3F 63
Bissextile Ho. SE8 ......2D 106
Bisson Rd. E15 ....2D 106
Bisterne Av. E17 ....3F 35
Bittacy Cl. NW7 ....6A 14
Bittacy Ct. NW7 ....7A 14
Bittacy Hill NW7 ....6A 14
Bittacy Pk. Av. NW7 .....5A 14
Bittacy Ri. NW7 ....6K 13
Bittacy Rd. NW7 ....6A 14
Bittern Cl. UB4: Hayes ...5B 60
Bittern Ct. NW9 ....2A 28
  SE8 ....6C 88
Bittern Ho. SE1 ....7C 168
  (off Gt. Suffolk St.)
Bittern Pl. N22 ....2K 31

Bittern St.—Bloemfontein Way

Bittern St. SE1 . . . . .2C 86 (7C 168)
Bittoms Ct. KT1: King T 3D 134
Bittoms, The KT1: King T . . .3D 134 (not continuous)
Bixley Cl. UB2: S'hall 4D 78
Blackall St. EC2 . . .4E 68 (3G 163)
Blackberry Cl. TW17: Shep 4G 131
Blackberry Farm Cl. TW5: Houn 7C 78
Blackberry Fld. BR5: Orp . . .7A 128
Blackbird Ct. NW9 . . . . .3K 45
Blackbird Hill NW9 . . . . .2J 45
Blackbird Yd. E2 . . .3F 69 (1K 163)
Blackborne Rd. RM10: Dag 6G 57
Black Boy La. N15 . . . . .5C 32
Blackbrook La.
BR1: Brom 5D 144
BR2: Short 5D 144
Blackburn NW9 . . . . .2B 28
Blackburne's M. W1 . . . . . . .7E 66 (2G 165)
Blackburn Rd. NW6 . . . . .6K 47
Blackbush Av. RM6: Chad H 5D 38
Blackbush Cl. SM2: Sutt . . .7K 149
Blackdown Cl. N2 . . . . .2A 30
Blackdown Ter. SE18 . . . . . .1D 108
Blackett St. SW15 . . . . .3F 101
Black Fan Cl. EN2: Enf 1H 7
BLACKFEN 7A 110
Blackfen Pde. DA15: Sidc 6A 110
Blackfen Rd. DA15: Sidc 5J 109
Blackford Cl. CR2: S Croy 7B 152
Blackford's Path SW15 . . . . .7C 100
Blackfriars Bri. SE1 . . . . .7B 68 (3A 168)
Blackfriars Ct. EC4 . . . . .2A 168
Black Friars La. EC4 . . . . .6B 68 (2A 168) (not continuous)
Blackfriars Pas. EC4 . . . . .7B 68 (2A 168)
Blackfriars Rd. SE1 . . . . .2B 86 (4A 168)
Blackfriars Underpass EC4 . . . . .7A 68 (2A 168)
Black Gates HA5: Pinn 3D 24
BLACKHEATH 2H 107
Blackheath Av. SE10 . . . . .7F 89
Blackheath Bus. Est. SE10 . . . . .1E 106 (off Blackheath Hill)
Blackheath Concert Halls 3H 107
Blackheath Gro. SE3 . . . . . .2H 107
Blackheath Hill SE10 . . . . . .1E 106
BLACKHEATH PARK 4J 107
Blackheath Pk. SE3 . . . . . . .3H 107
Blackheath Ri. SE13 . . . . . . .2E 106 (not continuous)
Blackheath Rd. SE10 . . . . . .1D 106
BLACKHEATH VALE 2H 107
Blackheath Va. SE3 . . . . . . .2G 107
Blackheath Village SE3 . . . .2H 107
Black Horse Ct. SE1 . . . . .3D 86 (off Gt. Dover St.)
Blackhorse La.
CR0: Croy 7G 141
E17 . . . . .2K 33
Blackhorse M. E17 . . . . .3K 33
Black Horse Pde. HA5: Pinn 5K 23
BLACKHORSE RD. 4K 33
Blackhorse Rd.
DA14: Sidc 4A 128
E17 . . . . .4K 33
SE8 . . . . .6A 88
Blacklands Dr. UB4: Hayes . . .4E 58
Blacklands Rd. SE6 . . . . . . .4E 124
Blacklands Ter. SW3 . . . . . . .4D 84 (4E 170)
Black Lion La. W6 . . . . .4C 82
Black Lion M. W6 . . . . .4C 82
Blackmans Yd. E2 . . . . .3K 163 (off Grimsby St.)
Blackmore Av. UB1: S'hall . . .1H 79
Blackmore Ho. N1 . . . . .1K 67 (off Barnsbury Est.)
Blackmore Rd. IG9: Buck H 1H 21
Blackmore's Gro. TW11: Tedd 6A 116
Blackmore Twr. W3 . . . . .3J 81 (off Stanley Rd.)
Blackness La. BR2: Kes 7B 156
Black Path E10 . . . . .7A 34
Blackpool Gdns. UB4: Hayes 4G 59
Blackpool Rd. SE15 . . . . . . .2H 105
BLACK PRINCE INTERCHANGE 6H 111
Black Prince Rd. SE1 . . . . .4K 85 (4G 173)
Black Rod Cl. UB3: Hayes 3H 77
Blackshaw Rd. SW17 . . . . . .4A 120
Blacksmiths Cl. RM6: Chad H 6C 38
Blacksmiths Ho. E17 . . . . . . .4C 34 (off Gillards M.)
Blacks Rd. W6 . . . . .5E 82
Blackstock M. N4 . . . . .2B 50
Blackstock Rd. N4 . . . . .2B 50
N5 . . . . .2B 50
Blackstone Est. E8 . . . . .7G 51
Blackstone Ho. SW1 . . . . . . .6A 172 (off Churchill Gdns.)
Blackstone Rd. NW2 . . . . . . .5E 46
Black Swan Yd. SE1 . . . . . . .2E 86 (6H 169)
Blackthorn Av. UB7: W Dray 4C 76
Blackthorn Ct. E11 . . . . .4F 53 (off Hall Rd.)
TW5: Houn 7C 78
Blackthorne Av. CR0: Croy 1J 153
Blackthorne Ct. SE15 . . . . . . .7F 87 (off Cator St.)
UB1: S'hall . . . . .1F 79 (off Dormer's Wells La.)
Blackthorne Dr. E4 . . . . .4A 20
Blackthorn Gro. DA7: Bex . . .3E 110
Blackthorn St. E3 . . . . .4C 70
Blacktree M. SW9 . . . . .3A 104
BLACKWALL 1E 88
Blackwall La. SE10 . . . . .5G 89
Blackwall Trad. Est. E14 . . . . .5F 71
Blackwall Tunnel E14 . . . . . . .1F 89 (not continuous)
Blackwall Tunnel App. E14 . . .6E 70
Blackwall Tunnel Northern App.
E3 . . . . .2C 70
E14 . . . . .4E 70
Blackwall Tunnel Southern App.
SE10 . . . . .3G 89
Blackwall Way E14 . . . . .1E 88
Blackwater Cl. E7 . . . . .4H 53
RM13: Rain 5K 75
Blackwater Ho. NW8 . . . . . .5B 158 (off Church St.)
Blackwater St. SE22 . . . . . . .5F 105
Blackwell Cl. E5 . . . . .4K 51
HA3: Harr 7C 10
Blackwell Gdns. HA8: Edg . . .4B 12
Blackwell Ho. SW4 . . . . . . .6H 103
Blackwood Av. N18 . . . . .5E 18
Blackwood Ho. E1 . . . . .4H 69 (off Collingwood St.)
Blackwood St. SE17 . . . . .5D 86
Blade M. SW15 . . . . .4H 101
Bladen Ho. E1 . . . . .6K 69 (off Dunelm St.)
Blades Ct. SW15 . . . . .4H 101
W6 . . . . .5D 82 (off Lower Mall)
Blades Ho. SE11 . . . . .7J 173 (off Kennington Oval)
Bladindon Dr. DA5: Bexl 7C 110
Bladon Ct. SW16 . . . . .6J 121
Bladon Gdns. HA2: Harr 6F 25
Blagdens Cl. N14 . . . . .2C 16
Blagdens La. N14 . . . . .2C 16
Blagdon Ct. W7 . . . . .7J 61
Blagdon Rd. KT3: N Mald . . .4B 136 (not continuous)
SE13 . . . . .6D 106
Blagdon Wlk. TW11: Tedd 6C 116
Blagrove Rd. W10 . . . . .5G 65
Blair Av. NW9 . . . . .7A 28
Blair Cl. DA15: Sidc 5J 109
N1 . . . . .6C 50
UB3: Hayes 4J 77
Blair Ct. BR3: Beck 1D 142
NW8 . . . . .1B 66
SE6 . . . . .1H 125
Blairderry Rd. SW2 . . . . . . .2J 121
Blair Ho. SW9 . . . . .2K 103
Blair St. E14 . . . . .6E 70
Blake Av. IG11: Bark 1J 73
Blake Cl. DA16: Well 1J 109
SM5: Cars 1C 150
Blake Ct. NW6 . . . . .3J 65 (off Malvern Rd.)
SE16 . . . . .5H 87 (off Stubbs Dr.)
Blakeden Dr. KT10: Esh 6A 146
Blake Gdns. SW6 . . . . .1K 101
Blake Hall Cres. E11 . . . . . . .1J 53
Blake Hall Rd. E11 . . . . .7J 35
Blakehall Rd. SM5: Cars . . .6D 150
Blake Ho. E14 . . . . .2C 88 (off Admirals Way)
SE1 . . . . .3A 86 (1J 173)
SE8 . . . . .6C 88 (off New King St.)
Blakeley Cotts. SE10 . . . . . . .2F 89
Blakemore Rd.
CR7: Thor H 5K 139
SW16 . . . . .3J 121
Blakemore Way DA17: Belv 3E 92
Blakeney Av. BR3: Beck 1B 142
Blakeney Cl. E8 . . . . .5G 51
N20 . . . . .1F 15
NW1 . . . . .7H 49
Blakeney Rd. BR3: Beck 7B 124
Blakenham Rd. SW17 . . . . .4D 120
Blaker Ct. SE7 . . . . .7A 90 (not continuous)
Blake Rd. CR0: Croy 2E 152
CR4: Mitc 3C 138
E16 . . . . .4H 71
N11 . . . . .7B 16
Blaker Rd. E15 . . . . .2E 70
Blakes Av. KT3: N Mald 5B 136
Blakes Cl. W10 . . . . .5E 64
Blake's Grn. BR4: W W'ck 1E 154
Blakes La. KT3: N Mald 5B 136
Blakesley Av. W5 . . . . .6C 62
Blakesley Wlk. SW20 . . . . .2H 137
Blake's Rd. SE15 . . . . .7E 86
Blakes Ter. KT3: N Mald 5C 136
Blakesware Gdns. N9 . . . . .7J 7
Blakewood Cl. TW13: Felt 4A 114
Blakewood Ct. SE20 . . . . . . .7H 123 (off Anerley Pk.)
Blanchard Cl. SE9 . . . . .3C 126
Blanchard Ho. TW1: Twick . . .6D 98 (off Clevedon Rd.)
Blanchard Way E8 . . . . .6G 51
Blanch Cl. SE15 . . . . .7J 87
Blanchedowne SE5 . . . . . . .4D 104
Blanche St. E16 . . . . .4H 71
Blanchland Rd. SM4: Mord 5K 137
Blandfield Rd. SW12 . . . . . .7E 102
Blandford Av. BR3: Beck . . .2A 142
TW2: Twick 1F 115
Blandford Cl. CR0: Croy 3J 151
N2 . . . . .4A 30
RM7: Mawney 4G 39
Blandford Ct. E8 . . . . .7E 50 (off St Peter's Way)
NW6 . . . . .7F 47
Blandford Cres. E4 . . . . .7K 9
Blandford Ho. SW8 . . . . .7K 85 (off Richborne Ter.)
Blandford Rd.
BR3: Beck 3J 141
TW11: Tedd 5H 115
UB2: S'hall 4E 78
W4 . . . . .3A 82
W5 . . . . .2D 80
Blandford Sq. NW1 . . . . . . .4C 66 (4D 158)
Blandford St. W1 . . .6D 66 (7F 159)
Blandford Waye UB4: Hayes 6A 60
Bland Ho. SE11 . . . . .5H 173
Bland St. SE9 . . . . .4B 108
Blaney Cres. E6 . . . . .3F 73
Blanmerle Rd. SE9 . . . . .1F 127
Blann Cl. SE9 . . . . .6B 108
Blantyre St. SW10 . . . . .7B 84
Blantyre Twr. SW10 . . . . .7B 84 (off Blantyre St.)
Blantyre Wlk. SW10 . . . . .7B 84 (off Worlds End Est.)
Blashford NW3 . . . . .7D 48 (off Adelaide Rd.)
Blashford St. SE13 . . . . .7F 107
Blasker Wlk. E14 . . . . .5D 88
Blawith Rd. HA1: Harr 4J 25
Blaxland Ho. W12 . . . . .7D 64 (off White City Est.)
Blaydon Cl. HA4: Ruis 7G 23
N17 . . . . .7C 18
Blaydon Ct. UB5: N'olt 6E 42
Blazer Ct. NW8 . . . . .2B 158
Bleak Hill La. SE18 . . . . .6K 91
Blean Gro. SE20 . . . . .7J 123
Bleasdale Av. UB6: G'frd 2A 62
Blechynden Ho. W10 . . . . . . .6F 65 (off Kingsdown Cl.)
Blechynden St. W10 . . . . .7F 65
Bledlow Cl. SE28 . . . . .7C 74
Bledlow Ho. NW8 . . . . .4B 158 (off Capland St.)
Bledlow Ri. UB6: G'frd 2G 61
Bleeding Heart Yd. EC1 . . . . .6K 161
Blegborough Rd. SW16 . . . .6G 121
Blemundsbury WC1 . . . . . . .5G 161 (off Dombey St.)
BLENDON 6D 110
Blendon Dr. DA5: Bexl 6D 110
Blendon Path BR1: Brom 7H 125
Blendon Rd. DA5: Bexl 6D 110
Blendon Row SE17 . . . . .4D 86 (off Townley St.)
Blendon Ter. SE18 . . . . .5G 91
Blenheim Av. IG2: Ilf 6E 36
Blenheim Cl. N21 . . . . .1H 17
RM7: Mawney 4J 39
SE12 . . . . .1K 125
SM6: Wall 7G 151
SW20 . . . . .3E 136
UB6: G'frd 2H 61
Blenheim Ct. BR2: Short . . .4H 143
DA14: Sidc 3H 127
Blenheim Ct. HA1: Harr 6A 26
IG8: Wfd G 7E 20
N19 . . . . .2J 49
SE16 . . . . .1K 87 (off King & Queen Wharf)
SM2: Sutt 6A 150
Blenheim Cres.
CR2: S Croy 7C 152
HA4: Ruis 2F 41
W11 . . . . .7G 65
Blenheim Dr. DA16: Well 1K 109
Blenheim Gdns.
HA9: Wemb 3E 44
KT2: King T 7H 117
NW2 . . . . .6E 46
SM6: Wall 6G 151
SW2 . . . . .6K 103
Blenheim Gro. SE15 . . . . . .2G 105
Blenheim Ho. E16 . . . . .7K 71 (off Constable Av.)
TW3: Houn 3E 96
Blenheim Pde. UB10: Uxb . . .4D 58
Blenheim Pk. Rd. CR2: S Croy 7C 152
Blenheim Pas. NW8 . . . . .2A 66 (not continuous)
Blenheim Ri. N15 . . . . .4F 33
Blenheim Rd. BR1: Brom . . .4C 144
DA15: Sidc 1C 128
E6 . . . . .3B 72
E15 . . . . .4G 53
E17 . . . . .3K 33
EN5: Barn 3A 4
HA2: Harr 6F 25
NW8 . . . . .2A 66
SE20 . . . . .7J 123
SM1: Sutt 3J 149
SW20 . . . . .3E 136
UB5: N'olt 6F 43
W4 . . . . .3A 82
Blenheim Shop. Cen. SE20 . . . . .7J 123
Blenheim St. W1 . . .6F 67 (1J 165)
Blenheim Ter. NW8 . . . . .2A 66
Blenheim Way TW7: Isle 1A 98
Blenkarne Rd. SW11 . . . . . .6D 102
Bleriot NW9 . . . . .2B 28 (off Belvedere Strand)
Bleriot Rd. TW5: Houn 7A 78
Blessbury Rd. HA8: Edg 1J 27
Blessington Cl. SE13 . . . . . .3F 107
Blessington Rd. SE13 . . . . . .3F 107
Blessing Way IG11: Bark 3C 74
Bletchingley Cl. CR7: Thor H 4B 140
Bletchley Ct. N1 . . . . .1E 162 (not continuous)
Bletchley St. N1 . . .2D 68 (1D 162)
Bletchmore Cl. UB3: Hayes 5F 77
Bletsoe Wlk. N1 . . . . .2C 68
Blewbury Ho. SE2 . . . . .2C 92 (Tavy Bri.)
SE2 . . . . .2D 92 (Tilehurst Point)
Blick Ho. SE16 . . . . .3J 87 (off Neptune St.)
Blincoe Cl. SW19 . . . . .2F 119
Bliss Cres. SE13 . . . . .2D 106
Blissett St. SE10 . . . . .1E 106
Bliss M. W10 . . . . .3G 65
Blisworth Cl. UB4: Hayes 4C 60
Blisworth Ho. E2 . . . . .1G 69 (off Whiston Rd.)
Blithbury Rd. RM9: Dag 6B 56
Blithdale Rd. SE2 . . . . .4A 92
Blithfield St. W8 . . . . .3K 83
Blockley Rd. HA0: Wemb 2B 44
Bloemfontein Av. W12 . . . . . .1D 82
Bloemfontein Rd. W12 . . . . . .7D 64
Bloemfontein Way W12 . . . . .1D 82

Blomfield Ct.—Boscombe Gdns.

Blomfield Ct. *W9* *3A 158*
(off Maida Va.)
Blomfield Mans. *W12* *1E 82*
(off Stanlake Rd.)
Blomfield Rd.
W9 . . . . 5K 65 (4A 158)
Blomfield St.
EC2 . . . . 5D 68 (6F 163)
Blomfield Vs. W2 . . . . 5K 65
Blomville Rd. RM8: Dag 3E 56
Blondel St. SW11 . . . . 2E 102
Blondin Av. W5 . . . . 4C 80
Blondin St. E3 . . . . 2C 70
Bloomburg St.
SW1 . . . . . . 4H 85 (4B 172)
Bloomfield Ct. N6 . . . . 6E 30
Bloomfield Cres. IG2: Ilf 6F 37
Bloomfield Ho. *E1* *5G 69*
(off Old Montague St.)
Bloomfield Pl. W1 . . . . 2K 165
Bloomfield Rd.
BR2: Short 5B 144
KT1: King T 4E 134
N6 . . . . 6E 30
SE18 . . . . 6F 91
Bloomfields, The
IG11: Bark 6G 55
Bloomfield Ter.
SW1 . . . . . . 5E 84 (5H 171)
Bloom Gro. SE27 . . . . 3B 122
Bloomhall Rd. SE19 . . . . . . 5D 122
Bloom Pk. Rd. SW6 . . . . 7H 83
BLOOMSBURY . . . 5J 67 (5E 160)
Bloomsbury Cl. NW7 . . . . 7H 13
W5 . . . . 7F 63
Bloomsbury Ct.
HA5: Pinn 3D 24
TW5: Houn 1K 95
WC1 . . . . 6F 161
Bloomsbury Ho. SW4 . . . . . . 6H 103
Bloomsbury Pl. SW18 . . . . 5A 102
WC1 . . . . . . 5J 67 (5F 161)
Bloomsbury Sq.
WC1 . . . . . . 5J 67 (6F 161)
Bloomsbury St.
WC1 . . . . . . 5H 67 (6D 160)
Bloomsbury Theatre 3C 160
Bloomsbury Way
WC1 . . . . . . 5J 67 (6E 160)
Blore Cl. SW8 . . . . 1H 103
Blore Ct. W1 . . . . 1C 166
Blossom Cl. CR2: S Croy . . . 5F 153
RM9: Dag 1F 75
W5 . . . . 2E 80
Blossom La. EN2: Enf 1H 7
Blossom St. E1 . . . . 4E 68 (4H 163)
Blossom Way
UB7: W Dray 4C 76
UB10: Uxb 7B 40
Blossom Waye TW5: Houn . . . 6C 78
Blount Ho. *E14* *5A 70*
(off Maroon St.)
Blount St. E14 . . . . 6A 70
Bloxam Gdns. SE9 . . . . 5C 108
Bloxhall Rd. E10 . . . . 1B 52
Bloxham Cres.
TW12: Hamp 7D 114
Bloxworth Cl. SM6: Wall . . . 3G 151
Blucher Rd. SE5 . . . . 7C 86
Blue Anchor All.
TW9: Rich 4E 98
Blue Anchor La. SE16 . . . . . 4G 87
Blue Anchor Yd.
E1 . . . . 7G 69 (2K 169)
Blue Ball Yd.
SW1 . . . . . . 1G 85 (5A 166)
Bluebell Av. E12 . . . . 5B 54
Bluebell Cl. E9 . . . . 1J 69
RM7: Rush G 2K 57
SE26 . . . . 4F 123
SM6: Wall 1F 151
Bluebell Way IG1: Ilf 6F 55
Blueberry Cl. IG8: Wfd G 6D 20
Bluebird La. RM10: Dag 7G 57
Bluebird Way SE28 . . . . 2H 91
Blue Elephant Theatre 7C 86
Bluefield Cl.
TW12: Hamp 5E 114
Bluegate M. E1 . . . . 7H 69
Bluegates KT17: Eps 7C 148
Bluehouse Rd. E4 . . . . 2B 20
Blue Lion Pl.
SE1 . . . . 3E 86 (7G 169)
Blue Riband Ind. Est.
CR0: Croy 2B 152
Blue Water SW18 . . . . 4K 101
Blundell Cl. E8 . . . . 5G 51
Blundell Rd. HA8: Edg 1K 27
Blundell St. N7 . . . . 7J 49
Blunden Cl. RM8: Dag 1C 56
Blunt Rd. CR2: S Croy 5D 152
Blunts Av. UB7: W Dray 7C 76
Blunts Rd. SE9 . . . . 5E 108
Blurton Rd. E5 . . . . 4J 51
Blydon Ct. *N21* *5E 6*
(off Chaseville Pk. Rd.)
Blyth Cl. E14 . . . . 4F 89
TW1: Twick 6K 97
Blyth Ct. *BR1: Brom* *1H 143*
(off Blyth Rd.)
Blythe Cl. SE6 . . . . 7B 106
BLYTHE HILL 7B 106
Blythe Hill BR5: Orp 1K 145
SE6 . . . . 7B 106
Blythe Hill La. SE6 . . . . 7B 106
Blythe Hill Pl. SE23 . . . . 7A 106
Blythe Ho. SE11 . . . . 6A 86 (7J 173)
Blythe M. W14 . . . . 3F 83
Blythendale Ho. *E2* *2G 69*
(off Mansford St.)
Blythe Rd. W14 . . . . 3F 83
(not continuous)
Blythe St. E2 . . . . 3H 69
Blythe Va. SE6 . . . . 1B 124
Blyth Hill Pl. *SE23* *7A 106*
(off Brockley Pk.)
Blyth Rd. BR1: Brom 1H 143
E17 . . . . 7B 34
SE28 . . . . 7C 74
UB3: Hayes 2G 77
Blyth's Wharf E14 . . . . 7A 70
Blythswood Rd. IG3: Ilf 1A 56
Blyth Wood Pk.
BR1: Brom 1H 143
Blythwood Rd. HA5: Pinn 1B 24
N4 . . . . 7J 31
Boades M. NW3 . . . . 4B 48
Boadicea St. N1 . . . . 1K 67
Boakes Cl. NW9 . . . . 4J 27
Boardman Av. E4 . . . . 5J 9
Boardman Cl. EN5: Barn 5B 4
Boardwalk Pl. E14 . . . . 1E 88
Boarhound *NW9* *2B 28*
(off Further Acre)
Boarley Ho. *SE17* *4E 86*
(off Massinger St.)
Boars Head Yd.
TW8: Bford 7D 80
Boathouse Cen., The *W10* . . . *4F 65*
(off Canal Cl.)
Boathouse Wlk. SE15 . . . . 7F 87
(not continuous)
Boat Lifter Way SE16 . . . . 4A 88
Bob Anker Cl. E13 . . . . 3J 71
Bobbin Cl. SW4 . . . . 3G 103
Bobby Moore Way N12 . . . . . . 7J 15
Bob Hope Theatre, The . . . 6D 108
Bob Marley Way SE24 . . . . . 4A 104
Bockhampton Rd.
KT2: King T 7F 117
Bocking St. E8 . . . . 1H 69
BOC Mus. 6D 160
(off Bedford Sq.)
Boddicott Cl. SW19 . . . . 2G 119
Boddington Ho. *SE14* *1J 105*
(off Pomeroy St.)
SW13 . . . . *6D 82*
(off Wyatt Dr.)
Boddy's Bri. *SE1* *4K 167*
(off Hatfields)
Bodeney Ho. *SE5* *1E 104*
(off Peckham Rd.)
Boden Ho. *E1* *5K 163*
(off Woodseer St.)
Bodiam Cl. EN1: Enf 2K 7
Bodiam Rd. SW16 . . . . 7H 121
Bodicea M. TW4: Houn 6D 96
Bodington Ct. W12 . . . . 2F 83
Bodley Cl. KT3: N Mald . . . 5A 136
Bodley Mnr. Way SW2 . . . . . 7A 104
Bodley Rd. KT3: N Mald 6K 135
Bodmin *NW9* *2B 28*
(off Further Acre)
Bodmin Cl. HA2: Harr 3D 42
Bodmin Gro. SM4: Mord . . . 5K 137
Bodmin Pl. SE27 . . . . 4B 122
Bodmin St. SW18 . . . . 1J 119
Bodnant Gdns. SW20 . . . . . . 3C 136
Bodney Rd. E8 . . . . 5H 51
Boeing Way UB2: S'hall 3K 77
Boevey Path DA17: Belv 5F 93
Bogart Ct. *E14* *7C 70*
(off Premiere Pl.)
Bogey La. BR6: Orp 7E 156
Bognor Rd. DA16: Well 1D 110
Bohemia Pl. E8 . . . . 6J 51
Bohn Rd. E1 . . . . 5A 70
Bohun Gro. EN4: Barn 6H 5
Boileau Pde. *W5* *6F 63*
(off Boileau Rd.)
Boileau Rd. SW13 . . . . 7C 82
W5 . . . . 6F 63
Boisseau Ho. *E1* *5J 69*
(off Stepney Way)
Bolden St. SE8 . . . . 2D 106
Boldero Pl. NW8 . . . . 4C 158
Bolderwood Way
BR4: W W'ck 2D 154
Boldmere Rd. HA5: Pinn 7A 24
Boleyn Av. EN1: Enf 1C 8
Boleyn Cl. E17 . . . . 4C 34
Boleyn Ct. IG9: Buck H 1D 20
Boleyn Dr. HA4: Ruis 2B 42
KT8: W Mole 3D 132
Boleyn Gdns.
BR4: W W'ck 2D 154
RM10: Dag 7J 57
Boleyn Gro. BR4: W W'ck . . . 2E 154
Boleyn Ho. *E16* *7J 71*
(off Southey M.)
Boleyn Rd. E6 . . . . 2B 72
E7 . . . . 7J 53
N16 . . . . 5E 50
Boleyn Way EN5: Barn 3F 5
Bolina Rd. SE16 . . . . 5J 87
Bolingbroke Gro. SW11 . . . . 4C 102
Bolingbroke Rd. W14 . . . . 3F 83
Bolingbroke Wlk. SW11 . . . . 1B 102
Bolingbroke Way
UB3: Hayes 1F 77
Bolliger Ct. NW10 . . . . 4J 63
Bollo Bri. Rd. W3 . . . . 3H 81
Bollo Ct. *W3* *3J 81*
(off Bollo Bri. Rd.)
Bollo La. W3 . . . . 2H 81
W4 . . . . 4J 81
Bolney Ga. SW7 . . 2C 84 (7C 164)
Bolney St. SW8 . . . . 7K 85
Bolney Way TW13: Felt 3C 114
Bolsover St. W1 . . . . 4F 67 (4K 159)
Bolstead Rd. CR4: Mitc 1F 139
Bolster Gro. N22 . . . . 7C 16
Bolt Ct. EC4 . . . . . . 6A 68 (1K 167)
Boltmore Cl. NW4 . . . . 3F 29
Bolton Cl. KT9: Chess 6D 146
SE20 . . . . 2G 141
Bolton Cres. SE5 . . . . 7B 86
Bolton Gdns. BR1: Brom . . . 6H 125
NW10 . . . . 2F 65
SW5 . . . . 5K 83
TW11: Tedd 6A 116
Bolton Gdns. M. SW10 . . . . . 5A 84
Bolton Ho. *SE10* *5G 89*
(off Trafalgar Rd.)
Bolton Pl. *NW8* *1K 65*
(off Bolton Rd.)
Bolton Rd. E15 . . . . 6H 53
HA1: Harr 4G 25
KT9: Chess 6D 146
N18 . . . . 5A 18
NW8 . . . . 1K 65
NW10 . . . . 1A 64
W4 . . . . 7J 81
Boltons Ct. *SW5* *5K 83*
(off Old Brompton Rd.)
Bolton's La. UB3: Hayes 7D 76
Boltons Pl. SW5 . . . . 5A 84
Boltons, The HA0: Wemb 4K 43
IG8: Wfd G 4D 20
SW10 . . . . 5A 84
Bolton St. W1 . . . . . 1F 85 (4K 165)
Bolton Studios SW10 . . . . 5A 84
Bolton Wlk. *N7* *2K 49*
(off Durham Rd.)
Bombay St. SE16 . . . . 4H 87
Bomer Cl. UB7: W Dray 7C 76
Bomore Rd. W11 . . . . 7G 65
Bonar Pl. BR7: Chst 7C 126
Bonar Rd. SE15 . . . . 7G 87
Bonchester Cl. BR7: Chst . . . 7E 126
Bonchurch Cl. SM2: Sutt . . . 7K 149
Bonchurch Rd. W10 . . . . 5G 65
W13 . . . . 1B 80
Bond Cl. UB7: W Dray 6B 58
Bond Ct. EC4 . . . . . . 7D 68 (2E 168)
Bondfield Av. UB4: Hayes 3J 59
Bondfield Rd. E6 . . . . 5D 72
Bond Gdns. SM6: Wall 4G 151
Bond Ho. *NW6* *2H 65*
(off Rupert Rd.)
SE14 . . . . *7A 88*
(off Goodwood Rd.)
Bonding Yd. Wlk. SE16 . . . . . 3A 88
Bond Rd. CR4: Mitc 2C 138
KT6: Surb 2F 147
Bond St. E15 . . . . 5G 53
W4 . . . . 4K 81
W5 . . . . 7D 62
Bondway SW8 . . . . 6J 85 (7F 173)
Boneta Rd. SE18 . . . . 3D 90
Bonfield Rd. SE13 . . . . 4E 106
Bonham Gdns. RM8: Dag 2D 56
Bonham Rd. RM8: Dag 2D 56
SW2 . . . . 5K 103
Bonheur Rd. W4 . . . . 2K 81
Bonhill St. EC2 . . . . 4D 68 (4F 163)
Boniface Gdns. HA3: Harr . . . 7A 10
Boniface Rd. UB10: Uxb 3D 40
Boniface Wlk. HA3: Harr 7A 10
Bonita M. SE4 . . . . 3K 105
Bon Marche Ter. M.
SE27 . . . . 4E 122
Bonner Hill Rd.
KT1: King T 2F 135
(not continuous)
Bonner Rd. E2 . . . . 2J 69
Bonnersfield Cl. HA1: Harr . . . 6K 25
Bonnersfield La.
HA1: Harr 6K 25
Bonner St. E2 . . . . 2J 69
Bonneville Gdns. SW4 . . . . . 6G 103
Bonnington Ct. *UB5: N'olt* . . . *2B 60*
(off Gallery Gdns.)
Bonnington Ho. N1 . . . . 2K 67
Bonnington Sq.
SW8 . . . . . . 6K 85 (7G 173)
Bonny St. NW1 . . . . 7G 49
Bonser Rd. TW1: Twick 2K 115
Bonsor Ho. SW8 . . . . 1G 103
Bonsor St. SE5 . . . . 7E 86
Bonville Gdns. NW4 . . . . 4D 28
Bonville Rd. BR1: Brom 5H 125
Bookbinders Cott. Homes
N20 . . . . 3J 15
Booker Cl. E14 . . . . 5B 70
Booker Rd. N18 . . . . 5B 18
Bookham Ct. SW19 . . . . 3B 138
Boone Ct. N9 . . . . 3D 18
Boones Rd. SE13 . . . . 4G 107
Boone St. SE13 . . . . 4G 107
Boord St. SE10 . . . . 3G 89
Boothby Ct. E4 . . . . 3K 19
Boothby Rd. N19 . . . . 2H 49
Booth Cl. E9 . . . . 1H 69
SE28 . . . . 1B 92
Booth Dr. TW18: Staines . . . 6A 112
Booth La. EC4 . . . . 2C 168
Boothman Ho. HA3: Harr 3D 26
Booth Rd. CR0: Croy 2B 152
NW9 . . . . 2K 27
Booth's Pl. W1 . . . . 5G 67 (6B 160)
Boot Pde. *HA8: Edg* *6B 12*
(off High St.)
Boot St. N1 . . . . . . 3E 68 (2G 163)
Bordars Rd. W7 . . . . 5J 61
Bordars Wlk. W7 . . . . 5J 61
Borden Av. EN1: Enf 6J 7
Border Cres. SE26 . . . . 5H 123
Border Gdns. CR0: Croy 4D 154
Bordergate CR4: Mitc 1C 138
Border Rd. SE26 . . . . 5H 123
Bordesley Rd.
SM4: Mord 5K 137
Bordeston Ct. *TW8: Bford* . . . *7C 80*
(off Augustus Cl.)
Bordon Wlk. SW15 . . . . 7C 100
Boreas Wlk. *N1* *1B 162*
(off Nelson Pl.)
Boreham Av. E16 . . . . 6J 71
Boreham Cl. E11 . . . . 1E 52
Boreham Rd. N22 . . . . 2C 32
Boreman Ho. *SE10* *6E 88*
(off Thames St.)
Borgard Rd. SE18 . . . . 4D 90
Borland Rd. SE15 . . . . 4J 105
TW11: Tedd 7B 116
Borneo St. SW15 . . . . 3E 100
Borough High St.
SE1 . . . . 2C 86 (7D 168)
Borough Hill CR0: Croy 3B 152
Borough Rd. CR4: Mitc 2C 138
KT2: King T 1G 135
SE1 . . . . 3B 86 (7B 168)
TW7: Isle 1J 97
Borough Sq. SE1 . . . . 7C 168
BOROUGH, THE . . . 2D 86 (7D 168)
Borrett Cl. SE17 . . . . 5C 86
Borrodaile Rd. SW18 . . . . . . 6K 101
Borrowdale *NW1* *2A 160*
(off Robert St.)
Borrowdale Av. HA3: Harr . . . 2A 26
Borrowdale Cl. IG4: Ilf 4C 36
Borrowdale Ct. EN2: Enf 1H 7
Borthwick M. E15 . . . . 4G 53
Borthwick Rd. E15 . . . . 4G 53
NW9 . . . . 6B 28
Borthwick St. SE8 . . . . 5C 88
Borwick Av. E17 . . . . 3B 34
Bosanquet Cl. UB8: Uxb 4A 58
Bosbury Rd. SE6 . . . . 3E 124
Boscastle Rd. NW5 . . . . 3F 49
Boscobel Cl. BR1: Brom . . . 2D 144
Boscobel Ho. E8 . . . . 6H 51
Boscobel Pl.
SW1 . . . . . . 4E 84 (3H 171)
Boscobel St.
NW8 . . . . . . 4B 66 (4B 158)
Boscombe Av. E10 . . . . 7F 35
Boscombe Cl. E5 . . . . 5A 52
Boscombe Gdns. SW16 . . . . 6J 121

Boscombe Ho. *CR0: Croy ... 1D 152*
(off Sydenham Rd.)
Boscombe Rd.
KT4: Wor Pk ... 1E 148
SW17 ... 6E 120
SW19 ... 1K 137
W12 ... 1C 82
Bose Cl. N3 ... 1G 29
Bosgrove E4 ... 2K 19
Boss Ho. *SE1 ... 6J 169*
(off Boss St.)
Boss St. SE1 ... 2F 87 (6J 169)
Bostall Hill SE2 ... 5A 92
Bostall La. SE2 ... 4B 92
Bostall Mnr. Way SE2 ... 4B 92
Bostall Pk. Av. DA7: Bex ... 7E 92
Bostall Rd. BR5: Orp ... 7B 128
Bostock Ho. TW5: Houn ... 6E 78
Boston Bus. Pk. W7 ... 3J 79
Boston Gdns. TW8: Bford ... 4A 80
W4 ... 6A 82
W7 ... 4A 80
Boston Gro. HA4: Ruis ... 6E 22
BOSTON MANOR ... 4A 80
Boston Manor House ... 5B 80
Boston Mnr. Rd.
TW8: Bford ... 4B 80
Boston Pde. W7 ... 3A 80
Boston Pk. Rd.
TW8: Bford ... 5C 80
Boston Pl. NW1 ... 4D 66 (4E 158)
Boston Rd. CR0: Croy ... 6K 139
E6 ... 3C 72
E17 ... 6C 34
HA8: Edg ... 7D 12
W7 ... 1J 79
Bostonthorpe Rd. W7 ... 2J 79
Boston Va. W7 ... 4A 80
Bosun Cl. E14 ... 2C 88
Boswell Ct. *KT2: King T ... 1F 135*
(off Clifton Rd.)
W14 ... 3F 83
(off Blythe Rd.)
WC1 ... 5J 67 (5F 161)
Boswell Ho. *WC1 ... 5F 161*
(off Boswell St.)
Boswell Path UB3: Hayes ... 4H 77
Boswell Rd. CR7: Thor H ... 4C 140
Boswell St. WC1 ... 5J 67 (5F 161)
Bosworth Cl. E17 ... 1B 34
Bosworth Ho. *W10 ... 4G 65*
(off Bosworth Rd.)
Bosworth Rd. EN5: Barn ... 3D 4
N11 ... 6C 16
RM10: Dag ... 3G 57
W10 ... 4G 65
Botany Bay La.
BR7: Chst ... 3G 145
Botany Cl. EN4: Barn ... 4H 5
Boteley Cl. E4 ... 2A 20
Botham Cl. HA8: Edg ... 7D 12
Botha Rd. E13 ... 5K 71
Bothwell Cl. E16 ... 5H 71
Bothwell St. W6 ... 6F 83
Botolph All. EC3 ... 2G 169
Botolph La.
EC3 ... 7E 68 (3G 169)
Botsford Rd. SW20 ... 2G 137
Botts M. W2 ... 6J 65
Botwell Comn. Rd.
UB3: Hayes ... 7F 59
Botwell Cres.
UB3: Hayes ... 6G 59
Botwell La. UB3: Hayes ... 7G 59
Boucher Cl. TW11: Tedd ... 5K 115
Bouchier Ho. N2 ... 2B 30
Boughton Av.
BR2: Short ... 7H 143
Boughton Ho. *SE1 ... 6E 168*
(off Tennis St.)
Boughton Rd. SE28 ... 3J 91
Boulcott St. E1 ... 6K 69
Boulevard, The HA5: Pinn ... 4E 24
(not continuous)
IG8: Ilf ... 6K 21
SW17 ... 2E 120
SW18 ... 4K 101
Boulogne Ho. *SE1 ... 7J 169*
(off Abbey St.)
Boulogne Rd. CR0: Croy ... 6C 140
Boulter Ho. *SE14 ... 1J 105*
(off Kender St.)
Boulton Ho. TW8: Bford ... 5E 80
Boulton Rd. RM8: Dag ... 2E 56
Boultwood Rd. E6 ... 6D 72
Bounces La. N9 ... 2C 18
Bounces Rd. N9 ... 2C 18
Boundaries Rd. SW12 ... 2D 120
TW13: Felt ... 1A 114
Boundary Av. E17 ... 7B 34
Boundary Bus. Ct.
CR4: Mitc ... 3B 138
Boundary Cl. EN5: Barn ... 1C 4
IG3: Ilf ... 4J 55
KT1: King T ... 3H 135
SE20 ... 2G 141
UB2: S'hall ... 5E 78
Boundary Ct. *N18 ... 6A 18*
(off Snells Pk.)
Boundary Ho. SE5 ... 7C 86
Boundary La. E13 ... 3B 72
SE5 ... 6C 86
Boundary M. *NW8 ... 1A 66*
(off Boundary Rd.)
Boundary Pas. E1 ... 4F 69 (3J 163)
Boundary Rd. DA15: Sidc ... 5J 109
E13 ... 2A 72
E17 ... 7B 34
HA5: Pinn ... 7B 24
HA9: Wemb ... 3E 44
IG11: Bark ... 2G 73
(Gascoigne Rd.)
IG11: Bark ... 1H 73
(King Edwards Rd.)
N2 ... 1B 30
N9 ... 6D 8
N22 ... 3B 32
NW8 ... 1K 65
SM5: Cars, Wall ... 6F 151
SM6: Wall ... 6F 151
SW19 ... 6B 120
Boundary Row
SE1 ... 2B 86 (6A 168)
Boundary St. E2 ... 3F 69 (2J 163)
Boundary Way CR0: Croy ... 5C 154
Boundfield Rd. SE6 ... 3G 125
BOUNDS GREEN ... 6C 16
Bounds Grn. Ct. *N11 ... 6C 16*
(off Bounds Grn. Rd.)
Bounds Grn. Ind. Est. N11 ... 6B 16
Bounds Grn. Rd. N11 ... 6B 16
N22 ... 6B 16
Bourbon Ho. SE6 ... 5E 124
Bourchier St.
W1 ... 7H 67 (2C 166)
(not continuous)
Bourdon Pl. W1 ... 2K 165
Bourdon Rd. SE20 ... 2J 141
Bourdon St. W1 ... 7F 67 (3J 165)
Bourke Cl. NW10 ... 6A 46
SW4 ... 6J 103
Bourlet Cl. W1 ... 5G 67 (6A 160)
Bourn Av. EN4: Barn ... 5G 5
N15 ... 4D 32
UB8: Uxb ... 4C 58
Bournbrook Rd. SE3 ... 3B 108
Bourne Av. HA4: Ruis ... 5A 42
N14 ... 2D 16
UB3: Hayes ... 3E 76
Bourne Cir. UB3: Hayes ... 3E 76
Bourne Ct. HA4: Ruis ... 5K 41
IG8: Wfd G ... 3B 36
W4 ... 6J 81
Bourne Dr. CR4: Mitc ... 2B 138
Bourne Est. EC1 ... 5A 68 (5J 161)
Bourne Gdns. E4 ... 4J 19
Bourne Hall Mus. ... 7B 148
Bourne Hill N13 ... 2D 16
Bourne Hill Cl. N13 ... 2E 16
Bourne Ho. IG9: Buck H ... 3G 21
Bourne Ind. Pk., The
DA1: Cray ... 5K 111
Bourne Mead DA5: Bexl ... 5J 111
Bournemead Av.
UB5: N'olt ... 2J 59
Bournemead Cl. UB5: N'olt ... 3J 59
Bournemead Way
UB5: N'olt ... 2K 59
Bourne M. W1 ... 6E 66 (1H 165)
Bournemouth Cl. SE15 ... 2G 105
Bournemouth Rd. SE15 ... 2G 105
SW19 ... 1J 137
Bourne Pde. DA5: Bexl ... 7H 111
Bourne Pl. W4 ... 5K 81
Bourne Rd. BR2: Short ... 4B 144
DA1: Cray ... 7H 111
DA5: Bexl ... 7H 111
E7 ... 3H 53
N8 ... 6J 31
Bournes Ho. *N15 ... 6E 32*
(off Chisley Rd.)
Bourneside Cres. N14 ... 1C 16
Bourneside Gdns. SE6 ... 5E 124
Bourne St. CR0: Croy ... 2B 152
SW1 ... 4E 84 (4G 171)
Bourne Ter. W2 ... 5K 65
Bourne, The N14 ... 1C 16
Bourne Va. BR2: Short ... 1H 155
Bournevale Rd. SW16 ... 4J 121
Bourne Vw. UB6: G'frd ... 6K 43
Bourne Way BR2: Short ... 2H 155
KT19: Eps ... 4J 147
SM1: Sutt ... 5H 149
Bournewood Rd. SE18 ... 7A 92
Bournville Rd. SE6 ... 7C 106
Bournwell Cl. EN4: Barn ... 3J 5
Bourton Cl. UB3: Hayes ... 1J 77
Bousfield Rd. SE14 ... 2K 105
Boutflower Rd. SW11 ... 4C 102
Boutique Hall SE13 ... 4E 106
Bouverie Gdns. HA3: Harr ... 6D 26
Bouverie M. N16 ... 2E 50
Bouverie Pl. W2 ... 6B 66 (7B 158)
Bouverie Rd. HA1: Harr ... 6G 25
N16 ... 1E 50
Bouverie St. EC4 ... 6A 68 (1K 167)
Bouvier Rd. EN3: Enf ... 1D 8
Boveney Rd. SE23 ... 7K 105
Bovill Rd. SE23 ... 7K 105
Bovingdon Av.
HA9: Wemb ... 6G 45
Bovingdon Cl. N19 ... 2G 49
Bovingdon La. NW9 ... 1A 28
Bovingdon Rd. SW6 ... 1K 101
Bovingdon Sq. CR4: Mitc ... 4J 139
BOW ... 3B 70
Bowater Cl. NW9 ... 5K 27
SW2 ... 6J 103
Bowater Gdns.
TW16: Sun T ... 2A 132
Bowater Ho. *EC1 ... 4C 162*
(off Golden La. Est.)
Bowater Pl. SE3 ... 7K 89
Bowater Rd. SE18 ... 3B 90
Bow Bri. Est. E3 ... 3D 70
Bow Brook, The *E2 ... 2K 69*
(off Mace St.)
Bow Chyd. EC4 ... 1D 168
BOW COMMON ... 5C 70
Bow Comn. La. E3 ... 4B 70
Bowden Cl. TW14: Felt ... 1G 113
Bowden St. SE11 ... 5A 86 (6K 173)
Bowditch SE8 ... 4B 88
(not continuous)
Bowdon Rd. E17 ... 7C 34
Bowen Dr. SE21 ... 3E 122
Bowen Rd. HA1: Harr ... 7G 25
Bowen St. E14 ... 6D 70
Bower Av. SE10 ... 1G 107
Bower Cl. RM5: Col R ... 1K 39
UB5: N'olt ... 2A 60
Bower Ct. *E4 ... 1K 19*
(off Ridgeway, The)
Bowerdean St. SW6 ... 1K 101
Bower Ho. *SE14 ... 1K 105*
(off Besson St.)
Bowerman Av. SE14 ... 6A 88
Bowerman Ct. *N19 ... 2H 49*
(off St John's Way)
Bower St. E1 ... 6K 69
Bowers Wlk. E6 ... 6D 72
Bowes Cl. DA15: Sidc ... 6B 110
Bowe's Ho. IG11: Bark ... 7F 55
Bowes-Lyon Hall *E16 ... 1J 89*
(off Wesley Av., not continuous)
BOWES PARK ... 6D 16
Bowes Rd. N11 ... 5B 16
N13 ... 5B 16
RM8: Dag ... 4C 56
W3 ... 7A 64
Bowfell Rd. W6 ... 6E 82
Bowford Av. DA7: Bex ... 1E 110
Bowhill Cl. SW9 ... 7A 86
Bowie Cl. SW4 ... 7H 103
Bow Ind. Pk. E15 ... 7C 52
Bow Interchange ... 2D 70
Bowland Rd. IG8: Wfd G ... 6F 21
SW4 ... 4H 103
Bowland Yd. SW1 ... 7F 165
Bow La. EC4 ... 6C 68 (1D 168)
N12 ... 7F 15
SM4: Mord ... 6G 137
Bowl Ct. EC2 ... 4E 68 (4H 163)
Bowles Rd. SE1 ... 6G 87
Bowley Cl. SE19 ... 6F 123
Bowley Ho. SE16 ... 3G 87
Bowley La. SE19 ... 5F 123
Bowling Cl. UB10: Uxb ... 1B 58
Bowling Grn. Cl.
SW15 ... 7D 100
Bowling Grn. Ct.
HA9: Wemb ... 2F 45
Bowling Grn. La.
EC1 ... 4A 68 (3K 161)
Bowling Grn. Pl.
SE1 ... 2D 86 (6E 168)
Bowling Grn. Row SE18 ... 3D 90
Bowling Grn. St.
SE11 ... 6A 86 (7J 173)
Bowling Grn. Wlk.
N1 ... 3E 68 (1G 163)
Bowls Cl. HA7: Stan ... 5G 11
Bowman Av. E16 ... 7H 71
Bowman M. SW18 ... 1H 119
Bowman's Bldgs. *NW1 ... 5C 158*
(off Penfold Pl.)
Bowmans Cl. W13 ... 1B 80
Bowmans Lea SE23 ... 7J 105
Bowmans Mdw.
SM6: Wall ... 3F 151
Bowman's M. E1 ... 7G 69
N7 ... 3J 49
Bowman's Pl. N7 ... 3J 49
Bowman Trad. Est. NW9 ... 4G 27
Bowmead SE9 ... 2D 126
Bowmore Wlk. NW1 ... 7H 49
Bowness Cl. *E8 ... 6F 51*
(off Beechwood Rd.)
Bowness Cres. SW15 ... 5A 118
Bowness Dr. TW4: Houn ... 4C 96
Bowness Ho. *SE15 ... 7J 87*
(off Hillbeck Cl.)
Bowness Rd. DA7: Bex ... 2H 111
SE6 ... 7D 106
Bowood Rd. EN3: Enf ... 2E 8
SW11 ... 5E 102
Bow Rd. E3 ... 3B 70
Bowrons Av. HA0: Wemb ... 7D 44
Bowry Ho. *E14 ... 5B 70*
(off Wallwood St.)
Bowsley Ct. TW13: Felt ... 2J 113
Bowsprit Point *E14 ... 3C 88*
(off Westferry Rd.)
Bow St. E15 ... 5G 53
WC2 ... 6J 67 (1F 167)
Bow Triangle Bus. Cen.
E3 ... 4C 70
Bowyer Cl. E6 ... 5D 72
Bowyer Ho. *N1 ... 1E 68*
(off Mill Row)
Bowyer Pl. SE5 ... 7C 86
Bowyer St. SE5 ... 7C 86
Boxall Rd. SE21 ... 6E 104
Boxelder Cl. HA8: Edg ... 5D 12
Boxgrove Rd. SE2 ... 3C 92
Box La. IG11: Bark ... 2B 74
Boxley Rd. SM4: Mord ... 4A 138
Boxley St. E16 ... 1K 89
Boxmoor Ho. *W11 ... 1F 83*
(off Queensdale Cres.)
Boxmoor Rd. HA3: Harr ... 4B 26
Boxoll Rd. RM9: Dag ... 4F 57
Boxted Cl. IG9: Buck H ... 1H 21
Box Tree Ho. SE8 ... 6A 88
Boxtree La. HA3: Harr ... 1G 25
Boxtree Rd. HA3: Harr ... 7C 10
Boxwood Cl. UB7: W Dray ... 2B 76
Boxworth Cl. N12 ... 5G 15
Boxworth Gro. N1 ... 1K 67
Boyard Rd. SE18 ... 5F 91
Boyce Ho. *W10 ... 3H 65*
(off Bruckner St.)
Boyce Way E13 ... 4J 71
Boycroft Av. NW9 ... 6J 27
Boyd Av. UB1: S'hall ... 1D 78
Boyd Cl. KT2: King T ... 7G 117
Boydell Ct. NW8 ... 7B 48
(not continuous)
Boyden Ho. E17 ... 3E 34
Boyd Rd. SW19 ... 6B 120
Boyd St. E1 ... 6G 69
Boyfield St. SE1 ... 2B 86 (7B 168)
Boyland Rd. BR1: Brom ... 5H 125
Boyle Av. HA7: Stan ... 6F 11
Boyle Cl. UB10: Uxb ... 2B 58
Boyle Farm Rd.
KT7: T Ditt ... 6A 134
Boyle St. W1 ... 7G 67 (2A 166)
Boyne Av. NW4 ... 4F 29
Boyne Rd. RM10: Dag ... 3G 57
SE13 ... 3E 106
Boyne Ter. M. W11 ... 1H 83
Boyseland Ct. HA8: Edg ... 2D 12
Boyson Rd. SE5 ... 6C 86
(not continuous)
Boyson Wlk. SE17 ... 6D 86
Boyton Cl. E1 ... 4J 69
N8 ... 3J 31
Boyton Ho. *NW8 ... 2B 66*
(off Wellington Rd.)
Boyton Rd. N8 ... 3J 31
Brabant Ct. EC3 ... 2G 169
Brabant Rd. N22 ... 2K 31
Brabazon Av. SM6: Wall ... 7J 151
Brabazon Rd. TW5: Houn ... 7A 78
UB5: N'olt ... 2E 60
Brabazon St. E14 ... 6D 70
Brabner Ho. *E2 ... 1K 163*
(off Wellington Row)
Brabourne Cl. SE19 ... 5E 122
Brabourne Cres. DA7: Bex ... 6F 93
Brabourne Hgts. NW7 ... 3F 13
Brabourne Ri. BR3: Beck ... 5E 142
Brabourn Gro. SE15 ... 2J 105
Brabrook Ct. SM6: Wall ... 4F 151
Brabstone Ho. UB6: G'frd ... 2K 61
Bracer Ho. *N1 ... 2E 68*
(off Whitmore Est.)
Bracewell Av. UB6: G'frd ... 5K 43
Bracewell Rd. W10 ... 5E 64

Bracewood Gdns.—Brantwood Cl.

Bracewood Gdns.
CR0: Croy 3F 153
Bracey M. N4 2J 49
Bracey St. N4 2J 49
Bracken Av. CR0: Croy 3C 154
SW12 6E 102
Brackenbridge Dr.
HA4: Ruis 3B 42
Brackenbridge Ho.
HA4: Ruis 4C 42
Brackenbury N4 1A 50
(off Osborne Rd.)
Brackenbury Gdns. W6 3D 82
Brackenbury Rd. N2 3A 30
W6 3D 82
Bracken Cl. E6 5D 72
TW2: Twick 7E 96
TW16: Sun T 6H 113
Brackendale N21 2E 16
Brackendale Cl.
TW3: Houn 1F 97
Brackendene DA5: Dart 4K 129
Bracken End TW7: Isle 5H 97
Brackenfield Cl. E5 3H 51
Bracken Gdns. SW13 2C 100
Brackenhill HA4: Ruis 4C 42
Bracken Hill Cl.
BR1: Brom 1H 143
Bracken Hill La.
BR1: Brom 1H 143
Bracken Ho. E3 5C 70
(off Devons Rd.)
Bracken Ind. Est. IG6: Ilf 1J 37
Bracken M. E4 1K 19
RM7: Rom 6H 39
Brackens BR3: Beck 7C 124
Brackens, The EN1: Enf 7K 7
Bracken, The E4 2K 19
Brackenwood
TW16: Sun T 1J 131
Brackenwood Lodge
EN5: Barn 4D 4
(off Prospect Rd.)
Brackley Cl. SM6: Wall 7J 151
Brackley Ct. NW8 3B 158
(off Pollitt Dr.)
Brackley Rd. BR3: Beck 7B 124
W4 5A 82
Brackley Sq. IG8: Wfd G 7G 21
Brackley St. EC1 4C 68 (5D 162)
Brackley Ter. W4 5A 82
Bracklyn Ct. N1 2D 68
Bracklyn St. N1 2D 68
Bracknell Cl. N22 1A 32
Bracknell Gdns. NW3 4K 47
Bracknell Ga. NW3 5K 47
Bracknell Way NW3 4K 47
Bracondale Rd. SE2 4A 92
Bradbeer Ho. E2 3J 69
(off Cornwall Av.)
Bradbourne Rd.
DA5: Bexl 7G 111
Bradbourne St. SW6 2J 101
Bradbury Cl. UB2: S'hall 4D 78
Bradbury M. N16 5E 50
(off Bradbury St.)
Bradbury St. N16 5E 50
Braddock Cl. TW7: Isle 2K 97
Braddon Ct. EN5: Barn 3B 4
Braddon Rd. TW9: Rich 3F 99
Braddyll St. SE10 5G 89
Bradenham SE17 6D 86
(off Bradenham Cl.)
Bradenham Av.
DA16: Well 4A 110
Bradenham Cl. SE17 6D 86
Bradenham Rd.
HA3: Harr 4B 26
UB4: Hayes 3G 59
Braden St. W9 4K 65
Bradfield Ct. NW1 7F 49
(off Hawley Rd.)
Bradfield Dr. IG11: Bark 5A 56
Bradfield Ho. IG8: Ilf 6K 21
Bradfield Rd. E16 2J 89
HA4: Ruis 5C 42
Bradford Cl. BR2: Short 1D 156
N17 6A 18
SE26 4H 123
Bradford Dr. KT19: Eps 6B 148
Bradford Ho. W14 3F 83
(off Spring Va. Ter.)
Bradford Rd. IG1: Ilf 1H 55
W3 2A 82
Bradgate Rd. SE6 6D 106
Brading Cres. E11 2K 53
Brading Rd. CR0: Croy 6K 139
SW2 7K 103
Brading Ter. W12 3C 82
Bradiston Rd. W9 3H 65
Bradley Cl. N7 6J 49
Bradley Gdns. W13 6B 62
Bradley Ho. E2 2G 69
(off Claredale St.)
IG8: Wfd G 7D 20
SE16 4J 87
(off Raymouth Rd.)
Bradley M. SW17 1D 120
Bradley Rd. N22 2K 31
SE19 6C 122
Bradley's Cl. N1 2A 68
Bradley Stone Rd. E6 5D 72
Bradman Row HA8: Edg 7D 12
Bradmead SW8 7F 85
Bradmore Pk. Rd. W6 4D 82
Bradshaw Cl. SW19 6J 119
Bradshawe Waye
UB8: Uxb 5B 58
Bradshaws Cl. SE25 3G 141
Bradstock Ho. E9 7K 51
Bradstock Rd. E9 6K 51
KT17: Eps 5C 148
Brad St. SE1 1A 86 (5K 167)
Bradwell Av. RM10: Dag 2G 57
Bradwell Cl. E18 4H 35
Bradwell Ho. NW6 1K 65
(off Mortimer Cres.)
Bradwell M. N18 4B 18
Bradwell Rd. IG9: Buck H 1H 21
Brady Ct. RM8: Dag 1D 56
Brady Ho. SW8 1G 103
(off Corunna Rd.)
Bradymead E6 6E 72
Brady St. E1 4H 69
Braeburn Ct. EN4: Barn 4G 5
Braemar Av. CR2: S Croy 7C 152
CR7: Thor H 3A 140
DA7: Bex 4J 111
HA0: Wemb 7D 44
N22 1J 31
NW10 3K 45
SW19 2J 119
Braemar Cl. SE16 5H 87
(off Masters Dr.)
Braemar Ct. SE6 1H 125
Braemar Gdns.
BR4: W W'ck 1E 154
DA15: Sidc 3H 127
NW9 1K 27
Braemar Ho. W9 3A 66
(off Maida Va.)
Braemar Rd. E13 4H 71
KT4: Wor Pk 3D 148
N15 5E 32
TW8: Bford 6D 80
Braeside BR3: Beck 5C 124
Braeside Av. SW19 1G 137
Braeside Cres. DA7: Bex 4J 111
Braeside Rd. SW16 7G 121
Braes St. N1 7B 50
Braesyde Cl. DA17: Belv 4F 93
Brafferton Rd. CR0: Croy 4C 152
Braganza St. SE17 5B 86
Bragg Cl. RM8: Dag 6B 56
Bragg Rd. TW11: Tedd 6J 115
Braham Ho.
SE11 5K 85 (6H 173)
Braham St. E1 6F 69 (1K 169)
Braid Av. W3 6A 64
Braid Cl. TW13: Felt 2D 114
Braid Ho. SE10 1E 106
(off Blackheath Hill)
Braidwood Pas. EC1 5C 162
(off Aldersgate St.)
Braidwood Rd. SE6 1F 125
Brailsford Cl. SW19 7C 120
Brailsford Rd. SW2 5A 104
Brainton Av. TW14: Felt 7K 95
Braintree Av. IG4: Ilf 4C 36
Braintree Ho. E1 4J 69
(off Malcolm Rd.)
Braintree Rd. HA4: Ruis 4K 41
RM10: Dag 3G 57
Braintree St. E2 3J 69
Braithwaite Av.
RM7: Rush G 7G 39
Braithwaite Gdns.
HA7: Stan 1C 26
Braithwaite Ho. E14 6F 71
EC1 3E 162
(off Bunhill Row)
Braithwaite Rd. EN3: Enf 3G 9
Braithwaite Twr. W2 5B 158
Bramah Grn. SW9 1A 104
Bramah Tea & Coffee Mus.
6K 169
Bramalea Cl. N6 6E 30
Bramall Cl. E15 5H 53
Bramall Ct. N7 5K 49
(off George's Rd.)
Bramber WC1 2E 160
Bramber Ct. W5 4E 80
Bramber Rd. N12 5H 15
W14 6H 83
Brambleacres Cl.
SM2: Sutt 7J 149
Bramblebury Rd. SE18 5G 91
Bramble Cl. BR3: Beck 5E 142
CR0: Croy 4C 154
HA7: Stan 7J 11
N15 4G 33
TW17: Shep 3F 131
UB8: Uxb 6B 58
Bramble Cft. DA8: Erith 4J 93
Brambledown Cl.
BR4: W W'ck 5G 143
Brambledown Rd.
CR2: S Croy 7E 152
SM5: Cars 7E 150
Bramble Gdns. W12 7B 64
Bramble Ho. E3 5C 70
(off Devons Rd.)
Bramble La.
TW12: Hamp 6D 114
Brambles Cl. TW7: Isle 7B 80
Brambles Farm Dr.
UB10: Uxb 3C 58
Brambles, The SW19 5H 119
(off Woodside)
UB7: W Dray 4A 76
Bramblewood Cl.
SM5: Cars 1C 150
Brambling Ct. SE8 6B 88
(off Abinger Gro.)
Bramblings, The E4 4A 20
Bramcote Av. CR4: Mitc 4D 138
Bramcote Gro. SE16 5J 87
Bramcote Rd. SW15 4D 100
Bramdean Cres. SE12 1J 125
Bramdean Gdns. SE12 1J 125
Bramerton NW6 7F 47
(off Willesden La.)
Bramerton Rd.
BR3: Beck 3B 142
Bramerton St.
SW3 6C 84 (7C 170)
Bramfield Ct. N4 2C 50
(off Queens Dr.)
Bramfield Rd. SW11 6C 102
Bramford Ct. N14 2C 16
Bramford Rd. SW18 4A 102
Bramham Gdns.
KT9: Chess 4D 146
SW5 5K 83
Bramham Ho. SE15 4E 104
Bramhope La. SE7 6K 89
Bramlands Cl. SW11 3C 102
Bramley Av. TW17: Shep 3G 131
Bramley Bank Nature Reserve
6J 153
Bramley Cl. BR6: Orp 7F 145
CR2: S Croy 5C 152
E17 2A 34
HA5: Pinn 3H 23
IG8: Wfd G 7F 21
N14 5A 6
TW2: Twick 6G 97
UB3: Hayes 7J 59
Bramley Ct. CR4: Mitc 2B 138
DA16: Well 1B 110
E4 1K 19
(off Ridgeway, The)
EN4: Barn 4H 5
UB1: S'hall 7G 61
(off Haldane Rd.)
Bramley Cres. IG2: Ilf 6E 36
SW8 7H 85
Bramley Hill CR2: S Croy 5B 152
Bramley Ho. SW15 6B 100
(off Tunworth Cres.)
TW4: Houn 4D 96
W10 6F 65
Bramleyhyrst
CR2: S Croy 4C 152
(off Bramley Hill)
Bramley Pde. N14 4B 6
Bramley Rd. N14 5A 6
SM1: Sutt 5B 150
SM2: Sutt 7F 149
W5 3C 80
W10 6F 65
(not continuous)
Bramley Way
BR4: W W'ck 2D 154
TW4: Houn 5D 96
Brampton WC1 6G 161
(off Red Lion Sq.)
Brampton Cl. E5 2H 51
Brampton Ct. NW4 4D 28
Brampton Gdns. N15 5C 32
Brampton Gro. HA3: Harr 4A 26
HA9: Wemb 1G 45
NW4 4D 28
Brampton La. NW4 4E 28
Brampton Pk. Rd. N8 3A 32
Brampton Rd. CR0: Croy 7F 141
DA7: Bex 3D 110
E6 3B 72
N15 5C 32
NW9 4G 27
SE2: Bex 6C 92
UB10: Uxb 2D 58
Bramshaw Ri.
KT3: N Mald 6A 136
Bramshaw Rd. E9 6K 51
Bramshill Gdns. NW5 3F 49
Bramshill Rd. NW10 2B 64
Bramshot Av. SE7 6J 89
Bramshurst NW8 1K 65
(off Abbey Rd.)
Bramston Rd. NW10 2C 64
SW17 3A 120
Bramwell Cl.
TW16: Sun T 2B 132
Bramwell Ho. SE1 3C 86
SW1 6A 172
(off Churchill Gdns.)
Bramwell M. N1 1K 67
Brancaster Dr. NW7 7H 13
Brancaster Ho. E1 3K 69
(off Moody St.)
Brancaster Rd. E12 4D 54
IG2: Ilf 6J 37
SW16 3J 121
Brancepeth Gdns.
IG9: Buck H 2D 20
Branch Hill NW3 3A 48
Branch Hill Ho. NW3 3K 47
Branch Pl. N1 1D 68
Branch Rd. E14 7A 70
Branch St. SE5 7E 86
Brancker Cl. SM6: Wall 7J 151
Brancker Rd. HA3: Harr 3D 26
Brancroft Way EN3: Enf 1F 9
Brand Cl. N4 1B 50
Brandesbury Sq. IG8: Ilf 7K 21
Brandlehow Rd. SW15 4H 101
Brandon NW9 2B 28
(off Further Acre)
Brandon Est. SE17 6B 86
Brandon Ho. BR3: Beck 5D 124
(off Beckenham Hill Rd.)
Brandon Mans. W14 6G 83
(off Queen's Club Gdns.)
Brandon M. EC2 6E 162
Brandon Rd. E17 4E 34
N7 7J 49
SM1: Sutt 4K 149
UB2: S'hall 5D 78
Brandon St. SE17 4C 86
(not continuous)
Brandram M. SE13 4G 107
(off Brandram Rd.)
Brandram Rd. SE13 3G 107
Brandreth Ct. HA1: Harr 6K 25
Brandreth Rd. E6 6D 72
SW17 2F 121
Brandries, The
SM6: Wall 3H 151
Brand St. SE10 7E 88
Brandville Gdns. IG6: Ilf 4F 37
Brandville Rd.
UB7: W Dray 2A 76
Brandy Way SM2: Sutt 7J 149
Brangbourne Rd.
BR1: Brom 5E 124
Brangton Rd.
SE11 5K 85 (6H 173)
Brangwyn Ct. W14 3G 83
(off Blythe Rd.)
Brangwyn Cres. SW19 1A 138
Branham Ho. SE18 5F 91
Branksea St. SW6 7G 83
Branksome Av. N18 6A 18
Branksome Cl.
TW11: Tedd 4H 115
Branksome Ho. SW8 7K 85
(off Meadow Rd.)
Branksome Rd. SW2 5J 103
SW19 1J 137
Branksome Way
HA3: Harr 6F 27
KT3: N Mald 1J 135
Branksone Ct. N2 3A 30
Bransby Rd. KT9: Chess 6E 146
Branscombe NW1 1G 67
(off Plender St.)
Branscombe Ct.
BR2: Short 5H 143
Branscombe Gdns. N21 7F 7
Branscombe St. SE13 3D 106
Bransdale Cl. NW6 1J 65
Bransgrove Rd.
HA8: Edg 1F 27
Branston Cres. BR5: Orp 7H 145
Branstone Rd. TW9: Rich 1F 99
Brants Wlk. W7 4J 61
Brantwood Av. DA8: Erith 7J 93
TW7: Isle 4A 98
Brantwood Cl. E17 3D 34

Brantwood Gdns.—Bridgeland Rd.

Brantwood Gdns. EN2: Enf 4D 6
IG4: Ilf 4C 36
Brantwood Ho. *SE5* *7C 86*
(off Wyndam Est.)
Brantwood Rd.
CR2: S Croy 7C 152
DA7: Bex 2H 111
N17 6B 18
SE24 5C 104
Branxholme Ct.
BR1: Brom *1H 143*
(off Highland Rd.)
Brasenose Dr. SW13 6E 82
Brasher Cl. UB6: G'frd 5H 43
Brassett Point *E15* *1G 71*
(off Abbey Rd.)
Brassey Cl. TW14: Felt 1J 113
Brassey Ho. *E14* *4D 88*
(off Cahir St.)
Brassey Rd. NW6 6H 47
Brassey Sq. SW11 3E 102
Brassie Av. W3 6A 64
Brass Talley All. SE16 2K 87
Brasted Cl. DA6: Bex 5D 110
SE26 4J 123
Brasted Lodge BR3: Beck 7C 124
Brathay *NW1* *1B 160*
(off Ampthill Est.)
Brathway Rd. SW18 7J 101
Bratley St. E1 4G 69
Bratten Ct. CR0: Croy 6D 140
Braund Av. UB6: G'frd 4F 61
Braundton Av.
DA15: Sidc 1K 127
Braunston Dr. UB4: Hayes 4C 60
Bravington Cl.
TW17: Shep 5B 130
Bravington Pl. W9 4H 65
Bravington Rd. W9 2H 65
Brawne Ho. *SE17* *6B 86*
(off Brandon Est.)
Braxfield Rd. SE4 4A 106
Braxted Pk. SW16 6K 121
Bray NW3 7C 48
Brayards Rd. SE15 2H 105
Brayards Rd. Est. *SE15* *2J 105*
(off Brayards Rd.)
Braybourne Dr. TW7: Isle 7K 79
Braybrooke Gdns. SE19 7E 122
Braybrook St. W12 5B 64
Brayburne Av. SW4 2G 103
Bray Ct. SW16 5J 121
Braycourt Av.
KT12: Walt T 7K 131
Bray Cres. SE16 2K 87
Braydon Rd. N16 1G 51
Bray Dr. E16 7H 71
Brayfield Ter. N1 7A 50
Brayford Sq. E1 6J 69
Bray Pas. E16 7J 71
Bray Pl. SW3 4D 84 (4E 170)
Bray Rd. NW7 6A 14
Brayton Gdns. EN2: Enf 4C 6
Braywood Rd. SE9 4H 109
Brazil Cl. CR0: Croy 7J 139
Breach La. RM9: Dag 3G 75
Bread St. EC4 6C 68 (1D 168)
(not continuous)
Breakspear Crematorium
HA4: Ruis 5E 22
Breakspear Ho. HA4: Ruis 5F 23
Breakspear M. UB9: Uxb 3A 22
Breakspear Rd.
HA4: Ruis 7D 22
Breakspear Rd. Nth.
UB9: Uxb 3A 22
Breakspear Rd. Sth.
UB9: Uxb 3B 40
UB10: Uxb 3B 40
Breakspears Dr.
BR5: Orp 7A 128
Breakspears M. SE4 2B 106
Breakspears Rd. SE4 4B 106
Bream Cl. N17 4H 33
Bream Gdns. E6 3E 72
Breamore Cl. SW15 1C 118
Breamore Ct. IG3: Ilf 2A 56
Breamore Ho. *SE15* *7G 87*
(off Friary Est.)
Breamore Rd. IG3: Ilf 2K 55
Bream's Bldgs.
EC4 6A 68 (7J 161)
Bream St. E3 7C 52
Breamwater Gdns.
TW10: Rich 3B 116
Brearley Cl. HA8: Edg 7D 12
UB8: Uxb 6A 40
Breasley Cl. SW15 4D 100
Breasy Pl. *NW4* *4D 28*
(off Burroughs Gdns.)
Brechin Pl. SW7 4A 84
Brecknock Rd. N7 5H 49
N19 4G 49
Brecknock Rd. Est. N19 4G 49
Breckonmead BR1: Brom 2A 144
Brecon Cl. CR4: Mitc 3J 139
KT4: Wor Pk 2E 148
Brecon Grn. NW9 6A 28
Brecon Ho. *W2* *6A 66*
(off Hallfield Est.)
Brecon M. NW5 5H 49
Brecon Rd. EN3: Enf 4D 8
W6 6G 83
Brede Cl. E6 3E 72
Bredel Ho. *E14* *5C 70*
(off St Paul's Way)
Bredgar SE13 5D 106
Bredgar Rd. N19 2G 49
Bredhurst Cl. SE20 6J 123
Bredin Ho. *SW10* *7K 83*
(off Coleridge Gdns.)
Bredo Ho. IG11: Bark 3B 74
Bredon Rd. CR0: Croy 7F 141
Breer St. SW6 3K 101
Breezers Ct. *E1* *7G 69*
(off Highway, The)
Breezer's Hill E1 7G 69
Brember Rd. HA2: Harr 2G 43
Bremer M. E17 4D 34
Bremner Rd.
SW7 3A 84 (1A 170)
Brenchley Cl. BR2: Short 6H 143
BR7: Chst 1E 144
Brenchley Gdns. SE23 6J 105
Brenchley Rd. BR5: Orp 2K 145
Brenda Rd. SW17 2D 120
Brende Gdns.
KT8: W Mole 4F 133
Brendon Av. NW10 4A 46
Brendon Cl. UB3: Hayes 7E 76
Brendon Ct. UB2: S'hall 4F 79
Brendon Gdns. HA2: Harr 4F 43
IG2: Ilf 5J 37
Brendon Gro. N2 2A 30
Brendon Rd. RM8: Dag 1F 57
SE9 2H 127
Brendon St. W1 6C 66 (7D 158)
Brendon Vs. N21 1H 17
Brendon Way EN1: Enf 7K 7
Brenley Cl. CR4: Mitc 3E 138
Brenley Gdns. SE9 4B 108
Brenley Ho. *SE1* *6E 168*
(off Tennis St.)
Brennand Ct. N19 3G 49
Brent Cl. DA5: Bexl 1E 128
Brentcot Cl. W13 4B 62
Brent Ct. NW11 7F 29
W7 7H 61
Brent Cres. NW10 2F 63
BRENT CROSS 7E 28
Brent Cross Fly-Over
NW2 7F 29
NW4 7F 29
Brent Cross Gdns. NW4 6F 29
Brent Cross Interchange
6E 28
Brent Cross Shop. Cen.
NW4 7E 28
Brentfield NW10 7H 45
Brentfield Cl. NW10 6K 45
Brentfield Gdns. NW2 7F 29
Brentfield Ho. NW10 7K 45
Brentfield Rd. NW10 6K 45
BRENTFORD 6D 80
Brentford Bus. Cen.
TW8: Bford 7C 80
Brentford Cl. UB4: Hayes 4B 60
BRENTFORD END 7B 80
Brentford Ho. TW1: Twick 7B 98
Brentford Musical Mus. *6E 80*
Brent Grn. NW4 5E 28
Brent Grn. Wlk.
HA9: Wemb 3J 45
Brentham Way W5 4D 62
Brent Ho. *E9* *6J 51*
(off Frampton Pk. Rd.)
Brenthouse Rd. E9 7J 51
Brenthurst Rd. NW10 6B 46
Brent Lea TW8: Bford 7C 80
Brentmead Cl. W7 7J 61
Brentmead Gdns. NW10 2F 63
Brentmead Pl. NW4 6F 29
NW11 6F 29
Brent New Ent. Cen.
NW10 6B 46
Brenton St. E14 6A 70
Brent Pk. Ind. Est.
UB2: S'hall 3K 77
Brent Pk. Rd. NW4 7D 28
Brent Pl. EN5: Barn 5C 4
Brent Rd. CR2: S Croy 7H 153
E16 6J 71
SE18 7F 91
TW8: Bford 6C 80
UB2: S'hall 3A 78
Brent Side TW8: Bford 6C 80
Brentside Cl. W13 4A 62
Brentside Executive Cen.
TW8: Bford 6B 80
Brent St. NW4 4E 28
Brent Ter. NW2 1E 46
(not continuous)
Brent Trad. Cen. NW10 5A 46
Brentvale Av. HA0: Wemb 1F 63
UB1: S'hall 1H 79
Brent Vw. Rd. NW9 6C 28
Brentwaters Bus. Pk.
TW8: Bford 7C 80
Brent Way HA9: Wemb 6H 45
N3 6D 14
TW8: Bford 7D 80
Brentwick Gdns.
TW8: Bford 4E 80
Brentwood Cl. SE9 1G 127
Brentwood Ho. *SE18* *7B 90*
(off Portway Gdns.)
Brentwood Lodge *NW4* *5F 29*
(off Holmdale Gdns.)
Brereton Rd. N17 7A 18
Bressenden Pl.
SW1 3F 85 (1K 171)
Bressey Av. EN1: Enf 1B 8
Bressey Gro. E18 2H 35
Breton Highwalk *EC2* *5D 162*
(off Golden La.)
Breton Ho. EC1 4D 162
SE1 *7J 169*
(off Abbey St.)
Brett Cl. N16 2E 50
UB5: N'olt 3B 60
Brett Ct. N9 2D 18
Brett Cres. NW10 1K 63
Brettell St. SE17 5D 86
Brettenham Av. E17 1C 34
Brettenham Rd. E17 2C 34
N18 4B 18
Brett Gdns. RM9: Dag 7E 56
Brett Ho. Cl. SW15 7F 101
Brettinghurst *SE1* *5G 87*
(off Avondale Sq.)
Brett Pas. E8 5H 51
Brett Rd. E8 5H 51
Brewer's Grn. SW1 1C 172
Brewer's Hall Gdn. *EC2* *6D 162*
(off London Wall)
Brewers La. TW9: Rich 5D 98
Brewer St. W1 7G 67 (2B 166)
Brewery Cl. HA0: Wemb 5A 44
Brewery Ind. Est., The
N1 *1D 162*
(off Wenlock Rd.)
Brewery La. TW1: Twick 7K 97
Brewery M. Cen.
TW7: Isle 3A 98
Brewery Rd. BR2: Short 1C 156
N7 7J 49
SE18 5H 91
Brewery Sq. SE1 5J 169
Brewery, The RM1: Rom 5K 39
Brewhouse La. E1 1H 87
SW15 3G 101
Brewhouse Rd. SE18 4D 90
Brewhouse Wlk. SE16 1A 88
Brewhouse Yd.
EC1 4B 68 (3A 162)
Brewin Ter. UB4: Hayes 5A 60
Brewood Rd. RM8: Dag 6B 56
Brewster Gdns. W10 5E 64
Brewster Ho. *E14* *7B 70*
(off Three Colt St.)
SE1 *4F 87*
(off Dunton Rd.)
Brewster Rd. E10 1D 52
Brian Rd. RM6: Chad H 5C 38
Briant Ho. SE1 2J 173
Briants Cl. HA5: Pinn 2D 24
Briant St. SE14 1K 105
Briar Av. SW16 7K 121
Briarbank Rd. W13 6A 62
Briar Cl. IG9: Buck H 2G 21
N2 3K 29
N13 3H 17
TW7: Isle 5K 97
TW12: Hamp 5D 114
Briar Ct. SM3: Sutt 4E 148
SW15 4D 100
Briar Cres. UB5: N'olt 6F 43
Briardale Gdns. NW3 3J 47
Briarfield Av. N2 3K 29
N3 2K 29
Briar Gdns. BR2: Short 1H 155
Briaris Cl. N17 7C 18
Briar La. CR0: Croy 4D 154
Briar Rd. DA5: Bexl 3K 129
HA3: Harr 5C 26
NW2 4E 46
SW16 3J 139
TW2: Twick 1J 115
TW17: Shep 5B 130
Briars, The WD23: Bush 1D 10
Briar Wlk. HA8: Edg 7D 12
SW15 4D 100
W10 4G 65
Briar Way UB7: W Dray 2C 76
Briarwood Cl. NW9 6J 27
TW13: Felt 4G 113
Briarwood Ct.
KT4: Wor Pk *1C 148*
(off Avenue, The)
Briarwood Dr. HA6: Nwood 2J 23
Briarwood Rd. KT17: Eps 6C 148
SW4 5H 103
Briary Cl. NW3 7C 48
Briary Ct. DA14: Sidc 5B 128
E16 6H 71
Briary Gdns. BR1: Brom 5K 125
Briary Gro. HA8: Edg 2H 27
Briary La. N9 3A 18
Briary Lodge BR3: Beck 1E 142
Brickbarn Cl. *SW10* *7A 84*
(off King's Barn)
Brick Ct. EC4 6A 68 (1J 167)
Brickett Cl. HA4: Ruis 5E 22
Brick Farm Cl.
TW9: Rich 1H 99
Brickfield Cl. TW8: Bford 7C 80
Brickfield Cotts.
BR7: Chst 5E 126
SE18 6K 91
Brickfield La. UB3: Hayes 6F 77
Brickfield Rd.
CR7: Thor H 1B 140
SW19 4K 119
Brickfields HA2: Harr 2H 43
(not continuous)
Brickfields Way
UB7: W Dray 3B 76
Brick La. E2 3F 69 (2K 163)
EN1: Enf 2C 8
EN3: Enf 2C 8
HA7: Stan 7J 11
Brick Lane Music Hall ***2H 163***
(off Curtain Rd.)
Bricklayer's Arms 4D 86
Bricklayers Arms Bus. Cen.
SE1 4E 86
Brick St. W1 1F 85 (5J 165)
Brickwall La. HA4: Ruis 1G 41
Brickwood Cl. SE26 3H 123
Brickwood Rd.
CR0: Croy 2E 152
Brideale Cl. SE15 6F 87
Bride Ct. EC4 1A 168
Bride La. EC4 6B 68 (1A 168)
Bridel M. *N1* *1B 68*
(off Colebrook Row)
Bride St. N7 6K 49
Bridewain St.
SE1 3F 87 (7J 169)
(not continuous)
Bridewell Pl. E1 1H 87
EC4 6B 68 (1A 168)
Bridewell, The (Theatre) ***1A 168***
(off Bridewell Pl.)
Bridford M. W1 5F 67 (5K 159)
Bridge App. NW1 7E 48
Bridge Av. W6 4E 82
W7 5H 61
Bridge Av. Mans. *W6* *5E 82*
(off Bridge Av.)
Bridge Cl. EN1: Enf 2C 8
KT12: Walt T 7H 131
TW11: Tedd 4K 115
W10 6F 65
Bridge Ct. E10 1B 52
Bridge Dr. N13 4E 16
Bridge End E17 1E 34
Bridgefield Rd.
SM1: Sutt 6J 149
Bridgefoot SE1 5J 85 (6F 173)
TW16: Sun T 1H 131
Bridge Gdns. KT8: E Mos 4H 133
N16 4D 50
TW15: Ashf 7E 112
Bridge Ga. N21 7H 7
Bridge Ho. *E9* *6K 51*
(off Shepherds La.)
NW3 *7E 48*
(off Adelaide Rd.)
NW10 *2F 65*
(off Chamberlayne Rd.)
SE4 4B 106
SM2: Sutt *6K 149*
(off Bridge Rd.)
SW1 *5J 171*
(off Ebury Bri.)
Bridgehouse Ct. *SE1* *7A 168*
(off Blackfriars Rd.)
Bridge Ho. Quay E14 1E 88
Bridgeland Rd. E16 7J 71

A-Z London 201

Bridge La.—Broadmead

Broadmead Av.
KT4: Wor Pk 7C 136
Broadmead Cen.
IG8: Wfd G 7F 21
(off Navestock Cres.)
Broadmead Cl. HA5: Pinn ...1C 24
TW12: Hamp 6E 114
Broadmead Ct.
IG8: Wfd G 6D 20
Broadmead Rd.
IG8: Wfd G 6D 20
(not continuous)
UB4: Hayes 4C 60
UB5: N'olt 4C 60
Broad Oak IG8: Wfd G 5E 20
Broadoak TW16: Sun T 6H 113
Broad Oak Cl. E4 ....5H 19
Broadoak Ct. SW9 ....3A 104
Broadoak Ho. *NW6.........1K 65*
(off Mortimer Cres.)
Broadoak Rd. DA8: Erith 7K 93
Broadoaks KT6: Surb 2H 147
Broadoaks Way
BR2: Short.........5H 143
Broad Sanctuary
SW1 ....2H 85 (7D 166)
Broadstone Ho. *SW8 ....7K 85*
(off Dorset Rd.)
Broadstone Pl.
W1 ....5E 66 (6G 159)
Broad St. RM10: Dag 7G 57
TW11: Tedd 6K 115
Broad St. Av.
EC2 ....5E 68 (6G 163)
Broad St. Mkt.
RM10: Dag 7G 57
Broad St. Pl. EC2 ....6F 163
Broad Vw. NW9 ....6G 27
Broadview Rd. SW16 ......7H 121
Broad Wlk. N21 ....2E 16
NW1 ....1E 66 (1H 159)
SE3 ....2A 108
TW5: Houn 1B 96
TW9: Rich 7F 81
W1 ....7D 66 (3F 165)
Broadwalk E18 ....3H 35
HA2: Harr 5E 24
Broadwalk Cl. *E14 ....1E 88*
(off Broadwalk Pl.)
Broadwalk Ct. *W8..........1J 83*
(off Palace Gdns. Ter.)
Broadwalk Ho.
EC2 ....4E 68 (5G 163)
SW7...............2A 84
(off Hyde Pk. Ga.)
Broad Wlk. La. NW11 ......7H 29
Broadwalk Shop. Cen.
HA8: Edg 6C 12
Broad Wlk., The
KT8: E Mos 4K 133
W8................1K 83
Broadwalk, The
HA6: Nwood.........2E 22
Broadwall SE1 .....1A 86 (4K 167)
Broadwater Farm Est.
N17 ....2D 32
Broadwater Rd. N17 ....1E 32
SE28 ....3H 91
SW17.............4C 120
Broadway DA6: Bex 4E 110
(not continuous)
E13 ....2K 71
E15................7F 53
IG11: Bark 1G 73
SW1 ....3H 85 (7C 166)
W7 ....1J 79
W13...............1A 80
Broadway Arc. *W6 ....4E 82*
(off Hammersmith B'way.)
Broadway Av. CR0: Croy ...5D 140
TW1: Twick 6B 98
Broadway Cen., The W6 ....4E 82
Broadway Chambers *W6 ....4E 82*
(off Hammersmith B'way.)
Broadway Cl. IG8: Wfd G 6E 20
Broadway Ct. BR3: Beck 3E 142
SW19 ....6J 119
Broadway Gdns.
CR4: Mitc 4C 138
IG8: Wfd G 6E 20
Broadway Ho. *BR1: Brom ...5F 125*
(off Bromley Rd.)
E8 ....1H 69
Broadway Mkt. E8 ....1H 69
IG6: Ilf 2H 37
(Forest Rd.)
IG6: Ilf 2G 37
(Greystone Gdns.)
SW17 ....4D 120
Broadway Mkt. M. E8 ......1G 69
Broadway M. N13 ....5E 16
N16 ....7F 33
N21 ....1G 17
Broadway Pde. E4 ....6K 19
HA2: Harr 5F 25
N8 ....6J 31
UB3: Hayes 1J 77
Broadway Pl. SW19 ....6H 119
Broadway Shop. Cen.
DA6: Bex 4G 111
Broadway Shop. Mall
SW1 ....3H 85 (1C 172)
Broadway Sq. DA6: Bex 4G 111
Broadway, The CR0: Croy ...4J 151
E4 ....6A 20
HA3: Harr 2J 25
HA6: Nwood 2J 23
HA7: Stan 5H 11
HA9: Wemb 3E 44
IG8: Wfd G 6E 20
KT7: T Ditt 7J 133
N8 ....6J 31
N9 ....3B 18
N11 ....5K 15
(off Stanford Rd.)
N14 ....1C 16
(off Southgate Cir.)
N22 ....2A 32
NW7 ....7H 13
(off Colenso Dr.)
NW7 ....5F 13
(Millway)
NW9 ....6B 28
RM8: Dag 1F 57
SM1: Sutt 5A 150
SM3: Sutt 6G 149
SW14.............2A 100
SW19 ....6H 119
UB1: S'hall 7B 60
UB6: G'frd 4G 61
W3.................2G 81
W5................7D 62
Broadwell Ct. *TW5: Houn 1B 96*
(off Springwell Rd.)
Broadwick St.
W1 ....7G 67 (2B 166)
Broadwood Av. HA4: Ruis ...6G 23
Broadwood Ter. *W14 ....4H 83*
(off Warwick Rd.)
Broad Yd. EC1 .....4B 68 (4A 162)
Brocas Cl. NW3 ....7C 48
Brockbridge Ho. SW15 .....6B 100
Brockdene Dr. BR2: Kes 4B 156
Brockdish Av. IG11: Bark 5K 55
Brockenhurst
KT8: W Mole 5D 132
Brockenhurst Av.
KT4: Wor Pk 1A 148
Brockenhurst Gdns.
IG1: Ilf 5G 55
NW7 ....5F 13
Brockenhurst M. N18 ....4B 18
Brockenhurst Rd.
CR0: Croy 7H 141
Brockenhurst Way SW16 ...2H 139
Brocket Ho. SW8 ....2H 103
Brockham Cl. SW19 ....5H 119
Brockham Cres.
CR0: Croy..........7F 155
Brockham Dr. IG2: Ilf 6F 37
SW2..............7K 103
Brockham Ho. *NW1 ....1G 67*
(off Bayham Pl.)
SW2..............7K 103
(off Brockham Dri.)
Brockham St.
SE1 ....3C 86 (7D 168)
Brockhurst Cl. HA7: Stan 6E 10
Brockill Cres. SE4 ....4A 106
Brocklebank Ho. *E16 ....1E 90*
(off Glenister St.)
Brocklebank Ind. Est. SE7 ...4J 89
Brocklebank Rd. SE7 ....4K 89
SW18.............7A 102
Brocklehurst St. SE14 ......7K 87
Brocklesby Rd. SE25 ......4H 141
BROCKLEY 4K 105
Brockley Av. HA7: Stan 3K 11
Brockley Cl. HA7: Stan 4K 11
Brockley Cres. RM5: Col R ...1J 39
Brockley Cross SE4 ....3A 106
Brockley Cross Bus. Cen.
SE4 ....3A 106
Brockley Footpath SE4 .....5A 106
(not continuous)
SE15 ....4J 105
Brockley Gdns. SE4 ....2B 106
Brockley Gro. SE4 ....5B 106
Brockley Hall Rd. SE4 .....5A 106
Brockley Hill HA7: Stan 1H 11
Brockley M. SE4 ....5A 106
Brockley Pk. SE23 ....7A 106
Brockley Ri. SE23 ....1A 124
Brockley Rd. SE4 ....3B 106
Brockley Side HA7: Stan 4K 11
Brockley Vw. SE23 ....7A 106
Brockley Way SE4 ....5K 105
Brockman Ri. BR1: Brom 4F 125
Brockmer Ho. *E1 ....7H 69*
(off Crowder St.)
Brock Pl. E3 ....4D 70
Brock Rd. E13.............5K 71
Brocks Dr. SM3: Sutt 3G 149
Brockshot Cl. TW8: Bford 5D 80
Brock St. SE15 ....3J 105
Brockway Cl. E11 ....2G 53
Brockweir *E2 ....2J 69*
(off Cyprus St.)
Brockwell Av. BR3: Beck ...5D 142
Brockwell Cl. BR5: Orp 5K 145
Brockwell Ct. SW2 ....5A 104
Brockwell Ho. *SE11 ....7H 173*
(off Vauxhall St.)
Brockwell Pk. Gdns.
SE24 ....7A 104
Brockwell Pk. Row SW2 ...7A 104
Brodia Rd. N16 ....3E 50
Brodie Ho. *SE1 ....5F 87*
(off Cooper's Rd.)
Brodie Rd. E4 ....1K 19
EN2: Enf 1H 7
Brodie St. SE1 ....5F 87
Brodlove La. E1 ....7K 69
Brodrick Gro. SE2 ....4B 92
Brodrick Rd. SW17 ....2C 120
Brograve Gdns.
BR3: Beck 2D 142
Broken Wharf
EC4 ....7C 68 (2C 168)
Brokesley St. E3 ....3B 70
Broke Wlk. E8 ....1F 69
Bromar Rd. SE5 ....3E 104
Bromefield HA7: Stan 1C 26
Bromell's Rd. SW4 ....4G 103
Brome Rd. SE9 ....3D 108
Bromfelde Rd. SW4 ....3H 103
Bromfelde Wlk. SW4 ......2H 103
Bromfield St. N1 ....1A 68
Bromhall Rd.
RM8: Dag 6B 56
Bromhead Rd. *E1 ....6J 69*
(off Jubilee St.)
Bromhead St. E1 ....6J 69
Bromhedge SE9 ....3D 126
Bromholm Rd. SE2 ....3B 92
Bromleigh Ct. SE23 ....2G 123
Bromleigh Ho. *SE1 ....7J 169*
(off Abbey St.)
BROMLEY
BR1 ....2J 143
E3 ....3D 70
Bromley Av. BR1: Brom 7G 125
BROMLEY COMMON 1C 156
Bromley Comn.
BR2: Short 4A 144
Bromley Cres.
BR2: Short.........3H 143
HA4: Ruis 4H 41
Bromley Gdns.
BR2: Short.........3H 143
Bromley Gro. BR2:
Short 2F 143
Bromley Hall Rd. E14 ....5E 70
Bromley High St. E3 ....3D 70
Bromley Hill BR1: Brom 6G 125
Bromley Ind. Cen.
BR1: Brom 3B 144
(off Waldo Rd.)
Bromley La. BR7: Chst 7G 127
BROMLEY PARK 1G 143
Bromley Pk. BR1: Brom 1H 143
Bromley Pl.
W1 ....5G 67 (5A 160)
Bromley Rd. BR1: Brom 1D 124
BR2: Short.........2D 142
BR3: Beck 1D 142
BR7: Chst..........1F 145
E10 ....6D 34
E17 ....3C 34
N17 ....1F 33
N18 ....3J 17
SE6 ....1D 124
Bromley St. E1 ....5K 69
BROMPTON 3C 84 (2D 170)
Brompton Arc. SW1 ....7E 164
Brompton Cl. SE20 ....2G 141
TW4: Houn 5D 96
Brompton Gro. N2 ....4C 30
Brompton Oratory
.........3C 84 (2C 170)
Brompton Pk. Cres. SW6 ....6K 83
Brompton Pl.
SW3 ....3C 84 (1D 170)
Brompton Rd.
SW3 ....4C 84 (3C 170)
Brompton Sq.
SW3 ....3C 84 (1C 170)
Brompton Ter. SE18 ....1D 108
Bromwich Av. N6 ....2E 48
Bromyard Av. W3 ....7A 64
Bromyard Ho. *SE15 ....7H 87*
(off Commercial Way)
Bron Ct. NW6 ....1J 65
BRONDESBURY 7H 47
Brondesbury Ct. NW2 ....6F 47
Brondesbury M. NW6 ....7J 47
BRONDESBURY PARK 1G 65
Brondesbury Pk. NW2 ......6D 46
Brondesbury Rd. NW6 ......2H 65
Brondesbury Vs. NW6 ......2H 65
Bronhill Ter. N17 ....1G 33
Bronsart Rd. SW6 ....7G 83
Bronson Rd. SW20 ....2F 137
Bronte Cl. DA8: Erith 7H 93
E7.................4J 53
IG2: Ilf 4E 36
Bronte Ct. *W14 ....3F 83*
(off Girdler's Rd.)
Bronte Ho. N16 ....5E 50
NW6 ....3J 65
SW4 ....7G 103
Bronti Cl. SE17 ....5C 86
Bronwen Ct. *NW8 ....2A 158*
(off Grove End Rd.)
Bronze Age Way
DA8: Erith 2H 93
DA17: Belv..........2H 93
Bronze St. SE8 ....7C 88
Brook Av. HA8: Edg 6C 12
HA9: Wemb 3G 45
RM10: Dag 7H 57
Brookbank Av. W7 ....5H 61
Brookbank Rd. SE13 ....3C 106
Brook Cl. HA4: Ruis 7G 23
NW7 ....7B 14
SW17.............2E 120
SW20 ....3D 136
TW19: Staines 7B 94
W3................1G 81
Brook Ct. BR3: Beck 1B 142
E11 ....3G 53
E15 ....5D 52
(off Clays La.)
E17 ....3A 34
HA8: Edg 5C 12
IG11: Bark 1K 73
SE12 ....3A 126
Brook Cres. E4 ....4H 19
N18 ....4C 18
Brookdale N11 ....4B 16
Brookdale Rd.
DA5: Bexl 6E 110
E17 ....3C 34
SE6 ....7D 106
(not continuous)
Brookdales NW4 ....4G 29
Brookdene Rd. SE18........4J 91
Brook Dr. HA1: Harr 4G 25
HA4: Ruis 7G 23
SE11 ....3A 86 (2K 173)
Brooke Av. HA2: Harr 3G 43
Brooke Cl. WD23: Bush 1B 10
Brooke Ho. SE14 ....1A 106
Brookehowse Rd. SE6 .....2C 124
Brookend Rd. DA15: Sidc ...1J 127
Brooke Rd. E5 ....3G 51
E17 ....4E 34
N16 ....3F 51
Brooke's Ct. EC1 ...5A 68 (6J 161)
Brooke's Mkt. EC1 ....5K 161
Brooke St. EC1 .....5A 68 (6J 161)
Brooke Way WD23: Bush 1B 10
Brookfield N6 ....3E 48
Brookfield Av. E17 ....4E 34
NW7...............6J 13
SM1: Sutt 4C 150
W5................4D 62
Brookfield Cl. NW7 ....6J 13
Brookfield Ct. UB6: G'frd 3G 61
Brookfield Cres. HA3: Harr ...5E 26
NW7...............6J 13
Brookfield Gdns.
KT10: Esh 6A 146
Brookfield Pk. NW5 ....3F 49
Brookfield Path
IG8: Wfd G..........6B 20
Brookfield Rd. E9 ....6A 52
N9 ....3B 18
W4................2K 81
Brookfields EN3: Enf 4E 8
Brookfields Av.
CR4: Mitc..........5C 138
Brook Gdns. E4 ....4J 19
KT2: King T 1J 135
SW13 ....3B 100
Brook Ga. W1 .....7D 66 (3F 165)
BROOK GREEN 4F 83
Brook Grn. W6 ....3F 83
Brook Grn. Flats *W14 ....3F 83*
(off Dunsany Rd.)

Brookhill Cl.—Brunswick Quay

Brookhill Cl. EN4: Barn . . . 5H **5**
SE18 . . . 5F **91**
Brookhill Rd. EN4: Barn . . . 5H **5**
SE18 . . . 6F **91**
Brook Ho's. *NW1* . . . *2G* ***67***
(off Cranleigh St.)
Brook Ho. *W6* . . . *4E* ***82***
(off Shepherd's Bush Rd.)
Brookhouse Gdns. E4 . . . 4B **20**
Brook Ind. Est.
UB4: Hayes . . . 1B **78**
Brooking Cl. RM8: Dag . . . 3C **56**
Brooking Rd. E7 . . . 5J **53**
Brookland Cl. NW11 . . . 4J **29**
Brookland Gth. NW11 . . . 4J **29**
Brookland Hill NW11 . . . 4K **29**
Brookland Ri. NW11 . . . 4J **29**
Brooklands App.
RM1: Rom . . . 4K **39**
Brooklands Av.
DA15: Sidc . . . 2H **127**
SW19 . . . 2K **119**
Brooklands Cl. RM7: Rom . . . 4K **39**
TW16: Sun T . . . 1G **131**
Brooklands Ct. CR4: Mitc . . . 2B **138**
KT1: King T . . . *4D* ***134***
(off Surbiton Rd.)
N21 . . . 5J **7**
NW6 . . . 7H **47**
Brooklands Dr. UB6: G'frd . . . 1C **62**
Brooklands La. RM7: Rom . . . 4K **39**
(not continuous)
Brooklands Pk. SE3 . . . 3J **107**
Brooklands Pas. SW8 . . . 1H **103**
Brooklands Rd.
KT7: T Ditt . . . 1A **146**
RM7: Rom . . . 4K **39**
Brooklands, The TW7: Isle . . . 1H **97**
Brook La. BR1: Brom . . . 6J **125**
(not continuous)
DA5: Bexl, Bex . . . 6D **110**
SE3 . . . 2K **107**
Brook La. Bus. Cen.
TW8: Bford . . . 5D **80**
Brook La. Nth. TW8: Bford . . . 5D **80**
(not continuous)
Brooklea Cl. NW9 . . . 1A **28**
Brook Lodge *RM7: Rom* . . . *4K* ***39***
(off Medora Rd.)
Brooklyn SE20 . . . 7G **123**
Brooklyn Av. SE25 . . . 4H **141**
Brooklyn Cl. SM5: Cars . . . 2C **150**
Brooklyn Gro. SE25 . . . 4H **141**
Brooklyn Rd. BR2: Short . . . 5B **144**
SE25 . . . 4H **141**
Brookmarsh Ind. Est. SE8 . . . 7D **88**
SE10 . . . 7D **88**
Brook Mead KT19: Eps . . . 6A **148**
Brookmead Av.
BR1: Brom . . . 5D **144**
Brookmead Ind. Est.
CR0: Croy . . . 6G **139**
Brook Mdw. N12 . . . 3E **14**
Brook Mdw. Cl.
IG8: Wfd G . . . 6B **20**
Brookmead Rd.
CR0: Croy . . . 6G **139**
Brook M. WC2 . . . 6H **67** (1D **166**)
Brook M. Nth.
W2 . . . 7A **66** (2A **164**)
Brookmill Rd. SE8 . . . 1C **106**
Brook Pde. IG7: Chig . . . 3K **21**
Brook Pk. Cl. N21 . . . 5G **7**
Brook Pl. EN5: Barn . . . 5D **4**
Brook Ri. IG7: Chig . . . 3K **21**
Brook Rd. CR7: Thor H . . . 4C **140**
IG2: Ilf . . . 6J **37**
IG9: Buck H, Wfd G . . . 2D **20**
KT6: Surb . . . 2E **146**
N2 . . . 7H **15**
N8 . . . 4J **31**
N22 . . . 3K **31**
Brook Rd. NW2 . . . 2B **46**
TW1: Twick . . . 6A **98**
Brook Rd. Sth.
TW8: Bford . . . 6D **80**
Brooks Av. E6 . . . 4D **72**
Brooksbank St. E9 . . . 6J **51**
Brooksby M. N1 . . . 7A **50**
Brooksby St. N1 . . . 7A **50**
Brooksby's Wlk. E9 . . . 5K **51**
Brooks Cl. SE9 . . . 2E **126**
Brooks Ct. SW8 . . . 7G **85**
Brookscroft *E17* . . . *3D* ***34***
(off Forest Rd.)
Brookscroft Rd. E17 . . . 1D **34**
(not continuous)
Brookshill HA3: Harr . . . 5C **10**
Brookshill Av. HA3: Harr . . . 5C **10**
Brookshill Dr. HA3: Harr . . . 5C **10**
Brookside BR6: Orp . . . 7K **145**
EN4: Barn . . . 6H **5**
N21 . . . 6E **6**
SM5: Cars . . . 5E **150**
UB10: Uxb . . . 7B **40**
Brookside Cl. EN5: Barn . . . 6B **4**
HA2: Harr . . . 4C **42**
HA3: Harr . . . 5D **26**
TW13: Felt . . . 3J **113**
Brookside Cres.
KT4: Wor Pk . . . 1C **148**
Brookside Rd. N9 . . . 4C **18**
(not continuous)
N19 . . . 2G **49**
NW11 . . . 6G **29**
UB4: Hayes . . . 7A **60**
Brookside Sth. EN4: Barn . . . 7K **5**
Brookside Wlk. N12 . . . 6D **14**
NW11 . . . 4G **29**
Brookside Way
CR0: Croy . . . 6K **141**
Brooks La. W4 . . . 6G **81**
Brooks Lodge *N1* . . . *2E* ***68***
(off Hoxton St.)
Brooks M. W1 . . . 7F **67** (2J **165**)
Brook Sq. SE18 . . . 1C **108**
Brooks Rd. E13 . . . 1J **71**
W4 . . . 5G **81**
Brook St. DA8: Erith . . . 5H **93**
DA17: Belv, Erith . . . 5H **93**
KT1: King T . . . 2E **134**
N17 . . . 2F **33**
W1 . . . 7F **67** (2J **165**)
W2 . . . 7B **66** (2B **164**)
Brooksville Av. NW6 . . . 1G **65**
Brooks Wlk. N3 . . . 3G **29**
Brook Va. DA8: Erith . . . 1H **111**
Brookview Ct. EN1: Enf . . . 5K **7**
Brookview Rd. SW16 . . . 5G **121**
Brookville Rd. SW6 . . . 7H **83**
Brook Wlk. HA8: Edg . . . 6E **12**
N2 . . . 1B **30**
Brook Way IG7: Chig . . . 3K **21**
Brookway SE3 . . . 3J **107**
Brookwood Av. SW13 . . . 2B **100**
Brookwood Cl.
BR2: Short . . . 4H **143**
Brookwood Ho. *SE1* . . . *7B* ***168***
(off Webber St.)
Brookwood Rd. SW18 . . . 1H **119**
TW3: Houn . . . 2F **97**
Broom Cl. BR2: Short . . . 6C **144**
TW11: Tedd . . . 7D **116**
Broomcroft Av. UB5: N'olt . . . 3A **60**
Broome Rd.
TW12: Hamp . . . 7D **114**
Broome Way SE5 . . . 7D **86**
Broomfield E17 . . . 7B **34**
NW1 . . . *7E* ***48***
(off Ferdinand St.)
TW16: Sun T . . . 1J **131**
Broomfield Av. N13 . . . 5E **16**
Broomfield Ct. *SE16* . . . *3G* ***87***
(off Ben Smith Way)
Broomfield Ho. *HA7: Stan* . . . *3F* ***11***
(off Stanmore Hill)
SE17 . . . *4E* ***86***
(off Massinger St.)
Broomfield La. N13 . . . 4D **16**
Broomfield Pl. W13 . . . 1B **80**
Broomfield Rd.
BR3: Beck . . . 3A **142**
DA6: Bex . . . 5G **111**
KT5: Surb . . . 1F **147**
N13 . . . 5D **16**
RM6: Chad H . . . 7D **38**
TW9: Rich . . . 1F **99**
TW11: Tedd . . . 6C **116**
W13 . . . 1B **80**
Broomfield St. E14 . . . 5C **70**
Broom Gdns. CR0: Croy . . . 3C **154**
Broomgrove Gdns.
HA8: Edg . . . 1G **27**
Broomgrove Rd. SW9 . . . 2K **103**
Broomhall Rd.
CR2: S Croy . . . 7D **152**
BROOM HILL . . . **7K 145**
Broomhill Ct. IG8: Wfd G . . . 6D **20**
Broom Hill Ri. DA6: Bex . . . 5G **111**
Broomhill Rd. BR6: Orp . . . 7K **145**
IG3: Ilf . . . 2A **56**
IG8: Wfd G . . . 6D **20**
(not continuous)
SW18 . . . 5J **101**
Broomhill Wlk.
IG8: Wfd G . . . 6C **20**
Broomhouse La. SW6 . . . 2J **101**
(not continuous)
Broomhouse Rd. SW6 . . . 2J **101**
Broomleigh *BR1: Brom* . . . *1J* ***143***
(off Tweedy Rd.)
Broomloan La. SM1: Sutt . . . 2J **149**
Broom Lock TW11: Tedd . . . 6C **116**
Broom Mead DA6: Bex . . . 6G **111**
Broom Pk. TW11: Tedd . . . 7D **116**
Broom Rd. CR0: Croy . . . 3C **154**
TW11: Tedd . . . 5B **116**
Broomsleigh Bus. Pk.
SE26 . . . 5B **124**
Broomsleigh St. NW6 . . . 5H **47**
Broom Water
TW11: Tedd . . . 6C **116**
Broom Water W.
TW11: Tedd . . . 5C **116**
Broomwood Cl.
CR0: Croy . . . 5K **141**
DA5: Bexl . . . 2K **129**
Broomwood Rd. SW11 . . . 6D **102**
Broseley Gro. SE26 . . . 5A **124**
Broster Gdns. SE25 . . . 3F **141**
Brougham Rd. E8 . . . 1G **69**
W3 . . . 6J **63**
Brougham St. SW11 . . . 2D **102**
Brough Cl. KT2: King T . . . 5D **116**
SW8 . . . 7J **85**
Broughton Av. N3 . . . 3G **29**
TW10: Rich . . . 3B **116**
Broughton Ct. W13 . . . 7B **62**
Broughton Dr. SW9 . . . 4A **104**
Broughton Gdns. N6 . . . 6G **31**
Broughton Rd.
CR7: Thor H . . . 6A **140**
SW6 . . . 2K **101**
W13 . . . 7B **62**
Broughton St. SW8 . . . 2E **102**
Broughton St. Ind. Est.
SW11 . . . 2E **102**
Brouncker Rd. W3 . . . 2J **81**
Browells La. TW13: Felt . . . 2K **113**
(not continuous)
Brown Bear Ct.
TW13: Felt . . . 4B **114**
Brown Cl. SM6: Wall . . . 7J **151**
Browne Ho. *SE8* . . . *7C* ***88***
(off Deptford Chu. St.)
Brownfield Area E14 . . . 6D **70**
Brownfield St. E14 . . . 6D **70**
Browngraves Rd.
UB3: Hayes . . . 7E **76**
Brown Hart Gdns.
W1 . . . 7E **66** (2H **165**)
Brownhill Rd. SE6 . . . 7D **106**
Browning Av. KT4:
Wor Pk . . . 1D **148**
SM1: Sutt . . . 4C **150**
W7 . . . 6K **61**
Browning Cl. DA16: Well . . . 1J **109**
E17 . . . 4E **34**
RM5: Col R . . . 1F **39**
TW12: Hamp . . . 4D **114**
W9 . . . 4A **66** (4A **158**)
Browning Ho. *SE14* . . . *1A* ***106***
(off Loring Rd.)
W12 . . . *6E* ***64***
(off Wood La.)
Browning M. W1 . . . 5F **67** (6H **159**)
Browning Rd. E11 . . . 7H **35**
E12 . . . 5D **54**
EN2: Enf . . . 1J **7**
Browning St. SE17 . . . 5C **86**
Browning Way TW5: Houn . . . 1B **96**
Brownlea Gdns. IG3: Ilf . . . 2A **56**
Brownlow Cl. EN4: Barn . . . 5G **5**
Brownlow Ct. N2 . . . 5A **30**
N11 . . . *6D* ***16***
(off Brownlow Rd.)
Brownlow Ho. *SE16* . . . *2G* ***87***
(off George Row)
Brownlow M.
WC1 . . . 4K **67** (4H **161**)
Brownlow Rd. CR0: Croy . . . 4E **152**
E7 . . . 4J **53**
E8 . . . 1F **69**
N3 . . . 7E **14**
N11 . . . 6D **16**
NW10 . . . 7A **46**
W13 . . . 1A **80**
Brownlow St.
WC1 . . . 5K **67** (6H **161**)
Brownrigg Rd.
TW15: Ashf . . . 4C **112**
Browns Arc. *W1* . . . *3B* ***166***
(off Regent St.)
Brown's Bldgs.
EC3 . . . 6E **68** (1H **169**)
Browns La. NW5 . . . 5F **49**
Brownspring Dr. SE9 . . . 4F **127**
Browns Rd. E17 . . . 3C **34**
KT5: Surb . . . 7F **135**
Brown St. W1 . . . 6D **66** (7E **158**)
Brownswell Rd. N2 . . . 2B **30**
BROWNSWOOD PARK . . . **2B 50**
Brownswood Rd. N4 . . . 3B **50**
Broxash Rd. SW11 . . . 6E **102**
Broxbourne Av. E18 . . . 4K **35**
Broxbourne Rd. BR6: Orp . . . 7K **145**
E7 . . . 3J **53**
Broxholme Ho. *SW6* . . . *1K* ***101***
(off Harwood Rd.)
Broxholm Rd. SW16 . . . 3A **122**
Broxted Rd. SE6 . . . 2B **124**
Broxwood Way NW8 . . . 1C **66**
Bruce Av. TW17: Shep . . . 6E **130**
Bruce Castle . . . ***1E 32***
Bruce Castle Ct. *N17* . . . *1F* ***33***
(off Lordship La.)
Bruce Castle Rd. N17 . . . 1F **33**
Bruce Cl. DA16: Well . . . 1B **110**
W10 . . . 5F **65**
Bruce Ct. DA15: Sidc . . . 4K **127**
Bruce Gdns. N20 . . . 3J **15**
Bruce Gro. N17 . . . 1E **32**
Bruce Hall M. SW17 . . . 4E **120**
Bruce Ho. W10 . . . 5F **65**
Bruce Rd. CR4: Mitc . . . 7E **120**
E3 . . . 3D **70**
EN5: Barn . . . 3B **4**
HA3: Harr . . . 2J **25**
Bruce Rd. NW10 . . . 7K **45**
SE25 . . . 4D **140**
Bruckner St. W10 . . . 3G **65**
Brudenell Rd. SW17 . . . 3D **120**
Bruffs Mdw. UB5: N'olt . . . 6C **42**
Bruges Pl. *NW1* . . . *7G* ***49***
(off Randolph St.)
Brumfield Rd.
KT19: Eps . . . 5J **147**
Brummel Cl. DA7: Bex . . . 3J **111**
Brune Ho. E1 . . . 6J **163**
Brunei Gallery . . . ***5H 67 (5D 160)***
Brunel Cl. SE19 . . . 6F **123**
TW5: Houn . . . 7K **77**
UB5: N'olt . . . 3D **60**
Brunel Est. W2 . . . 5J **65**
Brunel Ho. *E14* . . . *5D* ***88***
(off Ship Yd.)
Brunel Pl. UB1: S'hall . . . 6F **61**
Brunel Rd. E17 . . . 6A **34**
IG8: Wfd G . . . 5J **21**
SE16 . . . 2J **87**
W3 . . . 5A **64**
Brunel Science Pk.
UB8: Uxb . . . 3A **58**
Brunel St. E16 . . . 6H **71**
Brunel University . . . ***7J 79***
St Margaret's Rd. . . . ***4B 98***
Brunel University (Uxbridge)
. . . ***3A 58***
Brunel Wlk. N15 . . . 4E **32**
TW2: Twick . . . 7E **96**
Brune St. E1 . . . 5F **69** (6J **163**)
Brunlees Ho. *SE1* . . . *3C* ***86***
(off Bath Ter.)
Brunner Cl. NW11 . . . 5K **29**
Brunner Ho. SE6 . . . 4E **124**
Brunner Rd. E17 . . . 5A **34**
W5 . . . 4D **62**
Bruno Pl. NW9 . . . 2J **45**
Brunswick Av. N11 . . . 3K **15**
(not continuous)
Brunswick Cen.
WC1 . . . 4J **67** (3E **160**)
Brunswick Cl. DA6: Bex . . . 4D **110**
HA5: Pinn . . . 6C **24**
KT7: T Ditt . . . 1A **146**
TW2: Twick . . . 3H **115**
Brunswick Cl. Est.
EC1 . . . 3B **68** (2A **162**)
Brunswick Ct. *EC1* . . . *2A* ***162***
(off Tompion St.)
EN4: Barn . . . 5G **5**
SE1 . . . 2E **86** (7H **169**)
SM1: Sutt . . . 4K **149**
SW1 . . . *4D* ***172***
(off Regency St.)
Brunswick Cres. N11 . . . 3K **15**
Brunswick Gdns. IG6: Ilf . . . 1G **37**
W5 . . . 4E **62**
W8 . . . 1J **83**
Brunswick Gro. N11 . . . 3K **15**
Brunswick Ho. *E2* . . . *2F* ***69***
(off Thurtle Rd.)
N3 . . . 1H **29**
SE16 . . . *3A* ***88***
(off Brunswick Quay)
Brunswick Ind. Pk. N11 . . . 4A **16**
Brunswick Mans. *WC1* . . . *3F* ***161***
(off Handel St.)
Brunswick M. SW16 . . . 6H **121**
W1 . . . 6D **66** (7F **159**)
BRUNSWICK PARK . . . **3K 15**
Brunswick Pk. SE5 . . . 1E **104**
Brunswick Pk. Gdns.
N11 . . . 2K **15**
Brunswick Pk. Rd. N11 . . . 2K **15**
Brunswick Pl. N1 . . . 3D **68** (2F **163**)
NW1 . . . 4E **66** (4H **159**)
(not continuous)
SE19 . . . 7G **123**
Brunswick Quay SE16 . . . 3K **87**

Brunswick Rd. DA6: Bex ...4D **110**	
E10 ....1E **52**	
E14 ....6E **70**	

Brunswick Rd. DA6: Bex ...4D **110**
E10 ....1E **52**
E14 ....6E **70**
Brunswick Rd. EN3: Enf ...1H **9**
  KT2: King T ...1G **135**
  N15 ....4E **32**
  (not continuous)
  SM1: Sutt ...4K **149**
  W5 ....4D **62**
Brunswick Sq. N17 ......6A **18**
  WC1 ...4J **67** (3F **161**)
Brunswick St. E17 .....5E **34**
Brunswick Vs. SE5 ....1E **104**
Brunswick Way N11 ...4A **16**
Brunton Pl. E14 ....6A **70**
Brushfield St. E1 ..5E **68** (5H **163**)
  EC2 ....5E **68**
Brussels Rd. SW11 ....4B **102**
Bruton Cl. BR7: Chst ...7D **126**
Bruton La. W1 ...7F **67** (3K **165**)
Bruton Pl. W1 ...7F **67** (3K **165**)
Bruton Rd. SM4: Mord 4A **138**
Bruton St. W1 ...7F **67** (3K **165**)
Bruton Way W13 ....5A **62**
Brutus Ct. SE11 .....4B **86**
  (off Kennington La.)
Bryan Av. NW10 ....7D **46**
Bryan Cl. TW16: Sun T ...7J **113**
Bryan Ho. NW10 ....7D **46**
  SE16 ....2B **88**
Bryan Rd. SE16 ....2B **88**
Bryan's All. SW6 ......2K **101**
Bryanston Av.
  TW2: Twick ...1F **115**
Bryanston Cl. UB2: S'hall ...4D **78**
Bryanston Ct. W1 ......7E **158**
  (not continuous)
Bryanstone Ct. SM1: Sutt ...3A **150**
Bryanstone Rd. N8 ....6H **31**
Bryanston Mans. W1 .....5E **158**
  (off York St.)
Bryanston M. E.
  W1 ...5D **66** (6E **158**)
Bryanston M. W.
  W1 ...5D **66** (6E **158**)
Bryanston Pl.
  W1 ...5D **66** (6E **158**)
Bryanston Sq.
  W1 ...6D **66** (6E **158**)
Bryanston St.
  W1 ...6D **66** (1E **164**)
Bryant Cl. EN5: Barn 5C **4**
Bryant Ct. E2 .....2F **69**
  (off Whiston Rd., not continuous)
  W3 ....1K **81**
Bryant St. E15 ....7F **53**
Bryantwood Rd. N7 ....5A **50**
Brycedale Cres. N14 ...4B **16**
Bryce Ho. SE14 .....6K **87**
  (off John Williams Cl.)
Bryce Rd. RM8: Dag ...4C **56**
Brydale Ho. SE16 .....4K **87**
  (off Rotherhithe New Rd.)
Bryden Cl. SE26 ....5A **124**
Brydges Pl. WC2 ...7J **67** (3E **166**)
Brydges Rd. E15 ......5F **53**
Brydon Wlk. N1 ....1J **67**
Bryer Ct. EC2 ....5C **162**
Bryet Rd. N7 ....3J **49**
Bryher Ct. SE11 ......5J **173**
Brymay Cl. E3 ....2C **70**
Brynmaer Rd. SW11 ...1D **102**
Brynmawr Rd. EN1: Enf ...4A **8**
Bryony Cl. UB8: Uxb ...5B **58**
Bryony Rd. W12 ....7C **64**
Bryony Way TW16: Sun T ...6J **113**
Buccleugh Ho. E5 .....7G **33**
Buchanan Cl. N21 .....5E **6**
Buchanan Ct. SE16 .....4K **87**
  (off Worgan St.)
Buchanan Gdns. NW10 ...2D **64**

Buchan Rd. SE15 ......3J **105**
Bucharest Rd. SW18 ...7A **102**
Buckden Cl. N2 ....4D **30**
  SE12 ....6J **107**
Buckfast Ct. W13 .....7A **62**
Buckfast Rd.
  SM4: Mord ...4K **137**
Buckfast St. E2 ....3G **69**
Buck Hill Wlk.
  W2 ...7B **66** (3B **164**)
Buckhold Rd. SW18 ...6J **101**
Buckhurst Av. SM5: Cars ...1C **150**
Buckhurst Ct.
  IG9: Buck H ...2G **21**
  (off Albert Rd.)
  IG9: Buck H 1G **21**
  (Roding La.)
BUCKHURST HILL 2F **21**
Buckhurst Hill Ho.
  IG9: Buck H 2E **20**
Buckhurst Ho. N7 .....5H **49**
Buckhurst St. E1 .....4H **69**
Buckhurst Way
  IG9: Buck H 4G **21**
Buckingham Arc. WC2 ...3E **166**
Buckingham Av.
  CR7: Thor H ...1A **140**
  DA16: Well ...4J **109**
  KT8: W Mole ...2F **133**
  N20 ....7F **5**
  TW14: Felt ...6K **95**
  UB6: G'frd ...1A **62**
Buckingham Chambers
  SW1 .....3B **172**
  (off Greencoat Pl.)
Buckingham Cl. BR5: Orp ...7J **145**
  EN1: Enf 2K **7**
  TW12: Hamp ...5D **114**
  W5 ....5C **62**
Buckingham Ct. NW4 ...3C **28**
  UB5: N'olt ...2C **60**
  W7 ....4K **61**
  (off Copley Cl.)
Buckingham Dr.
  BR7: Chst ...4G **127**
Buckingham Gdns.
  CR7: Thor H ...2A **140**
  HA8: Edg ...7K **11**
  KT8: W Mole ...2F **133**
Buckingham Ga.
  SW1 ...3G **85** (1A **172**)
Buckingham Gro.
  UB10: Uxb ...2C **58**
Buckingham La. SE23 ...7A **106**
Buckingham Mans. NW6 ...5K **47**
  (off W. End La.)
Buckingham M. N1 .....6E **50**
  NW10 ....2B **64**
  SW1 ....1A **172**
Buckingham Palace
  ....2F **85** (7K **165**)
Buckingham Pal. Rd.
  SW1 ...4F **85** (4J **171**)
Buckingham Pde.
  HA7: Stan ...5H **11**
Buckingham Pl.
  SW1 ...3G **85** (1A **172**)
Buckingham Rd.
  CR4: Mitc ...4J **139**
  E10 ....3D **52**
  E11 ....5A **36**
  E15 ....5H **53**
  E18 ....1H **35**
  HA1: Harr ...5H **25**
  HA8: Edg ...7A **12**
  IG1: Ilf ...2H **55**
  KT1: King T ...4F **135**
  N1 ....6E **50**
  N22 ....1J **31**
  NW10 ....2B **64**
  TW10: Rich ...2D **116**
  TW12: Hamp ...4D **114**

Buckingham St.
  WC2 ...7J **67** (4F **167**)
Buckingham Way
  SM6: Wall ...7G **151**
Buckland Ct. N1 .....2E **68**
  (off St John's Est.)
  UB10: Uxb 2E **40**
Buckland Cres. NW3 ...7B **48**
Buckland Ri. HA5: Pinn ...1A **24**
Buckland Rd. E10 ....2E **52**
  KT9: Chess ...5F **147**
Bucklands Rd.
  TW11: Tedd ...6C **116**
Buckland St. N1 .....2D **68**
Buckland's Wharf
  KT1: King T ...2D **134**
Buckland Wlk.
  SM4: Mord ...4A **138**
  W3 ....2J **81**
Buckland Way
  KT4: Wor Pk ...1E **148**
Buck La. NW9 ....5K **27**
Bucklebury NW1 .....3A **160**
  (off Stanhope St.)
Buckleigh Av. SW20 ...3G **137**
Buckleigh Rd. SW16 ...6H **121**
Buckleigh Way SE19 ...7F **123**
Buckler Gdns. SE9 ...3D **126**
Bucklers All. SW6 ....6H **83**
  (not continuous)
Bucklersbury EC2 ...1E **168**
Bucklersbury Pas. EC2 ...6D **68**
Buckler's Way SM5: Cars ...3D **150**
Buckles Ct. DA17: Belv ...4F **69**
Buckle St. E1 ...6F **69** (7K **163**)
Buckley Cl. SE23 ....7H **105**
Buckley Ct. NW6 ....7H **47**
Buckmaster Cl. SW9 ...3A **104**
  (off Stockwell Pk. Rd.)
Buckmaster Ho. N7 ...4K **49**
Buckmaster Rd. SW11 ...4C **102**
Bucknall St. WC1 ....6J **67**
  WC2 ...6J **67** (7D **160**)
Bucknall Way BR3: Beck ...4D **142**
Bucknell Cl. SW2 ...4K **103**
Buckner Rd. SW2 ...4K **103**
Bucknill Ho. SW1 .....5J **171**
  (off Ebury Bri. Rd.)
Buckrell Rd. E4 ....2A **20**
Buckridge Ho. EC1 .....5J **161**
  (off Portpool La.)
Buckstone Cl. SE23 ...6J **105**
Buckstone Rd. N18 ....5B **18**
Buck St. NW1 ....7F **49**
Buckters Rents SE16 ...1A **88**
Buckthorne Rd. SE4 ...5A **106**
Buckthorn Ho. DA15: Sidc ...3K **127**
  (off Longlands Rd.)
Buck Wlk. E17 ......4F **35**
Buckwheat Ct.
  DA18: Erith ...3D **92**
Budd Cl. N12 ....4E **14**
Buddings Circ.
  HA9: Wemb ...3J **45**
Budd's All. TW1: Twick ...5C **98**
Bude Cl. E17 ....5B **34**
Budge La. CR4: Mitc ...7D **138**
Budge Row EC4 ...7D **68** (2E **168**)
Budge's Wlk. W2 ....1A **84**
  (off Broad Wlk., The)
Budleigh Cres.
  DA16: Well ...1C **110**
Budleigh Ho. SE15 .....7G **87**
  (off Bird in Bush Rd.)
Budoch Cl. IG3: Ilf ...2A **56**
Budoch Dr. IG3: Ilf ...2A **56**
Buer Rd. SW6 ....2G **101**
Bugsby's Way SE7 ....4H **89**
  SE10 ....4H **89**
Bugsby's Way Retail Est.
  SE7 ....4J **89**

Bulbarrow NW8 ......1K **65**
  (off Abbey Rd.)
Bulganak Rd.
  CR7: Thor H ...4C **140**
Bulinga St. SW1 ....4E **172**
Bullace Row SE5 ...1D **104**
Bull All. DA16: Well ...3B **110**
Bullard's Pl. E2 .....3K **69**
Bullbanks Rd. DA17: Belv ...4J **93**
Bulleid Way
  SW1 ...4F **85** (4K **171**)
Bullen Ho. E1 ....4H **69**
  (off Collingwood St.)
Bullen St. SW11 ....2C **102**
Buller Cl. SE15 ....7G **87**
Buller Ct. SE15 .....7G **87**
Buller Rd. CR7: Thor H ...2D **140**
  IG11: Bark ...7J **55**
  N17 ....2G **33**
  N22 ....2A **32**
  NW10 ....3F **65**
Bullers Cl. DA14: Sidc ...5E **128**
Bullers Wood Dr.
  BR7: Chst ...7D **126**
Bullescroft Rd. HA8: Edg ...3B **12**
Bullingham Mans. W8 .....2J **83**
  (off Pitt St.)
Bull Inn Ct. WC2 .....3E **166**
Bullivant St. E14 .....7E **70**
Bull La. BR7: Chst ...7H **127**
  N18 ....5K **17**
  RM10: Dag ...3H **57**
Bull Rd. E15 ....2H **71**
Bullrush Cl. CR0: Croy ...6E **140**
  SM5: Cars ...2C **150**
Bull's All. SW14 ....2K **99**
Bull's Bri. Cen.
  UB3: Hayes ...3K **77**
Bull's Bri. Ind. Est.
  UB2: S'hall ...4A **78**
Bullsbridge Rd.
  UB2: S'hall ...4A **78**
Bullsbrook Rd.
  UB4: Hayes ...1A **78**
Bulls Gdns. SW3 ...4C **84** (3D **170**)
  (not continuous)
Bulls Head Pas. EC3 ...1G **169**
Bull Wharf La.
  EC4 ...7C **68** (2D **168**)
Bull Yd. SE15 ....1G **105**
Bulmer Gdns. HA3: Harr ...7D **26**
Bulmer M. W11 ....7J **65**
Bulmer Pl. W11 ....1J **83**
Bulow Est. SW6 ....1K **101**
  (off Pearscroft Rd.)
Bulstrode Av. TW3: Houn ...2D **96**
Bulstrode Gdns.
  TW3: Houn ...3E **96**
Bulstrode Pl. W1 ...5E **66** (6H **159**)
Bulstrode Rd. TW3: Houn ...3E **96**
Bulstrode St. W1 ...6E **66** (7H **159**)
Bulwer Ct. E11 ....1F **53**
Bulwer Ct. Rd. E11 ...1F **53**
Bulwer Gdns. EN5: Barn ...4F **5**
Bulwer Rd. E11 ....7F **35**
  EN5: Barn ...4E **4**
  N18 ....4K **17**
Bulwer St. W12 .....1E **82**
Bunbury Ho. SE15 .....7G **87**
  (off Fenham Rd.)
Bunce's La. IG8: Wfd G ...7C **20**
Bungalow Rd. SE25 ...4E **140**
Bungalows, The E10 ...6E **34**
  IG6: Ilf ...1J **37**
  SM6: Wall ...5F **151**
  SW16 ....7F **121**
Bunhill Row EC1 ...4D **68** (3E **162**)
Bunhouse Pl.
  SW1 ...5E **84** (5H **171**)
Bunkers Hill DA14: Sidc ...3F **129**
  DA17: Belv ...4G **93**
  NW11 ....7A **30**

Bunning Way N7 .....7J **49**
Bunns La. NW7 ....6F **13**
  (not continuous)
Bunsen Ho. E3 ....2A **70**
  (off Grove Rd.)
Bunsen St. E3 ....2A **70**
Buntingbridge Rd. IG2: Ilf ...5H **37**
Bunting Cl. CR4: Mitc ...5D **138**
  N9 ....1E **18**
Bunting Ct. NW9 .....2A **28**
Bunton St. SE18 .....3E **90**
Bunyan Ct. EC2 .....5C **162**
Bunyan Rd. E17 .....3A **34**
Buonaparte M.
  SW1 ...5H **85** (5C **172**)
Burbage Cl. SE1 ....3D **86**
  UB3: Hayes ...6F **59**
Burbage Ho. N1 ......1D **68**
  (off Poole St.)
  SE14 ....6K **87**
  (off Samuel Cl.)
Burbage Rd. SE21 ...6C **104**
  SE24 ....6C **104**
Burberry Cl. KT3: N Mald ...2A **136**
Burbidge Rd.
  TW17: Shep ...4C **130**
Burbridge Way N17 ...2G **33**
Burcham St. E14 ....6D **70**
Burcharbro Rd. SE2 ...6D **92**
Burchell Cl. WD23: Bush ...1B **10**
Burchell Ho. SE11 .....5H **173**
  (off Jonathan St.)
Burchell Rd. E10 ....1D **52**
  SE15 ....1H **105**
Burchetts Way
  TW17: Shep ...6D **130**
Burchett Way
  RM6: Chad H ...6F **39**
Burchwall Cl. RM5: Col R ...1J **39**
Burcote Rd. SW18 ....7B **102**
Burden Cl. TW8: Bford ...5C **80**
Burden Ho. SW8 .....7J **85**
  (off Thorncroft St.)
Burdenshott Av.
  TW10: Rich ...4H **99**
Burden Way E11 ....2K **53**
Burder Cl. N1 ....6E **50**
Burder Rd. N1 ......6E **50**
Burdett Av. SW20 ....1C **136**
Burdett Cl. DA14: Sidc ...5E **128**
  W7 ....1K **79**
Burdett M. NW3 ....6B **48**
  W2 ....6K **65**
Burdett Rd. CR0: Croy ...6D **140**
  E3 ....4A **70**
  TW9: Rich ...2F **99**
Burdetts Rd. RM9: Dag ...1F **75**
Burdock Cl. CR0: Croy ...1K **153**
Burdock Rd. N17 ....3G **33**
Burdon La. SM2: Sutt ...7G **149**
Burdon Pk. SM2: Sutt ...7H **149**
Bure Ct. EN5: Barn 5E **4**
Burfield Cl. SW17 ...4B **120**
Burford Cl. IG6: Ilf ...4G **37**
  RM8: Dag ...3C **56**
  UB10: Uxb ...4A **40**
Burford Gdns. N13 ...3E **16**
Burford Ho. TW8: Bford ...5D **80**
Burford Rd. BR1: Brom ...4C **144**
  E6 ....3C **72**
  E15 ....1F **71**
  KT4: Wor Pk ...7B **136**
  SE6 ....2B **124**
  SM1: Sutt ...2J **149**
  TW8: Bford ...5E **80**
  SW16 ....7F **121**
Burford Wlk. SW6 ....7A **84**
Burford Way CR0: Croy ...6E **154**
Burge Rd. E7 ....4B **54**
Burges Gro. SW13 ...7D **82**
Burges Rd. E6 ......7C **54**
Burgess Av. NW9 ....6K **27**
Burgess Cl. TW13: Felt ...4C **114**

Burgess Ct. E6 7E 54
UB1: S'hall 6F 61
(off Fleming Rd.)
Burgess Hill NW2 4J 47
Burgess Ind. Pk. SE5 7D 86
Burgess M. SW19 6K 119
Burgess Pk. 6E 86
Burgess Rd. E6 7E 54
E15 4G 53
SM1: Sutt 4K 149
Burgess St. E14 5C 70
Burge St. SE1 3D 86
Burgh House 4B 48
Burghill Rd. SE26 4A 124
Burghley Av.
KT3: N Mald 1K 135
Burghley Hall Cl.
SW19 1G 119
Burghley Pl. CR4: Mitc 5D 138
Burghley Rd. E11 1G 53
N8 3A 32
NW5 4F 49
SW19 4F 119
Burghley Twr. W3 7B 64
Burgh St. N1 2B 68
Burgon St. EC4 6B 68 (1B 168)
Burgos Cl. CR0: Croy 6A 152
Burgos Gro. SE10 1D 106
Burgoyne Rd. N4 6B 32
SE25 4F 141
SW9 3K 103
TW16: Sun T 6H 113
Burham Cl. SE20 7J 123
Burhill Gro. HA5: Pinn 2C 24
Burke Cl. SW15 4A 100
Burke Lodge E13 3K 71
Burke St. E16 5H 71
(not continuous)
Burket Cl. UB2: S'hall 4C 78
Burland Rd. SW11 5D 102
Burleigh Av. DA15: Sidc 5K 109
SM6: Wall 3E 150
Burleigh Gdns. N14 1B 16
TW15: Ashf 5E 112
Burleigh Ho. SW3 7B 170
W10 5G 65
(off St Charles Sq.)
Burleigh Pde. N14 1C 16
Burleigh Pl. SW15 5F 101
Burleigh Rd. EN1: Enf 4K 7
SM3: Sutt 1G 149
UB10: Uxb 1D 58
Burleigh St.
WC2 7K 67 (2G 167)
Burleigh Wlk. SE6 1E 124
Burleigh Way EN2: Enf 3J 7
Burley Cl. E4 5H 19
SW16 2H 139
Burley Ho. E1 6K 69
(off Chudleigh St.)
Burley Rd. E16 6A 72
Burlington Arc.
W1 7G 67 (3A 166)
Burlington Av.
RM7: Rom 6H 39
TW9: Rich 1G 99
Burlington Cl. E6 6C 72
HA5: Pinn 3K 23
TW14: Felt 7F 95
W9 4J 65
Burlington Gdns.
RM6: Chad H 7E 38
SW6 2G 101
W1 7G 67 (3A 166)
W3 1J 81
W4 5J 81
Burlington La. W4 7J 81
Burlington M. SW15 5H 101
W3 1J 81
Burlington Pl. IG8: Wfd G 3E 20
SW6 2G 101
Burlington Ri. EN4: Barn 1H 15
Burlington Rd.
CR7: Thor H 2C 140
EN2: Enf 1J 7
KT3: N Mald 4B 136
N10 3E 30
N17 1G 33
SW6 2G 101
TW7: Isle 1H 97
W4 5J 81
Burma M. N16 4D 50
Burma Rd. N16 4D 50
Burmarsh Ct. SE20 1J 141
Burma Ter. SE19 5E 122
Burmester Rd. SW17 3A 120
Burnaby Cres. W4 6J 81
Burnaby Gdns. W4 6H 81
Burnaby St. SW10 7A 84
Burnand Ho. W14 3F 83
(off Redan St.)
Burnard Pl. N7 5K 49
Burnaston Ho. E5 3G 51
Burnbrae Cl. N12 6E 14
Burnbury Rd. SW12 1G 121
Burncroft Av. EN3: Enf 2D 8
Burndell Way UB4: Hayes 5B 60
Burne Jones Ho. W14 4G 83
Burnell Av. DA16: Well 2A 110
TW10: Rich 5C 116
Burnell Gdns. HA7: Stan 2D 26
Burnell Rd. SM1: Sutt 4K 149
Burnell Wlk. SE1 5F 87
(off Abingdon Cl.)
Burnels Av. E6 3E 72
Burness Cl. N7 6K 49
Burne St. NW1 5C 66 (5C 158)
Burnett Cl. E9 5J 51
Burnett Ho. SE13 2E 106
(off Lewisham Hill)
Burnett Rd. IG6: Ilf 7K 21
Burney Av. KT5: Surb 5F 135
Burney St. SE10 7E 88
Burnfoot Av. SW6 1G 101
Burnham NW3 7C 48
Burnham Av. UB10: Uxb 4E 40
Burnham Cl. EN1: Enf 1K 7
HA3: Harr 4A 26
NW7 7H 13
SE1 4F 87
Burnham Ct. W2 7K 65
(off Moscow Rd.)
Burnham Cres. E11 4A 36
Burnham Dr.
KT4: Wor Pk 2F 149
Burnham Est. E2 3J 69
(off Burnham St.)
Burnham Gdns.
CR0: Croy 7F 141
TW4: Houn 1K 95
UB3: Hayes 3F 77
Burnham Rd.
DA14: Sidc 2E 128
E4 5G 19
RM7: Rom 3K 39
RM9: Dag 7B 56
SM4: Mord 4K 137
Burnham St. E2 3J 69
KT2: King T 1G 135
Burnham Way SE26 5B 124
W13 4B 80
Burnhill Rd. BR3: Beck 2C 142
Burnley Rd. NW10 5B 46
SW9 2K 103
Burnsall St.
SW3 5C 84 (6D 170)
Burns Av. DA15: Sidc 6B 110
RM6: Chad H 7C 38
TW14: Felt 6J 95
UB1: S'hall 7E 60
Burns Cl. DA16: Well 1K 109
E17 4E 34
SW19 6B 120
UB4: Hayes 5H 59
Burns Ho. E2 3J 69
(off Cornwall Av.)
SE17 5B 86
(off Doddington Gro.)
Burnside Av. E4 6G 19
Burnside Cl. EN5: Barn 3D 4
SE16 1K 87
TW1: Twick 6A 98
Burnside Ct. SM6: Wall 3E 150
Burnside Cres.
HA0: Wemb 1D 62
Burnside Rd. RM8: Dag 2C 56
Burns Rd. HA0: Wemb 2E 62
NW10 1B 64
SW11 2D 102
W13 2B 80
Burns Way TW5: Houn 2B 96
Burnt Ash Hgts.
BR1: Brom 5K 125
Burnt Ash Hill SE12 6H 107
(not continuous)
Burnt Ash La. BR1: Brom 7J 125
Burnt Ash Rd. SE12 5H 107
Burnthwaite Rd. SW6 7H 83
BURNT OAK 2J 27
Burnt Oak B'way.
HA8: Edg 7C 12
Burnt Oak Flds. HA8: Edg 1J 27
Burnt Oak La. DA15: Sidc 6A 110
Burntwood Cl. SW18 1C 120
Burntwood Grange Rd.
SW18 1B 120
Burntwood La. SW17 3A 120
Burntwood Vw. SE19 5F 123
Buross St. E1 6H 69
Burpham Cl. UB4: Hayes 5B 60
Burrage Ct. SE16 4K 87
(off Worgan St.)
Burrage Gro. SE18 4G 91
Burrage Pl. SE18 5F 91
Burrage Rd. SE18 6G 91
Burrard Rd. E16 6K 71
NW6 5J 47
Burr Cl. DA7: Bex 3F 111
E1 1G 87 (4K 169)
Burrell Cl. CR0: Croy 6A 142
HA8: Edg 2C 12
Burrell Row
BR3: Beck 2C 142
Burrell St. SE1 1B 86 (4A 168)
Burrells Wharf Sq. E14 5C 88
Burrell Towers E10 7C 34
Burrhill Ct. SE16 3K 87
(off Worgan St.)
Burritt Rd. KT1: King T 2G 135
Burroughs Cotts. E14 5A 70
(off Halley St.)
Burroughs Gdns. NW4 4D 28
Burroughs Pde. NW4 4D 28
Burroughs, The NW4 4D 28
Burrow Ho. SW9 2A 104
(off Stockwell Pk. Rd.)
Burrow Rd. SE22 4E 104
Burrows M.
SE1 2B 86 (6A 168)
Burrows Rd. NW10 3E 64
Burrow Wlk. SE21 7C 104
Burr Rd. SW18 1J 119
Bursar St. SE1 1E 86 (5G 169)
Bursdon Cl. DA15: Sidc 2K 127
Bursland Rd. EN3: Enf 4E 8
Burslem St. E1 6G 69
Burstock Rd. SW15 4G 101
Burston Rd. SW15 5F 101
Burstow Rd. SW20 1G 137
Burtenshaw Rd.
KT7: T Ditt 7A 134
Burtley Cl. N4 1C 50
Burton Bank N1 7D 50
(off Yeate St.)
Burton Cl. CR7: Thor H 3D 140
KT9: Chess 7D 146
Burton Ct. SE20 2J 141
SW3 5F 171
(off Franklin's Row, not cont.)
Burton Gdns. TW5: Houn 1D 96
Burton Gro. SE17 5D 86
Burtonhole Cl. NW7 4A 14
Burtonhole La. NW7 5K 13
Burton Ho. SE16 2H 87
(off Cherry Garden St.)
Burton La. SW9 2A 104
(not continuous)
Burton M. SW1 4E 84 (4H 171)
Burton Pl. WC1 3H 67 (2D 160)
Burton Rd. E18 3K 35
KT2: King T 7E 116
NW6 7H 47
SW9 2B 104
(Akerman Rd.)
SW9 2A 104
(Evesham Wlk.)
Burton's Rd.
TW12: Hamp 4F 115
Burton St. WC1 3H 67 (2D 160)
Burtonwood Ho. N4 7D 32
Burt Rd. E16 1A 90
Burtt Ho. N1 1G 163
(off Aske St.)
Burtwell La. SE27 4D 122
Burwash Ho. SE1 7F 169
(off Kipling Est.)
Burwash Rd. SE18 5H 91
Burwell KT1: King T 2G 135
(off Excelsior Rd.)
Burwell Av. UB6: G'frd 6J 43
Burwell Cl. E1 6H 69
Burwell Rd. E10 1A 52
Burwell Rd. Ind. Est.
E10 1A 52
Burwell Wlk. E3 4C 70
Burwood Av. BR2: Short 2K 155
HA5: Pinn 5K 23
Burwood Cl. KT6: Surb 1G 147
Burwood Ho. SW9 4B 104
Burwood Pl. EN4: Barn 1F 5
W2 6C 66 (7D 158)
Bury Av. HA4: Ruis 6E 22
UB4: Hayes 2G 59
Bury Cl. SE16 1K 87
Bury Ct. EC3 6E 68 (7H 163)
Bury Gro. SM4: Mord 5K 137
Bury Hall Vs. N9 7A 8
Bury Pl. WC1 5J 67 (6E 160)
Bury Rd. E4 1B 20
N22 2A 32
RM10: Dag 5H 57
Buryside Cl. IG2: Ilf 4K 37
Bury Sq. WC1 5J 67
Bury St. EC3 6E 68 (1H 169)
HA4: Ruis 5E 22
N9 7A 8
SW1 1G 85 (4B 166)
Bury St. W. N9 7J 7
Bury Wlk. SW3 4C 84 (4C 170)
Busbridge Ho. E14 5C 70
(off Brabazon St.)
Busby M. NW5 6H 49
Busby Pl. NW5 6H 49
Busch Cl. TW7: Isle 1B 98
Bushbaby Cl. SE1 3E 86
Bushberry Rd. E9 6A 52
Bush Cl. IG2: Ilf 5H 37
Bush Cotts. SW18 5J 101
Bush Ct. N14 1C 16
W12 2F 83
Bushell Cl. SW2 2K 121
Bushell Grn.
WD23: Bush 2C 10
Bushell St. E1 1G 87
Bushell Way BR7: Chst 5E 126
BUSHEY 1C 10
Bushey Av. BR5: Orp 7H 145
E18 3H 35
Bushey Cl. E4 3K 19
UB10: Uxb 2C 40
Bushey Ct. SW20 3D 136
Bushey Down SW12 2F 121
BUSHEY HEATH 1C 10
Bushey Hill Rd. SE5 1E 104
Bushey La. SM1: Sutt 4J 149
BUSHEY MEAD 2F 137
Bushey Rd. CR0: Croy 2C 154
E13 2A 72
N15 6E 32
SM1: Sutt 4J 149
SW20 3D 136
UB3: Hayes 4G 77
UB10: Uxb 2C 40
Bushey Way BR3: Beck 6F 143
Bush Fair Ct. N14 6A 6
Bushfield Cl. HA8: Edg 2C 12
Bushfield Cres. HA8: Edg 2C 12
Bush Gro. HA7: Stan 1D 26
NW9 7J 27
Bushgrove Rd. RM8: Dag 4D 56
Bush Hill N21 7H 7
Bush Hill Pde. N9 7J 7
BUSH HILL PARK 6A 8
Bush Hill Rd. HA3: Harr 6F 27
N21 6J 7
Bush Ind. Est. N19 3G 49
NW10 4K 63
Bush La. EC4 7D 68 (2E 168)
Bushmead Cl. N15 4F 33
Bushmoor Cres. SE18 7F 91
Bushnell Rd. SW17 2F 121
Bush Rd. E8 1H 69
E11 7H 35
IG9: Buck H 4G 21
SE8 4K 87
TW9: Rich 6F 81
TW17: Shep 5B 130
Bushway RM8: Dag 4D 56
Bushwood E11 1H 53
Bushwood Dr. SE1 4F 87
Bushwood Rd.
TW9: Rich 6G 81
Bushy Ct. KT1: King T 1C 134
(off Up. Teddington Rd.)
Bushy Lees DA15: Sidc 6K 109
Bushy Pk. Gdns.
TW11: Tedd 5H 115
Bushy Pk. Rd.
TW11: Tedd 7B 116
(not continuous)
Bushy Rd. TW11: Tedd 6K 115
Butcher Row E1 6K 69
E14 7K 69
Butchers Rd. E16 6J 71
Bute Av. TW10: Rich 2E 116
Bute Ct. SM6: Wall 5G 151
Bute Gdns. SM6: Wall 5G 151
TW10: Rich 1E 116
W6 4F 83
Bute Gdns. W.
SM6: Wall 5G 151
Bute M. NW11 5A 30
Bute Rd. CR0: Croy 1A 152
IG6: Ilf 5F 37
SM6: Wall 4G 151
Bute St. SW7 4B 84 (3A 170)
Bute Wlk. N1 6D 50
Butfield Ho. E9 6J 51
(off Stevens Av.)
Butler Av. HA1: Harr 7H 25
Butler Ct. HA0: Wemb 4A 44
RM8: Dag 2G 57
(off Gosfield Rd.)
Butler Ho. E2 3J 69
(off Bacton St.)
E14 6B 70
(off Burdett St.)
SW9 1B 104
(off Lothian Rd.)
Butler Pl. SW1 1C 172

Butler Rd.—Calne Av.

Butler Rd. HA1: Harr 7G **25**
NW10 . . . . .7B **46**
RM8: Dag 4B **56**
Butlers & Colonial Wharf
SE1 . . . .*6K 169*
(off Shad Thames)
Butlers Dr. E4 . . . . .1K **9**
Butler St. E2 . . . . .3J **69**
UB10: Uxb 4D **58**
Butlers Wharf *SE1* *6K 169*
(off Gainsford St.)
Butley Ct. *E3* *2A 70*
(off Ford St.)
Butterfield Cl. N17 . . . . .6H **17**
SE16 . . . . .2H **87**
TW1: Twick 6K **97**
Butterfields E17 . . . . .5E **34**
Butterfield Sq. E6 . . . . .6D **72**
Butterfly La. SE9 . . . . .6F **109**
Butterfly Wlk. *SE5* *2D 104*
(off Denmark Hill)
Butter Hill
SM5: Cars, Wall 3E **150**
SM6: Wall 3E **150**
Butteridges Cl. RM9: Dag 1F **75**
Buttermere *NW1* *1K 159*
(off Augustus St.)
Buttermere Cl. E15 . . . . .4F **53**
SE1 . . . . .4F **87**
SM4: Mord 6F **137**
TW14: Felt 1H **113**
Buttermere Ct. *NW8* *1B 66*
(off Boundary Rd.)
Buttermere Dr. SW15 . . . . . .5G **101**
Buttermere Wlk. E8 . . . . .6F **51**
Butterwick W6 . . . . .4F **83**
Butterworth Gdns.
IG8: Wfd G 6D **20**
Buttesland St.
N1 . . . . .3D **68** (1F **163**)
Buttfield Cl. RM10: Dag 6H **57**
Buttmarsh Cl. SE18 . . . . .5F **91**
Buttsbury Rd. IG1: Ilf 5G **55**
Butts Cotts. TW13: Felt 3C **114**
Butts Cres. TW13: Felt 3E **114**
Buttsmead HA6: Nwood 1E **22**
Butts Piece UB5: N'olt 2K **59**
Butts Rd. BR1: Brom 5G **125**
Butts, The TW8: Bford 6C **80**
TW16: Sun T 3A **132**
Buxhall Cres. E9 . . . . .6B **52**
Buxted Rd. E8 . . . . .7F **51**
N12 . . . . .5H **15**
SE22 . . . . .4E **104**
Buxton Cl. IG8: Wfd G 6G **21**
N9 . . . . .2D **18**
Buxton Ct. E11 . . . . .7H **35**
N1 . . . . .1D **162**
Buxton Cres. SM3: Sutt 4G **149**
Buxton Dr. E11 . . . . .4G **35**
KT3: N Mald 2K **135**
Buxton Gdns. W3 . . . . .7H **63**
Buxton Ho. E11 . . . . .4G **35**
Buxton Rd. CR7: Thor H 5B **140**
DA8: Erith 7K **93**
E4 . . . . .1A **20**
E6 . . . . .3C **72**
E15 . . . . .5G **53**
E17 . . . . .4A **34**
(not continuous)
IG2: Ilf 6J **37**
N19 . . . . .1H **49**
NW2 . . . . .6D **46**
SW14 . . . . .3A **100**
TW15: Ashf 5A **112**
Buxton St. E1 . . . . . .4F **69** (4K **163**)
Buzzard Creek Ind. Est.
IG11: Bark 5A **74**
Byam St. SW6 . . . . .2A **102**
Byards Ct. *SE16* *4K 87*
(off Worgan St.)
Byards Cft. SW16 . . . . .1H **139**
Byatt Wlk. TW12: Hamp 6C **114**
Bychurch End
TW11: Tedd 5K **115**
Bycroft Rd. UB1: S'hall 4E **60**
Bycroft St. SE20 . . . . .7K **123**
Bycullah Av. EN2: Enf 3G **7**
Bycullah Rd. EN2: Enf 2G **7**
Byegrove Rd. SW19 . . . . . . .6B **120**
Byelands Cl. SE16 . . . . .1K **87**
Bye, The W3 . . . . .6A **64**
Byeways TW2: Twick 3F **115**
Byeways, The
KT5: Surb 5G **135**
Bye Way, The
HA3: Harr 1J **25**
Byeway, The SW14 . . . . .3J **99**
Byfeld Gdns. SW13 . . . . . . .1C **100**
Byfield Cl. SE16 . . . . .2B **88**
Byfield Pas. TW7: Isle 3A **98**
Byfield Rd. TW7: Isle 3A **98**
Byford Cl. E15 . . . . .7G **53**
Byford Ho. EN5: Barn 4A **4**
Bygrove CR0: Croy 6D **154**
Bygrove St. E14 . . . . .6D **70**
(not continuous)
Byland Cl. N21 . . . . .7E **6**
Bylands Cl. SE2 . . . . .3B **92**
Byne Rd. SE26 . . . . .6J **123**
SM5: Cars 2C **150**
Bynes Rd. CR2: S Croy 7D **152**
Byng Pl. WC1 . . . . .4H **67** (4D **160**)
Byng Rd. EN5: Barn 2A **4**
Byng St. E14 . . . . .2C **88**
Bynon Av. DA7: Bex 3F **111**
Byre Rd. N14 . . . . .6A **6**
Byrne Rd. SW12 . . . . .1F **121**
Byron Av. E12 . . . . .6C **54**
E18 . . . . .3H **35**
KT3: N Mald 5C **136**
NW9 . . . . .4H **27**
SM1: Sutt 4B **150**
TW4: Houn 2J **95**
Byron Av. E. SM1: Sutt 4B **150**
Byron Cl. E8 . . . . .1G **69**
KT12: Walt T 7C **132**
SE20 . . . . .3H **141**
SE26 . . . . .4A **124**
SE28 . . . . .1C **92**
SW16 . . . . .6J **121**
TW12: Hamp 4D **114**
Byron Ct. *E11* *4K 35*
(off Makepeace Rd.)
EN2: Enf 2G **7**
HA1: Harr 6J **25**
NW6 . . . .*7A 48*
(off Fairfax Rd.)
SE22 . . . . .1G **123**
W7 . . . .*4A 80*
(off Boston Rd.)
W9 . . . .*4J 65*
(off Lanhill Rd.)
WC1 . . . .*3G 161*
(off Mecklenburgh Sq.)
Byron Dr. DA8: Erith 7H **93**
N2 . . . . .6B **30**
Byron Gdns. SM1: Sutt 4B **150**
Byron Hill Rd.
HA2: Harr 1H **43**
Byron Ho. DA1: Cray 5K **111**
Byron M. NW3 . . . . .5D **48**
W9 . . . . .4J **65**
Byron Pde. UB10: Uxb 4E **58**
Byron Rd. E10 . . . . .1D **52**
E17 . . . . .3C **34**
HA0: Wemb 2C **44**
HA1: Harr 6J **25**
HA3: Harr 2K **25**
NW2 . . . . .2D **46**
NW7 . . . . .5H **13**
W5 . . . . .1F **81**
Byron St. E14 . . . . .6E **70**
Byron Ter. N9 . . . . .6D **8**
Byron Way UB4: Hayes 4H **59**
UB5: N'olt 3C **60**
UB7: W Dray 4B **76**
Bysouth Cl. IG5: Ilf 1F **37**
N15 . . . . .4D **32**
Bythorn St. SW9 . . . . .3K **103**
Byton Rd. SW17 . . . . .6D **120**
Byward Av. TW14: Felt 6A **96**
Byward St. EC3 . . . .7E **68** (3H **169**)
Bywater Ho. SE18 . . . . .3C **90**
Bywater Pl. SE16 . . . . .1A **88**
Bywater St. SW3 . . .5D **84** (5E **170**)
Byway E11 . . . . .5A **36**
Byway, The KT19: Eps 4B **148**
SM2: Sutt 7B **150**
Bywell Pl. W1 . . . . .6A **160**
Bywood Av. CR0: Croy 6J **141**
Byworth Wlk. N19 . . . . .1J **49**

C

Cabbell St. NW1 . . .5C **66** (6C **158**)
Cabinet War Rooms
. . . . .2H 85 (6D 166)
Cabinet Way E4 . . . . .6G **19**
Cable Ho. *WC1* *1J 161*
(off Gt. Percy St.)
Cable Pl. SE10 . . . . .1E **106**
Cables Cl. DA17: Erith 3J **93**
Cable St. E1 . . . . .7G **69**
Cable Trade Pk. SE7 . . . . .4A **90**
Cabot Ct. *SE16* *4K 87*
(off Worgan St.)
Cabot Sq. E14 . . . . .1C **88**
Cabot Way E6 . . . . .1B **72**
Cab Rd. SE1 . . . . .6J **167**
Cabul Rd. SW11 . . . . .2C **102**
Caci Ho. *W14* *4H 83*
(off Kensington Village)
Cactus Cl. SE15 . . . . .2E **104**
Cactus Wlk. W12 . . . . .6B **64**
Cadbury Cl. TW7: Isle 1A **98**
TW16: Sun T 7G **113**
Cadbury Rd.
TW16: Sun T 7G **113**
Cadbury Way SE16 . . . . .3F **87**
(not continuous)
Caddington Cl. EN4: Barn 5H **5**
Caddington Rd. NW2 . . . . . . .3G **47**
Caddis Cl. HA7: Stan 7E **10**
Cadell Cl. E2 . . . . . .2F **69** (1K **163**)
Cade Rd. SE10 . . . . .1F **107**
Cader Rd. SW18 . . . . .6A **102**
Cadet Dr. SE1 . . . . .4F **87**
Cadet Pl. SE10 . . . . .5G **89**
Cadiz Ct. RM10: Dag 7K **57**
Cadiz Rd. RM10: Dag 7J **57**
Cadiz St. SE17 . . . . .5C **86**
Cadley Ter. SE23 . . . . .2J **123**
Cadman Cl. SW9 . . . . .7B **86**
Cadman Ct. *W4* *5H 81*
(off Chaseley Dr.)
Cadmer Cl.
KT3: N Mald 4A **136**
Cadmore Ho. *N1* *7B 50*
(off Sutton Est., The)
Cadmus Cl. SW4 . . . . .3H **103**
Cadmus Ct. *SW9* *1A 104*
(off Southey Rd.)
Cadnam Lodge *E14* *3E 88*
(off Schooner Cl.)
Cadogan Cl. BR3: Beck 1F **143**
E9 . . . . .7B **52**
HA2: Harr 4F **43**
TW11: Tedd 5J **115**
Cadogan Ct. SM2: Sutt 6K **149**
SW3 . . . .*4E 170*
(off Draycott Av.)
Cadogan Gdns. E18 . . . . .3K **35**
N3 . . . . .1K **29**
N21 . . . . .5F **7**
Cadogan Gdns.
SW3 . . . . . . .4D **84** (3F **171**)
Cadogan Ga.
SW1 . . . . . . .4D **84** (3F **171**)
Cadogan Ho. IG8: Ilf 7K **21**
SW3 . . . . .7B **170**
Cadogan La.
SW1 . . . . . . .3E **84** (2G **171**)
Cadogan Mans. *SW3* *4F 171*
(off Cadogan Gdns.)
Cadogan Pl.
SW1 . . . . . . .3D **84** (1F **171**)
Cadogan Rd. KT6: Surb 5D **134**
SE18 . . . . .3G **91**
Cadogan Sq.
SW1 . . . . . . .3D **84** (2E **170**)
Cadogan St.
SW3 . . . . . . .4D **84** (4E **170**)
Cadogan Ter. E9 . . . . .6B **52**
Cadoxton Av. N15 . . . . .6F **33**
Cadwallon Rd. SE9 . . . . .2F **127**
Caedmon Rd. N7 . . . . .4K **49**
Caerleon Cl. DA14: Sidc 5C **128**
Caerleon Ter. SE2 . . . . .4B **92**
Caernafon Ho. HA7: Stan 5F **11**
Caernarvon Cl. CR4: Mitc . . .3J **139**
Caernarvon Dr. IG5: Ilf 1E **36**
Caernarvon Ho. *E16* *7K 71*
(off Audley Dr.)
W2 . . . .*6A 66*
(off Hallfield Est.)
Caesars Wlk. CR4: Mitc 5D **138**
Caesars Way
TW17: Shep 6F **131**
Café Gallery *. 3J 87*
Cahill St. EC1 . . . . .4C **68** (4D **162**)
Cahir St. E14 . . . . .4D **88**
Cain Ct. *W5* *5C 62*
(off Castlebar M.)
Caine Ho. *W3* *2H 81*
(off Hanbury Rd.)
Cain's La. TW14: Felt 5G **95**
Caird St. W10 . . . . .3G **65**
Cairn Av. W5 . . . . .1D **80**
Cairncross M. *N8* *6J 31*
(off Felix Av.)
Cairndale Cl.
BR1: Brom 7H **125**
Cairnfield Av. NW2 . . . . .3A **46**
Cairngorm Cl.
TW11: Tedd 5A **116**
Cairns Av. IG8: Wfd G 6H **21**
Cairns M. SE18 . . . . .1C **108**
Cairns Rd. SW11 . . . . .5C **102**
Cairn Way HA7: Stan 6E **10**
Cairo New Rd. CR0: Croy . . .2B **152**
Cairo Rd. E17 . . . . .4C **34**
Caister Ho. N7 . . . . .6K **49**
Caistor Ho. *E15* *1H 71*
(off Caistor Pk. Rd.)
Caistor M. SW12 . . . . .7F **103**
Caistor Pk. Rd. E15 . . . . .1H **71**
Caistor Rd. SW12 . . . . .7F **103**
Caithness Gdns.
DA15: Sidc 6K **109**
Caithness Ho. *N1* *1K 67*
(off Twyford St.)
Caithness Rd. CR4: Mitc 7F **121**
W14 . . . . .3F **83**
Calabria Rd. N5 . . . . .6B **50**
Calais Ga. SE5 . . . . .1B **104**
Calais St. SE5 . . . . .1B **104**
Calbourne Rd. SW12 . . . . . .7D **102**
Calcott Ct. *W14* *3G 83*
(off Blythe Rd.)
Calcott Wlk. SE9 . . . . .4C **126**
Calcraft Ho. *E2* *2J 69*
(off Bonner Rd.)
Caldbeck Av.
KT4: Wor Pk 2C **148**
Caldecote *KT1: King T* *2G 135*
(off Excelsior Cl.)
Caldecote Gdns.
WD23: Bush 1D **10**
CALDECOTE HILL **1E 10**
Caldecot Rd. SE5 . . . . .2C **104**
Caldecott Way E5 . . . . .3K **51**
Calder Av. UB6: G'frd 2K **61**
Calder Cl. EN1: Enf 3K **7**
Calder Ct. SE16 . . . . .1B **88**
Calder Gdns. HA8: Edg 3G **27**
Calderon Ho. *NW8* *2C 66*
(off Townshend Est.)
Calderon Pl. W10 . . . . .5E **64**
Calderon Rd. E11 . . . . .4E **52**
Calder Rd. SM4: Mord 5A **138**
Caldervale Rd. SW4 . . . . . .5H **103**
Calderwood St. SE18 . . . . . . .4E **90**
(not continuous)
Caldew Ct. NW7 . . . . .7H **13**
Caldew St. SE5 . . . . .7D **86**
Caldicot Grn. NW9 . . . . .6A **28**
Caldwell Ho. *SW13* *7E 82*
(off Trinity Chu. Rd.)
Caldwell St. SW9 . . . . .7K **85**
Caldy Rd. DA17: Belv 3H **93**
Caldy Wlk. N1 . . . . .7C **50**
Caleb St. SE1 . . . . .2C **86** (6C **168**)
Caledonia Ct. *IG11: Bark* *2C 74*
(off Keel Cl.)
Caledonia Ho. *E14* *6A 70*
(off Salmon La.)
Caledonian Cl. IG3: Ilf 1B **56**
Caledonian Rd.
N1 . . . . .2J **67** (1F **161**)
N7 . . . . .4K **49**
Caledonian Wharf E14 . . . . . .4F **89**
Caledonia Rd.
TW19: Staines 1A **112**
Caledonia St. N1 . . .2J **67** (1F **161**)
Caledon Rd. E6 . . . . .1D **72**
SM6: Wall 4E **150**
Cale St. SW3 . . . . . .5C **84** (5C **170**)
Caletock Way SE10 . . . . .5H **89**
Calgarth *NW1* *1B 160*
(off Ampthill Est.)
Calgary Ct. *SE16* *2J 87*
(off Canada Est.)
Caliban Twr. *N1* *2E 68*
(off Arden Est.)
Calico Ho. *EC4* *1D 168*
(off Well Ct.)
Calico Row SW11 . . . . .3A **102**
Calidore Cl. SW2 . . . . .6K **103**
California La.
WD23: Bush 1C **10**
California Pl. *WD23: Bush* . . .*1C 10*
(off High Rd.)
California Rd.
KT3: N Mald 4H **135**
Callaby Ter. N1 . . . . .6D **50**
Callaghan Cl. SE13 . . . . . . .4G **107**
Callahan Cotts. *E1* *5J 69*
(off Lindley St.)
Callander Rd. SE6 . . . . .2D **124**
Callanders, The
WD23: Bush 1D **10**
Callard Av. N13 . . . . .4G **17**
Callcott Ct. NW6 . . . . .7H **47**
Callcott Rd. NW6 . . . . .7H **47**
Callcott St. W8 . . . . .1J **83**
Callendar Rd.
SW7 . . . . . . .3B **84** (1A **170**)
Callenders Cotts.
DA17: Erith 2K **93**
Callingham Cl. E14 . . . . .5B **70**
Callis Farm Cl.
TW19: Staines 6A **94**
Callis Rd. E17 . . . . .6B **34**
Callonfield E17 . . . . .4K **33**
Callow St. SW3 . . . .6B **84** (7A **170**)
Calmington Rd. SE5 . . . . .6E **86**
Calmont Rd. BR1: Brom 6F **125**
Calne Av. IG5: Ilf 1F **37**

Calonne Rd.—Camp Vw.

Calonne Rd. SW19 . . . . .4F 119
Calshot Ho. *N1* *2K 67*
(*off Calshot St.*)
Calshot Rd. TW6: Houn 2C 94
(not continuous)
Calshot St. N1 . . . . .2K 67 (1G 161)
Calshot Way EN2: Enf 3G 7
TW6: Houn 2C 94
(not continuous)
Calstock *NW1* *1G 67*
(*off Royal College St.*)
Calstock Ho. SE11 . . . . .5K 173
Calthorpe Gdns. HA8: Edg . . .5K 11
SM1: Sutt 3A 150
Calthorpe St.
WC1 . . . . . . .4K 67 (3H 161)
Calton Av. SE21 . . . . .6E 104
Calton Rd. EN5: Barn 6F 5
Calverley Cl. BR3: Beck 6D 124
Calverley Cres.
RM10: Dag 2G 57
Calverley Gdns. HA3: Harr . . .7D 26
Calverley Gro. N19 . . . . .1H 49
Calverley Rd. KT17: Eps . . .6C 148
Calvert Av. E2 . . . . .3E 68 (2H 163)
Calvert Cl. DA14: Sidc 6E 128
DA17: Belv 4G 93
Calvert Dr. DA5: Bexl 2K 129
Calvert Ho. *W12* *7D 64*
(*off White City Est.*)
Calverton *SE17* *6E 86*
(*off Albany Rd.*)
Calverton Rd. E6 . . . . .1E 72
Calvert Rd. EN5: Barn 2A 4
SE10 . . . . .5H 89
Calvert's Bldgs.
SE1 . . . . .1D 86 (5E 168)
Calvert St. NW1 . . . . .1E 66
Calvin St. E1 . . . . . .4F 69 (4J 163)
Calydon Rd. SE7 . . . . .5K 89
Calypso Cres. SE15 . . . . .7F 87
Calypso Way SE16 . . . . .3B 88
Camac Rd. TW2: Twick 1H 115
Cambalt Rd. SW15 . . . . . . .5F 101
Cambay Ho. *E1* *4A 70*
(*off Harford St.*)
Camber Ho. SE15 . . . . .6J 87
Camberley Av. EN1: Enf 4K 7
SW20 . . . . .2D 136
Camberley Cl. SM3: Sutt . . .3F 149
Camberley Ho. NW1 . . . . . .1K 159
Camberley Rd.
TW6: Houn 3C 94
Cambert Way SE3 . . . . .4K 107
CAMBERWELL 1D 104
Camberwell Chu. St.
SE5 . . . . .1D 104
Camberwell Glebe SE5 . . . .1E 104
CAMBERWELL GREEN 1D 104
Camberwell Grn. SE5 . . . . .1D 104
Camberwell Gro. SE5 . . . . .1D 104
Camberwell New Rd. SE5 . . .6A 86
Camberwell Pl. SE5 . . . . . . .1C 104
Camberwell Rd. SE5 . . . . . . .6C 86
Camberwell Sta. Rd.
SE5 . . . . .1C 104
Camberwell Trad. Est.
SE5 . . . . .1B 104
Cambeys Rd. RM10: Dag 5H 57
Camborne Av. W13 . . . . .2B 80
Camborne Cl. TW6: Houn . . .3C 94
Camborne Rd. CR0: Croy . . .7G 141
DA14: Sidc 3C 128
DA16: Well 2J 109
SM2: Sutt 7J 149
SM4: Mord 5F 137
SW18 . . . . .7J 101
Camborne Way
TW5: Houn 1E 96
Cambourne Av. N9 . . . . .7E 8
Cambourne M. *W11* *6G 65*
(*off St Mark's Rd.*)
Cambourne Rd.
TW6: Houn 3C 94
Cambourne Wlk.
TW10: Rich 6D 98
Cambrai Ct. N13 . . . . .3D 16
Cambray Rd. BR6: Orp 7K 145
SW12 . . . . .1G 121
Cambria Cl. DA15: Sidc 1H 127
TW3: Houn 4E 96
Cambria Ct. TW14: Felt 7K 95
Cambria Gdns.
TW19: Staines 7A 94
(not continuous)
Cambria Ho. *E14* *6A 70*
(*off Salmon La.*)
SE26 . . . .*4G 123*
(*off High Level Dr.*)
Cambrian Av. IG2: Ilf 5J 37
Cambrian Cl. SE27 . . . . .3B 122
Cambrian Grn. *NW9* *5A 28*
(*off Snowden Dr.*)
Cambrian Rd. E10 . . . . .7C 34
TW10: Rich 6F 99
Cambria Rd. SE5 . . . . .3C 104
Cambria St. SW6 . . . . .7K 83
Cambridge Arc. *E9* *7J 51*
(*off Elsdale St.*)
Cambridge Av.
DA16: Well 4K 109
KT3: N Mald 3A 136
(not continuous)
NW6 . . . . .2J 65
NW10 . . . . .3E 64
UB6: G'frd 5K 43
Cambridge Barracks Rd.
SE18 . . . . .4D 90
Cambridge Cir.
WC2 . . . . . . .6H 67 (1D 166)
Cambridge Cl. E17 . . . . .6B 34
N22 . . . . .1A 32
NW10 . . . . .3J 45
SW20 . . . . .1D 136
TW4: Houn 4C 96
Cambridge Cotts.
TW9: Rich 6G 81
Cambridge Ct. *E2* *2H 69*
(*off Cambridge Heath Rd.*)
N15 . . . .*7E 32*
(*off Amhurst Pk.*)
N16 . . . .*7E 32*
(*off Amhurst Pk.*)
NW6 . . . . .2J 65
W2 . . . .*6C 158*
(*off Edgware Rd.*)
W6 . . . .*4E 82*
(*off Shepherd's Bush Rd.*)
Cambridge Cres. E2 . . . . .2H 69
TW11: Tedd 5A 116
Cambridge Dr.
HA4: Ruis 2A 42
SE12 . . . . .5J 107
Cambridge Gdns. EN1: Enf 2B 8
KT1: King T 2G 135
N10 . . . . .1E 30
N17 . . . . .7J 17
N21 . . . . .7J 7
NW6 . . . . .2J 65
W10 . . . . .6F 65
Cambridge Ga.
NW1 . . . . . . .4F 67 (3J 159)
Cambridge Ga. M.
NW1 . . . . . . .4F 67 (3K 159)
Cambridge Grn. SE9 . . . . . . .1F 127
Cambridge Gro. SE20 . . . . .1H 141
W6 . . . . .4D 82
Cambridge Gro. Rd.
KT1: King T 3G 135
(not continuous)
Cambridge Heath Rd. E1 . . . .5H 69
Cambridge Ho. *W6* *4D 82*
(*off Cambridge Gro.*)
W13 . . . . .6A 62
Cambridge Lodge Vs. E8 . . . .1H 69
Cambridge Pde.
EN1: Enf 1B 8
Cambridge Pk. E11 . . . . .7J 35
TW1: Twick 6C 98
Cambridge Pk. Ct.
TW1: Twick 7D 98
Cambridge Pl. W8 . . . . .2K 83
Cambridge Rd.
BR1: Brom 7J 125
CR4: Mitc 3G 139
DA14: Sidc 4J 127
E4 . . . . .1A 20
E11 . . . . .6H 35
HA2: Harr 5E 24
IG3: Ilf 1J 55
IG11: Bark 7G 55
KT1: King T 2F 135
KT3: N Mald 4K 135
KT8: W Mole 4D 132
KT12: Walt T 6K 131
NW6 . . . . .2J 65
(not continuous)
SE20 . . . . .3H 141
SM5: Cars 6C 150
SW11 . . . . .1D 102
SW13 . . . . .2B 100
SW20 . . . . .1C 136
TW1: Twick 6D 98
TW4: Houn 4C 96
TW9: Rich 7G 81
TW11: Tedd 4K 115
TW12: Hamp 7D 114
TW15: Ashf 7E 112
UB1: S'hall 1D 78
W7 . . . . .2K 79
Cambridge Rd. Nth.
W4 . . . . .5H 81
Cambridge Rd. Sth. W4 . . . . .5H 81
Cambridge Row SE18 . . . . . . .5F 91
Cambridge Sq.
W2 . . . . .6C 66 (7C 158)
Cambridge St.
SW1 . . . . . . .4F 85 (4K 171)
Cambridge Ter. N9 . . . . .7K 7
NW1 . . . . . . .3F 67 (2J 159)
Cambridge Ter. M.
NW1 . . . . . . .3F 67 (2K 159)
Cambridge Theatre 1E 166
(*off Earlham St.*)
Cambridge Yd. W7 . . . . .2K 79
Cambstone Cl. N11 . . . . .2K 15
Cambus Cl. UB4: Hayes 5C 60
Cambus Rd. E16 . . . . .5J 71
Cam Ct. SE15 . . . . .6F 87
Camdale Rd. SE18 . . . . .7K 91
Camden Arts Cen. 5K 47
Camden Av. TW13: Felt 1A 114
UB4: Hayes 7B 60
Camden Cl. BR7: Chst 1G 145
Camden Ct. DA17: Belv 5G 93
NW1 . . . .*7G 49*
(*off Rousden St.*)
Camden Gdns.
CR7: Thor H 3B 140
NW1 . . . . .7F 49
SM1: Sutt 5K 149
Camden Gro.
BR7: Chst 6F 127
Camden High St. NW1 . . . . . .7F 49
Camden Hill Rd. SE19 . . . . .6E 122
Camden Ho. SE8 . . . . .5B 88
Camdenhurst St. E14 . . . . . . .6A 70
Camden La. N7 . . . . .5H 49
Camden Lock Pl. NW1 . . . . . .7F 49
Camden Market 7F 49
Camden M. NW1 . . . . .7G 49
Camden Pk. Rd.
BR7: Chst 7D 126
NW1 . . . . .6H 49
Camden Pas. N1 . . . . .1B 68
(not continuous)
Camden Peoples Theatre
. . . . .3A 160
(*off Hampstead Rd.*)
Camden Rd. DA5: Bexl 1E 128
E11 . . . . .6K 35
E17 . . . . .6B 34
N7 . . . . .4J 49
NW1 . . . . .7G 49
SM1: Sutt 5K 149
SM5: Cars 4D 150
Camden Row HA5: Pinn 3A 24
SE3 . . . . .2G 107
Camden Sq. NW1 . . . . .7H 49
(not continuous)
Camden St. NW1 . . . . .7G 49
Camden Studios *NW1* *1G 67*
(*off Camden St.*)
Camden Ter. NW1 . . . . .6H 49
CAMDEN TOWN 1F 67
Camden Wlk. N1 . . . . .1B 68
(not continuous)
Camden Way BR7: Chst 7D 126
CR7: Thor H 3B 140
Cameford Ct. SW12 . . . . . . .7J 103
Camelford *NW1* *1G 67*
(*off Royal College St.*)
Camelford Ct. W11 . . . . .6G 65
Camelford Ho.
SE1 . . . . .5J 85 (5F 173)
Camelford Wlk. W11 . . . . . . .6G 65
Camel Gro. KT2: King T 5D 116
Camellia Ho. *SE8* *7B 88*
(*off Idonia St.*)
Camellia Pl. TW2: Twick 7F 97
Camellia St. SW8 . . . . .7J 85
Camelot Cl. SE28 . . . . .2H 91
SW19 . . . . .4H 119
Camelot Ho. NW1 . . . . .6H 49
Camel Rd. E16 . . . . .1B 90
Camera Pl.
SW10 . . . . . .6B 84 (7A 170)
Cameret Ct. *W14* *2F 83*
(*off Holland Rd.*)
Cameron Cl. DA5: Bexl 3K 129
N18 . . . . .4C 18
N20 . . . . .2G 15
Cameron Ho. *NW8* *2C 66*
(*off St John's Wood Ter.*)
SE5 . . . . .7C 86
Cameron Pl. E1 . . . . .6H 69
Cameron Rd. BR2: Short . . .5J 143
CR0: Croy 6B 140
IG3: Ilf 1J 55
SE6 . . . . .2B 124
Cameron Sq. CR4: Mitc 1C 138
Cameron Ter. SE12 . . . . .3K 125
Camerton Cl. E8 . . . . .6F 51
Camilla Cl. TW16: Sun T 6H 113
Camilla Rd. SE16 . . . . .4H 87
Camille Cl. SE25 . . . . .3G 141
Camlan Rd. BR1: Brom 4H 125
Camlet St. E2 . . . . . .4F 69 (3J 163)
Camlet Way EN4: Barn 2D 4
Camley St. NW1 . . . . .7H 49
Camm Gdns.
KT1: King T 2F 135
KT7: T Ditt 7K 133
Camomile Av. CR4: Mitc . . .1D 138
Camomile Rd.
RM7: Rush G 2K 57
Camomile St.
EC2 . . . . .6E 68 (7H 163)
Camomile Way
UB7: W Dray 6A 58
Campana Rd. SW6 . . . . .1J 101
Campania Bldg. *E1* *7K 69*
(*off Jardine Rd.*)
Campbell Av. IG6: Ilf 4F 37
Campbell Cl. HA4: Ruis 6J 23
SE18 . . . . .1E 108
Campbell Cl. SW16 . . . . . . .4H 121
TW2: Twick 1H 115
Campbell Ct. N17 . . . . .1F 33
SE21 . . . . .1G 123
SW7 . . . .*3A 84*
(*off Gloucester Rd.*)
Campbell Cft. HA8: Edg 5B 12
Campbell Gordon Way
NW2 . . . . .4D 46
Campbell Ho. *SW1* *6A 172*
(*off Churchill Gdns.*)
W12 . . . .*7D 64*
(*off White City Est.*)
Campbell Rd. CR0: Croy . . .7B 140
E3 . . . . .3C 70
E6 . . . . .1C 72
E15 . . . . .4H 53
E17 . . . . .4B 34
KT8: E Mos 3J 133
N17 . . . . .1F 33
TW2: Twick 2H 115
W7 . . . . .7J 61
Campbell Wlk. *N1* *1J 67*
(*off Outram Pl.*)
Campdale Rd. N7 . . . . .3H 49
Campden Cres.
HA0: Wemb 3B 44
RM8: Dag 4B 56
Campden Gro. W8 . . . . .2J 83
Campden Hill W8 . . . . .2J 83
Campden Hill Ct. W8 . . . . . . .2J 83
Campden Hill Gdns. W8 . . . . .1J 83
Campden Hill Ga. W8 . . . . . . .2J 83
Campden Hill Mans. *W8* *1J 83*
(*off Edge St.*)
Campden Hill Pl. W11 . . . . . .1H 83
Campden Hill Rd. W11 . . . . . .1J 83
Campden Hill Sq. W11 . . . . .1H 83
Campden Ho's. W8 . . . . .1J 83
Campden Ho. *NW6* *7B 48*
(*off Harben Rd.*)
W8 . . . .*1J 83*
(*off Sheffield Ter.*)
Campden Ho. Cl. W8 . . . . . . .2J 83
Campden Rd.
CR2: S Croy 5E 152
UB10: Uxb 3B 40
Campden St. W8 . . . . .1J 83
Campe Ho. N10 . . . . .7K 15
Campen Cl. SW19 . . . . .2G 119
Camperdown Ho.
SM6: Wall 6F 151
(*off Stanley Pk. Rd.*)
Camperdown St.
E1 . . . . .6F 69 (1K 169)
Campfield Rd. SE9 . . . . .7B 108
Campion Cl. CR2: S Croy . . .4E 152
E6 . . . . .7D 72
HA3: Harr 6F 27
RM7: Rush G 2K 57
UB8: Uxb 5B 58
Campion Ct. HA0: Wemb 2E 62
Campion Gdns.
IG8: Wfd G 5D 20
Campion Pl. SE28 . . . . .1A 92
Campion Rd. SW15 . . . . . . .4E 100
TW7: Isle 1K 97
Campion Ter. NW2 . . . . .3F 47
Campion Way HA8: Edg 4D 12
Camplin Rd. HA3: Harr 5E 26
Camplin St. SE14 . . . . .7K 87
Camp Rd. SW19 . . . . .5D 118
(not continuous)
Campsbourne Rd. N8 . . . . . . .3J 31
(not continuous)
Campsbourne, The N8 . . . . . .4J 31
Campsey Gdns. RM9: Dag . . .7B 56
Campsey Rd. RM9: Dag 7B 56
Campsfield Rd. N8 . . . . .3J 31
Campshill Pl. SE13 . . . . . . .5E 106
Campshill Rd. SE13 . . . . . . .5E 106
Campus Rd. E17 . . . . .6B 34
Campus Way NW4 . . . . .3D 28
Camp Vw. SW19 . . . . .5D 118

Cam Rd. E15 ....1F 71
Camrose Av. DA8: Erith 6H 93
  HA8: Edg 2F 27
  TW13: Felt 4A 114
Camrose Cl. CR0: Croy ..7A 142
  SM4: Mord 4J 137
Camrose St. SE2 ....5A 92
Canada Av. N18 ....6H 17
Canada Cres. W3 ....5J 63
Canada Est. SE16 ......3J 87
Canada Gdns. SE13 ....5E 106
Canada Ho. SE16 ......3A 88
  (off Brunswick Quay)
Canada Memorial 6A 166
  (off Green Pk.)
Canada Rd. W3 ....5J 63
Canada Sq. E14 ....1D 88
Canada St. SE16 ....2K 87
Canada Way W12 ......7D 64
Canada Wharf SE16 ....1B 88
Canadian Av. SE6 ......1D 124
Canal App. SE8 ....5A 68
CANAL BRIDGE 6G 87
Canal Bldg. N1 ....2C 68
  (off Shepherdess Wlk.)
Canal Cl. E1 ....4A 70
  W10 ....4F 65
Canal Gro. SE15 ....6H 87
Canal Path E2 ....1H 69
Canalside SE28 ....7D 74
Canal St. SE5 ....6D 86
Canal Wlk. CR0: Croy ..6E 140
  N1 ....1D 68
  NW10 ....7J 45
  (off Westend Cl.)
  SE26 ....5J 123
Canal Way W10 ....4F 65
Canary Wharf Pier E14 ..1B 88
  (off Westferry Cir.)
Canberra Cl. NW4 ......3C 28
  RM10: Dag 1K 75
Canberra Cres.
  RM10: Dag 7K 57
Canberra Dr. UB5: N'olt ..3A 60
Canberra Rd. DA7: Bex ..6D 92
  E6 ....1D 72
  SE7 ....3C 90
  TW6: Houn 3C 94
Canbury Av. KT2: King T ..1F 135
Canbury Bus. Cen.
  KT2: King T 1E 134
Canbury Bus. Pk.
  KT2: King T 1E 134
  (off Canbury Pk. Rd.)
Canbury M. SE26 ......3G 123
Canbury Pk. Rd.
  KT2: King T 1E 134
Canbury Pas.
  KT2: King T 1D 134
Cancell Rd. SW9 ......1A 104
Candahar Rd. SW11 ....2C 102
Candida Ct. NW1 ......7F 49
Candid Ho. NW10 ......3D 64
  (off Trenmar Gdns.)
Candler M. TW1: Twick ..7A 98
Candler St. N15 ....6D 32
Candover Cl. UB7: W Dray ..7A 76
Candover St. W1 ..5G 67 (6A 160)
Candy St. E3 ....1B 70
Caney M. NW2 ....2F 47
Canfield Dr. HA4: Ruis ..5K 41
Canfield Gdns. NW6 ....7K 47
Canfield Ho. N15 ......6E 32
  (off Albert Rd.)
Canfield Pl. NW6 ......6A 48
Canfield Rd. IG8: Wfd G ..7H 21
Canford Av. UB5: N'olt ..1D 60
Canford Cl. EN2: Enf 2F 7
Canford Gdns.
  KT3: N Mald 6A 136
Canford Pl. TW11: Tedd ..6C 116
Canford Rd. SW11 ......5E 102

Canham Rd. SE25 ......3E 140
  W3 ....2A 82
Canmore Gdns. SW16 ..7G 121
CANN HALL 4G 53
Cann Hall Rd. E11 ......4G 53
Cann Ho. W14 ....3G 83
  (off Russell Rd.)
Canning Cres. N22 ......1K 31
Canning Cross SE5 ....2E 104
Canning Ho. W12 ......7D 64
  (off Australia Rd.)
Canning Pas. W8 ......3A 84
  (not continuous)
Canning Pl. W8 ....3A 84
Canning Pl. M. W8 ....3A 84
  (off Canning Pl.)
Canning Rd. CR0: Croy ..2F 153
  E15 ....2G 71
  E17 ....4A 34
  HA3: Harr 3J 25
  N5 ....3B 50
Cannington Rd. RM9: Dag ..6C 56
CANNING TOWN 6H 71
Canning Town 6H 71
Cannizaro Rd. SW19 ..6E 118
Cannock Ho. N4 ......7C 32
Cannonbury Av. HA5: Pinn ..6B 24
Cannon Cl. SW20 ......3E 136
  TW12: Hamp ..6F 115
Cannon Dr. E14 ....7C 70
Cannon Hill N14 ......3D 16
  NW6 ....5J 47
Cannon Hill La. SW20 ..5F 137
Cannon Hill M. N14 ....3D 16
Cannon Ho. SE11 ......4H 173
Cannon La. HA5: Pinn ..5C 24
  NW3 ....3B 48
Cannon Pl. NW3 ......3B 48
  SE7 ....5C 90
Cannon Retail Pk. SE28 ..7A 74
Cannon Rd. DA7: Bex ..1E 110
  N14 ....5D 16
Cannon St. EC4 ..6C 68 (1C 168)
Cannon St. Rd. E1 ......6H 69
Cannon Trad. Est.
  HA9: Wemb 4H 45
Cannon Way
  KT8: W Mole ..4E 132
Cannon Wharf Bus. Cen.
  SE8 ....4A 88
Cannon Workshops E14 ..7C 70
  (off Cannon Dr.)
Canon All. EC4 ....1C 168
  (off Queen's Head Pas.)
Canon Av. RM6: Chad H ..5C 38
Canon Beck Rd. SE16 ..2J 87
Canonbie Rd. SE23 ....7J 105
CANONBURY 6C 50
Canonbury Bus. Cen. N1 ..1C 68
Canonbury Ct. N1 ......7B 50
  (off Hawes St.)
Canonbury Cres. N1 ....7C 50
Canonbury Gro. N1 ....7C 50
Canonbury Hgts. N1 ....6D 50
  (off Dove Rd.)
Canonbury La. N1 ......7B 50
Canonbury Pk. Nth. N1 ..6C 50
Canonbury Pk. Sth. N1 ..6C 50
Canonbury Pl. N1 ......6B 50
  (not continuous)
Canonbury Rd. EN1: Enf ..1K 7
  N1 ....6B 50
Canonbury Sq. N1 .....7B 50
Canonbury St. N1 ......7C 50
Canonbury Vs. N1 ......7B 50
Canon Mohan Cl. N14 ..6K 5
Canon Rd. BR1: Brom ..3A 144
Canon Row SW1 ..2J 85 (7E 166)
  (not continuous)
Canons Cl. HA8: Edg ..6A 12
  N2 ....7B 30
Canons Cnr. HA8: Edg ..4K 11

Canons Ct. E15 ....4G 53
  HA8: Edg 6A 12
Canons Dr. HA8: Edg ..6K 11
Canonsleigh Rd.
  RM9: Dag 7B 56
CANONS PARK 7J 11
Canons Pk. 6K 11
Canons Pk. HA7: Stan ..6J 11
Canons Pk. Cl.
  HA8: Edg 7K 11
Canon St. N1 ....1C 68
Canons Wlk. CR0: Croy ..3K 153
Canopus Way
  TW19: Staines ..7A 94
Canrobert St. E2 ......2H 69
Cantelowes Rd. NW1 ..6H 49
  (not continuous)
Canterbury Av.
  DA15: Sidc 2B 128
  IG1: Ilf 7C 36
Canterbury Cl. BR3: Beck ..1D 142
  E6 ....6D 72
  SE5 ....2C 104
  (off Lilford Rd.)
  UB6: G'frd 5F 61
Canterbury Ct. NW6 ....2J 65
  (off Canterbury Rd.)
  NW9 ....2A 28
  SE12 ....3K 125
Canterbury Cres. SW9 ..3A 104
Canterbury Gro. SE27 ..4A 122
Canterbury Ho.
  CR0: Croy 1D 152
  E10 ....7E 34
  (off Sydenham Rd.)
  IG11: Bark 7A 56
  (off Margaret Bondfield Av.)
  SE1 ......3K 85 (1H 173)
Canterbury Ind. Pk. SE15 ..6J 87
Canterbury Pl. SE17 ....5B 86
Canterbury Rd.
  CR0: Croy 7K 139
  E10 ....7E 34
  HA1: Harr 5F 25
  HA2: Harr 5F 25
  NW6 ....2H 65
  (not continuous)
  SM4: Mord 7K 137
  TW13: Felt 2C 114
Canterbury Ter. NW6 ..2J 65
Cantium Retail Pk. SE1 ..6G 87
Cantley Gdns. IG2: Ilf ..6G 37
  SE19 ....1F 141
Cantley Rd. W7 ....3A 80
Canton St. E14 ....6C 70
Cantrell Rd. E3 ....4B 70
Cantwell Rd. SE18 ....7F 91
Canute Gdns. SE16 ....4K 87
Canvey St. SE1 ..1C 86 (4C 168)
Cape Cl. IG11: Bark 7F 55
Cape Henry Ct. E14 ....7F 71
  (off Jamestown Way)
Cape Ho. E8 ....6F 51
  (off Dalston La.)
Capel Av. SM6: Wall ..5K 151
Capel Cl. BR2: Short ..1C 156
  N20 ....3F 15
Capel Ct. EC2 ....1F 169
  (off Bartholomew La.)
  SE20 ....1J 141
Capel Gdns. HA5: Pinn ..4D 24
  IG3: Bark, Ilf ..4K 55
Capel Ho. E9 ....7J 51
  (off Loddiges Rd.)
Capel Rd. E7 ....4K 53
  EN4: Barn 6H 5
Capern's Cl. SW1 ......7F 165
Capern Rd. SW18 ......1A 120
Capel Rd. N17 ....3G 33

Capital Ind. Est.
  CR4: Mitc 5D 138
  DA17: Belv 3H 93
Capital Interchange Way
  TW8: Bford 5G 81
Capital Pl. CR0: Croy ..5K 151
Capital Wharf E1 ......1G 87
Capitol Ind. Pk. NW9 ..3J 27
Capital Way NW9 .....3J 27
Capland Ho. NW8 .....3B 158
  (off Capland St.)
Capland St.
  NW8 ......4B 66 (3B 158)
Caple Ho. SW10 ......7A 84
  (off King's Rd.)
Caple Rd. NW10 ......2B 64
Capper St. WC1 ..4G 67 (4B 160)
Caprea Cl. UB4: Hayes ..5B 66
Capricorn Cen. RM8: Dag ..7F 39
Capri Ho. E17 ....2B 34
Capri Rd. CR0: Croy ..1F 153
Capstan Cl. RM6: Chad H ..6B 38
Capstan Ct. E1 ....7J 69
  (off Wapping Wall)
Capstan Ho. E14 ......7F 71
  (off Clove Cres.)
  E14 ....4E 88
  (off Stebondale St.)
Capstan Ride SE2: Enf ..2F 7
Capstan Rd. SE8 ......4B 88
Capstan Sq. E14 ......2E 88
Capstan Way SE16 ....1A 88
Capstone Rd.
  BR1: Brom 4H 125
Capthorne Av. HA2: Harr ..1C 42
Capuchin Cl. HA7: Stan ..6G 11
Capulet M. E16 ....1J 89
Capworth St. E10 ......1C 52
Caradoc Cl. W2 ....6J 65
Caradoc Evans Cl. N11 ..5A 16
  (off Springfield Rd.)
Caradoc St. SE10 ......5G 89
Caradon Cl. E11 ......1G 53
Caradon Way N15 ......4D 32
Caranday Villas W11 ....1F 83
  (off Norland Rd.)
Caravel Cl. E14 ....3C 88
Caravelle Gdns.
  UB5: N'olt 3B 60
Caravel M. SE8 ....6C 88
Caraway Cl. E13 ......5K 71
Caraway Hgts. E14 ....7E 70
  (off Poplar High St.)
Caraway Pl. SM6: Wall ..3F 151
Carberry Rd. SE19 ....6E 122
Carbery Av. W3 ....2F 81
Carbis Cl. E4 ....1A 20
Carbis Rd. E14 ....6B 70
Carbroke Ho. E9 ......1J 69
  (off Templecombe Rd.)
Carburton St.
  W1 ......5F 67 (5K 159)
Cardale St. E14 ....2E 88
Carden Rd. SE15 ......3H 105
Cardiff Ho. SE15 ......6G 87
  (off Friary Est.)
Cardiff Rd. EN3: Enf 4C 8
  W7 ....3A 80
Cardiff St. SE18 ......7J 91
Cardigan Cl. W4 ......4K 61
  (off Copley Cl.)
Cardigan Gdns. IG3: Ilf ..2A 56
Cardigan Pl. SE3 ......2F 107
Cardigan Rd. E3 ......2B 70
  SW13 ....2C 100
  SW19 ....6A 120
  TW10: Rich 6E 98
Cardigan St.
  SE11 ......5A 86 (5J 173)
Cardigan Wlk. N1 ......7C 50
  (off Ashby Gro.)

Cardinal Av.
  KT2: King T 5E 116
  SM4: Mord 6G 137
Cardinal Bourne St.
  SE1 ....3D 86
Cardinal Cap All. SE1 ..1C 86
Cardinal Cl. BR7: Chst ..1H 145
  HA8: Edg 7D 12
  KT4: Wor Pk ..4C 148
  SM4: Mord 6G 137
Cardinal Ct. E1 ....7G 69
  (off Thomas More St.)
Cardinal Cres.
  KT3: N Mald 2J 135
Cardinal Hinsley Cl.
  NW10 ....2C 64
Cardinal Rd. HA4: Ruis ..1B 42
  TW13: Felt 1K 113
Cardinals Wlk.
  TW12: Hamp ..7G 115
  TW16: Sun T ..6G 113
Cardinals Way N19 ....1H 49
Cardinal Way HA3: Harr ..3J 25
Cardine M. SE15 ......7H 87
Cardington St.
  NW1 ......3G 67 (1B 160)
Cardozo Rd. N7 ....5J 49
Cardrew Av. N12 ......5G 15
Cardrew Cl. N12 ......5H 15
Cardrew Cl. N12 ......5G 15
Cardross Ho. W6 .....3D 82
  (off Cardross St.)
Cardross St. W6 ......3D 82
Cardwell Rd. N7 ......4J 49
Career Cl. SE16 ......2K 87
  (off Christopher Cl.)
Carew Cl. N7 ....2K 49
Carew Ct. SE14 ....6K 87
  (off Samuel Cl.)
  SM2: Sutt 7K 149
Carew Manor & Dovecote
  ....3G 151
Carew Mnr. Cotts.
  SM6: Wall 3H 151
Carew Rd. CR4: Mitc ..2E 138
  CR7: Thor H 4B 140
  N17 ....2G 33
  SM6: Wall 6G 151
  TW15: Ashf 6E 112
  W13 ....2C 80
Carew St. SE5 ....2C 104
Carey Cl. DA6: Bex ..5H 111
  SE5 ....7C 86
Carey Gdns. SW8 ....1G 103
Carey La. EC2 ..6C 68 (7C 162)
Carey Mans. SW1 .....3C 172
  (off Rutherford St.)
Carey Pl. SW1 ..4H 85 (4C 172)
Carey St. WC2 ..6K 67 (1H 167)
Carey Way HA9: Wemb ..4H 45
Carfax Pl. SW4 ....4H 103
Carfax Rd. UB3: Hayes ..5H 77
Carfree Cl. N1 ....7A 50
Cargill Rd. SW18 ......1K 119
Cargreen Pl. SE25 ....4F 141
Cargreen Rd. SE25 ....4F 141
Cargrey Ho. HA7: Stan ..5H 11
Carholme Rd. SE23 ..1B 124
Carillon Ct. W5 ....7D 62
Carina M. SE27 ....4C 122
Carinthia Ct. SE16 ....4A 88
  (off Plough Way)
Carisbrooke Av.
  DA5: Bexl 1D 128
Carisbrooke Cl. EN1: Enf ..1A 8
  HA7: Stan 2D 26

Casson St.—Cedar Copse

Casson St. E1 .... 5G 69
Castalia Sq. E14 .... 2E 88
Castellain Mans. *W9* *4K 65*
(off Castellain Rd., not continuous)
Castellain Rd. W9 .... 4K 65
Castellane Cl. HA7: Stan 7E 10
Castell Ho. SE8 .... 7C 88
Castello Av. SW15 .... 5E 100
CASTELNAU 6D 82
Castelnau SW13 .... 1C 100
Castelnau Gdns. SW13 .... 6D 82
Castelnau Mans. *SW13* *6D 82*
(off Castelnau, not continuous)
Castelnau Row SW13 .... 6D 82
Casterbridge *NW6* *1K 65*
(off Abbey Rd.)
W11 .... *6H 65*
(off Dartmouth Clo.)
Casterbridge Rd. SE3 .... 3J 107
Casterton St. E8 .... 6H 51
Castile Rd. SE18 .... 4E 90
Castillon Rd. SE6 .... 2G 125
Castlands Rd. SE6 .... 2B 124
Castleacre *W2* *1C 164*
(off Hyde Pk. Cres.)
Castle Av. E4 .... 5A 20
KT17: Eps 7D 148
UB7: W Dray 7A 58
Castlebar Ct. W5 .... 5C 62
Castlebar Hill W5 .... 5C 62
Castlebar M. W5 .... 5C 62
Castlebar Pk. W5 .... 5B 62
Castlebar Rd. W5 .... 5C 62
Castle Baynard St.
EC4 .... 7B 68 (2B 168)
Castlebrook Ct. SE11 .... 4B 86
Castle Climbing Cen., The
.... *2C 50*
Castle Cl. BR2: Short 3G 143
E9 .... 5A 52
SW19 .... 3F 119
TW16: Sun T 7G 113
W3 .... 2H 81
Castlecombe Dr. SW19 .... 7F 101
Castlecombe Rd. SE9 .... 4C 126
Castle Ct. *EC3* *1F 169*
(off Birchin La.)
SE26 .... 4A 124
Castledine Rd. SE20 .... 7H 123
Castle Dr. IG4: Ilf 6C 36
Castleford Av. SE9 .... 1F 127
Castleford Cl. N17 .... 6A 18
Castleford Ct. *NW8* *3B 158*
(off Henderson Dr.)
Castlegate TW9: Rich 3F 99
Castlehaven Rd. NW1 .... 7F 49
Castle Hill Av. CR0: Croy 7D 154
Castle Hill Pde. *W13* *7B 62*
(off Avenue, The)
Castle Ho. *SE1* *4C 86*
(off Walworth Rd.)
SW8 .... *7J 85*
(off Sth. Lambeth Rd.)
Castle Ind. Est. SE17 .... 4C 86
Castle La. SW1 .... 3G 85 (1B 172)
Castleleigh Ct. EN2: Enf 5J 7
Castlemaine SW11 .... 2D 102
Castlemaine Av.
CR2: S Croy 5F 153
KT17: Eps 7D 148
Castle Mead SE5 .... 7C 86
Castle M. N12 .... 5F 15
NW1 .... 6F 49
Castle Pde. KT17: Eps 7C 148
Castle Pl. NW1 .... 6F 49
W4 .... 4A 82
Castle Point *E13* *2A 72*
(off Boundary Rd.)
Castlereagh Ho.
HA7: Stan 6G 11
Castlereagh St.
W1 .... 6D 66 (7E 158)
Castle Rd. EN3: Enf 1F 9
N12 .... 5F 15
NW1 .... 6F 49
RM9: Dag 1B 74
TW7: Isle 2K 97
UB2: S'hall 3D 78
UB5: N'olt 6F 43
Castle Row W4 .... 5K 81
Castle St. E6 .... 2A 72
KT1: King T 2E 134
Castleton Av. DA7: Bex 1K 111
HA9: Wemb 4E 44
Castleton Cl.
CR0: Croy 6A 142
Castleton Gdns.
HA9: Wemb 3E 44
Castleton Ho. *E14* *4E 88*
(off Pier St.)
Castleton Rd. CR4: Mitc 4H 139
(not continuous)
E17 .... 2F 35
HA4: Ruis 1B 42
IG3: Ilf 1A 56
SE9 .... 4B 126
Castletown Rd. W14 .... 5G 83
Castleview Cl. N4 .... 2C 50
Castleview Gdns. IG1: Ilf 6C 36
Castle Wlk.
TW16: Sun T 3A 132
Castle Way SW19 .... 3F 119
TW13: Felt 4A 114
Castle Wharf *E14* *7G 71*
(off Orchard Pl.)
Castlewood Dr. SE9 .... 2D 108
Castlewood Rd. EN4: Barn 3G 5
N15 .... 6G 33
N16 .... 6G 33
Castle Yd. N6 .... 7E 30
SE1 .... 1B 86 (4B 168)
TW10: Rich 5D 98
Castor La. E14 .... 7D 70
Catalina Rd. TW6: Houn 2D 94
Caterham Av. IG5: Ilf 2D 36
Caterham Rd. SE13 .... 3F 107
Catesby Ho. *E9* *7J 51*
(off Frampton Pk. Rd.)
Catesby St. SE17 .... 4D 86
CATFORD 7D 106
CATFORD GYRATORY 7D 106
Catford B'way. SE6 .... 7D 106
Catford Hill SE6 .... 1B 124
Catford Island SE6 .... 7D 106
Catford M. SE6 .... 7D 106
Catford Rd. SE6 .... 7C 106
Catford Stadium (Greyhound)
.... *6C 106*
Catford Trad. Est. SE6 .... 2D 124
Cathall Rd. E11 .... 2F 53
Cathay Ho. SE16 .... 2H 87
Cathay St. SE16 .... 2H 87
Cathay Wlk. *UB5: N'olt* *2E 60*
(off Brabazon Rd.)
Cathcart Dr. BR6: Orp 7J 145
Cathcart Hill N19 .... 3G 49
Cathcart Rd. SW10 .... 6K 83
Cathcart St. NW5 .... 6F 49
Cathedral Lodge *EC1* *5C 162*
(off Aldersgate St.)
Cathedral Mans. *SW1* *3A 172*
(off Vauxhall Bri. Rd.)
Cathedral Piazza
SW1 .... 3G 85 (2A 172)
Cathedral St.
SE1 .... 1D 86 (4E 168)
Catherall Rd. N5 .... 3C 50
Catherine Ct. IG2: Ilf 5G 37
N14 .... 5B 6
SW19 .... 5H 119
Catherine Dr. TW9: Rich 4E 98
TW16: Sun T 6H 113
Catherine Gdns.
TW3: Houn 4H 97
Catherine Griffiths Ct.
EC1 .... *3K 161*
(off Northampton Rd.)
Catherine Gro. SE10 .... 1D 106
Catherine Ho. *N1* *1E 68*
(off Whitmore Est.)
Catherine Howard Ct.
SE9 .... 6H 109
Catherine of Aragon Ct.
SE9 .... 6G 109
Catherine Parr Ct. SE9 .... 6H 109
Catherine Pl. HA1: Harr 5K 25
SW1 .... 3G 85 (1A 172)
Catherine Rd. KT6: Surb 5D 134
Catherine St.
WC2 .... 7K 67 (2G 167)
Catherine Wheel All.
EC2 .... 5E 68 (6H 163)
(not continuous)
Catherine Wheel Rd.
TW8: Bford 7D 80
Catherine Wheel Yd.
SW1 .... 5A 166
Catherwood Ct. *N1* *1E 162*
(off Murray Gro., not continuous)
Cat Hill EN4: Barn 6H 5
Cathles Rd. SW12 .... 6F 103
Cathnor Rd. W12 .... 2D 82
Catlin Cres. TW17: Shep 5F 131
Catling Cl. SE23 .... 3J 123
Catlin's La. HA5: Pinn 3K 23
Catlin St. SE16 .... 5G 87
Cator La. BR3: Beck 1B 142
Cato Rd. SW4 .... 3H 103
Cator Rd. SE26 .... 6K 123
SM5: Cars 5D 150
Cator St. SE15 .... 7F 87
(E. Surrey Gro.)
SE15 .... 6F 87
(Ebley Cl.)
Cato St. W1 .... 5C 66 (6D 158)
Catsey La. WD23: Bush 1B 10
Catsey Wood WD23: Bush 1B 10
Catterick Cl. N11 .... 6K 15
Cattistock Rd. SE9 .... 5C 126
Cattley Cl. EN5: Barn 4B 4
Catton St. WC1 .... 5K 67 (6G 161)
Caudwell Ter. SW18 .... 6B 102
Caughley Ho. SE11 .... 2J 173
Caulfield Rd. E6 .... 1C 72
SE15 .... 2H 105
Causeway, The
KT9: Chess 4E 146
KT10: Esh 7A 146
N2 .... 4C 30
SM2: Sutt 7A 150
SM5: Cars 3E 150
SW18 .... 5K 101
(not continuous)
SW19 .... 5E 118
TW11: Tedd 6K 115
TW14: Felt 4J 95
Causeyware Rd. N9 .... 7D 8
Causton Cotts. E14 .... 6A 70
Causton Ho. SE5 .... 6C 86
Causton Rd. N6 .... 7F 31
Causton Sq. RM10: Dag 7G 57
Causton St. SW1 .... 4H 85 (4D 172)
Cautley Av. SW4 .... 5G 103
Cavalier Cl. RM6: Chad H 4D 38
Cavalier Ct. KT5: Surb 6F 135
Cavalier Gdns. UB3: Hayes 6F 59
Cavalry Cres. TW4: Houn 4B 96
Cavalry Gdns. SW15 .... 5H 101
Cavan Ho. E3 .... 1B 70
Cavan Pl. HA5: Pinn 1D 24
Cavaye Pl.
SW10 .... 5A 84 (6A 170)
Cavell Dr. EN2: Enf 2F 7
Cavell Ho. *N1* *1E 68*
(off Colville Est.)
Cavell Rd. N17 .... 7J 17
Cavell St. E1 .... 5H 69
Cavendish Av. DA8: Erith 6J 93
DA15: Sidc 7A 110
DA16: Well 3K 109
HA1: Harr 4H 43
HA4: Ruis 5K 41
IG8: Wfd G 1K 35
KT3: N Mald 5C 136
N3 .... 2J 29
NW8 .... 2B 66 (1B 158)
W13 .... 5A 62
Cavendish Cl. N18 .... 5C 18
NW6 .... 6H 47
NW8 .... 3B 66 (1B 158)
TW16: Sun T 6H 113
UB4: Hayes 5G 59
Cavendish Ct. EC3 .... 7H 163
TW16: Sun T 6H 113
Cavendish Dr. E11 .... 1F 53
HA8: Edg 6A 12
Cavendish Gdns. IG1: Ilf 1E 54
IG11: Bark 5J 55
RM6: Chad H 5E 38
SW4 .... 6G 103
Cavendish Ho. *NW8* *1B 158*
(off Wellington Rd.)
Cavendish Mans. *EC1* *4J 161*
(off Rosebery Av.)
NW6 .... 5J 47
Cavendish M. Nth.
W1 .... 5F 67 (5K 159)
Cavendish M. Sth.
W1 .... 5F 67 (6K 159)
Cavendish Pde. *SW12* *6F 103*
(off Clapham Comn. Sth. Side)
TW4: Houn 2C 96
Cavendish Pl. SW4 .... 5H 103
W1 .... 6F 67 (7K 159)
Cavendish Rd. CR0: Croy 1B 152
E4 .... 6K 19
EN5: Barn 3A 4
KT3: N Mald 4B 136
N4 .... 6B 32
N18 .... 5C 18
NW6 .... 7G 47
SM2: Sutt 7A 150
SW12 .... 6F 103
SW19 .... 7B 120
TW16: Sun T 6H 113
W4 .... 1J 99
Cavendish Sq.
W1 .... 6F 67 (7K 159)
Cavendish St. N1 .... 2D 68
Cavendish Ter.
TW13: Felt 2J 113
Cavendish Way
BR4: W W'ck 1D 154
Cavenham Gdns. IG1: Ilf 3H 55
Caverleigh Way
KT4: Wor Pk 1C 148
Cave Rd. E13 .... 3K 71
TW10: Rich 4C 116
Caversham Av. N13 .... 3F 17
SM3: Sutt 2G 149
Caversham Ct. N11 .... 2K 15
Caversham Ho.
KT1: King T *2E 134*
(off Lady Booth Rd.)
N15 .... *4C 32*
(off Caversham Rd.)
SE15 .... *6G 87*
(off Haymerle Rd.)
Caversham Rd.
KT1: King T 2F 135
N15 .... 4C 32
NW5 .... 6G 49
Caversham St.
SW3 .... 6D 84 (7E 170)
Caverswall St. W12 .... 6E 64
Caveside Cl. BR7: Chst 1E 144
Cavour Ho. *SE17* *5B 86*
(off Alberta Est.)
Cawdor Cres. W7 .... 4A 80
Cawnpore St. SE19 .... 5E 122
Caxton Ct. SW11 .... 2C 102
Caxton Gro. E3 .... 3C 70
Caxton M. TW8: Bford 6D 80
Caxton Pl. IG1: Ilf 3E 54
Caxton Rd. N22 .... 2K 31
SW19 .... 5A 120
UB2: S'hall 3B 78
W12 .... 2F 83
Caxton St. SW1 .... 3G 85 (1C 172)
Caxton St. Nth. E16 .... 6H 71
Caxton Trad. Est.
UB3: Hayes 2G 77
Caxton Wlk.
WC2 .... 6H 67 (1D 166)
Caygill Cl. BR2: Short 4H 143
Cayley Cl. SM6: Wall 7J 151
Cayley Rd. UB2: S'hall 3F 79
Cayton Pl. EC1 .... 2E 162
Cayton Rd. UB6: G'frd 2J 61
Cayton St. EC1 .... 3D 68 (2E 162)
Cazenove Rd. E17 .... 1C 34
N16 .... 2F 51
Cearns Ho. E6 .... 1B 72
Cecil Av. EN1: Enf 4A 8
HA9: Wemb 5F 45
IG11: Bark 7H 55
Cecil Cl. KT9: Chess 4D 146
TW15: Ashf 7E 112
W5 .... 5D 62
Cecil Ct. EN2: Enf 4J 7
EN5: Barn 3A 4
NW6 .... 7K 47
SW10 .... *6A 84*
(off Fawcett St.)
WC2 .... 7J 67 (3E 166)
Cecile Pk. N8 .... 6J 31
Cecil Ho. E17 .... 1C 34
Cecilia Cl. N2 .... 3A 30
Cecilia Rd. E8 .... 5F 51
Cecil Pk. HA5: Pinn 4C 24
Cecil Pl. CR4: Mitc 5D 138
Cecil Rhodes Ho. *NW1* *2H 67*
(off Goldington St.)
Cecil Rd. CR0: Croy 6J 139
E11 .... 3H 53
E13 .... 1J 71
E17 .... 1C 34
EN2: Enf 3H 7
HA3: Harr 3J 25
IG1: Ilf 4F 55
N10 .... 2F 31
N14 .... 1B 16
NW9 .... 3A 28
NW10 .... 1A 64
RM6: Chad H 7D 38
SM1: Sutt 6H 149
SW19 .... 7K 119
TW3: Houn 2G 97
TW15: Ashf 7E 112
W3 .... 5J 63
Cecil Rosen Ct.
HA0: Wemb 3B 44
Cecil Way BR2: Short 1J 155
Cedar Av. DA15: Sidc 7A 110
EN3: Enf 2D 8
EN4: Barn 7H 5
HA4: Ruis 5A 42
RM6: Chad H 5E 38
TW2: Twick 6F 97
UB3: Hayes 6J 59
UB7: W Dray 7B 58
Cedar Cl. BR2: Short 3C 156
E3 .... 1B 70
IG9: Buck H 2G 21
KT8: E Mos 4J 133
RM7: Rom 4J 39
SE21 .... 1C 122
SM5: Cars 6D 150
SW15 .... 4K 117
Cedar Copse BR1: Brom 2D 144

Claxton Gro.—Clive Pas.

Claxton Gro. W6 . . . . . 5F **83**
Claxton Path *SE4* *4K 105*
(off Coston Wlk.)
Clay Av. CR4: Mitc 2F **139**
Claybank Gro. SE13 . . . . . 3D **106**
Claybourne M. SE19 . . . . . 7E **122**
Claybridge Rd. SE12 . . . . . 4A **126**
Claybrook Cl. N2 . . . . . 3B **30**
Claybrook Rd. W6 . . . . . 6F **83**
Claybury B'way. IG5: Ilf 3C **36**
Claybury Rd. IG8: Wfd G 7H **21**
Clay Ct. E17 . . . . . 3F **35**
Claydon *SE17* *4C 86*
(off Deacon Way)
Claydon Dr. CR0: Croy 4J **151**
Claydon Ho. *NW4* *2F 29*
(off Holders Hill Rd.)
Claydown M. SE18 . . . . . 5E **90**
Clay Farm Rd. SE9 . . . . . 2G **127**
Claygate Cres. CR0: Croy . . . 6E **154**
Claygate La. KT7: T Ditt 1A **146**
KT10: Esh 2A **146**
(not continuous)
Claygate Rd. W13 . . . . . 3B **80**
CLAYHALL **3C 36**
Clayhall Av. IG5: Ilf 3C **36**
Clay Hill EN2: Enf 1K **7**
Clayhill KT5: Surb 5G **135**
Clayhill Cres. SE9 . . . . . 4B **126**
Claylands Pl. SW8 . . . . . 7A **86**
Claylands Rd.
SW8 . . . . . 6K **85** (7H **173**)
Clay La. HA8: Edg 2B **12**
TW19: Staines 7B **94**
WD23: Bush 1D **10**
Claymore Cl. SM4: Mord . . . 7J **137**
Claypole Ct. *E17* *5C 34*
(off Yunus Khan Cl.)
Claypole Dr. TW5: Houn 1C **96**
Claypole Rd. E15 . . . . . 2E **70**
Clayponds Av. W5 . . . . . 4D **80**
Clayponds Gdns. W5 . . . . . 4D **80**
(not continuous)
Clayponds La. TW8: Bford . . . 5E **80**
(not continuous)
Clays La. E15 . . . . . 5D **52**
Clays La. Cl. E15 . . . . . 5D **52**
Clay St. W1 . . . . . 5D **66** (6F **159**)
Clayton Av. HA0: Wemb 7E **44**
Clayton Cl. E6 . . . . . 6D **72**
Clayton Ct. E17 . . . . . 2A **34**
Clayton Cres. N1 . . . . . 1J **67**
TW8: Bford 5D **80**
Clayton Dr. SE8 . . . . . 5A **88**
Clayton Fld. NW9 . . . . . 7F **13**
Clayton Ho. *E9* *7J 51*
(off Frampton Pk. Rd.)
SW13 . . . . . *7E 82*
(off Trinity Chu. Rd.)
Clayton M. SE10 . . . . . 1F **107**
Clayton Rd. KT9: Chess 4C **146**
RM7: Rush G 1J **57**
SE15 . . . . . 1G **105**
TW7: Isle 3J **97**
UB3: Hayes 2G **77**
Clayton St. SE11 . . . 6A **86** (7J **173**)
Clayton Ter. UB4: Hayes 5C **60**
Claytonville Ter.
DA17: Belv 2J **93**
Claywood Cl. BR6: Orp 7J **145**
Clayworth Cl. DA15: Sidc . . . 6B **110**
Cleanthus Cl. SE18 . . . . . 1F **109**
Cleanthus Rd. SE18 . . . . . 2F **109**
(not continuous)
Clearbrook Way E1 . . . . . 6J **69**
Clearwater Pl. KT6: Surb . . . 6C **134**
Clearwater Ter. *W11* *2G 83*
(off Lorne Gdns.)
Clearwell Dr. W9 . . . . . 4K **65**
Cleave Av. UB3: Hayes 4G **77**
Cleaveland Rd.
KT6: Surb 5D **134**
Cleaverholme Cl. SE25 . . . . 6H **141**
Cleaver Ho. *NW3* *7D 48*
(off Adelaide Rd.)
Cleaver Sq.
SE11 . . . . . 5A **86** (6K **173**)
Cleaver St. SE11 . . . 5A **86** (5K **173**)
Cleaves Almshouses
KT2: King T *2E 134*
(off London Rd.)
Cleeve Ct. TW14: Felt 1G **113**
Cleeve Hill SE23 . . . . . 1H **123**
Cleeve Pk. Gdns.
DA14: Sidc 2B **128**
Cleeve Way SW15 . . . . . 7B **100**
Cleeve Workshops *E1* *2H 163*
(off Boundary Rd.)
Clegg Ho. SE3 . . . . . 4K **107**
SE16 . . . . . *3J 87*
(off Moodkee St.)
Clegg St. E1 . . . . . 1H **87**
E13 . . . . . 2J **71**
Cleland Ho. *E9* *2J 69*
(off Sewardstone Rd.)
Clematis Gdns.
IG8: Wfd G 5D **20**
Clematis St. W12 . . . . . 7C **64**
Clem Attlee Ct. SW6 . . . . . 6H **83**
Clem Attlee Pde. *SW6* *6H 83*
(off Nth. End Rd.)
Clemence Rd. RM10: Dag . . . 1J **75**
Clemence St. E14 . . . . . 5B **70**
Clement Av. SW4 . . . . . 4H **103**
Clement Cl. NW6 . . . . . 7E **46**
W4 . . . . . 4K **81**
Clement Gdns.
UB3: Hayes 4G **77**
Clementhorpe Rd.
RM9: Dag 6C **56**
Clement Ho. SE8 . . . . . 4A **88**
W10 . . . . . *5E 64*
(off Dalgarno Gdns.)
Clementina Rd. E10 . . . . . 1B **52**
Clementine Cl. W13 . . . . . 2B **80**
Clement Rd. BR3: Beck 2K **141**
SW19 . . . . . 5G **119**
Clement's Av. E16 . . . . . 7J **71**
Clements Ct. IG1: Ilf 3F **55**
TW4: Houn 4B **96**
Clement's Inn
WC2 . . . . . 6K **67** (1H **167**)
Clement's Inn Pas. WC2 . . . 1H **167**
Clements La.
EC4 . . . . . 7D **68** (2F **169**)
IG1: Ilf 3F **55**
Clements Pl. TW8: Bford 5D **80**
Clements Rd. E6 . . . . . 7C **54**
IG1: Ilf 3F **55**
SE16 . . . . . 3G **87**
Clemson Ho. E8 . . . . . 1F **69**
Clendon Way SE18 . . . . . 4H **91**
Clennam St. SE1 . . . 2C **86** (6D **168**)
Clensham Ct. SM1: Sutt 2J **149**
Clensham La. SM1: Sutt 2J **149**
Clenston M. W1 . . . 6D **66** (7E **158**)
Cleopatra's Needle
. . . . . ***7K 67 (3G 167)***
Clephane Rd. N1 . . . . . 6C **50**
Clephane Rd. Nth. N1 . . . . . 6C **50**
Clere Pl. EC2 . . . . . 4D **68** (3F **163**)
Clere St. EC2 . . . . . 4D **68** (3F **163**)
Clerics Wlk. TW17: Shep . . . 7F **131**
CLERKENWELL . . . . **4A 68 (3J 161)**
Clerkenwell Cl.
EC1 . . . . . 4A **68** (3K **161**)
(not continuous)
Clerkenwell Grn.
EC1 . . . . . 4A **68** (4K **161**)
Clerkenwell Rd.
EC1 . . . . . 4A **68** (4J **161**)
Clermont Rd. E9 . . . . . 1J **69**
Clevedon Cl. N16 . . . . . 3F **51**
Clevedon Ct. CR2: S Croy . . . 5E **152**
Clevedon Gdns.
TW5: Houn 1K **95**
UB3: Hayes 3F **77**
Clevedon Mans. NW5 . . . . . 4E **48**
Clevedon Pas. N16 . . . . . 2F **51**
Clevedon Rd.
KT1: King T 2G **135**
SE20 . . . . . 1K **141**
TW1: Twick 6D **98**
(not continuous)
Cleve Ho. NW6 . . . . . 7K **47**
Cleveland Av. SW20 . . . . . 2H **137**
TW12: Hamp 7D **114**
W4 . . . . . 4B **82**
Cleveland Ct. W13 . . . . . 5B **62**
Cleveland Gdns.
KT4: Wor Pk 2A **148**
N4 . . . . . 5C **32**
NW2 . . . . . 2F **47**
SW13 . . . . . 2B **100**
W2 . . . . . 6A **66**
Cleveland Gro. E1 . . . . . 4J **69**
Cleveland Ho. *N2* *2B 30*
(off Grange, The)
Cleveland La. N9 . . . . . 7C **8**
Cleveland Mans. *SW9* *7A 86*
(off Mowll St.)
W9 . . . . . 4J **65**
Cleveland M.
W1 . . . . . 5G **67** (5A **160**)
Cleveland Pk.
TW19: Staines 6A **94**
Cleveland Pk. Av. E17 . . . . . 4C **34**
Cleveland Pk. Cres.
E17 . . . . . 4C **34**
Cleveland Pl.
SW1 . . . . . 1G **85** (4B **166**)
Cleveland Ri. SM4: Mord . . . 7F **137**
Cleveland Rd.
DA16: Well 2K **109**
E18 . . . . . 3J **35**
IG1: Ilf 3F **55**
KT3: N Mald 4A **136**
KT4: Wor Pk 2A **148**
N1 . . . . . 7D **50**
SW13 . . . . . 2B **100**
TW7: Isle 4A **98**
W4 . . . . . 3J **81**
W13 . . . . . 5A **62**
Cleveland Row
SW1 . . . . . 1G **85** (5A **166**)
Cleveland Sq. W2 . . . . . 6A **66**
Clevelands, The
IG11: Bark 6G **55**
Cleveland St.
W1 . . . . . 4F **67** (4K **159**)
Cleveland Ter. W2 . . . . . 6A **66**
Cleveland Way E1 . . . . . 4J **69**
Cleveley Cl. SE7 . . . . . 4B **90**
Cleveley Cres. W5 . . . . . 2E **62**
Cleveleys Rd. E5 . . . . . 3H **51**
Cleverly Est. W12 . . . . . 1C **82**
Cleve Rd. DA14: Sidc 3D **128**
NW6 . . . . . 7K **47**
Cleves Av. KT17: Eps 7D **148**
Cleves Ho. *E16* *7K 71*
(off Southey M.)
Cleves Rd. E6 . . . . . 1B **72**
TW10: Rich 3C **116**
Cleves Wlk. IG6: Ilf 1G **37**
Cleves Way HA4: Ruis 1B **42**
TW12: Hamp 7D **114**
TW16: Sun T 6H **113**
Clewer Ct. *E10* *1C 52*
(off Leyton Grange Est.)
Clewer Cres. HA3: Harr 1H **25**
Clewer Ho. *SE2* *2D 92*
(off Wolvercote Rd.)
Cley Ho. SE4 . . . . . 4K **105**
Clichy Est. E1 . . . . . 5J **69**
Clichy Ho. *E1* *5J 69*
(off Stepney Way)
Clifden Rd. E5 . . . . . 5J **51**
TW1: Twick 1K **115**
TW8: Bford 6D **80**
Cliffe Ho. *SE10* *5H 89*
(off Blackwall La.)
Cliffe Rd. CR2: S Croy 5D **152**
Cliffe Wlk. *SM1: Sutt* *5A 150*
(off Greyhound Rd.)
Clifford Av. BR7: Chst 6D **126**
IG5: Ilf 1F **37**
SM6: Wall 4G **151**
SW14 . . . . . 3H **99**
(not continuous)
Clifford Cl. UB5: N'olt 1C **60**
Clifford Ct. *W2* *5K 65*
(off Westbourne Pk. Vs.)
Clifford Dr. SW9 . . . . . 4B **104**
Clifford Gdns. NW10 . . . . . 2E **64**
UB3: Hayes 4G **77**
Clifford Gro. TW15: Ashf . . . 4C **112**
Clifford Haigh Ho. SW6 . . . . 7F **83**
Clifford Ho. *BR3: Beck* *6D 124*
(off Calverley Cl.)
W14 . . . . . *4H 83*
(off Edith Vs.)
Clifford Rd. E16 . . . . . 4H **71**
E17 . . . . . 2E **34**
EN5: Barn 3E **4**
HA0: Wemb 7D **44**
N1 . . . . . 1E **68**
N9 . . . . . 6D **8**
SE25 . . . . . 4G **141**
TW4: Houn 3B **96**
TW10: Rich 2D **116**
Clifford's Inn Pas.
WC2 . . . . . 6A **68** (1J **167**)
Clifford St. W1 . . . 7G **67** (3A **166**)
Clifford Way NW10 . . . . . 4B **46**
Cliff Rd. NW1 . . . . . 6H **49**
Cliffsend Ho. *SW9* *1A 104*
(off Cowley Rd.)
Cliff Ter. SE8 . . . . . 2C **106**
Cliffview Rd. SE13 . . . . . 3C **106**
Cliff Vs. NW1 . . . . . 6H **49**
Cliff Wlk. E16 . . . . . 5H **71**
Clifton Av. E17 . . . . . 3K **33**
HA3: Harr 2B **26**
HA9: Wemb 6F **45**
N3 . . . . . 1H **29**
TW13: Felt 3A **114**
W12 . . . . . 1B **82**
Clifton Ct. BR3: Beck 1D **142**
IG8: Wfd G 6D **20**
KT5: Surb 7F **135**
N4 . . . . . 2A **50**
NW8 . . . . . 3A **158**
SE15 . . . . . 7H **87**
TW19: Staines 6A **94**
Clifton Cres. SE15 . . . . . 7H **87**
Clifton Est. SE15 . . . . . 1H **105**
Clifton Gdns. EN2: Enf 4D **6**
N15 . . . . . 6F **33**
NW11 . . . . . 6H **29**
UB10: Uxb 2D **58**
W4 . . . . . 4K **81**
(not continuous)
W9 . . . . . 4A **66**
Clifton Gro. E8 . . . . . 6G **51**
Clifton Hill NW6 . . . . . 2K **65**
Clifton Ho. *E2* *3J 163*
(off Club Row)
E11 . . . . . 2G **53**
Clifton Pde. TW13: Felt 4A **114**
Clifton Pk. Av. SW20 . . . . . 2E **136**
Clifton Pl. SE16 . . . . . 2J **87**
W2 . . . . . 6B **66** (1B **164**)
Clifton Ri. SE14 . . . . . 7A **88**
(not continuous)
Clifton Rd. DA14: Sidc 4J **127**
DA16: Well 3C **110**
E7 . . . . . 6B **54**
E16 . . . . . 5G **71**
Clifton Rd. HA3: Harr 4F **27**
IG2: Ilf 6H **37**
KT2: King T 7F **117**
N3 . . . . . 1A **30**
N8 . . . . . 6H **31**
N22 . . . . . 1G **31**
NW10 . . . . . 2C **64**
SE25 . . . . . 4E **140**
SM6: Wall 5F **151**
SW19 . . . . . 6F **119**
TW7: Isle 2J **97**
TW11: Tedd 4J **115**
UB2: S'hall 4C **78**
UB6: G'frd 4G **61**
W9 . . . . . 4A **66** (3A **158**)
Clifton St. EC2 . . . . . 4E **68** (4G **163**)
Clifton Ter. N4 . . . . . 2A **50**
Clifton Vs. W9 . . . . . 5A **66**
Cliftonville Ct. SE12 . . . . . 1J **125**
Clifton Wlk. *W6* *4D 82*
(off King St.)
Clifton Way HA0: Wemb 1E **62**
SE15 . . . . . 7H **87**
TW6: Houn 3D **94**
Climsland Ho.
SE1 . . . . . 1A **86** (4K **167**)
Clinch Ct. *E16* *5J 71*
(off Plymouth Rd.)
Cline Rd. N11 . . . . . 6B **16**
Clinger Ct. *N1* *1E 68*
(off Hobbs Pl. Est.)
Clink Exhibition, The ***4E 168***
Clink St. SE1 . . . . . 1D **86** (4E **168**)
Clink Wharf *SE1* *4E 168*
(off Clink St.)
Clinton Av. DA16: Well 4A **110**
KT8: E Mos 4G **133**
Clinton Rd. E3 . . . . . 3A **70**
E7 . . . . . 4J **53**
N15 . . . . . 4D **32**
Clipper Cl. SE16 . . . . . 2K **87**
Clipper Ho. *E14* *5E 88*
(off Manchester Rd.)
Clipper Way SE13 . . . . . 4E **106**
Clippesby Cl.
KT9: Chess 6F **147**
Clipstone M. W1 . . . 5G **67** (5A **160**)
Clipstone Rd. TW3: Houn 3E **96**
Clipstone St. W1 . . . 5F **67** (5K **159**)
Clissold Cl. N2 . . . . . 3D **30**
Clissold Ct. N4 . . . . . 2C **50**
Clissold Cres. N16 . . . . . 3D **50**
Clissold Leisure Cen. ***3D 50***
Clissold Rd. N16 . . . . . 3D **50**
Clitheroe Av. HA2: Harr 1E **42**
Clitheroe Rd. SW9 . . . . . 2J **103**
Clitherow Av. W7 . . . . . 3A **80**
Clitherow Ct. TW8: Bford 5C **80**
Clitherow Pas.
TW8: Bford 5C **80**
Clitherow Rd.
TW8: Bford 5B **80**
Clitterhouse Cres. NW2 . . . . . 1E **46**
Clitterhouse Rd. NW2 . . . . . 1E **46**
Clive Av. N18 . . . . . 6B **18**
Clive Ct. *W9* *4A 66*
(off Maida Va.)
Cliveden Cl. N12 . . . . . 4F **15**
Cliveden Ho. *E16* *7J 71*
(off Fitzwilliam M.)
Cliveden Pl.
SW1 . . . . . 4E **84** (3G **171**)
TW17: Shep 6E **130**
Cliveden Rd. SW19 . . . . . 1H **137**
Clivedon Ct. W13 . . . . . 5B **62**
Clivedon Rd. E4 . . . . . 5B **20**
Clive Ho. *SE10* *6E 88*
(off Haddo St.)
Clive Lloyd Ho. *N15* *5C 32*
(off Woodlands Pk. Rd.)
Clive Lodge NW4 . . . . . 6F **29**
Clive Pas. SE21 . . . . . 3D **122**

A-Z London 219

Clive Rd.—Coleman Mans.

Clive Rd. DA17: Belv 4G 93
EN1: Enf 4B 8
SE21 ....3D 122
SW19 ....6C 120
TW1: Twick 4K 115
TW14: Felt 6J 95
Clivesdale Dr. UB3: Hayes 1K 77
Clive Way EN1: Enf 4B 8
Cloak La. EC4 ....7C 68 (2D 168)
Clochar Ct. NW10 ....1B 64
Clock Ct. E11 ....4K 35
Clock Ho. E3 ....3E 70
E17 ....4F 35
(off Wood St.)
Clockhouse Av. IG11: Bark 1G 73
Clockhouse Cl. SW19 ....2E 118
Clockhouse Ct.
BR3: Beck 2A 142
CLOCKHOUSE JUNCTION 5E 16
Clockhouse La.
RM5: Col R 1H 39
(not continuous)
TW14: Felt 4C 112
TW15: Ashf 4C 112
Clock Ho. Pde. E11 ....6K 35
Clockhouse Pde. N13 ....5F 17
Clockhouse Pl. SW15 ....6G 101
Clock Ho. Rd. BR3: Beck 3A 142
CLOCKHOUSE RDBT. 1D 112
Clock Mus., The 7D 162
Clock Pde. EN2: Enf 5J 7
Clock Pl. *SE11 ....4B 86*
(off Newington Butts)
Clock Twr. Ind. Est.
TW7: Isle 3K 97
Clock Twr. M. N1 ....1C 68
SE28 ....7B 74
Clock Twr. Pl. N7 ....6J 49
Clock Twr. Rd. TW7: Isle 3K 97
Cloister Cl. TW11: Tedd 5B 116
Cloister Gdns. HA8: Edg 5D 12
SE25 ....6H 141
Cloister Rd. NW2 ....3H 47
W3 ....5J 63
Cloisters Av. BR2: Short 5D 144
Cloisters Bus. Cen. *SW8 ....7F 85*
(off Battersea Pk. Rd.)
Cloisters Ct. DA7: Bex 3H 111
Cloisters Mall
KT1: King T 2E 134
Cloisters, The 1E 172
Cloisters, The E1 ....4J 163
SW9 ....1A 104
TW7: Isle 3A 98
(off Pulteney Cl.)
Clonard Way HA5: Pinn 6A 10
Clonbrock Rd. N16 ....4E 50
Cloncurry St. SW6 ....2F 101
Clonmel Cl. HA2: Harr 2H 43
Clonmell Rd. N17 ....3D 32
Clonmel Rd. SW6 ....7H 83
TW11: Tedd 4H 115
Clonmore St. SW18 ....1H 119
Clorane Gdns. NW3 ....3J 47
Close, The BR3: Beck 4A 142
BR5: Orp 6J 145
CR4: Mitc 4D 138
DA5: Bexl 6G 111
DA14: Sidc 4B 128
E4 ....7K 19
EN4: Barn 6J 5
HA0: Wemb 6E 44
HA3: Harr 2G 25
HA5: Pinn 7A 24
(North Vw.)
HA5: Pinn 7D 24
(Rayners La.)
HA9: Wemb 3J 45
IG2: Ilf 6J 37
KT3: N Mald 2J 135
KT6: Surb 6E 134
N10 ....2F 31
Close, The N14 ....2C 16
N20 ....2C 14
RM6: Chad H 6E 38
SE3 ....2F 107
SE25 ....6G 141
SM3: Sutt 7H 137
SM5: Cars 7C 150
TW7: Isle 2H 97
TW9: Rich 3H 99
UB10: Uxb 1C 58
Cloth Ct. EC1 ....6B 162
Cloth Fair EC1 ....5B 68 (6B 162)
Clothier St. E1 ....6E 68 (7H 163)
Cloth St. EC1 ....5C 68 (5C 162)
Clothworkers Rd. SE18 ....7H 91
Cloudesdale Rd. SW17 ....2F 121
Cloudesley Pl. N1 ....1A 68
Cloudesley Rd. DA7: Bex 1F 111
N1 ....1A 68
(not continuous)
Cloudesley Sq. N1 ....1A 68
Cloudesley St. N1 ....1A 68
Clouston Cl. SM6: Wall 5J 151
Clova Rd. E7 ....6H 53
Clove Cres. E14 ....7E 70
Clove Hitch Quay SW11 ....3A 102
Clovelly Av. NW9 ....4B 28
UB10: Uxb 4E 40
Clovelly Cl. HA5: Pinn 3K 23
UB10: Uxb 4E 40
Clovelly Gdns. EN1: Enf 7K 7
RM7: Mawney 1H 39
SE19 ....1F 141
Clovelly Ho. *W2 ....6A 66*
(off Hallfield Est.)
Clovelly Rd. DA7: Bex 6E 92
N8 ....4H 31
TW3: Houn 2E 96
W4 ....2K 81
W5 ....2C 80
Clovelly Way BR6: Orp 6K 145
E1 ....6J 69
HA2: Harr 2D 42
Clover Cl. E11 ....2F 53
Cloverdale Gdns.
DA15: Sidc 6K 109
Clover M. SW3 ....6D 84 (7F 171)
Clover Way SM6: Wall 1E 150
Clove St. E13 ....4J 71
Clowders Rd. SE6 ....3B 124
Clowser Cl. SM1: Sutt 5A 150
Cloysters Grn. E1 ....1G 87
Cloyster Wood HA8: Edg 7J 11
Club Gdns. Rd.
BR2: Short 7J 143
Club Row E2 ....4F 69 (3J 163)
Clumps, The TW15: Ashf 4F 113
Clunbury Av. UB2: S'hall 5D 78
Clunbury St. N1 ....2D 68
Cluny Est. SE1 ....3E 86 (7G 169)
Cluny M. SW5 ....4J 83
Cluny Pl. SE1 ....3E 86 (7G 169)
Cluse Ct. *N1 ....2C 68*
(off St Peters St., not continuous)
Clutton St. E14 ....5D 70
Clydach Rd. EN1: Enf 4A 8
Clyde Cir. N15 ....4E 32
Clyde Ct. *NW1 ....2H 67*
(off Hampden Cl.)
Clyde Flats *SW6 ....7H 83*
(off Rhylston Rd.)
Clyde Ho. KT1: King T 1D 134
Clyde Pl. E10 ....7D 34
Clyde Rd. CR0: Croy 2F 153
N15 ....4E 32
N22 ....1H 31
SM1: Sutt 5J 149
SM6: Wall 6G 151
TW19: Staines 1A 112
Clydesdale EN3: Enf 4E 8
Clydesdale Av. HA7: Stan 3D 26
Clydesdale Cl. TW7: Isle 3K 97
Clydesdale Ct. N20 ....1G 15
Clydesdale Gdns.
TW10: Rich 4H 99
Clydesdale Ho.
DA18: Erith 2E 92
(off Kale Rd.)
W11 ....6H 65
(off Clydesdale Rd.)
Clydesdale Rd. W11 ....6H 65
Clyde St. SE8 ....6B 88
Clyde Ter. SE23 ....2J 123
Clyde Va. SE23 ....2J 123
Clyde Way RM1: Rom 1K 39
Clyde Wharf E16 ....1J 89
Clydon Cl. DA8: Erith 6K 93
Clyfford Rd. HA4: Ruis 4H 41
Clymping Dene TW14: Felt 7K 95
Clynes Ho. *E2 ....3K 69*
(off Knottisford St.)
RM10: Dag 3G 57
(off Uvedale Rd.)
Clyston St. SW8 ....2G 103
Coach & Horses Yd.
W1 ....7G 67 (2K 165)
Coach Ho. La. N5 ....4B 50
SW19 ....4F 119
Coach Ho. M.
SE1 ....2E 86 (7G 169)
SE20 ....7H 123
SE23 ....6K 105
Coach Ho. Yd. *NW3 ....4A 48*
(off Heath St.)
SW18 ....4K 101
Coachmaker M. *SW4 ....3J 103*
(off Fenwick Pl.)
Coach Yd. M. N19 ....1J 49
Coaldale Wlk. SE21 ....7C 104
Coalecroft Rd. SW15 ....4E 100
Coalport Ho. SE11 ....2J 173
Coates Av. SW18 ....6C 102
Coates Hill Rd.
BR1: Brom 2E 144
Coate St. E2 ....2G 69
Coates Wlk. TW8: Bford 6E 80
Cobalt Sq. SW8 ....7G 173
Cobbett Rd. SE9 ....3C 108
TW2: Twick 1E 114
Cobbetts Av. IG4: Ilf 5B 36
Cobbett St. SW8 ....7K 85
Cobble La. N1 ....7B 50
Cobble M. N4 ....3C 50
Cobblers Wlk.
TW12: Hamp 1G 133
(not continuous)
Cobblestone Pl.
CR0: Croy 1C 152
Cobbold Ct. *SW1 ....3C 172*
(off Elverton St.)
Cobbold Ind. Est. NW10 ....6B 46
Cobbold M. W12 ....2B 82
Cobbold Rd. E11 ....3H 53
NW10 ....6B 46
W12 ....2A 82
Cobb's Ct. EC4 ....1B 168
Cobb's Hall *W6 ....6F 83*
(off Fulham Pal. Rd.)
Cobb's Rd. TW4: Houn 4D 96
Cobbsthorpe Vs. SE26 ....4K 123
Cobb St. E1 ....5F 69 (6J 163)
Cobden Ct. BR2: Short 4A 144
Cobden Ho. *E2 ....3G 69*
(off Nelson Gdns.)
NW1 ....2G 67
(off Arlington Rd.)
Cobden M. SE26 ....5H 123
Cobden Rd. E11 ....3G 53
SE25 ....5G 141
Cobham Av. KT3: N Mald 5C 136
Cobham Cl. BR2: Short 7C 144
DA15: Sidc 6B 110
EN1: Enf 3B 8
HA8: Edg 2H 27
Cobham Cl. SM6: Wall 6J 151
SW11 ....6C 102
Cobham Ct. CR4: Mitc 2B 138
Cobham Ho. IG11: Bark 1G 73
(not continuous)
Cobham M. NW1 ....7H 49
Cobham Pl. DA6: Bex 5D 110
Cobham Rd. E17 ....1E 34
IG3: Ilf 2J 55
KT1: King T 2G 135
N22 ....3B 32
TW5: Houn 7A 78
Cobland Rd. SE12 ....4A 126
Coborn Rd. E3 ....2B 70
Coborn St. E3 ....3B 70
Cobourg Rd. SE5 ....6F 87
Cobourg St.
NW1 ....3G 67 (2B 160)
Coburg Cl. SW1 ....3B 172
Coburg Cres. SW2 ....1K 121
Coburg Dwellings *E1 ....6J 69*
(off Hardinge St.)
Coburg Gdns. IG5: Ilf 2B 36
Coburg Rd. N22 ....3K 31
Cochrane Cl. NW8 ....1B 158
Cochrane Ct. *E10 ....1C 52*
(off Leyton Grange Est.)
Cochrane Ho. *E14 ....2C 88*
(off Admirals Way)
Cochrane M. NW8 ....2B 66
Cochrane Rd. SW19 ....7G 119
Cochrane St.
NW8 ....2B 66 (1B 158)
Cochrane Theatre, The 6F 161
(off Theobald's Rd.)
Cockburn Ho. *SW1 ....6D 172*
(off Aylesford St.)
COCKCROW HILL 1D 146
Cockerell Rd. E17 ....7A 34
COCKFOSTERS 4K 5
Cockfosters Pde. EN4: Barn 4K 5
Cockfosters Rd. EN4: Barn 1H 5
Cock Hill E1 ....5E 68 (6H 163)
Cock La. EC1 ....5B 68 (6A 162)
Cockpit Steps SW1 ....7C 166
Cockpit Theatre 4C 158
(off Gateforth St.)
Cockpit Yd. WC1 ....5K 67 (5H 161)
Cocks Cres.
KT3: N Mald 4B 136
Cockspur Ct.
SW1 ....1H 85 (4D 166)
Cockspur St.
SW1 ....1H 85 (4D 166)
Cocksure La. DA14: Sidc 3G 129
Coda Cen., The SW6 ....7G 83
Code St. E1 ....4F 69 (4K 163)
Codicote Ho. *SE8 ....4K 87*
(off Chilton Gro.)
Codicote Ter. N4 ....2C 50
Codling Cl. E1 ....1G 87
Codling Way HA0: Wemb 4D 44
Codrington Ct. E1 ....4H 69
SE16 ....7A 70
Codrington Hill SE23 ....7A 106
Codrington M. W11 ....6G 65
Cody Cl. HA3: Harr 3D 26
SM6: Wall 7H 151
Cody Rd. E16 ....4F 71
Coe Av. SE25 ....6G 141
Coe's All. EN5: Barn 4B 4
Cofers Circ. HA9: Wemb 2H 45
Coffey St. SE8 ....7C 88
Cogan Av. E17 ....1A 34
Coin St. SE1 ....1A 86 (4J 167)
(not continuous)
Coity Rd. NW5 ....6E 48
Cokers La. SE21 ....1D 122
Coke St. E1 ....6G 69
Colas M. NW6 ....1J 65
Colbeck M. SW5 ....4K 83
Colbeck Rd. HA1: Harr 7G 25
Colberg Pl. N16 ....7F 33
Colborne Ho. *E14 ....7C 70*
(off E. India Dock Rd.)
Colborne Way
KT4: Wor Pk 3E 148
Colbrook Av. UB3: Hayes 3F 77
Colbrook Cl. UB3: Hayes 3F 77
Colburn Way SM1: Sutt 3B 150
Colby M. SE19 ....5E 122
Colby Rd. KT12: Walt T 7J 131
SE19 ....5E 122
Colchester Av. E12 ....4D 54
Colchester Dr. HA5: Pinn 5B 24
Colchester Rd. E10 ....7E 34
E17 ....6C 34
HA6: Nwood 2J 23
HA8: Edg 7D 12
Colchester St.
E1 ....6F 69 (7K 163)
Coldbath Sq.
EC1 ....4A 68 (3J 161)
Coldbath St. SE13 ....1D 106
COLDBLOW 1J 129
Cold Blow Cres.
DA5: Bexl 1K 129
Cold Blow La. SE14 ....7K 87
(not continuous)
Cold Blows CR4: Mitc 3D 138
Coldershaw Rd. W13 ....1A 80
Coldfall Av. N10 ....2E 30
Coldham Ct. N22 ....1B 32
Coldharbour E14 ....2E 88
Coldharbour Crest SE9 ....3E 126
Coldharbour La. SW9 ....4A 104
UB3: Hayes 1J 77
Coldharbour Pl. SE5 ....2C 104
Coldharbour Rd.
CR0: Croy 5A 152
Coldharbour Way
CR0: Croy 5A 152
Coldstream Gdns. SW18 ....6H 101
Colebeck M. N1 ....6B 50
Colebert Av. E1 ....4J 69
Colebert Ho. *E1 ....4J 69*
(off Colebert Av.)
Colebrook Cl. NW7 ....6A 14
SW15 ....7F 101
Colebrook Ct. *SW3 ....4D 170*
(off Makins St.)
Colebrooke Av. W13 ....6B 62
Colebrooke Ct. DA14: Sidc 3B 128
Colebrooke Dr. E11 ....7A 36
Colebrooke Pl. N1 ....1B 68
Colebrooke Ri.
BR2: Short 2G 143
Colebrooke Row N1 ....2B 68
Colebrook Ho. *E14 ....6D 70*
(off Ellesmere St.)
Colebrook Rd. SW16 ....1J 139
Colebrook Way N11 ....5A 16
Coleby Path SE5 ....7D 86
Colechurch Ho. *SE1 ....5G 87*
(off Avondale Sq.)
Cole Cl. SE28 ....1B 92
Cole Ct. TW1: Twick 7A 98
Coledale Dr. HA7: Stan 1C 26
Coleford Rd. SW18 ....5A 102
Cole Gdns. TW5: Houn 7J 77
Colegrave Rd. E15 ....5F 53
Colegrove Rd. SE15 ....6F 87
Coleherne Ct. SW5 ....5K 83
Coleherne Mans. *SW5 ....5K 83*
(off Old Brompton Rd.)
Coleherne M. SW10 ....5K 83
Coleherne Rd. SW10 ....5K 83
Colehill Gdns. SW6 ....2G 101
Colehill La. SW6 ....1G 101
Cole Ho. *SE1 ....7J 167*
(off Baylis Rd.)
Coleman Cl. SE25 ....2G 141
Coleman Flds. N1 ....1C 68
Coleman Mans. N8 ....7J 31

Coleman Rd.—Combedale Rd.

Coleman Rd. DA17: Belv ... 4G 93
RM9: Dag ... 6E 56
SE5 ... 7E 86
Colemans Heath SE9 ... 3E 126
Coleman St. EC2 ... 6D 68 (7E 162)
Coleman St. Bldgs. EC2 ... 7E 162
Colenso Dr. NW7 ... 7H 13
Colenso Rd. E5 ... 4J 51
IG2: Ilf ... 1J 55
COLE PARK ... 6A 98
Cole Pk. Gdns.
TW1: Twick ... 5A 98
Cole Pk. Rd. TW1: Twick ... 5A 98
Cole Pk. Vw. TW1: Twick ... 6A 98
Colepits Wood Rd. SE9 ... 5H 109
Coleraine Rd. N8 ... 3A 32
SE3 ... 6H 89
Coleridge Av. E12 ... 6C 54
SM1: Sutt ... 4C 150
Coleridge Cl. SW8 ... 2F 103
Coleridge Ct. *EN5: Barn* ... *5E 4*
(off Station Rd.)
W14 ... *3F 83*
(off Blythe Rd.)
Coleridge Gdns. NW6 ... 7A 48
SW10 ... 7K 83
Coleridge Ho. *SE17* ... *5C 86*
(off Browning St.)
SW1 ... *6B 172*
(off Churchill Gdns.)
Coleridge La. N8 ... 6J 31
Coleridge Rd. CR0: Croy ... 7J 141
E17 ... 4B 34
N4 ... 2A 50
N8 ... 6H 31
N12 ... 5F 15
TW15: Ashf ... 4A 112
Coleridge Sq. W13 ... 6A 62
Coleridge Wlk. NW11 ... 4J 29
Coleridge Way UB4: Hayes ... 6J 59
UB7: W Dray ... 4A 76
Cole Rd. TW1: Twick ... 6A 98
Colesburg Rd. BR3: Beck ... 3B 142
Coles Cres. HA2: Harr ... 2F 43
Coles Grn. WD23: Bush ... 1B 10
Coles Grn. Ct. NW2 ... 2C 46
Coles Grn. Rd. NW2 ... 1C 46
Coleshill Flats SW1 ... 4H 171
Coleshill Rd.
TW11: Tedd ... 6J 115
Colestown St. SW11 ... 2C 102
Cole St. SE1 ... 2C 86 (7D 168)
Colesworth Ho. *HA8: Edg* ... *2J 27*
(off Burnt Oak B'way.)
Colet Cl. N13 ... 6G 17
Colet Ct. *W6* ... *4F 83*
(off Hammersmith Rd.)
Colet Gdns. W14 ... 4F 83
Colet Ho. *SE17* ... *5B 86*
(off Doddington Gro.)
Colette Ct. *SE16* ... *2K 87*
(off Eleanor Cl.)
Coley St. WC1 ... 4K 67 (4H 161)
Colfe & Hatcliffe Glebe
SE13 ... *5D 106*
(off Lewisham High St.)
Colfe Rd. SE23 ... 1A 124
Colham Av. UB7: W Dray ... 1A 76
COLHAM GREEN ... 5C 58
Colham Grn. Rd.
UB8: Uxb ... 5C 58
Colham Mill Rd.
UB7: W Dray ... 2A 76
Colham Rd. UB8: Uxb ... 4B 58
Colham Rdbt. UB8: Uxb ... 6C 58
Colina M. N15 ... 4B 32
Colina Rd. N8 ... 5B 32
Colin Cl. BR4: W W'ck ... 3H 155
CR0: Croy ... 3B 154
NW9 ... 4A 28
Colin Cres. NW9 ... 4B 28
COLINDALE ... 3K 27
Colindale Av. NW9 ... 3K 27
Colindale Bus. Pk. NW9 ... 3J 27
Colindeep Gdns. NW4 ... 4C 28
Colindeep La. NW9 ... 3A 28
Colin Dr. NW9 ... 5B 28
Colinette Rd. SW15 ... 4E 100
Colin Gdns. NW9 ... 4B 28
Colin Pde. NW9 ... 4A 28
Colin Pk. Rd. NW9 ... 4A 28
Colin Rd. NW10 ... 6C 46
Colinton Rd. IG3: Ilf ... 2B 56
Colin Winter Ho. *E1* ... *4J 69*
(off Nicholas Rd.)
Coliseum Theatre ... 3E 166
(off St Martin's La.)
Coliston Pas. SW18 ... 7J 101
Coliston Rd. SW18 ... 7J 101
Collamore Av. SW18 ... 1C 120
Collapit Cl. HA1: Harr ... 6F 25
Collard Pl. NW1 ... 7F 49
Collards Almshouses *E17* ... *5E 34*
(off Maynard Rd.)
College App. SE10 ... 6E 88
College Arts Collection, The
... 3C 160
(off Gower St.)
College Av. HA3: Harr ... 1J 25
College Cl. E9 ... 5J 51
HA3: Harr ... 7D 10
N18 ... 5A 18
TW2: Twick ... 1H 115
College Ct. EN3: Enf ... 5D 8
NW3 ... *6B 48*
(off College Cres.)
SW3 ... 6F 171
W5 ... 7E 62
W6 ... *5E 82*
(off Queen Caroline St.)
College Cres. NW3 ... 6A 48
Coll. Cross N1 ... 7A 50
College Dr. HA4: Ruis ... 7J 23
KT7: T Ditt ... 7J 133
College E. E1 ... 5F 69 (6K 163)
College Flds. Bus. Cen.
SW19 ... 1B 138
College Gdns. E4 ... 7J 9
EN2: Enf ... 1J 7
IG4: Ilf ... 5C 36
KT3: N Mald ... 5B 136
N18 ... 5A 18
SE21 ... 1E 122
SW17 ... 2C 120
(not continuous)
College Grn. SE19 ... 7E 122
College Gro. NW1 ... 1G 67
College Hall ... 4H 67 (4C 160)
College Hill EC4 ... 7C 68 (2D 168)
College Hill Rd. HA3: Harr ... 7D 10
College La. NW5 ... 4F 49
College Mans. *NW6* ... *1G 65*
(off Winchester Av.)
College M. *N1* ... *7A 50*
(off College Cross)
SW1 ... 1E 172
SW18 ... 5K 101
College of Arms ... 2C 168
College Pde. NW6 ... 1G 65
COLLEGE PARK ... 3D 64
College Pk. Cl. SE13 ... 4F 107
College Pk. Rd. N17 ... 6A 18
College Pl. E17 ... 4G 35
NW1 ... 1G 67
SW10 ... *7A 84*
(off Hortensia Rd.)
College Point E15 ... 6H 53
College Rd. BR1: Brom ... 1J 143
BR8: Swan ... 7K 129
CR0: Croy ... 2D 152
E17 ... 5E 34
EN2: Enf ... 2J 7
HA1: Harr ... 6J 25
HA3: Harr ... 1J 25
College Rd. HA9: Wemb ... 1D 44
N17 ... 6A 18
N21 ... 2F 17
NW10 ... 2E 64
SE19 ... 7E 104
SE21 ... 7E 104
SW19 ... 6B 120
TW7: Isle ... 1K 97
W13 ... 6B 62
College Rdbt.
KT1: King T ... 3E 134
College Row E9 ... 5K 51
College Slip BR1: Brom ... 1J 143
College St. EC4 ... 7C 68 (2D 168)
College Ter. E3 ... 3B 70
N3 ... 2H 29
College Vw. SE9 ... 1B 126
College Wlk. KT1: King T ... 3E 134
College Way TW15: Ashf ... 4B 112
UB3: Hayes ... 7J 59
College Yd. NW5 ... 4F 49
Collent St. E9 ... 6J 51
Collerston Ho. *SE10* ... *5H 89*
(off Armitage Rd.)
Colless Rd. N15 ... 5F 33
Collett Rd. SE16 ... 3G 87
Collett Way UB2: S'hall ... 2F 79
Collier Cl. E6 ... 7F 73
KT19: Eps ... 6G 147
Collier Dr. HA8: Edg ... 2G 27
COLLIER ROW ... 1H 39
Collier Row La.
RM5: Col R ... 1H 39
Collier Row Rd.
RM5: Col R ... 1F 39
Colliers Ct. *CR0: Croy* ... *4D 152*
(off St Peter's Rd.)
Colliers Shaw BR2: Kes ... 5B 156
Collier St. N1 ... 2K 67
Colliers Water La.
CR7: Thor H ... 5A 140
COLLIER'S WOOD ... 7B 120
Colliers Wood ... 7B 120
Collindale Av. DA8: Erith ... 7H 93
DA15: Sidc ... 1A 128
Collingbourne Rd. W12 ... 1D 82
Collingham Gdns. SW5 ... 4K 83
Collingham Pl. SW5 ... 4K 83
Collingham Rd. SW5 ... 4K 83
Collings Cl. N22 ... 6E 16
Collington St. SE10 ... 5F 89
Collingtree Rd. SE26 ... 4J 123
Collingwood Av.
EN3: Enf ... 3D 8
KT5: Surb ... 1J 147
N10 ... 3E 30
Collingwood Cl. SE20 ... 1H 141
TW2: Twick ... 7E 96
Collingwood Ct. EN5: Barn ... 5E 4
W5 ... 5F 63
Collingwood Ho. *E1* ... *4H 69*
(off Darling Row)
SE16 ... *2H 87*
(off Cherry Garden St.)
SW1 ... *6C 172*
(off Dolphin Sq.)
W1 ... *5A 160*
(off Clipstone St.)
Collingwood Rd.
CR4: Mitc ... 3C 138
E17 ... 6C 34
N15 ... 4E 32
SM1: Sutt ... 3J 149
UB8: Uxb ... 4D 58
Collingwood St. E1 ... 4H 69
Collins Av. HA7: Stan ... 2E 26
Collins Ct. E8 ... 6G 51
Collins Dr. HA4: Ruis ... 2A 42
Collins Ho. *E14* ... *7E 70*
(off Newby Pl.)
E15 ... *1H 71*
(off John St.)
Collins Ho. *SE10* ... *5H 89*
(off Armitage Rd.)
Collinson Ct. *SE1* ... *7C 168*
(off Gt. Suffolk St.)
Collinson Ho. *SE15* ... *7G 87*
(off Peckham Pk. Rd.)
Collinson St.
SE1 ... 2C 86 (7C 168)
Collinson Wlk.
SE1 ... 2C 86 (7C 168)
Collins Path
TW12: Hamp ... 6D 114
Collins Rd. N5 ... 4C 50
Collins Sq. SE3 ... 2H 107
Collins St. SE3 ... 2G 107
(not continuous)
Collin's Yd. N1 ... 1B 68
Collinwood Gdns.
IG5: Ilf ... 5D 36
Collis All. TW2: Twick ... 1J 115
Coll's Rd. SE15 ... 1J 105
Collyer Av. CR0: Croy ... 4J 151
Collyer Pl. SE15 ... 1G 105
Collyer Rd. CR0: Croy ... 4J 151
Colman Ct. HA7: Stan ... 6G 11
N12 ... 6F 15
Colman Pde. EN1: Enf ... 3K 7
Colman Rd. E16 ... 5A 72
Colmans Wharf *E14* ... *5D 70*
(off Morris Rd.)
Colmar Cl. E1 ... 4K 69
Colmer Pl. HA3: Harr ... 7C 10
Colmer Rd. SW16 ... 1J 139
Colmore M. SE15 ... 1H 105
Colmore Rd. EN3: Enf ... 4D 8
Colnbrook St. SE1 ... 3B 86
Colne Ct. KT19: Eps ... 4J 147
W7 ... *6H 61*
(off High La.)
Colnedale Rd. UB8: Uxb ... 5A 40
Colne Ho. IG11: Bark ... 7F 55
Colne Rd. E5 ... 4A 52
N21 ... 7J 7
TW2: Twick ... 1J 115
Colne St. E13 ... 3J 71
COLNEY HATCH ... 6J 15
Colney Hatch La. N10 ... 6J 15
N11 ... 6J 15
Cologne Rd. SW11 ... 4B 102
Colombo Rd. IG1: Ilf ... 1G 55
Colombo St. SE1 ... 1B 86 (5A 168)
Colomb St. SE10 ... 5G 89
Colonel's Wlk. EN2: Enf ... 3G 7
Colonial Av. TW2: Twick ... 6G 97
Colonial Ct. N7 ... 3K 49
Colonial Dr. W4 ... 4J 81
Colonial Rd. TW14: Felt ... 7G 95
Colonnade WC1 ... 4J 67 (4F 161)
Colonnades, The
CR0: Croy ... 6A 152
W2 ... 6K 65
Colonnade, The SE8 ... 4B 88
Colonnade Wlk.
SW1 ... 4F 85 (4J 171)
Colosseum Ter. NW1 ... 2K 159
Colour Ct. SW1 ... 5B 166
Colroy Ct. NW11 ... 5G 29
Colson Rd. CR0: Croy ... 2E 152
Colson Way SW16 ... 4G 121
Colstead Ho. *E1* ... *6H 69*
(off Watney Mkt.)
Colsterworth Rd. N15 ... 4F 33
(not continuous)
Colston Av. SM5: Cars ... 4C 150
Colston Ct. *SM5: Cars* ... *4D 150*
(off West St.)
Colston Rd. E7 ... 6B 54
SW14 ... 4J 99
Colthurst Cres. N4 ... 2B 50
Colthurst Dr. N9 ... 3C 18
Coltman Ho. *E14* ... *6A 70*
(off Maroon St.)
Coltman Ho. *SE10* ... *6E 88*
(off Welland St.)
Coltness Cres. SE2 ... 5B 92
Colton Gdns. N17 ... 3C 32
Colton Rd. HA1: Harr ... 5J 25
Coltsfoot Dr. UB7: W Dray ... 6A 58
Columbas Dr. NW3 ... 1B 48
Columbia Av. HA4: Ruis ... 1K 41
HA8: Edg ... 1H 27
KT4: Wor Pk ... 7B 136
Columbia Point *SE16* ... *3J 87*
(off Surrey Quays Rd.)
Columbia Rd. E2 ... 3F 69 (1J 163)
E13 ... 4H 71
Columbia Road Market ... 1K 163
(off Columbia Rd.)
Columbia Sq. SW14 ... 4J 99
Columbia Wharf EN3: Enf ... 6F 9
Columbine Av.
CR2: S Croy ... 7B 152
E6 ... 5C 72
Columbine Way SE13 ... 2E 106
Columbus Ct. *SE16* ... *1J 87*
(off Rotherhithe St.)
Columbus Ct. Yd. E14 ... 1C 88
Columbus Gdns.
HA6: Nwood ... 1J 23
Colva Wlk. N19 ... 2F 49
Colverson Ho. *E1* ... *5J 69*
(off Lindley St.)
Colvestone Cres. E8 ... 5F 51
Colview Ct. SE9 ... 1B 126
Colville Est. N1 ... 1E 68
Colville Est. W. *E2* ... *2K 163*
(off Turin St.)
Colville Gdns. W11 ... 6H 65
(not continuous)
Colville Ho's. W11 ... 6H 65
Colville Ho. *E2* ... *2J 69*
(off Waterloo Gdns.)
Colville M. W11 ... 6H 65
Colville Pl. W1 ... 5G 67 (6B 160)
Colville Rd. E11 ... 3E 52
E17 ... 2A 34
N9 ... 1C 18
W3 ... 3H 81
W11 ... 6H 65
Colville Sq. W11 ... 6H 65
Colville Ter. W11 ... 6H 65
Colvin Cl. SE26 ... 5J 123
Colvin Gdns. E4 ... 3K 19
E11 ... 4K 35
IG6: Ilf ... 1G 37
Colvin Rd. CR7: Thor H ... 5A 140
E6 ... 7C 54
Colwall Gdns. IG8: Wfd G ... 5D 20
Colwell Rd. SE22 ... 5F 105
Colwick Cl. N6 ... 7H 31
Colwith Rd. W6 ... 6E 82
Colwood Gdns. SW19 ... 7B 120
Colworth Gro. SE17 ... 4C 86
Colworth Rd. CR0: Croy ... 1G 153
E11 ... 6G 35
Colwyn Av. UB6: G'frd ... 2K 61
Colwyn Cl. SW16 ... 5G 121
Colwyn Cres. TW3: Houn ... 1G 97
Colwyn Grn. *NW9* ... *6A 28*
(off Snowdon Dr.)
Colwyn Ho. SE1 ... 3A 86 (2J 173)
Colwyn Rd. NW2 ... 3D 46
Colyer Cl. N1 ... 2K 67
SE9 ... 2F 127
Colyers Cl. DA8: Erith ... 1K 111
Colyers La. DA8: Erith ... 1J 111
Colyers Wlk. DA8: Erith ... 1K 111
Colyton Cl. DA16: Well ... 1D 110
HA0: Wemb ... 6C 44
Colyton La. SW16 ... 5A 122
Colyton Rd. SE22 ... 5H 105
Colyton Way N18 ... 5B 18
Combe Av. SE3 ... 7H 89
Combedale Rd. SE10 ... 5J 89

Combe Dene—Convent Cl.

Combe Dene
BR2: Short 4H **143**
(off Cumberland Rd.)
Combemartin Rd.
SW18 7G **101**
Combe M. SE3 7H **89**
Comber Cl. NW2 2D **46**
Comber Gro. SE5 7C **86**
Comber Ho. SE5 7C **86**
Combermere Rd.
SM4: Mord 6K **137**
SW9 3K **103**
Comberton *KT1: King T* *2G* ***135***
(off Eureka Rd.)
Comberton Rd. E5 2H **51**
Combeside SE18 7K **91**
Combe, The
NW1 3F **67** (2K **159**)
(not continuous)
Combwell Cres. SE2 3A **92**
Comedy Store *3C* ***166***
(off Oxendon St.)
Comedy Theatre *3C* ***166***
(off Panton St.)
Comely Bank Rd. E17 5E **34**
Comeragh M. W14 5G **83**
Comeragh Rd. W14 5G **83**
Comer Cres. *UB2: S'hall* *2G* ***79***
(off Windmill Av.)
Comerell Pl. SE10 5H **89**
Comerford Rd. SE4 4A **106**
Comet Cl. E12 4B **54**
Comet Pl. SE8 7C **88**
(not continuous)
Comet Rd.
TW19: Staines 7A **94**
Comet St. SE8 7C **88**
Comfort St. SE15 6E **86**
Commerce Rd. N22 1K **31**
TW8: Bford 6C **80**
Commerce Way
CR0: Croy 2K **151**
Commercial Dock Path
SE16 *3B* ***88***
(off Gulliver St.)
Commercial Rd.
E1 6G **69** (7K **163**)
E14 6A **70**
N18 5K **17**
Commercial Rd. Ind. Est.
N18 6A **18**
Commercial St.
E1 4F **69** (4J **163**)
Commercial Way NW10 2H **63**
SE15 7F **87**
Commerell St. SE10 5G **89**
Commodity Quay
E1 7F **69** (3K **169**)
Commodore Ct. *SE8* *1C* ***106***
(off Albyn Rd.)
Commodore Ho. *E14* *7E* ***70***
(off Poplar High St.)
Commodore Sq. SW10 1A **102**
Commodore St. E1 4A **70**
Commondale SW15 3E **100**
Commonfield La. SW17 5C **120**
Common La. KT10: Esh 7A **146**
Common Mile Cl. SW4 5H **103**
Common Rd. HA7: Stan 4C **10**
KT10: Esh 6A **146**
SW13 3D **100**
Commonside BR2: Kes 4A **156**
Commonside E.
CR4: Mitc 3E **138**
(not continuous)
Commonside W.
CR4: Mitc 3D **138**
Common, The E15 6G **53**
HA7: Stan 2D **10**
UB2: S'hall 4A **78**
W5 7E **62**
(not continuous)
Commonwealth Av.
UB3: Hayes 6F **59**
W12 7D **64**
(not continuous)
Commonwealth Conference Cen.
1G ***85*** *(5B* ***166****)*
Commonwealth Institute *3H* ***83***
Commonwealth Rd. N17 7B **18**
Commonwealth Way SE2 5B **92**
Community Cl.
TW5: Houn 1K **95**
UB10: Uxb 3D **40**
Community La. N7 5H **49**
Community Rd. E15 5F **53**
UB6: G'frd 1G **61**
Como Rd. SE23 2A **124**
Como St. RM7: Rom 5K **39**
Compass Ct. *SE1* *5J* ***169***
(off Shad Thames)
Compass Hill TW10: Rich 6D **98**
Compass Ho. SW18 4K **101**
Compass Point *E14* *7B* ***70***
(off Grenade St.)
Compayne Gdns. NW6 7K **47**
Compton Av. E6 2B **72**
HA0: Wemb 4C **44**
N1 6B **50**
N6 7C **30**
Compton Cl. E3 5C **70**
HA8: Edg 7D **12**
NW1 2K **159**
NW11 3F **47**
SE15 7G **87**
W13 6A **62**
Compton Ct. SE19 6E **122**
SM1: Sutt 4A **150**
Compton Cres.
KT9: Chess 5E **146**
N17 7H **17**
UB5: N'olt 1B **60**
W4 6J **81**
Compton Pas.
EC1 4B **68** (3B **162**)
Compton Pl.
WC1 4J **67** (3E **160**)
Compton Ri. HA5: Pinn 5C **24**
Compton Rd. CR0: Croy 1H **153**
N1 6B **50**
N21 1F **17**
NW10 3F **65**
SW19 6H **119**
UB3: Hayes 7G **59**
Compton St. EC1 4B **68** (3A **162**)
Compton Ter. N1 6B **50**
N21 1F **17**
Comreddy Cl. EN2: Enf 1G **7**
Comus Ho. *SE17* *4E* ***86***
(off Comus Pl.)
Comus Pl. SE17 4E **86**
Comyn Rd. SW11 4C **102**
Comyns Cl. E16 5H **71**
Comyns Rd. RM9: Dag 7G **57**
Comyns, The WD23: Bush 1B **10**
Conant Ho. *SE11* *7K* ***173***
(off St Agnes Pl.)
Conant M. E1 7G **69**
Concanon Rd. SW2 4K **103**
Concert Hall App.
SE1 1K **85** (5H **167**)
Concord Bus. Cen. W3 4H **63**
Concord Cl. UB5: N'olt 3B **60**
Concord Ct. *KT1: King T* *3F* ***135***
(off Winery La.)
Concorde Cl. TW3: Houn 2F **97**
UB10: Uxb 2A **58**
Concorde Dr. E6 5D **72**
Concord Ho. *N17* *7A* ***18***
(off Park La.)
Concordia Wharf *E14* *1E* ***88***
(off Coldharbour)
Concord Rd. EN3: Enf 5D **8**
W3 4H **63**
Concourse, The *N9* *2C* ***18***
(in Edmonton Grn. Shop. Cen.)
NW9 1A **28**
Condell Rd. SW8 1G **103**
Conder St. E14 6A **70**
Condor Path *UB5: N'olt* *2E* ***60***
(off Union Rd.)
Condover Cres. SE18 7F **91**
Condray Pl. SW11 7C **84**
Conduit Av. SE10 1F **107**
Conduit Ct. WC2 2E **166**
Conduit La. CR2: S Croy 5G **153**
(not continuous)
EN3: Enf 6F **9**
N18 5D **18**
Conduit M. SE18 5F **91**
W2 6B **66** (1A **164**)
Conduit Pas. W2 1A **164**
Conduit Pl. W2 6B **66** (1A **164**)
Conduit Rd. SE18 5F **91**
Conduit St. W1 7F **67** (2K **165**)
WC1 4K **67**
Conduit Way NW10 7J **45**
Conewood St. N5 3B **50**
Coney Acre SE21 1C **122**
Coney Burrows E4 2B **20**
Coney Gro. UB8: Uxb 3C **58**
Coneygrove Path
UB5: N'olt *6C* ***42***
(off Arnold Rd.)
CONEY HALL **3G 155**
Coney Hall Pde.
BR4: W W'ck 3G **155**
Coney Hill Rd.
BR4: W W'ck 2G **155**
Coney Way SW8 6K **85**
Conference Cl. E4 2K **19**
Conference Rd. SE2 4C **92**
Congers Ho. SE8 7C **88**
Congleton Gro. SE18 5G **91**
Congo Rd. SE18 5H **91**
Congress Rd. SE2 4C **92**
Congreve Ho. N16 5E **50**
Congreve Rd. SE9 3D **108**
Congreve St. SE17 4E **86**
Congreve Wlk. *E16* *5B* ***72***
(off Fulmer Rd.)
Conical Cnr. EN2: Enf 2H **7**
Conifer Gdns. EN1: Enf 6K **7**
SM1: Sutt 2K **149**
SW16 3J **121**
Conifer Ho. *SE4* *4B* ***106***
(off Brockley Rd.)
Conifers Cl. TW11: Tedd 7B **116**
Conifer Way HA0: Wemb 3C **44**
UB3: Hayes 7J **59**
Coniffe Ct. SE9 5F **109**
Coniger Rd. SW6 2J **101**
Coningham Ct. *SW10* *7A* ***84***
(off King's Rd.)
Coningham M. W12 1C **82**
Coningham Rd. W12 2D **82**
Coningsby Cotts. W5 2D **80**
Coningsby Gdns. E4 6J **19**
Coningsby Rd.
CR2: S Croy 7C **152**
N4 7B **32**
W5 2D **80**
Conington Rd. SE13 2D **106**
Conisbee Ct. N14 5B **6**
Conisborough Cres.
SE6 3E **124**
Conisbrough *NW1* *1G* ***67***
(off Bayham St.)
Coniscliffe Cl.
BR7: Chst 1E **144**
Coniscliffe Rd. N13 3H **17**
Coniston *NW1* *1A* ***160***
(off Harrington St.)
Coniston Av. DA16: Well 3J **109**
IG11: Bark 7J **55**
UB6: G'frd 3B **62**
Coniston Cl. DA7: Bex 1J **111**
DA8: Erith 7K **93**
IG11: Bark 7J **55**
N20 3F **15**
SM4: Mord 6F **137**
SW13 7B **82**
W4 7J **81**
Coniston Ct. *SE16* *2K* ***87***
(off Eleanor Cl.)
W2 *1D* ***164***
(off Kendal St.)
Conistone Way N7 7J **49**
Coniston Gdns. HA5: Pinn 4J **23**
HA9: Wemb 1C **44**
IG4: Ilf 4C **36**
N9 1D **18**
NW9 5K **27**
SM2: Sutt 6B **150**
Coniston Ho. *E3* *4B* ***70***
(off Southern Gro.)
SE5 *7C* ***86***
(off Wyndham Rd.)
Coniston Rd. BR1: Brom 6G **125**
CR0: Croy 7G **141**
DA7: Bex 1J **111**
N10 2F **31**
N17 6B **18**
TW2: Twick 6F **97**
Coniston Wlk. E9 5J **51**
Coniston Way KT9: Chess 3E **146**
Conlan St. W10 4G **65**
Conley Rd. NW10 6A **46**
Conley St. SE10 5G **89**
Connaught Av. E4 1A **20**
EN1: Enf 2K **7**
EN4: Barn 1J **15**
SW14 3J **99**
TW4: Houn 4C **96**
TW15: Ashf 4A **112**
Connaught Bri. E16 1B **90**
Connaught Bus. Cen.
CR4: Mitc 5D **138**
NW9 5B **28**
Connaught Cl. E10 2K **51**
EN1: Enf 2K **7**
SM1: Sutt 2B **150**
UB8: Uxb 4E **58**
W2 1D **164**
Connaught Ct. *E17* *4D* ***34***
(off Orford Rd.)
Connaught Dr. NW11 4J **29**
Connaught Gdns. N10 5F **31**
N13 4G **17**
SM4: Mord 4A **138**
Connaught Ho. *NW10* *3D* ***64***
(off Trenmar Gdns.)
W1 *3J* ***165***
(off Davies St.)
Connaught La. IG1: Ilf 2G **55**
Connaught Lodge *N4* *7A* ***32***
(off Connaught Rd.)
Connaught M. NW3 4C **48**
SE11 *3K* ***173***
(off Walcot Sq.)
SE18 5E **90**
SW6 1G **101**
Connaught Pl.
W2 7D **66** (2E **164**)
Connaught Rd. E4 1B **20**
E11 1F **53**
E16 1B **90**
(Camel Rd.)
E16 7B **72**
(Connaught Bri.)
E17 5C **34**
EN5: Barn 6A **4**
HA3: Harr 1K **25**
IG1: Ilf 2H **55**
KT3: N Mald 4A **136**
N4 7A **32**
NW10 1A **64**
SE18 5E **90**
Connaught Rd. SM1: Sutt 2B **150**
TW10: Rich 5F **99**
TW11: Tedd 5H **115**
W13 7B **62**
Connaught Sq.
W2 6D **66** (1D **164**)
Connaught St.
W2 6C **66** (1D **164**)
Connaught Way N13 4G **17**
Connell Ct. *SE14* *6K* ***87***
(off Myers La.)
Connell Cres. W5 4F **63**
Connett Ho. *E2* *2G* ***69***
(off Mansford St.)
Connington Cres. E4 3A **20**
Connor Cl. E11 7G **35**
IG6: Ilf 1G **37**
Connor Ct. SW11 1F **103**
Connor Rd. RM9: Dag 4F **57**
Connor St. E9 1K **69**
Conolly Rd. W7 1J **79**
Conrad Dr.
KT4: Wor Pk 1E **148**
Conrad Ho. *E14* *7A* ***70***
(off Victory Pl.)
E16 *7K* ***71***
(off Wesley Av.)
N16 *5E* ***50***
(off Matthias Rd.)
SW8 *7J* ***85***
(off Wyvil Rd.)
Conrad Twr. *W3* *3H* ***81***
(off Bollo La.)
Consfield Av.
KT3: N Mald 4C **136**
Consort Ho. *E14* *5D* ***88***
(off St Davids Sq.)
W2 *7K* ***65***
(off Queensway)
Consort Lodge *NW8* *1D* ***66***
(off Prince Albert Rd.)
Consort M. TW7: Isle 5H **97**
Consort Rd. SE15 1H **105**
Cons St. SE1 2A **86** (6K **167**)
Constable Av. E16 1K **89**
Constable Cl. NW11 6K **29**
UB4: Hayes 2E **58**
Constable Ct. *SE16* *5H* ***87***
(off Stubbs Dr.)
W4 *5H* ***81***
(off Chaseley Dr.)
Constable Cres. N15 5G **33**
Constable Gdns. HA8: Edg 1G **27**
TW7: Isle 5H **97**
Constable Ho. NW3 7D **48**
UB5: N'olt *2B* ***60***
(off Gallery Gdns.)
Constable M. RM8: Dag 4B **56**
Constable Wlk. SE21 3E **122**
Constance Allen Ho. *W10* *6F* ***65***
(off Bridge Cl.)
Constance Cres.
BR2: Short 7H **143**
Constance Rd. CR0: Croy 7B **140**
EN1: Enf 6K **7**
SM1: Sutt 4A **150**
TW2: Twick 7F **97**
Constance St. E16 1C **90**
Constant Ho. *E14* *7D* ***70***
(off Harrow La.)
Constantine Pl. UB10: Uxb 1B **58**
Constantine Rd. NW3 4C **48**
Constitution Hill
SW1 2F **85** (6J **165**)
Constitution Ri. SE18 1E **108**
Consul Av. RM9: Dag, Rain 3J **75**
RM13: Rain 3J **75**
Content St. SE17 4D **86**
Control Twr. Rd.
TW6: Houn 3C **94**
Convair Wlk. UB5: N'olt 3B **60**
Convent Cl. BR3: Beck 7E **124**

Courtlands Av.—Cranmer Rd.

Courtlands Av.
BR2: Short 1G 155
SE12 ....5K 107
TW9: Rich 2H 99
TW12: Hamp 6D 114
Courtlands Cl. HA4: Ruis 7H 23
Courtlands Dr. KT19: Eps ...6A 148
Courtlands Rd.
KT5: Surb 7G 135
Court La. SE21 ....6E 104
Court La. Gdns. SE21 ......7E 104
Courtleet Dr. DA8: Erith 1H 111
Courtleigh NW11 ....5H 29
Courtleigh Gdns. NW11 .....4G 29
Court Lodge DA17: Belv 5G 93
Courtman Rd. N17 ....7H 17
Court Mead UB5: N'olt 3D 60
Courtmead Cl. SE24 ....6C 104
Courtnell St. W2 ....6J 65
Courtney Cl. SE19 ....6E 122
Courtney Ct. N7 ....5A 50
Courtney Cres.
SM5: Cars 7D 150
Courtney Ho. *NW4* *3E 28*
(off Mulberry Cl.)
W14 ....*3G 83*
(off Russell Rd.)
Courtney Pl. CR0: Croy 3A 152
Courtney Rd. CR0: Croy 3A 152
N7 ....5A 50
SW19 ....7C 120
TW6: Houn 3C 94
Court Pde. HA0: Wemb 3B 44
(not continuous)
Courtrai Rd. SE23 ....6A 106
Court Rd. SE9 ....6D 108
SE25 ....2F 141
UB2: S'hall 4D 78
UB10: Uxb 5D 40
Courtside N8 ....6H 31
SE26 ....3H 123
Court St. BR1: Brom 2J 143
E1 ....5H 69
Court, The HA4: Ruis 4C 42
Court Theatre 2H 83
(in Holland Pk.)
Courtville Ho. *W10* *3G 65*
(off Third Av.)
Court Way IG6: Ilf 3G 37
IG8: Wfd G 5F 21
NW9 ....4A 28
TW2: Twick 7K 97
W3 ....5J 63
Court Wood La.
CR0: Croy 7B 154
Court Yd. SE9 ....6D 108
Courtyard, The E3 ....2C 70
N1 ....7K 49
NW1 ....7E 48
Courtyard Theatre 1F 161
(off York Way)
Cousin La. EC4 ....7D 68 (3E 168)
Cousins Cl. UB7: W Dray 7A 58
Couthurst Rd. SE3 ....6K 89
Coutts Av. KT9: Chess 5E 146
Coutt's Cres. NW5 ....3E 48
Couzens Ho. *E3* *5B 70*
(off Weatherley Cl.)
Coval Gdns. SW14 ....4H 99
Coval La. SW14 ....4H 99
Coval Pas. SW14 ....4J 99
Coval Rd. SW14 ....4H 99
Covelees Wall E6 ....6E 72
Covell Ct. *EN2: Enf* *1E 6*
(off Ridgeway, The)
SE8 ....7C 88
COVENT GARDEN
.........7J 67 (2F 167)
Covent Garden 7J 67 (2F 167)
Covent Gdn. WC2 ...7J 67 (2F 167)
Coventry Cl. E6 ....6D 72
NW6 ....2J 65
Coventry Cross E3 ....4E 70
Coventry Hall SW16 ....5J 121
Coventry Rd. E1 ....4H 69
IG1: Ilf 2F 55
SE25 ....4G 141
Coventry St. W1 ...7H 67 (3C 166)
Coverack Cl. CR0: Croy 7A 142
N14 ....6B 6
Coverdale Cl. HA7: Stan 5G 11
Coverdale Gdns.
CR0: Croy 3F 153
Coverdale Rd. N11 ....6K 15
NW2 ....7F 47
W12 ....2D 82
Coverdales, The
IG11: Bark 2H 73
Coverley Cl. E1 ....5G 69
Coverley Point SE11 ....4G 173
Coverton Rd. SW17 ....5C 120
Covert, The BR6: Orp 6J 145
HA6: Nwood 1E 22
SE19 ....*7F 123*
(off Fox Hill)
Covert Way EN4: Barn 2F 5
Covet Wood Cl. BR5: Orp ...6K 145
Covey Cl. SW19 ....2K 137
Covington Gdns. SW16 ....7B 122
Covington Way SW16 ......6K 121
(not continuous)
Cowan Cl. E6 ....5C 72
Cowan Ct. NW10 ....7K 45
Cowbridge La. IG11: Bark 7F 55
Cowbridge Rd. HA3: Harr 4F 27
Cowcross St.
EC1 ....5B 68 (5A 162)
Cowdenbeath Path N1 ......1K 67
Cowden Rd. BR6: Orp 7K 145
Cowden St. SE6 ....4C 124
Cowdray Rd. UB10: Uxb 1E 58
Cowdrey Cl. EN1: Enf 2K 7
Cowdrey Rd. SW19 ....5K 119
Cowen Av. HA2: Harr 2H 43
Cowgate Rd. UB6: G'frd 3H 61
Cowick Rd. SW17 ....4D 120
Cowings Mead UB5: N'olt 6C 42
Cowland Av. EN3: Enf 4D 8
Cow La. UB6: G'frd 2H 61
Cow Leaze E6 ....6E 72
Cowleaze Rd.
KT2: King T 1E 134
Cowley La. E11 ....3G 53
COWLEY PEACHEY 6A 58
Cowley Pl. NW4 ....5E 28
Cowley Rd. E11 ....5K 35
IG1: Ilf 7D 36
SW9 ....1A 104
(not continuous)
SW14 ....3A 100
W3 ....1B 82
Cowley St. SW1 ....3J 85 (1E 172)
Cowling Cl. W11 ....1G 83
Cowper Av. E6 ....7C 54
SM1: Sutt 4B 150
Cowper Cl. BR2: Short 4B 144
DA16: Well 5A 110
Cowper Gdns. N14 ....6A 6
SM6: Wall 6G 151
Cowper Ho. *SE17* *5C 86*
(off Browning St.)
SW1 ....*6C 172*
(off Aylesford St.)
Cowper Rd. BR2: Short 4B 144
DA17: Belv 4G 93
KT2: King T 5F 117
N14 ....1A 16
N16 ....5E 50
N18 ....5B 18
SW19 ....6A 120
W3 ....1K 81
W7 ....7K 61
Cowper's Ct. *EC3* *1F 169*
(off Birchin La.)
Cowper St. EC2 ....4D 68 (3F 163)
Cowper Ter. W10 ....5F 65
Cowslip Cl. UB10: Uxb 7A 40
Cowslip Rd. E18 ....2K 35
Cowthorpe Rd. SW8 ....1H 103
Cox Ct. EN4: Barn 4H 5
Coxe Pl. HA3: Harr 4A 26
Cox Ho. *W6* *6G 83*
(off Field Rd.)
Cox La. KT9: Chess 4F 147
KT19: Eps 5H 147
Coxmount Rd. SE7 ....5B 90
Coxs Av. TW17: Shep 3G 131
Cox's Ct. E1 ....6J 163
Coxson Way SE1 ..2F 87 (7J 169)
Cox's Wlk. SE21 ....1G 123
Coxwell Rd. SE18 ....5H 91
SE19 ....7E 122
Coxwold Path
KT9: Chess 7E 146
Crab Hill BR3: Beck 7F 125
Crabtree Av. HA0: Wemb 2E 62
RM6: Chad H 4D 38
Crabtree Cl. E2 ....2F 69
Crabtree Ct. E15 ....5D 52
EN5: Barn 4E 4
Crabtree La. SW6 ....7E 82
(not continuous)
Crabtree Manorway Nth.
DA17: Belv, Erith 2J 93
Crabtree Manorway Sth.
DA17: Belv 3J 93
Crabtree Wlk. CR0: Croy ...1G 153
SE15 ....*1F 105*
(off Peckham Rd.)
Crace St. NW1 ....3H 67 (1C 160)
Craddock Rd. EN1: Enf 3A 8
Craddock St. NW5 ....6E 48
Cradley Rd. SE9 ....1H 127
Crafts Council & Gallery 2A 68
Cragie Ho. *SE1* *4F 87*
(off Balaclava Rd.)
Craig Dr. UB8: Uxb 6D 58
Craigen Av. CR0: Croy 1H 153
Craigerne Rd. SE3 ....7K 89
Craig Gdns. E18 ....2H 35
Craigholm SE18 ....2E 108
Craigmore Ct.
HA6: Nwood 1G 23
Craigmuir Pk. HA0: Wemb ...1F 63
Craignair Rd. SW2 ....7A 104
Craignish Av. SW16 ....2K 139
Craig Pk. Rd. N18 ....4C 18
Craig Rd. TW10: Rich 4C 116
Craig's Ct. SW1 ....1J 85 (4E 166)
Craigton Rd. SE9 ....4D 108
Craigweil Cl. HA7: Stan 5J 11
Craigweil Dr. HA7: Stan 5J 11
Craigwell Av. TW13: Felt ...3J 113
Craik Ct. *NW6* *2H 65*
(off Carlton Va.)
Crail Row SE17 ....4D 86
Crales Ho. SE18 ....3C 90
Cramer St. W1 ....5E 66 (6H 159)
Crammond Cl. W6 ....6G 83
Cramond Ct. TW14: Felt 1G 113
Cramonde Ct. DA16: Well ...2A 110
Crampton Ho. SW8 ....1G 103
Crampton Rd. SE20 ....6J 123
Crampton St. SE17 ....4C 86
Cranberry Cl. UB5: N'olt 2B 60
Cranberry La. E16 ....4G 71
Cranborne Av. KT6: Surb ...3G 147
UB2: S'hall 4E 78
Cranborne Rd. IG11: Bark ...1H 73
Cranborne Waye
UB4: Hayes 6K 59
(not continuous)
Cranbourn All. *WC2* *2D 166*
(off Cranbourn St.)
Cranbourne Av. E11 ....4K 35
Cranbourne Cl. SW16 ......3J 139
Cranbourne Dr. HA5: Pinn ...5B 24
Cranbourne Gdns.
IG6: Ilf 3G 37
NW11 ....5G 29
Cranbourne Pas. SE16 ......2H 87
Cranbourne Rd. E12 ....5C 54
E15 ....4E 52
HA6: Nwood 3H 23
N10 ....2F 31
Cranbourn Ho. *SE16* *2H 87*
(off Marigold St.)
Cranbourn St.
WC2 ....7H 67 (2D 166)
CRANBROOK 1D 54
Cranbrook *NW1* *1G 67*
(off Camden St.)
Cranbrook Cl. BR2: Short ...6J 143
Cranbrook Ct. TW8: Bford ...6C 80
Cranbrook Dr. KT10: Esh ...7G 133
TW2: Twick 1F 115
Cranbrook Est. E2 ....2K 69
Cranbrook La. N11 ....4A 16
Cranbrook M. E17 ....5B 34
Cranbrook Pk. N22 ....1A 32
Cranbrook Ri. IG1: Ilf 6D 36
Cranbrook Rd.
CR7: Thor H 2C 140
DA7: Bex 1F 111
EN4: Barn 6G 5
IG1: Ilf 7E 36
IG2: Ilf 5E 36
IG6: Ilf 5E 36
SE8 ....1C 106
SW19 ....7G 119
TW4: Houn 4D 96
W4 ....5A 82
Cranbrook St. E2 ....2K 69
Cranbury Rd. SW6 ....2K 101
Crandley Ct. SE8 ....4A 88
Crane Av. TW7: Isle 5A 98
W3 ....7J 63
Cranebank M. TW1: Twick ...4A 98
Cranebrook TW2: Twick 2G 115
Crane Cl. HA2: Harr 3G 43
RM10: Dag 6G 57
Crane Ct. EC4 ....6A 68
KT19: Eps 4J 147
Craneford Cl. TW2: Twick 7K 97
Craneford Way TW2: Twick ...7J 97
Crane Gdns. UB3: Hayes 4H 77
Crane Gro. N7 ....6A 50
Crane Ho. *E3* *2A 70*
(off Roman Rd.)
SE15 ....1F 105
TW13: Felt 3E 114
Crane Lodge Rd.
TW5: Houn 6K 77
Crane Mead SE16 ....4K 87
Crane Mead Ct.
TW1: Twick 7K 97
Crane Pk. Island Nature Reserve
...............2D 114
Crane Pk. Rd.
TW2: Twick 2F 115
Crane Rd. TW2: Twick 1J 115
Cranesbill Cl. NW9 ....3K 27
Cranes Dr. KT5: Surb 4E 134
Cranes Pk. KT5: Surb 4E 134
Cranes Pk. Av. KT5: Surb ...4E 134
Cranes Pk. Cres.
KT5: Surb 4F 135
Crane St. SE10 ....5F 89
SE15 ....1F 105
Craneswater UB3: Hayes 7H 77
Craneswater Pk.
UB2: S'hall 5D 78
Crane Way TW2: Twick 7G 97
Cranfield Cl. SE27 ....3C 122
Cranfield Ct. W1 ....6D 158
Cranfield Dr. NW9 ....7F 13
Cranfield Ho. WC1 ....5E 160
Cranfield Rd. SE4 ....3B 106
Cranfield Rd. E.
SM5: Cars 7E 150
Cranfield Rd. W.
SM5: Cars 7D 150
Cranfield Row SE1 ....1K 173
CRANFORD 1J 95
Cranford Av. N13 ....5D 16
TW19: Staines 7A 94
Cranford Cl. SW20 ....7D 118
TW19: Staines 7A 94
Cranford Cotts. *E1* *7K 69*
(off Cranford St.)
Cranford Dr. UB3: Hayes 4H 77
Cranford La. TW5: Houn 7K 77
TW6: Houn 1H 95
(Bath Rd., not continuous)
TW6: Houn 3H 95
(Elmdon Rd.)
UB3: Hayes 6F 77
Cranford Pk. Rd.
UB3: Hayes 4H 77
Cranford St. E1 ....7K 69
Cranford Way N8 ....4K 31
Cranhurst Rd. NW2 ....5E 46
Cranleigh Cl. DA5: Bex 6H 111
SE20 ....2H 141
Cranleigh Ct. CR4: Mitc 3B 138
TW9: Rich 3G 99
UB1: S'hall 6D 60
Cranleigh Gdns.
HA3: Harr 5E 26
IG11: Bark 7H 55
Cranleigh Gdns.
KT2: King T 6F 117
N21 ....5F 7
SE25 ....3E 140
SM1: Sutt 2K 149
UB1: S'hall 6D 60
Cranleigh Gdns. Ind. Est.
UB1: S'hall 5D 60
Cranleigh Ho's. *NW1* *2G 67*
(off Cranleigh St.)
Cranleigh M. SW11 ....2C 102
Cranleigh Rd. N15 ....5C 32
SW19 ....3J 137
TW13: Felt 4H 113
Cranleigh St. NW1 ....2G 67
Cranley Dene Ct. N10 ....4F 31
Cranley Dr. HA4: Ruis 2H 41
IG2: Ilf 7G 37
CRANLEY GARDENS 4F 31
Cranley Gdns. N10 ....4F 31
N13 ....3E 16
SM6: Wall 7G 151
SW7 ....5A 84 (5A 170)
Cranley M.
SW7 ....5A 84 (5A 170)
Cranley Pde. *SE9* *4C 126*
(off Beaconsfield Rd.)
Cranley Pl. SW7 ...4B 84 (4A 170)
Cranley Rd. E13 ....5K 71
IG2: Ilf 6G 37
Cranmer Av. W13 ....3B 80
Cranmer Cl. HA4: Ruis 1B 42
HA7: Stan 7H 11
SM4: Mord 6F 137
Cranmer Ct. N3 ....2G 29
SW3 ....4C 84 (4D 170)
SW4 ....3H 103
Cranmere Ct. EN2: Enf 2F 7
SE5 ....1C 104
Cranmer Farm Cl.
CR4: Mitc 4D 138
Cranmer Gdns. RM10: Dag ...4J 57
Cranmer Ho. *SW9* *7A 86*
(off Brixton Rd.)
Cranmer Rd. CR0: Croy 3B 152
CR4: Mitc 4D 138
E7 ....4K 53
HA8: Edg 3C 12
KT2: King T 5E 116
SW9 ....7A 86

Cranmer Rd.
  TW12: Hamp 5F 115
  UB3: Hayes 6F 59
Cranmer Ter. SW17 .....5B 120
Cranmore Av. TW7: Isle 7G 79
Cranmore Rd.
  BR1: Brom 3H 125
  BR7: Chst 5D 126
Cranmore Way N10 .....4G 31
Cranston Cl. TW3: Houn 2C 96
  UB10: Uxb 2F 41
Cranston Est. N1 .....2D 68
Cranston Gdns. E4 .....6J 19
Cranston Rd. SE23 .....1A 124
Cranswick Rd. SE16 .....5H 87
Crantock Rd. SE6 .....2D 124
Cranwell Cl. E3 .....4D 70
Cranwell Gro.
  TW17: Shep 4B 130
Cranwell Rd. TW6: Houn 2D 94
Cranwich Av. N21 .....7J 7
Cranwich Rd. N16 .....7D 32
Cranwood Ct. EC1 .....2F 163
Cranwood St.
  EC1 .....3D 68 (2F 163)
Cranworth Cres. E4 .....1A 20
Cranworth Gdns. SW9 .....1A 104
Craster Rd. SW2 .....7K 103
Crathie Rd. SE12 .....6K 107
Cravan Av. TW13: Felt 2J 113
Craven Av. UB1: S'hall 5D 60
  W5 .....7C 62
Craven Cl. N16 .....7G 33
  UB4: Hayes 6J 59
Craven Ct. NW10 .....1A 64
  RM6: Chad H 6E 38
Craven Gdns. IG6: Ilf 2H 37
  IG11: Bark 2J 73
  SW19 .....5J 119
Craven Hill W2 .....7A 66
Craven Hill Gdns. W2 .....7A 66
  (not continuous)
Craven Hill M. W2 .....7A 66
Craven Ho. N2 .....2B 30
  (off Central Av.)
Craven Lodge W2 .....7A 66
  (off Craven Hill)
Craven M. SW11 .....3E 102
Craven Pk. NW10 .....1K 63
Craven Pk. M. NW10 .....7A 46
  NW10 .....1A 64
Craven Pk. Rd. N15 .....6F 33
  NW10 .....1A 64
Craven Pas. WC2 .....4E 166
  (off Craven St.)
Craven Rd. CR0: Croy 1H 153
  KT2: King T 1F 135
  NW10 .....1K 63
  W2 .....7A 66 (1A 66)
  W5 .....7C 62
Craven St. WC2 .....1J 85 (4E 166)
Craven Ter. W2 .....7A 66 (2A 164)
Craven Wlk. N16 .....7G 33
Crawford Av.
  HA0: Wemb 5D 44
Crawford Bldgs. W1 .....6D 158
  (off Homer St.)
Crawford Cl. TW7: Isle 2J 97
Crawford Est. SE5 .....2C 104
Crawford Gdns. N13 .....3G 17
  UB5: N'olt 3D 60
Crawford Mans. W1 .....6D 158
  (off Crawford St.)
Crawford M. W1 .....5D 66 (6E 158)
Crawford Pas.
  EC1 .....4A 68 (4K 161)
Crawford Pl.
  W2 .....6C 66 (7D 158)
Crawford Point E16 .....6H 71
  (off Wouldham Rd.)
Crawford Rd. SE5 .....1C 104
Crawford St.
  W1 .....5C 66 (6E 158)

Crawley Rd. E10 .....1D 52
  EN1: Enf 7K 7
  N22 .....2C 32
Crawshay Ct. SW9 .....1A 104
Crawthew Gro. SE22 .....4F 105
Craybrooke Rd.
  DA14: Sidc 4B 128
Craybury End SE9 .....2G 127
Crayford Cl. E6 .....6C 72
Crayford Greyhound Stadium
  .....6K 111
Crayford Ho. SE1 .....7F 169
  (off Long La.)
Crayford Rd. N7 .....4H 49
Crayle Hill KT9: Chess 7E 146
Crayle Ho. EC1 .....3B 162
  (off Malta St.)
Crayleigh Ter.
  DA14: Sidc 6C 128
Crayonne Cl.
  TW16: Sun T 1G 131
Cray Rd. DA14: Sidc 6C 128
  DA17: Belv 6G 93
Cray Valley Rd. BR5: Orp 5K 145
Crealock Gro. IG8: Wfd G 5C 20
Crealock St. SW18 .....6K 101
Creasy Est. SE1 .....3E 86
Crebor St. SE22 .....6G 105
Credenhall Dr.
  BR2: Short 1D 156
Credenhill Ho. SE15 .....7H 87
Credenhill St. SW16 .....6G 121
Crediton Hill NW6 .....5K 47
Crediton Rd. E16 .....6J 71
  NW10 .....1F 65
Crediton Way KT10: Esh 5A 146
Credon Rd. E13 .....2A 72
  SE16 .....5H 87
Creechurch La.
  EC3 .....6E 68 (1H 169)
  (not continuous)
Creechurch Pl. EC3 .....1H 169
Creed Ct. EC4 .....1B 168
Creed La. EC4 .....6B 68 (1B 168)
Creek Ho. W14 .....3G 83
  (off Russell Rd.)
CREEKMOUTH 4K 73
Creekmouth Ind. Pk.
  IG11: Bark 4K 73
Creek Rd. IG11: Bark 3K 73
  KT8: E Mos 4J 133
  SE8 .....6C 88
  SE10 .....6C 88
Creekside SE8 .....7D 88
Creek, The TW16: Sun T 5J 131
Creek Way RM13: Rain 5K 75
Creeland Gro. SE6 .....1B 124
Crefeld Cl. W6 .....6G 83
Creffield Rd. W5 .....7F 63
Creffield Way W3 .....7F 63
Creighton Av. E6 .....2B 72
  N2 .....3C 30
Creighton Cl. W12 .....7C 64
Creighton Rd. N17 .....7K 17
  NW6 .....2F 65
  W5 .....3D 80
Cremer Bus. Cen. E2 .....1J 163
  (off Cremer St.)
Cremer Ho. SE8 .....7C 88
  (off Deptford Chu. St.)
Cremer St. E2 .....2F 69 (1J 163)
Cremorne Est. SW10 .....6B 84
Cremorne Rd. SW10 .....7A 84
Creon Ct. SW9 .....7A 86
  (off Caldwell St.)
Crescent EC3 .....7F 69 (2J 169)
Crescent Arc. SE10 .....6E 88
  (off Creek Rd.)
Crescent Ct. KT6: Surb 5D 134
Crescent Ct. Bus. Cen.
  E16 .....4F 71
Crescent Dr. BR5: Orp 5F 145

Crescent E. EN4: Barn 1F 5
Crescent Gdns. HA4: Ruis 7K 23
  SW19 .....3J 119
Crescent Gro. CR4: Mitc 4C 138
  SW4 .....4G 103
Crescent Ho. EC1 .....4C 162
  (off Golden La. Est.)
  SE8 .....2D 106
  SE13 .....2D 106
Crescent La. SW4 .....4G 103
Crescent M. N22 .....1J 31
Crescent Pde. UB10: Uxb 3C 58
Crescent Pl.
  SW3 .....4C 84 (3D 170)
Crescent Ri. EN4: Barn 5H 5
  N3 .....1H 29
  N22 .....1H 31
Crescent Rd. BR1: Brom 7J 125
  BR3: Beck 2D 142
  DA15: Sidc 3K 127
  E4 .....1B 20
  E6 .....1A 72
  E10 .....2D 52
  E13 .....1J 71
  E18 .....1A 36
  EN2: Enf 4G 5
  EN4: Barn 4G 5
  KT2: King T 7G 117
  N3 .....1H 29
  N8 .....6H 31
  N9 .....1B 18
  N11 .....4J 15
  N15 .....3B 32
  N22 .....1H 31
  RM10: Dag 3H 57
  SE18 .....5F 91
  SW20 .....1F 137
  TW17: Shep 5E 130
Crescent Row
  EC1 .....4C 68 (4C 162)
Crescent Stables SW15 .....5G 101
Crescent St. N1 .....7K 49
Crescent, The
  BR3: Beck 1C 142
  BR4: W W'ck 6G 143
  CR0: Croy 5D 140
  DA5: Bexl 7C 110
  DA14: Sidc 4K 127
  E17 .....6A 34
  EN5: Barn 2E 4
  HA0: Wemb 2B 44
  HA2: Harr 1G 43
  IG2: Ilf 6E 36
  KT3: N Mald 3J 135
  KT6: Surb 5E 134
  KT8: W Mole 4E 132
  N9 .....2C 18
  N11 .....4J 15
  NW2 .....3D 46
  SM1: Sutt 5B 150
  SW13 .....2H 99
  SW19 .....3J 119
  TW15: Ashf 5B 112
  TW17: Shep 7H 131
  UB1: S'hall 2D 78
  UB3: Hayes 7F 77
  W3 .....6A 64
Crescent Way N12 .....6H 15
  SE4 .....3C 106
  SW16 .....6K 121
Crescent W. EN4: Barn 1F 5
Crescent Wharf E16 .....2K 89
  (off Nth. Woolwich Rd.)
Crescent Wood Rd.
  SE26 .....3G 123
Cresford Rd. SW6 .....1K 101
Crespigny Rd. NW4 .....6D 28
Cressage Cl. UB1: S'hall 4E 60
Cressage Ho. TW8: Bford 6E 80
  (off Ealing Rd.)
Cressall Ho. E14 .....3C 88
  (off Tiller Rd.)

Cresset Rd. E9 .....6J 51
Cresset St. SW4 .....3H 103
Cressfield Cl. NW5 .....5E 48
Cressida Rd. N19 .....1G 49
Cressingham Gdns. Est.
  SW2 .....7A 104
Cressingham Gro.
  SM1: Sutt 4A 150
Cressingham Rd.
  HA8: Edg 6E 12
  SE13 .....3E 106
Cressington Cl. N16 .....5E 50
Cress M. BR1: Brom 5F 125
Cresswell NW9 .....2B 28
Cresswell Gdns. SW5 .....5A 84
Cresswell Pk. SE3 .....3H 107
Cresswell Pl. SW10 .....5A 84
Cresswell Rd. SE25 .....4G 141
  TW1: Twick 6D 98
  TW13: Felt 3C 114
Cresswell Way N21 .....7F 7
Cressy Ct. E1 .....5J 69
  W6 .....3D 82
Cressy Ho's. E1 .....5J 69
  (off Hannibal Rd.)
Cressy Pl. E1 .....5J 69
Cressy Rd. NW3 .....5D 48
Cresta Ct. W5 .....4F 63
Cresta Ho. NW3 .....7B 48
  (off Finchley Rd.)
Crestbrook Av. N13 .....3G 17
Crestbrook Pl. N13 .....3G 17
  (off Green Lanes)
Crest Ct. NW4 .....5E 28
Crest Dr. EN3: Enf 1D 8
Crestfield St.
  WC1 .....3J 67 (1F 161)
Crest Gdns. HA4: Ruis 3A 42
Creston Way KT4: Wor Pk 1F 149
Crest Rd. BR2: Short 7H 143
  CR2: S Croy 7H 153
  NW2 .....3F 13
Crest, The KT5: Surb 5G 135
  N13 .....4F 17
  NW4 .....5E 28
Crest Vw. HA5: Pinn 4B 24
Crest Vw. Dr. BR5: Orp 5F 145
Crestway SW15 .....6C 100
Crestwood Way
  TW4: Houn 5C 96
Creswell Dr. BR3: Beck 5D 142
Creswick Cl. W3 .....7H 63
Creswick Rd. W3 .....7H 63
Creswick Wlk. E3 .....3C 70
  NW11 .....4H 29
Creton St. SE18 .....3C 90
Crewdson Rd. SW9 .....7A 86
Crewe Pl. NW10 .....3B 64
Crewkerne Ct. SW11 .....1B 102
  (off Bolingbroke Wlk.)
Crews St. E14 .....4C 88
Crewys Rd. NW2 .....2H 47
  SE15 .....2H 105
Crichton Av. SM6: Wall 5H 151
Crichton Ho. DA14: Sidc 6D 128
Crichton Rd. SM5: Cars 6D 150
Crichton St. SW8 .....2G 103
Cricketers Arms Rd.
  EN2: Enf 2H 7
Cricketers Cl. DA8: Erith 5K 93
  KT9: Chess 4D 146
  N14 .....7B 6
Cricketers Ct. SE11 .....4B 86
  (off Kennington La.)
Cricketers M. SW18 .....5K 101
Cricketers Ter. SM5: Cars 3C 150
Cricketers Wlk. SE26 .....5J 123
Cricketfield Rd. E5 .....4H 51
Cricket Grn. CR4: Mitc 3D 138
Cricket Ground Rd.
  BR7: Chst 1F 145
  (not continuous)

Cricket La. BR3: Beck 6A 124
Cricklade Av. SW2 .....2J 121
CRICKLEWOOD 3G 47
Cricklewood B'way. NW2 .....3E 46
Cricklewood La. NW2 .....4F 47
Cridland St. E15 .....1H 71
Crieff Ct. TW11: Tedd 7C 116
Crieff Rd. SW18 .....6A 102
Criffel Av. SW2 .....2H 121
Crimscott St. SE1 .....3E 86
Crimsworth Rd. SW8 .....1H 103
Crinan St. N1 .....2J 67
Cringle St. SW8 .....7G 85
Cripplegate St.
  EC2 .....5C 68 (5D 162)
Cripps Grn. UB4: Hayes 4K 59
Crispe Ho. IG11: Bark 2H 73
  N1 .....1K 67
  (off Barnsbury Est.)
Crispen Rd. TW13: Felt 4C 114
Crispian Cl. NW10 .....4A 46
Crispin Cl. CR0: Croy 2J 151
Crispin Cres. CR0: Croy 3H 151
Crispin Lodge N11 .....5J 15
Crispin Rd. HA8: Edg 6D 12
Crispin St. E1 .....5F 69 (6J 163)
Crisp Rd. W6 .....5E 82
Cristowe Rd. SW6 .....2H 101
Criterion Ct. E8 .....7F 51
  (off Middleton Rd.)
Criterion M. N19 .....2H 49
Criterion Theatre 3C 166
  (off Piccadilly)
CRITTALLS CORNER 7C 128
Crockerton Rd. SW17 .....2D 120
Crockham Way SE9 .....4E 126
Crocus Cl. CR0: Croy 1K 153
Crocus Fld. EN5: Barn 6C 4
Croft Av. BR4: W W'ck 1E 154
Croft Cl. BR7: Chst 5D 126
  DA17: Belv 5F 93
  NW7 .....3F 13
  UB3: Hayes 7E 76
  UB10: Uxb 7C 40
Croft Ct. HA4: Ruis 1H 41
  SE13 .....6E 106
Croftdown Rd. NW5 .....3E 48
Croft End Cl. KT9: Chess 3F 147
Crofters Cl. TW7: Isle 5H 97
Crofters Ct. SE8 .....4A 88
  (off Croft St.)
Crofters Mead CR0: Croy 7B 154
Crofters Way NW1 .....1H 67
Croft Gdns. HA4: Ruis 1G 41
  W7 .....2A 80
Croft Ho. E17 .....4D 34
  W10 .....3G 65
  (off Third Av.)
Croft Lodge Cl. IG8: Wfd G 6E 20
Croft M. N12 .....3F 15
Crofton Av. DA5: Bexl 7D 110
  W4 .....7K 81
Croftongate Way SE4 .....5A 106
Crofton Gro. E4 .....4A 20
Crofton La. BR5: Orp 7H 145
  BR6: Orp 7H 145
CROFTON PARK 5B 106
Crofton Pk. Rd. SE4 .....6B 106
Crofton Rd. BR6: Orp 3E 156
  E13 .....4K 71
  SE5 .....1E 104
Crofton Ter. E5 .....5A 52
  TW9: Rich 4F 99
Crofton Way EN2: Enf 2F 7
  EN5: Barn 6E 4
Croft Rd. BR1: Brom 6J 125
  EN3: Enf 1F 9
  SM1: Sutt 5C 150
  SW16 .....1A 140
  SW19 .....7A 120
Crofts Ho. E2 .....2G 69
  (off Teale St.)

Crowther Av.—Cyprus Rd.

Crowther Av. TW8: Bford 4E 80
Crowther Cl. SW6 ....6H 83
(off Bucklers All.)
Crowther Rd. SE25 ....5G 141
Crowthorne Cl. SW18 .....7H 101
Crowthorne Rd. W10 ....6F 65
Croxall Ho. KT12: Walt T ...6A 132
Croxden Cl. HA8: Edg 3G 27
Croxden Wlk. SM4: Mord ...6A 138
Croxford Gdns. N22 ....7G 17
Croxford Way
RM7: Rush G 1K 57
Croxley Grn. BR5: Orp 7B 128
Croxley Rd. W9 ....3H 65
Croxted Cl. SE21 ....7C 104
Croxted M. SE24 ....6C 104
Croxted Rd. SE21 ....6C 104
SE24 ....6C 104
Croxteth Ho. SW8 ....2H 103
Croyde Av. UB3: Hayes 4G 77
UB6: G'frd 3G 61
Croyde Cl. DA15: Sidc 7H 109
CROYDON 2C 152
Croydon N17 ....2D 32
(off Gloucester Rd.)
Croydon Clocktower 3C 152
(off Katherine St.)
Croydon Crematorium
CR0: Croy 5K 139
Croydon Flyover, The
CR0: Croy 3C 152
Croydon Gro. CR0: Croy 1B 152
Croydon Ho. SE1 ....6K 167
(off Wootton St.)
Croydon Rd. BR2: Short 3A 156
BR3: Beck 4K 141
BR4: W W'ck 3G 155
CR0: Croy 4E 138
(Mitcham)
CR0: Croy..........4F 151
(Wallington)
CR4: Mitc 4E 138
E13 ....4H 71
SE20 ....2H 141
SM6: Wall 4F 151
TW6: Houn 2D 94
Croydon Rd. Ind. Est.
BR3: Beck 4K 141
Croyland Rd. N9 ....1B 18
Croylands Dr. KT6: Surb 7E 134
Croysdale Av.
TW16: Sun T 3J 131
Crozier Ho. SE3 ....3K 107
SW8...............7K 85
(off Wilkinson St.)
Crozier Ter. E9 ....5K 51
Crucible Cl. RM6: Chad H ...6B 38
Crucifix La. SE1 ...2E 86 (6H 169)
Cruden Ho. SE5 ....6B 86
(off Brandon Est.)
Cruden St. N1 ....1B 68
Cruikshank Ho. NW8 ....2C 66
(off Townshend Rd.)
Cruikshank Rd. E15 ....4G 53
Cruikshank St.
WC1 ....3A 68 (1J 161)
Crummock Gdns. NW9 ......5A 28
Crumpsall St. SE2 ....4C 92
Crundale Av. NW9 ....5G 27
Crunden Rd. CR2: S Croy 7D 152
Crusader Gdns.
CR0: Croy 3E 152
Crusoe M. N16 ....2D 50
Crusoe Rd. CR4: Mitc 7D 120
DA8: Erith 5K 93
Crutched Friars
EC3 ....7E 68 (2H 169)
Crutchley Rd. SE6 ....2G 125
Crystal Ho. SE18 ....5K 91
CRYSTAL PALACE 6F 123
Crystal Palace F.C. (Selhurst Pk.)
...............4E 140
Crystal Palace Mus. 6F 123
Crystal Palace National Sports
Cen. 6G 123
Crystal Pal. Pde. SE19 .....6F 123
Crystal Pal. Pk. Rd.
SE26 ....5G 123
Crystal Pal. Rd. SE22 ......6F 105
Crystal Pal. Sta. Rd.
SE19 ....6G 123
Crystal Ter. SE19 ....6D 122
Crystal Vw. Ct.
BR1: Brom 4F 125
Crystal Way HA1: Harr 5K 25
RM8: Dag 1C 56
Crystal Wharf N1 ....2B 68
Cuba Dr. EN3: Enf 2D 8
Cuba St. E14 ....2C 88
Cube Ho. SE1 ....3F 87
Cubitt Ho. SW4 ....6G 103
Cubitt Sq. UB2: S'hall 1G 79
Cubitt Steps E14 ....1C 88
Cubitt St. WC1 ....3K 67 (2H 161)
Cubitt's Yd. WC2 ....2F 167
Cubitt Ter. SW4 ....3G 103
CUBITT TOWN 4E 88
Cuckoo Av. W7 ....4J 61
Cuckoo Dene W7 ....5H 61
Cuckoo Hall La. N9 ....7D 8
Cuckoo Hall Rd. N9 ....7D 8
Cuckoo Hill HA5: Pinn 3A 24
Cuckoo Hill Dr. HA5: Pinn ...3A 24
Cuckoo Hill Rd. HA5: Pinn ...4A 24
Cuckoo La. W7 ....7J 61
Cuckoo Pound
TW17: Shep 5G 131
Cudas Cl. KT19: Eps 4B 148
Cuddington SE17 ....4C 86
(off Deacon Way)
Cuddington Av.
KT4: Wor Pk 3B 148
Cudham St. SE6 ....7E 106
Cudworth Ho. SW8 ....1G 103
Cudworth St. E1 ....4H 69
Cuff Cres. SE9 ....6B 108
Cuffley Ho. W10 ....5E 64
(off Sutton Way)
Cuff Point E2 ....1J 163
(off Columbia Rd.)
Culford Gdns.
SW3 ....4D 84 (4F 171)
Culford Gro. N1 ....6E 50
Culford Mans. SW3 ....4D 84
Culford M. N1 ....6E 50
Culford Rd. N1 ....7E 50
Culgaith Gdns. EN2: Enf 4D 6
Culham Ho. E2 ....2J 163
(off Palissy St.)
Cullen Way NW10 ....4J 63
Culling Rd. SE16 ....3J 87
Cullington Cl. HA3: Harr 4A 26
Cullingworth Rd. NW10 .....5C 46
Culloden Cl. SE1 ....5G 87
Culloden Rd. EN2: Enf 2G 7
Cullum St. EC3 ....7E 68 (2G 169)
Cullum Welch Ct. N1 ......1F 163
(off Haberdasher St.)
Cullum Welch Ho. EC1 .....4C 162
(off Goswell Rd.)
Culmington Pde. W13 ......1C 80
(off Uxbridge Rd.)
Culmington Rd.
CR2: S Croy 7C 152
W13 ....1C 80
Culmore Rd. SE15 ....7H 87
Culmstock Rd. SW11 ......5E 102
Culpeper Ho. E14 ....6A 70
Culpepper Ct. SE11 ....3J 173
Culross Bldgs. NW1 ....2J 67
(off Battle Bri. Rd.)
Culross Cl. N15 ....4C 32
Culross Ho. W10 ....6F 65
(off Bridge Cl.)
Culross St. W1 ....7E 66 (3G 165)
Culsac Rd. KT6: Surb 2E 146
Culverden Rd. SW12 ......2G 121
Culver Gro. HA7: Stan 2C 26
Culverhouse WC1 ....6G 161
(off Red Lion Sq.)
Culverhouse Gdns.
SW16 ....3K 121
Culverlands Cl. HA7: Stan ...4G 11
Culverley Rd. SE6 ....1D 124
Culvers Av. SM5: Cars 2D 150
Culvers Retreat
SM5: Cars 1D 150
Culverstone Cl.
BR2: Short.........6H 143
Culvers Way SM5: Cars 2D 150
Culvert Pl. SW11 ....2E 102
Culvert Rd. N15 ....5E 32
SW11 ....2D 102
Culworth Ho. NW8 ....2C 66
(off Allitsen Rd.)
Culworth St. NW8 ....2C 66
Culzean Cl. SE27 ....3B 122
Cumberland Av.
DA16: Well 3J 109
NW10 ....3H 63
Cumberland Bus. Pk.
NW10 ....3H 63
Cumberland Cl. E8 ....6F 51
IG6: Ilf 1G 37
SW20 ....7F 119
TW1: Twick 6B 98
Cumberland Ct.
CR0: Croy 1D 152
DA16: Well 2J 109
HA1: Harr 3J 25
(off Princes Dri.)
SW1 ....5K 171
(off Cumberland St.)
Cumberland Cres. W14 .....4G 83
(not continuous)
Cumberland Dr. DA7: Bex 7E 92
KT9: Chess 3E 146
KT10: Esh 2A 146
Cumberland Gdns. NW4 ....2G 29
WC1 ....3A 68 (1J 161)
Cumberland Ga. W1 7D 66 (2E 164)
Cumberland Ho. E16 ....7J 71
(off Wesley Av.)
KT2: King T 7H 117
N9 ....1D 18
(off Cumberland Rd.)
SE28 ....2G 91
(off Erebus Dr.)
Cumberland Mans. W1 ....7E 158
Cumberland Mkt.
NW1 ....3F 67 (1K 159)
Cumberland Mills Sq. E14 ...5F 89
Cumberland Pk. W3 ....7J 63
Cumberland Pk. Ind. Est.
NW10 ....3C 64
Cumberland Pl.
NW1 ....3F 67 (1J 159)
SE6 ....1H 125
TW16: Sun T 4J 131
Cumberland Rd.
BR2: Short 4G 143
E12 ....4B 54
E13 ....5K 71
E17 ....2A 34
HA1: Harr 5F 25
HA7: Stan 3F 27
N9 ....1D 18
N22 ....2K 31
SE25 ....6H 141
SW13 ....1B 100
TW9: Rich 7G 81
TW15: Ashf 3A 112
W3 ....7J 63
W7 ....2K 79
Cumberland St.
SW1 ....5F 85 (5K 171)
Cumberland Ter.
NW1 ....2F 67 (1J 159)
Cumberland Ter. M. NW1 ...1J 159
Cumberland Vs. W3 ....7J 63
(off Cumberland Rd.)
Cumberlow Av. SE25 ......3F 141
Cumbernauld Gdns.
TW16: Sun T 5H 113
Cumberton Rd. N17 ....1D 32
Cumbrae Gdns.
KT6: Surb 2D 146
Cumbrian Gdns. NW2 ....2F 47
Cumbrian Way UB8: Uxb 7A 40
Cuming Mus. 4C 86
(off Walworth Rd.)
Cumming St. N1 ...2K 67 (1H 161)
Cumnor Cl. SW9 ....2K 103
(off Robsart St.)
Cumnor Gdns. KT17: Eps ...6C 148
Cumnor Rd. SM2: Sutt 6A 150
Cunard Cres. N21 ....6J 7
Cunard Pl. EC3 ....6E 68 (1H 169)
Cunard Rd. NW10 ....3K 63
Cunard Wlk. SE16 ....4K 87
Cundy Rd. E16 ....6A 72
Cundy St. SW1 ....4E 84 (4H 171)
Cunliffe Pde. KT19: Eps 4B 148
Cunliffe Rd. KT19: Eps 4B 148
Cunliffe St. SW16 ....6G 121
Cunningham Cl.
BR4: W W'ck 2D 154
RM6: Chad H 5C 38
Cunningham Ho. SE5 ....7D 86
(off Elmington Est.)
Cunningham Pk.
HA1: Harr 5G 25
Cunningham Pl.
NW8 ......4B 66 (3A 158)
Cunningham Rd. N15 ....4G 33
Cunnington St. W4 ....3J 81
Cupar Rd. SW11 ....1E 102
Cupola Cl. BR1: Brom 5K 125
Cureton St. SW1 ...4H 85 (4D 172)
Curfew Ho. IG11: Bark 1G 73
Curie Ct. HA1: Harr 7B 26
Curie Gdns. NW9 ....2A 28
Curlew Cl. SE28 ....7D 74
Curlew Ct. KT6: Surb 3G 147
W13 ....4K 61
Curlew Ho. SE4 ....4A 106
(off St Norbert Rd.)
SE15 ....1F 105
Curlew St. SE1 .....2F 87 (6K 169)
Curlew Way UB4: Hayes 5B 60
Curnick's La. SE27 ....4C 122
Curran Av. DA15: Sidc 5K 109
SM6: Wall 3E 150
Curran Ho. SW3 ....4C 170
(off Lucan Pl.)
Currey Rd. UB6: G'frd 6H 43
Curricle St. W3 ....1A 82
Currie Hill Cl. SW19 ......4H 119
Currie Ho. E14 ....6F 71
(off Abbott Rd.)
Curry Ri. NW7 ....6A 14
Cursitor St. WC2 ...6A 68 (7J 161)
Curtain Pl. EC2 ....3E 68 (3H 163)
Curtain Rd. EC2 ....4E 68 (2H 163)
Curthwaite Gdns. EN2: Enf 4C 6
Curtis Dr. W3 ....6K 63
Curtis Fld. Rd. SW16 ......4K 121
Curtis Ho. SE17 ....5D 86
(off Morecambe St.)
Curtis La. HA0: Wemb 5E 44
Curtis Rd. KT19: Eps 4J 147
TW4: Houn 7D 96
Curtis St. SE1 ....4F 87
Curtis Way SE1 ....4F 87
SE28 ....7B 74
Curtlington Ho. HA8: Edg 2J 27
(off Burnt Oak B'way.)
Curve, The W12 ....7C 64
Curwen Av. E7 ....4K 53
Curwen Rd. W12 ....2C 82
Curzon Av. EN3: Enf 5E 8
HA3: Harr 1A 26
Curzon Ct. SW6 ....1A 102
(off Imperial Rd.)
Curzon Cres. IG11: Bark 2K 73
NW10 ....7A 46
Curzon Ga. W1 ....1E 84 (5H 165)
Curzon Pl. HA5: Pinn 5A 24
Curzon Rd. CR7: Thor H 6A 140
N10 ....2F 31
W5 ....4B 62
Curzon Sq. W1 ....1E 84 (5H 165)
Curzon St. W1 .....1E 84 (5H 165)
Cusack Cl. TW1: Twick 4K 115
Custance Ho. N1 ....1E 162
(off Fairbank Est.)
Custance St. N1 ...3D 68 (1E 162)
CUSTOM HOUSE 6A 72
Custom House 7E 68 (3G 169)
Custom Ho. Reach SE16 ....2B 88
Custom Ho. Wlk.
EC3 ....7E 68 (3G 169)
Cutbush Ho. N7 ....5H 49
Cutcombe Rd. SE5 ....2C 104
Cuthberga Cl. IG11: Bark 7G 55
Cuthbert Gdns. SE25 ......3E 140
Cuthbert Harrowing Ho.
EC1 ....4C 162
(off Golden La. Est.)
Cuthbert Ho. W2 ....5A 158
(off Hall Pl.)
Cuthbert Rd. CR0: Croy 2B 152
E17 ....3E 34
N18 ....5B 18
Cuthbert St. W2 ....5B 66 (5A 158)
Cuthill Wlk. SE5 ....1D 104
Cutlers Gdns. E1 ....6H 163
Cutlers Sq. E14 ....4C 88
Cutler St. E1 ......6E 68 (7H 163)
Cut, The SE1 ......2A 86 (6K 167)
Cutthroat All.
TW10: Rich 2C 116
Cutty Sark 6E 88
Cutty Sark Gdns. SE10 ......6E 88
(off King William Wlk.)
Cuxton BR5: Orp 5G 145
Cuxton Cl. DA6: Bex 5E 110
Cyclamen Cl.
TW12: Hamp 6E 114
Cyclamen Way
KT19: Eps 5J 147
Cyclops M. E14 ....4C 88
Cygnet Av. TW14: Felt 7A 96
Cygnet Cl. NW10 ....5K 45
Cygnets, The TW13: Felt ...4C 114
Cygnet St. E1 ......4F 69 (3K 163)
Cygnet Way UB4: Hayes 5B 60
Cygnus Bus. Cen. NW10 ....5B 46
Cymbeline Ct. HA1: Harr 6K 25
(off Gayton Rd.)
Cynthia St. N1 .....2K 67 (1H 161)
Cyntra Pl. E8 ....7H 51
Cypress Av. TW2: Twick 7G 97
Cypress Gdns. SE4 ....5A 106
Cypress Ho. SE14 ....1K 105
SE16 ....2K 87
(off Woodland Cres.)
Cypress Pl. W1 ....4G 67 (4B 160)
Cypress Rd. HA3: Harr 2H 25
SE25 ....2E 140
Cypress Tree Cl.
DA15: Sidc 1K 127
CYPRUS 7E 72
Cyprus Av. N3 ....2G 29
Cyprus Cl. N4 ....6B 32
Cyprus Gdns. N3 ....2G 29
Cyprus Pl. E2 ....2J 69
E6 ....7E 72
Cyprus Rd. N3 ....2H 29
N9 ....2A 18

Cyprus St.—Darnley Ho.

Cyprus St. E2 2J 69
(not continuous)
Cyrena Rd. SE22 6F 105
Cyril Lodge DA14: Sidc 4A 128
Cyril Mans. SW11 1D 102
Cyril Rd. BR6: Orp 7K 145
DA7: Bex 2E 110
Cyrus Ho. EC1 3B 162
Cyrus St. EC1 3B 162
Czar St. SE8 6C 88

D

Dabbs Hill La.
UB5: N'olt 6D 42
(not continuous)
Dabbs La. *EC1* *4K 161*
(off Farringdon Rd.)
Dabin Cres. SE10 1E 106
Dacca St. SE8 6B 88
Dace Rd. E3 1C 70
Dacre Av. IG5: Ilf 2E 36
Dacre Cl. UB6: G'frd 2F 61
Dacre Gdns. SE13 4G 107
Dacre Ho. SW3 7B 170
Dacre Pk. SE13 3G 107
Dacre Pl. SE13 3G 107
Dacre Rd. CR0: Croy 7J 139
E11 1H 53
E13 1K 71
Dacres Ho. SW4 3F 103
Dacres Rd. SE23 2K 123
Dacre St. SW1 3H 85 (1C 172)
Dade Way UB2: S'hall 5D 78
Daerwood Cl. BR2: Short 1D 156
Daffodil Cl. CR0: Croy 1K 153
Daffodil Gdns. IG1: Ilf 5F 55
Daffodil Pl.
TW12: Hamp 6E 114
Daffodil St. W12 7B 64
Dafforne Rd. SW17 3E 120
Da Gama Pl. E14 5C 88
DAGENHAM 6G 57
Dagenham Av. RM9: Dag 1E 74
(not continuous)
Dagenham Leisure Pk.
RM9: Dag 1E 74
Dagenham Rd. E10 1B 52
RM7: Rush G 7K 39
RM10: Dag, Rush G 4J 57
RM13: Rain 7K 57
Dagmar Av. HA9: Wemb 4F 45
Dagmar Ct. E14 3E 88
Dagmar Gdns. NW10 2F 65
Dagmar M. *UB2: S'hall* *3C 78*
(off Dagmar Rd.)
Dagmar Pas. *N1* *1B 68*
(off Cross St.)
Dagmar Rd. KT2: King T 1F 135
N4 7A 32
N15 4D 32
N22 1H 31
RM10: Dag 7J 57
SE5 1E 104
SE25 5E 140
UB2: S'hall 3C 78
Dagmar Ter. N1 1B 68
Dagnall Pk. SE25 6E 140
Dagnall Rd. SE25 5E 140
Dagnall St. SW11 2D 102
Dagnan Rd. SW12 7F 103
Dagobert Ho. *E1* *5J 69*
(off Smithy St.)
Dagonet Gdns.
BR1: Brom 3J 125
Dagonet Rd. BR1: Brom 3J 125
Dahlia Gdns. CR4: Mitc 4H 139
IG1: Ilf 6F 55
Dahlia Rd. SE2 4B 92
Dahomey Rd. SW16 6G 121
Daimler Way SM6: Wall 7J 151

Dain Ct. *W8* *4J 83*
(off Lexham Gdns.)
Daines Cl. E12 3D 54
Dainford Cl. BR1: Brom 5F 125
Dainton Cl. BR1: Brom 1K 143
Daintry Cl. HA3: Harr 4A 26
Daintry Way E9 6B 52
Dairsie Ct. BR1: Brom 1A 144
Dairsie Rd. SE9 3E 108
Dairy Cl. BR1: Brom 7K 125
CR7: Thor H 2C 140
NW10 1C 64
Dairy La. SE18 4D 90
Dairyman Cl. NW2 3F 47
Dairy M. SW9 3J 103
Dairy Wlk. SW19 4G 119
Daisy Cl. CR0: Croy 1K 153
Daisy Dobbings Wlk. *N19* *7J 31*
(off Jessie Blythe La.)
Daisy La. SW6 3J 101
Daisy Rd. E16 4G 71
E18 2K 35
Dakota Cl. SM6: Wall 7K 151
Dakota Gdns. E6 4C 72
UB5: N'olt 3C 60
Dalberg Rd. SW2 4A 104
(not continuous)
Dalberg Way SE2 3D 92
Dalby Rd. SW18 4A 102
Dalbys Cres. N17 6K 17
Dalby St. NW5 6F 49
Dalcross Rd. TW4: Houn 2C 96
Dale Av. HA8: Edg 1F 27
TW4: Houn 3C 96
Dalebury Rd. SW17 2D 120
Dale Cl. EN5: Barn 6E 4
HA5: Pinn 1K 23
SE3 3J 107
Dale Ct. EN2: Enf 1H 7
KT2: King T *7F 117*
(off York Rd.)
Dale Dr. UB4: Hayes 4H 59
Dalefield *IG9: Buck H* *1F 21*
(off Roebuck La.)
Dale Gdns. IG8: Wfd G 4E 20
Dale Grn. Rd. N11 3A 16
Dale Gro. N12 5F 15
Daleham Dr. UB8: Uxb 6D 58
Daleham Gdns. NW3 5B 48
Daleham M. NW3 6B 48
Dalehead *NW1* *1A 160*
(off Hampstead Rd.)
Dale Ho. *NW8* *1A 66*
(off Boundary Rd.)
SE4 4A 106
Dale Lodge N6 6G 31
Dalemain M. E16 1J 89
Dale Pk. Av. SM5: Cars 2D 150
Dale Pk. Rd. SE19 1C 140
Dale Rd. KT12: Walt T 7H 131
NW5 5E 48
SE17 6B 86
SM1: Sutt 4H 149
TW16: Sun T 7H 113
UB6: G'frd 5F 61
Dale Row W11 6G 65
Daleside Rd. KT19: Eps 6K 147
SW16 5F 121
Dale St. W4 5A 82
Dale, The BR2: Kes 4B 156
Dale Vw. Av. E4 2K 19
Dale Vw. Cres. E4 2K 19
Dale Vw. Gdns. E4 3A 20
Daleview Rd. N15 6E 32
Dalewood Gdns.
KT4: Wor Pk 2D 148
Dale Wood Rd.
BR6: Orp 7J 145
Daley Ho. W12 6D 64
Daley St. E9 6K 51
Daley Thompson Way
SW8 2F 103

Dalgarno Gdns. W10 5E 64
Dalgarno Way W10 4E 64
Dalgleish St. E14 6A 70
Daling Way E3 1A 70
Dali Universe *2K 85 (6G 167)*
Dalkeith Ct. *SW1* *3D 172*
(off Vincent St.)
Dalkeith Gro. HA7: Stan 5J 11
Dalkeith Ho. *SW9* *1B 104*
(off Lothian Rd.)
Dalkeith Rd. IG1: Ilf 3G 55
SE21 1C 122
Dallas Rd. NW4 7C 28
SE26 3H 123
SM3: Sutt 6G 149
W5 5F 63
Dallas Ter. UB3: Hayes 3H 77
Dallega Cl. UB3: Hayes 7F 59
Dallinger Rd. SE12 6H 107
Dalling Rd. W6 4D 82
Dallington St.
EC1 4B 68 (3B 162)
Dallin Rd. DA6: Bex 4D 110
SE18 7F 91
Dalmain Rd. SE23 1K 123
Dalmally Rd. CR0: Croy 7F 141
Dalmeny Av. N7 4H 49
SW16 2A 140
Dalmeny Cl.
HA0: Wemb 6C 44
Dalmeny Cres.
TW3: Houn 4H 97
Dalmeny Rd. DA8: Erith 1H 111
EN5: Barn 6F 5
KT4: Wor Pk 3D 148
N7 3H 49
(not continuous)
SM5: Cars 7E 150
Dalmeyer Rd. NW10 6B 46
Dalmore Rd. SE21 2C 122
Dalo Lodge *E3* *5C 70*
(off Gale St.)
Dalrymple Cl. N14 7C 6
Dalrymple Rd. SE4 4A 106
DALSTON 6F 51
Dalston Gdns. HA7: Stan 1E 26
Dalston La. E8 6F 51
Dalton Av. CR4: Mitc 2C 138
Dalton Cl. UB4: Hayes 4F 59
Dalton Ho. HA7: Stan 5F 11
SE14 *6K 87*
(off John Williams Cl.)
SW1 *5J 171*
(off Ebury Bri. Rd.)
Dalton Rd. HA3: Harr 2H 25
Dalton St. SE27 2B 122
Dalwood St. SE5 1E 104
Daly Ct. E15 5D 52
Dalyell Rd. SW9 3K 103
Damascene Wlk. SE21 1C 122
Damask Cres. E16 4G 71
Damer Ter. SW10 7A 84
Dames Rd. E7 3J 53
Dame St. N1 2C 68
Damien Ct. *E1* *6H 69*
(off Damien St.)
Damien St. E1 6H 69
Damon Cl. DA14: Sidc 3B 128
Damory Ho. *SE16* *4H 87*
(off Abbeyfield Est.)
Damson Dr. UB3: Hayes 7J 59
Damsonwood Rd.
UB2: S'hall 3E 78
Danbrook Rd. SW16 1J 139
Danbury Cl. RM6: Chad H 3D 38
Danbury Mans. *IG11: Bark* *7F 55*
(off Whiting Av.)
Danbury M. SM6: Wall 4F 151
Danbury St. N1 2B 68
Danbury Way IG8: Wfd G 6F 21
Danby Ct. *EN2: Enf* *3H 7*
(off Horseshoe La.)

Danby Ho. *E9* *7J 51*
(off Frampton Pk. Rd.)
Danby St. SE15 3F 105
Dancer Rd. SW6 1H 101
TW9: Rich 3G 99
Dando Cres. SE3 3K 107
Dandridge Cl. SE10 5H 89
Dandridge Ho. *E1* *5J 163*
(off Lamb St.)
Danebury CR0: Croy 6E 154
Danebury Av. SW15 6A 100
(not continuous)
Daneby Rd. SE6 3D 124
Dane Cl. DA5: Bexl 7G 111
Danecourt Gdns.
CR0: Croy 3F 153
Danecroft Rd. SE24 5C 104
Danehill Wlk. DA14: Sidc 3A 128
Danehurst Gdns. IG4: Ilf 5C 36
Danehurst St. SW6 1G 101
Daneland EN4: Barn 6J 5
Danemead Gro. UB5: N'olt 5F 43
Danemere St. SW15 3E 100
Dane Pl. E3 2A 70
Dane Rd. IG1: Ilf 5G 55
N18 3D 18
SW19 1A 138
TW15: Ashf 6E 112
UB1: S'hall 7C 60
W13 1C 80
Danesbury Rd.
TW13: Felt 1K 113
Danescombe SE12 1J 125
Danes Ct. HA9: Wemb 3H 45
NW8 *1D 66*
(off St Edmund's Ter.)
Danescourt Cres.
SM1: Sutt 2A 150
Danescroft NW4 5F 29
Danescroft Av. NW4 5F 29
Danescroft Gdns. NW4 5F 29
Danesdale Rd. E9 6A 52
Danesfield *SE17* *6E 86*
(off Albany Rd.)
Danes Ga. HA1: Harr 3J 25
Danes Ho. *W10* *5E 64*
(off Sutton Way)
Danes Rd. RM7: Rush G 7J 39
Dane St. WC1 5K 67 (6G 161)
Daneswood Av. SE6 3E 124
Danethorpe Rd.
HA0: Wemb 6D 44
Danetree Cl. KT19: Eps 7J 147
Danetree Rd. KT19: Eps 7J 147
Danette Gdns. RM10: Dag 2G 57
Daneville Rd. SE5 1D 104
Dangan Rd. E11 6J 35
Daniel Bolt Cl. E14 5D 70
Daniel Cl. N18 4D 18
SW17 6C 120
TW4: Houn 7D 96
Daniel Ct. NW9 1A 28
Daniel Gdns. SE15 7F 87
Daniel Ho. *N1* *2D 68*
(off Cranston Est.)
Daniell Way CR0: Croy 1J 151
Daniel Pl. NW4 7D 28
Daniel Rd. W5 7F 63
Daniels Rd. SE15 3J 105
Danleigh Ct. N14 7C 6
Dan Leno Wlk. SW6 7K 83
Dansey Pl. W1 2C 166
Dansington Rd.
DA16: Well 4A 110
Danson Cres. DA16: Well 3B 110
DANSON INTERCHANGE 5D 110
Danson La. DA16: Well 4B 110
Danson Mead DA16: Well 3C 110
Danson Rd.
DA5: Bexl, Bex 6C 110
DA6: Bex 6C 110
SE17 5B 86

Danson Underpass
DA15: Sidc 6C 110
Dante Pl. *SE11* *4B 86*
(off Dante Rd.)
Dante Rd. SE11 4B 86
Danube Ct. *SE15* *7F 87*
(off Daniel Gdns.)
Danube St. SW3 5C 84 (5D 170)
Danvers Ho. *E1* *6G 69*
(off Christian St.)
Danvers Rd. N8 4H 31
Danvers St. SW3 6B 84 (7B 170)
Da Palma Ct. *SW6* *6J 83*
(off Anselm Rd.)
Daphne Ct. KT4: Wor Pk 2A 148
Daphne Gdns. E4 3K 19
Daphne Ho. *N22* *1A 32*
(off Acacia Rd.)
Daphne St. SW18 6A 102
Daplyn St. E1 5G 69 (5K 163)
D'Arblay St. W1 6G 67 (1B 166)
Darby Cres. TW16: Sun T 2A 132
Darby Gdns.
TW16: Sun T 2A 132
Darcy Av. SM6: Wall 4G 151
Darcy Cl. N20 2G 15
D'Arcy Dr. HA3: Harr 4D 26
D'Arcy Gdns. HA3: Harr 4E 26
Darcy Gdns. RM9: Dag 1F 75
Darcy Ho. *E8* *1H 69*
(off London Flds. E. Side)
D'Arcy Pl. BR2: Short 4J 143
D'Arcy Rd. SM3: Sutt 4F 149
Darcy Rd. SW16 2J 139
TW7: Isle 1A 98
Dare Ct. E10 7E 34
Dare Gdns. RM8: Dag 3E 56
Darell Rd. TW9: Rich 3G 99
Darent Ho. BR1: Brom 5F 125
NW8 *5B 158*
(off Church St. Est.)
Darenth Rd. DA16: Well 1A 110
N16 7F 33
Darfield *NW1* *1G 67*
(off Bayham St.)
Darfield Rd. SE4 5B 106
Darfield Way W10 6F 65
Darfur St. SW15 3F 101
Dargate Cl. SE19 7F 123
Darien Ho. *E1* *5K 69*
(off Shandy St.)
Darien Rd. SW11 3B 102
Daring Ho. *E3* *2A 70*
(off Roman Rd.)
Dark Ho. Wlk.
EC3 7D 68 (3G 169)
Darland Lake Nature Reserve
3B 14
Darlands Dr. EN5: Barn 5A 4
Darlan Rd. SW6 7H 83
Darlaston Rd. SW19 7F 119
Darley Cl. CR0: Croy 6A 142
Darley Dr. KT3: N Mald 2K 135
Darley Gdns. SM4: Mord 6A 138
Darley Ho. SE11 6G 173
Darley Rd. N9 1A 18
SW11 6D 102
Darling Ho. TW1: Twick 6D 98
Darling Rd. SE4 3C 106
Darling Row E1 4H 69
Darlington Ct. SE6 1H 125
Darlington Ho. *SW8* *7H 85*
(off Hemans St.)
Darlington Rd. SE27 5B 122
Darmaine Cl.
CR2: S Croy 7C 152
Darnall Ho. *SE10* *1E 106*
(off Royal Hill)
Darnay Ho. SE1 3G 87 (7K 169)
Darndale Cl. E17 2B 34
Darnley Ho. *E14* *6A 70*
(off Camdenhurst St.)

A-Z London 229

Defoe Pl.—Deroy Cl.

Defoe Pl. *EC2* *5C 162*
(off Beech St.)
SW17 4D **120**
Defoe Rd. N16 3E **50**
De Frene Rd. SE26 4K **123**
Degema Rd. BR7: Chst 5F **127**
Dehar Cres. NW9 7B **28**
De Havilland Cl.
UB5: N'olt 3B **60**
De Havilland Rd.
HA8: Edg 2H **27**
TW5: Houn 7A **78**
De Havilland Way
TW19: Staines 6A **94**
Dekker Ho. *SE5* *7D 86*
(off Elmington Est.)
Dekker Rd. SE21 6E **104**
Delacourt Rd. SE3 7K **89**
Delafield Ho. *E1* *6G 69*
(off Christian St.)
Delafield Rd. SE7 5K **89**
Delaford Rd. SE16 5H **87**
Delaford St. SW6 7G **83**
Delamare Cres.
CR0: Croy 6J **141**
Delamere Gdns. NW7 6E **12**
Delamere Rd. SW20 1F **137**
UB4: Hayes 7B **60**
W5 2E **80**
Delamere St. W2 5K **65**
Delamere Ter. W2 5K **65**
Delancey Pas. *NW1* *1F 67*
(off Delancey St.)
Delancey St. NW1 1F **67**
Delancey Studios NW1 1F **67**
Delany Ho. *SE10* *6E 88*
(off Thames St.)
Delarch Ho. SE1 7A **168**
De Laune St.
SE17 5B **86** (6K **173**)
Delaware Mans. *W9* *4K 65*
(off Delaware Rd.)
Delaware Rd. W9 4K **65**
Delawyk Cres. SE24 6C **104**
Delcombe Av.
KT4: Wor Pk 1E **148**
Delderfield Ho.
RM1: Rom *2K 39*
(off Portnoi Cl.)
Delft Ho. *KT2: King T* *7F 117*
(off Acre Rd.)
Delft Way SE22 5E **104**
Delhi Rd. EN1: Enf 7A **8**
Delhi St. N1 1J **67**
(not continuous)
Delia St. SW18 7K **101**
Delisle Rd. SE28 2J **91**
(not continuous)
Delius Gro. E15 2F **71**
Della Path E5 3G **51**
Dellbow Rd. TW14: Felt 5K **95**
Dell Cl. E15 1F **71**
IG8: Wfd G 3E **20**
SM6: Wall 4G **151**
Dell Farm Rd.
HA4: Ruis 5F **23**
Dellfield Cl. BR3: Beck 1E **142**
Dell La. KT17: Eps 5C **148**
Dellors Cl. EN5: Barn 5A **4**
Dellow Cl. IG2: Ilf 7H **37**
Dellow Ho. *E1* *7H 69*
(off Dellow St.)
Dellow St. E1 7H **69**
Dell Rd. KT17: Eps 6C **148**
UB7: W Dray 4B **76**
Dells Cl. E4 7J **9**
TW11: Tedd 6K **115**
Dell's M. SW1 4B **172**
Dell, The DA5: Bexl 1K **129**
HA0: Wemb 5B **44**
HA5: Pinn 2B **24**
IG8: Wfd G 3E **20**
Dell, The SE2 5A **92**
SE19 1F **141**
TW8: Bford 6C **80**
TW14: Felt 7K **95**
Dell Wlk. KT3: N Mald 2A **136**
Dell Way W13 6C **62**
Dellwood Gdns. IG5: Ilf 3E **36**
Delmaine Ho. *E14* *6A 70*
(off Maroon St.)
Delmare Cl. SW9 4K **103**
Delme Cres. SE3 2K **107**
Delmerend Ho. *SW3* *5C 170*
(off Ixworth Pl.)
Delmey Cl. CR0: Croy 3F **153**
Deloraine Ho. SE8 1C **106**
Delorme St. W6 6F **83**
Delroy Ct. N20 7F **5**
Delta Bldg. *E14* *6E 70*
(off Ashton St.)
Delta Cen. HA0: Wemb 1F **63**
Delta Cl. KT4: Wor Pk 3B **148**
Delta Ct. NW2 2C **46**
Delta Est. E2 3G **69**
Delta Gro. UB5: N'olt 3B **60**
Delta Pk. SW18 4K **101**
Delta Point *CR0: Croy* *1C 152*
(off Wellesley Rd.)
Delta Rd. KT4: Wor Pk 3A **148**
Delta St. E2 3G **69**
De Luci Rd. DA8: Erith 5J **93**
De Lucy St. SE2 4B **92**
Delvan Cl. SE18 7E **90**
Delvers Mead RM10: Dag 4J **57**
Delverton Ho. *SE17* *5B 86*
(off Delverton Rd.)
Delverton Rd. SE17 5B **86**
Delvino Rd. SW6 1J **101**
Demesne Rd. SM6: Wall 4H **151**
Demeta Cl. HA9: Wemb 3J **45**
De Montfort Pde. SW16 3J **121**
De Montfort Rd. SW16 3J **121**
De Morgan Rd. SW6 3K **101**
Dempster Cl. KT6: Surb 1C **146**
Dempster Rd. SW18 5A **102**
Denbar Pde.
RM7: Mawney 4J **39**
Denberry Dr.
DA14: Sidc 3B **128**
Denbigh Cl. BR7: Chst 6D **126**
HA4: Ruis 2H **41**
NW10 7A **46**
SM1: Sutt 5H **149**
UB1: S'hall 6D **60**
W11 7H **65**
Denbigh Ct. E6 3B **72**
W7 *5K 61*
(off Copley Cl.)
Denbigh Dr. UB3: Hayes 2E **76**
Denbigh Gdns.
TW10: Rich 5F **99**
Denbigh Ho. *SW1* *1F 171*
(off Hans Pl.)
W11 *7H 65*
(off Westbourne Gro.)
Denbigh M. SW1 4A **172**
Denbigh Pl.
SW1 5G **85** (5A **172**)
Denbigh Rd. E6 3B **72**
TW3: Houn 2F **97**
UB1: S'hall 6D **60**
W11 7H **65**
W13 7B **62**
Denbigh St.
SW1 4G **85** (4A **172**)
(not continuous)
Denbigh Ter. W11 7H **65**
Denbridge Rd.
BR1: Brom 2D **144**
Denby Ct. SE11 3H **173**
Dence Ho. *E2* *2K 163*
(off Turin St.)
Denchworth Ho. SW9 2A **104**
Dencliffe TW15: Ashf 5C **112**
Den Cl. BR3: Beck 3F **143**
Dene Av. DA15: Sidc 7B **110**
TW3: Houn 3D **96**
Dene Cl. BR2: Short 1H **155**
DA2: Dart 4K **129**
KT4: Wor Pk 2B **148**
SE4 3A **106**
Dene Ct. *CR2: S Croy* *5C 152*
(off Warham Rd.)
W5 5C **62**
Denecroft Cres.
UB10: Uxb 1D **58**
Dene Gdns. HA7: Stan 5H **11**
KT7: T Ditt 2A **146**
Dene Ho. N14 7C **6**
Denehurst Gdns.
IG8: Wfd G 4E **20**
NW4 6E **28**
TW2: Twick 7H **97**
TW10: Rich 4G **99**
W3 1H **81**
Dene Rd. IG9: Buck H 1G **21**
N11 1J **15**
Denesmead SE24 5C **104**
Dene, The CR0: Croy 4K **153**
HA9: Wemb 4E **44**
KT8: W Mole 5D **132**
W13 5B **62**
Denewood EN5: Barn 5F **5**
Denewood Rd. N6 6D **30**
Denford St. *SE10* *5H 89*
(off Glenforth St.)
Dengie Wlk. *N1* *1C 68*
(off Basire St.)
Denham Cl. DA16: Well 3C **110**
Denham Ct. *SE26* *3H 123*
(off Kirkdale)
UB1: S'hall *7G 61*
(off Baird Av.)
Denham Cres. CR4: Mitc 4D **138**
Denham Dr. IG2: Ilf 6G **37**
Denham Ho. *W12* *7D 64*
(off White City Est.)
Denham Rd. N20 3J **15**
TW14: Felt 7A **96**
Denham St. SE10 5J **89**
Denham Way IG11: Bark 1J **73**
Denholme Rd. W9 3H **65**
Denison Cl. N2 3A **30**
Denison Ho. *E14* *6C 70*
(off Farrance St.)
Denison Rd. SW19 6B **120**
TW13: Felt 4H **113**
W5 4C **62**
Deniston Av. DA5: Bexl 1E **128**
Denis Way SW4 3H **103**
Denland Ho. *SW8* *7K 85*
(off Dorset Rd.)
Denleigh Gdns.
KT7: T Ditt 6J **133**
N21 7F **7**
Denman Dr. KT10: Esh 5A **146**
NW11 5J **29**
TW15: Ashf 6D **112**
Denman Dr. Nth. NW11 5J **29**
Denman Dr. Sth. NW11 5J **29**
Denman Pl. W1 2C **166**
Denman Rd. SE15 1F **105**
Denman St. W1 7H **67** (3C **166**)
Denmark Av. SW19 7G **119**
Denmark Ct.
SM4: Mord 6J **137**
Denmark Gdns.
SM5: Cars 3D **150**
Denmark Gro. N1 2A **68**
Denmark Hill SE5 1D **104**
Denmark Hill Dr. NW9 3C **28**
Denmark Hill Est. SE5 4D **104**
Denmark Mans. *SE5* *2C 104*
(off Coldharbour La.)
Denmark Path SE25 5H **141**
Denmark Pl.
WC2 6H **67** (7D **160**)
Denmark Rd. BR1: Brom 1K **143**
KT1: King T 3E **134**
N8 4A **32**
NW6 2H **65**
(not continuous)
SE5 1C **104**
SE25 5G **141**
SM5: Cars 3D **150**
SW19 6F **119**
TW2: Twick 3H **115**
W13 7B **62**
Denmark St. E11 3G **53**
E13 5K **71**
N17 1H **33**
WC2 6H **67** (7D **160**)
Denmark Ter. N2 3D **30**
Denmark Wlk. SE27 4C **122**
Denmead Ho. *SW15* *6B 100*
(off Highcliffe Dr.)
Denmead Rd. CR0: Croy 1B **152**
Denmore Ct. SM6: Wall 5F **151**
Dennan Rd. KT6: Surb 1F **147**
Dennard Way BR6: Orp 4E **156**
Denner Rd. E4 2H **19**
Denne Ter. E8 1F **69**
Dennett Rd. CR0: Croy 1A **152**
Dennett's Gro. SE14 1J **105**
Denning Av. CR0: Croy 4A **152**
Denning Cl.
NW8 3A **66** (1A **158**)
TW12: Hamp 5D **114**
Denning Point *E1* *7K 163*
(off Commercial St.)
Denning Rd. NW3 4B **48**
Dennington Cl. E5 2J **51**
Dennington Pk. Rd. NW6 6J **47**
Denningtons, The
KT4: Wor Pk 2A **148**
Dennis Av. HA9: Wemb 5F **45**
Dennis Cl. TW15: Ashf 7F **113**
Dennis Gdns. HA7: Stan 5H **11**
Dennis Ho. SM1: Sutt 4J **149**
Dennis La. HA7: Stan 3G **11**
Dennison Point E15 7E **52**
Dennis Pde. N14 1C **16**
Dennis Pk. Cres. SW20 1G **137**
Dennis Reeve Cl.
CR4: Mitc 1D **138**
Dennis Rd. KT8: E Mos 4G **133**
Denny Cl. E6 5C **72**
Denny Cres.
SE11 5A **86** (5K **173**)
Denny Gdns. RM9: Dag 7B **56**
Denny Rd. N9 1C **18**
Denny St. SE11 5A **86** (5K **173**)
Den Rd. BR2: Short 3F **143**
Densham Ho. *NW8* *1B 158*
(off Cochrane St.)
Densham Rd. E15 1G **71**
Densole Cl. BR3: Beck 1A **142**
Denstone Ho. *SE15* *6G 87*
(off Haymerle Rd.)
Densworth Gro. N9 2D **18**
Den, The *5J 87*
Dent Ho. *SE17* *4E 86*
(off Tatum St.)
Denton NW1 6E **48**
Denton Ct. BR2: Short 7E **144**
Denton Ho. *N1* *7B 50*
(off Halton Rd.)
Denton Rd. DA5: Bexl 2K **129**
DA16: Well 7C **92**
N8 5K **31**
N18 4K **17**
TW1: Twick 6D **98**
Denton St. SW18 6K **101**
Denton Ter. DA5: Bexl 2K **129**
Denton Way E5 3K **51**
Dents Rd. SW11 6D **102**
Denver Cl. BR6: Orp 6J **145**
Denver Rd. N16 7E **32**
Denwood SE23 3K **123**
Denyer St. SW3 4C **84** (4D **170**)
Denys Ho. *EC1* *5J 161*
(off Bourne Est.)
Denziloe Av. UB10: Uxb 3D **58**
Denzil Rd. NW10 5B **46**
Deodar Rd. SW15 4G **101**
Deodora Cl. N20 3H **15**
Depot App. NW2 4F **47**
Depot Rd. TW3: Houn 3H **97**
W12 7E **64**
Depot St. SE5 6D **86**
Deptford Bri. SE8 1C **106**
Deptford B'way. SE8 1C **106**
Deptford Bus. Pk. SE15 6J **87**
Deptford Chu. St. SE8 6C **88**
Deptford Creek Bri. *SE8* *6D 88*
(off Creek Rd.)
Deptford Ferry Rd. E14 4C **88**
Deptford Grn. SE8 6C **88**
Deptford High St. SE8 6C **88**
Deptford Pk. Bus. Cen.
SE8 5A **88**
Deptford Strand SE8 4B **88**
Deptford Trad. Est. SE8 5A **88**
Deptford Wharf SE8 4B **88**
De Quincey Ho. *SW1* *6A 172*
(off Lupus St.)
De Quincey M. E16 1J **89**
De Quincey Rd. N17 1D **32**
Derby Av. HA3: Harr 1H **25**
N12 5F **15**
RM7: Rom 6J **39**
Derby Ga. SW1 2J **85** (6E **166**)
(not continuous)
Derby Hill SE23 2J **123**
Derby Hill Cres. SE23 2J **123**
Derby Ho. HA5: Pinn 2B **24**
SE11 3J **173**
Derby Lodge N3 2H **29**
WC1 *1G 161*
(off Britannia St.)
Derby Rd. CR0: Croy 1B **152**
E7 7B **54**
E9 1K **69**
E18 1H **35**
EN3: Enf 5C **8**
KT5: Surb 1G **147**
N18 5D **18**
SM1: Sutt 6H **149**
SW14 4H **99**
SW19 7J **119**
TW3: Houn 4F **97**
UB6: G'frd 1F **61**
Derbyshire St. E2 3G **69**
(not continuous)
Derby St. W1 1E **84** (5H **165**)
Dereham Ho. *SE4* *4K 105*
(off Frendsbury Rd.)
Dereham Pl. EC2 3E **68** (2H **163**)
Dereham Rd. IG11: Bark 5K **55**
Derek Av. HA9: Wemb 7H **45**
KT19: Eps 6G **147**
SM6: Wall 4F **151**
Derek Cl. KT19: Eps 5H **147**
Derek Walcott Cl. SE24 5B **104**
Dericote St. E8 1H **69**
Deridene Cl.
TW19: Staines 6A **94**
Derifall Cl. E6 5D **72**
Dering Pl. CR2: S Croy 4C **152**
Dering Rd. CR0: Croy 4C **152**
Dering St. W1 6F **67** (1J **165**)
Dering Yd. W1 6F **67** (1K **165**)
Derinton Rd. SW17 4D **120**
Derley Rd. UB2: S'hall 3A **78**
Dermody Gdns. SE13 5F **107**
Dermody Rd. SE13 5F **107**
Deronda Est. SW2 1B **122**
Deronda Rd. SE24 1B **122**
Deroy Cl. SM5: Cars 6D **150**

Derrick Gdns.—Ditton Grange Cl.

Derrick Gdns. SE7 3A **90**
Derrick Rd. BR3: Beck 3B **142**
Derry Rd. CR0: Croy 3J **151**
Derry St. W8 2K **83**
Dersingham Av. E12 4D **54**
Dersingham Rd. NW2 3G **47**
Derwent *NW1* *2A 160* *(off Robert St.)*
Derwent Av. EN4: Barn 1J **15**
N18 5J **17**
NW7 6E **12**
NW9 5A **28**
SW15 4A **118**
UB10: Uxb 2C **40**
Derwent Cl. TW14: Felt 1H **113**
Derwent Ct. *SE16* *2K 87* *(off Eleanor Cl.)*
Derwent Cres. DA7: Bex 2G **111**
HA7: Stan 2C **26**
N12 3F **15**
Derwent Dr. BR5: Orp 7H **145**
UB4: Hayes 5G **59**
Derwent Gdns.
HA9: Wemb 7C **26**
IG4: Ilf 4C **36**
Derwent Gro. SE22 4F **105**
Derwent Ho. *E3* *4B 70* *(off Southern Gro.)*
SE20 *2H 141* *(off Derwent Rd.)*
SW7 *3A 170* *(off Cromwell Rd.)*
Derwent Lodge
KT4: Wor Pk 2D **148**
TW7: Isle 2H **97**
Derwent Ri. NW9 6A **28**
Derwent Rd. N13 4E **16**
SE20 2G **141**
SW20 5F **137**
TW2: Twick 6F **97**
UB1: S'hall 6D **60**
W5 3C **80**
Derwent St. SE10 5G **89**
Derwent Wlk. SM6: Wall 7F **151**
Derwentwater Rd. W3 1J **81**
Derwent Yd. *W5* *3C 80* *(off Derwent Rd.)*
De Salis Rd. UB10: Uxb 4E **58**
Desborough Cl.
TW17: Shep 7C **130**
W2 5K **65**
Desborough Ho. *W14* *6H 83* *(off Nth. End Rd.)*
Desenfans Rd. SE21 6E **104**
Desford Ct. TW15: Ashf 2C **112**
Desford Rd. E16 4G **71**
Desford Way TW15: Ashf 2B **112**
Design Mus. ***2F 87 (6K 169)***
Desmond Ho. EN4: Barn 6H **5**
Desmond St. SE14 6A **88**
Despard Rd. N19 1G **49**
Dethick Ct. E3 1A **70**
Detling Ho. *SE17* *4E 86* *(off Congreve St.)*
Detling Rd. BR1: Brom 5J **125**
DA8: Erith 7K **93**
Detmold Rd. E5 2J **51**
Devalls Cl. E6 7F **73**
Devana End SM5: Cars 3D **150**
Devas Rd. SW20 1E **136**
Devas St. E3 4D **70**
Devenay Rd. E15 7H **53**
Devenish Rd. SE2 2A **92**
Deventer Cres. SE22 5E **104**
De Vere Gdns. IG1: Ilf 2D **54**
W8 2A **84**
Deverell St. SE1 3D **86**
De Vere M. *W8* *3A 84* *(off De Vere Gdns.)*
Devereux Ct. WC2 1J **167**
Devereux La. SW13 7D **82**
Devereux Rd. SW11 6D **102**
Deveron Way RM1: Rom 1K **39**
Deveroux Cl.
BR3: Beck 5E **142**
Devey Cl.
KT2: King T 7B **118**
Devitt Ho. *E14* *7D 70* *(off Wade's Pl.)*
Devizes St. N1 1D **68**
Devon Av. TW2: Twick 1G **115**
Devon Cl. IG9: Buck H 2E **20**
N17 3F **33**
UB6: G'frd 1C **62**
Devon Ct. TW12: Hamp 7E **114**
W7 *5K 61* *(off Copley Cl.)*
Devoncroft Gdns.
TW1: Twick 7A **98**
Devon Gdns. N4 6B **32**
Devon Ho. E17 2B **34**
Devonhurst Pl. W4 5K **81**
Devonia Gdns. N18 6H **17**
Devonia Rd. N1 2B **68**
Devon Mans. *HA3: Harr* *5C 26* *(off Woodcock Hill)*
SE1 *6J 169* *(off Tooley St.)*
Devon Pde. HA3: Harr 5C **26**
Devonport W2 6C **66** (1C **164**)
Devonport Gdns. IG1: Ilf 6D **36**
Devonport M. W12 2D **82**
Devonport Rd. W12 1D **82** (not continuous)
Devonport St. E1 6K **69**
Devon Ri. N2 4B **30**
Devon Rd. IG11: Bark 1J **73**
SM2: Sutt 7G **149**
Devons Est. E3 3D **70**
Devonshire Av.
SM2: Sutt 7A **150**
Devonshire Cl. E15 4G **53**
N13 3F **17**
W1 5F **67** (5J **159**)
Devonshire Ct. *E1* *3J 69* *(off Bancroft Rd.)*
HA5: Pinn *1D 24* *(off Devonshire Rd.)*
WC1 *5F 161* *(off Boswell St.)*
Devonshire Cres. NW7 7A **14**
Devonshire Dr.
KT6: Surb 1D **146**
SE10 7D **88**
Devonshire Gdns. N17 6H **17**
N21 7H **7**
W4 7J **81**
Devonshire Gro. SE15 6H **87**
Devonshire Hall *E9* *6J 51* *(off Frampton Pk. Rd.)*
Devonshire Hill La. N17 6G **17** (not continuous)
Devonshire Ho. IG8: Ilf 7K **21**
NW6 *6H 47* *(off Kilburn High Rd.)*
SE1 *3C 86* *(off Bath Ter.)*
SM2: Sutt 7A **150**
SW1 *5D 172* *(off Lindsay Sq.)*
Devonshire Ho. Bus. Cen.
BR2: Short *4K 143* *(off Devonshire Sq.)*
Devonshire M. N13 4F **17**
SW10 *7A 170* *(off Park Wlk.)*
W4 5A **82**
Devonshire M. Nth.
W1 5F **67** (5J **159**)
Devonshire M. Sth.
W1 5F **67** (5J **159**)
Devonshire M. W.
W1 4E **66** (4H **159**)
Devonshire Pas. W4 5A **82**
Devonshire Pl. NW2 3J **47**
W1 4E **66** (4H **159**)
W8 3K **83**
Devonshire Pl. M.
W1 5E **66** (4H **159**)
Devonshire Rd.
BR6: Orp 7K **145**
CR0: Croy 7D **140**
DA6: Bex 4E **110**
E16 6K **71**
E17 6C **34**
HA1: Harr 6H **25**
HA5: Pinn 6A **24** (Abbotsbury Gdns.)
HA5: Pinn 1D **24** (Wellington Rd.)
IG2: Ilf 7H **37**
N9 1D **18**
N13 4E **16**
N17 6H **17**
NW7 7A **14**
SE9 2C **126**
SE23 1J **123**
SM2: Sutt 7A **150**
SM5: Cars 4E **150**
SW19 7C **120**
TW13: Felt 3C **114**
UB1: S'hall 5E **60**
W4 5A **82**
W5 3C **80**
Devonshire Row
EC2 5E **68** (6H **163**)
Devonshire Row M. W1 4K **159**
Devonshire Sq.
BR2: Short 4K **143**
EC2 6E **68** (6H **163**)
Devonshire St.
W1 5E **66** (5H **159**)
W4 5A **82**
Devonshire Ter. W2 6A **66**
Devonshire Way
CR0: Croy 2A **154**
UB4: Hayes 6K **59**
Devons Rd. E3 3D **70**
Devon St. SE15 6H **87**
Devon Way KT9: Chess 5C **146**
KT19: Eps 5H **147**
UB10: Uxb 2B **58**
Devon Waye TW5: Houn 7D **78**
Devon Wharf *E14* *5E 70* *(off Leven Rd.)*
De Walden Ho. *NW8* *2C 66* *(off Allitsen Rd.)*
De Walden St.
W1 5E **66** (6H **159**)
Dewar St. SE15 3G **105**
Dewberry Gdns. E6 5C **72**
Dewberry St. E14 5E **70**
Dewey Rd. N1 2A **68**
RM10: Dag 6H **57**
Dewey St. SW17 5D **120**
Dewhurst Rd. W14 3F **83**
Dewsbury Cl. HA5: Pinn 6C **24**
Dewsbury Ct. W4 4J **81**
Dewsbury Gdns.
KT4: Wor Pk 3C **148**
Dewsbury Rd. NW10 5C **46**
Dewsbury Ter. NW1 1F **67**
Dexter Ho. *DA18: Erith* *3E 92* *(off Kale Rd.)*
Dexter Rd. EN5: Barn 6A **4**
Deyncourt Rd. N17 1C **32**
Deynecourt Gdns. E11 4A **36**
D'Eynsford Rd. SE5 1D **104**
Dhonau Ho. *SE1* *4F 87* *(off Longfield Est.)*
Diadem Ct. W1 7C **160**
Dial Wlk., The *W8* *2K 83* *(off Broad Wlk., The)*
Diameter Rd. BR5: Orp 7F **145**
Diamond Cl. RM8: Dag 1C **56**
Diamond Est. SW17 3C **120**
Diamond Ho. *E3* *2A 70* *(off Roman Rd.)*
Diamond Rd. HA4: Ruis 4B **42**
Diamond St. NW10 7K **45**
SE5 7E **86**
Diamond Ter. SE10 1E **106**
Diamond Way SE8 6C **88**
Diana Cl. E18 1K **35**
SE8 6B **88**
Diana Gdns. KT6: Surb 2F **147**
Diana Ho. SW13 1B **100**
Diana Rd. E17 3B **34**
Dianne Way EN4: Barn 4H **5**
Dianthus Cl. SE2 5B **92**
Dibden Ho. SE5 7E **86**
Dibden St. N1 1C **68**
Dibdin Cl. SM1: Sutt 3J **149**
Dibdin Ho. NW6 2K **65**
Dibdin Rd. SM1: Sutt 3J **149**
Dicey Av. NW2 4E **46**
Dickens Av. N3 1A **30**
UB8: Uxb 6D **58**
Dickens Cl. DA8: Erith 7H **93**
TW10: Rich 2E **116**
UB3: Hayes 4G **77**
Dickens Ct. *E11* *4J 35* *(off Makepeace Rd.)*
Dickens Dr. BR7: Chst 6G **127**
Dickens Est. SE1 2G **87**
SE16 3G **87**
Dickens House ***4K 67 (4H 161)***
Dickens Ho. *NW6* *3J 65* *(off Malvern Rd.)*
NW8 3B **158**
SE17 *5B 86* *(off Doddington Gro.)*
WC1 3E **160**
Dickens La. N18 5K **17**
Dickens M. *EC1* *5A 162* *(off Turnmill St.)*
Dickenson Cl. N9 1B **18**
Dickenson Ho. N8 6K **31**
Dickenson Rd. N8 7J **31**
TW13: Felt 5A **114**
Dickensons La. SE25 5G **141** (not continuous)
Dickensons Pl. SE25 6G **141**
Dickens Ri. IG7: Chig 3K **21**
Dickens Rd. E6 2B **72**
Dickens Sq. SE1 3C **86** (7D **168**)
Dickens St. SW8 2F **103**
Dickenswood Cl. SE19 7B **122**
Dickerage La.
KT3: N Mald 3J **135**
Dickerage Rd.
KT1: King T 1J **135**
Dicksee Ho. *NW8* *4A 158* *(off Lyons Pl.)*
Dickson Fold HA5: Pinn 4B **24**
Dickson Ho. *E1* *6H 69* *(off Philpot St.)*
Dickson Rd. SE9 3C **108**
Dick Turpin Way
TW14: Felt 4H **95**
Didsbury Cl. E6 1D **72**
Digby Bus. Cen. *E9* *6K 51* *(off Digby Rd.)*
Digby Cres. N4 2C **50**
Digby Gdns. RM10: Dag 1G **75**
Digby Mans. *W6* *5D 82* *(off Hammersmith Bri. Rd.)*
Digby Pl. CR0: Croy 3F **153**
Digby Rd. E9 6K **51**
IG11: Bark 7K **55**
Digby St. E2 3J **69**
Diggon St. E1 5K **69**
Dighton Ct. SE17 6C **86**
Dighton Rd. SW18 5A **102**
Dignum St. N1 2A **68**
Digswell St. N7 6A **50**
Dilhorne Cl. SE12 3K **125**
Dilke St. SW3 6D **84** (7F **171**)
Dilloway La. UB2: S'hall 2C **78**
Dillwyn Cl. SE26 4A **124**
Dilston Cl. UB5: N'olt 3A **60**
Dilston Gro. SE16 4J **87**
Dilton Gdns. SW15 1C **118**
Dilwyn Ct. E17 2A **34**
Dimes Pl. W6 4D **82**
Dimmock Dr. UB6: G'frd 5H **43**
Dimond Cl. E7 4J **53**
Dimsdale Dr. EN1: Enf 6B **8**
NW9 1J **45**
Dimsdale Wlk. E13 2J **71**
Dimson Cres. E3 3C **70**
Dingle Gdns. E14 7C **70**
Dingle Rd. TW15: Ashf 5D **112**
Dingles Ct. HA5: Pinn 1B **24**
Dingle, The UB10: Uxb 3D **58**
Dingley La. SW16 2H **121**
Dingley Pl. EC1 3C **68** (1D **162**)
Dingley Rd.
EC1 3C **68** (2C **162**)
Dingwall Av. CR0: Croy 2C **152**
Dingwall Gdns. NW11 6J **29**
Dingwall Rd. CR0: Croy 1D **152**
SM5: Cars 7D **150**
SW18 7A **102**
Dinmont Est. E2 2G **69**
Dinmont Ho. *E2* *2G 69* *(off Pritchard's Rd.)*
Dinmont St. E2 2H **69**
Dinmore Ho. *E9* *1J 69* *(off Templecombe Rd.)*
Dinnington Ho. *E1* *4H 69* *(off Coventry Rd.)*
Dinsdale Gdns. EN5: Barn 5E **4**
SE25 5E **140**
Dinsdale Rd. SE3 6H **89**
Dinsmore Rd. SW12 7F **103**
Dinton Ho. *NW8* *3D 158* *(off Lilestone St.)*
Dinton Rd. KT2: King T 7F **117**
SW19 6B **120**
Diploma Av. N2 4C **30**
Diploma Ct. N2 4C **30**
Dirleton Rd. E15 1H **71**
Disbrowe Rd. W6 6G **83**
Discovery Bus. Pk. *SE16* *3G 87* *(off St James's Rd.)*
Discovery Ho. *E14* *7E 70* *(off Newby Pl.)*
Discovery Wlk. E1 1H **87**
Dishforth La. NW9 7F **13**
Disley Ct. *UB1: S'hall* *6F 61* *(off Howard Rd.)*
Disney Pl. SE1 2C **86** (6D **168**)
Disney St. SE1 2C **86** (6D **168**)
Dison Cl. EN3: Enf 1E **8**
Disraeli Cl. SE28 1C **92**
W4 3K **81**
Disraeli Gdns. SW15 4H **101**
Disraeli Rd. E7 6J **53**
NW10 2K **63**
SW15 4G **101**
W5 1D **80**
Diss St. E2 3F **69** (1J **163**)
Distaff La. EC4 7C **68** (2C **168**)
Distillery La. W6 5E **82**
Distillery Rd. W6 5E **82**
Distillery Wlk. TW8: Bford 6E **80**
Distin St. SE11 4A **86** (4J **173**)
District Rd. HA0: Wemb 5B **44**
Ditch All. SE10 1D **106**
Ditchburn St. E14 7E **70**
Ditchfield Rd. UB4: Hayes 4C **60**
Ditchley Ct. *W7* *5K 61* *(off Templeman Rd.)*
Dittisham Rd. SE9 4C **126**
Ditton Cl. KT7: T Ditt 7A **134**
Dittoncroft Cl.
CR0: Croy 4E **152**
Ditton Grange Cl.
KT6: Surb 1D **146**

Ditton Grange Dr.—Douglas Dr.

Ditton Grange Dr.
KT6: Surb 1D 146
Ditton Hill KT6: Surb 1C 146
Ditton Hill Rd.
KT6: Surb 1C 146
Ditton Lawn KT7: T Ditt . . . 1A 146
Ditton Pl. SE20 . . . . 1H 141
Ditton Reach KT7: T Ditt . . . 6B 134
Ditton Rd. DA6: Bex 5D 110
KT6: Surb 2D 146
UB2: S'hall 5D 78
Divisional Rd. E12 . . . . 2B 54
Divis Way *SW15* *6D 100*
(off Dover Pk. Dr.)
Dixon Clark Ct. N1 . . . . 6B 50
Dixon Cl. E6 . . . . 6D 72
Dixon Ho. *W10* *6F 65*
(off Darfield Way)
Dixon Pl. BR4: W W'ck 1D 154
Dixon Rd. SE14 . . . . 1A 106
SE25 . . . . 3E 140
Dixon's All. SE16 . . . . 2H 87
Dobbin Cl. HA3: Harr 2A 26
Dobell Rd. SE9 . . . . 5D 108
Dobree Av. NW10 . . . . 7D 46
Dobson Cl. NW6 . . . . 7B 48
Dobson Ho. *SE5* *7D 86*
(off Edmund St.)
SE14 . . . . *6K 87*
(off John Williams Cl.)
Doby Ct. EC4 . . . . 2D 168
Dock Cotts. *E1* *7J 69*
(off Highway, The)
Dockers Tanner Rd. E14 . . . . . 3C 88
Dockett Eddy KT16: Chert . . . 7A 130
Dockett Eddy La.
TW17: Shep 7B 130
Dockhead SE1 . . . . 2F 87 (7K 169)
Dockhead Wharf *SE1* *7K 169*
(off Shad Thames)
Dock Hill Av. SE16 . . . . 1K 87
Dockland St. E16 . . . . 1E 90
(not continuous)
Dockley Rd. SE16 . . . . 3G 87
Dockley Rd. Ind. Est.
SE16 . . . . *3G 87*
(off Dockley Rd.)
Dock Offices *SE16* *3J 87*
(off Surrey Quays Rd.)
Dock Rd. E16 . . . . 7H 71
TW8: Bford 7D 80
Dockside Rd. E16 . . . . 7B 72
Dock St. E1 . . . . 7G 69
Dockwell Cl. TW14: Felt 4J 95
Doctor Johnson Av.
SW17 . . . . 3F 121
Doctors Cl. SE26 . . . . 5J 123
Docwra's Bldgs. N1 . . . . 6E 50
Dodbrooke Rd. SE27 . . . . . . 3A 122
Dodd Ho. *SE16* *4H 87*
(off Rennie Est.)
Doddington Gro. SE17 . . . . . . 6B 86
Doddington Pl. SE17 . . . . 6B 86
Dodsley Pl. N9 . . . . 3D 18
Dodson St. SE1 . . . . 2A 86 (7K 167)
Dod St. E14 . . . . 6B 70
Doebury Wlk. *SE18* *6A 92*
(off Prestwood Cl.)
Doel Cl. SW19 . . . . 7A 120
Dog & Duck Yd. WC1 . . . . . . 5G 161
Doggett Rd. SE6 . . . . 7C 106
Doggetts Courts EN4: Barn 5H 5
Doghurst Av. UB3: Hayes 7D 76
Doghurst Dr. UB7: W Dray . . . 7D 76
Dog Kennel Hill SE5 . . . . 3E 104
Dog Kennel Hill Est.
SE22 . . . . *3E 104*
(off Albrighton Rd.)
Dog La. NW10 . . . . 4A 46
Doherty Rd. E13 . . . . 4J 71
Dokal Ind. Est. UB2: S'hall . . . 3C 78
Dolben Ct. SE8 . . . . 4B 88
Dolben St. SE1 . . . . 1B 86 (5A 168)
(not continuous)
Dolby Rd. SW6 . . . . 2H 101
Dolland Ho. SE11 . . . . 6H 173
Dolland St. SE11 . . . 5K 85 (6H 173)
Dollar Bay Ct. *E14* *2E 88*
(off Lawn Ho. Clo)
Dollary Pde. *KT1: King T* . . . *3H 135*
(off Kingston Rd.)
Dollis Av. N3 . . . . 1H 29
Dollis Brook Wlk.
EN5: Barn 6B 4
Dollis Cres. HA4: Ruis 1A 42
Dolliscroft NW7 . . . . 7B 14
DOLLIS HILL 2D 46
Dollis Hill Av. NW2 . . . . 3D 46
Dollis Hill Est. NW2 . . . . 3C 46
Dollis Hill La. NW2 . . . . 4B 46
Dollis M. N3 . . . . 1J 29
Dollis Pk. N3 . . . . 1H 29
Dollis Rd. N3 . . . . 1G 29
NW7 . . . . 7B 14
Dollis Valley Dr.
EN5: Barn 6C 4
Dollis Valley Way
EN5: Barn 6C 4
Dolman Cl. N3 . . . . 1A 30
Dolman Rd. W4 . . . . 4K 81
Dolman St. SW4 . . . . 4K 103
Dolphin Cl. KT6: Surb 5D 134
SE16 . . . . 2K 87
SE28 . . . . 6D 74
Dolphin Ct. NW11 . . . . 6G 29
SE8 . . . . *6B 88*
(off Wotton Rd.)
Dolphin Est.
TW16: Sun T 1G 131
Dolphin Ho. SW18 . . . . 4K 101
Dolphin La. E14 . . . . 7D 70
Dolphin Rd.
TW16: Sun T 1G 131
UB5: N'olt 2D 60
Dolphin Rd. Nth.
TW16: Sun T 1G 131
Dolphin Rd. Sth.
TW16: Sun T 1G 131
Dolphin Rd. W.
TW16: Sun T 1G 131
Dolphin Sq.
SW1 . . . . . . 5G 85 (6B 172)
W4 . . . . 7A 82
Dolphin St. KT1: King T 2E 134
Dolphin Twr. *SE8* *6B 88*
(off Abinger Gro.)
Dombey Ho. *SE1* *7K 169*
(off Wolseley St.)
W11 . . . . *1F 83*
(off St Ann's Rd.)
Dombey St. WC1 . . . 5K 67 (5G 161)
(not continuous)
Domecq Ho. *EC1* *3B 162*
(off Dallington St.)
Dome Hill Pk. SE26 . . . . 4F 123
Domett Cl. SE5 . . . . 4D 104
Domfe Pl. E5 . . . . 4J 51
Domingo St. EC1 . . . 4C 68 (3C 162)
Dominica Cl. E6 . . . . 2B 72
Dominion Bus. Pk. N9 . . . . . . 2E 18
Dominion Cen., The
UB2: S'hall 2C 78
Dominion Ct. *E8* *7F 51*
(off Middleton Rd.)
Dominion Ho. *E14* *5D 88*
(off St Davids Sq.)
Dominion Pde. HA1: Harr 5K 25
Dominion Rd. CR0: Croy . . . 7F 141
UB2: S'hall 2C 78
Dominion St.
EC2 . . . . 5D 68 (5F 163)
Dominion Theatre 7D 160
(off Tottenham Ct. Rd.)
Domitian Pl. EN1: Enf 5A 8
Domonic Dr. SE9 . . . . 4F 127
Domville Cl. N20 . . . . 2G 15
Donald Dr. RM6: Chad H 5C 38
Donald Hunter Ho. *E7* *5K 53*
(off Post Office App.,
not continuous)
Donald Rd. CR0: Croy 7K 139
E13 . . . . 1K 71
Donaldson Rd. NW6 . . . . 1H 65
SE18 . . . . 1E 108
Donald Woods Gdns.
KT5: Surb 2H 147
Donato Dr. SE15 . . . . 6E 86
Doncaster Dr. UB5: N'olt 5D 42
Doncaster Gdns. N4 . . . . 6C 32
UB5: N'olt 5D 42
Doncaster Rd. N9 . . . . 7C 8
Donegal Ho. *E1* *4H 69*
(off Cambridge Heath Rd.)
Donegal St. N1 . . . . 2K 67
Doneraile Ho. *SW1* *5J 171*
(off Ebury Bri. Rd.)
Doneraile St. SW6 . . . . 2F 101
Dongola Rd. E1 . . . . 5A 70
E13 . . . . 3K 71
N17 . . . . 3E 32
Dongola Rd. W. E13 . . . . 3K 71
Donington Av. IG6: Ilf 5G 37
Donkey All. SE22 . . . . 7G 105
Donkey La. EN1: Enf 2B 8
Donkin Ho. *SE16* *4H 87*
(off Rennie Est.)
Donmar Warehouse Theatre
. . . . 1E 166
(off Earlham St.)
Donnatt's Rd. SE14 . . . . 1B 106
Donne Ct. SE24 . . . . 6C 104
Donnefield Av. HA8: Edg 7K 11
Donne Ho. *E14* *6C 70*
(off Dod St.)
SE14 . . . . *6K 87*
(off Samuel Cl.)
Donnelly Ct. *SW6* *7G 83*
(off Dawes Rd.)
Donne Pl. CR4: Mitc 4F 139
SW3 . . . . . . 4C 84 (3D 170)
Donne Rd. RM8: Dag 2C 56
Donnington Ct. *NW1* *7F 49*
(off Castlehaven Rd.)
NW10 . . . . 7D 46
Donnington Mans. *NW10* . . . *1E 64*
(off Donnington Rd.)
Donnington Rd.
HA3: Harr 5D 26
KT4: Wor Pk 2C 148
NW10 . . . . 7D 46
Donnybrook Rd. SW16 . . . . . 7G 121
Donoghue Cotts. *E14* *5A 70*
(off Galsworthy Av.)
Donovan Av. N10 . . . . 2F 31
Donovan Ct. NW10 . . . . 7J 45
SW10 . . . . *6A 170*
(off Drayton Gdns.)
Donovan Ho. *E1* *7J 69*
(off Cable St.)
Donovan Pl. N21 . . . . 5E 6
Don Phelan Cl. SE5 . . . . 1D 104
Doone Cl. TW11: Tedd 6A 116
Doon St. SE1 . . . . . 1A 86 (5J 167)
Dora Ho. *E14* *6B 70*
(off Rhodeswell Rd.)
W11 . . . . *7F 65*
(off St Ann's Rd.)
Doral Way SM5: Cars 5D 150
Doran Ct. E6 . . . . 2D 72
Dorando Cl. W12 . . . . 7D 64
Doran Gro. SE18 . . . . 7J 91
Doran Mnr. *N2* *5D 30*
(off Gt. North Rd.)
Doran Wlk. E15 . . . . 7E 52
Dora Rd. SW19 . . . . 5J 119
Dora St. E14 . . . . 6B 70
Dorchester Av.
DA5: Bexl 1D 128
HA2: Harr 6G 25
N13 . . . . 4H 17
Dorchester Cl. BR5: Orp 7B 128
UB5: N'olt 5F 43
Dorchester Ct. *E18* *1H 35*
(off Buckingham Rd.)
N1 . . . . *7E 50*
(off Englefield Rd.)
N10 . . . . 3F 31
N14 . . . . 7A 6
NW2 . . . . 3F 47
SE24 . . . . 5C 104
Dorchester Dr. SE24 . . . . . . 5C 104
TW14: Felt 6G 95
Dorchester Gdns. E4 . . . . 4H 19
NW11 . . . . 4J 29
Dorchester Gro. W4 . . . . 5A 82
Dorchester M.
KT3: N Mald 4K 135
TW1: Twick 6C 98
Dorchester Rd.
KT4: Wor Pk 1E 148
SM4: Mord 7K 137
UB5: N'olt 5F 43
Dorchester Ter. *NW2* *3F 47*
(off Gratton Ter.)
Dorchester Way HA3: Harr . . . 6F 27
Dorchester Waye
UB4: Hayes 6K 59
(not continuous)
Dorcis Av. DA7: Bex 2E 110
Dordrecht Rd. W3 . . . . 1A 82
Dore Av. E12 . . . . 5E 54
Doreen Av. NW9 . . . . 1K 45
Doreen Capstan Ho. *E11* *3G 53*
(off Apollo Pl.)
Dore Gdns. SM4: Mord 7K 137
Dorell Cl. UB1: S'hall 5D 60
Doria Rd. SW6 . . . . 2H 101
Doric Ho. *E2* *2K 69*
(off Mace St.)
Doric Way NW1 . . . . 3H 67 (1C 160)
Dorien Rd. SW20 . . . . 2F 137
Doris Av. DA8: Erith 1J 111
Doris Emmerton Ct.
SW11 . . . . 4A 102
Doris Rd. E7 . . . . 7J 53
TW15: Ashf 6F 113
Dorking Cl. KT4: Wor Pk . . . 2F 149
SE8 . . . . 6B 88
Dorking Ct. *N17* *1G 33*
(off Hampden La.)
Dorking Ho. SE1 . . . . 3D 86
Dorlcote Rd. SW18 . . . . 7C 102
Dorly Cl. TW17: Shep 5G 131
Dorman Pl. N9 . . . . 2B 18
Dormans Cl. HA6: Nwood 1F 23
Dorman Wlk. NW10 . . . . 5K 45
Dorman Way NW8 . . . . 1B 66
Dorma Trad. Pk. E10 . . . . 1K 51
Dormay St. SW18 . . . . 5K 101
Dormer Cl. E15 . . . . 6H 53
EN5: Barn 5A 4
Dormer's Av. UB1: S'hall 6E 60
Dormers Ri. UB1: S'hall 6F 61
DORMER'S WELLS 6E 60
Dormer's Wells La.
UB1: S'hall 6E 60
Dormstone Ho. *SE17* *4E 86*
(off Beckway St.)
Dormywood HA4: Ruis 5H 23
Dornberg Cl. SE3 . . . . 7J 89
Dornberg Rd. SE3 . . . . 7K 89
Dorncliffe Rd. SW6 . . . . 2G 101
Dorney NW3 . . . . 7C 48
Dorney Ri. BR5: Orp 4K 145
Dorney Way TW4: Houn 5C 96
Dornfell St. NW6 . . . . 5H 47
Dornton Rd. CR2: S Croy . . . 6D 152
SW12 . . . . 2F 121
Dorothy Av. HA0: Wemb 7E 44
Dorothy Evans Cl.
DA7: Bex 4H 111
Dorothy Gdns. RM8: Dag 4B 56
Dorothy Pettingell Ho.
SM1: Sutt *3K 149*
(off Angel Hill)
Dorothy Rd. SW11 . . . . 3D 102
Dorrell Pl. SW9 . . . . 3A 104
Dorrien Wlk. SW16 . . . . 2H 121
Dorrington Ct. SE25 . . . . . . 1E 140
Dorrington St.
EC1 . . . . 5A 68 (5J 161)
Dorrington Way
BR3: Beck 5E 142
Dorrit Ho. *W11* *1F 83*
(off St Ann's Rd.)
Dorrit St. SE1 . . . . . 2C 86 (6D 168)
Dorritt M. N18 . . . . 5K 17
Dorrit Way BR7: Chst 6G 127
Dorryn Ct. SE26 . . . . 5K 123
Dors Cl. NW9 . . . . 1K 45
Dorset Av. DA16: Well 4K 109
RM1: Rom 4K 39
UB2: S'hall 4E 78
UB4: Hayes 3G 59
Dorset Bldgs.
EC4 . . . . 6B 68 (1A 168)
Dorset Cl. NW1 . . . . 5D 66 (5E 158)
UB4: Hayes 3G 59
Dorset Ct. HA6: Nwood 1H 23
N1 . . . . *7E 50*
(off Hertford Rd.)
W7 . . . . *5K 61*
(off Copley Cl.)
Dorset Dr. HA8: Edg 6A 12
Dorset Gdns. CR4: Mitc 4K 139
Dorset Ho. *NW1* *5F 159*
(off Gloucester Pl.)
Dorset M. N3 . . . . 1J 29
Dorset Pl. E15 . . . . 6F 53
Dorset Ri. EC4 . . . . . 6B 68 (1A 168)
Dorset Rd. BR3: Beck 3K 141
CR4: Mitc 2C 138
E7 . . . . 7A 54
HA1: Harr 6G 25
N15 . . . . 4D 32
N22 . . . . 1J 31
SE9 . . . . 2C 126
SW8 . . . . 7J 85
SW19 . . . . 1J 137
TW15: Ashf 3A 112
W5 . . . . 3C 80
Dorset Sq. NW1 . . . . 4D 66 (4E 158)
Dorset St. W1 . . . . . 5D 66 (6F 159)
Dorset Way TW2: Twick 1H 115
UB10: Uxb 2B 58
Dorset Waye TW5: Houn 7D 78
Dorton Cl. SE15 . . . . 7E 86
Dorton Vs. UB7: W Dray 7C 76
Dorville Cres. W6 . . . . 3D 82
Dorville Rd. SE12 . . . . 5H 107
Dothill Rd. SE18 . . . . 7G 91
Douai Gro. TW12: Hamp . . . 1G 133
Doughty Ct. *E1* *1H 87*
(off Prusom St.)
Doughty Ho. *SW10* *6A 84*
(off Netherton Gro.)
Doughty M. WC1 . . . 4K 67 (4G 161)
Doughty St. WC1 . . . 4K 67 (3G 161)
Douglas Av. E17 . . . . 1B 34
HA0: Wemb 7E 44
KT3: N Mald 4D 136
Douglas Cl. HA7: Stan 5F 11
IG6: Ilf 7K 21
SM6: Wall 6J 151
Douglas Ct. *KT1: King T* *4E 134*
(off Geneva Rd.)
NW6 . . . . *7J 47*
(off Quex Rd.)
Douglas Cres. UB4: Hayes . . . 4A 60
Douglas Dr. CR0: Croy 3C 154

Dron Ho.—Dunstan's Rd.

Dron Ho. *E1* 5J 69
(off Adelina Gro.)
Droop St. W10 3F 65
Drovers Ct. *KT1: King T* 2E 134
(off Fairfield E.)
Drovers Pl. SE15 7J 87
Drovers Rd.
CR2: S Croy 5D 152
Druce Rd. SE21 6E 104
Druid St. SE1 2E 86 (6H 169)
Druids Way BR2: Short 4F 143
Drumaline Ridge
KT4: Wor Pk 2A 148
Drummond Av. RM7: Rom 4K 39
Drummond Cres.
NW1 3H 67 (1C 160)
Drummond Dr. HA7: Stan 7E 10
Drummond Ga.
SW1 5H 85 (5D 172)
Drummond Ho. *E2* 2G 69
(off Goldsmiths Row)
Drummond Pl. TW1: Twick 7B 98
Drummond Rd.
CR0: Croy 2C 152
(not continuous)
E11 6A 36
RM7: Rom 4K 39
SE16 3H 87
Drummonds, The
IG9: Buck H 2E 20
Drummond St.
NW1 4G 67 (3A 160)
Drum St. E1 6F 69 (7K 163)
Drury Cres. CR0: Croy 2A 152
Drury Ho. SW8 1G 103
Drury La. WC2 6J 67 (7F 161)
Drury Lane Theatre 1G 167
(off Catherine St.)
Drury Rd. HA1: Harr 7G 25
Drury Way NW10 5K 45
Drury Way Ind. Est. NW10 5J 45
Dryad St. SW15 3F 101
Dryburgh Gdns. NW9 3G 27
Dryburgh Ho. *SW1* 5K 171
(off Abbots Mnr.)
Dryburgh Rd. SW15 3D 100
Dryden Av. W7 6K 61
Dryden Ct. SE11 4B 86 (4K 173)
Dryden Mans. *W14* 6G 83
(off Queen's Club Gdns.)
Dryden Rd. DA16: Well 1K 109
EN1: Enf 6K 7
HA3: Harr 1K 25
SW19 6A 120
Dryden St. WC2 6J 67 (1F 167)
Dryfield Cl. NW10 6J 45
Dryfield Rd. HA8: Edg 6D 12
Dryfield Wlk. SE8 6C 88
Dryhill Rd. DA17: Belv 6F 93
Drylands Rd. N8 6J 31
Drysdale Av. E4 7J 9
Drysdale Cl. HA6: Nwood 1G 23
Drysdale Ho. *N1* 1H 163
(off Drysdale St.)
Drysdale Pl. N1 3E 68 (1H 163)
Drysdale St. N1 3E 68 (1H 163)
Dublin Av. E8 1G 69
Dublin Ct. *HA2: Harr* 2H 43
(off Northolt Rd.)
Du Burstow Ter. W7 2J 79
Ducal St. E2 3F 69 (2K 163)
Du Cane Cl. W12 6E 64
Du Cane Ct. SW17 1E 120
Du Cane Rd. W12 6B 64
Ducavel Ho. SW2 1K 121
Duchess Cl. N11 5A 16
SM1: Sutt 4A 150
Duchess Gro. IG9: Buck H 2E 20
Duchess M. W1 5F 67 (6K 159)
Duchess of Bedford Ho.
W8 2J 83
(off Duchess of Bedford's Wlk.)
Duchess of Bedford's Wlk.
W8 2J 83
Duchess St. W1 5F 67 (6K 159)
Duchess Theatre 2G 167
(off Catherine St.)
Duchy Rd. EN4: Barn 1G 5
Duchy St. SE1 1A 86 (4K 167)
(not continuous)
Ducie St. SW4 4K 103
Duckett M. N4 6B 32
Duckett Rd. N4 6A 32
Duckett St. E1 4K 69
Ducking Stool Ct.
RM1: Rom 4K 39
Duck La. W1 1C 166
Duck Lees La. EN3: Enf 4F 9
Duck's Hill Rd.
HA6: Nwood 2D 22
DUCKS ISLAND 6A 4
Ducks Wlk. TW1: Twick 5C 98
Du Cros Dr. HA7: Stan 6J 11
Du Cros Rd. W3 1A 82
DUDDEN HILL 5D 46
Dudden Hill La. NW10 4B 46
Dudden Hill Pde. NW10 4B 46
Duddington Cl. SE9 4B 126
Dudley Av. HA3: Harr 3C 26
Dudley Ct. NW11 4H 29
W1 1E 164
(off Up. Berkeley St.)
WC2 6J 67 (7E 160)
Dudley Dr. HA4: Ruis 5K 41
SM4: Mord 1G 149
Dudley Gdns. HA2: Harr 1H 43
W13 2B 80
Dudley Ho. *W2* 6A 158
(off Nth. Wharf Rd.)
Dudley M. SW2 6A 104
Dudley Pl. UB3: Hayes 4F 77
Dudley Rd. E17 2C 34
HA2: Harr 2G 43
IG1: Ilf 4F 55
KT1: King T 3F 135
KT12: Walt T 6J 131
N3 2K 29
NW6 2G 65
SW19 6J 119
TW9: Rich 2F 99
TW14: Felt 1E 112
TW15: Ashf 5B 112
UB2: S'hall 2B 78
Dudley St. W2 5B 66 (6A 158)
Dudlington Rd. E5 2J 51
Dudmaston M. SW3 5B 170
Dudrich M. EN2: Enf 1G 7
SE5 7C 86
(off Pitman St.)
Dudsbury Rd. DA14: Sidc 6B 128
Dudset La. TW5: Houn 1J 95
Duffell Ho. SE11 6H 173
Dufferin Av. EC1 4E 162
Dufferin Ct. *EC1* 4E 162
(off Dufferin St.)
Dufferin St. EC1 4C 68 (4D 162)
Duffield Cl. HA1: Harr 5K 25
Duffield Dr. N15 4F 33
Duff St. E14 6D 70
Dufour's Pl. W1 6G 67 (1B 166)
Dugard Way SE11 4B 86
Duke Gdns. IG6: Ilf 4H 37
Duke Humphrey Rd.
SE3 1G 107
Duke of Cambridge Cl.
TW2: Twick 6H 97
Duke of Edinburgh Rd.
SM1: Sutt 2B 150
Duke of Wellington Pl.
SW1 2E 84 (6H 165)
Duke of York Column (Memorial) 5D 166
Duke of York Sq.
SW3 4D 84 (4F 171)
Duke of York's Theatre 3E 166
(off St Martin's La.)
Duke of York St.
SW1 1G 85 (4B 166)
Duke Rd. IG6: Ilf 4H 37
W4 5K 81
Dukes Av. HA1: Harr 4J 25
HA5: Pinn 6D 24
HA8: Edg 6A 12
KT3: N Mald 3A 136
N3 1K 29
N10 3F 31
TW4: Houn 4C 96
TW10: Rich 4C 116
UB5: N'olt 7C 42
W4 5K 81
Dukes Cl. TW12: Hamp 5D 114
TW15: Ashf 4E 112
Dukes Ct. E6 1E 72
(not continuous)
SE13 2E 106
SW14 2K 99
Dukes Ga. W4 4J 81
Dukes Grn. Av. TW14: Felt 5J 95
Dukes Head Pas.
TW12: Hamp 7G 115
Duke's Head Yd. N6 1F 49
Duke Shore Wharf E14 7B 70
Duke's Ho. *SW1* 3D 172
(off Vincent St.)
Dukes La. W8 2K 83
Dukes M. N10 3F 31
W1 7H 159
Dukes Orchard DA5: Bexl 1J 129
Duke's Pas. E17 4E 34
Duke's Pl. EC3 6E 68 (1H 169)
Dukes Ride UB10: Uxb 4A 40
Dukes Rd. E6 1E 72
W3 4G 63
WC1 3H 67 (2D 160)
Dukesthorpe Rd. SE26 4K 123
Duke St. SM1: Sutt 4B 150
SW1 1G 85 (4B 166)
TW9: Rich 4D 98
W1 6E 66 (7H 159)
Duke St. Hill SE1 1D 86 (4F 169)
Duke St. Mans. *W1* 1H 165
(off Duke St.)
Dukes Way BR4: W W'ck 3G 155
Duke's Yd. W1 7E 66 (2H 165)
Dulas St. N4 1K 49
Dulford St. W11 7G 65
Dulka Rd. SW11 5D 102
Dulverton *NW1* 1G 67
(off Royal College St.)
Dulverton Mans. WC1 4H 161
Dulverton Rd. HA4: Ruis 1J 41
SE9 2G 127
DULWICH 2E 122
Dulwich Bus. Cen.
SE23 1K 123
Dulwich Comn. SE21 1E 122
Dulwich Lawn Cl. SE22 5F 105
Dulwich Oaks Pl. SE21 3E 122
Dulwich Picture Gallery 7D 104
Dulwich Ri. Gdns. SE22 5F 105
Dulwich Rd. SE24 5A 104
DULWICH VILLAGE 7E 104
Dulwich Village SE21 6D 104
Dulwich Wood Av. SE19 4E 122
Dulwich Wood Pk. SE19 4E 122
Dumain Ct. *SE11* 4B 86
(off Opal St.)
Dumbarton Ct. SW2 6J 103
Dumbarton Rd. SW2 6J 103
Dumbleton Cl.
KT1: King T 1H 135
Dumbreck Rd. SE9 4D 108
Dumont Rd. N16 3E 50
Dumpton Pl. NW1 7E 48
Dumsey Eyot
KT16: Chert 7A 130
Dunally Pk. TW17: Shep 7F 131
Dunbar Av. BR3: Beck 4A 142
RM10: Dag 3G 57
SW16 2A 140
Dunbar Cl. UB4: Hayes 6K 59
Dunbar Ct. *BR2: Short* 4J 143
(off Durham Rd.)
SM1: Sutt 5B 150
Dunbar Gdns. RM10: Dag 5G 57
Dunbar Rd. E7 6J 53
KT3: N Mald 4J 135
N22 1A 32
Dunbar St. SE27 3C 122
Dunbar Wharf *E14* 7B 70
(off Narrow St.)
Dunblane Cl. HA8: Edg 2C 12
Dunblane Rd. SE9 3C 108
Dunboe Pl. TW17: Shep 7E 130
Dunboyne Rd. NW3 5D 48
Dunbridge Ho. *SW15* 6B 100
(off Highcliffe Dr.)
Dunbridge St. E2 4G 69
Duncan Cl. EN5: Barn 4F 5
Duncan Ct. N21 1G 17
Duncan Gro. W3 6A 64
Duncan Ho. *NW3* 7D 48
(off Fellows Rd.)
SW1 6B 172
(off Dolphin Sq.)
Duncannon Ho. *SW1* 6D 172
(off Lindsay Sq.)
Duncannon St.
WC2 7J 67 (3E 166)
Duncan Rd. E8 1H 69
TW9: Rich 4E 98
Duncan St. N1 2B 68
Duncan Ter. N1 2B 68
(not continuous)
Dunch St. E1 6H 69
Duncombe Hill SE23 7A 106
Duncombe Rd. N19 1H 49
Duncrievie Rd. SE13 6F 107
Duncroft SE18 7J 91
Dundalk Ho. *E1* 6J 69
(off Clark St.)
Dundalk Rd. SE4 3A 106
Dundas Gdns.
KT8: W Mole 3F 133
Dundas Rd. SE15 2J 105
Dundee Ct. *E1* 1H 87
(off Wapping High St.)
Dundee Ho. *W9* 3A 66
(off Maida Va.)
Dundee Rd. E13 2K 71
SE25 5H 141
Dundee St. E1 1H 87
Dundee Way EN3: Enf 3F 9
Dundee Wharf E14 7B 70
Dundela Gdns.
KT4: Wor Pk 4D 148
Dundonald Cl. E6 6C 72
Dundonald Ho. *E14* 2D 88
(off Admirals Way)
Dundonald Rd. NW10 1F 65
SW19 7G 119
(not continuous)
Dundry Ho. SE26 3G 123
Dunedin Ho. *E16* 1D 90
(off Manwood St.)
Dunedin Rd. E10 3D 52
IG1: Ilf 1G 55
Dunedin Way UB4: Hayes 4A 60
Dunelm Gro. SE27 3C 122
Dunelm St. E1 6K 69
Dunfield Gdns. SE6 5D 124
Dunfield Rd. SE6 5D 124
(not continuous)
Dunford Ct. HA5: Pinn 1D 24
Dunford Rd. N7 4K 49
Dungarvan Av. SW15 4C 100
Dunheved Cl.
CR7: Thor H 6A 140
Dunheved Rd. Nth.
CR7: Thor H 6A 140
Dunheved Rd. Sth.
CR7: Thor H 6A 140
Dunheved Rd. W.
CR7: Thor H 6A 140
Dunholme Grn. N9 3A 18
Dunholme La. N9 3A 18
Dunholme Rd. N9 3A 18
Dunkeld Ho. *E14* 6F 71
(off Abbott Rd.)
Dunkeld Rd. RM8: Dag 2B 56
SE25 4D 140
Dunkery Rd. SE9 4B 126
Dunkirk St. SE27 4C 122
Dunlace Rd. E5 4J 51
Dunleary Cl. TW4: Houn 7D 96
Dunley Dr. CR0: Croy 7D 154
Dunlin Ho. *SE16* 4K 87
(off Tawny Way)
Dunloe Av. N17 3D 32
Dunloe Ct. E2 2F 69
Dunloe St. E2 2F 69
Dunlop Pl. SE16 3F 87
Dunmore Point *E2* 2J 163
(off Gascoigne Pl.)
Dunmore Rd. NW6 1G 65
SW20 1E 136
Dunmow Cl. RM6: Chad H 5C 38
TW13: Felt 3C 114
Dunmow Ho. RM9: Dag 1B 74
SE11 5H 173
(off Newburn St.)
Dunmow Rd. E15 4F 53
Dunmow Wlk. *N1* 1C 68
(off Popham St.)
Dunnage Cres. SE16 4A 88
(not continuous)
Dunnico Ho. *SE17* 5E 86
(off East St.)
Dunn Mead NW9 7G 13
Dunnock Cl. E6 6C 72
N9 1E 18
Dunn's Pas. WC1 7F 161
Dunn St. E8 5F 51
Dunollie Pl. NW5 5G 49
Dunollie Rd. NW5 5G 49
Dunoon Gdns. SE23 7K 105
Dunoon Ho. *N1* 1K 67
(off Bemerton Est.)
Dunoon Rd. SE23 7J 105
Dunoran Home
BR1: Brom 1C 144
Dunraven Dr. EN2: Enf 2F 7
Dunraven Rd. W12 1C 82
Dunraven St. W1 7D 66 (2F 165)
Dunsany Rd. W14 3F 83
Dunsfold Way CR0: Croy 7D 154
Dunsford Way SW15 6D 100
Dunsmore Cl. UB4: Hayes 4C 60
Dunsmore Rd.
KT12: Walt T 6K 131
Dunsmure Rd. N16 1E 50
Dunspring La. IG5: Ilf 2F 37
Dunstable M.
W1 5E 66 (5H 159)
Dunstable Rd.
KT8: W Mole 4D 132
TW9: Rich 4E 98
Dunstall Rd. SW20 6D 118
Dunstall Way
KT8: W Mole 3F 133
Dunstall Welling Est.
DA16: Well 2B 110
Dunstan Cl. N2 3A 30
Dunstan Glade
BR5: Orp 6H 145
Dunstan Ho's. *E1* 5J 69
(off Stepney Grn.)
Dunstan Rd. NW11 1H 47
Dunstan's Gro. SE22 6H 105
Dunstan's Rd. SE22 7G 105

Dunster Av.—Eastern Av.

Dunster Av. SM4: Mord 1F 149
Dunster Cl. EN5: Barn 4A 4
RM5: Col R 2J 39
Dunster Ct.
EC3 . . . . .7E 68 (2H 169)
Dunster Dr. NW9 . . . . .1J 45
Dunster Gdns. NW6 . . . . .7H 47
Dunster Ho. SE6 . . . . .3E 124
Dunstorville Way
SE1 . . . . .2D 86 (7F 169)
Dunster Way HA2: Harr 3C 42
SM6: Wall 1E 150
Dunston Rd. E8 . . . . .1F 69
SW11 . . . . .2E 102
Dunston St. E8 . . . . .1E 68
Dunton Cl. KT6: Surb 1E 146
Dunton Ct. SE23 . . . . .2H 123
Dunton Rd. E10 . . . . .7D 34
RM1: Rom 4K 39
SE1 . . . . .5F 87
Duntshill Rd. SW18 . . . . . . .1K 119
Dunvegan Cl.
KT8: W Mole 4F 133
Dunvegan Rd. SE9 . . . . .4D 108
Dunwich Rd. DA7: Bex 1F 111
Dunworth M. W11 . . . . .6H 65
Duplex Ride
SW1 . . . . . . .2D 84 (7F 165)
Dupont Rd. SW20 . . . . .2F 137
Duppas Av. CR0: Croy 4B 152
Duppas Cl.
TW17: Shep 5F 131
Duppas Ct. CR0: Croy 3B 152
(off Duppas Hill Ter.)
Duppas Hill La.
CR0: Croy 4B 152
Duppas Hill Rd.
CR0: Croy 4A 152
Duppas Hill Ter.
CR0: Croy 3B 152
Duppas Rd. CR0: Croy 3A 152
Dupree Rd. SE7 . . . . .5K 89
Duraden Cl. BR3: Beck 7D 124
Durand Cl. SM5: Cars 1D 150
Durand Gdns. SW9 . . . . .1K 103
Durands Wlk. SE16 . . . . .2B 88
Durand Way NW10 . . . . .7J 45
Durants Pk. Av. EN3: Enf 4E 8
Durants Rd. EN3: Enf 4D 8
Durant St. E2 . . . . .2G 69
Durban Ct. E7 . . . . .7B 54
Durban Gdns. RM10: Dag 7J 57
Durban Ho. W12 . . . . .7D 64
(off White City Est.)
Durban Rd. BR3: Beck 2B 142
E15 . . . . .3G 71
E17 . . . . .1B 34
IG2: Ilf 1J 55
N17 . . . . .6K 17
SE27 . . . . .4C 122
Durbin Rd. KT9: Chess 4E 146
Durdan Cotts.
UB1: S'hall 6D 60
(off Denbigh Rd.)
Durdans Ho. NW1 . . . . .7F 49
(off Farrier St.)
Durdans Rd. UB1: S'hall 6D 60
Durell Gdns. RM9: Dag 5D 56
Durell Ho. SE16 . . . . .2K 87
(off Wolfe Cres.)
Durell Rd. RM9: Dag 5D 56
Durfey Ho. SE5 . . . . .7D 86
(off Edmund St.)
Durford Cres. SW15 . . . . . . .1D 118
Durham Av. BR2: Short 4H 143
IG8: Buck H, Wfd G . . .5G 21
TW5: Houn 5D 78
Durham Cl. SW20 . . . . .2D 136
Durham Ct. NW6 . . . . .2J 65
(off Kilburn Pk. Rd.)
TW11: Tedd 4J 115
Durham Hill BR1: Brom 4H 125
Durham Ho. BR2: Short 4G 143
IG11: Bark 7A 56
(off Margaret Bondfield Av.)
RM10: Dag 5J 57
Durham Ho. St. WC2 . . . . . .3F 167
Durham Pl. IG1: Ilf 4G 55
SW3 . . . . . . .5D 84 (6E 170)
Durham Ri. SE18 . . . . .5G 91
Durham Rd. BR2: Short 3H 143
DA14: Sidc 5B 128
E12 . . . . .4B 54
E16 . . . . .4G 71
HA1: Harr 5F 25
N2 . . . . .3C 30
N7 . . . . .2K 49
N9 . . . . .2B 18
RM10: Dag 5J 57
SW20 . . . . .1D 136
TW14: Felt 7A 96
W5 . . . . .3D 80
Durham Row E1 . . . . .5K 69
Durham St.
SE11 . . . . . . .6K 85 (6G 173)
Durham Ter. W2 . . . . .6K 65
Durham Wharf TW8: Bford . . .7C 80
Durham Yd. E2 . . . . .3H 69
Durley Av. HA5: Pinn 7C 24
Durley Rd. N16 . . . . .7E 32
Durlston Rd. E5 . . . . .2G 51
KT2: King T 6E 116
Durnford Ho. SE6 . . . . .3E 124
Durnford St. N15 . . . . .5E 32
SE10 . . . . .6E 88
Durning Rd. SE19 . . . . .5D 122
Durnsford Av. SW19 . . . . . . .2J 119
Durnsford Rd. N11 . . . . .1H 31
SW19 . . . . .2J 119
Durrant Ct. HA3: Harr 2J 25
Durrell Rd. SW6 . . . . .1H 101
Durrell Way TW17: Shep . . .6F 131
Durrels Ho. W14 . . . . .4H 83
(off Warwick Gdns.)
Durrington Av. SW20 . . . . . .7E 118
Durrington Pk. Rd. SW20 . . .1E 136
Durrington Rd. E5 . . . . .4A 52
Durrington Twr. SW8 . . . . . .2G 103
Durrisdeer Ho. NW2 . . . . . . .4H 47
(off Lyndale)
Dursley Cl. SE3 . . . . .2A 108
Dursley Ct. SE15 . . . . .7E 86
(off Lydney Cl.)
Dursley Gdns. SE3 . . . . .1B 108
Dursley Rd. SE3 . . . . .2A 108
Durward St. E1 . . . . .5H 69
Durweston M. W1 . . . . .5F 159
Durweston St.
W1 . . . . . . .5D 66 (6F 159)
Dury Falls Ct. RM5: Col R . . .2J 39
Dury Rd. EN5: Barn 1C 4
Dutch Barn Cl.
TW19: Staines 6A 94
Dutch Gdns.
KT2: King T 6H 117
Dutch Yd. SW18 . . . . .5J 101
Dutton St. SE10 . . . . .1E 106
Duxberry Av. TW13: Felt 3A 114
Duxberry Cl. BR2: Short 5C 144
Duxford Ho. SE2 . . . . .2D 92
(off Wolvercote Rd.)
Dye Ho. La. E3 . . . . .1C 70
Dyer Ho. TW12: Hamp 1F 133
Dyer's Bldgs.
EC1 . . . . .5A 68 (6J 161)
Dyers Hall Rd. E11 . . . . .1G 53
Dyers Hill Rd. E11 . . . . .2F 53
Dyers La. SW15 . . . . .4D 100
Dykes Way BR2: Short 3H 143
Dykewood Cl. DA5: Bexl 3K 129
Dylan Rd. DA17: Belv 3G 93
SE24 . . . . .4B 104
Dylan Thomas Ho. N8 . . . . . .4K 31
Dylways SE5 . . . . .4D 104
Dymchurch Cl. IG5: Ilf 2E 36
Dymes Path SW19 . . . . .2F 119
Dymock Ct. SE15 . . . . .7E 86
(off Lydney Cl.)
Dymock St. SW6 . . . . .3K 101
Dyneley Rd. SE12 . . . . .3A 126
Dyne Rd. NW6 . . . . .7G 47
Dynevor Rd. N16 . . . . .3E 50
TW10: Rich 5E 98
Dynham Rd. NW6 . . . . .7J 47
Dyott St. WC1 . . . . .6H 67 (7D 160)
Dysart Av. KT2: King T 5C 116
Dysart St. EC2 . . . . .4D 68 (4G 163)
Dyson Ct. HA0: Wemb 4A 44
NW2 . . . . .1E 46
Dyson Ho. SE10 . . . . .5H 89
(off Blackwall La.)
Dyson Rd. E11 . . . . .6G 35
E15 . . . . .6H 53
Dysons Rd. N18 . . . . .5C 18

E

Eade Rd. N4 . . . . .7C 32
Eagans Cl. N2 . . . . .3B 30
Eagle Av. RM6: Chad H 6E 38
Eagle Cl. EN3: Enf 4D 8
SE16 . . . . .5J 87
SM6: Wall 6J 151
Eagle Ct. E11 . . . . .4J 35
EC1 . . . . .5B 68 (5A 162)
Eagle Dr. NW9 . . . . .2A 28
Eagle Hill SE19 . . . . .6D 122
Eagle Ho. E1 . . . . .4H 69
(off Headlam St.)
N1 . . . . .2D 68
(off Eagle Wharf Rd.)
Eagle La. E11 . . . . .4J 35
Eagle Lodge NW11 . . . . .7H 29
Eagle M. N1 . . . . .6E 50
Eagle Pl. SW10 . . . . .5A 84
(off Roland Way)
W1 . . . . .3B 166
Eagle Rd. HA0: Wemb 7D 44
TW6: Houn 3H 95
Eaglesfield Rd. SE18 . . . . . .1F 109
Eagle St. WC1 . . . . .5K 67 (6G 161)
Eagle Ter. IG8: Wfd G 7E 20
Eagle Trad. Est.
CR4: Mitc 6D 138
Eagle Wharf Ct. SE1 . . . . . . .5J 169
(off Lafone St.)
Eagle Wharf E. E14 . . . . .7A 70
(off Narrow St.)
Eagle Wharf Rd. N1 . . . . .2C 68
Eagle Wharf W. E14 . . . . .7A 70
(off Narrow St.)
Ealdham Sq. SE9 . . . . .4A 108
EALING 7D 62
Ealing B'way. Cen. W5 . . . . .7D 62
EALING COMMON 7F 63
Ealing Downs Ct.
UB6: G'frd 3A 62
Ealing Grn. W5 . . . . .1D 80
Ealing Pk. Gdns. W5 . . . . . . .4C 80
Ealing Rd. HA0: Wemb 6E 44
TW8: Bford 4D 80
UB5: N'olt 1E 60
Ealing Rd. Trad. Est.
TW8: Bford 5D 80
Ealing Village W5 . . . . .6E 62
Eamont Cl. HA4: Ruis 7D 22
Eamont Ct. NW8 . . . . .2C 66
(off Eamont St.)
Eamont St. NW8 . . . . .2C 66
Eardley Cres. SW5 . . . . .5J 83
Eardley Rd. DA17: Belv 5G 93
SW16 . . . . .5G 121
Earl Cl. N11 . . . . .5A 16
Earldom Rd. SW15 . . . . .4E 100
Earle Gdns. KT2: King T 7E 116
Earlham Ct. E11 . . . . .7H 35
Earlham Gro. E7 . . . . .5H 53
N22 . . . . .7E 16
Earlham St. WC2 . . .6J 67 (1D 166)
Earl Ho. NW1 . . . . .4D 158
(off Lisson Gro.)
Earlom Ho. WC1 . . . . .2J 161
(off Margery St.)
Earl Ri. SE18 . . . . .5H 91
Earl Rd. SW14 . . . . .4J 99
EARL'S COURT 5J 83
Earl's Court Exhibition Building
. . . . .5J 83
Earls Ct. Gdns. SW5 . . . . . . .4K 83
Earls Ct. Rd. W8 . . . . .3J 83
Earl's Ct. Sq. SW5 . . . . .5K 83
Earls Cres. HA1: Harr 4J 25
Earlsdown Ho.
IG11: Bark 2H 73
Earlsferry Way N1 . . . . .7J 49
(not continuous)
EARLSFIELD 1A 120
Earlsfield Rd. SW18 . . . . . . .1A 120
Earlshall Rd. SE9 . . . . .4D 108
Earlsmead HA2: Harr 4D 42
Earlsmead Rd. N15 . . . . .5F 33
NW10 . . . . .3E 64
Earls Ter. W8 . . . . .3H 83
Earlsthorpe M. SW12 . . . . . .6E 102
Earlsthorpe Rd. SE26 . . . . . .4K 123
Earlstoke St.
EC1 . . . . .3B 68 (1A 162)
Earlston Gro. E9 . . . . .1H 69
Earl St. EC2 . . . . . . .5D 68 (5G 163)
(not continuous)
Earls Wlk. RM8: Dag 4B 56
W8 . . . . .3J 83
Earlswood Av.
CR7: Thor H 5A 140
Earlswood Cl. SE10 . . . . .6G 89
Earlswood Gdns. IG5: Ilf 3E 36
Earlswood St. SE10 . . . . .5G 89
Early M. NW1 . . . . .1F 67
Earnshaw St.
WC2 . . . . . . .6H 67 (7D 160)
Earsby St. W14 . . . . .4G 83
(not continuous)
Easby Cres. SM4: Mord 6K 137
Easebourne Rd. RM8: Dag . . .5C 56
Easleys M. W1 . . . .6E 66 (7H 159)
EAST ACTON 7B 64
E. Acton Arc. W3 . . . . .6A 64
E. Acton Ct. W3 . . . . .7A 64
E. Acton La. W3 . . . . .1A 82
E. Arbour St. E1 . . . . .6K 69
East Av. E12 . . . . .7C 54
E17 . . . . .4D 34
N2 . . . . .4K 29
SM6: Wall 5K 151
UB1: S'hall 7D 60
UB3: Hayes 1H 77
East Bank N16 . . . . .7E 32
Eastbank Rd.
TW12: Hamp 5G 115
EAST BARNET 6H 5
E. Barnet Rd. EN4: Barn 4G 5
E. Beckton District Cen.
E6 . . . . .5D 72
EAST BEDFONT 7G 95
East Block SE1 . . . . .6H 167
(off York Rd.)
E. Boundary Rd. E12 . . . . . . .3D 54
Eastbourne Av. W3 . . . . .6K 63
Eastbourne Gdns. SW14 . . . . .3J 99
Eastbourne M.
W2 . . . . .6A 66 (7A 158)
Eastbourne Rd. E6 . . . . .3E 72
(not continuous)
E15 . . . . .1G 71
N15 . . . . .6E 32
SW17 . . . . .6E 120
TW8: Bford 5C 80
Eastbourne Rd. TW13: Felt . .2B 114
W4 . . . . .6J 81
Eastbourne Ter.
W2 . . . . .6A 66 (7A 158)
Eastbournia Av. N9 . . . . .3C 18
Eastbrook Av. N9 . . . . .7D 8
RM10: Dag 4J 57
Eastbrook Dr.
RM7: Rush G 3K 57
Eastbrook Rd. SE3 . . . . .1K 107
Eastbury Av. EN1: Enf 1A 8
IG11: Bark 1J 73
Eastbury Ct. EN5: Barn 5F 5
(off Lyonsdown Rd.)
IG11: Bark 1J 73
Eastbury Gro. W4 . . . . .5A 82
Eastbury Manor House 1K 73
Eastbury Rd. BR5: Orp 6H 145
E6 . . . . .4E 72
KT2: King T 7E 116
RM7: Rom 6K 39
Eastbury Sq. IG11: Bark 1K 73
Eastbury Ter. E1 . . . . .4K 69
Eastcastle St.
W1 . . . . .6G 67 (7A 160)
Eastcheap EC3 . . . . .7E 68 (2G 169)
E. Churchfield Rd. W3 . . . . . .1K 81
Eastchurch Rd.
TW6: Houn 2G 95
East Cl. EN4: Barn 4K 5
UB6: G'frd 2G 61
W5 . . . . .4G 63
Eastcombe Av. SE7 . . . . .6K 89
EASTCOTE 7K 23
Eastcote BR6: Orp 7K 145
Eastcote Av. HA2: Harr 2F 43
KT8: W Mole 5D 132
UB6: G'frd 5A 44
Eastcote Ind. Est.
HA4: Ruis 7A 24
Eastcote La. HA2: Harr 4C 42
UB5: N'olt 5D 42
(not continuous)
Eastcote La. Nth.
UB5: N'olt 6D 42
Eastcote Pl. HA5: Pinn 6K 23
Eastcote Rd. DA16: Well . . .2H 109
HA2: Harr 3G 43
HA4: Ruis 7G 23
HA5: Pinn 5B 24
Eastcote St. SW9 . . . . .2K 103
Eastcote Vw. HA5: Pinn 4A 24
EASTCOTE VILLAGE 5K 23
East Ct. HA0: Wemb 2C 44
East Cres. EN1: Enf 5A 8
N11 . . . . .4J 15
Eastcroft Rd. KT19: Eps 7A 148
E. Cross Cen. E15 . . . . .6C 52
E. Cross Route E3 . . . . .7B 52
E9 . . . . .5B 52
(Homerton)
E9 . . . . .7B 52
(Old Ford)
E15 . . . . .5B 52
Eastdown Ct. SE13 . . . . .4F 107
Eastdown Ho. E8 . . . . .4G 51
Eastdown Pk. SE13 . . . . .4F 107
East Dr. SM5: Cars 7C 150
E. Duck Lees La. EN3: Enf 4F 9
EAST DULWICH 4F 105
E. Dulwich Gro. SE22 . . . . . .5E 104
E. Dulwich Rd. SE22 . . . . . .4F 105
E. End Farm HA5: Pinn 3D 24
E. End Rd. N3 . . . . .2J 29
E. End Way HA5: Pinn 3C 24
East 10 Ent. Pk. E10 . . . . .1A 52
East Entrance RM10: Dag . . .2H 75
Eastern Av. E11 . . . . .6K 35
HA5: Pinn 7B 24
IG2: Ilf 6F 37
IG4: Ilf 6B 36
RM6: Chad H 4A 38

Eastern Av.—Edinburgh Cl.

Eastern Av. RM7: Mawney ... 4E 38
Eastern Av. E. RM1: Rom ... 3K 39
Eastern Av. W.
RM6: Chad H ... 4E 38
Eastern Ind. Est.
DA18: Erith ... 2G 93
Eastern Perimeter Rd.
TW6: Houn ... 2H 95
Eastern Quay Apartments
E16 ... 1K 89
(off Portsmouth M.)
Eastern Rd. E13 ... 2K 71
E17 ... 5E 34
N2 ... 3D 30
N22 ... 1J 31
SE4 ... 4C 106
Easternville Gdns. IG2: Ilf ... 6G 37
Eastern Way SE28 ... 2A 92
E. Ferry Rd. E14 ... 4D 88
Eastfield Gdns.
RM10: Dag ... 4G 57
Eastfield Rd. E17 ... 4C 34
EN3: Enf ... 1E 8
N8 ... 3J 31
RM9: Dag ... 4F 57
RM10: Dag ... 4G 57
Eastfields HA5: Pinn ... 5A 24
Eastfields Rd. CR4: Mitc ... 2E 138
W3 ... 5J 63
Eastfield St. E14 ... 5A 70
EAST FINCHLEY ... 4C 30
East Gdns. SW17 ... 6C 120
Eastgate Cl. SE28 ... 6D 74
Eastglade HA5: Pinn ... 3D 24
EAST HAM ... 2D 72
E. Ham & Barking By-Pass
IG11: Bark ... 2J 73
Eastham Cl. EN5: Barn ... 5C 4
E. Ham Ind. Est. E6 ... 4C 72
E. Ham Mnr. Way E6 ... 6E 72
East Ham Nature Reserve ... 4D 72
E. Harding St.
EC4 ... 6A 68 (7K 161)
E. Heath Rd. NW3 ... 3A 48
East Hill HA9: Wemb ... 2G 45
SW18 ... 5K 101
Eastholm NW11 ... 4K 29
East Holme DA8: Erith ... 1K 111
UB3: Hayes ... 1J 77
E. India Bldgs. E14 ... 7C 70
(off Saltwell St.)
E. India Dock Ho. E14 ... 6E 70
E. India Dock Rd. E14 ... 6C 70
East India Way CR0: Croy ... 1F 153
Eastlake Ho. NW8 ... 4B 158
Eastlake Rd. SE5 ... 2C 104
Eastlands Cres. SE21 ... 6F 105
East La. HA0: Wemb ... 3B 44
HA9: Wemb ... 3B 44
KT1: King T ... 3D 134
SE16 ... 2G 87
(Chambers St.)
SE16 ... 2G 87
(Scott Lidgett Cres.)
East La. Bus. Pk.
HA9: Wemb ... 2D 44
Eastlea M. E16 ... 4G 71
Eastleigh Av. HA2: Harr ... 2F 43
Eastleigh Cl. NW2 ... 3A 46
SM2: Sutt ... 7K 149
Eastleigh Rd. DA7: Bex ... 3J 111
E17 ... 2B 34
TW6: Houn ... 3H 95
Eastleigh Wlk. SW15 ... 7C 100
Eastleigh Way TW14: Felt ... 1J 113
East Lodge E16 ... 7J 71
(off Wesley Av.)
East London Crematorium
E13 ... 3H 71
Eastman Ho. SW4 ... 6G 103
Eastman Rd. W3 ... 2K 81
East Mascalls SE7 ... 6A 90
East Mead HA4: Ruis ... 3B 42
Eastmead Av. UB6: G'frd ... 3F 61
Eastmead Cl. BR1: Brom ... 2C 144
Eastmearn Rd. SE27 ... 2C 122
EAST MOLESEY ... 4H 133
Eastmoor Pl. SE7 ... 3B 90
Eastmoor St. SE7 ... 3B 90
E. Mount St. E1 ... 5H 69
(not continuous)
Eastney Rd. CR0: Croy ... 1B 152
Eastney St. SE10 ... 5F 89
Eastnor Rd. SE9 ... 1G 127
Easton St. WC1 ... 4A 68 (3J 161)
E. Park Cl.
RM6: Chad H ... 5D 38
East Parkside SE10 ... 2G 89
East Pas. EC1 ... 5C 162
East Pl. SE27 ... 4C 122
East Point SE1 ... 5G 87
E. Pole Cotts. EN4: Barn ... 4C 6
E. Poultry Av.
EC1 ... 5B 68 (6A 162)
East Ramp TW6: Houn ... 1D 94
East Rd. DA16: Well ... 2B 110
E15 ... 1J 71
EN3: Enf ... 1D 8
EN4: Barn ... 1K 15
HA1: Harr ... 7B 26
HA8: Edg ... 1H 27
KT2: King T ... 1E 134
N1 ... 3D 68 (2E 162)
N2 ... 1C 30
RM6: Chad H ... 5E 38
RM7: Rush G ... 7K 39
SW19 ... 6A 120
TW14: Felt ... 7F 95
UB7: W Dray ... 4B 76
E. Rochester Way
DA15: Bexl, Sidc ... 4J 109
East Row E11 ... 6J 35
W10 ... 4G 65
Eastry Av. BR2: Short ... 6H 143
Eastry Ho. SW8 ... 7J 85
(off Hartington Rd.)
Eastry Rd. DA8: Erith ... 7G 93
EAST SHEEN ... 4J 99
E. Sheen Av. SW14 ... 5K 99
Eastside Rd. NW11 ... 4H 29
East Smithfield
E1 ... 7F 69 (3K 169)
East St. BR1: Brom ... 2J 143
DA7: Bex ... 4G 111
IG11: Bark ... 1G 73
SE17 ... 5C 86
TW8: Bford ... 7C 80
E. Surrey Gro. SE15 ... 7F 87
E. Tenter St.
E1 ... 6F 69 (1K 169)
East Ter. DA15: Sidc ... 1J 127
E. Thamesmead Bus. Pk.
DA18: Erith ... 2F 93
East Towers HA5: Pinn ... 5B 24
East Va. W3 ... 1B 82
East Vw. E4 ... 5K 19
EN5: Barn ... 2C 4
Eastview Av. SE18 ... 7J 91
Eastville Av. NW11 ... 6H 29
East Wlk. EN4: Barn ... 7K 5
UB3: Hayes ... 1J 77
East Way BR2: Short ... 7J 143
CR0: Croy ... 2A 154
E11 ... 5K 35
HA4: Ruis ... 1J 41
UB3: Hayes ... 1J 77
Eastway E9 ... 6B 52
SM4: Mord ... 5F 137
SM6: Wall ... 4G 151
Eastwell Cl. BR3: Beck ... 7A 124
Eastwell Ho. SE1 ... 7F 169
E. W. Link Rd.
KT2: King T ... 1D 134
EAST WICKHAM ... 1C 110
Eastwood Cl. E18 ... 2J 35
N7 ... 5A 50
N17 ... 7C 18
Eastwood Rd. E18 ... 2J 35
IG3: Ilf ... 1A 56
N10 ... 2E 30
UB7: W Dray ... 2C 76
East Woodside DA5: Bexl ... 7E 110
Eastwood St. SW16 ... 6G 121
Eatington Rd. E10 ... 5F 35
Eaton Cl. HA7: Stan ... 4G 11
SW1 ... 4E 84 (4G 171)
Eaton Dr. KT2: King T ... 7G 117
RM5: Col R ... 1H 39
SW9 ... 4B 104
Eaton Gdns. RM9: Dag ... 7E 56
Eaton Ga. SW1 ... 4E 84 (3G 171)
Eaton Gro. N19 ... 3H 49
Eaton Ho. E14 ... 7B 70
(off Westferry Cir.)
SW11 ... 1B 102
Eaton La. SW1 ... 3F 85 (2K 171)
Eaton Mans. SW1 ... 4G 171
(off Bourne St.)
Eaton M. Nth.
SW1 ... 4E 84 (3G 171)
Eaton M. Sth.
SW1 ... 4E 84 (3H 171)
Eaton M. W.
SW1 ... 4E 84 (3H 171)
Eaton Pk. Rd. N13 ... 2F 17
Eaton Pl. SW1 ... 4E 84 (2G 171)
Eaton Ri. E11 ... 5A 36
W5 ... 5D 62
Eaton Rd. DA14: Sidc ... 2D 128
EN1: Enf ... 3K 7
NW4 ... 5E 28
SM2: Sutt ... 6A 150
TW3: Houn ... 4H 97
Eaton Row SW1 ... 3F 85 (2J 171)
Eatons Mead E4 ... 2H 19
Eaton Sq. SW1 ... 4E 84 (3G 171)
Eaton Ter. E3 ... 3A 70
SW1 ... 4E 84 (3G 171)
Eaton Ter. M. SW1 ... 3G 171
Eatonville Rd. SW17 ... 2D 120
Eatonville Vs. SW17 ... 2D 120
Ebbisham Dr.
SW8 ... 6K 85 (7G 173)
Ebbisham Rd.
KT4: Wor Pk ... 2E 148
Ebbsfleet Rd. NW2 ... 5G 47
Ebdon Way SE3 ... 3K 107
Ebenezer Ho.
SE11 ... 4B 86 (4K 173)
Ebenezer Mussel Ho. E2 ... 2J 69
(off Patriot Sq.)
Ebenezer St. N1 ... 3D 68 (1E 162)
Ebenezer Wlk. SW16 ... 1G 139
Ebley Cl. SE15 ... 6F 87
Ebner St. SW18 ... 5K 101
Ebor Cotts. SW15 ... 3A 118
Ebor St. E1 ... 4F 69 (3J 163)
Ebrington Rd. HA3: Harr ... 6D 26
Ebsworth St. SE23 ... 7K 105
Eburne Rd. N7 ... 3J 49
Ebury Bri. SW1 ... 5F 85 (5J 171)
Ebury Bri. Est.
SW1 ... 5F 85 (5J 171)
Ebury Bri. Rd.
SW1 ... 5E 84 (6H 171)
Ebury Cl. BR2: Kes ... 3C 156
Ebury M. SE27 ... 3B 122
SW1 ... 4F 85 (3J 171)
Ebury M. E. SW1 ... 3F 85 (2J 171)
Ebury Sq. SW1 ... 4E 84 (4H 171)
Ebury St. SW1 ... 4E 84 (4H 171)
Ecclesbourne Cl. N13 ... 5F 17
Ecclesbourne Gdns. N13 ... 5F 17
Ecclesbourne Rd.
CR7: Thor H ... 5C 140
N1 ... 7C 50
Eccleshill BR2: Short ... 4H 143
(off Durham Rd.)
Eccles Rd. SW11 ... 4D 102
Eccleston Bri.
SW1 ... 4F 85 (3K 171)
Eccleston Cl. EN4: Barn ... 4J 5
Eccleston Cres.
RM6: Chad H ... 7B 38
Ecclestone Ct. HA9: Wemb ... 5E 44
Ecclestone M. HA9: Wemb ... 5E 44
Ecclestone Pl. HA9: Wemb ... 5F 45
Eccleston Ho. SW2 ... 6A 104
Eccleston M.
SW1 ... 3E 84 (2H 171)
Eccleston Pl.
SW1 ... 4F 85 (3J 171)
Eccleston Rd. W13 ... 7A 62
Eccleston Sq.
SW1 ... 4F 85 (4K 171)
Eccleston Sq. M.
SW1 ... 4F 85 (4K 171)
Eccleston St.
SW1 ... 3F 85 (2J 171)
Echelforde Dr.
TW15: Ashf ... 4C 112
Echo Hgts. E4 ... 1J 19
Eckford St. N1 ... 2A 68
Eckington Ho. N15 ... 6D 32
(off Fladbury Rd.)
Eckstein Rd. SW11 ... 4C 102
Eclipse Rd. E13 ... 5K 71
Ecology Cen. and Arts Pavilion
... 3A 70
Ector Rd. SE6 ... 2G 125
Edam Ct. DA14: Sidc ... 3A 128
Edans Ct. W12 ... 2B 82
Edbrooke Rd. W9 ... 4J 65
Eddington St. N4 ... 1A 50
Eddisbury Ho. SE26 ... 3G 123
Eddiscombe Rd. SW6 ... 2H 101
Eddy Cl. RM7: Rom ... 6H 39
Eddystone Rd. SE4 ... 5A 106
Eddystone Twr. SE8 ... 5A 88
Eddystone Wlk.
TW19: Staines ... 7A 94
Ede Cl. TW3: Houn ... 3D 96
Edenbridge Cl. SE16 ... 5H 87
(off Masters Dr.)
Edenbridge Rd. E9 ... 7K 51
EN1: Enf ... 6K 7
Eden Cl. DA5: Bexl ... 4K 129
HA0: Wemb ... 1D 62
NW3 ... 2J 47
W8 ... 3J 83
Edencourt Rd. SW16 ... 6F 121
Edendale W3 ... 7H 63
Edendale Rd. DA7: Bex ... 1K 111
Edenfield Gdns.
KT4: Wor Pk ... 3B 148
Eden Gro. E17 ... 5D 34
N7 ... 5K 49
Edenham Way W10 ... 4H 65
Eden Ho. NW8 ... 4C 158
(off Church St.)
Edenhurst Av. SW6 ... 3H 101
Eden Lodge NW6 ... 7F 47
Eden M. SW17 ... 3A 120
EDEN PARK ... 5C 142
Eden Pk. Av. BR3: Beck ... 4A 142
(not continuous)
Eden Rd. BR3: Beck ... 4A 142
CR0: Croy ... 4D 152
DA5: Bexl ... 4J 129
E17 ... 5D 34
SE27 ... 4B 122
Edensor Gdns. W4 ... 7A 82
Edensor Rd. W4 ... 7A 82
Eden St. KT1: King T ... 2D 134
Edenvale Cl. CR4: Mitc ... 7E 120
Edenvale Rd. CR4: Mitc ... 7E 120
Edenvale St. SW6 ... 2A 102
Eden Wlk. KT1: King T ... 2E 134
Eden Way BR3: Beck ... 5B 142
Ederline Av. SW16 ... 3K 139
Edgar Ct. KT3: N Mald ... 2A 136
Edgar Ho. E9 ... 5A 52
(off Homerton Rd.)
E11 ... 7J 35
SW8 ... 7J 85
(off Wyvil Rd.)
Edgar Kail Way SE22 ... 4E 104
Edgarley Ter. SW6 ... 1G 101
Edgar Rd. E3 ... 3D 70
RM6: Chad H ... 7D 38
TW4: Houn ... 7D 96
UB7: W Dray ... 7A 58
Edgcott Ho. W10 ... 5E 64
(off Sutton Way)
Edgeborough Way
BR1: Brom ... 7B 126
Edgebury BR7: Chst ... 4F 127
Edgebury Wlk. BR7: Chst ... 4G 127
Edge Bus. Cen., The
NW2 ... 2D 46
Edgecombe Ho. SE5 ... 2E 104
Edgecoombe CR2: S Croy ... 7J 153
Edgecoombe Cl.
KT2: King T ... 7K 117
Edgecote Cl. W3 ... 1J 81
Edgecot Gro. N15 ... 5E 32
Edgefield Av. IG11: Bark ... 7K 55
Edgefield Ct. IG11: Bark ... 7K 55
(off Edgefield Av.)
Edge Hill SE18 ... 6F 91
SW19 ... 7F 119
Edge Hill Av. N3 ... 4J 29
Edge Hill Ct. DA14: Sidc ... 4K 127
SW19 ... 7F 119
Edgehill Gdns. RM10: Dag ... 4G 57
Edgehill Ho. SW9 ... 2B 104
Edgehill Rd. BR7: Chst ... 3G 127
CR4: Mitc ... 1F 139
W13 ... 5C 62
Edgeley La. SW4 ... 3H 103
Edgeley Rd. SW4 ... 3H 103
Edgel St. SW18 ... 4K 101
Edgepoint Cl. SE27 ... 5B 122
Edge St. W8 ... 1J 83
Edgewood Grn.
CR0: Croy ... 1K 153
Edgeworth Av. NW4 ... 5C 28
Edgeworth Cl. NW4 ... 5C 28
Edgeworth Ct. EN4: Barn ... 4H 5
(off Fordham Rd.)
Edgeworth Cres. NW4 ... 5C 28
Edgeworth Ho. NW8 ... 1A 66
(off Boundary Rd.)
Edgeworth Rd. EN4: Barn ... 4H 5
SE9 ... 4A 108
Edgington Rd. SW16 ... 6H 121
Edgington Way
DA14: Sidc ... 7C 128
Edgson Ho. SW1 ... 5J 171
(off Ebury Bri. Rd.)
EDGWARE ... 6B 12
EDGWARE BURY ... 3C 12
Edgwarebury Gdns.
HA8: Edg ... 5B 12
Edgwarebury La.
HA8: Edg ... 1A 12
(not continuous)
WD6: Bore ... 1A 12
(not continuous)
Edgwarebury Pk. ... 3A 12
Edgware Ct. HA8: Edg ... 6B 12
Edgware Rd. NW2 ... 1D 46
NW9 ... 2J 27
W2 ... 4B 66 (4A 158)
Edgware Way HA8: Edg ... 4A 12
NW7 ... 4A 12
WD6: Bore, Edg ... 1J 11
Edinburgh Cl. E2 ... 2J 69
HA5: Pinn ... 7B 24
UB10: Uxb ... 4D 40

A-Z London 237

Edinburgh Ct.—Elgin Rd.

Edinburgh Ct. DA8: Erith ... 7K **93**
KT1: King T ... *3E* ***134***
(off Watersplash Cl.)
SE16 ... *1K* ***87***
(off Rotherhithe St.)
SW20 ... 5F **137**
Edinburgh Dr. RM7: Rom ... 4J **39**
UB10: Uxb ... 4D **40**
Edinburgh Ga.
SW1 ... 2D **84** (6E **164**)
Edinburgh Ho. NW4 ... 3E **28**
W9 ... *3K* ***65***
(off Maida Va.)
Edinburgh Rd. E13 ... 2K **71**
E17 ... 5C **34**
(not continuous)
N18 ... 5B **18**
SM1: Sutt ... 2A **150**
W7 ... 2K **79**
Edington NW5 ... 6E **48**
Edington Rd. EN3: Enf ... 2D **8**
SE2 ... 3B **92**
Edison Bldg. E14 ... 2C **88**
Edison Cl. E17 ... 5C **34**
Edison Ct. SE10 ... 3H **89**
Edison Dr. HA9: Wemb ... 3E **44**
UB1: S'hall ... 6F **61**
Edison Gro. SE18 ... 7K **91**
Edison Ho. *HA9: Wemb* ... *3J* ***45***
(off Barnhill Rd.)
Edison Rd. BR2: Short ... 2J **143**
DA16: Well ... 1K **109**
EN3: Enf ... 2G **9**
N8 ... 6H **31**
Edis St. NW1 ... 1E **66**
Edith Brinson Ho. *E14* ... *6F* ***71***
(off Oban St.)
Edith Cavell Cl. N19 ... 7J **31**
Edith Gdns. KT5: Surb ... 7H **135**
Edith Gro. SW10 ... 6A **84**
Edith Ho. *W6* ... *5E* ***82***
(off Queen Caroline St.)
Edithna St. SW9 ... 3J **103**
Edith Neville Cotts.
NW1 ... *1C* ***160***
(off Drummond Cres.)
Edith Ramsay Ho. *E1* ... *5A* ***70***
(off Duckett St.)
Edith Rd. E6 ... 7B **54**
E15 ... 5F **53**
N11 ... 7C **16**
RM6: Chad H ... 7D **38**
SE25 ... 5D **140**
SW19 ... 6K **119**
W14 ... 4G **83**
Edith Row SW6 ... 1K **101**
Edith St. E2 ... 2G **69**
Edith Summerskill Ho.
SW6 ... *7H* ***83***
(off Clem Attlee Est.)
Edith Ter. SW10 ... 7A **84**
Edith Vs. W14 ... 4H **83**
Edith Yd. SW10 ... 7A **84**
Edmansons Cl. N17 ... 1F **33**
Edmeston Cl. E9 ... 6A **52**
Edmond Ct. SE14 ... 1J **105**
Edmonscote W13 ... 5A **62**
EDMONTON ... 3B 18
Edmonton Ct. *SE16* ... *3J* ***87***
(off Canada Est.)
Edmonton Grn. Shop. Cen.
N9 ... 2B **18**
Edmund Halley Way SE10 ... 2G **89**
Edmund Ho. SE17 ... 6B **86**
Edmund Hurst Dr. E6 ... 5F **73**
Edmund Rd. CR4: Mitc ... 3C **138**
DA16: Well ... 3A **110**
Edmundsbury Ct. Est.
SW9 ... 4K **103**
Edmunds Cl. UB4: Hayes ... 5A **60**
Edmund St. SE5 ... 7D **86**
Edmunds Wlk. N2 ... 4C **30**
Ednam Ho. *SE15* ... *6G* ***87***
(off Haymerle Rd.)
Edna Rd. SW20 ... 2F **137**
Edna St. SW11 ... 1C **102**
Edred Ho. *E9* ... *4A* ***52***
(off Lindisfarne Way)
Edrich Ho. SW4 ... 1J **103**
Edric Ho. *SW1* ... *3D* ***172***
(off Page St.)
Edrick Rd. HA8: Edg ... 6D **12**
Edrick Wlk. HA8: Edg ... 6D **12**
Edric Rd. SE14 ... 7K **87**
Edridge Rd. CR0: Croy ... 3C **152**
Edward Av. E4 ... 6J **19**
SM4: Mord ... 5B **138**
Edward Bond Ho. *WC1* ... *2F* ***161***
(off Cromer St.)
Edward Cl. N9 ... 7A **8**
NW2 ... 4F **47**
TW12: Hamp ... 5G **115**
UB5: N'olt ... 2A **60**
Edward Ct. E16 ... 5J **71**
Edward Dodd Ct. *N1* ... *1F* ***163***
(off Haberdasher St.)
Edward Edward's Ho.
SE1 ... 5A **168**
Edwardes Pl. W8 ... 3H **83**
Edwardes Sq. W8 ... 3H **83**
Edward Gro. EN4: Barn ... 5G **5**
Edward Ho. SE11 ... 5H **173**
Edward Mann Cl. *E1* ... *6K* ***69***
(off Caroline St.)
Edward VII Mans. *NW10* ... *3F* ***65***
(off Chamberlayne Rd.)
Edward M.
NW1 ... 3F **67** (1K **159**)
Edward Pl. SE8 ... 6B **88**
Edward Rd. BR1: Brom ... 7K **125**
BR7: Chst ... 5F **127**
CR0: Croy ... 7E **140**
E17 ... 4K **33**
EN4: Barn ... 5G **5**
HA2: Harr ... 3G **25**
RM6: Chad H ... 6E **38**
SE20 ... 7K **123**
TW12: Hamp ... 5G **115**
TW14: Felt ... 5F **95**
UB5: N'olt ... 2A **60**
Edward Robinson Ho.
SE14 ... *7K* ***87***
(off Reaston St.)
Edward's Av. HA4: Ruis ... 6K **41**
Edwards Cl. KT4: Wor Pk ... 2F **149**
Edward's Cotts. N1 ... 6B **50**
Edwards Ct. *CR2: S Croy* ... *4D* ***152***
(off Sth. Park Hill Rd.)
Edwards Dr. N11 ... 7C **16**
Edward's La. N16 ... 2D **50**
Edwards Mans. *IG11: Bark* ... *7K* ***55***
(off Upney La.)
Edwards M. N1 ... 7A **50**
W1 ... 6E **66** (1G **165**)
Edward Sq. N1 ... 1K **67**
SE16 ... 1A **88**
Edwards Rd. DA17: Belv ... 4G **93**
Edward St. E16 ... 4J **71**
(not continuous)
SE8 ... 7B **88**
SE14 ... 7A **88**
Edwards Yd. HA0: Wemb ... 1E **62**
Edward Temme Av. E15 ... 7H **53**
Edward Tyler Rd. SE12 ... 2A **126**
Edward Way TW15: Ashf ... 2B **112**
Edwina Gdns. IG4: Ilf ... 5C **36**
Edwin Arnold Ct.
DA14: Sidc ... 4K **127**
Edwin Av. E6 ... 2E **72**
(not continuous)
Edwin Cl. DA7: Bex ... 6F **93**
Edwin Ho. SE15 ... 7G **87**
Edwin Pl. *CR0: Croy* ... *1E* ***152***
(off Leslie Gro.)
Edwin Rd. HA8: Edg ... 6E **12**
TW2: Twick ... 1J **115**
(not continuous)
Edwin's Mead E9 ... 4A **52**
Edwinstray Ho.
TW13: Felt ... 2E **114**
Edwin St. E1 ... 4J **69**
E16 ... 5J **71**
Edwin Ware Ct.
HA5: Pinn ... 2A **24**
Edwyn Cl. EN5: Barn ... 6A **4**
Effie Pl. SW6 ... 7J **83**
Effie Rd. SW6 ... 7J **83**
Effingham Cl. SM2: Sutt ... 7K **149**
Effingham Lodge
KT1: King T ... 4D **134**
Effingham Rd.
CR0: Croy ... 7K **139**
KT6: Surb ... 7B **134**
N8 ... 5A **32**
SE12 ... 5G **107**
Effort St. SW17 ... 5C **120**
Effra Cl. SW19 ... 6K **119**
Effra Ct. *SW2* ... *5K* ***103***
(off Brixton Hill)
Effra Pde. SW2 ... 5A **104**
Effra Rd. SW2 ... 4A **104**
SW19 ... 6K **119**
Effra Rd. Retail Pk. SW2 ... 5A **104**
Egan Way UB3: Hayes ... 7G **59**
Egbert St. NW1 ... 1E **66**
Egbury Ho. *SW15* ... *6B* ***100***
(off Tangley Gro.)
Egerton Cl. HA5: Pinn ... 4J **23**
Egerton Ct. E11 ... 7F **35**
Egerton Cres.
SW3 ... 4C **84** (3D **170**)
Egerton Dr. SE10 ... 1D **106**
Egerton Gdns. IG3: Ilf ... 3K **55**
NW4 ... 4D **28**
NW10 ... 1E **64**
SW3 ... 4C **84** (2C **170**)
W13 ... 6B **62**
Egerton Gdns. M.
SW3 ... 3C **84** (2D **170**)
Egerton Pl. SW3 ... 3C **84** (2D **170**)
Egerton Rd. HA0: Wemb ... 7F **45**
KT3: N Mald ... 4B **136**
N16 ... 7F **33**
SE25 ... 3E **140**
TW2: Twick ... 7J **97**
Egerton Ter.
SW3 ... 3C **84** (2D **170**)
Egerton Way UB3: Hayes ... 7D **76**
Eggardon Ct. UB5: N'olt ... 6F **43**
Egham Cl. SM3: Sutt ... 2G **149**
SW19 ... 2G **119**
Egham Cres. SM3: Sutt ... 3G **149**
Egham Rd. E13 ... 5K **71**
Eglantine Rd. SW18 ... 5A **102**
Egleston Rd. SM4: Mord ... 6K **137**
Eglington Ct. SE17 ... 6C **86**
Eglington Rd. E4 ... 7K **9**
Eglinton Hill SE18 ... 6F **91**
Eglinton Rd. SE18 ... 6E **90**
Egliston M. SW15 ... 3E **100**
Egliston Rd. SW15 ... 3E **100**
Eglon M. NW1 ... 7D **48**
Egmont Av. KT6: Surb ... 1F **147**
Egmont Rd. KT3: N Mald ... 4B **136**
KT6: Surb ... 1F **147**
KT12: Walt T ... 7K **131**
SM2: Sutt ... 7A **150**
Egmont St. SE14 ... 7K **87**
Egremont Ho. *SE13* ... *2D* ***106***
(off Russett Way)
Egremont Rd. SE27 ... 3A **122**
Egret Ho. *SE16* ... *4K* ***87***
(off Tawny Way)
Egret Way UB4: Hayes ... 5B **60**
Eider Cl. E7 ... 5H **53**
UB4: Hayes ... 5B **60**
Eider Ct. *SE8* ... *6B* ***88***
(off Pilot Cl.)
Eighteenth Rd. CR4: Mitc ... 4J **139**
Eighth Av. E12 ... 4D **54**
UB3: Hayes ... 1J **77**
Eileen Rd. SE25 ... 5D **140**
Eindhoven Cl.
SM5: Cars ... 1E **150**
Einstein Ho. HA9: Wemb ... 3J **45**
Eisenhower Dr. E6 ... 5C **72**
Elaine Gro. NW5 ... 5E **48**
Elam Cl. SE5 ... 2B **104**
Elam St. SE5 ... 2B **104**
Elan Ct. E1 ... 5H **69**
Eland Ho. *SW1* ... *1A* ***172***
(off Bressenden Pl.)
Eland Pl. CR0: Croy ... 3B **152**
Eland Rd. CR0: Croy ... 3B **152**
SW11 ... 3D **102**
Elba Pl. SE17 ... 4C **86**
Elberon Av. CR0: Croy ... 6G **139**
Elbe St. SW6 ... 2A **102**
Elborough Rd. SE25 ... 5G **141**
Elborough St. SW18 ... 1J **119**
Elbourne Ct. *SE16* ... *3K* ***87***
(off Worgan St.)
Elbourne Trad. Est.
DA17: Belv ... 3H **93**
Elbourn Ho. *SW3* ... *5C* ***170***
(off Cale St.)
Elbury Dr. E16 ... 6J **71**
Elcho St. SW11 ... 7C **84**
Elcot Av. SE15 ... 7H **87**
Eldenwall Ind. Est.
RM8: Dag ... 1E **56**
Elder Av. N8 ... 5J **31**
Elderberry Gro. SE27 ... 4C **122**
Elderberry Rd. W5 ... 2E **80**
Elder Cl. DA15: Sidc ... 1K **127**
N20 ... 2E **14**
UB7: W Dray ... 7A **58**
Elder Ct. WD23: Bush ... 2D **10**
Elderfield Ho. E14 ... 7C **70**
Elderfield Pl. SW17 ... 4F **121**
Elderfield Rd. E5 ... 4K **51**
Elderfield Wlk. E11 ... 5K **35**
Elderflower Way E15 ... 7G **53**
Elder Gdns. SE27 ... 5C **122**
Elder Oak Cl. SE20 ... 1H **141**
Elder Oak Ct. *SE20* ... *1H* ***141***
(off Anerley Ct.)
Elder Rd. SE27 ... 4C **122**
Elderslie Cl. BR3: Beck ... 5C **142**
Elderslie Rd. SE9 ... 5E **108**
Elder St. E1 ... 4F **69** (5J **163**)
(not continuous)
Elderton Rd. SE26 ... 4A **124**
Eldertree Pl. CR4: Mitc ... 1G **139**
Eldertree Way CR4: Mitc ... 1G **139**
Elder Wlk. *N1* ... *1B* ***68***
(off Popham St.)
Elderwood Pl. SE27 ... 5C **122**
Eldon Av. CR0: Croy ... 2J **153**
TW5: Houn ... 7E **78**
Eldon Ct. NW6 ... 1J **65**
Eldon Gro. NW3 ... 5B **48**
Eldon Pk. SE25 ... 4H **141**
Eldon Rd. E17 ... 4B **34**
N9 ... 1D **18**
N22 ... 1B **32**
W8 ... 3K **83**
Eldon St. EC2 ... 5D **68** (6F **163**)
Eldon Way NW10 ... 3H **63**
Eldred Rd. IG11: Bark ... 1J **73**
Eldrick Ct. TW14: Felt ... 1F **113**
Eldridge Cl. TW14: Felt ... 1J **113**
Eldridge Ct. SE16 ... 3G **87**
Eleanor Cl. N15 ... 3F **33**
SE16 ... 2K **87**
Eleanor Cres. NW7 ... 5A **14**
Eleanor Gdns. EN5: Barn ... 5A **4**
RM8: Dag ... 2F **57**
Eleanor Gro. SW13 ... 3A **100**
UB10: Uxb ... 3D **40**
Eleanor Ho. *W6* ... *5E* ***82***
(off Queen Caroline St.)
Eleanor Rd. E8 ... 6H **51**
E15 ... 6H **53**
N11 ... 6D **16**
Eleanor's Station (Ruislip Lido Railway) ... 3G 23
Eleanor St. E3 ... 3C **70**
Eleanor Wlk. SE18 ... 4C **90**
Electra Av. TW6: Houn ... 3H **95**
Electra Bus. Pk. E16 ... 5F **71**
Electric Av. SW9 ... 4A **104**
Electric La. SW9 ... 4A **104**
(not continuous)
Electric Pde. *E18* ... *2J* ***35***
(off George La.)
IG3: Ilf ... 2J **55**
KT6: Surb ... 6D **134**
Elektron Ho. E14 ... 7F **71**
Eleonora Ter. *SM1: Sutt* ... *5A* ***150***
(off Lind Rd.)
ELEPHANT & CASTLE ... 3B 86
Elephant & Castle SE1 ... 4B **86**
Elephant La. SE16 ... 2J **87**
Elephant Rd. SE17 ... 4C **86**
Elers Rd. UB3: Hayes ... 4F **77**
W13 ... 2C **80**
Eley Rd. N18 ... 4D **18**
Eleys Est. N9 ... 3E **18**
N18 ... 4E **18**
(not continuous)
Elfindale Rd. SE24 ... 5C **104**
Elfin Gro. TW11: Tedd ... 5K **115**
Elford Cl. SE3 ... 4K **107**
Elford M. SW4 ... 5G **103**
Elfort Rd. N5 ... 4A **50**
Elfrida Cres. SE6 ... 4C **124**
Elf Row E1 ... 7J **69**
Elfwine Rd. W7 ... 5J **61**
Elgar *N8* ... *3J* ***31***
(off Boyton Cl.)
Elgar Av. KT5: Surb ... 1G **147**
NW10 ... 6K **45**
(not continuous)
SW16 ... 3J **139**
W5 ... 2E **80**
Elgar Cl. E13 ... 2A **72**
IG9: Buck H ... 2G **21**
SE8 ... 7C **88**
UB10: Uxb ... 2C **40**
Elgar Ct. *W14* ... *3G* ***83***
(off Blythe Rd.)
Elgar Ho. *NW6* ... *7A* ***48***
(off Fairfax Rd.)
SW1 ... *6K* ***171***
(off Churchill Gdns.)
Elgar St. SE16 ... 3A **88**
Elgin Av. HA3: Harr ... 2B **26**
TW15: Ashf ... 6E **112**
W9 ... 4H **65**
W12 ... 2D **82**
Elgin Ct. *CR2: S Croy* ... *4C* ***152***
(off Bramley Hill)
W9 ... 4K **65**
Elgin Cres. TW6: Houn ... 2G **95**
W11 ... 7G **65**
Elgin Dr. HA6: Nwood ... 1G **23**
Elgin Est. *W9* ... *4J* ***65***
(off Elgin Av.)
Elgin Ho. *E14* ... *6D* ***70***
(off Ricardo St.)
Elgin Mans. W9 ... 3K **65**
Elgin M. W11 ... 6G **65**
Elgin M. Nth. W9 ... 3K **65**
Elgin M. Sth. W9 ... 3K **65**
Elgin Rd. CR0: Croy ... 2F **153**
IG3: Ilf ... 1J **55**
N22 ... 2G **31**
SM1: Sutt ... 3A **150**
SM6: Wall ... 6G **151**

Elgood Cl.—Elm Rd.

Elgood Cl. W11 .....7G 65
Elgood Ho. NW8 .....2B 66
(off Wellington Rd.)
Elham Cl. BR1: Brom 7B 126
Elham Ho. E5 .....5H 51
Elia M. N1 .....2B 68 (1A 162)
Elias Pl. SW8 .....6A 86
Elia St. N1 .....2B 68 (1B 162)
Elibank Rd. SE9 .....4D 108
Elim Est. SE1 .....3E 86 (7G 169)
Elim St. SE1 .....7G 169
(not continuous)
Elim Way E13 .....3H 71
Eliot Bank SE23 .....2H 123
Eliot Cotts. SE3 .....2G 107
Eliot Dr. HA2: Harr 2F 43
Eliot Gdns. SW15 .....4C 100
Eliot Hill SE13 .....2E 106
Eliot M. NW8 .....2A 66
Eliot Pk. SE13 .....2E 106
Eliot Pl. SE3 .....2G 107
Eliot Rd. RM9: Dag 4D 56
Eliot Va. SE3 .....2F 107
Elis David Almshouses
CR0: Croy 3B 152
Elizabethan Cl.
TW19: Staines 7A 94
Elizabethan Way
TW19: Staines 7A 94
Elizabeth Av. EN2: Enf 3G 7
IG1: Ilf 2H 55
N1 .....1C 68
TW18: Staines 7A 112
Elizabeth Barnes Ct.
SW6 .....2K 101
(off Marinefield Rd.)
Elizabeth Blackwell Ho.
N22 .....1A 32
(off Progress Way)
Elizabeth Bri.
SW1 .....4F 85 (4J 171)
Elizabeth Cl. E14 .....6D 70
EN5: Barn 3A 4
RM7: Mawney 1H 39
SM1: Sutt 4H 149
W9 .....4A 66
Elizabeth Clyde Cl. N15 .....4E 32
Elizabeth Cotts. TW9: Rich 1F 99
Elizabeth Ct. BR1: Brom 1H 143
(off Highland Rd.)
E4 .....5G 19
IG8: Wfd G 7F 21
SW1 .....2D 172
SW10 .....6B 84
(off Milman's St.)
TW11: Tedd 5J 115
Elizabeth Fry Ho.
UB3: Hayes 4H 77
Elizabeth Fry M. E8 .....7H 51
Elizabeth Fry Pl. SE18 .....1C 108
Elizabeth Gdns.
HA7: Stan 6H 11
TW7: Isle 4A 98
TW16: Sun T 3A 132
W3 .....1B 82
Elizabeth Garrett Anderson Ho.
DA17: Belv 3G 93
(off Ambrook Rd.)
Elizabeth Ho. SE11 .....4K 173
(off Reedworth St.)
W6 .....5E 82
(off Queen Caroline St.)
Elizabeth Ind. Est. SE14 .....6K 87
Elizabeth M. HA1: Harr 6J 25
NW3 .....6C 48
Elizabeth Newcomen Ho.
SE1 .....6E 168
(off Newcomen St.)
Elizabeth Pl. N15 .....4D 32
Elizabeth Ride N9 .....7C 8
Elizabeth Rd. E6 .....1B 72
N15 .....5E 32
Elizabeth Sq. SE16 .....7A 70
(off Sovereign Cres.)
Elizabeth St.
SW1 .....4E 84 (3H 171)
Elizabeth Ter. SE9 .....6D 108
Elizabeth Way SE19 .....7D 122
TW13: Felt 4A 114
Elkanette M. N20 .....2F 15
Elkington Point SE11 .....4J 173
Elkington Rd. E13 .....4K 71
Elkstone Ct. SE15 .....6E 86
(off Birdlip Cl.)
Elkstone Rd. W10 .....5H 65
Ella Cl. BR3: Beck 2C 142
Ellaline Rd. W6 .....6F 83
Ella M. NW3 .....4D 48
Ellanby Cres. N18 .....4C 18
Elland Ho. E14 .....6B 70
(off Copenhagen Pl.)
Elland Rd. SE15 .....4J 105
Ella Rd. N8 .....7J 31
Ellement Cl. HA5: Pinn 5B 24
Ellena Ct. N14 .....3D 16
(off Conway Rd.)
Ellenborough Ho. W12 .....7D 64
(off White City Est.)
Ellenborough Pl. SW15 .....4C 100
Ellenborough Rd.
DA14: Sidc 5D 128
N22 .....1C 32
Ellenbridge Way
CR2: S Croy 7E 152
Ellen Cl. BR1: Brom 3B 144
Ellen Ct. E4 .....1K 19
(off Ridgeway, The)
N9 .....2D 18
Ellen St. E1 .....6G 69
Ellen Webb Dr. HA3: Harr 3J 25
Ellen Wilkinson Ho. E2 .....3K 69
(off Usk St.)
RM10: Dag 3G 57
SW6 .....6H 83
(off Clem Attlee Ct.)
Elleray Rd. TW11: Tedd 6K 115
Ellerby St. SW6 .....1F 101
Ellerdale Cl. NW3 .....4A 48
Ellerdale Rd. NW3 .....5A 48
Ellerdale St. SE13 .....4D 106
Ellerdine Rd. TW3: Houn 4G 97
Ellerker Gdns. TW10: Rich 6E 98
Ellerman Av. TW2: Twick 1D 114
Ellerslie Gdns. NW10 .....1C 64
Ellerslie Rd. W12 .....1D 82
Ellerslie Sq. Ind. Est.
SW2 .....5J 103
Ellerton Gdns. RM9: Dag 7C 56
Ellerton Lodge N3 .....2J 29
Ellerton Rd. KT6: Surb 2F 147
RM9: Dag 7C 56
SW13 .....1C 100
SW18 .....1B 120
SW20 .....7C 118
Ellery Ho. SE17 .....4D 86
Ellery Rd. SE19 .....7D 122
Ellery St. SE15 .....2H 105
Ellesmere Av. BR3: Beck 2D 142
NW7 .....3E 12
Ellesmere Cl. E11 .....5H 35
HA4: Ruis 7E 22
Ellesmere Ct. W4 .....5K 81
Ellesmere Gdns. IG4: Ilf 5C 36
Ellesmere Gro. EN5: Barn 5C 4
Ellesmere Rd. E3 .....2A 70
NW10 .....5C 46
TW1: Twick 6C 98
UB6: G'frd 4G 61
W4 .....6J 81
Ellesmere St. E14 .....6D 70
Elleswood Ct.
KT6: Surb 7D 134
Ellie M. TW15: Ashf 2A 112
Ellingfort Rd. E8 .....7H 51
Ellingham Rd. E15 .....4F 53
KT9: Chess 6D 146
W12 .....2C 82
Ellington Ct. N14 .....2C 16
Ellington Ho. SE1 .....3C 86
Ellington Rd. N10 .....4F 31
TW3: Houn 2F 97
TW13: Felt 4H 113
Ellington St. N7 .....6A 50
Elliot Cl. E15 .....7G 53
Elliot Ho. W1 .....6D 158
(off Cato St.)
Elliot Rd. NW4 .....6D 28
Elliott Av. HA4: Ruis 2K 41
Elliott Cl. HA9: Wemb 3G 45
Elliott Gdns. TW17: Shep 4C 130
Elliott Rd. BR2: Short 4B 144
CR7: Thor H 4B 140
HA7: Stan 6F 11
SW9 .....1B 104
W4 .....4A 82
Elliott's Pl. N1 .....1B 68
Elliott Sq. NW3 .....7C 48
Elliotts Row SE11 .....4B 86
Ellis Cl. HA8: Edg 6F 13
NW10 .....6D 46
SE9 .....2G 127
Elliscombe Mt. SE7 .....6A 90
Elliscombe Rd. SE7 .....6A 90
Ellis Ct. W7 .....5K 61
Ellisfield Dr. SW15 .....7C 100
Ellis Franklin Ct. NW8 .....2A 66
(off Abbey Rd.)
Ellis Ho. SE17 .....5D 86
(off Brandon St.)
Ellison Gdns. UB2: S'hall 4D 78
Ellison Ho. SE13 .....2D 106
(off Lewisham Rd.)
Ellison Rd. DA15: Sidc 1H 127
SW13 .....2B 100
SW16 .....7H 121
Ellis Rd. CR4: Mitc 6D 138
UB2: S'hall 1G 79
Ellis St. SW1 .....4E 84 (3F 171)
Ellora Rd. SW16 .....5H 121
Ellsworth St. E2 .....3H 69
Ellwood Ct. W9 .....4K 65
(off Clearwell Dr.)
Elmar Rd. N15 .....4D 32
Elm Av. HA4: Ruis 1J 41
TW19: Staines 2A 112
W5 .....1E 80
Elm Bank N14 .....7D 6
Elmbank Av. EN5: Barn 4A 4
Elm Bank Dr. BR1: Brom 2B 144
Elm Bank Gdns. SW13 .....2A 100
Elmbank Way W7 .....5H 61
Elmbourne Dr. DA17: Belv 4H 93
Elmbourne Rd. SW17 .....3F 121
Elmbridge Av.
KT5: Surb 5H 135
Elmbridge Cl. HA4: Ruis 6J 23
Elmbridge Dr. HA4: Ruis 5H 23
Elmbridge Wlk. E8 .....7G 51
Elmbrook Cl.
TW16: Sun T 1K 131
Elmbrook Gdns. SE9 .....4C 108
Elmbrook Rd. SM1: Sutt 4H 149
Elm Cl. CR2: S Croy 6E 152
E11 .....6K 35
HA2: Harr 6F 25
IG9: Buck H 2G 21
KT5: Surb 7J 135
N19 .....2G 49
NW4 .....5F 29
RM7: Mawney 1H 39
SM5: Cars 1D 150
SW20 .....4E 136
TW2: Twick 2F 115
UB3: Hayes 6J 59
Elmcote HA5: Pinn 2B 24
Elm Cotts. CR4: Mitc 2D 138
Elm Ct. EC4 .....1J 167
KT8: W Mole 4F 133
SE13 .....3F 107
W9 .....5J 65
(off Admiral Wlk.)
Elmcourt Rd. SE27 .....2B 122
Elm Cres. KT2: King T 1E 134
W5 .....1E 80
Elmcroft N6 .....7G 31
Elmcroft Av. DA15: Sidc 7K 109
E11 .....5K 35
N9 .....6C 8
NW11 .....7H 29
Elmcroft Cl. E11 .....4K 35
KT9: Chess 3E 146
N8 .....5K 31
TW14: Felt 6H 95
W5 .....6D 62
Elmcroft Cres. HA2: Harr 3E 24
NW11 .....7G 29
Elmcroft Dr. KT9: Chess 3E 146
TW15: Ashf 5C 112
Elmcroft Gdns. NW9 .....4G 27
Elmcroft St. E5 .....4J 51
Elmcroft Ter. UB8: Uxb 6C 58
Elmdale Rd. N13 .....5E 16
Elmdene KT5: Surb 1J 147
Elmdene Cl. BR3: Beck 6B 142
Elmdene Rd. SE18 .....5F 91
Elmdon Rd. TW4: Houn 2B 96
TW6: Houn 3H 95
Elm Dr. HA2: Harr 6F 25
TW16: Sun T 2A 132
Elmer Cl. EN2: Enf 3E 6
Elmer Gdns. HA8: Edg 7C 12
TW7: Isle 3H 97
Elmer Ho. NW8 .....5C 158
(off Broadley St.)
Elmer Rd. SE6 .....7E 106
Elmers Dr. TW11: Tedd 6B 116
ELMERS END 4A 142
Elmers End Rd. SE20 .....2J 141
Elmerside Rd. BR3: Beck 4A 142
Elmers Lodge BR3: Beck 4K 141
Elmers Rd. SE25 .....7G 141
Elmfield Av. CR4: Mitc 1E 138
N8 .....5J 31
TW11: Tedd 5K 115
Elmfield Cl. HA1: Harr 2J 43
Elmfield Ct. DA16: Well 1B 110
Elmfield Ho. N2 .....2B 30
(off Grange, The)
Elmfield Pk. BR1: Brom 3J 143
Elmfield Rd. BR1: Brom 2J 143
E4 .....2K 19
E17 .....6K 33
N2 .....3B 30
SW17 .....2E 120
UB2: S'hall 3C 78
Elmfield Way
CR2: S Croy 7F 153
W9 .....5J 65
Elm Friars Wlk. NW1 .....7H 49
Elm Gdns. CR4: Mitc 4H 139
KT10: Esh 6A 146
N2 .....3A 30
Elmgate Av. TW13: Felt 3K 113
Elmgate Gdns. HA8: Edg 5D 12
Elm Grn. W3 .....6A 64
Elm Gro. DA8: Erith 7K 93
HA2: Harr 7E 24
IG8: Wfd G 5C 20
KT2: King T 1E 134
N8 .....6J 31
NW2 .....4F 47
SE15 .....2F 105
SM1: Sutt 4K 149
SW19 .....7G 119
UB7: W Dray 7B 58
Elmgrove Cres. HA1: Harr 5K 25
Elmgrove Gdns. HA1: Harr 5A 26
Elm Gro. Pde. SM6: Wall 3E 150
Elm Gro. Rd. SW13 .....1C 100
W5 .....2E 80
Elmgrove Rd. CR0: Croy 7H 141
HA1: Harr 5K 25
HA3: Harr 5A 26
Elm Hall Gdns. E11 .....5K 35
(not continuous)
Elm Ho. E14 .....2E 88
(off E. Ferry Rd.)
KT2: King T 7F 117
(off Elm Rd.)
W10 .....4G 65
(off Briar Wlk.)
Elmhurst DA17: Belv 6E 92
Elmhurst Av. CR4: Mitc 7F 121
N2 .....3B 30
Elmhurst Ct. CR0: Croy 4D 152
Elmhurst Dr. E18 .....2J 35
Elmhurst Lodge
SM2: Sutt 7A 150
Elmhurst Mans. SW4 .....3H 103
Elmhurst Rd. E7 .....7K 53
N17 .....2F 33
SE9 .....2C 126
Elmhurst St. SW4 .....3H 103
Elmington Cl. DA5: Bexl 6H 111
Elmington Est. SE5 .....7D 86
Elmington Rd. SE5 .....7D 86
Elmira St. SE13 .....3D 106
Elm La. SE6 .....2B 124
Elm Lawn Cl. UB8: Uxb 7A 40
Elmlea Dr. UB3: Hayes 5G 59
Elm Lea Trad. Est. N17 .....6C 18
Elmlee Cl. BR7: Chst 6D 126
Elmley Cl. E6 .....5C 72
Elmley St. SE18 .....5H 91
(not continuous)
Elm Lodge SW6 .....1E 100
Elmore Cl. HA0: Wemb 2E 62
Elmore Ho. SW9 .....2B 104
Elmore Rd. E11 .....3E 52
EN3: Enf 1E 8
Elmore St. N1 .....7C 50
Elm Pde. DA14: Sidc 4A 128
Elm Pk. HA7: Stan 5G 11
SW2 .....6K 103
Elm Pk. Av. N15 .....5F 33
Elm Pk. Chambers SW10 .....6A 170
(off Fulham Rd.)
Elm Pk. Ct. HA5: Pinn 3A 24
Elm Pk. Gdns. NW4 .....5F 29
SW10 .....5B 84 (6A 170)
Elm Pk. Ho. SW10 .....5B 84
Elm Pk. La. SW3 .....5B 84 (6A 170)
Elm Pk. Mans. SW10 .....7A 170
Elm Pk. Rd. E10 .....1A 52
HA5: Pinn 2A 24
N3 .....7C 14
N21 .....7H 7
SE25 .....3F 141
SW3 .....6B 84 (7A 170)
Elm Pas. EN5: Barn 4C 4
Elm Pl. SW7 .....5B 84 (5A 170)
Elm Quay Ct.
SW8 .....6H 85 (7C 172)
Elm Rd. BR3: Beck 2B 142
CR7: Thor H 4D 140
DA14: Sidc 4A 128
E7 .....6H 53
E11 .....2F 53
E17 .....5E 34
EN5: Barn 4C 4
HA9: Wemb 5E 44
KT2: King T 1F 135
KT3: N Mald 2K 135
KT9: Chess 4E 146
KT17: Eps 6B 148
N22 .....1B 32
RM7: Mawney 2H 39
SM6: Wall 1E 150
SW14 .....3J 99
TW14: Felt 1F 113

Engadine Cl. CR0: Croy 3F 153
Engadine St. SW18 ....1H 119
Engate St. SE13 ....4E 106
Engel Pk. NW7 ....6K 13
Engine Ct. SW1 ....5B 166
  (off Ambassador's Ct.)
Engineer Cl. SE18 ....6E 90
Engineers Way
  HA9: Wemb 4G 45
England's La. NW3 ....6D 48
England Way
  KT3: N Mald 4H 135
Englefield NW1 ....2A 160
  (off Clarence Gdns.)
Englefield Cl. BR5: Orp ...5K 145
  CR0: Croy 6C 140
  EN2: Enf 2F 7
Englefield Cres. BR5: Orp..4K 145
Englefield Path BR5: Orp ..4K 145
Englefield Rd. N1 ....7D 50
Engleheart Dr. TW14: Felt ..6H 95
Engleheart Rd. SE6 ......7D 106
Englewood Rd. SW12 .....6F 103
English Grounds
  SE1 ....1E 86 (5G 169)
English St. E3 ....4B 70
Enid St. SE16 ....3F 87 (7K 169)
Enmore Av. SE25 ....5G 141
Enmore Gdns. SW14 ......5K 99
Enmore Rd. SE25 ....5G 141
  SW15 ....4E 100
  UB1: S'hall 4E 60
Ennerdale NW1 ....1A 160
  (off Varndell St.)
Ennerdale Av. HA7: Stan ...3C 26
Ennerdale Cl. SM1: Sutt ..4H 149
  TW14: Felt 1H 113
Ennerdale Ct. E11 ....7J 35
  (off Cambridge Rd.)
Ennerdale Dr. NW9 ....5A 28
Ennerdale Gdns.
  HA9: Wemb 1C 44
Ennerdale Ho. E3 ....4B 70
Ennerdale Rd. DA7: Bex ..1G 111
  TW9: Rich 2F 99
Ennersdale Rd. SE13 .....5F 107
Ennis Ho. E14 ....6D 70
  (off Vesey Path)
Ennismore Av. UB6: G'frd ..6J 43
  W4 ....4B 82
Ennismore Gdns.
  KT7: T Ditt 6J 133
  SW7 ....2C 84 (7C 164)
Ennismore Gdns. M.
  SW7 ....3C 84 (1C 170)
Ennismore M.
  SW7 ....3C 84 (7C 164)
Ennismore St.
  SW7 ....3C 84 (1C 170)
Ennis Rd. N4 ....1A 50
  SE18 ....6G 91
Ennor Ct. SM3: Sutt 4E 148
Ensbury Ho. SW8 ....7K 85
  (off Carroun Rd.)
Ensign Cl. TW19: Staines ..1A 112
Ensign Dr. N13 ....3H 17
Ensign Ho. E14 ....2C 88
  (off Admirals Way)
Ensign Ind. Cen. E1 ......7G 69
  (off Ensign St.)
Ensign St. E1 ....7G 69
Ensign Way SM6: Wall 7J 151
  TW19: Staines 1A 112
Enslin Rd. SE9 ....6E 108
Ensor M. SW7 .....5B 84 (5A 170)
Enstone Rd. EN3: Enf 3F 9
  UB10: Uxb 3B 40
Enterprise Bus. Pk. E14 ...2D 88
Enterprise Cen., The
  BR3: Beck 5A 124
  (off Cricket La.)
Enterprise Cl. CR0: Croy ..1A 152

Enterprise Ho. E4 ....7K 9
  E9 ....7J 51
  (off Tudor Gro.)
  E14 ....5D 88
  (off St Davids Sq.)
  IG11: Bark 3K 73
Enterprise Ind. Est. SE16 ..5J 87
Enterprise Way NW10 .....3B 64
  SW18 ....4J 101
  TW11: Tedd 6A 115
Enterprize Way SE8 ......4B 88
Epcot M. NW10 ....3F 65
Epirus M. SW6 ....7J 83
Epirus Rd. SW6 ....7H 83
Epping Cl. E14 ....4C 88
  RM7: Mawney 3H 39
Epping Glade E4 ....6K 9
Epping New Rd.
  IG9: Buck H 2E 20
Epping Pl. N1 ....6A 50
Epping Way E4 ....6J 9
Epple Rd. SW6 ....1H 101
Epsom Cl. DA7: Bex 3H 111
  UB5: N'olt 5D 42
Epsom Rd. CR0: Croy 4A 152
  E10 ....6E 34
  IG3: Ilf 6K 37
  SM3: Sutt 7H 137
Epsom Sq. TW6: Houn 2H 95
Epstein Rd. SE28 ....1A 92
Epworth Rd. TW7: Isle 7B 80
Epworth St. EC2 ...4D 68 (4F 163)
Equity Sq. E2 ....2K 163
  (off Shacklewell St.)
Erasmus St.
  SW1 ....4H 85 (4D 172)
Erconwald St. W12 ....6B 64
Erebus Dr. SE28 ....2G 91
Eresby Dr. BR3: Beck 1C 154
Eresby Ho. SW7 ....7D 164
  (off Rutland Ga.)
Eresby Pl. NW6 ....7J 47
Erica Gdns. CR0: Croy 3D 154
Erica Ho. N22 ....1A 32
  (off Acacia Rd.)
  SE4 ....3B 106
Erica St. W12 ....7C 64
Eric Clarke La. IG11: Bark ..4F 73
Eric Cl. E7 ....4J 53
Ericson Cl. SW18 ....5J 101
Eric Fletcher Ct. N1 .....7C 50
  (off Essex Rd.)
Eric Rd. E7 ....4J 53
  NW10 ....6B 46
  RM6: Chad H 7D 38
Ericson Ho. SE13 ....4F 107
  (off Blessington Rd.)
Eric St. E3 ....3B 70
  (not continuous)
Eric Wilkins Ho. SE1 .....5G 87
  (off Old Kent Rd.)
Eridge Rd. W4 ....3K 81
Erin Cl. BR1: Brom 7G 125
  IG3: Ilf 6A 38
Erindale SE18 ....6H 91
Erindale Ter. SE18 ......6H 91
Erith Cres. RM5: Col R ...1J 39
Erith Rd. DA7: Bex, Erith ..4H 111
  DA8: Erith 5G 93
  (Belvedere)
Erith Rd. DA8: Erith 4H 111
  (Bexleyheath)
  DA17: Belv, Erith 5G 93
Erlanger Rd. SE14 ....1K 105
Erlesmere Gdns. W13 .....3A 80
Erlich Cotts. E1 ....5J 69
  (off Sidney St.)
Ermine Cl. TW4: Houn 2A 96
Ermine Ho. N15 ....6F 33
  SE13 ....4D 106
Ermine Side EN1: Enf 5B 8
Ermington Rd. SE9 ......2G 127

Ernald Av. E6 ....2C 72
Erncroft Way TW1: Twick ..6K 97
Ernest Av. SE27 ....4B 122
Ernest Cl. BR3: Beck 5C 142
Ernest Cotts. KT17: Eps ...7B 148
Ernest Gdns. W4 ....6H 81
Ernest Gro. BR3: Beck ...5B 142
Ernest Harriss Ho. W9 ....4J 65
  (off Elgin Av.)
Ernest Rd. KT1: King T ...2H 135
Ernest Sq. KT1: King T ...2H 135
Ernest St. E1 ....4K 69
Ernle Rd. SW20 ....7D 118
Ernshaw Pl. SW15 ....5G 101
Eros 7H 67 (3C 166)
Eros Ho. Shops SE6 ......7D 106
  (off Brownhill Rd.)
Erpingham Rd. SW15 .....3E 100
Erridge Rd. SW19 ....2J 137
Errington Rd. W9 ....4H 65
Errol Gdns. KT3: N Mald ..4C 136
  UB4: Hayes 4K 59
Errol St. EC1 ....4C 68 (4D 162)
Erskine Cl. SM1: Sutt 3C 150
Erskine Cres. N17 ....4H 33
Erskine Hill NW11 ....4J 29
Erskine Ho. SW1 ....6A 172
  (off Churchill Gdns.)
Erskine M. NW3 ....7D 48
  (off Erskine Rd.)
Erskine Rd. E17 ....4B 34
  NW3 ....7D 48
  SM1: Sutt 4B 150
Erwood Rd. SE7 ....5C 90
Esam Way SW16 ....5A 122
Escot Rd. TW16: Sun T ...7H 113
Escott Gdns. SE9 ....4C 126
Escreet Gro. SE18 ....4E 90
Esher Av. KT12: Walt T ...7J 131
  RM7: Rom 6J 39
  SM3: Sutt 3F 149
Esher By-Pass
  KT9: Chess 7B 146
  KT10: Chess, Esh 7B 146
Esher Cl. DA5: Bexl 1E 128
Esher Cres. TW6: Houn ...2H 95
Esher Gdns. SW19 ....2F 119
Esher M. CR4: Mitc 3E 138
Esher Rd. IG3: Ilf 3J 55
  KT8: E Mos 6H 133
Eskdale NW1 ....1A 160
  (off Stanhope St.)
Eskdale Av. UB5: N'olt 1D 60
Eskdale Cl. HA9: Wemb ...2D 44
Eskdale Rd. DA7: Bex 2G 111
Eskmont Ridge SE19 .....7D 122
Esk Rd. E13 ....4J 71
Esk Way RM1: Rom 1K 39
Esmar Cres. NW9 ....7C 28
Esmeralda Rd. SE1 ......4G 87
Esmond Cl. W4 ....3K 83
  (off Thackeray St.)
Esmond Gdns. W4 ....4K 81
Esmond Rd. NW6 ....1H 65
  W4 ....4K 81
Esmond St. SW15 ....4G 101
Esparto St. SW18 ....7K 101
Esprit Ct. E1 ....6J 163
  (off Brune St.)
Essan Ho. W5 ....5B 62
Essenden Rd.
  CR2: S Croy 7E 152
  DA17: Belv 5G 93
Essendine Rd. W9 ....3J 65
Essex Av. TW7: Isle 3J 97
Essex Cl. E17 ....4A 34
  HA4: Ruis 1B 42
  RM7: Mawney 4H 39
  SM4: Mord 7F 137
Essex Ct. SW13 ....2B 100
  WC2 ....1J 167
Essex Gdns. N4 ....6B 32

Essex Gro. SE19 ....6D 122
Essex Hall E17 ....1K 33
Essex Ho. E14 ....6D 70
  (off Giraud St.)
Essex Mans. E11 ....7F 35
Essex Pk. N3 ....6E 14
Essex Pk. M. W3 ....1A 82
Essex Pl. W4 ....4J 81
  (not continuous)
Essex Pl. Sq. W4 ....4K 81
Essex Rd. E4 ....1B 20
  E10 ....6E 34
  E12 ....5C 54
  E17 ....6A 34
  E18 ....2K 35
  EN2: Enf 4J 7
  IG11: Bark 7H 55
  N1 ....1B 68
  NW10 ....7A 46
  RM6: Chad H 7C 38
  RM7: Mawney 4H 39
  RM10: Dag 5J 57
  W3 ....7J 63
  W4 ....4K 81
  (not continuous)
Essex Rd. Sth. E11 ......7F 35
Essex St. E7 ....5J 53
  WC2 ....6A 68 (1J 167)
Essex Twr. SE20 ....1H 141
  (off Jasmine Gro.)
Essex Vs. W8 ....2J 83
Essex Wharf E5 ....2K 51
Essian St. E1 ....4A 70
Essoldo Way HA8: Edg 3F 27
Estate Way E10 ....1B 52
Estcourt Rd. SE25 ......6H 141
  SW6 ....7H 83
Estella Av. KT3: N Mald ..4D 136
Estella Ho. W11 ....7F 65
  (off St Ann's Rd.)
Estelle Rd. NW3 ....4D 48
Esterbrooke St.
  SW1 ....4H 85 (4C 172)
Este Rd. SW11 ....3C 102
Esther Cl. N21 ....7F 7
Esther Rd. E11 ....7G 35
Estoria Cl. SW2 ....7A 104
Estorick Collection of Modern
  Italian Art 6B 50
Estreham Rd. SW16 ......6H 121
Estridge Cl. TW3: Houn ...4E 96
Estuary Cl. IG11: Bark ...3B 74
Eswyn Rd. SW17 ....4D 120
Etal Ho. N1 ....7B 50
  (off Sutton Est., The)
Etchingham Ct. N3 ......7E 14
Etchingham Pk. Rd. N3 ...7E 14
Etchingham Rd. E15 .....4E 52
Eternit Wlk. SW6 ....1E 100
Etfield Gro. DA14: Sidc ..5B 128
Ethelbert Cl. BR1: Brom ..2J 143
Ethelbert Ct. BR1: Brom ..3J 143
  (off Ethelbert Rd.)
Ethelbert Gdns. IG2: Ilf ..5D 36
Ethelbert Ho. E9 ....4A 52
  (off Ethelbert Rd.)
Ethelbert Rd. BR1: Brom ..3J 143
  DA8: Erith 7J 93
  SW20 ....1F 137
Ethelbert St. SW12 ......1F 121
Ethel Brooks Ho. SE18 ...6F 91
Etheldene Av. N10 ....4G 31
Ethelden Rd. W12 ....1D 82
Ethel Rd. E16 ....6K 71
  TW15: Ashf 5A 112
Ethel St. SE17 ....4C 86
Etheridge Rd. NW4 ......7E 28
  (not continuous)
Etherley Rd. N15 ....5C 32
Etherow St. SE22 ....7G 105
Etherstone Grn. SW16 ....4A 122

Etherstone Rd. SW16 .....4A 122
Ethnard Rd. SE15 ....6H 87
Ethronvi Rd. DA7: Bex ...3E 110
Etloe Ho. E10 ....1C 52
Etloe Rd. E10 ....2C 52
Eton Av. EN4: Barn 6H 5
  HA0: Wemb 4B 44
  KT3: N Mald 5K 135
  N12 ....7F 15
  NW3 ....7B 48
  TW5: Houn 6D 78
Eton Cl. SW18 ....7K 101
Eton Coll. Rd. NW3 ......6D 48
Eton Ct. HA0: Wemb 4C 44
  NW3 ....7B 48
  (off Eton Av.)
Eton Garages NW3 ....6C 48
Eton Gro. NW9 ....3G 27
  SE13 ....3G 107
Eton Hall NW3 ....6D 48
Eton Ho. N5 ....4B 50
  (off Leigh Rd.)
Eton Mnr. Ct. E10 ....2C 52
  (off Leyton Grange Est.)
Eton Pl. NW3 ....7E 48
Eton Ri. NW3 ....6D 48
Eton Rd. IG1: Ilf 4G 55
  NW3 ....7D 48
  UB3: Hayes 7H 77
Eton St. TW9: Rich 5C 98
Eton Vs. NW3 ....6D 48
Etta St. SE8 ....6A 88
Ettrick St. E14 ....6E 70
  (not continuous)
Etwell Pl. KT5: Surb 6F 135
Eugene Cotter Ho. SE17 ...4D 86
  (off Tatum St.)
Eugenia Rd. SE16 ....4J 87
Eugenie M. BR7: Chst 1F 145
Eureka Rd. KT1: King T ...2G 135
Euro Cl. NW10 ....6C 46
Eurolink Bus. Cen. SW2 ...5A 104
Europa Pl. EC1 ....3C 68 (2C 162)
Europa Trad. Est.
  DA8: Erith 5K 93
European Bus. Cen. NW9 ..3K 27
  NW9 ....3J 27
Europe Rd. SE18 ....3D 90
Eustace Ho. SE11 ....3G 173
Eustace Pl. SE18 ....4D 90
Eustace Rd. E6 ....3C 72
  RM6: Chad H 7D 38
  SW6 ....7J 83
EUSTON 3G 67
Euston Cen.
  NW1 ....4G 67 (3A 160)
  (not continuous)
Euston Gro. NW1 ....3G 67
  (off Euston Sq.)
Euston Rd. CR0: Croy 1A 152
  NW1 ....4F 67 (4A 160)
Euston Sq. NW1 ....3H 67
Euston Sta. Colonnade
  NW1 ....3H 67 (2C 160)
Euston St. NW1 ...3G 67 (2B 160)
Euston Twr. NW1 ..4G 67 (3A 160)
Euston Underpass
  ....4G 67 (3A 160)
Evandale Rd. SW9 ....2A 104
Evangelist Ho. EC4 ......1A 168
  (off Black Friars La.)
Evangelist Rd. NW5 ......4F 49
Evans Cl. E8 ....6F 51
Evans Gro. TW13: Felt ...2E 114
Evans Ho. SW8 ....7H 85
  (off Wandsworth Rd.)
  TW13: Felt 2E 114
  W12 ....7D 64
  (off White City Est.)
Evans Rd. SE6 ....2G 125
Evanston Av. E4 ....7K 19

Evanston Gdns.—Fairfields Rd.

Evanston Gdns. IG4: Ilf 6C 36
Eva Rd. RM6: Chad H 7C 38
Evelina Mans. SE5 7D 86
Evelina Rd. SE15 3J 105
SE20 7J 123
Eveline Rd. CR4: Mitc 1D 138
Evelyn Av. HA4: Ruis 7G 23
NW9 4K 27
Evelyn Cl. TW2: Twick 7F 97
Evelyn Ct. E8 4G 51
N1 1E 162
(off Evelyn Wlk., not continuous)
Evelyn Cres.
TW16: Sun T 1H 131
Evelyn Denington Ct. *N1* 7B 50
(off Sutton Est., The)
Evelyn Denington Rd. E6 4C 72
Evelyn Dr. HA5: Pinn 1B 24
Evelyn Fox Ct. W10 5E 64
Evelyn Gdns.
SW7 5A 84 (6A 170)
TW9: Rich 4E 98
Evelyn Gro. UB1: S'hall 6D 60
W5 1F 81
Evelyn Ho. *SE14* 1A 106
(off Loring Rd.)
W12 2B 82
(off Cobbold Rd.)
Evelyn Lowe Est. SE16 3G 87
Evelyn Mans. *SW1* 2A 172
(off Carlisle Pl.)
W14 6G 83
(off Queen's Club Gdns.)
Evelyn Rd. E16 1J 89
E17 4E 34
EN4: Barn 4J 5
SW19 5K 119
TW9: Rich 3E 98
TW10: Rich 3C 116
W4 3K 81
Evelyns Cl. UB8: Uxb 6C 58
Evelyn St. SE8 4A 88
Evelyn Ter. TW9: Rich 3E 98
Evelyn Wlk. N1 2D 68 (1E 162)
Evelyn Way SM6: Wall 4H 151
TW16: Sun T 1H 131
Evelyn Yd. W1 6H 67 (7C 160)
Evening Hill BR3: Beck 7E 124
Evenlode Ho. SE2 2C 92
Evenwood Cl. SW15 5G 101
Everard Av. BR2: Short 1J 155
Everard Ct. N13 3E 16
Everard Ho. *E1* 6G 69
(off Boyd St.)
Everard Way HA9: Wemb 3E 44
Everatt Cl. SW18 6H 101
Everdon Rd. SW13 6C 82
Everest Pl. E14 5E 70
Everest Rd. SE9 5D 108
TW19: Staines 7A 94
Everett Cl. HA5: Pinn 3H 23
WD23: Bush 1D 10
Everett Ho. *SE17* 5D 86
(off East St.)
Everett Wlk. *DA17: Belv* 5F 93
(off Osborne Rd.)
Everglade Ho. E17 2B 34
Everglade Strand NW9 1B 28
Evergreen Cl. SE20 7J 123
Evergreen Way
UB3: Hayes 7G 59
Everilda St. N1 1K 67
Evering Rd. N16 3F 51
Everington Rd. N10 2D 30
Everington St. W6 6F 83
(not continuous)
Everitt Rd. NW10 3K 63
Everleigh St. N4 1K 49
Eve Rd. E11 4G 53
E15 2G 71
N17 3E 32
TW7: Isle 4A 98
Eversfield Gdns.
HA8: Edg 6F 13
NW7 7F 13
Eversfield Rd. TW9: Rich 2F 99
Evershed Wlk. W4 3J 81
Eversholt St.
NW1 2G 67 (1B 160)
Evershot Rd. N4 1K 49
Eversleigh Rd. E6 1B 72
EN5: Barn 5F 5
N3 7C 14
SW11 3D 102
Eversley Av. DA7: Bex 2K 111
HA9: Wemb 2G 45
Eversley Cl. N21 6E 6
Eversley Cres. HA4: Ruis 2G 41
N21 6E 6
TW7: Isle 1H 97
Eversley Ho. *E2* 2K 163
(off Gossett St.)
Eversley Mt. N21 6E 6
Eversley Pk. SW19 6D 118
Eversley Pk. Rd. N21 6E 6
Eversley Rd. KT5: Surb 4F 135
SE7 6K 89
SE19 7D 122
Eversley Way CR0: Croy 4C 154
Everthorpe Rd. SE15 3F 105
Everton Bldgs.
NW1 3G 67 (2A 160)
Everton Dr. HA7: Stan 3E 26
Everton Rd. CR0: Croy 1G 153
Evesham Av. E17 2C 34
Evesham Cl. SM2: Sutt 7J 149
UB6: G'frd 2F 61
Evesham Ct. TW10: Rich 6F 99
W13 1A 80
(off Tewkesbury Rd.)
Evesham Grn.
SM4: Mord 6K 137
Evesham Ho. *E2* 2J 69
(off Old Ford Rd.)
NW8 1A 66
(off Abbey Rd.)
Evesham Rd. E15 7H 53
N11 5B 16
SM4: Mord 6K 137
Evesham St. W11 7F 65
Evesham Ter. KT6: Surb 6D 134
Evesham Wlk. SE5 2D 104
SW9 2A 104
Evesham Way IG5: Ilf 3E 36
SW11 3E 102
Evry Rd. DA14: Sidc 6C 128
Ewald Rd. SW6 2H 101
Ewanrigg Ter. IG8: Wfd G 5F 21
Ewart Gro. N22 1A 32
Ewart Pl. E3 2B 70
Ewart Rd. SE23 7K 105
Ewe Cl. N7 6J 49
EWELL 7B 148
Ewell By-Pass KT17: Eps 7C 148
Ewell Ct. Av. KT19: Eps 5A 148
Ewellhurst Rd. IG5: Ilf 2C 36
Ewell Pk. Gdns.
KT17: Eps 7C 148
Ewell Pk. Way KT17: Eps 6C 148
Ewell Rd. KT6: Surb 6E 134
(Surbiton Hill Rd.)
KT6: Surb 7B 134
(Thornhill Rd.)
SM3: Sutt 7F 149
Ewelme Rd. SE23 1J 123
Ewen Cres. SW2 7A 104
Ewen Ho. *N1* 1K 67
(off Barnsbury Est.)
Ewer St. SE1 1C 86 (5C 168)
Ewesdon Cl. N9 3C 18
Ewhurst Av. CR2: S Croy 7F 153
Ewhurst Cl. E1 5J 69
Ewhurst Ct. CR4: Mitc 3B 138
Ewhurst Rd. SE4 6B 106
Exbury Ho. E9 7J 51
SW1 5C 172
(off Rampayne St.)
Exbury Rd. SE6 2C 124
ExCeL 7K 71
Excel Ct. WC2 3D 166
Excelsior Cl.
KT1: King T 2G 135
Excelsior Gdns. SE13 2E 106
Excelsior Ind. Est.
SE15 6J 87
Exchange Arc.
EC2 5E 68 (5H 163)
Exchange Bldg. *E1* 4J 163
(off Commercial St.)
Exchange Cl. N11 2K 15
Exchange Ct.
WC2 7J 67 (3F 167)
Exchange Ho. EC2 5H 163
SW1 4C 172
(off Vauxhall Bri. Rd.)
Exchange Mans. NW11 7H 29
Exchange Pl.
EC2 5E 68 (5G 163)
Exchange Sq.
EC2 5E 68 (5G 163)
Exchange St.
EC1 3C 68 (2C 162)
RM1: Rom 5K 39
Exchange, The IG1: Ilf 2F 55
Exeforde Av.
TW15: Ashf 4C 112
Exeter Cl. E6 6D 72
Exeter Ct. *KT6: Surb* 5E 134
(off Maple Rd.)
NW6 2J 65
(off Cambridge Rd.)
Exeter Gdns. IG1: Ilf 1C 54
Exeter Ho. *IG11: Bark* 7A 56
(off Margaret Bondfield Av.)
SE15 6G 87
(off Friary Est.)
TW13: Felt 2D 114
(off Watermill Way)
W2 6A 66
(off Hallfield Est.)
Exeter Mans. NW2 6G 47
Exeter M. NW6 6K 47
SW6 7J 83
Exeter Rd. CR0: Croy 7E 140
DA16: Well 2K 109
E16 5J 71
E17 5C 34
EN3: Enf 3E 8
HA2: Harr 2C 42
N9 2D 18
N14 1A 16
NW2 5G 47
RM10: Dag 6H 57
TW6: Houn 3G 95
TW13: Felt 3D 114
Exeter St. WC2 7J 67 (2F 167)
Exeter Way SE14 7B 88
TW6: Houn 2G 95
Exford Gdns. SE12 1K 125
Exford Rd. SE12 2K 125
Exhibition Cl. W12 7E 64
Exhibition Rd.
SW7 2B 84 (7B 164)
Exmoor Cl. IG6: Ilf 1G 37
Exmoor Ho. *E3* 2A 70
(off Gernon Rd.)
Exmoor St. W10 4F 65
Exmouth Ho. *E14* 4D 88
(off Cahir St.)
EC1 3J 161
(off Pine St.)
Exmouth Mkt.
EC1 4A 68 (3J 161)
Exmouth M.
NW1 3G 67 (2B 160)
Exmouth Pl. E8 7H 51
Exmouth Rd. DA16: Well 1C 110
E17 5B 34
HA4: Ruis 3A 42
UB4: Hayes 3G 59
Exmouth St. E1 6J 69
Exning Rd. E16 4H 71
Exonbury *NW8* 1K 65
(off Abbey Rd.)
Exon St. SE17 5E 86
Explorer Av.
TW19: Staines 1A 112
Export Ho. *SE1* 7H 169
(off Tower Bri. Rd.)
Express Dr. IG3: Ilf 1B 56
Express Newspapers *SE1* 4A 168
(off Blackfriars Rd.)
Express Wharf E14 2C 88
Exton Cres. NW10 7J 45
Exton Gdns. RM8: Dag 5C 56
Exton St. SE1 1A 86 (5J 167)
Eyebright Cl. CR0: Croy 1K 153
Eyhurst Cl. NW2 2C 46
Eylewood Rd. SE27 5C 122
Eynella Rd. SE22 7F 105
Eynham Rd. W12 6E 64
Eynsford Cl. BR5: Orp 7G 145
Eynsford Cres. DA5: Bexl 1C 128
Eynsford Ho. *SE1* 7E 168
(off Crosby Row)
SE15 6J 87
SE17 4E 86
(off Beckway St.)
Eynsford Rd. IG3: Ilf 2J 55
Eynsford Ter. UB7: W Dray 6B 58
Eynsham Dr. SE2 4A 92
Eynswood Dr. DA14: Sidc 5B 128
Eyot Gdns. W6 5B 82
Eyot Grn. W4 5B 82
Eyre Ct. NW8 2B 66
Eyre St. Hill EC1 4A 68 (4J 161)
Eysham Ct. EN5: Barn 5E 4
Eythorne Rd. SW9 1A 104
Ezra St. E2 3F 69 (1K 163)

F

Faber Gdns. NW4 5C 28
Fabian Rd. SW6 7H 83
Fabian St. E6 4D 72
Facade, The SE23 2J 123
Factory La. CR0: Croy 1A 152
N17 2F 33
Factory Rd. E16 1B 90
Factory Sq. *SW16* 6J 121
(off Streatham High Rd.)
Factory Yd. W7 1J 79
Faggs Rd. TW14: Felt 4H 95
Fairacre KT3: N Mald 3A 136
Fairacre Ct. HA6: Nwood 1G 23
Fair Acres BR2: Short 5J 143
CR0: Croy 7B 154
Fairacres HA4: Ruis 7H 23
SW15 4B 100
Fairbairn Grn. SW9 1B 104
Fairbank Est. N1 2D 68 (1E 162)
Fairbanks Rd. N17 3F 33
Fairbourne Ho.
UB3: Hayes 3E 76
Fairbourne Rd. N17 3E 32
Fairbridge Rd. N19 2H 49
Fairbrook Cl. N13 5F 17
Fairbrook Rd. N13 6F 17
Fairburn Ct. SW15 5G 101
Fairburn Ho. *W14* 5H 83
(off Ivatt Pl.)
Fairby Ho. *SE1* 4F 87
(off Longfield Est.)
Fairby Rd. SE12 5K 107
Faircharm Trad. Est.
SE8 7D 88
Fairchild Cl. SW11 2B 102
Fairchild Ho. *E9* 7J 51
(off Frampton Pk. Rd.)
N1 1G 163
(off Fanshaw St.)
N3 1J 29
Fairchild Pl. EC2 4H 163
Fairchild St. EC2 4E 68 (3H 163)
Fair Cl. WD23: Bush 1A 10
Fairclough St. E1 6G 69
Faircroft Ct. TW11: Tedd 6A 116
FAIR CROSS 5J 55
Faircross Av. IG11: Bark 6G 55
RM5: Col R 1K 39
Faircross Pde. IG11: Bark 5J 55
Fairdale Gdns. SW15 4D 100
UB3: Hayes 2J 77
Fairey Av. UB3: Hayes 4H 77
Fairfax Av. KT17: Eps 7D 148
Fairfax Cl. KT12: Walt T 7K 131
Fairfax Gdns. SE3 1A 108
Fairfax Ho. *KT1: King T* 3F 135
(off Livesey Cl.)
Fairfax Mans. *NW3* 6A 48
(off Finchley Rd.)
Fairfax M. E16 1K 89
SW15 4E 100
Fairfax Pl. NW6 7A 48
W14 3G 83
Fairfax Rd. N8 4A 32
NW6 7A 48
TW11: Tedd 6A 116
W4 3A 82
Fairfax Way N10 7K 15
Fairfield *E1* 5J 69
(off Redman's Rd.)
EN5: Barn 7G 5
NW1 1G 67
(off Arlington Rd.)
Fairfield Av. HA4: Ruis 7E 22
HA8: Edg 6C 12
NW4 6D 28
TW2: Twick 1F 115
Fairfield Cl. CR4: Mitc 7C 120
DA15: Sidc 6K 109
EN3: Enf 4E 8
KT19: Eps 5A 148
N12 4F 15
Fairfield Ct. HA4: Ruis 1F 41
HA6: Nwood 2J 23
NW10 1C 64
Fairfield Cres. HA8: Edg 6C 12
Fairfield Dr. HA2: Harr 3G 25
SW18 5K 101
UB6: G'frd 1C 62
Fairfield E. KT1: King T 2E 134
Fairfield Gdns. N8 5J 31
Fairfield Gro. SE7 6B 90
Fairfield Halls 3D 152
Fairfield Ind. Est.
KT1: King T 3F 135
Fairfield Nth. KT1: King T 2E 134
Fairfield Path CR0: Croy 3D 152
Fairfield Pl. KT1: King T 3E 134
Fairfield Rd. BR1: Brom 7J 125
BR3: Beck 2C 142
BR5: Orp 6H 145
CR0: Croy 3D 152
DA7: Bex 2F 111
E3 2C 70
Fairfield Rd. E17 2A 34
IG1: Ilf 6F 55
IG8: Wfd G 6D 20
KT1: King T 2E 134
N8 5J 31
N18 4B 18
UB1: S'hall 6D 60
UB7: W Dray 7A 58
UB8: Uxb 6A 40
Fairfields Cl. NW9 5J 27
Fairfields Cres. NW9 4J 27
Fairfield Sth. KT1: King T 2E 134
Fairfields Rd. TW3: Houn 3G 97

Fairfield St.—Farm Wlk.

Fairfield St. SW18 . . . . .5K 101
Fairfield Way EN5: Barn 5D 4
KT19: Eps 5A 148
Fairfield W. KT1: King T 2E 134
Fairfoot Rd. E3 . . . . .4C 70
Fairford SE6 . . . . .1C 124
Fairford Av. CR0: Croy 5K 141
DA7: Bex 1K 111
Fairford Cl. CR0: Croy 5A 142
Fairford Ct. SM2: Sutt 7K 149
Fairford Gdns.
KT4: Wor Pk 2B 148
Fairford Ho.
SE11 . . . . . . .4A 86 (4K 173)
Fairgreen EN4: Barn 3J 5
Fairgreen Ct. EN4: Barn 3J 5
Fairgreen E. EN4: Barn 3J 5
Fairgreen Rd.
CR7: Thor H 5B 140
Fairhaven Av. CR0: Croy . . .6K 141
Fairhaven Ct.
CR2: S Croy 5C 152
(off Warham Rd.)
Fairhazel Gdns. NW6 . . . . . . .6K 47
Fairhazel Mans. *NW6* *7A 48*
(off Fairhazel Gdns.)
Fairholme TW14: Felt 7F 95
Fairholme Cl. N3 . . . . .4G 29
Fairholme Cres.
UB4: Hayes 4H 59
Fairholme Gdns. N3 . . . . .3G 29
Fairholme Rd. CR0: Croy . . .7A 140
HA1: Harr 5K 25
IG1: Ilf 7D 36
SM1: Sutt 6H 149
TW15: Ashf 5A 112
W14 . . . . .5G 83
Fairholt Cl. N16 . . . . .1E 50
Fairholt Rd. N16 . . . . .1D 50
Fairholt St. SW7 . . .3C 84 (1D 170)
Fairland Ho. BR2: Short 4K 143
Fairland Rd. E15 . . . . .6H 53
Fairlands Av.
CR7: Thor H 4K 139
IG9: Buck H 2D 20
SM1: Sutt 2J 149
Fairlands Ct. SE9 . . . . .6E 108
Fairlawn SE7 . . . . .7A 90
Fairlawn Av. DA7: Bex 2D 110
N2 . . . . .4C 30
W4 . . . . .4J 81
Fair Lawn Cl. KT10: Esh 6A 146
KT2: King T 6J 117
Fairlawn Cl. N14 . . . . .6B 6
TW13: Felt 4D 114
Fairlawn Ct. SE7 . . . . .7A 90
(not continuous)
W4 . . . . .4J 81
Fairlawn Dr. IG8: Wfd G 7D 20
Fairlawn Gdns.
UB1: S'hall 7D 60
Fairlawn Gro. W4 . . . . .4J 81
Fairlawn Mans. SE14 . . . . . .1K 105
Fairlawn Pk. SE26 . . . . .5A 124
Fairlawn Rd. SW19 . . . . . . .7H 119
Fairlawns HA5: Pinn 2B 24
SM6: Wall 5F 151
TW1: Twick 6C 98
Fairlawns TW16: Sun T 3H 131
Fairlea Pl. W5 . . . . .4C 62
Fairlie Gdns. SE23 . . . . .7J 105
Fairlight Av. E4 . . . . .2A 20
IG8: Wfd G 6D 20
NW10 . . . . .2A 64
(not continuous)
Fairlight Cl. E4 . . . . .2A 20
KT4: Wor Pk 4E 148
Fairlight Ct. NW10 . . . . .2A 64
UB6: G'frd 2G 61
Fairlight Rd. SW17 . . . . . . .4B 120
Fairline Ct. BR3: Beck 2E 142
FAIRLOP 1J 37
Fairlop Ct. E11 . . . . .1F 53
Fairlop Gdns. IG6: Ilf 1G 37
Fairlop Rd. E11 . . . . .7F 35
IG6: Ilf 2G 37
Fairlop Waters Country Pk.
. . . . .1K 37
Fairman Ter. HA3: Harr 4D 26
Fairmark Dr. UB10: Uxb 6C 40
Fairmead BR1: Brom 4D 144
KT5: Surb 1H 147
Fairmead Cl. BR1: Brom . . .4D 144
KT3: N Mald 3K 135
TW5: Houn 7B 78
Fairmead Ct. TW9: Rich 2H 99
Fairmead Cres. HA8: Edg . . .3D 12
Fairmead Gdns. IG4: Ilf 5C 36
Fairmead Ho. E9 . . . . .4A 52
Fairmead Rd. CR0: Croy . . .7K 139
N19 . . . . .3H 49
Fairmile Av. SW16 . . . . .5H 121
Fairmile Ho. TW11: Tedd . . .4A 116
Fairmont Cl. DA17: Belv 5F 93
Fairmount Rd. SW2 . . . . . . .6K 103
Fairoak Cl. BR5: Orp 7F 145
Fairoak Dr. SE9 . . . . .5H 109
Fairoak Gdns. RM1: Rom 2K 39
Fair Oak Pl. IG6: Ilf 2G 37
Fairseat Cl. WD23: Bush 2D 10
Fairstead Wlk. *N1* *1C 68*
(off Popham St.)
Fair St. SE1 . . . . . . .2E 86 (6H 169)
TW3: Houn 3G 97
Fairthorn Rd. SE7 . . . . .5J 89
Fairview HA4: Ruis 4A 42
Fairview Av. HA0: Wemb 6D 44
Fairview Cl. E17 . . . . .1A 34
SE26 . . . . .5A 124
Fairview Ct. NW4 . . . . .2F 29
TW15: Ashf 5C 112
Fairview Cres. HA2: Harr 1E 42
Fairview Dr. TW17: Shep . . .5B 130
Fairview Gdns.
IG8: Wfd G 1K 35
Fairview Ho. SW2 . . . . .7K 103
Fairview Ind. Pk.
RM13: Rain 5K 75
Fairview Pl. SW2 . . . . .7K 103
Fairview Rd. EN2: Enf 1F 7
N15 . . . . .5F 33
SM1: Sutt 5B 150
SW16 . . . . .1K 139
Fairview Vs. E4 . . . . .7J 19
Fairview Way HA8: Edg 4B 12
Fairwall Ho. SE5 . . . . .1E 104
Fairwater Av.
DA16: Well 4A 110
Fairwater Ho.
TW11: Tedd 4A 116
Fair Way IG8: Wfd G 5F 21
Fairway BR5: Orp 5H 145
DA6: Bex 5E 110
SW20 . . . . .3E 136
Fairway Av. NW9 . . . . .3H 27
Fairway Cl. CR0: Croy 5A 142
KT19: Eps 4J 147
NW11 . . . . .7A 30
TW4: Houn 5A 96
Fairway Ct. EN5: Barn 6E 4
NW7 . . . . .3E 12
SE16 . . . . .2K 87
(off Christopher Cl.)
Fairway Dr. SE28 . . . . .6D 74
UB6: G'frd 7F 43
Fairway Gdns.
BR3: Beck 6F 143
IG1: Ilf 5G 55
Fairways E17 . . . . .4E 34
HA7: Stan 2E 26
TW7: Isle 1H 97
TW11: Tedd 7D 116
TW15: Ashf 6D 112
Fairways Bus. Pk. E10 . . . . . .2A 52
Fairway, The BR1: Brom . . .5D 144
EN5: Barn 6E 4
HA0: Wemb 3B 44
HA4: Ruis 4A 42
KT3: N Mald 1K 135
KT8: W Mole 3F 133
N13 . . . . .3H 17
N14 . . . . .6A 6
NW7 . . . . .3E 12
UB5: N'olt 6G 43
UB10: Uxb 2B 58
W3 . . . . .6A 64
Fairweather Cl. N15 . . . . .4E 32
Fairweather Ct. N13 . . . . .4E 16
Fairweather Rd. N16 . . . . . . .6G 33
Fairwyn Rd. SE26 . . . . .4A 124
Fakenham Cl. NW7 . . . . .7H 13
UB5: N'olt 6D 42
Fakruddin St. E1 . . . . .4G 69
Falcon *WC1* *5F 161*
(off Old Gloucester St.)
Falcon Av. BR1: Brom 4C 144
Falconberg Ct.
W1 . . . . .6H 67 (7D 160)
Falconberg M.
W1 . . . . .6H 67 (7D 160)
Falcon Cl. HA6: Nwood 1G 23
SE1 . . . . .1B 86 (4B 168)
W4 . . . . .6J 81
Falcon Ct. *E18* *3K 35*
(off Albert Rd.)
EC4 . . . . .6A 68 (1K 167)
EN5: Barn 4F 5
HA4: Ruis 2G 41
N1 . . . . .1B 162
(off City Garden Row)
Falcon Cres. EN3: Enf 5E 8
Falcon Dr. TW19: Staines 6A 94
Falconer Ct. N17 . . . . .7H 17
Falconer Wlk. N7 . . . . .2K 49
Falconet Ct. *E1* *1H 87*
(off Wapping High St.)
Falcon Gro. SW11 . . . . .3C 102
Falcon Ho. *E14* *5D 88*
(off St Davids Sq.)
Falcon La. SW11 . . . . .3C 102
Falcon Lodge *W9* *5J 65*
(off Admiral Wlk.)
Falcon Pk. Ind. Est. NW10 . . .4A 46
Falcon Point
SE1 . . . . .7B 68 (3B 168)
Falcon Rd. EN3: Enf 5E 8
SW11 . . . . .2C 102
TW12: Hamp 7D 114
Falconry Ct. *KT1: King T 3E 134*
(off Fairfield Sth.)
Falcon St. E13 . . . . .4H 71
Falcon Ter. SW11 . . . . .3C 102
Falcon Way E11 . . . . .4J 35
E14 . . . . .4D 88
HA3: Harr 5E 26
NW9 . . . . .2A 28
TW14: Felt 5K 95
TW16: Sun T 2G 131
FALCONWOOD 4K 109
Falconwood 4H 109
Falconwood Av.
DA16: Well 2H 109
Falconwood Ct. *SE3* *2H 107*
(off Montpelier Row)
Falconwood Pde.
DA16: Well 4J 109
Falconwood Rd.
CR0: Croy 7B 154
Falcourt Cl. SM1: Sutt 5K 149
Falkirk Ct. *SE16* *1K 87*
(off Rotherhithe St.)
Falkirk Ho. *W9* *2K 65*
(off Maida Va.)
Falkirk St. N1 . . . . .2E 68 (1H 163)
Falkland Av. N3 . . . . .7D 14
N11 . . . . .4A 16
Falkland Ho. SE6 . . . . .4E 124
W8 . . . . .3K 83
W14 . . . . .5H 83
(off Edith Vs.)
Falkland Pk. Av. SE25 . . . . .3E 140
Falkland Pl. NW5 . . . . .5G 49
Falkland Rd. EN5: Barn 2B 4
N8 . . . . .4A 32
NW5 . . . . .5G 49
Fallaize Av. IG1: Ilf 4F 55
Falling La. UB7: W Dray 7A 58
Falloden Way NW11 . . . . .4J 29
Fallodon Ho. *W11* *5H 65*
(off Tavistock Cres.)
FALLOW CORNER 7F 15
Fallow Ct. *SE16* *5G 87*
(off Argyle Way)
Fallow Ct. Av. N12 . . . . .7F 15
Fallowfield HA7: Stan 4F 11
Fallowfield Ct. HA7: Stan 3F 11
Fallowfields Dr. N12 . . . . . . .6H 15
Fallowhurst Path N3 . . . . .7F 15
Fallows Cl. N2 . . . . .2B 30
Fallsbrook Rd. SW16 . . . . . .6F 121
Falman Cl. N9 . . . . .1B 18
Falmer Rd. E17 . . . . .3D 34
EN1: Enf 4K 7
N15 . . . . .5C 32
Falmouth Av. E4 . . . . .5A 20
Falmouth Cl. N22 . . . . .7E 16
SE12 . . . . .5H 107
Falmouth Gdns. IG4: Ilf 4B 36
Falmouth Ho. HA5: Pinn 1D 24
SE11 . . . . .5K 173
(off Seaton Clo.)
W2 . . . . .2C 164
(off Clarendon Pl.)
Falmouth Rd.
SE1 . . . . .3C 86 (7E 168)
Falmouth St. E15 . . . . .5F 53
Falmouth Way E17 . . . . .5B 34
Falstaff Cl. DA1: Cray 7K 111
Falstaff Ct. *SE11* *4B 86*
(off Opal St.)
Falstaff Ho. *N1* *1G 163*
(off Crondall St.)
Falstaff M. *TW12: Hamp . . .5H 115*
(off Parkside)
Fambridge Cl. SE26 . . . . . . .4B 124
Fambridge Ct.
RM7: Rom 5K 39
(off Marks Rd.)
Fambridge Rd. RM8: Dag . . .1G 57
Fane Ho. E2 . . . . .1J 69
Fane St. W14 . . . . .6H 83
Fan Mus., The 7E 88
Fann St. EC2 . . . . . .4C 68 (4C 162)
(not continuous)
Fanshawe Av. IG11: Bark 6G 55
Fanshawe Cres.
RM9: Dag 5E 56
Fanshawe Rd.
TW10: Rich 4C 116
Fanshaw St. N1 . . . .3E 68 (1G 163)
Fantail, The 3D 156
Fanthorpe St. SW15 . . . . . . .3E 100
Faraday Av. DA14: Sidc 2A 128
Faraday Cl. N7 . . . . .6K 49
Faraday Ho. *E14* *7B 70*
(off Brightlingsea Pl.)
HA9: Wemb 3J 45
SE1 . . . . .7D 168
(off Cole St.)
Faraday Lodge SE10 . . . . . . .3H 89
Faraday Mans. *W14* *6G 83*
(off Queen's Club Gdns.)
Faraday Mus. 7G 67 (3A 166)
Faraday Rd. DA16: Well 3A 110
E15 . . . . .6H 53
KT8: W Mole 4E 132
SW19 . . . . .6J 119
UB1: S'hall 7F 61
Faraday Rd. W3 . . . . .7J 63
W10 . . . . .5G 65
Faraday Way CR0: Croy 1K 151
SE18 . . . . .3B 90
Fareham Rd. TW14: Felt 7A 96
Fareham St.
W1 . . . . .6H 67 (7C 160)
Farewell Pl. CR4: Mitc 1C 138
Faringdon Av. BR2: Short . . .7E 144
Faringford Rd. E15 . . . . .7G 53
Farjeon Ho. *NW6* *7B 48*
(off Hilgrove Rd.)
Farjeon Rd. SE3 . . . . .1B 108
Farleigh Av. BR2: Short 7H 143
Farleigh Ct. CR2: S Croy . . .5C 152
Farleigh Pl. N16 . . . . .4F 51
Farleigh Rd. N16 . . . . .4F 51
Farley Ct. *NW1* *4G 159*
(off Allsop Pl.)
Farley Dr. IG3: Ilf 1J 55
Farley Ho. SE26 . . . . .3H 123
Farley Pl. SE25 . . . . .4G 141
Farley Rd. CR2: S Croy 7H 153
SE6 . . . . .7D 106
Farlington Pl. SW15 . . . . . .7D 100
Farlow Rd. SW15 . . . . .3F 101
Farlton Rd. SW18 . . . . .1K 119
Farman Gro. UB5: N'olt 3B 60
Farm Av. HA0: Wemb 6C 44
HA2: Harr 7D 24
NW2 . . . . .3G 47
SW16 . . . . .4J 121
Farmborough Cl.
HA1: Harr 7H 25
Farm Cl. BR4: W W'ck 3H 155
IG9: Buck H 3F 21
RM10: Dag 7J 57
SM2: Sutt 7B 150
SW6 . . . . .7J 83
TW17: Shep 7C 130
UB1: S'hall 7F 61
UB10: Uxb 2D 40
Farmcote Rd. SE12 . . . . .1J 125
Farm Ct. NW4 . . . . .3C 28
Farmdale Rd. SE10 . . . . .5J 89
SM5: Cars 7C 150
Farm Dr. CR0: Croy 2B 154
Farm End HA6: Nwood 1D 22
Farmer Rd. E10 . . . . .1D 52
Farmers Rd. SE5 . . . . .7B 86
Farmer St. W8 . . . . .1J 83
Farmfield Rd.
BR1: Brom 5G 125
Farm Ho. Ct. NW7 . . . . .7H 13
Farmhouse Rd. SW16 . . . . .7G 121
Farmilo Rd. E17 . . . . .7B 34
Farmington Av.
SM1: Sutt 3B 150
Farmlands EN2: Enf 1F 7
HA5: Pinn 4J 23
Farmlands, The UB5: N'olt . . .6D 42
Farmland Wlk. BR7: Chst . . .5F 127
Farm La. CR0: Croy 2B 154
N14 . . . . .6A 6
SW6 . . . . .6J 83
Farm La. Trad. Est. SW6 . . . .6J 83
Farmleigh N14 . . . . .7B 6
Farmleigh Ho. SW9 . . . . . . .5B 104
Farm M. CR4: Mitc 2F 139
Farm Pl. W8 . . . . .1J 83
Farm Rd. E12 . . . . .2C 54
HA8: Edg 6C 12
N21 . . . . .1H 17
NW10 . . . . .1K 63
SM2: Sutt 7B 150
SM4: Mord 5K 137
TW4: Houn 1C 114
Farmstead Rd. HA3: Harr 1H 25
SE6 . . . . .4D 124
Farm St. W1 . . . . . . .7F 67 (3J 165)
Farm Va. DA5: Bexl 6H 111
Farm Wlk. NW11 . . . . .5H 29

Farm Way IG9: Buck H 4F 21
  KT4: Wor Pk 3E 148
Farmway RM8: Dag 3C 56
Farnaby Ho. W10 . . . . .3H 65
  (off Bruckner St.)
Farnaby Rd. BR1: Brom 7F 125
  BR2: Short 7F 125
  SE9 . . . . .4A 108
Farnan Av. E17 . . . . .2C 34
Farnan Rd. SW16 . . . . .5J 121
Farnborough Av.
  CR2: S Croy 7K 153
  E17 . . . . .3A 34
Farnborough Cl.
  HA9: Wemb 2H 45
Farnborough Comn.
  BR6: Orp 3D 156
Farnborough Cres.
  BR2: Short 1H 155
  CR2: S Croy 7A 154
Farncombe St. SE16 . . . . . . .2G 87
Farndale Av. N13 . . . . .3G 17
Farndale Cl. SE18 . . . . .7C 90
Farndale Cres.
  UB6: G'frd 3G 61
Farndale Ho. NW6 . . . . .1K 65
  (off Kilburn Va.)
Farnell M. SW5 . . . . .5K 83
Farnell Pl. W3 . . . . .7H 63
Farnell Rd. TW7: Isle 3H 97
Farnham Cl. N20 . . . . .7F 5
Farnham Ct. SM3: Sutt 6G 149
  UB1: S'hall 7G 61
  (off Redcroft Rd.)
Farnham Gdns. SW20 . . . . . .2D 136
Farnham Ho. NW1 . . . . .4D 158
Farnham Pl. SE1 . . .1B 86 (5B 168)
Farnham Rd. DA16: Well 2C 110
  IG3: Ilf 7K 37
Farnham Royal
  SE11 . . . . .5K 85 (6H 173)
Farningham Ct. SW16 . . . . . .7H 121
Farningham Ho. N4 . . . . .7D 32
Farningham Rd. N17 . . . . . . .7B 18
Farnley Ho. SW8 . . . . .2H 103
Farnley Rd. E4 . . . . .1B 20
  SE25 . . . . .4D 140
Farnworth Ho. E14 . . . . .4F 89
  (off Manchester Rd.)
Faro Cl. BR1: Brom 2E 144
Faroe Rd. W14 . . . . .3F 83
Farorna Wlk. EN2: Enf 1F 7
Farquhar Rd. SE19 . . . . .5E 138
  SW19 . . . . .3J 119
Farquharson Rd.
  CR0: Croy 1C 152
Farrance Rd. RM6:
  Chad H 6E 38
Farrance St. E14 . . . . .6C 70
Farrans Ct. HA3: Harr 7B 26
Farrant Av. N22 . . . . .2A 32
Farr Av. IG11: Bark 2A 74
Farrell Ho. E1 . . . . .6J 69
  (off Ronald St.)
Farren Rd. SE23 . . . . .2A 140
Farrer Ct. TW1: Twick 7D 98
Farrer Ho. SE8 . . . . .7C 88
Farrer M. N8 . . . . .4G 31
Farrer Rd. HA3: Harr 5E 26
  N8 . . . . .4G 31
Farrer's Pl. CR0: Croy 4K 153
Farrier Cl. BR1: Brom 3B 144
  TW16: Sun T 3J 131
  UB8: Uxb 6C 58
Farrier Rd. UB5: N'olt 2E 60
Farriers Ho. EC1 . . . . .4D 162
  (off Errol St.)
Farriers M. SE15 . . . . .3J 105
Farrier St. NW1 . . . . .7F 49
Farrier Wlk. SW10 . . . . .6A 84
Farringdon La.
  EC1 . . . . .4A 68 (4K 161)

Farringdon Rd.
  EC1 . . . . .4A 68 (3J 161)
Farringdon St.
  EC4 . . . . .5B 68 (6A 162)
Farrington Pl.
  BR7: Chst 7H 127
Farrins Rents SE16 . . . . .1A 88
Farrow La. SE14 . . . . .7J 87
Farrow Pl. SE16 . . . . .3A 88
Farr Rd. EN2: Enf 1J 7
Farthingale Wlk. E15 . . . . . . .7F 53
Farthing All. SE1 . .2G 87 (7K 169)
Farthing Barn La.
  BR6: Orp 7E 156
Farthing Flds. E1 . . . . .1H 87
Farthings Cl. E4 . . . . .3B 20
  HA5: Pinn 6K 23
Farthings, The
  KT2: King T 1G 135
FARTHING STREET 7D 156
Farthing St. BR6: Orp 7D 156
Farwell Rd. DA14: Sidc 4B 128
Farwig La. BR1: Brom 1H 143
Fashion & Textile Mus.
  . . . . .2E 86 (6H 169)
Fashion St. E1 . . . . .5F 69 (6K 163)
Fashoda Rd. BR2: Short 4B 144
Fassett Rd. E8 . . . . .6G 51
  KT1: King T 4E 134
Fassett Sq. E8 . . . . .6G 51
Fauconberg Ct. W4 . . . . .6J 81
  (off Fauconberg Rd.)
Fauconberg Rd. W4 . . . . .6J 81
Faulkner Cl. RM8: Dag 7D 38
Faulkners All.
  EC1 . . . . .5B 68 (5A 162)
Faulkner St. SE14 . . . . .1J 105
Fauna Cl. RM6: Chad H 6C 38
Faunce Ho. SE17 . . . . .6B 86
  (off Doddington Gro.)
Faunce St. SE17 . . . . .5B 86
Faure Rd. SW6 . . . . .1J 101
Faversham Av. E4 . . . . .1B 20
  EN1: Enf 6J 7
Faversham Ho. NW1 . . . . . . .1G 67
  (off Bayham Pl.)
  SE17 . . . . .5E 86
  (off Kinglake St.)
Faversham Rd.
  BR3: Beck 2B 142
  SE6 . . . . .7B 106
  SM4: Mord 6K 137
Fawcett Cl. SW11 . . . . .2B 102
  SW16 . . . . .5A 122
Fawcett Est. E5 . . . . .1G 51
Fawcett Rd. CR0: Croy 3C 152
  NW10 . . . . .7B 46
Fawcett St. SW10 . . . . .6A 84
Fawe Pk. M. SW15 . . . . .4H 101
Fawe Pk. Rd. SW15 . . . . . . .4H 101
Fawe St. E14 . . . . .5D 70
Fawkham Ho. SE1 . . . . .4F 87
  (off Longfield Est.)
Fawley Lodge E14 . . . . .4F 89
  (off Millennium Dr.)
Fawley Rd. NW6 . . . . .5K 47
Fawnbrake Av. SE24 . . . . . . .5B 104
Fawn Rd. E13 . . . . .2A 72
Fawns Mnr. Cl.
  TW14: Felt 1E 112
Fawns Mnr. Rd.
  TW14: Felt 1F 113
Fawood Av. NW10 . . . . .7J 45
Faygate Cres. DA6: Bex 5G 111
Faygate Rd. SW2 . . . . .2K 121
Fayland Av. SW16 . . . . .5G 121
Fazeley Ct. W9 . . . . .5J 65
  (off Elmfield Way)
Fearnley Cres.
  TW12: Hamp 5C 114
Fearnley Ho. SE5 . . . . .2E 104
Fearon St. SE10 . . . . .5J 89

Featherbed La.
  CR0: Croy 7B 154
FELTHAM 2J 113
Feltham Av. KT8: E Mos 4J 133
Felthambrook Ind. Est.
  TW13: Felt 3K 113
Felthambrook Way
  TW13: Felt 3K 113
Feltham Bus. Complex
  TW13: Felt 1K 113
FELTHAMHILL 5H 113
Feltham Hill Rd.
  TW15: Ashf 5C 112
Felthamhill Rd.
  TW13: Felt 4J 113
Feltham Rd. CR4: Mitc 2D 138
  TW15: Ashf 4C 112
Felton Cl. BR5: Orp 6F 145
Felton Gdns. IG11: Bark 1J 73
Felton Ho. N1 . . . . .1D 68
  (off Branch Pl.)
  SE3 . . . . .4K 107
Felton Lea DA14: Sidc 5K 127
Felton Rd. IG11: Bark 2J 73
  W13 . . . . .2C 80
Felton St. N1 . . . . .1D 68
Fencepiece Rd. IG6: Ilf 1G 37
Fenchurch Av.
  EC3 . . . . .6E 68 (1G 169)
Fenchurch Bldgs.
  EC3 . . . . .6E 68 (1H 169)
Fenchurch Pl.
  EC3 . . . . .6E 68 (2H 169)
Fenchurch St.
  EC3 . . . . .7E 68 (2G 169)
Fen Ct. EC3 . . . . . . .6E 68 (2G 169)
Fendall Rd. KT19: Eps 5J 147
Fendall St. SE1 . . . . .3E 86
  (not continuous)
Fendt Cl. E16 . . . . .6H 71
Fendyke Rd. DA17: Belv 4D 92
Fenelon Pl. W14 . . . . .4H 83
Fen Gro. DA15: Sidc 5K 109
Fenham Rd. SE15 . . . . .7G 87
Fenman Ct. N17 . . . . .1H 33
Fenman Gdns. IG3: Ilf 1B 56
Fenn Cl. BR1: Brom 6J 125
Fennel Cl. CR0: Croy 1K 153
  E16 . . . . .4G 71
Fennells Mead
  KT17: Eps 7B 148
Fennell St. SE18 . . . . .6E 90
Fenner Cl. SE16 . . . . .4H 87
Fenner Ho. E1 . . . . .1H 87
  (off Watts St.)
Fenner Sq. SW11 . . . . .3B 102
Fenn Ho. TW7: Isle 1B 98
Fenning St.
  SE1 . . . . .2E 86 (6G 169)
Fenn St. E9 . . . . .5K 51
Fenstanton N4 . . . . .1K 49
  (off Marquis Rd.)
Fenstanton Av. N12 . . . . .6G 15
Fen St. E16 . . . . .7H 71
  (not continuous)
Fenswood Cl. DA6: Bex 6G 111
Fentiman Rd.
  SW8 . . . . . .6J 85 (7F 173)
Fenton Cl. BR7: Chst 5D 126
  E8 . . . . .6F 51
  SW9 . . . . .2K 103
Fenton House 4A 48
  (off Windmill Hill)
Fenton Ho. SE14 . . . . .7A 88
  TW5: Houn 6E 78
Fenton Rd. N17 . . . . .7H 17
Fentons Av. E13 . . . . .3K 71
Fenton St. E1 . . . . .6H 69
Fenwick Cl. SE18 . . . . .6E 90
Fenwick Gro. SE15 . . . . .3G 105
Fenwick Pl.
  CR2: S Croy 7B 152
  SW9 . . . . .3J 103
Fenwick Rd. SE15 . . . . .3G 105

Ferby Ct. DA14: Sidc 4K 127
  (off Main Rd.)
  SE9 . . . . .3H 127
  (off Main Rd.)
Ferdinand Ho. NW1 . . . . . . .7E 48
  (off Ferdinand Pl.)
Ferdinand Pl. NW1 . . . . .7E 48
Ferdinand St. NW1 . . . . .7E 48
Ferguson Av. KT5: Surb 5F 135
Ferguson Cen., The E17 . . . .6A 34
Ferguson Cl. BR2: Short 3F 143
  E14 . . . . .4C 88
Ferguson Dr. W3 . . . . .6K 63
Ferguson Ho. SE10 . . . . .1E 106
Fergus Rd. N5 . . . . .5B 50
Fermain Ct. E. N1 . . . . .1E 68
  (off De Beauvoir Est.)
Fermain Ct. Nth. N1 . . . . . . .1E 68
  (off De Beauvoir Est.)
Fermain Ct. W. N1 . . . . .1E 68
  (off De Beauvoir Est.)
Ferme Pk. Rd. N8 . . . . .5J 31
Fermor Rd. SE23 . . . . .1A 124
Fermoy Rd. UB6: G'frd 4F 61
  W9 . . . . .4H 65
Fern Av. CR4: Mitc 4H 139
Fernbank IG9: Buck H 1E 20
Fernbank Av. HA0: Wemb . . .4K 43
  KT12: Walt T 7C 132
Fernbank M. SW12 . . . . .6F 103
Fernbrook Av. DA15: Sidc . . .5J 109
Fernbrook Cres. SE13 . . . . . .6G 107
  (off Leahurst Rd.)
Fernbrook Dr. HA2: Harr 7F 25
Fernbrook Rd. SE13 . . . . . . .5G 107
Ferncliff Rd. E8 . . . . .5G 51
Fern Cl. N1 . . . . .2E 68
Fern Ct. DA7: Bex 4G 111
  SE14 . . . . .2K 105
Ferncroft Av. HA4: Ruis 2A 42
  N12 . . . . .6J 15
  NW3 . . . . .3J 47
Ferndale BR1: Brom 2A 144
Ferndale Av. E17 . . . . .5F 35
  TW4: Houn 3C 96
Ferndale Cl. DA7: Bex 1E 110
Ferndale Rd. E7 . . . . .7K 53
  E11 . . . . .2G 53
  N15 . . . . .6F 33
  RM5: Col R 2J 39
  SE25 . . . . .5H 141
  SW4 . . . . .4J 103
  SW9 . . . . .4J 103
  TW15: Ashf 5A 112
Ferndale St. E6 . . . . .7F 73
Ferndale Ter. HA1: Harr 4K 25
Ferndell Av. DA5: Bexl 3K 129
Fern Dene W13 . . . . .5B 62
Ferndene Rd. SE24 . . . . .4C 104
Ferndon Way RM7: Rom 6H 39
Ferndown HA6: Nwood 2J 23
Ferndown Av. BR6: Orp 7H 145
Ferndown Cl. HA5: Pinn 1C 24
  SM2: Sutt 6B 150
Ferndown Ct. UB1: S'hall 6G 61
  (off Haldane Rd.)
Ferndown Lodge E14 . . . . . . .3E 88
  (off Manchester Rd.)
Ferndown Rd. SE9 . . . . .7B 108
Ferney Meade Way
  TW7: Isle 2A 98
Ferney Rd. EN4: Barn 7K 5
Fern Gro. TW14: Felt 7K 95
Fernhall Dr. IG4: Ilf 5B 36
Fernham Rd.
  CR7: Thor H 3C 140
Fernhead Rd. W9 . . . . .2H 65
Fernheath Way DA2: Dart . . .5K 129
Fernhill Ct. E17 . . . . .2F 35
Fernhill Gdns.
  KT2: King T 5D 116
Fernhill St. E16 . . . . .1D 90

Fernholme Rd. SE15 ....5K 105
Fernhurst Gdns.
  HA8: Edg 6B 12
Fernhurst Rd. CR0: Croy ...7H 141
  SW6 ....1G 101
  TW15: Ashf 4E 112
Fern La. TW5: Houn 5D 78
Fernlea Rd. CR4: Mitc 2E 138
  SW12 ....1F 121
Fernleigh Cl. CR0: Croy ...4A 152
Fernleigh Ct. HA2: Harr ...2F 25
  HA9: Wemb 2E 44
  RM7: Rom 5J 39
Fernleigh Rd. N21 ....2F 17
Fernley Cl. HA5: Pinn 4J 23
Fernsbury St.
  WC1 ....3A 68 (2J 161)
Fernshaw Cl. SW10 ......6A 84
Fernshaw Rd. SW10 ......6A 84
Fernside IG9: Buck H 1E 20
  NW11 ....2J 47
Fernside Av. NW7 ....3E 12
  TW13: Felt 4K 113
Fernside Ct. NW4 ....2F 29
  (off Holders Hill Rd.)
Fernside Rd. SW12 ....1D 120
Ferns Rd. E15 ....6H 53
Fern St. E3 ....4C 70
Fernthorpe Rd. SW16 ....6G 121
Ferntower Rd. N5 ....5D 50
Fern Wlk. SE1 ....5G 87
  TW15: Ashf 5A 112
Fernways IG1: Ilf 4F 55
Fernwood CR0: Croy 7A 154
Fernwood Av.
  HA0: Wemb 6C 44
  SW16 ....4H 121
Fernwood Cl. BR1: Brom ..2A 144
Fernwood Cres. N20 .....3J 15
Ferny Hill EN4: Barn 1J 5
Ferranti Cl. SE18 ....3B 90
Ferraro Cl. TW5: Houn ...6E 78
Ferrers Av. SM6: Wall 4H 151
  UB7: W Dray 2A 76
Ferrers Rd. SW16 ....5H 121
Ferrestone Rd. N8 ....4K 31
Ferrey M. SW9 ....2A 104
Ferriby Cl. N1 ....7A 50
Ferrier Ind. Est. SW18 ....4K 101
  (off Ferrier St.)
Ferrier Point E16 ....5J 71
  (off Forty Acre La.)
Ferrier St. SW18 ....4K 101
Ferring Cl. HA2: Harr 1G 43
Ferrings SE21 ....3E 122
Ferris Av. CR0: Croy 3B 154
Ferris Rd. SE22 ....4G 105
Ferron Rd. E5 ....3H 51
Ferry App. SE18 ....3E 90
Ferrybridge Ho. SE11 ....2H 173
Ferrydale Lodge NW4 ....4E 28
  (off Church Rd.)
Ferry Ho. E5 ....1H 51
  (off Harrington Hill)
Ferry Island Retail Pk.
  N17 ....3G 33
Ferry La. N17 ....4G 33
  SW13 ....6B 82
  TW8: Bford 6E 80
  TW9: Rich 4E 80
  TW17: Shep 7C 130
Ferry La. Ind. Est. E17 ....4K 33
Ferrymead Av. UB6: G'frd ..3E 60
Ferrymead Dr. UB6: G'frd ..2E 60
Ferrymead Gdns.
  UB6: G'frd 2F 61
Ferrymoor TW10: Rich 3B 116
Ferry Pl. SE18 ....3E 90
Ferry Quays TW8: Bford ...7E 80
Ferry Rd. KT7: T Ditt 6B 134
  KT8: W Mole 3E 132
  SW13 ....7C 82

Ferry Rd. TW1: Twick 1B 116
  TW11: Tedd 5B 116
Ferry Sq. TW8: Bford 7E 80
  TW17: Shep 7D 130
Ferry St. E14 ....5E 88
Festing Rd. SW15 ....3F 101
Festival Cl. DA5: Bexl 1D 128
  UB10: Uxb 1D 58
Festival Ct. E8 ....7F 51
  (off Holly St.)
Festival Wlk. SM5: Cars ...5D 166
Fetter La. EC4 ......6A 68 (1K 167)
  (not continuous)
Fettes Ho. NW8 ....2B 66
  (off Wellington Rd.)
Ffinch St. SE8 ....7C 88
Field Cl. BR1: Brom 2A 144
  E4 ....6J 19
  HA4: Ruis 1E 40
  IG9: Buck H 3F 21
  KT8: W Mole 5F 133
  KT9: Chess 5C 146
  TW4: Houn 1K 95
  UB3: Hayes 7H 76
  UB10: Uxb 2D 40
FIELDCOMMON 7D 132
Fieldcommon La.
  KT12: Walt T 7C 132
Field Ct. SW19 ....3J 119
  WC1 ....5K 67 (6H 161)
Field End HA4: Ruis 6A 42
  UB5: N'olt 6C 42
Fieldend TW1: Twick 4K 115
Field End Rd. HA4: Ruis ...5K 23
  HA5: Pinn, Ruis 5K 23
Fieldend Rd. SW16 ......1G 139
Fielders Cl. EN1: Enf 4K 7
  HA2: Harr 1G 43
Fieldfare Rd. SE28 ....7C 74
Fieldgate La. CR4: Mitc ...2C 138
Fieldgate Mans. E1 ......5G 69
  (off Fieldgate St., not continuous)
Fieldgate St. E1 ....5G 69
Field Ho. NW6 ....3F 65
  (off Harvist Rd.)
Fieldhouse Cl. E18 ....1K 35
Fieldhouse Rd. SW12 ....1G 121
Fielding Av. TW2: Twick ...3G 115
Fielding Ho. NW6 ....3J 65
  W4 ....6A 82
  (off Devonshire Rd.)
Fielding M. SW13 ....6D 82
  (off Jenner Pl.)
Fielding Rd. W4 ....3K 81
  W14 ....3F 83
Fieldings, The SE23 .....1J 123
Fielding St. SE17 ....6C 86
Fielding Ter. W5 ....7F 63
Field La. TW8: Bford 7C 80
  TW11: Tedd 5A 116
Field Mead NW7 ....7F 13
Field Pl. KT3: N Mald 6B 136
Field Point E7 ....4J 53
  E7 ....4H 53
  N17 ....3D 32
Field Rd. TW14: Felt 6K 95
  W6 ....5G 83
Fieldsend Rd. SM3: Sutt ..5G 149
Fields Est. E8 ....7G 51
Fieldside Rd.
  BR1: Brom 5F 125
Fids. Park Cres.
  RM6: Chad H 5D 38
Fieldstile Rd. W13 ......1B 80
Field St. WC1 ....3K 67 (1G 161)
Fieldsway Ho. N5 ....5A 50
Field Vw. TW13: Felt 4F 113
Fieldview SW18 ....1B 120
Fieldview Cotts. N14 .....2C 16
  (off Balaams La.)
Field Way HA4: Ruis 1E 40
  NW10 ....7J 45
  UB6: G'frd 1F 61

Fieldway BR5: Orp 6H 145
  CR0: Croy 7D 154
  RM8: Dag 3C 56
Fieldway Cres. N5 ....5A 50
Fiennes Cl. RM8: Dag 1C 56
Fifehead Ct. TW15: Ashf ..6A 112
Fife Rd. E16 ....5J 71
  KT1: King T 2E 134
  (not continuous)
  N22 ....7G 17
  SW14 ....5J 99
Fife Ter. N1 ....2K 67
Fiffield Path SE23 ....3K 123
Fifth Av. E12 ....4D 54
  UB3: Hayes 1H 77
  W10 ....3G 65
Fifth Cross Rd.
  TW2: Twick 2H 115
Fifth Way HA9: Wemb 4H 45
Figges Rd. CR4: Mitc 7E 120
Fig Tree Cl. NW10 ....1A 64
Figure Ct. SW3 ....6F 171
Filanco Ct. W7 ....1K 79
  (off Uxbridge Rd.)
Filby Rd. KT9: Chess 6F 147
Filey Av. N16 ....1G 51
Filey Cl. SM2: Sutt 7A 150
Filey Waye HA4: Ruis 2J 41
Filigree Ct. SE16 ....1B 88
Fillebrook Av. EN1: Enf ...2K 7
Fillebrook Rd. E11 ....1F 53
Filmer Rd. SW6 ....1G 101
Filston Rd. DA8: Erith 5J 93
Filton Ct. SE14 ....7J 87
  (off Farrow La.)
Finborough Ho. SW10 ....6A 84
  (off Finborough Rd.)
Finborough Rd. SW10 ....5K 83
  SW17 ....6D 120
Finborough Theatre, The ...6K 83
  (off Finborough Rd.)
Finchale Rd. SE2 ....3A 92
Fincham Ct. UB10: Uxb ...3E 40
Finch Av. SE27 ....4D 122
Finch Cl. EN5: Barn 5D 4
  NW10 ....6K 45
Finch Ct. DA14: Sidc 3B 128
Finchdean Ho. SW15 .....7B 100
Finch Dr. TW14: Felt 7B 96
Finch Gdns. E4 ....5H 19
Finch Ho. SE8 ....7D 88
  (off Bronze St.)
Finchingfield Av.
  IG8: Wfd G 7F 21
Finch La. EC3 .....6D 68 (1F 169)
FINCHLEY 1J 29
Finchley Cl. N13 ....6E 14
Finchley La. NW4 ....4E 28
Finchley Pk. N12 ....4F 15
Finchley Pl. NW8 ....2B 66
Finchley Rd. NW3 ....4J 47
  NW8 ....1B 66
  NW11 ....4H 29
Finchley Way N3 ....7D 14
Finch Lodge W2 ....5J 65
  (off Admiral Wlk.)
Finch M. SE15 ....1F 105
Finch's Ct. E14 ....7D 70
Finden Rd. E7 ....5A 54
Findhorn Av. UB4: Hayes ..5K 59
Findhorn St. E14 ....6E 70
Findon Cl. HA2: Harr 3F 43
  SW18 ....6J 101
Findon Rd. N9 ....1C 18
  W12 ....2C 82
Fine Bush La. UB9: Uxb ...6D 22
Fingal St. SE10 ....5H 89
Fingest Ho. NW8 ....3C 158
  (off Lilestone St.)
Finians Cl. UB10: Uxb 7B 40
Finland Rd. SE4 ....3A 106

Finland St. SE16 ....3A 88
Finlays Cl. KT9: Chess ...5G 147
Finlay St. SW6 ....1F 101
Finmere Ho. N4 ....7C 32
Finnemore Ho. N1 ....1C 68
  (off Britannia Row)
Finney La. TW7: Isle 1A 96
Finn Ho. N1 ....1F 163
  (off Bevenden St.)
Finnis St. E2 ....3H 69
Finnymore Rd. RM9: Dag ..7E 56
FINSBURY 3A 68 (3C 162)
Finsbury Av. EC2 ...5D 68 (6F 163)
  (not continuous)
Finsbury Av. Sq. EC2 .....5G 163
Finsbury Cir. EC2 ...5D 68 (6F 163)
Finsbury Cotts. N22 ......7D 16
Finsbury Est.
  EC1 ....3A 68 (2K 161)
Finsbury Mkt.
  EC2 ....4E 68 (4G 163)
  (Clifton St.)
  EC2 ....5E 68
  (Pindar St.)
FINSBURY PARK 1A 50
Finsbury Pk. Av. N4 ......6C 32
Finsbury Pk. Rd. N4 ......2B 50
  (not continuous)
Finsbury Pavement
  EC2 ....5D 68 (5F 163)
Finsbury Rd. N22 ....7E 16
Finsbury Sq.
  EC2 ....4D 68 (4F 163)
Finsbury Way DA5: Bexl ...6F 111
Finsen Rd. SE5 ....4C 104
Finstock Rd. W10 ....6F 65
Fincuane Ri. WD23: Bush ..2B 10
Finwhale Ho. E14 ....3D 88
  (off Glengall Gro.)
Fiona Ct. EN2: Enf 3G 7
Firbank Cl. E16 ....5B 72
  EN2: Enf 4H 7
Firbank Rd. SE15 ....2H 105
Fir Cl. KT12: Walt T 7J 131
Fircroft Gdns. HA1: Harr ..3J 43
Fircroft Rd. KT9: Chess ...4F 147
  SW17 ....2D 120
Firdene KT5: Surb 1J 147
Fire Bell La. KT6: Surb 6E 134
Firecrest Dr. NW3 ....3K 47
Firefly Cl. SM6: Wall 7J 151
Firefly Gdns. E6 ....4C 72
Firemans Flats N22 ......7D 16
Firepower (Royal Artillery
  Mus.,The) 3F 91
Fire Sta. All. EN5: Barn ...3B 4
Fire Sta. M. BR3: Beck ...1C 142
Firethorn Cl. HA8: Edg ...4D 12
Fir Gro. KT3: N Mald 6B 136
Firhill Rd. SE6 ....4C 124
Fir Ho. W10 ....4G 65
  (off Droop St.)
Firle Ho. W10 ....5E 64
  (off Sutton Way)
Fir Rd. SM3: Sutt 1H 149
  TW13: Felt 5B 114
Firs Av. N10 ....3E 30
  N11 ....6J 15
  SW14 ....4J 99
Firsby Av. CR0: Croy 1K 153
Firsby Rd. N16 ....1G 51
Firs Cl. CR4: Mitc 1F 139
  N10 ....4E 30
  SE23 ....7A 106
Firscroft N13 ....3H 17
Firs Dr. TW5: Houn 7K 77
Firs Ho. N22 ....1A 32

Firside Gro. DA15: Sidc ...1K 127
Firs La. N13 ....3H 17
  N21 ....7H 7
Firs Pk. Av. N21 ....1H 17
Firs Pk. Gdns. N21 ......1H 17
First Av. DA7: Bex 7C 92
  E12 ....4C 54
  E13 ....3J 71
  E17 ....5C 34
  EN1: Enf 5A 8
  HA9: Wemb 2D 44
  KT8: W Mole 4D 132
  KT12: Walt T 6K 131
  KT19: Eps 7A 148
  N18 ....4D 18
  NW4 ....4E 28
  RM6: Chad H 5C 38
  RM10: Dag 2H 75
  SW14 ....3A 100
  UB3: Hayes 1H 77
  W3 ....1B 82
  W10 ....4H 65
First Bowl 7K 65
First Cl. KT8: W Mole 3G 133
First Cross Rd.
  TW2: Twick 2J 115
First Dr. NW10 ....7J 45
Firs, The DA5: Bexl 1K 129
  DA15: Sidc 2K 127
  E6 ....7C 54
  IG8: Wfd G 7F 21
  N20 ....1G 15
  SE26 ....5H 123
  (Border Rd.)
  SE26 ....5J 123
  (Waverley Ct.)
  W5 ....5D 62
First St. SW3 ......4C 84 (3D 170)
First Way HA9: Wemb 4H 45
Firstway SW20 ....2E 136
Firs Wlk. IG8: Wfd G 5D 20
Firswood Av. KT19: Eps ...5A 148
Firth Gdns. SW6 ....1G 101
Firth Ho. E2 ....3G 69
  (off Barnet Gro.)
Fir Tree Av. UB7: W Dray ..3C 76
Firtree Av. CR4: Mitc 2E 138
Fir Tree Cl. RM1: Rom 3K 39
  W5 ....6E 62
Firtree Cl. KT19: Eps 4B 148
  SW16 ....5G 121
Firtree Gdns. CR0: Croy ...4C 154
Fir Tree Gro. SM5: Cars ...7D 150
Fir Tree Ho. SE14 ....7J 87
  (off Avonley Rd.)
Fir Tree Pl. TW15: Ashf ...5C 112
Fir Tree Rd. TW4: Houn ...4C 96
Fir Trees Cl. SE16 ....1A 88
Fir Tree Wlk. EN1: Enf 3J 7
  RM10: Dag 3J 57
Fir Wlk. SM3: Sutt 6F 149
Fisher Cl. CR0: Croy 1F 153
  UB6: G'frd 3E 60
Fisher Ho. E1 ....7J 69
  (off Cable St.)
  N1 ....1A 68
  (off Barnsbury Est.)
Fisherman Cl. TW10: Rich ..4B 116
Fishermans Dr. SE16 .....2K 87
Fisherman's Pl. W4 ......6B 82
Fishermans Wlk. E14 .....1C 88
  SE28 ....2J 91
Fisher Rd. HA3: Harr 2K 25
Fishers Cl. SW16 ....3H 121
Fishers Ct. SE14 ....1K 105
Fishers Dene KT10: Esh ...7A 146
Fishers La. W4 ....4K 81
Fisher St. E16 ....5J 71
  WC1 ....5K 67 (6G 161)
Fishers Way DA17: Belv ...1J 93
Fisherton St.
  NW8 ....4B 66 (4A 158)

Fishguard Way—Fordham Rd.

Fishguard Way E16 ... 1F 91
(not continuous)
Fishmongers Hall Wharf
EC4 ... 3E 168
Fishponds Rd. BR2: Kes ... 5B 156
SW17 ... 4C 120
Fish St. Hill EC3 ... 7D 68 (3F 169)
Fish Wharf EC3 ... 3F 169
Fiske Ct. IG11: Bark ... 2H 73
N17 ... 1G 33
Fisons Rd. E16 ... 1J 89
Fitzalan Rd. N3 ... 3G 29
Fitzalan St.
SE11 ... 4A 86 (3H 173)
Fitzgeorge Av.
KT3: N Mald ... 1K 135
W14 ... 4G 83
Fitzgerald Av. SW14 ... 3A 100
Fitzgerald Ct. E10 ... 1D 52
(off Leyton Grange Est.)
Fitzgerald Ho. E14 ... 6D 70
(off E. India Dock Rd.)
SW9 ... 2A 104
Fitzgerald Rd. E11 ... 5J 35
KT7: T Ditt ... 6A 134
SW14 ... 3K 99
Fitzhardinge Ho. W1 ... 7G 159
(off Portman Sq.)
Fitzhardinge St.
W1 ... 6E 66 (7G 159)
Fitzhugh Gro. SW18 ... 6B 102
Fitzjames Av. CR0: Croy ... 2G 153
W14 ... 4G 83
Fitzjohn Av. EN5: Barn ... 5B 4
Fitzjohn's Av. NW3 ... 4A 48
Fitzmaurice Ho. SE16 ... 4H 87
(off Rennie Est.)
Fitzmaurice Pl.
W1 ... 1F 85 (4K 165)
Fitzneal St. W12 ... 6B 64
FITZROVIA ... 5F 67 (5K 159)
Fitzroy Cl. N6 ... 1D 48
Fitzroy Ct. CR0: Croy ... 7D 140
N6 ... 6G 31
W1 ... 4B 160
Fitzroy Cres. W4 ... 7K 81
Fitzroy Gdns. SE19 ... 7E 122
Fitzroy Ho. E14 ... 5B 70
(off Wallwood St.)
SE1 ... 5F 87
(off Coopers La.)
Fitzroy M. W1 ... 4A 160
Fitzroy Pk. N6 ... 1D 48
Fitzroy Rd. NW1 ... 1E 66
Fitzroy Sq. W1 ... 4G 67 (4A 160)
Fitzroy St. W1 ... 4G 67 (4A 160)
(not continuous)
Fitzroy Yd. NW1 ... 1E 66
Fitzsimmons Ct. NW10 ... 1K 63
Fitzstephen Rd. RM8: Dag ... 5B 56
Fitzwarren Gdns. N19 ... 1G 49
Fitzwilliam Av. TW9: Rich ... 2F 99
Fitzwilliam Hgts. SE23 ... 2J 123
Fitzwilliam Ho. TW9: Rich ... 4D 98
Fitzwilliam M. E16 ... 1J 89
Fitzwilliam Rd. SW4 ... 3G 103
Fitzwygram Cl.
TW12: Hamp ... 5G 115
Five Acre NW9 ... 2B 28
Fiveacre Cl. CR7: Thor H ... 6A 140
Five Bell All. E14 ... 6B 70
(off Three Colt St.)
Five Elms Rd.
BR2: Short ... 3K 155
RM9: Dag ... 3F 57
Fives Ct. SE11 ... 3B 86
FIVEWAYS ... 2F 127
Five Ways Bus. Cen.
TW13: Felt ... 3K 113
FIVEWAYS CORNER
WADDON ... 4A 152
HENDON ... 1C 28
Fiveways Rd. SW9 ... 2A 104
Flack Ct. E10 ... 7D 34
Fladbury Rd. N15 ... 6D 32
Fladgate Rd. E11 ... 6G 35
Flag Cl. CR0: Croy ... 1K 153
Flag Wlk. HA5: Pinn ... 6J 23
Flambard Rd. HA1: Harr ... 6A 26
Flamborough Ho. SE15 ... 1G 105
(off Clayton Rd.)
Flamborough Rd.
HA4: Ruis ... 3J 41
Flamborough St. E14 ... 6A 70
Flamborough Wlk. E14 ... 6A 70
(off Flamborough St.)
Flamingo Ct. SE8 ... 7C 88
(off Hamilton St.)
Flamingo Gdns. UB5: N'olt ... 3C 60
Flamstead Gdns.
RM9: Dag ... 7C 56
Flamstead Ho. SW3 ... 5C 170
(off Cale St.)
Flamstead Rd. RM9: Dag ... 7C 56
Flamsted Av. HA9: Wemb ... 6G 45
Flamsteed Rd. SE7 ... 5C 90
Flanchford Rd. W12 ... 3B 82
Flanders Ct. E17 ... 7A 34
Flanders Cres. SW17 ... 7D 120
Flanders Mans. W4 ... 4B 82
Flanders Rd. E6 ... 2D 72
W4 ... 4A 82
Flanders Way E9 ... 6K 51
Flandrian Cl. EN3: Enf ... 1J 9
Flank St. E1 ... 7G 69
Flansham Ho. E14 ... 6B 70
(off Clemence St.)
Flask Wlk. NW3 ... 4A 48
Flatford Ho. SE6 ... 4E 124
Flatiron Yd. SE1 ... 5D 168
(off Union St.)
Flavell M. SE10 ... 5G 89
Flaxen Cl. E4 ... 3J 19
Flaxen Rd. E4 ... 3J 19
Flaxley Rd. SM4: Mord ... 7K 137
Flaxman Ct. DA17: Belv ... 5G 93
(off Hoddesdon Rd.)
W1 ... 1C 166
WC1 ... 2D 160
(off Flaxman Ter.)
Flaxman Ho. W4 ... 5A 82
(off Devonshire St.)
Flaxman Rd. SE5 ... 3B 104
Flaxman Ter.
WC1 ... 3H 67 (2D 160)
Flaxton Rd. SE18 ... 1H 109
Flecker Cl. HA7: Stan ... 5E 10
Flecker Ho. SE5 ... 7D 86
(off Lomond Gro.)
Fleece Dr. N9 ... 4B 18
Fleece Rd. KT6: Surb ... 1C 146
Fleece Wlk. N7 ... 6J 49
Fleeming Cl. E17 ... 2B 34
Fleeming Rd. E17 ... 2B 34
Fleetbank Ho. EC4 ... 1K 167
(off Salisbury Sq.)
Fleet Bldg. EC4 ... 7A 162
Fleet Cl. HA4: Ruis ... 6E 22
KT8: W Mole ... 5D 132
Fleetfield WC1 ... 1F 161
(off Birkenhead St.)
Fleet Ho. E14 ... 7A 70
(off Victory Pl.)
Fleet La. KT8: W Mole ... 6D 132
Fleet Pl. EC4 ... 7A 162
(not continuous)
Fleet Rd. NW3 ... 5C 48
Fleetside KT8: W Mole ... 5D 132
Fleet Sq. WC1 ... 3K 67 (2H 161)
Fleet St. EC4 ... 6A 68 (1J 167)
Fleet St. Hill E1 ... 4G 69
Fleetway WC1 ... 1F 161
(off Birkenhead St.)
Fleetway Bus. Cen. NW2 ... 1B 46
Fleetway W. Bus. Pk.
UB6: G'frd ... 2B 62
Fleetwood Cl. CR0: Croy ... 3F 153
E16 ... 5B 72
KT9: Chess ... 7D 146
Fleetwood Ct. E6 ... 5D 72
(off Evelyn Dennington Rd.)
TW19: Staines ... 6A 94
Fleetwood Rd.
KT1: King T ... 3H 135
NW10 ... 5C 46
Fleetwood Sq.
KT1: King T ... 3H 135
Fleetwood St. N16 ... 2E 50
Fleming N8 ... 3J 31
(off Boyton Cl.)
Fleming Cl. W9 ... 4J 65
Fleming Ct. CR0: Croy ... 5A 152
W2 ... 5A 158
Fleming Dr. N21 ... 5E 6
Fleming Ho. HA9: Wemb ... 3J 45
(off Barnhill Rd.)
N4 ... 1C 50
SE16 ... 2G 87
(off George Row)
Fleming Lodge W2 ... 5J 65
(off Admiral Wlk.)
Fleming Mead CR4: Mitc ... 7C 120
Fleming Rd. SE17 ... 6B 86
UB1: S'hall ... 6F 61
Fleming Wlk. NW9 ... 3A 28
Fleming Way SE28 ... 7D 74
TW7: Isle ... 4K 97
Flemming Av. HA4: Ruis ... 1K 41
Flempton Rd. E10 ... 1A 52
Fletcher Bldgs. WC2 ... 1F 167
(off Martlett Ct.)
Fletcher Cl. E6 ... 6F 73
Fletcher Ho. SE15 ... 7J 87
(off Clifton Way)
Fletcher La. E10 ... 7E 34
Fletcher Path SE8 ... 7C 88
Fletcher Rd. W4 ... 3J 81
Fletchers Cl. BR2: Short ... 4K 143
Fletcher St. E1 ... 7G 69
Fletching Rd. E5 ... 3J 51
SE7 ... 6A 90
Fletton Rd. N11 ... 7D 16
Fleur-de-Lis St.
E1 ... 4F 69 (4H 163)
Fleur Gates SW19 ... 7F 101
Flexmere Gdns. N17 ... 1D 32
Flexmere Rd. N17 ... 1D 32
Flight App. NW9 ... 2B 28
Flimwell Cl. BR1: Brom ... 5G 125
Flinders Ho. E1 ... 1H 87
(off Green Bank)
Flintmill Cres. SE3 ... 2C 108
(not continuous)
Flinton St. SE17 ... 5E 86
Flint St. SE17 ... 4D 86
Flitcroft St. WC2 ... 6H 67 (1D 166)
Flitton Ho. N1 ... 7B 50
(off Sutton Est., The)
Floathaven Cl. SE28 ... 1A 92
Flock Mill Pl. SW18 ... 1K 119
Flockton St. SE16 ... 2G 87
Flodden Rd. SE5 ... 1C 104
Flood La. TW1: Twick ... 1A 116
Flood Pas. SE18 ... 3C 90
Flood St. SW3 ... 5C 84 (6D 170)
Flood Wlk.
SW3 ... 6C 84 (7D 170)
Flora Cl. E14 ... 6D 70
Flora Gdns. RM6: Chad H ... 6C 38
W6 ... 4D 82
(off Albion Gdns.)
Floral Pl. N1 ... 5D 50
Floral St. WC2 ... 7J 67 (2E 166)
Flora St. DA17: Belv ... 5F 93
Florence Av. EN2: Enf ... 3H 7
SM4: Mord ... 5A 138
Florence Cl.
KT12: Walt T ... 7K 131
Florence Ct. E5 ... 3G 51
E11 ... 4K 35
N1 ... 7B 50
(off Florence St.)
SW19 ... 6G 119
W9 ... 3A 66
(off Maida Va.)
Florence Dr. EN2: Enf ... 3H 7
Florence Elson Cl. E12 ... 4E 54
Florence Gdns. W4 ... 6J 81
Florence Ho.
KT2: King T ... 7F 117
(off Florence Rd)
SE16 ... 5H 87
(off Rotherhithe New Rd.)
W11 ... 7F 65
(off St Ann's Rd.)
Florence Mans. NW4 ... 5D 28
(off Vivian Av.)
Florence Nightingale Mus.
... 2K 85 (7G 167)
Florence Rd. BR1: Brom ... 1J 143
BR3: Beck ... 2A 142
CR2: S Croy ... 7D 152
E6 ... 1A 72
E13 ... 2J 71
KT2: King T ... 7F 117
KT12: Walt T ... 7K 131
N4 ... 7K 31
(not continuous)
SE2 ... 4D 92
SE14 ... 1B 106
SW19 ... 6K 119
TW13: Felt ... 1K 113
UB2: S'hall ... 4B 78
W4 ... 3K 81
W5 ... 7E 62
Florence St. E16 ... 4H 71
N1 ... 7B 50
NW4 ... 4E 28
Florence Ter. SE14 ... 1B 106
SW15 ... 3A 118
Florence Way SW12 ... 1D 120
Flores Ho. E1 ... 5K 69
(off Shandy St.)
Florey Lodge W9 ... 5J 65
(off Admiral Wlk.)
Florfield Pas. E8 ... 6H 51
(off Florfield Rd.)
Florfield Rd. E8 ... 6H 51
Florian SE5 ... 1E 104
Florian Av. SM1: Sutt ... 4B 150
Florian Rd. SW15 ... 4G 101
Florida Cl. WD23: Bush ... 2C 10
Florida Ct. BR2: Short ... 4H 143
(off Westmoreland Rd.)
Florida Rd. CR7: Thor H ... 1B 140
Florida St. E2 ... 3G 69
Florin Ct. N18 ... 4K 17
SE1 ... 7J 169
(off Tanner St.)
Floris Pl. SW4 ... 3G 103
Floriston Av. UB10: Uxb ... 7E 40
Floriston Cl. HA7: Stan ... 1B 26
Floriston Ct. UB5: N'olt ... 5F 43
Floriston Gdns. HA7: Stan ... 1B 26
Floss St. SW15 ... 2E 100
Flower & Dean Wlk.
E1 ... 5F 69 (6K 163)
Flower La. NW7 ... 5G 13
Flowerpot Cl. N15 ... 6F 33
Flowers Cl. NW2 ... 3C 46
Flowersmead SW17 ... 2E 120
Flowers M. N19 ... 2G 49
Flower Wlk., The
SW7 ... 2A 84 (6A 164)
Floyd Rd. SE7 ... 5A 90
Fludyer St. SE13 ... 4G 107
Flynn Ct. E14 ... 7C 70
(off Garford St.)
Foley Ho. E1 ... 6J 69
(off Tarling St.)
Foley St. W1 ... 5G 67 (6A 160)
Folgate St. E1 ... 5E 68 (5H 163)
(not continuous)
Foliot Ho. N1 ... 2K 67
(off Priory Grn. Est.)
Foliot St. W3 ... 6B 64
Folkestone Ct. UB5: N'olt ... 5F 43
(off Newmarket Av.)
Folkestone Rd. E6 ... 2E 72
E17 ... 4D 34
N18 ... 4B 18
Folkingham La. NW9 ... 1K 27
Folkington Cnr. N12 ... 5C 14
Folland NW9 ... 2B 28
(off Hundred Acre)
Follett Ho. SW10 ... 7B 84
(off Worlds End Est.)
Follett St. E14 ... 6E 70
Follingham Ct. N1 ... 1H 163
(off Drysdale Pl.)
Folly La. E17 ... 1A 34
(not continuous)
Folly M. W11 ... 6H 65
Folly Wall E14 ... 2E 88
Fonda Ct. E14 ... 7C 70
(off Premiere Pl.)
Fontaine Rd. SW16 ... 7K 121
Fontarabia Rd. SW11 ... 4E 102
Fontayne Av. RM1: Rom ... 2K 39
Fontenelle Gdns. SE5 ... 1E 104
Fontenoy Ho. SE11 ... 4B 86
(off Kennington La.)
Fontenoy Rd. SW12 ... 2F 121
Fonteyne Gdns. IG8:
Wfd G ... 2B 36
Fonthill Cl. SE20 ... 2G 141
Fonthill M. N4 ... 2K 49
Fonthill Rd. N4 ... 1K 49
Font Hills N2 ... 2A 30
Fontley Way SW15 ... 7C 100
Fontmell Cl. TW15: Ashf ... 5C 112
Fontmell Pk. TW15: Ashf ... 5B 112
Fontwell Cl. HA3: Harr ... 7D 10
UB5: N'olt ... 6E 42
Fontwell Dr. BR2: Short ... 5E 144
Football La. HA1: Harr ... 1K 43
Footpath, The SW15 ... 6C 100
FOOTS CRAY ... 6C 128
Foots Cray High St.
DA14: Sidc ... 6C 128
Foots Cray La.
DA14: Sidc ... 1C 128
Footscray Rd. SE9 ... 6E 108
Forber Ho. E2 ... 3J 69
(off Cornwall Av.)
Forbes Cl. NW2 ... 3C 46
Forbes St. E1 ... 6G 69
Forbes Way HA4: Ruis ... 2K 41
Forburg Rd. N16 ... 1G 51
Fordbridge Ct.
TW15: Ashf ... 6A 112
Fordbridge Pk.
TW16: Sun T ... 6H 131
Fordbridge Rd.
TW15: Ashf ... 6A 112
TW16: Sun T ... 6G 131
TW17: Shep ... 6G 131
FORDBRIDGE RDBT. ... 6A 112
Ford Cl. CR7: Thor H ... 5B 140
E3 ... 2A 70
HA1: Harr ... 7H 25
TW15: Ashf ... 6A 112
TW17: Shep ... 4C 130
Forde Av. BR1: Brom ... 3A 144
Fordel Rd. SE6 ... 1E 124
Ford End IG8: Wfd G ... 6E 20
Fordham KT1: King T ... 2G 135
(off Excelsior Cl.)
Fordham Cl. EN4: Barn ... 3H 5
Fordham Rd. EN4: Barn ... 3G 5

Fordham St.—Fox La.

Fordham St. E1 6G **69**
Fordhook Av. W5 1F **81**
Ford Ho. EN5: Barn 5E **4**
Ford Ind. Pk. RM9: Dag 4H **75**
Fordingley Rd. W9 3H **65**
Fordington Ho. SE26 3G **123**
Fordington Rd. N6 5D **30**
Fordmill Rd. SE6 2C **124**
Ford Rd. E3 2B **70**
RM9: Dag 7F **57**
TW15: Ashf 4B **112**
Fords Gro. N21 1H **17**
Fords Pk. Rd. E16 5J **71**
Ford Sq. E1 5H **69**
Ford St. E3 1A **70**
E16 6H **71**
Fordview Ind. Est.
RM13: Rain 3K **75**
Fordwich Cl. BR6: Orp 7K **145**
Fordwych Rd. NW2 4G **47**
Fordyce Rd. SE13 6E **106**
Fordyke Rd. RM8: Dag 2F **57**
Foreign St. SE5 2B **104**
Foreland Ct. NW4 1F **29**
Foreland Ho. *W11 7G **65***
(off Walmer Rd.)
Foreland St. SE18 4H **91**
Foreman Ct. TW1: Twick 1K **115**
Foreshore SE8 4B **88**
Forest App. E4 1B **20**
IG8: Wfd G 7D **20**
Forest Av. E4 1B **20**
IG7: Chig 5K **21**
Forest Bus. Pk. E10 7K **33**
Forest Cl. BR7: Chst 1E **144**
E11 5J **35**
IG8: Wfd G 3E **20**
N10 1F **31**
Forest Ct. E4 1C **20**
E11 4G **35**
N12 5E **14**
Forest Cft. SE23 2H **123**
FORESTDALE 7B **154**
Forestdale N14 4C **16**
Forestdale Cen., The
CR0: Croy 7B **154**
Forest Dene Ct.
SM2: Sutt 6A **150**
Forest Dr. BR2: Kes 4C **156**
E12 3B **54**
IG8: Wfd G 7A **20**
TW16: Sun T 7H **113**
Forest Dr. E. E11 7F **35**
Forest Dr. W. E11 7E **34**
Forest Edge IG9: Buck H 4F **21**
Forester Rd. SE15 3H **105**
Foresters Cl. SM6: Wall 7H **151**
Foresters Cres. DA7: Bex 4H **111**
Foresters Dr. E17 4F **35**
SM6: Wall 7H **151**
Forest Gdns. N17 2F **33**
FOREST GATE 5J **53**
Forest Ga. NW9 4A **28**
Forest Glade E4 4B **20**
E11 6G **35**
Forest Gro. E8 6F **51**
Forest Hgts. IG9: Buck H 2D **20**
FOREST HILL 2J **123**
Forest Hill Bus. Cen.
*SE23 2J **123***
(off Clyde Va.)
Forest Hill Ind. Est.
SE23 2J **123**
Forest Hill Rd. SE22 5H **105**
Forestholme Cl. SE23 2J **123**
Forest Ind. Pk. IG6: Ilf 1J **37**
Forest La. E7 5H **53**
E15 5G **53**
IG7: Chig 5K **21**
Forest Lodge *SE26 3J **123***
(off Dartmouth Rd.)
Forest Mt. Rd. IG8: Wfd G 7A **20**
Forest Point *E7 5K **53***
(off Windsor Rd.)
Fore St. EC2 5C **68** (6D **162**)
HA5: Pinn 3H **23**
N9 4B **18**
N18 6A **18**
Fore St. Av. EC2 5D **68** (6E **162**)
Forest Ridge BR2: Kes 4C **156**
BR3: Beck 3C **142**
Forest Ri. E17 3F **35**
(not continuous)
Forest Rd. E7 4J **53**
E8 6F **51**
E11 7F **35**
E17 4J **33**
IG6: Chig, Ilf 2H **37**
IG8: Wfd G 3D **20**
N9 1C **18**
N17 4J **33**
RM7: Mawney 3H **39**
SM3: Sutt 1J **149**
TW9: Rich 7G **81**
TW13: Felt 2A **114**
Forest Side E4 1C **20**
E7 4K **53**
IG9: Buck H 1F **21**
KT4: Wor Pk 1B **148**
Forest St. E7 5J **53**
Forest Ter. IG7: Chig 5K **21**
Forest, The E11 4G **35**
Forest Trad. Est. E17 3K **33**
Forest Vw. E4 1B **20**
E11 7H **35**
Forest Vw. Av. E10 5F **35**
Forest Vw. Rd. E12 4C **54**
E17 1E **34**
Forest Wlk. N10 1F **31**
Forest Way BR5: Orp 5K **145**
DA15: Sidc 7H **109**
IG8: Wfd G 4E **20**
N19 2G **49**
Forest Works Ind. Est.
E17 3K **33**
Forfar Rd. N22 1B **32**
SW11 1E **102**
Forge Cl. BR2: Short 1J **155**
UB3: Hayes 6F **77**
Forge Cotts. W5 1D **80**
Forge Dr. KT10: Esh 7A **146**
Forge La. HA6: Nwood 1G **23**
SM3: Sutt 7G **149**
TW13: Felt 5C **114**
TW16: Sun T 3J **131**
Forge M. CR0: Croy 5C **154**
Forge Pl. NW1 6E **48**
Forges Rd. E12 2B **54**
Forman Pl. N16 4F **51**
Formation, The *E16 2F **91***
(off Woolwich Mnr. Way)
Formby Av. HA7: Stan 3C **26**
Formby Ct. *N7 5A **50***
(off Morgan Rd.)
Formosa Ho. *E1 4A **70***
(off Ernest St.)
Formosa St. W9 4K **65**
Formunt Cl. E16 5H **71**
Forres Gdns. NW11 6J **29**
Forrester Path SE26 4J **123**
Forrest Gdns. SW16 3K **139**
Forris Av. UB3: Hayes 1H **77**
Forset Ct. *W2 7D **158***
(off Edgware Rd.)
Forset St. W1 6C **66** (7D **158**)
Forstal Cl. BR2: Short 3J **143**
Forster Cl. E4 7A **20**
Forster Ho. BR1: Brom 4F **125**
Forster Rd. BR3: Beck 3A **142**
E17 6A **34**
N17 3F **33**
SW12 7J **103**
Forsters Cl. RM6: Chad H 6F **39**
Forsters Way UB4: Hayes 6K **59**
Forston St. N1 2C **68**
Forsyte Cres. SE19 1E **140**
Forsythe Shades Ct.
BR3: Beck 1E **142**
Forsyth Gdns. SE17 6B **86**
Forsyth Ho. *E9 7J **51***
(off Frampton Pk. Rd.)
*SW1 5B **172***
(off Tachbrook St.)
Forsythia Cl. IG1: Ilf 5F **55**
Forsyth Pl. EN1: Enf 5K **7**
Forterie Gdns.
IG3: Bark, Ilf 3A **56**
Fortescue Av. E8 7H **51**
TW2: Twick 3G **115**
Fortescue Rd. HA8: Edg 1K **27**
SW19 7B **120**
Fortess Gro. NW5 5G **49**
Fortess Rd. NW5 5F **49**
Fortess Wlk. NW5 5F **49**
Fortess Yd. NW5 4F **49**
Forthbridge Rd. SW11 4E **102**
Fortis Cl. E16 6A **72**
Fortis Ct. N10 3E **30**
FORTIS GREEN 4D **30**
Fortis Grn. N2 4C **30**
N10 4C **30**
Fortis Grn. Av. N2 3D **30**
Fortis Grn. Rd. N10 3E **30**
Fortismere Av. N10 3E **30**
Fortnam Rd. N19 2H **49**
Fortnum's Acre HA7: Stan 6E **10**
Fort Rd. SE1 4F **87**
UB5: N'olt 7E **42**
Fortrose Gdns. SW2 1J **121**
Fort St. E1 5E **68** (6H **163**)
E16 1K **89**
Fortuna Cl. N7 6K **49**
Fortune Ct. IG11: Bark 2C **74**
Fortunegate Rd. NW10 1A **64**
FORTUNE GREEN 4J **47**
Fortune Grn. Rd. NW6 4J **47**
Fortune Ho. *EC1 4D **162***
(off Fortune St.)
SE11 4J **173**
Fortunes Mead UB5: N'olt 6C **42**
Fortune St. EC1 4C **68** (4D **162**)
Fortune Theatre** 1F **167
(off Russell St.)
Fortune Wlk. *SE28 3H **91***
(off Broadwater Rd.)
Fortune Way NW10 3C **64**
Forty Acre La. E16 5J **71**
Forty Av. HA9: Wemb 3F **45**
Forty Cl. HA9: Wemb 3F **45**
Forty Footpath SW14 3J **99**
Forty Foot Way SE9 7G **109**
FORTY HILL 1K **7**
Forty Hill EN2: Enf 1K **7**
Forty La. HA9: Wemb 2H **45**
Forum Magnum Sq. *SE1 6H **167***
(off York Rd.)
Forumside HA8: Edg 6B **12**
Forum, The KT8: W Mole 4F **133**
Forum Way HA8: Edg 6B **12**
Forval Cl. CR4: Mitc 5D **138**
Forward Bus. Cen., The
E16 4F **71**
Forward Dr. HA3: Harr 4K **25**
Fosbrooke Ho. *SW8 7J **85***
(off Davidson Gdns.)
Fosbury M. W2 7K **65**
Foscote Ct. *W9 4J **65***
(off Foscote M.)
Foscote M. W9 4J **65**
Foscote Rd. NW4 6D **28**
Foskett Ho. N2 2B **30**
Foskett Rd. SW6 2H **101**
Foss Av. CR0: Croy 5A **152**
Fossdene Rd. SE7 5K **89**
Fossdyke Cl. UB4: Hayes 5C **60**
Fosset Lodge DA7: Bex 1J **111**
Fosse Way W13 5A **62**
Fossil Rd. SE13 3C **106**
Fossington Rd.
DA17: Belv 4D **92**
Foss Rd. SW17 4B **120**
Fossway RM8: Dag 2C **56**
Foster Ct. *E16 7H **71***
(off Tarling Rd.)
*NW1 7G **49***
(off Royal College St.)
NW4 4E **28**
Foster Ho. SE14 1B **106**
Foster La. EC2 6C **68** (7C **162**)
Foster Rd. E13 4J **71**
W3 7A **64**
W4 5K **81**
Fosters Cl. BR7: Chst 5D **126**
E18 1K **35**
Foster St. NW4 4E **28**
Foster's Way SW18 1K **119**
Foster Wlk. NW4 4E **28**
Fothergill Cl. E13 2J **71**
Fothergill Dr. N21 5D **6**
Fotheringham Rd. EN1: Enf 4A **8**
(not continuous)
Foubert's Pl. W1 6G **67** (1A **166**)
Foulden Rd. N16 4F **51**
Foulden Ter. N16 4F **51**
Foulis Ter. SW7 5B **84** (5B **170**)
Foulser Rd. SW17 3D **120**
Foulsham Rd.
CR7: Thor H 3C **140**
Founder Cl. E6 6F **73**
Founders Ct. EC2 7E **162**
Founders Gdns. SE19 7C **122**
Founders Ho. *SW1 6C **172***
(off Aylesford St.)
Foundling Ct. *WC1 3E **160***
(off Brunswick Cen.)
Foundling Mus., The
4J 67 (3F 161)
Foundry Cl. SE16 1A **88**
Foundry Ho. *E14 5D **70***
(off Morris Rd.)
Foundry M. NW1 3B **160**
Foundry Pl. SW18 7K **101**
Fountain Cl. UB8: Uxb 5E **58**
Fountain Ct. DA15: Sidc 6B **110**
EC4 7A **68** (2J **167**)
SE23 2K **123**
*SW1 4J **171***
(off Buckingham Pal. Rd.)
Fountain Dr. SE19 4F **123**
SM5: Cars 7D **150**
Fountain Grn. Sq. SE16 2G **87**
Fountain Ho. NW6 7G **47**
*W1 4G **165***
(off Park St.)
Fountain M. *N5 4C **50***
(off Highbury Grange)
NW3 6D **48**
Fountain Pl. SW9 1A **104**
Fountain Rd.
CR7: Thor H 3C **140**
SW17 5B **120**
Fountain Rdbt.
KT3: N Mald 4A **136**
Fountains Av. TW13: Felt 3D **114**
Fountains Cl. TW13: Felt 2D **114**
(not continuous)
Fountains Cres. N14 7D **6**
Fountain Sq.
SW1 4F **85** (3K **171**)
Fountains, The *N3 7E **14***
(off Ballards La.)
Fountayne Bus. Cen. N15 4G **33**
Fountayne Rd. N15 4G **33**
N16 2G **51**
Fount St. SW8 7H **85**
Fouracres EN3: Enf 1F **9**
*NW1 2A **160***
(off Stanhope St.)
Fourland Wlk. HA8: Edg 6D **12**
Fournier St. E1 5F **69** (5J **163**)
Four Seasons Cl. E3 2C **70**
Four Seasons Cres.
SM3: Sutt 2H **149**
Four Sq. Ct. TW4: Houn 6E **96**
Fourth Av. E12 4D **54**
RM7: Rush G 1K **57**
UB3: Hayes 1H **77**
W10 4G **65**
Fourth Cross Rd.
TW2: Twick 2H **115**
Fourth Way HA9: Wemb 4H **45**
Four Wents, The E4 2A **20**
Fovant Ct. SW8 2G **103**
Fowey Av. IG4: Ilf 5B **36**
Fowey Cl. E1 1H **87**
Fowey Ho. SE11 5K **173**
Fowler Cl. SW11 3B **102**
Fowler Ho. *N15 5D **32***
(off South Gro.)
Fowler Rd. CR4: Mitc 2E **138**
E7 4J **53**
N1 1B **68**
Fowlers Cl. DA14: Sidc 5E **128**
Fowlers M. *N19 2G **49***
(off Holloway Rd.)
Fowler's Wlk. W5 4D **62**
Fownes St. SW11 3C **102**
Fox & Knot St. EC1 5B **162**
Foxberry Rd. SE4 3A **106**
Foxborough Gdns. SE4 5C **106**
Foxbourne Rd. SW17 2E **120**
Foxbury Av. BR7: Chst 6H **127**
Foxbury Cl. BR1: Brom 6K **125**
Foxbury Rd. BR1: Brom 6J **125**
Fox Cl. E1 4J **69**
E16 5J **71**
Foxcombe CR0: Croy 6D **154**
(not continuous)
Foxcombe Cl. E6 2B **72**
Foxcombe Rd. SW15 1C **118**
Foxcote SE5 5E **86**
Foxcroft *WC1 1H **161***
(off Penton Ri.)
Foxcroft Rd. SE18 1F **109**
Foxearth Spur
CR2: S Croy 7J **153**
Foxes Dale BR2: Short 3F **143**
SE3 3J **107**
Foxfield *NW1 1F **67***
(off Arlington Rd.)
Foxglove Cl. UB1: S'hall 7C **60**
Foxglove Ct. HA0: Wemb 2E **62**
Foxglove Gdns. E11 4A **36**
Foxglove La. KT9: Chess 4G **147**
Foxglove Rd.
RM7: Rush G 2K **57**
Foxglove St. W12 7B **64**
Foxglove Way
SM6: Wall 1F **151**
Fox Gro. KT12: Walt T 7K **131**
Foxgrove N14 3D **16**
Foxgrove Av. BR3: Beck 7D **124**
Foxgrove Rd. BR3: Beck 7D **124**
Foxham Rd. N19 3H **49**
Fox Hill BR2: Kes 5A **156**
SE19 7F **123**
Fox Hill Gdns. SE19 7F **123**
Foxhole Rd. SE9 5C **108**
Fox Hollow Cl. SE18 5J **91**
Fox Hollow Dr. DA7: Bex 3D **110**
Foxholt Gdns. NW10 7J **45**
Foxhome Cl. BR7: Chst 6E **126**
Fox Ho. Rd. DA17: Belv 5H **93**
(not continuous)
Foxlands Cres. RM10: Dag 5J **57**
Foxlands La. RM10: Dag 5K **57**
Foxlands Rd. RM10: Dag 5J **57**
Fox La. BR2: Kes 5K **155**
N13 2E **16**
W5 4E **62**

Foxleas Ct.—Frobisher Pas.

Foxleas Ct. BR1: Brom ... 7G 125
Foxlees HA0: Wemb ... 4A 44
Foxley Cl. E8 ... 5G 51
Foxley Ct. SM2: Sutt ... 7A 150
Foxley Rd.
CR7: Thor H ... 4B 140
SW9 ... 7A 86
Foxley Sq. SW9 ... 1B 104
Foxmead Cl. EN2: Enf ... 3E 6
Foxmore St. SW11 ... 1D 102
Fox Rd. E16 ... 5H 71
Fox's Path CR4: Mitc ... 2C 138
Foxton Gro. CR4: Mitc ... 2B 138
Foxton Ho. *E16 ... 2E 90*
(off Albert Rd.)
Foxwarren KT10: Esh ... 7A 146
Foxwell M. SE4 ... 3A 106
Foxwell St. SE4 ... 3A 106
Foxwood Cl. NW7 ... 4F 13
TW13: Felt ... 3K 113
Foxwood Grn. Cl. EN1: Enf ... 6K 7
Foxwood Rd. SE3 ... 4H 107
Foyle Rd. N17 ... 1G 33
SE3 ... 6H 89
Framfield Cl. N12 ... 3D 14
Framfield Ct. *EN1: Enf ... 6K 7*
(off Queen Annes Gdns.)
Framfield Rd. CR4: Mitc ... 7E 120
N5 ... 5B 50
W7 ... 6J 61
Framlingham Cl. E5 ... 2J 51
Framlingham Cres. SE9 ... 4C 126
Frampton *NW1 ... 7H 49*
(off Wrotham Rd.)
Frampton Cl. SM2: Sutt ... 7J 149
Frampton Ct. *W3 ... 2J 81*
(off Avenue Rd.)
Frampton Ho. *NW8 ... 4B 158*
(off Frampton St.)
Frampton Pk. Est. E9 ... 7J 51
Frampton Pk. Rd. E9 ... 6J 51
Frampton Rd. TW4: Houn ... 5C 96
Frampton St.
NW8 ... 4B 66 (4B 158)
Francemary Rd. SE4 ... 5C 106
Frances Ct. E17 ... 6C 34
Frances Rd. E4 ... 6H 19
Frances St. SE18 ... 3D 90
Franche Ct. Rd. SW17 ... 3A 120
Francis Av. DA7: Bex ... 2G 111
IG1: Ilf ... 2H 55
TW13: Felt ... 3J 113
Francis Barber Cl.
SW16 ... 5K 121
Franciscan Rd. SW17 ... 5D 120
Francis Chichester Way
SW11 ... 1E 102
Francis Cl. E14 ... 4F 89
KT19: Eps ... 4K 147
TW17: Shep ... 4C 130
Francis Ct. EC1 ... 5A 162
KT5: Surb ... 4E 134
(off Cranes Pk. Av.)
NW7 ... 5G 13
(off Watford Way)
SE14 ... 6K 87
(off Myers La.)
Francis Gro. SW19 ... 6H 119
(not continuous)
Francis Ho. E17 ... 6B 34
N1 ... 1E 68
(off Colville Est.)
Francis M. SE12 ... 7J 107
Francis Rd. CR0: Croy ... 7B 140
E10 ... 1E 52
HA1: Harr ... 5A 26
HA5: Pinn ... 5A 24
IG1: Ilf ... 2H 55
N2 ... 4D 30
SM6: Wall ... 6G 151
TW4: Houn ... 2B 96
UB6: G'frd ... 2B 62
Francis St. E15 ... 5G 53
IG1: Ilf ... 2H 55
SW1 ... 4G 85 (3A 172)
Francis Ter. N19 ... 3G 49
Francis Wlk. N1 ... 1K 67
Francklyn Gdns. HA8: Edg ... 3B 12
Franconia Rd. SW4 ... 5H 103
Frank Bailey Wlk. E12 ... 5E 54
Frank Beswick Ho. *SW6 ... 6H 83*
(off Clem Attlee Ct.)
Frank Burton Cl. SE7 ... 5K 89
Frank Dixon Cl. SE21 ... 7E 104
Frank Dixon Way SE21 ... 1E 122
Frankfurt Rd. SE24 ... 5C 104
Frank Godley Ct.
DA14: Sidc ... 5B 128
Frankham Ho. *SE8 ... 7C 88*
(off Frankham St.)
Frankham St. SE8 ... 7C 88
Frank Ho. *SW8 ... 7J 85*
(off Wyvil Rd.)
Frankland Cl. IG8: Wfd G ... 5F 21
SE16 ... 3H 87
Frankland Rd. E4 ... 5H 19
SW7 ... 3B 84 (2A 170)
Franklin Bldg. E14 ... 2C 88
Franklin Cl. KT1: King T ... 3G 135
N20 ... 7F 5
SE13 ... 1D 106
SE27 ... 3B 122
Franklin Cotts. HA7: Stan ... 4G 11
Franklin Cres. CR4: Mitc ... 4G 139
Franklin Ho. BR2: Short ... 3G 143
E1 ... 1H 87
(off Watts St.)
Franklin Ind. Est. *SE20 ... 1J 141*
(off Franklin Rd.)
Franklin Pas. SE9 ... 3C 108
Franklin Pl. SE10 ... 1D 106
Franklin Rd. DA7: Bex ... 1E 110
SE20 ... 7J 123
Franklins M. HA2: Harr ... 2G 43
Franklin Sq. W14 ... 5H 83
Franklin's Row
SW3 ... 5D 84 (5F 171)
Franklin St. E3 ... 3D 70
N15 ... 6E 32
Franklin Way CR0: Croy ... 7J 139
Franklyn Rd.
KT12: Walt T ... 6J 131
NW10 ... 6B 46
Franks Av. KT3: N Mald ... 4J 135
Frank Soskice Ho. *SW6 ... 6H 83*
(off Clem Attlee Ct.)
Frank St. E13 ... 4J 71
Franks Wood Av.
BR5: Orp ... 5F 145
Frankswood Av.
UB7: W Dray ... 6B 58
Frank Towell Ct.
TW14: Felt ... 7J 95
Frank Welsh Ct. HA5: Pinn ... 4A 24
Frank Whymark Ho. *SE16 ... 2J 87*
(off Rupack St.)
Franlaw Cres. N13 ... 4H 17
Fransfield Gro. SE26 ... 3H 123
Frans Hals Ct. E14 ... 3F 89
Frant Cl. SE20 ... 7J 123
Franthorne Way SE6 ... 2D 124
Frant Rd. CR7: Thor H ... 5B 140
Fraser Cl. DA5: Bexl ... 1J 129
E6 ... 6C 72
Fraser Ct. *E14 ... 5E 88*
(off Ferry St.)
Fraser Ho. TW8: Bford ... 5F 81
Fraser Rd. DA8: Erith ... 5K 93
E17 ... 5D 34
N9 ... 3C 18
UB6: G'frd ... 1B 62
Fraser St. W4 ... 5A 82
Frating Cres. IG8: Wfd G ... 6E 20
Frazer Av. HA4: Ruis ... 5A 42
Frazier St. SE1 ... 2A 86 (7J 167)
Frean St. SE16 ... 3G 87
Frearson Ho. *WC1 ... 1H 161*
(off Penton Ri.)
Freda Corbett Cl. SE15 ... 7G 87
Frederica Rd. E4 ... 1A 20
Frederica St. N7 ... 7K 49
Frederick Charrington Ho.
E1 ... 4J 69
(off Wickford St.)
Frederick Cl. SM1: Sutt ... 4H 149
W2 ... 7D 66 (2D 164)
Frederick Ct. *SW3 ... 4F 171*
(off Duke of York Sq.)
Frederick Cres. EN3: Enf ... 2D 8
SW9 ... 7B 86
Frederick Gdns. CR0: Croy ... 6B 140
SM1: Sutt ... 5H 149
Frederick Pl. SE18 ... 5F 91
Frederick Rd. RM13: Rain ... 2K 75
SE17 ... 6B 86
SM1: Sutt ... 5H 149
Fredericks Pl.
EC2 ... 6D 68 (1E 168)
N12 ... 4F 15
Frederick Sq. *SE16 ... 7A 70*
(off Sovereign Cres.)
Frederick's Row
EC1 ... 3B 68 (1A 162)
Frederick St.
WC1 ... 3K 67 (2G 161)
Frederick Ter. E8 ... 7F 51
Frederic M. SW1 ... 7F 165
Frederic St. E17 ... 5A 34
Fredora Av. UB4: Hayes ... 4H 59
Fred Styles Ho. SE7 ... 6A 90
Fred White Wlk. N7 ... 6J 49
Freedom Cl. E17 ... 4K 33
Freedom Rd. N17 ... 2D 32
Freedom St. SW11 ... 2D 102
Freegrove Rd. N7 ... 5J 49
(not continuous)
Freehold Ind. Est.
TW4: Houn ... 5A 96
Freeland Ct. DA15: Sidc ... 3A 128
Freeland Pk. NW4 ... 2G 29
Freeland Rd. W5 ... 7F 63
Freelands Av.
CR2: S Croy ... 7K 153
Freelands Gro.
BR1: Brom ... 1K 143
Freelands Rd.
BR1: Brom ... 1K 143
Freeling Ho. *NW8 ... 1B 66*
(off Dorman Way)
Freeling St. N1 ... 7K 49
(Carnoustie Dr.)
N1 ... 7J 49
(Pembroke St.)
Freeman Cl. TW17: Shep ... 4G 131
UB5: N'olt ... 7C 42
Freeman Dr.
KT8: W Mole ... 4D 132
Freeman Rd. SM4: Mord ... 5B 138
Freemans La. UB3: Hayes ... 7G 59
Freemantle Av. EN3: Enf ... 5E 8
Freemantle St. SE17 ... 5E 86
Freemasons Rd.
CR0: Croy ... 1E 152
E16 ... 5K 71
Freethorpe Cl. SE19 ... 7D 122
Free Trade Wharf E1 ... 7K 69
Freezeland Way
UB10: Uxb ... 6D 40
Freke Rd. SW11 ... 3E 102
Fremantle Ho. *E1 ... 4H 69*
(off Somerford St.)
Fremantle Rd. DA17: Belv ... 4G 93
IG6: Ilf ... 2F 37
Fremont St. E9 ... 1H 69
(not continuous)
French Ordinary Ct. EC3 ... 2H 169
French Pl. E1 ... 3E 68 (2H 163)
French St. TW16: Sun T ... 2A 132
Frendsbury Rd. SE4 ... 4A 106
Frensham Cl. UB1: S'hall ... 4D 60
Frensham Dr. CR0: Croy ... 7E 154
SW15 ... 3B 118
(not continuous)
Frensham Rd. SE9 ... 2H 127
Frensham St. SE15 ... 6G 87
Frere St. SW11 ... 2C 102
Fresham Ho.
BR2: Short ... 3H 143
(off Durham Rd.)
Freshfield Av. E8 ... 7F 51
Freshfield Cl. SE13 ... 4F 107
Freshfield Dr. N14 ... 7A 6
Freshfields CR0: Croy ... 1B 154
Freshford St. SW17 ... 3A 120
Freshwater Cl. SW17 ... 6E 120
Freshwater Ct. UB1: S'hall ... 3E 60
W1 ... 6D 158
(off Crawford St.)
Freshwater Rd. RM8: Dag ... 1D 56
SW17 ... 6E 120
Freshwell Av.
RM6: Chad H ... 4B 38
Fresh Wharf Rd.
IG11: Bark ... 1F 73
Freshwood Cl. BR3: Beck ... 1D 142
Freshwood Way
SM6: Wall ... 7F 151
Freston Gdns. EN4: Barn ... 5K 5
Freston Pk. N3 ... 2H 29
Freston Rd. W10 ... 7F 65
Freswick Ho. *SE8 ... 4K 87*
(off Chilton Gro.)
Freta Rd. DA6: Bex ... 5F 111
Freud Mus., The ... 6A 48
Frewell Ho. *EC1 ... 5J 161*
(off Bourne Est.)
Frewing Cl. BR7: Chst ... 6D 126
Frewin Rd. SW18 ... 1B 120
Friar M. SE27 ... 3B 122
Friar Rd. BR5: Orp ... 5K 145
UB4: Hayes ... 4B 60
Friars Av. N20 ... 3H 15
SW15 ... 3B 118
Friars Cl. E4 ... 3K 19
SE1 ... 5B 168
UB5: N'olt ... 3B 60
Friars Ct. E17 ... 1B 34
Friars Gdns. W3 ... 6K 63
Friars Ga. Cl. IG8: Wfd G ... 4D 20
Friars La. TW9: Rich ... 5D 98
Friars Mead E14 ... 3E 88
Friars M. SE9 ... 5E 108
Friars Pl. La. W3 ... 7K 63
Friars Rd. E6 ... 1B 72
Friars Stile Pl.
TW10: Rich ... 6E 98
Friars Stile Rd.
TW10: Rich ... 6E 98
Friar St. EC4 ... 6B 68 (1B 168)
Friars Wlk. N14 ... 7A 6
SE2 ... 5D 92
Friars Way W3 ... 6K 63
Friarswood CR0: Croy ... 7A 154
Friary Cl. N12 ... 5H 15
Friary Ct. SW1 ... 5B 166
Friary Est. SE15 ... 6G 87
(not continuous)
Friary La. IG8: Wfd G ... 4D 20
Friary Pk. Ct. W3 ... 6J 63
Friary Rd. N12 ... 4G 15
SE15 ... 7G 87
W3 ... 6J 63
Friary Way N12 ... 4H 15
FRIDAY HILL ... 2B 20
Friday Hill E4 ... 2B 20
Friday Hill E. E4 ... 3B 20
(not continuous)
Friday Hill W. E4 ... 2B 20
Friday Rd. CR4: Mitc ... 7D 120
DA8: Erith ... 5K 93
Friday St. EC4 ... 7C 68 (2C 168)
Frideswide Pl. NW5 ... 5G 49
Friendly Pl. SE13 ... 1D 106
Friendly St. SE8 ... 2C 106
Friendly St. M. SE8 ... 2C 106
Friendship Ho. *SE1 ... 7B 168*
(off Belvedere Pl.)
Friendship Wlk. UB5: N'olt ... 3B 60
Friends Rd. CR0: Croy ... 3D 152
Friend St. EC1 ... 3B 68 (1A 162)
FRIERN BARNET ... 5J 15
Friern Barnet La. N20 ... 2G 15
Friern Barnet Rd. N11 ... 5J 15
Friern Bri. Retail Pk. N11 ... 6A 16
Friern Ct. N20 ... 3G 15
Friern Mt. Dr. N20 ... 7F 5
Friern Pk. N12 ... 5F 15
Friern Rd. SE22 ... 7G 105
Friern Watch Av. N12 ... 4F 15
Frigate Ho. *E14 ... 4E 88*
(off Stebondale St.)
Frigate M. SE8 ... 6C 88
Frimley Av. SM6: Wall ... 5J 151
Frimley Cl. CR0: Croy ... 7E 154
SW19 ... 2G 119
Frimley Ct. DA14: Sidc ... 5C 128
Frimley Cres. CR0: Croy ... 7E 154
Frimley Gdns. CR4: Mitc ... 3C 138
Frimley Rd. IG3: Ilf ... 3J 55
KT9: Chess ... 5D 146
Frimley St. *E1 ... 4K 69*
(off Frimley Way)
Frimley Way E1 ... 4K 69
Fringewood Cl.
HA6: Nwood ... 1D 22
Frinstead Ho. *W10 ... 7F 65*
(off Freston Rd.)
Frinsted Rd. DA8: Erith ... 7K 93
Frinton Ct. *W13 ... 5B 62*
(off Hardwick Grn.)
Frinton Dr. IG8: Wfd G ... 7A 20
Frinton M. IG2: Ilf ... 6E 36
Frinton Rd. DA14: Sidc ... 2E 128
E6 ... 3B 72
N15 ... 6E 32
SW17 ... 6E 120
Friston St. SW6 ... 2K 101
Friswell Pl. DA6: Bex ... 4G 111
Fritham Cl. KT3: N Mald ... 6A 136
Frith Ct. NW7 ... 7B 14
Frith Ho. *NW8 ... 4B 158*
(off Frampton St.)
Frith La. NW7 ... 7B 14
Frith Rd. CR0: Croy ... 2C 152
E11 ... 4E 52
Frith St. W1 ... 6H 67 (1C 166)
Frithville Ct. *W12 ... 1E 82*
(off Frithville Gdns.)
Frithville Gdns. W12 ... 1E 82
Frizlands La.
RM10: Dag ... 2H 57
Frobisher Cl. HA5: Pinn ... 7B 24
Frobisher Ct. NW9 ... 2A 28
SE10 ... 6F 89
(off Old Woolwich Rd.)
SE23 ... 2H 123
SM3: Sutt ... 7G 149
W12 ... 2E 82
(off Lime Gro.)
Frobisher Cres. *EC2 ... 5D 162*
(off Beech St.)
TW19: Staines ... 7A 94
Frobisher Gdns. E10 ... 7D 34
TW19: Staines ... 7A 94
Frobisher Ho. *E1 ... 1H 87*
(off Watts St.)
SW1 ... 7C 172
(off Dolphin Sq.)
Frobisher M. EN2: Enf ... 4J 7
Frobisher Pas. E14 ... 1C 88

Frobisher Pl. Pioneer Cen.—Galway Cl.

Frobisher Pl. Pioneer Cen.
SE15 ... 1J 105
Frobisher Rd. E6 ... 6D 72
N8 ... 4A 32
Frobisher St. SE10 ... 6G 89
Frog La. RM13: Rain ... 6K 75
Frogley Rd. SE22 ... 4F 105
Frogmore SW18 ... 5J 101
Frogmore Av.
UB4: Hayes ... 4G 59
Frogmore Cl. SM3: Sutt ... 3F 149
Frogmore Ct. UB2: S'hall ... 4D 78
Frogmore Gdns.
SM3: Sutt ... 4G 149
UB4: Hayes ... 4G 59
Frogmore Ind. Est. N5 ... 5C 50
NW10 ... 3J 63
UB3: Hayes ... 2G 77
Frognal NW3 ... 4A 48
Frognal Av. DA14: Sidc ... 5A 128
HA1: Harr ... 4K 25
Frognal Cl. NW3 ... 5A 48
FROGNAL CORNER ... 6K 127
Frognal Ct. NW3 ... 6A 48
Frognal Gdns. NW3 ... 4A 48
Frognal La. NW3 ... 5K 47
Frognal Pde. NW3 ... 6A 48
Frognal Pl. DA14: Sidc ... 6A 128
Frognal Ri. NW3 ... 3A 48
Frognal Way NW3 ... 4A 48
Froissart Rd. SE9 ... 5B 108
Frome Ho. SE15 ... 4H 105
Frome Rd. N15 ... 3B 32
Frome St. N1 ... 2C 68
Fromondes Rd.
SM3: Sutt ... 5G 149
Frontenac NW10 ... 7D 46
Frostic Wlk. E1 ... 5G 69 (6K 163)
Froude St. SW8 ... 2F 103
Fruen Rd. TW14: Felt ... 7H 95
Fruiterers Pas. *EC4* ... *3D 168*
(off Queen St. Pl.)
Fryatt Rd. N17 ... 7J 17
(not continuous)
Fryent Cl. NW9 ... 6G 27
Fryent Country Pk. ... *7G 27*
Fryent Cres. NW9 ... 6A 28
Fryent Flds. NW9 ... 6A 28
Fryent Gro. NW9 ... 6A 28
Fryent Way NW9 ... 5G 27
Fry Ho. E7 ... 7A 54
Frying Pan All. E1 ... 6J 163
Fry Rd. E6 ... 7B 54
NW10 ... 1B 64
TW15: Ashf ... 4A 112
Fryston Av. CR0: Croy ... 2G 153
Fuchsia Cl. RM7: Rush G ... 2K 57
Fuchsia St. SE2 ... 5B 92
Fulbeck Dr. NW9 ... 1A 28
Fulbeck Ho. *N7* ... *6K 49*
(off Sutterton St.)
Fulbeck Rd. N19 ... 4G 49
Fulbeck Wlk. HA8: Edg ... 2C 12
Fulbeck Way HA2: Harr ... 2G 25
Fulbourn *KT1: King T* ... *2G 135*
(off Eureka Rd.)
Fulbourne Rd. E17 ... 1E 34
Fulbourne St. E1 ... 5H 69
Fulbrook M. N19 ... 4G 49
Fulcher Ho. *N1* ... *1E 68*
(off Colville Est.)
SE8 ... 5B 88
Fulford Ho. KT19: Eps ... 7K 147
Fulford Rd. KT19: Eps ... 7K 147
Fulford St. SE16 ... 2H 87
FULHAM ... 2G 101
FULHAM BROADWAY ... 7J 83
Fulham B'way. SW6 ... 7J 83
Fulham Cl. UB10: Uxb ... 4E 58
Fulham Ct. SW6 ... 1J 101
Fulham F.C. Ground
(Craven Cottage) ... *1F 101*
Fulham F.C. (Loftus Road)
... *1D 82*
Fulham High St. SW6 ... 2G 101
Fulham Palace ... *2G 101*
Fulham Pal. Rd. SW6 ... 6F 83
W6 ... 5E 82
Fulham Pk. Gdns. SW6 ... 2H 101
Fulham Pk. Rd. SW6 ... 2H 101
Fulham Rd. SW3 ... 7K 83 (6A 170)
SW6 ... 2G 101
(not continuous)
SW10 ... 7K 83 (7A 170)
Fullbrooks Av.
KT4: Wor Pk ... 1B 148
Fuller Cl. E2 ... 3K 163
Fuller Rd. RM8: Dag ... 3B 56
Fullers Av. IG8: Wfd G ... 7C 20
KT6: Surb ... 2F 147
Fullers Cl. RM5: Col R ... 1J 39
Fuller's Griffin Brewery &
Vis. Cen. ... *6B 82*
Fullers La. RM5: Col R ... 1J 39
Fullers Rd. E18 ... 7C 20
Fuller St. NW4 ... 4E 28
Fullers Way Nth.
KT6: Surb ... 3F 147
Fullers Way Sth.
KT9: Chess ... 4E 146
Fuller's Wood CR0: Croy ... 5C 154
Fullerton Ct.
TW11: Tedd ... 6A 116
Fullerton Rd. CR0: Croy ... 7F 141
SM5: Cars ... 7C 150
SW18 ... 5K 101
Fuller Way UB3: Hayes ... 5H 77
Fullwell Av. IG5: Ilf ... 1D 36
IG6: Ilf ... 1F 37
FULLWELL CROSS ... 1G 37
Fullwell Cross IG6: Ilf ... 2H 37
Fullwell Pde. IG5: Ilf ... 1E 36
Fullwood's M.
N1 ... 3D 68 (1F 163)
Fulmar Ct. KT5: Surb ... 6F 135
Fulmar Ho. *SE16* ... *4K 87*
(off Tawny Way)
Fulmead St. SW6 ... 1K 101
Fulmer Cl. TW12: Hamp ... 5C 114
Fulmer Ho. *NW8* ... *4D 158*
(off Mallory St.)
Fulmer Rd. E16 ... 5B 72
Fulmer Way W13 ... 3B 80
Fulneck *E1* ... *5J 69*
(off Mile End Rd.)
Fulready Rd. E10 ... 5F 35
Fulstone Cl. TW4: Houn ... 4D 96
Fulthorp Rd. SE3 ... 2H 107
Fulton M. *W2* ... *7A 66*
(off Porchester Ter.)
Fulton Rd. HA9: Wemb ... 3G 45
FULWELL ... 4H 115
Fulwell Ct. *UB1: S'hall* ... *7G 61*
(off Baird Av.)
Fulwell Pk. Av.
TW2: Twick ... 2F 115
Fulwell Rd. TW11: Tedd ... 4H 115
Fulwood Av. HA0: Wemb ... 2F 63
Fulwood Cl. UB3: Hayes ... 6H 59
Fulwood Ct. HA3: Harr ... 6A 26
Fulwood Gdns.
TW1: Twick ... 6K 97
Fulwood Pl.
WC1 ... 5K 67 (6H 161)
Fulwood Wlk. SW19 ... 1G 119
Furber St. W6 ... 3D 82
Furham Fld. HA5: Pinn ... 7A 10
Furley Ho. *SE15* ... *7G 87*
(off Peckham Pk. Rd.)
Furley Rd. SE15 ... 7G 87
Furlong Cl. SM6: Wall ... 1F 151
Furlong Path *UB5: N'olt* ... *6C 42*
(off Cowings Mead)
Furlong Rd. N7 ... 6A 50
Furmage St. SW18 ... 7K 101
Furneaux Av. SE27 ... 5B 122
Furness Ho. *SW1* ... *5J 171*
(off Abbots Mnr.)
Furness Rd. HA2: Harr ... 7F 25
NW10 ... 2C 64
SM4: Mord ... 6K 137
SW6 ... 2K 101
Furnival Mans. *W1* ... *6A 160*
(off Wells St.)
Furnival St.
EC4 ... 6A 68 (7J 161)
Furrow La. E9 ... 5J 51
Fursby Av. N3 ... 6D 14
Fursecroft W1 ... 7E 158
Further Acre NW9 ... 2B 28
Furtherfield Cl.
CR0: Croy ... 6A 140
Further Grn. Rd. SE6 ... 7G 107
FURZEDOWN ... 5F 121
Furzedown Dr. SW17 ... 5F 121
Furzedown Rd. SW17 ... 5F 121
Furze Farm Cl.
RM6: Chad H ... 2E 38
Furzefield Cl. BR7: Chst ... 6F 127
Furzefield Rd. SE3 ... 6K 89
Furzeground Way
UB11: Uxb ... 1E 76
Furzeham Rd.
UB7: W Dray ... 2A 76
Furze Rd. CR7: Thor H ... 3C 140
Furze St. E3 ... 5C 70
Furzewood TW16: Sun T ... 1J 131
Fye Foot La. *EC4* ... *2C 168*
(off Queen Victoria St., not continuous)
Fyfe Way BR1: Brom ... 2J 143
Fyfield *N4* ... *2A 50*
(off Six Acres Est.)
Fyfield Cl. BR2: Short ... 4F 143
Fyfield Ct. E7 ... 6J 53
Fyfield Ho. *E6* ... *1C 72*
(off Ron Leighton Way)
Fyfield Rd. E17 ... 3F 35
EN1: Enf ... 3K 7
IG8: Wfd G ... 7F 21
SW9 ... 3A 104
Fynes St. SW1 ... 4H 85 (3C 172)

G

Gable Cl. HA5: Pinn ... 1E 24
Gable Ct. SE26 ... 4H 123
Gables Av. TW15: Ashf ... 5B 112
Gables Cl. SE5 ... 1E 104
SE12 ... 1J 125
Gables Lodge EN4: Barn ... 1F 5
Gables, The BR1: Brom ... 7K 125
HA9: Wemb ... 3G 45
IG11: Bark ... 6G 55
N10 ... *3E 30*
(off Fortis Grn.)
Gabriel Cl. TW13: Felt ... 4C 114
Gabriel Ho.
SE11 ... 4K 85 (3G 173)
Gabrielle Cl. HA9: Wemb ... 3F 45
Gabrielle Ct. NW3 ... 6B 48
Gabriel St. SE23 ... 7K 105
Gabriels Wharf
SE1 ... 1A 86 (4J 167)
Gad Cl. E13 ... 3K 71
Gaddesden Av.
HA9: Wemb ... 6F 45
Gaddesden Ho. *EC1* ... *2F 163*
(off Cranwood St.)
Gadebridge Ho. *SW3* ... *5C 170*
(off Cale St.)
Gade Cl. UB3: Hayes ... 1K 77
Gadesden Rd. KT19: Eps ... 6J 147
(not continuous)
Gadsbury Cl. NW9 ... 6B 28
Gadsden Ho. *W10* ... *4G 65*
(off Hazlewood Cres.)
Gadwall Cl. E16 ... 6K 71
Gadwall Way SE28 ... 2H 91
Gage Brown Ho. *W10* ... *6F 65*
(off Bridge Cl.)
Gage Rd. E16 ... 5G 71
Gage St. WC1 ... 5J 67 (5F 161)
Gainford Ho. *E2* ... *3H 69*
(off Ellsworth St.)
Gainford St. N1 ... 1A 68
Gainsboro Gdns.
UB6: G'frd ... 5J 43
Gainsborough Av. *E12* ... *6E 54*
(off Barrington Rd.)
E12 ... 5E 54
(Church Rd.)
Gainsborough Cl.
BR3: Beck ... 7C 124
KT10: Esh ... 7J 133
Gainsborough Ct.
BR2: Short ... 4A 144
N12 ... 5E 14
SE16 ... *5H 87*
(off Stubbs Dr.)
SE21 ... 2E 122
W4 ... *5H 81*
(off Chaseley Dr.)
W12 ... 2E 82
Gainsborough Gdns.
HA8: Edg ... 2F 27
NW3 ... 3B 48
NW11 ... 7H 29
TW7: Isle ... 5H 97
Gainsborough Ho. *E14* ... *7A 70*
(off Victory Pl.)
RM8: Dag ... *4B 56*
(off Earl's Wlk.)
SW1 ... *4D 172*
(off Erasmus St.)
Gainsborough Lodge
HA1: Harr ... *5K 25*
(off Hindes Rd.)
Gainsborough Mans. *W14* ... *6G 83*
(off Queen's Club Gdns.)
Gainsborough M. SE26 ... 3H 123
Gainsborough Rd. E11 ... 7G 35
E15 ... 3G 71
IG8: Wfd G ... 6H 21
KT3: N Mald ... 6K 135
N12 ... 5E 14
Gainsborough Rd. RM8: Dag . 4B 56
TW9: Rich ... 2F 99
UB4: Hayes ... 2E 58
W4 ... 4B 82
Gainsborough Sq.
DA6: Bex ... 3D 110
Gainsborough St. E9 ... 6B 52
Gainsborough Ter.
SM2: Sutt ... *7H 149*
(off Belmont Ri.)
Gainsborough Twr.
UB5: N'olt ... *2B 60*
(off Academy Gdns.)
Gainsfield Ct. E11 ... 3G 53
Gainsford Rd. E17 ... 4B 34
Gainsford St. SE1 ... 2F 87 (6J 169)
Gairloch Ho. *NW1* ... *7H 49*
(off Stratford Vs.)
Gairloch Rd. SE5 ... 2E 104
Gaisford St. NW5 ... 6G 49
Gaitskell Ct. SW11 ... 2C 102
Gaitskell Ho. E6 ... 1B 72
E17 ... 3D 34
SE17 ... *6E 86*
(off Villa St.)
Gaitskell Rd. SE9 ... 1G 127
Galahad Rd. BR1: Brom ... 4J 125
Galata Rd. SW13 ... 7C 82
Galatea Sq. SE15 ... 3H 105
Galaxy Bldg. *E14* ... *4C 88*
(off Crews St.)
Galaxy Ho. *EC2* ... *3F 163*
(off Leonard St.)
Galba Ct. TW8: Bford ... 7D 80
Galbraith St. E14 ... 3E 88
Galdana Av. EN5: Barn ... 3F 5
Galeborough Av.
IG8: Wfd G ... 7A 20
Gale Cl. CR4: Mitc ... 3B 138
TW12: Hamp ... 6C 114
Galena Ho. *SE18* ... *5K 91*
(off Grosmont Rd.)
W6 ... *4D 82*
(off Galena Rd.)
Galena Rd. W6 ... 4D 82
Galen Pl. WC1 ... 5J 67 (6F 161)
Galesbury Rd. SW18 ... 6A 102
Gales Gdns. E2 ... 3H 69
Gale St. E3 ... 5C 70
RM9: Dag ... 5C 56
Gales Way IG8: Wfd G ... 7H 21
Galgate Cl. SW19 ... 1F 119
Gallants Farm Rd.
EN4: Barn ... 7H 5
Galleon Cl. DA8: Erith ... 4K 93
SE16 ... 2K 87
Galleon Ho. *E14* ... *4E 88*
(off Glengarnock Av.)
Galleons Dr. IG11: Bark ... 3A 74
Gallery Ct. *SE1* ... *7E 168*
(off Pilgrimage St.)
SW10 ... *6A 84*
(off Gunter Gro.)
Gallery Gdns. UB5: N'olt ... 2B 60
Gallery Rd. SE21 ... 1D 122
Galleywall Rd. SE16 ... 4H 87
Galleywall Rd. Trad. Est.
SE16 ... *4H 87*
(off Galleywall Rd.)
Galleywood Ho. *W10* ... *5E 64*
(off Sutton Way)
Galliard Cl. N9 ... 6D 8
Galliard Ct. N9 ... 6B 8
Galliard Rd. N9 ... 7B 8
Gallia Rd. N5 ... 5B 50
Gallions Cl. IG11: Bark ... 3A 74
Gallions Entrance E16 ... 1G 91
Gallions Reach Shop. Pk.
E6 ... 5G 73
Gallions Rd. SE7 ... 4K 89
Gallions Rdbt. E16 ... 7F 73
Gallions Vw. Rd. SE28 ... 2J 91
Galliver Pl. E5 ... 4H 51
Gallon Cl. SE7 ... 4A 90
Gallop, The CR2: S Croy ... 7H 153
SM2: Sutt ... 7B 150
Gallosson Rd. SE18 ... 4J 91
Galloway Path CR0: Croy ... 4D 152
Galloway Rd. W12 ... 1C 82
Gallus Cl. N21 ... 6E 6
Gallus Sq. SE3 ... 3K 107
Galpin's Rd. CR7: Thor H ... 5J 139
Galsworthy Av. E14 ... 5A 70
RM6: Chad H ... 7B 38
Galsworthy Cl. NW2 ... 4G 47
SE28 ... 1B 92
Galsworthy Ct. *W3* ... *3H 81*
(off Bollo Bri. Rd.)
Galsworthy Cres. SE3 ... 1A 108
Galsworthy Ho. *W11* ... *6G 65*
(off Elgin Cres.)
Galsworthy Rd.
KT2: King T ... 7H 117
NW2 ... 4G 47
Galsworthy Ter. N16 ... 3E 50
Galton St. W10 ... 3G 65
Galva Cl. EN4: Barn ... 4K 5
Galvani Way CR0: Croy ... 1K 151
Galveston Ho. *E1* ... *4A 70*
(off Harford St.)
Galveston Rd. SW15 ... 5H 101
Galway Cl. *SE16* ... *5H 87*
(off Masters Dr.)

Galway Ho.—Geddes Pl.

Galway Ho. *E1* 5K 69
(off White Horse La.)
EC1 2D 162
Galway St. EC1 3C 68 (2D 162)
Galy NW9 2B 28
Gambetta St. SW8 2F 103
Gambia St. SE1 1B 86 (5B 168)
Gambier Ho. *EC1* 2D 162
(off Mora St.)
Gambole Rd. SW17 4C 120
Games Rd. EN4: Barn 3J 5
Gamlen Rd. SW15 4F 101
Gamuel Cl. E17 6C 34
Gander Grn. Cres.
TW12: Hamp 1E 132
Gander Grn. La.
SM1: Sutt 3H 149
SM3: Sutt 2G 149
Gandhi Cl. E17 6C 34
Gandolfi St. SE15 6E 86
Ganton St. W1 7G 67 (2A 166)
GANTS HILL 6E 36
Gants Hill 6E 36
Gantshill Cres. IG2: Ilf 5E 36
Gants Hill Cross IG2: Ilf 6E 36
Gap Rd. SW19 5J 119
Garage Rd. W3 6G 63
Garbett Ho. *SE17* 6B 86
(off Doddington Gro.)
Garbutt Pl. W1 5E 66 (5H 159)
Garden Av. CR4: Mitc 7F 121
DA7: Bex 3F 111
Garden City HA8: Edg 6B 12
Garden Cl. E4 5H 19
HA4: Ruis 2G 41
SE12 3K 125
SM6: Wall 5J 151
SW15 7E 100
TW12: Hamp 5D 114
TW15: Ashf 6E 112
UB5: N'olt 1C 60
Garden Ct. CR0: Croy 2F 153
HA7: Stan 5H 11
TW9: Rich 1F 99
TW12: Hamp 5D 114
W4 3J 81
WC2 2J 167
Gardener Gro.
TW13: Felt 2D 114
Gardeners Cl. N11 2K 15
Gardeners Rd. CR0: Croy 1B 152
Garden Ho. *N2* 2B 30
(off Grange, The)
Gardenia Rd. EN1: Enf 6K 7
Gardenia Way IG8: Wfd G 6D 20
Garden La. BR1: Brom 6K 125
SW2 1K 121
Garden M. W2 7J 65
Garden Pl. E8 1F 69
Garden Rd. BR1: Brom 7K 125
KT12: Walt T 6K 131
NW8 3A 66 (1A 158)
SE20 1J 141
TW9: Rich 3G 99
Garden Row SE1 3B 86
Gardens, The BR3: Beck 1E 142
HA1: Harr 6G 25
HA5: Pinn 6D 24
N8 4J 31
(not continuous)
SE22 4G 105
TW14: Felt 5F 95
UB10: Uxb 2A 40
Garden St. E1 5K 69
Gardens Way E12 3C 54
Garden Ter. SW1 5H 85 (5C 172)
SW7 7D 164
Garden Vw. E7 4A 54
Garden Wlk. BR3: Beck 1B 142
EC2 3E 68 (2G 163)
Garden Way NW10 6J 45
Gardiner Av. NW2 5E 46
Gardiner Cl. EN3: Enf 6E 8
RM8: Dag 4D 56
Gardiner Ct. CR2: S Croy 6C 152
NW10 1K 63
Gardner Cl. E11 6K 35
Gardner Ho. TW13: Felt 2D 114
UB1: S'hall 7B 60
(off Broadway, The)
Gardner Ind. Est. SE26 5B 124
Gardner Pl. TW14: Felt 6K 95
Gardner Rd. E13 4K 71
Gardners La.
EC4 7C 68 (2C 168)
Gardnor Rd. NW3 4B 48
Gard St. EC1 3B 68 (1B 162)
Garendon Gdns.
SM4: Mord 7K 137
Garendon Rd.
SM4: Mord 7K 137
Garenne Ct. E4 1K 19
Gareth Cl. KT4: Wor Pk 2F 149
Gareth Ct. SW16 3H 121
Gareth Gro. BR1: Brom 4J 125
Garfield *EN1: Enf* 5J 7
(off Private Rd.)
Garfield Ct. *NW6* 7G 47
(off Willesden La.)
Garfield M. SW11 3E 102
Garfield Rd. E4 1A 20
E13 4H 71
EN3: Enf 4D 8
SW11 3E 102
SW19 5A 120
TW1: Twick 1A 116
Garford St. E14 7C 70
Garganey Ct. *NW10* 6K 45
(off Elgar Av.)
Garganey Wlk. SE28 7C 74
Garibaldi St. SE18 4J 91
Garland Ct. *E14* 7C 70
(off Premiere Pl.)
Garland Rd. HA7: Stan 1E 26
SE18 7H 91
Garlands Ct. *CR0: Croy* 4D 152
(off Chatsworth Rd.)
Garlick Hill EC4 7C 68 (2D 168)
Garlies Rd. SE23 3A 124
Garlinge Rd. NW2 6H 47
Garman Cl. N18 5J 17
Garman Rd. N17 7D 18
Garnault M. EC1 2K 161
Garnault Pl. EC1 3A 68 (2K 161)
Garnault Rd. EN1: Enf 1A 8
Garner Cl. RM8: Dag 1D 56
Garner Rd. E17 1E 34
Garner St. E2 2G 69
Garnet Ho. *E1* 1J 87
(off Garnet St.)
Garnet Rd. CR7: Thor H 4C 140
NW10 6A 46
Garnet St. E1 7J 69
Garnett Cl. SE9 3D 108
Garnett Rd. NW3 5D 48
Garnett Way *E17* 1A 34
(off Swansland Gdns.)
Garnet Wlk. E6 5C 72
Garnham Cl. N16 2F 51
Garnham St. N16 2F 51
Garnies Cl. SE15 7F 87
Garrad's Rd. SW16 3H 121
Garrard Cl. BR7: Chst 5F 127
DA7: Bex 3G 111
Garrard Wlk. NW10 6A 46
Garratt Cl. CR0: Croy 4J 151
Garratt Ct. SW18 7K 101
Garratt La. SW17 3A 120
SW18 6K 101
Garratt Rd. HA8: Edg 7B 12
Garratts Rd. WD23: Bush 1B 10
Garratt Ter. SW17 4C 120
Garraway Ct. *SW13* 7E 82
(off Wyatt Dr.)
Garrett Cl. W3 5K 63
Garrett Ho. *W12* 6D 64
(off Du Cane Rd.)
Garrett St.
EC1 4C 68 (3D 162)
Garrick Av. NW11 6G 29
Garrick Cl. SW18 4A 102
TW9: Rich 5D 98
W5 4E 62
Garrick Cres. CR0: Croy 2E 152
Garrick Dr. NW4 2E 28
SE28 3H 91
Garrick Gdns.
KT8: W Mole 3E 132
Garrick Ho. *KT1: King T* 4E 134
(off Surbiton Rd.)
W1 1F 85 (5J 165)
W4 6A 82
Garrick Ind. Est. NW9 5B 28
Garrick Pk. NW4 2F 29
Garrick Rd. NW9 6B 28
TW9: Rich 2G 99
UB6: G'frd 4F 61
Garricks Ho. *KT1: King T* 2D 134
(off Wadbrook St.)
Garrick St. WC2 7J 67 (2E 166)
Garrick Theatre 3E 166
(off Charing Cross Rd.)
Garrick Way NW4 4F 29
Garrick Yd. WC2 2E 166
Garrison Cl. SE18 7E 90
TW4: Houn 5D 96
Garrison La. KT9: Chess 7D 146
Garrowsfield EN5: Barn 6C 4
Garry Way RM1: Rom 1K 39
Garsdale Cl. N11 6K 15
Garsdale Ter. *W14* 5H 83
(off Aisgill Av.)
Garside Cl. SE28 3H 91
TW12: Hamp 6F 115
Garsington M. SE4 3B 106
Garson Ho. *W2* 2A 164
(off Gloucester Ter.)
Garston Ho. *N1* 7B 50
(off Sutton Est., The)
Garter Way SE16 2K 87
Garth Cl. HA4: Ruis 1B 42
KT2: King T 5F 117
Garth Cl. SM4: Mord 7F 137
W4 5K 81
Garth Ct. *HA1: Harr* 6K 25
(off Northwick Pk. Rd.)
W4 5K 81
Garth M. W5 4E 62
Garthorne Rd. SE23 7K 105
Garth Rd. KT2: King T 5F 117
NW2 2H 47
SM4: Mord 6E 136
W4 5K 81
Garth Rd. Ind. Est.
SM4: Mord 1F 149
Garthside TW10: Rich 5E 116
Garth, The HA3: Harr 6F 27
TW12: Hamp 6F 115
Garthway N12 6H 15
Gartmoor Gdns. SW19 1H 119
Gartmore Rd. IG3: Ilf 2K 55
Garton Pl. SW18 6A 102
Gartons Cl. EN3: Enf 4D 8
Gartons Way SW11 3A 102
Garvary Rd. E16 6K 71
Garway Rd. W2 6K 65
Garwood Cl. N17 1H 33
Gascoigne Gdns.
IG8: Wfd G 7B 20
Gascoigne Pl. E2 3F 69 (1J 163)
(not continuous)
Gascoigne Rd. CR0: Croy 7F 155
IG11: Bark 1G 73
Gascony Av. NW6 7J 47
Gascoyne Ho. E9 7A 52
Gascoyne Rd. E9 7K 51
Gaselee St. *E14* 1E 88
(off Baffin Way)
Gaskarth Rd. HA8: Edg 1J 27
SW12 6F 103
Gaskell Rd. N6 6D 30
Gaskell St. SW4 2J 103
Gaskin St. N1 1B 68
Gaspar Cl. *SW5* 4K 83
(off Courtfield Gdns.)
Gaspar M. SW5 4K 83
Gassiot Rd. SW17 4D 120
Gassiot Way SM1: Sutt 3B 150
Gasson Ho. *SE14* 6K 87
(off John Williams Cl.)
Gastein Rd. W6 6F 83
Gastigny Ho. EC1 2D 162
Gaston Bell Cl. TW9: Rich 3F 99
Gaston Bri. Rd.
TW17: Shep 6F 131
Gaston Rd. CR4: Mitc 3E 138
Gaston Way TW17: Shep 5F 131
Gataker Ho. *SE16* 3H 87
(off Slippers Pl.)
Gataker St. SE16 3H 87
Gatcombe Ct. BR3: Beck 7C 124
Gatcombe Ho. SE22 3E 104
Gatcombe M. W5 7F 63
Gatcombe Rd. E16 1J 89
N19 3H 49
Gatcombe Way EN4: Barn 3J 5
Gateacre Ct. DA14: Sidc 4B 128
Gate Cen., The
TW8: Bford 7A 80
Gateforth St.
NW8 4C 66 (4C 158)
Gate Hill Ct. *W11* 1H 83
(off Ladbroke Ter.)
Gatehouse Cl.
KT2: King T 7J 117
Gatehouse Sq. SE1 4D 168
Gateley Ho. *SE4* 4K 105
(off Coston Wlk.)
Gateley Rd. SW9 3K 103
Gate Lodge *W9* 5J 65
(off Admiral Wlk.)
Gate M. SW7 7D 164
Gater Dr. EN2: Enf 1J 7
Gates NW9 2B 28
Gatesborough St.
EC2 4E 68 (3G 163)
Gates Ct. SE17 5C 86
Gatesden WC1 3J 67 (2G 161)
Gates Grn. Rd. BR2: Kes 3H 155
BR4: W W'ck 3H 155
Gateside Rd. SW17 3D 120
Gatestone Rd. SE19 6E 122
Gate St. WC2 6K 67 (7G 161)
Gate Theatre, The 1J 83
(off Pembridge Rd.)
Gateway SE17 6C 86
Gateway Arc. *N1* 2B 68
(off Upper St.)
Gateway Ho. IG11: Bark 1G 73
Gateway Ind. Est. NW10 3B 64
Gateway M. E8 5F 51
Gateway Retail Pk. E6 4F 73
Gateway Rd. E10 3D 52
Gateways *KT6: Surb* 5E 134
(off Surbiton Hill Rd.)
Gateways Ct. SM6: Wall 5F 151
Gateways, The SW3 4D 170
TW9: Rich 4D 98
(off Park La.)
Gatfield Gro. TW13: Felt 2E 114
Gatfield Ho. TW13: Felt 2D 114
Gathorne Rd. N22 2A 32
Gathorne St. E2 2K 69
Gatley Av. KT19: Eps 5H 147
Gatliff Cl. SW1 6H 171
Gatliff Rd. SW1 5F 85 (6J 171)
(not continuous)
Gatling Rd. SE2 5A 92
Gatonby St. SE15 1F 105
Gatting Cl. HA8: Edg 7D 12
Gatting Way UB8: Uxb 6A 40
Gattis Wharf *N1* 2J 67
(off New Wharf Rd.)
Gatton Rd. SW17 4C 120
Gattons Way DA14: Sidc 4F 129
Gatward Cl. N21 6G 7
Gatward Grn. N9 2A 18
Gatwick Ho. *E14* 6B 70
(off Clemence St.)
Gatwick Rd. SW18 7H 101
Gauden Cl. SW4 3H 103
Gauden Rd. SW4 2H 103
Gaugin Ct. *SE16* 5H 87
(off Stubbs Dr.)
Gaumont Ter. *W12* 2E 82
(off Lime Gro.)
Gauntlet Cl. UB5: N'olt 7C 42
Gauntlets *NW9* 2B 28
(off Five Acre)
Gauntlett Ct. HA0: Wemb 5B 44
Gauntlett Rd. SM1: Sutt 5B 150
Gaunt St. SE1 3C 86
Gautrey Rd. SE15 2J 105
Gautrey Sq. E6 6D 72
Gavel St. SE17 4D 86
Gaverick M. E14 4C 88
Gavestone Cres. SE12 7K 107
Gavestone Rd. SE12 7K 107
Gaviller Pl. E5 4H 51
Gavina Cl. SM4: Mord 5C 138
Gavin Ho. SE18 4J 91
Gawber St. E2 3J 69
Gawsworth Cl. E15 5H 53
Gawthorne Av. NW7 5B 14
Gay Cl. NW2 5D 46
Gaydon Ho. *W2* 5K 65
(off Bourne Ter.)
Gaydon La. NW9 1A 28
Gayfere Rd. IG5: Ilf 3D 36
KT17: Eps 5C 148
Gayfere St. SW1 3J 85 (2E 172)
Gayford Rd. W12 2B 82
Gay Gdns. RM10: Dag 4J 57
Gay Ho. N16 5E 50
Gayhurst *SE17* 6D 86
(off Hopwood Rd.)
Gayhurst Ct. UB5: N'olt 3A 60
Gayhurst Ho. *NW8* 3C 158
(off Mallory St.)
Gayhurst Rd. E8 7G 51
Gaylor Rd. UB5: N'olt 5D 42
Gaymead *NW8* 1K 65
(off Abbey Rd.)
Gaynesford Rd. SE23 2K 123
SM5: Cars 7D 150
Gaynes Hill Rd.
IG8: Wfd G 6H 21
Gay Rd. E15 2F 71
Gaysham Av. IG2: Ilf 5E 36
Gaysham Hall IG5: Ilf 3F 37
Gaysley Ho. SE11 4J 173
Gay St. SW15 3F 101
Gayton Ct. HA1: Harr 6K 25
Gayton Cres. NW3 4B 48
Gayton Rd. HA1: Harr 6K 25
NW3 4B 48
SE2 3C 92
Gayville Rd. SW11 6D 102
Gaywood Cl. SW2 1K 121
Gaywood Rd. E17 3C 34
Gaywood St. SE1 3B 86
Gaza St. SE17 5B 86
Gaze Ho. *E14* 6F 71
(off Blair St.)
Gean Ct. E11 4F 53
Geariesville Gdns. IG6: Ilf 4F 37
Geary Rd. NW10 5C 46
Geary St. N7 5K 49
Geddes Pl. *DA6: Bex* 4G 111
(off Arnsberga Way)

Gedeney Rd.—Glade Cl.

Gedeney Rd. N17 ... 1C 32
Gedling Pl. SE1 ... 3F 87 (7K 169)
Geere Rd. E15 ... 1H 71
Gees Ct. W1 ... 6E 66 (1H 165)
Gee St. EC1 ... 4C 68 (3C 162)
Geffery's Ct. SE9 ... 3C 126
Geffrye Ct. N1 ... 2E 68
Geffrye Est. N1 ... 2E 68
Geffrye Mus. ... 2F 69 (1J 163)
Geffrye St. E2 ... 2F 69 (1J 163)
Geldart Rd. SE15 ... 7H 87
Geldeston Rd. E5 ... 2G 51
Gellatly Rd. SE14 ... 2J 105
Gell Cl. UB10: Uxb ... 3B 40
Gelsthorpe Rd. RM5: Col R ... 1H 39
Gemini Bus. Cen. E16 ... 4F 71
Gemini Bus. Est. SE14 ... 5K 87
Gemini Ct. E1 ... 7G 69 (off Vaughan Way)
Gemini Gro. UB5: N'olt ... 3C 60
General Gordon Pl. SE18 ... 4F 91
General Wolfe Rd. SE10 ... 1F 107
Genesis Cl. TW19: Staines ... 1B 112
Genesta Rd. SE18 ... 6F 91
Geneva Cl. TW17: Shep ... 2G 131
Geneva Ct. NW9 ... 5B 28
Geneva Dr. SW9 ... 4A 104
Geneva Gdns. RM6: Chad H ... 5E 38
Geneva Rd. CR7: Thor H ... 5C 140
KT1: King T ... 4E 134
Genever Cl. E4 ... 5H 19
Genista Rd. N18 ... 5C 18
Genoa Av. SW15 ... 5E 100
Genoa Ho. E1 ... 4K 69 (off Ernest St.)
Genoa Rd. SE20 ... 1J 141
Genotin Rd. EN1: Enf ... 3J 7
Genotin Ter. EN2: Enf ... 4J 7
Gentlemans Row EN2: Enf ... 3H 7
Gentry Gdns. E13 ... 4J 71
Geoffrey Cl. SE5 ... 2C 104
Geoffrey Ct. SE4 ... 2B 106
Geoffrey Gdns. E6 ... 2C 72
Geoffrey Ho. SE1 ... 7F 169 (off Pardoner St.)
Geoffrey Jones Ct. NW10 ... 1C 64
Geoffrey Rd. SE4 ... 3B 106
Geographers' A-Z Shop ... 5A 68 (5J 161)
George V Av. HA5: Pinn ... 2D 24
George V Cl. HA5: Pinn ... 3E 24
George V Way UB6: G'frd ... 1B 62
George Beard Rd. SE8 ... 4B 88
George Belt Ho. E2 ... 3K 69 (off Smart St.)
George Comberton Wlk. E12 ... 5E 54
George Ct. WC2 ... 3F 167
George Cres. N10 ... 7K 15
George Davies Lodge IG2: Ilf ... 5G 37 (off Veronique Gdns.)
George Downing Est. N16 ... 2F 51
George Eliot Ho. SW1 ... 4B 172 (off Vauxhall Bri. Rd.)
George Elliston Ho. SE1 ... 5G 87 (off Old Kent Rd.)
George Eyre Ho. NW8 ... 2B 66 (off Cochrane St.)
George Gange Way HA3: Harr ... 3J 25
George Gillett Ct. EC1 ... 3D 162
George Gro. Rd. SE20 ... 1G 141
George Inn Yd. SE1 ... 1D 86 (5E 168)
George La. BR2: Short ... 1K 155
E18 ... 2J 35
(not continuous)
SE13 ... 6D 106
George Lansbury Ho. N22 ... 1A 32 (off Progress Way)
NW10 ... 7A 46
George Lindgren Ho. SW6 ... 7H 83 (off Clem Attlee Ct.)
George Loveless Ho. E2 ... 1K 163 (off Diss St.)
George Lowe Ct. W2 ... 5K 65 (off Bourne Ter.)
George Mathers Rd. SE11 ... 4B 86
George M. EN2: Enf ... 3J 7 (off Town, The)
NW1 ... 2B 160
George Peabody Ct. NW1 ... 5C 158 (off Burne St.)
George Pl. N17 ... 3E 32
George Potter Ho. SW11 ... 2B 102 (off George Potter Way)
George Potter Way SW11 ... 2B 102
George Rd. E4 ... 6H 19
KT2: King T ... 7H 117
(not continuous)
KT3: N Mald ... 4B 136
George Row SE16 ... 2G 87
George Sq. SW19 ... 3J 137
George's Rd. N7 ... 5K 49
George's Sq. SW6 ... 6H 83 (off Nth. End Rd.)
George St. CR0: Croy ... 2C 152
E16 ... 6H 71
IG11: Bark ... 7G 55
TW3: Houn ... 2D 96
TW9: Rich ... 5D 98
UB2: S'hall ... 4C 78
W1 ... 6D 66 (7E 158)
W7 ... 1J 79
George Tingle Ho. SE1 ... 3F 87 (off Grange Wlk.)
Georgetown Cl. SE19 ... 5E 122
Georgette Pl. SE10 ... 7E 88
Georgeville Gdns. IG6: Ilf ... 4F 37
George Walter Ct. SE16 ... 4J 87 (off Millender Wlk.)
George Wyver Cl. SW19 ... 7G 101
George Yd. EC3 ... 6D 68 (1F 169)
W1 ... 7E 66 (2H 165)
Georgiana St. NW1 ... 1G 67
Georgian Cl. BR2: Short ... 1K 155
HA7: Stan ... 7F 11
UB10: Uxb ... 4A 40
Georgian Ct. CR0: Croy ... 1D 152 (off Cross Rd.)
E9 ... 1J 69
EN5: Barn ... 4F 5
HA9: Wemb ... 6G 45
N3 ... 1H 29
NW4 ... 5D 28
SW16 ... 4J 121
Georgian Ho. E16 ... 7J 71 (off Capulet M.)
Georgian Way HA1: Harr ... 2H 43
Georgia Rd. CR7: Thor H ... 1B 140
KT3: N Mald ... 4J 135
Georgina Gdns. E2 ... 3F 69 (1K 163)
Geraint Rd. BR1: Brom ... 4J 125
Geraldine Rd. SW18 ... 5A 102
W4 ... 6G 81
Geraldine St. SE11 ... 3B 86 (2K 173)
Gerald M. SW1 ... 3H 171
Gerald Rd. E16 ... 4H 71
RM8: Dag ... 2F 57
SW1 ... 4E 84 (3H 171)
Gerard Av. TW4: Houn ... 7E 96
Gerard Gdns. RM13: Rain ... 2K 75
Gerard Rd. HA1: Harr ... 6A 26
SW13 ... 1B 100
Gerards Cl. SE16 ... 5J 87
Gerda Rd. SE9 ... 2G 127
Germander Way E15 ... 3G 71
Gernon Rd. E3 ... 2A 70
Geron Way NW2 ... 2D 46
Gerrard Gdns. HA5: Pinn ... 5J 23
Gerrard Ho. SE14 ... 7J 87 (off Briant St.)
Gerrard Pl. W1 ... 7H 67 (2D 166)
Gerrard Rd. N1 ... 2B 68
Gerrards Cl. N14 ... 5B 6
Gerrards Ct. W5 ... 3D 80
Gerrard St. W1 ... 7H 67 (2D 166)
Gerridge Ct. SE1 ... 1K 173 (off Gerridge St.)
Gerridge St. SE1 ... 3A 86 (1K 173)
Gerry Raffles Sq. E15 ... 7F 53
Gertrude Rd. DA17: Belv ... 4G 93
Gertrude St. SW10 ... 6A 84 (7A 170)
Gervase Cl. HA9: Wemb ... 3J 45
Gervase Rd. HA8: Edg ... 1J 27
Gervase St. SE15 ... 7H 87
Gervis Ct. TW7: Isle ... 7G 79
Ghent St. SE6 ... 2C 124
Ghent Way E8 ... 6F 51
Giant Arches Rd. SE24 ... 7C 104
Giant Tree Hill WD23: Bush ... 1C 10
Gibbfield Cl. RM6: Chad H ... 3E 38
Gibbings Ho. SE1 ... 7B 168 (off King James St.)
Gibbins Rd. E15 ... 7E 52
Gibbon Ho. NW8 ... 4B 158
Gibbon Rd. KT2: King T ... 1E 134
SE15 ... 2J 105
W3 ... 7A 64
Gibbon's Rents SE1 ... 5G 169
Gibbons Rd. NW10 ... 6A 46
Gibbon Wlk. SW15 ... 4C 100
Gibbs Av. SE19 ... 5D 122
Gibbs Cl. SE19 ... 6D 122
Gibbs Grn. HA8: Edg ... 4D 12
W14 ... 5H 83
(not continuous)
Gibbs Grn. Cl. W14 ... 5H 83
Gibbs Ho. BR1: Brom ... 1H 143 (off Longfield)
Gibb's Rd. N18 ... 4D 18
Gibbs Sq. SE19 ... 5D 122
Gibney Ter. BR1: Brom ... 4H 125
Gibraltar Wlk. E2 ... 2K 163
Gibson Cl. E1 ... 4J 69
KT9: Chess ... 5C 146
N21 ... 6F 7
TW7: Isle ... 3J 97
Gibson Gdns. N16 ... 2F 51
Gibson Ho. SM1: Sutt ... 4J 149
Gibson M. TW1: Twick ... 6C 98
Gibson Rd. RM8: Dag ... 1C 56
SE11 ... 4K 85 (4H 173)
SM1: Sutt ... 5K 149
UB10: Uxb ... 4B 40
Gibsons Hill SW16 ... 7A 122
Gibson Sq. N1 ... 1A 68
Gibson St. SE10 ... 5G 89
Gideon Cl. DA17: Belv ... 4H 93
Gideon M. W5 ... 2D 80
Gideon Rd. SW11 ... 3E 102
Gielgud Theatre ... 2C 166 (off Shaftesbury Av.)
Giesbach Rd. N19 ... 2H 49
Giffard Rd. N18 ... 6K 17
Giffen Sq. Mkt. SE8 ... 7C 88 (off Giffen St.)
Giffin St. SE8 ... 7C 88
Gifford Gdns. W7 ... 5H 61
Gifford Ho. SE10 ... 5F 89 (off Eastney St.)
SW1 ... 6A 172 (off Churchill Gdns.)
Gifford St. N1 ... 7J 49
Gift La. E15 ... 1G 71
GIGGSHILL ... 7A 134
Giggs Hill BR5: Orp ... 2K 145
Giggshill Gdns. KT7: T Ditt ... 1A 146
Giggshill Rd. KT7: T Ditt ... 7A 134
Gilbert Bri. EC2 ... 5D 162 (off Gilbert Ho.)
Gilbert Cl. SE18 ... 1D 108
SW19 ... 7K 119 (off High Path)
Gilbert Collection ... 2H 167 (off Lancaster Pl.)
Gilbert Ct. W5 ... 6F 63 (off Green Va.)
Gilbert Gro. HA8: Edg ... 1K 27
Gilbert Ho. E2 ... 3K 69 (off Usk St.)
E17 ... 3D 34
EC2 ... 5D 162
SE8 ... 6C 88
SW1 ... 6K 171 (off Churchill Gdns.)
SW8 ... 7J 85 (off Wyvil Rd.)
SW13 ... 7D 82 (off Trinity Chu. Rd.)
Gilbert Pl. WC1 ... 5J 67 (6E 160)
Gilbert Rd. BR1: Brom ... 7J 125
DA17: Belv ... 3G 93
HA5: Pinn ... 4B 24
SE11 ... 4A 86 (4K 173)
SW19 ... 7A 120
UB9: Uxb ... 2A 22
Gilbert Sheldon Ho. W2 ... 5B 158 (off Edgware Rd.)
Gilbertson Ho. E14 ... 3C 88 (off Mellish St.)
Gilbert St. E15 ... 4G 53
TW3: Houn ... 3G 97
W1 ... 6E 66 (1H 165)
Gilbert Way CR0: Croy ... 2K 151
Gilbey Cl. UB10: Uxb ... 4D 40
Gilbey Rd. SW17 ... 4C 120
Gilbeys Yd. NW1 ... 7E 48
Gilbourne Rd. SE18 ... 6K 91
Gilby Ho. E9 ... 6K 51
Gilda Av. EN3: Enf ... 5F 9
Gilda Ct. NW7 ... 1C 28
Gilda Cres. N16 ... 1G 51
Gildea Cl. HA5: Pinn ... 1E 24
Gildea St. W1 ... 5F 67 (6K 159)
Gilden Cres. NW5 ... 5E 48
Gildersome St. SE18 ... 6E 90
Gilders Rd. KT9: Chess ... 7F 147
Giles Coppice SE19 ... 4F 123
Giles Ho. SE16 ... 7K 169
Gilesmead SE5 ... 1D 104
Gilfrid Cl. UB8: Uxb ... 6D 58
Gilkes Cres. SE21 ... 6E 104
Gilkes Pl. SE21 ... 6E 104
Gillam Ho. SE16 ... 4J 87 (off Silwood St.)
Gillan Ct. SE12 ... 3K 125
Gillan Grn. WD23: Bush ... 2B 10
Gillards M. E17 ... 4C 34
Gillards Way E17 ... 4C 34
Gill Av. E16 ... 6J 71
Gillender St. E3 ... 4E 70
Gillespie Rd. N5 ... 3A 50
Gillett Av. E6 ... 2C 72
GILLETTE CORNER ... 7A 80
Gillett Ho. N8 ... 3J 31 (off Campsfield Rd.)
Gillett Pl. N16 ... 5E 50
Gillett Rd. CR7: Thor H ... 4D 140
Gillett St. N16 ... 5E 50
Gillfoot NW1 ... 1A 160 (off Hampstead Rd.)
Gillham Ter. N17 ... 6B 18
Gillian Ho. HA3: Harr ... 6D 10
Gillian Pk. Rd. SM3: Sutt ... 1H 149
Gillian St. SE13 ... 5D 106
Gillies St. NW5 ... 5E 48
Gilling Ct. NW3 ... 6C 48
Gillingham M. SW1 ... 4G 85 (3A 172)
Gillingham Rd. NW2 ... 3G 47
Gillingham Row SW1 ... 4G 85 (3A 172)
Gillingham St. SW1 ... 4G 85 (3A 172)
Gillings Ct. EN5: Barn ... 4B 4 (off Wood St.)
Gillison Wlk. SE16 ... 3H 87
Gillman Dr. E15 ... 1H 71
Gillman Ho. E2 ... 2G 69 (off Pritchard's Rd.)
Gill St. E14 ... 6B 70
Gillum Cl. EN4: Barn ... 1J 15
Gilmore Cl. UB10: Uxb ... 3C 40
Gilmore Ct. N11 ... 5J 15
Gilmore Cres. TW15: Ashf ... 5C 112
Gilmore Rd. SE13 ... 4F 107
Gilpin Av. SW14 ... 4K 99
Gilpin Cl. CR4: Mitc ... 2C 138
Gilpin Cres. N18 ... 5A 18
TW2: Twick ... 7F 97
Gilpin Rd. E5 ... 4A 52
Gilpin Way UB3: Hayes ... 7F 77
Gilray Ho. W2 ... 2A 164 (off Gloucester Ter.)
Gilsland Rd. CR7: Thor H ... 4D 140
Gilstead Ho. IG11: Bark ... 2B 74
Gilstead Rd. SW6 ... 2K 101
Gilston Rd. SW10 ... 5A 84 (7A 170)
Gilton Rd. SE6 ... 3G 125
Giltspur St. EC1 ... 6B 68 (7B 162)
Gilwell Cl. E4 ... 4J 9
Gilwell La. E4 ... 4J 9
(not continuous)
GILWELL PARK ... 4K 9
Gilwell Pk. E4 ... 3K 9
Ginsburg Yd. NW3 ... 4A 48
Gippeswyck Cl. HA5: Pinn ... 1B 24
Gipsy Hill SE19 ... 4E 122
Gipsy La. SW15 ... 3D 100
Gipsy Moth IV ... 6E 88
Gipsy Rd. DA16: Well ... 7D 92
SE27 ... 4C 122
Gipsy Rd. Gdns. SE27 ... 4C 122
Giralda Cl. E16 ... 5B 72
Giraud St. E14 ... 6D 70
Girdler's Rd. W14 ... 4F 83
Girdlestone Wlk. N19 ... 2G 49
Girdwood Rd. SW18 ... 7G 101
Girling Ho. N1 ... 1E 68 (off Colville Est.)
Girling Way TW14: Felt ... 3J 95
Gironde Rd. SW6 ... 7H 83
Girtin Ho. UB5: N'olt ... 2B 60 (off Academy Gdns.)
Girton Av. NW9 ... 3G 27
Girton Cl. UB5: N'olt ... 6G 43
Girton Gdns. CR0: Croy ... 3C 154
Girton Rd. SE26 ... 5K 123
UB5: N'olt ... 6G 43
Girton Vs. W10 ... 6F 65
Gisbourne Cl. SM6: Wall ... 3H 151
Gisburn Ho. SE15 ... 6G 87 (off Friary Est.)
Gisburn Rd. N8 ... 4K 31
Gissing Wlk. N1 ... 7A 50
Gittens Cl. BR1: Brom ... 4H 125
Given Wilson Wlk. E13 ... 2H 71
Glacier Way HA0: Wemb ... 2D 62
Gladbeck Way EN2: Enf ... 4G 7
Gladding Rd. E12 ... 4B 54
Glade Cl. KT6: Surb ... 2D 146

Glenwood Gdns.—Goodyer Ho.

Glenwood Gdns. IG2: Ilf 5E **36**
Glenwood Gro. NW9 . . . . .1J **45**
Glenwood Rd. KT17: Eps . . .6C **148**
N15 . . . . .5B **32**
NW7 . . . . .3F **13**
SE6 . . . . .1B **124**
TW3: Houn 3H **97**
Glenwood Way
CR0: Croy 6K **141**
Glenworth Av. E14 . . . . .4F **89**
Gliddon Dr. E5 . . . . .4G **51**
Gliddon Rd. W14 . . . . .4G **83**
Glimpsing Grn.
DA18: Erith 3E **92**
Glisson Rd. UB10: Uxb 2C **58**
Global App. E3 . . . . .2D **70**
Globe Pond Rd. SE16 . . . . . . .1A **88**
Globe Rd. E2 . . . . .3J **69**
(not continuous)
E15 . . . . .5H **53**
IG8: Wfd G 6F **21**
Globe Rope Wlk. *E14* *4D 88*
(off E. Ferry Rd.)
Globe St. SE1 . . . . .3D **86** (7E **168**)
Globe Ter. E2 . . . . .3J **69**
GLOBE TOWN **3K 69**
Globe Town Mkt. E2 . . . . .3K **69**
Globe Wharf SE16 . . . . .7K **69**
Globe Yd. W1 . . . . .1J **165**
Glossop Rd. CR2: S Croy . . .7D **152**
Gloster Rd. KT3: N Mald . . .4A **136**
Gloucester Arc. SW7 . . . . . . .4A **84**
Gloucester Av.
DA15: Sidc 2J **127**
DA16: Well 4K **109**
NW1 . . . . .7E **48**
Gloucester Cir. SE10 . . . . . . .7E **88**
Gloucester Cl.
KT7: T Ditt 1A **146**
NW10 . . . . .7K **45**
Gloucester Ct. CR4: Mitc . . .5J **139**
EC3 . . . . .7E **68** (3H **169**)
HA1: Harr 3J **25**
NW11 . . . .*7H 29*
(off Golders Grn. Rd.)
TW9: Rich 7G **81**
W7 . . . .*5K 61*
(off Copley Cl.)
Gloucester Cres. NW1 . . . . . .1F **67**
TW18: Staines 6A **112**
Gloucester Dr. N4 . . . . .2B **50**
NW11 . . . . .4J **29**
Gloucester Gdns. EN4: Barn . . .4K **5**
IG1: Ilf 7C **36**
NW11 . . . . .7H **29**
SM1: Sutt 2K **149**
W2 . . . . .6A **66**
Gloucester Ga. NW1 . . . . .2F **67**
(not continuous)
Gloucester Ga. M. NW1 . . . . .2F **67**
Gloucester Gro. HA8: Edg . . .1K **27**
Gloucester Ho. *E16* *7J 71*
(off Gatcombe Rd.)
NW6 . . . .*2J 65*
(off Cambridge Rd.)
SE5 . . . . .7A **86**
TW10: Rich 5G **99**
Gloucester M. E10 . . . . .7C **34**
W2 . . . . .6A **66** (1A **164**)
Gloucester M. W. W2 . . . . . . .6A **66**
Gloucester Pde.
DA15: Sidc 5A **110**
UB3: Hayes 3E **76**
Gloucester Pl.
NW1 . . . . . . .4D **66** (4E **158**)
W1 . . . . .5D **66** (4E **158**)
Gloucester Pl. M.
W1 . . . . .5D **66** (6F **159**)
Gloucester Rd.
CR0: Croy 1D **152**
DA17: Belv 5F **93**
E10 . . . . .7C **34**
Gloucester Rd. E11 . . . . .5K **35**
E12 . . . . .3D **54**
E17 . . . . .2K **33**
EN2: Enf 1H **7**
EN5: Barn 5E **4**
HA1: Harr 5F **25**
KT1: King T 2G **135**
N17 . . . . .2D **32**
N18 . . . . .5A **18**
SW7 . . . . . . .3A **84** (4A **170**)
TW2: Twick 1G **115**
TW4: Houn 4C **96**
TW9: Rich 7G **81**
TW11: Tedd 5J **115**
TW12: Hamp 7F **115**
TW13: Felt 1A **114**
W3 . . . . .2J **81**
W5 . . . . .2C **80**
Gloucester Sq. E2 . . . . .1G **69**
W2 . . . . .6B **66** (1B **164**)
Gloucester St.
SW1 . . . . . . .5G **85** (6A **172**)
Gloucester Ter. *N14* *1C 16*
(off Crown La.)
W2 . . . . .6K **65** (1A **164**)
Gloucester Wlk. W8 . . . . .2J **83**
Gloucester Way
EC1 . . . . . . .3A **68** (2K **161**)
Glover Cl. SE2 . . . . .4C **92**
Glover Dr. N18 . . . . .6D **18**
Glover Ho. *NW6* *7A 48*
(off Harben Rd.)
SE15 . . . . .4H **105**
Glover Rd. HA5: Pinn 6B **24**
Glovers Gro. HA4: Ruis 7D **22**
Gloxinia Wlk.
TW12: Hamp 6E **114**
Glycena Rd. SW11 . . . . .3D **102**
Glyn Av. EN4: Barn 4G **5**
Glyn Cl. SE25 . . . . .2E **140**
Glyn Ct. SW16 . . . . .3A **122**
Glyndale Grange
SM2: Sutt 6K **149**
Glyndebourne Ct.
UB5: N'olt *3A 60*
(off Canberra Dr.)
Glynde M. SW3 . . . . .2D **170**
Glynde Reach WC1 . . . . .2F **161**
Glynde Rd. DA7: Bex 3D **110**
Glynde St. SE4 . . . . .6B **106**
Glyndon Rd. SE18 . . . . .4G **91**
(not continuous)
Glyn Dr. DA14: Sidc 4B **128**
Glynfield Rd. NW10 . . . . .7A **46**
Glynne Rd. N22 . . . . .2A **32**
Glyn Rd. E5 . . . . .3K **51**
EN3: Enf 4D **8**
KT4: Wor Pk 2F **149**
Glyn St. SE11 . . . . .5K **85** (6G **173**)
Glynwood Ct. SE23 . . . . .2J **123**
Goater's All. *SW6* *7H 83*
(off Dawes Rd.)
Goat Ho. Bri. SE25 . . . . .3G **141**
Goat La. EN1: Enf 1A **8**
Goat Rd. CR4: Mitc 7E **138**
Goat Wharf TW8: Bford 6E **80**
Gobions Av. RM5: Col R 1K **39**
Godalming Av. SM6: Wall . . .5J **151**
Godalming Rd. E14 . . . . .5D **70**
Godbold Rd. E15 . . . . .4G **71**
Goddard Cl. TW17: Shep 3B **130**
Goddard Ct. HA3: Harr 2A **26**
Goddard Pl. N19 . . . . .3G **49**
Goddard Rd. BR3: Beck 4K **141**
Goddards Way IG1: Ilf 1H **55**
Goddarts Ho. E17 . . . . .3C **34**
Godfree Ct. *SE1* *6E 168*
(off Long La.)
Godfrey Av. TW2: Twick 7H **97**
UB5: N'olt 1C **60**
Godfrey Hill SE18 . . . . .4C **90**
Godfrey Ho. EC1 . . . . .2E **162**
Godfrey Rd. SE18 . . . . .4D **90**
Godfrey St. E15 . . . . .2E **70**
SW3 . . . . . . .5C **84** (5D **170**)
Godfrey Way TW4: Houn 7C **96**
Goding St. SE11 . . . .5J **85** (5F **173**)
Godley Rd. SW18 . . . . .1B **120**
Godliman St.
EC4 . . . . .6B **68** (1B **168**)
Godman Rd. SE15 . . . . .2H **105**
Godolphin Cl. N13 . . . . .6G **17**
Godolphin Ho. *NW3* *7C 48*
(off Fellows Rd.)
Godolphin Pl. W3 . . . . .7K **63**
Godolphin Rd. W12 . . . . .1D **82**
(not continuous)
Godric Cres. CR0: Croy 7F **155**
Godson Rd. CR0: Croy 3A **152**
Godstone Ho. *SE1* *7F 169*
(off Pardoner St.)
Godstone Rd. SM1: Sutt 4A **150**
TW1: Twick 6B **98**
Godstow Rd. SE2 . . . . .2B **92**
Godwin Cl. E4 . . . . .1K **9**
KT19: Eps 6J **147**
N1 . . . . .2C **68**
Godwin Ct. *NW1* *2G 67*
(off Chalton St.)
Godwin Ho. *NW6* *2K 65*
(off Tollgate Gdns., not continuous)
Godwin Rd. BR2: Short 3A **144**
E7 . . . . .4K **53**
Goffers Rd. SE3 . . . . .1G **107**
Goffs Rd. TW15: Ashf 6F **113**
Goidel Cl. SM6: Wall 4H **151**
Golborne Gdns. W10 . . . . . . .4G **65**
Golborne Ho. *W10* *4G 65*
(off Adair Rd.)
Golborne M. W10 . . . . .5G **65**
Golborne Rd. W10 . . . . .5G **65**
Golda Cl. EN5: Barn 6A **4**
Golda Ct. N3 . . . . .2H **29**
Goldbeaters Gro.
HA8: Edg 6F **13**
Goldcliff Cl. SM4: Mord 7J **137**
Goldcrest Cl. E16 . . . . .5B **72**
SE28 . . . . .7C **74**
Goldcrest M. W5 . . . . .5D **62**
Goldcrest Way CR0: Croy . . .7F **155**
WD23: Bush 1B **10**
Golden Ct. EN4: Barn 4H **5**
TW9: Rich 5D **98**
Golden Cres. UB3: Hayes 1H **77**
Golden Cross M. *W11* *6H 65*
(off Portobello Rd.)
Golden Hinde Educational Mus.
. . . .***1D 86 (4E 168)***
Golden Hind Pl. *SE8* *4B 88*
(off Grove St.)
Golden La. EC1 . . . .4C **68** (3C **162**)
Golden La. Est.
EC1 . . . . .4C **68** (4C **162**)
Golden Mnr. W7 . . . . .7J **61**
Golden M. SE20 . . . . .1J **141**
Golden Pde. *E17* *3E 34*
(off Wood St.)
Golden Plover Cl. E16 . . . . . . .6J **71**
Golden Sq. W1 . . . .7G **67** (2B **166**)
Golden Yd. *NW3* *4A 48*
(off Holly Mt.)
Golders Cl. HA8: Edg 5C **12**
Golders Ct. NW11 . . . . .7H **29**
Golders Gdns. NW11 . . . . . . .7G **29**
GOLDERS GREEN **6G 29**
Golders Green Crematorium
NW11 . . . . .7J **29**
Golders Grn. Cres. NW11 . . .7H **29**
Golders Grn. Rd. NW11 . . . . .6G **29**
Goldersiea NW11 . . . . .1J **47**
Golders Mnr. Dr. NW11 . . . . .6F **29**
Golders Pk. Cl. NW11 . . . . . . .1J **47**
Golders Ri. NW4 . . . . .5F **29**
Golders Way NW11 . . . . .7H **29**
Golderton *NW4* *4D 28*
(off Prince of Wales Cl.)
Goldfinch Rd. SE28 . . . . .3H **91**
Goldhawk Ind. Est. W6 . . . . .3D **82**
Goldhawk M. W12 . . . . .2D **82**
Goldhawk Rd. W6 . . . . .4B **82**
Goldhaze Cl. IG8: Wfd G 7F **21**
Gold Hill HA8: Edg 6E **12**
Goldhurst Ter. NW6 . . . . .7K **47**
Goldie Ho. N19 . . . . .7H **31**
Golding Cl. KT9: Chess 6C **146**
Golding Ct. IG1: Ilf 3E **54**
Golding St. E1 . . . . .6G **69**
Golding Ter. E1 . . . . .6G **69**
SW11 . . . . .2E **102**
Goldington Ct. *NW1* *1H 67*
(off Royal College St.)
Goldington Cres. NW1 . . . . . .2H **67**
Goldington St. NW1 . . . . .2H **67**
Gold La. HA8: Edg 6E **12**
Goldman Cl. E2 . . . .4G **69** (3K **163**)
Goldmark Ho. SE3 . . . . .3K **107**
Goldney Rd. W9 . . . . .4J **65**
Goldrill Dr. N11 . . . . .2K **15**
Goldsboro' Rd. SW8 . . . . . .1H **103**
Goldsborough Cres. E4 . . . . . .2J **19**
Goldsborough Ho. *E14* *5D 88*
(off St Davids Sq.)
Goldsdown Cl. EN3: Enf 2F **9**
Goldsdown Rd. EN3: Enf 2E **8**
Goldsmid St. SE18 . . . . .5J **91**
Goldsmith Av. E12 . . . . .6C **54**
NW9 . . . . .5A **28**
Goldsmith Av. RM7: Rush G .7G **39**
W3 . . . . .7K **63**
Goldsmith Cl. HA2: Harr 1F **43**
Goldsmith Ct. *WC2* *7F 161*
(off Stukeley St.)
Goldsmith La. NW9 . . . . .4H **27**
Goldsmith Rd. E10 . . . . .1C **52**
E17 . . . . .2K **33**
N11 . . . . .5J **15**
SE15 . . . . .1G **105**
W3 . . . . .1K **81**
Goldsmith's Bldgs. W3 . . . . .1K **81**
Goldsmiths Cl. W3 . . . . .1K **81**
Goldsmith's Pl. *NW6* *1K 65*
(off Springfield La.)
Goldsmith's Row E2 . . . . .2G **69**
Goldsmith's Sq. E2 . . . . .2G **69**
Goldsmith St.
EC2 . . . . .6C **68** (7D **162**)
Goldsworthy Gdns. SE16 . . . .5J **87**
Goldthorpe *NW1* *1G 67*
(off Camden St.)
Goldwell Ho. SE22 . . . . .3E **104**
Goldwell Rd.
CR7: Thor H 4K **139**
Goldwin Cl. SE14 . . . . .1J **105**
Goldwing Cl. E16 . . . . .6J **71**
Golf Cl. CR7: Thor H 1A **140**
HA7: Stan 7H **11**
Golf Club Dr. KT2: King T . . .7K **117**
Golfe Rd. IG1: Ilf 3H **55**
Golf Rd. BR1: Brom 3E **144**
W5 . . . . .6F **63**
Golf Side TW2: Twick 3H **115**
Golfside Cl. KT3: N Mald . . .2A **136**
N20 . . . . .3H **15**
Goliath Cl. SM6: Wall 7J **151**
Gollogly Ter. SE7 . . . . .5A **90**
Gomer Gdns.
TW11: Tedd 6A **116**
Gomer Pl. TW11: Tedd 6A **116**
Gomm Rd. SE16 . . . . .3J **87**
Gomshall Av. SM6: Wall 5J **151**
Gondar Gdns. NW6 . . . . .5H **47**
Gonson St. SE8 . . . . .6D **88**
Gonston Cl. SW19 . . . . .2G **119**
Gonville Cres. UB5: N'olt 6F **43**
Gonville Rd. CR7: Thor H . . .5K **139**
Gonville St. SW6 . . . . .3G **101**
Gooch Ho. E5 . . . . .3H **51**
EC1 . . . .*5J 161*
(off Portpool La.)
Goodall Ho. SE4 . . . . .4K **105**
Goodall Rd. E11 . . . . .3E **52**
Gooden Ct. HA1: Harr 3J **43**
Goodenough Rd. SW19 . . . .7H **119**
Goodey Rd. IG11: Bark 7K **55**
Goodfaith Ho. *E14* *7D 70*
(off Simpson's Rd.)
Goodge Pl. W1 . . . .5G **67** (6B **160**)
Goodge St. W1 . . . .5G **67** (6B **160**)
Goodhall Cl. HA7: Stan 6G **11**
Goodhall St. NW10 . . . . .3B **64**
(not continuous)
Goodhart Pl. E14 . . . . .7A **70**
Goodhart Way
BR4: W W'ck 7G **143**
Goodhew Rd. CR0: Croy . . .6G **141**
Goodhope Ho. *E14* *7D 70*
(off Poplar High St.)
Gooding Cl. KT3: N Mald . . .4J **135**
Goodinge Cl. N7 . . . . .6J **49**
Gooding Ho. SE7 . . . . .5A **90**
Goodman Cres. SW2 . . . . . .2J **121**
Goodman Rd. E10 . . . . .7E **34**
Goodmans Ct. E1 . . . . .2J **169**
HA0: Wemb 4D **44**
Goodman's Stile E1 . . . . .6G **69**
Goodmans Yd.
EC3 . . . . . . .7F **69** (2J **169**)
GOODMAYES **1A 56**
Goodmayes Av. IG3: Ilf 1A **56**
Goodmayes La. IG3: Ilf 4A **56**
Goodmayes Retail Pk.
RM6: Chad H 1B **56**
Goodmayes Rd. IG3: Ilf 1A **56**
Goodrich Ct. W10 . . . . .6F **65**
Goodrich Ho. *E9* *2J 69*
(off Sewardstone Rd.)
Goodrich Rd. SE22 . . . . .6F **105**
Goodson Rd. NW10 . . . . .7A **46**
Goodson St. N1 . . . . .2A **68**
Goodspeed Ho. *E14* *7D 70*
(off Simpson's Rd.)
Goods Way NW1 . . . . .2J **67**
Goodway Gdns. E14 . . . . .6F **71**
Goodwill Ho. *E14* *7D 70*
(off Simpson's Rd.)
Goodwin Cl. CR4: Mitc 3B **138**
SE16 . . . . .3F **87**
Goodwin Ct. EN4: Barn 6H **5**
N8 . . . .*3J 31*
(off Campsbourne Rd.)
SW19 . . . . .7C **120**
Goodwin Dr. DA14: Sidc 3D **128**
Goodwin Gdns.
CR0: Croy 6B **152**
Goodwin Ho. N9 . . . . .1D **18**
Goodwin Rd. CR0: Croy 5B **152**
N9 . . . . .1E **18**
W12 . . . . .2C **82**
Goodwins Ct.
WC2 . . . . . . .7J **67** (2E **166**)
Goodwin St. N4 . . . . .2A **50**
Goodwood Cl. HA7: Stan 5H **11**
SM4: Mord 4J **137**
Goodwood Ct. *W1* *5K 159*
(off Devonshire St.)
Goodwood Dr. UB5: N'olt 6E **42**
Goodwood Ho. *SE14* *1A 106*
(off Goodwood St.)
Goodwood Pde.
BR3: Beck 4A **142**
Goodwood Rd. SE14 . . . . . . .7A **88**
Goodwyn Av. NW7 . . . . .5F **13**
Goodwyns Va. N10 . . . . .1E **30**
Goodyear Ho. *N2* *2B 30*
(off Grange, The)
Goodyear Pl. SE5 . . . . .6C **86**
Goodyer Ho. *SW1* *5C 172*
(off Tachbrook St.)

Goodyers Gdns. NW4 . . . 5F 29
Goosander Way SE28 . . . 3H 91
Gooseacre La. HA3: Harr . . . 5D 26
Goose Grn. Trad. Est.
SE22 . . . 4F 105
Gooseley La. E6 . . . 4F 73
(Claps Ga. La.)
E6 . . . 3E 72
(Vicarage La.)
Goosens Cl. SM1: Sutt . . . 5A 150
Goose Sq. E6 . . . 6D 72
Gophir La. EC4 . . . 7D 68 (2E 168)
Gopsall St. N1 . . . 1D 68
Gordon Av. E4 . . . 6B 20
HA7: Stan . . . 7E 10
SW14 . . . 4A 100
TW1: Twick . . . 5A 98
Gordonbrock Rd. SE4 . . . 5C 106
Gordon Cl. E17 . . . 6C 34
N19 . . . 1G 49
Gordon Ct. HA8: Edg . . . 5K 11
W12 . . . 6E 64
Gordon Cres. CR0: Croy . . . 1E 152
UB3: Hayes . . . 4J 77
Gordondale Rd. SW19 . . . 2J 119
Gordon Dr. TW17: Shep . . . 7F 131
Gordon Gdns. HA8: Edg . . . 2H 27
Gordon Gro. SE5 . . . 2B 104
Gordon Hill EN2: Enf . . . 1H 7
Gordon Ho. *E1* . . . *7J 69*
(off Glamis Rd.)
Gordon Ho. *SE10* . . . *7D 88*
(off Tarves Way)
W5 . . . 3E 62
Gordon Ho. Rd. NW5 . . . 4E 48
Gordon Mans. *W14* . . . *3F 83*
(off Addison Gdns.)
WC1 . . . *4C 160*
(off Torrington Pl.)
Gordon Pl. W8 . . . 2J 83
Gordon Rd. BR3: Beck . . . 3B 142
DA15: Sidc . . . 5J 109
DA17: Belv . . . 4J 93
E4 . . . 1B 20
E11 . . . 6J 35
E15 . . . 4E 52
E18 . . . 1K 35
EN2: Enf . . . 1H 7
HA3: Harr . . . 3J 25
IG1: Ilf . . . 3H 55
IG11: Bark . . . 1J 73
KT2: King T . . . 1F 135
KT5: Surb . . . 7F 135
N3 . . . 7C 14
N9 . . . 2C 18
N11 . . . 7C 16
RM6: Chad H . . . 6F 39
SE15 . . . 2H 105
SM5: Cars . . . 6D 150
TW3: Houn . . . 4G 97
TW9: Rich . . . 2F 99
TW15: Ashf . . . 3A 112
TW17: Shep . . . 6F 131
UB2: S'hall . . . 4C 78
UB7: W Dray . . . 7A 58
W4 . . . 6H 81
W5 . . . 7B 62
W13 . . . 7B 62
Gordon Sq. WC1 . . . 4H 67 (3C 160)
Gordon St. E13 . . . 3J 71
WC1 . . . 4H 67 (3C 160)
Gordon Way BR1: Brom . . . 1J 143
EN5: Barn . . . 4C 4
Gore Ct. NW9 . . . 5G 27
Gorefield Ho. *NW6* . . . *2J 65*
(off Gorefield Pl.)
Gorefield Pl. NW6 . . . 2J 65
Gore Rd. E9 . . . 1J 69
SW20 . . . 2E 136
GORESBROOK INTERCHANGE
. . . 2F 75
Goresbrook Rd. RM9: Dag . . . 1B 74
Gore St. SW7 . . . 3A 84
Gorham Ho. *SE16* . . . *2K 87*
(off Wolfe Cres.)
Gorham Pl. W11 . . . 7G 65
Goring Cl. RM5: Col R . . . 1J 39
Goring Gdns. RM8: Dag . . . 4C 56
Goring Rd. N11 . . . 6D 16
RM10: Dag . . . 6K 57
Goring St. EC3 . . . 7H 163
Goring Way UB6: G'frd . . . 2G 61
Gorleston Rd. N15 . . . 5D 32
Gorleston St. W14 . . . 4G 83
(not continuous)
Gorman Rd. SE18 . . . 4D 90
Gorringe Pk. Av.
CR4: Mitc . . . 7D 120
Gorse Cl. E16 . . . 6J 71
Gorsefield Ho. *E14* . . . *7C 70*
(off E. India Dock Rd.)
Gorse Ri. SW17 . . . 5E 120
Gorse Rd. CR0: Croy . . . 4C 154
Gorse Wlk. UB7: W Dray . . . 6A 58
Gorseway RM7: Rush G . . . 1K 57
Gorst Rd. NW10 . . . 4J 63
SW11 . . . 6D 102
Gorsuch Pl. E2 . . . 3F 69 (1J 163)
Gorsuch St. E2 . . . 2F 69 (1J 163)
Gosberton Rd. SW12 . . . 1D 120
Gosbury Hill KT9: Chess . . . 4E 146
Gosfield Rd. RM8: Dag . . . 2G 57
Gosfield St. W1 . . . 5G 67 (6A 160)
Gosford Gdns. IG4: Ilf . . . 5D 36
Goshawk Gdns.
UB4: Hayes . . . 3G 59
Goslett Yd. WC2 . . . 6H 67 (1D 166)
Gosling Cl. UB6: G'frd . . . 3E 60
Gosling Ho. *E1* . . . *7J 69*
(off Sutton St.)
Gosling Way SW9 . . . 1A 104
Gospatrick Rd. N17 . . . 7H 17
GOSPEL OAK . . . 4E 48
Gospel Oak Est. NW5 . . . 5D 48
Gosport Rd. E17 . . . 5B 34
Gosport Wlk. N17 . . . 4H 33
Gossage Rd. SE18 . . . 5H 91
UB10: Uxb . . . 7B 40
Gosset St. E2 . . . 3F 69 (1K 163)
Gosshill Rd. BR7: Chst . . . 2E 144
Gossington Cl. BR7: Chst . . . 4F 127
Gosterwood St. SE8 . . . 6A 88
Gostling Rd. TW2: Twick . . . 1E 114
Goston Gdns.
CR7: Thor H . . . 3A 140
Goswell Pl. EC1 . . . 2B 162
Goswell Rd. EC1 . . . 2B 68 (1A 162)
Gothic Cotts. *EN2: Enf* . . . *2H 7*
(off Chase Grn. Av.)
Gothic Ct. *SE5* . . . *7C 86*
(off Wyndham Rd.)
UB3: Hayes . . . 6F 77
Gothic Rd. TW2: Twick . . . 2H 115
Gottfried M. NW5 . . . 4G 49
Goudhurst Rd.
BR1: Brom . . . 5G 125
Gough Ho. *KT1: King T* . . . *2E 134*
(off Eden St.)
N1 . . . *1B 68*
(off Windsor St.)
Gough Rd. E15 . . . 4H 53
EN1: Enf . . . 2C 8
Gough Sq. EC4 . . . 6A 68 (7K 161)
Gough St. WC1 . . . 4K 67 (3H 161)
Gough Wlk. E14 . . . 6C 70
Goulden Ho. SW11 . . . 2C 102
Goulden Ho. App. SW11 . . . 2C 102
Goulding Gdns.
CR7: Thor H . . . 2C 140
Gouldman Ho. *E1* . . . *4J 69*
(off Wyllen Cl.)
Gould Rd. TW2: Twick . . . 1J 115
TW14: Felt . . . 7G 95
GOULDS GREEN . . . 6D 58
Gould's Grn. UB8: Uxb . . . 7D 58
Gould Ter. E8 . . . 5H 51
Goulston St. E1 . . . 6F 69 (7J 163)
Goulton Rd. E5 . . . 4H 51
Gourley Pl. N15 . . . 5E 32
Gourley St. N15 . . . 5E 32
Gourock Rd. SE9 . . . 5E 108
Govan St. E2 . . . 1G 69
Gover Ct. SW4 . . . 2J 103
Govett Av. TW17: Shep . . . 5E 130
Govier Cl. E15 . . . 7G 53
Gowan Av. SW6 . . . 1G 101
Gowan Ho. *E2* . . . *2K 163*
(off Chambord St.)
Gowan Rd. NW10 . . . 6D 46
Gower Cl. SW4 . . . 6G 103
Gower Ct. WC1 . . . 4H 67 (3C 160)
Gower Ho. E17 . . . 3D 34
SE17 . . . *5C 86*
(off Morecambe St.)
Gower M. WC1 . . . 5H 67 (6D 160)
Gower M. Mans. *WC1* . . . *5D 160*
(off Gower M.)
Gower Pl. WC1 . . . 4H 67 (3B 160)
Gower Rd. E7 . . . 6J 53
TW7: Isle . . . 6K 79
Gower St.
WC1 . . . 4G 67 (3B 160)
Gower's Wlk. E1 . . . 6G 69
Gowland Pl. BR3: Beck . . . 2B 142
Gowlett Rd. SE15 . . . 3G 105
Gowlland Cl. CR0: Croy . . . 7G 141
Gowrie Rd. SW11 . . . 3E 102
Graburn Way KT8: E Mos . . . 3H 133
Grace Av. DA7: Bex . . . 2F 111
Gracechurch St.
EC3 . . . 7D 68 (2F 169)
Grace Cl. HA8: Edg . . . 7D 12
SE9 . . . 3B 126
Grace Ct. *CR0: Croy* . . . *3B 152*
(off Waddon Rd.)
Gracedale Rd. SW16 . . . 5F 121
Gracefield Gdns. SW16 . . . 3J 121
Gracehill *E1* . . . *5J 69*
(off Hannibal Rd.)
Grace Ho. SE11 . . . 7H 173
Grace Jones Cl. E8 . . . 6G 51
Grace M. *SE20* . . . *2J 141*
(off Marlow Rd.)
Grace Path SE26 . . . 4J 123
Grace Pl. E3 . . . 3D 70
Grace Rd. CR0: Croy . . . 6C 140
Graces All. E1 . . . 7G 69
Graces M. NW8 . . . 2A 66
SE5 . . . 2D 104
Grace's Rd. SE5 . . . 2E 104
Grace St. E3 . . . 3D 70
Gradient, The SE26 . . . 4G 123
Graduate Pl. SE1 . . . 7G 169
Graeme Rd. EN1: Enf . . . 2J 7
Graemesdyke Av. SW14 . . . 3H 99
Grafton Cl. KT4: Wor Pk . . . 3A 148
TW4: Houn . . . 1C 114
W13 . . . 6A 62
Grafton Ct. TW14: Felt . . . 1F 113
Grafton Cres. NW1 . . . 6F 49
Grafton Gdns. N4 . . . 6C 32
RM8: Dag . . . 2E 56
Grafton Ho. SE8 . . . 5B 88
Grafton M. *N1* . . . *2C 68*
(off Frome St.)
W1 . . . 4G 67 (4A 160)
Grafton Pk. Rd.
KT4: Wor Pk . . . 2A 148
Grafton Pl.
NW1 . . . 3H 67 (2D 160)
Grafton Rd. CR0: Croy . . . 1A 152
EN2: Enf . . . 3E 6
HA1: Harr . . . 5G 25
KT3: N Mald . . . 3A 136
KT4: Wor Pk . . . 3K 147
NW5 . . . 5E 48
Grafton Rd. RM8: Dag . . . 2E 56
W3 . . . 7J 63
Grafton Sq. SW4 . . . 3G 103
Graftons, The NW2 . . . 3J 47
Grafton St. W1 . . . 7F 67 (3K 165)
Grafton Ter. NW5 . . . 5D 48
Grafton Way
KT8: W Mole . . . 4D 132
W1 . . . 4G 67 (4A 160)
WC1 . . . 4G 67 (4A 160)
Grafton Yd. NW5 . . . 6F 49
Graham Av. CR4: Mitc . . . 1E 138
W13 . . . 2B 80
Graham Cl. CR0: Croy . . . 2C 154
Graham Ct. *SE14* . . . *6K 87*
(off Myers La.)
UB5: N'olt . . . 5D 42
GRAHAME PARK . . . 1B 28
Grahame Pk. Est. NW9 . . . 1A 28
Grahame Pk. Way NW7 . . . 7G 13
Grahame White Ho.
HA3: Harr . . . 3D 26
Graham Gdns.
KT6: Surb . . . 1E 146
Graham Ho. *N9* . . . *1D 18*
(off Cumberland Rd.)
Graham Lodge NW4 . . . 6D 28
Graham Mans. *IG11: Bark* . . . *7A 56*
(off Lansbury Av.)
Graham Rd. CR4: Mitc . . . 1E 138
DA6: Bex . . . 4F 111
E8 . . . 6G 51
E13 . . . 4J 71
HA3: Harr . . . 3J 25
N15 . . . 3B 32
NW4 . . . 6D 28
SW19 . . . 7H 119
TW12: Hamp . . . 4E 114
W4 . . . 3K 81
Graham St. N1 . . . 2B 68 (1B 162)
Graham Ter. *DA15: Sidc* . . . *6B 110*
(off Westerham Dr.)
SW1 . . . 4E 84 (4G 171)
Grainger Cl. UB5: N'olt . . . 5F 43
Grainger Ct. SE5 . . . 7C 86
Grainger Rd. N22 . . . 1C 32
TW7: Isle . . . 2K 97
Gramer Cl. E11 . . . 2F 53
Gramophone La.
UB3: Hayes . . . 2G 77
Grampian Cl. BR6: Orp . . . 6K 145
SM2: Sutt . . . 7A 150
UB3: Hayes . . . 7F 77
Grampian Gdns. NW2 . . . 1G 47
Grampians, The *W6* . . . *2F 83*
(off Shepherd's Bush Rd.)
Granada St. SW17 . . . 5C 120
Granard Av. SW15 . . . 5D 100
Granard Bus. Cen. NW7 . . . 6F 13
Granard Ho. E9 . . . 6K 51
Granard Rd. SW12 . . . 7D 102
Granary Cl. N9 . . . 7D 8
Granary Mans. *SE28* . . . *2G 91*
(off Erebus Dr.)
Granary Rd. E1 . . . 4H 69
Granary Sq. N1 . . . 6A 50
Granary St. NW1 . . . 1H 67
Granby Pl. *SE1* . . . *7J 167*
(off Station App. Rd.)
Granby Rd. SE9 . . . 2D 108
Granby St. E2 . . . 4G 69 (3K 163)
(not continuous)
Granby Ter. NW1 . . . 2G 67 (1A 160)
Grand Arc. N12 . . . 5F 15
Grand Av. EC1 . . . 5B 68 (5B 162)
(not continuous)
HA9: Wemb . . . 5G 45
KT5: Surb . . . 5H 135
N10 . . . 4E 30
Grand Av. E. HA9: Wemb . . . 5H 45
Grand Central Hgts. *EC1* . . . *1C 162*
(off Central St.)
Grand Dpt. Rd. SE18 . . . 5E 90
Grand Dr. SW20 . . . 2E 136
UB2: S'hall . . . 2G 79
Granden Rd. SW16 . . . 2J 139
Grandfield Ct. W4 . . . 6K 81
Grandison Rd.
KT4: Wor Pk . . . 2E 148
SW11 . . . 5D 102
Grand Junc. Wharf N1 . . . 2C 68
Grand Pde. HA9: Wemb . . . 2G 45
KT6: Surb . . . 1G 147
N4 . . . 5B 32
SW14 . . . *4J 99*
(off Up. Richmond Rd. W.)
Grand Pde. M. SW15 . . . 5G 101
Grand Union Cen. *W10* . . . *4F 65*
(off West Row)
Grand Union Cl. W9 . . . 5H 65
Grand Union Cres. E8 . . . 1G 69
Grand Union Ent. Pk.
UB2: S'hall . . . 3E 78
Grand Union Ind. Est.
NW10 . . . 2H 63
Grand Union Wlk. *NW1* . . . *7F 49*
(off Kentish Town Rd.)
Grand Union Way
UB2: S'hall . . . 2E 78
(Bridge Rd.)
Grand Vitesse Ind. Cen.
SE1 . . . *5B 168*
(off Dolben St.)
Grand Wlk. E1 . . . 4A 70
Granfield St. SW11 . . . 1B 102
Grange Av. EN4: Barn . . . 1H 15
HA3: Harr . . . 2B 26
IG8: Wfd G . . . 6D 20
N12 . . . 5F 15
N20 . . . 7B 4
SE25 . . . 2E 140
TW2: Twick . . . 2J 115
Grangecliffe Gdns. SE25 . . . 2E 140
Grange Cl. DA15: Sidc . . . 3A 128
HA8: Edg . . . 5D 12
IG8: Wfd G . . . 7D 20
KT8: W Mole . . . 4F 133
TW5: Houn . . . 6D 78
UB3: Hayes . . . 5G 59
Grange Ct. HA0: Wemb . . . 3K 43
HA5: Pinn . . . 3C 24
NW10 . . . *3A 46*
(off Neasden La.)
SM2: Sutt . . . 7K 149
TW17: Shep . . . 4C 130
UB5: N'olt . . . 2A 60
WC2 . . . 6K 67 (1H 167)
Grangecourt Rd. N16 . . . 1E 50
Grange Cres. SE28 . . . 6C 74
Grangedale Cl.
HA6: Nwood . . . 1G 23
Grange Dr. BR7: Chst . . . 6C 126
Grange Farm Cl.
HA2: Harr . . . 2G 43
Grangefield *NW1* . . . *7H 49*
(off Marquis Rd.)
Grange Gdns. HA5: Pinn . . . 3C 24
N14 . . . 1C 16
NW3 . . . 3K 47
SE25 . . . 2E 140
Grange Gro. N1 . . . 6C 50
Grange Hill HA8: Edg . . . 5D 12
SE25 . . . 2E 140
Grangehill Pl. SE9 . . . 3D 108
Grangehill Rd. SE9 . . . 4D 108
Grange Ho. NW10 . . . 7D 46
SE1 . . . 3F 87
Grange La. SE21 . . . 2F 123
Grange Lodge SW19 . . . 6F 119
Grange Mans.
KT17: Eps . . . 7B 148
Grange M. TW13: Felt . . . 4J 113
Grangemill Rd. SE6 . . . 3C 124
Grangemill Way SE6 . . . 2C 124

Grange Mus. of Community History—Gt. Trinity La.

Grange Mus. of Community
History 4A 46
GRANGE PARK 6G 7
Grange Pk. W5 ....1E 80
Grange Pk. Av. N21 ....6H 7
Grange Pk. Pl. SW20 ....7D 118
Grange Pk. Rd.
CR7: Thor H 4D 140
E10 ....1D 52
Grange Pl. NW6 ....7J 47
Grange Rd.
CR2: S Croy 7C 152
CR7: Thor H 4D 140
E10 ....1C 52
E13 ....3H 71
E17 ....5A 34
(not continuous)
HA1: Harr 5A 26
HA2: Harr 2H 43
HA8: Edg 6E 12
IG1: Ilf 4F 55
KT1: King T 3E 134
KT8: W Mole 4F 133
KT9: Chess 4E 146
N6 ....6E 30
N17 ....6B 18
NW10 ....6D 46
SE1 ....3E 86
SE19 ....4D 140
SE25 ....4D 140
SM2: Sutt 7J 149
SW13 ....1C 100
UB1: S'hall 2C 78
UB3: Hayes 6G 59
W4 ....5H 81
W5 ....1D 80
Grange St. N1 ....1D 68
Grange, The CR0: Croy 2B 154
E17 ....5A 34
(off Grange Rd.)
HA0: Wemb 7G 45
KT3: N Mald 5B 136
KT4: Wor Pk 4K 147
N2 ....2B 30
N20 ....1F 15
(Grangeview Rd.)
N20 ....1G 15
(Oxford Gdns.)
SE1 ....3F 87
SW19 ....6F 119
W3 ....2H 81
W4 ....5H 81
W13 ....5C 62
W14 ....4H 83
Grange Va. SM2: Sutt 7K 149
Grangeview Rd. N20 ....1F 15
Grange Wlk. SE1 ....3E 86
Grange Wlk. M. SE1 ....3E 86
(off Grange Wlk.)
Grange Way IG8: Wfd G 4F 21
N12 ....4E 14
NW6 ....7J 47
Grangeway Gdns.
IG4: Ilf 5C 36
Grangeway, The N21 ....6G 7
Grangewood DA5: Bexl 1F 129
Grangewood Cl.
HA5: Pinn 5J 23
Grangewood Dr.
TW16: Sun T 7H 113
Grangewood La.
BR3: Beck 6B 124
Grangewood St. E6 ....1B 72
Grangewood Ter. SE25 ....2D 140
Grange Yd. SE1 ....3F 87
Granham Gdns. N9 ....2A 18
Granite St. SE18 ....5K 91
Granleigh Rd. E11 ....2G 53
Gransden Av. E8 ....7H 51
Gransden Ho. SE8 ....5B 88
Gransden Rd. W12 ....2B 82
Grantbridge St. N1 ....2B 68
Grantchester
KT1: King T 2G 135
(off St Peters Rd.)
Grantchester Cl.
HA1: Harr 3K 43
Grant Cl. N14 ....7B 6
TW17: Shep 6D 130
Grant Ct. E4 ....1K 19
(off Ridgeway, The)
NW9 ....2B 28
(off Hazel Cl.)
Grantham Cl. HA8: Edg 3K 11
Grantham Ct.
KT2: King T 5D 116
RM6: Chad H 7F 39
SE16 ....2K 87
(off Eleanor Cl.)
Grantham Gdns.
RM6: Chad H 6F 39
Grantham Ho. SE15 ....6G 87
(off Friary Est.)
Grantham Pl. W1 ....1F 85 (5J 165)
Grantham Rd. E12 ....4E 54
SW9 ....2J 103
W4 ....7A 82
Grantley Ho. SE14 ....6K 87
(off Myers La.)
Grantley Rd. TW4: Houn 2A 96
Grantley St. E1 ....3K 69
Grant Mus. of Zoology &
Comparative Anatomy
....4C 160
Grantock Rd. E17 ....1F 35
Granton Rd. DA14: Sidc 6C 128
IG3: Ilf 1A 56
SW16 ....1G 139
Grant Pl. CR0: Croy 1F 153
Grant Rd. CR0: Croy 1F 153
HA3: Harr 3K 25
SW11 ....4B 102
Grants Cl. NW7 ....7K 13
Grants Quay Wharf
EC3 ....7D 68 (3F 169)
Grant St. E13 ....3J 71
N1 ....2A 68
Grantully Rd. W9 ....3K 65
Grant Way TW7: Isle 6A 80
Granville Arc. SW9 ....4A 104
Granville Av. N9 ....3D 18
TW4: Houn 5E 96
TW13: Felt 2J 113
Granville Cl. CR0: Croy 2E 152
Granville Ct. N1 ....1E 68
SE14 ....7A 88
(off Nynehead St.)
Granville Gdns. SW16 ....1K 139
W5 ....1F 81
Granville Gro. SE13 ....3E 106
Granville Ho. E14 ....6C 70
(off E. India Dock Rd.)
Granville Mans. W12 ....2E 82
(off Shepherd's Bush Grn.)
Granville M. DA14: Sidc 4A 128
Granville Pk. SE13 ....3E 106
Granville Pl. HA5: Pinn 3B 24
N12 ....7F 15
SW6 ....7K 83
W1 ....6E 66 (1G 165)
Granville Point NW2 ....2H 47
Granville Rd. DA14: Sidc 4A 128
DA16: Well 3C 110
E17 ....6D 34
E18 ....2K 35
EN5: Barn 4A 4
IG1: Ilf 1F 55
N4 ....6K 31
N12 ....7F 15
N13 ....6E 16
N22 ....1B 32
NW2 ....2H 47
NW6 ....2J 65
(not continuous)
Granville Rd. SW18 ....7H 101
SW19 ....7J 119
UB3: Hayes 4H 77
UB10: Uxb 6D 40
Granville Sq. SE15 ....7E 86
WC1 ....3K 67 (2H 161)
Granville St.
WC1 ....3K 67 (2H 161)
Granwood Ct. TW7: Isle 1J 97
Grape St. WC2 ....6J 67 (7E 160)
Graphite Sq.
SE11 ....5K 85 (5G 173)
Grapsome Cl.
KT9: Chess 7C 146
Grasdene Rd. SE18 ....7A 92
Grasgarth Cl. W3 ....7J 63
Grasmere NW1 ....2K 159
(off Osnaburgh St.)
Grasmere Av. HA4: Ruis 7E 22
HA9: Wemb 7C 26
SW15 ....4K 117
SW19 ....3J 137
TW3: Houn 6F 97
W3 ....7K 63
Grasmere Cl.
TW14: Felt 1H 113
Grasmere Ct. N22 ....6E 16
SE26 ....5G 123
SM2: Sutt 6A 150
Grasmere Ct. SW13 ....6C 82
(off Verdun Rd.)
Grasmere Gdns.
HA3: Harr 2A 26
IG4: Ilf 5D 36
Grasmere Point SE15 ....7J 87
(off Old Kent Rd.)
Grasmere Rd.
BR1: Brom 1H 143
DA7: Bex 2J 111
E13 ....2J 71
N10 ....1F 31
N17 ....6B 18
SE25 ....6H 141
SW16 ....5K 121
Grasshaven Way SE28 ....1K 91
(not continuous)
Grassington Cl. N11 ....6K 15
Grassington Rd.
DA14: Sidc 4A 128
Grassmount SE23 ....2H 123
Grass Pk. N3 ....1H 29
Grass Way SM6: Wall 4G 151
Grasvenor Av. EN5: Barn 5D 4
Gratton Rd. W14 ....3G 83
Gratton Ter. NW2 ....3F 47
Gravel Hill CR0: Croy 6K 153
DA6: Bex 4H 111
N3 ....2H 29
UB8: Uxb 5A 40
Gravel Hill Cl. DA6: Bex 5H 111
Gravel La. E1 ....6F 69 (7J 163)
Gravel Pit La. SE9 ....5F 109
Gravel Rd. BR2: Short 3C 156
TW2: Twick 1J 115
Gravelwood Cl.
BR7: Chst 3G 127
Gravely Ho. SE8 ....4A 88
(off Chilton Gro.)
Gravenel Gdns. SW17 ....5C 120
(off Nutwell St.)
Graveney Gro. SE20 ....7J 123
Graveney Rd. SW17 ....4C 120
Gravesend Rd. W12 ....7C 64
Gray Av. RM8: Dag 1F 57
Grayham Cres.
KT3: N Mald 4K 135
Grayham Rd.
KT3: N Mald 4K 135
Gray Ho. SE17 ....5C 86
(off King & Queen St.)
Grayland Cl. BR1: Brom 1B 144
Grayling Cl. E16 ....4G 71
Grayling Ct. W5 ....1D 80
(off Grange Rd.)
Grayling Rd. N16 ....2D 50
Grayling Sq. E2 ....3G 69
(off Nelson Gdns.)
Grays Ct. RM10: Dag 7H 57
Grayscroft Rd. SW16 ....7H 121
Grays Farm Production Village
BR5: Orp 7B 128
Grays Farm Rd.
BR5: Orp 7B 128
Grayshott Rd. SW11 ....2E 102
Gray's Inn 5K 67 (5H 161)
Gray's Inn Bldgs. EC1 ....4J 161
(off Rosebery Av.)
Gray's Inn Pl.
WC1 ....5K 67 (6H 161)
Gray's Inn Rd.
WC1 ....3J 67 (1F 161)
Gray's Inn Sq.
WC1 ....5K 67 (5J 161)
Grays La. TW15: Ashf 4D 112
Grayson Ho. EC1 ....2D 162
Grays Rd. UB10: Uxb 2A 58
Gray St. SE1 ....2A 86 (7K 167)
Grayswood Gdns. SW20 ....2D 136
Gray's Yd. W1 ....1H 165
Graywood Ct. N12 ....7F 15
Grazebrook Rd. N16 ....2D 50
Grazeley Cl. DA6: Bex 5J 111
Grazeley Ct. SE19 ....5E 122
Gt. Acre Ct. SW4 ....4H 103
Gt. Arthur Ho. EC1 ....4C 162
(off Golden La. Est.)
Gt. Bell All.
EC2 ....6D 68 (7E 162)
Great Benty UB7: W Dray 4A 76
Great Brownings SE21 ....4F 123
Gt. Bushey Dr. N20 ....1E 14
Gt. Cambridge Ind. Est.
EN1: Enf 5C 8
GREAT CAMBRIDGE JUNCTION
....4J 17
Gt. Cambridge Rd.
EN1: Enf, Walt C 6B 8
N9: Enf 4J 17
N18 ....4J 17
Gt. Castle St. W1 ....6F 67 (7K 159)
Gt. Central Av. HA4: Ruis 5A 42
Gt. Central St.
NW1 ....5D 66 (5E 158)
Gt. Central Way
HA9: Wemb 4J 45
NW10 ....4J 45
Gt. Chapel St.
W1 ....6H 67 (7C 160)
Gt. Chertsey Rd.
TW13: Felt 3D 114
W4 ....2J 99
Gt. Church La. W6 ....4F 83
Gt. College St.
SW1 ....3J 85 (1E 172)
Great Cft. WC1 ....2F 161
(off Cromer St.)
Gt. Cross Av. SE10 ....7F 89
(not continuous)
Gt. Cumberland M.
W1 ....6D 66 (1E 164)
Gt. Cumberland Pl.
W1 ....6D 66 (7E 158)
Gt. Dover St.
SE1 ....2C 86 (7D 168)
Greatdown Rd. W7 ....4K 61
Gt. Eastern Bldgs. E1 ....5G 69
(off Fieldgate St.)
Gt. Eastern Ent. Cen. E14 ....2D 88
Gt. Eastern Rd. E15 ....7F 53
Gt. Eastern St.
EC2 ....3E 68 (2G 163)
Gt. Eastern Wlk. EC2 ....6H 163
Gt. Eastern Wharf SW11 ....7C 84
Gt. Elms Rd. BR2: Short 4A 144
Great Fld. NW9 ....1A 28
Greatfield Av. E6 ....4D 72
Greatfield Cl. N19 ....4G 49
SE4 ....4C 106
Greatfields Dr. UB8: Uxb 5C 58
Greatfields Rd. IG11: Bark 1H 73
Gt. Fleete Way IG11: Bark 2C 74
Gt. Galley Cl. IG11: Bark 3B 74
Gt. Gatton Cl. CR0: Croy 7A 142
Gt. George St.
SW1 ....2H 85 (7D 166)
Gt. Guildford Bus. Sq.
SE1 ....5C 168
Gt. Guildford St.
SE1 ....1C 86 (4C 168)
Great Hall
Royal Hospital Chelsea
....5D 84 (6F 171)
Greatham Wlk. SW15 ....1C 118
Gt. Harry Dr. SE9 ....3E 126
Gt. James St.
WC1 ....5K 67 (5G 161)
Gt. Marlborough St.
W1 ....6G 67 (1A 166)
Gt. Maze Pond
SE1 ....2D 86 (5F 169)
(not continuous)
Gt. Newport St.
WC2 ....7J 67 (2E 166)
Gt. New St. EC4 ....6A 68 (7K 161)
Gt. Nth. Leisure Pk. N12 ....7G 15
Gt. North Rd. EN5: Barn 5D 4
(Barnet Vale)
EN5: Barn 2C 4
(Monken Hadley)
N2 ....5C 30
Gt. North Way NW4 ....2D 28
Greatorex Ho. E1 ....5G 69
(off Spelman St.)
Greatorex St. E1 ....5G 69
Gt. Ormond St.
WC1 ....5J 67 (5F 161)
Gt. Owl Rd. IG7: Chig 3K 21
Gt. Percy St.
WC1 ....3K 67 (1H 161)
Gt. Peter St.
SW1 ....3H 85 (2C 172)
Gt. Portland St.
W1 ....4F 67 (4K 159)
Gt. Pulteney St.
W1 ....7G 67 (2B 166)
Gt. Queen St.
WC2 ....6J 67 (1F 167)
Gt. Russell St.
WC1 ....6H 67 (7D 160)
Gt. St Helen's
EC2 ....6E 68 (7G 163)
Gt. St Thomas Apostle
EC4 ....7C 68 (2D 168)
Gt. Scotland Yd.
SW1 ....1J 85 (5E 166)
Gt. Smith St.
SW1 ....3H 85 (1D 172)
Gt. South W. Rd.
TW4: Houn 4H 95
TW14: Felt 7E 94
Great Spilmans SE22 ....5E 104
Great Strand NW9 ....1B 28
Gt. Suffolk St.
SE1 ....1B 86 (5B 168)
Gt. Sutton St.
EC1 ....4B 68 (4B 162)
Gt. Swan All.
EC2 ....6D 68 (7E 162)
(not continuous)
Great Thrift BR5: Orp 4G 145
Gt. Titchfield St.
W1 ....4F 67 (4K 159)
Gt. Tower St.
EC3 ....7E 68 (2G 169)
Gt. Trinity La.
EC4 ....7C 68 (2D 168)

Great Turnstile—Greenways, The

Great Turnstile
WC1 . . . . . . .5K 67 (6H 161)
Gt. Western Ind. Pk.
UB2: S'hall 2F 79
Gt. Western Rd. W9 . . . . .5H 65
Gt. West Rd. TW5: Houn 2B 96
TW7: Isle 7A 80
W4 . . . . .5B 82
W6 . . . . .5B 82
Gt. West Trad. Est.
TW8: Bford 6B 80
Gt. Winchester St.
EC2 . . . . .6D 68 (7F 163)
Gt. Windmill St.
W1 . . . . .7H 67 (2C 166)
Greatwood BR7: Chst 7E 126
Great Yd. SE1 . . . . .6H 169
Greaves Cl. IG11: Bark 7H 55
Greaves Cotts. E14 . . . . .5A 70
Greaves Pl. SW17 . . . . .4C 120
Greaves Twr. *SW10* *7A 84*
(off Worlds End Est.)
Grebe Av. UB4: Hayes 6B 60
Grebe Cl. E7 . . . . .5H 53
E17 . . . . .7F 19
IG11: Bark 4A 74
Grebe Ct. *E14* *2E 88*
(off River Barge Cl.)
SE8 . . . .*6B 88*
(off Dorking Cl.)
SM1: Sutt 5H 149
Grebe Ter. KT1: King T 3E 134
Grecian Cres. SE19 . . . . . . .6B 122
Greek Ct. W1 . . . . .6H 67 (1D 166)
Greek St. W1 . . . . .6H 67 (1D 166)
Greenacre Cl. EN5: Barn 1C 4
UB5: N'olt 5D 42
Greenacre Gdns. E17 . . . . . . .4E 34
Greenacre Pl. SM6: Wall . . .2F 151
Green Acres CR0: Croy 3F 153
Greenacres DA14: Sidc 4A 128
N3 . . . . .2H 29
SE9 . . . . .6E 108
WD23: Bush 2C 10
Greenacres Av. UB10: Uxb . . .3B 40
Greenacres Dr. HA7: Stan . . .6G 11
Greenacre Sq. SE16 . . . . .2K 87
Greenacre Wlk. N14 . . . . .3C 16
Grn. Arbour Ct. *EC4* *7A 162*
(off Old Bailey)
Green Av. NW7 . . . . .4E 12
W13 . . . . .3B 80
Greenaway Av. N18 . . . . .6E 18
Greenaway Gdns. NW3 . . . . .4K 47
Greenaway Ho. *NW8* *1A 66*
(off Boundary Rd.)
WC1 . . . .*2J 161*
(off Fernsbury St.)
Green Bank E1 . . . . .1H 87
Greenbank N12 . . . . .4E 14
Greenbank Av.
HA0: Wemb 5A 44
Grn. Bank Cl. E4 . . . . .2K 19
Greenbank Cres. NW4 . . . . . .4G 29
Greenbank Lodge
BR7: Chst *2E 144*
(off Forest Cl.)
Greenbanks HA1: Harr 4J 43
Greenbay Rd. SE7 . . . . .7B 90
Greenberry St.
NW8 . . . . . .2C 66 (1C 158)
Greenbrook Av. EN4: Barn 1F 5
Green Cl. BR2: Short 3G 143
E15 . . . . .1G 71
NW9 . . . . .6J 27
NW11 . . . . .7A 30
SM5: Cars 2D 150
TW13: Felt 5C 114
Greencoat Mans. *SW1* *2B 172*
(off Greencoat Row)
Greencoat Pl.
SW1 . . . . . . .4G 85 (3B 172)
Greencoat Row
SW1 . . . . . . .3G 85 (2B 172)
Greencourt Av.
CR0: Croy 2H 153
HA8: Edg 1H 27
Greencourt Gdns.
CR0: Croy 1H 153
Greencourt Ho. *E1* *4K 69*
(off Mile End Rd.)
Greencourt Rd. BR5: Orp . . .5H 145
Greencrest Pl. NW2 . . . . .3C 46
Greencroft HA8: Edg 5D 12
Greencroft Av. HA4: Ruis 2A 42
Greencroft Cl. E6 . . . . .5B 72
Greencroft Gdns. EN1: Enf 3K 7
NW6 . . . . .7K 47
Greencroft Rd.
TW5: Houn 1D 96
Green Dale SE5 . . . . .4D 104
SE22 . . . . .5E 104
Greendale NW7 . . . . .4F 13
Grn. Dale Cl. SE22 . . . . .5E 104
Grn. Dragon Ct. SE1 . . . . . . .4E 168
Grn. Dragon La. N21 . . . . .6F 7
TW8: Bford 5E 80
Grn. Dragon Yd.
E1 . . . . .5G 69 (6K 163)
Green Dr. UB1: S'hall 1E 78
Greene Ct. *SE14* *6K 87*
(off Samuel Cl.)
Greene Ho. *SE1* *3D 86*
(off Burbage Cl.)
Green End KT9: Chess 4E 146
N21 . . . . .2G 17
Greenend Rd. W4 . . . . .2A 82
Greener Ho. SW4 . . . . .3H 103
Greenfell Mans. SE8 . . . . . . .6D 88
Greenfield Av.
KT5: Surb 7H 135
Greenfield Dr.
BR1: Brom 2A 144
N2 . . . . .4D 30
Greenfield Gdns.
BR5: Orp 7H 145
NW2 . . . . .2G 47
RM9: Dag 1D 74
Greenfield Rd. DA2: Dart . . .5K 129
E1 . . . . .5G 69
N15 . . . . .5E 32
RM9: Dag 7C 56
Greenfields UB1: S'hall 6E 60
Greenfield Way HA2: Harr . . .3F 25
GREENFORD 3E 60
Greenford Av. UB1: S'hall 7D 60
W7 . . . . .4J 61
Greenford Bus. Cen.
UB6: G'frd 7H 43
Greenford Gdns.
UB6: G'frd 3F 61
GREENFORD GREEN 6J 43
Greenford Ind. Est.
UB6: G'frd 7F 43
Greenford Rd. HA1: Harr 7J 43
SM1: Sutt 4K 149
(not continuous)
UB1: S'hall 1G 79
UB6: G'frd 7G 61
GREENFORD RDBT. 2H 61
Greengate UB6: G'frd 6B 44
Greengate Lodge *E13* *2K 71*
(off Hollybush St.)
Greengate Pde. IG2: Ilf 6H 37
Greengate St. E13 . . . . .2K 71
Greenhalgh Wlk. N2 . . . . .4A 30
Greenham Cl.
SE1 . . . . .2A 86 (7J 167)
Greenham Cres. E4 . . . . .6G 19
Greenham Ho. *E9* *1J 69*
(off Templecombe Rd.)
TW3: Houn 3H 97
Greenham Rd. N10 . . . . .2E 30
Greenhaven Dr. SE28 . . . . . . .6B 74
Greenheath Bus. Cen. *E2* . . .*4H 69*
(off Three Colts La.)
Green Hedge TW1: Twick 5C 98
Greenheys Cl.
HA6: Nwood 1G 23
Greenheys Dr. E18 . . . . .3H 35
Green Hill SE18 . . . . .5D 90
GREENHILL 5J 25
Greenhill HA9: Wemb 2H 45
IG9: Buck H 1F 21
NW3 . . . . .4B 48
Greenhill SM1: Sutt 2A 150
Greenhill Ct. EN5: Barn 5E 4
SE18 . . . . .5D 90
Greenhill Gdns. UB5: N'olt . . .2D 60
Greenhill Gro. E12 . . . . .4C 54
Greenhill Pde. EN5: Barn 5E 4
Greenhill Pk. EN5: Barn 5E 4
NW10 . . . . .1A 64
Greenhill Rd. HA1: Harr 6J 25
NW10 . . . . .1A 64
Greenhill's Rents
EC1 . . . . .5B 68 (5A 162)
Greenhills Ter. N1 . . . . .6D 50
Greenhill Ter. SE18 . . . . .5D 90
UB5: N'olt 2D 60
Greenhill Way
HA1: Harr 6J 25
HA9: Wemb 2H 45
Greenhithe Cl.
DA15: Sidc 7J 109
Greenholm Rd. SE9 . . . . . . .5F 109
Grn. Hundred Rd.
SE15 . . . . .6G 87
Greenhurst Rd. SE27 . . . . . .5A 122
Greening St. SE2 . . . . .4C 92
Greenland Cres.
UB2: S'hall 3A 78
Greenland Ho. *E1* *4A 70*
(off Ernest St.)
Greenland M. SE8 . . . . .5K 87
Greenland Pl. NW1 . . . . .1F 67
Greenland Quay SE16 . . . . . .4K 87
Greenland Rd. EN5: Barn 6A 4
NW1 . . . . .1G 67
Greenland St. NW1 . . . . .1F 67
Greenland Way
CR0: Croy 7H 139
Green La. BR7: Chst 2F 127
CR7: Thor H 1A 140
HA1: Harr 3J 43
HA7: Stan 4G 11
HA8: Edg 4A 12
IG1: Ilf 2H 55
IG3: Ilf 1B 56
KT3: N Mald 5J 135
KT4: Wor Pk 1C 148
KT8: W Mole 5F 133
KT9: Chess 7D 146
NW4 . . . . .4F 29
RM8: Dag 2A 56
SE9: Chst 1F 127
SE20 . . . . .7K 123
SM4: Mord 6J 137
(Central Rd.)
SM4: Mord 7E 136
(Lwr. Morden La.)
SW16 . . . . .7K 121
TW4: Houn 3K 95
TW13: Felt 5C 114
TW16: Sun T 7H 113
TW17: Shep 6E 130
UB8: Uxb 5E 58
W7 . . . . .2J 79
Green La. Bus. Pk. SE9 . . . .2E 126
Green La. Cotts.
HA7: Stan 4G 11
Green La. Gdns.
CR7: Thor H 2C 140
Green Lanes KT19: Eps 7A 148
(not continuous)
N8 . . . . .3B 32
Green Lanes N13 . . . . .6E 16
N16 . . . . .1C 50
N21 . . . . .3F 17
Greenlaw Ct. *W5* *6D 62*
(off Mt. Park Rd.)
Greenlaw Gdns.
KT3: N Mald 7B 136
Green Lawns HA4: Ruis 1A 42
Greenlawns N12 . . . . .6E 14
Greenlaw St. SE18 . . . . .3E 90
Grn. Leaf Av. SM6: Wall 4H 151
Greenleaf Cl. SW2 . . . . .7A 104
Greenleafe Dr. IG6: Ilf 3F 37
Greenleaf Rd. E6 . . . . .1A 72
E17 . . . . .3B 34
Green Leas *KT1: King T* *3E 134*
(off Mill St.)
TW16: Sun T 6H 113
Grn. Leas Cl.
TW16: Sun T 6H 113
Greenleaves Ct.
TW15: Ashf 6D 112
Grn. Man Gdns. W13 . . . . . . .7A 62
Grn. Man La. TW14: Felt 4J 95
(not continuous)
W13 . . . . .7A 62
Green Man Pas. W13 . . . . . . .7B 62
(not continuous)
GREEN MAN RDBT. 7H 35
Greenman St. N1 . . . . .7C 50
Greenmead DA18: Erith 3E 92
Greenmead Cl. SE25 . . . . . .5G 141
Green Moor Link N21 . . . . .7G 7
Greenmoor Rd. EN3: Enf 2D 8
Greenoak Pl. EN4: Barn 2J 5
Green Oaks UB2: S'hall 4B 78
Greenoak Way SW19 . . . . . .4F 119
Greenock Rd. SW16 . . . . . . .1H 139
W3 . . . . .3H 81
Greeno Cres.
TW17: Shep 5C 130
Green Pde. TW3: Houn 5F 97
Green Pk. . . . .*2F 85 (6K 165)*
Greenpark Ct. HA0: Wemb . . .7C 44
Grn. Park Way UB6: G'frd 7J 43
(not continuous)
Green Point E15 . . . . .6G 53
Grn. Pond Cl. E17 . . . . .3A 34
Grn. Pond Rd. E17 . . . . .3A 34
Green Rd. N14 . . . . .6A 6
N20 . . . . .3F 15
Greenroof Way *SE10* *3H 89*
(off W. Parkside)
Greenscape SE10 . . . . .3H 89
Green's Ct. W1 . . . . .2C 166
Green's End SE18 . . . . .4F 91
Greenshank Cl. E17 . . . . .7F 19
Greenshields Ind. Est. E16 . . .2J 89
Green Side RM8: Dag 1C 56
Greenside DA5: Bexl 1E 128
Greenside Cl. N20 . . . . .2G 15
SE6 . . . . .2F 125
Greenside Rd. CR0: Croy . . .7A 140
W12 . . . . .3C 82
Greenslade Rd.
IG11: Bark 7H 55
Grn. Slip Rd. EN5: Barn 2C 4
Greenstead Av. IG8: Wfd G . . .7F 21
Greenstead Cl. IG8: Wfd G . . .6F 21
Greenstead Gdns.
IG8: Wfd G 6F 21
SW15 . . . . .5D 100
Greensted Rd.
IG10: Lough 1H 21
Greenstone M. E11 . . . . .6J 35
Green St. E7 . . . . .6K 53
E13 . . . . .6A 54
EN3: Enf 2D 8
TW16: Sun T 1J 131
W1 . . . . .7E 66 (2G 165)
Greenstreet Hill SE14 . . . . .2K 105
Green Ter. EC1 . . . .3A 68 (2K 161)
Green, The BR1: Brom 3J 125
(not continuous)
BR2: Short 7J 143
BR5: Orp 7B 128
CR0: Croy 7B 154
DA7: Bex 1G 111
DA14: Sidc 4A 128
DA16: Well 4J 109
E4 . . . . .1K 19
E11 . . . . .6K 35
E15 . . . . .6G 53
HA0: Wemb 2A 44
IG8: Wfd G 5D 20
IG9: Buck H 1E 20
KT3: N Mald 3K 135
N9 . . . . .2B 18
N14 . . . . .2C 16
(not continuous)
N17 . . . . .6H 17
N21 . . . . .7F 7
SM1: Sutt 3K 149
SM4: Mord 4G 137
SM5: Cars 4E 150
SW19 . . . . .5F 119
TW2: Twick 1J 115
TW5: Houn 6E 78
TW9: Rich 5D 98
TW13: Felt 2K 113
TW17: Shep 4G 131
UB2: S'hall 3C 78
UB7: W Dray 3A 76
UB10: Uxb 2E 40
W3 . . . . .6A 64
W5 . . . . .1D 80
Green Va. DA6: Bex 5D 110
W5 . . . . .6F 63
Greenvale Rd. SE9 . . . . .4D 108
Green Verges HA7: Stan 7J 11
Green Vw. KT9: Chess 7F 147
Greenview Av.
BR3: Beck 6A 142
CR0: Croy 6A 142
Greenview Cl. W3 . . . . .1A 82
Greenview Ct.
TW15: Ashf 4B 112
Green Wlk. HA4: Ruis 1H 41
IG8: Wfd G 6H 21
IG10: Buck H 1H 21
NW4 . . . . .5F 29
SE1 . . . . .3E 86
TW12: Hamp 6D 114
UB2: S'hall 5E 78
Green Wlk., The E4 . . . . .1A 20
Green Way BR2: Short 6C 144
IG8: Wfd G 5F 21
SE9 . . . . .5B 108
SM6: Wall 4G 151
TW16: Sun T 4J 131
Greenway BR7: Chst 5E 126
HA3: Harr 5E 26
HA5: Pinn 2K 23
N14 . . . . .2D 16
N20 . . . . .2D 14
RM8: Dag 2C 56
SW20 . . . . .4E 136
UB4: Hayes 3J 59
Greenway Av. E17 . . . . .4F 35
Greenway Cl. N4 . . . . .2C 50
N11 . . . . .6K 15
N15 . . . . .4F 33
N20 . . . . .2D 14
NW9 . . . . .2K 27
Greenway Ct. IG1: Ilf 1E 54
Greenway Gdns.
CR0: Croy 3B 154
HA3: Harr 2J 25
NW9 . . . . .2K 27
UB6: G'frd 3E 60
Greenways BR3: Beck 3C 142
Greenways, The
TW1: Twick 6A 98

Grove Cl.—Hadfield Ho.

Grove Cl. TW13: Felt 4C 114
UB10: Uxb 5C 40
Grove Cotts. W4 6A 82
Grove Ct. KT1: King T 3E 134
(off Grove Cres.)
KT8: E Mos 4H 133
NW8 1A 158
SW10 6A 170
(off Drayton Gdns.)
TW3: Houn 4E 96
W5 1E 80
Grove Cres. E18 2H 35
KT1: King T 3E 134
KT12: Walt T 7K 131
NW9 4J 27
TW13: Felt 4C 114
Grove Cres. Rd. E15 6F 53
Grovedale Rd. N19 2H 49
Grove Dwellings E1 5J 69
Grove End E18 2H 35
NW5 4F 49
Grove End Gdns. NW8 2B 66
Grove End Ho. NW8 2A 158
Grove End La. KT10: Esh 7H 133
Grove End Rd.
NW8 2B 66 (1A 158)
Grovefield N11 4A 16
(off Coppies Gro.)
Grove Footpath
KT5: Surb 4E 134
Grove Gdns. EN3: Enf 1E 8
NW4 5C 28
NW8 3C 66 (2D 158)
RM10: Dag 3J 57
TW10: Rich 6F 99
TW11: Tedd 4A 116
Grove Grn. Rd. E10 3E 52
Grove Hall Ct.
NW8 3A 66 (1A 158)
Grove Hill E18 2H 35
HA1: Harr 7J 25
Grovehill Ct. BR1: Brom 6H 125
Grove Hill Rd. HA1: Harr 7K 25
SE5 3E 104
Grove Ho. SW3 7D 170
(off Chelsea Mnr. St.)
Grove Ho. Rd. N8 4J 31
Groveland Av. SW16 7K 121
Groveland Ct. EC4 1D 168
Groveland Rd. BR3: Beck 3B 142
Grovelands KT1: King T 4D 134
(off Palace Rd.)
KT8: W Mole 4E 132
Grovelands Cl. HA2: Harr 3F 43
SE5 2E 104
Grovelands Ct. N14 7C 6
Grovelands Rd. BR5: Orp 7A 128
N13 4E 16
N15 6G 33
Groveland Way
KT3: N Mald 5J 135
Grove La. KT1: King T 4E 134
SE5 1D 104
UB8: Uxb 4B 58
Grove La. Ter SE5 2D 104
Groveley Rd. TW13: Felt 5H 113
TW16: Sun T 5H 113
Grove Mans. W6 2E 82
(off Hammersmith Gro.)
Grove Mkt. Pl. SE9 6D 108
Grove M. W6 3E 82
Grove Mill Pl. SM5: Cars 3E 150
Grove Nature Reserve, The
4B 58
GROVE PARK 1J 99
3K 125
Grove Pk. E11 6K 35
NW9 4J 27
SE5 2E 104
Gro. Park Av. E4 7J 19
Gro. Park Bri. W4 7J 81
Gro. Park Gdns. W4 7H 81
Gro. Park Ind. Est. NW9 4K 27
Gro. Park M. W4 7J 81
Gro. Park Rd. N15 4E 32
SE9 3A 126
W4 7H 81
Gro. Park Ter. W4 7H 81
(not continuous)
Grove Pas. E2 2H 69
Grove Pl. IG11: Bark 7G 55
NW3 3B 48
SW12 7F 103
W3 1J 81
Grover Ct. SE13 2D 106
Grover Ho. SE11 5K 85 (6H 173)
Grove Rd. CR4: Mitc 3E 138
(not continuous)
CR7: Thor H 4A 140
DA7: Bex 4J 111
DA17: Belv 6F 93
E3 1K 69
E4 4K 19
E11 7H 35
E17 6D 34
E18 2H 35
EN4: Barn 3H 5
HA5: Pinn 5D 24
HA8: Edg 6B 12
KT6: Surb 5D 134
KT8: E Mos 4H 133
N11 5A 16
N12 5G 15
N15 5E 32
NW2 6E 46
RM6: Chad H 7B 38
SM1: Sutt 6J 149
SW13 2B 100
SW19 7A 120
TW2: Twick 3H 115
TW3: Houn 4E 96
TW7: Isle 1J 97
TW8: Bford 5C 80
TW10: Rich 6F 99
TW17: Shep 6E 130
UB8: Uxb 7A 40
W3 1J 81
W5 7D 62
Groveside Cl. SM5: Cars 2C 150
W3 5G 63
Groveside Rd. E4 2B 20
Grovestile Waye
TW14: Felt 7F 95
Grove St. N18 5A 18
SE8 4B 88
Grove Ter. NW5 3F 49
TW11: Tedd 4A 116
UB1: S'hall 7E 60
Grove Ter. M. NW5 3F 49
Grove, The 1G 123
Grove, The BR4: W W'ck 3D 154
DA6: Bex 4D 110
DA14: Sidc 5E 128
E15 6G 53
EN2: Enf 2F 7
HA7: Stan 2F 11
HA8: Edg 4C 12
KT12: Walt T 7K 131
N3 1J 29
N4 7K 31
N6 1E 48
N8 5H 31
N13 4F 17
(not continuous)
N14 5B 6
NW9 5K 27
NW11 7G 29
TW1: Twick 6B 98
TW7: Isle 1J 97
TW11: Tedd 4A 116
UB6: G'frd 6G 61
UB8: Uxb 4B 58
UB10: Uxb 5C 40
W5 1D 80
Grove Va. BR7: Chst 6E 126
SE22 4F 105
Grove Vs. E14 7D 70
Grove Way HA9: Wemb 5H 45
KT10: Esh 7G 133
UB8: Uxb 7A 40
Groveway RM8: Dag 4D 56
SW9 1K 103
Grovewood TW9: Rich 1G 99
Grovewood Pl. IG8: Wfd G 6J 21
Grummant Rd. SE15 1F 105
Grundy St. E14 6D 70
Gruneisen Rd. N3 7E 14
Guardian Ct. SE12 5G 107
Guards Memorial
1H 85 (5D 166)
Guards' Mus. 2G 85 (7B 166)
Gubyon Av. SE24 5B 104
Guerin Sq. E3 3B 70
Guernsey Cl. TW5: Houn 7E 78
Guernsey Gro. SE24 7C 104
Guernsey Ho. EN3: Enf 1E 8
(off Eastfield Rd.)
N1 6C 50
(off Douglas Rd. Nth.)
Guernsey Rd. E11 1F 53
N1 6C 50
Guibal Rd. SE12 7K 107
Guildersfield Rd. SW16 7J 121
Guildford Av. TW13: Felt 2H 113
Guildford Ct. SW8 7J 85
(off Guildford Rd.)
Guildford Gro. SE10 1D 106
Guildford Rd. CR0: Croy 6D 140
E6 6D 72
E17 1E 34
IG3: Ilf 2J 55
SW8 1J 103
Guildford Way SM6: Wall 5J 151
Guildhall
City 6C 68 (7D 162)
Westminster 7E 166
(off Lit. George St.)
Guildhall Art Gallery
6D 68 (7E 162)
Guildhall Bldgs. EC2 7E 162
Guildhall Library
6C 68 (7D 162)
Guildhall Offices EC2 7D 162
Guildhall School of Music &
Drama 5D 162
(off Silk St.)
Guildhall Yd.
EC2 6C 68 (7D 162)
Guildhouse St.
SW1 4G 85 (3A 172)
Guildown Av. N12 4E 14
Guild Rd. SE7 6B 90
Guildsway E17 1B 34
Guilford Av. KT5: Surb 5F 135
Guilford Pl. WC1 4K 67 (4G 161)
Guilford St. WC1 4J 67 (4E 160)
Guilfoyle NW9 2B 28
Guillemot Pl. N22 2K 31
Guilsborough Cl. NW10 7A 46
Guinness Cl. E9 7A 52
UB3: Hayes 3F 77
Guinness Ct. CR0: Croy 2F 153
E1 1J 169
EC1 2D 162
NW8 1C 66
SE1 6G 169
SW3 4D 84 (4E 170)
Guinness Sq. SE1 4E 86
Guinness Trust Bldgs.
SE17 5B 86
W6 5F 83
(off Fulham Pal. Rd.)
Guinness Trust Est. E15 1H 71
(off John St.)
N16 1E 50
Guion Rd. SW6 2H 101
Gulland Wlk. N1 7C 50
(off Church Rd.)
Gull Cl. SM6: Wall 7J 151
Gulliver Cl. UB5: N'olt 1D 60
Gulliver Rd. DA15: Sidc 2H 127
Gulliver's Ho. EC1 4C 162
Gulliver St. SE16 3A 88
Gulston Wlk. SW3 4F 171
Gumleigh Rd. W5 4C 80
Gumley Gdns. TW7: Isle 3A 98
Gundulph Rd.
BR2: Short 3A 144
Gun Ho. E1 1H 87
(off Wapping High St.)
Gunmaker's La. E3 1A 70
E9 1A 70
Gunnell Cl. CR0: Croy 6F 141
SE26 4G 123
Gunner La. SE18 5E 90
GUNNERSBURY 5H 81
Gunnersbury Av. W3 1F 81
W5 1F 81
Gunnersbury Cl. W4 5H 81
Gunnersbury Ct. W3 2H 81
Gunnersbury Cres. W3 2G 81
Gunnersbury Dr. W5 2F 81
Gunnersbury Gdns. W3 2G 81
Gunnersbury La. W3 3G 81
Gunnersbury Mnr. W5 1F 81
Gunnersbury M. W4 5H 81
GUNNERSBURY PARK 3G 81
Gunnersbury Pk. Mus. 3G 81
Gunnersbury Triangle Nature
Reserve 4J 81
(off Chiswick High Rd.)
Gunners Gro. E4 3K 19
Gunners Rd. SW18 2B 120
Gunnery Ter. SE18 3G 91
Gunning St. SE18 4J 91
Gunpowder Sq. EC4 7K 161
(off Gough Sq., not continuous)
Gunstor Rd. N16 4E 50
Gun St. E1 5F 69 (6J 163)
Gunter Gro. HA8: Edg 1K 27
SW10 6A 84
Gunterstone Rd. W14 4G 83
Gunthorpe St. E1 5F 69 (6K 163)
Gunton Rd. E5 3H 51
SW17 6E 120
Gunwhale Cl. SE16 1K 87
Gun Wharf E1 1J 87
(off Wapping High St.)
Gun Wharf Bus. Cen.
E3 1A 70
(off Old Ford Rd.)
Gurdon Ho. E14 6C 70
(off Dod St.)
Gurdon Rd. SE7 5J 89
Gurnard Cl. UB7: W Dray 7A 58
Gurnell Gro. W13 4K 61
Gurney Cl. E15 5G 53
E17 1K 33
IG11: Bark 6F 55
Gurney Cres. CR0: Croy 1K 151
Gurney Dr. N2 4A 30
Gurney Ho. E2 2G 69
(off Goldsmiths Row)
UB3: Hayes 5G 77
Gurney Rd. E15 5G 53
SM5: Cars 4E 150
SW6 3A 102
UB5: N'olt 3K 59
Guthrie Ct. SE1 7K 167
Guthrie St. SW3 5B 84 (5C 170)
Gutter La. EC2 6C 68 (7C 162)
Guyatt Gdns. CR4: Mitc 2E 138
Guy Barnett Gro. SE3 3J 107
Guy Rd. SM6: Wall 3H 151
Guyscliff Rd. SE13 5E 106
Guys Retreat IG9: Buck H 1F 21
Guy St. SE1 2D 86 (6F 169)
Gwalior Rd. SW15 4F 101
Gwendolen Av. SW15 4F 101
Gwendolen Cl. SW15 5F 101
Gwendoline Av. E13 1K 71
Gwendwr Rd. W14 5G 83
Gweneth Cotts. HA8: Edg 6B 12
Gwent Ct. SE16 1K 87
(off Rotherhithe St.)
Gwillim Cl. DA15: Sidc 5A 110
Gwilym Maries Ho. E2 3H 69
(off Blythe St.)
Gwydor Rd. BR3: Beck 3K 141
Gwydyr Rd. BR2: Short 3H 143
Gwyn Cl. SW6 7A 84
Gwynne Av. CR0: Croy 7K 141
Gwynne Cl. W4 6B 82
Gwynne Ho. E1 5H 69
(off Turner St.)
WC1 2J 161
(off Lloyd Baker St.)
Gwynne Pk. Av.
IG8: Wfd G 6J 21
Gwynne Pl. WC1 3K 67 (2H 161)
Gwynne Rd. SW11 2B 102
Gylcote Cl. SE5 4D 104
Gyles Pk. HA7: Stan 1C 26
Gyllyngdune Gdns.
IG3: Ilf 2K 55
GYPSY CORNER 5K 63

H

Haarlem Rd. W14 3F 83
Haberdasher Est.
N1 3D 68 (1F 163)
Haberdasher Pl. N1 1F 163
Haberdashers Ct. SE14 3K 105
Haberdasher St.
N1 3D 68 (1F 163)
Habington Ho. SE5 7D 86
(off Notley St.)
Haccombe Rd. SW19 6A 120
HACKBRIDGE 1E 150
Hackbridge Grn.
SM6: Wall 2E 150
Hackbridge Pk. Gdns.
SM5: Cars 2D 150
Hackbridge Rd.
SM6: Wall 2E 150
Hackford Rd. SW9 1K 103
Hackford Wlk. SW9 1K 103
Hackington Cres.
BR3: Beck 6C 124
HACKNEY 6H 51
Hackney Gro. E8 6H 51
Hackney Rd. E2 3F 69 (2J 163)
HACKNEY WICK 6B 52
HACKNEY WICK 6A 52
Hadar Cl. N20 1D 14
Hadden Rd. SE28 3J 91
Hadden Way UB6: G'frd 6H 43
Haddington Ct. SE10 7D 88
(off Tarves Way)
Haddington Rd.
BR1: Brom 3F 125
Haddo Ho. SE10 6D 88
(off Haddo St.)
Haddon Cl. EN1: Enf 6B 8
KT3: N Mald 5B 136
Haddon Ct. NW4 3E 28
W3 7B 64
Haddonfield SE8 4K 87
Haddon Gro. DA15: Sidc 7K 109
Haddon Hall St. SE1 3D 86
(off Rephidim St.)
Haddon Rd. SM1: Sutt 4K 149
Haddo St. SE10 6D 88
Haden Ct. N4 2A 50
Haden La. N11 4B 16
Hadfield Cl. UB1: S'hall 3D 60
Hadfield Ho. E1 6G 69
(off Ellen St.)

Hadleigh Cl. E1	4J 69
SW20	2H 137
Hadleigh Ct. E4	1B 20
Hadleigh Ho. E1	4J 69
(off Hadleigh Cl.)	
Hadleigh Rd. N9	7C 8
Hadleigh St. E2	3J 69
Hadleigh Wlk. E6	6C 72
HADLEY	3B 4
Hadley Cl. N21	6F 7
Hadley Comn. EN5: Barn	2D 4
Hadley Ct. EN5: Barn	3E 4
N16	1G 51
Hadley Gdns. UB2: S'hall	5D 78
W4	5K 81
Hadley Grn. Rd. EN5: Barn	2C 4
Hadley Grn. W. EN5: Barn	2C 4
Hadley Gro. EN5: Barn	2B 4
Hadley Highstone EN5: Barn	1C 4
Hadley Mnr. Trad. Est. EN5: Barn	3C 4
Hadley M. EN5: Barn	3C 4
Hadley Pde. EN5: Barn	3B 4
(off High St.)	
Hadley Ridge EN5: Barn	3C 4
Hadley Rd. CR4: Mitc	4H 139
DA17: Belv	4F 93
EN2: Enf	1A 6
EN4: Barn	1K 5
EN5: Barn	2E 4
Hadley St. NW1	6F 49
(not continuous)	
Hadley Way N21	6F 7
HADLEY WOOD	1F 5
Hadley Wood Rd. EN4: Barn	2F 5
Hadlow Ho. SE17	5E 86
(off Kinglake Est.)	
Hadlow Pl. SE19	7G 123
Hadlow Rd. DA14: Sidc	4A 128
DA16: Well	7C 92
Hadrian Cl. TW19: Staines	7A 94
Hadrian Ct. SM2: Sutt	7K 149
Hadrian Est. E2	2G 69
Hadrians Ride EN1: Enf	5A 8
Hadrian St. SE10	5G 89
Hadrian Way TW19: Staines	7A 94
(not continuous)	
Hadstock Ho. NW1	1D 160
(off Ossulston St.)	
Hadyn Pk. Ct. W12	2C 82
(off Curwen Rd.)	
Hadyn Pk. Rd. W12	2C 82
Hafer Rd. SW11	4D 102
Hafst Way BR8: Swan	7J 129
Hafton Rd. SE6	1G 125
Haggard Rd. TW1: Twick	7B 98
Hagger Ct. E17	3F 35
HAGGERSTON	7F 51
Haggerston Rd. E8	7F 51
Hague St. E2	3G 69
Ha Ha Rd. SE18	6D 90
Haig Ho. E2	1K 163
(off Shipton St.)	
Haig Pl. SM4: Mord	6J 137
Haig Rd. HA7: Stan	5H 11
UR8: Uxb	5D 58
Haig Rd. E. E13	3A 72
Haig Rd. W. E13	3A 72
Haigville Gdns. IG6: Ilf	4F 37
Hailes Cl. SW19	6A 120
Haileybury Av. EN1: Enf	6A 8
Haileybury Rd. E8: Erith	2G 93
Hailey Rd. Bus. Pk. DA18: Erith	2G 93
Hailsham Av. SW2	2K 121
Hailsham Cl. KT6: Surb	7D 134
Hailsham Dr. HA1: Harr	3H 25
Hailsham Rd. SW17	6E 120
Hailsham Ter. N18	5J 17
Haimo Rd. SE9	5B 108

Hainault Ct. E17	4F 35
Hainault Gore RM6: Chad H	5E 38
Hainault Rd. E11	1E 52
RM5: Col R, Rom	2J 39
RM6: Chad H	1B 38
(Forest Rd.)	
RM6: Chad H	6F 39
(High Rd.)	
Hainault St. IG1: Ilf	2G 55
SE9	1F 127
Haines St. SW8	7G 85
Haines Wlk. SM4: Mord	7K 137
Hainford Cl. SE4	4K 105
Haining Cl. W4	5G 81
Hainthorpe Rd. SE27	3B 122
Hainton Cl. E1	6H 69
Halberd M. E5	2H 51
Halbut Gdns. RM9: Dag	3F 57
Halbutt St. RM9: Dag	4F 57
Halcomb St. N1	1E 68
Halcot Av. DA6: Bex	5H 111
Halcrow St. E1	5H 69
Halcyon EN1: Enf	5K 7
(off Private Rd.)	
Halcyon Wharf E1	1G 87
(off Hermitage Wall)	
Haldane Cl. N10	7A 16
Haldane Pl. SW18	1K 119
Haldane Rd. E6	3B 72
SE28	2D 74
SW6	7H 83
UB1: S'hall	7G 61
Haldan Rd. E4	6K 19
Haldon Rd. SW18	6H 101
Hale Cl. E4	3K 19
HA8: Edg	5D 12
Hale Ct. HA8: Edg	5D 12
Hale Dr. NW7	6D 12
HALE END	6B 20
Hale End Cl. HA4: Ruis	6J 23
Hale End Rd. E4	6A 20
E17	1E 34
IG8: Wfd G	7A 20
Halefield Rd. N17	1H 33
Hale Gdns. N17	4G 33
W3	1G 81
Hale Ho. SW1	5D 172
(off Lindsay Sq.)	
Hale La. HA8: Edg	5C 12
NW7	5E 12
Hale Path SE27	4B 122
Hale Rd. E6	4C 72
N17	3G 33
Halesowen Rd. SM4: Mord	7K 137
Hales Prior N1	1G 161
(off Calshot St.)	
Hales St. SE8	7C 88
Hale St. E14	7D 70
Halesworth Cl. E5	2J 51
Halesworth Rd. SE13	3D 106
HALE, THE	5D 12
Hale, The E4	7A 20
N17	4G 33
Hale Wlk. W7	5J 61
Haley Rd. NW4	6E 28
Half Acre HA7: Stan	6H 11
TW8: Bford	6D 80
Half Acre Rd. W7	1J 79
Half Moon Ct. EC1	6C 162
Half Moon Cres. N1	2K 67
(not continuous)	
Half Moon La. SE24	6C 104
Half Moon Pas. E1	6F 69 (1K 169)
Half Moon St. W1	1F 85 (4K 165)
Halford Cl. HA8: Edg	2H 27

Halford Rd. E10	5F 35
SW6	6J 83
TW10: Rich	5E 98
UB10: Uxb	4C 40
Halfway St. DA15: Sidc	7H 109
Haliburton Rd. TW1: Twick	5A 98
Haliday Ho. N1	6D 50
(off Mildmay St.)	
Haliday Wlk. N1	6D 50
Halidon Cl. E9	5J 51
Halifax Cl. TW11: Tedd	6J 115
Halifax Rd. EN2: Enf	2H 7
UB6: G'frd	1F 61
Halifax St. SE26	3H 123
Halifield Dr. DA17: Belv	3E 92
Haling Down Pas. CR2: S Croy	7C 152
(not continuous)	
Haling Gro. CR2: S Croy	7C 152
Haling Pk. Gdns. CR2: S Croy	6B 152
Haling Pk. Rd. CR2: S Croy	5B 152
Haling Rd. CR2: S Croy	6D 152
Hallwell Ho. NW6	1K 65
(off Mortimer Cres.)	
Halkin Arc. SW1	3D 84 (1F 171)
(not continuous)	
Halkin M. SW1	3E 84 (1G 171)
Halkin Pl. SW1	3E 84 (1G 171)
Halkin St. SW1	2E 84 (7H 165)
Hallam Cl. BR7: Chst	5D 126
Hallam Ct. W1	5K 159
(off Hallam St.)	
Hallam Gdns. HA5: Pinn	1C 24
Hallam Ho. SW1	6B 172
(off Churchill Gdns.)	
Hallam M. W1	5F 67 (5K 159)
Hallam Rd. N15	4B 32
SW13	3D 100
Hallam St. W1	4F 67 (4K 159)
Hallane Ho. SE27	5C 122
Hall Cl. W5	5E 62
Hall Ct. TW11: Tedd	5K 115
Hall Dr. SE26	5J 123
W7	6J 61
Halley Gdns. SE13	4F 107
Halley Ho. E2	2G 69
SE10	5H 89
(off Armitage Rd.)	
Halley Rd. E7	6A 54
E12	6A 54
Halley St. E14	5A 70
Hall Farm Cl. HA7: Stan	4G 11
Hall Farm Dr. TW2: Twick	7H 97
Hallfield Est. W2	6A 66
(not continuous)	
Hall Gdns. E4	3A 20
Hall Ga. NW8	3B 66 (1A 158)
Halliards, The KT12: Walt T	6J 131
Halliday Sq. UB2: S'hall	1H 79
Halliford Cl. TW17: Shep	4F 131
Halliford Rd. TW16: Sun T	5G 131
TW17: Shep, Sun T	5G 131
Halliford St. N1	7C 50
Hallingbury Ct. E17	3D 34
Halliwell Cl. SE22	5G 105
Halliwell Rd. SW2	6K 103
Hallowell Cl. Pde. N12	6J 15
(off Woodhouse Rd.)	
Halliwick Rd. N10	1E 30
Hall La. E4	5F 19
NW4	1C 28
UB3: Hayes	7F 77

Hall Lane Junction	5E 18
Hallmark Trad. Cen. HA9: Wemb	4J 45
Hallmead Rd. SM1: Sutt	3K 149
Hall Oak Wlk. NW6	6H 47
Hallowell Av. CR0: Croy	4J 151
Hallowell Cl. CR4: Mitc	3E 138
Hallowell Rd. HA6: Nwood	1G 23
Hallowfield Way CR4: Mitc	3C 138
Hall Pl. W2	4B 66 (4A 158)
(not continuous)	
Hall Place & Visitors Cen.	6J 111
Hall Pl. Cres. DA5: Bexl	5J 111
Hall Place Gardens	6J 111
Hall Rd. E6	1D 72
E15	4F 53
NW8	3A 66 (1A 158)
RM6: Chad H	6C 38
SM6: Wall	7F 151
TW7: Isle	5H 97
Hallside Rd. EN1: Enf	1A 8
Hall St. EC1	3B 68 (1B 162)
N12	5F 15
Hallsville Rd. E16	6H 71
Hallswelle Pde. NW11	5H 29
Hallswelle Rd. NW11	5H 29
Hall, The SE3	3J 107
Hall Twr. W2	5B 158
Hall Vw. SE9	2B 126
Hallywell Cres. E6	5D 72
Halons Rd. SE9	7E 108
Halpin Pl. SE17	4D 86
Halsbrook Rd. SE3	3A 108
Halsbury Cl. HA7: Stan	4G 11
Halsbury Ho. N7	5G 11
Halsbury Rd. W12	1D 82
Halsbury Rd. E. UB5: N'olt	4G 43
Halsbury Rd. W. UB5: N'olt	5F 43
Halsend UB3: Hayes	1K 77
Halsey M. SW3	4D 84 (3E 170)
Halsey St. SW3	4D 84 (3E 170)
Halsham Cres. IG11: Bark	5K 55
Halsmere Rd. SE5	1B 104
Halstead Cl. CR0: Croy	3C 152
Halstead Ct. E17	7B 34
N1	1E 163
(off Fairbank Est.)	
Halstead Gdns. N21	1J 17
Halstead Rd. E11	5J 35
EN1: Enf	4K 7
N21	1J 17
Halston Cl. SW11	6D 102
Halstow Rd. NW10	3F 65
SE10	5J 89
Halsway UB3: Hayes	1J 77
Halton Cl. N11	6J 15
Halton Cross St. N1	1B 68
Halton Mans. N1	7B 50
Halton Pl. N1	1C 68
Halton Rd. N1	7B 50
Halt Robin La. DA17: Belv	4H 93
Halt Robin Rd. DA17: Belv	4G 93
(not continuous)	
Halyard Ho. E14	3E 88
HAM	3C 116
Hamara Ghar E13	1A 72
Hambalt Rd. SW4	5G 103
Hamble Cl. HA4: Ruis	2G 41
Hambledon SE17	6D 86
(off Villa St.)	
Hambledon Cl. UB8: Uxb	4D 58
Hambledon Ct. SE22	4E 104
Hambledon Gdns. SE25	3F 141
Hambledon Pl. SE21	1E 122
Hambledon Rd. SW18	7H 101
Hambledown Rd. DA15: Sidc	7H 109

Hamblehyrst BR3: Beck	2D 142
Hamble St. SW6	3K 101
Hambleton Cl. KT4: Wor Pk	2E 148
Hamble Wlk. UB5: N'olt	2E 60
(off Brabazon Rd.)	
Hambley Ho. SE16	4H 87
(off Camilla Rd.)	
Hamblin Ho. UB1: S'hall	7C 60
(off Broadway, The)	
Hambridge Way SW2	7A 104
Hambro Av. BR2: Short	1J 155
Hambro Rd. SE25	3H 141
Hambro Rd. SW16	6H 121
Hambrough Ho. UB4: Hayes	5A 60
Hambrough Rd. UB1: S'hall	1C 78
Ham Cl. TW10: Rich	3C 116
(not continuous)	
Ham Comn. TW10: Rich	3D 116
Ham Ct. NW9	2A 28
Hamden Cres. RM10: Dag	3H 57
Hamel Cl. HA3: Harr	4D 26
Hamey Way E6	4E 72
Ham Farm Rd. TW10: Rich	4D 116
Hamfrith Rd. E15	6H 53
Ham Ga. Av. TW10: Rich	3D 116
Ham House	1C 116
Hamilton Av. IG6: Ilf	4F 37
KT6: Surb	2G 147
N9	7B 8
RM1: Rom	2K 39
SM3: Sutt	2G 149
Hamilton Bldgs. EC2	4H 163
Hamilton Cl. EN4: Barn	4H 5
HA7: Stan	2D 10
N17	3F 33
NW8	3B 66 (2A 158)
SE16	2A 88
TW13: Felt	5H 113
Hamilton Ct. CR0: Croy	1G 153
SE6	1H 125
SW15	3G 101
W5	7E 62
W9	3A 66
(off Maida Va.)	
Hamilton Cres. HA2: Harr	3D 42
N13	4F 17
TW3: Houn	5F 97
Hamilton Gdns. NW8	3A 66 (1A 158)
Hamilton Ho. E14	5D 88
(off St Davids Sq.)	
E14	7B 70
(off Victory Pl.)	
NW8	1A 158
W4	6A 82
Hamilton La. N5	4B 50
Hamilton Lodge E1	4J 69
(off Cleveland Gro.)	
Hamilton M. SW18	1J 119
SW19	7J 119
W1	2F 85 (6J 165)
Hamilton Pde. TW13: Felt	4H 113
Hamilton Pk. N5	4B 50
Hamilton Pk. W. N5	4B 50
Hamilton Pl. TW16: Sun T	7K 113
W1	1E 84 (5H 165)
Hamilton Rd. CR7: Thor H	3D 140
DA7: Bex	2E 110
DA15: Sidc	4A 128
E15	3G 71
E17	2A 34
EN4: Barn	4H 5
HA1: Harr	5J 25
IG1: Ilf	4F 55
N2	3A 30

Hamilton Rd.—Harbury Rd.

Hamilton Rd. N9 7B 8
NW10 5C 46
NW11 7F 29
SE27 4D 122
SW19 7K 119
TW2: Twick 1J 115
TW8: Bford 6D 80
TW13: Felt 4H 113
UB1: S'hall 1D 78
UB3: Hayes 7K 59
W4 2A 82
W5 7E 62
Hamilton Rd. Ind. Est.
SE27 4D 122
(off Hamilton Rd.)
Hamilton Rd. M. SW19 7K 119
Hamilton Sq. N12 6G 15
SE1 6F 169
Hamilton St. SE8 6C 88
Hamilton Ter.
NW8 2K 65 (2A 158)
Hamilton Way N3 6D 14
N13 4G 17
SM6: Wall 7H 151
Hamlea Cl. SE12 5J 107
Hamlet Cl. RM5: Col R 1G 39
SE13 4G 107
Hamlet Ct. EN1: Enf 5K 7
SE11 5B 86
(off Opal St.)
W6 4C 82
Hamlet Gdns. W6 4C 82
Hamlet Ind. Est. E9 7C 52
Hamlet International Trad. Est.
DA8: Erith 5K 93
Hamlet Rd. RM5: Col R 1G 39
SE19 7F 123
Hamlet Sq. NW2 3G 47
Hamlets Way E3 4B 70
Hamlet, The SE5 3D 104
Hamlet Way SE1 2D 86 (6F 169)
Hamlin Cres. HA5: Pinn 5A 24
Hamlyn Cl. HA8: Edg 3K 11
Hamlyn Gdns. SE19 7E 122
Hammelton Ct.
BR1: Brom 1H 143
(off London Rd.)
Hammelton Grn. SW9 1B 104
Hammelton Rd.
BR1: Brom 1H 143
Hammerfield Ho. SW3 5D 170
(off Cale St.)
Hammers La. NW7 5H 13
Hammersley Ho. SE14 7J 87
(off Pomeroy St.)
HAMMERSMITH 4E 82
Hammersmith Bri. SW13 6D 82
Hammersmith Bri. Rd.
W6 5E 82
Hammersmith Broadway
4E 82
(off Hammersmith Rd.)
Hammersmith B'way. W6 4E 82
Hammersmith Flyover 5E 82
Hammersmith Flyover W6 5E 82
Hammersmith Gro. W6 2E 82
Hammersmith Ind. Est.
W6 6E 82
Hammersmith Rd. W6 4F 83
W14 4F 83
Hammersmith Ter. W6 5C 82
Hammet Cl. UB4: Hayes 5B 60
Hammett St.
EC3 7F 69 (2J 169)
Hammond Av. CR4: Mitc 2F 139
Hammond Cl. EN5: Barn 5B 4
TW12: Hamp 1E 132
UB6: G'frd 5H 43
Hammond Ct. E10 2D 52
(off Crescent Rd.)
E17 5A 34
(off Maude Rd.)
Hammond Ho. E14 3C 88
(off Tiller Rd.)
SE14 7J 87
(off Lubbock St.)
Hammond Lodge W9 5J 65
(off Admiral Wlk.)
Hammond Rd. EN1: Enf 2C 8
UB2: S'hall 3C 78
Hammonds Cl. RM8: Dag 3C 56
Hammond St. NW5 6G 49
Hammond Way SE28 7B 74
Hamond Cl. CR2: S Croy 7B 152
Hamonde Cl. HA8: Edg 2C 12
Hamond Sq. N1 2E 68
(off Hoxton St.)
Ham Pk. Rd. E7 7H 53
E15 7H 53
Hampden Av. BR3: Beck 2A 142
Hampden Cl. NW1 2H 67
Hampden Ct. N10 7K 15
Hampden Gurney St.
W1 6D 66 (1E 164)
Hampden Ho. SW9 2A 104
Hampden La. N17 1F 33
Hampden Rd. BR3: Beck 2A 142
HA3: Harr 1G 25
KT1: King T 3G 135
N8 4A 32
N10 7K 15
N17 1G 33
N19 2H 49
RM5: Col R 1H 39
Hampden Sq. N14 1A 16
Hampden Way N14 1A 16
Hampshire Cl. N18 5C 18
Hampshire Hog La. W6 5D 82
Hampshire Rd. N22 7E 16
Hampshire St. NW5 6H 49
Hampson Way SW8 1K 103
HAMPSTEAD 4B 48
Hampstead Av.
IG8: Wfd G 7K 21
Hampstead Cl. SE28 1B 92
Hampstead Gdns. NW11 6J 29
RM6: Chad H 5B 38
HAMPSTEAD GARDEN SUBURB
5A 30
Hampstead Grn. NW3 5C 48
Hampstead Gro. NW3 3A 48
Hampstead Heath 7K 29
2B 48
Hampstead Heath Info. Cen.
4E 48
Hampstead Hgts. N2 3A 30
Hampstead High St. NW3 4B 48
Hampstead Hill Gdns.
NW3 4B 48
Hampstead La. N6 7B 30
NW3 1B 48
Hampstead Mus. 4B 48
(in Burgh House)
Hampstead Rd.
NW1 2G 67 (1A 160)
Hampstead Sq. NW3 3A 48
Hampstead Theatre Club
7B 48
(off Avenue Rd.)
Hampstead Wlk. E3 1B 70
Hampstead Way NW11 5H 29
Hampstead W. NW6 6J 47
HAMPTON 1F 133
Hampton Cl. N11 5A 16
NW6 3J 65
SW20 7E 118
HAMPTON COURT 4J 133
Hampton Court 3J 133
Hampton Ct. N1 6B 50
N22 1G 31
SE16 7K 69
(off King & Queen Wharf)
Hampton Ct. Av.
KT8: E Mos 6H 133
Hampton Ct. Bri.
KT8: E Mos 4J 133
Hampton Ct. Cres.
KT8: E Mos 3H 133
Hampton Court Palace 4K 133
Hampton Ct. Pde.
KT8: E Mos 4J 133
Hampton Ct. Rd.
KT1: King T 3A 134
KT8: E Mos 3K 133
TW12: Hamp 2G 133
Hampton Court Way
KT7: E Mos, T Ditt 7J 133
KT8: E Mos 7J 133
Hampton Farm Ind. Est.
TW13: Felt 3C 114
HAMPTON HILL 5G 115
Hampton Ho. DA7: Bex 2H 111
(off Erith Rd.)
Hampton La. TW13: Felt 4C 114
Hampton M. NW10 3K 63
Hampton Ri. HA3: Harr 6E 26
Hampton Rd. CR0: Croy 6C 140
E4 5G 19
E7 5K 53
E11 1F 53
IG1: Ilf 4G 55
KT4: Wor Pk 2C 148
TW2: Twick 3H 115
TW11: Tedd 5H 115
Hampton Rd. E.
TW13: Felt 4D 114
Hampton Rd. W.
TW13: Felt 3C 114
Hampton St. SE1 4B 86
SE17 4B 86
HAMPTON WICK 1C 134
Ham Ridings TW10: Rich 5F 117
Hamshades Cl.
DA15: Sidc 3K 127
Ham St. TW10: Rich 1B 116
Ham, The TW8: Bford 7C 80
Ham Vw. CR0: Croy 6A 142
Ham Yd. W1 7H 67 (2C 166)
Hanah Ct. SW19 7F 119
Hanameel St. E16 1J 89
Hana M. E5 4H 51
Hanbury Cl. NW4 3E 28
Hanbury Ct. HA1: Harr 6K 25
Hanbury Dr. E11 7H 35
N21 5E 6
Hanbury Ho. E1 5G 69
(off Hanbury St.)
SW8 7J 85
(off Regent's Bri. Gdns.)
Hanbury M. N1 1C 68
Hanbury Rd. N17 2H 33
W3 2H 81
Hanbury St. E1 5F 69 (5K 163)
Hanbury Wlk. DA5: Bexl 3K 129
Hancock Nunn Ho. NW3 6D 48
(off Fellows Rd.)
Hancock Rd. E3 3E 70
SE19 6D 122
Handa Wlk. N1 6D 50
Hand Ct. WC1 5K 67 (6H 161)
Handcroft Rd. CR0: Croy 7B 140
Handel Cl. HA8: Edg 6A 12
Handel House Mus. 2J 165
(off Brook St.)
Handel Mans. SW13 7E 82
WC1 3F 161
(off Handel St.)
Handel Pde. HA8: Edg 7B 12
(off Whitchurch La.)
Handel Pl. NW10 6K 45
Handels Bus. Cen.
SW8 6J 85 (7E 172)
Handel St.
WC1 4J 67 (3E 160)
Handel Way HA8: Edg 7B 12
Handen Rd. SE12 5G 107
Handforth Rd. IG1: Ilf 3F 55
SW9 7A 86
Handley Gro. NW2 3F 47
Handley Page Rd.
SM6: Wall 7K 151
Handley Rd. E9 7J 51
Handowe Cl. NW4 4C 28
Handside Cl.
KT4: Wor Pk 1F 149
Hands Wlk. E16 6J 71
Handsworth Av. E4 6A 20
Handsworth Rd. N17 3D 32
Handtrough Way
IG11: Bark 2F 73
Hanford Cl. SW18 1J 119
Hanford Row SW19 6E 118
Hanger Ct. W5 4F 63
Hanger Grn. W5 4G 63
HANGER HILL 4F 63
Hanger Lane 3E 62
Hanger La. W5 2E 62
Hanger Va. La. W5 6F 63
(not continuous)
Hanger Vw. Way W3 6G 63
Hanging Sword All.
EC4 1K 167
Hankey Pl. SE1 2D 86 (7F 169)
Hankins La. NW7 2F 13
Hanley Gdns. N4 1K 49
Hanley Pl. BR3: Beck 7C 124
Hanley Rd. N4 1J 49
Hanmer Wlk. N7 2K 49
Hannah Barlow Ho. SW8 1K 103
Hannah Cl. BR3: Beck 3E 142
NW10 4J 45
Hannah Mary Way SE1 4G 87
Hannah M. SM6: Wall 7G 151
Hannay La. N8 7H 31
Hannay Wlk. SW16 2H 121
Hannell Rd. SW6 7G 83
Hannen Rd. SE27 3B 122
Hannibal Rd. E1 5J 69
TW19: Staines 7A 94
Hannibal Way CR0: Croy 5K 151
Hannington Point E9 6B 52
(off Eastway)
Hannington Rd. SW4 3F 103
Hanover Av. E16 1J 89
TW13: Felt 1J 113
Hanover Circ. UB3: Hayes 6E 58
Hanover Cl. SM3: Sutt 4G 149
TW9: Rich 7G 81
Hanover Ct. HA4: Ruis 3J 41
NW9 3A 28
SE19 7F 123
(off Anerley Va.)
SW15 4B 100
W12 1C 82
(off Uxbridge Rd.)
Hanover Dr. BR7: Chst 4G 127
Hanover Flats W1 2H 165
(off Binney St., not continuous)
Hanover Gdns. IG6: Ilf 1G 37
SE11 6A 86
Hanover Ga.
NW1 3C 66 (2D 158)
Hanover Ga. Mans. NW1 4C 66
Hanover Ho. E14 1B 88
(off Westferry Cir.)
NW8 1C 158
SW9 3A 104
Hanover Mans. SW2 5A 104
Hanover Mead NW11 5G 29
Hanover Pk. SE15 1G 105
Hanover Pl. E3 3B 70
WC2 6J 67 (1F 167)
Hanover Rd. N15 4F 33
NW10 7E 46
SW19 7A 120
Hanover Sq.
W1 6F 67 (1K 165)
Hanover Steps W2 1D 164
Hanover St. CR0: Croy 3B 152
W1 6F 67 (1K 165)
Hanover Ter.
NW1 3C 66 (2E 158)
TW7: Isle 1A 98
Hanover Ter. M.
NW1 3C 66 (2D 158)
Hanover Trad. Est. N7 5J 49
Hanover Way DA6: Bex 3D 110
Hanover W. Ind. Est.
NW10 3K 63
Hanover Yd. N1 2C 68
(off Noel Rd.)
Hansard M. W14 2F 83
(not continuous)
Hansart Way EN2: Enf 1F 7
Hanscomb M. SW4 4G 103
Hans Cres. SW1 3D 84 (1E 170)
Hanselin Cl. HA7: Stan 5E 10
Hansen Dr. N21 5E 6
Hanshaw Dr. HA8: Edg 1K 27
Hansler Gro. KT8: E Mos 4H 133
Hansler Rd. SE22 5F 105
Hansol Rd. DA6: Bex 5E 110
Hansom Ter. BR1: Brom 1K 143
(off Freelands Gro.)
Hanson Cl. BR3: Beck 6D 124
SW12 7F 103
SW14 3J 99
UB7: W Dray 3B 76
Hanson Ct. E17 6D 34
Hanson Gdns. UB1: S'hall 2C 78
Hanson St. W1 5G 67 (5A 160)
Hans Pl. SW1 3D 84 (1F 171)
Hans Rd. SW3 3D 84 (1E 170)
Hans St. SW1 3D 84 (2F 171)
Hanway Pl. W1 6H 67 (7C 160)
Hanway Rd. W7 6H 61
Hanway St. W1 6H 67 (7C 160)
HANWELL 1K 79
HANWORTH 5C 114
Hanworth Ho. SE5 7B 86
(not continuous)
Hanworth Rd.
TW4: Houn 1C 114
TW12: Hamp 4D 114
TW13: Felt 1K 113
TW16: Sun T 7J 113
(not continuous)
Hanworth Ter. TW3: Houn 4F 97
Hanworth Trad. Est.
TW13: Felt 3C 114
Hapgood Cl. UB6: G'frd 5H 43
Harad's Pl. E1 7G 69
Harben Pde. NW3 7A 48
(off Finchley Rd.)
Harben Rd. NW6 7A 48
Harberson Rd. E15 1H 71
SW12 1F 121
Harberton Rd. N19 1G 49
Harbet Rd. N18 5F 19
W2 5B 66 (6B 158)
Harbex Cl. DA5: Bexl 7H 111
Harbinger Rd. E14 4D 88
Harbledown Ho. SE1 7E 168
(off Manciple St.)
Harbledown Rd. SW6 1J 101
Harbord Cl. SE5 2D 104
Harbord Ho. SE16 4K 87
(off Cope St.)
Harbord St. SW6 1F 101
Harborough Av.
DA15: Sidc 7J 109
Harborough Rd. SW16 4K 121
Harbour Av. SW10 1A 102
Harbour Exchange Sq.
E14 2D 88
Harbour Quay E14 1E 88
Harbour Rd. SE5 3C 104
Harbour Yd. SW10 1A 102
Harbridge Av. SW15 7B 100
Harbury Rd. SM5: Cars 7C 150

260 A-Z London

Harbut Rd.—Harrow Rd.

Harbut Rd. SW11 . . . . 4B 102
(not continuous)
Harcombe Rd. N16 . . . . 3E 50
Harcourt Av. DA15: Sidc 6C 110
E12 . . . . 4D 54
HA8: Edg 3D 12
SM6: Wall 4F 151
Harcourt Bldgs. EC4 . . . . 2J 167
Harcourt Cl. TW7: Isle 3A 98
Harcourt Fld. SM6: Wall . . . 4F 151
Harcourt Lodge
SM6: Wall 4F 151
Harcourt Rd.
CR7: Thor H 6K 139
DA6: Bex 4E 110
E15 . . . . 2H 71
N22 . . . . 1H 31
SE4 . . . . 3B 106
SM6: Wall 4F 151
SW19 . . . . 7J 119
Harcourt St. W1 . . . 5C 66 (6D 158)
Harcourt Ter. SW10 . . . . 5K 83
Hardcastle Cl. CR0: Croy . . . 6G 141
Hardcastle Ho. SE14 . . . . . . 1A 106
(off Loring Rd.)
Hardcourts Cl.
BR4: W W'ck 3D 154
Hardel Ri. SW2 . . . . 1B 122
Hardel Wlk. SW2 . . . . 7A 104
Harden Ct. SE7 . . . . 4C 90
Harden Ho. SE5 . . . . 2E 104
Harden's Manorway SE7 . . . . 3B 90
(not continuous)
Harders Rd. SE15 . . . . 2H 105
Hardess St. SE24 . . . . 3C 104
Hardie Cl. NW10 . . . . 5K 45
Hardie Rd. RM10: Dag 3J 57
Harding Cl. CR0: Croy 3F 153
SE17 . . . . 6C 86
Hardinge Cl. UB8: Uxb 5D 58
Hardinge Cres. SE18 . . . . 3G 91
Hardinge La. E1 . . . . 6J 69
(not continuous)
Hardinge Rd. N18 . . . . 6K 17
NW10 . . . . 1D 64
Harding Ho. SW13 . . . . 6D 82
(off Wyatt Dr.)
UB3: Hayes 6K 59
Harding Rd. DA7: Bex 2F 111
Harding's Cl. KT2: King T . . . 1F 135
Hardings La. SE20 . . . . 6K 123
Hardington NW1 . . . . 7E 48
(off Belmont St.)
Hardman Rd. KT2: King T . . . 2E 134
SE7 . . . . 5K 89
Hardwick Cl. HA7: Stan 5H 11
Hardwick Ct. DA8: Erith 6K 93
Hardwicke Av. TW5: Houn . . . 1E 96
Hardwicke M. WC1 . . . . 2H 161
Hardwicke Rd. N13 . . . . 6D 16
TW10: Rich 4C 116
W4 . . . . 4K 81
Hardwicke St. IG11: Bark 1G 73
Hardwick Grn. W13 . . . . 5B 62
Hardwick Ho. NW8 . . . . 3D 158
(off Lilestone St.)
Hardwick St.
EC1 . . . . 3A 68 (2K 161)
Hardwicks Way SW18 . . . . . . 5J 101
Hardwidge St.
SE1 . . . . 2E 86 (6G 169)
Hardy Av. E16 . . . . 1J 89
HA4: Ruis 5K 41
Hardy Cl. EN5: Barn 6B 4
HA5: Pinn 7B 24
SE16 . . . . 2K 87
Hardy Cotts. SE10 . . . . 6F 89
Hardy Ho. SW4 . . . . 7G 103
Hardying Ho. E17 . . . . 4A 34
Hardy Rd. E4 . . . . 6G 19
SE3 . . . . 7H 89
SW19 . . . . 7K 119
Hardys Cl. KT8: E Mos 4J 133
Hardy Way EN2: Enf 1F 7
Hare & Billet Rd. SE3 . . . . . . 1F 107
Harebell Dr. E6 . . . . 5E 72
Harecastle Cl.
UB4: Hayes 4C 60
Hare Ct. EC4 . . . . . . 6A 68 (1J 167)
(off Kale Rd.)
Harecourt Rd. N1 . . . . 6C 50
Haredale Rd. SE24 . . . . 4C 104
Haredon Cl. SE23 . . . . 7K 105
HAREFIELD 1A 22
Harefield Cl. EN2: Enf 1F 7
Harefield Grn. NW7 . . . . 6K 13
Harefield M. SE4 . . . . 3B 106
Harefield Rd. DA14: Sidc . . . 2D 128
N8 . . . . 5H 31
SE4 . . . . 3B 106
SW16 . . . . 7K 121
UB8: Uxb 5A 40
Hare Marsh E2 . . . . 4G 69
Hare Pl. EC4 . . . . 1K 167
(off Pleydell St.)
Hare Row E2 . . . . 2H 69
Haresfield Rd. RM10: Dag . . . 6G 57
Hare St. SE18 . . . . 3E 90
Hare Wlk. N1 . . . . 2E 68
(not continuous)
Harewood Av.
NW1 . . . . 4C 66 (4D 158)
UB5: N'olt 7D 42
Harewood Cl. UB5: N'olt 7D 42
Harewood Dr. IG5: Ilf 2D 36
Harewood Pl.
W1 . . . . 6F 67 (1K 165)
Harewood Rd.
CR2: S Croy 6E 152
SW19 . . . . 6C 120
TW7: Isle 7K 79
Harewood Row
NW1 . . . . 5C 66 (5D 158)
Harewood Ter. UB2: S'hall . . . 4D 78
Harfield Gdns. SE5 . . . . 3E 104
Harfield Rd.
TW16: Sun T 2B 132
Harfleur Ct. SE11 . . . . 4B 86
(off Opal St.)
Harford Cl. E4 . . . . 7J 9
Harford Ho. SE5 . . . . 6C 86
(off Bethwin Rd.)
W11 . . . . 5H 65
Harford M. N19 . . . . 3H 49
Harford Rd. E4 . . . . 7J 9
Harford St. E1 . . . . 4A 70
Harford Wlk. N2 . . . . 4B 30
Hargood Cl. HA3: Harr 6E 26
Hargood Rd. SE3 . . . . 1A 108
Hargrave Mans. N19 . . . . 2H 49
Hargrave Pk. N19 . . . . 2G 49
Hargrave Pl. NW5 . . . . 5H 49
Hargrave Rd. N19 . . . . 2G 49
Hargraves Ho. W12 . . . . 7D 64
(off White City Est.)
Hargwyne St. SW9 . . . . 3K 103
Haringey Mus. 1E 32
Haringey Pk. N8 . . . . 6J 31
Haringey Pas. N8 . . . . 4A 32
Haringey Rd. N8 . . . . 4J 31
Harington Ter. N13 . . . . 3J 17
Harkett Cl. HA3: Harr 2K 25
Harkett Ct. HA3: Harr 2K 25
Harkness Ho. E1 . . . . 6G 69
(off Christian St.)
Harland Av. CR0: Croy 3F 153
DA15: Sidc 3H 127
Harland Cl. SW19 . . . . 3K 137
Harland Rd. SE12 . . . . 1J 125
Harlech Gdns. HA5: Pinn 1B 42
TW5: Houn 6A 78
Harlech Rd. N14 . . . . 3D 16
Harlech Twr. W3 . . . . 2J 81
Harlequin Av. TW8: Bford . . . 6A 80
Harlequin Cen. UB2: S'hall . . . 4A 78
Harlequin Cl. TW7: Isle 5J 97
UB4: Hayes 5B 60
Harlequin Ct. NW10 . . . . 6K 45
(off Mitchellbrook Way)
W5 . . . . 7C 62
Harlequin Ho. DA18: Erith . . . 3E 92
(off Kale Rd.)
Harlequin Rd.
TW11: Tedd 7B 116
Harlequins R.U.F.C. (Stoop Memorial Ground) . . . 7J 97
Harlescott Rd. SE15 . . . . 4K 105
HARLESDEN 2B 64
Harlesden Gdns. NW10 . . . . . 1B 64
Harlesden La. NW10 . . . . 1C 64
Harlesden Plaza NW10 . . . . . 2B 64
Harlesden Rd. NW10 . . . . 1C 64
Harleston Cl. E5 . . . . 2J 51
Harley Cl. HA0: Wemb 6D 44
Harley Ct. E11 . . . . 7J 35
HA1: Harr 4H 25
N20 . . . . 3F 15
Harley Cres. HA1: Harr 4H 25
Harleyford BR1: Brom 1K 143
Harleyford Ct. SE11 . . . . 7G 173
Harleyford Mnr. W3 . . . . 1J 81
(off Edgecote Cl.)
Harleyford Rd.
SE11 . . . . 6K 85 (7G 173)
Harleyford St.
SE11 . . . . 6A 86 (7J 173)
Harley Gdns. SW10 . . . . 5A 84
Harley Gro. E3 . . . . 3B 70
Harley Ho. E11 . . . . 7F 35
NW1 . . . . 4H 159
Harley Pl. W1 . . . . . 5F 67 (6J 159)
Harley Rd. HA1: Harr 4H 25
NW3 . . . . 7B 48
NW10 . . . . 2A 64
Harley St. W1 . . . . . . 4F 67 (4J 159)
Harley Vs. NW10 . . . . 2A 64
Harling Ct. SW11 . . . . 2D 102
Harlinger St. SE18 . . . . 3C 90
HARLINGTON 6F 77
Harlington Cl. UB3: Hayes . . . 7E 76
HARLINGTON CORNER 1F 95
Harlington Rd. DA7: Bex . . . 3E 110
UB8: Uxb 3C 58
Harlington Rd. E.
TW13: Felt 1A 114
TW14: Felt 7K 95
Harlington Rd. W.
TW14: Felt 6K 95
Harlowe Cl. E8 . . . . 1G 69
Harlowe Ho. E8 . . . . 1F 69
(off Clarissa St.)
Harlow Mans. IG11: Bark 7F 55
(off Whiting Av.)
Harlow Rd. N13 . . . . 3J 17
Harlyn Dr. HA5: Pinn 3K 23
Harlynwood SE5 . . . . 7C 86
(off Wyndham Rd.)
Harman Av. IG8: Wfd G 6C 20
Harman Cl. E4 . . . . 4A 20
NW2 . . . . 3G 47
SE1 . . . . 5G 87
Harman Dr. DA15: Sidc 6K 109
NW2 . . . . 3G 47
Harman Rd. EN1: Enf 5A 8
HARMONDSWORTH 6A 76
Harmondsworth La.
UB7: W Dray 6A 76
Harmondsworth Rd.
UB7: W Dray 5A 76
Harmon Ho. SE8 . . . . 4B 88
Harmont Ho. W1 . . . . 6J 159
(off Harley St.)
Harmony Cl. NW11 . . . . 5G 29
SM6: Wall 7H 151
Harmony Way BR2: Short . . . 2J 143
NW4 . . . . 4E 28
Harmood Gro. NW1 . . . . 7F 49
Harmood Ho. NW1 . . . . 7F 49
(off Harmood St.)
Harmood Pl. NW1 . . . . 7F 49
Harmood St. NW1 . . . . 6F 49
Harmsworth M.
SE1 . . . . 3A 86 (2K 173)
Harmsworth St.
SE17 . . . . 5B 86 (6K 173)
Harmsworth Way N20 . . . . . 1C 14
Harness Rd. SE28 . . . . 2A 92
Harold Av. DA17: Belv 5F 93
UB3: Hayes 3H 77
Harold Ct. SE16 . . . . 2K 87
(off Christopher Cl.)
Harold Est. SE1 . . . . 3E 86
Harold Gibbons Ct. SE7 . . . . . 6A 90
Harold Ho. E2 . . . . 2K 69
(off Mace St.)
Harold Laski Ho. EC1 . . . . . . 2B 162
(off Percival St.)
Harold Maddison Ho.
SE17 . . . . 5B 86
(off Penton Pl.)
Harold Pl. SE11 . . . . 5A 86 (6J 173)
Harold Rd. E4 . . . . 4K 19
E11 . . . . 1G 53
E13 . . . . 1K 71
IG8: Wfd G 1J 35
N8 . . . . 5K 31
N15 . . . . 5F 33
NW10 . . . . 3K 63
SE19 . . . . 7D 122
SM1: Sutt 4B 150
Haroldstone Rd. E17 . . . . 5K 33
Harold Wilson Ho. SE28 . . . . 1B 92
SW6 . . . . 6H 83
(off Clem Attlee Ct.)
Harp All. EC4 . . . . . 6B 68 (7A 162)
Harp Bus. Cen. NW2 . . . . 1C 46
(off Apsley Way)
Harpenden Rd. E12 . . . . 2A 54
SE27 . . . . 3B 122
Harpenmead Point NW2 . . . . 2H 47
Harper Cl. N14 . . . . 5B 6
Harper Ho. SW9 . . . . 3B 104
Harper M. SW17 . . . . 3A 120
Harper Rd. E6 . . . . 6D 72
SE1 . . . . 3C 86 (7C 168)
Harper's Yd. N17 . . . . 1F 33
Harp Island Cl. NW10 . . . . . . 2K 45
Harp La. EC3 . . . . . 7E 68 (3G 169)
Harpley Sq. E1 . . . . 4J 69
Harpour Rd. IG11: Bark 6G 55
Harp Rd. W7 . . . . 4K 61
Harpsden St. SW11 . . . . 1E 102
Harpur M. WC1 . . . . 5K 67 (5G 161)
Harpur St. WC1 . . . . 5K 67 (5G 161)
Harraden Rd. SE3 . . . . 1A 108
Harrier Av. E11 . . . . 6K 35
Harrier Ct. TW4: Houn 3C 96
Harrier M. SE28 . . . . 2H 91
Harrier Rd. NW9 . . . . 2A 28
Harriers Cl. W5 . . . . 7E 62
Harrier Way E6 . . . . 5D 72
Harries Rd. UB4: Hayes 4A 60
Harriet Cl. E8 . . . . 1G 69
Harriet Gdns. CR0: Croy . . . 2G 153
Harriet Ho. SW6 . . . . 7K 83
(off Wandon Rd.)
Harriet St. SW1 . . . 2D 84 (7F 165)
Harriet Tubman Cl.
SW2 . . . . 7K 103
Harriet Wlk.
SW1 . . . . 2D 84 (7F 165)
Harriet Way WD23: Bush 1C 10
HARRINGAY 5B 32
Harringay Gdns. N8 . . . . 4B 32
Harringay Rd. N15 . . . . 5B 32
(not continuous)
Harrington Cl.
CR0: Croy 2J 151
NW10 . . . . 3K 45
Harrington Ct.
CR0: Croy 2D 152
W10 . . . . 3H 65
Harrington Gdns. SW7 . . . . . 4K 83
Harrington Hill E5 . . . . 1H 51
Harrington Ho. NW1 . . . . 1A 160
(off Harrington St.)
UB10: Uxb 4D 40
Harrington Rd. E11 . . . . 1G 53
SE25 . . . . 4G 141
SW7 . . . . 4B 84 (3A 170)
Harrington Sq. NW1 . . . . 2G 67
Harrington St.
NW1 . . . . 2G 67 (1A 160)
(not continuous)
Harrington Way SE18 . . . . 3B 90
Harriott Cl. SE10 . . . . 4H 89
Harriott Ho. E1 . . . . 5J 69
(off Jamaica St.)
Harris Bldgs. E1 . . . . 6G 69
(off Burslem St.)
Harris Cl. EN2: Enf 1G 7
TW3: Houn 1E 96
Harris Ct. HA9: Wemb 3F 45
Harris Ho. SW9 . . . . 3A 104
(off St James's Cres.)
Harris Lodge SE6 . . . . 1E 124
Harrison Cl. N20 . . . . 1H 15
Harrison Ct. TW17: Shep . . . 5D 130
Harrison Ho. SE17 . . . . 5D 86
(off Brandon St.)
Harrison Rd. RM10: Dag 6H 57
Harrisons Ct. SE14 . . . . 6K 87
(off Myers La.)
Harrison's Ri. CR0: Croy . . . 3B 152
Harrison St. WC1 . . . 3J 67 (2F 161)
Harris Rd. DA7: Bex 1E 110
RM9: Dag 5F 57
Harris St. E17 . . . . 7B 34
SE5 . . . . 7D 86
Harris Way TW16: Sun T . . . 1G 131
Harrods 3D 84 (1E 170)
Harrogate Ct. N11 . . . . 6K 15
SE12 . . . . 7J 107
SE26 . . . . 3G 123
(off Droitwich Cl.)
Harrold Ho. NW3 . . . . 7B 48
Harrold Rd. RM8: Dag 5B 56
Harrovian Bus. Village
HA1: Harr 7J 25
HARROW 6J 25
Harrow Av. EN1: Enf 6A 8
Harroway Rd. SW11 . . . . 2B 102
Harrowby St. W2 . . . 6C 66 (7D 158)
Harrow Cl. KT9: Chess 7D 146
Harrowdene Cl.
HA0: Wemb 4D 44
Harrowdene Gdns.
TW11: Tedd 6A 116
Harrowdene Rd.
HA0: Wemb 3D 44
Harrow Dr. N9 . . . . 1A 18
Harrowes Meade
HA8: Edg 3B 12
Harrow Flds. Gdns.
HA1: Harr 3J 43
Harrowgate Ho. E9 . . . . 6K 51
Harrowgate Rd. E9 . . . . 6A 52
Harrow Grn. E11 . . . . 3G 53
Harrow La. E14 . . . . 7D 70
Harrow Lodge NW8 . . . . 3A 158
(off Northwick Ter.)
Harrow Mnr. Way SE2 . . . . . . 1C 92
SE28 . . . . 7C 74
Harrow Mus. & Heritage Cen. 3G 25
HARROW ON THE HILL 1J 43
Harrow Pk. HA1: Harr 2J 43
Harrow Pl. E1 . . . . 6E 68 (7H 163)
HARROW ROAD 7H 45
Harrow Rd. E6 . . . . 1C 72
E11 . . . . 3G 53

Harrow Rd.—Havelock Wlk.

Harrow Rd. HA0: Wemb 4K 43
(not continuous)
HA9: Wemb 5G 45
IG1: Ilf 4G 55
IG11: Bark 1J 73
NW10 ....3C 64
SM5: Cars 6C 150
TW14: Felt 2C 112
W2 ....5A 66 (6A 158)
(not continuous)
W9 ....4F 65
W10...............4G 65
Harrow Rd. Bri. W2 ....5A 66
Harrow School Old Speech Room Gallery
in Harrow School 1J 43
(off High St.)
Harrow St. NW1 ....5D 158
Harrow Vw. HA2: Harr 2G 25
UB3: Hayes 6J 59
UB10: Uxb 3E 58
Harrow Vw. Rd. W5 ....4B 62
Harrow Way TW17: Shep ...2E 130
HARROW WEALD 1J 25
Harrow Weald Pk.
HA3: Harr 6C 10
Harrrow Rd. W2 ....4F 65
Harry Hinkins Ho. SE17 .....5C 86
(off Bronti Cl.)
Harry Lambourn Ho. SE15 ...7H 87
(off Gervase St.)
Hartcliff Ct. W7 ....2K 79
Hart Ct. E6 ....7E 54
Harte Rd. TW3: Houn 2D 96
Hartfield Av. UB5: N'olt 2K 59
Hartfield Cres.
BR4: W W'ck 3J 155
SW19 ....7H 119
Hartfield Gro. SE20 ....1J 141
Hartfield Ho. UB5: N'olt 2K 59
(off Hartfield Av.)
Hartfield Rd.
BR4: W W'ck 4J 155
KT9: Chess 5D 146
SW19 ....7H 119
Hartfield Ter. E3 ....2C 70
Hartford Av. HA3: Harr 3A 26
Hartford Rd. DA5: Bexl 6G 111
KT19: Eps 6H 147
Hart Gro. UB1: S'hall 5E 60
W5 ....1G 81
Hart Gro. Ct. W5 ....1G 81
Hartham Cl. N7 ....5J 49
TW7: Isle 1A 98
Hartham Rd. N7 ....5J 49
N17 ....2F 33
TW7: Isle 1K 97
Harting Rd. SE9 ....3C 126
Hartington Cl. HA1: Harr 4J 43
Hartington Ct. SW8 ....1J 103
W4 ....7H 81
Hartington Ho. SW1 ....5D 172
(off Drummond Ga.)
Hartington Rd. E16 ....6K 71
E17 ....6A 34
SW8 ....1J 103
TW1: Twick 7B 98
UB2: S'hall 3C 78
W4 ....7H 81
W13 ....7B 62
Hartismere Rd. SW6 ....7H 83
Hartlake Rd. E9 ....6K 51
Hartland NW1 ....1G 67
(off Royal College St.)
Hartland Cl. HA8: Edg 2B 12
N21 ....6H 7
Hartland Ct. N11 ....5J 15
(off Hartland Rd.)
Hartland Dr. HA4: Ruis 3K 41
HA8: Edg 2B 12
Hartland Rd. E15 ....7H 53
N11 ....5J 15
Hartland Rd. NW1 ....7F 49
NW6 ....2H 65
SM4: Mord 7J 137
TW7: Isle 3A 98
TW12: Hamp 4F 115
Hartlands Cl. DA5: Bexl 6F 111
Hartlands, The TW5: Houn ...6K 77
Hartland Way CR0: Croy ...3A 154
SM4: Mord 7H 137
Hartlepool Ct. E16 ....1F 91
Hartley Av. E6 ....1C 72
NW7 ....5G 13
Hartley Cl. BR1: Brom 2D 144
NW7 ....5G 13
Hartley Ho. SE1 ....4F 87
(off Longfield Est.)
Hartley Rd. CR0: Croy 7C 140
DA16: Well 7C 92
E11 ....1H 53
Hartley St. E2 ....3J 69
(not continuous)
Hart Lodge EN5: Barn 3B 4
Hartmann Rd. E16 ....1B 90
Hartnoll St. N7 ....5K 49
Harton Cl. BR1: Brom 1B 144
Harton Rd. N9 ....2C 18
Harton St. SE8 ....1C 106
Hartop Point SW6 ....7G 83
(off Pellant Rd.)
Hartsbourne Av.
WD23: Bush 2B 10
Hartsbourne Cl.
WD23: Bush 2C 10
Hartsbourne Ct.
UB1: S'hall 6G 61
(off Fleming Rd.)
Hartsbourne Pk.
WD23: Bush 2D 10
Hartsbourne Rd.
WD23: Bush 2C 10
Harts Gro. IG8: Wfd G 5D 20
Hartshill Cl. UB10: Uxb 7D 40
Hartshorn All. EC3 ....1H 169
Hartshorn Gdns. E6 ....4E 72
Harts La. IG11: Bark 6F 55
SE14 ....1A 106
Hartslock Dr. SE2 ....2D 92
Hartsmead Rd. SE9 ....2D 126
Hart St. EC3 ....7E 68 (2H 169)
Hartsway EN3: Enf 4D 8
Hartswood Gdns. W12 ......3B 82
Hartswood Rd. W12 ....2B 82
Hartsworth Cl. E13 ....2H 71
Hartville Rd. SE18 ....4J 91
Hartwell Dr. E4 ....6K 19
Hartwell Ho. SE7 ....5K 89
(off Troughton Rd.)
Hartwell St. E8 ....6F 51
Hartwood Grn.
WD23: Bush 2C 10
Harvard Ct. NW6 ....5K 47
Harvard Hill W4 ....6H 81
Harvard Ho. SE17 ....6B 86
(off Doddington Gro.)
Harvard La. W4 ....5J 81
Harvard Rd. SE13 ....5E 106
TW7: Isle 1J 97
W4 ....5H 81
Harvel Cl. BR5: Orp 3K 145
Harvel Cres. SE2 ....5D 92
Harvest Bank Rd.
BR4: W W'ck 3H 155
Harvest Ct. TW17: Shep 4C 130
Harvesters Cl. TW7: Isle 5H 97
Harvest La. KT7: T Ditt 6A 134
Harvest Rd. TW13: Felt 4J 113
Harvey Ct. E17 ....5C 34
Harvey Dr. TW12: Hamp 1F 133
Harvey Gdns. E11 ....1H 53
SE7 ....5A 90
Harvey Ho. E1 ....4H 69
(off Brady St.)
Harvey Ho. N1 ....1D 68
(off Colville Est.)
RM6: Chad H 4D 38
SW1 ....6D 172
(off Aylesford St.)
Harvey Ho. TW8: Bford 5E 80
Harvey Lodge W9 ....5J 65
(off Admiral Wlk.)
Harvey Point E16 ....5J 71
(off Fife Rd.)
Harvey Rd. E11 ....1G 53
IG1: Ilf 5F 55
KT12: Walt T 7H 131
N8 ....5K 31
SE5 ....1D 104
(not continuous)
TW4: Houn 7D 96
UB5: N'olt 7A 42
UB10: Uxb 2C 58
Harvey's Bldgs.
WC2 ....7J 67 (3F 167)
Harveys La. RM7: Rush G ...2K 57
Harvey St. N1 ....1D 68
Harvill Rd. DA14: Sidc 5E 128
Harvil Rd. UB9: Uxb 6A 22
Harvington Wlk. E8 ....7G 51
Harvist Est. N7 ....4A 50
Harvist Rd. NW6 ....2F 65
Harwell Cl. HA4: Ruis 1F 41
Harwell Pas. N2 ....4D 30
Harwood Av. BR1: Brom 2K 143
CR4: Mitc 3C 138
Harwood Cl. HA0: Wemb 4D 44
N12 ....6H 15
Harwood Ct. N1 ....1D 68
(off Colville Est.)
SW15 ....4E 100
Harwood Dr. UB10: Uxb 1B 58
Harwood M. SW6 ....7J 83
Harwood Point SE16 ....2B 88
Harwood Rd. SW6 ....7J 83
Harwoods Yd. N21 ....7F 7
Harwood Ter. SW6 ....1K 101
Haselbury Rd. N9 ....4K 17
N18 ....4K 17
Haseley End SE23 ....7J 105
Haselrigge Rd. SW4 ......4H 103
Haseltine Rd. SE26 ....4B 124
Haselwood Dr. EN2: Enf 4G 7
Haskard Rd. RM9: Dag 4D 56
Hasker St. SW3 ....4C 84 (3D 170)
Haslam Av. SM3: Sutt 1G 149
Haslam Cl. N1 ....7A 50
UB10: Uxb 2E 40
Haslam Ct. N11 ....4A 16
Haslam St. SE15 ....7F 87
Haslemere and Heathrow Est., The
TW4: Houn 2K 95
Haslemere Av. CR4: Mitc ...2B 138
EN4: Barn 1J 15
NW4 ....6F 29
SW18 ....2K 119
TW5: Houn 2A 96
W7 ....3A 80
W13 ....3A 80
Haslemere Bus. Cen.
EN1: Enf 4C 8
Haslemere Cl. SM6: Wall ...5J 151
TW12: Hamp 5D 114
Haslemere Gdns. N3 ....3H 29
Haslemere Ind. Est.
SW18 ....2K 119
Haslemere Rd.
CR7: Thor H 5B 140
DA7: Bex 2F 111
IG3: Ilf 2K 55
N8 ....7H 31
N21 ....2G 17
Hasler Cl. SE28 ....7B 74
Haslers Wharf E3 ....1A 70
(off Old Ford Rd.)
Haslett Rd. TW17: Shep 2G 131
Hasluck Gdns. EN5: Barn 6E 4
Hassard St. E2 .....2F 69 (1K 163)
Hassendean Rd. SE3 ....6K 89
Hassett Rd. E9 ....6K 51
Hassocks Cl. SE26 ....3H 123
Hassocks Rd. SW16 ....1H 139
Hassock Wood
BR2: Kes 4B 156
Hassop Rd. NW2 ....4F 47
Hassop Wlk. SE9 ....4C 126
Hasted Rd. SE7 ....5B 90
Haste Hill Station (Ruislip Lido
Railway) 3G 23
Hastings Av. IG6: Ilf 4G 37
Hastings Cl. EN5: Barn 4F 5
HA0: Wemb 4C 44
SE15 ....7G 87
Hastings Ct. TW11: Tedd ...5H 115
Hastings Dr. KT6: Surb 6C 134
Hastings Ho. SE18 ....4D 90
(off Mulgrave Rd.)
W12 ....7D 64
(off White City Est.)
W13 ....7B 62
WC1 ....2E 160
(off Hastings St.)
Hastings Rd. BR2: Short ...1C 156
CR0: Croy 1F 153
N11 ....5B 16
N17 ....3D 32
W13 ....7B 62
Hastings St. SE18 ....3G 91
WC1 ....3J 67 (2E 160)
Hastingwood Ct. E17 ....5D 34
Hastingwood Trad. Est.
N18 ....6E 18
Hastoe Cl. UB4: Hayes 4C 60
Hat & Mitre Ct. EC1 ....4B 162
Hatcham M. Bus. Cen.
SE14 ....1K 105
Hatcham Pk. M. SE14 .....1K 105
Hatcham Pk. Rd. SE14 .....1K 105
Hatcham Rd. SE15 ....6J 87
Hatchard Rd. N19 ....2H 49
Hatchcroft NW4 ....3D 28
HATCH END 7A 10
Hatchers M. SE1 ....7H 169
Hatchett Rd. TW14: Felt 1E 112
Hatchfield Ho. N15 ....6E 32
(off Albert Rd.)
Hatch Gro. RM6: Chad H 4E 38
Hatch La. E4 ....4A 20
(not continuous)
UB7: W Dray 7A 76
Hatch Pl. KT2: King T 5F 117
Hatch Rd. SW16 ....2J 139
Hatch Side IG7: Chig 5K 21
Hatch, The EN3: Enf 1E 8
Hatchwood Cl. IG8: Wfd G ...4C 20
Hatcliffe Almshouses
SE10 ....5G 89
(off Tuskar St.)
Hatcliffe Cl. SE3 ....3H 107
Hatcliffe St. SE10 ....5H 89
Hatfield Cl. CR4: Mitc 4B 138
IG6: Ilf 3F 37
SE14 ....7K 87
Hatfield Ct. SE3 ....7J 89
UB5: N'olt 3A 60
(off Canberra Dr.)
Hatfield Ho. EC1 ....4C 162
Hatfield Mead
SM4: Mord 5J 137
Hatfield Rd. E15 ....5G 53
RM9: Dag 6E 56
W4 ....2K 81
W13 ....1A 80
Hatfields SE1 ......1A 86 (4K 167)
Hathaway Cl. BR2: Short ...1D 156
HA4: Ruis 4H 41
HA7: Stan 5F 11
Hathaway Cres. E12 ....6D 54
Hathaway Gdns.
RM6: Chad H 5D 38
W13 ....5A 62
Hathaway Ho.
N1 ....2E 68 (1G 163)
Hathaway Rd. CR0: Croy ...7B 140
Hatherleigh Cl.
KT9: Chess 5D 146
SM4: Mord 4J 137
Hatherleigh Rd.
HA4: Ruis 2J 41
Hatherley Ct. W2 ....6K 65
(off Hatherley Gro.)
Hatherley Cres.
DA14: Sidc 2A 128
Hatherley Gdns. E6 ....3B 72
N8 ....6J 31
Hatherley Gro. W2 ....6K 65
Hatherley Ho. E17 ....4C 34
Hatherley M. E17 ....4C 34
Hatherley Rd.
DA14: Sidc 4A 128
E17 ....4B 34
TW9: Rich 1F 99
Hatherley St.
SW1 ....4G 85 (4B 172)
Hathern Gdns. SE9 ....4E 126
Hatherop Rd.
TW12: Hamp 7D 114
Hathersage Ct. N1 ....5D 50
Hathorne Cl. SE15 ....2H 105
Hathway St. SE15 ....2K 105
Hathway Ter. SE14 ....2K 105
(off Hathway St.)
Hatley Av. IG6: Ilf 4G 37
Hatley Cl. N11 ....5J 15
Hatley Rd. N4 ....2K 49
Hatteraick St. SE16 ....2J 87
Hattersfield Cl.
DA17: Belv 4F 93
HATTON 4H 95
Hatton Cl. SE18 ....7H 91
HATTON CROSS 4H 95
Hatton Gdn.
EC1 ....5A 68 (5K 161)
Hatton Gdns. CR4: Mitc 5D 138
Hatton Grn. TW14: Felt 4J 95
Hatton Gro. UB7: W Dray 2A 76
Hatton Ho. KT1: King T 2F 135
(off Victoria Rd.)
Hatton Pl. EC1 .....5A 68 (5K 161)
Hatton Rd. CR0: Croy 1A 152
TW14: Felt 7E 94
Hatton Rd. Sth.
TW6: Houn 4H 95
Hatton Row NW8 ....4B 158
Hatton St. NW8 ....4B 66 (4B 158)
Hatton Wall EC1 ....5A 68 (5K 161)
Haughmond N12 ....4E 14
Haunch of Venison Yd.
W1 ....6F 67 (1J 165)
Hauteville Ct. Gdns. W6 ....3B 82
(off South Side)
Havana Rd. SW19 ....2J 119
Havannah St. E14 ....2C 88
Havant Rd. E17 ....3E 34
Havelock Cl. W12 ....7D 64
Havelock Ct. UB2: S'hall 3D 78
(off Havelock Rd.)
Havelock Ho. SE23 ....1J 123
Havelock Pl. HA1: Harr 6J 25
Havelock Rd. BR2: Short ...4A 144
CR0: Croy 2F 153
DA17: Belv 4F 93
HA3: Harr 3J 25
N17 ....2G 33
SW19 ....5A 120
UB2: S'hall 3C 78
Havelock St. IG1: Ilf 2F 55
N1 ....1J 67
Havelock Ter. SW8 ....1F 103
Havelock Wlk. SE23 ....1J 123

Haven Cl.—Hazelmere Rd.

Haven Cl. DA14: Sidc 6C 128
SE9 ......3D 126
SW19 ......3F 119
UB4: Hayes 4G 59
Haven Ct. BR3: Beck 2E 142
KT5: Surb 6F 135
Haven Grn. W5 ......6D 62
Haven Grn. Ct. W5 ......6D 62
Havenhurst Ri. EN2: Enf 2F 7
Haven La. W5 ......6E 62
Haven Lodge *EN1: Enf* *6K 7*
(off Village Rd.)
Haven M. E3 ......5B 70
N1 ......7A 50
Haven Pl. W5 ......7D 62
Havenpool *NW8* *1K 65*
(off Abbey Rd.)
Haven Rd. TW15: Ashf 3D 112
Haven St. NW1 ......7F 49
Haven, The N14 ......6A 6
TW9: Rich 3G 99
TW16: Sun T 7J 113
Haven Wood HA9: Wemb 3H 45
Haverfield Gdns.
TW9: Rich 7G 81
Haverfield Rd. E3 ......3A 70
Haverford Way HA8: Edg 1F 27
Haverhill Rd. E4 ......1K 19
SW12 ......1G 121
Havering *NW1* *7F 49*
(off Castlehaven Rd.)
Havering Dr. RM1: Rom 4K 39
Havering Gdns.
RM6: Chad H 5C 38
Havering St. E1 ......6K 69
Havering Way IG11: Bark 3B 74
Haversham Cl.
TW1: Twick 6D 98
Haversham Ct.
UB6: G'frd 6K 43
Haversham Pl. N6 ......2D 48
Haverstock Hill NW3 ......5C 48
Haverstock Pl. *N1* *1B 162*
(off Haverstock St.)
Haverstock Rd. NW5 ......5E 48
Haverstock St.
N1 ......2B 68 (1B 162)
Havil St. SE5 ......7E 86
Havisham Ho. SE16 ......2G 87
Havisham Pl. SE19 ......7B 122
Hawarden Gro. SE24 ......7C 104
Hawarden Hill NW2 ......3C 46
Hawarden Rd. E17 ......4K 33
Hawbridge Rd. E11 ......1F 53
Hawes Ho. E17 ......4K 33
Hawes La. BR4: W W'ck 1E 154
Hawes Rd. BR1: Brom 1K 143
(not continuous)
N18 ......6C 18
Hawes St. N1 ......7B 50
Hawgood St. E3 ......5C 70
Hawkdene E4 ......6J 9
Hawke Ct. *UB4: Hayes* *4A 60*
(off Perth Av.)
Hawke Ho. *E1* *4K 69*
(off Ernest St.)
Hawke Pk. Rd. N22 ......3B 32
Hawke Pl. SE16 ......2K 87
Hawker Ct. *KT1: King T* *2F 135*
(off Church Rd.)
Hawke Rd. SE19 ......6D 122
Hawkesbury Rd. SW15 ......5D 100
Hawkesfield Rd. SE23 ......2A 124
Hawkesley Cl.
TW1: Twick 4A 116
Hawkes Rd. CR4: Mitc 1D 138
TW14: Felt 7J 95
Hawkesworth Cl.
HA6: Nwood 1G 23
Hawke Twr. SE14 ......6A 88
Hawkewood Rd.
TW16: Sun T 3J 131
Hawkfield Ct. TW7: Isle 2J 97
Hawkhurst Gdns.
KT9: Chess 4E 146
Hawkhurst Rd. SW16 ......1H 139
Hawkhurst Way
BR4: W W'ck 2D 154
KT3: N Mald 5K 135
Hawkinge *N17* *2D 32*
(off Gloucester Rd.)
Hawkins Cl. HA1: Harr 7H 25
NW7 ......5E 12
Hawkins Ct. SE18 ......4C 90
Hawkins Ho. *SE8* *6C 88*
(off New King St.)
SW1 ......*7B 172*
(off Dolphin Sq.)
Hawkins Rd. TW11: Tedd 6B 116
Hawkins Way SE6 ......5C 124
Hawkley Gdns. SE27 ......2B 122
Hawkridge Cl.
RM6: Chad H 6C 38
Hawksbrook La.
BR3: Beck 6D 142
(not continuous)
Hawkshaw Cl. SW2 ......7J 103
Hawkshead NW1 ......1A 160
Hawkshead Cl.
BR1: Brom 7G 125
Hawkshead Rd. NW10 ......7B 46
W4 ......2A 82
Hawkslade Rd. SE15 ......5K 105
Hawksley Rd. N16 ......3E 50
Hawks M. SE10 ......7E 88
Hawksmoor Cl. E6 ......6C 72
SE18 ......5J 91
Hawksmoor Ho. *E14* *5A 70*
(off Aston St.)
Hawksmoor M. E1 ......7H 69
Hawksmoor Pl. *E2* *3K 163*
(off Cheshire St.)
Hawksmoor St. W6 ......6F 83
Hawksmouth E4 ......7K 9
Hawks Pas. *KT1: King T* *2F 135*
(off Minerva Rd.)
Hawks Rd. KT1: King T 2F 135
Hawkstone Rd. SE16 ......4J 87
Hawkwell Ct. E4 ......3K 19
Hawkwell Ho. RM8: Dag 1G 57
Hawkwell Wlk. *N1* *1C 68*
(off Maldon Cl.)
Hawkwood Cres. E4 ......6J 9
Hawkwood La. BR7: Chst 1G 145
Hawkwood Mt. E5 ......1H 51
Hawlands Dr. HA5: Pinn 7C 24
Hawley Cl.
TW12: Hamp 6D 114
Hawley Cres. NW1 ......7F 49
Hawley M. NW1 ......7F 49
Hawley Rd. N18 ......5E 18
NW1 ......7F 49
(not continuous)
Hawley St. NW1 ......7F 49
Hawley Way TW15: Ashf 5C 112
Hawstead Rd. SE6 ......6D 106
Hawsted IG9: Buck H 1E 20
Hawter NW9 ......1B 28
Hawthorn Av.
CR7: Thor H 1B 140
E3 ......1B 70
N13 ......5D 16
Hawthorn Cen. HA1: Harr 5K 25
Hawthorn Cl. BR5: Orp 6H 145
TW5: Houn 7K 77
TW12: Hamp 5E 114
Hawthorn Cotts.
DA16: Well *3A 110*
(off Hook La.)
Hawthorn Ct. *HA5: Pinn* *2A 24*
(off Rickmansworth Rd.)
TW9: Rich 1H 99
Hawthorn Cres. SW17 ......5E 120
Hawthornden Cl. N12 ......6H 15
Hawthorndene Cl.
BR2: Short 2H 155
Hawthorndene Rd.
BR2: Short 2H 155
Hawthorn Dr.
BR4: W W'ck 4G 155
HA2: Harr 6E 24
Hawthorne Av. CR4: Mitc 2B 138
HA3: Harr 6A 26
HA4: Ruis 6K 23
SM5: Cars 7E 150
Hawthorne Cl.
BR1: Brom 3D 144
N1 ......6E 50
SM1: Sutt 2A 150
Hawthorne Ct.
HA6: Nwood 2J 23
W5 ......1E 80
Hawthorne Cres.
UB7: W Dray 2B 76
Hawthorne Farm Av.
UB5: N'olt 1C 60
Hawthorne Gro. NW9 ......7J 27
Hawthorne Ho. *SW1* *6B 172*
(off Churchill Gdns.)
Hawthorne M. UB6: G'frd 6G 61
Hawthorne Pl. UB3: Hayes 7H 59
Hawthorne Rd.
BR1: Brom 3C 144
E17 ......3C 34
Hawthorn Gdns. W5 ......3D 80
Hawthorn Gro. EN2: Enf 1J 7
SE20 ......7H 123
Hawthorn Hatch
TW8: Bford 7B 80
Hawthorn M. NW7 ......1G 29
Hawthorn Pl. DA8: Erith 5J 93
Hawthorn Rd. DA6: Bex 4F 111
IG9: Buck H 4G 21
N8 ......3H 31
N18 ......6A 18
NW10 ......7C 46
SM1: Sutt 6C 150
SM6: Wall 7F 151
TW8: Bford 7B 80
TW13: Felt 1J 113
Hawthorns *CR2: S Croy* *4B 152*
(off Bramley Hill)
IG8: Wfd G 3D 20
Hawthorns, The
KT17: Eps 7B 148
Hawthorn Ter.
DA15: Sidc 5K 109
Hawthorn Wlk. W10 ......4G 65
Hawthorn Way N9 ......2K 17
TW17: Shep 4F 131
Hawtrey Av. UB5: N'olt 2B 60
Hawtrey Dr. HA4: Ruis 7J 23
Hawtrey Rd. NW3 ......7C 48
Haxted Rd. BR1: Brom 1K 143
Hay Cl. E15 ......7G 53
Haycroft Gdns. NW10 ......1C 64
Haycroft Rd. KT6: Surb 2D 146
SW2 ......5J 103
Hay Currie St. E14 ......6D 70
Hayday Rd. E16 ......5J 71
(not continuous)
Haydens M. W3 ......6J 63
Hayden's Pl. W11 ......6H 65
Hayden Way RM5: Col R 2J 39
Haydock Av. UB5: N'olt 6E 42
Haydock Grn. UB5: N'olt 6E 42
Haydock Grn. Flats
UB5: N'olt *6E 42*
(off Haydock Grn.)
Haydon Cl. EN1: Enf 6K 7
NW9 ......4J 27
Haydon Dr. HA5: Pinn 4J 23
Haydon Pk. Rd. SW19 ......5J 119
Haydon Rd. RM8: Dag 2C 56
Haydons Rd. SW19 ......5K 119
Haydon St. EC3 ......7F 69 (2J 169)
Haydon Wlk. E1 ......6F 69 (1K 169)
Haydon Way SW11 ......4B 102
HAYES
BR2 ......1J 155
UB3 ......6G 59
Hayes Bri. Retail Pk.
UB4: Hayes 7A 60
Hayes Chase
BR4: W W'ck 6F 143
Hayes Cl. BR2: Short 2J 155
Hayes Ct. *SE5* *7C 86*
(off Camberwell New Rd.)
SW2 ......1J 121
Hayes Cres. NW11 ......5H 29
SM3: Sutt 4F 149
HAYES END 5F 59
Hayes End Cl. UB4: Hayes 5F 59
Hayes End Dr. UB4: Hayes 4F 59
Hayes End Rd. UB4: Hayes 4F 59
Hayesford Pk. Dr.
BR2: Short 5H 143
Hayes Gdn. BR2: Short 2J 155
Hayes Gro. SE15 ......3F 105
Hayes Hill BR2: Short 1G 155
Hayes Hill Rd.
BR2: Short 1H 155
Hayes La. BR2: Short 5J 143
BR3: Beck 3E 142
Hayes Mead Rd.
BR2: Short 1G 155
Hayes Metro Cen.
UB4: Hayes 7A 60
Hayes Pl. NW1 ......4C 66 (4D 158)
Hayes Rd. BR2: Short 4J 143
UB2: S'hall 4K 77
Hayes St. BR2: Short 1K 155
HAYES TOWN 2H 77
Hayes Way BR3: Beck 4E 142
Hayes Wood Av.
BR2: Short 1K 155
Hayfield Pas. E1 ......4J 69
Hayfield Yd. E1 ......4J 69
Haygarth Pl. SW19 ......5F 119
Haygreen Cl. KT2: King T 6H 117
Hay Hill W1 ......7F 67 (3K 165)
Hayland Cl. NW9 ......4K 27
Hay La. NW9 ......4J 27
Hayles Bldgs. *SE11* *4B 86*
(off Elliotts Row)
Hayles St. SE11 ......4B 86
Haylett Gdns.
KT1: King T 4D 134
Hayling Av. TW13: Felt 3J 113
Hayling Cl. N16 ......5E 50
Hayling Ct. SM3: Sutt 4E 148
Haymaker Cl. UB10: Uxb 7B 40
Hayman Cres. UB4: Hayes 2F 59
Haymans Point
SE11 ......4K 85 (5G 173)
Hayman St. N1 ......7B 50
Haymarket SW1 ......7H 67 (3C 166)
Haymarket Arc. SW1 ......3C 166
Haymarket Theatre Royal
......*3D 166*
(off Haymarket)
Haymer Gdns.
KT4: Wor Pk 3C 148
Haymerle Ho. *SE15* *6G 87*
(off Haymerle Rd.)
Haymerle Rd. SE15 ......6G 87
Haymill Cl. UB6: G'frd 3K 61
Hayne Ho. *W11* *1G 83*
(off Penzance Pl.)
Hayne Rd. BR3: Beck 2B 142
Haynes Cl. N11 ......3K 15
N17 ......7C 18
SE3 ......3G 107
Haynes Dr. N9 ......3C 18
Haynes La. SE19 ......6E 122
Haynes Rd. HA0: Wemb 7E 44
Hayne St. EC1 ......5B 68 (5B 162)
Haynt Wlk. SW20 ......3G 137
Hay's Galleria
SE1 ......1E 86 (4G 169)
Hays La. SE1 ......1E 86 (4G 169)
Haysleigh Gdns. SE20 ......2G 141
Hay's M. W1 ......1F 85 (4J 165)
Haysoms Cl. RM1: Rom 4K 39
Haystall Cl. UB4: Hayes 2G 59
Hay St. E2 ......1G 69
Hayter Ct. E11 ......2K 53
Hayter Rd. SW2 ......5J 103
Hayton Cl. E8 ......6F 51
Hayward Cl. DA1: Cray 5K 111
SW19 ......7K 119
Hayward Ct. *SW9* *2J 103*
(off Clapham Rd.)
Hayward Gallery *5H 167*
Hayward Gdns. SW15 ......6E 100
Hayward Rd. KT7: T Ditt 7K 133
N20 ......2F 15
Haywards Cl.
RM6: Chad H 5B 38
Hayward's Pl.
EC1 ......4B 68 (3A 162)
Haywards Yd. *SE4* *5B 106*
(off Lindal Rd.)
Haywood Cl. HA5: Pinn 2B 24
Haywood Lodge *N11* *6D 16*
(off Oak La.)
Haywood Rd. BR2: Short 4B 144
Hayworth Cl. EN3: Enf 2F 9
Hazel Av. UB7: W Dray 3C 76
Hazel Bank KT5: Surb 1J 147
SE25 ......2E 140
Hazelbank Rd. SE6 ......2F 125
Hazelbourne Rd. SW12 ......6F 103
Hazelbury Cl. SW19 ......2J 137
Hazelbury Grn. N9 ......3K 17
Hazelbury La. N9 ......3K 17
Hazel Cl. CR0: Croy 7K 141
CR4: Mitc 4H 139
N13 ......3J 17
N19 ......2G 49
NW9 ......2A 28
SE15 ......2G 105
TW2: Twick 7G 97
TW8: Bford 7B 80
Hazel Ct. W5 ......7E 62
Hazel Cres. RM5: Col R 1H 39
Hazel Cft. HA5: Pinn 6A 10
Hazelcroft Cl. UB10: Uxb 7B 40
Hazeldean Rd. NW10 ......7K 45
Hazeldene Dr. HA5: Pinn 3A 24
Hazeldene Gdns.
UB10: Uxb 1E 58
Hazeldene Rd.
DA16: Well 2C 110
IG3: Ilf 2B 56
Hazeldon Rd. SE4 ......5A 106
Hazeleigh Gdns.
IG8: Wfd G 5H 21
Hazel Gdns. HA8: Edg 4C 12
Hazelgreen Cl. N21 ......1G 17
Hazel Gro. EN1: Enf 6B 8
HA0: Wemb 1E 62
RM6: Chad H 3E 38
SE26 ......4K 123
TW13: Felt 1J 113
Hazelhurst BR3: Beck 1F 143
Hazelhurst Ct. *SE6* *5E 124*
(off Beckenham Hill Rd.)
Hazelhurst Rd. SW17 ......4A 120
Hazel La. IG6: Ilf 6K 21
TW10: Rich 2E 116
Hazellville Rd. N19 ......7H 31
Hazelmere Cl. TW14: Felt 6G 95
UB5: N'olt 2D 60
Hazelmere Ct. SW2 ......1K 121
Hazelmere Dr. UB5: N'olt 2D 60
Hazelmere Rd.
BR5: Orp 4G 145
NW6 ......1H 65
UB5: N'olt 2D 60

Hazelmere Wlk.—Helen Gladstone Ho.

Hazelmere Wlk.
UB5: N'olt 2D **60**
(not continuous)
Hazelmere Way
BR2: Short 6J **143**
Hazel Rd. E15 5G **53**
NW10 3D **64**
(not continuous)
Hazeltree La. UB5: N'olt 3C **60**
Hazel Wlk. BR2: Short 6E **144**
Hazel Way E4 6G **19**
SE1 4F **87**
Hazelwood Av.
SM4: Mord 4K **137**
Hazelwood Cl. HA2: Harr 4F **25**
W5 2E **80**
Hazelwood Ct. KT6: Surb 6E **134**
*N13 4F **17***
(off Hazelwood La.)
NW10 3A **46**
Hazelwood Cres. N13 4F **17**
Hazelwood Dr. HA5: Pinn 2K **23**
Hazelwood Ho's.
BR2: Short 3G **143**
Hazelwood Ho. SE8 4A **88**
Hazelwood La. N13 4F **17**
Hazelwood Rd. E17 5A **34**
EN1: Enf 6A **8**
Hazlebury Rd. SW6 2K **101**
Hazledean Rd.
CR0: Croy 2D **152**
Hazledene Rd. W4 6J **81**
Hazlemere Gdns.
KT4: Wor Pk 1C **148**
Hazlewell Rd. SW15 5E **100**
Hazlewood Cl. E5 3A **52**
Hazlewood Cres. W10 4G **65**
Hazlewood Twr. *W10 4G **65***
(off Golborne Gdns.)
Hazlitt Cl. TW13: Felt 4C **114**
Hazlitt M. W14 3G **83**
Hazlitt Rd. W14 3G **83**
Heacham Av. UB10: Uxb 3E **40**
Headbourne Ho.
SE1 3D **86** (7F **169**)
Headcorn Pl.
CR7: Thor H 4K **139**
Headcorn Rd. BR1: Brom 5H **125**
CR7: Thor H 4K **139**
N17 7A **18**
Headfort Pl.
SW1 2E **84** (7H **165**)
Headington Ct.
*CR0: Croy 4C **152***
(off Tanfield Rd.)
Headington Rd. SW18 2A **120**
Headlam Rd. SW4 6H **103**
(not continuous)
Headlam St. E1 4H **69**
Headley App. IG2: Ilf 5F **37**
Headley Av. SM6: Wall 5K **151**
Headley Cl. KT19: Eps 6G **147**
Headley Ct. SE26 5J **123**
Headley Dr. CR0: Croy 7D **154**
IG2: Ilf 6F **37**
Head's M. W11 6J **65**
HEADSTONE **3H 25**
Headstone Dr. HA1: Harr 3H **25**
Headstone Gdns.
HA2: Harr 4G **25**
Headstone La. HA3: Harr 7A **10**
Headstone Pde. HA1: Harr 4H **25**
Headstone Rd. HA1: Harr 5J **25**
Head St. E1 6K **69**
(not continuous)
Headway Cl. TW10: Rich 4C **116**
Heald St. SE14 1C **106**
Healey Ho. SW9 7A **86**
Healey St. NW1 6F **49**
Hearne Rd. W4 6G **81**
Hearn Ri. UB5: N'olt 1B **60**
Hearn's Bldgs. SE17 4D **86**
Hearnshaw Ho. *E14 5A **70***
(off Halley St.)
Hearn St. EC2 4E **68** (4H **163**)
Hearnville Rd. SW12 1E **120**
Heatham Pk.
TW2: Twick 7K **97**
Heath Av. DA7: Bex 6D **92**
Heathbourne Rd.
WD23: Bush 1D **10**
Heath Brow NW3 3A **48**
Heath Bus. Cen.
TW3: Houn 4G **97**
Heath Cl. NW11 7K **29**
UB3: Hayes 7F **77**
W5 4F **63**
Heathcock Ct. *WC2 3F **167***
(off Exchange Ct.)
Heathcote Av. IG5: Ilf 2D **36**
Heathcote Ct. IG5: Ilf 1D **36**
(Glade Ct.)
IG5: Ilf 2D **36**
(Heathcote Av.)
Heathcote Gro. E4 3K **19**
Heathcote Rd.
TW1: Twick 6B **98**
Heathcote St.
WC1 4K **67** (3G **161**)
Heath Ct. *CR0: Croy 4D **152***
(off Heathfield Rd.)
TW4: Houn 4D **96**
UB8: Uxb 7A **40**
Heathcroft NW11 1K **47**
W5 4F **63**
Heathcroft Av.
TW16: Sun T 7H **113**
Heathcroft Gdns. E17 1F **35**
Heathdale Av. TW4: Houn 3C **96**
Heathdene Dr. DA17: Belv 4H **93**
Heathdene Rd.
SM6: Wall 7F **151**
SW16 7K **121**
Heath Dr. NW3 4K **47**
SM2: Sutt 7A **150**
SW20 4E **136**
Heathedge SE26 2H **123**
Heath End Rd.
DA5: Bexl 1K **129**
Heather Av. RM1: Rom 2K **39**
Heatherbank BR7: Chst 2E **144**
SE9 2D **108**
Heather Cl. E6 6E **72**
N7 3K **49**
RM1: Rom 1K **39**
SE13 7F **107**
SW8 3F **103**
TW7: Isle 5H **97**
TW12: Hamp 1D **132**
UB8: Uxb 5B **58**
Heather Ct. DA14: Sidc 6D **128**
Heatherdale Cl.
KT2: King T 6G **117**
Heatherdene Cl.
CR4: Mitc 4B **138**
N12 7F **15**
Heather Dr. EN2: Enf 2G **7**
RM1: Rom 2K **39**
Heatherfold Way
HA5: Pinn 3H **23**
Heather Gdns. NW11 6G **29**
RM1: Rom 2K **39**
SM2: Sutt 6J **149**
Heather Glen
RM1: Rom 2K **39**
Heather Ho. *E14 6E **70***
(off Dee St.)
Heatherlands
TW16: Sun T 6J **113**
Heather La. UB7: W Dray 6A **58**
Heatherley Ct. E5 3G **51**
Heatherley Dr. IG5: Ilf 3C **36**
Heather Pk. Dr.
HA0: Wemb 7G **45**
Heather Pk. Pde.
*HA0: Wemb 7F **45***
(off Heather Pk. Dr.)
Heather Rd. E4 6G **19**
NW2 2B **46**
SE12 2J **125**
Heatherset Gdns. SW16 7K **121**
Heatherside Rd.
DA14: Sidc 3C **128**
KT19: Eps 7K **147**
Heathers, The
TW19: Staines 7B **94**
Heatherton Ter. N3 2K **29**
Heather Wlk. HA8: Edg 5C **12**
*TW2: Twick 7E **96***
(off Stephenson Rd.)
W10 4G **65**
Heather Way
CR2: S Croy 7K **153**
HA7: Stan 6E **10**
RM1: Rom 2K **39**
Heatherwood Cl. E12 2A **54**
Heatherwood Dr.
UB4: Hayes 2F **59**
Heathfield BR7: Chst 6G **127**
E4 3K **19**
HA1: Harr 7K **25**
Heathfield Av. SW18 7B **102**
Heathfield Cl. BR2: Kes 5A **156**
E16 5B **72**
Heathfield Ct. SE20 7J **123**
W4 5K **81**
Heathfield Dr. CR4: Mitc 1C **138**
Heathfield Gdns.
CR0: Croy 4D **152**
NW11 6F **29**
*SE3 2G **107***
(off Baizdon Rd.)
SW18 6B **102**
W4 5J **81**
Heathfield Ho. SE3 2G **107**
Heathfield La. BR7: Chst 6F **127**
Heathfield Nth.
TW2: Twick 7J **97**
Heathfield Pk. NW2 6E **46**
Heathfield Pk. Dr.
RM6: Chad H 5B **38**
Heathfield Ri. HA4: Ruis 7E **22**
Heathfield Rd.
BR1: Brom 7H **125**
BR2: Kes 5A **156**
CR0: Croy 4D **152**
DA6: Bex 4F **111**
SW18 6A **102**
W3 2H **81**
Heathfields Ct.
TW4: Houn 5C **96**
Heathfield Sth.
TW2: Twick 7K **97**
Heathfield Sq. SW18 7B **102**
Heathfield St. *W11 7G **65***
(off Portland Rd.)
Heathfield Ter. SE18 6J **91**
W4 5J **81**
Heathfield Va.
CR2: S Croy 7K **153**
Heath Gdns. TW1: Twick 1K **115**
Heathgate NW11 6K **29**
Heathgate Pl. NW3 5D **48**
Heath Gro. SE20 7J **123**
TW16: Sun T 7H **113**
Heath Ho. DA15: Sidc 4K **127**
Heath Hurst Rd. NW3 4C **48**
Heathland Rd. N16 1E **50**
Heathlands Cl.
TW1: Twick 2K **115**
TW16: Sun T 2J **131**
Heathlands Way
TW4: Houn 5C **96**
Heath La. SE3 2F **107**
(not continuous)
Heathlee Rd. SE3 4H **107**
Heathley End BR7: Chst 6G **127**
Heath Lodge WD23: Bush 1D **10**
Heathmans Rd. SW6 1H **101**
Heath Mead SW19 3F **119**
Heath Pk. Dr. BR1: Brom 3C **144**
Heath Pas. NW3 2K **47**
Heathpool Ct. E1 4H **69**
Heath Ri. BR2: Short 6H **143**
SW15 6F **101**
Heath Rd. CR7: Thor H 3C **140**
DA5: Bexl 1J **129**
HA1: Harr 7G **25**
RM6: Chad H 7D **38**
SW8 2F **103**
TW1: Twick 1K **115**
TW2: Twick 1K **115**
TW3: Houn 4F **97**
UB10: Uxb 4E **58**
Heathrow Blvd.
UB7: W Dray 7B **76**
(not continuous)
Heathrow C'way. Cen.
TW14: Felt 3J **95**
Heathrow Corporate Pk.
TW4: Houn 3A **96**
Heathrow Interchange
UB4: Hayes 1A **78**
Heathrow Intl. Trad. Est.
TW4: Houn 3K **95**
***Heathrow Visitors Cen.* 1E 94**
Heaths Cl. EN1: Enf 2K **7**
Heath Side NW3 4B **48**
Heathside BR5: Orp 7G **145**
NW11 1J **47**
SE13 2E **106**
TW4: Houn 7D **96**
Heathside Av. DA7: Bex 1E **110**
Heathside Cl. IG2: Ilf 5H **37**
Heathstan Rd. W12 6C **64**
Heath St. NW3 3A **48**
Heath, The W7 1J **79**
Heathurst Rd.
CR2: S Croy 7E **152**
Heath Vw. N2 4A **30**
Heathview NW5 4E **48**
Heath Vw. Cl. N2 4A **30**
Heathview Dr. SE2 6D **92**
Heathview Gdns. SW15 7E **100**
Heathview Rd.
CR7: Thor H 4A **140**
Heath Vs. NW3 3B **48**
SE18 5K **91**
Heathville Rd. N19 7J **31**
Heathwall St. SW11 3D **102**
Heath Way DA8: Erith 1J **111**
IG8: Wfd G 5F **21**
HEATHWAY **1G 75**
Heathway CR0: Croy 3B **154**
RM9: Dag 3F **57**
RM10: Dag 3F **57**
SE3 7J **89**
UB2: S'hall 4B **78**
Heathway Ct. NW11 2J **47**
Heathway Ind. Est.
RM10: Dag 4H **57**
Heathwood Gdns. SE7 4C **90**
Heathwood Point SE23 3K **123**
Heathwood Wlk.
DA5: Bexl 1K **129**
Heaton Cl. E4 3K **19**
Heaton Rd. CR4: Mitc 7E **120**
SE15 2H **105**
Heaven Tree Cl. N1 6C **50**
Heaver Rd. SW11 3B **102**
Heavitree Cl. SE18 5H **91**
Heavitree Rd. SE18 5H **91**
(not continuous)
Hebden Ct. E2 1F **69**
Hebden Ter. N17 6K **17**
Hebdon Rd. SW17 3C **120**
Heber Mans. *W14 6G **83***
(off Queen's Club Gdns.)
Heber Rd. NW2 5F **47**
SE22 6F **105**
Hebron Rd. W6 3E **82**
Hecham Cl. E17 2A **34**
Heckfield Pl. SW6 7J **83**
Heckford Ho. *E14 6D **70***
(off Grundy St.)
Heckford St. E1 7K **69**
Hector *NW9 1B **28***
(off Five Acre)
Hector Ct. *SW9 7A **86***
(off Caldwell St.)
Hector Ho. *E2 2H **69***
(off Old Bethnal Grn. Rd.)
Hector St. SE18 4J **91**
Heddington Gro. N7 5K **49**
Heddon Cl. TW7: Isle 4A **98**
Heddon Ct. Av. EN4: Barn 5J **5**
Heddon Ct. Pde.
EN4: Barn 5K **5**
Heddon Rd. EN4: Barn 5J **5**
Heddon St. W1 7G **67** (2A **166**)
(not continuous)
Hedgegate Ct. W11 6H **65**
Hedge Hill EN2: Enf 1G **7**
Hedge La. N13 3G **17**
Hedgemans Rd.
RM9: Dag 7D **56**
Hedgemans Way
RM9: Dag 6E **56**
Hedgerley Gdns.
UB6: G'frd 2G **61**
Hedgers Gro. E9 6A **52**
Hedger St. SE11 4B **86**
Hedge Wlk. SE6 5D **124**
Hedgewood Gdns. IG5: Ilf 5E **36**
Hedgley IG4: Ilf 4D **36**
Hedgley M. SE12 5H **107**
Hedgley St. SE12 5H **107**
Hedingham Cl. N1 7C **50**
Hedingham Rd.
RM8: Dag 5B **56**
Hedley Ho. *E14 3E **88***
(off Stewart St.)
Hedley Rd. TW2: Twick 7E **96**
Hedley Row N5 5D **50**
Hedley St. RM1: Rom 5K **39**
Hedsor Ho. *E2 3J **163***
(off Ligonier St.)
Heenan Cl. IG11: Bark 6G **55**
Heene Rd. EN2: Enf 1J **7**
Hega Ho. *E14 5E **70***
(off Ullin St.)
Heidegger Cres. SW13 7D **82**
Heigham Rd. E6 7C **54**
Heighton Gdns.
CR0: Croy 5B **152**
Heights Cl. SW20 7D **118**
Heights, The BR3: Beck 7E **124**
(not continuous)
SE7 5A **90**
UB5: N'olt 5D **42**
Heiron St. SE17 6B **86**
Helby Rd. SW4 6H **103**
Heldar Ct. SE1 2D **86** (7F **169**)
Helder Gro. SE12 7H **107**
Helder St. CR2: S Croy 6D **152**
Heldmann Cl. TW7: Isle 4H **97**
Helena Ct. W5 5D **62**
Helena Pl. E9 1H **69**
Helena Rd. E13 2H **71**
E17 5C **34**
NW10 5D **46**
W5 5D **62**
Helena Sq. *SE16 7A **70***
(off Sovereign Cres.)
Helen Av. TW14: Felt 7K **95**
Helen Cl. KT8: W Mole 4F **133**
N2 3A **30**
Helen Gladstone Ho.
*SE1 6A **168***
(off Surrey Row)

Helen Ho. E2 ......2H 69
(off Old Bethnal Grn. Rd.)
Helen Mackay Ho. E14 ....6F 71
(off Blair St.)
Helen Peele Cotts. SE16 ....3J 87
(off Lower Rd.)
Helenslea Av. NW11 ....1J 47
Helen's Pl. E2 ......3J 69
Helen St. SE18 ......4F 91
Helen Taylor Ho. SE16 ....3G 87
(off Evelyn Lowe Est.)
Helford Cl. HA4: Ruis 2G 41
Helgiford Gdns.
TW16: Sun T 7G 113
Helios Rd. SM6: Wall 1E 150
Heliport Ind. Est. SW11 ....2B 102
Helix Gdns. SW2 ......6K 103
Helix Rd. SW2 ......6K 103
Hellings St. E1 ......1G 87
Helme Cl. SW19 ......5H 119
Helmet Row EC1 ....4C 68 (2D 162)
Helmore Rd. IG11: Bark 7K 55
Helmsdale Cl.
UB4: Hayes 4C 60
Helmsdale Ho. NW6 ....2K 65
(off Carlton Va.)
Helmsdale Rd. SW16 ....1H 139
Helmsley Pl. E8 ......7H 51
Helmsley St. E8 ......7H 51
Helperby Rd. NW10 ....7A 46
Helsby Ct. NW8 ......3A 158
(off Pollitt Dr.)
Helsinki Sq. SE16 ......3A 88
Helston NW1 ......1G 67
(off Camden St.)
Helston Cl. HA5: Pinn 1D 24
Helston Ct. N15 ......5E 32
(off Culvert Rd.)
Helston Ho. SE11 ......5K 173
(off Kennings Way)
Helvetia St. SE6 ......2B 124
Helwys Ct. E4 ......6J 19
Hemans St. SW8 ......7H 85
Hemans St. Est. SW8 ....7H 85
Hemberton Rd. SW9 ....3J 103
Hemery Rd. UB6: G'frd 5H 43
Hemingford Cl. N12 ....5G 15
Hemingford Rd. N1 ....1K 67
SM3: Sutt 4E 148
Heming Rd. HA8: Edg 7C 12
Hemington Av. N11 ....5J 15
Hemingway Cl. NW5 ....4E 48
Hemlington Ho. E14 ....5A 70
(off Aston St.)
Hemlock Rd. W12 ......7B 64
(not continuous)
Hemmen La. UB3: Hayes 6H 59
Hemming Cl.
TW12: Hamp 1E 132
Hemmings Cl.
DA14: Sidc 2B 128
Hemming St. E1 ......4G 69
Hempstead Cl.
IG9: Buck H 2D 20
Hempstead Rd. E17 ....3F 35
Hemp Wlk. SE17 ......4D 86
Hemsby Rd. KT9: Chess 6F 147
Hemstal Rd. NW6 ......7J 47
Hemsted Rd. DA8: Erith 7K 93
Hemswell Dr. NW9 ....1A 28
Hemsworth Cl. N1 ......2E 68
Hemsworth St. N1 ......2E 68
Hemus Pl. SW3 ....5C 84 (6D 170)
Hen & Chicken Ct. EC4 ....1J 167
(off Fleet St.)
Henchman St. W12 ......6B 64
Hendale Av. NW4 ......3D 28
Henderson Cl. NW10 ....6J 45
Henderson Ct. SE14 ....6K 87
(off Myers La.)
Henderson Dr.
NW8 ......4B 66 (3A 158)

Henderson Ho.
RM10: Dag 3G 57
(off Kershaw Rd.)
Henderson Rd.
CR0: Croy 6D 140
E7 ......6A 54
N9 ......1C 18
SW18 ......7C 102
UB4: Hayes 3J 59
Hendham Rd. SW17 ....2C 120
HENDON 5D 28
Hendon Av. N3 ......1G 29
Hendon Crematorium
NW4 ......1F 29
Hendon Hall Ct. NW4 ....3F 29
Hendon Ho. NW4 ......5F 29
Hendon La. N3 ......3G 29
Hendon Lodge NW4 ....3D 28
Hendon Pk. Mans. NW4 ....5E 28
Hendon Pk. Row NW11 ....6H 29
Hendon Rd. N9 ......2B 18
Hendon Way NW2 ......7F 29
NW4 ......6D 28
Hendon Wood La. NW7 ....1G 13
Hendren Cl. UB6: G'frd 5H 43
Hendre Rd. SE1 ......4E 86
Hendrick Av. SW12 ....7D 102
Heneage La.
EC3 ......6E 68 (1H 169)
Heneage Pl. EC3 ....6E 68 (1H 169)
Heneage St. E1 ....5F 69 (5K 163)
Henfield Cl. DA5: Bexl 6G 111
N19 ......1G 49
Henfield Rd. SW19 ....1H 137
Hengelo Gdns. CR4: Mitc 4B 138
Hengist Rd. DA8: Erith 7H 93
SE12 ......7K 107
Hengist Way BR2: Short 4G 143
Hengrave Rd. SE23 ....6J 105
Hengrove Ct. DA5: Bexl 1E 128
Hengrove Cres.
TW15: Ashf 3A 112
Henham Ct. RM5: Col R 1J 39
Henley Av. SM3: Sutt 3G 149
Henley Cl. SE16 ......2J 87
(off St Marychurch St.)
TW7: Isle 1K 97
UB6: G'frd 2G 61
Henley Cl. N14 ......7B 6
NW2 ......6F 47
Henley Dr. KT2: King T 7B 118
SE1 ......4F 87
SE16 ......4F 87
Henley Gdns. HA5: Pinn 3K 23
RM6: Chad H 5E 38
Henley Ho. E2 ......3K 163
(off Swanfield St.)
Henley Prior N1 ......1G 161
(off Affleck St.)
Henley Rd. E16 ......2D 90
IG1: Ilf 4G 55
N18 ......4K 17
NW10 ......1E 64
Henley St. SW11 ......2E 102
Henley Way TW13: Felt 5B 114
Henlow Pl.
TW10: Rich 2D 116
Henlys Corner 4H 29
HENLYS ROBT. 2A 96
Hennel Cl. SE23 ......3J 123
Hennessey Rd. N9 ......2D 18
Henniker Gdns. E6 ......3B 72
Henniker M.
SW3 ......5B 84 (7A 170)
Henniker Point E15 ......5G 53
(off Leytonstone Rd.)
Henniker Rd. E15 ......5F 53
Henningham Rd. N17 ....1D 32
Henning St. SW11 ......1C 102
Henrietta Cl. SE8 ......6C 88
Henrietta Ct. TW1: Twick 7C 98
(off Richmond Rd.)

Henrietta Ho. N15 ......6E 32
(off St Ann's Rd.)
W6 ......5E 82
(off Queen Caroline St.)
Henrietta M.
WC1 ......4J 67 (3F 161)
Henrietta Pl. W1 ....6F 67 (1J 165)
Henrietta St. E15 ......5E 52
WC2 ......7J 67 (2F 167)
Henriques St. E1 ......6G 69
Henry Addington Cl. E6 ....5F 73
Henry Cl. EN2: Enf 1K 7
Henry Cooper Way SE9 ....3B 126
Henry Darlot Dr. NW7 ....5A 14
Henry Dickens Ct. W11 ....7F 65
Henry Doulton Dr. SW17 ....4E 120
Henry Hatch Wlk.
SM2: Sutt 7A 150
Henry Ho. SE1 ....1A 86 (5J 167)
SW8 ......7J 85
(off Wyvil Rd.)
Henry Jackson Rd. SW15 ....3F 101
Henry Macaulay Av.
KT2: King T 1D 134
Henry Peters Dr.
TW11: Tedd 5J 115
(off Somerset Gdns.)
Henry Purcell Ho. E16 ....7K 71
(off Evelyn Rd.)
Henry Rd. E6 ......2C 72
EN4: Barn 5G 5
N4 ......1C 50
Henrys Av. IG8: Wfd G 5C 20
Henryson Rd. SE4 ......5C 106
Henry St. BR1: Brom 1K 143
Henry's Wlk. IG6: Ilf 1H 37
Henry Tate M. SW16 ....5A 122
Henry Tudor Ct. SE9 ....7G 109
Henry Wise Ho. SW1 ....4B 172
(off Vauxhall Bri. Rd.)
Hensford Gdns. SE26 ....4H 123
Henshall St. N1 ......6D 50
Henshawe Rd. RM8: Dag 3D 56
Henshaw St. SE17 ......4D 86
Henslowe Rd. SE22 ....5G 105
Henslow Ho. SE15 ......7G 87
(off Peckham Pk. Rd.)
Henson Av. NW2 ......5E 46
Henson Path HA3: Harr 3D 26
Henson Pl. UB5: N'olt 1A 60
Henstridge Pl. NW8 ......1C 66
Henty Cl. SW11 ......7C 84
Henty Wlk. SW15 ......5D 100
Henville Rd. BR1: Brom 1K 143
Henwick Rd. SE9 ......3B 108
Henwood Side IG8: Wfd G 6J 21
Hepburn Gdns.
BR2: Short 1G 155
Hepburn M. SW11 ......5D 102
Hepple Cl. TW7: Isle 2B 98
Hepplestone Cl. SW15 ....6D 100
Hepscott Rd. E9 ......6C 52
Hepworth Ct. N1 ......1B 68
(off Gaskin St.)
NW3 ......5C 48
SM3: Sutt 1J 149
Hepworth Gdns.
IG11: Bark 5A 56
Hepworth Rd. SW16 ....7J 121
Hepworth Way
KT12: Walt T 7H 131
Heracles NW9 ......1B 28
(off Five Acre)
Heracles Cl. SM6: Wall 7J 151
Hera Ct. E14 ......4C 88
(off Homer Dr.)
Herald Gdns. SM6: Wall 2F 151
Herald's Pl.
SE11 ......4B 86 (3K 173)
Herald St. E2 ......4H 69
Herbal Hill EC1 ....4A 68 (4K 161)
Herbal Hill Gdns. EC1 ....4A 68

Herbal Pl. EC1 ......4K 161
Herbert Cres.
SW1 ......3D 84 (1F 171)
Herbert Gdns. NW10 ....2D 64
RM6: Chad H 7D 38
W4 ......6H 81
Herbert Ho. E1 ......7J 163
(off Old Castle St.)
Herbert M. SW2 ......6A 104
Herbert Morrison Ho.
SW6 ......6H 83
(off Clem Attlee Ct.)
Herbert Pl. SE18 ......6F 91
Herbert Rd.
BR2: Short 5B 144
DA7: Bex 2E 110
E12 ......4C 54
E17 ......7B 34
IG3: Ilf 2J 55
KT1: King T 3F 135
N11 ......7D 16
N15 ......5F 33
NW9 ......6C 28
SE18 ......7E 90
(not continuous)
SW19 ......7H 119
(not continuous)
UB1: S'hall 1D 76
Herbert St. E13 ......2J 71
NW5 ......6E 48
Herbrand Est.
WC1 ......4J 67 (3E 160)
Herbrand St.
WC1 ......4J 67 (3E 160)
Hercies Rd. UB10: Uxb 7B 40
Hercules Cl. SE14 ......6A 88
Hercules Pl. N7 ......3J 49
(not continuous)
Hercules Rd.
SE1 ......3K 85 (2H 173)
Hercules St. N7 ......3J 49
Hercules Wharf E14 ....7G 71
(off Orchard Pl.)
Hercules Yd. N7 ......3J 49
Hereford Av. EN4: Barn 1J 15
Hereford Bldgs. SW3 ....7B 170
(off Old Chu. St.)
Hereford Ct. HA1: Harr 4J 25
SM2: Sutt 7J 149
W7 ......5K 61
(off Copley Cl.)
Hereford Gdns. HA5: Pinn 5C 24
IG1: Ilf 7C 36
SE13 ......5G 107
TW2: Twick 1G 115
Hereford Ho. NW6 ......2J 65
(off Carlton Va.)
SW3 ......1D 170
(off Ovington Gdns.)
SW10 ......7K 83
(off Fulham Rd.)
Hereford M. W2 ......6J 65
Hereford Pl. SE14 ......7B 88
Hereford Retreat SE15 ....7G 87
Hereford Rd. E11 ......5K 35
TW13: Felt 1A 114
W2 ......6J 65
W3 ......7H 63
W5 ......3C 80
Hereford Sq. SW7 ......4A 84
Hereford St. E2 ......4G 69
Hereford Way
KT9: Chess 5C 146
Herent Dr. IG5: Ilf 4C 36
Hereward Gdns. N13 ....5F 17
Hereward Rd. SW17 ....4D 120
Herga Ct. HA1: Harr 3J 43
Herga Rd. HA3: Harr 4K 25
Heriot Av. E4 ......2H 19
Heriot Rd. NW4 ......5E 28
Heriots Cl. HA7: Stan 4F 11
Heritage Cl. SW9 ......3B 104

Heritage Ct. SE8 ......5K 87
(off Trundley's Rd.)
Heritage Hill BR2: Kes 5A 156
Heritage Vw. HA1: Harr 3K 43
Herlwyn Av. HA4: Ruis 2G 41
Herlwyn Gdns. SW17 ....4D 120
Her Majesty's Theatre 4C 166
(off Haymarket)
Herm Cl. TW7: Isle 7G 79
Hermes Cl. W9 ......4J 65
Hermes Ct. SW9 ......1A 104
(off Southey Rd.)
Hermes St. N1 ....2A 68 (1J 161)
Hermes Wlk. UB5: N'olt 2E 60
Hermes Way SM6: Wall 7H 151
Herm Ho. EN3: Enf 1E 8
N1 ......6C 50
Hermiston Av. N8 ......5J 31
Hermitage Cl. E18 ......4H 35
EN2: Enf 2G 7
KT10: Esh 6A 146
TW17: Shep 4C 130
Hermitage Ct. E1 ......1G 87
(off Knighten St.)
E18 ......4J 35
NW2 ......3J 47
Hermitage Gdns. NW2 ....3J 47
SE19 ......7C 122
Hermitage Grn. SW16 ....1J 139
Hermitage La. N18 ......5J 17
NW2 ......3J 47
SE25 ......6G 141
(not continuous)
SW16 ......7K 121
Hermitage Path SW16 ....1J 139
Hermitage Rd. N4 ......7B 32
SE19 ......7C 122
Hermitage Rooms 2H 167
(off Embankment)
Hermitage Row SE8 ......5G 51
Hermitage St.
W2 ......5B 66 (6A 158)
Hermitage, The
KT1: King T 4D 134
SE13 ......2E 106
SE23 ......1J 123
SW13 ......1B 100
TW10: Rich 5E 98
TW13: Felt 3H 113
UB8: Uxb 6A 40
Hermitage Wlk. E18 ......4H 35
Hermitage Wall E1 ......1G 87
Hermitage Waterside E1 ....1G 87
(off Thomas More St.)
Hermitage Way HA7: Stan 1A 26
Hermit Pl. NW6 ......1K 65
Hermit Rd. E16 ......5H 71
Hermit St. EC1 ......3B 68 (1A 162)
Hermon Gro. UB3: Hayes 1J 77
Hermon Hill E11 ......5J 35
E18 ......5J 35
Herndon Rd. SW18 ....5A 102
Herne Cl. NW10 ......5K 45
Herne Ct. WD23: Bush 1B 10
HERNE HILL 5C 104
Herne Hill SE24 ......6C 104
Herne Hill Ho. SE24 ......6B 104
(off Railton Rd.)
Herne Hill Rd. SE24 ......3C 104
Herne Hill Stadium 6D 104
Herne M. N18 ......4B 18
Herne Pl. SE24 ......5B 104
Herne Rd. KT6: Surb 2D 146
Heron Cl. E17 ......2B 34
IG9: Buck H 1D 20
NW10 ......6A 46
SM1: Sutt 5H 149
Heron Ct. BR2: Short 4A 144
E14 ......3E 88
(off New Union Cl.)
HA4: Ruis 2F 41
KT1: King T 3E 134

Heron Cres.—Highlever Rd.

Heron Cres. DA14: Sidc 3J 127
Herondale Av. SW18 .... 1B 120
Heron Dr. N4 .... 2C 50
Herongate Cl. EN1: Enf 2A 8
Herongate Rd. E12 .... 2A 54
Heron Hill DA17: Belv 5F 93
Heron Ho. DA14: Sidc 3B 128
E6 .... 7C 54
NW8 .... *1C 158*
(off Newcourt St.)
SW11 .... *7C 84*
(off Searles Cl.)
W13 .... 4A 62
Heron Ind. Est. E15 .... 2D 70
Heron Mead EN3: Enf 1H 9
Heron M. IG1: Ilf 2F 55
Heron Pl. SE16 .... 1A 88
W1 .... *7H 159*
(off Thayer St.)
Heron Quay E14 .... 1C 88
Heron Rd. CR0: Croy 2E 152
SE24 .... 4C 104
TW1: Twick 4A 98
Heronsforde W13 .... 6C 62
Heronsgate HA8: Edg 5B 12
Heron's Lea N6 .... 6D 30
Heronslea Dr. HA7: Stan 5K 11
Heron's Pl. TW7: Isle 3B 98
Heron Sq. TW9: Rich 5D 98
Herons Ri. EN4: Barn 4H 5
Herons, The E11 .... 6H 35
Heron Trad. Est. W3 .... 5H 63
Heron Way IG8: Wfd G 4F 21
TW14: Felt 4J 95
Herrick Ho. *SE5* *7D 86*
(off Elmington Est.)
Herrick Rd. N5 .... 3C 50
Herrick St. SW1 .... 4H 85 (4D 172)
Herries St. W10 .... 2G 65
Herringham Rd. SE7 .... 3A 90
Herron Ct. BR2: Short 4H 143
Hersant Cl. NW10 .... 1C 64
Herschell M. SE5 .... 3C 104
Herschell Rd. SE23 .... 7A 106
Hersham Cl. SW15 .... 7C 100
Hershell Ct. SW14 .... 4H 99
Hertford Av. SW14 .... 5K 99
Hertford Cl. EN4: Barn 3G 5
Hertford Ct. *E6* *3D 72*
(off Vicarage La.)
N13 .... 3F 17
Hertford Pl. W1 .... 4G 67 (4B 160)
Hertford Rd.
EN3: Enf, Walt C 4D 8
EN4: Barn 3F 5
IG2: Ilf 6J 37
IG11: Bark 7E 54
N1 .... 1E 68
(not continuous)
N2 .... 3C 30
N9 .... 2C 18
Hertford Sq. CR4: Mitc 4J 139
Hertford St. W1 .... 1F 85 (5J 165)
Hertford Wlk. DA17: Belv 5G 93
Hertford Way CR4: Mitc 4J 139
Hertslet Rd. N7 .... 3K 49
Hertsmere Ho. *E14* *7C 70*
(off Hertsmere Rd.)
Hertsmere Rd. E14 .... 1C 88
Hertswood Ct. EN5: Barn 4B 4
Hervey Cl. N3 .... 1J 29
Hervey Pk. Rd. E17 .... 4A 34
Hervey Rd. SE3 .... 1K 107
Hervey Way N3 .... 1J 29
Hesa Rd. UB3: Hayes 6J 59
Hesewall Cl. SW4 .... 2G 103
Hesketh Pl. W11 .... 7G 65
Hesketh Rd. E7 .... 3J 53
Heslop Rd. SW12 .... 1D 120
Hesper M. SW5 .... 4K 83
Hesperus Cl. E14 .... 4D 88
Hesperus Cres. E14 .... 4D 88
Hessel Rd. W13 .... 2A 80
Hessel St. E1 .... 6H 69
Hestercombe Av. SW6 .... 2G 101
Hesterman Way
CR0: Croy 1K 151
Hester Rd. N18 .... 5B 18
SW11 .... 7C 84
Hester Ter. TW9: Rich 3G 99
HESTON 7E 78
Heston Av. TW5: Houn 6C 78
Heston Cen., The
TW5: Houn 5A 78
Heston Grange
TW5: Houn 6D 78
Heston Grange La.
TW5: Houn 6D 78
Heston Ho. SE8 .... 1C 106
Heston Ind. Cen.
TW5: Houn 6A 78
Heston Ind. Mall
TW5: Houn 7D 78
Heston Rd. TW5: Houn 7E 78
Heston St. SE14 .... 1C 106
Hetherington Rd. SW4 .... 4J 103
TW17: Shep 2E 130
Hetherington Way
UB10: Uxb 4A 40
Hethpool Ho. W2 .... 4A 158
Hetley Gdns. SE19 .... 7F 123
Hetley Rd. W12 .... 1D 82
Heton Gdns. NW4 .... 4D 28
Hevelius Cl. SE10 .... 5H 89
Hever Cft. SE9 .... 4E 126
Hever Gdns. BR1: Brom 2E 144
Heverham Rd. SE18 .... 4J 91
Hever Ho. *SE15* *6K 87*
(off Lovelinch Cl.)
Heversham Ho. SE15 .... 6J 87
Heversham Rd. DA7: Bex 2G 111
Hewens Rd. UB10: Uxb 4E 58
Hewer St. W10 .... 5F 65
Hewett Cl. HA7: Stan 4G 11
Hewett Rd. RM8: Dag 5D 56
Hewett St. EC2 .... 4E 68 (4H 163)
Hewish Rd. N18 .... 4K 17
Hewison St. E3 .... 2B 70
Hewitt Av. N22 .... 2B 32
Hewitt Cl. CR0: Croy 3C 154
Hewitt Rd. N8 .... 5A 32
Hewlett Ho. *SW8* *7F 85*
(off Havelock Ter.)
Hewlett Rd. E3 .... 2A 70
Hexagon, The N6 .... 1D 48
Hexal Rd. SE6 .... 3G 125
Hexham Gdns. TW7: Isle 7A 80
Hexham Rd. EN5: Barn 4E 4
SE27 .... 2C 122
SM4: Mord 1K 149
Heybourne Rd. N17 .... 7C 18
Heybridge *NW1* *6F 49*
(off Lewis St.)
Heybridge Av. SW16 .... 7J 121
Heybridge Dr. IG6: Ilf 2H 37
Heybridge Way E10 .... 7A 34
Heydon Ho. *SE14* *1J 105*
(off Kender St.)
Heyford Av. SW8 .... 7J 85
SW20 .... 3H 137
Heyford Rd. CR4: Mitc 2C 138
Heyford Ter. SW8 .... 7J 85
Heygate St. SE17 .... 4C 86
Heylyn Sq. E3 .... 3B 70
Heynes Rd. RM8: Dag 4C 56
Heysham La. NW3 .... 3K 47
Heysham Rd. N15 .... 6D 32
Heythorp St. SW18 .... 1H 119
Heythrop College
University of London
.... *3K 83*
(off Kensington Sq.)
Heythrop Dr. UB10: Uxb 4B 40
Heywood Av. NW9 .... 1A 28
Heywood Ct. HA7: Stan 5H 11
Heywood Ho. *SE14* *6K 87*
(off Myers La.)
Heyworth Rd. E5 .... 4H 51
E15 .... 5H 53
Hibbert Ho. *E14* *3C 88*
(off Tiller Rd.)
Hibbert Rd. E17 .... 7B 34
HA3: Harr 2K 25
Hibbert St. SW11 .... 3B 102
Hibernia Gdns.
TW3: Houn 4E 96
Hibernia Point *SE2* *2D 92*
(off Wolvercote Rd.)
Hibernia Rd.
W3: Houn 4E 96
Hibiscus Cl. HA8: Edg 4D 12
Hichisson Rd. SE15 .... 5J 105
Hickes Ho. NW6 .... 7B 48
Hickey's Almshouses
TW9: Rich 4F 99
Hickin Cl. SE7 .... 4B 90
Hickin St. E14 .... 3E 88
Hickleton *NW1* *1G 67*
(off Camden St.)
Hickling Ho. *SE16* *3H 87*
(off Slippers Pl.)
Hickling Rd. IG1: Ilf 5F 55
Hickman Av. E4 .... 6K 19
Hickman Cl. E16 .... 5B 72
Hickman Rd.
RM6: Chad H 7C 38
Hickmore Wlk. SW4 .... 3H 103
Hickory Cl. N9 .... 7B 8
Hicks Av. UB6: G'frd 3H 61
Hicks Cl. SW11 .... 3C 102
Hicks Ct. RM10: Dag 3H 57
Hicks St. SE8 .... 5A 88
Hidcote Gdns. SW20 .... 3D 136
Hide E6 .... 6E 72
Hide Pl. SW1 .... 4H 85 (4C 172)
Hider Ct. SE3 .... 7A 90
Hide Rd. HA1: Harr 4G 25
Hides St. N7 .... 6K 49
Hide Twr. *SW1* *4C 172*
(off Regency St.)
Higgins Ho. *N1* *1E 68*
(off Colville Est.)
Higginson Ho. *NW3* *7D 48*
(off Fellows Rd.)
Higgins Wlk.
TW12: Hamp *6C 114*
(off Abbott Cl.)
Higgs Ind. Est. SE24 .... 3B 104
High Acres EN2: Enf 3G 7
HIGHAM HILL 2A 34
Higham Hill Rd. E17 .... 1A 34
Higham Path E17 .... 3A 34
Higham Pl. E17 .... 3A 34
Higham Rd. IG8: Wfd G 6D 20
N17 .... 3D 32
Highams Ct. E4 .... 3A 20
Highams Lodge Bus. Cen.
E17 .... 3K 33
HIGHAMS PARK 6A 20
Highams Pk. Ind. Est. E4 .... 6K 19
Higham Sta. Av. E4 .... 6H 19
Highams, The E17 .... 1E 34
Higham St. E17 .... 3A 34
Highbanks Cl.
DA16: Well 7B 92
Highbanks Rd. HA5: Pinn 6A 10
Highbank Way N8 .... 6A 32
HIGH BARNET 2A 4
Highbarrow Rd.
CR0: Croy 1G 153
High Beech CR2: S Croy 7E 152
N21 .... 6E 6
High Beeches DA14: Sidc 5E 128
High Birch Ct. *EN4: Barn* *4H 5*
(off Park Rd.)
High Bri. SE10 .... 5F 89
Highbridge Ct. *SE14* *7J 87*
(off Farrow La.)
Highbridge Rd. IG11: Bark 1F 73
High Bri. Wharf *SE10* *5F 89*
(off High Bri.)
Highbrook Rd. SE3 .... 3B 108
High Broom Cres.
BR4: W W'ck 7D 142
HIGHBURY 4B 50
Highbury *3B 50*
Highbury Av.
CR7: Thor H 2A 140
Highbury Barn N5 .... 4C 50
Highbury Cl.
BR4: W W'ck 2D 154
KT3: N Mald 4J 135
HIGHBURY CORNER 6B 50
Highbury Cres. N5 .... 5B 50
Highbury Est. N5 .... 5C 50
Highbury Gdns. IG3: Ilf 2J 55
Highbury Grange N5 .... 4C 50
Highbury Gro. N5 .... 5B 50
Highbury Gro. Ct. N5 .... 6C 50
Highbury Hill N5 .... 3A 50
Highbury New Pk. N5 .... 5C 50
Highbury Pk. N5 .... 3B 50
Highbury Pk. M. N5 .... 4C 50
Highbury Pl. N5 .... 6B 50
Highbury Quad. N5 .... 3C 50
Highbury Rd. SW19 .... 5G 119
Highbury Sta. Rd. N1 .... 6A 50
Highbury Ter. N5 .... 5B 50
Highbury Ter. M. N5 .... 5B 50
High Cedar Dr. SW20 .... 7E 118
Highclere Rd.
KT3: N Mald 3K 135
Highclere St. SE26 .... 4A 124
Highcliffe *W13* *5B 62*
(off Clivedon Ct.)
Highcliffe Dr. SW15 .... 6B 100
(not continuous)
Highcliffe Gdns. IG4: Ilf 5C 36
Highcombe SE7 .... 6K 89
Highcombe Cl. SE9 .... 1B 126
High Coombe Pl.
KT2: King T 6K 117
Highcroft NW9 .... 5A 28
Highcroft Av. HA0: Wemb 7G 45
Highcroft Est. N19 .... 7J 31
Highcroft Gdns. NW11 .... 6H 29
Highcroft Rd. N19 .... 7J 31
High Cross Cen., The N15 .... 4G 33
High Cross Rd. N17 .... 3G 33
Highcross Way SW15 .... 1C 118
Highdaun Dr. SW16 .... 4K 139
Highdown KT4: Wor Pk 2A 148
Highdown Rd. SW15 .... 6D 100
High Dr. KT3: N Mald 1J 135
High Elms IG8: Wfd G 5D 20
Highfield WD23: Bush 2D 10
Highfield Av. DA8: Erith 6H 93
HA5: Pinn 5D 24
HA9: Wemb 3F 45
NW9 .... 5J 27
NW11 .... 7F 29
UB6: G'frd 5J 43
Highfield Cl. HA6: Nwood 1G 23
KT6: Surb 1C 146
N22 .... 1A 32
NW9 .... 5J 27
SE13 .... 6F 107
Highfield Ct. N14 .... 6B 6
NW11 .... 6G 29
Highfield Cres.
HA6: Nwood 1G 23
Highfield Dr.
BR2: Short 4G 143
BR4: W W'ck 2D 154
KT19: Eps 6B 148
UB10: Uxb 4A 40
Highfield Gdns. NW11 .... 6G 29
Highfield Hill SE19 .... 7D 122
Highfield Rd. BR1: Brom 4D 144
BR7: Chst 3K 145
DA6: Bex 5F 111
HA6: Nwood 1G 23
IG8: Wfd G 7H 21
KT5: Surb 7J 135
KT12: Walt T 7J 131
N21 .... 2G 17
NW11 .... 6G 29
SM1: Sutt 5C 150
TW7: Isle 1K 97
TW13: Felt 1J 113
(Hazel Gro.)
TW13: Felt 2J 113
(Tiley Rd.)
TW16: Sun T 5H 131
W3 .... 5H 63
Highfields SM1: Sutt 2J 149
Highfields Gro. N6 .... 1D 48
High Foleys KT10: Esh 7B 146
High Gables BR2: Short 2G 143
HIGHGATE 1F 49
Highgate Av. N6 .... 7F 31
Highgate Cemetery N6 .... 1E 48
Highgate Cl. N6 .... 7E 30
Highgate Edge N2 .... 5C 30
Highgate Hgts. N6 .... 6G 31
Highgate High St. N6 .... 1E 48
Highgate Hill N6 .... 1F 49
N19 .... 1F 49
Highgate Ho. SE26 .... 3G 123
Highgate Rd. NW5 .... 3E 48
Highgate Spinney N8 .... 6H 31
Highgate Wlk. SE23 .... 2J 123
Highgate W. Hill N6 .... 2E 48
High Gro. BR1: Brom 1B 144
SE18 .... 7H 91
Highgrove Cl. BR7: Chst 1C 144
N11 .... 5K 15
Highgrove Ct. BR3: Beck 7C 124
SM1: Sutt 6J 149
Highgrove M. SM5: Cars 3D 150
Highgrove Rd. RM8: Dag 5C 56
Highgrove Way HA4: Ruis 6J 23
High Hill Est. E5 .... 1H 51
High Hill Ferry E5 .... 1H 51
High Holborn
WC1 .... 6J 67 (7E 160)
Highland Av. RM10: Dag 3J 57
(not continuous)
W7 .... 6J 61
Highland Cotts.
SM6: Wall 4G 151
Highland Ct. E18 .... 1K 35
Highland Cft. BR3: Beck 5D 124
Highland Dr. WD23: Bush 1A 10
Highland Pk. TW13: Felt 4H 113
Highland Rd. BR1: Brom 1H 143
BR2: Short 1H 143
DA6: Bex 5G 111
HA6: Nwood 2H 23
SE19 .... 6E 122
Highlands N20 .... 2G 15
Highlands Av. N21 .... 5E 6
W3 .... 7J 63
Highlands Cl. N4 .... 7J 31
TW3: Houn 1F 97
Highlands Ct. SE19 .... 6E 122
Highlands Gdns. IG1: Ilf 1D 54
Highlands Heath SW15 .... 7E 100
Highlands Rd. EN5: Barn 5D 4
Highlands, The EN5: Barn 4D 4
HA8: Edg 2H 27
HIGHLANDS VILLAGE 5D 6
Highland Ter. *SE13* *3D 106*
(off Algernon Rd.)
High La. W7 .... 5H 61
(not continuous)
Highlawn Hall HA1: Harr 3J 43
Highlea Cl. NW9 .... 7F 13
High Level Dr. SE26 .... 4G 123
Highlever Rd. W10 .... 5E 64

266 A-Z London

High Mead—Hillside Dr.

High Mead
BR4: W W'ck 2F **155**
HA1: Harr 5J **25**
Highmead *N18* *5B 18*
(off Alpha Rd.)
SE18 .... 7K **91**
Highmead Cres.
HA0: Wemb 7F **45**
High Mdw. Cl. HA5: Pinn 4A **24**
High Mdw. Cres. NW9 ...... 5K **27**
High Meads Rd. E16 .... 6B **72**
Highmore Rd. SE3 .... 7G **89**
High Mt. NW4 .... 6C **28**
High Oaks EN2: Enf 1E **6**
High Pde., The SW16 ...... 3J **121**
High Pk. Av. TW9: Rich 1G **99**
High Pk. Rd. TW9: Rich 1G **99**
High Path SW19 .... 1K **137**
High Point SE9 .... 3F **127**
Highpoint N6 .... 7E **30**
High Ridge N10 .... 1F **31**
High Ridge Pl. *EN2: Enf* *1E 6*
(off Oak Av.)
High Rd. E18 .... 1J **35**
HA0: Wemb 5D **44**
HA3: Harr 7D **10**
HA5: Pinn 6J **23**
HA9: Wemb 5D **44**
IG1: Ilf 3F **55**
(not continuous)
IG3: Chad H, Ilf 1K **55**
IG7: Chig 5K **21**
IG9: Buck H 2E **20**
IG9: Buck H, Lough ... 2E **20**
N11 .... 5A **16**
N15 .... 5F **33**
N22 .... 1K **31**
NW10 .... 6A **46**
RM6: Chad H 7D **38**
UB4: Hayes 5G **59**
UB10: Uxb 3E **40**
WD23: Bush 1C **10**
High Rd. E. Finchley N2 .... 1B **30**
High Rd. Leyton E10 .... 6D **34**
E15 .... 2D **52**
High Rd. Leytonstone E11 .... 4G **53**
High Rd. Nth. Finchley
N12 .... 3F **15**
High Rd. Whetstone N20 ..... 7F **5**
High Rd. Woodford Grn.
E18 .... 7C **20**
IG8: Wfd G 6C **20**
High Sheldon N6 .... 6D **30**
Highshore Rd. SE15 .... 2F **105**
(not continuous)
Highstead Cres.
DA8: Erith 1K **111**
Highstone Av. E11 .... 6J **35**
Highstone Ct. *E11* *6H 35*
(off New Wanstead)
Highstone Mans. *NW1* *7G 49*
(off Camden Rd.)
High St. BR1: Brom 2J **143**
(not continuous)
BR3: Beck 2C **142**
BR4: W W'ck 1D **154**
BR7: Chst 6F **127**
CR0: Croy 2C **152**
(not continuous)
CR7: Thor H 4C **140**
E11 .... 5J **35**
E13 .... 2J **71**
E15 .... 2E **70**
E17 .... 5A **34**
EN3: Enf 6D **8**
EN5: Barn 3B **4**
HA1: Harr 1J **43**
HA3: Harr 2J **25**
(not continuous)
HA4: Ruis 7G **23**
HA5: Pinn 3C **24**
HA6: Nwood 1H **23**
High St. HA8: Edg 6B **12**
HA9: Wemb 4F **45**
IG6: Ilf 3G **37**
KT1: King T 3D **134**
(Portsmouth Rd.)
KT1: King T 1C **134**
(Up. Teddington Rd.)
KT3: N Mald 4A **136**
KT7: T Ditt 6A **134**
KT8: W Mole 4E **132**
KT12: Walt T 7J **131**
KT17: Eps 7B **148**
N14 .... 1C **16**
NW7 .... 5J **13**
RM1: Rom 5K **39**
SE20 .... 6J **123**
SE25 .... 4F **141**
SM1: Sutt 4K **149**
SM3: Sutt 6G **149**
SM5: Cars 5E **150**
SW19 .... 5F **119**
TW2: Twick 7G **97**
TW3: Houn 3F **97**
(not continuous)
TW5: Houn 1J **95**
TW8: Bford 7C **80**
TW11: Tedd 5K **115**
TW12: Hamp 1G **133**
TW13: Felt 3H **113**
TW17: Shep 6D **130**
TW19: Staines 6A **94**
UB1: S'hall 1D **78**
UB3: Hayes 6F **77**
UB7: W Dray 6A **76**
(Harmondsworth)
UB7: W Dray 7A **58**
(Yiewsley)
UB8: Uxb 1A **58**
(Harefield Rd., not continuous)
W3 .... 1H **81**
W5 .... 1D **80**
High St. Colliers Wood
SW19 .... 7B **120**
High St. Harlesden NW10 ... 2B **64**
High St. Hornsey N8 .... 4J **31**
High St. M. SW19 .... 5G **119**
High St. Nth. E6 .... 5C **54**
E12 .... 5C **54**
High St. Sth. E6 .... 2D **72**
High Timber St.
EC4 .... 7C **68** (2C **168**)
High Tor Cl. BR1: Brom 7K **125**
High Tor Vw. SE28 .... 1J **91**
High Trees CR0: Croy 1A **154**
EN4: Barn 5H **5**
N20 .... 3F **15**
SW2 .... 1A **122**
Hightrees Ct. W7 .... 7J **61**
High Vw. HA5: Pinn 4A **24**
Highview N6 .... 6G **31**
NW7 .... 3E **12**
UB5: N'olt 3C **60**
Highview Av. HA8: Edg 4D **12**
SM6: Wall 5K **151**
High Vw. Cl. SE19 .... 2F **141**
High Vw. Ct. HA3: Harr 7D **10**
Highview Gdns. HA8: Edg ... 4D **12**
N3 .... 3G **29**
N11 .... 5B **16**
Highview Ho.
RM6: Chad H 4E **38**
Highview Lodge *EN2: Enf* *3G 7*
(off Ridgeway, The)
High Vw. Pde. IG4: Ilf 5D **36**
High Vw. Rd.
DA14: Sidc 4B **128**
E18 .... 2H **35**
N2 .... 1D **30**
Highview Rd. SE19 .... 6D **122**
W13 .... 5A **62**
Highway Bus. Pk., The *E1* ... *7K 69*
(off Heckford St.)
Highway, The E1 .... 7G **69**
HA3: Harr 1K **25**
SM2: Sutt 7A **150**
Highway Trad. Cen., The
E1 .... *7K 69*
(off Heckford St.)
Highwood BR2: Short 3F **143**
Highwood Av. N12 .... 4F **15**
Highwood Ct. EN5: Barn 5D **4**
N12 .... 3F **15**
Highwood Gdns. IG5: Ilf 5D **36**
Highwood Gro. NW7 .... 5E **12**
HIGHWOOD HILL **3G 13**
Highwood Hill NW7 .... 2G **13**
Highwood Rd. N19 .... 3J **49**
High Worple HA2: Harr 7D **24**
Highworth Rd. N11 .... 6C **16**
Highworth St. NW1 .... 5D **158**
Hi-Gloss Cen. SE8 .... 5A **88**
Hilary Av. CR4: Mitc 3E **138**
Hilary Cl. DA8: Erith 1H **111**
SW6 .... 7K **83**
Hilary Dennis Ct. E11 .... 4J **35**
Hilary Rd. W12 .... 6B **64**
(not continuous)
Hilbert Rd. SM3: Sutt 3F **149**
Hilborough Ct. E8 .... 7F **51**
Hilda Ct. KT6: Surb 7D **134**
Hilda Rd. E6 .... 7B **54**
E16 .... 4G **71**
(not continuous)
Hilda Ter. SW9 .... 2A **104**
Hilda Va. Rd. BR6: Orp 4E **156**
Hildenborough Gdns.
BR1: Brom 6G **125**
Hildenborough Ho.
BR3: Beck *7B 124*
(off Bethersden Cl.)
Hildenlea Pl. BR2: Short ... 2F **143**
Hilderley Ho. *KT1: King T* ... *3F 135*
(off Winery La.)
Hildreth St. SW12 .... 1F **121**
Hildyard Rd. SW6 .... 6J **83**
Hiley Rd. NW10 .... 3E **64**
Hilgrove Rd. NW6 .... 7A **48**
Hiliary Gdns. HA7: Stan 2C **26**
Hillary *N8* *3J 31*
(off Boyton Cl.)
Hillary Ct. *W12* *2E 82*
(off Titmuss St.)
Hillary Cres.
KT12: Walt T 7A **132**
Hillary Dr. TW7: Isle 5K **97**
Hillary Ri. EN5: Barn 4D **4**
Hillary Rd. UB2: S'hall 3E **78**
Hillbeck Cl. SE15 .... 7J **87**
Hillbeck Ho. *SE15* *6J 87*
(off Hillbeck Cl.)
Hillbeck Way UB6: G'frd 1H **61**
Hillborne Cl. UB3: Hayes 5J **77**
Hillboro Ct. E11 .... 7F **35**
Hillborough Cl. SW19 ..... 7A **120**
Hillbrook Rd. SW17 .... 3D **120**
Hill Brow BR1: Brom 1B **144**
Hillbrow KT3: N Mald 3B **136**
Hill Brow Cl. DA5: Bexl 4K **129**
Hillbrow Rd. BR1: Brom ... 7G **125**
Hillbury Av. HA3: Harr 5B **26**
Hillbury Rd. SW17 .... 3F **121**
Hill Cl. BR7: Chst 5F **127**
HA1: Harr 3J **43**
HA7: Stan 4G **11**
NW2 .... 3D **46**
NW11 .... 6J **29**
Hillcote Av. SW16 .... 7A **122**
Hill Ct. EN4: Barn 4H **5**
UB5: N'olt 5E **42**
W5 .... 4F **63**
Hillcourt Av. N12 .... 6E **14**
Hillcourt Est. N16 .... 1D **50**
Hillcourt Rd. SE22 .... 6H **105**
Hill Cres. DA5: Bexl 1J **129**
Hill Cres. HA1: Harr 5A **26**
KT4: Wor Pk 2E **148**
KT5: Surb 5F **135**
N20 .... 2E **14**
KT6: Surb 7E **134**
Hillcrest DA15: Sidc 7A **110**
N6 .... 7E **30**
N21 .... 7F **7**
SE5 .... 4D **104**
Hillcrest Av. HA5: Pinn 4B **24**
HA8: Edg 4C **12**
NW11 .... 5H **29**
Hillcrest Cl. BR3: Beck 6B **142**
SE26 .... 4G **123**
Hillcrest Ct. RM5: Col R 1K **39**
SM2: Sutt 6B **150**
Hill Crest Gdns. NW2 .... 3C **46**
Hillcrest Gdns.
KT10: Esh 3A **146**
N3 .... 4G **29**
Hillcrest Rd. BR1: Brom 5J **125**
E17 .... 2F **35**
E18 .... 2H **35**
W3 .... 1H **81**
W5 .... 5E **62**
Hillcrest Vw. BR3: Beck 6B **142**
Hillcroft Av. HA5: Pinn 6D **24**
Hillcroft Cres. HA4: Ruis 3B **42**
HA9: Wemb 4F **45**
W5 .... 6E **62**
Hillcroft Rd. E6 .... 5F **73**
Hillcroome Rd.
SM2: Sutt 6B **150**
Hillcross Av. SM4: Mord 6F **137**
Hilldale Rd. SM1: Sutt 4H **149**
Hilldown Ct. SW16 .... 7J **121**
Hilldown Rd. BR2: Short ... 1G **155**
SW16 .... 7J **121**
Hill Dr. NW9 .... 1J **45**
SW16 .... 3K **139**
Hilldrop Cres. N7 .... 5H **49**
Hilldrop Est. N7 .... 4H **49**
Hilldrop La. N7 .... 5H **49**
Hilldrop Rd. BR1: Brom 6K **125**
N7 .... 5H **49**
Hillend SE18 .... 1E **108**
Hillersden Ho. *SW1* *5J 171*
(off Ebury Bri. Rd.)
Hillersdon Av. HA8: Edg 5A **12**
SW13 .... 2C **100**
Hillery Cl. SE17 .... 4D **86**
Hill Farm Cotts. HA4: Ruis ... 7E **22**
Hill Farm Rd. UB10: Uxb 4F **41**
W10 .... 5E **64**
Hillfield Av. HA0: Wemb 7E **44**
N8 .... 5J **31**
NW9 .... 5A **28**
SM4: Mord 6C **138**
Hillfield Cl. HA2: Harr 4G **25**
Hillfield Ct. NW3 .... 5C **48**
Hillfield Ho. N5 .... 5C **50**
Hillfield Pk. N10 .... 4F **31**
N21 .... 2F **17**
Hillfield Pk. M. N10 .... 4F **31**
Hill Fld. Rd.
TW12: Hamp 7D **114**
Hillfield Rd. NW6 .... 5H **47**
Hillfoot Av. RM5: Col R 1J **39**
Hillfoot Rd. RM5: Col R 1J **39**
Hillgate Pl. SW12 .... 7F **103**
W8 .... 1J **83**
Hillgate St. W11 .... 1J **83**
Hill Gro. RM1: Rom 3K **39**
TW13: Felt 2D **114**
Hill Ho. BR2: Short 2H **143**
E5 .... *1H 51*
(off Harrington Hill)
Hillhouse Av. HA7: Stan 7E **10**
Hill Ho. Cl. N21 .... 7F **7**
Hill Ho. Dr.
TW12: Hamp 1E **132**
Hill Ho. Rd. SW16 .... 5K **121**
Hilliard Ho. *E1* *1H 87*
(off Prusom St.)
Hilliard Rd. HA6: Nwood 1H **23**
Hilliards Ct. E1 .... 1J **87**
Hillier Cl. EN5: Barn 6E **4**
Hillier Gdns. CR0: Croy 5A **152**
Hillier Ho. *NW1* *7H 49*
(off Camden Sq.)
Hillier Lodge
TW11: Tedd 5H **115**
Hillier Pl. KT9: Chess 6D **146**
Hillier Rd. SW11 .... 6D **102**
Hilliers Av. UB8: Uxb 3C **58**
Hilliers La. CR0: Croy 3J **151**
HILLINGDON **3C 58**
Hillingdon Av.
TW19: Staines 1A **112**
Hillingdon Cir. UB10: Uxb ... 6D **40**
Hillingdon Ct. HA3: Harr 4D **26**
HILLINGDON HEATH **4D 58**
Hillingdon Hill UB10: Uxb ... 2A **58**
Hillingdon Rd. DA7: Bex 2J **111**
UB8: Uxb 1A **58**
UB10: Uxb 1A **58**
Hillingdon St. SE5 .... 6B **86**
(not continuous)
SE17 .... 6B **86**
Hillington Gdns.
IG8: Wfd G 2B **36**
Hill La. HA4: Ruis 1E **40**
Hillman Cl. UB8: Uxb 5A **40**
Hillman Dr. W10 .... 4E **64**
Hillman St. E8 .... 6H **51**
Hillmarton Rd. N7 .... 5J **49**
Hillmead Dr. SW9 .... 4B **104**
Hillmore Ct. *SE13* *3F 107*
(off Belmont Hill)
Hillmore Gro. SE26 .... 5A **124**
Hill Path SW16 .... 5K **121**
Hillreach SE18 .... 5D **90**
Hill Ri. HA4: Ruis 1E **40**
KT10: Esh 2B **146**
KT12: Walt T 7H **131**
N9 .... 6C **8**
NW11 .... 4K **29**
SE23 .... 1H **123**
TW10: Rich 5D **98**
UB6: G'frd 7G **43**
Hillrise Mans. *N19* *7J 31*
(off Warltersville Rd.)
Hillrise Rd. N19 .... 7J **31**
Hill Rd. CR4: Mitc 1F **139**
HA0: Wemb 3B **44**
HA1: Harr 5A **26**
HA5: Pinn 5C **24**
N10 .... 1D **30**
NW8 .... 3A **66**
SM1: Sutt 5K **149**
SM5: Cars 6C **150**
Hillsboro' Rd. SE22 .... 5E **104**
Hillsborough Ct. *NW6* *1K 65*
(off Mortimer Cres.)
Hillsgrove Cl. DA16: Well ... 7C **92**
HILLSIDE **4J 93**
Hillside DA8: Erith 4J **93**
EN5: Barn 5F **5**
N8 .... 6H **31**
NW5 .... 3E **48**
NW9 .... 4K **27**
NW10 .... 7J **45**
SE10 .... *7F 89*
(off Crooms Hill)
SW19 .... 6F **119**
Hillside Av. HA9: Wemb 4F **45**
IG8: Wfd G 6F **21**
N11 .... 6J **15**
Hillside Cl. IG8: Wfd G 5F **21**
NW8 .... 2K **65**
SM4: Mord 4G **137**
Hillside Cres. HA2: Harr 1G **43**
HA6: Nwood 1J **23**
Hillside Dr. HA8: Edg 6B **12**

Hillside Est.—Hollingsworth Ct.

Hillside Est. N15 ....6F 33
Hillside Gdns. E17 ....3F 35
EN5: Barn 4B 4
HA3: Harr 7E 26
HA6: Nwood 1J 23
HA8: Edg 4A 12
N6 ....6F 31
N11 ....6B 16
SM6: Wall 7G 151
SW2 ....2A 122
Hillside Gro. N14 ....7C 6
NW7 ....7H 13
Hillside Ho. *CR0: Croy* *4B 152*
(off Violet La.)
Hillside La. BR2: Short 2H 155
(not continuous)
Hillside Mans. EN5: Barn 4C 4
Hillside Pas. SW16 ....2K 121
Hillside Ri. HA6: Nwood 1J 23
Hillside Rd. BR2: Short 3H 143
CR0: Croy 5B 152
HA5: Pinn 1K 23
HA6: Nwood 1J 23
KT5: Surb 4F 135
SM2: Sutt 7H 149
SW2 ....2K 121
UB1: S'hall 4E 60
W5 ....5E 62
Hills La. HA6: Nwood 1G 23
Hillsleigh Rd. W8 ....1H 83
Hills M. W5 ....7E 62
Hills Pl. W1 ....6G 67 (1A 166)
Hills Rd. IG9: Buck H 1E 20
Hillstowe St. E5 ....3J 51
Hill St. TW9: Rich 5D 98
W1 ....1E 84 (4H 165)
Hill Top SM3: Sutt 7H 137
SM4: Mord 6J 137
Hilltop E17 ....3D 34
NW11 ....4K 29
Hill Top Ct. IG8: Wfd G 6J 21
Hilltop Ct. *NW8* *7A 48*
(off Alexandra Rd.)
Hilltop Gdns. NW4 ....2D 28
Hilltop Rd. NW6 ....7J 47
Hill Top Vw. IG8: Wfd G 6J 21
Hilltop Way HA7: Stan 3F 11
Hillview SW20 ....7D 118
Hillview Av. HA3: Harr 5E 26
Hillview Cl. HA9: Wemb 2F 45
Hill Vw. Cres. IG1: Ilf 6D 36
Hill Vw. Dr. DA16: Well 2J 109
SE28 ....1J 91
Hill Vw. Gdns. NW9 ....5K 27
Hillview Gdns. HA5: Pinn 3E 24
NW4 ....4F 29
Hill Vw. Rd. KT10: Esh 7A 146
TW1: Twick 6A 98
Hillview Rd. BR7: Chst 5E 126
HA5: Pinn 1D 24
NW7 ....4A 14
SM1: Sutt 3A 150
Hillway N6 ....2E 48
NW9 ....1A 46
Hill-Wood Ho. *NW1* *1B 160*
(off Polygon Rd.)
Hillworth BR3: Beck 2D 142
Hillworth Rd. SW2 ....7A 104
Hillyard Ho. SW9 ....1A 104
Hillyard Rd. W7 ....5J 61
Hillyard St. SW9 ....1A 104
Hillyfield E17 ....2A 34
Hillyfield Cl. *E9* *6A 52*
(off Red Path)
Hilly Flds. Cres. SE4 ....3C 106
Hilsea St. E5 ....4J 51
Hilton Av. N12 ....5G 15
Hilton Ho. SE4 ....4K 105
Hilton Wharf *SE10* *6D 88*
(off Norman Rd.)
Hilversum Cres. SE22 ....5E 104
Himley Rd. SW17 ....5C 120
Hinchinbrook Ho. *NW6* *1K 65*
(off Mortimer Cres.)
Hinchley Cl. KT10: Esh 4A 146
Hinchley Dr. KT10: Esh 3A 146
Hinchley Way KT10: Esh 3A 146
HINCHLEY WOOD 3A 146
Hinckley Rd. SE15 ....4G 105
Hind Ct. EC4 ....6A 68 (1K 167)
Hind Cres. DA8: Erith 6K 93
Hinde Ho. *W1* *7H 159*
(off Hinde St.)
Hinde M. W1 ....7H 159
Hindes Rd. HA1: Harr 5H 25
Hinde St. W1 ....6E 66 (7H 159)
Hind Gro. E14 ....6C 70
Hindhead Cl. N16 ....1E 50
UB8: Uxb 5D 58
Hindhead Gdns. UB5: N'olt 1C 60
Hindhead Way SM6: Wall 5J 151
Hind Ho. *SE14* *6K 87*
(off Myers La.)
Hindlip Ho. SW8 ....1H 103
Hindmans Rd. SE22 ....5G 105
Hindmans Way RM9: Dag 4F 75
Hindmarsh Cl. E1 ....7G 69
Hindrey Rd. E5 ....5H 51
Hindsley's Pl. SE23 ....2J 123
Hinkler Rd. HA3: Harr 3D 26
Hinksey Path SE2 ....2D 92
Hinstock *NW6* *1K 65*
(off Belsize Rd.)
Hinstock Rd. SE18 ....6G 91
Hinton Av. TW4: Houn 4B 96
Hinton Cl. SE9 ....1C 126
Hinton Ct. *E10* *2D 52*
(off Leyton Grange Est.)
Hinton Ho. W5 ....6C 62
Hinton Rd. N18 ....4K 17
SM6: Wall 6G 151
SW9 ....3B 104
Hippodrome M. W11 ....7G 65
Hippodrome Pl. W11 ....7G 65
Hiroshima Prom. SE7 ....3A 90
Hissocks Ho. NW10 ....7J 45
Hitcham Rd. E17 ....7B 34
Hitchcock Cl.
TW17: Shep 3B 130
Hitchin Sq. E3 ....2A 70
Hitherbroom Rd.
UB3: Hayes 1J 77
Hither Farm Rd. SE3 ....3A 108
Hitherfield Rd. RM8: Dag 2E 56
SW16 ....2K 121
HITHER GREEN 6G 107
Hither Grn. La. SE13 ....5E 106
Hitherwell Dr. HA3: Harr 1H 25
Hitherwood Dr. SE19 ....4F 123
Hive Cl. WD23: Bush 2C 10
Hive Rd. WD23: Bush 2C 10
(not continuous)
HMS Belfast ....*1E 86 (4G 169)*
Hoadly Rd. SW16 ....3H 121
Hobart Cl. N20 ....2H 15
UB4: Hayes 4B 60
Hobart Ct. *CR2: S Croy* *5D 152*
(off Sth. Park Hill Rd.)
Hobart Dr. UB4: Hayes 4B 60
Hobart Gdns.
CR7: Thor H 3D 140
Hobart La. UB4: Hayes 4B 60
Hobart Pl. SW1 ....3F 85 (1J 171)
TW10: Rich 7F 99
Hobart Rd. IG6: Ilf 2G 37
KT4: Wor Pk 3D 148
RM9: Dag 4D 56
UB4: Hayes 4B 60
Hobbayne Rd. W7 ....6H 61
Hobbes Wlk. SW15 ....5D 100
Hobbs Ct. *SE1* *6K 169*
(off Mill St.)
Hobbs Grn. N2 ....3A 30
Hobbs M. IG3: Ilf 2K 55
Hobbs Pl. N1 ....1E 68
Hobbs Pl. Est. *N1* *2E 68*
(off Hobbs Pl.)
Hobbs Rd. SE27 ....4C 122
Hobday St. E14 ....6D 70
Hobill Wlk. KT5: Surb 6F 135
Hoblands End BR7: Chst 6J 127
Hobson's Pl. E1 ....5G 69
Hobury St. SW10 ....6A 84 (7A 170)
Hocker St. E2 ....3F 69 (2J 163)
Hockett Cl. SE8 ....4A 88
Hockington Ct. EN5: Barn 4E 4
Hockley Av. E6 ....2C 72
Hockley Ct. E18 ....1J 35
Hockley M. IG11: Bark 3J 73
Hockliffe Ho. *W10* *5E 64*
(off Sutton Way)
Hockney Ct. *SE16* *5H 87*
(off Rossetti Rd.)
Hocroft Av. NW2 ....3H 47
Hocroft Ct. NW2 ....3H 47
Hocroft Rd. NW2 ....3H 47
Hocroft Wlk. NW2 ....3H 47
Hodder Dr. UB6: G'frd 2K 61
Hoddesdon Rd.
DA17: Belv 5G 93
Hodes Row NW3 ....4E 48
Hodford Rd. NW11 ....1H 47
Hodgkin Cl. SE28 ....7D 74
Hodgkins M. HA7: Stan 5G 11
Hodister Cl. SE5 ....7C 86
Hodnet Gro. SE16 ....4K 87
Hodson Cl. HA2: Harr 3D 42
Hoecroft Ct. *EN3: Enf* *1D 8*
(off Hoe La.)
Hoe La. EN1: Enf 1B 8
Hoe St. E17 ....4C 34
Hoever Ho. SE6 ....4E 124
Hofland Rd. W14 ....3G 83
Hogan M. W2 ....5A 66 (5A 158)
Hogan Way E5 ....2G 51
Hogarth Av. TW15: Ashf 6E 112
Hogarth Bus. Cen. W4 ....6A 82
Hogarth Cl. E16 ....5B 72
W5 ....5E 62
Hogarth Ct. *E1* *6G 69*
(off Batty St.)
EC3 ....6E 68 (2H 169)
NW1 ....*7G 49*
(off St Pancras Way)
SE19 ....4F 123
TW5: Houn 7C 78
Hogarth Cres. CR0: Croy 7C 140
SW19 ....1B 138
Hogarth Gdns.
TW5: Houn 7E 78
Hogarth Hill NW11 ....4H 29
Hogarth Ho. *SW1* *4D 172*
(off Erasmus St.)
UB5: N'olt *2B 60*
(off Gallery Gdns.)
Hogarth Ind. Est. NW10 ....4C 64
Hogarth La. W4 ....6A 82
Hogarth Pl. *SW5* *4K 83*
(off Hogarth Rd.)
Hogarth Rd. HA8: Edg 2G 27
RM8: Dag 5B 56
SW5 ....4K 83
HOGARTH RDBT. 6A 82
Hogarth's House *6A 82*
(off Hogarth La.)
Hogarth Ter. W4 ....6A 82
Hogarth Way
TW12: Hamp 1G 133
Hog Hill Rd. RM5: Col R 1F 39
Hogshead Pas. *E1* *7H 69*
(off Reunion Row)
Hogsmill Ho. *KT1: King T* *3F 135*
(off Vineyard Cl.)
Hogsmill Wlk.
KT1: King T *3E 134*
(off Penrhyn Rd.)
Hogsmill Way KT19: Eps 5J 147
Holbeach Gdns.
DA15: Sidc 6J 109
Holbeach M. SW12 ....1F 121
Holbeach Rd. SE6 ....7C 106
Holbeck Row SE15 ....7G 87
Holbein Ho. *SW1* *5G 171*
(off Holbein M.)
Holbein M. SW1 ....5E 84 (5G 171)
Holbein Pl. SW1 ....4E 84 (4G 171)
Holbein Ter. *RM8: Dag* *4C 56*
(off Marlborough Rd.)
Holberton Gdns. NW10 ....3D 64
HOLBORN 5A 68 (6G 161)
Holborn EC1 ....5A 68 (6J 161)
Holborn Cir. EC1 ....5A 68 (6K 161)
Holborn Pl. WC1 ....6G 161
Holborn Rd. E13 ....4K 71
Holborn Viaduct
EC4 ....5A 68 (6K 161)
Holborn Way CR4: Mitc 2D 138
Holbrook Cl. EN1: Enf 1A 8
N19 ....1F 49
Holbrooke Ct. N7 ....3J 49
Holbrooke Pl. TW10: Rich 5D 98
Holbrook Ho. BR7: Chst 1H 145
Holbrook La. BR7: Chst 7H 127
Holbrook Rd. E15 ....2H 71
Holbrook Way
BR2: Short 6D 144
Holburne Cl. SE3 ....1A 108
Holburne Gdns. SE3 ....1B 108
Holburne Rd. SE3 ....1A 108
Holcombe Hill NW7 ....3H 13
Holcombe Ho. *SW9* *3J 103*
(off Landor Rd.)
Holcombe Pl. *SE4* *3A 106*
(off St Asaph Rd.)
Holcombe Rd. IG1: Ilf 7E 36
N17 ....3F 33
(not continuous)
Holcombe St. W6 ....4D 82
Holcote Cl. DA17: Belv 3E 92
Holcroft Ct. W1 ....5A 160
Holcroft Ho. SW11 ....3B 102
Holcroft Rd. E9 ....7J 51
Holden Av. N12 ....5E 14
NW9 ....1J 45
Holdenby Rd. SE4 ....5A 106
Holden Cl. RM8: Dag 3B 56
Holden Ho. *N1* *1C 68*
(off Prebend St.)
SE8 ....7C 88
Holdenhurst Av. N12 ....7F 15
Holden Rd. N12 ....5E 14
Holden St. SW11 ....2E 102
Holder Cl. N3 ....7E 14
Holdernesse Cl. TW7: Isle 1A 98
Holdernesse Rd. SW17 ....3D 120
Holderness Ho. SE5 ....3E 104
Holderness Way SE27 ....5B 122
HOLDERS HILL 2F 29
Holder's Hill Av. NW4 ....2F 29
Holders Hill Cir. NW7 ....7B 14
Holders Hill Cres. NW4 ....2F 29
Holders Hill Dr. NW4 ....3F 29
Holder's Hill Gdns. NW4 ....2G 29
Holders Hill Pde. NW4 ....1G 29
Holders Hill Rd. NW4 ....2F 29
NW7 ....2F 29
Holford Ho. *SE16* *4H 87*
(off Camilla Rd.)
Holford M. WC1 ....1J 161
Holford Pl. WC1 ....3K 67 (1H 161)
Holford Rd. NW3 ....3A 48
Holford St. WC1 ....3K 67 (1J 161)
Holford Yd. *WC1* *1J 161*
(off Cruikshank St.)
Holgate Av. SW11 ....3B 102
Holgate Gdns. RM10: Dag 6G 57
Holgate Rd. RM10: Dag 5G 57
Holgate St. SE7 ....3B 90
Hollam Ho. N8 ....4K 31
Holland Av. SM2: Sutt 7J 149
SW20 ....1B 136
Holland Cl. BR2: Short 2H 155
EN5: Barn 7G 5
HA7: Stan 5G 11
RM7: Rom 5J 39
Holland Ct. *E17* *4E 34*
(off Evelyn Rd.)
KT6: Surb 7D 134
NW7 ....6H 13
Holland Dr. SE23 ....3A 124
Holland Gdns. W14 ....3G 83
Holland Gro. SW9 ....7A 86
Holland Ho. E4 ....4A 20
NW10 ....*2D 64*
(off Holland Rd.)
HOLLAND PARK 1H 83
Holland Pk. *2H 83*
Holland Pk. W11 ....1G 83
Holland Pk. Av. IG3: Ilf 6J 37
W11 ....2G 83
Holland Pk. Gdns. W14 ....2G 83
Holland Pk. M. W11 ....1G 83
Holland Pk. Rd. W14 ....3H 83
HOLLAND PARK RDBT. 2G 83
Holland Pk. Theatre
Open Air *2H 83*
(in Holland Pk.)
Holland Pas. *N1* *1C 68*
(off Basire St.)
Holland Pl. *W8* *2K 83*
(off Kensington Chu. St.)
Holland Pl. Chambers *W8* *2K 83*
(off Holland Pl.)
Holland Ri. Ho. *SW9* *7K 85*
(off Clapham Rd.)
Holland Rd. E6 ....1D 72
E15 ....3G 71
HA0: Wemb 6D 44
NW10 ....1C 64
SE25 ....5G 141
W14 ....2F 83
Hollands, The
KT4: Wor Pk 1B 148
TW13: Felt 4B 114
Holland St. SE1 ....1B 86 (4B 168)
W8 ....2J 83
Holland Vs. Rd. W14 ....2G 83
Holland Wlk. HA7: Stan 5F 11
N19 ....1H 49
W8 ....*1H 83*
(off Holland Pk. Av.)
Holland Way BR2: Short 2H 155
Hollar Rd. N16 ....3F 51
Hollen St. W1 ....6H 67 (7C 160)
Holles Cl. TW12: Hamp 6E 114
Holles Ho. SW9 ....2A 104
Holles St. W1 ....6F 67 (7K 159)
Holley Rd. W3 ....2A 82
Hollick Wood Av. N12 ....6J 15
Holliday Sq. *SW11* *3B 102*
(off Fowler Cl.)
Hollidge Way RM10: Dag 7H 57
Hollies Av. DA15: Sidc 2K 127
Hollies Cl. SW16 ....6A 122
TW1: Twick 2K 115
Hollies End NW7 ....5J 13
Hollies Rd. W5 ....4C 80
Hollies, The *E11* *5J 35*
(off New Wanstead)
HA3: Harr 4A 26
N20 ....1G 15
Hollies Way SW12 ....7E 102
Holligrave Rd.
BR1: Brom 1J 143
Hollingbourne Av.
DA7: Bex 1F 111
Hollingbourne Gdns. W13 ....5B 62
Hollingbourne Rd. SE24 ....5C 104
Hollingsworth Ct.
KT6: Surb 7D 134

Hollingsworth Rd.—Honey La.

Hollingsworth Rd.
CR0: Croy ... 6H 153
Hollington Ct. BR7: Chst ... 6F 127
Hollington Cres.
KT3: N Mald ... 6B 136
Hollington Rd. E6 ... 3D 72
N17 ... 2G 33
Hollingworth Cl.
KT8: W Mole ... 4D 132
Hollingworth Rd.
BR5: Orp ... 6F 145
Hollins Ho. N7 ... 4J 49
Hollisfield *WC1* ... *2F 161*
(off Cromer St.)
Hollman Gdns. SW16 ... 6B 122
HOLLOWAY ... 3J 49
Holloway Cl. UB7: W Dray ... 5A 76
Holloway Ho. *NW2* ... *3E 46*
(off Stoll Cl.)
Holloway La.
UB7: W Dray ... 6A 76
Holloway Rd. E6 ... 3D 72
E11 ... 3F 53
N7 ... 4K 49
N19 ... 2H 49
Holloway St. TW3: Houn ... 3F 97
Hollowfield Wlk.
UB5: N'olt ... 7C 42
Hollows, The TW8: Bford ... 6F 81
Hollow, The IG8: Wfd G ... 4C 20
Holly Av. HA7: Stan ... 2E 26
KT12: Walt T ... 7B 132
Hollybank Cl.
TW12: Hamp ... 5E 114
Hollyberry La. NW3 ... 4A 48
Hollybrake Cl. BR7: Chst ... 7H 127
Hollybush Cl. E11 ... 5J 35
HA3: Harr ... 1J 25
Hollybush Gdns. E2 ... 3H 69
Hollybush Hill E11 ... 6H 35
NW3 ... 4A 48
Hollybush Ho. E2 ... 3H 69
Holly Bush La.
TW12: Hamp ... 7D 114
Hollybush Pl. E2 ... 3H 69
Hollybush Rd.
KT2: King T ... 5E 116
Hollybush Steps *NW3* ... *4A 48*
(off Holly Mt.)
Hollybush St. E13 ... 3K 71
Holly Bush Va. NW3 ... 4A 48
Hollybush Wlk. SW9 ... 4B 104
Holly Cl. BR3: Beck ... 4E 142
IG9: Buck H ... 3G 21
NW10 ... 7A 46
SM6: Wall ... 7F 151
TW13: Felt ... 5C 114
Holly Cott. M. UB8: Uxb ... 5C 58
Holly Ct. *DA14: Sidc* ... *4B 128*
(off Sidcup Hill)
N15 ... 4E 32
SM2: Sutt ... 7J 149
Holly Cres. BR3: Beck ... 5B 142
IG8: Wfd G ... 7A 20
Hollycroft Av. HA9: Wemb ... 2F 45
NW3 ... 3J 47
Hollycroft Cl.
CR2: S Croy ... 5E 152
UB7: W Dray ... 6C 76
Hollycroft Gdns.
UB7: W Dray ... 6C 76
Hollydale Cl. UB5: N'olt ... 4F 43
Hollydale Dr.
BR2: Short ... 3D 156
Hollydale Rd. SE15 ... 1J 105
Holly Dene SE15 ... 1H 105
Hollydene *BR2: Short* ... *1H 143*
(off Beckenham Rd.)
Hollydown Way E11 ... 3F 53
Holly Dr. E4 ... 7J 9
Holly Farm Rd.
UB2: S'hall ... 5C 78
Hollyfield Av. N11 ... 5J 15
Hollyfield Rd. KT6: Surb ... 7F 135
Holly Gdns. DA7: Bex ... 4J 111
UB7: W Dray ... 2B 76
Holly Gro. HA5: Pinn ... 1C 24
NW9 ... 7J 27
SE15 ... 2F 105
Hollygrove WD23: Bush ... 1C 10
Hollygrove Cl. TW3: Houn ... 4D 96
Holly Hedge Ter. SE13 ... 5F 107
Holly Hill N21 ... 6E 6
NW3 ... 4A 48
Holly Hill Rd. DA8: Erith ... 5J 93
DA17: Belv, Erith ... 5H 93
Holly Ho. TW8: Bford ... 6C 80
W10 ... *4G 65*
(off Hawthorn Wlk.)
Holly Lodge HA1: Harr ... 5H 25
Holly Lodge Gdns. N6 ... 2E 48
Holly Lodge Mans. N6 ... 2E 48
Hollymead SM5: Cars ... 3D 150
Holly M. SW10 ... 6A 170
Holly Mt. NW3 ... 4A 48
Hollymount Cl. SE10 ... 1E 106
Holly Pk. N3 ... 3H 29
N4 ... 7J 31
(not continuous)
Holly Pk. Est. N4 ... 7K 31
Holly Pk. Gdns. N3 ... 3J 29
Holly Pk. Rd. N11 ... 5K 15
W7 ... 1K 79
Holly Pl. *NW3* ... *4A 48*
(off Holly Berry La.)
Holly Rd. E11 ... 7H 35
TW1: Twick ... 1K 115
TW3: Houn ... 4F 97
TW12: Hamp ... 6G 115
W4 ... 4K 81
Holly St. E8 ... 7F 51
Holly Ter. N6 ... 1E 48
N20 ... 2F 15
Holly Tree Cl. SW19 ... 1F 119
Holly Tree Ho. *SE4* ... *3B 106*
(off Brockley Rd.)
Hollytree Pde.
DA14: Sidc ... *6C 128*
(off Sidcup Hill)
Holly Vw. Cl. NW4 ... 6C 28
Holly Village N6 ... 2F 49
Holly Wlk. EN2: Enf ... 3H 7
NW3 ... 4A 48
Holly Way CR4: Mitc ... 4H 139
Hollywood Ct. W5 ... 7F 63
Hollywood Gdns.
UB4: Hayes ... 6K 59
Hollywood M. SW10 ... 6A 84
Hollywood Rd. E4 ... 5F 19
SW10 ... 6A 84
Hollywood Way
IG8: Wfd G ... 7A 20
Holman Ct. KT17: Eps ... 7C 148
Holman Ho. *E2* ... *3K 69*
(off Roman Rd.)
Holman Hunt Ho. *W6* ... *5G 83*
(off Field Rd.)
Holman Rd. KT19: Eps ... 5J 147
SW11 ... 2B 102
Holmbank Dr.
TW17: Shep ... 4G 131
Holmbridge Gdns. EN3: Enf ... 4E 8
Holmbrook *NW1* ... *2G 67*
(off Eversholt St.)
Holmbrook Dr. NW4 ... 5F 29
Holmbury Ct.
CR2: S Croy ... 5E 152
SW17 ... 3D 120
Holmbury Gdns.
UB3: Hayes ... 1H 77
Holmbury Gro. CR0: Croy ... 7B 154
Holmbury Ho. SE24 ... 5B 104
Holmbury Mnr.
DA14: Sidc ... 4A 128
Holmbury Pk. BR1: Brom ... 7C 126
Holmbury Vw. E5 ... 1H 51
Holmbush Rd. SW15 ... 6G 101
Holmcote Gdns. N5 ... 5C 50
Holm Ct. SE12 ... 3K 125
Holmcroft Ho. E17 ... 4D 34
Holmcroft Way
BR2: Short ... 5D 144
Holmdale Gdns. NW4 ... 5F 29
Holmdale Rd. BR7: Chst ... 5G 127
NW6 ... 5J 47
Holmdale Ter. N15 ... 7E 32
Holmdene N12 ... 5E 14
Holmdene Av. HA2: Harr ... 3F 25
NW7 ... 6H 13
SE24 ... 5C 104
Holmdene Cl. BR3: Beck ... 2E 142
Holmdene Ct. BR1: Brom ... 3C 144
Holmead Rd. SW6 ... 7K 83
Holmebury Cl.
WD23: Bush ... 2D 10
Holme Lacey Rd. SE12 ... 6H 107
Holme Rd. E6 ... 1C 72
Holmes Av. E17 ... 3B 34
NW7 ... 5B 14
Holmesdale Av. SW14 ... 3H 99
Holmesdale Cl. SE25 ... 3F 141
Holmesdale Ho. *NW6* ... *1J 65*
(off Kilburn Va.)
Holmesdale Rd.
CR0: Croy ... 5D 140
DA7: Bex ... 2D 110
N6 ... 7F 31
SE25 ... 5D 140
TW9: Rich ... 1F 99
TW11: Tedd ... 7C 116
Holmesley Rd. SE23 ... 6A 106
Holmes Pl. SW10 ... 6A 84
Holmes Rd. NW5 ... 5F 49
SW19 ... 7A 120
TW1: Twick ... 2K 115
Holmes Ter. SE1 ... 6J 167
Holmeswood SM2: Sutt ... 6K 149
Holmeswood Ct. N22 ... 2A 32
Holme Way HA7: Stan ... 6E 10
Holmewood Gdns. SW2 ... 7K 103
Holmewood Rd. SE25 ... 3E 140
SW2 ... 7J 103
Holmfield Av. NW4 ... 5F 29
Holmfield Ct. NW3 ... 5C 48
Holm Gro. UB10: Uxb ... 7C 40
Holmhurst Rd. DA17: Belv ... 5H 93
Holmlea Ct. *CR0: Croy* ... *4D 152*
(off Chatsworth Rd.)
Holmleigh Ct. EN3: Enf ... 4D 8
Holmleigh Rd. N16 ... 1E 50
Holmleigh Rd. Est. N16 ... 1E 50
Holmoak Cl. SW15 ... 6H 101
Holm Oak M. SW4 ... 5J 103
Holmoaks Ho. BR3: Beck ... 2E 142
Holmsdale Ho. *E14* ... *7D 70*
(off Poplar High St.)
N11 ... *4A 16*
(off Coppies Gro.)
Holmshaw Cl. SE26 ... 4A 124
Holmside Rd. SW12 ... 6E 102
Holmsley Cl.
KT3: N Mald ... 6B 136
Holmsley Ho. *SW15* ... *7B 100*
(off Tangley Gro.)
Holmstall Av. HA8: Edg ... 3J 27
Holmstall Pde. HA8: Edg ... 2J 27
Holm Wlk. SE3 ... 2J 107
Holmwood Cl. HA2: Harr ... 3G 25
SM2: Sutt ... 7F 149
UB5: N'olt ... 6F 43
Holmwood Gdns. N3 ... 2J 29
SM6: Wall ... 6F 151
Holmwood Gro. NW7 ... 5E 12
Holmwood Rd. IG3: Ilf ... 2J 55
KT9: Chess ... 5D 146
SM2: Sutt ... 7E 148
Holmwood Vs. SE7 ... 5J 89
Holne Chase N2 ... 6A 30
SM4: Mord ... 6H 137
Holness Rd. E15 ... 6H 53
Holroyd Rd. KT10: Esh ... 7A 146
SW15 ... 4E 100
Holst Ct. *SE1* ... *1J 173*
(off Westminster Bri. Rd.)
Holstein Way DA18: Erith ... 3D 92
Holst Mans. SW13 ... 6E 82
Holstock Rd. IG1: Ilf ... 2G 55
Holsworth Cl. HA2: Harr ... 5G 25
Holsworthy Sq. WC1 ... 4H 161
Holsworthy Way
KT9: Chess ... 5C 146
Holt Cl. N10 ... 4E 30
SE28 ... 7B 74
Holt Ct. E15 ... 5E 52
Holt Ho. SW2 ... 6A 104
Holton St. E1 ... 4K 69
Holt Rd. E16 ... 1C 90
HA0: Wemb ... 3B 44
Holt, The SM4: Mord ... 4J 137
SM6: Wall ... 4G 151
Holtwhites Av. EN2: Enf ... 2H 7
Holtwhite's Hill EN2: Enf ... 1G 7
Holwell Pl. HA5: Pinn ... 4C 24
Holwood Pk. Av.
BR6: Orp ... 4D 156
Holwood Pl. SW4 ... 4H 103
Holybourne Av. SW15 ... 7C 100
Holyhead Cl. E3 ... 3C 70
E6 ... 5D 72
Holyhead Ct. *KT1: King T* ... *4D 134*
(off Anglesea Rd.)
Holyoake Ct. SE16 ... 2B 88
Holyoake Ho. W5 ... 4C 62
Holyoake Wlk. N2 ... 3A 30
W5 ... 4C 62
Holyoak Rd. SE11 ... 4B 86
Holyport Rd. SW6 ... 7F 83
Holyrood Av. HA2: Harr ... 4C 42
Holyrood Gdns. HA8: Edg ... 3H 27
Holyrood M. *E16* ... *1J 89*
(off Badminton M.)
Holyrood Rd. EN5: Barn ... 6F 5
Holyrood St.
SE1 ... 1E 86 (5G 169)
Holywell Cen. ... *3G 163*
(off Phipp St.)
Holywell Cl. SE3 ... 6J 89
SE16 ... 5H 87
TW19: Staines ... 1A 112
Holywell La. EC2 ... 4E 68 (3H 163)
Holywell Row
EC2 ... 4E 68 (4G 163)
Holywell Way
TW19: Staines ... 1A 112
Homan Ct. N12 ... 4G 15
Homebush Ho. E4 ... 7J 9
Home Cl. SM5: Cars ... 2D 150
UB5: N'olt ... 3D 60
Home Ct. KT6: Surb ... 5D 134
Homecroft Rd. N22 ... 1C 32
SE26 ... 5J 123
Home Farm Cl.
KT7: T Ditt ... 7K 133
TW17: Shep ... 4G 131
Homefarm Rd. W7 ... 6J 61
Home Fld. EN5: Barn ... 5C 4
Homefield SM4: Mord ... 4J 137
Homefield Av. IG2: Ilf ... 5J 37
Homefield Cl. NW10 ... 6J 45
UB4: Hayes ... 4B 60
Homefield Ct. SW16 ... 3J 121
Homefield Gdns.
CR4: Mitc ... 2A 138
N2 ... 3B 30
Homefield Ho. SE23 ... 3K 123
Homefield M.
BR3: Beck ... 1C 142
Homefield Pk. SM1: Sutt ... 6K 149
Homefield Rd.
BR1: Brom ... 1A 144
HA0: Wemb ... 4A 44
HA8: Edg ... 6E 12
KT12: Walt T ... 7C 132
SW19 ... 6F 119
W4 ... 4B 82
Homefield St.
N1 ... 2E 68 (1G 163)
Homefirs Ho. HA9: Wemb ... 3F 45
Home Gdns. RM10: Dag ... 3J 57
Homeheather Ho. IG4: Ilf ... 5D 36
Homeland Dr. SM2: Sutt ... 7K 149
Homelands Dr. SE19 ... 7E 122
Homeleigh Rd. SE15 ... 5K 105
Home Mead HA7: Stan ... 1C 26
Homemead Rd.
BR2: Short ... 5D 144
CR0: Croy ... 6G 139
Home Pk. Ct.
KT1: King T ... *4D 134*
(off Palace Rd.)
Home Pk. Pde.
KT1: King T ... *2D 134*
(off High St.)
Home Pk. Rd. SW19 ... 4H 119
Home Pk. Ter.
KT1: King T ... *2D 134*
(off Hampton Ct. Rd.)
Home Pk. Wlk.
KT1: King T ... 4D 134
Homer Cl. DA7: Bex ... 1J 111
Homer Dr. E14 ... 4C 88
Home Rd. SW11 ... 2C 102
Homer Rd. CR0: Croy ... 6K 141
E9 ... 6A 52
Homer Row W1 ... 5C 66 (6D 158)
Homersham Rd.
KT1: King T ... 2G 135
Homer St. W1 ... 5C 66 (6D 158)
HOMERTON ... 5K 51
Homerton Gro. E9 ... 5K 51
Homerton High St. E9 ... 5K 51
Homerton Rd. E9 ... 5A 52
Homerton Row E9 ... 5J 51
Homerton Ter. E9 ... 6J 51
(not continuous)
Homesdale Cl. E11 ... 5J 35
Homesdale Rd.
BR1: Brom ... 4A 144
BR2: Short ... 4A 144
BR5: Orp ... 7J 145
Homesfield NW11 ... 5J 29
Homestall Rd. SE22 ... 5J 105
Homestead Ct. EN5: Barn ... 5D 4
Homestead Paddock N14 ... 5A 6
Homestead Pk. NW2 ... 3B 46
Homestead Rd. RM8: Dag ... 2F 57
SW6 ... 7H 83
Homesteads, The N11 ... 4A 16
Homewaters Av.
TW16: Sun T ... 1H 131
Homewillow Cl. N21 ... 6G 7
Homewood Cl.
TW12: Hamp ... 6D 114
Homewood Cres.
BR7: Chst ... 6J 127
Homewoods SW12 ... 7G 103
Homildon Ho. SE26 ... 3G 123
Honduras St.
EC1 ... 4C 68 (3C 162)
Honeybourne Rd. NW6 ... 5K 47
Honeybourne Way
BR5: Orp ... 7H 145
Honeybrook Rd. SW12 ... 7G 103
Honey Cl. RM10: Dag ... 6H 57
Honeycroft Hill
UB10: Uxb ... 7A 40
Honeyden Rd.
DA14: Sidc ... 6E 128
Honey Hill UB10: Uxb ... 7B 40
Honey La. EC2 ... 1D 168

Honeyman Cl. NW6 ....7F **47**
(not continuous)
Honeymead N8 ....3J **31**
(off Campsfield Rd.)
Honeypot Bus. Cen.
HA7: Stan 1E **26**
Honeypot Cl. NW9 ....4F **27**
Honeypot La. HA7: Stan ...7J **11**
NW9 ....1D **26**
Honeysett Rd. N17 ....2F **33**
Honeysuckle Cl.
UB1: S'hall 7C **60**
Honeysuckle Ct. E12: Ilf 6F **55**
Honeysuckle Gdns.
CRO: Croy 7K **141**
Honeysuckle La. N22 ....2C **32**
Honeywell Rd. SW11 ......6D **102**
Honeywood Heritage Cen.
.................4D **150**
Honeywood Rd. NW10 .....2B **64**
TW7: Isle 4A **98**
Honeywood Wlk.
SM5: Cars 4D **150**
Honister Cl. HA7: Stan 1B **26**
Honister Gdns.
HA7: Stan 7G **11**
Honister Pl. HA7: Stan 1B **26**
Honiton Gdns. NW7 ....7A **14**
SE15 ....2J **105**
(off Gibbon Rd.)
Honiton Rd. DA16: Well 2K **109**
NW6 ....2H **65**
RM7: Rom 6X **39**
Honley Rd. SE6 ....7D **106**
Honnor Gdns. TW7: Isle 2H **97**
HONOR OAK 6J **105**
Honor Oak Crematorium
SE23 ....5A **106**
HONOR OAK PARK 7A **106**
Honor Oak Pk. SE23 ....6J **105**
Honor Oak Ri. SE23 ....6J **105**
Honor Oak Rd. SE23 ....1J **123**
Hood Av. N14 ....6A **6**
SW14 ....5J **99**
Hood Cl. CRO: Croy 1B **152**
Hoodcote Gdns. N21 ......7G **7**
Hood Ct. EC4 ....1K **167**
Hood Ho. SE5 ....7D **86**
(off Elmington Est.)
SW1 ....6C **172**
(off Dolphin Sq.)
Hood Rd. SW20 ....7B **118**
Hood Wlk. RM7: Mawney ...1H **39**
HOOK 5D **146**
Hooke Ho. E3 ....2A **70**
(off Gernon Rd.)
Hookers Rd. E17 ....3K **33**
Hook Farm Rd.
BR2: Short 5B **144**
Hookham Cl. SW8 ....1H **103**
Hooking Grn. HA2: Harr 5F **25**
HOOK JUNCTION 3E **146**
Hook La. DA16: Well 4K **109**
Hook Ri. Bus. Cen.
KT9: Chess 3G **147**
Hook Ri. Nth. KT6: Surb 3E **146**
Hook Ri. Sth. KT6: Surb 3E **146**
Hook Ri. Sth. Ind. Pk.
KT9: Chess 3F **147**
Hook Rd. KT9: Chess 5D **146**
KT19: Eps 7J **147**
Hooks Cl. SE15 ....1H **105**
Hookshall Dr. RM10: Dag ...3J **57**
Hookstone Way
IG8: Wfd G 7G **21**
Hook, The EN5: Barn 6G **5**
Hook Wlk. HA8: Edg 6D **12**
Hooper Dr. UB8: Uxb 5D **58**
Hooper Rd. E16 ....6J **71**
Hooper's Ct.
SW3 ....2D **84** (7E **164**)
Hooper's M. W3 ....1J **81**

Hooper Sq. E1 ....6G **69**
(off Hooper St.)
Hooper St. E1 ....6G **69**
Hoop La. NW11 ....7H **29**
(not continuous)
Hope Cl. IG8: Wfd G 6F **21**
N1 ....6C **50**
RM6: Chad H 4D **38**
SE12 ....3K **125**
SM1: Sutt 5A **150**
TW8: Bford 5E **80**
Hope Ct. NW10 ....3F **65**
(off Chamberlayne Rd.)
Hopedale Rd. SE7 ....6K **89**
Hopefield Av. NW6 ....2G **65**
Hope Ho. CRO: Croy 4E **152**
(off Steep Hill)
Hope Pk. BR1: Brom 7H **125**
Hopes Cl. TW5: Houn 6E **78**
Hope St. SW11 ....3B **102**
Hopetown St. E1 ...5F **69** (6K **163**)
Hopewell St. SE5 ....7D **86**
Hopewell Yd. SE5 ....7D **86**
(off Hopewell St.)
Hope Wharf SE16 ....2J **87**
Hop Gdns. WC2 ....7J **67** (3E **166**)
Hopgood St. W12 ....1E **82**
Hopkins Cl. N10 ....7K **15**
Hopkins Ho. E14 ....4C **70**
(off Canton St.)
Hopkins M. E15 ....1H **71**
Hopkinsons Pl. NW1 ......1E **66**
Hopkins St. W1 ....6G **67** (1B **166**)
Hoppers Rd. N21 ....2F **17**
Hoppett Rd. E4 ....2B **20**
Hopping La. N1 ....6B **50**
Hoppingwood Av.
KT3: N Mald 3A **136**
Hoppner Rd. UB4: Hayes ...2F **59**
Hop St. SE10 ....4H **89**
(off W. Parkside)
Hopton Cl. BR2: Short 1K **155**
Hopton Gdns.
KT3: N Mald 6C **136**
Hopton Rd. SE18 ....3F **91**
SW16 ....5J **121**
Hopton's Gdns. SE1 ......4B **168**
Hopton St. SE1 ...1B **86** (4B **168**)
Hoptree Cl. N12 ....5E **14**
Hopwood Cl. SW17 ......3A **120**
Hopwood Rd. SE17 ......6D **86**
Hopwood Wlk. E8 ....7G **51**
Horace Av. RM7: Rush G ...1J **57**
Horace Rd. E7 ....4K **53**
IG6: Ilf 3G **37**
KT1: King T 3F **135**
Horatio Ct. SE16 ....1J **87**
(off Rotherhithe St.)
Horatio Ho. E2 ....2F **69**
(off Horatio St.)
W6 ....5F **83**
(off Fulham Pal. Rd.)
Horatio Pl. E14 ....1E **88**
(off Preston's Rd.)
SW19 ....1J **137**
Horatio St. E2 ....2F **69**
Horatius Way CRO: Croy ...5K **151**
Horbury Cres. W11 ....7J **65**
Horbury M. W11 ....7H **65**
Hordean Ho. SW6 ....1G **101**
Hordle Prom. E. SE15 .....7F **87**
Hordle Prom. Sth. SE15 ....7F **87**
(off Quarley Way)
Horizon Bldg. E14 ....7C **70**
(off Hertsmere Rd.)
E14 ....7C **70**
(off Hertsmere Rd.)
Horizon Way SE7 ....4K **89**
Horle Wlk. SW9 ....2B **104**
Horley Cl. DA6: Bex 5G **111**
Horley Rd. SE9 ....4C **126**
Hormead Rd. W9 ....4H **65**

Hornbeam Cl. IG1: Ilf 5H **55**
IG9: Buck H 3G **21**
IG11: Bark 3A **74**
NW7 ....3G **13**
SE11 ....4A **86** (3J **173**)
UB5: N'olt 5D **42**
Hornbeam Cres.
TW8: Bford 7B **80**
Hornbeam Gro. E4 ....3B **20**
Hornbeam Ho.
IG9: Buck H 3H **21**
Hornbeam La. DA7: Bex ...2J **111**
Hornbeam Rd.
IG9: Buck H 3G **21**
UB4: Hayes 5A **60**
Hornbeams Ri. N11 ......6K **15**
Hornbeam Ter.
SM5: Cars 1C **150**
Hornbeam Wlk.
TW10: Rich 2F **117**
Hornbeam Way
BR2: Short 6E **144**
Hornblower Cl. SE16 ......3A **88**
Hornbuckle Cl. HA2: Harr ...2H **43**
Hornby Cl. NW3 ....7B **48**
Hornby Ho. SE11 ....7J **173**
Horncastle Cl. SE12 ......7J **107**
Horncastle Rd. SE12 ......7J **107**
Hornchurch N17 ....2D **32**
(off Gloucester Rd.)
Hornchurch Cl.
KT2: King T 4D **116**
Horndean Cl. SW15 ......1C **118**
Horndon Cl. RM5: Col R ...1J **39**
Horndon Grn. RM5: Col R ...1J **39**
Horndon Rd. RM5: Col R ...1J **39**
Horner Ho. N1 ....1E **68**
(off Whitmore Est.)
Horner La. CR4: Mitc 2B **138**
Horne Rd. TW17: Shep 4C **130**
Horne Way SW15 ....2E **100**
Hornfair Rd. SE7 ....6A **90**
Horniman Dr. SE23 ......1H **123**
Horniman Mus. 1H **123**
Horning Cl. SE9 ....4C **126**
Horn La. IG8: Wfd G 6D **20**
SE10 ....5J **89**
(not continuous)
W3 ....7J **63**
(not continuous)
Horn Link Way SE10 ......4J **89**
HORN PARK 5K **107**
Horn Pk. Cl. SE12 ....5K **107**
Horn Pk. La. SE12 ....5K **107**
Hornpark La. SE12 ....5K **107**
Horns End Pl. HA5: Pinn ...4A **24**
HORNSEY 4J **31**
Hornsey La. N6 ....1F **49**
Hornsey La. Est. N19 .....7H **31**
Hornsey La. Gdns. N6 .....7G **31**
Hornsey Pk. Rd. N8 ......3K **31**
Hornsey Ri. N19 ....7H **31**
Hornsey Ri. Gdns. N19 ....7H **31**
Hornsey Rd. N7 ....1J **49**
N19 ....1J **49**
Hornsey St. N7 ....5K **49**
HORNSEY VALE 5K **31**
Hornshay St. SE15 ....6J **87**
Horns Rd. IG2: Ilf 5G **37**
IG6: Ilf 4H **37**
Hornton Ct. W8 ....2J **83**
(off Kensington High St.)
Hornton Pl. W8 ....2K **83**
Hornton St. W8 ....2J **83**
Horsa Rd. DA8: Erith 7H **93**
SE12 ....7A **108**
Horse & Dolphin Yd. W1 ...2D **166**
Horsebridge Cl. RM9: Dag ...1E **74**
Horsecroft Rd. HA8: Edg ...7E **12**
Horse Fair KT1: King T 2D **134**
Horseferry Pl. SE10 ......6E **88**
Horseferry Rd. E14 ....7A **70**
SW1 ....3H **85** (2C **172**)

Horseferry Rd. Est. SW1 ...2C **172**
Horseguards Av.
SW1 ....1J **85** (5E **166**)
Horse Guards Parade
.............1J **85** (5E **166**)
Horse Guards Rd.
SW1 ....1H **85** (5D **166**)
Horse Leaze E6 ....6E **72**
Horsell Rd. BR5: Orp 7B **128**
N5 ....2B **66**
(not continuous)
Horselydown La.
SE1 ....2F **87** (6J **169**)
Horselydown Mans. SE1 ...6J **169**
(off Lafone St.)
Horsemongers M. SE1 ....7D **168**
Horsenden Av. UB6: G'frd ...5K **43**
Horsenden Cres.
UB6: G'frd 5K **43**
Horsenden La. Nth.
UB6: G'frd 6J **43**
Horsenden La. Sth.
UB6: G'frd 1A **62**
Horse Ride SW1 ...1G **85** (5C **166**)
Horseshoe Cl. E14 ....5E **88**
NW2 ....2D **46**
Horse Shoe Cres.
UB5: N'olt 2E **60**
Horseshoe Dr. UB8: Uxb ...6C **58**
Horse Shoe Grn.
SM1: Sutt 2K **149**
Horseshoe La. EN2: Enf ...3H **7**
N20 ....1A **14**
Horseshoe Wharf SE1 .....4E **168**
(off Clink St.)
Horse Yd. N1 ....1B **68**
(off Essex Rd.)
Horsfeld Gdns. SE9 ......5C **108**
Horsfeld Rd. SE9 ....5B **108**
Horsfield Ho. N1 ....7C **50**
(off Northampton St.)
Horsford Rd. SW2 ....5K **103**
Horsham Av. N12 ....5H **15**
Horsham Ct. N17 ....1G **33**
(off Lansdowne Rd.)
Horsham Rd. DA6: Bex ...5G **111**
TW14: Felt 6E **94**
TW14: Felt 1B **114**
TW14: Felt 1K **113**
Hounslow Urban Farm ...5J **95**
HOUNSLOW WEST 2C **96**
Houseman Way SE5 ......7D **86**
Houses of Parliament
.............3J **85** (1F **173**)
Houston Bus. Pk.
UB4: Hayes 1A **78**
Houston Pl. KT10: Esh 7H **133**
Houston Rd. KT6: Surb 6B **134**
SE23 ....2A **124**
Houstoun Ct.
TW5: Houn 7D **78**
Hove Av. E17 ....5B **34**
Hoveden Rd. NW2 ....5G **47**
Hove Gdns. SM1: Sutt 1K **149**
Hove St. SE15 ....7J **87**
(off Culmore Rd.)
Hoveton Rd. SE28 ....6C **74**
Hoveton Way IG6: Ilf 1F **37**
Howard Av. DA5: Bexl 1C **128**
Howard Cl. N11 ....2K **15**
NW2 ....4G **47**
TW12: Hamp 7G **115**
TW16: Sun T 6H **113**
W3 ....6H **63**
WD23: Bush 1D **10**
Howard Ct. IG11: Bark 1H **73**
Howard Ho. E16 ....7K **71**
(off Wesley Av.)
SE8 ....6B **88**
(off Evelyn St.)
SW1 ....6B **172**
(off Dolphin Sq.)
SW9 ....3B **104**
(off Barrington Rd.)

Horwood Ho. E2 ....3H **69**
(off Pott St.)
NW8 ....3D **158**
(off Paveley St.)
Hosack Rd. SW17 ....2E **120**
Hoser Av. SE12 ....2J **125**
Hosier La. EC1 ....5B **68** (6A **162**)
Hoskins Cl. E16 ....6A **72**
UB3: Hayes 5H **77**
Hoskins St. SE10 ....5F **89**
Hospital Bri. Rd.
TW2: Twick 7F **97**
Hospital Bridge Robt.
.................2F **115**
Hospital Rd. E9 ....5K **51**
TW3: Houn 3E **96**
Hospital Way SE13 ....6F **107**
Hotham Cl. KT8: W Mole ...3E **132**
Hotham Rd. SW15 ....3E **100**
SW19 ....7A **120**
Hotham Rd. M. SW19 ....7A **120**
Hotham St. E15 ....1G **71**
Hothfield Pl. SE16 ....3J **87**
Hotspur Ind. Est. N17 .....6C **18**
Hotspur Rd. UB5: N'olt 2E **60**
Hotspur St. SE11 ...4A **86** (5J **173**)
Houblon Rd. TW10: Rich ...5E **98**
Houghton Cl. E8 ....6F **51**
TW12: Hamp 6C **114**
Houghton Rd. N15 ......4F **33**
Houghton St.
WC2 ....6K **67** (1H **167**)
(not continuous)
Houlder Cres. CRO: Croy ...6B **152**
Houndsden Rd. N21 ......6E **6**
Houndsditch EC3 ...6E **68** (7H **163**)
Houndsfield Rd. N9 ......7C **8**
HOUNSLOW 3F **97**
Hounslow Av. TW3: Houn ...5F **97**
Hounslow Bus. Pk.
TW3: Houn 4E **96**
Hounslow Cen. TW3: Houn ...3F **97**
Hounslow Gdns.
TW3: Houn 5F **97**
Hounslow Rd. TW2: Twick ...6F **97**

Howard Ho.—Huxley Gdns.

Howard Ho. W1 . . . . 4K 159
(off Cleveland St.)
Howard M. N5 . . . . 4B 50
Howard Rd. BR1: Brom 7J 125
E6 . . . . 2D 72
E11 . . . . 3G 53
E17 . . . . 3C 34
IG1: Ilf 4F 55
IG11: Bark 1H 73
KT3: N Mald 3A 136
KT5: Surb 6F 135
N15 . . . . 6E 32
N16 . . . . 4D 50
NW2 . . . . 4F 47
SE20 . . . . 1J 141
SE25 . . . . 5G 141
TW7: Isle 3K 97
TW15: Ashf 4A 112
UB1: S'hall 6F 61
Howards Cl. HA5: Pinn 2K 23
Howards Crest Cl.
BR3: Beck 2E 142
Howard's La. SW15 . . . . 4D 100
Howards Rd. E13 . . . . 3J 71
Howard St. KT7: T Ditt 7B 134
Howard Wlk. N2 . . . . 4A 30
Howard Way EN5: Barn 5A 4
Howarth Ct. E15 . . . . 5E 52
(off Clays La.)
Howarth Rd. SE2 . . . . 5A 92
Howberry Cl. HA8: Edg 6J 11
Howberry Rd.
CR7: Thor H 1D 140
HA7: Edg, Stan 6J 11
HA8: Edg 6J 11
Howbury Rd. SE15 . . . . 3J 105
Howcroft Cres. N3 . . . . 7D 14
Howcroft La. UB6: G'frd 3H 61
Howden Cl. SE28 . . . . 7D 74
Howden Ho. TW4: Houn 7C 96
Howden Rd. SE25 . . . . 2F 141
Howden St. SE15 . . . . 3G 105
Howe Cl. RM7: Mawney 1G 39
Howell Cl. RM6: Chad H 5D 38
Howell Ct. E10 . . . . 7D 34
Howell Wlk. SE17 . . . . 4B 86
Howerd Way SE18 . . . . 1C 108
(not continuous)
Howes Cl. N3 . . . . 3J 29
Howeth Ct. N11 . . . . 6J 15
(off Ribblesdale Av.)
Howfield Pl. N17 . . . . 3F 33
Howgate Rd. SW14 . . . . 3K 99
Howick Pl. SW1 . . . 3G 85 (2B 172)
Howie St. SW11 . . . . 7C 84
Howitt Cl. N16 . . . . 4E 50
NW3 . . . . 6C 48
Howitt Rd. NW3 . . . . 6C 48
Howland Est. SE16 . . . . 3J 87
Howland Ho. SW16 . . . . 3J 121
Howland M. E.
W1 . . . . 5G 67 (5B 160)
Howland St. W1 . . . 5G 67 (5A 160)
Howland Way SE16 . . . . 2A 88
Howletts La. HA4: Ruis 5E 22
Howlett's Rd. SE24 . . . . 6C 104
Howley Pl. W2 . . . . 5A 66 (5A 158)
Howley Rd. CR0: Croy 3B 152
Howsman Rd. SW13 . . . . 6C 82
Howson Rd. SE4 . . . . 4A 106
Howson Ter. TW10: Rich 6E 98
How's St. E2 . . . . 2F 69
Howton Pl. WD23: Bush 1C 10
HOXTON 2E 68
Hoxton Hall Theatre 2E 68
(off Hoxton Rd.)
Hoxton Mkt. N1 . . . . 2G 163
Hoxton Sq. N1 . . . . . 3E 68 (2G 163)
Hoxton St. N1 . . . . . 1E 68 (2H 163)
Hoylake Cres. UB10: Uxb 2C 40
Hoylake Gdns. CR4: Mitc . . . 3G 139
HA4: Ruis 1K 41
Hoylake Rd. W3 . . . . 6A 64
Hoyland Cl. SE15 . . . . 7H 87
Hoyle Rd. SW17 . . . . 5C 120
Hoy St. E16 . . . . 6H 71
Hubbard Dr. KT9: Chess 6D 146
Hubbard Rd. SE27 . . . . 4C 122
Hubbards Cl. UB8: Uxb 6D 58
Hubbard St. E15 . . . . 1G 71
Huberd Ho. SE1 . . . . 7F 169
(off Manciple St.)
Hubert Cl. SW19 . . . . 1A 138
(off Nelson Gro. Rd.)
Hubert Gro. SW9 . . . . 3J 103
Hubert Ho. NW8 . . . . 4C 158
(off Ashbridge St.)
Hubert Rd. E6 . . . . 3B 72
Hucknall Ct. NW8 . . . . 3A 158
(off Cunningham Pl.)
Huddart St. E3 . . . . 5B 70
(not continuous)
Huddleston Cl. E2 . . . . 2J 69
Huddlestone Rd. E7 . . . . 4H 53
NW2 . . . . 6D 46
Huddleston Rd. N7 . . . . 3G 49
Hudson NW9 . . . . 1B 28
(off Near Acre)
Hudson Cl. W12 . . . . 7D 64
Hudson Ct. E14 . . . . 5C 88
(off Maritime Quay)
Hudson Pl. SE18 . . . . 5G 91
Hudson Rd. DA7: Bex 2F 111
UB3: Hayes 6F 77
Hudson's Pl. SW1 . . . . 3A 172
Hudson Way N9 . . . . 3D 18
Huggin Ct. EC4 . . . . 2D 168
Huggin Hill EC4 . . . . 7C 68 (2D 168)
Huggins Pl. SW2 . . . . 1K 121
Hughan Rd. E15 . . . . 5F 53
Hugh Astor Ct. SE1 . . . . 7B 168
(off Keyworth St.)
Hugh Clark Ho. W13 . . . . 1A 80
(off Singapore Rd.)
Hugh Dalton Av. SW6 . . . . 6H 83
Hughenden Av. HA3: Harr . . . 5B 26
Hughenden Gdns.
UB5: N'olt 3A 60
(not continuous)
Hughenden Ho. NW8 . . . . . . 3C 158
Hughenden Rd.
KT4: Wor Pk 7C 136
Hughendon EN5: Barn 4E 4
Hughendon Ter. E15 . . . . 4E 52
Hughes Cl. N12 . . . . 5F 15
Hughes Ct. N7 . . . . 5H 49
Hughes Ho. E2 . . . . 3J 69
(off Sceptre Ho.)
SE8 . . . . 6C 88
(off Benbow St.)
Hughes Ho. SE17 . . . . 4B 86
(off Peacock St.)
Hughes Mans. E1 . . . . 4G 69
Hughes M. SW11 . . . . 5D 102
Hughes Rd.
TW15: Ashf 6E 112
UB3: Hayes 7K 59
Hughes Ter. E16 . . . . 5H 71
(off Clarkson Rd.)
Hughes Wlk. CR0: Croy 7C 140
Hugh Gaitskell Cl. SW6 . . . . . 6H 83
Hugh Gaitskell Ho. N16 . . . . . 2F 51
Hugh Herland Ho.
KT1: King T 3E 134
Hugh M. SW1 . . . . . 4F 85 (4K 171)
Hugh Platt Ho. E2 . . . . 2H 69
(off Patriot Sq.)
Hugh St. SW1 . . . . . 4F 85 (4K 171)
Hugon Rd. SW6 . . . . 3K 101
Hugo Rd. N19 . . . . 4G 49
Huguenot Pl. E1 . . . . 5F 69 (5K 163)
SW18 . . . . 5A 102
Huguenot Sq. SE15 . . . . 3H 105
Hullbridge M. N1 . . . . 1D 68
Hull Cl. SE16 . . . . 2K 87
Hull Pl. E16 . . . . 1G 91
Hull St. EC1 . . . . . . 3C 68 (2C 162)
Hulme Pl. SE1 . . . . . 2C 86 (7D 168)
Hulse Av. IG11: Bark 6H 55
RM7: Mawney 1H 39
Hulverston Cl.
SM2: Sutt 7K 149
Humber Cl. UB7: W Dray 1A 76
Humber Ct. W7 . . . . 6H 61
(off Hobbayne Rd.)
Humber Dr. W10 . . . . 4F 65
Humber Rd. NW2 . . . . 2D 46
SE3 . . . . 6H 89
Humberstone Rd. E13 . . . . . . 3A 72
Humberton Cl. E9 . . . . 5A 52
Humbolt Rd. W6 . . . . 6G 83
Hume Ct. N1 . . . . 7B 50
(off Hawes St.)
Hume Ho. W11 . . . . 1F 83
(off Queensdale Cres.)
Humes Av. W7 . . . . 3J 79
Hume Ter. E16 . . . . 5K 71
Hume Way HA4: Ruis 6J 23
Humphrey Cl. IG5: Ilf 1D 36
Humphrey St. SE1 . . . . 5F 87
Humphries Cl. RM9: Dag 4F 57
Hundred Acre NW9 . . . . 2B 28
Hungerdown E4 . . . . 1K 19
Hungerford Ho. SW1 . . . . . . 7B 172
(off Churchill Gdns.)
Hungerford La. WC2 . . . . 4F 167
(not continuous)
Hungerford Rd. N7 . . . . 6H 49
Hungerford St. E1 . . . . 6H 69
Hunsdon Cl. RM9: Dag 6E 56
Hunsdon Rd. SE14 . . . . 7K 87
Hunslett St. E2 . . . . 3J 69
Hunstanton Ho. NW1 . . . . . . 5D 158
(off Cosway St.)
Hunston Rd. SM4: Mord 1K 149
Hunt Ct. N14 . . . . 7A 6
UB5: N'olt 2B 60
(off Gallery Gdns.)
Hunter Cl. SE1 . . . . 3D 86
SM6: Wall 7J 151
Hunter Ho. SE1 . . . . 7B 168
(off Lancaster St.)
SW5 . . . . 5J 83
(off Old Brompton Rd.)
SW8 . . . . 7H 85
(off Fount St.)
WC1 . . . . 3F 161
(off Hunter St.)
Hunterian Mus., The 7H 161
(off Portugal St.)
Hunter Lodge W9 . . . . 5J 65
(off Admiral Wlk.)
Hunter Rd. CR7: Thor H 3D 140
IG1: Ilf 5F 55
SW20 . . . . 1E 136
Hunters Cl. DA5: Bexl 3K 129
SW12 . . . . 1E 120
Hunters Ct. TW9: Rich 5D 98
Hunters Gro. HA3: Harr 4C 26
UB3: Hayes 1J 77
Hunters Hall Rd.
RM10: Dag 4G 57
Hunters Hill HA4: Ruis 3A 42
Hunters Mdw. SE19 . . . . 4E 122
Hunter's Rd. KT9: Chess 3E 146
Hunters Sq. RM10: Dag 4G 57
Hunter St. WC1 . . . . 4J 67 (3F 161)
Hunters Way CR0: Croy 4E 152
EN2: Enf 1F 7
Hunter Wlk. E13 . . . . 2J 71
Huntingdon Cl. CR4: Mitc . . . 3J 139
Huntingdon Gdns.
KT4: Wor Pk 3E 148
W4 . . . . 7J 81
Huntingdon Rd. N2 . . . . 3C 30
N9 . . . . 1D 18
Huntingdon St. E16 . . . . 6H 71
N1 . . . . 7K 49
Huntingfield CR0: Croy 7B 154
Huntingfield Rd. SW15 . . . . 4C 100
Hunting Ga. Cl. EN2: Enf 3F 7
Hunting Ga. Dr.
KT9: Chess 7E 146
Hunting Ga. M.
SM1: Sutt 3K 149
TW2: Twick 1J 115
Huntings Farm IG1: Ilf 2J 55
Huntings Rd. RM10: Dag 6G 57
Huntley Dr. N3 . . . . 6D 14
Huntley St. WC1 . . . 4G 67 (4B 160)
Huntley Way SW20 . . . . 2C 136
Huntly Rd. SE25 . . . . 4E 140
Hunton St. E1 . . . . . 5G 69 (4K 163)
Hunt Rd. UB2: S'hall 3E 78
Hunt's Cl. SE3 . . . . 2J 107
Hunt's Ct. WC2 . . . . 7H 67 (3D 166)
Hunts La. E15 . . . . 2E 70
Huntsmans Cl.
TW13: Felt 4K 113
Huntsman St. SE17 . . . . 4E 86
Hunts Mead EN3: Enf 3E 8
Huntsmead Cl.
BR7: Chst 7D 126
Huntsmoor Rd.
KT19: Eps 5K 147
Huntspill St. SW17 . . . . 3A 120
Hunts Slip Rd. SE21 . . . . . . 3E 122
Hunt St. W11 . . . . 1F 83
Huntsworth M.
NW1 . . . . . . 4D 66 (3E 158)
Hurdwick Pl. NW1 . . . . 2G 67
(off Hampstead Rd.)
Hurleston Ho. SE8 . . . . 5B 88
Hurley Ct. W5 . . . . 6C 62
Hurley Cres. SE16 . . . . 2K 87
Hurley Ho. SE11 . . . 4B 86 (4K 173)
Hurley Rd. UB6: G'frd 6F 61
HURLINGHAM 3K 101
Hurlingham Bus. Pk.
SW6 . . . . 3J 101
Hurlingham Ct. SW6 . . . . . . 3H 101
Hurlingham Gdns. SW6 . . . . 3H 101
Hurlingham Retail Pk.
SW6 . . . . 3K 101
Hurlingham Rd. DA7: Bex 7F 93
SW6 . . . . 2H 101
Hurlingham Sq. SW6 . . . . . . 3J 101
Hurlock St. N5 . . . . 3B 50
Hurlstone Rd. SE25 . . . . 5E 140
Hurn Ct. TW4: Houn 2B 96
Hurn Ct. Rd. TW4: Houn 2B 96
Huron Rd. SW17 . . . . 2E 120
Huron University 3B 84
Hurren Cl. SE3 . . . . 3G 107
Hurricane Rd. SM6: Wall 7J 151
Hurry Cl. E15 . . . . 7G 53
Hurst Av. E4 . . . . 4H 19
N6 . . . . 6G 31
Hurstbourne KT10: Esh 6A 146
Hurstbourne Gdns.
IG11: Bark 6J 55
Hurstbourne Ho. SW15 . . . . 6B 100
(off Tangley Gro.)
Hurstbourne Rd. SE23 . . . . . 1A 124
Hurst Cl. BR2: Short 1H 155
E4 . . . . 3H 19
KT9: Chess 5G 147
NW11 . . . . 6K 29
UB5: N'olt 6D 42
Hurstcombe IG9: Buck H 2D 20
Hurst Ct. DA15: Sidc 2A 128
E6 . . . . 5B 72
(off Tollgate Rd.)
Hurstcourt Rd. SM1: Sutt . . . 2K 149
Hurstdene Av.
BR2: Short 1H 155
Hurstdene Gdns. N15 . . . . 7E 32
Hurstfield BR2: Short 5J 143
Hurstfield Cres.
UB4: Hayes 4G 59
Hurstfield Rd.
KT8: W Mole 3E 132
Hurst Gro. KT12: Walt T 7H 131
Hurst Ho. WC1 . . . . 1H 161
(off Penton Ri.)
Hurst La. KT8: E Mos 4G 133
SE2 . . . . 5D 92
Hurst La. Est. SE2 . . . . 5D 92
Hurstleigh Gdns. IG5: Ilf 1D 36
Hurstmead Ct. HA8: Edg 4C 12
HURST PARK 2G 133
Hurst Pl. HA6: Nwood 1D 22
Hurst Ri. EN5: Barn 3D 4
Hurst Rd. CR0: Croy 5D 152
DA5: Bexl 1D 128
DA8: Erith 1J 111
DA15: Bexl, Sidc 2A 128
E17 . . . . 3D 34
IG9: Buck H 1G 21
KT8: E Mos 3F 133
KT8: W Mole 3C 132
KT12: Walt T, W Mole
. . . . 5A 132
N21 . . . . 1F 17
Hurst Springs DA5: Bexl 1E 128
Hurst St. SE24 . . . . 6B 104
Hurstview Grange
CR2: S Croy 7B 152
Hurst Vw. Rd.
CR2: S Croy 7E 152
Hurst Way CR2: S Croy 6E 152
Hurstway Rd. W11 . . . . 7F 65
Hurstway Wlk. W11 . . . . 7F 65
Hurstwood Av. DA5: Bexl . . . 1E 128
E18 . . . . 4K 35
Hurstwood Ct. N12 . . . . 6H 15
NW11 . . . . 4H 29
(off Finchley Rd.)
Hurstwood Dr.
BR1: Brom 3D 144
Hurstwood Rd. NW11 . . . . . . 4G 29
Hurtwood Rd.
KT12: Walt T 7D 132
Husborne Ho. SE8 . . . . 4A 88
(off Chilton Gro.)
Huson Cl. NW3 . . . . 7C 48
Hussain Cl. HA1: Harr 4K 43
Hussars Cl. TW4: Houn 3C 96
Husseywell Cres.
BR2: Short 1J 155
Hutchings St. E14 . . . . 2C 88
Hutchings Wlk. NW11 . . . . . . 4K 29
Hutchings Wharf E14 . . . . 2C 88
(off Hutchings St.)
Hutchins Cl. E15 . . . . 7E 52
Hutchinson Ct.
RM6: Chad H 4D 38
Hutchinson Ho. NW3 . . . . 7D 48
SE14 . . . . 7J 87
Hutchinson Ter.
HA9: Wemb 3D 44
Hutchins Rd. SE28 . . . . 7A 74
Hutton Cl. IG8: Wfd G 6E 20
UB6: G'frd 5H 43
Hutton Ct. N4 . . . . 1K 49
(off Victoria Rd.)
N9 . . . . 7D 8
(off Tramway Av.)
W5 . . . . 5B 62
Hutton Gdns. HA3: Harr 7B 10
Hutton Gro. N12 . . . . 5E 14
Hutton La. HA3: Harr 7B 10
Hutton Row HA8: Edg 7D 12
Hutton St. EC4 . . . . . 6B 68 (2K 167)
Hutton Wlk. HA3: Harr 7B 10
Huxbear St. SE4 . . . . 5B 106
Huxley Cl. UB5: N'olt 2C 60
UB8: Uxb 4A 58
Huxley Dr. RM6: Chad H 7B 38
Huxley Gdns. NW10 . . . . 3F 63

Huxley Ho.—Inverness Ter.

Huxley Ho. *NW8* ... *4B* ***158***
(off Fisherton St.)
Huxley Pde. N18 ... 5J **17**
Huxley Pl. N13 ... 3G **17**
Huxley Rd. DA16: Well ... 3K **109**
E10 ... 2E **52**
N18 ... 4J **17**
Huxley Sayze N18 ... 5J **17**
Huxley Sth. N18 ... 5J **17**
Huxley St. W10 ... 3G **65**
Hyacinth Cl. IG1: Ilf ... 6F **55**
TW12: Hamp ... 6E **114**
Hyacinth Dr. UB10: Uxb ... 7A **40**
Hyacinth Rd. SW15 ... 1C **118**
Hyde Cl. E13 ... 2J **71**
EN5: Barn ... 3C **4**
TW15: Ashf ... 6G **113**
Hyde Ct. N20 ... 3G **15**
Hyde Cres. NW9 ... 5A **28**
Hyde Est. Rd. NW9 ... 5B **28**
Hyde Farm M. SW12 ... 1H **121**
Hydefield Cl. N21 ... 1J **17**
Hydefield Ct. N9 ... 2K **17**
Hyde Ind. Est., The
NW9 ... 5B **28**
Hyde La. SW11 ... 1C **102**
Hyde Pk. ... ***1C 84 (4D 164)***
Hyde Pk. Av. N21 ... 2H **17**
HYDE PARK CORNER
... **2F 85 (6H 165)**
Hyde Pk. Cnr.
W1 ... 2E **84** (6H **165**)
Hyde Pk. Cres.
W2 ... 6C **66** (1C **164**)
Hyde Pk. Gdns. N21 ... 1H **17**
W2 ... 7B **66** (2B **164**)
Hyde Pk. Gdns. M.
W2 ... 7B **66** (2B **164**)
(not continuous)
Hyde Pk. Ga. SW7 ... 2A **84**
(not continuous)
Hyde Pk. Ga. M. SW7 ... 2A **84**
Hyde Pk. Mans. *NW1* ... *6C* ***158***
(off Cabbell St., not continuous)
Hyde Pk. Pl. W2 ... 7C **66** (2D **164**)
Hyde Pk. Sq. W2 ... 6C **66** (1C **164**)
Hyde Pk. Sq. M. W2 ... 1C **164**
Hyde Pk. St. W2 ... 6C **66** (1C **164**)
Hyde Pk. Towers W2 ... 7A **66**
Hyderabad Way E15 ... 7G **53**
Hyde Rd. DA7: Bex ... 2F **111**
N1 ... 1E **68**
TW10: Rich ... 5F **99**
Hydeside Gdns. N9 ... 2A **18**
Hyde's Pl. N1 ... 7B **50**
Hyde St. SE8 ... 6C **88**
Hyde Ter. TW15: Ashf ... 6G **113**
HYDE, THE ... **5B 28**
Hyde, The NW9 ... 5A **28**
Hydethorpe Av. N9 ... 2A **18**
Hydethorpe Rd. SW12 ... 1G **121**
Hyde Va. SE10 ... 7E **88**
Hyde Wlk. SM4: Mord ... 7J **137**
Hyde Way N9 ... 2A **18**
UB3: Hayes ... 4H **77**
Hydon Ct. N11 ... 5J **15**
Hydra Bldg., The EC1 ... 2K **161**
Hylands Rd. E17 ... 2F **35**
Hylton St. SE18 ... 4K **91**
Hyndewood SE23 ... 3K **123**
Hyndman Ho.
RM10: Dag ... *3G* ***57***
(off Kershaw Rd.)
Hyndman St. SE15 ... 6H **87**
Hynton Rd. RM8: Dag ... 2C **56**
Hyperion Ho. *E3* ... *2A* ***70***
(off Arbery Rd.)
SW2 ... 6K **103**
Hyrstdene CR2: S Croy ... 4B **152**
Hyson Rd. SE16 ... 5H **87**
Hythe Av. DA7: Bex ... 7E **92**
Hythe Cl. N18 ... 4B **18**
Hythe Ho. *SE16* ... *2J* ***87***
(off Swan Rd.)
W6 ... *4E* ***82***
(off Shepherd's Bush Rd.)
Hythe Rd. CR7: Thor H ... 2D **140**
NW10 ... 3B **64**
Hythe Rd. Ind. Est.
NW10 ... 3C **64**

I

Ian Bowater Ct. *N1* ... *1F* ***163***
(off East Rd.)
Ian Ct. SE23 ... 2J **123**
Ian Sq. EN3: Enf ... 1E **8**
Ibberton Ho. *SW8* ... *7K* ***85***
(off Meadow Rd.)
W14 ... *3G* ***83***
(off Russell Rd.)
Ibbotson Av. E16 ... 6H **71**
Ibbott St. E1 ... 4J **69**
Iberia Ho. N19 ... 7H **31**
Iberian Av. SM6: Wall ... 4H **151**
Ibis Ct. *SE8* ... *6B* ***88***
(off Edward Pl.)
Ibis La. W4 ... 1J **99**
Ibis Way UB4: Hayes ... 6B **60**
Ibrox Ct. IG9: Buck H ... 2F **21**
Ibscott Cl. RM10: Dag ... 6J **57**
Ibsley Gdns. SW15 ... 1C **118**
Ibsley Way EN4: Barn ... 5H **5**
Iceland Rd. E3 ... 1C **70**
Iceni Ct. IG9: Buck H ... 1E **20**
Ice Wharf Marina *N1* ... *2J* ***67***
(off New Wharf Rd.)
Ickburgh Est. E5 ... 2H **51**
Ickburgh Rd. E5 ... 3H **51**
ICKENHAM ... **3D 40**
Ickenham Cl. HA4: Ruis ... 2F **41**
Ickenham Grn. UB10: Uxb ... 1D **40**
Ickenham Rd. HA4: Ruis ... 2E **40**
Ickleton Rd. SE9 ... 4C **126**
Icknield Dr. IG2: Ilf ... 5F **37**
Icknield Ho. *SW3* ... *5D* ***170***
(off Cale St.)
Ickworth Pk. Rd. E17 ... 4A **34**
Ida Rd. N15 ... 4D **32**
Ida St. E14 ... 6E **70**
(not continuous)
Iden Cl. BR2: Short ... 3G **143**
Idlecombe Rd. SW17 ... 6E **120**
Idmiston Rd. E15 ... 4H **53**
KT4: Wor Pk ... 7B **136**
SE27 ... 3C **122**
Idmiston Sq.
KT4: Wor Pk ... 7B **136**
Idol La. EC3 ... 7E **68** (3G **169**)
Idonia St. SE8 ... 7C **88**
Iffley Cl. UB8: Uxb ... 7A **40**
Iffley Rd. W6 ... 3D **82**
Ifield Rd. SW10 ... 6K **83**
Ifor Evans Pl. E1 ... 4K **69**
Ightham Ho. *BR3: Beck* ... *7B* ***124***
(off Bethersden Cl.)
SE17 ... *4E* ***86***
(off Beckway St.)
Ightham Rd. DA7: Erith ... 7G **93**
Ilbert St. W10 ... 3F **65**
Ilchester Gdns. W2 ... 7K **65**
Ilchester Pl. W14 ... 3H **83**
Ilchester Rd. RM8: Dag ... 5B **56**
Ildersly Gro. SE21 ... 2D **122**
Ilderton Rd. SE16 ... 5J **87**
Ilderton Wharf *SE15* ... *6J* ***87***
(off Rollins St.)
Ilex Cl. TW16: Sun T ... 2A **132**
Ilex Rd. NW10 ... 6B **46**
Ilex Way SW16 ... 5A **122**
ILFORD ... **3F 55**
Ilford Hill IG1: Ilf ... 3E **54**
Ilford Ho. *N1* ... *6D* ***50***
(off Dove Rd.)
Ilford La. IG1: Bark, Ilf ... 3F **55**
Ilfracombe Flats *SE1* ... *6D* ***168***
(off Marshalsea Rd.)
Ilfracombe Gdns. R
M6: Chad H ... 7B **38**
Ilfracombe Rd.
BR1: Brom ... 3H **125**
Iliffe St. SE17 ... 5B **86**
Iliffe Yd. *SE17* ... *5B* ***86***
(off Crampton St.)
Ilkeston Ct. *E5* ... *4K* ***51***
(off Overbury St.)
Ilkley Cl. SE19 ... 6D **122**
Ilkley Rd. E16 ... 5A **72**
Illingworth Cl. CR4: Mitc ... 3B **138**
Illingworth Way EN1: Enf ... 5K **7**
Ilmington Rd. HA3: Harr ... 6D **26**
Ilminster Gdns. SW11 ... 4C **102**
Imani Mans. SW11 ... 2B **102**
Imber Cl. N14 ... 7B **6**
Imber Ct. Trad. Est.
KT8: E Mos ... 6H **133**
Imber Cross KT7: T Ditt ... 6K **133**
Imber Gro. KT10: Esh ... 7H **133**
Imber Pk. Rd.
KT10: Esh ... 7H **133**
Imber St. N1 ... 1D **68**
Impact Bus. Pk.
UB6: G'frd ... 2B **62**
Impact Ct. SE20 ... 2H **141**
Imperial Av. N16 ... 4E **50**
Imperial Cl. HA2: Harr ... 6E **24**
Imperial College
... ***3B 84 (1A 170)***
Imperial Coll. Rd.
SW7 ... 3B **84** (2A **170**)
Imperial Ct. HA2: Harr ... 7E **24**
N6 ... 6G **31**
N20 ... 3F **15**
NW8 ... *2C* ***66***
(off Prince Albert Rd.)
SE11 ... 5A **86** (6J **173**)
Imperial Dr. HA2: Harr ... 7E **24**
Imperial Gdns.
CR4: Mitc ... 3F **139**
Imperial Ho. *E3* ... *3A* ***70***
(off Grove Rd.)
E14 ... *7B* ***70***
(off Victory Pl.)
Imperial M. E6 ... 2B **72**
Imperial Pde. *EC4* ... *1A* ***168***
(off New Bri. St.)
Imperial Pl. BR7: Chst ... 1E **144**
Imperial Rd. N22 ... 7D **16**
SW6 ... 1K **101**
TW14: Felt ... 7G **95**
Imperial Sq. SW6 ... 1K **101**
Imperial St. E3 ... 3E **70**
Imperial War Mus.
... ***3A 86 (2K 173)***
Imperial Way BR7: Chst ... 3G **127**
CR0: Croy ... 6K **151**
HA3: Harr ... 6E **26**
Imre Cl. W12 ... 1D **82**
Inca Dr. SE9 ... 7F **109**
Inchmery Rd. SE6 ... 2D **124**
Inchwood CR0: Croy ... 4D **154**
Independent Ind. Est.
UB7: W Dray ... 1A **76**
Independent Pl. E8 ... 5F **51**
Independents Rd. SE3 ... 3H **107**
Inderwick Rd. N8 ... 5K **31**
Indescon Ct. E14 ... 2C **88**
India Pl. WC2 ... 2G **167**
India St. EC3 ... 6F **69** (1J **169**)
India Way W12 ... 7D **64**
Indigo M. E14 ... 7E **70**
N16 ... 3D **50**
Indus Rd. SE7 ... 7A **90**
Infirmary Ct. SW3 ... 7F **171**
Ingal Rd. E13 ... 4J **71**
Ingate Pl. SW8 ... 1F **103**
Ingatestone Rd. E12 ... 1A **54**
IG8: Wfd G ... 7E **20**
SE25 ... 4H **141**
Ingelow Ho. *W8* ... *2K* ***83***
(off Holland St.)
Ingelow Rd. SW8 ... 2F **103**
Ingersoll Rd. EN3: Enf ... 1D **8**
W12 ... 1D **82**
Ingestre Pl. W1 ... 6G **67** (1B **166**)
Ingestre Rd. E7 ... 4J **53**
NW5 ... 4F **49**
Ingham Cl. CR2: S Croy ... 7K **153**
Ingham Rd. CR2: S Croy ... 7J **153**
NW6 ... 4J **47**
Inglebert St. EC1 ... 3A **68** (1J **161**)
Ingleborough Ct. N17 ... 3F **33**
Ingleborough St. SW9 ... 2A **104**
Ingleby Dr. HA1: Harr ... 3H **43**
Ingleby Rd. IG1: Ilf ... 1F **55**
N7 ... 3J **49**
RM10: Dag ... 6H **57**
Ingleby Way BR7: Chst ... 5E **126**
SM6: Wall ... 7H **151**
Ingle Cl. HA5: Pinn ... 3C **24**
Ingledew Rd. SE18 ... 5H **91**
Inglefield Sq. *E1* ... *1H* ***87***
(off Prusom St.)
Inglehurst Gdns. IG4: Ilf ... 5D **36**
Inglemere Rd. CR4: Mitc ... 7D **120**
SE23 ... 3K **123**
Inglesham Wlk. E9 ... 6B **52**
Ingleside Cl. BR3: Beck ... 7C **124**
Ingleside Gro. SE3 ... 6H **89**
Inglethorpe St. SW6 ... 1F **101**
Ingleton Av. DA16: Well ... 5A **110**
Ingleton Rd. N18 ... 6B **18**
SM5: Cars ... 7C **150**
Ingleton St. SW9 ... 2A **104**
Ingleway N12 ... 6G **15**
Inglewood CR0: Croy ... 7A **154**
Inglewood Cl. E14 ... 4C **88**
Inglewood Copse
BR1: Brom ... 2C **144**
Inglewood Rd. DA7: Bex ... 4K **111**
NW6 ... 5J **47**
Inglis Rd. CR0: Croy ... 1F **153**
W5 ... 7F **63**
Inglis St. SE5 ... 1B **104**
Ingoldisthorpe Gro. SE15 ... 6F **87**
Ingram Av. NW11 ... 7A **30**
Ingram Cl. HA7: Stan ... 5H **11**
SE11 ... 4K **85** (3H **173**)
Ingram Ho. E3 ... 1A **70**
Ingram Rd. CR7: Thor H ... 1C **140**
N2 ... 4C **30**
Ingram Way UB6: G'frd ... 1H **61**
Ingrave Ho. RM9: Dag ... 1B **74**
Ingrave Rd. RM1: Rom ... 4K **39**
Ingrave St. SW11 ... 3B **102**
Ingrebourne Ct. E4 ... 3J **19**
Ingrebourne Ho.
BR1: Brom ... *5F* ***125***
(off Brangbourne Rd.)
NW8 ... *5B* ***158***
(off Broadley St.)
Ingress St. W4 ... 5A **82**
Inigo Jones Rd. SE7 ... 7C **90**
Inigo Pl. WC2 ... 2E **166**
Inkerman Rd. NW5 ... 6F **49**
Inkerman Ter. *W8* ... *3J* ***83***
(off Allen St.)
Inks Grn. E4 ... 5K **19**
Inkwell Cl. N12 ... 3F **15**
Inman Rd. NW10 ... 1A **64**
SW18 ... 7A **102**
Inmans Row IG8: Wfd G ... 4D **20**
Inner Circ. NW1 ... 3E **66** (2G **159**)
Inner London Sessions House
... ***3C 86 (7C 168)***
Inner Pk. Rd. SW19 ... 1F **119**
Inner Ring E. TW6: Houn ... 3D **94**
Inner Ring W.
TW6: Houn ... 3C **94**
Inner Temple Hall ... ***1J 167***
Inner Temple La.
EC4 ... 6A **68** (1J **167**)
Innes Cl. SW20 ... 2G **137**
Innes Gdns. SW15 ... 6D **100**
Innes Yd. CR0: Croy ... 3C **152**
Innis Ho. *SE17* ... *5E* ***86***
(off East St.)
Inniskilling Rd. E13 ... 2A **72**
Innis St. SE15 ... 7E **86**
Inn of Court & City Yeomanry
Mus. ... ***6H 161***
(off Chancery La.)
Innovation Cen., The *E14* ... *2E* ***88***
(off Marsh Wall)
Innovation Cl. HA0: Wemb ... 1E **62**
Inskip Cl. E10 ... 2D **52**
Inskip Rd. RM8: Dag ... 1D **56**
Institute for English Studies
... ***5H 67 (5D 160)***
Institute of Archaeology ... ***3C 160***
(off Gordon Sq.)
Institute of Classical Studies
... ***5H 67***
Institute of Commonwealth
Studies ... ***5D 160***
Institute of Contemporary Arts
... ***5D 166***
Institute of Education ... ***4D 160***
Institute of Germanic Studies
... ***5E 160***
(off Russell Sq.)
Institute of Historical Research
... ***5H 67 (5D 160)***
Institute of Latin American
Studies ... ***4H 67***
Institute of Romance Studies
... ***5H 67 (5D 160)***
Institute of United States
Studies ... ***5H 67 (5D 160)***
Institute Pl. E8 ... 5H **51**
Integer Gdns. E11 ... 7F **35**
Interface Ho. *TW3: Houn* ... *3E* ***96***
(off Staines Rd.)
International Av.
TW5: Houn ... 5A **78**
International Ho. *E1* ... *3K* ***169***
(off St Katharine's Way)
International Trad. Est.
UB2: S'hall ... 3K **77**
International Way
TW16: Sun T ... 1G **131**
Inverary Pl. SE18 ... 6H **91**
Inver Cl. E5 ... 2J **51**
Inverclyde Gdns.
RM6: Chad H ... 4C **38**
(not continuous)
Inver Ct. W2 ... 6K **65**
Inveresk Gdns.
KT4: Wor Pk ... 3C **148**
Inverforth Cl. NW3 ... 2A **48**
Inverforth Rd. N11 ... 5A **16**
Invergarry Ho. *W9* ... *2K* ***65***
(off Carlton Va.)
Inverine Rd. SE7 ... 5K **89**
Invermore Pl. SE18 ... 4G **91**
Inverness Av. EN1: Enf ... 1K **7**
Inverness Ct. SE6 ... 1H **125**
Inverness Gdns. W8 ... 1K **83**
Inverness M. E16 ... 1G **91**
W2 ... 7K **65**
Inverness Pl. W2 ... 7K **65**
Inverness Rd.
KT4: Wor Pk ... 1F **149**
N18 ... 5C **18**
TW3: Houn ... 4D **96**
UB2: S'hall ... 4C **78**
Inverness St. NW1 ... 1F **67**
Inverness Ter. W2 ... 6K **65**

272 A-Z London

Inverton Rd.—Jardine Rd.

Inverton Rd. SE15 4K 105
Invicta Cen., The
IG11: Bark 1A 74
Invicta Cl. BR7: Chst 5E 126
TW14: Felt 1H 113
Invicta Gro. UB5: N'olt 3D 60
Invicta Pde. DA14: Sidc 4B 128
Invicta Plaza
SE1 1B 86 (4A 168)
Invicta Rd. SE3 7J 89
Inville Rd. SE17 5D 86
Inville Wlk. SE17 5D 86
Inwen Ct. SE8 5A 88
Inwood Av. TW3: Houn 3G 97
Inwood Cl. CR0: Croy 2A 154
Inwood Ct. *NW1 7G 49*
(off Rochester Sq.)
Inwood Rd. TW3: Houn 4F 97
Inworth St. SW11 2C 102
Inworth Wlk. *N1 1C 68*
(off Popham St.)
Iona Cl. SE6 7C 106
SM4: Mord 7K 137
Ion Ct. E2 2G 69
Ionian Bldg. E14 7A 70
Ionian Ho. *E1 4K 69*
(off Duckett St.)
Ion Sq. E2 2G 69
Ipsden Bldgs. SE1 5K 167
Ipswich Ho. SE4 5K 105
Ipswich Rd. SW17 6E 120
Ireland Cl. E6 5D 72
Ireland Pl. N22 7D 16
Ireland Yd. EC4 6B 68
Irene M. *W7 1K 79*
(off Uxbridge Rd.)
Irene Rd. BR6: Orp 7K 145
SW6 1J 101
Ireton Cl. N10 7K 15
Ireton St. E3 4C 70
Iris Av. DA5: Bexl 5E 110
Iris Cl. CR0: Croy 1K 153
E6 5C 72
KT6: Surb 7F 135
Iris Ct. *SE14 1J 105*
(off Briant St.)
Iris Cres. DA7: Bex 6F 93
Iris Rd. KT19: Eps 5H 147
Iris Wlk. HA8: Edg 4D 12
Iris Way E4 6G 19
Irkdale Av. EN1: Enf 1A 8
Iron Bri. Cl. NW10 5A 46
Ironbridge Cl. UB2: S'hall 1G 79
Iron Bri. Ho. NW1 7D 48
Iron Bri. Rd. UB7: W Dray 1C 76
Iron Mill Pl. SW18 6K 101
Iron Mill Rd. SW18 6K 101
Ironmonger La.
EC2 6C 68 (1D 168)
Ironmonger Pas. *EC1 2D 162*
(off Ironmonger Row)
Ironmonger Row
EC1 3C 68 (2D 162)
Ironmongers Pl. E14 4C 88
Ironside Cl. SE16 2K 87
Ironside Ho. E9 4A 52
Irons Way RM5: Col R 1J 39
Irvine Av. HA3: Harr 3A 26
Irvine Cl. N20 2H 15
Irvine Ho. *E14 5D 70*
(off Uamvar St.)
N7 6K 49
(off Caledonian Rd.)
Irvine Way BR6: Orp 7K 145
Irving Av. UB5: N'olt 1B 60
Irving Gro. SW9 2K 103
Irving Ho. *SE17 5B 86*
(off Doddington Gro.)
Irving Mans. *W14 6G 83*
(off Queen's Club Gdns.)
Irving M. N1 6C 50
Irving Rd. W14 3F 83
Irving St. WC2 7H 67 (3D 166)
Irving Way NW9 5C 28
Irwell Ct. *W7 6H 61*
(off Hobbayne Rd.)
Irwell Est. SE16 3J 87
Irwin Av. SE18 7J 91
Irwin Cl. UB10: Uxb 3C 40
Irwin Gdns. NW10 1D 64
Isabel Hill Cl.
TW12: Hamp 2F 133
Isabella Cl. N14 7B 6
Isabella Ct. *TW10: Rich 6F 99*
(off Kings Mead)
Isabella Ho. SE11 5K 173
W6 5E 82
(off Queen Caroline St.)
Isabella Plantation ***4H 117***
Isabella Rd. E9 5J 51
Isabella St. SE1 1B 86 (5A 168)
Isabel St. SW9 1K 103
Isambard M. E14 3E 88
Isambard Pl. SE16 1J 87
Isard Ho. BR2: Short 1K 155
Isel Way SE22 5E 104
Isham Rd. SW16 2J 139
Isis Cl. HA4: Ruis 6E 22
SW15 4E 100
Isis Ct. W4 7H 81
Isis Ho. N18 6A 18
NW8 4B 158
(off Church St. Est.)
Isis St. SW18 2A 120
Island Farm Av.
KT8: W Mole 5D 132
Island Farm Rd.
KT8: W Mole 5D 132
Island Rd. CR4: Mitc 7D 120
Island Row E14 6B 70
Island, The KT7: T Ditt 6A 134
Isla Rd. SE18 6G 91
Islay Gdns. TW4: Houn 5B 96
Isleden Ho. *N1 1C 68*
(off Prebend St.)
Isledon Rd. N7 3A 50
ISLEDON VILLAGE 3A 50
Islehurst Cl. BR7: Chst 1E 144
ISLEWORTH 3A 98
Isleworth Bus. Complex
TW7: Isle 2K 97
Isleworth Prom.
TW1: Twick 4B 98
Isley Ct. SW8 2G 103
ISLINGTON 7B 50
Islington Crematorium
N2 1D 30
Islington Grn. N1 1B 68
Islington High St. N1 2A 68
(not continuous)
Islington Pk. M. N1 7B 50
Islington Pk. St. N1 7A 50
Islip Gdns. HA8: Edg 7E 12
UB5: N'olt 7C 42
Islip Mnr. Rd.
UB5: N'olt 7C 42
Islip St. NW5 5G 49
Ismailia Rd. E7 7K 53
Isobel Ho. HA1: Harr 5K 25
Isom Cl. E13 3K 71
Itaska Cotts.
WD23: Bush 1D 10
Ivanhoe Cl. UB8: Uxb 5A 58
Ivanhoe Dr. HA3: Harr 3A 26
Ivanhoe Ho. *E3 2A 70*
(off Grove Rd.)
Ivanhoe Rd. SE5 3F 105
TW4: Houn 3B 96
Ivatt Pl. W14 5H 83
Ivatt Way N17 3B 32
Iveagh Av. NW10 2G 63
Iveagh Cl. E9 1K 69
HA6: Nwood 1D 22
NW10 2G 63
Iveagh Ct. BR3: Beck 3E 142
EC3 1J 169
Iveagh Ho. SW9 2B 104
SW10 7A 84
(off King's Rd.)
Iveagh Ter. *NW10 2G 63*
(off Iveagh Av.)
Ivedon Rd.
DA16: Well 2C 110
Ive Farm Cl. E10 2C 52
Ive Farm La. E10 2C 52
Iveley Rd. SW4 2G 103
Ivere Dr. EN5: Barn 6E 4
Iverhurst Cl. DA6: Bex 5D 110
Iverna Ct. W8 3J 83
Iverna Gdns. TW14: Felt 5F 95
W8 3J 83
Iverson Rd. NW6 6H 47
Ivers Way CR0: Croy 7D 154
Ives Rd. E16 5G 71
Ives St. SW3 4C 84 (3D 170)
Ivestor Ter. SE23 7J 105
Ivimey St. E2 3G 69
Ivinghoe Cl. EN1: Enf 1K 7
Ivinghoe Ho. N7 5H 49
Ivinghoe Rd.
RM8: Dag 5B 56
Ivor Ct. N8 6J 31
NW1 3E 158
(off Gloucester Pl.)
Ivor Gro. SE9 1F 127
Ivories, The *N1 7C 50*
(off Northampton St.)
Ivor Pl. NW1 4D 66 (4E 158)
Ivor St. NW1 7G 49
Ivory Ct. TW13: Felt 2J 113
Ivorydown BR1: Brom 4J 125
Ivory Ho. E1 1F 87 (3K 169)
Ivory Sq. SW11 3A 102
Ivybridge Cl.
TW1: Twick 7A 98
UB8: Uxb 3A 58
Ivybridge Ct. *BR7: Chst 1E 144*
(off Old Hill)
NW1 7F 49
(off Lewis St.)
Ivybridge La.
WC2 7J 67 (3F 167)
Ivy Bri. Retail Pk.
TW7: Isle 5K 97
Ivychurch Cl. SE20 7J 123
Ivychurch La. SE17 5F 87
Ivy Cl. HA2: Harr 4D 42
HA5: Pinn 7A 24
TW16: Sun T 2A 132
Ivy Cotts. E14 7E 70
UB10: Uxb 3C 58
Ivy Ct. *SE16 5G 87*
(off Argyle Way)
Ivy Cres. W4 4J 81
Ivydale Rd. SE15 3K 105
SM5: Cars 2D 150
Ivyday Gro. SW16 3K 121
Ivydene KT8: W Mole 5D 132
Ivydene Cl. SM1: Sutt 4A 150
Ivy Gdns. CR4: Mitc 3H 139
N8 6J 31
Ivyhouse Rd. RM9: Dag 6D 56
UB10: Uxb 3D 40
Ivy La. TW4: Houn 4D 96
Ivymount Rd. SE27 3A 122
Ivy Rd. E16 6J 71
E17 6C 34
KT6: Surb 1G 147
N14 7B 6
NW2 4E 46
SE4 4B 106
SW17 5C 120
TW3: Houn 4F 97
Ivy St. N1 2E 68
Ivy Wlk. HA6: Nwood 1G 23
RM9: Dag 6E 56
Ixworth Pl.
SW3 5C 84 (5C 170)
Izane Rd. DA6: Bex 4F 111

J

Jacaranda Cl.
KT3: N Mald 3A 136
Jacaranda Gro. E8 7F 51
Jackass La. BR2: Kes 5K 155
Jack Barnett Way N22 2K 31
Jack Clow Rd. E15 2G 71
Jack Cook Ho. IG11: Bark 7F 55
Jack Cornwell St. E12 4E 54
Jack Dash Ho. *E14 2E 88*
(off Lawn Ho. Cl.)
Jack Dash Way E6 4C 72
Jackets La. HA6: Nwood 1D 22
Jack Goodchild Way
KT1: King T 3H 135
Jacklin Grn. IG8: Wfd G 4D 20
Jackman Ho. *E1 1H 87*
(off Watts St.)
Jackman M. NW2 3A 46
Jackman St. E8 1H 69
Jackson Cl. E9 7J 51
UB10: Uxb 7A 40
Jackson Ct. E7 6K 53
Jackson Rd. BR2: Short 2D 156
EN4: Barn 6H 5
IG11: Bark 1H 73
N7 4K 49
UB10: Uxb 7A 40
Jacksons La. N6 7E 30
Jacksons Pl. CR0: Croy 1D 152
Jackson St. SE18 6E 90
Jackson's Way
CR0: Croy 3C 154
Jackson Way UB2: S'hall 2F 79
Jack Walker Ct. N5 4B 50
Jacob Ho. *DA18: Erith 2D 92*
(off Kale Rd.)
Jacobin Lodge N7 5J 49
Jacobs Cl. RM10: Dag 4H 57
Jacobs Ho. *E13 3A 72*
(off New City Rd.)
Jacob St. SE1 2G 87 (6K 169)
Jacob's Well M.
W1 5E 66 (6H 159)
Jacotts Ho. *W10 4E 64*
(off Sutton Way)
Jacqueline Cl. UB5: N'olt 1C 60
Jacqueline Creft Ter. *N6 6E 30*
(off Grange Rd.)
Jacqueline Vs. *E17 5E 34*
(off Shernhall St.)
Jade Cl. E16 6B 72
NW2 7F 29
RM8: Dag 1C 56
Jade Ter. NW6 7A 48
Jaffe Rd. IG1: Ilf 1H 55
Jaffray Pl. SE27 4B 122
Jaffray Rd. BR2: Short 4B 144
Jaggard Way SW12 7D 102
Jagger Ho. *SW11 1D 102*
(off Rosenau Rd.)
Jago Cl. SE18 6G 91
Jago Wlk. SE5 7D 86
Jamaica Rd.
CR7: Thor H 6B 140
SE1 2F 87 (7K 169)
SE16 2F 87 (7K 169)
Jamaica St. E1 6J 69
James Anderson Ct. *E2 2E 68*
(off Kingsland Rd.)
James Av. NW2 5E 46
RM8: Dag 1F 57
James Bedford Cl.
HA5: Pinn 2A 24
James Boswell Cl.
SW16 4K 121
James Brine Ho. *E2 1K 163*
(off Ravenscroft St.)
James Campbell Ho. *E2 2J 69*
(off Old Ford Rd.)
James Cl. E13 2J 71
NW11 6G 29
James Collins Cl. W9 4H 65
James Ct. HA6: Nwood 1H 23
N1 1C 68
(off Raynor Pl.)
NW9 2A 28
UB5: N'olt 2C 60
(off Church Rd.)
James Docherty Ho. *E2 2H 69*
(off Patriot Sq.)
James Dudson Ct. NW10 7J 45
James Est. CR4: Mitc 2D 138
James Gdns. N22 7G 17
James Hammett Ho.
E2 1K 163
(off Ravenscroft St.)
James Ho. *E1 4A 70*
(off Solebay St.)
SE16 2K 87
(off Wolfe Cres.)
James Joyce Wlk. SE24 4B 104
James La. E10 7E 34
E11 6F 35
James Lind Ho. *SE8 4B 88*
(off Grove St.)
James Middleton Ho. *E2 3H 69*
(off Middleton St.)
James Newman Ct. SE9 3E 126
Jameson Cl. W3 2J 81
Jameson Ct. *E2 2J 69*
(off Russia La.)
Jameson Ho. *SE11 5G 173*
(off Glasshouse Wlk.)
Jameson Lodge N6 6G 31
Jameson St. W8 1J 83
James Pl. N17 1F 33
James's Cotts. TW9: Rich 7G 81
James Stewart Ho. NW6 7H 47
James St. EN1: Enf 5A 8
IG11: Bark 7G 55
TW3: Houn 3H 97
W1 6E 66 (1H 165)
WC2 7J 67 (1F 167)
James Stroud Ho.
SE17 5C 86
(off Bronti Cl.)
James Ter. *SW14 3K 99*
(off Church Path)
James Terry Ct.
CR2: S Croy 5C 152
(off Warham Rd.)
Jamestown Rd. NW1 1F 67
Jamestown Way E14 7F 71
James Yd. E4 6A 20
Jamieson Ho. TW4: Houn 6D 96
Jamilah Ho. *E16 7E 72*
(off University Way)
Jamuna Cl. E14 5A 70
Jane Austen Hall *E16 1K 89*
(off Wesley Av.)
Jane Austen Ho. *SW1 6A 172*
(off Churchill Gdns.)
Jane Seymour Ct.
SE9 7H 109
Jane St. E1 6H 69
Janet St. E14 3C 88
Janeway Pl. SE16 2H 87
Janeway St. SE16 2G 87
Janice M. IG1: Ilf 2F 55
Jansen Wlk. SW11 3B 102
Janson Cl. E15 5G 53
NW10 3A 46
Janson Rd. E15 5G 53
Jansons Rd. N15 3E 32
Japan Cres. N4 1K 49
Japan Rd. RM6: Chad H 6D 38
Jardine Rd. E1 7K 69

Jarman Ho.—Jones Wlk.

Jarman Ho. E1 5J 69
(off Jubilee St.)
SE16 4K 87
(off Hawkstone Rd.)
Jarrett Cl. SW2 1B 122
Jarrow Cl.
SM4: Mord 5K 137
Jarrow Rd. N17 4H 33
RM6: Chad H 6C 38
SE16 4J 87
Jarrow Way E9 4B 52
Jarvis Cl. EN5: Barn 5A 4
IG11: Bark 1H 73
Jarvis Rd. CR2: S Croy 6D 152
SE22 4E 104
Jashoda Ho. SE18 5E 90
(off Connaught M.)
Jasmin Cl. HA6: Nwood 1H 23
Jasmin Ct. SE12 6H 107
Jasmine Cl. IG1: Ilf 5F 55
UB1: S'hall 7C 60
Jasmine Ct. SW19 5J 119
Jasmine Gdns.
CR0: Croy 3D 154
HA2: Harr 2E 42
Jasmine Gro. SE20 1H 141
Jasmine Rd. RM7: Rush G 2K 57
Jasmine Ter. UB7: W Dray 2C 76
Jasmine Way KT8: E Mos 4J 133
Jasmin Lodge SE16 5H 87
(off Sherwood Gdns.)
Jasmin Rd. KT19: Eps 5H 147
Jason Ct. SW9 1A 104
(off Southey Rd.)
W1 7H 159
Jason Wlk. SE9 4E 126
Jasper Cl. EN3: Enf 1D 8
Jasper Pas. SE19 6F 123
Jasper Rd. E16 6B 72
SE19 5F 123
Jasper Wlk. N1 3D 68
Java Wharf SE1 6K 169
(off Shad Thames)
Javelin Way UB5: N'olt 3B 60
Jaycroft EN2: Enf 1F 7
Jay Gdns. BR7: Chst 4D 126
Jay M. SW7 2A 84 (7A 164)
Jazzfern Ter. HA0: Wemb 5A 44
Jean Batten Cl.
SM6: Wall 7K 151
Jean Darling Ho. SW10 6B 84
(off Milman's St.)
Jean Pardies Ho. E1 5J 69
(off Jubilee St.)
Jebb Av. SW2 6J 103
(not continuous)
Jebb St. E3 2C 70
Jedburgh Rd. E13 3A 72
Jedburgh St. SW11 4E 102
Jeddo M. W3 2B 82
Jeddo Rd. W12 2B 82
Jefferson Bldg. E14 2C 88
Jefferson Cl. IG2: Ilf 5F 37
W13 3B 80
Jefferson Wlk. SE18 6E 90
Jeffrey Row SE12 5K 107
Jeffrey's Pl. NW1 7G 49
Jeffreys Rd. EN3: Enf 4F 9
SW4 2J 103
Jeffrey's St. NW1 7G 49
Jeffries Ho. NW10 7K 45
Jeffs Cl. TW12: Hamp 6F 115
Jeffs Rd. SM1: Sutt 4H 149
Jeger Av. E2 1F 69
Jeken Rd. SE9 4A 108
Jelf Rd. SW2 5A 104
Jellicoe Gdns. HA7: Stan 6E 10
Jellicoe Ho. E2 2G 69
(off Ropley St.)
NW1 4F 67
Jellicoe Rd. E13 4J 71
N17 7J 17
Jemmett Cl.
KT2: King T 1H 135
Jemotts Ct. SE14 6K 87
(off Myers La.)
Jem Paterson Ct.
HA1: Harr 4J 43
Jengar Cl. SM1: Sutt 4K 149
Jenkins La. IG11: Bark 2G 73
Jenkinson Ho. E2 3K 69
(off Usk St.)
Jenkins Rd. E13 4K 71
Jenner Av. W3 5K 63
Jenner Ho. SE3 6G 89
(off Restell Cl.)
WC1 3F 161
(off Hunter St.)
Jenner Pl. SW13 6D 82
Jenner Rd. N16 3F 51
Jennett Rd. CR0: Croy 3A 152
Jennifer Ho. SE11 4K 173
(off Reedworth St.)
Jennifer Rd. BR1: Brom 3H 125
Jenningsbury Ho. SW3 5D 170
(off Cale St.)
Jennings Cl. KT6: Surb 7C 134
Jennings Ho. SE10 5F 89
(off Old Woolwich Rd.)
Jennings Rd. SE22 6F 105
Jennings Way EN5: Barn 3A 4
Jenningtree Way
DA17: Belv 2J 93
Jenny Hammond Cl. E11 3H 53
Jenson Way SE19 7F 123
Jenton Av. DA7: Bex 1E 110
Jephson Ct. SW4 2J 103
Jephson Ho. SE17 6B 86
(off Doddington Gro.)
Jephson Rd. E7 7A 54
Jephson St. SE5 1D 104
Jephtha Rd. SW18 6J 101
Jeppos La. CR4: Mitc 4D 138
Jepson Ho. SW6 1K 101
(off Pearscroft Rd.)
Jerdan Pl. SW6 7J 83
Jeremiah St. E14 6D 70
Jeremy Bentham Ho. E2 3G 69
(off Mansford St.)
Jeremy's Grn. N18 4C 18
Jermyn St.
SW1 1G 85 (4A 166)
Jermyn Street Theatre 3C 166
(off Jermyn St.)
Jerningham Av. IG5: Ilf 2F 37
Jerningham Ct. SE14 1A 106
Jerningham Rd. SE14 2A 106
Jerome Cres.
NW8 4C 66 (3C 158)
Jerome Ho. KT1: King T 2D 134
(off Old Bri. St.)
NW1 5D 158
(off Lisson Gro.)
SW7 3A 170
(off Glendower Pl.)
Jerome St. E1 4F 69 (5J 163)
Jerome Twr. W3 2H 81
Jerrard St. SE13 3D 106
Jerrold St. N1 2E 68 (1H 163)
Jersey Av. HA7: Stan 2B 26
Jersey Dr. BR5: Orp 6H 145
Jersey Ho. EN3: Enf 1E 8
(off Eastfield Rd.)
N1 6C 50
Jersey Rd. E11 1F 53
E16 6A 72
IG1: Ilf 4F 55
N1 6C 50
SW17 6F 121
TW3: Houn 1F 97
W7 2A 80
Jersey St. E2 3H 69
Jerusalem Pas.
EC1 4B 68 (4A 162)
Jervis Bay Ho. E14 6F 71
(off Blair St.)
Jervis Ct. RM10: Dag 6H 57
SE10 1E 106
(off Blissett St.)
W1 1K 165
Jerviston Gdns. SW16 6A 122
Jerwood Space Art Gallery
6C 168
Jesmond Av. HA9: Wemb 6F 45
Jesmond Cl. CR4: Mitc 3F 139
Jesmond Rd. CR0: Croy 7F 141
Jesmond Way HA7: Stan 5K 11
Jessam Av. E5 1H 51
Jessamine Rd. W7 1K 79
Jessel Ho. SW1 3D 172
(off Page St.)
WC1 2E 160
(off Judd St.)
Jessel Mans. W14 6G 83
(off Queen's Club Gdns.)
Jesse Rd. E10 1E 52
Jessett Cl. DA8: Erith 4K 93
Jessica Rd. SW18 6A 102
Jessie Blythe La. N19 7J 31
Jessie Wood Ct. SW9 7A 86
(off Caldwell St.)
Jessiman Ter.
TW17: Shep 5C 130
Jesson Ho. SE17 4D 86
(off Orb St.)
Jessop Av. UB2: S'hall 4D 78
Jessop Ct. N1 2B 68
Jessop Rd. SE24 4B 104
Jessop Sq. E14 1C 88
(off Heron Quay)
Jessops Way CR0: Croy 6G 139
Jessup Cl. SE18 4G 91
Jetstar Way UB5: N'olt 3C 60
Jevington Way SE12 1K 125
Jewel House
in Tower of London, The
7F 69
Jewel Rd. E17 3C 34
Jewel Tower 1E 172
(off College M.)
Jewish Mus.
Albert St. 1F 67
E. End Rd. 2K 29
Jewry St. EC3 6F 69 (1J 169)
Jew's Row SW18 4K 101
Jews' Wlk. SE26 4H 123
Jeymer Av. NW2 5D 46
Jeymer Dr. UB6: G'frd 1F 61
(not continuous)
Jeypore Pas. SW18 6A 102
Jeypore Rd. SW18 7A 102
Jillian Cl. TW12: Hamp 7E 114
Jim Bradley Cl. SE18 4E 90
Jim Griffiths Ho. SW6 6H 83
(off Clem Attlee Ct.)
Joan Bicknell Cen., The 2B 120
Joan Cres. SE9 7B 108
Joan Gdns. RM8: Dag 2E 56
Joanna Ho. W6 5E 82
(off Queen Caroline St.)
Joan Rd. RM8: Dag 2E 56
Joan St. SE1 1B 86 (5A 168)
Jocelin Ho. N1 1K 67
(off Barnsbury Est.)
Jocelyn Rd. TW9: Rich 3E 98
Jocelyn St. SE15 1G 105
Jockey's Flds.
WC1 5K 67 (5H 161)
Jodane St. SE8 4B 88
Jodrell Cl. TW7: Isle 1A 98
Jodrell Rd. E3 1B 70
Joe Hunte Ct. SE27 5B 122
Joel St. HA5: Pinn 3J 23
HA6: Nwood, Pinn 2J 23
Johanna St. SE1 2A 86 (7J 167)
John Adams Ct. N9 2A 18
John Adam St.
WC2 7J 67 (3F 167)
John Aird Ct. W2 5A 158
(not continuous)
John Archer Way SW18 6B 102
John Ashby Cl. SW2 6J 103
John Austin Cl.
KT2: King T 1F 135
John Baird Ct. SE26 4J 123
John Barker Ct. NW6 7G 47
(off Brondesbury Pk.)
John Barnes Wlk. E15 6H 53
John Betts' Ho. W12 3B 82
John Bradshaw Rd. N14 1C 16
John Brent Ho. SE8 4K 87
(off Bush Rd.)
John Buck Ho. NW10 1B 64
John Burns Dr. IG11: Bark 7J 55
John Campbell Rd. N16 5E 50
John Carpenter St.
EC4 7B 68 (2A 168)
John Cartwright Ho. E2 3H 69
(off Old Bethnal Grn. Rd.)
John Drinkwater Cl. E11 7H 35
John Felton Rd. SE16 2G 87
John Fielden Ho. E2 3H 69
(off Canrobert St.)
John Fisher St.
E1 7G 69 (2K 169)
John Goddard Way
TW13: Felt 2K 113
John Gooch Dr. EN2: Enf 1G 7
John Harrison Way SE10 3H 89
John Islip St.
SW1 4H 85 (5D 172)
John Kennedy Ct. N1 6D 50
(off Newington Grn. Rd.)
John Kennedy Ho. SE16 4K 87
(off Rotherhithe Old Rd.)
John Kirk Ho. E6 6E 72
(off Pearl Cl.)
John Knight Lodge SW6 7J 83
John Lamb Ct. HA3: Harr 1J 25
John McDonald Ho. E14 3E 88
(off Glengall Gro.)
John McKenna Wlk. SE16 3G 87
John Masefield Ho. N15 6D 32
(off Fladbury Rd.)
John Maurice Cl. SE17 4D 86
John Newton Ct.
DA16: Well 3B 110
John Orwell Sports Cen. 1H 87
John Parker Cl.
RM10: Dag 7H 57
John Parker Sq. SW11 3B 102
John Parry Ct. N1 2E 68
(off Hare Wlk.)
John Penn Ho. SE14 7B 88
(off Amersham Va.)
John Penn St. SE13 1D 106
John Perrin Pl. HA3: Harr 7E 26
John Pound Ho. SW18 7K 101
John Prince's St.
W1 6F 67 (7K 159)
John Pritchard Ho. E1 4G 69
(off Buxton St.)
John Ratcliffe Ho. NW6 3J 65
(off Chippenham Gdns.)
John Rennie Wlk. E1 7H 69
John Roll Way SE16 3G 87
John Ruskin St. SE5 7B 86
John's Av. NW4 4E 28
John's Cl. TW15: Ashf 4E 112
John's Ct. SM2: Sutt 6K 149
John Scurr Ho. E14 6A 70
(off Ratcliffe La.)
John Silkin La. SE8 5K 87
John's La. SM4: Mord 5A 138
John's M. WC1 4K 67 (4H 161)
John Smith Av. SW6 7H 83
John Smith M. E14 7F 71
Johnson Cl. E8 1G 69
Johnson Ho. E2 3G 69
(off Roberta St.)
NW1 2G 67
(off Cranleigh St.)
NW3 7D 48
(off Adelaide Rd.)
SW1 4H 171
(off Cundy St.)
SW8 7H 85
(off Wandsworth Rd.)
Johnson Lodge W2 5J 65
(off Admiral Wlk.)
Johnson Mans. W14 6G 83
(off Queen's Club Gdns.)
Johnson Rd. BR2: Short 5B 144
CR0: Croy 7D 140
NW10 1K 63
TW5: Houn 7A 78
Johnsons Cl. SM5: Cars 2D 150
Johnson's Ct. EC4 6A 68
Johnsons Dr.
TW12: Hamp 1G 133
Johnsons Ind. Est.
UB3: Hayes 2H 77
Johnson's Pl.
SW1 5G 85 (6A 172)
Johnson St. E1 7J 69
UB2: S'hall 3A 78
Johnsons Way NW10 4H 63
John Spencer Sq. N1 6B 50
John's Pl. E1 6H 69
John's Ter. CR0: Croy 1E 152
Johnston Cl. SW9 1K 103
Johnstone Ho. SE13 3F 107
(off Belmont Hill)
Johnstone Rd. E6 3D 72
Johnston Rd. IG8: Wfd G 6D 20
Johnston Ter. NW2 3F 47
John Strachey Ho. SW6 6H 83
(off Clem Attlee Ct.)
John St. E15 1H 71
EN1: Enf 5A 8
SE25 4G 141
TW3: Houn 2C 96
WC1 4K 67 (4H 161)
John Strype Ct. E10 1D 52
John Trundle Ct. EC2 5C 162
John Trundle Highwalk
EC2 5C 162
(off Beech St.)
John Tucker Ho. E14 3C 88
(off Mellish St.)
John Watkin Cl.
KT19: Eps 7H 147
John Wesley Ct.
TW1: Twick 1A 116
John Wesley Highwalk
EC1 6C 162
(off Barbican)
John Wheatley Ho. SW6 6H 83
(off Clem Attlee Ct.)
John Williams Cl.
KT2: King T 1D 134
SE14 6K 87
John Wilson St. SE18 3E 90
John Woolley Cl. SE13 4G 107
Joiners Arms Yd. SE5 1D 104
Joiners Pl. N5 4D 50
Joiner St. SE1 1D 86 (5F 169)
Joiners Yd. N1 1F 161
(off Caledonia St.)
Joint Rd. N2 1C 30
Jollys La. HA2: Harr 1H 43
UB4: Hayes 5B 60
Jonathan St.
SE11 5K 85 (5G 173)
Jones Ho. E14 6F 71
(off Blair St.)
Jones M. SW15 4G 101
Jones Rd. E13 4K 71
Jones St. W1 7F 67 (3J 165)
Jones Wlk. TW10: Rich 6F 99

274 A-Z London

Jonquil Gdns.—Kelvi

Jonquil Gdns.
TW12: Hamp 6E 114
Jonson Cl. CR4: Mitc 4F 139
UB4: Hayes 5J 59
Jonson Ho. SE1 ....3D 86
(off Burbage Cl.)
Jordan Cl. HA2: Harr 3D 42
RM10: Dag 4H 57
Jordan Ho. N1 ....1D 68
(off Colville Est.)
SE4 ....4K 105
(off St Norbert Rd.)
Jordan Rd. UB6: G'frd 1B 62
Jordans Cl. TW7: Isle 1J 97
Jordans Ho. NW8 ....3B 158
Jordans M. TW2: Twick 2J 115
Joscoyne Ho. E1 ....6H 69
(off Philpot St.)
Joseph Av. W3 ....6K 63
Joseph Conrad Ho. SW1 ....4B 172
(off Tachbrook St.)
Joseph Ct. N15 ....6E 32
(off Amhurst Pk.)
N16 ....7E 32
(off Amhurst Pk.)
Joseph Hardcastle Cl.
SE14 ....7K 87
Josephine Av. SW2 ....5K 103
Joseph Irwin Ho. E14 ....7B 70
(off Gill St.)
Joseph Lister Ct. E7 ....7J 53
Joseph Powell Cl. SW12 ....6F 103
Joseph Priestley Ho. E2 ....3H 69
(off Canrobert St.)
Joseph Ray Rd. E11 ....2G 53
Joseph St. E3 ....4B 70
Joseph Trotter Cl. EC1 ....2K 161
Joshua Cl. CR2: S Croy 7B 152
Joshua St. E14 ....6E 70
Joslings Cl. W12 ....7C 64
Joslyn Cl. EN3: Enf 1H 9
Josseline Ct. E3 ....2A 70
(off Ford St.)
Joubert St. SW11 ....2D 102
Jowett St. SE15 ....7F 87
Jowitt Ho. E2 ....3K 69
(off Morpeth St.)
Joyce Av. N18 ....5A 18
Joyce Butler Ho. N22 ....1K 31
Joyce Dawson Way SE28 ....7A 74
Joyce Page Cl. SE7 ....6B 90
Joyce Wlk. SW2 ....6A 104
JOYDENS WOOD 4K 129
Joydens Wood (Nature Reserve)
....4H 129
Joydens Wood Rd.
DA5: Bexl 4K 129
Joydon Dr. RM6: Chad H 6B 38
Joyners Cl. RM9: Dag 4F 57
Joystone Ct. EN4: Barn 4H 5
(off Park Rd.)
Jubb Powell Ho. N15 ....6E 32
Jubilee Av. E4 ....6K 19
RM7: Rom 5H 39
TW2: Twick 1G 115
Jubilee Bldgs. NW8 ....1B 66
Jubilee Cl. HA5: Pinn 2A 24
KT1: King T 1C 134
NW9 ....6K 27
RM7: Rom 5H 39
Jubilee Ct. HA3: Harr 7E 26
N10 ....3E 30
TW3: Houn 3G 97
(off Bristow Rd.)
Jubilee Cres. E14 ....3E 88
N9 ....1B 18
Jubilee Dr. HA4: Ruis 4B 42
Jubilee Gdns. UB1: S'hall 5E 60
Jubilee Ho. HA7: Stan 5J 11
SE11 ....4K 173
(off Reedworth St.)
WC1 ....3G 161
Jubilee Mans. E1 ....6J 69
(off Jubilee St.)
Jubilee Mkt. IG8: Wfd G 6F 21
Jubilee Pde. IG8: Wfd G 6F 21
Jubilee Pl.
SW3 ....5C 84 (5D 170)
Jubilee Rd. SM3: Sutt 7F 149
UB6: G'frd 1B 62
Jubilee St. E1 ....6J 69
Jubilee, The SE10 ....7D 88
Jubilee Vs. KT10: Esh 7H 133
Jubilee Walkway
SE1 ....7B 68 (3B 168)
Jubilee Way
DA14: Sidc 2A 128
KT9: Chess 4G 147
SW19 ....1K 137
TW14: Felt 1J 113
Jubilee Yd. SE1 ....6J 169
Judd St. WC1 ....3J 67 (2E 160)
Jude St. E16 ....6H 71
Judge Heath La.
UB3: Hayes 6E 58
Judges Wlk. NW3 ....3A 48
Juer Ho. SW11 ....7C 84
(off Juer St.)
Juer St. SW11 ....7C 84
Jules Thorn Av. EN1: Enf 4B 8
Julia Ct. E17 ....5D 34
Julia Gdns. IG11: Bark 2D 74
Julia Garfield M. E16 ....1K 89
Juliana Cl. N2 ....2A 30
Julian Av. W3 ....7H 63
Julian Cl. EN5: Barn 3E 4
Julian Hill HA1: Harr 2J 43
Julian Pl. E14 ....5D 88
Julian Taylor Path SE23 ....2H 123
Julia St. NW5 ....4E 48
Julien Rd. W5 ....3C 80
Juliet Ho. N1 ....2E 68
(off Arden Est.)
Juliette Rd. E13 ....2J 71
Julius Nyerere Cl. N1 ....1K 67
(off Copenhagen St.)
Junction App. SE13 ....3E 106
SW11 ....3C 102
Junction Av. NW10 ....4E 64
Junction M. W2 ....6C 66 (7C 158)
Junction Pl. W2 ....7B 158
Junction Rd.
CR2: S Croy 5D 152
E13 ....2K 71
HA1: Harr 6J 25
Junction Rd. N9 ....1B 18
N17 ....3G 33
N19 ....4G 49
TW15: Ashf 5E 112
W5 ....4C 80
Junction Rd. E.
RM6: Chad H 7E 38
Junction Rd. W.
RM6: Chad H 7E 38
Juniper Cl. EN5: Barn 5A 4
HA9: Wemb 5G 45
KT9: Chess 5F 147
Juniper Ct. HA3: Harr 1K 25
HA6: Nwood 1J 23
RM6: Chad H 6B 38
TW3: Houn 4F 97
(off Grove Rd.)
W8 ....3K 83
(off St Mary's Pl.)
Juniper Cres. NW1 ....7E 48
Juniper Gdns. SW16 ....1G 139
TW16: Sun T 6H 113
Juniper Ho. SE15 ....7J 87
W10 ....4G 65
(off Fourth Av.)
Juniper La. E6 ....5C 72
Juniper Rd. IG1: Ilf 3E 54
Juniper St. E1 ....7J 69
Juniper Way UB3: Hayes 7F 59
Juno Ct. SW9 ....7A 86
(off Caldwell St.)
Juno Way SE14 ....6K 87
Juno Way Ind. Est. SE14 ....6K 87
Jupiter Ct. SW9 ....7A 86
(off Caldwell St.)
UB5: N'olt 3B 60
(off Seasprite Cl.)
Jupiter Hgts. UB10: Uxb 1B 58
Jupiter Ho. E14 ....5D 88
(off St Davids Sq.)
Jupiter Way N7 ....6K 49
Jupp Rd. E15 ....7F 53
Jupp Rd. W. E15 ....1F 71
Jura Ho. SE16 ....4K 87
(off Plough Way)
Jurston Ct. SE1 ....7K 167
Justice Wlk. SW3 ....7C 170
Justin Cl. TW8: Bford 7D 80
Justin Rd. E4 ....6G 19
Jute La. EN3: Enf 2F 9
(not continuous)
Jutland Cl. N19 ....1J 49
Jutland Ho. SE5 ....2C 104
Jutland Rd. E13 ....4J 71
SE6 ....7E 106
Jutsums Av. RM7: Rom 6H 39
Jutsums Ct. RM7: Rom 6H 39
Jutsums La.
RM7: Rom, Rush G 6H 39
Juxon Cl. HA3: Harr 1F 25
Juxon St. SE11 ....4K 85 (3H 173)
JVC Bus. Pk. NW2 ....1C 46

K

Kaduna Cl. HA5: Pinn 5J 23
Kale Rd. DA18: Erith 2D 92
Kambala Rd. SW11 ....3B 102
Kangley Bri. Rd. SE26 ....6B 124
Kangley Bus. Cen. SE26 ....5B 124
Kaplan Dr. N21 ....5E 6
Kara Way NW2 ....4F 47
Karen Ct. BR1: Brom 1H 143
Karen Ter. E11 ....2H 53
Kariba Cl. N9 ....3D 18
Karoline Gdns.
UB6: G'frd 2H 61
Kashgar Rd. SE18 ....4K 91
Kashmir Rd. SE7 ....7B 90
Kassala Rd. SW11 ....1D 102
Katella Trad. Est.
IG11: Bark 3J 73
Katharine Ho. CR0: Croy 3C 152
(off Katharine St.)
Katharine St. CR0: Croy 3C 152
Katherine Cl. SE16 ....1K 87
Katherine Ct. SE23 ....1H 123
Katherine Gdns. SE9 ....4B 108
Katherine Rd. E6 ....5A 54
E7 ....5A 54
TW1: Twick 1A 116
Katherine Sq. W11 ....1G 83
Kathleen Av. HA0: Wemb 7E 44
W3 ....5J 63
Kathleen Godfree Ct.
SW19 ....6J 119
Kathleen Rd. SW11 ....3D 102
Kayemoor Rd. SM2: Sutt 6B 150
Kay Rd. SW9 ....2J 103
Kay St. DA16: Well 1B 110
E2 ....2G 69
E15 ....7F 53
Kay Ter. E18 ....1H 35
Kay Way SE10 ....7E 88
(off Greenwich High Rd.)
Kean Ho. SE17 ....6B 86
TW1: Twick 6D 98
(off Arosa Rd.)
Kean St. WC2 ....6K 67 (1G 167)
Keatley Grn. E4 ....6G 19
Keats Av. E16 ....1K 89
Keats Cl. E11 ....5K 35
EN3: Enf 5E 8
NW3 ....4C 48
SE1 ....4F 87
SW19 ....6B 120
UB4: Hayes 5J 59
Keat's Gro. NW3 ....4C 48
Keats House 4C 48
Keats Ho. DA1: Cray 5K 111
E2 ....3J 69
(off Roman Rd.)
SE5 ....7C 86
(off Elmington Est.)
SW1 ....7B 172
(off Churchill Gdns.)
Keats Pde. N9 ....2B 18
(off Church St.)
Keats Pl. EC2 ....6E 162
(off Moorfields)
Keats Rd. DA16: Well 1J 109
DA17: Belv 3J 93
Keats Way CR0: Croy 6J 141
UB6: G'frd 5F 61
UB7: W Dray 4B 76
Kebbell Ter. E7 ....5K 53
(off Claremont Rd.)
Keble Cl. KT4: Wor Pk 1B 148
UB5: N'olt 5G 43
Keble Pl. SW13 ....6D 82
Keble St. SW17 ....4A 120
Kechill Gdns. BR2: Short 7J 143
Kedeston Ct. SM1: Sutt 1K 149
Kedge Ho. E14 ....3C 88
(off Tiller Rd.)
Kedleston Dr. BR5: Orp 6K 145
Kedleston Wlk. E2 ....3H 69
Kedyngton Ho. HA8: Edg 2J 27
(off Burnt Oak B'way.)
Keeble Cl. SE18 ....6F 91
Keedonwood Rd.
BR1: Brom 5G 125
Keel Cl. IG11: Bark 2C 74
SE16 ....1K 87
Keeley Rd. CR0: Croy 2C 152
Keeley St. WC2 ....6K 67 (1G 167)
Keeling Ho. E2 ....2H 69
(off Claredale St.)
Keeling Rd. SE9 ....5B 108
Keely Cl. EN4: Barn 5H 5
Keemor Cl. SE18 ....7E 90
Keens Cl. SW16 ....5H 121
Keens Rd. CR0: Croy 4C 152
Keen's Yd. N1 ....6B 50
Keepers Ct.
CR2: S Croy 5C 152
(off Warham Rd.)
Keepers M. TW11: Tedd 6C 116
Keepier Wharf E14 ....7K 69
(off Narrow St.)
Keep, The KT2: King T 6F 117
SE3 ....2J 107
Keeton's Rd. SE16 ....3H 87
(not continuous)
Keevil Dr. SW19 ....7F 101
Keighley Cl. N7 ....5J 49
Keightley Dr. SE9 ....1G 127
Keilder Cl. UB10: Uxb 2C 58
Keildon Rd. SW11 ....4D 102
Keir Hardie Ct. NW10 ....7B 46
Keir Hardie Est. E5 ....1H 51
Keir Hardie Ho. N19 ....7H 31
W6 ....6F 83
(off Fulham Pal. Rd.)
Keir Hardie Way
IG11: Bark 7A 56
UB4: Hayes 3J 59
Keir, The SW19 ....5E 118
Keith Connor Cl. SW8 ....3F 103
Keith Gro. W12 ....2C 82
Keith Ho. W9 ....3K 65
(off Carlton Va.)
Keith Pk. Rd. UB10: Uxb ..
Keith Rd. E17 ....
IG11: Bark 2H 73
UB3: Hayes 3G 77
Kelbrook Rd. SE3 ....2C 108
Kelby Ho. N7 ....6K 49
(off Sutterton St.)
Kelby Path SE9 ....3F 127
Kelceda Cl. NW2 ....2C 46
Kelf Gro. UB3: Hayes 6H 59
Kelfield Ct. W10 ....6F 65
Kelfield Gdns. W10 ....6E 64
Kelfield M. W10 ....6F 65
Kelland Cl. N8 ....5H 31
Kelland Rd. E13 ....4J 71
Kellaway Rd. SE3 ....2B 108
Keller Cres. E12 ....4B 54
Kellerton Rd. SE13 ....5G 107
Kellet Ho's. WC1 ....2F 161
(off Tankerton St.)
Kellett Ho. N1 ....1E 68
(off Colville Est.)
Kellett Rd. SW2 ....4A 104
Kelling Gdns. CR0: Croy 7B 140
Kellino St. SW17 ....4D 120
Kellner Rd. SE28 ....3K 91
Kellogg Twr. UB6: G'frd 5J 43
Kellow Ho. SE1 ....6E 168
(off Tennis St.)
Kell St. SE1 ....3B 86 (7B 168)
Kelly Av. SE15 ....7F 87
Kelly Cl. NW10 ....3K 45
TW17: Shep 2G 131
Kelly Ct. E14 ....7C 70
(off Garford St.)
Kelly M. W9 ....4H 65
Kelly Rd. NW7 ....6B 14
Kelly St. NW1 ....6F 49
Kelly Way RM6: Chad H 5E 38
Kelman Cl. SW4 ....2H 103
Kelmore Gro. SE22 ....4G 105
Kelmscott Cl. E17 ....1B 34
Kelmscott Gdns. W12 ....3C 82
Kelmscott Rd. SW11 ....5C 102
Kelross Pas. N5 ....4C 50
Kelross Rd. N5 ....4C 50
Kelsall Cl. SE3 ....2K 107
Kelsey Ga. BR3: Beck 2D 142
Kelsey La. BR3: Beck 2C 142
(not continuous)
Kelsey Pk. Av. BR3: Beck 2D 142
(not continuous)
Kelsey Pk. Rd.
BR3: Beck 2C 142
Kelsey Sq. BR3: Beck 2C 142
Kelsey St. E2 ....4G 69
Kelsey Way BR3: Beck 3C 142
Kelson Ho. E14 ....3E 88
Kelso Pl. W8 ....3K 83
Kelso Rd. SM5: Cars 7A 138
Kelston Rd. IG6: Ilf 2F 37
Kelvedon Cl. KT2: King T 6G 117
Kelvedon Ho. SW8 ....1J 103
Kelvedon Rd. SW6 ....7H 83
Kelvedon Way IG8: Wfd G 6J 21
Kelvin Av. N13 ....6E 16
TW11: Tedd 6J 115
Kelvinbrook KT8: W Mole 3F 133
Kelvin Cl. KT19: Eps 6G 147
Kelvin Ct. SE20 ....1H 141
TW7: Isle 2J 97
W11 ....7J 65
Kelvin Cres. HA3: Harr 7D 10
Kelvin Dr. TW1: Twick 6B 98
Kelvin Gdns. CR0: Croy 7J 139
UB1: S'hall 6E 60
Kelvin Gro. KT9: Chess 3D 146
SE26 ....3H 123
Kelvington Cl. CR0: Croy 7A 142
Kelvington Rd. SE15 ....5K 105
Kelvin Rd. DA16: Well 3A 110
N5 ....4C 50

Kember St.—Kentwell Cl.

Kember St. N1 ....7K **49**
Kemble Ct. *SE15* *7E 86*
(off Lydney Cl.)
Kemble Dr. BR2: Short 3C **156**
Kemble Ho. *SW9* *3B 104*
(off Barrington Rd.)
Kemble Rd. CR0: Croy 3B **152**
N17 ....1G **33**
SE23 ....1K **123**
Kemble St.
WC2 ....6K **67** (1G **167**)
Kemerton Rd.
BR3: Beck 2D **142**
CR0: Croy 7F **141**
SE5 ....3C **104**
Kemeys St. E9 ....5A **52**
Kemnal Rd. BR7: Chst 4H **127**
(not continuous)
Kemp *NW9* *1B 28*
(off Concourse, The)
Kemp Ct. *SW8* *7J 85*
(off Hartington Rd.)
Kempe Ho. *SE1* *3D 86*
(off Burge St.)
Kempe Rd. NW6 ....2F **65**
Kemp Gdns. CR0: Croy 6C **140**
Kemp Ho. E6 ....6E **54**
E9 ....*2K 69*
(off Sewardstone Rd.)
W1 ....*2C 166*
(off Berwick St.)
Kempis Way SE22 ....5E **104**
Kemplay Rd. NW3 ....4B **48**
Kemp Rd. RM8: Dag 1D **56**
Kemps Ct. *W1* *1C 166*
(off Hopkins St.)
Kemps Dr. E14 ....7C **70**
HA6: Nwood 1H **23**
Kempsford Gdns. SW5 ....5J **83**
Kempsford Rd.
SE11 ....4A **86** (4K **173**)
(not continuous)
Kemps Gdns. SE13 ....5E **106**
Kempshott Rd. SW16 ....7H **121**
Kempson Rd. SW6 ....1J **101**
Kempthorne Rd. SE8 ....4B **88**
Kempton Av.
TW16: Sun T 1K **131**
UB5: N'olt 6E **42**
Kempton Cl. DA8: Erith 6J **93**
UB10: Uxb 4E **40**
Kempton Ct. E1 ....5H **69**
TW16: Sun T 1K **131**
Kempton Park Racecourse
****....7A 114****
Kempton Rd. E6 ....1D **72**
TW12: Hamp 2D **132**
(not continuous)
Kempton Wlk. CR0: Croy 6A **142**
Kempt St. SE18 ....6E **90**
Kemsing Cl. BR2: Short 2H **155**
CR7: Thor H 4C **140**
DA5: Bexl 7E **110**
Kemsing Ho. *SE1* *7F 169*
(off Long La.)
Kemsing Rd. SE10 ....5J **89**
Kemsley SE13 ....5D **106**
Kemsley Ct. W13 ....1C **80**
Kenbrook Ho. W14 ....3H **83**
Kenbury Cl. UB10: Uxb 3C **40**
Kenbury Gdns. SE5 ....2C **104**
Kenbury Mans. *SE5* *2C 104*
(off Kenbury St.)
Kenbury St. SE5 ....2C **104**
Kenchester Cl. SW8 ....7J **85**
Kencot Way DA18: Erith 2F **93**
Kendal *NW1* *1K 159*
(off Augustus St.)
Kendal Av. IG11: Bark 1J **73**
N18 ....4J **17**
W3 ....4G **63**
(not continuous)
Kendal Cl. IG8: Wfd G 2C **20**
SW9 ....7B **86**
TW14: Felt 1H **113**
UB4: Hayes 2G **59**
Kendal Ct. W3 ....5G **63**
Kendale Rd. BR1: Brom 5G **125**
Kendal Gdns. N18 ....4J **17**
SM1: Sutt 2A **150**
Kendal Ho. E9 ....1J **69**
N1 ....*2K 67*
(off Priory Grn. Est.)
SE20 ....*2G 141*
(off Derwent Rd.)
Kendall Av. BR3: Beck 2A **142**
CR2: S Croy 7D **152**
Kendall Ct. DA15: Sidc 3A **128**
SW19 ....6B **120**
Kendall Lodge
BR1: Brom *1K 143*
(off Willow Tree Wlk.)
Kendall Pl. W1 ....5E **66** (6G **159**)
Kendall Rd. BR3: Beck 2A **142**
SE18 ....1C **108**
TW7: Isle 2A **98**
Kendalmere Cl. N10 ....1F **31**
Kendal Pde. N18 ....4J **17**
Kendal Pl. *SE5* *7B 86*
(off Kendal Clo.)
SW15 ....5H **101**
Kendal Rd. NW10 ....4C **46**
Kendal Steps W2 ....1D **164**
Kendal St. W2 ....6C **66** (1D **164**)
Kender Est. *SE14* *1J 105*
(off Queen's Rd.)
Kender St. SE14 ....7J **87**
Kendoa Rd. SW4 ....4H **103**
Kendon Cl. E11 ....5K **35**
Kendra Hall Rd.
CR2: S Croy 7B **152**
Kendrey Gdns.
TW2: Twick 7J **97**
Kendrick Ct. *SE15* *1H 105*
(off Woods Rd.)
Kendrick M.
SW7 ....4B **84** (3A **170**)
Kendrick Pl.
SW7 ....4B **84** (4A **170**)
Kenelm Cl. HA1: Harr 3A **44**
Kenerne Dr. EN5: Barn 5B **4**
Kenilford Rd. SW12 ....7F **103**
Kenilworth Av. E17 ....2C **34**
HA2: Harr 4D **42**
SW19 ....5J **119**
Kenilworth Cres. EN1: Enf 1K **7**
Kenilworth Gdns. IG3: Ilf 2K **55**
SE18 ....2F **109**
UB1: S'hall 3D **60**
UB4: Hayes 5H **59**
Kenilworth Rd. BR5: Orp 6G **145**
E3 ....2A **70**
HA8: Edg 3D **12**
KT17: Eps 5C **148**
NW6 ....1H **65**
SE20 ....1K **141**
TW15: Ashf 3A **112**
W5 ....1E **80**
Kenley Av. NW9 ....1A **28**
Kenley Cl. BR7: Chst 3J **145**
DA5: Bexl 7G **111**
EN4: Barn 4H **5**
Kenley Gdns.
CR7: Thor H 4B **140**
Kenley Rd. KT1: King T 2H **135**
SW19 ....2J **137**
TW1: Twick 6B **98**
Kenley Wlk. SM3: Sutt 4F **149**
W11 ....7G **65**
Kenlor Rd. SW17 ....5B **120**
Kenmare Dr. CR4: Mitc 7D **120**
Kenmare Gdns. N13 ....4H **17**
Kenmare Rd.
CR7: Thor H 6A **140**
Kenmere Gdns.
HA0: Wemb 1G **63**
Kenmere Rd. DA16: Well 2C **110**
Kenmont Gdns. NW10 ....3D **64**
Kenmore Av. HA3: Harr 4A **26**
Kenmore Cl. TW9: Rich 7G **81**
Kenmore Cres.
UB4: Hayes 3H **59**
Kenmore Gdns.
HA8: Edg 2H **27**
Kenmore Rd. HA3: Harr 3D **26**
Kenmure Rd. E8 ....5H **51**
Kenmure Yd. E8 ....5H **51**
Kennacraig Cl. E16 ....1J **89**
Kennard Ho. SW11 ....2E **102**
Kennard Rd. E15 ....7F **53**
N11 ....5J **15**
Kennard St. E16 ....1D **90**
SW11 ....1E **102**
Kennedy Av. EN3: Enf 6D **8**
Kennedy Cl. BR5: Orp 7H **145**
CR4: Mitc 1E **138**
E13 ....2J **71**
Kennedy Ct. WD23: Bush 2C **10**
Kennedy Cox Ho. *E16* *5H 71*
(off Burke St.)
Kennedy Ho. *SE11* *5G 173*
(off Vauxhall Wlk.)
Kennedy Path W7 ....4K **61**
Kennedy Rd. IG11: Bark 1J **73**
W7 ....5J **61**
Kennedy Wlk. *SE17* *4D 86*
(off Elsted St.)
Kennet Cl. SW11 ....4B **102**
Kennet Ct. *W9* *5J 65*
(off Elmfield Way)
Kenneth Av. IG1: Ilf 4F **55**
Kenneth Campbell Ho.
NW8 ....*3B 158*
(off Orchardson St.)
Kenneth Ct.
SE11 ....4A **86** (3K **173**)
Kenneth Cres. NW2 ....5D **46**
Kenneth Gdns. HA7: Stan 6F **11**
Kenneth More Rd. IG1: Ilf 3F **55**
Kenneth More Theatre 3F 55
Kennet Ho. *NW8* *4B 158*
(off Church St. Est.)
Kenneth Rd. RM6: Chad H 7D **38**
Kenneth Robbins Ho. N17 ....7C **18**
Kenneth Younger Ho.
SW6 ....*6H 83*
(off Clem Attlee Ct.)
Kennet Rd. TW7: Isle 3K **97**
W9 ....4H **65**
Kennet Sq. SW19 ....1B **138**
Kennet St. E1 ....1G **87**
Kennett Ct. W4 ....7H **81**
Kennett Dr. UB4: Hayes 5C **60**
Kennett Wharf La.
EC4 ....7C **68** (2D **168**)
KENNINGHALL JUNCTION 5D 18
Kenninghall Rd. E5 ....3G **51**
N18 ....5D **18**
Kenning Ho. *N1* *1E 68*
(off Colville Est.)
Kenning St. SE16 ....2J **87**
Kennings Way
SE11 ....5A **86** (5K **173**)
KENNINGTON 6A 86 (7K 173)
Kennington Grn.
SE11 ....5A **86** (6J **173**)
Kennington Gro.
SE11 ....6K **85** (7H **173**)
Kennington La.
SE11 ....5K **85** (6G **173**)
KENNINGTON OVAL
....6A 86 (7J 173)
Kennington Oval
SE11 ....6K **85** (7H **173**)
Kennington Pal. Ct.
SE11 ....5J **173**
Kennington Pk. Gdns.
SE11 ....6B **86** (7K **173**)
Kennington Pk. Ho. SE11 ....6K **173**
Kennington Pk. Pl.
SE11 ....6A **86** (7K **173**)
Kennington Pk. Rd.
SE11 ....6A **86** (7K **173**)
Kennington Rd.
SE1 ....3A **86** (1J **173**)
SE11 ....3A **86** (1J **173**)
Kennistoun Ho. NW5 ....5G **49**
Kenny Dr. SM5: Cars 7E **150**
Kennyland Ct. *NW4* *6D 28*
(off Hendon Way)
Kenny Rd. NW7 ....6B **14**
Kenrick Pl. W1 ....5E **66** (6G **159**)
KENSAL GREEN 3E 64
Kensal Ho. *W10* *4F 65*
(off Ladbroke Gro.)
KENSAL RISE 2F 65
Kensal Rd. W10 ....4G **65**
KENSAL TOWN 4G 65
KENSINGTON 2K 83
Kensington Arc. *W8* *2K 83*
(off Kensington High St.)
Kensington Av.
CR7: Thor H 1A **140**
E12 ....6C **54**
Kensington Cen. W14 ....4G **83**
(not continuous)
Kensington Chu. Ct. W8 ....2K **83**
Kensington Chu. St. W8 ....1J **83**
Kensington Chu. Wlk. W8 ....2K **83**
(not continuous)
Kensington Cl. N11 ....6K **15**
Kensington Ct. *SE16* *1K 87*
(off King & Queen Wharf)
W8 ....2K **83**
Kensington Ct. Gdns. *W8* *3K 83*
(off Kensington Ct. Pl.)
Kensington Ct. M. *W8* *3K 83*
(off Kensington Ct. Pl.)
Kensington Ct. Pl. W8 ....3K **83**
Kensington Dr. IG8: Wfd G 2B **36**
Kensington Gardens
....1A 84 (4A 164)
Kensington Gdns. IG1: Ilf 1D **54**
KT1: King T 3D **134**
(not continuous)
Kensington Gdns. Sq. W2 ....6K **65**
(not continuous)
Kensington Ga. W8 ....3A **84**
Kensington Gore
SW7 ....2A **84** (7A **164**)
Kensington Hall Gdns.
W14 ....5H **83**
Kensington Hgts.
HA1: Harr *6K 25*
(off Sheepcote Rd.)
W8 ....1J **83**
Kensington High St. W8 ....3H **83**
W14 ....3H **83**
Kensington Ho. IG8: Ilf 7K **21**
W14 ....2F **83**
Kensington Mall W8 ....1J **83**
Kensington Mans. *SW5* *5J 83*
(off Trebovir Rd., not continuous)
Kensington Memorial Pk. 5F 65
Kensington Palace 2K 83
Kensington Pal. Gdns. W8 ....1K **83**
Kensington Pk. Gdns.
W11 ....7H **65**
Kensington Pk. M. W11 ....6H **65**
Kensington Pk. Rd. W11 ....6H **65**
Kensington Pl. W8 ....1J **83**
Kensington Rd. RM7: Rom 6J **39**
SW7 ....2A **84**
UB5: N'olt 3E **60**
W8 ....2A **84**
Kensington Sq. W8 ....3K **83**
Kensington Ter.
CR2: S Croy 7D **152**
Kensington Village W14 ....4H **83**
Kensington W. W14 ....4G **83**
Kensworth Ho. *EC1* *2F 163*
(off Cranwood St.)
Kent Av. DA16: Well 5K **109**
RM9: Dag 4G **75**
W13 ....5B **62**
Kent Cl. CR4: Mitc 4J **139**
Kent Ct. E2 ....2F **69**
NW9 ....2A **28**
Kent Dr. EN4: Barn 4K **5**
TW11: Tedd 5J **115**
Kentford Way UB5: N'olt 1C **60**
Kent Gdns. HA4: Ruis 6J **23**
W13 ....5B **62**
Kent Ga. Way
CR0: Croy 6B **154**
Kent Ho. SE1 ....5F **87**
SW1 ....*5C 172*
(off Aylesford St.)
W4 ....*5A 82*
(off Devonshire St.)
Kent Ho. La. BR3: Beck 6A **124**
Kent Ho. Rd. SE26 ....5A **124**
Kentish Bldgs.
SE1 ....2D **86** (5E **168**)
Kentish Rd. DA17: Belv 4G **93**
KENTISH TOWN 5F 49
Kentish Town Ind. Est.
NW5 ....5F **49**
Kentish Town Rd. NW1 ....7F **49**
Kentish Way BR1: Brom 2J **143**
BR2: Short 2K **143**
Kentlea Rd. SE28 ....2J **91**
Kentmere Ho. SE15 ....6J **87**
Kentmere Mans. W5 ....4B **62**
Kentmere Rd. SE18 ....4J **91**
KENTON 5C 26
Kenton Av. HA1: Harr 7K **25**
TW16: Sun T 2B **132**
UB1: S'hall 7E **60**
Kenton Ct. HA3: Harr 6B **26**
SE26 ....*4A 124*
(off Adamsrill Rd.)
TW1: Twick 6D **98**
W14 ....3H **83**
Kentone Ct. SE25 ....4H **141**
Kenton Gdns. HA3: Harr 5C **26**
Kenton Ho. *E1* *4J 69*
(off Mantus Cl.)
Kenton La. HA3: Harr 6E **10**
Kenton Pk. Av. HA3: Harr 4D **26**
Kenton Pk. Cl. HA3: Harr 4C **26**
Kenton Pk. Cres.
HA3: Harr 4D **26**
Kenton Pk. Mans.
HA3: Harr *5C 26*
(off Kenton Rd.)
Kenton Pk. Pde.
HA3: Harr 5C **26**
Kenton Pk. Rd. HA3: Harr 4C **26**
Kenton Rd. E9 ....6K **51**
HA1: Harr 7K **25**
Kenton St. WC1 ....4J **67** (3E **160**)
Kenton Way UB4: Hayes 3G **59**
Kent Pk. Ind. Est. SE15 ....6H **87**
Kent Pas. NW1 ....4D **66** (3E **158**)
Kent Rd. BR4: W W'ck 1D **154**
KT1: King T 3D **134**
KT8: E Mos 4G **133**
N21 ....1J **17**
RM10: Dag 5H **57**
TW9: Rich 7G **81**
W4 ....3J **81**
Kent's Pas. TW12: Hamp 1D **132**
Kent St. E2 ....2F **69**
E13 ....3A **72**
Kent Ter. NW1 ....3C **66** (2D **158**)
Kent Vw. Gdns. IG3: Ilf 2J **55**
Kent Wlk. SW9 ....4B **104**
Kent Way KT6: Surb 3E **146**
Kentwell Cl. SE4 ....4A **106**

Kent Wharf SE8 ....7D 88
(off Creekside)
Kentwode Grn. SW13 ......7C 82
Kent Yd. SW7 ...2C 84 (7D 164)
Kenver Av. N12 ....6G 15
Kenward Rd. SE9 ....5A 108
Kenward Way SW11 ......2E 102
Ken Way HA9: Wemb 3J 45
Kenway RM5: Col R 2J 39
Kenway Rd. SW5 ....4K 83
Ken Wilson Ho. E2 ....2G 69
(off Pritchards Rd.)
Kenwood Av. N14 ....5C 6
Kenwood Cl. NW3 ....1B 48
UB7: W Dray 6C 76
Kenwood Dr. BR3: Beck ...3E 142
Kenwood Gdns. E18 ......3K 35
IG2: Ilf 5E 36
IG5: Ilf 4E 36
Kenwood House 1C 48
Kenwood Ho. SW9 ....4B 104
Kenwood Rd. N6 ....6D 30
N9 ....1B 18
Kenworthy Rd. E9 ....5A 52
Kenwick Ho. N1 ....1K 67
(off Barnsbury Est.)
Kenwyn Dr. NW2 ....2A 46
Kenwyn Lodge N2 ....4D 30
Kenwyn Rd. SW4 ....4H 103
SW20 ....1E 136
Kenya Rd. SE7 ....7B 90
Kenyngton Ct.
TW16: Sun T 5J 113
Kenyngton Dr.
TW16: Sun T 5J 113
Kenyngton Pl. HA3: Harr ...5C 26
Kenyon Mans. W14 ....6G 83
(off Queen's Club Gdns.)
Kenyon St. SW6 ....1F 101
Keogh Rd. E15 ....6G 53
Kepler Ho. SE10 ....5H 89
(off Armitage Rd.)
Kepler Rd. SW4 ....4J 103
Keppel Ho. SE8 ....5B 88
Keppel Rd. E6 ....7D 54
RM9: Dag 4E 56
Keppel Row SE1 ...1C 86 (5C 168)
Keppel St. WC1 ..5H 67 (5D 160)
Kerbela St. E2 ....4G 69 (3K 163)
Kerbey St. E14 ....6D 70
Kerfield Cres. SE5 ....1D 104
Kerfield Pl. SE5 ....1D 104
Kerridge Ct. N1 ....6E 50
(off Balls Pond Rd.)
Kerrington Ct. W12 ....2E 82
(off Uxbridge Rd.)
Kerrison Pl. W5 ....1D 80
Kerrison Rd. E15 ....1F 71
SW11 ....3C 102
W5 ....1D 80
Kerrison Vs. W5 ....1D 80
Kerry N7 ....6J 49
Kerry Av. HA7: Stan 4H 11
Kerry Cl. E16 ....6K 71
N13 ....2E 16
Kerry Ct. HA7: Stan 4J 11
Kerry Ho. E1 ....6J 69
(off Sidney St.)
Kerry Path SE14 ....6B 88
Kerry Rd. SE14 ....6B 88
Kersey Gdns. SE9 ....4C 126
Kersfield Rd. SW15 ....6F 101
Kershaw Cl. SW18 ....6B 102
Kershaw Rd. RM10: Dag ...3G 57
Kersley M. SW11 ....1D 102
Kersley Rd. N16 ....2E 50
Kersley St. SW11 ....2D 102
Kerstin Cl. UB3: Hayes ...7H 59
Kerswell Cl. N15 ....5E 32
Kerwick Cl. N7 ....7J 49
Keslake Mans. NW10 ......2F 65
(off Station Ter.)

Keslake Rd. NW6 ....2F 65
Kessock Cl. N17 ....5H 33
Kestlake Rd. DA5: Bexl ...6C 110
KESTON 5A 156
Keston Av. BR2: Kes 5A 156
Keston Cl. DA16: Well ...7C 92
N18 ....3J 17
Keston Ct. DA5: Bexl 7F 111
KT5: Surb 5F 135
(off Cranes Pk.)
Keston Gdns. BR2: Kes ...4A 156
Keston Ho. SE17 ....5E 86
(off Kinglake St.)
Keston Mark 4C 156
KESTON MARK 3C 156
Keston Pk. Cl. BR2: Kes ...3D 156
Keston Rd. CR7: Thor H ..6A 140
N17 ....3D 32
SE15 ....3G 105
Kestrel Av. E6 ....5C 72
SE24 ....5B 104
Kestrel Cl. KT2: King T ...4D 116
NW9 ....2A 28
NW10 ....5K 45
Kestrel Ct. CR2: S Croy ...6C 152
E17 ....2K 33
HA4: Ruis 2F 41
Kestrel Ho. EC1 ....1C 162
(off Pickard St.)
EN3: Enf 5F 9
Kestrel Pl. SE14 ....6A 88
Kestrel Way CR0: Croy ...7F 155
UB3: Hayes 2F 77
Keswick Av. SW15 ....5A 118
SW19 ....3J 137
TW17: Shep 3G 131
Keswick Cl. SM1: Sutt ...4A 150
Keswick Ct. BR2: Short ...4H 143
SE6 ....1H 125
SE13 ....5D 106
Keswick Gdns. HA4: Ruis ..6F 23
HA9: Wemb 4E 44
IG4: Ilf 4C 36
Keswick Ho. SE5 ....2C 104
Keswick M. W5 ....1E 80
Keswick Rd.
BR4: W W'ck 2G 155
BR6: Orp 7K 145
DA7: Bex 1G 111
SW15 ....5G 101
TW2: Twick 6G 97
Kettering St. SW16 ......6G 121
Kett Gdns. SW2 ....5K 103
Kettlebaston Rd. E10 .....1B 52
Kettleby Ho. SW9 ....3B 104
(off Barrington Rd.)
Kettlewell Cl. N11 ....6K 15
Ketton Ho. W10 ....4E 64
(off Sutton Way)
Kevan Ct. E17 ....4C 34
Kevan Ho. SE5 ....7C 86
Kevelioc Rd. N17 ....1C 32
Kevin Cl. TW4: Houn 2B 96
Kevington Cl. BR5: Orp ...4K 145
Kevington Dr. BR5: Orp ...4K 145
BR7: Chst 4J 145
KEW 7G 81
Kew Bridge 5F 81
Kew Bri. TW8: Bford 6F 81
Kew Bri. Arches
TW9: Rich 6G 81
Kew Bri. Ct. W4 ....5G 81
Kew Bri. Distribution Cen.
TW8: Bford 5F 81
Kew Bri. Rd. TW8: Bford ..6F 81
Kew Bridge Steam Mus. ...5F 81
Kew Cres. SM3: Sutt 3G 149
Kew Foot Rd. TW9: Rich ...4E 98
Kew Gardens 7E 80
Kew Gardens Plants & People
Exhibition 7F 81
Kew Gdns. Rd. TW9: Rich ..7F 81

Kew Green 7G 81
Kew Grn. TW9: Rich 6F 81
Kew Mdw. Path
TW9: Rich 2J 99
(Chiswick Bri.)
TW9: Rich 1H 99
(W. Park Av.)
Kew Palace 6E 80
Kew Retail Pk. TW9: Rich ..1H 99
Kew Riverside Pk.
TW9: Rich 1H 99
Kew Rd. TW9: Rich 6G 81
Keybridge Ho. SW8 ......7F 173
(off Miles St.)
Key Cl. E1 ....4J 69
Keyes Ho. SW1 ....6C 172
(off Dolphin Sq.)
Keyes Rd. NW2 ....5F 47
Key Ho. SE11 ....6A 86 (7K 173)
Keymer Rd. SW2 ....2K 121
Keynes Cl. N2 ....4D 30
Keynes Ct. SE28 ....7B 74
(off Attlee Rd.)
Keynsham Av. IG8: Wfd G ..4B 20
Keynsham Gdns. SE9 ....5C 108
Keynsham Rd. SE9 ......5B 108
SM4: Mord 1K 149
Keynsham Wlk.
SM4: Mord 1K 149
Keys Cl. CR0: Croy 3D 152
(off Beech Ho. Rd.)
Keyse Rd. SE1 ....3F 87
Keysham Av. TW5: Houn ...1J 95
Keystone Cres.
N1 ....2J 67 (1F 161)
Keywood Dr.
TW16: Sun T 6J 113
Keyworth Cl. E5 ....4A 52
Keyworth Pl. SE1 ....7B 168
Keyworth St.
SE1 ....3B 86 (7B 168)
Kezia St. SE8 ....5A 88
Khama Rd. SW17 ....4C 120
Khartoum Rd. E13 ....3K 71
IG1: Ilf 5F 55
SW17 ....4B 120
Khyber Rd. SW11 ....2C 102
Kibworth St. SW8 ....7K 85
KIDBROOKE 2K 107
Kidbrooke Est. SE3 ....3A 108
Kidbrooke Gdns. SE3 .....2J 107
Kidbrooke Green Nature Reserve
.................3A 108
Kidbrooke Gro. SE3 ......1J 107
Kidbrooke La. SE9 ....4C 108
Kidbrooke Pk. Cl. SE3 ....1K 107
Kidbrooke Pk. Rd. SE3 ...1K 107
Kidbrooke Way SE3 ......2K 107
Kidderminster Pl.
CR0: Croy 1B 152
Kidderminster Rd.
CR0: Croy 1B 152
Kidderpore Av. NW3 ......4J 47
Kidderpore Gdns. NW3 ....4J 47
Kidd Pl. SE7 ....5C 90
Kidlington Way NW9 ......2K 27
Kierbeck Bus. Complex
E16 ....2K 89
Kiffen St. EC2 ....4D 68 (3F 163)
Kilberry Cl. TW7: Isle 1H 97
Kilbrennan Ho. E14 ......6E 70
(off Findhorn St.)
KILBURN 2H 65
Kilburn Bri. NW6 ....1J 65
Kilburn Ga. NW6 ....2K 65
Kilburn High Rd. NW6 ....7H 47
Kilburn Ho. NW6 ....2H 65
(off Malvern Pl.)
Kilburn La. W10 ....3F 65
Kilburn Pk. Rd. NW6 .....3J 65
Kilburn Pl. NW6 ....1J 65
Kilburn Priory NW6 ......1K 65

Kilburn Mill Cl.
SM6: Wall 2F 151
Kilburn Sq. NW6 ....1J 65
Kilburn Va. NW6 ....1K 65
Kilburn Va. Est. NW6 .....1K 65
(off Kilburn Va.)
Kildare Cl. HA4: Ruis 1A 42
Kildare Gdns. W2 ....6J 65
Kildare Rd. E16 ....5J 71
Kildare Ter. W2 ....6J 65
Kildare Wlk. E14 ....6C 70
Kildoran Rd. SW2 ....5J 103
Kildowan Rd. IG3: Ilf 1A 56
Kilgour Rd. SE23 ....6A 106
Kilkie St. SW6 ....2A 102
Killarney Rd. SW18 ......6A 102
Killearn Rd. SE6 ....1F 125
Killester Gdns.
KT4: Wor Pk 4D 148
Killick Ho. SM1: Sutt 4K 149
Killick St. N1 .....2K 67 (1G 161)
Killieser Av. SW2 ....2J 121
Killigarth Cl.
DA14: Sidc 4A 128
Killip Cl. E16 ....6H 71
Killoran Ho. E14 ....3E 88
(off Galbraith St.)
Killowen Av. UB5: N'olt ...5G 43
Killowen Rd. E9 ....6K 51
Killyon Rd. SW8 ....2G 103
Killyon Ter. SW8 ....2G 103
Kilmaine Rd. SW6 ....7G 83
Kilmarnock Gdns.
RM8: Dag 3C 56
Kilmarsh Rd. W6 ....4E 82
Kilmartin Av. SW16 ......3A 140
Kilmartin Rd. IG3: Ilf 2A 56
Kilmington Rd. SW13 .....6C 82
Kilmiston Av.
TW17: Shep 6E 130
Kilmore Ho. E14 ....6D 70
(off Vesey Path)
Kilmorey Gdns.
TW1: Twick 5B 98
Kilmorey Rd. TW1: Twick ..4B 98
Kilmorie Rd. SE23 ......1A 124
Kilmuir Ho. SW1 ....4H 171
(off Bury St.)
Kiln Cl. UB3: Hayes 6F 77
Kiln Ct. E14 ....7B 70
(off Newell St.)
Kilner Ho. E16 ....5K 71
(off Freemasons Rd.)
SE11 ....7J 173
Kilner St. E14 ....5C 70
Kiln M. SW17 ....5B 120
Kiln Pl. NW5 ....5E 48
Kilnside KT10: Esh 7A 146
Kilpatrick Way UB4: Hayes .5C 60
Kilravock St. W10 ....3G 65
Kilronan W3 ....6K 63
Kilross Rd. TW14: Felt ...1F 113
Kilsby Wlk. RM9: Dag 6B 56
Kilsha Rd. KT12: Walt T ..6A 132
Kimbell Gdns. SW6 ....1G 101
Kimbell Pl. SE3 ....4A 108
Kimberley Av. E6 ....2C 72
IG2: Ilf 7H 37
RM7: Rom 6J 39
SE15 ....2H 105
Kimberley Dr.
DA14: Sidc 2D 128
Kimberley Gdns. EN1: Enf ..3A 8
N4 ....5B 32
Kimberley Ga.
BR1: Brom 7G 125
Kimberley Ho. E14 ......3E 88
(off Galbraith St.)
Kimberley Ind. Est. E17 ...1B 34
Kimberley Rd. BR3: Beck ..2K 141
CR0: Croy 6B 140
E4 ....1B 20

Kimberley Rd. E11 ......2F 53
E16 ....4H 71
E17 ....1A 34
N17 ....2G 33
N18 ....6C 18
NW6 ....1G 65
SW9 ....2J 103
Kimberley Wlk.
KT12: Walt T 7K 131
Kimberley Way E4 ....1B 20
Kimber Rd. SW18 ....7J 101
Kimble Cres. WD23: Bush ..1B 10
Kimble Ho. NW8 ....3D 158
Kimble Rd. SW19 ....6B 120
Kimbolton Cl. SE12 ......6H 107
Kimbolton Ct. SW3 ......4C 170
(off Fulham Rd.)
Kimbolton Row SW3 .....4C 170
(off Fulham Rd.)
Kimmeridge Gdns. SE9 ...4C 126
Kimmeridge Rd. SE9 .....4C 126
Kimpton Ind. Est. SM3: Sutt .2H 149
Kimpton Rd. SE5 ....1D 104
SM3: Sutt 2H 149
Kinburn St. SE16 ....2K 87
Kincaid Rd. SE15 ....7H 87
Kincardine Gdns. W9 ....4J 65
(off Harrow Rd.)
Kincha Lodge
KT2: King T 1F 135
(off Elm Rd.)
Kinch Gro. HA3: Harr 7F 27
Kinder Cl. SE28 ....7D 74
Kinder Ho. N1 ....2D 68
(off Cranston Est.)
Kindersley Ho. E1 ....6G 69
(off Pinchin St.)
Kinder St. E1 ....6H 69
Kinefold Ho. N7 ....6J 49
Kinfauns Rd. IG3: Ilf 1A 56
SW2 ....2A 122
King Alfred Av. SE6 ......4C 124
(not continuous)
King & Queen Cl. SE9 ....4C 126
King & Queen St. SE17 ...5C 86
King & Queen Wharf
SE16 ....1K 87
King Arthur Cl. SE15 .....7J 87
King Charles I Island
SW1 ....4E 166
King Charles Ct. SE17 ....6B 86
(off Royal Rd.)
King Charles Cres.
KT5: Surb 7F 135
King Charles Ho. SW6 ....7K 83
(off Wandon Rd.)
King Charles Rd.
KT5: Surb 5F 135
King Charles's Cl. SE10 ...6B 88
(off Park Row)
King Charles St.
SW1 ....2H 85 (6D 166)
King Charles Ter. E1 .....7H 69
(off Sovereign Cl.)
King Charles Wlk. SW19 ..1G 119
King Ct. E10 ....7D 34
Kingcup Cl. CR0: Croy 7K 141
King David La. E1 ....7J 69
Kingdon Ho. E14 ....3E 88
(off Galbraith St.)
Kingdon Rd. NW6 ....6J 47
King Edward III M. SE16 ..2H 87
King Edward Bldg. EC1 ....6B 68
King Edward Dr.
KT9: Chess 3E 146
King Edward Mans. E8 ....1H 69
(off Mare St.)
King Edward M. SW13 ....1C 100
King Edward Rd. E10 .....1E 52
E17 ....3A 34
EN5: Barn 4D 4
King Edward's Gdns. W3 ..1G 81

King Edwards Gro.
TW11: Tedd 6B 116
King Edwards Mans. SW6 ....7J 83
(off Fulham Rd.)
King Edward's Pl. W3 ......1G 81
King Edwards Rd. E9 ......1H 69
EN3: Enf 4E 8
HA4: Ruis 1F 41
IG11: Bark 1H 73
N9 ....7C 8
King Edward St.
EC1 ....6C 68 (7C 162)
King Edward Wlk.
SE1 ....3A 86 (1K 173)
Kingfield Rd. W5 ....4D 62
Kingfield St. E14 ....4E 88
Kingfisher Av. E11 ....6K 35
Kingfisher Cl. HA3: Harr 7E 10
HA6: Nwood 1D 22
SE28 ....7C 74
Kingfisher Ct. E14 ....2E 88
(off River Barge Cl.)
EN2: Enf 1E 6
SM1: Sutt 5H 149
SW19 ....2F 119
TW3: Houn 5F 97
Kingfisher Dr.
TW10: Rich 4B 116
Kingfisher M. SE13 ....4C 106
Kingfisher Pl. N22 ....2K 31
Kingfisher Sq. SE8 ....6B 88
(off Clyde St.)
Kingfisher St. E6 ....5C 72
Kingfisher Wlk. NW9 ......2A 28
Kingfisher Way
BR3: Beck 5K 141
NW10 ....6K 45
King Frederick IX Twr.
SE16 ....3B 88
King Gdns. CR0: Croy 5B 152
King George VI Av.
CR4: Mitc 4D 138
King George VI Memorial
..............1H 85 (5C 166)
King George Av. E16 ......6A 72
IG2: Ilf 5H 37
King George Cl.
RM7: Mawney 3J 39
TW16: Sun T 5G 113
King George's Dr.
UB1: S'hall 5D 60
King George Sq.
TW10: Rich 6F 99
King George's Trad. Est.
KT9: Chess 4G 147
King George St. SE10 ....7E 88
Kingham Cl. SW18 ....7A 102
W11 ....2G 83
(off Holland Pk. Av.)
King Harolds Way
DA7: Belv, Bex 7D 92
DA17: Belv 7D 92
King Henry's Dr.
CR0: Croy 7D 154
King Henry's Reach W6 ...6E 82
King Henry's Rd.
KT1: King T 3H 135
NW3 ....7C 48
King Henry St. N16 ......5E 50
King Henry's Wlk. N1 .....6E 50
King Henry Ter. E1 ....7H 69
(off Sovereign Cl.)
Kinghorn St. EC1 ..5C 68 (6C 162)
King Ho. W12 ....6D 64
King James Ct. SE1 ......7B 168
King James St.
SE1 ....2B 86 (7B 168)
King John Ct.
EC2 ....4E 68 (3H 163)
King John St. E1 ....5K 69
King John's Wlk. SE9 .....7C 108
(not continuous)

Kinglake Est. SE17 ......5E 86
Kinglake St. SE17 ....5E 86
(not continuous)
Kingly Ct. W1 ....2B 166
Kingly St. W1 ....6G 67 (1A 166)
Kingsand Rd. SE12 ......2J 125
Kings Arbour UB2: S'hall ...5C 78
King's Arms All.
TW8: B'ford 6D 80
Kings Arms Ct. E1 ....5G 69
Kings Arms Yd.
EC2 ....6D 68 (7E 162)
Kingsash Dr.
UB4: Hayes 4C 60
Kings Av. BR1: Brom 6H 125
IG8: Wfd G 6E 20
IG9: Buck H 2G 21
(Queen's Rd.)
IG9: Buck H 6E 20
(Station Way)
KT3: N Mald 4A 136
N10 ....3E 30
N21 ....1G 17
RM6: Chad H 6F 39
SM5: Cars 7C 150
SW4 ....7H 103
SW12 ....1H 121
TW3: Houn 1F 97
TW16: Sun T 5H 113
UB6: G'frd 5F 61
W5 ....6D 62
King's Bench St.
SE1 ....2B 86 (6B 168)
King's Bench Wlk.
EC4 ....6A 68 (1K 167)
Kingsbridge Av. W3 ......2F 81
Kingsbridge Ct. E14 .....3C 88
(off Dockers Tanner Rd.)
NW1 ....7F 49
(off Castlehaven Rd.)
Kingsbridge Cres.
UB1: S'hall 5D 60
Kingsbridge Dr. NW7 ....7A 14
Kingsbridge Rd.
IG11: Bark 2H 73
KT12: Walt T 7K 131
SM4: Mord 6F 137
UB2: S'hall 4D 78
W10 ....6E 64
Kingsbridge Way
UB4: Hayes 3G 59
Kingsbridge Wharf
IG11: Bark 3J 73
KINGSBURY 7K 27
Kingsbury Circ. NW9 .....5G 27
KINGSBURY GREEN 5J 27
Kingsbury Rd. N1 ....6E 50
NW9 ....5G 27
Kingsbury Ter. N1 ....6E 50
Kingsbury Trad. Est. NW9 ..6K 27
Kings Chase KT8: E Mos ...3G 133
Kings Chase Vw. EN2: Enf ..2F 7
Kingsclere Cl. SW15 .....7C 100
Kingsclere Ct. N12 ......5H 15
Kingsclere Pl. EN2: Enf 2H 7
Kingscliffe Gdns. SW19 ...1H 119
Kings Cl. DA1: Cray 4K 111
E10 ....7D 34
KT7: T Ditt 6A 134
KT12: Walt T 7K 131
NW4 ....4F 29
TW18: Staines 7A 112
Kings Coll. Ct. NW3 .....7C 48
King's College London
Chelsea Campus
.........5B 84 (6B 170)
Strand Campus
.........7K 67 (2H 167)
Waterloo Campus
.........5J 167
King's College London Dental
Institute 2D 104

Kings Coll. Rd. HA4: Ruis ...6H 23
NW3 ....7C 48
King's College School of Medicine
& Dentistry 2C 104
Kings College University
(Hampstead Campus)
.........4J 47
Kingscote Rd. CR0: Croy ...7H 141
KT3: N Mald 3K 135
W4 ....3K 81
Kingscote St.
EC4 ....7B 68 (2A 168)
Kings Ct. E13 ....1K 71
IG9: Buck H 2G 21
N7 ....2K 49
(off Caledonian Rd.)
NW8 ....1D 66
(off Prince Albert Rd.)
SE1 ....2B 86 (6B 168)
W6 ....4C 82
Kings Ct. Nth.
SW3 ....5C 84 (6C 170)
Kingscourt Rd. SW16 ....3H 121
Kings Ct. Sth. SW3 ......6C 170
King's Cres. N4 ....3C 50
Kings Cres. Est. N4 .....2C 50
Kingscroft SW4 ....6J 103
Kingscroft Rd. NW2 .....6H 47
King's Cross 2J 67 (1F 161)
King's Cross Bri. WC1 ....1F 161
King's Cross Rd.
WC1 ....3K 67 (1G 161)
Kingsdale Gdns. W11 ....1F 83
Kingsdale Rd. SE18 .....7K 91
SE20 ....7K 123
Kingsdown Av.
CR2: S Croy 7C 152
W3 ....7A 64
W13 ....2B 80
Kingsdown Cl. SE16 .....5H 87
(off Masters Dr.)
W10 ....6F 65
Kingsdowne Rd.
KT6: Surb 7E 134
Kingsdown Ho. E8 ....5G 51
Kingsdown Rd. E11 ......3G 53
N19 ....2J 49
SM3: Sutt 5G 149
Kingsdown Way
BR2: Short 7J 143
Kings Dr. HA8: Edg 4A 12
HA9: Wemb 2H 45
KT5: Surb 7G 135
KT7: T Ditt 7B 134
TW11: Tedd 5H 115
Kingsend HA4: Ruis 1F 41
Kingsend Ct. HA4: Ruis ...1G 41
Kings Farm E17 ....1D 34
Kings Farm Av.
TW10: Rich 4G 99
Kingsfield Av. HA2: Harr ...4F 25
Kingsfield Ho. SE9 ......3B 126
Kingsfield Rd. HA1: Harr ...7H 25
Kingsfield Ter. HA1: Harr ...1H 43
Kingsford St. NW5 ......5D 48
Kingsford Way E6 ....5D 72
Kings Gdns. IG1: Ilf 1H 55
NW6 ....7J 47
Kings Gth. M. SE23 .....2J 123
Kingsgate HA9: Wemb 3J 45
Kingsgate Av. N3 ....3J 29
Kingsgate Bus. Cen.
KT2: King T 1E 134
(off Kingsgate Rd.)
Kingsgate Cl.
DA7: Bex 1E 110
KT2: King T 7E 134
Kingsgate Ho. SW9 .....1A 104
Kingsgate Mans. WC1 ....6G 161
(off Red Lion Sq.)
Kingsgate Pde. SW1 .....2B 172
Kingsgate Pl. NW6 ......7J 47

Kingsgate Rd.
KT1: King T 1E 134
NW6 ....7J 47
Kingsground SE9 ....7B 108
King's Gro. SE15 ....7H 87
(not continuous)
Kings Hall Leisure Cen. ...5J 51
Kingshall M. SE13 ......3E 106
Kings Hall Rd.
BR3: Beck 7A 124
Kings Head Hill E4 ......7J 9
Kings Head Pas. SW4 ....4H 103
(off Clapham Pk. Rd.)
Kings Head Theatre 1B 68
(off Upper St.)
King's Head Yd.
SE1 ....1D 86 (5E 168)
King's Highway SE18 ....6J 91
Kingshill SE17 ....7C 86
Kingshill Av. HA3: Harr 4B 26
KT4: Wor Pk 7C 136
UB4: Hayes 3G 59
UB5: N'olt 3G 59
Kingshill Cl. UB4: Hayes ...3J 59
Kingshill Ct. EN5: Barn ...4B 18
Kingshill Dr. HA3: Harr 2B 26
Kingshold Rd. E9 ....7J 51
Kingsholm Gdns. SE9 ....4B 108
Kings Ho. SW8 ....7J 85
(off Sth. Lambeth Rd.)
Kingshurst Rd. SE12 ....7J 107
Kingside Bus. Pk. SE18 ...3C 90
Kings Keep BR2: Short ...3G 143
KT1: King T 4E 134
SW15 ....5F 101
KINGSLAND 6E 50
Kingsland NW8 ....1C 66
(off Kingsmill Ter.)
Kingsland Grn. E8 ......6E 50
Kingsland High St. E8 ...6F 51
Kingsland Pas. E8 ......6E 50
Kingsland Rd.
E2 ....3E 68 (2H 163)
E13 ....3A 72
Kingsland Shop. Cen. E8 ...6F 51
Kings La. SM1: Sutt 6B 150
Kingslawn Cl. SW15 .....5D 100
Kingsleigh Pl. CR4: Mitc ...3D 138
Kingsleigh Wlk.
BR2: Short 4H 143
(off Stamford Dr.)
Kingsley Av. SM1: Sutt ...4B 150
TW3: Houn 2G 97
UB1: S'hall 7E 60
W13 ....5A 62
Kingsley Cl. N2 ....5A 30
RM10: Dag 4H 57
Kingsley Ct. DA6: Bex ...4G 111
HA8: Edg 3C 12
KT4: Wor Pk 2B 148
(off Avenue, The)
NW2 ....6D 46
SM2: Sutt 7K 149
Kingsley Dr. KT4: Wor Pk ...2B 148
Kingsley Flats SE1 ......4E 88
(off Old Kent Rd.)
Kingsley Gdns. E4 ......5H 19
Kingsley Ho. SW3 ....6B 84
(off Beaufort St.)
Kingsley Mans. W14 ....6G 83
(off Greyhound Rd.)
Kingsley M. BR7: Chst 6E 127
E1 ....7H 69
W8 ....3K 83
Kingsley Pl. N6 ....7E 30
Kingsley Rd. CR0: Croy ...1A 152
E7 ....7J 53
E17 ....2E 34
HA2: Harr 4G 43
HA5: Pinn 4D 24
IG6: Ilf 3F 37
N13 ....4F 17

Kingsley Rd. NW6 ....1H 65
SW19 ....5K 119
TW3: Houn 1F 97
Kingsley St. SW11 ......3D 102
Kingsley Way N2 ....6A 30
Kingsley Wood Dr. SE9 ...3D 126
Kingslyn Cres. SE19 ....1E 140
Kings Mall W6 ....4E 82
Kingsman Pde. SE18 ....3D 90
Kingsman St. SE18 .....3D 90
Kings Mead TW10: Rich ...6F 99
Kingsmead EN5: Barn 4D 4
Kingsmead Av.
CR4: Mitc 3G 139
KT4: Wor Pk 2D 148
KT6: Surb 2G 147
N9 ....1C 18
NW9 ....7K 27
TW16: Sun T 2A 132
Kingsmead Cl.
DA15: Sidc 2A 128
E18 ....7K 147
TW11: Tedd 6B 116
Kingsmead Cotts.
BR2: Short 1C 156
Kingsmead Ct. N6 ....1J 49
Kingsmead Dr. UB5: N'olt ...7D 42
Kingsmead Ho. E9 ......4A 52
Kingsmead Rd. SW2 ....2A 122
King's Mead Way E9 .....4A 52
Kingsmere Cl. SW15 ....3F 101
Kingsmere Pk. NW9 .....1H 45
Kingsmere Pl. N16 .....1D 50
Kingsmere Rd. SW19 ....2F 119
King's M. SW4 ....5J 103
WC1 ....4K 67 (4H 161)
Kingsmill NW8 ....2B 66
(off Kingsmill Ter.)
Kingsmill Bus. Pk.
KT1: King T 3F 135
Kingsmill Gdns.
RM9: Dag 2F 57
Kingsmill Ho. SW3 ......5D 170
(off Cale St.)
Kingsmill Rd. RM9: Dag ...5F 57
Kingsmill Ter. NW8 ......2B 66
Kingsnorth Ho. W10 .....6F 65
Kingsnympton Pk.
KT2: King T 7H 117
Kings Oak RM7: Mawney ...3G 39
King's Orchard SE9 .....6C 108
King's Paddock
TW12: Hamp 1G 133
Kings Pde. HA8: Edg 5B 12
(off Edgwarebury La.)
N17 ....3F 33
NW10 ....1E 64
SM5: Cars 3D 150
(off Wrythe La.)
W12 ....3C 82
Kingspark Ct. E18 ......3J 35
Kings Pas. E11 ....7G 35
KT1: King T 2D 134
KT2: King T 1D 134
Kings Pl. IG9: Buck H 2F 21
Kings Pl. SE1 ...2C 86 (7C 168)
W4 ....4J 81
King Sq. EC1 ...3C 68 (2C 162)
King's Quay SW10 ......1A 102
(off Chelsea Harbour Dr.)
Kings Reach Twr. SE1 ....4K 167
Kings Ride Ga.
TW10: Rich 4G 99
Kingsridge SW19 ....2G 119
Kings Rd. CR4: Mitc 3E 138
E4 ....1A 20
E6 ....1A 72
E11 ....7G 35
EN5: Barn 3A 4
HA2: Harr 2D 42
IG11: Bark 7G 55
KT2: King T 7E 116

Knightsbridge Grn. SW1 2D 84 (7E 164) (not continuous)
Knights Cl. E9 5J 51
Knightscote Farm & Agricultural Mus. 2A 22
Knights Ct. BR1: Brom 3H 125
KT1: King T 3E 134
Knights Hill SE27 5B 122
Knight's Hill Sq. SE27 4B 122
Knights Ho. *SW8* 7J 85 (off Sth. Lambeth Rd.)
Knights La. N9 3B 18
Knight's Pk. KT1: King T 3E 134
Knight's Pl. TW2: Twick 1J 115
Knights Rd. E16 2J 89
HA7: Stan 4H 11
Knight's Wlk. SE11 4B 86 (4K 173) (not continuous)
Knightswood Cl. HA8: Edg 2D 12
Knightswood Ct. N6 7H 31
Knightswood Ho. N12 6F 15
Knightwood Cres. KT3: N Mald 6A 136
Knivet Rd. SW6 6J 83
Knobs Hill Rd. E15 1D 70
Knockholt Rd. SE9 5B 108
Knole Cl. CR0: Croy 6J 141
Knole Ct. *UB5: N'olt* 3A 60 (off Broomcroft Av.)
Knole Ga. DA15: Sidc 3J 127
Knole, The BR7: Chst 4E 126
Knoll Cres. HA6: Nwood 1G 23 (not continuous)
Knoll Dr. N14 7K 5
Knoll Ho. *NW8* 2A 66 (off Carlton Hill)
Knollmead KT5: Surb 1J 147
Knoll Ri. BR6: Orp 7K 145
Knoll Rd. DA5: Bexl 7G 111
DA14: Sidc 5B 128
SW18 5A 102
Knolls Cl. KT4: Wor Pk 3D 148
Knoll, The BR2: Short 2J 155
BR3: Beck 1D 142
W13 5C 62
Knollys Cl. SW16 3A 122
Knolly's Ho. *WC1* 3E 160 (off Tavistock Pl.)
Knollys Rd. SW16 3K 121
Knottisford St. E2 3J 69
Knotts Grn. M. E10 6D 34
Knotts Grn. Rd. E10 6D 34
Knowlden Ho. *E1* 7J 69 (off Cable St.)
Knowle Av. DA7: Bex 7E 92
Knowle Cl. SW9 3A 104
Knowle Rd. BR2: Short 2D 156
TW2: Twick 1J 115
Knowles Cl. UB7: W Dray 1A 76
Knowles Ct. *HA1: Harr* 6K 25 (off Gayton Rd.)
Knowles Hill Cres. SE13 5F 107
Knowles Wlk. SW4 3G 103
Knowlton Grn. BR2: Short 5H 143
Knowlton Ho. *SW9* 1A 104 (off Cowley Rd.)
Knowsley Av. UB1: S'hall 1F 79
Knowsley Rd. SW11 2D 102
Knox Ct. SW4 2J 103
Knox Rd. E7 6H 53
Knox St. NW1 5D 66 (5E 158)
Knoyle St. SE14 6A 88
Koblenz Ho. *N8* 3J 31 (off Newland Rd.)
Kohat Rd. SW19 5K 119
Korda Cl. TW17: Shep 3B 130
Kossuth St. SE10 5G 89
Kotree Way SE1 4G 87
Kramer M. SW5 5J 83
Kreedman Wlk. E8 5G 51
Kreisel Wlk. TW9: Rich 6F 81
Kristina Ct. *SM2: Sutt* 6J 149 (off Overton Rd.)
Krupnik Pl. EC2 2H 163
Kuala Gdns. SW16 1K 139
Kubrick Bus. Est. *E7* 4K 53 (off Station App.)
Kuhn Way E7 5J 53
Kwame Ho. *E16* 7E 72 (off University Way)
Kydbrook Cl. BR5: Orp 7G 145
Kylemore Cl. E6 2B 72
Kylemore Rd. NW6 7J 47
Kylestrome Ho. *SW1* 4H 171 (off Cundy St.)
Kymberley Rd. HA1: Harr 6J 25
Kymes Ct. HA2: Harr 2H 43
Kynance Gdns. HA7: Stan 1C 26
Kynance M. SW7 3K 83
Kynance Pl. W8 3A 84
Kynaston Av. CR7: Thor H 5C 140
N16 3F 51
Kynaston Cl. HA3: Harr 7C 10
Kynaston Cres. CR7: Thor H 5C 140
Kynaston Rd. BR1: Brom 5J 125
CR7: Thor H 5C 140
EN2: Enf 1J 7
N16 3E 50
Kynaston Wood HA3: Harr 7C 10
Kynnersley Cl. SM5: Cars 3D 150
Kynoch Rd. N18 4D 18
Kyrle Rd. SW11 6E 102
Kyverdale Rd. N16 7F 33

L

Laburnum Av. N9 2A 18
N17 7J 17
SM1: Sutt 3C 150
UB7: W Dray 7B 58
Laburnum Cl. E4 6G 19
HA0: Wemb 1G 63
N11 6K 15
SE15 7J 87
Laburnum Ct. E2 1F 69
HA1: Harr 6F 25
HA7: Stan 4H 11
SE16 2J 87 (off Albion St.)
SE19 1F 141
Laburnum Cres. TW16: Sun T 1K 131
Laburnum Gdns. CR0: Croy 7K 141
N21 2H 17
Laburnum Gro. HA4: Ruis 6F 23
KT3: N Mald 2K 135
N21 2H 17
NW9 7J 27
TW3: Houn 4D 96
UB1: S'hall 4D 60
Laburnum Ho. BR2: Short 1F 143
Laburnum Lodge N3 2H 29
Laburnum Pl. SE9 5E 108
Laburnum Rd. CR4: Mitc 2E 138
SW19 7A 120
UB3: Hayes 4H 77
Laburnums, The E6 4C 72
Laburnum St. E2 1F 69
SE16 2J 87 (off Albion St.)
Laburnum Way BR2: Short 7E 144
TW19: Staines 1B 112
La Caye Apartments *E14* 4F 89 (off Glenaffric Av.)
Lacebark Cl. DA15: Sidc 7K 109
Lacey Cl. N9 2B 18
Lacey Dr. HA8: Edg 4A 12
TW12: Hamp 1D 132
Lacey Wlk. E3 2C 70
Lacine Ct. *SE16* 2K 87 (off Christopher Cl.)
Lackington St. EC2 5D 68 (5F 163)
Lackland Ho. *SE1* 5F 87 (off Rowcross St.)
Lacland Ho. *SW10* 7B 84 (off Worlds End Est.)
Lacock Cl. SW19 6A 120
Lacock Ct. *W13* 1A 80 (off Tewkesbury Rd.)
Lacon Ho. *WC1* 5G 161 (off Theobalds Rd.)
Lacon Rd. SE22 4G 105
Lacrosse Way SW16 1H 139
Lacy Dr. RM8: Dag 3C 56
Lacy Rd. SW15 4F 101 (not continuous)
Ladas Rd. SE27 4C 122
Ladbroke Cres. W11 6G 65
Ladbroke Gdns. W11 7H 65
Ladbroke Gro. W10 4F 65
Ladbroke Gro. Ho. *W11* 7H 65 (off Ladbroke Gro.)
Ladbroke M. W11 1G 83
Ladbroke Rd. EN1: Enf 6A 8
W11 1H 83
Ladbroke Sq. W11 7H 65
Ladbroke Ter. W11 7H 65
Ladbroke Wlk. W11 1H 83
Ladbrook Cl. HA5: Pinn 5D 24
Ladbrooke Cres. DA14: Sidc 3D 128
Ladbrook Rd. SE25 4D 140
Ladderstile Ride TW10: Rich 5H 117
Ladderswood Way N11 5B 16
Ladlands SE22 7G 105
Lady Aylesford Av. HA7: Stan 5F 11
Lady Booth Rd. KT1: King T 2E 134
Ladycroft Rd. SE13 3D 106
Ladycroft Wlk. HA7: Stan 1D 26
Lady Dock Wlk. SE16 2A 88
Lady Elizabeth Ho. SW14 3J 99
Lady Forsdyke Way KT19: Eps 7G 147
Ladygate La. HA4: Ruis 6D 22
Lady Harewood Way KT19: Eps 7G 147
Lady Hay KT4: Wor Pk 2B 148
Lady Margaret Rd. NW5 5G 49
UB1: S'hall 7D 60
Lady Micos Almshouses *E1* 6J 69 (off Aylward St.)
Lady Sarah Ho. *N11* 6J 15 (off Asher Loftus Way)
Lady Shaw Ct. N13 2E 16
Ladyship Ter. SE22 7G 105
Ladysmith Av. E6 2C 72
IG2: Ilf 7H 37
Ladysmith Cl. NW7 7H 13
Ladysmith Rd. E16 3H 71
EN1: Enf 3K 7 (not continuous)
HA3: Harr 2J 25
N17 2G 33
N18 5C 18
SE9 6E 108
Lady Somerset Rd. NW5 4F 49
LADYWELL 5D 106
Ladywell Cl. SE4 5C 106
Ladywell Hgts. SE4 6B 106
Ladywell Rd. SE13 5C 106
Ladywell St. E15 1H 71
Ladywood Av. BR5: Orp 5J 145
Ladywood Rd. KT6: Surb 2G 147
Lafone Av. TW13: Felt 2A 114
Lafone St. SE1 2F 87 (6J 169)
Lagado M. SE16 1K 87
Laidlaw Dr. N21 5E 6
Laing Dean UB5: N'olt 1A 60
Laing Ho. SE5 7C 86
Laings Av. CR4: Mitc 2D 138
Lainlock Pl. TW3: Houn 1F 97
Lainson St. SW18 7J 101
Lairdale Cl. SE21 1C 122
Laird Ho. *SE5* 7C 86 (off Redcar St.)
Lairs Cl. N7 5J 49
Laitwood Rd. SW12 1F 121
Lakanal *SE5* 1E 104 (off Dalwood St.)
Lake Av. BR1: Brom 6J 125
Lake Bus. Cen. N17 7B 18
Lake Cl. RM8: Dag 3D 56
SW19 5H 119
Lakedale Rd. SE18 6J 91
Lake Dr. WD23: Bush 2C 10
Lakefield Cl. SE20 7H 123
Lakefield Rd. N22 2B 32
Lake Footpath SE2 2D 92
Lake Gdns. RM10: Dag 5G 57
SM6: Wall 3F 151
TW10: Rich 2B 116
Lakehall Gdns. CR7: Thor H 5B 140
Lakehall Rd. CR7: Thor H 5B 140
Lake Ho. *SE1* 7C 168 (off Southwark Bri. Rd.)
Lake Ho. Rd. E11 3J 53
Lakehurst Rd. KT19: Eps 5A 148
Lakeland Cl. HA3: Harr 6C 10
Lakenheath N14 5C 6
Laker Ct. SW4 1J 103
Laker Ind. Est. *SE26* 5A 124 (off Kent Ho. La.)
Lake Rd. CR0: Croy 2B 154
RM6: Chad H 4D 38
RM9: Dag 3H 75
SW19 5H 119
Laker Pl. SW15 6G 101
Lakeside BR3: Beck 3D 142
EN2: Enf 4C 6
KT19: Eps 6A 148
N3 2K 29
SM6: Wall 4F 151
W13 6C 62
Lakeside Av. IG4: Ilf 4B 36
SE28 1A 92
Lakeside Cl. DA15: Sidc 5C 110
HA4: Ruis 4E 22
SE25 2G 141
Lakeside Ct. N4 2C 50
Lakeside Cres. EN4: Barn 5J 5
Lakeside Dr. BR2: Short 3C 156
Lakeside Rd. N13 4E 16
W14 3F 83
Lakeside Station (Ruislip Lido Railway) 4F 23
Lakeside Ter. EC2 5D 162
Lakeside Way HA9: Wemb 4G 45
Lakes Rd. BR2: Kes 5A 156
Lakeswood Rd. BR5: Orp 6F 145
Lake, The WD23: Bush 1C 10
Lake Vw. HA8: Edg 5A 12
Lake Vw. Ct. *SW1* 1K 171 (off Bressenden Pl.)
Lake Vw. Est. E3 2A 70
Lakeview Rd. DA16: Well 4B 110
SE27 5A 122
Lake Vw. Ter. *N18* 4A 18 (off Sweet Briar Wlk.)
Lakis Cl. NW3 4A 48
Laleham Av. NW7 3E 12
Laleham Ho. *E2* 3J 163 (off Camlet St.)
Laleham Rd. SE6 7E 106
TW17: Shep 4B 130
Lalor St. SW6 2G 101
Lambarde Av. SE9 4E 126
Lambard Ho. *SE10* 7E 88 (off Langdale Rd.)
Lamb Ct. *E14* 7A 70 (off Narrow St.)
Lamberhurst Ho. SE15 6J 87
Lamberhurst Rd. RM8: Dag 1F 57
SE27 4A 122
Lambert Av. TW9: Rich 3G 99
Lambert Ct. *DA8: Erith* 6J 93 (off Park Cres.)
Lambert Jones M. EC2 5C 162
Lambert Lodge *TW8: Bford* 5D 80 (off Layton Rd.)
Lambert Rd. E16 6K 71
N12 5G 15
SW2 5J 103
Lambert's Pl. CR0: Croy 1D 152
Lamberts Rd. KT5: Surb 5E 134
Lambert St. N1 7A 50
Lambert Wlk. HA9: Wemb 3D 44
Lambert Way N12 5F 15
LAMBETH 3K 85 (3G 173)
Lambeth Bri. SW1 4J 85 (3F 173)
Lambeth Crematorium SW17 4A 120
Lambeth High St. SE1 4K 85 (4G 173)
Lambeth Hill EC4 7C 68 (2C 168)
Lambeth Palace 3K 85 (2G 173)
Lambeth Pal. Rd. SE1 3K 85 (2G 173)
Lambeth Rd. CR0: Croy 7A 140
SE1 4K 85 (3G 173)
Lambeth Towers SE1 2J 173
Lambeth Wlk. SE11 4K 85 (4H 173) (not continuous)
Lambfold Ho. N7 6J 49
Lamb Ho. *SE5* 7C 86 (off Elmington Est.)
SE10 6E 88 (off Haddo St.)
Lamb La. E8 7H 51
Lamble St. NW5 5E 48
Lambley Rd. RM9: Dag 6B 56
Lambolle Pl. NW3 6C 48
Lambolle Rd. NW3 6C 48
Lambourn Cl. CR2: S Croy 7B 152
NW5 4G 49
W7 2K 79
Lambourne Av. SW19 4H 119
Lambourne Ct. IG8: Wfd G 7F 21
Lambourne Gdns. E4 2H 19
EN1: Enf 2A 8
IG11: Bark 7K 55
Lambourne Ho. *NW8* 5B 158 (off Broadley St.)
SE16 4K 87
Lambourne Pl. SE3 1K 107
Lambourne Rd. E11 7E 34
IG3: Ilf 2J 55
IG11: Bark 7J 55
Lambourn Gro. KT1: King T 2H 135
Lambourn Rd. SW8 3F 103
Lambrook Ho. SE15 1G 105
Lambrook Ter. SW6 1G 101
Lamb's Bldgs. EC1 4D 68 (4E 162)
Lamb's Cl. N9 2B 18

Lavender Pond Nature Pk.—Lees Av.

Lavender Pond Nature Pk. 1A 88
Lavender Ri. UB7: W Dray 2C 76
Lavender Rd. CR0: Croy 6K 139
EN2: Enf 1J 7
KT19: Eps 5H 147
SE16 1A 88
SM1: Sutt 4B 150
SM5: Cars 4E 150
SW11 3B 102
UB8: Uxb 5B 58
Lavender Sq. E11 3F 53
Lavender St. E15 6G 53
Lavender Sweep SW11 4D 102
Lavender Ter. SW11 3C 102
Lavender Va. SM6: Wall 6H 151
Lavender Wlk. CR4: Mitc 3E 138
SW11 4D 102
Lavender Way CR0: Croy 6K 141
Lavendon Ho. NW8 3D 158 (off Paveley St.)
Lavengro Rd. SE27 2C 122
Lavenham Rd. SW18 2H 119
Lavernock Rd. DA7: Bex 2G 111
Lavers Rd. N16 3E 50
Laverstoke Gdns. SW15 7B 100
Laverton M. SW5 4K 83
Laverton Pl. SW5 4K 83
Lavidge Rd. SE9 2C 126
Lavina Gro. N1 2K 67
Lavington Cl. E9 6B 52
Lavington Rd.
CR0: Croy 3K 151
W13 1B 80
Lavington St.
SE1 1B 86 (5B 168)
Lavisham Ho. BR1: Brom 5J 125
Lawdons Gdns.
CR0: Croy 4B 152
Lawford Cl. SM6: Wall 7J 151
Lawford Rd. N1 7E 50
NW5 6G 49
W4 7J 81
Law Ho. IG11: Bark 2A 74
Lawless Ho. E14 7E 70 (off Bazely St.)
Lawless St. E14 7D 70
Lawley Ho. TW1: Twick 6D 98
Lawley Rd. N14 7A 6
Lawley St. E5 4J 51
Lawn Cl. BR1: Brom 7K 125
HA4: Ruis 3H 41
KT3: N Mald 2A 136
N9 7A 8
Lawn Cres. TW9: Rich 2G 99
Lawn Dr. E7 4B 54
Lawn Farm Gro.
RM6: Chad H 4E 38
Lawn Gdns. W7 1J 79
Lawn Ho. Cl. E14 2E 88
Lawn La. SW8 6J 85 (7F 173)
Lawn Rd. BR3: Beck 7B 124
NW3 5D 48
Lawns Ct. HA9: Wemb 2F 45
Lawnside SE3 4H 107
Lawns, The DA14: Sidc 4B 128
E4 5H 19
HA5: Pinn 7A 10
SE3 3H 107
SE19 1D 140
SM2: Sutt 7G 149
SW19 5H 119
Lawns Way RM5: Col R 1J 39
Lawnswood EN5: Barn 5B 4
Lawn Ter. SE3 3G 107
Lawn, The UB2: S'hall 5E 78
Lawn Va. HA5: Pinn 2C 24
Lawrence Av. E12 4E 54
E17 1K 33
KT3: N Mald 6K 135
N13 4G 17
NW7 4F 13
Lawrence Bldgs. N16 3F 51
Lawrence Campe Cl. N20 3G 15
Lawrence Cl. E3 3C 70
N15 4E 32
W12 7D 64
Lawrence Ct. N10 3G 31
NW7 5F 13
W3 3J 81 (off Stanley Rd.)
Lawrence Cres. HA8: Edg 2G 27
RM10: Dag 3H 57
Lawrence Dr. UB10: Uxb 4E 40
Lawrence Est. TW4: Houn 4A 96
Lawrence Gdns. NW7 3G 13
Lawrence Hill E4 2H 19
Lawrence Ho. SW1 4D 172 (off Cureton St.)
Lawrence La.
EC2 6C 68 (7D 162)
Lawrence Pde. TW7: Isle 3B 98 (off Lower Sq.)
Lawrence Pl. N1 1J 67 (off Brydon Wlk.)
Lawrence Rd. BR4: W W'ck 4J 155
DA8: Erith 7H 93
E6 1C 72
E13 1K 71
HA5: Pinn 6B 24
N15 4E 32
N18 4C 18 (not continuous)
SE25 4F 141
TW4: Houn 4A 96
TW10: Rich 4C 116
TW12: Hamp 7D 114
UB4: Hayes 2E 58
W5 4D 80
Lawrence St. E16 5H 71
NW7 4G 13
SW3 6C 84 (7C 170)
Lawrence Trad. Est. SE10 4G 89
Lawrence Way NW10 3K 45
Lawrence Weaver Cl.
SM4: Mord 6J 137
Lawrence Yd. N15 4E 32
Lawrie Pk. Av. SE26 5H 123
Lawrie Pk. Cres. SE26 5H 123
Lawrie Pk. Gdns. SE26 4H 123
Lawrie Pk. Rd. SE26 6H 123
Laws Cl. SE25 4D 140
Lawson Cl. E16 5A 72
SW19 3F 119
Lawson Ct. KT6: Surb 7D 134
N4 1K 49 (off Lorne Rd.)
Lawson Gdns. HA5: Pinn 3K 23
Lawson Ho. SE18 6E 90 (off Nightingale Pl.)
W12 7D 64 (off White City Est.)
Lawson Rd. EN3: Enf 1D 8
UB1: S'hall 4E 60
Law St. SE1 3D 86
Lawton Rd. E3 3A 70 (not continuous)
EN4: Barn 3G 5
E10 1E 52
Laxcon Cl. NW10 5K 45
Laxfield Ct. E8 1G 69 (off Pownall Rd.)
Laxford Ho. SW1 4H 171 (off Cundy St.)
Laxley Cl. SE5 7B 86
Laxton Pl. NW1 4F 67 (3K 159)
Layard Rd. CR7: Thor H 2D 140
EN1: Enf 1A 8
SE16 4H 87
Layard Sq. SE16 4H 87
Laybourne Ho. E14 2C 88 (off Admirals Way)
Laybrook Lodge E18 4H 35
Laycock St. N1 6A 50
Layer Gdns. W3 7G 63
Layfield Cl. NW4 7D 28
Layfield Cres. NW4 7D 28
Layfield Ho. SE10 5J 89 (off Kemsing Rd.)
Layfield Rd. NW4 7D 28
Layhams Rd. BR2: Kes 3F 155
BR4: W W'ck 3F 155
Laymarsh Cl. DA17: Belv 3F 93
Laymead Cl. UB5: N'olt 6C 42
Laystall Ct. WC1 4J 161 (off Mount Pleasant)
Laystall St. EC1 4A 68 (4J 161)
Layton Ct. TW8: Bford 5D 80
Layton Cres. CR0: Croy 5A 152
Layton Pl. TW9: Rich 1G 99
Layton Rd. TW3: Houn 4F 97
TW8: Bford 5D 80
Layton's Bldgs.
SE1 2D 86 (6E 168)
Layton's La.
TW16: Sun T 2H 131
Layzell Wlk. SE9 1B 126
Lazar Wlk. N7 2K 49
Lazenby Ct. WC2 2E 166
Leabank Cl. HA1: Harr 3J 43
Leabank Sq. E9 6C 52
Leabank Vw. N15 6G 33
Lea Bon Ct. E15 1H 71 (off Plaistow Gro.)
Leabourne Rd. N16 7G 33
LEA BRIDGE 3K 51
Lea Bri. Ind. Cen. E10 1A 52
Lea Bridge Rd. E5 3J 51
E10 3J 51
E17 5F 35
Lea Cl. TW2: Twick 7D 96
Lea Ct. E4 2K 19
E13 3J 71
Lea Cres. HA4: Ruis 4H 41
Leacroft Av. SW12 7D 102
Leacroft Cl. UB7: W Dray 6A 58
Leadale Av. E4 2H 19
Leadale Rd. N15 6G 33
Leadbeaters Cl. N11 5J 15
Leadbetter Ct. NW10 7K 45 (off Melville Rd.)
Leadenhall Market 6E 68 (1G 169)
Leadenhall Pl.
EC3 6E 68 (1G 169)
Leadenhall St.
EC3 6E 68 (1G 169)
Leadenham Ct. E3 4C 70
Leader Av. E12 5E 54
Leadings, The HA9: Wemb 3J 45
Leaf Cl. HA6: Nwood 1F 23
KT7: T Ditt 5J 133
Leaf Gro. SE27 5A 122
Leaf Ho. HA1: Harr 5K 25 (off Catherine Pl.)
Leafield Cl. SW16 6B 122
Leafield La. DA14: Sidc 3F 129
Leafield Rd. SM1: Sutt 2J 149
SW20 3H 137
Leafy Gro. BR2: Kes 5A 156
Leafy Oak Rd. SE12 4A 126
Leafy Way CR0: Croy 2F 153
Lea Gdns. HA9: Wemb 4F 45
Leagrave St. E5 3J 51
Lea Hall Gdns. E10 1C 52
Lea Hall Rd. E10 1C 52
Leaholme Way HA4: Ruis 6E 22
Lea Ho. NW8 4C 158 (off Salisbury St.)
Leahurst Rd. SE13 5F 107 (not continuous)
Lea Interchange 5C 52
Leake Ct. SE1 2K 85 (7H 167)
Leake St. SE1 2K 85 (6H 167) (not continuous)
Lealand Rd. N15 6F 33
Leamington Av.
BR1: Brom 5A 126
E17 5C 34
SM4: Mord 4G 137
Leamington Cl.
BR1: Brom 4A 126
E12 5C 54
TW3: Houn 5G 97
Leamington Cres.
HA2: Harr 3C 42
Leamington Gdns.
IG3: Ilf 2K 55
Leamington Ho.
HA8: Edg 5A 12
Leamington Pk. W3 5K 63
Leamington Pl.
UB4: Hayes 4H 59
Leamington Rd.
UB2: S'hall 4B 78
Leamington Rd. Vs.
W11 5H 65
Leamore St. W6 4E 82
LEAMOUTH 7G 71
Leamouth Rd. E6 5C 72
E14 6F 71
Leander Ct. KT6: Surb 7D 134
NW9 1A 28
SE8 1C 106
Leander Rd. CR7: Thor H 4K 139
SW2 6K 103
UB5: N'olt 2E 60
Lea Pk. Trad. Est. E10 1B 52 (off Warley Cl.)
Leapold M. E9 1J 69
Learner Dr. HA2: Harr 2E 42
Lea Rd. BR3: Beck 2C 142
EN2: Enf 1J 7
UB2: S'hall 4C 78
Learoyd Gdns. E6 7E 72
Leary Ho. SE11 5K 85
Leas Cl. KT9: Chess 7F 147
Leas Dale SE9 3E 126
Leas Grn. BR7: Chst 6K 127
Leaside Av. N10 3E 30
Leaside Bus. Cen.
EN3: Enf 2G 9
Leaside Ct. UB10: Uxb 3D 58
Leaside Mans. N10 3E 30 (off Fortis Grn.)
Leaside Rd. E5 1J 51
Leasowes Rd. E10 1C 52
Leatherbottle Grn.
DA18: Erith 3F 93
Leather Bottle La.
DA17: Belv 4E 92
Leather Cl. CR4: Mitc 2E 138
Leatherdale St. E1 4J 69
Leather Gdns. E15 1G 71
Leatherhead Cl. N16 1F 51
Leatherhead Rd.
KT9: Chess 7D 146
Leather La. EC1 5A 68 (5J 161) (not continuous)
Leathermarket Ct.
SE1 2E 86 (7G 169)
Leathermarket St.
SE1 2E 86 (7G 169)
Leathersellers Cl.
EN5: Barn 3B 4
Leather St. E1 7K 69
Leathsail Rd. HA2: Harr 3F 43
Leathwaite Rd. SW11 4D 102
Leathwell Rd. SE8 2D 106
Lea Va. DA1: Cray 4K 111
Lea Valley Rd. E4 5F 9
EN3: Enf 5F 9
Lea Valley Trad. Est. N18 6E 18
Lea Valley Viaduct E4 5E 18
N18 5E 18
Leaveland Cl. BR3: Beck 4C 142
Leaver Gdns. UB6: G'frd 2H 61
Leavesden Rd. HA7: Stan 6F 11
Leaves Grn. Rd.
BR2: Kes 7B 156
Lea Vw. Ho. E5 1H 51
Leaway E10 1K 51
Lebanon Av. TW13: Felt 5B 114
Lebanon Gdns. SW18 6J 101
Lebanon Pk. TW1: Twick 7B 98
Lebanon Rd. CR0: Croy 1E 152
SW18 5J 101
Lebrun Sq. SE3 4K 107
Lebus Ho. NW8 1C 158 (off Cochrane St.)
Le Chateau CR0: Croy 3D 152 (off Chatsworth Rd.)
Lechmere App.
IG8: Wfd G 2A 36
Lechmere Av. IG8: Wfd G 2B 36
Lechmere Rd. NW2 6D 46
Leckford Rd. SW18 2A 120
Leckhampton Pl. SW2 7A 104
Leckwith Av. DA7: Bex 6E 92
Lecky St. SW7 5B 84 (5A 170)
Leclair Ho. SE3 3K 107
Leconfield Av. SW13 3B 100
Leconfield Ho. SE5 4E 104
Leconfield Rd. N5 4D 50
Leda Av. EN3: Enf 1E 8
Leda Ct. SW9 7A 86 (off Caldwell St.)
Ledam Ho. EC1 5J 161 (off Bourne Est.)
Leda Rd. SE18 3D 90
Ledbury Ho. SE22 3E 104
W11 6H 65 (off Colville Rd.)
Ledbury M. Nth. W11 7J 65
Ledbury M. W. W11 7J 65
Ledbury Pl. CR0: Croy 4C 152
Ledbury Rd. CR0: Croy 4D 152
W11 6H 65
Ledbury St. SE15 7G 87
Ledrington Rd. SE19 6G 123
Ledway Dr. HA9: Wemb 7F 27
LEE 6J 107
Lee Av. RM6: Chad H 6E 38
Lee Bri. SE13 3E 106
Leechcroft Av.
DA15: Sidc 5K 109
Leechcroft Rd. SM6: Wall 3E 150
Lee Chu. St. SE13 4G 107
Lee Cl. E17 1K 33
EN5: Barn 4F 5
Lee Conservancy Rd. E9 5B 52
Lee Ct. SE13 4F 107 (off Lee High Rd.)
Leecroft Rd. EN5: Barn 5B 4
Leeds Pl. N4 1K 49
Leeds Rd. IG1: Ilf 1H 55
Leeds St. N18 5B 18
Leefern Rd. W12 2C 82
Leegate SE12 5H 107
Lee Green 5H 107
Lee Gro. IG7: Chig 2K 21
Lee High Rd. SE12 3E 106
SE13 3E 106
Lee Ho. EC2 6D 162 (off Monkwell Sq.)
Leeke St. WC1 3K 67 (1G 161)
Leeland Rd. W13 1A 80
Leeland Ter. W13 1A 80
Leeland Way NW10 4B 46
Leemount Ho. NW4 4F 29
Lee Pk. SE3 4H 107
Lee Pk. Way N9 4E 18
N18 4E 18
Leerdam Dr. E14 3E 88
Lee Rd. EN1: Enf 6B 8
NW7 7A 14
SE3 3H 107
SW19 1K 137
UB6: G'frd 1C 62
Lees Av. HA6: Nwood 1H 23

Leyburn Gdns.—Lind Rd.

Leyburn Gdns. CR0: Croy 2E 152
Leyburn Gro. N18 6B 18
Leyburn Rd. N18 6B 18
Leydenhatch La.
BR8: Dart 7J 129
Leyden Mans. N19 7J 31
Leyden St. E1 5F 69 (6J 163)
Leydon Cl. SE16 1K 87
Leyes Rd. E16 7B 72
Leyfield KT4: Wor Pk 1A 148
Leyland Av. EN3: Enf 2F 9
Leyland Gdns. IG8: Wfd G 5F 21
Leyland Ho. *E14* *7D 70*
(off Hale St.)
Leyland Rd. SE12 5J 107
Leylang Rd. SE14 7K 87
Leys Av. RM10: Dag 1J 75
Leys Cl. HA1: Harr 5H 25
Leys Ct. SW9 2A 104
Leysdown Av. DA7: Bex 4J 111
Leysdown Ho. *SE17* *5E 86*
(off Madron St.)
Leysdown Rd. SE9 2C 126
Leysfield Rd. W12 3C 82
Leys Gdns. EN4: Barn 5K 5
Leyspring Rd. E11 1H 53
Leys Rd. E. EN3: Enf 1F 9
Leys Rd. W. EN3: Enf 1F 9
Leys Sq. N3 1K 29
Leys, The HA3: Harr 6F 27
N2 4A 30
Ley St. IG1: Ilf 2F 55
IG2: Ilf 2G 55
Leyswood Dr. IG2: Ilf 5J 37
Leythe Rd. W3 2J 81
LEYTON 2E 52
Leyton Bus. Cen. E10 2C 52
Leyton Ct. SE23 1J 123
Leyton Grange Est. E10 2C 52
Leyton Grn. Rd. E10 6E 34
Leyton Grn. Twr. *E10* *6E 34*
(off Leyton Grn. Rd.)
Leyton Ind. Village E10 7K 33
Leyton Orient F.C. (Matchroom Stadium) *2D 52*
Leyton Pk. Rd. E10 3E 52
Leyton Rd. E15 5E 52
SW19 7A 120
LEYTONSTONE 3G 53
Leytonstone Ho. *E11* *7H 35*
(off Hanbury Dr.)
Leytonstone Rd. E15 4G 53
Leyton Way E11 7G 35
Leywick St. E15 2G 71
Liardet St. SE14 6A 88
Liberia Rd. N5 6B 50
Liberty Av. SW19 1A 138
Liberty Ct. IG11: Bark 2B 74
Liberty M. N22 1B 32
SW12 6F 103
Liberty St. SW9 1K 103
Libra Rd. E3 2B 70
E13 2J 71
Library Ct. N17 3F 33
Library Mans. *W12* *2E 82*
(off Pennard Rd.)
Library Pde. *NW10* *1A 64*
(off Craven Pk. Rd.)
Library Pl. E1 7H 69
Library St. SE1 2B 86 (7A 168)
Library Way TW2: Twick 7G 97
Libro Ct. E4 4H 19
Lichfield Cl. EN4: Barn 3J 5
Lichfield Ct. *KT6: Surb* *5E 134*
(off Claremont Rd.)
TW9: Rich 4E 98
Lichfield Gdns. TW9: Rich 4E 98
Lichfield Gro. N3 1J 29
Lichfield Rd. E3 3A 70
E6 3B 72
HA6: Nwood 3J 23
IG8: Wfd G 4B 20
Lichfield Rd. N9 2B 18
NW2 4G 47
RM8: Dag 4B 56
TW4: Houn 3A 96
TW9: Rich 1F 99
Lichfield Ter. TW9: Rich 5E 98
Lickey Ho. *W14* *6H 83*
(off Nth. End Rd.)
Lidbury Rd. NW7 6B 14
Lidcote Gdns. SW9 2K 103
Liddall Way UB7: W Dray 1B 76
Liddell Cl. HA3: Harr 3D 26
Liddell Gdns. NW10 2E 64
Liddell Rd. NW6 6J 47
Lidding Rd. HA3: Harr 5D 26
Liddington Rd. E15 1H 71
Liddon Rd. BR1: Brom 3A 144
E13 3K 71
Liden Cl. E17 7B 34
Lidfield Rd. N16 4D 50
Lidgate Rd. SE15 7F 87
Lidiard Rd. SW18 2A 120
Lidlington Pl. NW1 2G 67
Lido Sq. N17 2D 32
Lidyard Rd. N19 1G 49
Lifetimes Mus. *3C 152*
(off High St.)
Liffler Rd. SE18 5J 91
Liffords Pl. SW13 2B 100
Lifford St. SW15 4F 101
Lightcliffe Rd. N13 4F 17
Lighter Cl. SE16 4A 88
Lighterman Ho. E14 7E 70
Lighterman M. E1 6K 69
Lightermans Rd. E14 2C 88
Lightermans Wlk. SW18 4J 101
Lightfoot Rd. N8 5J 31
Light Horse Ct. SW3 6G 171
Lightley Cl. HA0: Wemb 1E 62
Ligonier St. E2 4F 69 (3J 163)
Lilac Cl. E4 6G 19
Lilac Ct. E13 1A 72
TW11: Tedd 4K 115
Lilac Gdns. CR0: Croy 3C 154
RM7: Rush G 1K 57
UB3: Hayes 6G 59
W5 3D 80
Lilac Ho. SE4 3C 106
Lilac Pl. SE11 4K 85 (4G 173)
UB7: W Dray 7B 58
Lilac St. W12 7C 64
Lilburne Gdns. SE9 5C 108
Lilburne Rd. SE9 5C 108
Lilburne Wlk. NW10 6J 45
Lile Cres. W7 5J 61
Lilestone Ho. *NW8* *3B 158*
(off Frampton St.)
Lilestone St.
NW8 4C 66 (3C 158)
Lilford Ho. SE5 2C 104
Lilford Rd. SE5 2B 104
Lilian Barker Cl. SE12 5J 107
Lilian Board Way
UB5: N'olt 5H 43
UB6: G'frd 5H 43
Lilian Cl. N16 3E 50
Lilian Gdns. IG8: Wfd G 1K 35
Lilian Rd. SW16 1G 139
Lillechurch Rd. RM8: Dag 6B 56
Lilleshall Rd. SM4: Mord 6B 138
Lilley Cl. E1 1G 87
Lilley La. NW7 5E 12
Lillian Av. W3 2G 81
Lillian Rd. SW13 6C 82
Lillie Mans. *SW6* *6G 83*
(off Lillie Rd.)
Lillie Rd. SW6 6G 83
Lillieshall Rd. SW4 3F 103
Lillie Yd. SW6 6J 83
Lillington Gdns. Est.
SW1 4B 172
Lilliput Av. UB5: N'olt 1C 60
Lilliput Ct. SE12 5K 107
Lilliput Rd. RM7: Rush G 7K 39
Lily Cl. W14 4F 83
(not continuous)
Lily Gdns. HA0: Wemb 2C 62
Lily Nichols Ho. *E16* *1B 90*
(off Connaught Rd.)
Lily Pl. EC1 5A 68 (5K 161)
Lily Rd. E17 6C 34
Lilyville Rd. SW6 1H 101
Limberg Ho. SE8 4B 88
Limborough Ho. *E14* *5C 70*
(off Thomas Rd.)
Limbourne Av. RM8: Dag 7F 39
Limburg Rd. SW11 4C 102
Lime Av. UB7: W Dray 7B 58
Limeburner La.
EC4 6B 68 (1A 168)
Lime Cl. BR1: Brom 4C 144
E1 1G 87
HA3: Harr 2A 26
HA5: Pinn 3H 23
IG9: Buck H 2G 21
RM7: Rom 4J 39
SM5: Cars 2D 150
Lime Ct. CR4: Mitc 2B 138
E11 *2G 53*
(off Trinity Cl.)
E17 5E 34
HA1: Harr 6K 25
SE9 2F 127
Lime Cres. TW16: Sun T 2A 132
Limecroft Cl. KT19: Eps 7K 147
Limedene Cl. HA5: Pinn 1B 24
Lime Gro. DA15: Sidc 6K 109
E4 6G 19
HA4: Ruis 6K 23
KT3: N Mald 3K 135
N20 1C 14
TW1: Twick 6K 97
UB3: Hayes 7F 59
W12 2E 82
Limeharbour E14 3D 88
LIMEHOUSE 6B 70
Lime Ho. TW9: Rich 1H 99
Limehouse C'way. E14 7B 70
Limehouse Ct. E14 6C 70
Limehouse Cut *E14* *5D 70*
(off Morris Rd.)
Limehouse Flds. Est. E14 5A 70
Limehouse Link E14 6A 70
Lime Kiln Dr. SE7 6K 89
Limekiln Pl. SE19 7F 123
Limerick Cl. SW12 7G 103
Lime Rd. TW9: Rich 4F 99
Lime Row DA18: Erith 3F 93
Limerston St.
SW10 6A 84 (7A 170)
Limes Av. CR0: Croy 3A 152
E11 4K 35
E12 3C 54
N12 4F 15
NW7 6F 13
NW11 7G 29
SE20 7H 123
SM5: Cars 1D 150
SW13 2B 100
Limes Av., The N11 5A 16
Limes Cl. N11 5B 16
TW15: Ashf 5C 112
Limes Ct. *NW6* *7G 47*
(off Brondesbury Pk.)
Limesdale Gdns. HA8: Edg 2J 27
Limes Fld. Rd. SW14 3A 100
Limesford Rd. SE15 4K 105
Limes Gdns. SW18 6J 101
Limes Gro. SE13 4E 106
Limes Pl. CR0: Croy 7D 140
Limes Rd. BR3: Beck 2D 142
CR0: Croy 6D 140
Limes, The BR2: Short 2C 156
KT8: W Mole 4F 133
Limes, The SW18 6J 101
W2 7J 65
Limestone Wlk.
DA18: Erith 2D 92
Lime St. E17 4A 34
EC3 7E 68 (2G 169)
Lime St. Pas.
EC3 6E 68 (1G 169)
Limes Wlk. SE15 4J 105
W5 2D 80
Lime Ter. W7 7J 61
Lime Tree Av. KT10: Esh 7H 133
Limetree Cl. SW2 1K 121
Lime Tree Ct.
CR2: S Croy 6C 152
Lime Tree Gro.
CR0: Croy 3B 154
Lime Tree Pl. CR4: Mitc 1F 139
Lime Tree Rd.
TW5: Houn 1F 97
Limetree Ter. DA16: Well 3A 110
SE6 1B 124
Lime Tree Wlk. BR4:
W W'ck 4H 155
EN2: Enf 1H 7
WD23: Bush 1D 10
Limetree Wlk. SW17 5E 120
Lime Wlk. E15 1G 71
Limewood Cl. BR3: Beck 5E 142
E17 4B 34
W13 6B 62
Limewood Ct. IG4: Ilf 5D 36
Limewood Rd. DA8: Erith 7J 93
Limpsfield Av.
CR7: Thor H 5K 139
SW19 2F 119
Linacre Cl. SE15 3H 105
Linacre Ct. W6 5F 83
Linacre Rd. NW2 6D 46
Linale Ho. N1 1E 162
Linberry Wlk. SE8 4B 88
Linchmere Rd. SE12 7H 107
Lincoln Av. N14 3B 16
RM7: Rush G 2K 57
SW19 3F 119
TW2: Twick 2G 115
Lincoln Cl. HA2: Harr 5D 24
SE25 6G 141
UB6: G'frd 1G 61
Lincoln Ct. *CR2: S Croy* *5C 152*
(off Warham Rd.)
N16 7D 32
SE12 3A 126
Lincoln Cres. EN1: Enf 5K 7
Lincoln Gdns. IG1: Ilf 7C 36
Lincoln Grn. Rd.
BR5: Orp 5K 145
Lincoln Ho. SW3 2D 84
SW9 7A 86
Lincoln M. NW6 1H 65
SE21 2D 122
Lincoln Pde. N2 3C 30
Lincoln Rd. CR4: Mitc 5J 139
DA14: Sidc 5B 128
E7 6B 54
E13 4K 71
E18 1J 35
EN1: Enf 4K 7
EN3: Enf 5B 8
HA0: Wemb 6D 44
HA2: Harr 5D 24
HA6: Nwood 3H 23
KT3: N Mald 3J 135
KT4: Wor Pk 1D 148
N2 3C 30
SE25 3H 141
TW13: Felt 3D 114
Lincolns Inn Flds.
WC2 6K 67 (7G 161)
Lincoln's Inn Hall
6K 67 (7H 161)
Lincolns, The NW7 3G 13
Lincoln St. E11 2G 53
SW3 4D 84 (4E 170)
Lincoln Way EN1: Enf 5C 8
TW16: Sun T 1G 131
Lincombe Rd.
BR1: Brom 3H 125
Lindal Cres. EN2: Enf 4D 6
Lindal Rd. SE4 5B 106
Lindbergh Rd. SM6: Wall 7J 151
Linden Av. CR7: Thor H 4B 140
EN1: Enf 1B 8
HA4: Ruis 1J 41
HA9: Wemb 5F 45
NW10 2F 65
TW3: Houn 5F 97
Linden Cl. HA4: Ruis 1J 41
HA7: Stan 5G 11
KT7: T Ditt 7K 133
N14 6B 6
Linden Ct. DA14: Sidc 4J 127
W12 1E 82
Linden Cres. IG8: Wfd G 6E 20
KT1: King T 2F 135
UB6: G'frd 6K 43
Lindenfield BR7: Chst 2F 145
Linden Gdns. EN1: Enf 1B 8
W2 7J 65
W4 5A 82
Linden Gro. KT3: N Mald 3A 136
SE15 3H 105
SE26 6J 123
TW11: Tedd 5K 115
Linden Ho. *SE8* *6B 88*
(off Abinger Gro.)
SE15 3H 105
TW12: Hamp 6E 114
Linden Lawns HA9: Wemb 4F 45
Linden Lea N2 5A 30
Linden Leas
BR4: W W'ck 2F 155
Linden M. N1 5D 50
W2 7J 65
Linden Pl. CR4: Mitc 4C 138
Linden Rd. N10 4F 31
N11 2J 15
N15 4C 32
TW12: Hamp 7E 114
Lindens, The CR0: Croy 6E 154
E17 *4D 34*
(off Prospect Hill)
N12 5G 15
W4 1J 99
Linden St. RM7: Rom 4K 39
Linden Wlk. N19 2G 49
Linden Way N14 6B 6
TW17: Shep 5E 130
Lindeth Cl. HA7: Stan 6G 11
Lindfield Gdns. NW3 5K 47
Lindfield Rd. CR0: Croy 6F 141
W5 4C 62
Lindfield St. E14 6C 70
Lindhill Cl. EN3: Enf 2E 8
Lindholme Ct. *NW9* *1A 28*
(off Pageant Av.)
Lindisfarne Rd. RM8: Dag 3C 56
SW20 7C 118
Lindisfarne Way E9 4A 52
Lindley Ct. KT1: King T 1C 134
Lindley Est. SE15 7G 87
Lindley Ho. *E1* *5J 69*
(off Lindley St.)
SE15 *7G 87*
(off Peckham Pk. Rd.)
Lindley Pl. TW9: Rich 1G 99
Lindley Rd. E10 2E 52
Lindley St. E1 5J 69
Lindop Ho. *E1* *4A 70*
(off Mile End Rd.)
Lindore Rd. SW11 4D 102
Lindores Rd. SM5: Cars 7A 138
Lindo St. SE15 2J 105
Lind Rd. SM1: Sutt 5A 150

Littleton La.—Longfield

Littleton La. TW17: Shep 6A 130
Littleton Rd. HA1: Harr 2K 43
TW15: Ashf 7E 112
Littleton St. SW18 2A 120
Lit. Trinity La.
EC4 7C 68 (2D 168)
Little Turnstile
WC1 5K 67 (6G 161)
Lit. Warkworth Ho.
TW7: Isle 2B 98
Littlewood SE13 6E 106
Littlewood Cl. W13 3B 80
Lit. Wood St.
KT1: King T 2D 134
Livermere Ct. *E8* *1F 69*
(off Queensbridge Rd.)
Livermere Rd. E8 1F 69
Liverpool Gro. SE17 5C 86
Liverpool Rd.
CR7: Thor H 3C 140
E10 6E 34
E16 5G 71
KT2: King T 7G 117
N1 5A 50
N7 5A 50
W5 2D 80
Liverpool St.
EC2 5E 68 (6G 163)
Livesey Cl. KT1: King T 3F 135
SE28 2G 91
Livesey Mus. *6H 87*
Livesey Pl. SE15 6G 87
Livingstone Ct. E10 6E 34
HA3: Harr 3K 25
Livingstone Ho. NW10 7K 45
SE5 *7C 86*
(off Wyndham Rd.)
Livingstone Lodge *W2* *5J 65*
(off Admiral Wlk.)
Livingstone Mans. *W14* *6G 83*
(off Queen's Club Gdns.)
Livingstone Pl. E14 5E 88
Livingstone Rd.
CR7: Thor H 2C 140
E15 1E 70
E17 6D 34
N13 6D 16
SW11 3B 102
TW3: Houn 4G 97
UB1: S'hall 7B 60
Livonia St. W1 6G 67 (1B 166)
Lizard St. EC1 3C 68 (2D 162)
Lizban St. SE3 7K 89
Llandovery Ho. *E14* *2E 88*
(off Chipka St.)
Llanelly Rd. NW2 2H 47
Llanover Rd. HA9: Wemb 3D 44
SE18 6E 90
Llanthony Rd.
SM4: Mord 5B 138
Llanvanor Rd. NW2 2H 47
Llewellyn Ct. SE20 1J 141
Llewellyn St. SE16 2G 87
Lloyd Av. SW16 1J 139
Lloyd Baker St.
WC1 3K 67 (2H 161)
(not continuous)
Lloyd Ct. HA5: Pinn 5B 24
Lloyd Ho. BR3: Beck 6D 124
Lloyd M. EN3: Enf 1H 9
Lloyd Pk. Av. CR0: Croy 4F 153
Lloyd Pk. Ho. E17 3C 34
Lloyd Rd. E6 1D 72
E17 4K 33
KT4: Wor Pk 3E 148
RM9: Dag 6F 57
Lloyd's Av. EC3 6E 68 (1H 169)
Lloyds Building *6E 68 (1G 169)*
Lloyd's Pl. SE3 2G 107
Lloyd Sq. WC1 3A 68 (1J 161)
Lloyd's Row EC1 3A 68 (2K 161)
Lloyd St. WC1 3A 68 (1J 161)
Lloyds Way BR3: Beck 5A 142
Lloyds Wharf SE1 6K 169
Lloyd Thomas Ct. N22 7E 16
Lloyd Vs. *SE4* *2C 106*
(off Lewisham Way)
Loampit Hill SE13 2C 106
LOAMPIT VALE 3E 106
Loampit Va. SE13 3D 106
Loanda Cl. E8 1F 69
Loats Rd. SW2 6J 103
Lobelia Cl. E6 5C 72
Locarno Ct. SW16 5G 121
Locarno Rd. UB6: G'frd 4H 61
W3 1J 81
Lochaber Rd. SE13 4G 107
Lochaline St. W6 6E 82
Lochan Cl. UB4: Hayes 4C 60
Lochinvar St. SW12 7F 103
Lochleven Ho. *N2* *2B 30*
(off Grange, The)
Lochmere Cl. DA8: Erith 6H 93
Lochmore Ho. *SW1* *4H 171*
(off Cundy St.)
Lochnagar St. E14 5E 70
Lockbridge Ct. *W9* *5J 65*
(off Woodfield Rd.)
Lock Chase SE3 3G 107
Lock Cl. UB2: S'hall 2G 79
Locke Ho. *SW8* *1G 103*
(off Wadhurst Rd.)
Lockesley Dr. BR5: Orp 6K 145
Lockesley Sq. KT6: Surb 6D 134
Locket Rd. HA3: Harr 3J 25
Lockfield Av. EN3: Enf 2F 9
Lockgate Cl. E9 5B 52
Lockhart Cl. EN3: Enf 5C 8
N7 6K 49
Lockhart Ho. *SE10* *7D 88*
(off Tarves Way)
Lockhart St. E3 4B 70
Lockhurst St. E5 4K 51
Lockie Pl. SE25 3G 141
Lockier Wlk. HA9: Wemb 3D 44
Lockington Rd. SW8 1F 103
Lock Keepers Quay *SE16* *3K 87*
(off Brunswick Quay)
Lockmead Rd. N15 6G 33
SE13 3E 106
Lock Rd. TW10: Rich 4C 116
LOCKSBOTTOM 3E 156
Locksfield Pl. E14 5D 88
Locksfields *SE17* *4D 86*
(off Catesby St.)
Lockside *E14* *7A 70*
(off Narrow St.)
Locks La. CR4: Mitc 1E 138
Locksley Est. E14 6B 70
Locksley St. E14 5B 70
Locksmeade Rd.
TW10: Rich 4C 116
Lockswood Cl. EN4: Barn 4J 5
Lock Vw. Ct. *E14* *7A 70*
(off Narrow St.)
Lockwood Cl. SE26 4K 123
Lockwood Ho.
SE11 6A 86 (7J 173)
Lockwood Ind. Pk. N17 3H 33
Lockwood Sq. SE16 3H 87
Lockwood Way E17 2K 33
KT9: Chess 5G 147
Lockyer Est. SE1 7F 169
(not continuous)
Lockyer Ho. *SE10* *5H 89*
(off Armitage Rd.)
SW8 *7H 85*
(off Wandsworth Rd.)
SW15 3F 101
Lockyer M. EN3: Enf 1J 9
Lockyer St. SE1 2D 86 (7F 169)
Locomotive Dr.
TW14: Felt 1J 113
Locton Grn. E3 1B 70
Loddiges Ho. E9 7J 51
Loddiges Rd. E9 7J 51
Loder St. SE15 7J 87
Lodge Av. CR0: Croy 3A 152
HA3: Harr 4E 26
RM8: Dag 6B 56
RM9: Dag 1A 74
SW14 3A 100
Lodge Cl. HA8: Edg 6A 12
N18 5H 17
SM6: Wall 1E 150
TW7: Isle 1B 98
Lodge Ct. HA0: Wemb 6E 44
Lodge Dr. N13 4F 17
Lodge Gdns. BR3: Beck 5B 142
Lodge Hill DA16: Well 7B 92
IG4: Ilf 4C 36
Lodgehill Pk. Cl.
HA2: Harr 2F 43
Lodge La. CR0: Croy 6C 154
DA5: Bexl 6D 110
N12 5F 15
RM5: Col R 1G 39
Lodge Pl. SM1: Sutt 5K 149
Lodge Rd. BR1: Brom 7K 125
CR0: Croy 6B 140
NW4 4E 28
NW8 3B 66 (2B 158)
SM6: Wall 5F 151
Lodge Vs. IG8: Wfd G 6C 20
Lodge Way TW15: Ashf 2A 112
TW17: Shep 2E 130
Lodore Gdns. NW9 5A 28
Lodore Grn. UB10: Uxb 3A 40
Lodore St. E14 6E 70
Loft Ho. Pl. KT9: Chess 6C 146
Loftie St. SE16 2G 87
Lofting Rd. N1 7K 49
Loftus Road *1D 82*
Loftus Rd. W12 1D 82
Logan Cl. EN3: Enf 1E 8
TW4: Houn 3D 96
Logan Ct. RM1: Rom 5K 39
Logan M. RM1: Rom 5K 39
W8 4J 83
Logan Pl. SW5 4J 83
Logan Rd. HA9: Wemb 2D 44
N9 2C 18
Loggetts SE21 2E 122
Logs Hill BR1: Brom 1C 144
BR7: Chst 7C 126
Logs Hill Cl. BR7: Chst 1C 144
Lohmann Ho. SE11 7J 173
Lois Dr. TW17: Shep 5D 130
Lolesworth Cl. E1 5F 69 (6J 163)
Lollard St. SE11 4K 85 (3H 173)
(not continuous)
Loman St. SE1 2B 86 (6B 168)
Lomas Cl. CR0: Croy 7E 154
Lomas St. E1 5G 69
Lombard Av. EN3: Enf 1D 8
IG3: Ilf 1J 55
Lombard Bus. Cen., The
SW11 2B 102
Lombard Bus. Pk.
CR0: Croy 7K 139
Lombard Ct. EC3 7D 68 (2F 169)
RM7: Rom 4J 39
W3 1H 81
Lombard La.
EC4 6A 68 (1K 167)
Lombard Rd. N11 5A 16
SW11 2B 102
SW19 2K 137
LOMBARD RDBT. 7K 139
Lombard St.
EC3 6D 68 (1F 169)
Lombard Trad. Est. SE7 4K 89
Lombard Wall SE7 3K 89
(not continuous)
Lombardy Cl. IG6: Ilf 7K 21
Lombardy Pl. W2 7K 65
Lombardy Retail Pk.
UB3: Hayes 7K 59
Lomond Cl. HA0: Wemb 7F 45
N15 5E 32
Lomond Gdns.
CR2: S Croy 7A 154
Lomond Gro. SE5 7D 86
Lomond Ho. SE5 7D 86
Loncroft Rd. SE5 6E 86
Londesborough Rd.
N16 4E 50
Londinium Twr. *E1* *2K 169*
(off W. Tenter St.)
London Academy of Music & Dramatic Art *4J 83*
(off Cromwell Rd.)
London Aquarium
2K 85 (6G 167)
London Arena *3D 88*
London Bri. SE1 1D 86 (4F 169)
London Bri. St.
SE1 1D 86 (5F 169)
London Bri. Wlk. *SE1* *4F 169*
(off Duke St. Hill)
London Broncos Rugby League Football Club *6D 80*
London Business School
4D 66 (3E 158)
London Butterfly House *1B 98*
London Canal Mus. *2J 67*
LONDON CITY AIRPORT 7C 72
London City College in Schiller University
1A 86 (5J 167)
London Coliseum *3E 166*
(off St Martin's La.)
London College of Fashion
3H 163
Baltic St. E.
4C 68 (4C 162)
Londonderry Pde.
DA8: Erith 7K 93
London Dungeon *5F 169*
London Eye *2K 85 (6G 167)*
London Flds. E. Side E8 7H 51
London Flds. W. Side E8 7G 51
London Fruit Exchange
E1 *6J 163*
(off Brushfield St.)
London Gas Mus., The *4F 71*
London Guildhall University
1J 169
(off Jewry St.)
Castle St. *7K 163*
6G 69
(off Coke St.)
Goulston St. *6F 69*
Minories *7F 69*
Moorgate *5D 68 (6F 163)*
LONDON HEATHROW AIRPORT
3D 94
London Ho. *NW8* *2C 66*
(off Avenue Rd.)
WC1 4K 67 (3G 161)
London Ind. Pk., The E6 5F 73
London La. BR1: Brom 7H 125
E8 7H 51
London Master Bakers
Almshouses E10 6D 34
London Metropolitan University
5A 50
London M. W2 6B 66 (7B 158)
London Motorcycle Mus.
3G 61
London Palladium *1A 166*
(off Argyll St.)
London Planetarium
4E 66 (4G 159)
London Rd. BR1: Brom 7H 125
CR0: Croy 7B 140
CR4: Mitc 7E 138
(Carshalton Rd.)
London Rd. CR4: Mitc 5C 138
(Bishopsford Rd.)
CR4: Mitc 2D 138
(Holborn Way)
CR7: Thor H 7B 140
DA1: Bexl, Cray 5K 111
E13 2J 71
EN2: Enf 3J 7
HA1: Harr 2J 43
HA7: Stan 5H 11
HA9: Wemb 5E 44
IG11: Bark 7F 55
(Nth. Circular Rd.)
KT2: King T 2F 135
(not continuous)
KT17: Eps 7B 148
RM7: Chad H, Rom 6G 39
SE1 3B 86 (7A 168)
SE23 1H 123
SM4: Mord 5J 137
SW16 1K 139
SW17 7D 120
TW3: Houn 3G 97
TW7: Isle 5A 98
TW14: Felt 2A 112
TW15: Ashf 2A 112
LONDON ROAD RDBT. 6A 98
London School of Economics & Politics, The
6K 67 (1H 167)
London Stile W4 5G 81
London St. EC3 7E 68 (2H 169)
W2 6B 66 (7A 158)
London Ter. E2 2G 69
London Transport Mus.
7J 67 (2F 167)
London Underwriting Cen.
EC3 7E 68 (2H 169)
London Wall EC2 5C 68 (6D 162)
London Wall Bldgs. EC2 6F 163
London Welsh R.U.F.C.
(Old Deer Pk.) *3E 98*
London Westland Heliport
2B 102
London Wetland Cen. *1D 100*
London Wharf *E2* *1H 69*
(off Wharf Pl.)
London Wildlife Trust *1H 67*
London Zoo *2E 66*
LONESOME 1G 139
Lonesome Way SW16 1F 139
Long Acre WC2 7J 67 (2E 166)
Longacre Cl. EN2: Enf 3H 7
Long Acre Ct. W13 5A 62
Longacre Pl. SM5: Cars 6E 150
Longacre Rd. E17 1F 35
Longbeach Rd. SW11 3D 102
Longberrys NW2 3H 47
Longboat Row UB1: S'hall 6D 60
Longbridge Ho. *RM8: Dag* *4B 56*
(off Gainsborough Rd.)
Longbridge Rd.
IG11: Bark 6H 55
RM8: Dag 4A 56
Longbridge Way SE13 5E 106
Longcroft SE9 3D 126
Longcrofte Rd. HA8: Edg 7J 11
Long Deacon Rd. E4 1B 20
LONG DITTON 1C 146
Longdon Wood
BR2: Kes 3C 156
Longdown Rd. SE6 4C 124
Long Dr. HA4: Ruis 5A 42
UB6: G'frd 1F 61
UB7: W Dray 2A 76
W3 6A 64
Long Elmes HA3: Harr 1F 25
Longfellow Rd. E17 6B 34
KT4: Wor Pk 2C 148
Longfellow Way SE1 4F 87
Long Fld. NW9 7F 13
Longfield BR1: Brom 1H 143

A-Z London 287

Longfield Av. E17 ....4A 34
HA9: Wemb 1E 44
NW7 ....7H 13
SM6: Wall 1E 150
W5 ....7C 62
Longfield Cres. SE26 ....3J 123
Longfield Dr. CR4: Mitc 7C 120
SW14 ....5H 99
Longfield Est. SE1 ....4F 87
Longfield Rd. W5 ....6C 62
Longfield St. SW18 ....7J 101
Longfield Wlk. W5 ....6C 62
Longford Av. TW14: Felt 6G 95
TW19: Staines 1A 112
UB1: S'hall 7F 61
Longford Cl.
TW12: Hamp 4E 114
TW13: Felt 3C 114
UB4: Hayes 7B 60
Longford Ct. KT19: Eps 4J 147
NW4 ....4F 29
UB1: S'hall 1E 78
(off Uxbridge Rd.)
Longford Gdns.
SM1: Sutt 3A 150
UB4: Hayes 7B 60
Longford Ho. *BR1: Brom 5F 125*
(off Brangbourne Rd.)
E1 ....6J 69
(off Jubilee St.)
TW12: Hamp 4E 114
Longford Rd. TW2: Twick 1E 114
Longford St.
NW1 ....4F 67 (3K 159)
Longford Wlk. SW2 ....7A 104
Longford Way
TW19: Staines 1A 112
Longhayes Av.
RM6: Chad H 4D 38
Longhayes Ct.
RM6: Chad H 4D 38
Longheath Gdns.
CR0: Croy 5J 141
Longhedge Ho. *SE26 ....4G 123*
(off High Level Dr.)
Long Hedges TW3: Houn 2E 96
Longhedge St. SW11 ....2E 102
Longhill Rd. SE6 ....2F 125
Longhook Gdns.
UB5: N'olt 2J 59
Longhope Cl. SE15 ....6E 86
Longhurst Rd. CR0: Croy 6H 141
SE13 ....5F 107
Longland Ct. SE1 ....5G 87
Longland Dr. N20 ....3E 14
LONGLANDS 3G 127
Longlands Ct.
DA15: Sidc 2K 127
W11 ....7H 65
(off Westbourne Gro.)
Longlands Pk. Cres.
DA15: Sidc 3J 127
Longlands Rd.
DA15: Sidc 3J 127
Long La. CR0: Croy 6H 141
DA7: Bex 7D 92
EC1 ....5B 68 (6B 162)
N3 ....1K 29
(not continuous)
SE1 ....2D 86 (7E 168)
TW19: Staines 2B 112
UB10: Uxb 3C 58
Longleat Ho. *SW1 ....5C 172*
(off Rampayne St.)
Longleat Rd. EN1: Enf 5K 7
Longleat Way TW14: Felt 7F 95
Longleigh Ho. *SE5 ....1E 104*
(off Peckham Rd.)
Longleigh La. SE2 ....6C 92
Long Lents Ho. NW10 ....1K 63
Longley Av. HA0: Wemb 1F 63
Longley Ct. SW8 ....1J 103
Longley Rd. CR0: Croy 7B 140
HA1: Harr 5G 25
SW17 ....6C 120
Long Leys E4 ....6J 19
Longley St. SE1 ....4G 87
Longley Way NW2 ....3E 46
Longman Ho. *E2 ....2K 69*
(off Mace St.)
E8 ....1F 69
(off Haggerston Rd.)
Long Mark Rd. E16 ....5B 72
Longmarsh La. SE28 ....1J 91
Long Mead NW9 ....1B 28
Longmead BR7: Chst 2E 144
Longmead Dr.
DA14: Sidc 2D 128
Longmead Ho. SE27 ....5C 122
Long Mdw. NW5 ....5H 49
Long Mdw. Cl.
BR4: W W'ck 7E 142
Longmeadow Rd.
DA15: Sidc 1J 127
Longmead Rd.
KT7: T Ditt 7J 133
SW17 ....5D 120
UB3: Hayes 7H 59
Longmore Av. EN4: Barn 6F 5
EN5: Barn 6F 5
Longmore Gdns. Est.
SW1 ....4B 172
Longmore St.
SW1 ....4G 85 (4A 172)
Longnor Est. E1 ....3K 69
Longnor Rd. E1 ....3K 69
Long Pond Rd. SE3 ....1G 107
Longreach Ct. IG11: Bark 2H 73
Long Reach Rd.
IG11: Bark 4K 73
Longridge Ho. SE1 ....3C 86
Longridge La. UB1: S'hall 6F 61
Longridge Rd. IG11: Bark 7G 55
SW5 ....4J 83
Long Ridges *N10 ....3E 30*
(off Fortis Grn.)
Long Rd. SW4 ....4F 103
Longs Ct. TW9: Rich 4F 99
WC2 ....3D 166
Longshaw Rd. E4 ....3A 20
Longshore SE8 ....4B 88
Longshott Ct. *SW5 ....4J 83*
(off W. Cromwell Rd.)
Longstaff Cres. SW18 ....6J 101
Longstaff Rd. SW18 ....6J 101
Longstone Av. NW10 ....7B 46
Longstone Ct. *SE1 ....7E 168*
(off Gt. Dover St.)
Longstone Rd. SW17 ....5F 121
Long St. E2 ....3F 69 (1J 163)
Longthornton Rd.
SW16 ....2G 139
Longton Av. SE26 ....4G 123
Longton Gro. SE26 ....4H 123
Longview Vs. RM5: Col R 1F 39
Longview Way
RM5: Col R 1K 39
Longville Rd. SE11 ....4B 86
Long Wlk. KT3: N Mald 3J 135
SE1 ....3E 86
SE18 ....6F 91
SW13 ....2A 100
Longwalk Rd.
UB11: Uxb 1D 76
Long Wall E15 ....3F 71
Longwater Ho.
KT1: King T 3D 134
(off Portsmouth Rd.)
Longwood Dr. SW15 ....6C 100
Longwood Gdns. IG5: Ilf 4D 36
IG6: Ilf 4D 36
Longworth Cl. SE28 ....6D 74
Long Yd. WC1 ....4K 67 (4G 161)
Loning, The NW9 ....4B 28
Lonsdale Av. E6 ....4B 72
HA9: Wemb 5E 44
RM7: Rom 6J 39
Lonsdale Cl. E6 ....4C 72
HA5: Pinn 1C 24
HA8: Edg 5A 12
SE9 ....3B 126
UB8: Uxb 5E 58
Lonsdale Ct.
KT6: Surb 7D 134
Lonsdale Cres. IG2: Ilf 6F 37
Lonsdale Dr. EN2: Enf 4C 6
Lonsdale Gdns.
CR7: Thor H 4K 139
Lonsdale Ho. *W11 ....6H 65*
(off Lonsdale Rd.)
Lonsdale M. TW9: Rich 1G 99
W11 ....6H 65
(off Lonsdale Rd.)
Lonsdale Pl. N1 ....7A 50
Lonsdale Rd. DA7: Bex 2F 111
E11 ....6H 35
NW6 ....1H 65
SE25 ....4H 141
SW13 ....1B 100
UB2: S'hall 3B 78
W4 ....4B 82
W11 ....6H 65
Lonsdale Sq. N1 ....7A 50
Lonsdale Yd. W11 ....7J 65
Loobert Rd. N15 ....3E 32
Looe Gdns. IG6: Ilf 3F 37
Loop Rd. BR7: Chst 6G 127
Lopen Rd. N18 ....4K 17
Lopez Ho. SW9 ....3J 103
Lorac Ct. SM2: Sutt 7J 149
Loraine Cl. EN3: Enf 5D 8
Loraine Ct. BR7: Chst 5F 127
Loraine Ho. SM6: Wall 4F 151
Loraine Rd. N7 ....4K 49
W4 ....6H 81
Lord Amory Way E14 ....2E 88
Lord Av. IG5: Ilf 4D 36
Lord Chancellor Wlk.
KT2: King T 1J 135
Lord Ct. IG5: Ilf 4D 36
Lordell Pl. SW19 ....6E 118
Lorden Wlk.
E2 ....3G 69 (2K 163)
Lord Gdns. IG5: Ilf 4D 36
Lord Hills Bri. W2 ....5K 65
Lord Hills Rd. W2 ....5K 65
Lord Holland La. SW9 ....2A 104
Lord Knyvetts Ct.
TW19: Staines 6A 94
Lord Napier Pl. W6 ....5C 82
Lord Nth. St.
SW1 ....3J 85 (2E 172)
Lord Roberts M. SW6 ....7K 83
Lord Robert's Ter. SE18 ....5E 90
Lords Cl. SE21 ....2C 122
TW13: Felt 2C 114
Lord's Cricket Ground
Marylebone & Middlesex County
Cricket Clubs
..........3B 66 (2B 158)
Lordship Gro. N16 ....2D 50
Lordship La. N22 ....2A 32
SE22 ....4F 105
Lordship La. Est. SE21 ....7G 105
Lordship Pk. N16 ....2C 50
Lordship Pk. M. N16 ....2C 50
Lordship Pl.
SW3 ....6C 84 (7C 170)
Lordship Rd. N16 ....1D 50
UB5: N'olt 7C 42
Lordship Ter. N16 ....2D 50
Lordsmead Rd. N17 ....1E 32
Lord St. E16 ....1C 90
Lords Vw. NW8 ....3B 66 (2C 158)
Lord Warwick St. SE18 ....3D 90
Loreburn Ho. N7 ....4K 49
Lorenzo St.
WC1 ....3K 67 (1G 161)
Loretto Gdns. HA3: Harr 4E 26
Lorian Cl. N12 ....4E 14
Lorimar Bus. Cen.
RM13: Rain 5K 75
Loring Rd. N20 ....2H 15
SE14 ....1A 106
TW7: Isle 2K 97
Loris Rd. W6 ....3E 82
Lorn Ct. SW9 ....2A 104
Lorne Av. CR0: Croy 7K 141
Lorne Cl. NW8 ....3C 66 (2D 158)
Lorne Gdns. CR0: Croy 7K 141
E11 ....4A 36
W11 ....2F 83
Lorne Ho. *E1 ....5A 70*
(off Ben Jonson Rd.)
Lorne Rd. E7 ....4K 53
E17 ....5C 34
HA3: Harr 2K 25
N4 ....1K 49
TW10: Rich 5F 99
Lorne Ter. N3 ....2H 29
Lorn Rd. SW9 ....2K 103
Lorraine Ct. NW1 ....7F 49
Lorraine Pk. HA3: Harr 7D 10
Lorrimore Rd. SE17 ....6B 86
Lorrimore Sq. SE17 ....6B 86
Lorton Ho. *NW6 ....1J 65*
(off Kilburn Va.)
Lothair Rd. W5 ....2D 80
Lothair Rd. Nth. N4 ....6B 32
Lothair Rd. Sth. N4 ....7A 32
Lothbury EC2 ....6D 68 (7E 162)
Lothian Av. UB4: Hayes 5K 59
Lothian Cl. HA0: Wemb 4A 44
Lothian Rd. SW9 ....1B 104
Lothrop St. W10 ....3G 65
Lots Rd. SW10 ....7A 84
Lotus Cl. SE21 ....3D 122
Loubet St. SW17 ....6D 120
Loudoun Av. IG6: Ilf 5F 37
Loudoun Rd. NW8 ....1A 66
Loudwater Cl.
TW16: Sun T 4J 131
Loudwater Rd.
TW16: Sun T 4J 131
Loughboro' St.
SE11 ....5K 85 (5H 173)
Loughborough Est. SW9 ....3B 104
Loughborough Pk. SW9 ....4B 104
Loughborough Rd. SW9 ....2A 104
Lough Rd. N7 ....5K 49
Loughton Way
IG9: Buck H 1G 21
Louisa Cl. E9 ....1K 69
Louisa Ct. TW2: Twick 2J 115
Louisa Gdns. E1 ....4K 69
Louisa St. E1 ....4K 69
Louise Bennett Cl. SE24 ....4B 104
Louise Ct. N22 ....1A 32
Louise De Marillac Ho. *E1 ....5J 69*
(off Smithy St.)
Louise Rd. E15 ....6G 53
Louise White Ho. N19 ....1H 49
Louis Gdns. BR7: Chst 4D 126
Louis M. N10 ....1F 31
Louisville Rd. SW17 ....3E 120
Lousada Lodge *N14 ....6B 6*
(off Avenue Rd.)
Louvaine Rd. SW11 ....4B 102
Lovage App. E6 ....5C 72
Lovat Cl. NW2 ....3B 46
Lovat La. EC3 ....7E 68 (2G 169)
(not continuous)
Lovatt Cl. HA8: Edg 6C 12
Lovatt Ct. SW12 ....1F 121
Lovatt Dr. HA4: Ruis 5J 23
Lovat Wlk. TW5: Houn 7C 78
Loveday Rd. W13 ....2B 80
Lovegrove St. SE1 ....5G 87
Lovegrove Wlk. E14 ....1E 88
Lovekyn Cl. KT2: King T 2E 134
Lovelace Av. BR2: Short 6E 144
Lovelace Gdns.
IG11: Bark 4A 56
KT6: Surb 7D 134
Lovelace Grn. SE9 ....3D 108
Lovelace Ho. *E8 ....1F 69*
(off Haggerston Rd.)
Lovelace Rd. EN4: Barn 7H 5
KT6: Surb 7C 134
SE21 ....2C 122
Loveland Mans.
IG11: Bark 7K 55
(off Upney La.)
Love La. *BR1: Brom 3K 143*
(off Elmfield Rd., not continuous)
CR4: Mitc 3C 138
(not continuous)
DA5: Bexl 6F 111
(not continuous)
EC2 ....6C 68 (7D 162)
HA5: Pinn 2B 24
IG8: Wfd G 6J 21
KT6: Surb 2C 146
N17 ....7A 18
SE18 ....4E 90
SE25 ....3H 141
(not continuous)
SM3: Sutt 6G 149
SM4: Mord 7J 137
Lovel Av. DA16: Well 2A 110
Lovelinch Cl. SE15 ....6J 87
Lovell Ho. *E8 ....1G 69*
(off Shrubland Rd.)
Lovell Pl. SE16 ....3A 88
Lovell Rd. TW10: Rich 3C 116
UB1: S'hall 6F 61
Loveridge M. NW6 ....6H 47
Loveridge Rd. NW6 ....6H 47
Lovers Wlk. N3 ....7D 14
NW7 ....6C 14
SE10 ....6F 89
W1 ....1E 84 (4G 165)
Lovett Dr. SM5: Cars 7A 138
Lovett Way NW10 ....5J 45
Love Wlk. SE5 ....2D 104
Lovibonds Av.
UB7: W Dray 6B 58
Lowbrook Rd. IG1: Ilf 4F 55
Low Cross Wood La.
SE21 ....3F 123
Lowdell Cl. UB7: W Dray 6A 58
Lowden Rd. N9 ....1C 18
SE24 ....4B 104
UB1: S'hall 7C 60
Lowder Ho. *E1 ....1H 87*
(off Wapping La.)
Lowe Av. E16 ....5J 71
Lowell Ho. *SE5 ....7C 86*
(off Wyndham Est.)
Lowell St. E14 ....6A 70
Lowen Rd. RM13: Rain 2K 75
Lwr. Addiscombe Rd.
CR0: Croy 1E 152
Lwr. Addison Gdns. W14 ....2G 83
Lwr. Belgrave St.
SW1 ....3F 85 (2J 171)
Lwr. Boston Rd. W7 ....1J 79
Lwr. Broad St.
RM10: Dag 1G 75
Lower Camden
BR7: Chst 7D 126
Lwr. Church St.
CR0: Croy 2B 152
LOWER CLAPTON 4H 51
Lwr. Clapton Rd. E5 ....3H 51
Lwr. Clarendon Wlk. *W11 ....6G 65*
(off Clarendon Rd.)
Lwr. Common Sth. SW15 ....3D 100
Lwr. Coombe St.
CR0: Croy 4C 152

Lwr. Downs Rd.—Lynchen Cl.

Lwr. Downs Rd. SW20 .....1F 137
Lwr. Drayton Pl.
CR0: Croy 2B 152
LOWER EDMONTON 2B 18
LOWER FELTHAM 3H 113
Lwr. Fosters NW4 ....5E 28
(off New Brent St.)
Lwr. George St.
TW9: Rich 5D 98
Lwr. Gravel Rd.
BR2: Short 1C 156
Lwr. Green Gdns.
KT4: Wor Pk 1C 148
Lwr. Green W.
CR4: Mitc 3C 138
Lwr. Grosvenor Pl.
SW1 ....3F 85 (1K 171)
Lwr. Grove Rd.
TW10: Rich 6F 99
LOWER HALLIFORD 6F 131
Lwr. Hall La. E4 ....5F 19
(not continuous)
Lwr. Hampton Rd.
TW16: Sun T 3A 132
Lwr. Ham Rd.
KT2: King T 5D 116
LOWER HOLLOWAY 5K 49
Lwr. James St.
W1 ....7G 67 (2B 166)
Lwr. John St.
W1 ....7G 67 (2B 166)
Lwr. Kenwood Av.
EN2: Enf 5D 6
Lwr. King's Rd. ....
KT2: King T 1E 134
Lwr. Lea Crossing E14 ......7G 71
Lwr. Maidstone Rd. N11 ....6B 16
Lower Mall W6 ....5E 82
(off Hammersmith Bri. Rd.)
W6 ....5D 82
(Gt. West Rd., not continuous)
Lwr. Mardyke Av.
RM13: Rain 2J 75
Lower Marsh
SE1 ....2A 86 (7J 167)
Lwr. Marsh La. ....
KT1: King T 4F 135
(not continuous)
Lwr. Merton Ri. NW3 ....7C 48
Lower Mill KT17: Eps 7B 148
Lwr. Morden La.
SM4: Mord 6E 136
Lwr. Mortlake Rd. ....
TW9: Rich 4E 98
Lwr. Park Rd. DA17: Belv 4G 93
N11 ....5B 16
Lwr. Park Trad. Est. W3 .....4J 63
LOWER PLACE 2J 63
Lwr. Place Bus. Cen.
NW10 ....2K 63
(off Steele Rd.)
Lwr. Queen's Rd.
IG9: Buck H 2G 21
Lwr. Richmond Rd.
SW15 ....3D 100
TW9: Rich 3G 99
Lower Rd. DA8: Erith 3H 93
DA17: Belv 3H 93
HA2: Harr 1H 43
SE1 ....2A 86 (6J 167)
SE16 ....2J 87
(not continuous)
SM1: Sutt 4A 150
Lwr. Sloane St.
SW1 ....4E 84 (4G 171)
Lower Sq. TW7: Isle 3B 98
Lower Sq., The
SM1: Sutt 5K 149
Lower Strand NW9 ....2B 28
Lwr. Sunbury Rd.
TW12: Hamp 2D 132
LOWER SYDENHAM 4K 123
Lwr. Sydenham Ind. Est.
SE26 ....5B 124
Lwr. Teddington Rd.
KT1: King T 1D 134
Lower Ter. NW3 ....3A 48
SE27 ....5B 122
(off Woodcote Pl.)
Lwr. Thames St.
EC3 ....7D 68 (3F 169)
Lowerwood Ct. W11 ....6G 65
(off Westbourne Pk. Rd.)
Lwr. Wood Rd.
KT10: Esh 6B 146
Lowestoft Cl. E5 ....2J 51
(off Mundford Rd.)
Lowestoft M. E16 ....2F 91
Loweswater Cl.
HA9: Wemb 2D 44
Loweswater Ho. E3 ....4B 70
Lowfield Rd. NW6 ....7J 47
W3 ....6H 63
Low Hall Cl. E4 ....7J 9
Low Hall La. E17 ....6A 34
Low Hall Mnr. Bus. Cen.
E17 ....6A 34
Lowick Rd. HA1: Harr 4J 25
Lowlands Gdns.
RM7: Rom 6H 39
Lowlands Rd. HA1: Harr 6J 25
HA5: Pinn 7A 24
Lowman Rd. N7 ....4K 49
Lowndes Cl.
SW1 ....3E 84 (2H 171)
Lowndes Ct.
SW1 ....3D 84 (1F 171)
W1 ....1A 166
Lowndes Pl.
SW1 ....3E 84 (2G 171)
Lowndes Sq.
SW1 ....2D 84 (7F 165)
Lowndes St.
SW1 ....3E 84 (1F 171)
Lownds Ct. BR1: Brom 2J 143
Lowood Ho. E1 ....7J 69
(off Bewley St.)
Lowood St. E1 ....7H 69
Lowry Cl. DA8: Erith 4K 93
Lowry Ct. SE16 ....5H 87
(off Stubbs Dr.)
Lowry Cres. CR4: Mitc 2C 138
Lowry Ho. N17 ....1F 33
(off Pembury Rd.)
Lowry Rd. RM8: Dag 5B 56
Lowshoe La. RM5: Col R 1G 39
Lowswood Cl.
HA6: Nwood 1E 22
Lowther Dr. EN2: Enf 4D 6
Lowther Gdns.
SW7 ....2B 84 (1B 170)
Lowther Hill SE23 ....7A 106
Lowther Ho. E8 ....1F 69
(off Clarissa St.)
SW1 ....6B 172
(off Churchill Gdns.)
Lowther Rd. E17 ....2A 34
HA7: Stan 3F 27
KT2: King T 1F 135
N7 ....5A 50
SW13 ....1B 100
Lowth Rd. SE5 ....1C 104
LOXFORD 5G 55
Loxford Av. E6 ....2B 72
Loxford La. IG1: Ilf 5G 55
IG3: Ilf 5G 55
Loxford Rd. IG11: Bark 6F 55
Loxford Ter. IG11: Ilf 6G 55
Loxham Rd. E4 ....7J 19
Loxham St. WC1 ...3J 67 (2F 161)
Loxley Cl. SE26 ....5K 123
Loxley Rd. SW18 ....1B 120
TW12: Hamp 4D 114
Loxton Rd. SE23 ....1K 123
Loxwood Cl. TW14: Felt 1F 113
Loxwood Rd. N17 ....3E 32
Lubbock Ho. E14 ....7D 70
(off Poplar High St.)
Lubbock Rd. BR7: Chst 7D 126
Lubbock St. SE14 ....7J 87
Lucan Ho. N1 ....1D 68
(off Colville Est.)
Lucan Pl. SW3 ....4C 84 (4C 170)
Lucan Rd. EN5: Barn 3B 4
Lucas Av. E13 ....1K 71
HA2: Harr 2E 42
Lucas Cl. NW10 ....7C 46
Lucas Ct. SE26 ....5A 124
SW11 ....1E 102
Lucas Gdns. N2 ....2A 30
Lucas Rd. SE20 ....6J 123
Lucas Sq. NW11 ....6J 29
Lucas St. SE8 ....1C 106
Lucerne Cl. N13 ....3D 16
Lucerne Ct. DA18: Erith 3E 92
Lucerne Gro. E17 ....4F 35
Lucerne M. W8 ....1J 83
Lucerne Rd. BR6: Orp 7K 145
CR7: Thor H 5B 140
N5 ....4B 50
Lucey Rd. SE16 ....3G 87
Lucey Way SE16 ....3G 87
(not continuous)
Lucie Av. TW15: Ashf 6D 112
Lucien Rd. SW17 ....4E 120
SW19 ....2K 119
Lucinda Ct. EN1: Enf 5K 7
Lucknow St. SE18 ....7J 91
Lucorn Cl. SE12 ....6H 107
Luctons Av. IG9: Buck H 1F 21
Lucy Brown Ho. SE1 ......5D 168
Lucy Cres. W3 ....5J 63
Lucy Gdns. RM8: Dag 3F 57
Luddesdon Rd. DA8: Erith ...7G 93
Ludford Cl. CR0: Croy 3B 152
NW9 ....2A 28
Ludgate B'way.
EC4 ....6B 68 (1A 168)
Ludgate Cir. EC4 ...6B 68 (1A 168)
Ludgate Hill
EC4 ....6B 68 (1A 168)
Ludgate Sq.
EC4 ....6B 68 (1B 168)
Ludham Cl. IG6: Ilf 1G 37
SE28 ....6C 74
Ludlow Cl. BR2: Short 3J 143
HA2: Harr 4D 42
Ludlow Ct. W3 ....2J 81
Ludlow Rd. TW13: Felt 4J 113
W5 ....4C 62
Ludlow St. EC1 ....4C 68 (3C 162)
Ludlow Way N2 ....4A 30
Ludovick Wlk. SW15 ......4A 100
Ludwick M. SE14 ....7A 88
Luffield Rd. SE2 ....3B 92
Luffman Rd. SE12 ....3K 125
Lugard Ho. W12 ....1D 82
Lugard Rd. SE15 ....2H 105
Lugg App. E12 ....3E 54
Luke Ho. E1 ....6H 69
(off Tillman St.)
Luke St. EC2 ......4E 68 (3G 163)
Lukin Cres. E4 ....3A 20
Lukin St. E1 ....6J 69
Lullingstone Cl.
BR5: Orp 7B 128
Lullingstone Cres.
BR5: Orp 7A 128
Lullingstone Ho. SE15 ......6J 87
(off Lovelinch Cl.)
Lullingstone La. SE13 .....6F 107
Lullingstone Rd.
DA17: Belv 6F 93
Lullington Gth.
BR1: Brom 7G 125
N12 ....5C 14
Lullington Rd.
RM9: Dag 7E 56
SE20 ....7G 123
Lulot Gdns. N19 ....2F 49
Lulworth NW1 ....7H 49
(off Wrotham Rd.)
SE17 ....5D 86
(off Portland St.)
Lulworth Av. HA9: Wemb 7C 26
TW5: Houn 1F 97
Lulworth Cl. HA2: Harr 3D 42
Lulworth Ct. N1 ....7E 50
(off St Peter's Way)
Lulworth Cres. CR4: Mitc ...2C 138
Lulworth Dr. HA5: Pinn 6B 24
Lulworth Gdns. HA2: Harr ...2C 42
Lulworth Ho. SW8 ....7K 85
Lulworth Rd. DA16: Well ...2K 109
SE9 ....2C 126
SE15 ....2H 105
Lulworth Waye
UB4: Hayes 6K 59
Lumen Rd. HA9: Wemb 2D 44
Lumiere Bldg., The E7 ......5B 54
(off Romford Rd.)
Lumiere Ct. SW17 ....2E 120
Lumley Cl. DA17: Belv 5G 93
Lumley Ct. WC2 ....7J 67 (3F 167)
Lumley Flats SW1 ....5G 171
(off Holbein Pl.)
Lumley Gdns. SM3: Sutt 5G 149
Lumley Rd. SM3: Sutt 5G 149
Lumley St. W1 ....6E 66 (1H 165)
Lumsdon NW8 ....1K 65
(off Abbey Rd.)
Luna Rd. CR7: Thor H 3C 140
Lund Point E15 ....1E 70
Lundy Dr. UB3: Hayes 4G 77
Lundy Wlk. N1 ....6C 50
Lunham Rd. SE19 ....6E 122
Luntley Pl. E1 .....5G 69 (6K 163)
Lupin Cl. CR0: Croy 1K 153
RM7: Rush G 2K 57
SW2 ....2B 122
Lupin Cres. IG1: Ilf 6F 55
Lupin Point SE1 ....7K 169
Lupton Cl. SE12 ....3K 125
Lupton St. NW5 ....4G 49
(not continuous)
Lupus St. SW1 .....5F 85 (6K 171)
Luralda Gdns. E14 ....5F 89
Lurgan Av. W6 ....6F 83
Lurline Gdns. SW11 ....1E 102
Luscombe Ct. BR2: Short ...2G 143
Luscombe Way SW8 ....7J 85
Lushington Ho.
KT12: Walt T 6A 132
Lushington Rd. NW10 ......2D 64
SE6 ....4D 124
Lushington Ter. E8 ....5G 51
(off Wayland Av.)
Lutea Ho. SM2: Sutt 7A 150
(off Walnut M.)
Luther Cl. HA8: Edg 2D 12
Luther King Cl. E17 ....6B 34
Luther M. TW11: Tedd 5K 115
Luther Rd. TW11: Tedd 5K 115
Luton Ho. E13 ....4J 71
(off Luton Rd.)
Luton Pl. SE10 ....7E 88
Luton Rd. DA14: Sidc 3C 128
E13 ....4J 71
E17 ....3B 34
Luton St. NW8 .....4B 66 (4B 158)
Lutton Ter. NW3 ....4A 48
(off Lakis Cl.)
Luttrell Av. SW15 ....5D 100
Lutwyche Rd. SE6 ....2B 124
Lutyens Ho. SW1 ....6A 172
(off Churchill Gdns.)
Luxborough Ho. W1 ....5G 159
(off Luxborough St.)
Luxborough La. IG7: Chig ...3H 21
Luxborough St.
W1 ....5E 66 (5G 159)
Luxborough Twr. W1 ......5G 159
Luxemburg Gdns. W6 ....4F 83
Luxfield Rd. SE9 ....1C 126
Luxford St. SE16 ....4K 87
Luxmore St. SE4 ....1B 106
Luxor St. SE5 ....3C 104
Lyall Av. SE21 ....4E 122
Lyall M. SW1 ......3E 84 (2G 171)
Lyall M. W. SW1 ...3E 84 (2G 171)
Lyall St. SW1 .....3E 84 (2G 171)
Lyal Rd. E3 ....2A 70
Lycett Pl. W12 ....2C 82
Lyceum Theatre 2G 167
Lychgate Mnr. HA1: Harr 7J 25
Lych Ga. Wlk. UB3: Hayes ...7H 59
(not continuous)
Lyconby Gdns. CR0: Croy ...7A 142
Lydd Cl. DA14: Sidc 3J 127
Lydden Ct. SE9 ....6J 109
Lydden Gro. SW18 ....7K 101
Lydden Rd. SW18 ....7K 101
Lydd Rd. DA7: Bex 7F 93
Lydeard Rd. E6 ....7D 54
Lydford NW1 ....1G 67
(off Royal College St.)
Lydford Cl. N16 ....5E 50
(off Pellerin Rd.)
Lydford Rd. N15 ....5D 32
NW2 ....6E 46
W9 ....4H 65
Lydhurst Av. SW2 ....2K 121
Lydia Ct. N12 ....6F 15
Lydney Cl. SE15 ....7E 86
SW19 ....2G 119
Lydon Rd. SW4 ....3G 103
Lydstep Rd. BR7: Chst 4E 126
Lyford Rd. SW18 ....7B 102
Lyford St. SE7 ....4C 90
Lygon Ho. E2 ....1K 163
(off Gosset St.)
SW6 ....1G 101
(off Fulham Pal. Rd.)
Lygon Pl. SW1 .....3F 85 (2J 171)
Lyham Cl. SW2 ....6J 103
Lyham Rd. SW2 ....5J 103
Lyle Cl. CR4: Mitc 7E 138
Lyly Ho. SE1 ....3D 86
(off Burbage Cl.)
Lyme Farm Rd. SE12 ......4J 107
Lyme Gro. E9 ....7J 51
Lyme Gro. Ho. E9 ....7J 51
(off Lyme Gro.)
Lymer Av. SE19 ....5F 123
Lyme Rd. DA16: Well 1B 110
Lymescote Gdns.
SM1: Sutt 2J 149
Lyme St. NW1 ....7G 49
Lyme Ter. NW1 ....7G 49
Lyminge Cl. DA14: Sidc 4K 127
Lyminge Gdns. SW18 ......1C 120
Lymington Av. N22 ....2A 32
Lymington Cl. E6 ....5D 72
SW16 ....2H 139
Lymington Ct. SM1: Sutt ...3K 149
Lymington Dr. HA4: Ruis 2F 41
Lymington Gdns.
KT19: Eps 5B 148
Lymington Lodge E14 ....3F 89
(off Schooner Cl.)
Lymington Rd. NW6 ....6K 47
RM8: Dag 1D 56
Lyminster Cl. UB4: Hayes 5C 60
Lympne N17 ....2D 32
(off Gloucester Rd.)
Lympstone Gdns. SE15 .....7G 87
Lynbridge Gdns. N13 ....4G 17
Lynbrook Cl. RM13: Rain 2K 75
Lynch Cl. SE3 ....2H 107
Lynchen Cl. TW5: Houn 1K 95

Lynch Wlk.—Madison Ho.

Lynch Wlk. *SE8* *6B* ***88***
(off Dacca St.)
Lyncott Cres. SW4 4F **103**
Lyncourt SE3 2F **107**
Lyncroft Av. HA5: Pinn 5C **24**
Lyncroft Gdns. NW6 5J **47**
TW3: Houn 5G **97**
W13 2C **80**
Lyncroft Mans. NW6 5J **47**
Lyndale KT7: T Ditt 7J **133**
NW2 4H **47**
Lyndale Av. NW2 3H **47**
Lyndale Cl. SE3 6H **89**
Lyndean Ind. Est. SE2 3C **92**
Lynde Ho. KT12: Walt T 6A **132**
SW4 3H **103**
Lynden Hyrst CR0: Croy 2F **153**
Lyndhurst Av. HA5: Pinn 1K **23**
KT5: Surb 1H **147**
N12 6J **15**
NW7 6F **13**
SW16 2H **139**
TW2: Twick 1D **114**
TW16: Sun T 3J **131**
UB1: S'hall 1F **79**
Lyndhurst Cl. CR0: Croy 3F **153**
DA7: Bex 3H **111**
NW10 3K **45**
Lyndhurst Ct. E18 1J **35**
NW8 *1B* ***66***
(off Finchley Rd.)
SM2: Sutt *7J* ***149***
(off Grange Rd.)
Lyndhurst Dr. E10 7E **34**
KT3: N Mald 7A **136**
Lyndhurst Gdns. EN1: Enf 4K **7**
HA5: Pinn 1K **23**
IG2: Ilf 6H **37**
IG11: Bark 6J **55**
N3 1G **29**
NW3 5B **48**
Lyndhurst Gro. SE15 2E **104**
Lyndhurst Lodge *E14* *4F* ***89***
(off Millennium Dr.)
Lyndhurst Ri. IG7: Chig 4K **21**
Lyndhurst Rd.
CR7: Thor H 4A **140**
DA7: Bex 3H **111**
E4 7K **19**
N18 4B **18**
N22 6F **17**
NW3 5B **48**
UB6: G'frd 4F **61**
Lyndhurst Sq. SE15 1F **105**
Lyndhurst Ter. NW3 5B **48**
Lyndhurst Way SE15 1F **105**
SM2: Sutt 7J **149**
Lyndon Av. DA15: Sidc 5K **109**
SM6: Wall 3E **150**
Lyndon Rd. DA17: Belv 4G **93**
Lyne Cres. E17 1B **34**
Lynegrove Av.
TW15: Ashf 5E **112**
Lyneham Wlk. E5 5A **52**
HA5: Pinn 3H **23**
Lynette Av. SW4 6F **103**
Lynford Cl. HA8: Edg 1J **27**
Lynford Ct. *CR0: Croy* *4E* ***152***
(off Coombe Rd.)
Lynford Gdns. HA8: Edg 3C **12**
IG3: Ilf 2K **55**
Lynford Ter. N9 1A **18**
Lynhurst Cres.
UB10: Uxb 7E **40**
Lynhurst Rd. UB10: Uxb 7E **40**
Lynmere Rd.
DA16: Well 2B **110**
Lyn M. E3 3B **70**
N16 4E **50**
Lynmouth Av. EN1: Enf 6A **8**
SM4: Mord 6F **137**
Lynmouth Dr. HA4: Ruis 2K **41**
Lynmouth Gdns.
TW5: Houn 7B **78**
UB6: G'frd 1B **62**
Lynmouth Rd. E17 6A **34**
N2 3D **30**
N16 1F **51**
UB6: G'frd 1B **62**
Lynn Cl. HA3: Harr 2H **25**
TW15: Ashf 5F **113**
Lynne Cl. SE23 7B **106**
Lynne Ct. *CR2: S Croy* *4E* ***152***
(off Birdhurst Rd.)
Lynnett Rd. RM8: Dag 2D **56**
Lynne Way UB5: N'olt 2B **60**
Lynn Ho. *SE15* *6H* ***87***
(off Friary Est.)
Lynn M. E11 2G **53**
Lynn Rd. E11 2G **53**
IG2: Ilf 7H **37**
SW12 7F **103**
Lynn St. EN2: Enf 1J **7**
Lynscott Way
CR2: S Croy 7B **152**
Lynstead Ct. BR3: Beck 2A **142**
Lynsted Cl. BR1: Brom 2A **144**
DA6: Bex 5H **111**
Lynsted Gdns. SE9 3B **108**
Lynton Av. N12 4G **15**
NW9 4B **28**
RM7: Mawney 1G **39**
W13 6A **62**
Lynton Cl. KT9: Chess 4E **146**
NW10 5A **46**
TW7: Isle 4K **97**
Lynton Cres. IG2: Ilf 6F **37**
Lynton Est. SE1 4G **87**
Lynton Gdns. EN1: Enf 7K **7**
N11 6C **16**
Lynton Grange N2 3D **30**
Lynton Ho. IG1: Ilf 2G **55**
W2 *6A* ***66***
(off Hallfield Est.)
Lynton Mans. *SE1* *1J* ***173***
(off Kennington Rd.)
Lynton Mead N20 3D **14**
Lynton Rd. CR0: Croy 6A **140**
E4 5J **19**
HA2: Harr 2C **42**
KT3: N Mald 5K **135**
N8 5H **31**
(not continuous)
NW6 2H **65**
SE1 4F **87**
W3 7G **63**
Lynton Ter. W3 6J **63**
Lynton Wlk. UB4: Hayes 3G **59**
Lynwood Cl. E18 1A **36**
HA2: Harr 3C **42**
Lynwood Ct.
KT1: King T 2H **135**
Lynwood Dr.
HA6: Nwood 1H **23**
KT4: Wor Pk 2C **148**
Lynwood Gdns.
CR0: Croy 4K **151**
UB1: S'hall 6D **60**
Lynwood Gro. BR6: Orp 7J **145**
N21 1F **17**
Lynwood Rd. KT7: T Ditt 2A **146**
SW17 3D **120**
W5 3D **62**
Lyon Bus. Pk. IG11: Bark 2J **73**
Lyon Ct. HA4: Ruis 1H **41**
Lyon Ho. *NW8* *4C* ***158***
(off Broadley St.)
Lyon Ind. Est. NW2 2D **46**
Lyon Meade HA7: Stan 1C **26**
Lyon Pk. Av. HA0: Wemb 6E **44**
(not continuous)
Lyon Rd. HA1: Harr 6K **25**
SW19 1A **138**
LYONSDOWN 5F **5**
Lyonsdown Av. EN5: Barn 6F **5**
Lyonsdown Rd. EN5: Barn 6F **5**
Lyons Pl. NW8 4B **66** (4A **158**)
Lyon St. N1 7K **49**
Lyons Wlk. W14 4G **83**
Lyon Way UB6: G'frd 1J **61**
Lyric Dr. UB6: G'frd 4F **61**
Lyric M. SE26 4J **123**
Lyric Rd. SW13 1B **100**
Lyric Theatre
2C 166
(off Shaftesbury Av.)
Lysander NW9 1B **28**
Lysander Gdns.
KT6: Surb 6F **135**
Lysander Gro. N19 1H **49**
Lysander Ho. *E2* *2H* ***69***
(off Temple St.)
Lysander M. N19 1G **49**
Lysander Rd. CR0: Croy 6K **151**
HA4: Ruis 2F **41**
Lysia Ct. *SW6* *7F* ***83***
(off Lysia St.)
Lysias Rd. SW12 6F **103**
Lysia St. SW6 7F **83**
Lysons Wlk. SW15 4C **100**
Lytchet Rd. BR1: Brom 7J **125**
Lytchet Way EN3: Enf 1D **8**
Lytchgate Cl.
CR2: S Croy 7E **152**
Lytcott Dr. KT8: W Mole 3D **132**
Lytcott Gro. SE22 5E **104**
Lytham Cl. SE28 6E **74**
Lytham Ct. *UB1: S'hall* *6F* ***61***
(off Whitecote Rd.)
Lytham Gro. W5 3F **63**
Lytham St. SE17 5D **86**
Lyttelton Cl. NW3 7C **48**
Lyttelton Ct. N2 5A **30**
Lyttelton Ho. *E9* *7J* ***51***
(off Well St.)
Lyttelton Rd. E10 3D **52**
N2 5A **30**
Lyttelton Theatre ***4J 167***
(in Royal National Theatre)
Lyttleton Ct. *UB4: Hayes* *4A* ***60***
(off Dunedin Way)
Lyttleton Rd. N8 3A **32**
Lytton Av. EN3: Enf 1F **9**
N13 2F **17**
Lytton Cl. N2 6B **30**
UB5: N'olt 7D **42**
Lytton Gdns. SM6: Wall 4H **151**
Lytton Gro. SW15 5F **101**
Lytton Rd. E11 7G **35**
EN5: Barn 4F **5**
HA5: Pinn 1C **24**
Lytton Strachey Path SE28 7B **74**
Lyveden Rd. SE3 7K **89**
SW17 6D **120**

M

Mabbett Ho. *SE18* *6E* ***90***
(off Nightingale Pl.)
Mabel Evetts Ct.
UB3: Hayes 7K **59**
Maberley Cres. SE19 7G **123**
Maberley Rd. BR3: Beck 3K **141**
SE19 1F **141**
Mabledon Ct. *WC1* *2D* ***160***
(off Mabledon Pl.)
Mabledon Pl.
WC1 3H **67** (2D **160**)
Mablethorpe Rd. SW6 7G **83**
Mabley St. E9 5A **52**
Mablin Lodge IG9: Buck H 1F **21**
McAdam Dr. EN2: Enf 2G **7**
Macaret Cl. N20 7E **4**
Macarthur Cl. E7 6J **53**
Macarthur Ter. SE7 6B **90**
Macartney Ho. *SE10* *7F* ***89***
(off Chesterfield Wlk.)
SW9 *1A* ***104***
(off Gosling Way)
Macaulay Ct. SW4 3F **103**
Macaulay Rd. E6 2B **72**
SW4 3F **103**
Macaulay Sq. SW4 4F **103**
Macaulay Way SE28 1B **92**
McAuley Cl. SE1 3A **86** (1J **173**)
SE9 5F **109**
Macauley M. SE13 1E **106**
Macbean St. SE18 3F **91**
Macbeth Ho. N1 2E **68**
Macbeth St. W6 5D **82**
McCall Cl. SW4 2J **103**
McCall Cres. SE7 5C **90**
McCall Ho. N7 4J **49**
McCarthy Rd. TW13: Felt 5B **114**
Macclesfield Ho. *EC1* *2C* ***162***
(off Central St.)
Macclesfield Rd.
EC1 3C **68** (1C **162**)
SE25 5J **141**
Macclesfield St.
W1 7H **67** (2D **166**)
McCoid Way SE1 2C **86** (7C **168**)
McCrone M. NW3 6B **48**
McCullum Rd. E3 1B **70**
McDermott Cl. SW11 3C **102**
McDermott Rd. SE15 3G **105**
Macdonald Av.
RM10: Dag 3H **57**
Macdonald Rd. E7 4J **53**
E17 2E **34**
N11 5J **15**
N19 2G **49**
McDonough Cl.
KT9: Chess 4E **146**
McDowall Cl. E16 5H **71**
McDowall Rd. SE5 1C **104**
Macduff Rd. SW11 1E **102**
Mace Cl. E1 1H **87**
Mace Gateway E16 7J **71**
McEntee Av. E17 1A **34**
Mace St. E2 2K **69**
McEwen Way E15 1F **71**
Macey St. *SE10* *6E* ***88***
(off Thames St.)
Macfarlane La. TW7: Isle 6K **79**
Macfarlane Rd. W12 1E **82**
Macfarren Pl.
NW1 4E **66** (4H **159**)
McGlashon Ho. *E1* *4K* ***163***
(off Hunton St.)
McGrath Rd. E15 5H **53**
McGregor Ct. N1 1H **163**
MacGregor Rd. E16 5A **72**
McGregor Rd. W11 6H **65**
Machell Rd. SE15 3J **105**
McIndoe Ct. *N1* *1D* ***68***
(off Sherborne St.)
McIntosh Cl. RM1: Rom 3K **39**
SM6: Wall 7J **151**
McIntosh Ho. *SE16* *4J* ***87***
(off Millender Wlk.)
Macintosh Ho. *W1* *5H* ***159***
(off Beaumont St.)
McIntosh Rd. RM1: Rom 3K **39**
McIntyre Ct. *SE18* *4C* ***90***
(off Prospect Va.)
Mackay Ho. *W12* *7D* ***64***
(off White City Est.)
Mackay Rd. SW8 3F **103**
McKay Rd. SW20 7D **118**
McKay Trad. Est. W10 4G **65**
McKellar Cl. WD23: Bush 2B **10**
Mackennal St. NW8 2C **66**
Mackenzie Cl. W12 7D **64**
Mackenzie Ho. NW2 3C **46**
Mackenzie Rd. BR3: Beck 2J **141**
N7 6K **49**
Mackenzie Wlk. E14 1C **88**
McKerrell Rd. SE15 1G **105**
Mackeson Rd. NW3 4D **48**
Mackie Rd. SW2 7A **104**
McKillop Way
DA14: Sidc 7C **128**
Mackintosh La. E9 5K **51**
Macklin St. WC2 6J **67** (7F **161**)
Mackonochie Ho. *EC1* *5J* ***161***
(off Baldwins Gdns.)
Mackrow Wlk. E14 7E **70**
Mack's Rd. SE16 4G **87**
Mackworth Ho. *NW1* *1A* ***160***
(off Augustus St.)
Mackworth St.
NW1 3G **67** (1A **160**)
Maclaren M. SW15 4E **100**
Maclean Rd. SE23 6A **106**
McLeod Ct. SE22 1G **123**
Macleod Rd. N21 5D **6**
McLeod Rd. SE2 4B **92**
Macleod St. SE17 5C **86**
McLeod's M. SW7 4K **83**
(not continuous)
Maclise Ho. *SW1* *4E* ***172***
(off Marsham St.)
Maclise Rd. W14 3G **83**
Macmillan Ct. HA2: Harr 1E **42**
McMillan Ho. *SE4* *3A* ***106***
(off Arica Rd.)
SE14 1A **106**
McMillan St. SE8 6C **88**
Macmillan Way SW17 4F **121**
McNair Rd. UB2: S'hall 3F **79**
Macnamara Ho. *SW10* *7B* ***84***
(off Worlds End Est.)
McNeil Rd. SE5 2E **104**
McNicol Dr. NW10 2J **63**
Macoma Rd. SE18 6H **91**
Macoma Ter. SE18 6H **91**
Maconochies Rd. E14 5D **88**
Macquarie Way E14 4D **88**
McRae La. CR4: Mitc 7D **138**
Macready Ho. *W1* *6E* ***158***
(off Crawford St.)
Macready Pl. N7 4J **49**
Macroom Rd. W9 3H **65**
Macs Ho. E17 3D **34**
Mac's Pl. EC4 7J **161**
Madame Tussaud's
4E 66 (4G 159)
Maddams St. E3 4D **70**
Maddison Cl.
TW11: Tedd 6K **115**
Maddocks Cl.
DA14: Sidc 5E **128**
Maddocks Ho. *E1* *7H* ***69***
(off Cornwall St.)
Maddock Way SE17 6B **86**
Maddox St. W1 7F **67** (2K **165**)
Madeira Av. BR1: Brom 7G **125**
Madeira Gro. IG8: Wfd G 6F **21**
Madeira Rd.
CR4: Mitc 4D **138**
E11 1F **53**
N13 4G **17**
SW16 5J **121**
Madeleine Cl.
RM6: Chad H 6C **38**
Madeley Rd. W5 6D **62**
Madeline Gro. IG1: Ilf 5H **55**
Madeline Rd. SE20 7G **123**
Madge Gill Way *E6* *1C* ***72***
(off High St. Nth.)
Madge Hill W7 7H **61**
Madinah Rd. E8 6G **51**
Madison Cres. DA7: Bex 7C **92**
Madison Gdns.
BR2: Short 3H **143**
DA7: Bex 7C **92**
Madison Ho. *E14* *7B* ***70***
(off Victory Pl.)

Madison, The—Mandeville Dr.

Madison, The *SE1* *6E 168*
(*off Long La.*)
Madras Pl. N7 ....6A 50
Madras Rd. IG1: Ilf 4F 55
Madrid Rd. SW13 ....1C 100
Madrigal La. SE5 ....7B 86
Madron St. SE17 ....5E 86
Mafeking Av. E6 ....2C 72
IG2: Ilf 7H 37
TW8: Bford 6E 80
Mafeking Rd. E16 ....4H 71
EN1: Enf 3A 8
N17 ....2G 33
Magdala Av. N19 ....2G 49
Magdala Rd.
CR2: S Croy 7D 152
TW7: Isle 3A 98
Magdalene Cl. SE15 ......2H 105
Magdalene Gdns. E6 ....4E 72
Magdalene Rd.
TW17: Shep 4B 130
Magdalen Ho. *E16* *7K 71*
(*off Keats Av.*)
Magdalen Pas.
E1 ....7F 69 (2K 169)
Magdalen Rd. SW18 ......1A 120
Magdalen St.
SE1 ....1E 86 (5G 169)
Magee St. SE11 ....6A 86 (7J 173)
Magellan Ct. *NW10* *7K 45*
(*off Brentfield Rd.*)
Magellan Ho. *E1* *4K 69*
(*off Ernest St.*)
Magellan Pl. E14 ....4C 88
Magnaville Rd.
WD23: Bush 1D 10
Magnet Rd. HA9: Wemb 2D 44
Magnin Cl. E8 ....1G 69
Magnolia Cl. E10 ....2C 52
KT2: King T 6H 117
Magnolia Ct. HA3: Harr 7F 27
SM2: Sutt *7J 149*
(*off Grange Rd.*)
SM6: Wall 5F 151
TW9: Rich 1H 99
TW13: Felt *1J 113*
(*off Plum Cl.*)
UB5: N'olt 4C 60
UB10: Uxb 6D 40
Magnolia Gdns. E10 ....2C 52
HA8: Edg 4D 12
Magnolia Ho. *SE8* *6B 88*
(*off Evelyn St.*)
Magnolia Lodge E4 ....3J 19
W8 ....*3K 83*
(*off St Mary's Ga.*)
Magnolia Pl. SW4 ....5J 103
W5 ....5D 62
Magnolia Rd. W4 ....6H 81
Magnolia St. UB7: W Dray ...4A 76
Magnolia Way
KT19: Eps 5J 147
Magpie All.
EC4 ....6A 68 (1K 167)
Magpie Cl. E7 ....5H 53
EN1: Enf 1B 8
NW9 ....2A 28
Magpie Hall Cl.
BR2: Short 6C 144
Magpie Hall La.
BR2: Short 5D 144
Magpie Hall Rd.
WD23: Bush 2D 10
Magpie Pl. SE14 ....6A 88
Magri Wlk. E1 ....5J 69
Maguire Dr. TW10: Rich 4C 116
Maguire St. SE1 ...2F 87 (6K 169)
Mahatma Gandhi Ind. Est.
SE24 ....4B 104
Mahlon Av. HA4: Ruis 5K 41
Mahogany Cl. SE16 ....1A 88
Mahon Cl. EN1: Enf 1A 8
Maida Av. E4 ....7J 9
W2 ....5A 66 (4A 158)
MAIDA HILL 4H 65
Maida Rd. DA17: Belv 3G 93
MAIDA VALE 3K 65
Maida Va. W9 .....2K 65 (3A 158)
Maida Way E4 ....7J 9
Maiden Erlegh Av.
DA5: Bexl 1E 128
Maiden La. NW1 ....7H 49
SE1 ....1C 86 (5D 168)
WC2 ....7J 67 (3F 167)
Maiden Pl. NW5 ....3G 49
Maiden Rd. E15 ....7G 53
Maidenstone Hill SE10 .....1E 106
Maids of Honour Row
TW9: Rich 5D 98
Maidstone Av. RM5: Col R ...2J 39
Maidstone Bldgs.
SE1 ....1C 86 (5D 168)
Maidstone Ho. *E14* *6D 70*
(*off Carmen St.*)
Maidstone Rd.
DA14: Sidc, Swan ...6D 128
N11 ....6B 16
Mail Coach Yd.
E2 ....3E 68 (1H 163)
N1 ....3E 68
Main Av. EN1: Enf 5A 8
Main Dr. HA9: Wemb 3D 44
Mainridge Rd. BR7: Chst ...4E 126
Main Rd. DA14: Sidc 3H 127
Main St. TW13: Felt 5B 114
Mais Ho. SE26 ....2H 123
Maismore St. SE15 ....6G 87
Maisonettes, The
SM1: Sutt 5H 149
Maitland Cl. SE10 ....7D 88
TW4: Houn 3D 96
Maitland Ct. *W2* *2A 164*
(*off Lancaster Ter.*)
Maitland Ho. *E2* *2J 69*
(*off Waterloo Gdns.*)
SW1 ....*7A 172*
(*off Churchill Gdns.*)
Maitland Pk. Est. NW3 .....6D 48
Maitland Pk. Rd. NW3 ......6D 48
Maitland Pk. Vs. NW3 ......6D 48
Maitland Pl. E5 ....4H 51
Maitland Rd. E15 ....6H 53
SE26 ....6K 123
Maitland Yd. W13 ....1A 80
Maize Row E14 ....7B 70
Majendie Rd. SE18 ....5H 91
Majestic Way CR4: Mitc 2D 138
Major Rd. E15 ....5F 53
SE16 ....3G 87
Makepeace Av. N6 ....2E 48
Makepeace Mans. N6 ......2E 48
Makepeace Rd. E11 ....4J 35
UB5: N'olt 2C 60
Makinen Ho. IG9: Buck H 1F 21
Makins St. SW3 ...4C 84 (4D 170)
Malabar Ct. *W12* *7D 64*
(*off India Way*)
Malabar St. E14 ....2C 88
Malam Ct. SE11 ....4A 86 (4J 173)
Malam Gdns. E14 ....7D 70
Malbrook Rd. SW15 ....4D 100
Malcolm Ct. E7 ....6H 53
HA7: Stan 5H 11
NW4 ....6C 28
Malcolm Cres. NW4 ....6C 28
Malcolm Dr. KT6: Surb 1D 146
Malcolm Ho. *N1* *2E 68*
(*off Arden Est.*)
Malcolm Pl. E2 ....4J 69
Malcolm Rd. E1 ....4J 69
SE20 ....7J 123
SE25 ....6G 141
SW19 ....6G 119
UB10: Uxb 4B 40
Malcolm Sargent Ho. *E16* ...*7K 71*
(*off Evelyn Rd.*)
Malcolmson Ho. *SW1* *6C 172*
(*off Aylesford St.*)
Malcolm Way E11 ....5J 35
Malcombs Way N14 ....5B 6
Malden Av. SE25 ....4H 141
UB6: G'frd 5J 43
Malden Ct. KT3: N Mald 3D 136
N4 ....6C 32
Malden Cres. NW1 ....6E 48
MALDEN GREEN 1C 148
Malden Grn. Av.
KT4: Wor Pk 1B 148
Malden Hill KT3: N Mald ...3B 136
Malden Hill Gdns.
KT3: N Mald 3B 136
MALDEN JUNCTION 5B 136
Malden Pk. KT3: N Mald ...6B 136
Malden Pl. NW5 ....5E 48
Malden Rd. KT3: N Mald ...5A 136
NW5 ....5D 48
SM3: Sutt 4E 148
Malden Way KT3: N Mald ...6K 135
Maldon Cl. E15 ....5G 53
N1 ....1C 68
SE5 ....3E 104
Maldon Ct. E6 ....1E 72
SM6: Wall 5G 151
Maldon Rd. N9 ....3A 18
RM7: Rush G 7J 39
SM6: Wall 5F 151
W3 ....7J 63
Maldon Wlk. IG8: Wfd G 6F 21
Malet Pl. WC1 .....4H 67 (4C 160)
Malet St. WC1 .....4H 67 (4C 160)
Maley Av. SE27 ....2B 122
Malford Ct. E18 ....2J 35
Malford Gro. E18 ....4H 35
Malfort Rd. SE5 ....3E 104
Malham Cl. N11 ....6K 15
Malham Rd. SE23 ....1K 123
Malham Ter. *N18* *6C 18*
(*off Dysons Rd.*)
Malibu Ct. SE26 ....3H 123
Mallams M. SW9 ....3B 104
Mallard Cl. E9 ....6B 52
EN5: Barn 6G 5
NW6 ....2J 65
TW2: Twick 7E 96
W7 ....2J 79
Mallard Ct. E17 ....3F 35
Mallard Ho. *NW8* *2C 66*
(*off Barrow Hill Est.*)
Mallard Path *SE28* *3H 91*
(*off Goosander Way*)
Mallard Pl. N22 ....2K 31
TW1: Twick 3A 116
Mallards *E11* *7J 35*
(*off Blake Hall Rd.*)
Mallards Rd. IG8: Wfd G 7E 20
IG11: Bark 3A 74
Mallard Wlk. BR3: Beck 5K 141
DA14: Sidc 6C 128
Mallard Way NW9 ....7J 27
SM6: Wall 7G 151
Mall Chambers *W8* *1J 83*
(*off Kensington Mall*)
Mallet Dr. UB5: N'olt 5D 42
Mallet Rd. SE13 ....6F 107
Mall Galleries *4D 166*
Mall Gallery *WC2* *1E 166*
(*in Thomas Neals Shop. Mall*)
Malling SE13 ....5D 106
Malling Cl. CR0: Croy 6J 141
Malling Gdns.
SM4: Mord 6A 138
Malling Way BR2: Short ...7H 143
Mallinson Rd. CR0: Croy ...3H 151
SW11 ....5C 102
Mallon Gdns. *E1* *7K 163*
(*off Commercial St.*)
Mallord St. SW3 ...6B 84 (7B 170)
Mallory Cl. SE4 ....4A 106
Mallory Gdns. EN4: Barn 7K 5
Mallory Ho. *E14* *5D 70*
(*off Teviot St.*)
Mallory St. NW8 ...4C 66 (3D 158)
Mallow Cl. CR0: Croy 1K 153
Mallow Mead NW7 ....7B 14
Mallows, The UB10: Uxb 3D 40
Mallow St.
EC1 ....4D 68 (3E 162)
Mall Rd. W6 ....5D 82
Mall, The BR1: Brom 3J 143
CR0: Croy 2C 152
DA6: Bex 4G 111
E15 ....7F 53
HA3: Harr 6F 27
KT6: Surb 5D 134
N14 ....3D 16
RM10: Dag 6G 57
SW1 ....2G 85 (5D 166)
SW14 ....5J 99
TW8: Bford 6D 80
W5 ....7E 62
Malmains Cl. BR3: Beck 4F 143
Malmains Way
BR3: Beck 4E 142
Malmesbury *E2* *2J 69*
(*off Cyprus St.*)
Malmesbury Cl.
HA5: Pinn 4H 23
Malmesbury Rd. E3 ....3B 70
E16 ....5G 71
E18 ....1H 35
SM4: Mord 7A 138
Malmesbury Ter. E16 ....5H 71
Malmsey Ho.
SE11 ....5K 85 (5H 173)
Malory Cl. BR3: Beck 2A 142
Malpas Dr. HA5: Pinn 5B 24
Malpas Rd. E8 ....5H 51
RM9: Dag 6D 56
SE4 ....2B 106
Malsmead Ho. *E9* *5B 52*
(*off King's Mead Way*)
Malta Rd. E10 ....1C 52
Malta St. EC1 .....4B 68 (3A 162)
Maltby Cl. BR6: Orp 7K 145
Maltby Dr. EN1: Enf 1C 8
Maltby Rd. KT9: Chess 6G 147
Maltby St. SE1 .....2F 87 (7J 169)
Malthouse Dr. TW13: Felt ...5B 114
W4 ....6B 82
Malthouse Pas. *SW13* *2B 100*
(*off Maltings Cl.*)
Malthus Path SE28 ....1C 92
Malting Ho. *E14* *7B 70*
(*off Oak La.*)
Maltings W4 ....5G 81
Maltings Cl. SW13 ....2B 100
Maltings Lodge *W4* *6A 82*
(*off Corney Reach Way*)
Maltings M. DA15: Sidc 3A 128
Maltings Pl. SE1 ....7H 169
SW6 ....1K 101
Malting Way TW7: Isle 3K 97
Malton M. SE18 ....6J 91
W10 ....6G 65
Malton Rd. W10 ....6G 65
Malton St. SE18 ....6J 91
Maltravers St.
WC2 ....7K 67 (2H 167)
Malt St. SE1 ....6G 87
Malva Cl. SW18 ....5K 101
Malvern Av. DA7: Bex 7E 92
E4 ....7A 20
HA2: Harr 3C 42
Malvern Cl. CR4: Mitc 3G 139
KT6: Surb 1E 146
SE20 ....2G 141
UB10: Uxb 2C 40
W10 ....5H 65
Malvern Ct. SM2: Sutt 7J 149
SW7 ....*3B 170*
(*off Onslow Sq.*)
W12 ....*2C 82*
(*off Hadyn Pk. Rd.*)
Malvern Dr. IG3: Bark, Ilf 4K 55
IG8: Wfd G 5F 21
TW13: Felt 5B 114
Malvern Gdns. HA3: Harr 4E 26
NW2 ....2G 47
Malvern Ho. N16 ....1F 51
Malvern M. NW6 ....3J 65
Malvern Pl. NW6 ....3H 65
Malvern Rd. CR7: Thor H ...4A 140
E6 ....1C 72
E8 ....7G 51
E11 ....2G 53
KT6: Surb 2E 146
N8 ....3A 32
N17 ....3G 33
NW6 ....2H 65
(not continuous)
TW12: Hamp 7E 114
UB3: Hayes 7G 77
Malvern Ter. N1 ....1A 68
N9 ....1A 18
Malvern Way W13 ....5B 62
Malwood Rd. SW12 ....6F 103
Malyons Rd. SE13 ....6D 106
Malyons Ter. SE13 ....5D 106
Malyons, The
TW17: Shep 6F 131
Managers St. E14 ....1E 88
Manatee Pl. SM6: Wall 3H 151
Manaton Cl. SE15 ....3H 105
Manaton Cres. UB1: S'hall ...6E 60
Manbey Gro. E15 ....6G 53
Manbey Pk. Rd. E15 ....6G 53
Manbey Rd. E15 ....6G 53
Manbey St. E15 ....6G 53
Manbre Rd. W6 ....6E 82
Manbrough Av. E6 ....3E 72
Manchester Ct. *E16* *6K 71*
(*off Garvary Rd.*)
Manchester Dr. W10 ....4G 65
Manchester Gro. E14 ....5E 88
Manchester Ho. SE17 ......5C 86
Manchester M. W1 ....6G 159
Manchester Rd.
CR7: Thor H 3C 140
E14 ....5E 88
N15 ....6D 32
Manchester Sq.
W1 ....6E 66 (7G 159)
Manchester St.
W1 ....5E 66 (6G 159)
Manchester Way
RM10: Dag 4H 57
Manchuria Rd. SW11 ......6E 102
Manciple St.
SE1 ....2D 86 (7E 168)
Mandalay Rd. SW4 ....5G 103
Mandarin Ct. *NW10* *6K 45*
(*off Mitchellbrook Way*)
SE8 ....6B 88
Mandarin St. E14 ....7C 70
Mandarin Way UB4: Hayes ...6C 60
Mandela Cl. NW10 ....7J 45
W12 ....7D 64
Mandela Ho. *E2* *2J 163*
(*off Virginia Rd.*)
SE5 ....2B 104
Mandela Rd. E16 ....6J 71
Mandela St. NW1 ....1G 67
SW9 ....7A 86
(not continuous)
Mandela Way SE1 ....4E 86
Mandeville Cl. SE3 ....7H 89
SW19 ....7G 119
Mandeville Ct. E4 ....5F 19
Mandeville Dr.
KT6: Surb 1D 146

Mandeville Ho.—Mapleleafe Gdns.

Mandeville Ho. *SE1* 5F 87
(off Rolls Rd.)
SW4 5G 103
Mandeville M. SW4 4H 103
Mandeville Pl.
W1 6E 66 (7H 159)
Mandeville Rd. N14 2A 16
TW7: Isle 2A 98
TW17: Shep 5C 130
UB5: N'olt 7E 42
Mandeville St. E5 3A 52
Mandrake Rd. SW17 3D 120
Mandrake Way E15 7G 53
Mandrell Rd. SW2 5J 103
Manesty Ct. *N14* 7C 6
(off Ivy Rd.)
Manette St. W1 6H 67 (1D 166)
Manfred Rd. SW15 5H 101
Manger Rd. N7 6J 49
Mangold Way DA18: Erith 3D 92
Manilla St. E14 2C 88
Man in the Moon Theatre 7A 170
(off King's Rd.)
Manister Rd. SE2 3A 92
Manitoba Ct. *SE16* 2J 87
(off Canada Est.)
Manley Ct. N16 3F 51
Manley Ho. SE11 4A 86 (5J 173)
Manley St. NW1 1E 66
Mann Cl. CR0: Croy 3C 152
Manneby Prior *N1* 1H 161
(off Cumming St.)
Manning Ct. *SE28* 1B 92
(off Titmuss Av.)
Manningford Cl.
EC1 3B 68 (1A 162)
Manning Gdns. HA3: Harr 7D 26
Manning Pl. TW10: Rich 6F 99
Manning Rd. E17 5A 34
RM10: Dag 6G 57
Manningtree Cl. SW19 1G 119
Manningtree Rd.
HA4: Ruis 4K 41
Manningtree St. E1 6G 69
Mannin Rd. RM6: Chad H 7B 38
Mannock Rd. N22 3B 32
Mann's Cl. TW7: Isle 5K 97
Manns Rd. HA8: Edg 6B 12
Manny Shinwell Ho. *SW6* 6H 83
(off Clem Attlee Ct.)
Manoel Rd. TW2: Twick 3G 115
Manor Av. E7 4A 54
SE4 2B 106
TW4: Houn 3B 96
UB5: N'olt 7D 42
Manor Brook SE3 4J 107
MANOR CIRCUS 3G 99
Manor Cl. DA1: Cray 4K 111
E17 1A 34
EN5: Barn 4B 4
HA4: Ruis 1H 41
KT4: Wor Pk 1A 148
NW7 5E 12
NW9 5H 27
RM10: Dag 6K 57
SE28 7C 74
Manor Cotts. HA6: Nwood 1H 23
N2 2A 30
(off Manor Cotts. App.)
Manor Cotts. App. N2 2A 30
Manor Ct. BR4: W W'ck 1D 154
DA7: Bex 4H 111
E4 1B 20
E10 1D 52
HA1: Harr 6K 25
HA9: Wemb 5E 44
IG11: Bark 7K 55
KT2: King T 1G 135
KT8: W Mole 4E 132
N2 5D 30
(off Aylmer Rd.)
Manor Ct. N14 2C 16
N20 3J 15
(off York Way)
SM6: Wall 3E 150
SW2 5K 103
SW6 1K 101
SW16 3J 121
TW2: Twick 2G 115
W3 4G 81
Manor Ct. Rd. W7 7J 61
Manor Cres. KT5: Surb 6G 135
Manor Dene SE28 6C 74
Manordene Cl.
KT7: T Ditt 1A 146
Manordene Rd. SE28 6C 74
Manor Dr. HA9: Wemb 4F 45
KT5: Surb 6F 135
KT10: Esh 2A 146
KT19: Eps 6A 148
N14 1A 16
N20 4J 15
NW7 5E 12
TW13: Felt 5B 114
TW16: Sun T 2J 131
Manor Dr. Nth.
KT3: N Mald 7K 135
Manor Dr., The
KT4: Wor Pk 1A 148
Manor Est. SE16 4H 87
Mnr. Farm Av.
TW17: Shep 6D 130
Mnr. Farm Cl.
KT4: Wor Pk 1A 148
Mnr. Farm Ct. *E6* 3D 72
(off Holloway Rd.)
Mnr. Farm Dr. E4 3B 20
Mnr. Farm Rd.
HA0: Wemb 2D 62
SW16 2A 140
Manorfield Cl. *N19* 4G 49
(off Fulbrook M.)
Manor Flds. SW15 6F 101
Manorfields Cl.
BR7: Chst 3K 145
Manor Gdns. CR2: S Croy 6F 153
HA4: Ruis 5A 42
N7 3J 49
SW4 2G 103
(off Larkhall Ri.)
SW20 2H 137
TW9: Rich 4F 99
TW12: Hamp 7F 115
TW16: Sun T 1J 131
W3 4G 81
W4 5A 82
Manor Ga. UB5: N'olt 7C 42
Manorgate Rd.
KT2: King T 1G 135
Manor Gro. BR3: Beck 2D 142
SE15 6J 87
TW9: Rich 4G 99
Mnr. Hall Av. NW4 2F 29
Mnr. Hall Dr. NW4 2F 29
Manorhall Gdns. E10 1C 52
Manor Ho. *NW1* 5D 158
(off Marylebone Rd.)
UB2: S'hall 3C 78
Manor Ho. Ct.
TW17: Shep 7D 130
W9 4A 66
(off Warrington Gdns.)
Manor House Dr.
HA6: Nwood 1D 22
NW6 7F 47
Manor Ho. Est. HA7: Stan 6G 11
Mnr. House Gdn. E11 6K 35
Manor Ho. Way TW7: Isle 3B 98
Manor La. SE12 5G 107
SE13 5G 107
SM1: Sutt 5A 150
TW13: Felt 2J 113
TW16: Sun T 2J 131
Manor La. UB3: Hayes 6F 77
Manor La. Ter. SE13 4G 107
Manor M. *NW6* 2J 65
(off Cambridge Av.)
SE4 2B 106
Manor Mt. SE23 1J 123
Manor Pde. HA1: Harr 6K 25
N16 2F 51
NW10 2B 64
(off High St. Harlesden)
MANOR PARK 4B 54
Manor Pk. BR7: Chst 2H 145
SE13 4F 107
TW9: Rich 4F 99
Mnr. Park Cl.
BR4: W W'ck 1D 154
Manor Park Crematorium
E7 4A 54
Mnr. Park Cres. HA8: Edg 6B 12
Mnr. Park Dr. HA2: Harr 3F 25
Mnr. Park Gdns. HA8: Edg 5B 12
Mnr. Park Pde. *SE13* 4F 107
(off Lee High Rd.)
Mnr. Park Rd.
BR4: W W'ck 1D 154
BR7: Chst 1G 145
E12 4B 54
(not continuous)
N2 3A 30
NW10 1B 64
SM1: Sutt 5A 150
Manor Pl. BR7: Chst 2H 145
CR4: Mitc 3G 139
KT12: Walt T 7J 131
(off Thames St., not continuous)
SE17 5B 86
SM1: Sutt 4K 149
TW14: Felt 1J 113
Manor Rd. BR3: Beck 2D 142
BR4: W W'ck 2D 154
CR4: Mitc 4G 139
DA1: Cray 4K 111
DA5: Bexl 1H 129
DA15: Sidc 3K 127
E10 7C 34
E15 2G 71
E16 4G 71
E17 2A 34
EN2: Enf 2H 7
EN5: Barn 4B 4
HA1: Harr 6A 26
HA4: Ruis 1F 41
IG7: Chig 6J 21
IG8: Wfd G 6J 21
IG11: Bark 6K 55
KT8: E Mos 4H 133
KT12: Walt T 7H 131
N16 2D 50
N17 1G 33
N22 6D 16
RM6: Chad H 6D 38
RM10: Dag 6J 57
SE25 4G 141
SM2: Sutt 7H 149
SM6: Wall 4F 151
SW20 2H 137
TW2: Twick 2G 115
TW9: Rich 4G 99
TW11: Tedd 5A 116
(not continuous)
TW15: Ashf 5B 112
UB3: Hayes 6J 59
W13 7A 62
Manor Rd. Ho.
HA1: Harr 6A 26
Manor Rd. Nth.
KT10: Esh 3A 146
SM6: Wall 4F 151
Manorside EN5: Barn 4B 4
Manorside Cl. SE2 4C 92
Manor Sq. RM8: Dag 2C 56
Manor Va. TW8: Bford 5C 80
Manor Vw. N3 2K 29
Manor Way BR2: Short 6C 144
BR3: Beck 2C 142
BR5: Orp 4G 145
CR2: S Croy 6E 152
CR4: Mitc 3G 139
DA5: Bexl 1G 129
DA7: Bex 3K 111
E4 4A 20
HA2: Harr 4F 25
HA4: Ruis 7G 23
IG8: Wfd G 5F 21
KT4: Wor Pk 1A 148
NW9 4A 28
RM13: Rain 4K 75
SE3 4H 107
UB2: S'hall 4B 78
Manorway EN1: Enf 7K 7
Manor Way Bus. Cen.
RM13: Rain 5K 75
Manor Waye UB8: Uxb 1A 58
Manor Way, The
SM6: Wall 4F 151
Manpreet Ct. E12 5D 54
Manresa Rd.
SW3 5C 84 (6C 170)
Mansard Beeches SW17 5E 120
Mansard Cl. HA5: Pinn 3B 24
Manse Cl. UB3: Hayes 6F 77
Mansel Gro. E17 1C 34
Mansell Rd. UB6: G'frd 5F 61
W3 2K 81
Mansell St. E1 6F 69 (1K 169)
Mansel Rd. SW19 6G 119
Mansergh Cl. SE18 7C 90
Manse Rd. N16 3F 51
Manser Rd. RM13: Rain 3K 75
Mansfield Av. EN4: Barn 6J 5
HA4: Ruis 1K 41
N15 4D 32
Mansfield Cl. N9 6B 8
Mansfield Ct. *E2* 1F 69
(off Whiston Rd.)
Mansfield Dr. UB4: Hayes 4G 59
Mansfield Hgts. N2 5C 30
Mansfield Hill E4 7J 9
Mansfield M. W1 5F 67 (6J 159)
Mansfield Pl.
CR2: S Croy 6D 152
NW3 4A 48
Mansfield Rd.
CR2: S Croy 6D 152
E11 6K 35
E17 4B 34
IG1: Ilf 2E 54
KT9: Chess 5C 146
NW3 5D 48
W3 4H 63
Mansfield St. W1 5F 67 (6J 159)
Mansford St. E2 2G 69
Manship Rd. CR4: Mitc 7E 120
Mansion Cl. SW9 1A 104
(not continuous)
Mansion Cottage Vis. Info. Cen. 1C 48
Mansion Gdns. NW3 3K 47
Mansion House 6D 68 (1E 168)
Mansion Ho. Pl.
EC4 6D 68 (1E 168)
Mansion Ho. St. EC2 1E 168
Mansions, The SW5 5K 83
Manson M. SW7 4B 84 (4A 170)
Manson Pl. SW7 4B 84 (4A 170)
Mansted Gdns.
RM6: Chad H 7C 38
Manston *N17* 2D 32
(off Adams Rd.)
NW1 7G 49
(off Agar Gro.)
Manston Av. UB2: S'hall 4E 78
Manston Cl. SE20 1J 141
Manstone Rd. NW2 5G 47
Manston Gro.
KT2: King T 5D 116
Manston Ho. *W14* 3G 83
(off Russell Rd.)
Manthorp Rd. SE18 5G 91
Mantilla Rd. SW17 4E 120
Mantle Rd. SE4 3A 106
Mantlet Cl. SW16 7G 121
Mantle Way E15 7G 53
Manton Av. W7 2K 79
Manton Cl. UB3: Hayes 7G 59
Manton Rd. EN3: Enf 1H 9
SE2 4A 92
Manton Way EN3: Enf 1J 9
Mantua St. SW11 3B 102
Mantus Cl. E1 4J 69
Mantus Rd. E1 4J 69
Manus Way N20 2F 15
Manville Gdns. SW17 3F 121
Manville Rd. SW17 2E 120
Manwood Rd. SE4 5B 106
Manwood St. E16 1D 90
Manygate La.
TW17: Shep 7E 130
Manygate Mobile Home Est.
TW17: Shep 6F 131
(off Mitre Cl.)
Manygates SW12 2F 121
Mapesbury M. NW4 6C 28
NW9 6C 28
Mapesbury Rd. NW2 7G 47
Mapeshill Pl. NW2 6E 46
Mapes Ho. NW6 7G 47
Mape St. E2 4H 69
Maple Av. E4 5G 19
HA2: Harr 2F 43
UB7: W Dray 7A 58
W3 1A 82
Maple Cl. BR5: Orp 5H 145
CR4: Mitc 1F 139
HA4: Ruis 6K 23
IG9: Buck H 3G 21
N3 6D 14
N16 6G 33
SW4 6H 103
TW12: Hamp 6C 114
UB4: Hayes 3B 60
Maple Ct. *CR0: Croy* 4C 152
(off Lwr. Coombe St.)
CR0: Croy 4C 152
(off Waldrons, The)
E6 5E 72
KT3: N Mald 3K 135
SE6 1D 124
TW15: Ashf 7F 113
Maple Cres. DA15: Sidc 6A 110
Maplecroft Cl. E6 6B 72
Mapledale Av. CR0: Croy 2G 153
Mapledene BR7: Chst 5G 127
Mapledene Est. E8 7G 51
Mapledene Rd. E8 7F 51
Maple Gdns. HA8: Edg 7F 13
TW19: Staines 2A 112
Maple Gro. NW9 7J 27
TW8: Bford 7B 80
UB1: S'hall 5D 60
W5 3D 80
Maple Gro. Bus. Cen.
TW4: Houn 4A 96
Maple Ho. E17 3D 34
KT1: King T 5E 134
(off Maple Rd.)
SE8 7B 88
(off Idonia St.)
Maplehurst BR2: Short 2G 143
Maplehurst Cl.
KT1: King T 4E 134
Maple Ind. Est.
TW13: Felt 3J 113
Maple Leaf Dr.
DA15: Sidc 1K 127
Mapleleafe Gdns. IG6: Ilf 3F 37

Maple Leaf Sq. SE16 .....2K 87
Maple Lodge W8 .....3K 83
(off Abbots Wlk.)
Maple M. NW6 .....2K 65
SW16 .....5K 121
Maple Pl. N17 .....7B 18
UB7: W Dray 1A 76
W1 .....4G 67 (5B 160)
Maple Rd. E11 .....6G 35
KT6: Surb 6D 134
SE20 .....1H 141
UB4: Hayes 3A 60
Maples Pl. E1 .....5H 69
Maplestead Rd. RM9: Dag 1B 74
SW2 .....7K 103
Maples, The KT10: Esh 7A 146
TW11: Tedd 7C 116
Maple St. RM7: Rom 4J 39
W1 .....5G 67 (5A 160)
Maplethorpe Rd.
CR7: Thor H 4A 140
Mapleton Cl. BR2: Short 6J 143
Mapleton Cres. EN3: Enf 1D 8
SW18 .....6K 101
Mapleton Rd. E4 .....3K 19
EN1: Enf 2C 8
SW18 .....6J 101
(not continuous)
Maple Wlk. W10 .....3F 65
Maple Way TW13: Felt 3J 113
Maplin Cl. N21 .....6E 6
Maplin Ho. SE2 .....2D 92
(off Wolvercote Rd.)
Maplin Rd. E16 .....6J 71
Maplin St. E3 .....3B 70
Mapperley Cl. E11 .....6H 35
Mapperley Dr. IG8: Wfd G 7B 20
Maran Way DA18: Erith 2D 92
Marathon Ho. NW1 .....5E 158
(off Marylebone Rd.)
Marathon Way SE28 .....2K 91
Marban Rd. W9 .....3H 65
Marble Arch 2F 165
MARBLE ARCH 7D 66 (2E 164)
Marble Arch W1 .....7D 66 (2E 164)
Marble Arch Apartments
W1 .....7E 158
(off Harrowby St.)
Marble Cl. W3 .....1H 81
Marble Dr. NW2 .....1F 47
Marble Hill Cl.
TW1: Twick 7B 98
Marble Hill Gdns.
TW1: Twick 7B 98
Marble Hill House 7C 98
Marble Ho. SE18 .....5K 91
W9 .....4H 65
Marble Quay E1 .....1G 87 (4K 169)
Marbrook Cl. SE12 .....3A 126
Marcella Rd. SW9 .....2A 104
March NW9 .....1B 28
(off Concourse, The)
Marchant Cl. SE1 .....5F 87
Marchant Rd. E11 .....2F 53
Marchant St. SE14 .....6A 88
Marchbank Rd. W14 .....6H 83
March Cl. SW15 .....4D 100
Marchmont Rd.
SM6: Wall 7G 151
TW10: Rich 5F 99
Marchmont St.
WC1 .....4J 67 (3E 160)
March Rd. TW1: Twick 7A 98
Marchside Cl. TW5: Houn 1B 96
Marchwood Cl. SE5 .....7E 86
Marchwood Cres. W5 .....6C 62
Marcia Rd. SE1 .....4E 86
Marcilly Rd. SW18 .....5B 102
Marcon Cl. E8 .....5H 51
(off Amhurst Rd.)
Marconi Pl. N11 .....4A 16
Marconi Rd. E10 .....1C 52

Marconi Way UB1: S'hall 6F 61
Marcon Pl. E8 .....5H 51
Marco Polo Ho. SW8 .....7F 85
Marco Rd. W6 .....3E 82
Marcourt Lawns W5 .....4E 62
Marcus Cl. E15 .....1G 71
Marcus Garvey M.
SE22 .....6H 105
Marcus Garvey Way
SE24 .....4A 104
Marcus St. E15 .....1H 71
SW18 .....6K 101
Marcus Ter. SW18 .....6K 101
Mardale Cl. NW7 .....7H 13
Mardale Dr. NW9 .....5K 27
Mardell Rd. CR0: Croy 5K 141
Marden Av. BR2: Short 6H 143
Marden Cres. CR0: Croy 6K 139
DA5: Bexl 5J 111
Marden Ho. E5 .....5H 51
Marden Rd. CR0: Croy 6K 139
N17 .....2E 32
Marden Sq. SE16 .....3H 87
Marder Rd. W13 .....2A 80
Mardyke Cl. RM13: Rain 2J 75
Mardyke Ho. RM13: Rain 2K 75
SE17 .....4D 86
(off Mason St.)
Mareschal Niel Av.
DA15: Sidc 3H 127
Mareschal Niel Pde.
DA14: Sidc 3H 127
(off Main Rd.)
Maresby Ho. E4 .....2J 19
Mares Fld. CR0: Croy 3E 152
Maresfield Gdns. NW3 .....5A 48
Mare St. E8 .....5H 51
Marfleet Cl. SM5: Cars 2C 150
Margaret Av. E4 .....6J 9
Margaret Bondfield Av.
IG11: Bark 7A 56
Margaret Bldgs. N16 .....1F 51
Margaret Cl. EN4: Barn 4G 5
W1 .....7A 160
Margaret Gardner Dr.
SE9 .....2D 126
Margaret Herbison Ho.
SW6 .....6H 83
(off Clem Attlee Ct.)
Margaret Ho. W6 .....5E 82
(off Queen Caroline St.)
Margaret Ingram Cl. SW6 .....6H 83
(off Rylston Rd.)
Margaret Lockwood Cl.
KT1: King T 4F 135
Margaret Rd. DA5: Bexl 6D 110
EN4: Barn 4G 5
N16 .....1F 51
Margaret St. W1 .....6F 67 (7K 159)
Margaretta Ter.
SW3 .....6C 84 (7C 170)
Margaretting Rd. E12 .....1A 54
Margaret Way IG4: IIf 6C 36
Margaret White Ho.
NW1 .....1D 160
(off Chalton St.)
Margate Rd. SW2 .....5J 103
Margery Fry Ct. N7 .....3J 49
Margery Pk. Rd. E7 .....6J 53
Margery Rd. RM8: Dag 3D 56
Margery St. WC1 .....3A 68 (2J 161)
Margin Dr. SW19 .....5F 119
Margravine Gdns. W6 .....5F 83
Margravine Rd. W6 .....5F 83
Marham Gdns.
SM4: Mord 6A 138
SW18 .....1C 120
Maria Cl. SE1 .....4H 87
Marian Cl. UB4: Hayes 4B 60
Marian Ct. E9 .....5J 51
SM1: Sutt 5K 149
Marianne North Gallery 2F 99

Marian Pl. E2 .....2H 69
Marian Rd. SW16 .....1G 139
Marian Sq. E2 .....2H 69
Marian St. E2 .....2H 69
Marian Way NW10 .....7B 46
Maria Ter. E1 .....5K 69
Maria Theresa Cl.
KT3: N Mald 5K 135
Maribor SE10 .....7E 88
(off Burney St.)
Maricas Av. HA3: Harr 1H 25
Marie Curie SE5 .....1E 104
Marie Lloyd Gdns. N19 .....7J 31
Marie Lloyd Ho. N1 .....1E 162
(off Murray Gro.)
Marie Lloyd Wlk. E8 .....6F 51
Mariette Way SM6: Wall 7J 151
Marigold All. SE1 .....3A 168
Marigold Cl. UB1: S'hall 7C 60
Marigold Rd. N17 .....7D 18
Marigold St. SE16 .....2H 87
Marigold Way CR0: Croy 1K 153
Marina App. UB4: Hayes 5C 60
Marina Av. KT3: N Mald 5D 136
Marina Cl. BR2: Short 3J 143
Marina Dr. DA16: Well 2J 109
Marina Gdns. RM7: Rom 5H 39
Marina Ho. IG11: Bark 4A 74
SE18 .....4D 90
Marinefield Rd. SW6 .....2K 101
Marine Ho. SE5 .....7C 86
Mariner Gdns.
TW10: Rich 3C 116
Mariner Rd. E12 .....4E 54
Mariners M. E14 .....4F 89
Marine St. SE16 .....3G 87
Marine Twr. SE8 .....6B 88
(off Abinger Gro.)
Marion Av. TW17: Shep 5D 130
Marion Gro. IG8: Wfd G 5B 20
Marion Rd. CR7: Thor H 5C 140
NW7 .....5K 13
Marischal Rd. SE13 .....3F 107
Maritime Ind. Est. SE7 .....4K 89
Maritime Quay E14 .....5C 88
Maritime St. E3 .....4B 70
Marius Pas. SW17 .....2E 120
Marius Rd. SW17 .....2E 120
Marjorie Gro. SW11 .....4D 102
Marjorie M. E1 .....6K 69
Mark Av. E4 .....6J 9
Mark Cl. DA7: Bex 1E 110
UB1: S'hall 7F 61
Marke Cl. BR2: Kes 4K 156
Market Cen., The
UB2: S'hall 4K 77
Market Chambers EN2: Enf 3J 7
(off Church St.)
Market Ct. W1 .....7A 160
Market Entrance SW8 .....7G 85
Market Est. N7 .....6J 49
Market Hill SE18 .....3E 90
Market La. HA8: Edg 1J 27
Market Link RM1: Rom 4K 39
Market M. W1 .....1F 85 (5J 165)
Market Pde.
BR1: Brom 1J 143
(off East St.)
DA14: Sidc 4B 128
E10 .....6E 34
(off High Rd.)
E17 .....3B 34
(off Forest Rd.)
N9 .....2B 18
(off Winchester Rd.)
TW13: Felt 1C 114
Market Pav. E10 .....3C 52
Market Pl. DA6: Bex 4G 111
EN2: Enf 3J 7
KT1: King T 2D 134
N2 .....3C 30

Market Pl. NW11 .....4K 29
SE16 .....4G 87
(not continuous)
TW8: Bford 7C 80
UB1: S'hall 1D 78
W1 .....6G 67 (7A 160)
W3 .....1J 81
Market Rd. N7 .....6J 49
TW9: Rich 3G 99
Market Row SW9 .....4A 104
Market Sq. BR1: Brom 2J 143
(not continuous)
E14 .....6D 70
Market Sq., The N9 .....2C 18
(off Plevna Rd.)
Market St. E6 .....2D 72
SE18 .....4E 90
Market Ter. TW8: Bford 6E 80
(off Albany Rd.)
Market, The SM1: Sutt 1A 166
Market Way E14 .....6D 70
HA0: Wemb 5E 44
Market Yd. M.
SE1 .....2E 86 (7G 169)
Markfield Beam Engine & Mus.
.....5G 33
Markfield Gdns. E4 .....7J 9
Markfield Rd. N15 .....4G 33
Markham Ho.
RM10: Dag 3G 57
(off Uvedale Rd.)
Markham Pl.
SW3 .....5D 84 (5E 170)
Markham Sq.
SW3 .....5D 84 (5E 170)
Markham St.
SW3 .....5C 84 (5D 170)
Markhole Cl.
TW12: Hamp 7D 114
Mark Ho. E2 .....2K 69
(off Sewardstone Rd.)
Markhouse Av. E17 .....6A 34
Markhouse Pas. E17 .....6B 34
(off Markhouse Rd.)
Markhouse Rd. E17 .....6B 34
Markland Ho. W10 .....7F 65
(off Darfield Way)
Mark La. EC3 .....7E 68 (2H 169)
Mark Lodge EN4: Barn 4H 5
(off Edgeworth Rd.)
Markmanor Av. E17 .....7A 34
Mark Rd. N22 .....1B 32
Marksbury Av. TW9: Rich 3G 99
Marks Lodge RM7: Rom 5K 39
Marks Rd. RM7: Rom 5J 39
(not continuous)
Markstone Ho. SE1 .....7A 168
(off Lancaster St.)
Mark St. E15 .....7G 53
EC2 .....4E 68 (3G 163)
Mark Wade Cl. E12 .....1B 54
Markway TW16: Sun T 2A 132
Markwell Cl. SE26 .....4H 123
Markyate Ho. W10 .....4E 64
(off Sutton Way)
Markyate Rd. RM8: Dag 5B 56
Marlands Rd. IG5: IIf 3C 36
Marlborough Av. E8 .....1G 69
(not continuous)
HA4: Ruis 6E 22
HA8: Edg 3C 12
N14 .....3B 16
Marlborough Cl.
BR6: Orp 6K 145
N20 .....3J 15
SE17 .....4C 86
SW19 .....6C 120
Marlborough Ct.
CR2: S Croy 4E 152
(off Birdhurst Rd.)

Marlborough Ct. EN1: Enf 5K 7
HA1: Harr 4H 25
HA6: Nwood 1H 23
IG9: Buck H 2F 21
SM6: Wall 7G 151
W1 .....2A 166
W8 .....4J 83
(off Pembroke Rd.)
Marlborough Cres.
UB3: Hayes 7F 77
W4 .....3K 81
Marlborough Dr. IG5: IIf 3C 36
Marlborough Flats SW3 .....3D 170
Marlborough Gdns.
KT6: Surb 7D 134
N20 .....3J 15
Marlborough Gro. SE1 .....5G 87
Marlborough Hill
HA1: Harr 4H 25
NW8 .....2A 66
Marlborough House
.....1G 85 (5B 166)
Marlborough Ho. E16 .....7J 71
(off Hardy Av.)
NW1 .....3K 159
(off Osnaburgh St.)
Marlborough La. SE7 .....6A 90
Marlborough Mans. NW6 .....5K 47
(off Canon Hill)
Marlborough M. SW2 .....4K 103
Marlborough Pde.
HA8: Edg 3C 12
(off Marlborough Av.)
UB10: Uxb 4D 58
Marlborough Pk. Av.
DA15: Sidc 7A 110
Marlborough Pl. NW8 .....2A 66
Marlborough Rd.
BR2: Short 4A 144
CR2: S Croy 7C 152
DA7: Bex 3D 110
E4 .....6J 19
E7 .....7A 54
E15 .....4G 53
E18 .....2J 35
N9 .....1B 18
N19 .....2H 49
(not continuous)
N22 .....7D 16
RM7: Mawney 4G 39
RM8: Dag 4B 56
SE18 .....3F 91
SM1: Sutt 3J 149
SW1 .....1G 85 (5B 166)
SW19 .....6C 120
TW7: Isle 1B 98
TW10: Rich 6F 99
TW12: Hamp 6E 114
TW13: Felt 2B 114
TW15: Ashf 5A 112
UB2: S'hall 3A 78
UB10: Uxb 4D 58
W4 .....5J 81
W5 .....2D 80
Marlborough St.
SW3 .....4C 84 (4C 170)
Marlborough Yd. N19 .....2H 49
Marlbury NW8 .....1K 65
(off Abbey Rd.)
Marler Rd. SE23 .....1A 124
Marley Av. DA7: Bex 6D 92
Marley Cl. N15 .....4B 32
UB6: G'frd 3E 60
Marley Ho. W11 .....7F 65
(off St Ann's Rd.)
Marley Wlk. NW2 .....5E 46
Marlfield Cl.
KT4: Wor Pk 1C 148
Marlin Cl. TW16: Sun T 6G 113
Marlingdene Cl.
TW12: Hamp 6E 114
Marlings Cl. BR7: Chst 4J 145

Marlings Pk. Av.—Mason Rd.

Marlings Pk. Av.
BR7: Chst 4J **145**
Marlins Cl. SM1: Sutt 5A **150**
Marloes Cl. HA0: Wemb 4D **44**
Marloes Rd. W8 3K **83**
Marlow Cl. SE20 3H **141**
Marlow Ct. N14 7B **6**
NW6 7F **47**
NW9 3B **28**
Marlow Cres. TW1: Twick 6K **97**
Marlow Dr. SM3: Sutt 2F **149**
Marlowe Bus. Cen *SE14 7A **88***
(off Batavia Rd.)
Marlowe Cl. BR7: Chst 6H **127**
IG6: Ilf 1G **37**
Marlowe Ct. *SW3 4D **170***
(off Petyward)
Marlowe Gdns. SE9 6E **108**
Marlowe Ho. IG8: Wfd G 7K **21**
*KT1: King T 4D **134***
(off Portsmouth Rd.)
*SE8 5B **88***
(off Bowditch)
Marlowe Rd. E17 4E **34**
Marlowe Sq. CR4: Mitc 4G **139**
Marlowes, The
DA1: Cray 4K **111**
NW8 1B **66**
Marlowe Way CR0: Croy 2J **151**
Marlow Gdns. UB3: Hayes 3F **77**
Marlow Ho. *E2 2J **163***
(off Calvert Av.)
*KT5: Surb 5E **134***
(off Cranes Pk.)
*SE1 7J **169***
(off Maltby St.)
TW11: Tedd 4A **116**
*W2 6K **65***
(off Hallfield Est.)
Marlow Rd. E6 3D **72**
SE20 3H **141**
UB2: S'hall 3D **78**
Marlow Way SE16 2K **87**
Marl Rd. SW18 4A **102**
Marlton St. SE10 5H **89**
Marlwood Cl. DA15: Sidc 2J **127**
Marmadon Rd. SE18 4K **91**
Marmion App. E4 4H **19**
Marmion Av. E4 4G **19**
Marmion Cl. E4 4G **19**
Marmion M. SW11 3E **102**
Marmion Rd. SW11 4E **102**
Marmont Rd. SE15 1G **105**
Marmora Ho. *E1 5A **70***
(off Ben Jonson Rd.)
Marmora Rd. SE22 6J **105**
Marmot Rd. TW4: Houn 3B **96**
Marne Av. DA16: Well 3A **110**
N11 4A **16**
Marnell Way TW4: Houn 3B **96**
Marne St. W10 3G **65**
Marney Rd. SW11 4E **102**
Marnfield Cres. SW2 1A **122**
Marnham Av. NW2 4G **47**
Marnham Ct. HA0: Wemb 5C **44**
Marnham Cres. UB6: G'frd 3F **61**
Marnock Ho. *SE17 5D **86***
(off Brandon St.)
Marnock Rd. SE4 5B **106**
Maroon Ho. E14 5A **70**
Maroon St. E14 5A **70**
Maroons Way SE6 5C **124**
Marqueen Towers SW16 7K **121**
Marquess Rd. N1 6D **50**
Marquess Rd. Nth. N1 6D **50**
Marquess Rd. Sth. N1 6C **50**
Marquis Cl. HA0: Wemb 7F **45**
Marquis Ct. IG11: Bark 5J **55**
*KT1: King T 4D **134***
(off Anglesea Rd.)
*N4 1K **49***
(off Marquis Rd.)
Marquis Rd. N4 1K **49**
N22 6E **16**
NW1 6H **49**
Marrabon Cl. DA15: Sidc 1A **128**
Marrick Cl. SW15 4C **100**
Marrick Ho. *NW6 1K **65***
(off Mortimer Cres.)
Marriett Ho. SE6 4E **124**
Marrilyne Av. EN3: Enf 1G **9**
Marriner Ct. *UB3: Hayes 7G **59***
(off Barra Hall Rd.)
Marriott Cl. TW14: Felt 6F **95**
Marriott Rd. E15 1G **71**
EN5: Barn 3A **4**
N4 1K **49**
N10 1D **30**
Marriotts Cl. NW9 6B **28**
Marryat Cl. TW4: Houn 4D **96**
Marryat Ho. *SW1 6A **172***
(off Churchill Gdns.)
Marryat Pl. SW19 4G **119**
Marryat Rd. SW19 5F **119**
Marryat Sq. SW6 1G **101**
Marsala Rd. SE13 4D **106**
Marsden Rd. N9 2C **18**
SE15 3F **105**
Marsden St. NW5 6E **48**
(not continuous)
Marshall Cl. HA1: Harr 7H **25**
SW18 6A **102**
TW4: Houn 5D **96**
Marshall Dr. UB4: Hayes 5H **59**
Marshall Est. NW7 4H **13**
Marshall Ho. *N1 2D **68***
(off Cranston Est.)
*NW6 2H **65***
(off Albert Rd.)
*SE1 3E **86***
(off Page's Wlk.)
*SE17 5D **86***
(off East St.)
Marshall Path SE28 7B **74**
Marshall Rd. E10 3D **52**
N17 1D **32**
Marshalls Cl. N11 4A **16**
Marshalls Dr. RM1: Rom 3K **39**
Marshalls Gro. SE18 4C **90**
Marshall's Pl. SE16 3F **87**
Marshalls Rd. RM7: Rom 4K **39**
SM1: Sutt 4K **149**
Marshall St. W1 6G **67** (1B **166**)
Marshall Way E10 3D **52**
Marshalsea Rd.
SE1 2C **86** (6D **168**)
Marsham Cl. BR7: Chst 5F **127**
Marsham Ct.
SW1 4H **85** (3D **172**)
Marsham St.
SW1 3H **85** (2D **172**)
Marsh Av. CR4: Mitc 2D **138**
Marshbrook Cl. SE3 3B **108**
Marsh Cen., The *E1 7K **163***
(off Whitechapel High St.)
Marsh Cl. NW7 3G **13**
Marsh Ct. *E8 6G **51***
(off St Philip's Rd.)
Marsh Dr. NW9 6B **28**
Marsh Farm Rd.
TW2: Twick 1K **115**
Marshfield St. E14 3E **88**
Marsh Ga. Bus. Cen.
E15 1E **70**
Marshgate Cen., The
E15 1D **70**
Marshgate La. E15 7D **52**
Marshgate Path SE28 3G **91**
Marshgate Trad. Est.
E15 7D **52**
Marsh Grn. Rd.
RM10: Dag 1G **75**
Marsh Hall HA9: Wemb 3F **45**
Marsh Hill E9 5A **52**
Marsh Ho. *SW1 6D **172***
(off Aylesford St.)
SW8 1G **103**
Marsh La. E10 2B **52**
HA7: Stan 5H **11**
N17 1H **33**
NW7 3F **13**
Marsh Rd. HA0: Wemb 3D **62**
HA5: Pinn 4C **24**
Marshside Cl. N9 1D **18**
Marsh St. E14 4D **88**
Marsh Wall E14 1C **88**
Marsh Way
RM13: Dag, Rain 3K **75**
(not continuous)
Marshwood Ho. *NW6 1J **65***
(off Kilburn Va.)
Marsland Cl. SE17 5B **86**
Marsom Ho. *N1 1E **162***
(off Fairbank Est.)
Marston Av. KT9: Chess 6E **146**
RM10: Dag 2G **57**
Marston Cl. NW6 7A **48**
RM10: Dag 3G **57**
Marston Ho. SW9 2A **104**
Marston Rd. IG5: Ilf 1C **36**
TW11: Tedd 5B **116**
Marston Way SE19 7B **122**
Marsworth Av. HA5: Pinn 1B **24**
Marsworth Cl.
UB4: Hayes 5C **60**
Marsworth Ho. *E2 1G **69***
(off Whiston Rd.)
Martaban Rd. N16 2F **51**
Martara M. SE17 5C **86**
Martello St. E8 7H **51**
Martello Ter. E8 7H **51**
Martell Rd. SE21 3D **122**
Martel Pl. E8 6F **51**
Marten Rd. E17 2C **34**
Martens Av. DA7: Bex 4H **111**
Martens Cl. DA7: Bex 4J **111**
Martha Ct. E2 2H **69**
Martham Cl. IG6: Ilf 1F **37**
SE28 7D **74**
Martha Rd. E15 6G **53**
Martha's Bldgs.
EC1 4D **68** (3E **162**)
Martha St. E1 6J **69**
Marthorne Cres.
HA3: Harr 2H **25**
Martin Bowes Rd. SE9 3D **108**
Martinbridge Trad. Est.
EN1: Enf 5B **8**
Martin Cl. N9 1E **18**
UB10: Uxb 2A **58**
Martin Ct. *CR2: S Croy 5D **152***
(off Birdhurst Rd.)
*E14 2E **88***
(off River Barge Cl.)
Martin Cres. CR0: Croy 1A **152**
Martindale SW14 5J **99**
Martindale Av. E16 7J **71**
Martindale Ho. *E14 7D **70***
(off Poplar High St.)
Martin Dale Ind. Est.
EN1: Enf 3C **8**
Martindale Rd. SW12 7F **103**
TW4: Houn 3C **96**
Martin Dene DA6: Bex 5F **111**
Martin Dr. UB5: N'olt 5D **42**
Martineau Est. E1 7J **69**
Martineau Ho. *SW1 6A **172***
(off Churchill Gdns.)
Martineau M. N5 4B **50**
Martineau Rd. N5 4B **50**
Martingale Cl.
TW16: Sun T 4J **131**
Martingales Cl.
TW10: Rich 3D **116**
Martin Gdns. RM8: Dag 4C **56**
Martin Gro. SM4: Mord 3J **137**
Martin Ho. SE1 3C **86**
*SW8 7J **85***
(off Wyvil Rd.)
Martin La. EC4 7D **68** (2F **169**)
(not continuous)
Martin Pl. *SE28 1J **91***
(off Martin St.)
Martin Ri. DA6: Bex 5F **111**
Martin Rd. RM8: Dag 4C **56**
Martins Cl. BR4: W W'ck 1F **155**
Martinside *NW9 1B **28***
(off Quakers Course)
Martins Mt. EN5: Barn 4D **4**
Martin's Rd. BR2: Short 2G **143**
Martins, The HA9: Wemb 3F **45**
Martin St. SE28 1J **91**
Martins Wlk. N10 1E **30**
Martin Wlk. *SE28 1J **91***
(off Martin St.)
Martin Way SW20 2F **137**
Martlesham *N17 2E **32***
(off Adams Rd.)
Martlet Gro. UB5: N'olt 3B **60**
Martlett Ct. WC2 6J **67** (1F **167**)
Martley Dr. IG2: Ilf 5F **37**
Martock Cl. HA3: Harr 4A **26**
Martock Gdns. N11 5J **15**
Marton Cl. SE6 3C **124**
Marton Rd. N16 2E **50**
Martynside NW9 1B **28**
Martys Yd. NW3 4B **48**
Marvell Av. UB4: Hayes 5J **59**
Marvell Ho. *SE5 7D **86***
(off Camberwell Rd.)
Marvels Cl. SE12 2K **125**
Marvels La. SE12 2K **125**
(not continuous)
Marville Rd. SW6 7H **83**
Marvin St. E8 6H **51**
Marwell Cl.
BR4: W W'ck 2H **155**
Marwood Cl. DA16: Well 3B **110**
Marwood Dr. NW7 7A **14**
Mary Adelaide Cl. SW15 4A **118**
Mary Ann Gdns. SE8 6C **88**
Mary Ann Pl. *SE8 6C **88***
(off Mary Ann Gdns.)
Maryatt Av. HA2: Harr 2F **43**
Mary Bank SE18 4D **90**
Mary Cl. HA7: Stan 4F **27**
Mary Datchelor Cl. SE5 1D **104**
Maryfield Cl. DA5: Bexl 3K **129**
Mary Flux Ct. *SW5 5K **83***
(off Bramham Gdns.)
Mary Grn. NW8 1K **65**
Mary Ho. *W6 5E **82***
(off Queen Caroline St.)
Mary Jones Ho. *E14 7C **70***
(off Garford St.)
Maryland Ind. Est. *E15 5G **53***
(off Maryland Rd.)
Maryland Pk. E15 5G **53**
Maryland Point *E15 6G **53***
(off Grove, The)
Maryland Rd.
CR7: Thor H 1B **140**
E15 5F **53**
N22 6E **16**
Maryland Sq. E15 5G **53**
Marylands Rd. W9 4J **65**
Maryland St. E15 5F **53**
Maryland Wlk. *N1 1C **68***
(off Popham St.)
Maryland Way
TW16: Sun T 2J **131**
Mary Lawrenson Pl. SE3 7J **89**
MARYLEBONE 5E **66** (5H **159**)
Marylebone Cricket Club
Lord's Cricket Ground
3B 66 (1B 158)
MARYLEBONE FLYOVER
5B **66** (6C **158**)
Marylebone Fly-Over
W2 5B **66** (6C **158**)
Marylebone High St.
W1 5E **66** (5H **159**)
Marylebone La.
W1 5E **66** (6H **159**)
Marylebone M.
W1 5F **67** (6J **159**)
Marylebone Pas.
W1 6G **67** (7B **160**)
Marylebone Rd.
NW1 5C **66** (5D **158**)
Marylebone St.
W1 5E **66** (6H **159**)
Marylee Way
SE11 4K **85** (4H **173**)
Mary MacArthur Ho. *E2 3K **69***
(off Warley St.)
*RM10: Dag 3G **57***
(off Wythenshawe Rd.)
W6 6G **83**
Maryon Gro. SE7 4C **90**
Maryon M. NW3 4C **48**
Maryon Rd. SE7 4C **90**
SE18 4C **90**
Mary Peters Dr.
UB6: G'frd 5H **43**
Mary Pl. W11 7G **65**
Mary Rose Cl.
TW12: Hamp 1E **132**
Mary Rose Mall E6 5D **72**
Mary Rose Way N20 1G **15**
Mary Seacole Cl. E8 1F **69**
Mary Smith Ct. *SW5 4J **83***
(off Trebovir Rd.)
Marysmith Ho. *SW1 5D **172***
(off Cureton St.)
Mary's Ter. TW1: Twick 7A **98**
(not continuous)
Mary St. E16 5H **71**
N1 1C **68**
Mary Ter. NW1 1F **67**
Maryville DA16: Well 2K **109**
Mary Wharrie Ho. *NW3 7D **48***
(off Fellows Rd.)
Marzena Ct. TW3: Houn 6G **97**
Masault Ct. *TW9: Rich 4E **98***
(off Kew Foot Rd.)
Masbro' Rd. W14 3F **83**
Mascalls Ct. SE7 6A **90**
Mascalls Rd. SE7 6A **90**
Mascotte Rd. SW15 4F **101**
Mascotts Cl. NW2 3D **46**
Masefield Av. HA7: Stan 5E **10**
UB1: S'hall 7E **60**
Masefield Ct. EN5: Barn 4F **5**
KT6: Surb 7D **134**
Masefield Cres. N14 5B **6**
Masefield Gdns. E6 4E **72**
Masefield Ho. *NW6 3J **65***
(off Stafford Rd.)
Masefield La. UB4: Hayes 4K **59**
Masefield Rd.
TW12: Hamp 4D **114**
Masefield Way
TW19: Staines 1B **112**
Masham Ho. *DA18: Erith 2D **92***
(off Kale Rd.)
Mashie Rd. W3 6A **64**
Mashiters Hill RM1: Rom 1K **39**
Maskall Cl. SW2 1A **122**
Maskani Wlk. SW16 7G **121**
Maskell Rd. SW17 3A **120**
Maskelyne Cl. SW11 1C **102**
Mason Cl. DA7: Bex 3H **111**
E16 7J **71**
SE16 5G **87**
TW12: Hamp 1D **132**
Mason Ho. *E9 7J **51***
(off Frampton Pk. Rd.)
Mason Rd. IG8: Wfd G 4B **20**
SM1: Sutt 5K **149**

Mason's Arms M.—McGregor Ct.

Mason's Arms M.
W1 ... 6F **67** (1K **165**)
Masons Av. CR0: Croy ... 3C **152**
EC2 ... 6D **68** (7E **162**)
HA3: Harr ... 4K **25**
Masons Grn. La. W3 ... 4G **63**
(not continuous)
W3 ... 5G **63**
Masons Hill BR2: Short ... 3J **143**
SE18 ... 4F **91**
Masons Pl. CR4: Mitc ... 1D **138**
EC1 ... 3C **68** (1B **162**)
Mason St. SE17 ... 4D **86**
Mason's Yd.
SW1 ... 1G **85** (4B **166**)
SW19 ... 5F **119**
Massey Cl. N11 ... 5A **16**
Massey Ct. *E6* ... *1A* ***72***
(off Florence Rd.)
Massie Rd. E8 ... 6G **51**
Massingberd Way SW17 ... 4F **121**
Massinger St. SE17 ... 4E **86**
Massingham St. E1 ... 4K **69**
Masson Av. HA4: Ruis ... 6A **42**
Mast Ct. *SE16* ... *4A* ***88***
(off Boat Lifter Way)
Master Brewer ... **5D 40**
Master Gunners Pl. SE18 ... 7C **90**
Masterman Ho. *SE5* ... *7D* ***86***
(off Elmington Est.)
Masterman Rd. E6 ... 3C **72**
Masters Cl. SW16 ... 6G **121**
Masters Dr. SE16 ... 5H **87**
Masters Lodge *E1* ... *6J* ***69***
(off Johnson St.)
Masters St. E1 ... 5K **69**
Mast Ho. Ter. E14 ... 4C **88**
(not continuous)
Mastmaker Ct. E14 ... 2C **88**
Mastmaker Rd. E14 ... 2C **88**
MASWELL PARK ... **5G 97**
Maswell Pk. Cres.
TW3: Houn ... 5G **97**
Maswell Pk. Rd.
TW3: Houn ... 5F **97**
Matcham Ct. *TW1: Twick* ... *6D* ***98***
(off Clevedon Rd.)
Matcham Rd. E11 ... 3G **53**
Matchless Dr. SE18 ... 7E **90**
Matchroom Stadium ... ***2D 52***
Matfield Cl. BR2: Short ... 5J **143**
Matfield Rd. DA17: Belv ... 6G **93**
Matham Gro. SE22 ... 4F **105**
Matham Rd. KT8: E Mos ... 5H **133**
Matheson Lang Ho. SE1 ... 7J **167**
Matheson Rd. W14 ... 4H **83**
Mathews Av. E6 ... 2E **72**
Mathews Pk. Av. E15 ... 6H **53**
Mathews Yd.
WC2 ... 6J **67** (1E **166**)
Mathieson Ct. *SE1* ... *7B* ***168***
(off King James St.)
Mathison Ho. *SW10* ... *7A* ***84***
(off Coleridge Gdns.)
Matilda Cl. SE19 ... 7D **122**
Matilda Ho. *E1* ... *1G* ***87***
(off St Katherine's Way)
Matilda St. N1 ... 1K **67**
Matisse Ct. EC1 ... 4D **68** (3E **162**)
Matlock Cl. EN5: Barn ... 5A **4**
SE24 ... 4C **104**
Matlock Ct. SE5 ... 4D **104**
Matlock Cres. SM3: Sutt ... 4G **149**
Matlock Gdns. SM3: Sutt ... 4G **149**
Matlock Pl. SM3: Sutt ... 4G **149**
Matlock Rd. E10 ... 6E **34**
Matlock St. E14 ... 6A **70**
Matlock Way
KT3: N Mald ... 1K **135**
Maton Ho. *SW6* ... *7H* ***83***
(off Estcourt Rd.)
Matrimony Pl. SW4 ... 2G **103**
Matson Ct. IG8: Wfd G ... 7B **20**
Matson Ho. SE16 ... 3H **87**
Matthew Cl. W10 ... 4F **65**
Matthew Ct. CR4: Mitc ... 5H **139**
E17 ... 3E **34**
Matthew Parker St.
SW1 ... 2H **85** (7D **166**)
Matthews Ct. *E17* ... *1C* ***34***
(off Chingford Rd.)
Matthews Ho. *E14* ... *5C* ***70***
(off Burgess St.)
Matthews Rd. UB6: G'frd ... 5H **43**
Matthews St. SW11 ... 2D **102**
Matthias Rd. N16 ... 5E **50**
Mattison Rd. N4 ... 6A **32**
Mattock La. W5 ... 1B **80**
W13 ... 1B **80**
Maud Cashmore Way
SE18 ... 3D **90**
Maude Ho. *E2* ... *2G* ***69***
(off Ropley St.)
Maude Rd. E17 ... 5A **34**
SE5 ... 1E **104**
Maude Ter. E17 ... 5A **34**
Maud Gdns. E13 ... 1H **71**
IG11: Bark ... 2K **73**
Maudlins Grn.
E1 ... 1G **87** (4K **169**)
Maud Rd. E10 ... 3E **52**
E13 ... 2H **71**
Maudslay Rd. SE9 ... 3D **108**
Maudsley Ho. TW8: Bford ... 5E **80**
Maud St. E16 ... 5H **71**
Maudsville Cotts. W7 ... 1J **79**
Maud Wilkes Cl. NW5 ... 5G **49**
Maugham Ct. *W3* ... *3J* ***81***
(off Palmerston Rd.)
Mauleverer Rd. SW2 ... 5J **103**
Maundeby Wlk. NW10 ... 6A **46**
Maunder Rd. W7 ... 1K **79**
Maunsel St.
SW1 ... 4H **85** (3C **172**)
Maureen Ct. BR3: Beck ... 2J **141**
Mauretania Bldg. *E1* ... *7K* ***69***
(off Jardine Rd.)
Maurice Av. N22 ... 2B **32**
Maurice Bishop Ter. *N6* ... *6E* ***30***
(off View Rd.)
Maurice Brown Cl. NW7 ... 5A **14**
Maurice Ct. TW8: Bford ... 7D **80**
Maurice Drummond Ho.
SE10 ... *1D* ***106***
(off Catherine Gro.)
Maurice St. W12 ... 6D **64**
Maurice Wlk. NW11 ... 4A **30**
Maurier Cl. UB5: N'olt ... 1A **60**
Mauritius Rd. SE10 ... 4G **89**
Maury Rd. N16 ... 2G **51**
Mauveine Gdns.
TW3: Houn ... 4E **96**
Mavelstone Cl.
BR1: Brom ... 1C **144**
Mavelstone Rd.
BR1: Brom ... 1B **144**
Maverton Rd. E3 ... 1C **70**
Mavis Av. KT19: Eps ... 5A **148**
Mavis Cl. KT19: Eps ... 5A **148**
Mavis Wlk. *E6* ... *5C* ***72***
(off Greenwich Cres.)
Mavor Ho. *N1* ... *1K* ***67***
(off Barnsbury Est.)
Mawbey Ho. SE1 ... 5F **87**
Mawbey Pl. SE1 ... 5F **87**
Mawbey Rd. SE1 ... 5F **87**
Mawbey St. SW8 ... 7J **85**
Mawdley Ho. SE1 ... 7A **168**
MAWNEY ... **4J 39**
Mawney Cl.
RM7: Mawney ... 2H **39**
Mawney Rd.
RM7: Mawney ... 2H **39**
Mawson Cl. SW20 ... 2G **137**
Mawson Ho. *EC1* ... *5J* ***161***
(off Baldwins Gdns.)
Mawson La. W4 ... 6B **82**
Maxden Ct. SE15 ... 3F **105**
Maxey Gdns. RM9: Dag ... 4E **56**
Maxey Rd. RM9: Dag ... 5E **56**
SE18 ... 4G **91**
Maxfield Cl. N20 ... 7F **5**
Maxilla Wlk. *W10* ... *6F* ***65***
(off Westway)
Maximfeldt Rd. DA8: Erith ... 5K **93**
Maxim Rd. DA8: Erith ... 4K **93**
N21 ... 6F **7**
Maxted Pk. HA1: Harr ... 7J **25**
Maxted Rd. SE15 ... 3F **105**
Maxwell Cl. CR0: Croy ... 1J **151**
UB3: Hayes ... 7J **59**
Maxwell Ct. SE22 ... 1G **123**
SW4 ... 5H **103**
Maxwell Rd. DA16: Well ... 3K **109**
HA6: Nwood ... 1F **23**
SW6 ... 7K **83**
TW15: Ashf ... 6E **112**
UB7: W Dray ... 4B **76**
Maxwelton Av. NW7 ... 5E **12**
Maxwelton Cl. NW7 ... 5E **12**
Maya Angelou Ct. E4 ... 4K **19**
Maya Cl. SE15 ... 2H **105**
Mayall Cl. EN3: Enf ... 1H **9**
Mayall Rd. SE24 ... 5B **104**
Maya Rd. N2 ... 4A **30**
Maybank Av. E18 ... 2K **35**
HA0: Wemb ... 5K **43**
Maybank Gdns. HA5: Pinn ... 5J **23**
Maybank Rd. E18 ... 1K **35**
May Bate Av.
KT2: King T ... 1D **134**
Maybells Commercial Est.
IG11: Bark ... 2D **74**
Mayberry Ct. *BR3: Beck* ... *7B* ***124***
(off Copers Cope Rd.)
Mayberry Pl. KT5: Surb ... 7F **135**
Maybourne Cl. SE26 ... 6H **123**
Maybury Cl. BR5: Orp ... 5F **145**
EN1: Enf ... 1C **8**
Maybury Ct. *CR2: S Croy* ... *5B* ***152***
(off Haling Pk. Rd.)
HA1: Harr ... 6H **25**
W1 ... *6H* ***159***
(off Marylebone St.)
Maybury Gdns. NW10 ... 6D **46**
Maybury M. N6 ... 7G **31**
Maybury Rd. E13 ... 4A **72**
IG11: Bark ... 2K **73**
Maybury St. SW17 ... 5C **120**
Maychurch Cl. HA7: Stan ... 7J **11**
May Cl. KT9: Chess ... 6F **147**
Maycroft HA5: Pinn ... 2K **23**
Maycross Av. SM4: Mord ... 4H **137**
Mayday Gdns. SE3 ... 2C **108**
Mayday Rd.
CR7: Thor H ... 6B **140**
Maydew Ho. *SE16* ... *4J* ***87***
(off Abbeyfield Est.)
Maydwell Ho. *E14* ... *5C* ***70***
(off Thomas Rd.)
Mayerne Rd. SE9 ... 5B **108**
Mayesbrook Rd. IG3: Ilf ... 3A **56**
IG11: Bark ... 1K **73**
RM8: Dag ... 3B **56**
Mayesford Rd.
RM6: Chad H ... 7C **38**
Mayes Rd. N22 ... 2K **31**
Mayeswood Rd. SE12 ... 4A **126**
MAYFAIR ... **7F 67 (3J 165)**
Mayfair Av. DA7: Bex ... 1D **110**
IG1: Ilf ... 2D **54**
KT4: Wor Pk ... 1C **148**
RM6: Chad H ... 6D **38**
TW2: Twick ... 7G **97**
Mayfair Cl. BR3: Beck ... 1D **142**
KT6: Surb ... 1E **146**
Mayfair Gdns.
IG8: Wfd G ... 7D **20**
N17 ... 6H **17**
Mayfair M. *NW1* ... *7D* ***48***
(off Regents Pk. Rd.)
Mayfair Pl. W1 ... 1F **85** (4K **165**)
Mayfair Ter. N14 ... 7C **6**
Mayfield DA7: Bex ... 3F **111**
Mayfield Av. BR6: Orp ... 7K **145**
HA3: Harr ... 5B **26**
IG8: Wfd G ... 6D **20**
N12 ... 4F **15**
N14 ... 2C **16**
W4 ... 4A **82**
W13 ... 3B **80**
Mayfield Cl. E8 ... 6F **51**
KT7: T Ditt ... 1B **146**
SE20 ... 1H **141**
SW4 ... 5H **103**
TW15: Ashf ... 6D **112**
UB10: Uxb ... 3D **58**
Mayfield Cres.
CR7: Thor H ... 4K **139**
N9 ... 6C **8**
Mayfield Dr. HA5: Pinn ... 4D **24**
Mayfield Gdns. NW4 ... 6F **29**
W7 ... 6H **61**
Mayfield Ho. *E2* ... *2H* ***69***
(off Cambridge Heath Rd.)
Mayfield Rd. BR1: Brom ... 5C **144**
CR2: S Croy ... 7D **152**
CR7: Thor H ... 4K **139**
DA17: Belv ... 4J **93**
E4 ... 2K **19**
E8 ... 7F **51**
E13 ... 4H **71**
E17 ... 2A **34**
EN3: Enf ... 2E **8**
N8 ... 5K **31**
RM8: Dag ... 1C **56**
SM2: Sutt ... 6B **150**
SW19 ... 1H **137**
W3 ... 7H **63**
W12 ... 2A **82**
Mayfield Rd. Flats N8 ... 6K **31**
Mayfields HA9: Wemb ... 2G **45**
Mayfields Cl. HA9: Wemb ... 2G **45**
Mayfield Vs. DA14: Sidc ... 6C **128**
Mayflower Cl. HA4: Ruis ... 6E **22**
SE16 ... 4K **87**
Mayflower Ho. *IG11: Bark* ... *1H* ***73***
(off Westbury Rd.)
Mayflower Rd. SW9 ... 3J **103**
Mayflower St. SE16 ... 2J **87**
Mayfly Cl. HA5: Pinn ... 7A **24**
Mayfly Gdns. UB5: N'olt ... 3B **60**
Mayford NW1 ... 2G **67**
(not continuous)
Mayford Cl. BR3: Beck ... 3K **141**
SW12 ... 7D **102**
Mayford Rd. SW12 ... 7D **102**
May Gdns. HA0: Wemb ... 3C **62**
Maygood St. N1 ... 2A **68**
Maygrove Rd. NW6 ... 6H **47**
Mayhew Cl. E4 ... 3H **19**
Mayhew Ct. SE5 ... 4D **104**
Mayhill Rd. EN5: Barn ... 6B **4**
SE7 ... 6K **89**
Mayland Mans. *IG11: Bark* ... *7F* ***55***
(off Whiting Av.)
Maylands Dr. DA14: Sidc ... 3D **128**
Maylands Ho. *SW3* ... *4D* ***170***
(off Elystan St.)
Maynard Cl. N15 ... 5E **32**
SW6 ... 7K **83**
Maynard Path E17 ... 5E **34**
Maynard Rd. E17 ... 5E **34**
Maynards Quay E1 ... 7J **69**
Mayne Ct. SE26 ... 5H **123**
Maynooth Gdns.
SM5: Cars ... 7D **138**
Mayo Ct. W13 ... 3B **80**
Mayo Ho. *E1* ... *5J* ***69***
(off Lindley St.)
Mayola Rd. E5 ... 4J **51**
Mayo Rd. CR0: Croy ... 5D **140**
KT12: Walt T ... 7J **131**
NW10 ... 6A **46**
Mayow Rd. SE23 ... 4K **123**
SE26 ... 4K **123**
Mayplace Cl. DA7: Bex ... 3H **111**
Mayplace La. SE18 ... 6F **91**
(not continuous)
Mayplace Rd. E.
DA1: Cray ... 4K **111**
DA7: Bex ... 3H **111**
Mayplace Rd. W.
DA7: Bex ... 4G **111**
MAYPOLE ... **2K 129**
Maypole Ct. *UB2: S'hall* ... *2D* ***78***
(off Merrick Rd.)
May Rd. E4 ... 6H **19**
E13 ... 2J **71**
TW2: Twick ... 1J **115**
Mayroyd Av. KT6: Surb ... 2G **147**
May's Bldgs. M. SE10 ... 7E **88**
Mays Ct. SE10 ... 7F **89**
WC2 ... 7J **67** (3E **166**)
Mays Hill Rd. BR2: Short ... 2G **143**
Mays La. EN5: Barn ... 1H **13**
Maysoule Rd. SW11 ... 4B **102**
Mays Rd. TW11: Tedd ... 5H **115**
Mayston M. *SE10* ... *5J* ***89***
(off Ormiston Rd.)
May St. W14 ... 5H **83**
Mayswood Gdns.
RM10: Dag ... 6J **57**
Mayton St. N7 ... 3K **49**
Maytree Cl. HA8: Edg ... 3D **12**
Maytree Ct. UB5: N'olt ... 3C **60**
Maytree Gdns. W5 ... 2D **80**
May Tree Ho. *SE4* ... *3B* ***106***
(off Wickham Rd.)
Maytree La. HA7: Stan ... 7F **11**
Maytree Wlk. SW2 ... 2A **122**
Mayville Est. N16 ... 5E **50**
Mayville Rd. E11 ... 2G **53**
IG1: Ilf ... 5F **55**
May Wlk. E13 ... 2K **71**
Mayward Ho. *SE5* ... *1E* ***104***
(off Peckham Rd.)
Maywood Cl. BR3: Beck ... 7D **124**
May Wynne Ho. *E16* ... *7K* ***71***
(off Murray Sq.)
Maze Hill SE3 ... 6G **89**
SE10 ... 6G **89**
Maze Hill Lodge *SE10* ... *6F* ***89***
(off Park Vista)
Mazenod Av. NW6 ... 7J **47**
Maze Rd. TW9: Rich ... 7G **81**
McAdam Dr. EN2: Enf ... 2G **7**
McAuley Cl. SE1 ... 3A **86** (1J **173**)
SE9 ... 5F **109**
McCall Cl. SW4 ... 2J **103**
McCall Cres. SE7 ... 5C **90**
McCall Ho. N7 ... 4J **49**
McCarthy Rd. TW13: Felt ... 5B **114**
M.C.C. Cricket Mus. & Tours
... ***3B 66 (2A 158)***
McCoid Way SE1 ... 2C **86** (7C **168**)
McCrone M. NW3 ... 6B **48**
McCullum Rd. E3 ... 1B **70**
McDermott Cl. SW11 ... 3C **102**
McDermott Rd. SE15 ... 3G **105**
McDonough Cl.
KT9: Chess ... 4E **146**
McDowall Cl. E16 ... 5H **71**
McDowall Rd. SE5 ... 1C **104**
McEntee Av. E17 ... 1A **34**
McEwen Way E15 ... 1F **71**
McGlashon Ho. *E1* ... *4K* ***163***
(off Hunton St.)
McGrath Rd. E15 ... 5H **53**
McGregor Ct. N1 ... 1H **163**

McGregor Rd.—Melrose Ho.

McGregor Rd. W11 ....6H 65
McIndoe Ct. N1 ....1D 68
(off Sherborne St.)
McIntosh Cl. RM1: Rom 3K 39
SM6: Wall 7J 151
McIntosh Ho. SE16 ....4J 87
(off Millender Wlk.)
McIntosh Rd. RM1: Rom 3K 39
McIntyre Ct. SE18 ....4C 90
(off Prospect Va.)
McKay Rd. SW20 ....7D 118
McKay Trad. Est. W10 ....4G 65
McKellar Cl.
WD23: Bush 2B 10
McKerrell Rd. SE15 ....1G 105
McKillop Way
DA14: Sidc 7C 128
McLeod Ct. SE22 ....1G 123
McLeod Rd. SE2 ....4B 92
McLeod's M. SW7 ....4K 83
(not continuous)
McMillan Ho. SE4 ....3A 106
(off Arica Rd.)
SE14 ....1A 106
McMillan St. SE8 ....6C 88
McNair Rd. UB2: S'hall 3F 79
McNeil Rd. SE5 ....2E 104
McNicol Dr. NW10 ....2J 63
McRae La. CR4: Mitc 7D 138
Mead Cl. HA3: Harr 1H 25
NW1 ....6E 48
Mead Ct. NW9 ....5J 27
Mead Cres. E4 ....4K 19
SM1: Sutt 3C 150
Meadcroft Rd.
SE11 ....6B 86 (7K 173)
(not continuous)
Meade Cl. W4 ....6G 81
Meader Ct. SE14 ....7K 87
Mead Fld. HA2: Harr 3D 42
Meadfield HA8: Edg 2C 12
(not continuous)
Meadfield Grn. HA8: Edg 2C 12
Meadfoot Rd. SW16 ....7G 121
Meadgate Av. IG8: Wfd G 5H 21
Mead Gro. RM6: Chad H 3D 38
Mead Ho. W11 ....1H 83
(off Ladbroke Rd.)
Mead Ho. La. UB4: Hayes 4F 59
Meadhurst Pk.
TW16: Sun T 6G 113
Meadlands Dr.
TW10: Rich 2D 116
Mead Lodge W4 ....2K 81
Meadow Av. CR0: Croy 6K 141
Meadow Bank N21 ....6E 6
SE3 ....3H 107
Meadowbank KT5: Surb 6F 135
NW3 ....7D 48
Meadowbank Cl. SW6 ....7E 82
Meadowbank Gdns.
TW5: Houn 1J 95
Meadowbank Rd. NW9 ....7K 27
Meadowbrook Ct.
TW7: Isle 3J 97
Meadow Cl. BR7: Chst 5F 127
DA6: Bex 5F 111
E4 ....1J 19
E9 ....5B 52
EN3: Enf 1F 9
EN5: Barn 6C 4
HA4: Ruis 6H 23
KT10: Esh 3A 146
SE6 ....5C 124
SM1: Sutt 2A 150
SW20 ....4E 136
TW4: Houn 6E 96
TW10: Rich 1E 116
UB5: N'olt 2E 60
Meadow Ct. N1 ....2E 68
TW3: Houn 6F 97
Meadowcourt Rd. SE3 ....4H 107
Meadowcroft BR1: Brom 3D 144
W4 ....5G 81
(off Brooks Rd.)
Meadowcroft Cl. N13 ....2F 17
Meadowcroft Rd. N13 ....2F 17
Meadow Dr. N10 ....3F 31
NW4 ....2E 28
Meadowford Cl. SE28 ....7A 74
Meadow Gdns. HA8: Edg 6C 12
Meadow Gth. NW10 ....6J 45
(not continuous)
Meadow Hill
KT3: N Mald 6A 136
Meadow La. SE12 ....3K 125
Meadowlea Cl.
UB7: W Dray 6A 76
Meadow M. SW8 ....6K 85
Meadow Pl. SW8 ....7J 85
W4 ....7A 82
Meadow Rd. BR2: Short 2G 143
HA5: Pinn 4B 24
IG11: Bark 7K 55
RM7: Rush G 1J 57
RM9: Dag 6F 57
SM1: Sutt 4C 150
SW8 ....7K 85 (7H 173)
SW19 ....7A 120
TW13: Felt 2C 114
TW15: Ashf 5F 113
UB1: S'hall 7D 60
Meadow Row SE1 ....3C 86
Meadows Cl. E10 ....2C 52
Meadows Ct. DA14: Sidc 6B 128
Meadows End
TW16: Sun T 1J 131
Meadowside SE9 ....4A 108
TW1: Twick 7D 98
Meadow Stile CR0: Croy 3C 152
Meadowsweet Cl. E16 ....5B 72
SW20 ....4E 136
Meadow, The BR7: Chst 6G 127
N10 ....3E 30
Meadow Vw. DA15: Sidc 7B 110
HA1: Harr 1J 43
Meadow Vw. Rd.
CR7: Thor H 5B 140
UB4: Hayes 4F 59
Meadowview Rd.
DA5: Bexl 6E 110
KT19: Eps 7A 148
SE6 ....5B 124
Meadow Wlk. E18 ....4J 35
KT17: Eps 7B 148
KT19: Eps 6A 148
(not continuous)
RM9: Dag 6F 57
SM6: Wall 3F 151
Meadow Way BR6: Orp 3E 156
HA4: Ruis 6K 23
HA9: Wemb 4D 44
KT9: Chess 5E 146
NW9 ....5K 27
Meadow Waye TW5: Houn 6C 78
Meadow Way, The
HA3: Harr 1J 25
Mead Path SW17 ....4A 120
Mead Pl. CR0: Croy 1C 152
E9 ....6J 51
Mead Plat NW10 ....6J 45
Mead Rd. BR7: Chst 6G 127
HA8: Edg 6B 12
TW10: Rich 3C 116
Mead Row SE1 ....3A 86 (1J 173)
Meads Ct. E15 ....6H 53
Meadside Cl. BR3: Beck 1A 142
Meads La. IG3: Ilf 7J 37
Meads Rd. EN3: Enf 1F 9
N22 ....2B 32
Meads, The HA8: Edg 6E 12
SM3: Sutt 3G 149
SM4: Mord 5C 138
UB8: Uxb 4A 58
Mead Ter. HA9: Wemb 4D 44
Mead, The BR3: Beck 1E 142
BR4: W W'ck 1F 155
N2 ....2A 30
SM6: Wall 6H 151
UB10: Uxb 2C 40
W13 ....5B 62
Meadvale Rd.
CR0: Croy 7F 141
W5 ....4B 62
Mead Way BR2: Short 6H 143
CR0: Croy 2A 154
HA4: Ruis 6F 23
IG8: Wfd G 5F 21
SW20 ....4E 136
Meadway BR3: Beck 1E 142
EN5: Barn 4D 4
IG3: Bark, Ilf 4J 55
KT5: Surb 1J 147
N14 ....2C 16
NW11 ....6J 29
TW2: Twick 1H 115
TW15: Ashf 4C 112
Meadway Cl. EN5: Barn 4D 4
HA5: Pinn 6A 10
NW11 ....6K 29
Meadway Ct. NW11 ....6K 29
RM8: Dag 2F 57
TW11: Tedd 5C 116
W5 ....4F 63
Meadway Gdns.
HA4: Ruis 6F 23
Meadway Ga. NW11 ....6J 29
Meadway, The
IG9: Buck H 1G 21
SE3 ....2F 107
Meaford Way SE20 ....7H 123
Meakin Est. SE1 ....3E 86
Meanley Rd. E12 ....4C 54
Meard St. W1 ....6H 67 (1C 166)
(not continuous)
Meath Rd. E15 ....2H 71
IG1: Ilf 3G 55
Meath St. SW11 ....1F 103
Mechanic's Path SE8 ....7C 88
(off Deptford High St.)
Mecklenburgh Pl.
WC1 ....4K 67 (3G 161)
Mecklenburgh Sq.
WC1 ....4K 67 (3G 161)
Mecklenburgh St.
WC1 ....4K 67 (3G 161)
Medburn St. NW1 ....2H 67
Medcroft Gdns. SW14 ....4J 99
Medebourne Cl. SE3 ....3J 107
Mede Ho. BR1: Brom 5K 125
(off Pike Cl.)
Medesenge Way N13 ....6G 17
Medfield St. SW15 ....7C 100
Medhurst Cl. E3 ....2A 70
(not continuous)
Median Rd. E5 ....5J 51
Medina Gro. N7 ....3A 50
Medina Rd. N7 ....3A 50
Medland Cl. SM6: Wall 1E 150
Medland Ho. E14 ....7A 70
Medlar Cl. UB5: N'olt 2B 60
Medlar Ho. DA15: Sidc 3A 128
Medlar St. SE5 ....1C 104
Medley Rd. NW6 ....6J 47
Medora Rd. RM7: Rom 4K 39
SW2 ....7K 103
Medusa Rd. SE6 ....6D 106
Medway Bldgs. E3 ....2A 70
(off Medway Rd.)
Medway Cl. CR0: Croy 6J 141
IG1: Ilf 5G 55
Medway Ct. WC1 ....2E 160
(off Judd St.)
Medway Dr. UB6: G'frd 2K 61
Medway Gdns.
HA0: Wemb 4A 44
Medway Ho. KT1: King T 1D 134
NW8 ....4C 158
(off Penfold St.)
SE1 ....7F 169
(off Hankey Pl.)
Medway M. E3 ....2A 70
Medway Pde. UB6: G'frd 2K 61
Medway Rd. E3 ....2A 70
Medway St.
SW1 ....3H 85 (2D 172)
Medwin St. SW4 ....4K 103
Meerbrook Rd. SE3 ....3A 108
Meeson Rd. E15 ....7H 53
Meeson St. E5 ....4A 52
Meesons Wharf E15 ....2E 70
Meeting Fld. Path E9 ....6J 51
Meeting Ho. All. E1 ....1H 87
Meeting Ho. La. SE15 ....1H 105
Megabowl Croydon 2K 151
Mehetabel Rd. E9 ....5J 51
Meister Cl. IG1: Ilf 1H 55
Melancholy Wlk.
TW10: Rich 2C 116
Melanda Cl. BR7: Chst 5D 126
Melanie Cl. DA7: Bex 1E 110
Melba Way SE13 ....1D 106
Melbourne Av. HA5: Pinn 3F 25
N13 ....6E 16
W13 ....1A 80
Melbourne Cl. BR6: Orp 7J 145
SE20 ....7G 123
SM6: Wall 5G 151
UB10: Uxb 4C 40
Melbourne Ct. N10 ....7A 16
W9 ....4A 66
(off Randolph Av.)
Melbourne Gdns.
RM6: Chad H 5E 38
Melbourne Gro. SE22 ....4E 104
Melbourne Ho.
UB4: Hayes 4A 60
W8 ....1J 83
(off Kensington Pl.)
Melbourne Mans. W6 ....6G 83
(off Musard Rd.)
Melbourne M. SE6 ....7E 106
SW9 ....1A 104
Melbourne Pl.
WC2 ....6K 67 (1H 167)
Melbourne Rd. E6 ....2D 72
E10 ....7D 34
E17 ....4A 34
IG1: Ilf 1F 55
SM6: Wall 5F 151
SW19 ....1J 137
TW11: Tedd 6C 116
Melbourne Sq. SW9 ....1A 104
Melbourne Ter. SW6 ....7K 83
(off Moore Pk. Rd.)
Melbourne Way EN1: Enf 6A 8
Melbray M. SW6 ....2H 101
Melbreak Ho. SE22 ....3E 104
Melbury Av. UB2: S'hall 3F 79
Melbury Cl. BR7: Chst 6C 126
KT10: Esh 6B 146
Melbury Ct. W8 ....3H 83
Melbury Dr. SE5 ....7E 86
Melbury Gdns. SW20 ....1D 136
Melbury Ho. SW8 ....7K 85
(off Richborne Ter.)
Melbury Rd. HA3: Harr 5F 27
W14 ....3H 83
Melbury Ter.
NW1 ....4C 66 (4D 158)
Melchester W11 ....6H 65
(off Ledbury Rd.)
Melchester Ho. N19 ....3H 49
(off Wedmore St.)
Melcombe Ct. NW1 ....5E 158
(off Melcombe Pl.)
Melcombe Gdns.
HA3: Harr 6F 27
Melcombe Ho. SW8 ....7K 85
(off Dorset Rd.)
Melcombe Pl.
NW1 ....5D 66 (5E 158)
Melcombe Regis Ct.
W1 ....6H 159
(off Weymouth St.)
Melcombe St.
NW1 ....4D 66 (4F 159)
Meldex Cl. NW7 ....6K 13
(off Prince of Wales Cl.)
Meldon Cl. SW6 ....1K 101
Meldone Cl. KT5: Surb 7H 135
Meldrum Rd. IG3: Ilf 2A 56
Melfield Gdns. SE6 ....4E 124
Melford Av. IG11: Bark 6J 55
Melford Cl. KT9: Chess 5F 147
Melford Ct. SE1 ....3E 86
(off Fendall St.)
SE22 ....1G 123
Melford Pas. SE22 ....7G 105
Melford Rd. E6 ....4D 72
E11 ....2G 53
E17 ....4A 34
IG1: Ilf 2H 55
SE22 ....7G 105
Melfort Av. CR7: Thor H 3B 140
Melfort Rd.
CR7: Thor H 3B 140
Melgund Rd. N5 ....5A 50
Melina Cl. UB3: Hayes 5F 59
Melina Ct. SW15 ....3C 100
Melina Pl. NW8 ....3B 66 (2A 158)
Melina Rd W12 ....2D 82
Melior Ct. N6 ....6G 31
Melior Pl. SE1 ....2E 86 (6G 169)
Melior St. SE1 ....2E 86 (6G 169)
Meliot Rd. SE6 ....2F 125
Meller Cl. CR0: Croy 3J 151
Melling Dr. EN1: Enf 1B 8
Melling St. SE18 ....6J 91
Mellish Cl. IG11: Bark 1K 73
Mellish Flats E10 ....7C 34
Mellish Gdns. IG8: Wfd G 5D 20
Mellish Ho. E1 ....6H 69
(off Varden St.)
Mellish Ind. Est. SE18 ....3B 90
Mellish St. E14 ....3C 88
Mellison Rd. SW17 ....5C 120
Melliss Av. TW9: Rich 1H 99
Mellitus St. W12 ....5B 64
Mellor Cl. KT12: Walt T 7D 132
Mellow La. E. UB4: Hayes 3E 58
Mellow La. W. UB10: Uxb 3E 58
Mellows Rd. IG5: Ilf 3D 36
SM6: Wall 5H 151
Mells Cres. SE9 ....4D 126
Mell St. SE10 ....5G 89
Melody La. N5 ....5C 50
Melody Rd. SW18 ....5A 102
Melon Pl. W8 ....2J 83
Melon Rd. E11 ....3G 53
SE15 ....1G 105
Melrose Av. CR4: Mitc 7F 121
DA1: Cray 7K 111
N22 ....1B 32
NW2 ....5D 46
SW16 ....3K 139
SW19 ....2H 119
TW2: Twick 7F 97
UB6: G'frd 2F 61
Melrose Cl. SE12 ....1J 125
UB4: Hayes 5J 59
UB6: G'frd 2F 61
Melrose Dr. UB1: S'hall 1E 78
Melrose Gdns. HA8: Edg 3H 27
KT3: N Mald 3K 135
W6 ....3E 82
Melrose Ho. E14 ....3D 88
(off Lanark Sq.)
NW6 ....3J 65
(off Carlton Va.)

Melrose Rd.—Midcroft

Melrose Rd. HA5: Pinn 4D 24
SW13 ....2B 100
SW18 ....6H 101
SW19 ....2J 137
W3 ....3J 81
Melrose Ter. W6 ....3E 82
Melrose Tudor *SM6: Wall* ...*5J 151*
(off Plough La.)
Melsa Rd. SM4: Mord 6A 138
Melthorne Dr. HA4: Ruis 3A 42
Melthorpe Gdns. SE3 ......1C 108
Melton Cl. HA4: Ruis 1A 42
Melton Ct. SM2: Sutt 7A 150
SW7 ....4B 84 (4B 170)
(not continuous)
Melton St. NW1 ...3G 67 (2B 160)
Melville Av. CR2: S Croy 5F 153
SW20 ....7C 118
UB6: G'frd 5K 43
Melville Cl. UB10: Uxb 2F 41
Melville Ct. SE8 ....4A 88
W12 ....*3D 82*
(off Goldhawk Rd.)
Melville Gdns. N13 ....5G 17
Melville Ho. EN5: Barn 5G 5
SE10 ....1E 106
Melville Pl. N1 ....7C 50
Melville Rd. DA14: Sidc 2C 128
E17 ....3B 34
NW10 ....7K 45
RM5: Col R 1H 39
SW13 ....1C 100
Melville Vs. Rd. W3 ....1J 81
Melvin Rd. SE20 ....1J 141
Melwood Ho. *E1* *6H 69*
(off Watney Mkt.)
Melyn Cl. N7 ....4G 49
Memel Ct. EC1 ....4C 162
Memel St. EC1 ....4C 68 (4C 162)
Memess Path SE18 ....6E 90
Memorial Av. E12 ....2C 54
E15 ....3G 71
Memorial Cl. TW5: Houn 6D 78
Mendham Ho. *SE1* *7G 169*
(off Cluny Pl.)
Mendip Cl. KT4: Wor Pk 1E 148
SE26 ....4J 123
SW19 ....2G 119
UB3: Hayes 7F 77
Mendip Ct. *SE14* *6J 87*
(off Avonley Rd.)
SW11 ....3A 102
Mendip Dr. NW2 ....2G 47
Mendip Ho's. *E2* *3J 69*
(off Welwyn St.)
Mendip Rd. DA7: Erith 1K 111
IG2: Ilf 5J 37
SW11 ....3A 102
Mendora Rd. SW6 ....7G 83
Menelik Rd. NW2 ....4G 47
Menlo Gdns. SE19 ....7D 122
Menlo Lodge *N13* *3E 16*
(off Crothall Cl.)
Menon Dr. N9 ....3C 18
Menotti St. E2 ....4G 69
Menteath Ho. *E14* *6C 70*
(off Dod St.)
Mentmore Cl. HA3: Harr 6C 26
Mentmore Ter. E8 ....7H 51
Meon Ct. TW7: Isle 2J 97
Meon Rd. W3 ....2J 81
Meopham Rd. CR4: Mitc 1G 139
Mepham Cres. HA3: Harr 7B 10
Mepham Gdns. HA3: Harr ...7B 10
Mepham St. SE1 ...1A 86 (5J 167)
Mera Dr. DA7: Bex 4G 111
Merantun Way SW19 ....1K 137
Merbury Cl. SE13 ....5E 106
Merbury Rd. SE28 ....2J 91
Mercator Pl. E14 ....5C 88
Mercator Rd. SE13 ....4F 107
Mercer Cl. KT7: T Ditt 7A 134
Mercer Ho. *SW1* *5J 171*
(off Ebury Bri. Rd.)
Merceron Ho's. *E2* *3J 69*
(off Globe Rd.)
Merceron St. E1 ....4H 69
Mercer Pl. HA5: Pinn 2A 24
Mercers Cl. SE10 ....4H 89
Mercers Cotts. *E1* *6A 70*
(off White Horse Rd.)
Mercers Pl. W6 ....4F 83
Mercers Rd. N19 ....3H 49
(not continuous)
Mercer St. WC2 ....6J 67 (1E 166)
Merchant Ct. *E1* *1J 87*
(off Wapping Wall)
Merchant Ind. Ter. NW10 ....4J 63
Merchants Cl. SE25 ....4G 141
Merchants Lodge *E17* *4C 34*
(off Westbury Rd.)
Merchant St. E3 ....3B 70
Merchiston Rd. SE6 ....2F 125
Merchland Rd. SE9 ....1G 127
Mercia Gro. SE13 ....4E 106
Mercia Ho. *SE5* *2C 104*
(off Denmark Rd.)
Mercier Rd. SW15 ....5G 101
Mercury *NW9* *1B 28*
(off Concourse, The)
Mercury Cen. TW14: Felt 5J 95
Mercury Ct. *E14* *4C 88*
(off Homer Dr.)
Mercury Ho. *TW8: Bford* *6C 80*
(off Glenhurst Rd.)
Mercury Rd. TW8: Bford 6C 80
Mercury Way SE14 ....6K 87
Mercy Ter. SE13 ....5D 106
Merebank La. CR0: Croy ...5K 151
Mere Cl. BR6: Orp 2E 156
SW15 ....7F 101
Meredith Av. NW2 ....5E 46
Meredith Cl. HA5: Pinn 1B 24
Meredith Ho. N16 ....5E 50
Meredith M. SE4 ....4B 106
Meredith St. E13 ....3J 71
EC1 ....3B 68 (2A 162)
Meredyth Rd. SW13 ....2C 100
Mere End CR0: Croy 7K 141
Mere Rd. TW17: Shep 6D 130
Mere Side BR6: Orp 2E 156
Meretone Cl. SE4 ....4A 106
Merevale Cres.
SM4: Mord 6A 138
Mereway Rd.
TW2: Twick 1H 115
Merewood Cl. BR1: Brom ...2E 144
Merewood Rd. DA7: Bex 2J 111
Mereworth Cl.
BR2: Short 5H 143
Mereworth Dr. SE18 ....7F 91
Mereworth Ho. SE15 ....6J 87
Merganser Ct. *SE8* *6B 88*
(off Edward St.)
Merganser Gdns. SE28 .....3H 91
Meriden Cl. BR1: Brom 7B 126
IG6: Ilf 1G 37
Meriden Ct. SW3 ....6C 170
Meridian Ga. E14 ....2E 88
Meridian Ho. *SE10* *7E 88*
(off Royal Hill)
SE10 ....*4G 89*
(off Azof St.)
Meridian Pl. E14 ....2D 88
Meridian Rd. SE7 ....7B 90
Meridian Sq. E15 ....7F 53
Meridian Trad. Est. SE7 .....4K 89
Meridian Wlk. N17 ....6K 17
Meridian Way EN3: Enf 4D 18
N9 ....4D 18
N18 ....5D 18
Merifield Rd. SE9 ....4A 108
Merino Cl. E11 ....4A 36
Merino Pl. DA15: Sidc 6A 110
Merioneth Ct. *W7* *5K 61*
(off Copley Cl.)
Merivale Rd. HA1: Harr 7G 25
SW15 ....4G 101
Merlewood Dr.
BR7: Chst 1D 144
Merley Ct. NW9 ....1J 45
Merlin *NW9* *1B 28*
(off Concourse, The)
Merlin Cl. CR0: Croy 4E 152
CR4: Mitc 3C 138
SM6: Wall 6K 151
UB5: N'olt 3A 60
Merlin Ct. BR2: Short 3H 143
HA4: Ruis 2F 41
Merlin Cres. HA8: Edg 1F 27
Merlin Gdns. BR1: Brom ...3J 125
Merling Cl. KT9: Chess 5C 146
Merlin Gro. BR3: Beck 4B 142
Merlin Rd. DA16: Well 4A 110
E12 ....2B 54
Merlin Rd. Nth.
DA16: Well 4A 110
Merlins Av. HA2: Harr 3D 42
Merlins Ct. *WC1* *2J 161*
(off Margery St.)
Merlin St. WC1 ....3A 68 (2J 161)
Mermaid Ct. *E8* *7F 51*
(off Celandine Dr.)
SE1 ....2D 86 (6E 168)
SE16 ....1B 88
Mermaid Ho. *E14* *7E 70*
(off Bazely St.)
Mermaid Twr. *SE8* *6B 88*
(off Abinger Gro.)
Meroe Ct. N16 ....2E 50
Merredene St. SW2 ....6K 103
Merriam Av. E9 ....6B 52
Merriam Cl. E4 ....5K 19
Merrick Rd. UB2: S'hall 2D 78
Merrick Sq. SE1 ...3D 86 (7E 168)
Merridene N21 ....6G 7
Merrielands Cres.
RM9: Dag 2F 75
Merrielands Retail Pk.
RM9: Dag 1F 75
Merrilands Rd.
KT4: Wor Pk 1E 148
Merrilees Rd. DA15: Sidc ...7J 109
Merrilyn Cl. KT10: Esh 6A 146
Merriman Rd. SE3 ....1A 108
Merrington Rd. SW6 ....6J 83
Merrion Av. HA7: Stan 5J 11
Merritt Gdns. KT9: Chess ...6C 146
Merritt Rd. SE4 ....5B 106
Merritts Bldgs. EC2 ....4G 163
Merrivale N14 ....6C 6
NW1 ....*1G 67*
(off Camden St.)
Merrivale Av. IG4: Ilf 4B 36
Merrow Ct. CR4: Mitc 2B 138
Merrow Rd. SM2: Sutt 7F 149
Merrow St. SE17 ....5D 86
Merrow Wlk. SE17 ....5D 86
Merrow Way CR0: Croy 6E 154
Merrydown Way
BR7: Chst 1C 144
Merryfield SE3 ....2H 107
Merryfield Gdns.
HA7: Stan 5H 11
Merryfield Ho. *SE9* *3A 126*
(off Grove Pk. Rd.)
Merryfields UB8: Uxb 2A 58
(not continuous)
Merryfields Way SE6 ......7D 106
MERRY HILL 1A 10
Merryhill Cl. E4 ....7J 9
Merry Hill Mt.
WD23: Bush 1A 10
Merry Hill Rd.
WD23: Bush 1A 10
Merryhills Ct. N14 ....5B 6
Merryhills Dr. EN2: Enf 4C 6
Merryweather Ct.
KT3: N Mald 5A 136
N19 ....3G 49
Mersea Ho. IG11: Bark 6F 55
Mersey Ct. KT2: King T 1D 134
Mersey Rd. E17 ....3B 34
Mersey Wlk. UB5: N'olt 2E 60
Mersham Dr. NW9 ....5G 27
Mersham Pl. SE20 ....1H 141
Mersham Rd.
CR7: Thor H 3D 140
Merten Rd. RM6: Chad H 7E 38
Merthyr Ter. SW13 ....6D 82
MERTON 7A 120
Merton Av. UB5: N'olt 5G 43
UB10: Uxb 7D 40
W4 ....4B 82
Merton Ct. DA16: Well 2B 110
IG1: Ilf 6C 36
Merton Gdns. BR5: Orp 5F 145
Merton Hall Gdns.
SW20 ....1G 137
Merton Hall Rd. SW19 .....7G 119
Merton High St. SW19 .....7K 119
Merton Ind. Pk. SW19 .....1K 137
Merton La. N6 ....2D 48
Merton Lodge EN5: Barn 5F 5
Merton Mans. *SE8* *1C 106*
(off Brookmill Rd.)
SW20 ....2F 137
MERTON PARK 2J 137
Merton Pk. Pde. SW19 ....1H 137
Merton Pl. *SW19* *1A 138*
(off Nelson Gro. Rd.)
Merton Ri. NW3 ....7C 48
(not continuous)
Merton Rd. E17 ....5E 34
EN2: Enf 1J 7
HA2: Harr 1G 43
IG3: Ilf 7K 37
IG11: Bark 7K 55
SE25 ....5G 141
SW18 ....6J 101
SW19 ....7K 119
Merton Way KT8: W Mole ...4F 133
UB10: Uxb 7D 40
Mertoun Ter. *W1* *7E 158*
(off Seymour Pl.)
Merttins Rd. SE4 ....5K 105
SE15 ....5K 105
Meru Cl. NW5 ....4E 48
Mervan Rd. SW2 ....4A 104
Mervyn Av. SE9 ....3G 127
Mervyn Rd. TW17: Shep 7E 130
W13 ....3A 80
Messaline Av. W3 ....6J 63
Messent Rd. SE9 ....5A 108
Messeter Pl. SE9 ....6E 108
Messina Av. NW6 ....7J 47
Messiter Ho. *N1* *1K 67*
(off Barnsbury Est.)
Metcalf Rd. TW15: Ashf 5D 112
Metcalf Wlk. TW13: Felt 4C 114
Meteor St. SW11 ....4E 102
Meteor Way SM6: Wall 7J 151
Metheringham Way NW9 ....1A 28
Methley St.
SE11 ....5A 86 (6K 173)
Methuen Cl. HA8: Edg 7B 12
Methuen Pk. N10 ....3F 31
Methuen Rd. DA6: Bex 4F 111
DA17: Belv 4H 93
HA8: Edg 7B 12
Methwold Rd. W10 ....5F 65
Metro Bus. Cen., The
SE26 ....6B 124
Metro Central Hgts. *SE1* *3C 86*
(off Newington C'way.)
Metro Ind. Cen. TW7: Isle ...2J 97
Metropolis *SE11* *3B 86*
(off Oswin St.)
Metropolitan Bus. Cen.
N1 ....*7E 50*
(off Enfield Rd.)
Metropolitan Cl. E14 ....5C 70
Metropolitan Wharf E1 ......1J 87
Metro Trad. Est.
HA9: Wemb 4H 45
Mews Pl. IG8: Wfd G 4D 20
Mews St. E1 ......1G 87 (4K 169)
Mews, The DA14: Sidc 4A 128
IG4: Ilf 5B 36
N1 ....1C 68
N8 ....3A 32
RM1: Rom 4K 39
SE22 ....5G 105
TW1: Twick 6B 98
Mexborough NW1 ....1G 67
Mexfield Rd. SW15 ....5H 101
Meyer Grn. EN1: Enf 1B 8
Meyer Rd. DA8: Erith 6K 93
Meymott St. SE1 ...1B 86 (5A 168)
Meynell Cres. E9 ....7K 51
Meynell Gdns. E9 ....7K 51
Meynell Rd. E9 ....7K 51
Meyrick Ho. *E14* *5C 70*
(off Burgess St.)
Meyrick Rd. NW10 ....6C 46
SW11 ....3B 102
Miah Ter. E1 ....1G 87
Miall Wlk. SE26 ....4A 124
Micawber Av. UB8: Uxb 4C 58
Micawber Ct. *N1* *1D 162*
(off Windsor Ter.)
Micawber Ho. *SE16* *2G 87*
(off Llewellyn St.)
Micawber St. N1 ...3C 68 (1D 162)
Michael Cliffe Ho. EC1 ......2A 162
Michael Faraday Ho. *SE17* ...*5E 86*
(off Beaconsfield Rd.)
Michael Gaynor Cl. W7 .....1K 79
Michael Manley Ind. Est.
SW8 ....*2G 103*
(off Clyston St.)
Michaelmas Cl. SW20 .....3E 136
Michael Rd. E11 ....1H 53
SE25 ....3E 140
SW6 ....1K 101
Michaels Cl. SE13 ....4G 107
Michael Stewart Ho. *SW6* ...*6H 83*
(off Clem Attlee Ct.)
Michelangelo Ct. *SE16* *5H 87*
(off Stubbs Dr.)
Micheldever Rd. SE12 .....6G 107
Michelham Gdns.
TW1: Twick 3K 115
Michelle Ct. *BR1: Brom* *1H 143*
(off Blyth Rd.)
N12 ....5F 15
W3 ....7K 63
Michelsdale Dr.
TW9: Rich 4E 98
Michelson Ho. SE11 ......4H 173
Michels Row *TW9: Rich* *4E 98*
(off Michelsdale Dr.)
Michigan Av. E12 ....4D 54
Michigan Ho. E14 ....3C 88
Michleham Down N12 ......4C 14
Mickledore *NW1* *1B 160*
(off Ampthill Est.)
Mickleham Cl. BR5: Orp ...2K 145
Mickleham Gdns.
SM3: Sutt 6G 149
Mickleham Rd. BR5: Orp ...1K 145
Mickleham Way
CR0: Croy 7F 155
Micklethwaite Rd. SW6 .....6J 83
Midas Bus. Cen.
RM10: Dag 4H 57
Midas Metropolitan Ind. Est.
SM4: Mord 7E 136
MID BECKTON 6D 72
Midcroft HA4: Ruis 1G 41

Milne Ho.—Monks Av.

Milne Ho. SE18 ... 4D 90
(off Ogilby St.)
Milner Dr. TW2: Twick ... 7H 97
Milner Pl. N1 ... 1A 68
SM5: Cars ... 4E 150
Milner Rd. CR7: Thor H ... 3D 140
E15 ... 3G 71
KT1: King T ... 3D 134
RM8: Dag ... 2C 56
SM4: Mord ... 5B 138
SW19 ... 1K 137
Milner Sq. N1 ... 7B 50
Milner St. SW3 ... 4D 84 (3E 170)
Milner Wlk. DA15: Sidc ... 2H 127
Milnthorpe Rd. W4 ... 6K 81
Milo Gdns. SE22 ... 6F 105
Milo Rd. SE22 ... 6F 105
Milrood Ho. E1 ... 5K 69
(off Stepney Grn.)
Milroy Wlk.
SE1 ... 1B 86 (4A 168)
Milson Rd. W14 ... 3F 83
Milstead Ho. E5 ... 5H 51
Milton Av. CR0: Croy ... 7D 140
E6 ... 7B 54
EN5: Barn ... 5C 4
N6 ... 7G 31
NW9 ... 3J 27
NW10 ... 1J 63
SM1: Sutt ... 3B 150
Milton Cl. N2 ... 5A 30
SE1 ... 4F 87
SM1: Sutt ... 3B 150
UB4: Hayes ... 6J 59
Milton Ct. E17 ... 4C 34
EC2 ... 5D 68 (5E 162)
RM6: Chad H ... 7C 38
SE14 ... 6B 88
SW18 ... 5J 101
TW2: Twick ... 3J 115
UB10: Uxb ... 3D 40
Milton Ct. Highwalk
EC2 ... 5E 162
(off Silk St.)
Milton Ct. Rd. SE14 ... 6A 88
Milton Cres. IG2: Ilf ... 7F 37
Milton Dr. TW17: Shep ... 4A 130
Milton Gdn. Est. N16 ... 4D 50
Milton Gdns.
TW19: Staines ... 1B 112
Milton Gro. N11 ... 5B 16
N16 ... 4D 50
Milton Ho. E2 ... 3J 69
(off Roman Rd.)
E17 ... 4C 34
SE5 ... 7D 86
(off Elmington Est.)
SM1: Sutt ... 3J 149
Milton Lodge
DA14: Sidc ... 4A 128
TW2: Twick ... 7K 97
Milton Mans. W14 ... 6G 83
(off Queen's Club Gdns.)
Milton Pk. N6 ... 7G 31
Milton Pl. E5 ... 4G 51
N7 ... 5A 50
(off Eastwood Cl.)
Milton Rd. CR0: Croy ... 1D 152
CR4: Mitc ... 7E 120
DA16: Well ... 1K 109
DA17: Belv ... 4G 93
E17 ... 4C 34
HA1: Harr ... 4J 25
N6 ... 7G 31
N15 ... 4B 32
NW7 ... 5H 13
NW9 ... 7C 28
SE24 ... 5B 104
SM1: Sutt ... 3J 149
SM6: Wall ... 6G 151
SW14 ... 3K 99
SW19 ... 6A 120
Milton Rd. TW12: Hamp ... 7E 114
UB10: Uxb ... 4D 40
W3 ... 1K 81
W7 ... 7K 61
Milton St. EC2 ... 5D 68 (5E 162)
Milton Way UB7: W Dray ... 4B 76
Milverton Dr. UB10: Uxb ... 4E 40
Milverton Gdns. IG3: Ilf ... 2K 55
Milverton Ho. SE23 ... 3A 124
Milverton Rd. NW6 ... 7E 46
Milverton St. SE11 ... 5A 86 (6K 173)
Milverton Way SE9 ... 4E 126
Milward Wlk. E1 ... 5H 69
SE18 ... 6E 90
Mimosa Ho. UB4: Hayes ... 5A 60
Mimosa Lodge NW10 ... 5B 46
Mimosa Rd. UB4: Hayes ... 5A 60
Mimosa St. SW6 ... 1H 101
Minard Rd. SE6 ... 7G 107
Mina Rd. SE17 ... 5E 86
SW19 ... 1J 137
Minchenden Ct. N14 ... 2C 16
Minchenden Cres. N14 ... 3B 16
Minchin Ho. E14 ... 6C 70
(off Dod St.)
Mincing La. EC3 ... 7E 68 (2G 169)
Minden Rd. SE20 ... 1H 141
SM3: Sutt ... 2H 149
Minehead Rd. HA2: Harr ... 3E 42
SW16 ... 5K 121
Mineral St. SE18 ... 4J 91
Minera M. SW1 ... 4E 84 (3G 171)
Minerva Cl. DA14: Sidc ... 3J 127
SW9 ... 7A 86
(not continuous)
Minerva Rd. E4 ... 7J 19
KT1: King T ... 2F 135
NW10 ... 4J 63
Minerva St. E2 ... 2H 69
Minerva Wlk.
EC1 ... 6B 68 (7B 162)
Minet Av. NW10 ... 2A 64
Minet Dr. UB3: Hayes ... 1J 77
Minet Gdns. NW10 ... 2A 64
UB3: Hayes ... 1K 77
Minet Rd. SW9 ... 2B 104
Minford Gdns. W14 ... 2F 83
Minford Ho. W14 ... 2F 83
(off Minford Gdns.)
Mingard Wlk. N7 ... 2K 49
Ming St. E14 ... 7C 70
Minimax Cl. TW14: Felt ... 6J 95
Ministry Way SE9 ... 2D 126
Miniver Pl. EC4 ... 2D 168
Mink Ct. TW4: Houn ... 2A 96
Minniedale KT5: Surb ... 5F 135
Minnow St. SE17 ... 4E 86
Minnow Wlk. SE17 ... 4E 86
Minories EC3 ... 6F 69 (1J 169)
Minshaw Ct. DA14: Sidc ... 4K 127
Minshill St. SW8 ... 1H 103
Minshull Pl. BR3: Beck ... 7C 124
Minson Rd. E9 ... 1K 69
Minstead Gdns. SW15 ... 7B 100
Minstead Way
KT3: N Mald ... 6A 136
Minster Av. SM1: Sutt ... 2J 149
Minster Ct. EC3 ... 2H 169
W5 ... 4E 62
Minster Dr. CR0: Croy ... 4E 152
Minster Gdns.
KT8: W Mole ... 4D 132
Minsterley Av.
TW17: Shep ... 4G 131
Minster Pavement EC3 ... 2H 169
(off Mincing La.)
Minster Rd. BR1: Brom ... 7K 125
NW2 ... 5G 47
Minster Wlk. N8 ... 4J 31
Minstrel Gdns. KT5: Surb ... 4F 135
Mint Bus. Pk. E16 ... 5K 71
Mint Cl. UB10: Uxb ... 3D 58
Mintern Cl. N13 ... 3G 17
Minterne Av. UB2: S'hall ... 4E 78
Minterne Rd. HA3: Harr ... 5F 27
Minterne Waye
UB4: Hayes ... 6A 60
Mintern St. N1 ... 2D 68
Minton Ho. SE11 ... 3J 173
Minton M. NW6 ... 6K 47
Mint Rd. SM6: Wall ... 4F 151
Mint St. SE1 ... 2C 86 (6C 168)
Mint Wlk. CR0: Croy ... 3C 152
Mirabel Rd. SW6 ... 7H 83
Miranda Cl. E1 ... 5J 69
Miranda Ct. W3 ... 6F 63
Miranda Rd. N19 ... 1G 49
Mirfield St. SE7 ... 4B 90
Miriam Rd. SE18 ... 5J 91
Mirravale Trad. Est.
RM8: Dag ... 7E 38
Mirren Cl. HA2: Harr ... 4D 42
Mirror Path SE9 ... 3A 126
Misbourne Rd. UB10: Uxb ... 1C 58
Missenden SE17 ... 5D 86
(off Roland Way)
Missenden Cl.
TW14: Felt ... 1H 113
Missenden Gdns.
SM4: Mord ... 6A 138
Missenden Ho. NW8 ... 3C 158
Mission Gro. E17 ... 5A 34
Mission Pl. SE15 ... 1G 105
Mission Sq. TW8: Bford ... 6E 80
Mission, The E14 ... 6B 70
(off Commercial Rd.)
Mistletoe Cl. CR0: Croy ... 1K 153
Mistral SE5 ... 1E 104
Mistys Fld. KT12: Walt T ... 7A 132
Mitali Pas. E1 ... 6G 69
(not continuous)
MITCHAM ... 3D 138
Mitcham Gdn. Village
CR4: Mitc ... 5E 138
Mitcham Ho. SE5 ... 1C 104
Mitcham Ind. Est.
CR4: Mitc ... 1F 139
Mitcham La. SW16 ... 6G 121
Mitcham Pk. CR4: Mitc ... 4C 138
Mitcham Rd. CR0: Croy ... 6J 139
E6 ... 3C 72
IG3: Ilf ... 7K 37
SW17 ... 5D 120
Mitchell NW9 ... 1B 28
(off Concourse, The)
Mitchellbrook Way NW10 ... 6K 45
Mitchell Cl. DA17: Belv ... 3J 93
SE2 ... 4C 92
Mitchell Ho. W12 ... 7D 64
(off White City Est.)
Mitchell Rd. N13 ... 5H 17
Mitchells Pl. SE21 ... 6E 104
(off Aysgarth Rd.)
Mitchell St. EC1 ... 4C 68 (3C 162)
(not continuous)
Mitchell Wlk. E6 ... 5C 72
(off Neats Ct. Rd.)
E6 ... 5D 72
(Elmley Cl.)
Mitchell Way BR1: Brom ... 1J 143
NW10 ... 6J 45
Mitchison Rd. N1 ... 6D 50
Mitchley Rd. N17 ... 3G 33
Mitford Cl. KT9: Chess ... 6C 146
Mitford Rd. N19 ... 2J 49
Mitre Av. E17 ... 3C 34
Mitre Bri. Ind. Pk. NW10 ... 4D 64
Mitre Cl. BR2: Short ... 2H 143
SM2: Sutt ... 7A 150
TW17: Shep ... 6F 131
Mitre Ct. EC2 ... 7D 162
Mitre Rd. E15 ... 2G 71
SE1 ... 2A 86 (6K 167)
Mitre Sq. EC3 ... 6E 68 (1H 169)
Mitre St. EC3 ... 6E 68 (1H 169)
Mitre, The E14 ... 7B 70
Mitre Way NW10 ... 4D 64
W10 ... 4D 64
Mitre Yd. SW3 ... 4C 84 (3D 170)
Moat Ct. DA15: Sidc ... 3K 127
SE9 ... 6D 108
Moat Cres. N3 ... 3K 29
Moat Cft. DA16: Well ... 3C 110
Moat Dr. E13 ... 2A 72
HA1: Harr ... 4G 25
HA4: Ruis ... 7G 23
Moat Farm Rd. UB5: N'olt ... 6D 42
Moatfield NW6 ... 7G 47
Moatlands Ho. WC1 ... 2F 161
(off Cromer St.)
Moat Mount Open Space ... 1F 13
Moat Pl. SW9 ... 3K 103
W3 ... 6H 63
Moat Side EN3: Enf ... 4E 8
TW13: Felt ... 4A 114
Moat, The KT3: N Mald ... 1A 136
Moberley Rd. SW4 ... 7H 103
Mobil Ct. WC2 ... 1H 167
(off Clement's Inn)
Mobile Way W3 ... 5K 63
Moby Dick ... 4E 38
Mocatta Ho. E1 ... 4H 69
(off Brady St.)
Modbury Gdns. NW5 ... 6E 48
Modder Pl. SW15 ... 4F 101
Model Bldgs. WC1 ... 2H 161
Model Cotts. SW14 ... 4J 99
W13 ... 2B 80
Model Farm Cl. SE9 ... 3C 126
Modern Ct. EC4 ... 7A 162
Modling Ho. E2 ... 2K 69
(off Mace St.)
Moelwyn N7 ... 5H 49
Moelyn M. HA1: Harr ... 5A 26
Moffat Ct. SW19 ... 5J 119
Moffat Ho. SE5 ... 7C 86
Moffat Rd. CR7: Thor H ... 2C 140
N13 ... 6D 16
SW17 ... 4D 120
Mogden La. TW7: Isle ... 5K 97
Mohammedi Pk.
UB5: N'olt ... 1E 60
Mohawk Ho. E3 ... 2A 70
(off Gernon Rd.)
Mohmmad Khan Rd. E11 ... 1H 53
Moineau NW9 ... 1B 28
(off Concourse, The)
Moira Cl. N17 ... 2E 32
Moira Rd. SE9 ... 4D 108
Mokswell Ct. N10 ... 1E 30
Moland Mead SE16 ... 5K 87
(not continuous)
Molasses Ho. SW11 ... 3A 102
(off Clove Hitch Quay)
Molasses Row SW11 ... 3A 102
Mole Abbey Gdns.
KT8: W Mole ... 3F 133
Mole Ct. KT19: Eps ... 4J 147
Molember Ct.
KT8: E Mos ... 4J 133
Molember Rd.
KT8: E Mos ... 5J 133
Molescroft SE9 ... 3G 127
Molesey Av.
KT8: W Mole ... 5D 132
Molesey Dr. SM3: Sutt ... 2G 149
Molesey Pk. Av.
KT8: W Mole ... 5F 133
Molesey Pk. Cl.
KT8: E Mos ... 5G 133
Molesey Pk. Rd.
KT8: E Mos, W Mole
... 5F 133
Molesey Rd.
KT12: Walt T ... 7C 132
Molesford Rd. SW6 ... 1J 101
Molesham Cl.
KT8: W Mole ... 3F 133
Molesham Way
KT8: W Mole ... 3F 133
Molesworth Ho. SE17 ... 6B 86
(off Brandon Est.)
Molesworth St. SE13 ... 4E 106
Moliner Ct. BR3: Beck ... 7C 124
Mollis Ho. E3 ... 5C 70
(off Gale St.)
Mollison Av.
EN3: Enf, Walt A, Walt C
... 5F 9
Mollison Dr. SM6: Wall ... 7H 151
Mollison Sq. SM6: Wall ... 7H 151
(off Mollison Dr.)
Mollison Way HA8: Edg ... 2F 27
Molly Huggins Cl. SW12 ... 7G 103
Molton Ho. N1 ... 1K 67
(off Barnsbury Est.)
Molyneux Dr. SW17 ... 4F 121
Molyneux St.
W1 ... 5C 66 (6D 158)
Monarch Cl.
BR4: W W'ck ... 4H 155
TW14: Felt ... 7G 95
Monarch Ct. N2 ... 5B 30
Monarch Dr. E16 ... 5B 72
Monarch M. E17 ... 6D 34
SW16 ... 5A 122
Monarch Pde. CR4: Mitc ... 2D 138
Monarch Pl. IG9: Buck H ... 2F 21
Monarch Rd. DA17: Belv ... 3G 93
Monarchs Way HA4: Ruis ... 1F 41
Mona Rd. SE15 ... 2J 105
Monastery Gdns. EN2: Enf ... 2J 7
Mona St. E16 ... 5H 71
Monaveen Gdns.
KT8: W Mole ... 3F 133
Moncks Row SW18 ... 6H 101
Monck St. SW1 ... 3H 85 (2D 172)
Monclar Rd. SE5 ... 4D 104
Moncorvo Cl. SW7 ... 7C 164
Moncrieff Cl. E6 ... 6C 72
Moncrieff Pl. SE15 ... 2G 105
Moncrieff St. SE15 ... 2G 105
Mondial Way UB3: Hayes ... 7E 76
Monega Rd. E7 ... 6A 54
E12 ... 6B 54
Monet Ct. SE16 ... 5H 87
(off Stubbs Dr.)
Moneyer Ho. N1 ... 1E 162
(off Fairbank Est.)
Money La. UB7: W Dray ... 3A 76
Mongers Almshouses E9 ... 7K 51
(off Church Cres.)
Monica Ct. EN1: Enf ... 5K 7
Monica James Ho.
DA14: Sidc ... 3A 128
Monica Shaw Ct. NW1 ... 1D 160
(off Purchese St., not continuous)
Monier Rd. E3 ... 7C 52
Monivea Rd. BR3: Beck ... 7B 124
Monk Ct. W12 ... 1C 82
Monk Dr. E16 ... 7J 71
MONKEN HADLEY ... 2B 4
Monkfrith Av. N14 ... 6A 6
Monkfrith Cl. N14 ... 7A 6
Monkfrith Way N14 ... 7K 5
Monkhams Av.
IG8: Wfd G ... 5E 20
Monkhams Dr.
IG8: Wfd G ... 5E 20
Monkhams La.
IG8: Wfd G ... 5D 20
IG9: Buck H ... 3E 20
Monkleigh Rd.
SM4: Mord ... 3G 137
Monk Pas. E16 ... 7J 71
(off Monk Dr.)
Monks Av. EN5: Barn ... 6F 5
KT8: W Mole ... 5D 132

Monks Cl.—Moreton Rd.

Monks Cl. EN2: Enf 2H 7
HA2: Harr 2E 42
HA4: Ruis 4B 42
SE2 4D 92
Monks Cres.
KT12: Walt T 7K 131
Monksdene Gdns.
SM1: Sutt 3K 149
Monks Dr. W3 5G 63
MONKS ORCHARD 7A 142
Monks Orchard Rd.
BR3: Beck 1C 154
Monks Pk. HA9: Wemb 6H 45
Monks Pk. Gdns.
HA9: Wemb 7H 45
Monks Rd. EN2: Enf 2G 7
Monk St. SE18 4E 90
Monks Way BR3: Beck 6C 142
BR5: Orp 7G 145
NW11 4H 29
UB7: W Dray 6A 76
Monkswood Gdns. IG5: Ilf 3E 36
Monkton Ho. E5 5H 51
SE16 *2K 87*
(off Wolfe Cres.)
Monkton Rd. DA16: Well 2K 109
Monkton St.
SE11 4A 86 (3K 173)
Monkville Av. NW11 4H 29
Monkville Pde. NW11 4H 29
Monkwell Sq.
EC2 5C 68 (6D 162)
Monmouth Av. E18 3K 35
KT1: King T 7C 116
Monmouth Cl.
CR4: Mitc 4J 139
DA16: Well 4A 110
W4 3J 81
Monmouth Ct. *W7* *5K 61*
(off Copley Cl.)
Monmouth Gro. W5 4E 80
Monmouth Pl. *W2* *6K 65*
(off Monmouth Rd.)
Monmouth Rd. E6 3D 72
N9 2C 18
RM9: Dag 5F 57
UB3: Hayes 4G 77
W2 6J 65
Monmouth St.
WC2 6J 67 (1E 166)
Monnery Rd. N19 3G 49
Monnow Rd. SE1 5G 87
Mono La. TW13: Felt 2K 113
Monoux Almshouses E17 4D 34
Monoux Gro. E17 1C 34
Monroe Cres. EN1: Enf 1C 8
Monroe Dr. SW14 5H 99
Monro Gdns. HA3: Harr 7D 10
Monsell Ct. N4 3B 50
Monsell Rd. N4 3A 50
Monson Rd. NW10 2C 64
SE14 7K 87
Mons Way BR2: Short 6C 144
Montacute Rd.
CR0: Croy 7E 154
SE6 7B 106
SM4: Mord 6B 138
WD23: Bush 1E 10
Montagu Cres. N18 4C 18
Montague Av. SE4 4B 106
W7 1K 79
Montague Cl.
KT12: Walt T 7K 131
SE1 1D 86 (4E 168)
Montague Ct.
DA15: Sidc 3A 128
Montague Gdns. W3 7G 63
Montague Ho. *E16* *7K 71*
(off Wesley Av.)
Montague Pas. UB8: Uxb 7A 40
Montague Pl.
WC1 5H 67 (5D 160)
Montague Rd. CR0: Croy 1B 152
E8 5G 51
E11 2H 53
N8 5K 31
N15 4G 33
SW19 7K 119
TW3: Houn 3F 97
TW10: Rich 6E 98
UB2: S'hall 4C 78
UB8: Uxb 7A 40
W7 1K 79
W13 6B 62
Montague Sq. SE15 7J 87
Montague St.
EC1 5C 68 (6C 162)
WC1 5J 67 (5E 160)
Montague Ter.
BR2: Short 4H 143
Montague Waye
UB2: S'hall 3C 78
Montagu Gdns. N18 4C 18
SM6: Wall 4G 151
Montagu Mans.
W1 5D 66 (5F 159)
Montagu M. Nth.
W1 5D 66 (6F 159)
Montagu M. Sth.
W1 6D 66 (7F 159)
Montagu M. W.
W1 6D 66 (7F 159)
Montagu Pl. W1 5D 66 (6E 158)
Montagu Rd. N9 4C 18
N18 5C 18
NW4 6C 28
Montagu Rd. Ind. Est.
N18 4D 18
Montagu Row
W1 5D 66 (6F 159)
Montagu Sq. W1 5D 66 (6F 159)
Montagu St. W1 6D 66 (7F 159)
Montalt Rd. IG8: Wfd G 4C 20
Montana Gdns. SE26 5B 124
SM1: Sutt 5A 150
Montana Rd. SW17 3E 120
SW20 1E 136
Montbelle Rd. SE9 3F 127
Montcalm Cl. BR2: Short 6J 143
UB4: Hayes 3K 59
Montcalm Ho. E14 4B 88
Montcalm Rd. SE7 7B 90
Montclare St. E2 4F 69 (3J 163)
Monteagle Av. IG11: Bark 6G 55
Monteagle Ct. N1 2E 68
Monteagle Way E5 3G 51
SE15 3H 105
Montefiore St. SW8 2F 103
Montego Cl. SE24 4A 104
Montem Rd. KT3: N Mald 4A 136
SE23 7B 106
Montem St. N4 1K 49
Montenotte Rd. N8 5G 31
Monterey Cl. DA5: Bexl 2J 129
Monterey Pl. Shop. Cen.
NW7 5F 13
Montesole Ct. HA5: Pinn 2A 24
Montesquieu Ter. *E16* *6H 71*
(off Clarkson Rd.)
Montevetro SW11 1B 102
Montford Pl.
SE11 5A 86 (6J 173)
Montford Rd.
TW16: Sun T 4J 131
Montfort Ho. *E2* *3J 69*
(off Victoria Pk. Sq.)
E14 *3E 88*
(off Galbraith St.)
Montfort Pl. SW19 1F 119
Montgolfier Wlk.
UB5: N'olt 3C 60
Montgomery Cl.
CR4: Mitc 4J 139
DA15: Sidc 6K 109
Montgomery Ct.
CR2: S Croy *5E 152*
(off Birdhurst Rd.)
W4 7J 81
Montgomery Lodge *E1* *4J 69*
(off Cleveland Gro.)
Montgomery Rd.
HA8: Edg 6A 12
W4 4J 81
Montholme Rd. SW11 6D 102
Monthope Rd.
E1 5G 69 (6K 163)
Montolieu Gdns. SW15 5D 100
Montpelier Av.
DA5: Bexl 7D 110
W5 5C 62
Montpelier Cl. UB10: Uxb 1C 58
Montpelier Ct.
BR2: Short *4H 143*
(off Westmoreland Rd.)
W5 5D 62
Montpelier Gdns. E6 3B 72
RM6: Chad H 7C 38
Montpelier Gro. NW5 5G 49
Montpelier M.
SW7 3C 84 (1D 170)
Montpelier Pl. E1 6J 69
SW7 3C 84 (1D 170)
Montpelier Ri.
HA9: Wemb 1D 44
NW11 7G 29
Montpelier Rd. N3 1A 30
SE15 1H 105
SM1: Sutt 4A 150
W5 5D 62
Montpelier Row SE3 2H 107
TW1: Twick 7C 98
Montpelier Sq.
SW7 2C 84 (7D 164)
Montpelier St.
SW7 3C 84 (1D 170)
Montpelier Ter.
SW7 2C 84 (7D 164)
Montpelier Va. SE3 2H 107
Montpelier Wlk.
SW7 3C 84 (1D 170)
Montpelier Way NW11 7G 29
Montrave Rd. SE20 6J 123
Montreal Pl.
WC2 7K 67 (2G 167)
Montreal Rd. IG1: Ilf 7G 37
Montrell Rd. SW2 1J 121
Montrose Av. DA15: Sidc 7A 110
DA16: Well 3H 109
HA8: Edg 2J 27
NW6 2G 65
TW2: Twick 7F 97
Montrose Cl. DA16: Well 3K 109
IG8: Wfd G 4D 20
TW15: Ashf 6E 112
Montrose Ct. HA1: Harr 5F 25
NW9 2J 27
NW11 4H 29
SE6 1H 125
SW7 2B 84 (7B 164)
Montrose Cres.
HA0: Wemb 6E 44
N12 6F 15
Montrose Gdns.
CR4: Mitc 2D 138
SM1: Sutt 2K 149
Montrose Ho. E14 3C 88
Montrose Pl.
SW1 2E 84 (7H 165)
Montrose Rd. HA3: Harr 2J 25
TW14: Felt 6F 95
Montrose Wlk. HA7: Stan 6G 11
Montrose Way SE23 1K 123
Montserrat Av. IG8: Wfd G 7A 20
Montserrat Cl. SE19 5D 122
Montserrat Rd. SW15 4G 101
Monument Gdns. SE13 5E 106
Monument St.
EC3 7D 68 (2F 169)
Monument, The *2F 169*
(off Monument St.)
Monument Way N17 3F 33
Monza St. E1 7J 69
Moodkee St. SE16 3J 87
Moody Rd. SE15 1F 105
Moody St. E1 3K 69
Moon Ct. SE12 4J 107
Moon La. EN5: Barn 3C 4
Moon St. N1 1B 68
Moorcroft HA8: Edg 1H 27
Moorcroft Gdns.
BR2: Short 5C 144
Moorcroft La. UB8: Uxb 5C 58
Moorcroft Rd. SW16 3J 121
Moorcroft Way HA5: Pinn 5C 24
Moordown SE18 7F 91
Moore Cl. CR4: Mitc 2F 139
SM6: Wall 7J 151
SW14 3J 99
Moore Ct. *N1* *1B 68*
(off Gaskin St.)
Moore Cres. RM9: Dag 1B 74
Moorehead Way SE3 3J 107
Moore Ho. *E1* *7J 69*
(off Cable St.)
E2 *3J 69*
(off Roman Rd.)
N8 *4J 31*
(off Pembroke Rd.)
SE10 *5H 89*
(off Armitage Rd.)
Mooreland Rd.
BR1: Brom 7H 125
Moore Pk. Ct. *SW6* *7K 83*
(off Fulham Rd.)
Moore Pk. Rd. SW6 7J 83
Moore Rd. SE19 6C 122
Moore St. SW3 4D 84 (3E 170)
Moore Wlk. E7 4J 53
Moore Way SM2: Sutt 7J 149
Moorey Cl. E15 1H 71
Moorfield Av. W5 4D 62
Moorfield Rd. EN3: Enf 1D 8
KT9: Chess 5E 146
N17 2F 33
UB8: Uxb 6A 58
Moorfields EC2 5D 68 (6E 162)
Moorfields Highwalk *EC2* *6E 162*
(off Moorfields, not continuous)
Moorgate EC2 6D 68 (7E 162)
Moorgate Pl. EC2 7E 162
Moorgreen Ho. EC1 1A 162
Moorhouse NW9 1B 28
Moorhouse Rd. HA3: Harr 3D 26
W2 6J 65
Moorings, The *E16* *5A 72*
(off Prince Regent La.)
Moorland Cl. RM5: Col R 1H 39
TW2: Twick 7E 96
Moorland M. N1 7A 50
Moorland Rd. SW9 4B 104
Moorlands UB5: N'olt 1C 60
Moorlands Av. NW7 6J 13
Moor La. EC2 5D 68 (6E 162)
(not continuous)
KT9: Chess 4E 146
Moormead Dr. KT19: Eps 5A 148
Moor Mead Rd.
TW1: Twick 6A 98
Moor Pk. Gdns.
KT2: King T 7A 118
Moor Pl. EC2 5D 68 (6E 162)
Moorside Rd. BR1: Brom 3G 125
Moor St. W1 6H 67 (1D 166)
Moot Ct. NW9 5G 27
Moran Ho. *E1* *1H 87*
(off Wapping La.)
Morant Pl. N22 1K 31
Morant St. E14 7C 70
Mora Rd. NW2 4E 46
Mora St. EC1 3C 68 (2D 162)
Morat St. SW9 1K 103
Moravian Cl.
SW10 6B 84 (7A 170)
Moravian Pl. SW10 6B 84
Moravian St. E2 2J 69
Moray Av. UB3: Hayes 1H 77
Moray Cl. HA8: Edg 2C 12
RM1: Rom 1K 39
Moray Ct. *CR2: S Croy* *5C 152*
(off Warham Rd.)
Moray Ho. *E1* *4A 70*
(off Harford St.)
Moray M. N7 2K 49
Moray Rd. N4 2K 49
Moray Way RM1: Rom 1K 39
Mordaunt Gdns. RM9: Dag 7E 56
Mordaunt Ho. NW10 1K 63
Mordaunt Rd. NW10 1K 63
Mordaunt St. SW9 3K 103
MORDEN 3K 137
Morden Ct. SM4: Mord 4K 137
Morden Ct. Pde.
SM4: Mord 4K 137
Morden Gdns. CR4: Mitc 4B 138
UB6: G'frd 5K 43
Morden Hall Rd.
SM4: Mord 3K 137
Morden Hill SE13 2E 106
(not continuous)
Morden La. SE13 1E 106
MORDEN PARK 6G 137
Morden Rd. CR4: Mitc 4A 138
RM6: Chad H 7E 38
SE3 2J 107
SM4: Mord 4A 138
SW19 1K 137
Morden Rd. M. SE3 2J 107
Morden St. SE13 1D 106
Morden Way SM3: Sutt 7J 137
Morden Wharf Rd. SE10 3G 89
Mordern Ho. NW1 3D 158
Mordon Rd. IG3: Ilf 7K 37
Mordred Rd. SE6 2G 125
Morecambe Cl. E1 5K 69
Morecambe Gdns.
HA7: Stan 4J 11
Morecambe St. SE17 4C 86
Morecambe Ter. *N18* *4J 17*
(off Gt. Cambridge Rd.)
More Cl. E16 6H 71
W14 4F 83
Morecoombe Cl.
KT2: King T 7H 117
Moree Way N18 4B 18
Moreland Ct. NW2 3J 47
Moreland St.
EC1 3B 68 (1B 162)
Moreland Way E4 3J 19
Morella Rd. SW12 7D 102
Morello Av. UB8: Uxb 5D 58
Moremead Rd. SE6 4B 124
Morena St. SE6 7D 106
Moresby Av. KT5: Surb 7H 135
Moresby Rd. E5 1H 51
Moresby Wlk. SW8 2G 103
Mores Gdn. *SW3* *6B 84*
(off Cheyne Wlk.)
Moreton Av. TW7: Isle 1J 97
Moreton Cl. E5 2H 51
N15 6D 32
NW7 6K 13
SW1 5B 172
Moreton Gdns. IG8: Wfd G 5H 21
Moreton Ho. SE16 3H 87
Moreton Pl.
SW1 5G 85 (5B 172)
Moreton Rd. CR2: S Croy 5D 152
KT4: Wor Pk 2C 148
N15 6D 32

Moreton St.—Mount Rd.

Moreton St. SW1 . . .5G 85 (5B 172)
Moreton Ter.
SW1 . . . . . . .5G 85 (5B 172)
Moreton Ter. M. Nth.
SW1 . . . . . . .5G 85 (5B 172)
Moreton Ter. M. Sth.
SW1 . . . . . . .5G 85 (5B 172)
Moreton Twr. W3 . . . . .1H 81
Morford Cl. HA4: Ruis 7K 23
Morford Way HA4: Ruis 7K 23
Morgan Av. E17 . . . . .4F 35
Morgan Cl. RM10: Dag 7G 57
Morgan Ct. SM5: Cars 4D 150
TW15: Ashf 5D 112
Morgan Ho. *SW1 . . . . .4B 172*
(off Vauxhall Bri. Rd.)
SW8 . . . . .1G 103
(off Wadhurst Rd.)
Morgan Mans. *N7 . . . . .5A 50*
(off Morgan Rd.)
Morgan Rd. BR1: Brom 7J 125
N7 . . . . .5A 50
TW11: Tedd 6J 115
W10 . . . . .5H 65
Morgans La.
SE1 . . . . .1E 86 (5G 169)
UB3: Hayes 5F 59
Morgan St. E3 . . . . .3A 70
E16 . . . . .5H 71
Morgan Wlk. BR3: Beck 4D 142
Morgan Way IG8: Wfd G 6H 21
Moriatry Cl. N7 . . . . .4J 49
Morie St. SW18 . . . . .5K 101
Morieux Rd. E10 . . . . .1B 52
Moring Rd. SW17 . . . . .4E 120
Morkyns Wlk. SE21 . . . . . . .3E 122
Morland Av. CR0: Croy 1E 152
Morland Cl. CR4: Mitc 3C 138
NW11 . . . . .1K 47
TW12: Hamp 5D 114
Morland Ct. *W12 . . . . .2D 82*
(off Coningham Rd.)
Morland Est. E8 . . . . .7G 51
Morland Gdns. NW10 . . . . . . .7K 45
UB1: S'hall 1F 79
Morland Ho. *NW1 . . . . .1B 160*
(off Werrington St.)
NW6 . . . . .1J 65
SW1 . . . . .3E 172
(off Marsham St.)
W11 . . . . .6G 65
(off Lancaster Rd.)
Morland Rd. CR0: Croy 1E 152
E17 . . . . .5K 33
HA3: Harr 5E 26
IG1: Ilf 2F 55
RM10: Dag 7G 57
SE20 . . . . .6K 123
SM1: Sutt 5A 150
Morley Av. E4 . . . . .7A 20
N18 . . . . .4B 18
N22 . . . . .2A 32
Morley Ct. BR2: Short 4H 143
E4 . . . . .5G 19
Morley Cres. HA4: Ruis 2A 42
HA8: Edg 2D 12
Morley Cres. E. HA7: Stan . . .2C 26
Morley Cres. W.
HA7: Stan 3C 26
Morley Hill EN2: Enf 1J 7
Morley Ho. N16 . . . . .2G 51
Morley Rd. BR7: Chst 1G 145
E10 . . . . .1E 52
E15 . . . . .2H 71
IG11: Bark 1H 73
RM6: Chad H 5E 38
SE13 . . . . .4E 106
SM3: Sutt 1H 149
TW1: Twick 6D 98
Morley St. SE1 . . . .3A 86 (1K 173)
Morna Rd. SE5 . . . . .2C 104
Morning La. E9 . . . . .6J 51
Morningside Rd.
KT4: Wor Pk 2D 148
Mornington Av.
BR1: Brom 3A 144
IG1: Ilf 7E 36
W14 . . . . .4H 83
Mornington Cl.
IG8: Wfd G 4D 20
Mornington Ct. DA5: Bexl . . .1K 129
NW1 . . . . .2G 67
(off Mornington Cres.)
Mornington Cres. NW1 . . . . .2G 67
TW5: Houn 1K 95
Mornington Gro. E3 . . . . .3C 70
Mornington M. SE5 . . . . . . .1C 104
Mornington Pl. NW1 . . . . . . .2G 67
SE8 . . . . .7B 88
(off Mornington Rd.)
Mornington Rd. E4 . . . . .7K 9
E11 . . . . .7H 35
(not continuous)
IG8: Wfd G 4C 20
SE8 . . . . .7B 88
TW15: Ashf 5E 112
UB6: G'frd 5F 61
Mornington St. NW1 . . . . .2F 67
Mornington Ter. NW1 . . . . . . .1F 67
Mornington Wlk.
TW10: Rich 4C 116
Morocco St. SE1 . . .2E 86 (7G 169)
Morpeth Gro. E9 . . . . .1K 69
Morpeth Mans. *SW1 . . . . . .2A 172*
(off Morpeth Ter.)
Morpeth Rd. E9 . . . . .1K 69
Morpeth St. E2 . . . . .3J 69
Morpeth Ter.
SW1 . . . . . . .3G 85 (2A 172)
Morpeth Wlk. N17 . . . . .7C 18
Morrab Gdns. IG3: Ilf 3K 55
Morrel Ct. *E2 . . . . .2G 69*
(off Goldsmiths Row)
Morrell Cl. EN5: Barn 3F 5
Morris Av. E12 . . . . .5D 54
Morris Blitz Ct. N16 . . . . .4F 51
Morris Cl. CR0: Croy 5A 142
Morris Ct. E4 . . . . .3J 19
Morris Gdns. SW18 . . . . . . .7J 101
Morris Ho. *E2 . . . . .3J 69*
(off Roman Rd.)
NW8 . . . . .4C 158
(off Salisbury St.)
Morrish Rd. SW2 . . . . .7J 103
Morrison Av. E4 . . . . .6H 19
N17 . . . . .3E 32
Morrison Bldgs. Nth. *E1 . . . .6G 69*
(off Commercial Rd.)
Morrison Bldgs. Sth. *E1 . . . .6G 69*
(off Commercial Rd.)
Morrison Ct. *EN5: Barn 4B 4*
(off Manor Way)
Morrison Rd. IG11: Bark 2E 74
RM9: Bark, Dag 2E 74
UB4: Hayes 3K 59
Morrison St. SW11 . . . . .3E 102
Morris Pl. N4 . . . . .2A 50
Morris Rd. E14 . . . . .5D 70
E15 . . . . .4G 53
RM8: Dag 2F 57
TW7: Isle 3K 97
Morriss Ho. *SE16 . . . . .2H 87*
(off Cherry Garden St.)
Morris St. E1 . . . . .6H 69
Morritt Ho. *HA0: Wemb 5D 44*
(off Talbot Rd.)
Morse Cl. E13 . . . . .3J 71
Morshead Mans. *W9 . . . . . . .3J 65*
(off Morshead Rd.)
Morshead Rd. W9 . . . . .3J 65
Morson Rd. EN3: Enf 6F 9
Morston Gdns. SE9 . . . . . . .4D 126
Mortain Ho. *SE16 . . . . .4H 87*
(off Roseberry St.)
Morten Cl. SW4 . . . . .6H 103
Morteyne Rd. N17 . . . . .1D 32
Mortgramit Sq. SE18 . . . . . . .3E 90
Mortham St. E15 . . . . .1G 71
Mortimer Cl. NW2 . . . . .2H 47
SW16 . . . . .2H 121
Mortimer Ct. *NW8 . . . . .1A 158*
(off Abbey Rd.)
Mortimer Cres.
KT4: Wor Pk 3K 147
NW6 . . . . .1K 65
Mortimer Dr. EN1: Enf 6J 7
Mortimer Est. *NW6 . . . . .1K 65*
(off Mortimer Pl.)
Mortimer Ho. W11 . . . . .1F 83
W14 . . . . .4G 83
(off Nth. End Rd.)
Mortimer Mkt. *WC1 . . . . . . .4B 160*
(off Capper St.)
WC1 . . . . . . .4G 67 (4B 160)
Mortimer Pl. NW6 . . . . .1K 65
Mortimer Rd. CR4: Mitc 1D 138
DA8: Erith 6K 93
E6 . . . . .3D 72
N1 . . . . .7E 50
(not continuous)
NW10 . . . . .3E 64
W13 . . . . .6C 62
Mortimer Sq. W11 . . . . .7F 65
Mortimer St. W1 . . .6G 67 (7K 159)
Mortimer Ter. NW5 . . . . .4F 49
MORTLAKE **3K 99**
Mortlake Cl. CR0: Croy 3J 151
Mortlake Crematorium
TW9: Rich 2H 99
Mortlake Dr. CR4: Mitc 1C 138
Mortlake High St. SW14 . . . .3K 99
Mortlake Rd. E16 . . . . .6K 71
IG1: Ilf 4G 55
TW9: Rich 7G 81
Mortlake Ter. *TW9: Rich 7G 81*
(off Mortlake Rd.)
Mortlock Cl. SE15 . . . . .1H 105
Mortlock Ct. E7 . . . . .4B 54
Morton Cl. SM6: Wall 7K 151
Morton Ct. UB5: N'olt 5G 43
Morton Cres. N14 . . . . .4C 16
Morton Gdns. SM6: Wall . . .5G 151
Morton M. SW5 . . . . .4K 83
Morton Pl. SE1 . . . .3A 86 (2J 173)
Morton Rd. E15 . . . . .7H 53
N1 . . . . .7C 50
SM4: Mord 5B 138
Morton Way N14 . . . . .3B 16
Morvale Cl. DA17: Belv 4F 93
Morval Rd. SW2 . . . . .5A 104
Morven Rd. SW17 . . . . .3D 120
Morville St. E3 . . . . .2C 70
Morwell St. WC1 . . .5H 67 (6C 160)
Moscow Pl. W2 . . . . .7K 65
Moscow Rd. W2 . . . . .7J 65
Mosedale *NW1 . . . . .2K 159*
(off Cumberland Mkt.)
Moseley Row *SE10 . . . . .4H 89*
(off W. Parkside)
Moselle Av. N22 . . . . .2A 32
Moselle Cl. N8 . . . . .3K 31
Moselle Ho. *N17 . . . . .7A 18*
(off William St.)
Moselle Pl. N17 . . . . .7A 18
Moselle St. N17 . . . . .7A 18
Mosque Ter. *E1 . . . . .5G 69*
(off Fieldgate St.)
Mosque Twr. *E1 . . . . .5G 69*
(off Fieldgate St.)
E3 . . . . .2A 70
(off Ford St.)
Mossborough Cl. N12 . . . . . . .6E 14
Mossbury Rd. SW11 . . . . . .3C 102
Moss Cl. E1 . . . . .5G 69
HA5: Pinn 2D 24
Mossdown Cl. DA17: Belv . . .4G 93
Mossford Ct. IG6: Ilf 2F 37
Mossford Grn. IG6: Ilf 3F 37
Mossford La. IG6: Ilf 2F 37
Mossford St. E3 . . . . .4B 70
Moss Gdns.
CR2: S Croy 7K 153
TW13: Felt 2J 113
Moss Hall Ct. N12 . . . . .6E 14
Moss Hall Cres. N12 . . . . . . .6E 14
Moss Hall Gro. N12 . . . . .6E 14
Mossington Gdns. SE16 . . . . .4J 87
Moss La. HA5: Pinn 1C 24
Mosslea Rd. BR2: Short 5B 144
SE20 . . . . .6J 123
(not continuous)
Mossop St. SW3 . . .4C 84 (3D 170)
Moss Rd. RM10: Dag 7G 57
Mossville Gdns.
SM4: Mord 3H 137
Mosswell Ho. N10 . . . . .1E 30
Moston Cl. UB3: Hayes 5H 77
Mostyn Av. HA9: Wemb 5F 45
Mostyn Gdns. NW10 . . . . .3F 65
Mostyn Gro. E3 . . . . .2C 70
Mostyn Rd. HA8: Edg 7F 13
SW9 . . . . .1A 104
SW19 . . . . .1H 137
Mosul Way BR2: Short 6C 144
Motcomb St.
SW1 . . . . . . .3E 84 (1G 171)
Moth Cl. SM6: Wall 7J 151
Mothers Sq. *E5 . . . . .4H 51*
(off Hana M.)
Motley Av. EC2 . . . . .4G 163
Motley St. SW8 . . . . .2G 103
MOTSPUR PARK **6C 136**
Motspur Pk.
KT3: N Mald 6B 136
MOTTINGHAM **2C 126**
Mottingham Gdns. SE9 . . . .1B 126
Mottingham La. SE9 . . . . . .1A 126
SE12 . . . . .1A 126
Mottingham Rd. N9 . . . . .6E 8
SE9 . . . . .2C 126
Mottisfont Rd. SE2 . . . . .3A 92
Mott St. E4: Lough 1K 9
Moules Ct. SE5 . . . . .7C 86
Moulins Rd. E9 . . . . .7J 51
Moulsford Ho. N7 . . . . .5H 49
Moulton Av. TW3: Houn 2C 96
Moundfield Rd. N16 . . . . .6G 33
Mound, The SE9 . . . . .3E 126
Mounsey Ho. *W10 . . . . .3G 65*
(off Third Av.)
Mountacre Cl. SE26 . . . . . . .4F 123
Mt. Adon Pk. SE22 . . . . .7G 105
Mountague Pl. E14 . . . . .7E 70
Mountain Ho.
SE11 . . . . . . .4K 85 (4H 173)
Mt. Angelus Rd. SW15 . . . . .7B 100
Mt. Ararat Rd. TW10: Rich . . .5E 98
Mount Arlington
BR2: Short 2G 143
(off Pk. Hill Rd.)
Mt. Ash Rd. SE26 . . . . .3H 123
Mount Av. E4 . . . . .3H 19
UB1: S'hall 6E 60
W5 . . . . .5C 62
Mountbatten Cl. SE18 . . . . . . .6J 91
SE19 . . . . .5E 122
Mountbatten Ct.
IG9: Buck H 2G 21
SE16 . . . . .1J 87
(off Rotherhithe St.)
Mountbatten Gdns.
BR3: Beck 4A 142
Mountbatten Ho. *N6 . . . . .7E 30*
(off Hillcrest)
Mountbatten M. SW18 . . . . .7A 102
Mountbel Rd. HA7: Stan 1A 26
Mt. Carmel Chambers *W8 . . .2J 83*
(off Dukes La.)
Mount Cl. BR1: Brom 1C 144
EN4: Barn 4K 5
SM5: Cars 7E 150
W5 . . . . .5C 62
Mountcombe Cl.
KT6: Surb 7E 134
Mount Ct. BR4: W W'ck 2G 155
SW15 . . . . .3G 101
Mt. Culver Av.
DA14: Sidc 6D 128
Mount Dr. DA6: Bex 5E 110
HA2: Harr 5D 24
HA9: Wemb 2J 45
Mountearl Gdns. SW16 . . . .3K 121
Mt. Eaton Ct. *W5 . . . . .5C 62*
(off Mount Av.)
Mt. Echo Av. E4 . . . . .2J 19
Mt. Echo Dr. E4 . . . . .1J 19
Mt. Ephraim La. SW16 . . . .3H 121
Mt. Ephraim Rd. SW16 . . . .3H 121
Mount Felix
KT12: Walt T 7H 131
Mountfield Cl. SE6 . . . . .7F 107
Mountfield Rd. E6 . . . . .2E 72
N3 . . . . .3H 29
W5 . . . . .6D 62
Mountford Rd. E8 . . . . .5G 51
Mountford St. E1 . . . . .6G 69
Mountfort Cres. N1 . . . . .7A 50
Mountfort Ter. N1 . . . . .7A 50
Mount Gdns. SE26 . . . . .3H 123
Mount Gro. HA8: Edg 3D 12
Mountgrove Rd. N5 . . . . .3B 50
Mounthurst Rd.
BR2: Short 7H 143
Mountington Pk. Cl.
HA3: Harr 6D 26
Mountjoy Cl. *EC2 . . . . .6D 162*
(off Thomas More Highwalk)
SE2 . . . . .2B 92
Mountjoy Ho. EC2 . . . . .6C 162
Mount Lodge N6 . . . . .6G 31
Mount M. TW12: Hamp 1F 133
Mount Mills
EC1 . . . . .3B 68 (2B 162)
Mt. Nod Rd. SW16 . . . . .3K 121
Mt. Olive Ct. W7 . . . . .2J 79
Mount Pde. EN4: Barn 4H 5
Mount Pk. SM5: Cars 7E 150
Mount Pk. Av.
CR2: S Croy 7B 152
HA1: Harr 2H 43
Mount Pk. Cres. W5 . . . . .6D 62
Mount Pk. Rd. HA1: Harr 3H 43
HA5: Pinn 5J 23
W5 . . . . .5D 62
Mount Pl. W3 . . . . .1H 81
Mt. Pleasant EN4: Barn 4H 5
HA0: Wemb 1E 62
HA4: Ruis 2A 42
IG1: Ilf 5G 55
N14 . . . . .7C 6
(off Wells, The)
SE27 . . . . .4C 122
WC1 . . . . . . .4A 68 (4J 161)
Mt. Pleasant Cres. N4 . . . . . .1K 49
Mt. Pleasant Hill E5 . . . . .2H 51
Mt. Pleasant La. E5 . . . . .1H 51
Mt. Pleasant Pl. SE18 . . . . . .4H 91
Mt. Pleasant Rd. E17 . . . . . . .2A 34
KT3: N Mald 3J 135
N17 . . . . .2E 32
NW10 . . . . .7E 46
SE13 . . . . .6D 106
W5 . . . . .4C 62
Mt. Pleasant Vs. N4 . . . . .7K 31
Mt. Pleasant Wlk.
DA5: Bexl 5J 111
Mount Rd. CR4: Mitc 2B 138
EN4: Barn 5H 5
KT3: N Mald 3K 135
KT9: Chess 5F 147

Mount Rd.—Napier Av.

Mount Rd. NW2 . . . . .3D 46
NW4 . . . . .6C 28
RM8: Dag 1F 57
SW19 . . . . .2J 119
TW13: Felt 3C 114
UB3: Hayes 2J 77
Mount Row W1 . . . . .7F 67 (3J 165)
Mountsfield Ct. SE13 . . . . . .6F 107
Mountside HA7: Stan 1K 25
Mounts Pond Rd. SE3 . . . . . .2F 107
(not continuous)
Mount Sq., The NW3 . . . . . . .3A 48
Mounts Rd. DA6: Bex 5D 110
Mt. Stewart Av. HA3: Harr . . .7D 26
Mount St. W1 . . . . .7E 66 (3G 165)
Mount St. M. W1 . . .7F 67 (3J 165)
Mount Ter. E1 . . . . .5H 69
Mount, The CR2: S Croy 5C 152
(off Warham Rd.)
DA6: Bex 5H 111
E5 . . . . .2H 51
(Alcester Cres.)
E5 . . . . .2H 51
(Muston Rd.)
HA9: Wemb 2H 45
KT3: N Mald 3B 136
KT4: Wor Pk 4D 148
N20 . . . . .2F 15
NW3 . . . . .3A 48
UB5: N'olt 5F 43
W3 . . . . .1J 81
Mount Vernon NW3 . . . . .4A 48
Mount Vw. EN2: Enf 1E 6
NW7 . . . . .3E 12
UB2: S'hall 4B 78
W5 . . . . .4D 62
Mountview Cl. NW11 . . . . . . .1K 47
Mountview Ct. N8 . . . . .4B 32
Mount Vw. Rd. E4 . . . . .7K 9
KT10: Esh 7B 146
N4 . . . . .7J 31
NW9 . . . . .5K 27
Mountview Rd. BR6: Orp . . .7K 145
(not continuous)
Mount Vs. SE27 . . . . .3B 122
Mount Way SM5: Cars 7E 150
Mount Wood
KT8: W Mole 3F 133
Movers Lane 2J 73
Movers La. IG11: Bark 1H 73
Mowat Ct. KT4: Wor Pk 2B 148
(off Avenue, The)
Mowatt Cl. N19 . . . . .2H 49
Mowbray Ct. N22 . . . . .1A 32
SE19 . . . . .7F 123
Mowbray Gdns. UB5: N'olt . . .1E 60
Mowbray Ho. N2 . . . . .2B 30
(off Grange, The)
Mowbray Pde. HA8: Edg 4B 12
UB5: N'olt 1E 60
Mowbray Rd. EN5: Barn 5F 5
HA8: Edg 4B 12
NW6 . . . . .7G 47
SE19 . . . . .1F 141
TW10: Rich 3C 116
Mowbrays Cl. RM5: Col R . . .1J 39
Mowbrays Rd. RM5: Col R . . .2J 39
Mowlem St. E2 . . . . .2H 69
Mowlem Trad. Est. N17 . . . . .7D 18
Mowll St. SW9 . . . . .7A 86
Moxon Cl. E13 . . . . .2H 71
Moxon St. EN5: Barn 3C 4
W1 . . . . . . .5E 66 (6G 159)
Moye Cl. E2 . . . . .2G 69
Moyers Rd. E10 . . . . .7E 34
Moylan Rd. W6 . . . . .6G 83
Moyle Ho. SW1 . . . . .6B 172
(off Churchill Gdns.)
Moyne Ho. SW9 . . . . .5B 104
Moyne Pl. NW10 . . . . .2G 63
Moynihan Dr. N21 . . . . .5D 6
Moys Cl. CR0: Croy 6J 139
Moyser Rd. SW16 . . . . .5F 121
Mozart St. W10 . . . . .3H 65
Mozart Ter. SW1 . . .4E 84 (4H 171)
Muchelney Rd.
SM4: Mord 6A 138
Mudlarks Blvd. SE10 . . . . . . .3H 89
Mudlarks Way SE7 . . . . .3J 89
SE10 . . . . .3H 89
(not continuous)
Muggeridge Cl.
CR2: S Croy 5D 152
Muggeridge Rd.
RM10: Dag 4H 57
Muirdown Av. SW14 . . . . .4K 99
Muir Dr. SW18 . . . . .6C 102
Muirfield W3 . . . . .6A 64
Muirfield Cl. SE16 . . . . .5H 87
Muirfield Cres. E14 . . . . .3D 88
Muirkirk Rd. SE6 . . . . .1E 124
Muir Rd. E5 . . . . .4G 51
Muir St. E16 . . . . .1C 90
(not continuous)
Mulberry Av.
TW19: Staines 1A 112
Mulberry Bus. Cen. SE16 . . . .2K 87
Mulberry Cl. E4 . . . . .2H 19
EN4: Barn 4G 5
N8 . . . . .5J 31
NW3 . . . . .4B 48
NW4 . . . . .3E 28
SE7 . . . . .6B 90
SE22 . . . . .5G 105
SW3 . . . . . . .6B 84 (7B 170)
SW16 . . . . .4G 121
UB5: N'olt 2C 60
Mulberry Ct. E11 . . . . .4F 53
(off Langthorne Rd.)
EC1 . . . . .2B 162
(off Tompion St.)
IG11: Bark 6K 55
KT6: Surb 7D 134
TW1: Twick 3K 115
Mulberry Cres.
TW8: Bford 7B 80
UB7: W Dray 2C 76
Mulberry Ho. BR2: Short . . .1G 143
E2 . . . . .3J 69
(off Victoria Pk. Sq.)
SE8 . . . . .6B 88
Mulberry Housing Co-operative
SE1 . . . . .4K 167
Mulberry La. CR0: Croy 1F 153
Mulberry M. SE14 . . . . .1B 106
SM6: Wall 6G 151
Mulberry Pde.
UB7: W Dray 3C 76
Mulberry Pl. E14 . . . . .7E 70
(off Clove Cres.)
W6 . . . . .5C 82
Mulberry Rd. E8 . . . . .7F 51
Mulberry St. E1 . . . . .6G 69
Mulberry Trees
TW17: Shep 7F 131
Mulberry Wlk.
SW3 . . . . . . .6B 84 (7B 170)
Mulberry Way DA17: Belv 2J 93
E18 . . . . .2K 35
IG6: Ilf 4G 37
Mulgrave Ct. SM2: Sutt 6K 149
(off Mulgrave Rd.)
Mulgrave Rd. CR0: Croy . . .3D 152
HA1: Harr 2A 44
NW10 . . . . .4B 46
SE18 . . . . .4D 90
SM2: Sutt 7H 149
SW6 . . . . .6H 83
W5 . . . . .3D 62
Mulholland Cl. CR4: Mitc . . .2F 139
Mulkern Rd. N19 . . . . .1H 49
Mullards Cl. CR4: Mitc 1D 150
Mullen Twr. WC1 . . . . .4J 161
(off Mount Pleasant)
Muller Ho. SE18 . . . . .5E 90
Muller Rd. SW4 . . . . .6H 103
Mullet Gdns. E2 . . . . .3G 69
Mulletsfield WC1 . . . . .2F 161
(off Cromer St.)
Mullins Path SW14 . . . . .3K 99
Mullion Cl. HA3: Harr 1F 25
Mull Wlk. N1 . . . . .6C 50
(off Clephane Rd.)
N1 . . . . .6D 50
(off Marquess Rd. Nth.)
Mulready Ho. SW1 . . . . . . .4E 172
(off Marsham St.)
Mulready St.
NW8 . . . . . . .4C 66 (4C 158)
Multimedia Ho. NW10 . . . . . .4J 63
Multi Way W3 . . . . .2A 82
Multon Ho. E9 . . . . .7J 51
Multon Rd. SW18 . . . . .7B 102
Mulvaney Way
SE1 . . . . . . .2D 86 (7F 169)
(not continuous)
Mumford Ct. EC2 . . .6C 68 (7D 162)
Mumford Rd. SE24 . . . . .5B 104
Muncaster Cl.
TW15: Ashf 4C 112
Muncaster Rd. SW11 . . . . . .5D 102
TW15: Ashf 5D 112
Muncies M. SE6 . . . . .2E 124
Mundania Rd. SE22 . . . . . . .6H 105
Munday Ho. SE1 . . . . .3D 86
(off Deverell St.)
Munday Rd. E16 . . . . .7J 71
Munden St. W14 . . . . .4G 83
Mundford Rd. E5 . . . . .2J 51
Mundon Gdns. IG1: Ilf 1H 55
Mund St. W14 . . . . .5H 83
Mundy Ho. W10 . . . . .3G 65
Mundy St. N1 . . . . .3E 68 (1G 163)
Mungo Pk. Cl.
WD23: Bush 2B 10
Munnery Way BR6: Orp 3E 156
Munnings Gdns. TW7: Isle . . .5H 97
Munnings Ho. E16 . . . . .7K 71
(off Portsmouth M.)
Munro Dr. N11 . . . . .6B 16
Munro Ho. SE1 . . . .2A 86 (7J 167)
Munro M. W10 . . . . .5G 65
(not continuous)
Munro Ter. SW10 . . . . .7B 84
Munro Way E5 . . . . .4G 51
Munslow Gdns.
SM1: Sutt 4B 150
Munster Av. TW4: Houn 5C 96
Munster Ct. SW6 . . . . .2H 101
TW11: Tedd 6C 116
Munster Gdns. N13 . . . . .4G 17
Munster M. SW6 . . . . .7G 83
Munster Rd. SW6 . . . . .7G 83
TW11: Tedd 6B 116
Munster Sq.
NW1 . . . . . . .3F 67 (2K 159)
Munton Rd. SE17 . . . . .4C 86
Murchison Av. DA5: Bexl . . .1D 128
Murchison Rd. E10 . . . . .2E 52
Murdoch Ho. SE16 . . . . .3J 87
(off Moodkee St.)
Murdock Cl. E16 . . . . .6H 71
Murdock St. SE15 . . . . .6H 87
Murfett Cl. SW19 . . . . .2G 119
Muriel Ct. E10 . . . . .7D 34
Muriel St. N1 . . . . .2K 67
(not continuous)
Murillo Rd. SE13 . . . . .4F 107
Murphy Ho. SE1 . . . . .7B 168
(off Borough Rd.)
Murphy St. SE1 . . . .2A 86 (7J 167)
Murray Av. BR1: Brom 3K 143
TW3: Houn 5F 97
Murray Ct. HA1: Harr 6K 25
TW2: Twick 2H 115
Murray Cres. HA5: Pinn 1B 24
Murray Gro. N1 . . . .2C 68 (1D 162)
Murray Ho. SE18 . . . . .4D 90
(off Rideout St.)
Murray M. NW1 . . . . .7H 49
Murray Rd. HA6: Nwood 1G 23
SW19 . . . . .6F 119
TW10: Rich 2B 116
W5 . . . . .4C 80
Murray Sq. E16 . . . . .6J 71
Murray St. NW1 . . . . .7G 49
Murray Ter. NW3 . . . . .4A 48
W5 . . . . .4D 80
Mursell Est. SW8 . . . . .1K 103
Musard Rd. W6 . . . . .6G 83
Musbury St. E1 . . . . .6J 69
Muscal W6 . . . . .6G 83
(off Field Rd.)
Muscatel Pl. SE5 . . . . .1E 104
Muschamp Rd. SE15 . . . . . .3F 105
SM5: Cars 2C 150
Muscovy Ho. DA18: Erith 2E 92
(off Kale Rd.)
Muscovy St.
EC3 . . . . .7E 68 (2H 169)
Museum Chambers WC1 . . .6E 160
(off Bury Pl.)
Mus. in Docklands 7C 70
Museum La. SW7 . . . . .2B 170
Mus. of Artillery in the Rotunda
. . . . .5D 90
Mus. of Classical Archaeology
. . . . .3C 160
(off Gower Pl.)
Mus. of Garden History
. . . . .3K 85 (2G 173)
Mus. of London . . .5C 68 (6C 162)
Mus. of Richmond 5D 98
(off Whittaker Av.)
Mus. of Rugby, The 6J 97
(in Twickenham Rugby Football Ground)
Mus. of the Order of St John, The
. . . . .4A 162
(off St John's La.)
Museum Pas. E2 . . . . .3J 69
Museum St. WC1 . . .5J 67 (6E 160)
Musgrave Cl. EN4: Barn 1F 5
Musgrave Ct. SW11 . . . . . . .1C 102
Musgrave Cres. SW6 . . . . . . .7J 83
Musgrave Rd. TW7: Isle 1K 97
Musgrove Rd. SE14 . . . . . . .1K 105
Musjid Rd. SW11 . . . . .2B 102
Musket Cl. EN4: Barn 6G 5
Musquash Way
TW4: Houn 2A 96
Muston Rd. E5 . . . . .2H 51
Mustow Pl. SW6 . . . . .2H 101
Muswell Av. N10 . . . . .1F 31
MUSWELL HILL 3F 31
Muswell Hill N10 . . . . .3F 31
Muswell Hill B'way. N10 . . . .3F 31
Muswell Hill Pl. N10 . . . . . . .4F 31
Muswell Hill Rd. N6 . . . . .6E 30
Muswell M. N10 . . . . .3F 31
Muswell Rd. N10 . . . . .3F 31
Mutrix Rd. NW6 . . . . .1J 65
Mutton Pl. NW1 . . . . .6E 48
Muybridge Rd.
KT3: N Mald 2J 135
Myatt Rd. SW9 . . . . .1B 104
Myatts Flds. Sth. SW9 . . . . .2A 104
(off St Lawrence Way)
Mycenae Rd. SE3 . . . . .7J 89
Myddelton Av. EN1: Enf 1K 7
Myddelton Cl. EN1: Enf 1A 8
Myddelton Gdns. N21 . . . . . . .7H 7
Myddelton Pk. N20 . . . . .3G 15
Myddelton Pas.
EC1 . . . . .3A 68 (1K 161)
Myddelton Rd. N8 . . . . .4J 31
Myddelton Sq.
EC1 . . . . .3A 68 (1K 161)
Myddelton St.
EC1 . . . . .3A 68 (2K 161)
Myddleton Av. N4 . . . . .2C 50
Myddleton Ho. WC1 . . . . . . .1J 161
Myddleton M. N22 . . . . .7D 16
Myddleton Rd. N22 . . . . .7D 16
Myers La. SE14 . . . . .6K 87
Mylis Cl. SE26 . . . . .4H 123
Mylius Cl. SE14 . . . . .7J 87
Myline Cl. W6 . . . . .5C 82
Mylne St. EC1 . . . . .3A 68 (1J 161)
Myra St. SE2 . . . . .4A 92
Myrdle St. E1 . . . . .5G 69
Myrna Cl. SW19 . . . . .7C 120
Myron Pl. SE13 . . . . .3E 106
Myrtle Av. HA4: Ruis 7J 23
TW14: Felt 5G 95
Myrtleberry Cl. E8 . . . . .6F 51
(off Beechwood Rd.)
Myrtle Cl. EN4: Barn 1J 15
UB7: W Dray 3B 76
UB8: Uxb 5B 58
Myrtledene Rd. SE2 . . . . .5A 92
Myrtle Gdns. W7 . . . . .1J 79
Myrtle Gro. EN2: Enf 1J 7
KT3: N Mald 2J 135
Myrtle Rd. CR0: Croy 3C 154
E6 . . . . .1D 72
E17 . . . . .6A 34
IG1: Ilf 2F 55
N13 . . . . .3H 17
SM1: Sutt 5A 150
TW3: Houn 2G 97
TW12: Hamp 6G 115
W3 . . . . .1J 81
Myrtle Wlk. N1 . . . .2E 68 (1G 163)
Mysore Rd. SW11 . . . . .3D 102
Myton Rd. SE21 . . . . .3D 122
Mytton Ho. SW8 . . . . .7K 85
(off St Stephens Ter.)

N

Nadine Ct. SM6: Wall 7G 151
Nadine St. SE7 . . . . .5A 90
Nagasaki Wlk. SE7 . . . . .3K 89
Nagle Cl. E17 . . . . .2F 35
Nag's Head 3J 49
Nags Head Ct. EC1 . . . . .4D 162
Nags Head La.
DA16: Well 3B 110
Nags Head Rd. EN3: Enf 4D 8
Nags Head Shop. Cen. N7 . . .4K 49
Nailsworth Ct. SE15 . . . . .6E 86
(off Birdlip Cl.)
Nainby Ho. SE11 . . . . .4J 173
Nairne Gro. SE24 . . . . .5D 104
Nairn Rd. HA4: Ruis 6A 42
Nairn St. E14 . . . . .5E 70
Naish Ct. N1 . . . . .1J 67
(not continuous)
Naldera Gdns. SE3 . . . . .6J 89
Nallhead Rd. TW13: Felt 5A 114
Namba Roy Cl. SW16 . . . . . .4K 121
Namton Dr.
CR7: Thor H 4K 139
Nan Clarks La. NW7 . . . . .2F 13
Nankin St. E14 . . . . .6C 70
Nansen Ho. NW10 . . . . .7K 45
(off Stonebridge Pk.)
Nansen Rd. SW11 . . . . .3E 102
Nansen Village N12 . . . . .4E 14
Nant Ct. NW2 . . . . .2H 47
Nantes Cl. SW18 . . . . .4A 102
Nantes Pas. E1 . . . . .5F 69 (5J 163)
Nant Rd. NW2 . . . . .2H 47
Nant St. E2 . . . . .3H 69
Naoroji St. WC1 . . . .3A 68 (2J 161)
Napier NW9 . . . . .1B 28
Napier Av. E14 . . . . .5C 88
SW6 . . . . .3H 101

302 A-Z London

Napier Cl.—New Bri. St.

Napier Cl. SE8 . . . . 7B **88**
UB7: W Dray 3B **76**
W14 . . . . 3G **83**
Napier Ct. *N1* *2D **68***
(off Cropley St.)
SE12 . . . . 3K **125**
SW6 . . . . *3H **101***
(off Ranelagh Gdns.)
UB4: Hayes *4A **60***
(off Dunedin Way)
Napier Gro. N1 . . . . 2C **68**
Napier Pl. W14 . . . . 3H **83**
Napier Rd. BR2: Short 4K **143**
CR2: S Croy 7D **152**
DA17: Belv 4F **93**
E6 . . . . 1E **72**
E11 . . . . 4G **53**
E15 . . . . 2G **71**
(not continuous)
EN3: Enf 5E **8**
HA0: Wemb 6D **44**
N17 . . . . 3E **32**
NW10 . . . . 3D **64**
SE25 . . . . 4H **141**
TW6: Houn 1A **94**
TW7: Isle 4A **98**
TW15: Ashf 7F **113**
W14 . . . . 3H **83**
Napier St. *SE8* *7B **88***
(off Napier Cl.)
Napier Ter. N1 . . . . 7B **50**
Napier Wlk. TW15: Ashf 7F **113**
Napoleon Rd. E5 . . . . 3H **51**
TW1: Twick 7B **98**
Napton Cl. UB4: Hayes 4C **60**
Narbonne Av. SW4 . . . . 5G **103**
Narborough Cl. UB10: Uxb . . . 2E **40**
Narborough St. SW6 . . . . . . 2K **101**
Narcissus Rd. NW6 . . . . 5J **47**
Nardini *NW9* *1B **28***
(off Concourse, The)
Naresby Fold HA7: Stan 6H **11**
Narford Rd. E5 . . . . 3G **51**
Narrow Boat Cl. SE28 . . . . . . 2H **91**
Narrow St. *E14* *7K **69***
(off Highway, The)
W3 . . . . 1H **81**
Narrow Way BR2: Short 6C **144**
Narvic Ho. SE5 . . . . 2C **104**
Narwhal Inuit Art Gallery** . . . 5K **81
Nascot St. W12 . . . . 6E **64**
Naseby Cl. NW6 . . . . 7A **48**
TW7: Isle 1J **97**
Naseby Ct. DA14: Sidc 4K **127**
Naseby Rd. IG5: Ilf 1D **36**
RM10: Dag 3G **57**
SE19 . . . . 6D **122**
NASH **6J 155**
Nash Cl. SM1: Sutt 3B **150**
Nash Ct. *E14* *1D **88***
(off Nash Pl.)
HA3: Harr 6B **26**
Nashe Ho. *SE1* *3D **86***
(off Burbage Cl.)
Nash Grn. BR1: Brom 6J **125**
Nash Ho. E17 . . . . 3D **34**
SW1 . . . . *6K **171***
(off Lupus St.)
Nash La. BR2: Kes 7J **155**
Nash Pl. E14 . . . . 1D **88**
Nash Rd. N9 . . . . 2D **18**
RM6: Chad H 4D **38**
SE4 . . . . 4A **106**
Nash St. NW1 . . . . . 3F **67** (1K **159**)
Nash Way HA3: Harr 6B **26**
Nasmyth St. W6 . . . . 3D **82**
Nassau Path SE28 . . . . 1C **92**
Nassau Rd. SW13 . . . . 1B **100**
Nassau St. W1 . . . . 5G **67** (6A **160**)
Nassington Rd. NW3 . . . . 4D **48**
Natalie Cl. TW14: Felt 7F **95**
Natalie M. TW12: Hamp . . . 3H **115**
Natal Rd. CR7: Thor H 3D **140**
IG1: Ilf 4F **55**
N11 . . . . 6D **16**
SW16 . . . . 6H **121**
Nathan Ct. *N9* *7D **8***
(off Causeyware Rd.)
Nathan Ho. *SE11* *4K **173***
(off Reedworth St.)
Nathaniel Cl. E1 . . . 5F **69** (6K **163**)
Nathaniel Ct. E17 . . . . 7A **34**
Nathans Rd. HA0: Wemb 1C **44**
Nathan Way SE28 . . . . 4J **91**
National Army Mus.
*. . . . . 6D **84** (7F **171**)*
National Film Theatre, The
*. 4H **167***
***National Gallery** . . . 7H **67** (3D **166**)*
National Gallery (Sainsbury Wing)
*. 3D **166***
(in National Gallery)
National Maritime Mus.** 6F **89
National Portrait Gallery** . . . 3D **166
Nation Way E4 . . . . 1K **19**
Natural History Mus.
*. . . . . 3B **84** (2A **170**)*
Nautilus Bldg., The *EC1* *1K **161***
(off Myddelton Pas.)
Naval Ho. *E14* *7F **71***
(off Quixley St.)
Naval Row E14 . . . . 7E **70**
Naval Wlk. *BR1: Brom* *2J **143***
(off Mitre Cl.)
Navarino Gro. E8 . . . . 6G **51**
Navarino Mans. E8 . . . . 6G **51**
Navarino Rd. E8 . . . . 6G **51**
Navarre Rd. E6 . . . . 2C **72**
Navarre St. E2 . . . . . 4F **69** (3J **163**)
Navenby Wlk. E3 . . . . 4C **70**
Navestock Cl. E4 . . . . 3K **19**
Navestock Cres.
IG8: Wfd G 7F **21**
Navestock Ho. IG11: Bark . . . 2B **74**
Navigation Dr. EN3: Enf 1H **9**
Navigator Dr. UB2: S'hall . . . 2G **79**
Navy St. SW4 . . . . 3H **103**
Naxos Bldg. E14 . . . . 2B **88**
Nayland Ho. SE6 . . . . 4E **124**
Naylor Gro. EN3: Enf 5E **8**
Naylor Ho. W10 . . . . 3G **65**
Naylor Rd. N20 . . . . 2F **15**
SE15 . . . . 7H **87**
Nazareth Gdns. SE15 . . . . . 2H **105**
Nazrul St. E2 . . . . . 3F **69** (1J **163**)
Neagle Ho. *NW2* *3E **46***
(off Stoll Cl.)
Neal Av. UB1: S'hall 4D **60**
Neal Cl. HA6: Nwood 1J **23**
Nealden St. SW9 . . . . 3K **103**
Neale Cl. N2 . . . . 3A **30**
Neal St. WC2 . . . . . . 6J **67** (1E **166**)
Neals Yd. WC2 . . . . . . 6J **67** (1E **166**)
Near Acre NW9 . . . . 1B **28**
NEASDEN **3A 46**
Neasden Cl. NW10 . . . . 5A **46**
NEASDEN JUNCTION **4A 46**
Neasden La. NW10 . . . . 3A **46**
(not continuous)
Neasden La. Nth. NW10 . . . . 3K **45**
Neasham Rd. RM8: Dag 5B **56**
Neate St. SE5 . . . . 6E **86**
(not continuous)
Neath Gdns. SM4: Mord 6A **138**
Neath Ho. *SE24* *6B **104***
(off Dulwich Rd.)
Neathouse Pl.
SW1 . . . . . . 4G **85** (3A **172**)
Neats Acre HA4: Ruis 7F **23**
Neatscourt Rd. E6 . . . . 5B **72**
Nebraska St.
SE1 . . . . 2D **86** (7E **168**)
Neckinger SE1 . . . . . 3F **87** (7K **169**)
Neckinger Est. SE16 . . . . 3F **87**
Neckinger St.
SE1 . . . . 2F **87** (7K **169**)
Nectarine Way SE13 . . . . . . 2D **106**
Needham Ho. SE11 . . . . 4J **173**
Needham Rd. W11 . . . . 6J **65**
Needham Ter. NW2 . . . . 3F **47**
Needleman St. SE16 . . . . 2K **87**
Needwood Ho. N4 . . . . 1C **50**
Neela Cl. UB10: Uxb 4D **40**
Neeld Cres. HA9: Wemb 5G **45**
NW4 . . . . 5D **28**
Neeld Pde. HA9: Wemb 5F **45**
Neil Cl. TW15: Ashf 5E **112**
Neil Wates Cres. SW2 . . . . . 1A **122**
Nelgarde Rd. SE6 . . . . 7C **106**
Nella Rd. W6 . . . . 6F **83**
Nelldale Rd. SE16 . . . . 4J **87**
Nellgrove Rd. UB10: Uxb 4D **58**
Nell Gwynne Av.
TW17: Shep 6F **131**
Nello James Gdns. SE27 . . . 4D **122**
Nelson Cl. CR0: Croy 1B **152**
KT12: Walt T 7K **131**
NW6 . . . . *3J **65***
(off Cambridge Rd.)
RM7: Mawney 1H **39**
TW14: Felt 1H **113**
UB10: Uxb 3D **58**
Nelson Ct. SE1 . . . . 2B **86** (6B **168**)
SE16 . . . . *1J **87***
(off Brunel Rd.)
Nelson Gdns. E2 . . . . 3G **69**
TW3: Houn 6E **96**
Nelson Gro. Rd. SW19 . . . . . 1A **138**
Nelson Ho. *SW1* *7B **172***
(off Dolphin Sq.)
Nelson Ind. Est. SW19 . . . . . 1K **137**
Nelson La. UB10: Uxb 3D **58**
Nelson Mandela Cl. N10 . . . . 2E **30**
Nelson Mandela Rd. SE3 . . . 3A **108**
Nelson Pas. EC1 . . . 3C **68** (1D **162**)
Nelson Pl. DA14: Sidc 4A **128**
N1 . . . . 2B **68** (1B **162**)
Nelson Rd. BR2: Short 4A **144**
DA14: Sidc 4A **128**
DA17: Belv 5F **93**
E4 . . . . 6J **19**
E11 . . . . 4J **35**
EN3: Enf 6E **8**
HA1: Harr 1H **43**
HA7: Stan 6H **11**
KT3: N Mald 5K **135**
N8 . . . . 5K **31**
N9 . . . . 2C **18**
N15 . . . . 4E **32**
SE10 . . . . 6E **88**
SW19 . . . . 7K **119**
TW2: Twick 6E **96**
TW4: Houn 6E **96**
TW6: Houn 1B **94**
TW15: Ashf 5A **112**
UB10: Uxb 3D **58**
Nelson Rd. M. SW19 . . . . . . 7K **119**
***Nelson's Column** . . . 1J **85** (4E **166**)*
Nelson Sq. SE1 . . . . 2B **86** (6A **168**)
Nelsons Row SW4 . . . . 4H **103**
Nelson St. E1 . . . . 6H **69**
E6 . . . . 2D **72**
(not continuous)
E16 . . . . 7H **71**
(not continuous)
Nelsons Yd. *NW1* *2G **67***
(off Mornington Cres.)
Nelson Ter. N1 . . . . 2B **68** (1B **162**)
Nelson Wlk. KT19: Eps 7G **147**
SE16 . . . . 1A **88**
Nemoure Rd. W3 . . . . 7J **63**
Nene Gdns. TW13: Felt 2D **114**
Nene Rd. TW6: Houn 1D **94**
Nene Rd. Rdbt.
TW6: Houn 1D **94**
Nepaul Rd. SW11 . . . . 2C **102**
Nepean St. SW15 . . . . 6C **100**
Neptune Ct. *E14* *4C **88***
(off Homer Dr.)
Neptune Ho. *SE16* *3J **87***
(off Moodkee St.)
Neptune Rd. HA1: Harr 6H **25**
TW6: Houn 1E **94**
Neptune St. SE16 . . . . 3J **87**
Neptune Wlk. DA8: Erith 4K **93**
Nero Ct. TW8: Bford 7D **80**
Nesbit Rd. SE9 . . . . 4B **108**
Nesbitt Cl. SE3 . . . . 3G **107**
Nesbitts All. EN5: Barn 3C **4**
Nesbitt Sq. SE19 . . . . 7E **122**
Nesham St. E1 . . . . 7G **69**
Ness St. SE16 . . . . 3G **87**
Nesta Rd. IG8: Wfd G 6B **20**
Nestles Av. UB3: Hayes 3H **77**
Nestor Av. N21 . . . . 6G **7**
Nestor Ho. *E2* *2H **69***
(off Old Bethnal Grn. Rd.)
Netheravon Rd. W4 . . . . 4B **82**
W7 . . . . 1K **79**
Netheravon Rd. Sth. W4 . . . . 5B **82**
Netherbury Rd. W5 . . . . 3D **80**
Netherby Gdns. EN2: Enf 4D **6**
Netherby Rd. SE23 . . . . 7J **105**
Nether Cl. N3 . . . . 7D **14**
Nethercourt Av. N3 . . . . 6D **14**
Netherfield Gdns.
IG11: Bark 6H **55**
Netherfield Rd. N12 . . . . 5E **14**
SW17 . . . . 3E **120**
Netherford Rd. SW4 . . . . . . 2G **103**
Netherhall Gdns. NW3 . . . . . . 6A **48**
Netherhall Way NW3 . . . . 5A **48**
Netherlands Rd. EN5: Barn . . . 6G **5**
Netherleigh Cl. N6 . . . . 1F **49**
Nether St. N3 . . . . 1J **29**
Netherton Gro. SW10 . . . . 6A **84**
Netherton Rd. N15 . . . . 6D **32**
TW1: Twick 5A **98**
Netherwood N2 . . . . 2B **30**
Netherwood Pl. *W14* *3F **83***
(off Netherwood Rd.)
Netherwood Rd. W14 . . . . 3F **83**
Netherwood St. NW6 . . . . 7H **47**
Nethewode Ct. *DA17: Belv* . . . *3H **93***
(off Lwr. Park Rd.)
Netley *SE5* *1E **104***
(off Redbridge Gdns.)
Netley Cl. CR0: Croy 7E **154**
SM3: Sutt 5F **149**
Netley Dr. KT12: Walt T 7D **132**
Netley Gdns. SM4: Mord . . . 7A **138**
Netley Rd. E17 . . . . 5B **34**
IG2: Ilf 5H **37**
SM4: Mord 7A **138**
TW8: Bford 6E **80**
Netley St. NW1 . . . . 3G **67** (2A **160**)
Nettlecombe *NW1* *7H **49***
(off Agar Gro.)
Nettleden Av. HA9: Wemb . . . 6G **45**
Nettleden Ho. *SW3* *4D **170***
(off Marlborough St.)
Nettlefold Pl. SE27 . . . . 3B **122**
Nettlestead Cl.
BR3: Beck 7B **124**
Nettleton Ct. *EC2* *6C **162***
(off London Wall)
Nettleton Rd. SE14 . . . . 1K **105**
TW6: Houn 1D **94**
UB10: Uxb 4B **40**
Nettlewood Rd. SW16 . . . . . 7H **121**
Neuchatel Rd. SE6 . . . . 2B **124**
Nevada Cl. KT3: N Mald 4J **135**
Nevada St. SE10 . . . . 6E **88**
Nevern Mans. *SW5* *5J **83***
(off Warwick Rd.)
Nevern Pl. SW5 . . . . 4J **83**
Nevern Rd. SW5 . . . . 4J **83**
Nevern Sq. SW5 . . . . 4J **83**
Nevil Ho. *SW9* *2B **104***
(off Loughborough Est.)
Nevill Ct. EC4 . . . . 7K **161**
Neville Av. KT3: N Mald 1K **135**
Neville Cl. DA15: Sidc 4K **127**
E11 . . . . 3H **53**
NW1 . . . . 2H **67**
NW6 . . . . 2H **65**
SE15 . . . . 1G **105**
TW3: Houn 2F **97**
W3 . . . . 2J **81**
Neville Ct. NW8 . . . . 1A **158**
Neville Dr. N2 . . . . 6A **30**
Neville Gdns. RM8: Dag 3D **56**
Neville Gill Cl. SW18 . . . . . . 6J **101**
Neville Ho. N11 . . . . 4K **15**
N22 . . . . *1K **31***
(off Neville Pl.)
Neville Ho. Yd.
KT1: King T 2E **134**
Neville Pl. N22 . . . . 1K **31**
Neville Rd. CR0: Croy 7D **140**
E7 . . . . 7J **53**
IG6: Ilf 1G **37**
KT1: King T 2G **135**
NW6 . . . . 2H **65**
RM8: Dag 2D **56**
TW10: Rich 3C **116**
W5 . . . . 4D **62**
Nevilles Ct. NW2 . . . . 3C **46**
Neville St. SW7 . . . . 5B **84** (5A **170**)
Neville Ter. SW7 . . . 5B **84** (5A **170**)
Neville Wlk. SM5: Cars 7C **138**
Nevill Rd. N16 . . . . 4E **50**
Nevin Dr. E4 . . . . 1J **19**
Nevin Ho. UB3: Hayes 3E **76**
Nevinson Cl. SW18 . . . . 6B **102**
Nevis Rd. SW17 . . . . 2E **120**
Nevitt Ho. *N1* *2D **68***
(off Cranston Est.)
New Acres Rd. SE28 . . . . 2J **91**
(not continuous)
Newall Ho. *SE1* *3C **86***
(off Bath Ter.)
Newall Rd. TW6: Houn 1E **94**
Newark Cres. NW10 . . . . 3K **63**
Newarke Ho. SW9 . . . . 2B **104**
Newark Knok E6 . . . . 6E **72**
Newark Pde. NW4 . . . . 3C **28**
Newark Rd. CR2: S Croy . . . 6D **152**
Newark St. E1 . . . . 5H **69**
(not continuous)
Newark Way NW4 . . . . 4C **28**
New Ash Cl. N2 . . . . 3B **30**
New Atlas Wharf *E14* *3C **88***
(off Arnhem Pl.)
New Baltic Wharf *SE8* *5A **88***
(off Evelyn St.)
New Barn Cl. SM6: Wall 6K **151**
NEW BARNET **4G 5**
New Barn Rd. BR8: Swan . . . 7K **129**
New Barns Av. CR4: Mitc . . . 4H **139**
(not continuous)
New Barn St. E13 . . . . 4J **71**
New Barns Way IG7: Chig . . . 3K **21**
NEW BECKENHAM **6B 124**
New Bentham Ct. *N1* *7C **50***
(off Ecclesbourne Rd.)
Newbery Ho. *N1* *7C **50***
(off Northampton St.)
Newbold Cotts. E1 . . . . 6J **69**
Newbolt Av. SM3: Sutt 5E **148**
Newbolt Ho. *SE17* *5D **86***
(off Brandon St.)
Newbolt Rd. HA7: Stan 5E **10**
New Bond St. W1 . . . 6F **67** (1J **165**)
Newborough Grn.
KT3: N Mald 4K **135**
New Brent St. NW4 . . . . 5E **28**
Newbridge Point *SE23* *3K **123***
(off Windrush La.)
New Bri. St. EC4 . . . 6B **68** (1A **168**)

A-Z London 303

New Broad St.—New St. Hill

New Broad St. EC2 5E **68** (6G **163**)
New B'way. TW12: Hamp 5H **115**
UB10: Uxb 3D **58**
W5 7D **62**
Newburgh Rd. W3 1J **81**
Newburgh St. W1 6G **67** (1B **166**)
New Burlington M. W1 7G **67** (2A **166**)
New Burlington Pl. W1 7G **67** (2A **166**)
New Burlington St. W1 7G **67** (2A **166**)
Newburn Ho. *SE11 5H 173* *(off Newburn St.)*
Newburn St. SE11 5K **85** (5H **173**)
Newbury Cl. UB5: N'olt 6D **42**
Newbury Ct. DA14: Sidc 4K **127**
Newbury Gdns. KT19: Eps 4B **148**
Newbury Ho. N22 1J **31**
SW9 2B **104**
W2 6K 65 *(off Hallfield Est.)*
Newbury M. NW5 6E **48**
NEWBURY PARK 5H **37**
Newbury Rd. BR2: Short 3J **143**
E4 6K **19**
IG2: Ilf 6J **37**
TW6: Houn 1B **94**
Newbury St. EC1 5C **68** (6C **162**)
Newbury Way UB5: N'olt 6C **42**
New Bus. Cen., The NW10 3B **64**
New Butt La. SE8 7C **88**
New Butt La. Nth. *SE8 7C 88* *(off Hales St.)*
New B'way Bldgs. W5 7D **62**
Newby *NW1 2A 160* *(off Robert St.)*
Newby Cl. EN1: Enf 2K **7**
Newby Ho. *E14 7E 70* *(off Newby Pl.)*
Newby Pl. E14 7E **70**
Newby St. SW8 3F **103**
New Caledonian Wharf SE16 3B **88**
Newcastle Cl. EC4 6B **68** (7A **162**)
Newcastle Ct. *EC4 2D 168* *(off College Hill)*
Newcastle Ho. *W1 5G 159* *(off Luxborough St.)*
Newcastle Pl. W2 5B **66** (5B **158**)
Newcastle Row EC1 4A **68** (4K **161**)
New Cavendish St. W1 5E **66** (6H **159**)
New Change EC4 6C **68** (1C **168**)
New Chapel Sq. TW13: Felt 1K **113**
New Charles St. EC1 3B **68** (1B **162**)
NEW CHARLTON 4A **90**
New Chu. Rd. SE5 7C **86** (not continuous)
New City Rd. E13 3A **72**
New Cl. SW19 3A **138**
TW13: Felt 5C **114**
New Colebrooke Ct. *SM5: Cars 7E 150* *(off Stanley Rd.)*
New College Ct. *NW3 6A 48* *(off Finchley Rd.)*
New College M. N1 7A **50**
New College Pde. *NW3 6B 48* *(off College Cres.)*
Newcombe Gdns. SW16 4J **121**
TW4: Houn 4D **96**
Newcombe Pk. HA0: Wemb 1F **63**
NW7 5F **13**
Newcombe Ri. UB7: W Dray 6A **58**
Newcombe St. W8 1J **83**
Newcomen Rd. E11 3H **53**
SW11 3B **102**
Newcomen St. SE1 2D **86** (6E **168**)
New Compton St. WC2 6H **67** (1D **166**)
New Concordia Wharf SE1 2G **87** (6K **169**)
New Ct. EC4 2J **167**
UB5: N'olt 5F **43**
Newcourt Ho. *E2 3H 69* *(off Pott St.)*
Newcourt St. NW8 2C **66** (1C **158**)
***New Covent Garden Market* 7H 85 (7D 172)**
New Coventry St. W1 7H **67** (3D **166**)
New Crane Pl. E1 1J **87**
New Crane Wharf *E1 1J 87* *(off New Crane Pl.)*
New Cres. Yd. NW10 2B **64**
Newcroft Cl. UB8: Uxb 5B **58**
NEW CROSS 7B **88**
New Cross 1B **106**
NEW CROSS GATE 1K **105**
New Cross Gate 1K **105**
New Cross Rd. SE14 7J **87**
SE15 7J **87**
Newdales Cl. N9 2B **18**
Newdene Av. UB5: N'olt 2B **60**
Newdigate Ho. *E14 6B 70* *(off Norbiton Rd.)*
Newell St. E14 6B **70**
NEW ELTHAM 2G **127**
New End NW3 4A **48**
New End Sq. NW3 4B **48**
New England Ind. Est. IG11: Bark 2G **73**
Newent Cl. SE15 7E **86**
New Era Est. *N1 1E 68* *(off Phillipp St.)*
New Farm Av. BR2: Short 4J **143**
New Farm La. HA6: Nwood 1G **23**
New Fetter La. EC4 6A **68** (7K **161**)
Newfield Cl. TW12: Hamp 1E **132**
Newfield Ri. NW2 3D **46**
New Fieldways EN5: Barn 6C **4**
New Forest La. IG7: Chig 6K **21**
Newgale Gdns. HA8: Edg 1F **27**
New Gdn. Dr. UB7: W Dray 2A **76**
Newgate CR0: Croy 1C **152**
Newgate Cl. TW13: Felt 2C **114**
Newgate St. E4 3B **20** (not continuous)
EC1 6B **68** (7B **162**)
New Globe Wlk. SE1 1C **86** (4C **168**)
New Goulston St. E1 6F **69** (7J **163**)
New Grn. Pl. SE19 6E **122**
***Newham College of Futher Education (Stratford Campus)* 7G 53**
Newham Grn. N22 1A **32**
Newhams Row SE1 2E **86** (7H **169**)
Newham Way E6 5A **72**
E16 5H **71**
Newhaven Cl. UB3: Hayes 4H **77**
Newhaven Cres. TW15: Ashf 5F **113**
Newhaven Gdns. SE9 4B **108**
Newhaven La. E16 4H **71**
Newhaven Rd. SE25 5D **140**
New Heston Rd. TW5: Houn 7D **78**
New Horizons Ct. TW8: Bford 6C **80**
Newhouse Av. RM6: Chad H 3D **38**
Newhouse Cl. KT3: N Mald 7A **136**
Newhouse Wlk. SM4: Mord 7A **138**
Newick Cl. DA5: Bexl 6H **111**
Newick Rd. E5 4H **51**
Newing Grn. BR1: Brom 7B **126**
NEWINGTON 3C **86**
Newington Barrow Way N7 3K **49**
Newington Butts SE11 4B **86**
Newington C'way. SE1 3B **86** (7C **168**)
Newington Ct. Bus. Cen. SE1 7C **168**
Newington Grn. N16 5D **50**
Newington Grn. Mans. N16 5D **50**
Newington Grn. Rd. N1 6D **50**
Newington Ind. Est. *SE17 4C 86* *(off Crampton St.)*
New Inn B'way. EC2 4E **68** (3H **163**)
New Inn Pas. WC2 1H **167**
New Inn Sq. EC2 3H **163**
New Inn St. EC2 4E **68** (3H **163**)
New Inn Yd. EC2 4E **68** (3H **163**)
New Jubilee Ct. IG8: Wfd G 7D **20**
New Jubilee Wharf *E1 1J 87* *(off Wapping Wall)*
New Kelvin Av. TW11: Tedd 6J **115**
New Kent Rd. SE1 3C **86**
New Kings Rd. SW6 2H **101**
New King St. SE8 6C **88**
Newland Ct. EC1 2E **162**
Newland Dr. EN1: Enf 1C **8**
Newland Gdns. W13 2A **80**
Newland Ho. *N8 3J 31* *(off Newland Rd.)*
SE14 6K 87 *(off John Williams Cl.)*
Newland Rd. N8 3J **31**
NEWLANDS
BROCKLEY 5K **105**
EDGWARE 3K **11**
Newlands *NW1 1A 160* *(off Harrington St.)*
Newlands Av. KT7: T Ditt 7J **133**
Newlands Cl. HA0: Wemb 6C **44**
HA8: Edg 3K **11**
UB2: S'hall 5C **78**
Newlands Ct. SE9 6E **108**
Newlands Pk. SE26 6J **123**
Newlands Pl. EN5: Barn 5A **4**
Newlands Quay E1 7J **69**
Newlands Rd. IG8: Wfd G 2C **20**
SW16 2J **139**
Newlands, The SM6: Wall 7G **151**
Newland St. E16 1C **90**
Newlands Way KT9: Chess 5C **146**
Newlands Wood CR0: Croy 7B **154**
Newling Cl. E6 6D **72**
New London St. EC3 2H **169**
New London Theatre* 7F 161** ***(off Drury La.)
New Lydenburg Commercial Est. SE7 3A **90**
New Lydenburg St. SE7 3A **90**
Newlyn *NW1 1G 67* *(off Plender St.)*
Newlyn Cl. UB8: Uxb 5C **58**
Newlyn Gdns. HA2: Harr 7D **24**
Newlyn Ho. HA5: Pinn 1D **24**
Newlyn Rd. DA16: Well 2K **109**
EN5: Barn 4C **4**
N17 1F **33**
NEW MALDEN 4A **136**
Newman Pas. W1 5G **67** (6B **160**)
Newman Rd. BR1: Brom 1J **143**
CR0: Croy 1K **151**
E13 3K **71**
E17 5K **33**
UB3: Hayes 7K **59**
Newman Rd. Ind. Est. CR0: Croy 7K **139**
Newmans Ct. EC3 1F **169**
Newmans La. KT6: Surb 6D **134**
Newmans Row WC2 5K **67** (6H **161**)
Newman St. W1 5G **67** (6B **160**)
Newmans Way EN4: Barn 1F **5**
Newman Yd. W1 6G **67** (7C **160**)
Newmarket Av. UB5: N'olt 5E **42**
Newmarket Grn. SE9 7B **108**
Newmarsh Rd. SE28 1K **91**
Newmill Ho. E3 4E **70**
Newminster Rd. SM4: Mord 6A **138**
New Mt. St. E15 7F **53**
Newnes Path SW15 4D **100**
Newnet Cl. SM5: Cars 1D **150**
Newnham Av. HA4: Ruis 1A **42**
Newnham Cl. CR7: Thor H 2C **140**
UB5: N'olt 6G **43**
Newnham Gdns. UB5: N'olt 6G **43**
Newnham Lodge *DA17: Belv 5G 93* *(off Erith Rd.)*
Newnham M. N22 7E **16**
Newnham Rd. N22 1K **31**
Newnhams Cl. BR1: Brom 3D **144**
Newnham Ter. SE1 3A **86** (1J **173**)
Newnham Way HA3: Harr 5E **26**
New Nth. Pl. EC2 4E **68** (3G **163**)
New Nth. Rd. IG6: Ilf 1G **37**
N1 7C **50** (1F **163**)
New Nth. St. WC1 5K **67** (5G **161**)
Newnton Cl. N4 7D **32** (not continuous)
New Oak Rd. N2 2A **30**
New Orleans Wlk. N19 7H **31**
New Oxford St. WC1 6H **67** (7D **160**)
New Pde. TW15: Ashf 4B **112**
UB7: W Dray 1A **76**
New Pk. Av. N13 3H **17**
New Pk. Cl. UB5: N'olt 6C **42**
New Pk. Est. N18 5D **18**
New Pk. Ho. N13 4E **16**
New Pk. Pde. *SW2 7J 103* *(off New Pk. Rd.)*
New Pk. Rd. SW2 1H **121**
TW15: Ashf 5E **112**
New Pl. CR0: Croy 6C **154**
New Pl. Sq. SE16 3H **87**
New Plaistow Rd. E15 1G **71**
New Pond Pde. HA4: Ruis 3J **41**
Newport Av. E13 4K **71**
E14 7F **71**
Newport Ct. WC2 7H **67** (2D **166**)
Newport Ho. *E3 3A 70* *(off Strahan Rd.)*
Newport Lodge *EN1: Enf 5K 7* *(off Village Rd.)*
Newport Pl. WC2 7H **67** (2D **166**)
Newport Rd. E10 2E **52**
E17 4A **34**
SW13 1C **100**
TW6: Houn 1C **94**
UB4: Hayes 5F **59**
Newport St. SE11 4K **85** (4G **173**)
New Priory Ct. *NW6 7J 47* *(off Mazenod Av.)*
Newquay Cres. HA2: Harr 2C **42**
Newquay Ho. SE11 5A **86** (5J **173**)
Newquay Rd. SE6 2D **124**
New Quebec St. W1 6D **66** (1F **165**)
New Ride SW7 2C **84** (6C **164**)
New River Ct. N5 4C **50**
New River Cres. N13 4G **17**
New River Head EC1 3A **68** (1K **161**)
New River Wlk. N1 6C **50**
New River Way N4 7D **32**
New Rd. CR4: Mitc 1D **150**
DA16: Well 2B **110**
E1 5H **69**
E4 4J **19**
E12 2C **54**
HA1: Harr 4K **43**
IG3: Ilf 2J **55**
KT2: King T 7G **117**
KT8: W Mole 4E **132**
N8 5J **31**
N9 3B **18**
N17 1F **33**
N22 1C **32**
NW7 7B **14** (Bittacy Hill)
RM9: Dag 2G **75**
RM10: Dag 2G **75**
SE2 4D **92**
TW3: Houn 4F **97**
TW8: Bford 6D **80**
TW10: Rich 4C **116**
TW13: Felt 5C **114**
TW14: Felt 6F **95** (North Rd.)
TW14: Felt 1K **113** (Station Est. Rd.)
TW17: Shep 3C **130**
UB3: Hayes 7E **76**
UB8: Uxb 4E **58**
New Rd. Hill BR2: Kes 7C **156**
BR6: Orp 7D **156**
New Rochford St. NW5 5D **48**
New Row WC2 7J **67** (2E **166**)
Newry Rd. TW1: Twick 5A **98**
Newsam Av. N15 5D **32**
Newsholme Dr. N21 5E **6**
NEW SOUTHGATE 5A **16**
New Southgate Crematorium N11 3A **16**
New Southgate Ind. Est. N11 5B **16**
New Spitalfields Mkt. E10 3D **52**
New Spring Gdns. Wlk. SE1 5J **85**
SE11 5J **85** (6F **173**)
New Sq. TW14: Felt 1E **112**
WC2 6A **68** (7J **161**)
New Sq. Pas. WC2 7J **161**
Newstead Cl. N12 6H **15**
Newstead Ct. UB5: N'olt 3C **60**
Newstead Rd. SE12 7H **107**
Newstead Wlk. SM5: Cars 7A **138**
Newstead Way SW19 4F **119**
New St. EC2 5E **68** (6H **163**)
New St. Hill BR1: Brom 5K **125**

304 A-Z London

New St. Sq.—Normanton Rd.

New St. Sq.
EC4 6A 68 (7K 161)
Newton Av. N10 1E 30
W3 2J 81
Newton Cl. E17 6A 34
HA2: Harr 2E 42
Newton Gro. W4 4A 82
Newton Ho. E1 7H 69
(off Cornwall St.)
E17 3D 34
(off Prospect Hill)
NW8 1K 65
(off Abbey Rd.)
SE20 7K 123
Newton Ind. Est.
RM6: Chad H 4D 38
Newton Mans. W14 6G 83
(off Queen's Club Gdns.)
Newton Pl. E14 4C 88
Newton Point E16 6H 71
(off Clarkson Rd.)
Newton Rd. DA16: Well 3A 110
E15 5F 53
HA0: Wemb 7F 45
HA3: Harr 2J 25
N15 5G 33
NW2 4E 46
SW19 7G 119
TW6: Houn 1A 94
TW7: Isle 2K 97
W2 6K 65
Newton St. WC2 6J 67 (7F 161)
Newtons Yd. SW18 5J 101
Newton Ter. BR2: Short 6B 144
Newton Wlk. HA8: Edg 1H 27
Newton Way N18 5H 17
New Twr. Bldgs. E1 1H 87
Newtown St. SW11 1F 103
New Trinity Rd. N2 3B 30
New Turnstile WC1 6G 161
New Union Cl. E14 3E 88
New Union St.
EC2 5D 68 (6E 162)
New Wanstead E11 6H 35
New Way Rd. NW9 4A 28
New Wharf Rd. N1 2J 67
NEWYEARS GREEN 7B 22
Newyears Grn. La.
UB9: Uxb 6A 22
New Zealand Av.
KT12: Walt T 7H 131
New Zealand Way W12 7D 64
Niagara Av. W5 4C 80
Niagra Cl. N1 2C 68
Niagra Ct. SE16 3J 87
(off Canada Est.)
Nibthwaite Rd. HA1: Harr 5J 25
Nicholas Cl. UB6: G'frd 2F 61
Nicholas Ct. W4 6A 82
(off Corney Reach Way)
Nicholas Gdns. W5 2D 80
Nicholas La. EC4 7D 68 (2F 169)
(not continuous)
Nicholas M. W4 6A 82
Nicholas Pas. EC4 1F 169
Nicholas Rd. CR0: Croy 4J 151
E1 4J 69
RM8: Dag 2F 57
Nicholas Stacey Ho. SE7 5K 89
(off Frank Burton Cl.)
Nicholas Way
HA6: Nwood 1E 22
Nicholay Rd. N19 1H 49
Nichol Cl. N14 1C 16
Nicholes Rd. TW3: Houn 4E 96
Nichol La. BR1: Brom 7J 125
Nicholl Ho. N4 1C 50
Nicholls Av. UB8: Uxb 4C 58
Nichollsfield Wlk. N7 5K 49
Nicholls Point E13 1J 71
(off Park Gro.)
Nicholl St. E2 1G 69
Nichols Cl. KT9: Chess 6C 146
N4 1A 50
(off Osborne Rd.)
Nichols Ct. E2 1J 163
(off Cremer St.)
Nichols Grn. W5 5E 62
Nicholson Ct. E17 4A 34
Nicholson Dr.
WD23: Bush 1B 10
Nicholson Ho. SE17 5D 86
Nicholson M. KT1: King T 4E 134
Nicholson Rd. CR0: Croy 1F 153
Nicholson St.
SE1 1B 86 (5A 168)
Nickelby Cl. SE28 6C 74
Nickleby Cl. UB8: Uxb 6D 58
Nickleby Ho. SE16 7K 169
(off Parkers Row)
Nickols Wlk. SW18 4K 101
Nicola Cl. CR2: S Croy 6C 152
HA3: Harr 2H 25
Nicola Ter. DA7: Bex 1E 110
Nicol Cl. TW1: Twick 6B 98
Nicoll Ct. N10 7A 16
NW10 1A 64
Nicoll Pl. NW4 6D 28
Nicoll Rd. NW10 1A 64
Nicolson NW9 1A 28
Nicosia Rd. SW18 7C 102
Niederwald Rd. SE26 4A 124
Nield Rd. UB3: Hayes 2H 77
Nigel Cl. UB5: N'olt 1C 60
Nigel Ct. N3 7E 14
Nigel Fisher Way
KT9: Chess 7C 146
Nigel Ho. EC1 5J 161
(off Portpool La.)
Nigel M. IG1: Ilf 4F 55
Nigel Playfair Av. W6 4D 82
Nigel Rd. E7 5A 54
SE15 3G 105
Nigeria Rd. SE7 7A 90
Nighthawk NW9 1B 28
Nightingale Av. E4 5B 20
HA1: Harr 1B 44
Nightingale Cl. E4 4A 20
HA5: Pinn 5A 24
SM5: Cars 2E 150
W4 6J 81
Nightingale Ct.
BR2: Short 2G 143
E14 2E 88
(off Ovex Cl.)
N4 2K 49
(off Tollington Pk.)
SW6 1K 101
(off Maltings Pl.)
Nightingale Dr.
KT19: Eps 6H 147
Nightingale Gro. SE13 5F 107
Nightingale Hgts. SE18 6F 91
Nightingale Ho. E1 1G 87
(off Thomas More St.)
N1 1E 68
(off Wilmer Gdns.)
SE18 5E 90
(off Connaught M.)
W12 6E 64
(off Du Cane Rd.)
Nightingale La.
BR1: Brom 2A 144
E11 4K 35
N8 4J 31
SW12 7D 102
TW10: Rich 7E 98
Nightingale Lodge W9 5J 65
(off Admiral Wlk.)
Nightingale M. E3 2K 69
E11 5J 35
KT1: King T 3D 134
(off South La.)
SE11 4B 86 (3K 173)
Nightingale Pl. SE18 6E 90
SW10 6A 84 (7A 170)
Nightingale Rd.
BR5: Orp 6G 145
E5 3H 51
KT8: W Mole 5F 133
KT12: Walt T 7A 132
N9 6D 8
N22 7D 16
NW10 2B 64
SM5: Cars 3D 150
TW12: Hamp 5E 114
W7 1K 79
Nightingale Sq. SW12 7E 102
Nightingales, The
TW19: Staines 1B 112
Nightingale Va. SE18 6E 90
Nightingale Wlk. SW4 6F 103
Nightingale Way E6 5C 72
Nile Cl. N16 3F 51
Nile Dr. N9 2D 18
Nile Path SE18 6E 90
Nile Rd. E13 2A 72
Nile St. N1 3C 68 (1D 162)
Nile Ter. SE15 5F 87
Nimegen Way SE22 5E 104
Nimmo Dr. WD23: Bush 1C 10
Nimrod NW9 1A 28
Nimrod Cl. UB5: N'olt 3B 60
Nimrod Ho. E16 5K 71
(off Vanguard Cl.)
Nimrod Pas. N1 6E 50
Nimrod Rd. SW16 6F 121
Nina Mackay Cl. E15 1G 71
Nine Acres Cl. E12 5C 54
NINE ELMS 7G 85
Nine Elms Cl. TW14: Felt 1H 113
Nine Elms La.
SW8 7G 85 (7C 172)
Nineteenth Rd. CR4: Mitc 4J 139
Ninhams Wood BR6: Orp 4E 156
Ninth Av. UB3: Hayes 7J 59
Nirvana Apartments N1 1B 68
(off Islington Grn.)
Nita Ct. SE12 1J 125
Nithdale Rd. SE18 7F 91
Nithsdale Gro. UB10: Uxb 3E 40
Niton Cl. EN5: Barn 6A 4
Niton Rd. TW9: Rich 3G 99
Niton St. SW6 7F 83
Nobel Dr. UB3: Hayes 1F 95
Nobel Ho. SE5 2C 104
Nobel Rd. N18 4D 18
Noble Cnr. TW5: Houn 1E 96
Noble Ct. CR4: Mitc 2B 138
E1 7H 69
Noblefield Hgts. N2 5C 30
Noble M. N16 3D 50
(off Albion Rd.)
Noble St. EC2 6C 68 (7C 162)
Noel NW9 1A 28
Noel Ct. TW4: Houn 3D 96
Noel Coward Ho. SW1 4B 172
(off Vauxhall Bri. Rd.)
Noel Ho. NW6 7B 48
(off Harben Rd.)
NOEL PARK 2B 32
Noel Pk. Rd. N22 2A 32
Noel Rd. E6 4C 72
N1 2B 68
W3 7G 63
Noel Sq. RM8: Dag 4C 56
Noel St. W1 6G 67 (1B 166)
Noel Ter. DA14: Sidc 4B 128
SE23 2J 123
Nolan Way E5 4G 51
Nolton Pl. HA8: Edg 1F 27
Nonsuch Pl. SM3: Sutt 7F 149
Nonsuch Wlk. SM2: Sutt 7F 149
(not continuous)
Nora Gdns. NW4 4F 29
NORBITON 2G 135
Norbiton Av. KT1: King T 1G 135
Norbiton Comn. Rd.
KT1: King T 3H 135
Norbiton Hall KT2: King T 2F 135
Norbiton Rd. E14 6B 70
Norbreck Gdns. NW10 3F 63
Norbreck Pde. NW10 3E 62
Norbroke St. W12 7B 64
Norburn St. W10 5G 65
NORBURY 2K 139
Norbury Av. CR7: Thor H 1A 140
SW16: Thor H 1K 139
TW3: Houn 4H 97
Norbury Cl. SW16 1A 140
Norbury Ct. Rd. SW16 3J 139
Norbury Cres. SW16 1K 139
Norbury Cross SW16 3J 139
Norbury Gdns.
RM6: Chad H 5D 38
Norbury Gro. NW7 3F 13
Norbury Hill SW16 7A 122
Norbury Ri. SW16 3J 139
Norbury Rd. CR7: Thor H 2C 140
E4 5H 19
Norbury Trad. Est. SW16 2K 139
Norcombe Gdns.
HA3: Harr 6C 26
Norcombe Ho. N19 3H 49
(off Wedmore St.)
Norcott Cl. UB4: Hayes 4A 60
Norcott Rd. N16 2G 51
Norcroft Gdns. SE22 7G 105
Norcutt Rd. TW2: Twick 1J 115
Nordenfeldt Rd. DA8: Erith 5K 93
Norden Ho. E2 3H 69
(off Pott St.)
Norfield Rd. DA2: Dart 4J 129
Norfolk Av. N13 6G 17
N15 6F 33
Norfolk Cl. EN4: Barn 4K 5
N2 3C 30
N13 6G 17
TW1: Twick 6B 98
Norfolk Ct. EN5: Barn 4B 4
Norfolk Cres. DA15: Sidc 7J 109
W2 6C 66 (7C 158)
Norfolk Gdns. DA7: Bex 1F 111
TW4: Houn 5D 96
Norfolk Ho. SE3 6G 89
(off Restell Cl.)
SE8 1C 106
SE20 1J 141
SW1 3D 172
(off Page St.)
Norfolk Ho. Rd. SW16 3H 121
Norfolk Mans. SW11 1D 102
(off Prince of Wales Dr.)
Norfolk M. W10 5H 65
(off Blagrove Rd.)
Norfolk Pl. DA16: Well 2A 110
W2 6B 66 (7B 158)
(not continuous)
Norfolk Rd. CR7: Thor H 3C 140
E6 1D 72
E17 2K 33
EN3: Enf 6C 8
EN5: Barn 3D 4
HA1: Harr 5F 25
IG3: Ilf 1J 55
IG11: Bark 7J 55
NW8 1B 66
NW10 7A 46
RM7: Rom 6J 39
RM10: Dag 5H 57
SW19 7C 120
TW13: Felt 1A 114
UB8: Uxb 6A 40
Norfolk Row SE1 4K 85 (3G 173)
(not continuous)
Norfolk Sq. W2 6B 66 (1B 164)
Norfolk Sq. M. W2 1B 164
Norfolk St. E7 5J 53
Norfolk Ter. W6 5G 83
Norgrove St. SW12 7E 102
Norhyrst Av. SE25 3F 141
Norland Ho. W11 1F 83
(off Queensdale Cres.)
Norland Pl. W11 1G 83
Norland Rd. W11 1F 83
(off Queensdale Cres.)
Norlands Cres. BR7: Chst 1F 145
Norland Sq. W11 1G 83
Norland Sq. Mans. W11 1G 83
(off Norland Sq.)
Norley Va. SW15 1C 118
Norlington Rd. E10 1E 52
E11 1E 52
Norman Av. N22 1B 32
TW1: Twick 7C 98
TW13: Felt 2C 114
UB1: S'hall 7C 60
Normanby Cl. SW15 5H 101
Normanby Rd. NW10 4B 46
Norman Cl. N22 1C 32
RM5: Col R 1H 39
Norman Ct. BR1: Brom 1J 143
(off Tweedy Rd.)
IG2: Ilf 7H 37
N4 7A 32
NW10 7C 46
W13 1B 80
(off Kirkfield Cl.)
Norman Cres. HA5: Pinn 1A 24
TW5: Houn 7B 78
Normand Gdns. W14 6G 83
(off Greyhound Rd.)
Normand M. W14 6G 83
Normand Rd. W14 6H 83
Normandy Av. EN5: Barn 5C 4
Normandy Cl. SE26 3A 124
Normandy Dr. UB3: Hayes 6E 58
Normandy Ho. E14 2E 88
(off Plevna St.)
Normandy Rd. SW9 1A 104
Normandy Ter. E16 6K 71
Normandy Way
DA8: Erith 1K 111
Norman Gro. E3 2A 70
Norman Hay Ind. Est.
UB7: W Dray 7B 76
Norman Ho. SW8 7J 85
(off Wyvil Rd.)
TW13: Felt 2D 114
(off Watermill Way)
Normanhurst TW15: Ashf 5C 112
Normanhurst Av.
DA7: Bex 1D 110
DA16: Bex, Well 1D 110
Normanhurst Dr.
TW1: Twick 5A 98
Normanhurst Rd. SW2 2K 121
Norman Pde. DA14: Sidc 2D 128
Norman Rd. CR7: Thor H 5B 140
DA17: Belv 3H 93
(not continuous)
E6 4D 72
E11 2F 53
IG1: Ilf 5F 55
N15 5F 33
SE10 7D 88
SM1: Sutt 5J 149
SW19 7A 120
TW15: Ashf 6F 113
Normans Cl. NW10 6K 45
UB8: Uxb 4B 58
Normansfield Av.
TW11: Tedd 7C 116
Normanshire Dr. E4 4H 19
Normans Mead NW10 6K 45
Norman St. EC1 3C 68 (2D 162)
Normanton Av. SW19 2J 119
Normanton Pk. E4 2B 20
Normanton Rd.
CR2: S Croy 5E 152

Old Bexley—Onslow Pde.

OLD BEXLEY 7H 111
Old Bexley Bus. Pk. DA5: Bexl 7H 111
Old Bexley La. DA5: Bexl, Dart .... 2K 129 (not continuous)
Old Billingsgate Mkt. EC3 .... 3F 169 (off Lwr. Thames St.)
Old Billingsgate Wlk. EC3 .... 7E 68 (3G 169)
Old Bond St. W1 .... 7G 67 (3A 166)
Oldborough Rd. HA0: Wemb 3C 44
OLD BRENTFORD 7D 80
Old Brewers Yd. WC2 .... 6J 67 (1E 166)
Old Brewery M. NW3 .... 4B 48
Old Bri. Cl. UB5: N'olt 2E 60
Old Bri. St. KT1: King T 2D 134
Old Broad St. EC2 .... 6D 68 (7F 163)
Old Bromley Rd. BR1: Brom 5F 125
Old Brompton Rd. SW5 .... 5J 83
SW7 .... 5A 84 (4A 170)
Old Bldgs. WC2 .... 7J 161
Old Burlington St. W1 .... 7G 67 (2A 166)
Oldbury Pl. W1 .... 5E 66 (5H 159)
Oldbury Rd. EN1: Enf 2B 8
Old Canal M. SE15 .... 5F 87 (off Trafalgar Av.)
Old Castle St. E1 .... 6F 69 (7J 163)
Old Cavendish St. W1 .... 6F 67 (7J 159)
Old Change Ct. EC4 .... 1C 168
Old Chapel Pl. SW9 .... 2A 104
Old Charlton Rd. TW17: Shep 5E 130
Old Chelsea M. SW3 .... 6C 84 (7C 170)
Old Chiswick Yd. W4 .... 6A 82 (off Pumping Sta. Rd.)
Old Church Ct. N11 .... 5A 16
Oldchurch Gdns. RM7: Rush G 7K 39
Old Church La. HA7: Stan 5G 11
NW9 .... 2K 45
UB6: G'frd 3A 62
Oldchurch Ri. RM7: Rush G 7K 39
Old Church Rd. E1 .... 6K 69
E4 .... 4H 19
Oldchurch Rd. RM7: Rush G 7K 39
Old Church St. SW3 .... 5B 84 (6B 170)
Old Claygate La. KT10: Esh 6A 146
Old Clem Sq. SE18 .... 6E 90
Old Coal Yd. SE28 .... 4H 91
Old Compton St. W1 .... 7H 67 (2C 166)
Old Cote Dr. TW5: Houn 6E 78
Old Ct. Ho. W8 .... 2K 83 (off Old Ct. Pl.)
Old Ct. Pl. W8 .... 2K 83
Old Courtyard, The BR1: Brom 1K 143
Old Curiosity Shop .... 1H 167 (off Portsmouth St.)
Old Dairy M. NW5 .... 6F 49
SW12 .... 1E 120
Old Deer Pk. Gdns. TW9: Rich 3E 98
Old Devonshire Rd. SW12 .... 7F 103
Old Dock Cl. TW9: Rich 6G 81
Old Dover Rd. SE3 .... 7J 89
Oldegate Ho. E6 .... 7B 54
Old Farm Av. DA15: Sidc 1H 127
N14 .... 7B 6
Old Farm Cl. SW17 .... 2C 120
TW4: Houn 4D 96
Old Farm Pas. TW12: Hamp 1G 133
Old Farm Rd. N2 .... 1B 30
TW12: Hamp .... 6D 114 (not continuous)
UB7: W Dray 2A 76
Old Farm Rd. E. DA15: Sidc 2A 128
Old Farm Rd. W. DA15: Sidc 2K 127
Oldfield Cl. BR1: Brom 4D 144
HA7: Stan 5F 11
UB6: G'frd 5J 43
Oldfield Ct. KT5: Surb .... 4F 135 (off Cranes Pk. Cres.)
Oldfield Farm Gdns. UB6: G'frd 1H 61
Oldfield Gro. SE16 .... 4K 87
Oldfield Ho. W4 .... 5A 82 (off Devonshire Rd.)
Oldfield La. Nth. UB6: G'frd 2H 61
Oldfield La. Sth. UB6: G'frd 4G 61
Oldfield M. N6 .... 7G 31
Oldfield Rd. BR1: Brom 4D 144
DA7: Bex 2E 110
N16 .... 3E 50
NW10 .... 7B 46
SW19 .... 6G 119
TW12: Hamp 1D 132
W3 .... 2B 82
Oldfields Cir. UB5: N'olt 6G 43
Oldfields Rd. SM1: Sutt 3H 149
Oldfields Trad. Est. SM1: Sutt 3J 149
Old Fire Sta., The SE18 .... 7F 91
Old Fish St. Hill EC4 .... 2C 168 (off Victoria St.)
Old Fleet La. EC4 .... 6B 68 (7A 162)
Old Fold Cl. EN5: Barn 1C 4
Old Fold La. EN5: Barn 1C 4
Old Fold Vw. EN5: Barn 3A 4
OLD FORD 1C 70
Old Ford Rd. E2 .... 3J 69
Old Forge Cl. HA7: Stan 4F 11
Old Forge Cres. TW17: Shep 6D 130
Old Forge M. W12 .... 2D 82
Old Forge Rd. EN1: Enf 1A 8
Old Forge Way DA14: Sidc 4B 128
Old Gloucester St. WC1 .... 5J 67 (5F 161)
Old Hall Cl. HA5: Pinn 1C 24
Old Hall Dr. HA5: Pinn 1C 24
Oldham Ter. W3 .... 1J 81 (not continuous)
Old Hatch Mnr. HA4: Ruis 7H 23
Old Hill BR7: Chst 1E 144
Oldhill St. N16 .... 1G 51
Old Homesdale Rd. BR2: Short 4A 144
Old Hospital Cl. SW17 .... 1D 120
Old Ho. Cl. SW19 .... 5G 119
Old Ho. Gdns. TW1: Twick 6C 98
Old Howletts La. HA4: Ruis 6F 23
OLD ISLEWORTH 3B 98
Old Jamaica Rd. SE16 .... 3G 87 (7K 169)
Old James St. SE15 .... 3H 105
Old Jewry EC2 .... 6D 68 (1E 168)
Old Kenton La. NW9 .... 5H 27
Old Kent Rd. SE1 .... 4E 86
SE15 .... 4E 86
Old Kingston Rd. KT4: Wor Pk 2J 147
Old Laundry, The BR7: Chst 1G 145
Old Lodge Pl. TW1: Twick 6B 98
Old Lodge Way HA7: Stan 5F 11
Old London Rd. DA14: Sidc, Swan 7G 129
KT2: King T 2E 134
Old Maidstone Rd. DA14: Sidc 7F 129
OLD MALDEN 1A 148
Old Malden La. KT4: Wor Pk 2K 147
Old Mnr. Ct. NW8 .... 2A 66
Old Mnr. Dr. TW7: Isle 6G 97
Old Mnr. Ho. M. TW17: Shep 3C 130
Old Mnr. Rd. UB2: S'hall 4B 78
Old Mnr. Way BR7: Chst 5D 126
DA7: Bex 2K 111
Old Mnr. Yd. SW5 .... 4K 83
Old Market Ct. SM1: Sutt 4K 149
Old Mkt. Sq. E2 .... 3F 69 (1J 163)
Old Marylebone Rd. NW1 .... 5C 66 (6D 158)
Oldmead Ho. RM10: Dag 6H 57
Old M. HA1: Harr 5J 25
Old Mill Cl. E18 .... 3A 36
Old Mill Pl. RM7: Rom 6K 39
Old Mill Rd. SE18 .... 6H 91
Old Mitre Ct. EC4 .... 6A 68 (1K 167)
Old Montague St. E1 .... 5G 69 (6K 163)
Old Nichol St. E2 .... 4F 69 (3J 163)
Old Nth. St. WC1 .... 5G 161
Old Nursery Pl. TW15: Ashf 5D 112
Old Oak Cl. KT9: Chess 4F 147
OLD OAK COMMON 4A 64
Old Oak Comn. La. NW10 .... 5A 64
W3 .... 5A 64
Old Oak La. NW10 .... 3A 64
Old Oak Rd. W3 .... 7B 64
Old Orchard TW16: Sun T 2A 132
Old Orchard Cl. EN4: Barn 1G 5
UB8: Uxb 6C 58
Old Orchard, The NW3 .... 4D 48
Old Pal. La. TW9: Rich 5C 98
Old Pal. Rd. CR0: Croy 3B 152
Old Pal. Ter. TW9: Rich 5D 98
Old Pal. Yd. SW1 .... 3J 85 (1E 172)
TW9: Rich 5C 98
Old Paradise St. SE1 .... 4K 85 (3G 173)
Old Pk. Av. EN2: Enf 5H 7
SW12 .... 6E 102
Old Pk. Gro. EN2: Enf 4H 7
Old Pk. La. W1 .... 1F 85 (5J 165)
Old Pk. M. TW5: Houn 7D 78
Old Pk. Ridings N21 .... 6G 7
Old Pk. Rd. EN2: Enf 3G 7
N13 .... 4E 16
SE2 .... 5A 92
Old Pk. Rd. Sth. EN2: Enf 4G 7
Old Pk. Vw. EN2: Enf 3F 7
Old Perry St. BR7: Chst 6J 127
Old Post Office La. SE3 .... 3K 107
Old Pound Cl. TW7: Isle 2A 98
Old Pye St. SW1 .... 3H 85 (1C 172)
Old Pye St. Est. SW1 .... 2C 172 (off Old Pye St.)
Old Quebec St. W1 .... 6D 66 (1F 165)
Old Queen St. SW1 .... 2H 85 (7D 166)
Old Rectory Gdns. HA8: Edg 6B 12
Old Redding HA3: Harr 5A 10
Old Red Lion Theatre .... 1K 161 (off St John St.)
Oldridge Rd. SW12 .... 7E 102
Old River Works N17 .... 6H 17
Old Rd. DA1: Cray 5K 111
EN3: Enf 1D 8
SE13 .... 4G 107
Old Royal Free Pl. N1 .... 1A 68
Old Royal Free Sq. N1 .... 1A 68
Old Royal Naval College 5F 89
Old Ruislip Rd. UB5: N'olt 2A 60
Old School Cl. BR3: Beck 2K 141
SE10 .... 3G 89
SW19 .... 2J 137
Old School Ct. N17 .... 3F 33
Old School Cres. E7 .... 6J 53
Old School Pl. CR0: Croy 4A 152
Old School Rd. UB8: Uxb 4B 58
Old Schools La. KT17: Eps 7B 148
Old School Sq. E14 .... 6C 70 (off Pelling St.)
KT7: T Ditt 6K 133
Old Seacoal La. EC4 .... 6B 68 (1A 168)
Old Sth. Cl. HA5: Pinn 1B 24
Old Sth. Lambeth Rd. SW8 .... 7J 85
Old Spitalfields Market 5F 69 (5J 163)
Old Sq. WC2 .... 6K 67 (7J 161)
Old Stable M. N5 .... 3C 50
Old Sta. Gdns. TW11: Tedd .... 6A 116 (off Victoria Rd.)
Old Sta. Rd. UB3: Hayes 3H 77
Oldstead Rd. BR1: Brom 4E 124
Old Stockley Rd. UB7: W Dray 2D 76
OLD STREET 4D 68 (3F 163)
Old St. E13 .... 2K 71
EC1 .... 4C 68 (3C 162)
Old Sungate Cotts. RM5: Col R 1F 39
Old Sun Wharf E14 .... 7A 70 (off Narrow St.)
Old Swan Wharf SW11 .... 1B 102
Old Swan Yd. SM5: Cars 4D 150
Old Thackeray School SW8 .... 2F 103
Old Theatre Ct. SE1 .... 4D 168 (off Porter St.)
Old Town CR0: Croy 3B 152
SW4 .... 3G 103
Old Tramyard SE18 .... 4J 91
Old Vic Theatre, The .... 6K 167 (off Cut, The)
Old Woolwich Rd. SE10 .... 6F 89
Old York Rd. SW18 .... 5K 101
O'Leary Sq. E1 .... 5J 69
Olga St. E3 .... 2A 70
Olinda Rd. N16 .... 6F 33
Oliphant St. W10 .... 3F 65
Oliver Av. SE25 .... 3F 141
Oliver Bus. Pk. NW10 .... 2J 63
Oliver Cl. W4 .... 6H 81
Oliver Ct. SE18 .... 4G 91
Oliver Gdns. E6 .... 5C 72
Oliver Goldsmith Est. SE15 .... 1G 105
Oliver Gro. SE25 .... 4F 141
Oliver Ho. SE16 .... 2G 87 (off George Row)
SW8 .... 7J 85 (off Wyvil Rd.)
Oliver M. SE15 .... 2G 105
Olive Rd. E13 .... 3A 72
NW2 .... 4E 46
SW19 .... 7A 120
W5 .... 3D 80
Oliver Rd. E10 .... 2D 52
E17 .... 5E 34
KT3: N Mald 2J 135
NW10 .... 2J 63
SM1: Sutt 4B 150
Olivers Wharf E1 .... 1H 87 (off Wapping High St.)
Olivers Yd. EC1 .... 4D 68 (3F 163)
Olive St. RM7: Rom 5K 39
Olive Tree Ho. SE15 .... 6J 87 (off Sharratt St.)
Olivette St. SW15 .... 3F 101
Olive Waite Ho. NW6 .... 7J 47
Olivia Ct. EN2: Enf .... 1H 7 (off Chase Side)
Olivier Theatre .... 1A 86 (4J 167) (in Royal National Theatre)
Ollerton Grn. E3 .... 1B 70
Ollerton Rd. N11 .... 5C 16
Olley Cl. SM6: Wall 7J 151
Ollgar Cl. W12 .... 1B 82
Olliffe St. E14 .... 3E 88
Olmar St. SE1 .... 6G 87
Olney Ho. NW8 .... 3D 158 (off Tresham Cres.)
Olney Rd. SE17 .... 6B 86 (not continuous)
Olron Cres. DA6: Bex 5D 110
Olven Rd. SE18 .... 6G 91
Olveston Wlk. SM5: Cars 6B 138
Olwen M. HA5: Pinn 2B 24
Olyffe Av. DA16: Well 1A 110
Olympia 3G 83
Olympia Ind. Est. N22 .... 3K 31
Olympia M. W2 .... 7K 65
Olympian Ct. E14 .... 4C 88 (off Homer Dr.)
Olympia Way W14 .... 3G 83
Olympic Way HA9: Wemb .... 3G 45 (not continuous)
UB6: G'frd 1G 61
Olympus Sq. E5 .... 3G 51
O'Mahoney Ct. SW17 .... 3A 120
Oman Av. NW2 .... 4E 46
O'Meara St. SE1 .... 1C 86 (5D 168)
Omega Cl. E14 .... 3D 88
Omega Pl. N1 .... 1F 161
Omega St. SE14 .... 1C 106
Ommaney Rd. SE14 .... 1K 105
Omnibus Way E17 .... 2C 34
Ondine Rd. SE15 .... 4F 105
Onega Ga. SE16 .... 3A 88
O'Neill Ho. NW8 .... 1B 158 (off Cochrane St.)
O'Neill Path SE18 .... 6E 90
One Owen St. EC1 .... 1A 162 (off Goswell St.)
One Tree Cl. SE23 .... 6J 105
Ongar Cl. RM6: Chad H 5C 38
Ongar Rd. SW6 .... 6J 83
Onra Rd. E17 .... 7C 34
Onslow Av. TW10: Rich 5E 98
Onslow Cl. E4 .... 2K 19
KT7: T Ditt 7J 133
W10 .... 3H 65
Onslow Cres. BR7: Chst 1F 145
Onslow Dr. DA14: Sidc 2D 128
Onslow Gdns. E18 .... 3K 35
KT7: T Ditt 7J 133
N10 .... 5F 31
N21 .... 5F 7
SM6: Wall 6G 151
SW7 .... 4B 84 (4A 170)
Onslow Ho. KT2: King T .... 1F 135 (off Acre Rd.)
Onslow M. E. SW7 .... 4B 84 (4A 170)
Onslow M. W. SW7 .... 4B 84 (4A 170)
Onslow Pde. N14 .... 1A 16

A-Z London 309

Onslow Rd.—Osmond Cl.

Onslow Rd. CR0: Croy ... 7K 139
KT3: N Mald ... 4C 136
TW10: Rich ... 5E 98
Onslow Sq.
SW7 ... 4B 84 (4B 170)
Onslow St. EC1 ... 4A 68 (4K 161)
Onslow Way KT7: T Ditt ... 7J 133
Ontario St. SE1 ... 3B 86
Ontario Way E14 ... 7C 70
(not continuous)
Opal Cl. E16 ... 6B 72
Opal M. IG1: Ilf ... 2F 55
NW6 ... 1H 65
Opal St. SE11 ... 5B 86 (5K 173)
Openshaw Rd. SE2 ... 4B 92
Open University, The
(Parsifal College) ... 4J 47
Openview SW18 ... 1A 120
Opera Ct. *N19 ... 3H 49*
(off Wedmore St.)
Operating Theatre Mus. ... 5F 169
Ophelia Gdns. NW2 ... 3G 47
Ophelia Ho. *W6 ... 5F 83*
(off Fulham Pal. Rd.)
Ophir Ter. SE15 ... 1G 105
Opie Ho. *NW8 ... 2C 66*
(off Townshend Est.)
Opossum Way
TW4: Houn ... 3A 96
Oppenheim Rd. SE13 ... 2E 106
Oppidans Rd. NW3 ... 7D 48
Orange Ct. La. BR6: Orp ... 7E 156
Orange Gro. E11 ... 3G 53
(not continuous)
Orange Hill Rd. HA8: Edg ... 7D 12
Orange Pl. SE16 ... 3J 87
Orangery La. SE9 ... 5D 108
Orangery, The ... 1K 83
(in Kensington Gardens)
Orangery, The
TW10: Rich ... 2C 116
Orange St. SW1 ... 7H 67 (3D 166)
Orange Tree Ct. *SE5 ... 7E 86*
(off Havil St.)
Orange Yd. W1 ... 1D 166
Oransay Rd. N1 ... 6C 50
Oratory La. SW3 ... 5B 170
Orbain Rd. SW6 ... 7G 83
Orbel St. SW11 ... 1C 102
Orbital Cen., The
IG8: Wfd G ... 2B 36
Orb St. SE17 ... 4D 86
Orchard Av. CR0: Croy ... 2A 154
CR4: Mitc ... 1E 150
DA17: Belv ... 6E 92
KT3: N Mald ... 2A 136
KT7: T Ditt ... 1A 146
N3 ... 3J 29
N14 ... 6B 6
N20 ... 2G 15
TW5: Houn ... 7C 78
TW14: Felt ... 5F 95
TW15: Ashf ... 6E 112
UB1: S'hall ... 1D 78
Orchard Bus. Cen. SE26 ... 5B 124
Orchard Cl. DA7: Bex ... 1E 110
E4 ... 4H 19
E11 ... 4K 35
HA0: Wemb ... 1E 62
HA4: Ruis ... 7E 22
HA8: Edg ... 6K 11
KT7: T Ditt ... 1B 146
KT12: Walt T ... 7K 131
KT19: Eps ... 6H 147
N1 ... 7C 50
NW2 ... 3C 46
SE23 ... 6J 105
SW20 ... 4E 136
TW15: Ashf ... 6E 112
UB5: N'olt ... 6G 43
W10 ... 5H 65
WD23: Bush ... 1C 10
Orchard Cotts.
KT2: King T ... 1F 135
UB3: Hayes ... 2G 77
Orchard Ct. E10 ... 1D 52
EN5: Barn ... 3E 4
HA8: Edg ... 5A 12
KT4: Wor Pk ... 1C 148
N14 ... 6B 6
SM6: Wall ... 5F 151
TW2: Twick ... 2H 115
TW7: Isle ... 7H 79
Orchard Cres. EN1: Enf ... 1A 8
HA8: Edg ... 5D 12
Orchard Dr. HA8: Edg ... 5A 12
SE3 ... 2F 107
TW17: Shep ... 3G 131
Orchard Gdns.
KT9: Chess ... 4E 146
SM1: Sutt ... 5J 149
Orchard Ga. KT10: Esh ... 7H 133
NW9 ... 4A 28
UB6: G'frd ... 6B 44
Orchard Gro.
CR0: Croy ... 7A 142
HA3: Harr ... 5F 27
HA8: Edg ... 1G 27
SE20 ... 7G 123
Orchard Hill DA1: Cray ... 5K 111
SE13 ... 2D 106
SM5: Cars ... 5D 150
Orchard Ho. *SE5 ... 1C 104*
(off County Gro.)
SE16 ... 3J 87
SW6 ... 7H 83
(off Varna Rd.)
W1 ... 7G 159
(off Fitzhardinge St.)
W12 ... 1C 82
Orchard La. IG8: Wfd G ... 4F 21
KT8: E Mos ... 6H 133
SW20 ... 1D 136
Orchardleigh Av. EN3: Enf ... 2D 8
Orchard Mead Ho. NW2 ... 2J 47
Orchardmede N21 ... 6J 7
Orchard M. N1 ... 7D 50
Orchard Pl. BR2: Kes ... 7A 156
E5 ... 5H 51
E14 ... 7G 71
(not continuous)
N17 ... 7A 18
Orchard Ri. CR0: Croy ... 1A 154
HA5: Pinn ... 3H 23
KT2: King T ... 1J 135
TW10: Rich ... 4H 99
Orchard Ri. E.
DA15: Sidc ... 5J 109
Orchard Ri. W.
DA15: Sidc ... 5J 109
Orchard Rd. BR1: Brom ... 1A 144
CR4: Mitc ... 1E 150
DA14: Sidc ... 4J 127
DA16: Well ... 3B 110
DA17: Belv ... 4G 93
EN3: Enf ... 5D 8
EN5: Barn ... 4C 4
KT1: King T ... 2E 134
KT9: Chess ... 4E 146
N6 ... 7F 31
RM7: Mawney ... 1H 39
RM10: Dag ... 1G 75
SE3 ... 2G 107
SE18 ... 4H 91
SM1: Sutt ... 5J 149
TW1: Twick ... 5A 98
TW4: Houn ... 5D 96
TW8: Bford ... 6C 80
TW9: Rich ... 3G 99
TW12: Hamp ... 7D 114
TW13: Felt ... 1J 113
TW16: Sun T ... 7K 113
UB3: Hayes ... 7J 59
Orchardson Ho. NW8 ... 4A 158
Orchardson St.
NW8 ... 4B 66 (4A 158)
Orchard Sq. W14 ... 5H 83
Orchard St. E17 ... 4A 34
W1 ... 6E 66 (1G 165)
Orchard Studios *W6 ... 4F 83*
(off Brook Grn.)
Orchard Ter. EN1: Enf ... 6B 8
Orchard, The KT17: Eps ... 7B 148
(Meadow Wlk.)
N14 ... 5A 6
N21 ... 6J 7
NW11 ... 5J 29
SE3 ... 2F 107
TW3: Houn ... 2G 97
W4 ... 4K 81
W5 ... 5D 62
(off Montpelier Rd.)
Orchard Vs. DA14: Sidc ... 6C 128
Orchard Way BR3: Beck ... 7A 142
CR0: Croy ... 1A 154
EN1: Enf ... 3K 7
SM1: Sutt ... 4B 150
TW15: Ashf ... 2B 112
Orchard Waye UB8: Uxb ... 2A 58
Orchard Wharf *E14 ... 7G 71*
(off Orchard Pl.)
Orchid Cl. E6 ... 5C 72
KT9: Chess ... 7C 146
UB1: S'hall ... 7C 60
Orchid Ct. HA9: Wemb ... 2E 44
Orchid Grange N14 ... 7B 6
Orchid Rd. N14 ... 7B 6
Orchid St. W12 ... 7C 64
Orde NW9 ... 1B 28
Orde Hall St.
WC1 ... 4K 67 (4G 161)
Ordell Rd. E3 ... 2B 70
Ordnance Cl. TW13: Felt ... 2J 113
Ordnance Cres. SE10 ... 2F 89
Ordnance Hill NW8 ... 1B 66
Ordnance M. NW8 ... 2B 66
Ordnance Rd. E16 ... 5H 71
SE18 ... 6E 90
Oregano Cl. UB7: W Dray ... 6A 58
Oregano Dr. E14 ... 6F 71
Oregon Av. E12 ... 4D 54
Oregon Cl. KT3: N Mald ... 4J 135
Orestes M. NW6 ... 5J 47
Orford Ct. HA7: Stan ... 6H 11
SE27 ... 2B 122
Orford Gdns. TW1: Twick ... 2K 115
Orford Rd. E17 ... 5C 34
E18 ... 3K 35
SE6 ... 3D 124
ORGAN CROSSROADS ... 7C 148
Organ La. E4 ... 2K 19
(not continuous)
Oriana Ho. *E14 ... 7B 70*
(off Victory Pl.)
Oriel Cl. CR4: Mitc ... 4H 139
Oriel Ct. CR0: Croy ... 1D 152
NW3 ... 4A 48
Oriel Dr. SW13 ... 6E 82
Oriel Gdns. IG5: Ilf ... 3D 36
Oriel Pl. *NW3 ... 4A 48*
(off Heath St.)
Oriel Rd. E9 ... 6K 51
Oriel Way UB5: N'olt ... 7F 43
Oriental Rd. E16 ... 1B 90
Oriental St. *E14 ... 7C 70*
(off Pennyfields)
Orient Ind. Pk. E10 ... 2C 52
Orient St. SE11 ... 4B 86
Orient Way E5 ... 3K 51
E10 ... 1A 52
Orient Wharf *E1 ... 1J 87*
(off Wapping High St.)
Oriole Way SE28 ... 7B 74
Orion Bus. Cen. SE14 ... 5K 87
Orion Cen., The
CR0: Croy ... 2J 151
Orion Ho. *E1 ... 4H 69*
(off Coventry Rd.)
Orion Rd. N11 ... 7K 15
Orissa Rd. SE18 ... 5J 91
Orkney Ho. *N1 ... 1K 67*
(off Bemerton Est.)
Orkney St. SW11 ... 2E 102
Orlando Rd. SW4 ... 3G 103
Orleans Ct. TW1: Twick ... 7B 98
Orleans House Gallery ... 1B 116
Orleans Rd. SE19 ... 6D 122
TW1: Twick ... 7B 98
Orleston M. N7 ... 6A 50
Orleston Rd. N7 ... 6A 50
Orley Ct. HA1: Harr ... 4K 43
Orley Farm Rd. HA1: Harr ... 3J 43
Orlop St. SE10 ... 5G 89
Ormanton Rd. SE26 ... 4G 123
Orme Ct. W2 ... 7K 65
Orme Ct. M. *W2 ... 7K 65*
(off Orme La.)
Orme Ho. E8 ... 1F 69
Orme La. W2 ... 7K 65
Ormeley Rd. SW12 ... 1F 121
Orme Rd. KT1: King T ... 2H 135
SM1: Sutt ... 6K 149
Ormerod Gdns.
CR4: Mitc ... 2E 138
Ormesby Cl. SE28 ... 7D 74
Ormesby Way HA3: Harr ... 6F 27
Orme Sq. W2 ... 7K 65
Ormiston Gro. W12 ... 1D 82
Ormiston Rd. SE10 ... 5J 89
Ormond Av. TW10: Rich ... 5D 98
TW12: Hamp ... 1F 133
Ormond Cl. WC1 ... 5J 67 (5F 161)
Ormond Cres.
TW12: Hamp ... 1F 133
Ormond Dr. TW12: Hamp ... 7F 115
Ormonde Ct. SW15 ... 4E 100
Ormonde Ga.
SW3 ... 5D 84 (6F 171)
Ormonde Pl. SW1 ... 4E 84 (4G 171)
Ormonde Ri. IG9: Buck H ... 1F 21
Ormonde Rd. SW14 ... 3J 99
Ormonde Ter. NW8 ... 1D 66
Ormond M. WC1 ... 4J 67 (4F 161)
Ormond Rd. N19 ... 1J 49
TW10: Rich ... 5D 98
Ormond Yd.
SW1 ... 1G 85 (4B 166)
Ormsby SM2: Sutt ... 7K 149
Ormsby Gdns. UB6: G'frd ... 2G 61
Ormsby Lodge W4 ... 3A 82
Ormsby Pl. N16 ... 3F 51
Ormsby St. E2 ... 2F 69
Ormside St. SE15 ... 6J 87
Ornan Rd. NW3 ... 5C 48
Orpen Wlk. N16 ... 3E 50
Orpheus St. SE5 ... 1D 104
ORPINGTON ... 7K 145
Orpington Gdns. N18 ... 3K 17
Orpington Mans. N21 ... 1G 17
Orpington Rd. BR7: Chst ... 3J 145
N21 ... 1G 17
Orpwood Cl.
TW12: Hamp ... 6D 114
Orsett M. W2 ... 6K 65
(not continuous)
Orsett St. SE11 ... 5K 85 (5H 173)
Orsett Ter. IG8: Wfd G ... 7F 21
W2 ... 6K 65
Orsman Rd. N1 ... 1E 68
Orton St. E1 ... 1G 87
Orville Rd. SW11 ... 2B 102
Orwell Cl. RM13: Rain ... 5K 75
UB3: Hayes ... 7G 59
Orwell Ct. *E8 ... 1G 69*
(off Pownall Rd.)
N5 ... 4C 50
Orwell Rd. E13 ... 2A 72
Osbaldeston Rd. N16 ... 2G 51
Osberton Rd. SE12 ... 5J 107
Osbert St. SW1 ... 4H 85 (4C 172)
Osborn Cl. E8 ... 1G 69
Osborne Av.
TW19: Staines ... 1B 112
Osborne Cl. BR3: Beck ... 4A 142
EN4: Barn ... 3J 5
TW13: Felt ... 5B 114
Osborne Ct. E10 ... 7D 34
W5 ... 5E 62
Osborne Gdns.
CR7: Thor H ... 2C 140
Osborne Gro. E17 ... 4B 34
N4 ... 1A 50
Osborne Ho. *E16 ... 7J 71*
(off Wesley Av.)
Osborne M. E17 ... 4B 34
Osborne Pl. SM1: Sutt ... 5B 150
Osborne Rd. CR7: Thor H ... 2C 140
DA17: Belv ... 5F 93
E7 ... 5K 53
E9 ... 6B 52
E10 ... 2D 52
EN3: Enf ... 2F 9
IG9: Buck H ... 1E 20
KT2: King T ... 7E 116
KT12: Walt T ... 7J 131
N4 ... 1A 50
N13 ... 3F 17
NW2 ... 6D 46
RM9: Dag ... 5F 57
TW3: Houn ... 3D 96
UB1: S'hall ... 6G 61
W3 ... 3H 81
Osborne Sq. RM9: Dag ... 4F 57
Osborne Ter. *SW17 ... 5D 120*
(off Church La.)
Osborne Way *KT9: Chess ... 5F 147*
(off Bridge Rd.)
Osborn Gdns. NW7 ... 7A 14
Osborn La. SE23 ... 7A 106
Osborn St. E1 ... 5F 69 (6K 163)
Osborn Ter. SE3 ... 4H 107
Osbourne Ct. HA2: Harr ... 4F 25
Osbourne Ho. IG8: Wfd G ... 7K 21
TW2: Twick ... 2G 115
Oscar Faber Pl. N1 ... 7E 50
Oscar St. SE8 ... 2C 106
(Lewisham Way)
SE8 ... 1C 106
(Thornville St.)
Oseney Cres. NW5 ... 5G 49
O'Shea Gro. E3 ... 1B 70
OSIDGE ... 1A 16
Osidge La. N14 ... 1K 15
Osier Ct. *E1 ... 4K 69*
(off Osier St.)
RM7: Rom ... 6K 39
TW8: Bford ... 6E 80
(off Ealing Rd.)
Osier Cres. N10 ... 1D 30
Osier La. *SE10 ... 3H 89*
(off W. Parkside)
Osier M. W4 ... 6A 82
Osiers Ct. *KT1: King T ... 1D 134*
(off Steadfast Rd.)
Osiers Rd. SW18 ... 4J 101
Osier St. E1 ... 4J 69
Osier Way CR4: Mitc ... 5D 138
E10 ... 3D 52
Oslac Rd. SE6 ... 5D 124
Oslo Ct. *NW8 ... 2C 66*
(off Prince Albert Rd.)
Oslo Ho. *SE5 ... 2C 104*
(off Carew St.)
Oslo Sq. SE16 ... 3A 88
Osman Cl. N15 ... 6D 32
Osman Rd. N9 ... 3B 18
W6 ... 3E 82
Osmington Ho. *SW8 ... 7K 85*
(off Dorset Rd.)
Osmond Cl. HA2: Harr ... 2G 43

Osmond Gdns.—Paget Ri.

Osmond Gdns. SM6: Wall . .5G 151
Osmund St. W12 . . . . .5B 64
Osnaburgh St.
NW1 . . . . . .4F 67 (4K 159)
(Longford St.)
NW1 . . . . .2K 159
(Robert St.)
Osnaburgh Ter.
NW1 . . . . . .4F 67 (3K 159)
Osney Ho. SE2 . . . . .2D 92
Osney Wlk. SM5: Cars 6B 138
Osprey NW9 . . . . .1B 28
Osprey Cl. E6 . . . . .5C 72
E11 . . . . .4J 35
E17 . . . . .7F 19
E18 . . . . .4J 35
SM1: Sutt 5H 149
UB7: W Dray 2A 76
Osprey Ct. BR3: Beck 7C 124
Osprey Ho. *E14* *7A 70*
(off Victory Pl.)
Osprey M. EN3: Enf 5D 8
Ospringe Cl. SE20 . . . . .7J 123
Ospringe Ct. SE9 . . . . .6H 109
Ospringe Ho. *SE1* *6K 167*
(off Wootton St.)
Ospringe Rd. NW5 . . . . .4G 49
Osram Ct. W6 . . . . .3E 82
Osram Rd. HA9: Wemb 3D 44
Osric Path N1 . . . . .2E 68
Ossian M. N4 . . . . .7K 31
Ossian Rd. N4 . . . . .7K 31
Ossington Bldgs.
W1 . . . . . . .5E 66 (5G 159)
Ossington Cl. W2 . . . . .7J 65
Ossington St. W2 . . . . .7J 65
Ossory Rd. SE1 . . . . .6G 87
Ossulston St.
NW1 . . . . . . .2H 67 (1C 160)
Ossulton Pl. N2 . . . . .3A 30
Ossulton Way N2 . . . . .4A 30
Ostade Rd. SW2 . . . . .7K 103
Ostell Cres. EN3: Enf 1H 9
Ostend Pl. SE1 . . . . .4C 86
Osten M. SW7 . . . . .3K 83
OSTERLEY 7H 79
Osterley Av. TW7: Isle 7H 79
Osterley Cl. BR5: Orp 1K 145
Osterley Ct. TW7: Isle 1H 97
UB5: N'olt *3A 60*
(off Canberra Dr.)
Osterley Cres. TW7: Isle 1J 97
Osterley Gdns.
CR7: Thor H 2C 140
UB2: S'hall 2G 79
Osterley Ho. *E14* *6D 70*
(off Girauld St.)
Osterley La. UB2: S'hall 5E 78
(not continuous)
Osterley Lodge *TW7: Isle* *7J 79*
(off Church Rd.)
Osterley Pk. *6G 79*
Osterley Pk. House *6G 79*
Osterley Pk. Rd.
UB2: S'hall 3D 78
Osterley Pk. Vw. Rd. W7 . . . .2J 79
Osterley Rd. N16 . . . . .4E 50
TW7: Isle 7J 79
Osterley Views UB2: S'hall . . .1G 79
Oster Ter. E17 . . . . .5K 33
Ostlers Dr. TW15: Ashf 5E 112
Ostliffe Rd. N13 . . . . .5H 17
Oswald Rd. UB1: S'hall 1C 78
Oswalds Mead E9 . . . . .4A 52
Oswald St. E5 . . . . .3K 51
Oswald Ter. NW2 . . . . .3E 46
Osward Pl. N9 . . . . .2C 18
Osward Rd. SW17 . . . . .2D 120
Oswell Ho. *E1* *1H 87*
(off Farthing Flds.)
Oswin St. SE11 . . . . .4B 86
Oswyth Rd. SE5 . . . . .2E 104
Otford Cl. BR1: Brom 3E 144
DA5: Bexl 6H 111
SE20 . . . . .1J 141
Otford Cres. SE4 . . . . .6B 106
Otford Ho. *SE1* *7F 169*
(off Staple St.)
SE15 . . . .*6J 87*
(off Lovelinch Cl.)
Othello Cl. SE11 . . .5B 86 (5K 173)
Otho Ct. TW8: Bford 7D 80
Otis St. E3 . . . . .3E 70
Otley App. IG2: Ilf 6F 37
Otley Dr. IG2: Ilf 5F 37
Otley Ho. N5 . . . . .3A 50
Otley Rd. E16 . . . . .6A 72
Otley Ter. E5 . . . . .3K 51
Ottawa Gdns. RM10: Dag 7K 57
Ottaway Ct. E5 . . . . .3G 51
Ottaway St. E5 . . . . .3G 51
Otterbourne Rd.
CR0: Croy 2C 152
E4 . . . . .3A 20
Otterburn Gdns. TW7: Isle . . .7A 80
Otterburn Ho. *SE5* *7C 86*
(off Sultan St.)
Otterburn St. SW17 . . . . . . .6D 120
Otterden St. SE6 . . . . .4C 124
Otterfield Rd.
UB7: W Dray 7A 58
Otter Rd. UB6: G'frd 4G 61
Otto Cl. SE26 . . . . .3H 123
Otto St. SE17 . . . . .6B 86
Otway Gdns. WD23: Bush . . .1D 10
Oulton Cl. E5 . . . . .2J 51
SE28 . . . . .6C 74
Oulton Cres. IG11: Bark 5K 55
Oulton Rd. N15 . . . . .5D 32
Ouseley Rd. SW12 . . . . .1D 120
Outer Circ. NW1 . . .2C 66 (1D 158)
Outgate Rd. NW10 . . . . .7B 46
Outram Pl. N1 . . . . .1J 67
Outram Rd. CR0: Croy 2F 153
E6 . . . . .1C 72
N22 . . . . .1H 31
Outwich St. EC3 . . . . .7H 163
Outwood Ho. *SW2* *7K 103*
(off Deepdene Gdns.)
Oval Ct. HA8: Edg 7D 12
Oval Cricket Ground
(Surrey County Cricket Club)
. . . . .6K 85 (7H 173)
Oval Ho. *CR0: Croy* *1E 152*
(off Oval Rd.)
Oval House Theatre *6A 86*
(off Kennington Oval)
Oval Mans.
SE11 . . . . . . .6K 85 (7H 173)
Oval Pl. SW8 . . . . .7K 85
Oval Rd. CR0: Croy 2D 152
NW1 . . . . .1F 67
Oval Rd. Nth. RM10: Dag 1H 75
Oval Rd. Sth. RM10: Dag 2H 75
Oval, The DA15: Sidc 7A 110
E2 . . . . .2H 69
Oval Way SE11 . . . .5K 85 (6H 173)
Overbrae BR3: Beck 6C 124
Overbrook Wlk. HA8: Edg 7B 12
(not continuous)
Overbury Av. BR3: Beck 3D 142
Overbury Rd. N15 . . . . .6D 32
Overbury St. E5 . . . . .4K 51
Overcliff Rd. SE13 . . . . .3C 106
Overcourt Cl. DA15: Sidc . . .6B 110
Overdale Av. KT3: N Mald . . .2J 135
Overdale Rd. W5 . . . . .3C 80
Overdown Rd. SE6 . . . . .4C 124
Overhill Rd. SE22 . . . . .7G 105
Overhill Way BR3: Beck 5F 143
Overlea Rd. E5 . . . . .7G 33
Overmead DA15: Sidc 7H 109
Oversley Ho. *W2* *5J 65*
(off Alfred Rd.)
Overstand Cl. BR3: Beck . . .5C 142
Overstone Gdns.
CR0: Croy 7B 142
Overstone Ho. *E14* *6C 70*
(off E. India Dock Rd.)
Overstone Rd. W6 . . . . .3E 82
Overstrand Mans. SW11 . . .1D 102
Overton Cl. NW10 . . . . .6J 45
TW7: Isle 1K 97
Overton Ct. E11 . . . . .7J 35
SM2: Sutt 7J 149
Overton Dr. E11 . . . . .7J 35
RM6: Chad H 7C 38
Overton Ho. *SW15* *7B 100*
(off Tangley Gro.)
Overton Rd. E10 . . . . .1A 52
N14 . . . . .5D 6
SE2 . . . . .3C 92
SM2: Sutt 6J 149
SW9 . . . . .2A 104
Overton Rd. E. SE2 . . . . .3D 92
Overtons Yd. CR0: Croy 3C 152
Overy Ho. SE1 . . . . .2B 86 (7A 168)
Ovesdon Av. HA2: Harr 1D 42
Ovett Cl. SE19 . . . . .6E 122
Ovex Cl. E14 . . . . .2E 88
Ovington Gdns.
SW3 . . . . . . .3C 84 (2D 170)
Ovington M. SW3 . . . . .2D 170
Ovington Sq.
SW3 . . . . . . .3C 84 (2D 170)
Ovington St.
SW3 . . . . . . .4C 84 (3D 170)
Owen Cl. CR0: Croy 6D 140
SE28 . . . . .1C 92
UB4: Hayes 3K 59
Owen Gdns. IG8: Wfd G 6H 21
Owen Ho. TW1: Twick 7B 98
Owenite St. SE2 . . . . .4B 92
Owen Mans. *W14* *6G 83*
(off Queen's Club Gdns.)
Owen Rd. N13 . . . . .5H 17
UB4: Hayes 3K 59
Owens Ct. EC1 . . . . .3B 68 (1A 162)
Owens Row EC1 . . .3B 68 (1A 162)
Owen St. EC1 . . . . .2B 68 (1A 162)
(not continuous)
Owens Way SE23 . . . . .7A 106
Owen Wlk. SE20 . . . . .1G 141
Owen Way NW10 . . . . .6J 45
Owgan Cl. SE5 . . . . .7D 86
Oxberry Av. SW6 . . . . .2G 101
Oxendon St. W1 . . .7H 67 (3C 166)
Oxenford St. SE15 . . . . .3F 105
Oxenham Ho. *SE8* *6C 88*
(off Benbow St.)
Oxenholme *NW1* *1A 160*
(off Hampstead Rd.)
Oxenpark Av.
HA9: Wemb 7E 26
Oxestalls Rd. SE8 . . . . .5A 88
Oxford & Cambridge Mans.
NW1 . . . .*6D 158*
(off Old Marylebone Rd.)
Oxford Av. NW10 . . . . .3D 64
SW20 . . . . .2G 137
TW5: Houn 5E 78
UB3: Hayes 7H 77
Oxford Cir. W1 . . . . .1A 166
Oxford Cir. Av.
W1 . . . . . . .6G 67 (1A 166)
Oxford Cl. CR4: Mitc 3G 139
N9 . . . . .2C 18
TW15: Ashf 7E 112
Oxford Ct. EC4 . . . . .2E 168
TW13: Felt 4B 114
W3 . . . . .6G 63
W4 . . . . .5H 81
W7 . . . .*5K 61*
(off Copley Cl.)
W9 . . . .*5J 65*
(off Elmfield Way)
Oxford Cres. KT3: N Mald . . .6K 135
Oxford Dr. HA4: Ruis 2A 42
SE1 . . . . .1E 86 (5G 169)
Oxford Gdns. N20 . . . . .1G 15
N21 . . . . .7H 7
W4 . . . . .5G 81
W10 . . . . .6E 64
Oxford Ga. W6 . . . . .4F 83
Oxford M. DA5: Bexl 7G 111
Oxford Pl. *NW10* *3K 45*
(off Press Rd.)
Oxford Rd. DA14: Sidc 5B 128
E15 . . . . .6F 53
(not continuous)
EN3: Enf 5C 8
HA1: Harr 6G 25
HA3: Harr 3K 25
IG1: Ilf 5G 55
IG8: Wfd G 5G 21
N4 . . . . .1A 50
N9 . . . . .2C 18
NW6 . . . . .2J 65
SE19 . . . . .6D 122
SM5: Cars 6C 150
SM6: Wall 5G 151
SW15 . . . . .4G 101
TW11: Tedd 5H 115
W5 . . . . .7D 62
Oxford Rd. Nth. W4 . . . . .5H 81
Oxford Rd. Sth. W4 . . . . .5G 81
Oxford Sq. W2 . . . . .6C 66 (1D 164)
Oxford St. W1 . . . . .6E 66 (1G 165)
Oxford Wlk. UB1: S'hall 1D 78
Oxford Way TW13: Felt 4B 114
Oxgate Cen. NW2 . . . . .2D 46
Oxgate Ct. NW2 . . . . .2C 46
Oxgate Gdns. NW2 . . . . .3D 46
Oxgate La. NW2 . . . . .2D 46
Oxgate Pde. NW2 . . . . .2C 46
Oxhawth Cres.
BR2: Short 5E 144
Oxhey La. HA5: Pinn 5A 10
Oxleas E6 . . . . .6F 73
Oxleas Cl. DA16: Well 2H 109
Oxleay Rd. HA2: Harr 1E 42
Oxleigh Cl. KT3: N Mald 5A 136
Oxley Cl. SE1 . . . . .5F 87
Oxleys Rd. NW2 . . . . .3D 46
Oxlip Cl. CR0: Croy 1K 153
Oxlow La. RM9: Dag 4F 57
RM10: Dag 4G 57
Oxonian St. SE22 . . . . .4F 105
Oxo Tower Wharf
. . . . .7A 68 (3K 167)
Oxted Cl. CR4: Mitc 3B 138
Oxtoby Way SW16 . . . . .1H 139
Oystercatchers Cl. E16 . . . . . .6K 71
Oystergate Wlk. EC4 . . . . . .3E 168
Oyster Row E1 . . . . .6J 69
Ozolins Way E16 . . . . .6J 71

P

Pablo Neruda Cl. SE24 . . . .4B 104
Pace Pl. E1 . . . . .6H 69
Pacific Cl. TW14: Felt 1H 113
Pacific Ho. *E1* *4K 69*
(off Ernest St.)
Pacific Rd. E16 . . . . .6J 71
Pacific Wharf SE16 . . . . .1K 87
Packenham Ho. *E2* *1K 163*
(off Wellington Row)
Packington Rd. W3 . . . . .3J 81
Packington Sq. N1 . . . . .1C 68
(not continuous)
Packington St. N1 . . . . .1B 68
Packmores Rd. SE9 . . . . . . .5H 109
Padbury *SE17* *5E 86*
(off Bagshot St.)
Padbury Cl. TW14: Felt 1F 113
Padbury Ct. E2 . . . . .3F 69 (2K 163)
Padbury Ho. *NW8* *3D 158*
(off Tresham Cres.)
Padcroft Rd. UB7: W Dray . . .1A 76
Paddenswick Rd. W6 . . . . . . .3C 82
PADDINGTON 6B 66 (1A 164)
Paddington Cl.
UB4: Hayes 4B 60
Paddington Ct. *W7* *5K 61*
(off Copley Cl.)
Paddington Grn.
W2 . . . . .5B 66 (5A 158)
Paddington St.
W1 . . . . .5E 66 (5G 159)
Paddock Cl. KT4: Wor Pk . . .1A 148
SE3 . . . . .2J 107
SE26 . . . . .4K 123
UB5: N'olt 2E 60
Paddock Gdns. SE19 . . . . . .6E 122
Paddock Lodge *EN1: Enf* *5K 7*
(off Village Rd.)
Paddock Mobile Home Pk.
BR2: Kes 7C 156
Paddock Pas. *SE19* *6E 122*
(off Paddock Gdns.)
Paddock Rd. DA6: Bex 4E 110
HA4: Ruis 3B 42
NW2 . . . . .3C 46
Paddocks Cl. HA2: Harr 4F 43
Paddocks Grn. NW9 . . . . .1H 45
Paddocks, The CR0: Croy . . .6C 154
EN4: Barn 3J 5
HA9: Wemb 2H 45
W5 . . . .*3D 80*
(off Popes La.)
Paddock, The NW9 . . . . .5G 27
UB10: Uxb 4D 40
Paddock Way BR7: Chst 7H 127
SW15 . . . . .7E 100
Padfield Ct. HA9: Wemb 3F 45
Padfield Rd. SE5 . . . . .3C 104
Padley Cl. KT9: Chess 5F 147
Padnall Ct. RM6: Chad H 3D 38
Padnall Rd. RM6: Chad H . . .3D 38
Padstow Ho. *E14* *7B 70*
(off Three Colt St.)
Padstow Rd. EN2: Enf 1G 7
Padstow Wlk. TW14: Felt . . .1H 113
Padua Rd. SE20 . . . . .1J 141
Pagden St. SW8 . . . . .1F 103
Pageant Av. NW9 . . . . .1K 27
Pageant Cres. SE16 . . . . .1A 88
Pageantmaster Ct. EC4 . . . .1A 168
Pageant Wlk. CR0: Croy 3E 152
Page Av. HA9: Wemb 3J 45
Page Cl. HA3: Harr 6F 27
RM9: Dag 5E 56
TW12: Hamp 6C 114
Page Cres. CR0: Croy 5B 152
Page Grn. Rd. N15 . . . . .5G 33
Page Grn. Ter. N15 . . . . .5F 33
Page Heath La.
BR1: Brom 3B 144
Page Heath Vs.
BR1: Brom 3B 144
Page Ho. *SE10* *6E 88*
(off Welland St.)
Pagehurst Rd. CR0: Croy . . .7H 141
Page Mdw. NW7 . . . . .7J 13
Page Rd. TW14: Felt 6F 95
Pages Hill N10 . . . . .2E 30
Pages La. N10 . . . . .2E 30
Page St. NW7 . . . . .1C 28
SW1 . . . . . .4H 85 (3D 172)
Pages Wlk. SE1 . . . . .4E 86
Pages Yd. W4 . . . . .6B 82
Paget Av. SM1: Sutt 3B 150
Paget Cl. TW12: Hamp 4H 115
Paget Gdns. BR7: Chst 1F 145
Paget La. TW7: Isle 3H 97
Paget Pl. KT2: King T 6J 117
KT7: T Ditt 1A 146
Paget Ri. SE18 . . . . .6E 90

Parke Rd. SW13 1C **100**
TW16: Sun T 4J **131**
Parker Rd. CR0: Croy 4C **152**
Parkers Row SE1 2G **87** (7K **169**)
Parker St. E16 1C **90**
WC2 6J **67** (7F **161**)
Pk. Farm Cl. HA5: Pinn 5K **23**
N2 3A **30**
Pk. Farm Ct. UB3: Hayes 7G **59**
Pk. Farm Rd. BR1: Brom 1B **144**
KT2: King T 7E **116**
Parkfield TW7: Isle 1J **97**
Parkfield Av. HA2: Harr 2G **25**
SW14 4A **100**
TW13: Felt 3J **113**
UB5: N'olt 2B **60**
UB10: Uxb 3D **58**
Parkfield Cl. HA8: Edg 6C **12**
UB5: N'olt 2C **60**
Parkfield Ct. *SE14 1B 106*
(off Parkfield Rd.)
Parkfield Cres. HA2: Harr 2G **25**
HA4: Ruis 2C **42**
TW13: Felt 3J **113**
Parkfield Dr. UB5: N'olt 2B **60**
Parkfield Gdns. HA2: Harr 3F **25**
Parkfield Ho. HA2: Harr 1F **25**
Parkfield Ind. Est. SW11 2E **102**
Parkfield Pde. TW13: Felt 3J **113**
Parkfield Rd. HA2: Harr 3G **43**
NW10 7D **46**
SE14 1B **106**
TW13: Felt 3J **113**
UB5: N'olt 2C **60**
UB10: Uxb 2D **40**
Parkfields CR0: Croy 1B **154**
SW15 4E **100**
Parkfields Av. NW9 1K **45**
SW20 1D **136**
Parkfields Cl. SM5: Cars 4E **150**
Parkfields Rd.
KT2: King T 5F **117**
Parkfield St. N1 2A **68**
Parkfield Way
BR2: Short 6D **144**
Park Gdns. DA8: Erith 4K **93**
E10 1C **52**
KT2: King T 5F **117**
NW9 3H **27**
Park Ga. N2 3B **30**
N21 7E **6**
SE3 3H **107**
W5 5D **62**
Parkgate Av. EN4: Barn 1F **5**
Pk. Gate Cl. KT2: King T 6H **117**
Pk. Gate Ct.
TW12: Hamp 6G **115**
Parkgate Cres. EN4: Barn 1F **5**
Parkgate Gdns. SW14 5K **99**
Parkgate M. N6 7G **31**
Parkgate Rd. SM6: Wall 5E **150**
SW11 7C **84**
Park Gates HA2: Harr 4E **42**
Park Gro. BR1: Brom 1K **143**
DA7: Bex 4J **111**
E15 1J **71**
HA8: Edg 5A **12**
N11 7C **16**
Park Gro. Rd. E11 2G **53**
Park Hall *SE10 7F 89*
(off Crooms Hill)
Pk. Hall Rd. SE21 3C **122**
Parkhall Rd. N2 4C **30**
Pk. Hall Trad. Est. SE21 3C **122**
Parkham Ct. BR2: Short 2G **143**
Parkham St. SW11 1C **102**
Park Hill BR1: Brom 4C **144**
SE23 2H **123**
SM5: Cars 6C **150**
SW4 5H **103**
TW10: Rich 6F **99**
W5 5D **62**
Pk. Hill Cl. SM5: Cars 5C **150**
Pk. Hill Ct. SW17 3D **120**
Pk. Hill M. CR2: S Croy 5D **152**
Pk. Hill Ri. CR0: Croy 2E **152**
Pk. Hill Rd. BR2: Short 2G **143**
CR0: Croy 2E **152**
DA15: Sidc 3J **127**
SM6: Wall 7F **151**
Parkhill Rd. DA5: Bexl 7F **111**
E4 1K **19**
NW3 5D **48**
Parkhill Wlk. NW3 5D **48**
Parkholme Rd. E8 6F **51**
Park Ho. *E9 7J 51*
(off Shore Rd.)
N21 7E **6**
Park Ho. Gdns.
TW1: Twick 5C **98**
Park Ho. Pas. N6 7E **30**
Parkhouse St. SE5 7D **86**
Parkhurst Ct. N7 4J **49**
Parkhurst Gdns.
DA5: Bexl 7G **111**
Parkhurst Rd. DA5: Bexl 7G **111**
E12 4E **54**
E17 4A **34**
N7 4J **49**
N11 5K **15**
N17 2G **33**
N22 6E **16**
SM1: Sutt 4B **150**
Parkinson Ho. *E9 7J 51*
(off Frampton Pk. Rd.)
SW1 5C 172
(off Tachbrook St.)
Parkland Ct. *E15 5G 53*
(off Maryland Pk.)
Parkland Gdns. SW19 1F **119**
Parkland Gro.
TW15: Ashf 4C **112**
Parkland Rd. IG8: Wfd G 7E **20**
N22 2K **31**
TW15: Ashf 4C **112**
Parklands KT5: Surb 5F **135**
N6 1F **49**
Parklands Cl. EN4: Barn 1G **5**
IG2: Ilf 7G **37**
SW14 5J **99**
Parklands Ct. TW5: Houn 2B **96**
Parklands Dr. N3 3G **29**
Parklands Gro. TW7: Isle 1K **97**
Parklands Pde.
TW5: Houn 2B **96**
Parklands Rd. SW16 5F **121**
Parklands Way
KT4: Wor Pk 2A **148**
Park La. CR0: Croy 3D **152**
E15 1F **71**
HA2: Harr 3F **43**
HA7: Stan 3F **11**
HA9: Wemb 5E **44**
N9 3K **17**
N17 7A **18**
(not continuous)
RM6: Chad H 6D **38**
SM3: Sutt 6G **149**
SM5: Cars, Wall 4E **150**
SM6: Wall 5E **150**
TW5: Houn 7J **77**
TW9: Rich 4D **98**
TW11: Tedd 6K **115**
UB4: Hayes 5G **59**
W1 7D **66** (2F **165**)
Park La. Cl. N17 7B **18**
Park La. Mans.
CR0: Croy 3D 152
(off Edridge Rd.)
PARK LANGLEY 4E **142**
Park Lawns HA9: Wemb 4F **45**
Parklea Cl. NW9 1A **28**
Pk. Lee Ct. N16 7E **32**
Parkleigh Rd. SW19 2K **137**
Parkleys TW10: Rich 4D **116**
Parkleys Pde.
KT2: King T 4D **116**
Park Lodge NW8 7B **48**
Park Lofts *SW2 5J 103*
(off Mandrell Rd.)
Park Lorne *NW8 2D 158*
(off Park Rd.)
Park Mnr. *SM2: Sutt 7A 150*
(off Christchurch Pk.)
Park Mans. NW4 5D **28**
NW8 2C 66
(off Allitsen Rd.)
SW1 7E 164
(off Knightsbridge)
SW8 6J **85** (7F **173**)
SW11 1D 102
(off Prince of Wales Dr.)
Park Mead DA15: Sidc 5B **110**
HA2: Harr 3F **43**
Parkmead SW15 6D **100**
Parkmead Gdns. NW7 6G **13**
Park M. BR7: Chst 6F **127**
SE24 7C **104**
TW19: Staines 7B **94**
W10 2G **65**
Parkmore Cl. IG8: Wfd G 4D **20**
Park Pde. NW10 2B **64**
UB3: Hayes 6G **59**
W5 3G **81**
Park Pl. *BR1: Brom 1K 143*
(off Park Rd.)
E14 1C **88**
HA9: Wemb 4F **45**
SW1 1G **85** (5A **166**)
TW12: Hamp 6G **115**
W3 4G **81**
W5 1D **80**
Park Pl. Vs. W2 5A **66** (5A **158**)
Park Ridings N8 3A **32**
Park Ri. HA3: Harr 1J **25**
SE23 1A **124**
Park Ri. Rd. SE23 1A **124**
Park Rd. BR1: Brom 1K **143**
BR3: Beck 7B **124**
BR7: Chst 6F **127**
E6 1A **72**
E10 1C **52**
E12 1K **53**
E15 1J **71**
E17 5B **34**
EN4: Barn 4G **5**
EN5: Barn 4C **4**
HA0: Wemb 6E **44**
IG1: Ilf 3H **55**
KT1: King T 1C **134**
KT2: King T 5F **117**
KT3: N Mald 4K **135**
KT5: Surb 6F **135**
KT8: E Mos 4G **133**
N2 3B **30**
N8 4G **31**
N8 4B **32**
N11 7C **16**
N14 1C **16**
N18 4B **18**
NW1 3C **66** (2D **158**)
NW4 7C **28**
NW8 3C **66** (2D **158**)
NW9 7K **27**
NW10 1A **64**
SE25 4E **140**
SM3: Sutt 6G **149**
SM6: Wall 5F **151**
(Clifton Rd.)
SM6: Wall 2F **151**
(Elmwood Cl.)
SW19 6B **120**
TW1: Twick 6C **98**
TW3: Houn 5F **97**
TW7: Isle 1B **98**
TW10: Rich 6F **99**
Park Rd. TW11: Tedd 6K **115**
TW12: Hamp 4F **115**
TW13: Felt 4B **114**
TW15: Ashf 5D **112**
TW16: Sun T 7K **113**
UB4: Hayes 5G **59**
UB8: Uxb 7A **40**
W4 7J **81**
W7 7K **61**
Park Rd. E. UB10: Uxb 2A **58**
W3 2H **81**
Park Rd. Ho. KT2: King T 7G **117**
Park Rd. Nth. W3 2H **81**
W4 5K **81**
Park Row SE10 5F **89**
PARK ROYAL 3H **63**
Park Royal Junction 1G **63**
Pk. Royal Metro Cen.
NW10 4H **63**
Pk. Royal Rd. NW10 3J **63**
W3 3J **63**
Pk. Royal Sth. Leisure Complex
W3 4G **63**
Parkshot TW9: Rich 4D **98**
Parkside DA14: Sidc 2B **128**
IG9: Buck H 2E **20**
N3 1K **29**
NW2 3C **46**
NW7 6H **13**
SE3 7H **89**
SM3: Sutt 6G **149**
SW1 6F **165**
SW19 3F **119**
TW12: Hamp 5H **115**
UB3: Hayes 7G **59**
W3 1A **82**
W5 7E **62**
Parkside Av. BR1: Brom 4C **144**
DA7: Bex 2K **111**
RM1: Rom 3K **39**
SW19 5F **119**
Parkside Bus. Est. SE8 6A **88**
(Blackhorse Rd.)
SE8 6A **88**
(Childers St.)
Parkside Cl. SE20 7J **123**
Parkside Ct. *E11 6J 35*
(off Wanstead Pl.)
N22 6E **16**
Parkside Cres.
KT5: Surb 6J **135**
N7 3A **50**
Parkside Cross DA7: Bex 2K **111**
Parkside Dr. HA8: Edg 3B **12**
Parkside Est. E9 1J **69**
Parkside Gdns. EN4: Barn 1J **15**
SW19 4F **119**
Parkside Ho. RM10: Dag 3J **57**
Parkside Lodge
DA17: Belv 5J **93**
Parkside Rd. DA17: Belv 4H **93**
SW11 1E **102**
TW3: Houn 5F **97**
Parkside Ter. N18 4J **17**
Parkside Way HA2: Harr 4F **25**
Park Sq. E.
NW1 4F **67** (3J **159**)
Park Sq. M. NW1 4J **159**
Park Sq. W.
NW1 4F **67** (3J **159**)
Parkstead Rd. SW15 5C **100**
Park Steps W2 2D **164**
Parkstone Av. N18 6A **18**
Parkstone Rd. E17 3E **34**
SE15 2G **105**
Park St. CR0: Croy 2C **152**
SE1 1C **86** (4C **168**)
TW11: Tedd 6J **115**
W1 7E **66** (2G **165**)
Park Ter. EN3: Enf 1F **9**
KT4: Wor Pk 1C **148**
SM5: Cars 3C **150**
Park, The DA14: Sidc 5A **128**
N6 6E **30**
NW11 1K **47**
SE19 7E **122**
SE23 1J **123**
SM5: Cars 5D **150**
W5 1D **80**
Parkthorne Cl. HA2: Harr 6F **25**
Parkthorne Dr.
HA2: Harr 6E **24**
Parkthorne Rd. SW12 7H **103**
Park Towers *W1 5J 165*
(off Brick St.)
Parkview DA18: Erith 3D **92**
Park Vw. HA5: Pinn 1D **24**
HA9: Wemb 5H **45**
KT3: N Mald 3B **136**
N5 4C **50**
N21 7E **6**
RM6: Chad H 6D **38**
UB7: W Dray 7A **58**
W3 5J **63**
Parkview *UB6: G'frd 3A 62*
(off Perivale La.)
Pk. View Ct. N12 4H **15**
SE20 1H **141**
Parkview Ct. HA3: Harr 7D **10**
IG2: Ilf 6J **37**
SW6 2G **101**
SW18 5J **101**
Pk. View Cres. N11 4A **16**
Pk. View Est. E2 2K **69**
Pk. View Gdns. IG4: Ilf 4D **36**
IG11: Bark 2J **73**
N22 1A **32**
NW4 5E **28**
Pk. View Ho. E4 5H **19**
SE24 6B 104
(off Hurst St.)
Parkview Ho. N9 7C **8**
Pk. View Mans. N4 7B **32**
Park Vw. M. SW9 2K **103**
Pk. View Rd. CR0: Croy 1G **153**
DA16: Well 3C **110**
N3 1K **29**
N17 3G **33**
NW10 4B **46**
UB1: S'hall 1E **78**
UB8: Uxb 6B **58**
W5 5E **62**
Parkview Rd. SE9 1F **127**
Pk. Village E.
NW1 2F **67** (1K **159**)
Pk. Village W. NW1 2F **67**
Park Vs. RM6: Chad H 6D **38**
Parkville Rd. SW6 7H **83**
Park Vista SE10 6F **89**
Park Wlk. EN4: Barn 3G **5**
IG1: Ilf 2F 55
(in Exchange, The)
N6 7E **30**
SE10 7F **89**
SW10 6A **84** (7A **170**)
Park Way EN2: Enf 2F **7**
HA4: Ruis 1J **41**
HA8: Edg 1H **27**
IG8: Wfd G 5F **21**
KT8: W Mole 3F **133**
N20 4J **15**
NW11 5G **29**
TW14: Felt 7K **95**
Parkway DA18: Erith 3E **92**
IG3: Ilf 3K **55**
N14 2D **16**
NW1 1F **67**
SW20 4F **137**
UB10: Uxb 7C **40**
Pk. Way Ct. HA4: Ruis 1H **41**
Parkway, The TW5: Houn 5J **77**
UB2: S'hall 5J **77**
UB3: Hayes 3K **77**
UB4: Hayes 7A **60**

Pearson Cl.—Penrose Ho.

Pearson Cl. SE5 . . . . . 1C 104
(off Camberwell New Rd.)
Pearson M. SW4 . . . . . 3H 103
(off Slievemore Cl.)
Pearsons Av. SE14 . . . . . 1C 106
Pearson St. E2 . . . . . 2F 69
Pears Rd. TW3: Houn 3G 97
Peartree SE26 . . . . . 5A 124
Pear Tree Av.
UB7: W Dray 6B 58
Peartree Av. SW17 . . . . . 3A 120
Pear Tree Cl. E2 . . . . . 1F 69
KT9: Chess 5G 147
Peartree Cl. CR4: Mitc 2C 138
DA8: Erith 1K 111
Pear Tree Ct. E18 . . . . . 1K 35
EC1 . . . . . 4A 68 (4K 161)
Peartree Gdns.
RM7: Mawney 2H 39
RM8: Dag 4B 56
Pear Tree Ho. SE4 . . . . . 3B 106
Peartree La. E1 . . . . . 7J 69
Pear Tree Rd.
TW15: Ashf 5E 112
Peartree Rd. EN1: Enf 3K 7
Peartrees UB7: W Dray 7A 58
Pear Tree St.
EC1 . . . . . 4C 68 (3B 162)
Peartree Way SE10 . . . . . 4J 89
Peary Ho. NW10 . . . . . 7K 45
Peary Pl. E2 . . . . . 3J 69
Peas Mead Ter. E4 . . . . . 4K 19
Peatfield Cl. DA15: Sidc 3J 127
Pebble Way W3 . . . . . 1H 81
(off Steyne Rd.)
Pebworth Rd. HA1: Harr 2A 44
Peckarmans Wood
SE26 . . . . . 3G 123
Peckett Sq. N5 . . . . . 4C 50
Peckford Pl. SW9 . . . . . 2A 104
PECKHAM 1G 105
Peckham Gro. SE15 . . . . . 7E 86
Peckham High St. SE15 . . . . . 1G 105
Peckham Hill St. SE15 . . . . . 7G 87
Peckham Pk. Rd. SE15 . . . . . 7G 87
Peckham Rd. SE5 . . . . . 1E 104
SE15 . . . . . 1E 104
Peckham Rye SE15 . . . . . 3G 105
SE22 . . . . . 4G 105
Peckham Sq. SE15 . . . . . 1G 105
Pecks Yd. E1 . . . . . 5J 163
(off Hanbury St.)
Peckwater St. NW5 . . . . . 5G 49
Pedhoulas N14 . . . . . 3D 16
Pedlars Wlk. N7 . . . . . 5K 49
Pedley Rd. RM8: Dag 1C 56
Pedley St. E1 . . . . . 4F 69 (4K 163)
Pedro St. E5 . . . . . 3K 51
Pedworth Gdns. SE16 . . . . . 4J 87
Peebles Ct. UB1: S'hall 6G 61
(off Haldane Rd.)
Peek Cres. SW19 . . . . . 5F 119
Peel Cl. E4 . . . . . 2J 19
N9 . . . . . 3B 18
Peel Dr. IG5: Ilf 3C 36
Peel Gro. E2 . . . . . 2J 69
(not continuous)
Peel La. NW9 . . . . . 3C 28
Peel Pas. W8 . . . . . 1J 83
(off Peel St.)
Peel Pl. IG5: Ilf 2C 36
Peel Pct. NW6 . . . . . 2J 65
Peel Rd. E18 . . . . . 1H 35
HA3: Harr 3K 25
(not continuous)
HA9: Wemb 3D 44
Peel St. W8 . . . . . 1J 83
Peel Way UB8: Uxb 5A 58
Peerglow Est. EN3: Enf 5D 8
Peerless St. EC1 . . . 3D 68 (2E 162)
Pegamoid Rd. N18 . . . . . 3D 18
Pegasus Cl. N16 . . . . . 4D 50
Pegasus Ct. KT1: King T . . . 3D 134
NW10 . . . . . 3D 64
(off Trenmar Gdns.)
TW8: Bford 5F 81
W3 . . . . . 6J 63
(off Horn La.)
Pegasus Ho. E1 . . . . . 4K 69
(off Beaumont Sq.)
Pegasus Pl.
SE11 . . . . . 6A 86 (7J 173)
SW6 . . . . . 1J 101
Pegasus Way N11 . . . . . 6A 16
Peggotty Way UB8: Uxb 6D 58
Pegg Rd. TW5: Houn 7B 78
Pegley Gdns. SE12 . . . . . 2J 125
Pegwell St. SE18 . . . . . 7J 91
Pekin Cl. E14 . . . . . 6C 70
(off Pekin St.)
Pekin St. E14 . . . . . 6C 70
Pelabon Ho. TW1: Twick 6D 98
(off Clevedon Rd.)
Peldon Ct. TW9: Rich 4F 99
Peldon Pas. TW10: Rich 4F 99
Peldon Wlk. N1 . . . . . 1B 68
(off Popham St.)
Pelham Av. IG11: Bark 1K 73
Pelham Cl. SE5 . . . . . 3E 104
Pelham Cotts. DA5: Bexl . . . 1H 129
Pelham Ct. DA14: Sidc 3A 128
SW3 . . . . . 4C 170
(off Fulham Rd.)
Pelham Cres.
SW7 . . . . . 4C 84 (4C 170)
Pelham Ho. W14 . . . . . 4H 83
(off Mornington Av.)
Pelham Pl. SW7 . . . 4C 84 (3C 170)
W13 . . . . . 4K 61
Pelham Rd. BR3: Beck 2J 141
DA7: Bex 3G 111
E18 . . . . . 3K 35
IG1: Ilf 2H 55
N15 . . . . . 4F 33
N22 . . . . . 2A 32
SW19 . . . . . 7J 119
Pelham St. SW7 . . . 4B 84 (3B 170)
Pelican Est. SE15 . . . . . 1F 105
Pelican Ho. SE8 . . . . . 4B 88
Pelican Pas. E1 . . . . . 4J 69
Pelican Wlk. SW9 . . . . . 4B 104
Pelican Wharf E1 . . . . . 1J 87
(off Wapping Wall)
Pelier St. SE17 . . . . . 6C 86
Pelinore Rd. SE6 . . . . . 2G 125
Pella Ho. SE11 . . . . 5K 85 (5H 173)
Pellant Rd. SW6 . . . . . 7G 83
Pellatt Gro. N22 . . . . . 1A 32
Pellatt Rd. HA9: Wemb 2D 44
(not continuous)
SE22 . . . . . 5F 105
Pellerin Rd. N16 . . . . . 5E 50
Pellew Ho. E1 . . . . . 4H 69
(off Somerford St.)
Pelling St. E14 . . . . . 6C 70
Pellipar Cl. N13 . . . . . 3F 17
Pellipar Gdns. SE18 . . . . . 5D 90
Pellipar Rd. SE18 . . . . . 5D 90
Pelly Rd. E13 . . . . . 1J 71
(not continuous)
Pelter St. E2 . . . . . 3F 69 (1J 163)
(not continuous)
Pelton Rd. SE10 . . . . . 5G 89
Pembar Av. E17 . . . . . 3A 34
Pemberley Chase
KT19: Eps 5H 147
Pemberley Cl. KT19: Eps . . . 5H 147
Pember Rd. NW10 . . . . . 3F 65
Pemberton Ct. E1 . . . . . 3K 69
(off Portelet Rd.)
Pemberton Gdns. N19 . . . . . 3G 49
RM6: Chad H 5E 38
Pemberton Ho. SE26 . . . . . 4G 123
(off High Level Dr.)
Pemberton Pl. E8 . . . . . 7H 51
Pemberton Rd.
KT8: E Mos 4G 133
N4 . . . . . 5A 32
Pemberton Row
EC4 . . . . . 6A 68 (7K 161)
Pemberton Ter. N19 . . . . . 3G 49
Pembridge Av.
TW2: Twick 1D 114
Pembridge Cres. W11 . . . . . 7J 65
Pembridge Gdns. W2 . . . . . 7J 65
Pembridge M. W11 . . . . . 7J 65
Pembridge Pl. SW15 . . . . . 5J 101
W2 . . . . . 7J 65
Pembridge Rd. W11 . . . . . 7J 65
Pembridge Sq. W2 . . . . . 7J 65
Pembridge Vs. W11 . . . . . 7J 65
Pembroke Av. EN1: Enf 1C 8
HA3: Harr 3A 26
HA5: Pinn 1B 42
KT5: Surb 5H 135
N1 . . . . . 1J 67
Pembroke Bldgs. NW10 . . . . . 3C 64
Pembroke Cen., The
HA4: Ruis 1H 41
Pembroke Cl.
SW1 . . . . . 2E 84 (7H 165)
Pembroke Cotts. W8 . . . . . 3J 83
(off Pembroke Sq.)
Pembroke Ct. W7 . . . . . 6K 61
(off Copley Cl.)
Pembroke Gdns.
RM10: Dag 3H 57
W14 . . . . . 4H 83
Pembroke Gdns. Cl. W8 . . . . . 3J 83
Pembroke Hall NW4 . . . . . 3E 28
(off Mulberry Cl.)
Pembroke Ho. W2 . . . . . 6K 65
(off Hallfield Est.)
W3 . . . . . 2J 81
(off Park Rd. E.)
Pembroke Lodge
HA7: Stan 6H 11
Pembroke M. E3 . . . . . 3A 70
N10 . . . . . 1F 31
W8 . . . . . 3J 83
Pembroke Pde.
DA8: Erith 5J 93
Pembroke Pl. HA8: Edg 7B 12
TW7: Isle 2J 97
W8 . . . . . 3J 83
Pembroke Rd.
BR1: Brom 2A 144
CR4: Mitc 2E 138
DA8: Erith 5J 93
E6 . . . . . 5D 72
E17 . . . . . 5D 34
HA4: Ruis 1G 41
HA9: Wemb 3D 44
IG3: Ilf 1K 55
N8 . . . . . 4J 31
N10 . . . . . 1E 30
N13 . . . . . 3H 17
N15 . . . . . 5F 33
SE25 . . . . . 4E 140
UB6: G'frd 4F 61
W8 . . . . . 4H 83
Pembroke Sq. W8 . . . . . 3J 83
Pembroke St. N1 . . . . . 7J 49
(not continuous)
Pembroke Vs. TW9: Rich . . . 4D 98
W8 . . . . . 4J 83
Pembroke Wlk. W8 . . . . . 4J 83
Pembroke Way
UB3: Hayes 3E 76
Pembrook M. SW11 . . . . . 4B 102
Pembry Cl. SW9 . . . . . 1A 104
Pembury Av.
KT4: Wor Pk 1C 148
Pembury Cl. BR2: Short . . . 7H 143
E5 . . . . . 5H 51
Pembury Ct. UB3: Hayes 6F 77
Pembury Cres.
DA14: Sidc 2E 128
Pembury Pl. E5 . . . . . 5H 51
Pembury Rd. DA7: Bex 7E 92
E5 . . . . . 5H 51
N17 . . . . . 1F 33
SE25 . . . . . 4G 141
Pemdevon Rd. CR0: Croy . . . 7A 140
Pemell Cl. E1 . . . . . 4J 69
Pemell Ho. E1 . . . . . 4J 69
(off Pemell Cl.)
Pemerich Cl. UB3: Hayes . . . 5H 77
Pempath Pl. HA9: Wemb . . . 2D 44
Penally Pl. N1 . . . . . 1D 68
Penang Ho. E1 . . . . . 1H 87
(off Prusom St.)
Penang St. E1 . . . . . 1H 87
Penard Rd. UB2: S'hall 3F 79
Penarth Cen. SE15 . . . . . 6J 87
Penarth St. SE15 . . . . . 6J 87
Penberth Rd. SE6 . . . . . 2E 124
Penbury Rd. UB2: S'hall 4D 78
Pencombe M. W11 . . . . . 7H 65
Pencraig Way SE15 . . . . . 6H 87
Pendall Cl. EN4: Barn 4H 5
Penda Rd. DA8: Erith 7H 93
Pendarves Rd. SW20 . . . . . 1E 136
Pendas Mead E9 . . . . . 4A 52
Pendell Av. UB3: Hayes 7H 77
Pendennis Ho. SE8 . . . . . 4A 88
Pendennis Rd. N17 . . . . . 3D 32
SW16 . . . . . 4J 121
Penderel Rd. TW3: Houn . . . 5E 96
Penderry Ri. SE6 . . . . . 2F 125
Penderyn Way N7 . . . . . 4H 49
Pendlebury Ct. KT5: Surb . . . 4E 134
(off Cranes Pk.)
Pendle Ct. UB10: Uxb 1D 58
Pendle Ho. SE26 . . . . . 3G 123
Pendle Rd. SW16 . . . . . 6F 121
Pendlestone Rd. E17 . . . . . 5D 34
Pendragon Rd.
BR1: Brom 3H 125
Pendragon Wlk. NW9 . . . . . 6A 28
Pendrell Ho. WC2 . . . . . 1D 166
(off New Compton St.)
Pendrell Rd. SE4 . . . . . 2A 106
Pendrell St. SE18 . . . . . 6H 91
Pendula Dr. UB4: Hayes 4B 60
Pendulum M. E8 . . . . . 5F 51
Penerley Rd. SE6 . . . . . 1D 124
Penfield Lodge W9 . . . . . 5J 65
(off Admiral Wlk.)
Penfields Ho. N7 . . . . . 6J 49
Penfold Cl. CR0: Croy 3A 152
Penfold La. DA5: Bexl 2D 128
(Cotleigh Av.)
DA5: Bexl 1D 128
(Stansted Cres.)
Penfold Pl. NW1 . . . 5C 66 (5C 158)
Penfold Rd. N9 . . . . . 1E 18
Penfold St. NW1 . . . 5C 66 (4B 158)
NW8 . . . . . 4B 66 (4B 158)
Penford Gdns. SE9 . . . . . 3B 108
Penford St. SE5 . . . . . 2B 104
Pengarth Rd. DA5: Bexl . . . 5D 110
PENGE 7J 123
Penge Ho. SW11 . . . . . 3B 102
Penge La. SE20 . . . . . 7J 123
Penge Rd. E13 . . . . . 1A 72
SE25 . . . . . 3G 141
Penhall Rd. SE7 . . . . . 4B 90
Penhill Rd. DA5: Bexl 6C 110
Penhurst Pl. SE1 . . . . . 1H 173
Penhurst Rd. IG6: Ilf 1F 37
Penifather La. UB6: G'frd . . . 3H 61
Peninsula Ct. E14 . . . . . 3D 88
(off E. Ferry Rd.)
Peninsula Hgts.
SE1 . . . . . 5J 85 (5F 173)
Peninsula Pk. SE7 . . . . . 4J 89
Peninsula Pk. Rd. SE7 . . . . . 4J 89
Peninsular Cl. TW14: Felt 6F 95
Penistone Rd. SW16 . . . . . 7J 121
Penketh Dr. HA1: Harr 3H 43
Penley Ct. WC2 . . . . 7K 67 (2H 167)
Penmayne Ho. SE11 . . . . . 5K 173
(off Kennings Way)
Penmon Rd. SE2 . . . . . 3A 92
Pennack Rd. SE15 . . . . . 6F 87
Penn Almshouses SE10 . . . . . 1E 106
(off Greenwich Sth. St.)
Pennant M. W8 . . . . . 4K 83
Pennant Ter. E17 . . . . . 2B 34
Pennard Mans. W12 . . . . . 2E 82
(off Goldhawk Rd.)
Pennard Rd. W12 . . . . . 2E 82
Pennards, The
TW16: Sun T 3A 132
Penn Cl. HA3: Harr 4C 26
UB6: G'frd 2F 61
Penn Ct. NW9 . . . . . 3K 27
Penner Cl. SW19 . . . . . 2G 119
Penners Gdns.
KT6: Surb 7E 134
Pennethorne Cl. E9 . . . . . 1J 69
Pennethorne Ho. SW11 . . . . 3B 102
Pennethorne Rd. SE15 . . . . . 7H 87
Penn Gdns. BR7: Chst 2F 145
RM5: Col R 1G 39
Penn Ho. NW8 . . . . . 4C 158
(off Mallory St.)
Pennine Dr. NW2 . . . . . 2F 47
Pennine La. NW2 . . . . . 2G 47
Pennine Pde. NW2 . . . . . 2G 47
Pennine Way DA7: Bex 1K 111
UB3: Hayes 7F 77
Pennington Cl. SE27 . . . . . 4D 122
Pennington Ct. SE16 . . . . . 1A 88
Pennington Dr. N21 . . . . . 5D 6
Pennington Lodge
KT5: Surb 5E 134
(off Cranes Dr.)
Pennington St. E1 . . . . . 7H 69
Pennington Way SE12 . . . . . 2K 125
Penniston Cl. N17 . . . . . 2C 32
Penn La. DA5: Bexl 5D 110
(not continuous)
Penn Rd. N7 . . . . . 5J 49
Penn St. N1 . . . . . 1D 68
Pennycroft CR0: Croy 7A 154
Pennyfather La. EN2: Enf 3H 7
Pennyfields E14 . . . . . 7C 70
(not continuous)
Pennyford Ct. NW8 . . . . . 3A 158
(off St John's Wood Rd.)
Penny La. TW17: Shep 7G 131
Penny M. SW12 . . . . . 7F 103
Pennymoor Wlk. W9 . . . . . 4H 65
(off Ashmore Rd.)
Penny Rd. NW10 . . . . . 3H 63
Penny Royal SM6: Wall . . . 6H 151
Pennyroyal Av. E6 . . . . . 6E 72
Penpoll Rd. E8 . . . . . 6H 51
Penpool La. DA16: Well . . . 3B 110
Penrhyn Av. E17 . . . . . 1B 34
Penrhyn Cres. E17 . . . . . 1C 34
SW14 . . . . . 4J 99
Penrhyn Gdns.
KT1: King T 4D 134
Penrhyn Gro. E17 . . . . . 1C 34
Penrhyn Rd.
KT1: King T 4E 134
Penrith Cl. BR3: Beck 1D 142
SW15 . . . . . 5G 101
UB8: Uxb 7A 40
Penrith Pl. SE27 . . . . . 2B 122
Penrith Rd. CR7: Thor H . . . 2C 140
KT3: N Mald 4K 135
N15 . . . . . 5D 32
Penrith St. SW16 . . . . . 6G 121
Penrose Gro. SE17 . . . . . 5C 86
Penrose Ho. SE17 . . . . . 5C 86
(not continuous)

Penrose St.—Philip Ct.

Penrose St. SE17 5C 86
Penryn Ho. *SE11* *5A 86*
(off Seaton Cl.)
Penryn St. NW1 2H 67
Penry St. SE1 4E 86
Pensbury Pl. SW8 2G 103
Pensbury St. SW8 2G 103
Pensford Av. TW9: Rich 2G 99
Penshurst NW5 6E 48
Penshurst Av.
DA15: Sidc 6A 110
Penshurst Gdns. HA8: Edg 5C 12
Penshurst Grn.
BR2: Short 5H 143
Penshurst Ho. *SE15* *6J 87*
(off Lovelinch Cl.)
Penshurst Rd.
CR7: Thor H 5B 140
DA7: Bex 1F 111
E9 7K 51
N17 7A 18
Penshurst Wlk.
BR2: Short 5H 143
Penshurst Way SM2: Sutt 7J 149
Pensilver Cl. EN4: Barn 4H 5
Penstemon Cl. N3 6D 14
Pentagon, The W13 7A 62
Pentavia Retail Pk. NW7 7G 13
Pentelow Gdns.
TW14: Felt 6J 95
Pentire Rd. E17 1F 35
Pentland Av. HA8: Edg 2C 12
TW17: Shep 5C 130
Pentland Cl. N9 2D 18
NW11 2G 47
Pentland Gdns. SW18 6A 102
Pentland Pl. UB5: N'olt 1C 60
Pentlands Cl. CR4: Mitc 3F 139
Pentland St. SW18 6A 102
Pentland Way UB10: Uxb 3E 40
Pentlow St. SW15 3E 100
Pentlow Way IG9: Buck H 1H 21
Pentney Rd. E4 1A 20
SW12 1G 121
SW20 1G 137
Penton Gro. N1 2A 68
Penton Ho. *N1* *1J 161*
(off Pentonville Rd.)
SE2 1D 92
Penton Pl. SE17 5B 86
Penton Ri. WC1 3K 67 (1H 161)
Penton St. N1 2A 68
PENTONVILLE 2K 67
Pentonville Rd.
N1 2K 67 (1F 161)
Pentrich Av. EN1: Enf 1B 8
Pentridge St. SE15 7F 87
Pentyre Av. N18 5J 17
Penwerris Av. TW7: Isle 7G 79
Penwerris Ct. TW5: Houn 7G 79
Penwith Rd. SW18 2J 119
Penwood Ct. HA5: Pinn 4D 24
Penwood Ho. SW15 6B 100
Penwortham Ct. N22 2K 31
Penwortham Rd. SW16 6F 121
Penylan Pl. HA8: Edg 7B 12
Penywern Rd. SW5 5J 83
Penzance Ho. *SE11* *5K 173*
(off Seaton Cl.)
Penzance Pl. W11 1G 83
Penzance St. W11 1G 83
Peony Ct. IG8: Wfd G 7B 20
Peony Gdns. W12 7C 64
Peperfield *WC1* *2G 161*
(off Cromer St.)
Pepler Ho. *W10* *4G 65*
(off Wornington Rd.)
Pepler M. SE5 5F 87
Peploe Rd. NW6 2F 65
(not continuous)
Peplow Cl. UB7: W Dray 1A 76
Pepper Cl. E6 5D 72
Peppercorn Cl.
CR7: Thor H 2D 140
Peppermead Sq. SE4 5C 106
Peppermint Cl.
CR0: Croy 7J 139
Peppermint Pl. E11 3G 53
Pepper St. E14 3D 88
SE1 2C 86 (6C 168)
Peppie Cl. N16 2E 50
Pepys Cl. UB10: Uxb 4D 40
Pepys Cres. E16 1J 89
EN5: Barn 5A 4
Pepys Ho. *E2* *3J 69*
(off Kirkwall Pl.)
Pepys Rd. SE14 1K 105
SW20 1E 136
Pepys St. EC3 7E 68 (2H 169)
Perceval Av. NW3 5C 48
Perceval Ct. UB5: N'olt 5E 42
Perceval Ho. W5 7C 62
Percheron Cl. TW7: Isle 3K 97
Perch St. E8 4F 51
Percival Ct. N17 7A 18
Percival David Foundation of Chinese Art ***3D 160***
Percival Gdns.
RM6: Chad H 6C 38
Percival Rd. EN1: Enf 4A 8
SW14 4J 99
TW13: Felt 2H 113
Percival St. EC1 4B 68 (3A 162)
Percival Way KT19: Eps 4K 147
Percy Av. TW15: Ashf 5C 112
Percy Bryant Rd.
TW16: Sun T 7G 113
Percy Bush Rd.
UB7: W Dray 3B 76
Percy Cir. WC1 3K 67 (1H 161)
Percy Gdns. EN3: Enf 5E 8
KT4: Wor Pk 1A 148
TW7: Isle 3A 98
UB4: Hayes 3G 59
Percy M. W1 6C 160
Percy Pas. W1 6C 160
Percy Rd. CR4: Mitc 7E 138
DA7: Bex 2E 110
E11 7G 35
E16 5G 71
IG3: Ilf 7A 38
N12 5F 15
N21 7H 7
RM7: Mawney 3H 39
SE20 1K 141
SE25 5G 141
TW2: Twick 1F 115
TW7: Isle 4A 98
TW12: Hamp 7E 114
W12 2C 82
(not continuous)
Percy St. W1 5H 67 (6C 160)
Percy Way TW2: Twick 1G 115
Percy Yd. WC1 3K 67 (1H 161)
Peregrine Cl. NW10 5K 45
Peregrine Ct. DA16: Well 1K 109
SE8 *6C 88*
(off Edward St.)
SW16 4K 121
Peregrine Gdns.
CR0: Croy 2A 154
Peregrine Ho. EC1 1B 162
Peregrine Rd.
TW16: Sun T 2H 131
Peregrine Way SW19 7E 118
Perham Rd. W14 5G 83
Peridot St. E6 5C 72
Perifield SE21 1C 122
Perimeade Rd. UB6: G'frd 2C 62
Periton Rd. SE9 4B 108
PERIVALE 1C 62
Perivale Gdns. W13 4B 62
Perivale Grange
UB6: G'frd 3A 62
Perivale Ind. Pk.
UB6: G'frd 2B 62
Perivale La. UB6: G'frd 3A 62
Perivale Lodge *UB6: G'frd* *3A 62*
(off Perivale La.)
Perivale New Bus. Cen.
UB6: G'frd 2C 62
Perkin Cl. HA0: Wemb 5B 44
TW3: Houn 4E 96
Perkins Ct. TW15: Ashf 5B 112
Perkins Ho. *E14* *5B 70*
(off Wallwood St.)
Perkins Rents
SW1 3H 85 (2C 172)
Perkins Rd. IG2: Ilf 5H 37
Perkins Sq. SE1 1C 86 (4D 168)
Perks Cl. SE3 3G 107
Perley Ho. *E3* *5B 70*
(off Weatherley Cl.)
Perpins Rd. SE9 6J 109
Perran Rd. SW2 1B 122
Perran Wlk. TW8: Bford 5E 80
Perren St. NW5 6F 49
Perrers Rd. W6 4D 82
Perrin Cl. TW15: Ashf 5B 112
Perrin Ct. TW15: Ashf 4C 112
Perring Est. *E3* *5C 70*
(off Gale St.)
Perrin Ho. NW6 3J 65
Perrin Rd. HA0: Wemb 4B 44
Perrins Ct. NW3 4A 48
Perrins La. NW3 4A 48
Perrins Wlk. NW3 4A 48
Perronet Ho. *SE1* *3B 86*
(off Princess St.)
Perrott St. SE18 4G 91
Perry Av. W3 6K 63
Perry Cl. RM13: Rain 2K 75
UB8: Uxb 6D 58
Perry Ct. *E14* *5C 88*
(off Maritime Quay)
N15 6E 32
Perryfield Way NW9 6B 28
TW10: Rich 3B 116
Perry Gdns. N9 3J 17
Perry Gth. UB5: N'olt 1A 60
Perry Hall Rd. BR6: Orp 6K 145
Perry Hill SE6 3B 124
Perry Ho. RM13: Rain 2K 75
Perry How KT4: Wor Pk 1B 148
Perry Lodge E12 1B 54
Perrymans Farm Rd.
IG2: Ilf 6H 37
Perry Mead EN2: Enf 2G 7
Perrymead St. SW6 1J 101
Perryn Ct. TW1: Twick 6A 98
Perryn Ho. W3 7A 64
Perryn Rd. SE16 3H 87
W3 1K 81
Perry Ri. SE23 3A 124
Perry Rd. RM9: Dag 5F 75
Perrys Pl. W1 6H 67 (7C 160)
Perry St. BR7: Chst 6H 127
DA1: Cray 4K 111
Perry St. Gdns.
BR7: Chst 6J 127
Perry St. Shaw BR7: Chst 7J 127
Perry Va. SE23 2J 123
Persant Rd. SE6 2G 125
Perseverance Pl. SW9 7A 86
TW9: Rich 4E 98
Perseverance Works *E2* *1H 163*
(off Kingsland Rd.)
Pershore Cl. IG2: Ilf 5F 37
Pershore Gro. SM5: Cars 6B 138
Pert Cl. N10 7A 16
Perth Av. NW9 7K 27
UB4: Hayes 4A 60
Perth Cl. SE5 4D 104
SW20 2B 136
Perth Ho. *N1* *7K 49*
(off Bemerton Est.)
Perth Rd. BR3: Beck 2E 142
E10 1A 52
E13 2K 71
IG2: Ilf 6E 36
IG11: Bark 2H 73
N4 1A 50
N22 1B 32
Perth Ter. IG2: Ilf 7G 37
Perwell Av. HA2: Harr 1D 42
Perystreete SE23 2J 123
Petavel Rd. TW11: Tedd 6J 115
Peter Av. NW10 7D 46
Peter Best Ho. *E1* *6H 69*
(off Nelson St.)
Peterboat Cl. SE10 4G 89
Peterborough Ct.
EC4 6A 68 (1K 167)
Peterborough Gdns.
IG1: Ilf 7C 36
Peterborough M. SW6 2J 101
Peterborough Rd. E10 5E 34
HA1: Harr 1J 43
SM5: Cars 6C 138
SW6 2J 101
Peterborough Vs. SW6 1K 101
Peter Butler Ho. *SE1* *7K 169*
(off Wolseley St.)
Peterchurch Ho. *SE15* *6H 87*
(off Commercial Way)
Petergate SW11 4A 102
Peterhead Ct. *UB1: S'hall* *6G 61*
(off Osborne Rd.)
Peter Heathfield Ho. *E15* *1F 71*
(off Wise Rd.)
Peter Ho. *SW8* *7J 85*
(off Luscombe Way)
Peter James Bus. Cen.
UB3: Hayes 2J 77
Peter James Ent. Cen.
NW10 3J 63
Peter Kennedy Ct.
CR0: Croy 6B 142
Peterley Bus. Cen. E2 2H 69
Peter Pan Statue ***1B 84 (4A 164)***
Peters Cl. DA16: Well 2J 109
HA7: Stan 6J 11
RM8: Dag 1D 56
Peter Scott Vis. Cen., The ***1D 100***
Peters Ct. *W2* *6K 65*
(off Porchester Rd.)
Petersfield Cl. N18 5H 17
Petersfield Ri. SW15 1D 118
Petersfield Rd. W3 2J 81
PETERSHAM 1E 116
Petersham Cl. SM1: Sutt 5H 149
TW10: Rich 2D 116
Petersham Dr. BR5: Orp 2K 145
Petersham Gdns.
BR5: Orp 2K 145
Petersham Ho. *SW7* *3A 170*
(off Kendrick M.)
Petersham La. SW7 3A 84
Petersham M. SW7 3A 84
Petersham Pl. SW7 3A 84
Petersham Rd.
TW10: Rich 6D 98
Petersham Ter.
CR0: Croy *3J 151*
(off Richmond Grn.)
Peters Hill EC4 7C 68 (2C 168)
Peter Shore Ct. *E1* *5K 69*
(off Beaumont Sq.)
Peters La. EC1 5B 68 (5B 162)
Peters Path SE26 4H 123
Peterstone Rd. SE2 2B 92
Peterstow Cl. SW19 2G 119
Peter St. W1 7H 67 (2C 166)
Peterwood Pk. CR0: Croy 2K 151
Peterwood Way
CR0: Croy 2K 151
Petherton Ct. *HA1: Harr* *6K 25*
(off Gayton Rd.)
NW10 *1F 65*
(off Tiverton Rd.)
Petherton Ho. *N4* *1C 50*
(off Woodberry Down Est.)
Petherton Rd. N5 5C 50
Petiver Cl. E9 7J 51
Petley Rd. W6 6F 83
Peto Pl. NW1 4F 67 (3K 159)
Peto St. Nth. E16 6H 71
Petrie Cl. NW2 6G 47
Petrie Ho. *SE18* *6E 90*
(off Woolwich Comn.)
Petrie Mus. of Egyptian Archaeology ***4H 67 (4C 160)***
Petros Gdns. NW3 6A 48
Petticoat La. E1 5E 68 (6J 163)
Petticoat Lane Market ***7J 163***
(off Middlesex St.)
Petticoat Sq. E1 6F 69 (7J 163)
Petticoat Twr. E1 7J 163
Pettits Cl. RM1: Rom 2K 39
Pettits La. Nth. RM1: Rom 1K 39
Pettits Pl. RM10: Dag 5G 57
Pettits Rd. RM10: Dag 5G 57
Pettiward Cl. SW15 4E 100
Pettley Gdns. RM7: Rom 5K 39
Pettman Cres. SE28 3H 91
Pettsgrove Av.
HA0: Wemb 5C 44
Petts Hill UB5: N'olt 5F 43
Petts La. TW17: Shep 4C 130
Pett St. SE18 4C 90
PETTS WOOD 5G 145
Petts Wood Rd.
BR5: Orp 5G 145
Petty France
SW1 3G 85 (1B 172)
Petworth Cl. UB5: N'olt 7D 42
Petworth Gdns. SW20 3D 136
UB10: Uxb 1E 58
Petworth Rd. DA6: Bex 5G 111
N12 5H 15
Petworth St. SW11 1C 102
Petyt Pl. SW3 6C 84
Petyward SW3 4C 84 (4D 170)
Pevensey Av. EN1: Enf 2K 7
N11 5C 16
Pevensey Cl. TW7: Isle 7G 79
Pevensey Ct. W3 2H 81
Pevensey Ho. *E1* *5K 69*
(off Ben Jonson Rd.)
Pevensey Rd. E7 4H 53
SW17 4B 120
TW13: Felt 1C 114
Peverel E6 6E 72
Peverel Ho. RM10: Dag 2G 57
Peveret Cl. N11 5A 16
Peveril Dr. TW11: Tedd 5H 115
Peveril Ho. *SE1* *3D 86*
(off Rephidim St.)
Pewsey Cl. E4 5H 19
Peyton Pl. SE10 7E 88
Pharamond NW2 6F 47
Pharaoh Cl. CR4: Mitc 7D 138
Pheasant Cl. E16 6K 71
Phelp St. SE17 6D 86
Phelps Way UB3: Hayes 4H 77
Phene St. SW3 6C 84 (7D 170)
Philadelphia Ct. *SW10* *7A 84*
(off Uverdale Rd.)
Philbeach Gdns. SW5 5J 83
Phil Brown Pl. *SW8* *3F 103*
(off Wandsworth Rd.)
Philchurch Pl. E1 6G 69
Philimore Cl. SE18 5J 91
Philip Av. RM7: Rush G 1K 57
Philip Cl. RM7: Rush G 1K 57
Philip Ct. *W2* *5A 158*
(off Hall Pl.)

Plane St.—Porchester Rd.

Plane St. SE26 3H 123
Planetree Ct. W6 4F 83
(off Brook Grn.)
Plane Tree Cres.
TW13: Felt 3K 113
Plane Tree Ho. SE8 6A 88
(off Etta St.)
Plane Tree Wlk. N2 3C 30
SE19 6E 122
Plantagenet Cl.
KT4: Wor Pk 4K 147
Plantagenet Gdns.
RM6: Chad H 7D 38
Plantagenet Ho. SE18 3D 90
(off Leda Rd.)
Plantagenet Pl.
RM6: Chad H 7D 38
Plantagenet Rd. EN5: Barn 4F 5
Plantain Gdns. E11 3F 53
(off Hollydown Way)
Plantain Pl. SE1 2D 86 (6E 168)
Plantation, The SE3 2J 107
Plantation Wharf SW11 3A 102
Plasel Ct. E13 1K 71
(off Pawsey Cl.)
PLASHET 6C 54
Plashet Gro. E6 1A 72
Plashet Rd. E13 1J 71
Plassy Rd. SE6 7D 106
Plate Ho. E14 5D 88
(off Burrells Wharf Sq.)
Platina St. EC2 3F 163
Plato Rd. SW2 4J 103
Platt Halls NW9 2B 28
Platts La. NW3 4J 47
Platts Rd. EN3: Enf 1D 8
Platt St. NW1 2H 67
Platt, The SW15 3F 101
Plawsfield Rd.
BR3: Beck 1K 141
Plaxtol Cl. BR1: Brom 1A 144
Plaxtol Rd. DA8: Erith 7G 93
Plaxton Ct. E11 3H 53
Players Theatre 4F 167
(off Villiers St.)
Playfair Ho. E14 6C 70
(off Saracen St.)
Playfair Mans. W14 6G 83
(off Queen's Club Gdns.)
Playfair St. W6 5E 82
Playfield Av. RM5: Col R 1J 39
Playfield Cres. SE22 5F 105
Playfield Rd. HA8: Edg 2J 27
Playford Rd. N4 2K 49
(not continuous)
Playgreen Way SE6 3C 124
Playground Cl.
BR3: Beck 2K 141
Playhouse, The 7H 131
Playhouse Theatre 4F 167
(off Northumberland Av.)
Playhouse Yd.
EC4 6B 68 (1A 168)
Plaza Bus. Cen. EN3: Enf 2F 9
Plaza Pde. NW6 2K 65
Plaza Shop. Cen., The
W1 6G 67 (7B 160)
Pleasance Rd. SW15 5D 100
Pleasance, The SW15 4D 100
Pleasant Gro. CR0: Croy 3B 154
Pleasant Pl. HA2: Harr 1H 43
N1 7B 50
Pleasant Row NW1 1F 67
Pleasant Way HA0: Wemb 2C 62
Plender Pl. NW1 1G 67
(off Plender St.)
Plender St. NW1 1G 67
Pleshey Rd. N7 4H 49
Plesman Way SM6: Wall 7J 151
Plevna Cres. N15 6E 32
Plevna Rd. N9 3B 18
TW12: Hamp 1F 133
Plevna St. E14 3E 88
Pleydell Av. SE19 7F 123
W6 4B 82
Pleydell Ct. EC4 1K 167
(off Lombard La.)
Pleydell Est. EC1 2D 162
Pleydell St. EC4 1K 167
Plimsoll Cl. E14 6D 70
Plimsoll Rd. N4 3A 50
Plough Ct. EC3 7D 68 (2F 169)
Plough Farm Cl. HA4: Ruis 6F 23
Plough La. SE22 6F 105
SM6: Wall 4J 151
(Croydon Rd.)
SM6: Wall 7J 151
(Foresters Dr.)
SW17 5K 119
SW19 5K 119
TW11: Tedd 5A 116
Plough La. Cl. SM6: Wall 5J 151
Ploughmans Cl. NW1 1H 67
Ploughmans End
TW7: Isle 5H 97
Ploughmans Wlk. N2 2A 30
(off Long La.)
Plough Pl. EC4 6A 68 (7K 161)
Plough Rd. KT19: Eps 7K 147
SW11 3B 102
Plough St. E1 6F 69 (7K 163)
Plough Ter. SW11 4B 102
Plough Way SE16 4K 87
Plough Yd. EC2 4E 68 (4H 163)
Plover Ho. SW9 7A 86
(off Brixton Rd.)
Plover Way SE16 3A 88
UB4: Hayes 6B 60
Plowden Bldgs. EC4 2J 167
Plowman Cl. N18 5J 17
Plowman Way RM8: Dag 1C 56
Plumbers Row E1 5G 69
Plumbridge St. SE10 1E 106
Plum Cl. TW13: Felt 1J 113
Plume Ho. SE10 6D 88
(off Creek Rd.)
Plum Gth. TW8: Bford 4D 80
Plum La. SE18 7F 91
Plummer La. CR4: Mitc 2D 138
Plummer Rd. SW4 7H 103
Plumpton Cl. UB5: N'olt 6E 42
Plumpton Way
SM5: Cars 3C 150
PLUMSTEAD 4J 91
PLUMSTEAD COMMON 6G 91
Plumstead Comn. Rd.
SE18 6F 91
Plumstead High St. SE18 4H 91
Plumstead Rd. SE18 4F 91
Plumtree Cl. RM10: Dag 6H 57
SM6: Wall 7H 151
Plumtree Ct. EC4 6B 68 (7A 162)
Plymouth Ct. KT5: Surb 4E 134
(off Cranes Pk. Av.)
Plymouth Ho. IG11: Bark 7A 56
(off Keir Hardie Way)
SE10 1D 106
(off Devonshire Dr.)
Plymouth Rd. BR1: Brom 1K 143
E16 5J 71
Plymouth Wharf E14 4F 89
Plympton Av. NW6 7H 47
Plympton Cl. DA17: Belv 3E 92
Plympton Pl.
NW8 4C 66 (4C 158)
Plympton Rd. NW6 7H 47
Plympton St.
NW8 4C 66 (4C 158)
Plymstock Rd. DA16: Well 7C 92
Pocklington Cl. NW9 2A 28
W12 3C 82
(off Ashchurch Pk. Vs.)
Pocklington Lodge W12 3C 82
Pocock Av. UB7: W Dray 3B 76
Pocock St. SE1 2B 86 (6A 168)
Podmore Rd. SW18 4A 102
Poets Rd. N5 5D 50
Poets Way HA1: Harr 4J 25
Pointalls Cl. N3 2A 30
Point Cl. SE10 1E 106
Pointer Cl. SE28 6D 74
Pointers Cl. E14 5D 88
Pointers Cotts.
TW10: Rich 2C 116
Point Hill SE10 7E 88
Point Pl. HA9: Wemb 7H 45
Point Pleasant SW18 4J 101
Point Ter. E7 5K 53
(off Claremont Rd.)
Point, The HA4: Ruis 4J 41
Point West W8 4K 83
Point Wharf TW8: Bford 7E 80
Poland St. W1 6G 67 (1B 166)
Polebrook Rd. SE3 3A 108
Pole Cat All.
BR2: Short 2H 155
Polecroft La. SE6 2B 124
Polehamptons, The
TW12: Hamp 7G 115
Pole Hill Rd. E4 7K 9
UB10: Uxb 4D 58
Polesden Gdns. SW20 2D 136
Polesworth Ho. W2 5J 65
(off Alfred Rd.)
Polesworth Rd. RM9: Dag 7D 56
Police Sta. La.
WD23: Bush 1A 10
Polish War Memorial 7A 42
Pollard Cl. E16 7J 71
N7 4K 49
Pollard Ho. N1 1G 161
(off Northdown St.)
Pollard Rd. N20 2H 15
SM4: Mord 5B 138
Pollard Row E2 3G 69
Pollards Cres. SW16 3J 139
Pollards Hill E. SW16 3K 139
Pollards Hill Nth. SW16 3J 139
Pollards Hill Sth. SW16 3J 139
Pollards Hill W. SW16 3K 139
Pollard St. E2 3G 69
Pollards Wood Rd. SW16 3J 139
Pollard Wlk. DA14: Sidc 6C 128
Pollen St. W1 6G 67 (1A 166)
Pollitt Dr. NW8 4B 66 (3B 158)
Pollock Ho. W10 4G 65
(off Kensal Rd.)
Pollock's Toy Mus.
5G 67 (5B 160)
Polperro Cl. BR6: Orp 6K 145
Polperro M.
SE11 4B 86 (3K 173)
Polsted Rd. SE6 7B 106
Polthorne Gro. SE18 4G 91
Polworth Rd. SW16 5J 121
Polygon Rd.
NW1 2H 67 (1C 160)
Polygon, The NW8 1B 66
(off Avenue Rd.)
SW4 4G 103
Polytechnic St. SE18 4E 90
Pomell Way E1 6F 69 (7K 163)
Pomeroy Ho. E2 2K 69
(off St James's Av.)
W11 6G 65
(off Lancaster Rd.)
Pomeroy St. SE14 7J 87
Pomfret Rd. SE5 3B 104
Pomoja La. N19 2J 49
Pomona Ho. SE8 4A 88
(off Evelyn St.)
Pond Cl. N12 6H 15
SE3 2J 107
Pond Cott. La. BR3: Beck 1C 154
Pond Cotts. SE21 1E 122
PONDERS END 5D 8
Ponders End Ind. Est.
EN3: Enf 5F 9
Ponder St. N7 7K 49
(not continuous)
Pond Farm Est. E5 3J 51
Pondfield Ho. SE27 5C 122
Pondfield Rd. BR2: Short 1G 155
RM10: Dag 5H 57
Pond Grn. HA4: Ruis 2G 41
Pond Hill Gdns.
SM3: Sutt 6G 149
Pond Ho. HA7: Stan 6G 11
SW3 4C 84
Pond Lees Cl. RM10: Dag 7K 57
Pond Mead SE21 6D 104
Pond Path BR7: Chst 6F 127
Pond Pl. SW3 4C 84 (4C 170)
Pond Rd. E15 2G 71
SE3 2H 107
Pondside Cl. UB3: Hayes 6F 77
Pond Sq. N6 1E 48
Pond St. NW3 5C 48
Pond Way TW11: Tedd 6C 116
Pondwood Ri. BR6: Orp 7J 145
Ponler St. E1 6H 69
Ponsard Rd. NW10 3D 64
Ponsford St. E9 6J 51
Ponsonby Pl.
SW1 5H 85 (5D 172)
Ponsonby Rd. SW15 7D 100
Ponsonby Ter.
SW1 5H 85 (5D 172)
Pontefract Ct. UB5: N'olt 5F 43
(off Newmarket Av.)
Pontefract Rd.
BR1: Brom 5H 125
Ponton Rd. SW8 7H 85 (7D 172)
Pont St. SW1 3D 84 (2E 170)
Pont St. M. SW1 3D 84 (2E 170)
Pontypool Pl.
SE1 2B 86 (6A 168)
Pool Cl. BR3: Beck 5C 124
KT8: W Mole 5D 132
Pool Ct. SE6 2C 124
Poole Cl. HA4: Ruis 2G 41
Poole Ct. N1 7E 50
(off St Peter's Way)
TW5: Houn 2C 96
Poole Ct. Rd. TW4: Houn 2C 96
Poole Ho. SE11 2H 173
POOL END 5C 130
Pool End Cl. TW17: Shep 5C 130
Poole Rd. E9 6K 51
KT19: Eps 6K 147
Pooles Bldgs. WC1 4J 161
Pooles Cotts.
TW10: Rich 2D 116
Pooles La. SW10 7A 84
Pooles Pk. N4 2A 50
Poole St. N1 1D 68
Poole Way UB4: Hayes 3G 59
Pool Ho. NW8 5C 158
(off Penfold St.)
Poolmans St. SE16 2K 87
Pool Rd. HA1: Harr 7H 25
KT8: W Mole 5D 132
Poolsford Rd. NW9 4A 28
Poonah St. E1 6J 69
Pope Cl. SW19 6B 120
TW14: Felt 1H 113
Pope Ho. SE5 7D 86
(off Elmington Est.)
SE16 4H 87
(off Manor Est.)
Pope Rd. BR2: Short 5B 144
Popes Av. TW2: Twick 2J 115
Popes Ct. TW2: Twick 2J 115
Popes Dr. N3 1J 29
Popes Gro. CR0: Croy 3B 154
TW2: Twick 2J 115
Popes Head All.
EC3 6D 68 (1F 169)
Popes La. W5 3D 80
Popes Rd. SW9 3A 104
Pope St. SE1 2E 86 (7H 169)
Popham Cl. TW13: Felt 3D 114
Popham Gdns. TW9: Rich 3G 99
Popham Rd. N1 1C 68
Popham St. N1 1B 68
(not continuous)
Pop-In Commercial Cen.
HA9: Wemb 5H 45
Popinjays Row SM3: Sutt 5F 149
(off Netley Cl.)
POPLAR 7D 70
Poplar Av. CR4: Mitc 1D 138
UB2: S'hall 3F 79
UB7: W Dray 7B 58
Poplar Bath St. E14 6D 70
Poplar Bus. Pk. E14 7E 70
Poplar Cl. E9 5B 52
HA5: Pinn 1B 24
Poplar Ct. SW19 5J 119
TW1: Twick 6C 98
UB5: N'olt 2A 60
Poplar Cres. KT19: Eps 6J 147
Poplar Farm Cl.
KT19: Eps 6J 147
Poplar Gdns.
KT3: N Mald 2K 135
SE28 7C 74
Poplar Gro. HA9: Wemb 3J 45
KT3: N Mald 2K 135
N11 6K 15
W6 2E 82
Poplar High St. E14 7D 70
Poplar Ho. SE4 4B 106
(off Wickham Rd.)
SE16 2K 87
(off Woodland Cres.)
Poplar M. W12 1E 82
Poplar Mt. DA17: Belv 4H 93
Poplar Pl. SE28 7C 74
UB3: Hayes 7J 59
W2 7K 65
Poplar Rd. E12 2C 54
SE24 4C 104
SM3: Sutt 1H 149
SW19 2J 137
TW15: Ashf 5E 112
Poplar Rd. Sth. SW19 3J 137
Poplars Av. NW2 6E 46
Poplars Cl. HA4: Ruis 1G 41
Poplars Rd. E17 6D 34
Poplars, The N14 5A 6
Poplar St. RM7: Rom 4J 39
Poplar Vw. HA9: Wemb 2D 44
Poplar Wlk. CR0: Croy 2C 152
SE24 3C 104
(not continuous)
Poplar Way IG6: Ilf 4G 37
TW13: Felt 3J 113
Poppins Ct. EC4 6B 68 (1A 168)
Poppleton Rd. E11 6G 35
Poppy Cl. DA17: Belv 3H 93
SM6: Wall 1E 150
Poppy La. CR0: Croy 7J 141
Porchester Cl. SE5 4C 104
Porchester Ct. W2 7K 65
(off Porchester Gdns.)
Porchester Gdns. W2 7K 65
Porchester Gdns. M. W2 6K 65
Porchester Ga. W2 7K 65
(off Bayswater Rd., not continuous)
Porchester Ho. E1 6H 69
(off Philpot St.)
Porchester Mead
BR3: Beck 6C 124
Porchester M. W2 6K 65
Porchester Pl.
W2 6C 66 (1D 164)
Porchester Rd.
KT1: King T 2H 135
W2 6K 65

Porchester Sq.—Pricklers Hill

Porchester Sq. W2 . . . . 6K **65**
Porchester Ter. W2 . . . . 7A **66**
Porchester Ter. Nth. W2 . . . . . 6K **65**
Porch Way N20 . . . . 3J **15**
Porcupine Cl. SE9 . . . . 2C **126**
Porden Rd. SW2 . . . . 4K **103**
Porlock Av. HA2: Harr 1G **43**
Porlock Ho. SE26 . . . . 3G **123**
Porlock Rd. EN1: Enf 7A **8**
W10 . . . . 4F **65**
Porlock St. SE1 . . . . 2D **86** (6F **169**)
Porrington Cl. BR7: Chst . . . 1D **144**
Porson Ct. SE13 . . . . 3D **106**
Portal Cl. HA4: Ruis 4J **41**
(not continuous)
SE27 . . . . 3A **122**
UB10: Uxb 7A **40**
(not continuous)
Portbury Cl. SE15 . . . . 1G **105**
Port Cres. E13 . . . . 4K **71**
Portcullis Ho. SW1 . . . . 7E **166**
Portcullis Lodge Rd.
EN1: Enf 3J **7**
Portelet Ct. *N1* *1E* ***68***
(off De Beauvoir Est.)
Portelet Rd. E1 . . . . 3K **69**
Porten Ho's. *W14* *3G* ***83***
(off Porten Rd.)
Porten Rd. W14 . . . . 3G **83**
Porter Rd. E6 . . . . 6D **72**
Porters & Walters Almshouses
N22 . . . . *7E* ***16***
(off Nightingale Rd.)
Porters Av. RM8: Dag 6B **56**
RM9: Dag 6B **56**
Porter Sq. N19 . . . . 1J **49**
Porter St. SE1 . . . . . 1C **86** (4D **168**)
W1 . . . . 5D **66** (5F **159**)
Porters Wlk. *E1* *7H* ***69***
(off Balkan Wlk.)
Porters Way
UB7: W Dray 3B **76**
Porteus Rd. W2 . . . . 5A **66** (5A **158**)
Portgate Cl. W9 . . . . 4H **65**
Porthcawe Rd. SE26 . . . . . . 4A **124**
Porthkerry Av.
DA16: Well 4A **110**
Port Ho. *E14* *5D* ***88***
(off Burrells Wharf Sq.)
Portia Ct. IG11: Bark 7A **56**
SE11 . . . . *5B* ***86***
(off Opal St.)
Portia Way E3 . . . . 4B **70**
Porticos, The SW3 . . . . 7A **170**
Portinscale Rd. SW15 . . . . . 5G **101**
Portland Av. DA15: Sidc 6A **110**
KT3: N Mald 7B **136**
N16 . . . . 7F **33**
Portland Cl. RM6: Chad H . . . 5E **38**
Portland Commercial Est.
IG11: Bark 2C **74**
Portland Ct. *N1* *7E* ***50***
(off St Peter's Way)
SE1 . . . . *3D* ***86***
(off Gt. Dover St.)
SE14 . . . . *6A* ***88***
(off Whitcher Cl.)
Portland Cres. HA7: Stan 2D **26**
SE9 . . . . 2C **126**
TW13: Felt 4F **113**
UB6: G'frd 4F **61**
Portland Dr. EN2: Enf 1K **7**
Portland Gdns. N4 . . . . 6B **32**
RM6: Chad H 5D **38**
Portland Gro. SW8 . . . . 1K **103**
Portland Ho. SW1 . . . . 2A **172**
Portland M. W1 . . . . 6G **67** (1B **166**)
Portland Pl. *SE25* *4G* ***141***
(off Sth. Norwood Hill)
W1 . . . . 4F **67** (4J **159**)
Portland Ri. N4 . . . . 1B **50**
Portland Ri. Est. N4 . . . . 1C **50**
Portland Rd. BR1: Brom 4A **126**
CR4: Mitc 2C **138**
KT1: King T 3E **134**
N15 . . . . 4F **33**
SE9 . . . . 2C **126**
SE25 . . . . 4G **141**
TW15: Ashf 3A **112**
UB2: S'hall 3D **78**
UB4: Hayes 3G **59**
W11 . . . . 7G **65**
Portland Sq. E1 . . . . 1H **87**
Portland St. SE17 . . . . 5D **86**
Portland Ter. TW9: Rich 4D **98**
Portland Wlk. SE17 . . . . 6D **86**
Portman Av. SW14 . . . . 3K **99**
Portman Cl. DA5: Bexl 1K **129**
DA7: Bex 3E **110**
W1 . . . . 6D **66** (7F **159**)
Portman Dr. IG8: Wfd G 2B **36**
Portman Gdns. NW9 . . . . 2K **27**
UB10: Uxb 7C **40**
Portman Ga. NW1 . . . . 4D **158**
Portman Mans. *W1* *5F* ***159***
(off Chiltern St.)
Portman M. Sth.
W1 . . . . 6E **66** (1G **165**)
Portman Pl. E2 . . . . 3J **69**
Portman Rd. KT1: King T . . . 2F **135**
Portman Sq. W1 . . . 6E **66** (7G **159**)
Portman St. W1 . . . . 6E **66** (1G **165**)
Portman Towers
W1 . . . . 6D **66** (7F **159**)
Portmeadow Wlk. SE2 . . . . . . 2D **92**
Port Meers Cl. E17 . . . . 6B **34**
Portnall Rd. W9 . . . . 2H **65**
Portnoi Cl. RM1: Rom 2K **39**
Portobello Ct. Est. W11 . . . . . 6H **65**
Portobello M. W11 . . . . 7J **65**
Portobello Rd. W10 . . . . 5G **65**
W11 . . . . 6H **65**
Portobello Road Market *5G* ***65***
Portpool La. EC1 . . . 5A **68** (5J **161**)
Portree Cl. N22 . . . . 7E **16**
Portree St. E14 . . . . 6F **71**
Portrush Ct. *UB1: S'hall* *6G* ***61***
(off Whitecote Rd.)
Portsdown HA8: Edg 5B **12**
Portsdown Av. NW11 . . . . 6H **29**
Portsdown M. NW11 . . . . 6H **29**
Portsea Hall *W2* *1D* ***164***
(off Portsea Pl.)
Portsea M. W2 . . . . 1D **164**
Portsea Pl. W2 . . . . 6C **66** (1D **164**)
Portslade Rd. SW8 . . . . 2G **103**
Portsmouth Av.
KT7: T Ditt 7A **134**
Portsmouth M. E16 . . . . 1K **89**
Portsmouth Rd.
KT6: Surb 7A **134**
KT7: Surb, T Ditt 1A **146**
SW15 . . . . 7D **100**
Portsmouth St.
WC2 . . . . 6K **67** (1G **167**)
Portsoken St.
EC3 . . . . 7F **69** (2J **169**)
Portswood Pl. SW15 . . . . . . 6B **100**
Portugal Gdns.
TW2: Twick 2G **115**
Portugal St.
WC2 . . . . 6K **67** (1G **167**)
Portway E15 . . . . 1H **71**
Portway Gdns. SE18 . . . . 7B **90**
Pory Ho. SE11 . . . . 4K **85**
Poseidon Ct. *E14* *4C* ***88***
(off Homer Dr.)
Postern Grn. EN2: Enf 2F **7**
Postern, The EC2 . . . . 6D **162**
Post La. TW2: Twick 1H **115**
Postmill Cl. CR0: Croy 3J **153**
Post Office All.
TW12: Hamp 2F **133**
Post Office App. E7 . . . . 5K **53**
Post Office Ct. *EC4* *1F* ***169***
(off Barbican)
Post Office Way SW8 . . . . . . 7H **85**
Post Rd. UB2: S'hall 3F **79**
Postway M. IG1: Ilf 3F **55**
(not continuous)
Potier St. SE1 . . . . 3D **86**
Potter Cl. CR4: Mitc 2F **139**
Potteries, The EN5: Barn 5D **4**
Potterne Cl. SW19 . . . . 7F **101**
Potters Cl. CR0: Croy 1A **154**
Potters Fld. *EN1: Enf* *4K* ***7***
(off Lincoln Rd.)
Potters Flds.
SE1 . . . . 1E **86** (5H **169**)
Potters Gro. KT3: N Mald . . . 4J **135**
Potters Hgts. Cl.
HA5: Pinn 1K **23**
Potters La. EN5: Barn 4D **4**
SW16 . . . . 6H **121**
Potters Lodge *E14* *5E* ***88***
(off Manchester Rd.)
Potters Rd. EN5: Barn 4E **4**
SW6 . . . . 2A **102**
Potter St. HA5: Pinn 1K **23**
HA6: Nwood 1J **23**
Potter St. Hill HA5: Pinn 1K **23**
Pottery La. W11 . . . . 1G **83**
Pottery Rd. DA5: Bexl 2J **129**
TW8: Bford 6E **80**
Pottery St. SE16 . . . . 2H **87**
Pott St. E2 . . . . 3H **69**
Poulett Gdns.
TW1: Twick 1A **116**
Poulett Rd. E6 . . . . 2D **72**
Poulters Wood BR2: Kes 5B **156**
Poulton Av. SM1: Sutt 3B **150**
Poulton Cl. E8 . . . . 6H **51**
Poultry EC2 . . . . 6D **68** (1E **168**)
Pound Cl. KT6: Surb 1C **146**
Pound Grn. DA5: Bexl 7G **111**
Pound La. NW10 . . . . 6C **46**
Pound Pk. Rd. SE7 . . . . 4B **90**
Pound Pl. SE9 . . . . 6E **108**
Pound St. SM5: Cars 5D **150**
Pound Way BR7: Chst 7G **127**
Pountney Rd. SW11 . . . . 3E **102**
POVEREST **4K 145**
Poverest Rd. BR5: Orp 5K **145**
Povey Ho. *SE17* *4E* ***86***
(off Tatum St.)
Powder Mill La.
TW2: Twick 7D **96**
Powell Cl. HA8: Edg 6A **12**
KT9: Chess 5D **146**
SM6: Wall 7J **151**
Powell Ct. *CR2: S Croy* *4B* ***152***
(off Bramley Hill)
E17 . . . . 3D **34**
Powell Gdns. RM10: Dag 4G **57**
Powell Rd. E5 . . . . 3H **51**
IG9: Buck H 1F **21**
Powells Wlk. W4 . . . . 6A **82**
Powergate Bus. Pk. NW10 . . . 3K **63**
Power Rd. W4 . . . . 4G **81**
Powers Ct. TW1: Twick 7D **98**
Powerscroft Rd.
DA14: Sidc 6C **128**
(not continuous)
E5 . . . . 4J **51**
Powis Ct. *W11* *6H* ***65***
(off Powis Gdns.)
WD23: Bush *1C* ***10***
(off Rutherford Way)
Powis Gdns. NW11 . . . . 7H **29**
W11 . . . . 6H **65**
Powis M. W11 . . . . 6H **65**
Powis Pl. WC1 . . . . . 4J **67** (4F **161**)
Powis Rd. E3 . . . . 3D **70**
Powis Sq. W11 . . . . 6H **65**
(not continuous)
Powis St. SE18 . . . . 3E **90**
Powis Ter. W11 . . . . 6H **65**
Powlett Ho. *NW1* *6F* ***49***
(off Powlett Pl.)
Powlett Pl. NW1 . . . . 7E **48**
(not continuous)
Pownall Gdns. TW3: Houn . . . 4F **97**
Pownall Rd. E8 . . . . 1F **69**
TW3: Houn 4F **97**
Pownsett Ter. IG1: Ilf 5G **55**
Powster Rd. BR1: Brom 5J **125**
Powys Cl. DA7: Bex 6D **92**
Powys Ct. N11 . . . . 5D **16**
Powys La. N11 . . . . 5D **16**
N13 . . . . 4D **16**
N14 . . . . 4D **16**
Poynders Ct. SW4 . . . . 6G **103**
Poynders Gdns. SW4 . . . . . . 7G **103**
Poynders Rd. SW4 . . . . 6G **103**
Poynings Rd. N19 . . . . 3G **49**
Poynings Way N12 . . . . 5D **14**
Poyntell Cres. BR7: Chst . . . 1H **145**
Poynter Ct. *UB5: N'olt* *2B* ***60***
(off Gallery Gdns.)
Poynter Ho. *NW8* *3A* ***158***
(off Fisherton St.)
W11 . . . . *1F* ***83***
(off Queensdale Cres.)
Poynter Rd. EN1: Enf 5A **8**
Poynton Rd. N17 . . . . 2G **33**
Poyntz Rd. SW11 . . . . 2D **102**
Poyser St. E2 . . . . 2H **69**
Praed M. W2 . . . . . 6B **66** (7B **158**)
Praed St. W2 . . . . . 6B **66** (1A **164**)
Pragel St. E13 . . . . 2A **72**
Pragnell Rd. SE12 . . . . 2K **125**
Prague Pl. SW2 . . . . 5J **103**
Prah Rd. N4 . . . . 2A **50**
Prairie St. SW8 . . . . 2E **102**
Pratt M. NW1 . . . . 1G **67**
Pratts Pas. KT1: King T 2E **134**
Pratt St. NW1 . . . . 1G **67**
Pratt Wlk. SE11 . . . . 4K **85** (3H **173**)
Prayle Gro. NW2 . . . . 1F **47**
Preachers Ct. *EC1* *5B* ***162***
(off Charterhouse Sq.)
Prebend Gdns. W6 . . . . 4B **82**
(not continuous)
Prebend Mans. *W4* *4B* ***82***
(off Chiswick High Rd.)
Prebend St. N1 . . . . 1C **68**
Precinct Rd. UB3: Hayes 7J **59**
Precincts, The
SM4: Mord 6J **137**
Precinct, The
KT8: W Mole 3F **133**
N1 . . . . 1C **68**
(not continuous)
Premier Cnr. W9 . . . . 2H **65**
Premier Ct. EN3: Enf 1D **8**
Premiere Pl. E14 . . . . 7C **70**
Premier Ho. *N1* *7B* ***50***
(off Waterloo Ter.)
Premier Pk. NW10 . . . . 1H **63**
Premier Pk. Rd. NW10 . . . . . 2H **63**
Premier Pl. SW15 . . . . 4G **101**
Prendergast Rd. SE3 . . . . . . 3G **107**
Prentice Ct. SW19 . . . . 5H **119**
Prentis Rd. SW16 . . . . 4H **121**
Prentiss Ct. SE7 . . . . 4B **90**
Presburg Rd.
KT3: N Mald 5A **136**
Presburg St. E5 . . . . 3K **51**
Prescelly Pl. HA8: Edg 1F **27**
Prescot St. E1 . . . . . 7F **69** (2K **169**)
Prescott Av. BR5: Orp 6F **145**
Prescott Cl. SW16 . . . . 7J **121**
Prescott Ho. *SE5* *6B* ***86***
(off Hillingdon St.)
Prescott Pl. SW4 . . . . 3H **103**
Presentation M. SW2 . . . . . . 2K **121**
Preshaw Cres. CR4: Mitc . . . 3C **138**
President Dr. E1 . . . . 1H **87**
President Ho.
EC1 . . . . 3B **68** (2B **162**)
President Quay E1 . . . . 4K **169**
President St. EC1 . . . . 1C **162**
Prespa Cl. N9 . . . . 2D **18**
Press Ho. NW10 . . . . 3K **45**
Press Rd. NW10 . . . . 3K **45**
Prestage Way E14 . . . . 7E **70**
Prestbury Rd. E7 . . . . 7A **54**
Prestbury Sq. SE9 . . . . 4D **126**
Prested Rd. SW11 . . . . 4C **102**
Prestige Way NW4 . . . . 5E **28**
PRESTON **1E 44**
Preston Av. E4 . . . . 6A **20**
Preston Cl. SE1 . . . . 4E **86**
TW2: Twick 3J **115**
Preston Ct. *DA14: Sidc* *4K* ***127***
(off Crescent, The)
EN5: Barn 4F **5**
Preston Dr. DA7: Bex 1D **110**
E11 . . . . 5A **36**
KT19: Eps 6A **148**
Preston Gdns. IG1: Ilf 6C **36**
NW10 . . . . 6B **46**
Preston Hill HA3: Harr 7E **26**
Preston Ho. *RM10: Dag* *3G* ***57***
(off Uvedale Rd.)
SE1 . . . . *7J* ***169***
(off Stanworth St.)
SE17 . . . . *4E* ***86***
(off Preston Cl.)
Preston Pl. NW2 . . . . 6C **46**
TW10: Rich 5E **98**
Preston Rd. E11 . . . . 6G **35**
HA9: Harr, Wemb 1E **44**
SE19 . . . . 6B **122**
SW20 . . . . 7B **118**
TW17: Shep 5C **130**
Prestons Rd. BR2: Short 3J **155**
E14 . . . . 7E **70**
Preston St. E2 . . . . 2K **69**
Preston Waye HA3: Harr 1E **44**
Prestwich Ter. SW4 . . . . 5G **103**
Prestwick Cl. UB2: S'hall 5C **78**
Prestwick Ct. *UB1: S'hall* *7G* ***61***
(off Baird Av.)
Prestwood Av.
HA3: Harr 4B **26**
Prestwood Cl. HA3: Harr 4B **26**
SE18 . . . . 6A **92**
Prestwood Gdns.
CR0: Croy 7C **140**
Prestwood Ho. *SE16* *3H* ***87***
(off Drummond Rd.)
Prestwood St.
N1 . . . . 2C **68** (1D **162**)
Pretoria Av. E17 . . . . 4A **34**
Pretoria Cl. N17 . . . . 7A **18**
Pretoria Cres. E4 . . . . 1K **19**
Pretoria Rd. E4 . . . . 1K **19**
E11 . . . . 1F **53**
E16 . . . . 4H **71**
IG1: Ilf 5F **55**
N17 . . . . 7A **18**
RM7: Rom 4J **39**
SW16 . . . . 6F **121**
Pretoria Rd. Nth. N18 . . . . . . 6A **18**
N18 . . . . 6A **18**
Prevost Rd. N11 . . . . 2K **15**
Priam Ho. *E2* *2H* ***69***
(off Old Bethnal Grn. Rd.)
Price Cl. NW7 . . . . 6B **14**
SW17 . . . . 3D **120**
Price Ct. SW11 . . . . 3B **102**
Price Ho. *N1* *1C* ***68***
(off Britannia Row)
Price Rd. CR0: Croy 5B **152**
Prices St. SE1 . . . . . 1B **86** (5B **168**)
Prices Yd. N1 . . . . 1K **67**
Price Way TW12: Hamp 6C **114**
Prichard Ct. N7 . . . . 6K **49**
Pricklers Hill EN5: Barn 6E **4**

Queen Margaret Flats—Radlett Cl.

Queen Margaret Flats E2 . . . 3H 69
(off St Jude's Rd.)
Queen Margarets Gro.
N1 . . . 5E 50
Queen Mary Av.
SM4: Mord . . . 5F 137
Queen Mary Cl.
KT6: Surb . . . 3H 147
Queen Mary Ho. E16 . . . 7K 71
(off Wesley Av.)
Queen Mary Rd. SE19 . . . 6B 122
TW17: Shep . . . 2E 130
Queen Marys Av.
SM5: Cars . . . 7D 150
Queen Marys Bldgs.
SW1 . . . 3B 172
(off Stillington St.)
Queen Marys Ct. SE10 . . . 6F 89
(off Park Row)
Queen of Denmark Ct.
SE16 . . . 3B 88
Queens Acre SM3: Sutt . . . 7F 149
Queens Av. HA7: Stan . . . 3C 26
IG8: Wfd G . . . 5E 20
N3 . . . 7F 15
N10 . . . 3E 30
N20 . . . 2G 15
N21 . . . 1G 17
TW13: Felt . . . 4A 114
UB6: G'frd . . . 6F 61
Queensberry M. W.
SW7 . . . 4B 84 (3A 170)
Queensberry Pl. E12 . . . 5B 54
SW7 . . . 4B 84 (3A 170)
Queensberry Way
SW7 . . . 4B 84 (3A 170)
Queensborough Ct. NW11 . . . 4H 29
(off Nth. Circular Rd.)
Queensborough M. W2 . . . 7A 66
Queensborough Pas. W2 . . . 7A 66
(off Queensborough M.)
Queensborough Studios
W2 . . . 7A 66
(off Queensborough M.)
Queensborough Ter. W2 . . . 7K 65
Queensbridge Ct. E2 . . . 1F 69
(off Queensbridge Rd.)
Queensbridge Pk.
TW7: Isle . . . 5J 97
Queensbridge Rd. E2 . . . 1F 69
E8 . . . 6F 51
QUEENSBURY . . . 3E 26
Queensbury Circ. Pde.
HA3: Harr . . . 3E 26
Queensbury Ho.
TW9: Rich . . . 5C 98
Queensbury Rd.
HA0: Wemb . . . 2F 63
NW9 . . . 7K 27
Queensbury Sta. Pde.
HA8: Edg . . . 3F 27
Queensbury St. N1 . . . 7C 50
Queen's Chapel of the Savoy, The
. . . 7K 67
Queens Cir. SW8 . . . 7F 85
Queens Cl. HA8: Edg . . . 5B 12
SM6: Wall . . . 5F 151
Queens Club Gdns. W14 . . . 6G 83
Queen's Club (Tennis) . . . 5G 83
Queens Ct. CR2: S Croy . . . 5C 152
(off Warham Rd.)
HA3: Harr . . . 2B 26
IG9: Buck H . . . 2G 21
NW6 . . . 5K 47
NW8 . . . 2B 66
(off Queen's Ter.)
NW11 . . . 5H 29
SE23 . . . 2H 123
TW10: Rich . . . 6F 99
W2 . . . 7K 65
(off Queensway)
Queenscourt HA9: Wemb . . . 4E 44
Queens Cres. NW5 . . . 6E 48
TW10: Rich . . . 5F 99
Queenscroft Rd. SE9 . . . 5B 108
Queensdale Cres. W11 . . . 1F 83
Queensdale Pl. W11 . . . 1G 83
Queensdale Rd. W11 . . . 1F 83
Queensdale Wlk. W11 . . . 1G 83
Queensdown Rd. E5 . . . 4H 51
Queens Dr. E10 . . . 7C 34
KT5: Surb . . . 7G 135
KT7: T Ditt . . . 6A 134
N4 . . . 2B 50
W5 . . . 6F 63
Queens Elm Pde. SW3 . . . 5B 170
(off Old Chu. St.)
Queens Elm Sq.
SW3 . . . 5B 84 (6A 170)
Queens Ferry Wlk. N17 . . . 4H 33
Queensfield Ct.
SM3: Sutt . . . 4E 148
Queens Gallery . . . 2F 85 (7A 166)
Queens Gdns. NW4 . . . 5E 28
RM13: Rain . . . 2K 75
TW5: Houn . . . 1C 96
W2 . . . 7A 66
W5 . . . 4C 62
Queens Ga.
SW7 . . . 2A 84 (7A 164)
Queens Ga. Gdns. SW7 . . . 3A 84
SW15 . . . 4D 100
Queensgate Gdns.
BR7: Chst . . . 1H 145
Queens Ga. M. E9 . . . 7A 52
SW7 . . . 3A 84
Queens Ga. Pl. SW7 . . . 3A 84
Queensgate Pl. NW6 . . . 7J 47
Queens Ga. Pl. M.
SW7 . . . 3A 84 (2A 170)
Queens Ga. Ter.
SW7 . . . 3A 84 (1A 170)
Queens Gro. NW8 . . . 1B 66
Queens Gro. Rd. E4 . . . 1A 20
Queens Gro. Studios NW8 . . . 1B 66
Queens Head Pas.
EC4 . . . 6C 68 (7C 162)
Queens Head St. N1 . . . 1B 68
Queens Head Yd. SE1 . . . 5E 168
Queens Ho. SW8 . . . 7J 85
(off Sth. Lambeth Rd.)
TW11: Tedd . . . 6K 115
Queen's House, The . . . 6F 89
Queens Keep TW1: Twick . . . 6C 98
Queensland Av. N18 . . . 6H 17
SW19 . . . 1K 137
Queensland Cl. E17 . . . 2B 34
Queensland Ho. E16 . . . 1E 90
(off Rymill St.)
Queensland Pl. N7 . . . 4A 50
Queensland Rd. N7 . . . 4A 50
Queens La. N10 . . . 3F 31
TW15: Ashf . . . 4B 112
Queens Mans. W6 . . . 4F 83
(off Brook Grn.)
Queens Mkt. E13 . . . 1A 72
Queensmead NW8 . . . 1B 66
Queens Mead Rd.
BR2: Short . . . 2H 143
Queensmere Cl. SW19 . . . 2F 119
Queensmere Ct. SW13 . . . 7B 82
Queensmere Rd. SW19 . . . 2F 119
Queens M. W2 . . . 7K 65
(not continuous)
Queensmill Rd. SW6 . . . 7F 83
Queens Pde. N8 . . . 4B 32
Queens Pde. N11 . . . 5J 15
(off Friern Barnet Rd.)
NW2 . . . 6E 46
(off Willesden La.)
NW4 . . . 5E 28
(off Queens Rd.)
W5 . . . 6F 63
Queens Pde. Cl. N11 . . . 5J 15
Queens Pk. Ct. W10 . . . 3F 65
Queens Pk. Gdns.
TW13: Felt . . . 3H 113
Queens Pk. Rangers F.C.
(Loftus Road) . . . 1D 82
Queens Pas. BR7: Chst . . . 6F 127
Queens Pl. SM4: Mord . . . 4J 137
Queens Prom.
KT1: King T . . . 4D 134
Queen Sq.
WC1 . . . 4J 67 (4F 161)
Queen Sq. Pl. WC1 . . . 4F 161
Queens Quay EC4 . . . 2C 168
(off Up. Thames St.)
Queens Reach
KT1: King T . . . 2D 134
KT8: E Mos . . . 4J 133
Queens Ride SW13 . . . 3C 100
SW15 . . . 3D 100
Queens Ri. TW10: Rich . . . 6F 99
Queens Rd.
BR1: Brom . . . 2J 143
BR3: Beck . . . 2A 142
BR7: Chst . . . 6F 127
CR0: Croy . . . 6B 140
DA16: Well . . . 2B 110
E11 . . . 7F 35
E13 . . . 1K 71
E17 . . . 6B 34
EN1: Enf . . . 4K 7
EN5: Barn . . . 3A 4
IG9: Buck H . . . 2E 20
IG11: Bark . . . 6G 55
KT2: King T . . . 7G 117
KT3: N Mald . . . 4B 136
KT7: T Ditt . . . 5K 133
N3 . . . 1A 30
N9 . . . 3C 18
N11 . . . 7D 16
NW4 . . . 5E 28
SE14 . . . 1J 105
SE15 . . . 1H 105
SM4: Mord . . . 4J 137
SM6: Wall . . . 5F 151
SW14 . . . 3K 99
SW19 . . . 6H 119
TW1: Twick . . . 1A 116
TW3: Houn . . . 3F 97
TW10: Rich . . . 7F 99
TW11: Tedd . . . 6K 115
TW12: Hamp . . . 4F 115
TW13: Felt . . . 1K 113
UB2: S'hall . . . 2B 78
UB3: Hayes . . . 6G 59
UB7: W Dray . . . 2B 76
W5 . . . 6E 62
Queens Rd. W. E13 . . . 2J 71
Queens Row SE17 . . . 6D 86
Queens Ter. E1 . . . 4J 69
E13 . . . 1K 71
NW8 . . . 1B 66
Queens Ter. TW7: Isle . . . 4A 98
Queens Ter. Cotts. W7 . . . 2J 79
Queen's Theatre
Westminster . . . 2C 166
(off Shaftesbury Av.)
Queensthorpe Rd.
SE26 . . . 4K 123
Queenstown M. SW11 . . . 2F 103
Queenstown Rd.
SW8 . . . 6F 85 (7J 171)
Queen St. CR0: Croy . . . 4C 152
DA7: Bex . . . 3F 111
EC4 . . . 7C 68 (2D 168)
(not continuous)
N17 . . . 6K 17
RM7: Rom . . . 6K 39
W1 . . . 1F 85 (4J 165)
Queen St. Pl.
EC4 . . . 7C 68 (2D 168)
Queensville Rd.
SW12 . . . 7H 103
Queens Wlk. E4 . . . 1A 20
HA1: Harr . . . 4J 25
HA4: Ruis . . . 2A 42
NW9 . . . 2J 45
SW1 . . . 1G 85 (5A 166)
TW15: Ashf . . . 4A 112
W5 . . . 4C 62
Queens Wlk. Ter.
HA4: Ruis . . . 3A 42
Queens Wlk., The
SE1 . . . 1E 86 (4F 169)
(Morgan's La.)
SE1 . . . 7A 68
(Oxo Tower Wharf)
SE1 . . . 1K 85 (4H 167)
(Waterloo Rd.)
Queens Way NW4 . . . 5E 28
TW13: Felt . . . 4A 114
Queensway BR4: W W'ck . . . 3G 155
BR5: Orp . . . 5G 145
CR0: Croy . . . 6K 151
EN3: Enf . . . 4C 8
TW16: Sun T . . . 2K 131
W2 . . . 6K 65
Queensway Bus. Cen.
EN3: Enf . . . 4C 8
Queensway Ind. Est.
EN3: Enf . . . 4D 8
Queenswell Av. N20 . . . 3H 15
Queens Wharf W6 . . . 5E 82
Queenswood Av.
CR7: Thor H . . . 5A 140
E17 . . . 1E 34
SM6: Wall . . . 4H 151
TW3: Houn . . . 2D 96
TW12: Hamp . . . 6F 115
Queenswood Ct. SE27 . . . 4D 122
SW4 . . . 5J 103
Queenswood Gdns. E11 . . . 1K 53
Queenswood Pk. N3 . . . 2G 29
Queenswood Rd.
DA15: Sidc . . . 5K 109
SE23 . . . 3K 123
Queens Wood Rd. N10 . . . 6F 31
Queens Yd.
WC1 . . . 5G 67 (4B 160)
QUEEN VICTORIA . . . 4E 148
Queen Victoria Av.
HA0: Wemb . . . 7D 44
Queen Victoria Memorial
. . . 2G 85 (7A 166)
Queen Victoria Seamans Rest
E14 . . . 6D 70
(off E. India Dock Rd.)
Queen Victoria St.
EC4 . . . 7B 68 (2A 168)
Queen Victoria Ter. E1 . . . 7H 69
(off Sovereign Cl.)
Quemerford Rd. N7 . . . 5K 49
Quendon Ho. W10 . . . 4E 64
(off Sutton Way)
Quenington Ct. SE15 . . . 6F 87
Quentin Ho. SE1 . . . 6A 168
(off Chaplin Cl.)
SE1 . . . 7K 167
(off Gray St., not continuous)
Quentin Pl. SE13 . . . 3G 107
Quentin Rd. SE13 . . . 3G 107
Quernmore Cl.
BR1: Brom . . . 6J 125
Quernmore Rd.
BR1: Brom . . . 6J 125
N4 . . . 6A 32
Querrin St. SW6 . . . 2A 102
Quested Ct. E8 . . . 5H 51
(off Brett Rd.)
Quex M. NW6 . . . 1J 65
Quex Rd. NW6 . . . 1J 65
Quick Rd. W4 . . . 5A 82
Quicks Rd. SW19 . . . 7K 119
Quick St. N1 . . . 2B 68
Quick St. M. N1 . . . 2B 68
Quickswood NW3 . . . 7C 48
Quiet Nook BR2: Kes . . . 3B 156
Quill La. SW15 . . . 4F 101
Quill St. N4 . . . 3A 50
W5 . . . 2E 62
Quilp St. SE1 . . . 2C 86 (6C 168)
(not continuous)
Quilter Ho. W10 . . . 3H 65
(off Dart St.)
Quilter St. E2 . . . 3G 69 (1K 163)
SE18 . . . 5K 91
Quilting Ct. SE16 . . . 2K 87
(off Garter Way)
Quinta Dr. EN5: Barn . . . 5A 4
Quintin Av. SW20 . . . 1H 137
Quintin Cl. HA5: Pinn . . . 4K 23
Quinton Cl. BR3: Beck . . . 3E 142
SM6: Wall . . . 4F 151
TW5: Houn . . . 7K 77
Quinton Ho. SW8 . . . 7J 85
(off Wyvil Rd.)
Quinton Rd. KT7: T Ditt . . . 1A 146
Quinton St. SW18 . . . 2A 120
Quixley St. E14 . . . 7F 71
Quorn Rd. SE22 . . . 4E 104

R

Rabbit Row W8 . . . 1J 83
Rabbits Rd. E12 . . . 4C 54
Rabournmead Dr.
UB5: N'olt . . . 5C 42
Raby Rd. KT3: N Mald . . . 4K 135
Raby St. E14 . . . 6A 70
Raccoon Way TW4: Houn . . . 2A 96
Rachel Cl. IG6: Ilf . . . 3H 37
Rachel Point E5 . . . 4G 51
Racine SE5 . . . 1E 104
(off Peckham Rd.)
Rackham Cl. DA16: Well . . . 2B 110
Rackham M. SW16 . . . 6G 121
Rackstraw Ho. NW3 . . . 7D 48
Racton Rd. SW6 . . . 6J 83
R.A.D.A. . . . 5C 160
(off Chenies St.)
Gower St. . . . 5C 160
Radbourne Av. W5 . . . 4C 80
Radbourne Cl. E5 . . . 4K 51
Radbourne Ct. HA3: Harr . . . 6B 26
Radbourne Cres. E17 . . . 2F 35
Radbourne Rd. SW12 . . . 7G 103
Radcliffe Av. EN2: Enf . . . 1H 7
NW10 . . . 2C 64
Radcliffe Gdns.
SM5: Cars . . . 7C 150
Radcliffe Ho. SE16 . . . 4H 87
(off Anchor St.)
Radcliffe M.
TW12: Hamp . . . 5G 115
Radcliffe Path SW8 . . . 2F 103
Radcliffe Rd. CR0: Croy . . . 2F 153
HA3: Harr . . . 2A 26
N21 . . . 1G 17
SE1 . . . 3E 86
Radcliffe Sq. SW15 . . . 6F 101
Radcliffe Way UB5: N'olt . . . 3B 60
Radcot Point SE23 . . . 3K 123
Radcot St. SE11 . . . 5A 86 (6K 173)
Raddington Rd. W10 . . . 5G 65
Radfield Way DA15: Sidc . . . 7H 109
(not continuous)
Radford Ho. E14 . . . 5D 70
(off St Leonard's Rd.)
N7 . . . 5K 49
Radford Rd. SE13 . . . 6E 106
Radford Way IG11: Bark . . . 3K 73
Radipole Rd. SW6 . . . 1H 101
Radius Pk. TW14: Felt . . . 4H 95
Radland Rd. E16 . . . 6H 71
Radlet Av. SE26 . . . 3H 123
Radlett Cl. E7 . . . 6H 53

Radlett Pl.—Raven Ho.

Radlett Pl. NW8 ... 1C 66
Radley Av. IG3: Bark, Ilf ... 4A 56
Radley Cl. TW14: Felt ... 1H 113
Radley Ct. SE16 ... 2K 87
Radley Gdns. HA3: Harr ... 4E 26
Radley Ho. *NW1 ... 3E 158*
(off Gloucester Pl.)
SE2 ... 2D 92
(off Wolvercote Rd.)
Radley M. W8 ... 3J 83
Radley Rd. N17 ... 2E 32
Radleys La. E18 ... 2J 35
Radleys Mead
RM10: Dag ... 6H 57
Radley Sq. E5 ... 2J 51
Radley Ter. *E16 ... 5H 71*
(off Hermit Rd.)
Radlix Rd. E10 ... 1C 52
Radnor Av. DA16: Well ... 5B 110
HA1: Harr ... 5J 25
Radnor Cl. BR7: Chst ... 6J 127
CR4: Mitc ... 4J 139
Radnor Ct. HA3: Harr ... 1K 25
W7 ... 6K 61
(off Copley Cl.)
Radnor Cres. IG4: Ilf ... 5D 36
SE18 ... 7A 92
Radnor Gdns. EN1: Enf ... 1K 7
TW1: Twick ... 2K 115
Radnor Gro. UB10: Uxb ... 2C 58
Radnor M. W2 ... 6B 66 (1B 164)
Radnor Pl. W2 ... 6C 66 (1C 164)
Radnor Rd. HA1: Harr ... 5H 25
NW6 ... 1G 65
SE15 ... 7G 87
TW1: Twick ... 1K 115
Radnor St.
EC1 ... 3C 68 (2D 162)
Radnor Ter. SM2: Sutt ... 7J 149
W14 ... 4H 83
Radnor Wlk. CR0: Croy ... 6A 142
E14 ... 4C 88
(off Barnsdale Av.)
SW3 ... 5C 84 (6D 170)
Radnor Way NW10 ... 4H 63
Radstock Av. HA3: Harr ... 3A 26
Radstock Cl. N11 ... 6K 15
Radstock St. SW11 ... 7C 84
(not continuous)
Raeburn Av. KT5: Surb ... 1H 147
Raeburn Cl. KT1: King T ... 7D 116
NW11 ... 6A 30
Raeburn Ho. *UB5: N'olt ... 2B 60*
(off Academy Gdns.)
Raeburn Rd. DA15: Sidc ... 6J 109
HA8: Edg ... 1G 27
UB4: Hayes ... 2F 59
Raeburn St. SW2 ... 4J 103
Raffles Ct. NW4 ... 4D 28
Rafford Way BR1: Brom ... 2K 143
R.A.F. Mus. Hendon ... *2C 28*
RAF NORTHOLT AERODROME
... 6H 41
Ragged School Mus. ... *5A 70*
Raggleswood BR7: Chst ... 1E 144
Raglan Cl. TW4: Houn ... 5D 96
Raglan Ct. CR2: S Croy ... 5B 152
HA9: Wemb ... 4F 45
SE12 ... 5J 107
Raglan Rd. BR2: Short ... 4A 144
DA17: Belv ... 4F 93
E17 ... 5E 34
EN1: Enf ... 7A 8
SE18 ... 5G 91
Raglan St. NW5 ... 6F 49
Raglan Ter. HA2: Harr ... 4F 43
Raglan Way UB5: N'olt ... 6G 43
Ragley Cl. W3 ... 2J 81
Raider Cl. RM7: Mawney ... 1G 39
Railey M. NW5 ... 5G 49
Railshead Rd. TW7: Isle ... 4B 98
Railton Rd. SE24 ... 4A 104
Railway App. HA1: Harr ... 4K 25
N4 ... 6A 32
SE1 ... 1D 86 (5F 169)
SM6: Wall ... 5F 151
TW1: Twick ... 7A 98
Railway Arches *E7 ... 4J 53*
(off Winchelsea Rd.)
E10 ... 7D 34
(off Capworth St.)
E11 ... 2G 53
(off Leytonstone High Rd.)
E11 ... 1F 53
(off Sidings, The)
E17 ... 5C 34
(off Yunus Khan Cl.)
W12 ... 2E 82
(off Shepherd's Bush Mkt.)
Railway Av. SE16 ... 2J 87
(not continuous)
Railway Children Wlk.
BR1: Brom ... 2J 125
SE12 ... 2J 125
Railway Cotts. SW19 ... 4K 119
TW2: Twick ... 6E 96
W6 ... 2E 82
(off Sulgrave Rd.)
Railway Gro. SE14 ... 7B 88
Railway M. *E3 ... 3C 70*
(off Wellington Way)
W11 ... 6G 65
Railway Pas.
TW11: Tedd ... 6A 116
Railway Pl.
DA17: Belv ... 3G 93
SW19 ... 6H 119
Railway Ri. SE22 ... 4E 104
Railway Rd.
TW11: Tedd ... 4J 115
Railway Side SW13 ... 3A 100
(not continuous)
Railway St. N1 ... 2J 67
RM6: Chad H ... 7C 38
Railway Ter. E17 ... 1E 34
SE13 ... 5D 106
TW13: Felt ... 1J 113
Rainborough Cl. NW10 ... 6J 45
Rainbow Av. E14 ... 5D 88
Rainbow Ct. *SE14 ... 6A 88*
(off Chipley St.)
Rainbow Ind. Est.
UB7: W Dray ... 7A 58
Rainbow Quay SE16 ... 3A 88
(not continuous)
Rainbow St. SE5 ... 7E 86
Raine St. E1 ... 1H 87
Rainham Cl. SE9 ... 6J 109
SW11 ... 6C 102
Rainham Ho. *NW1 ... 1G 67*
(off Bayham Pl.)
Rainham Rd. NW10 ... 3E 64
Rainham Rd. Nth.
RM10: Dag ... 2G 57
Rainham Rd. Sth.
RM10: Dag ... 4H 57
Rainhill Way E3 ... 3C 70
(not continuous)
Rainsborough Av. SE8 ... 4A 88
Rainsford Cl. HA7: Stan ... 4H 11
Rainsford Rd. NW10 ... 2H 63
(not continuous)
Rainsford St.
W2 ... 6C 66 (7C 158)
Rainton Rd. SE7 ... 5J 89
Rainville Rd. W6 ... 6E 82
Raisins Hill HA5: Pinn ... 3A 24
Raith Av. N14 ... 3C 16
Raleana Rd. E14 ... 1E 88
Raleigh Av. SM6: Wall ... 4H 151
UB4: Hayes ... 5K 59
Raleigh Cl. HA4: Ruis ... 2H 41
HA5: Pinn ... 7B 24
NW4 ... 5E 28
Raleigh Ct. BR3: Beck ... 1D 142
SE16 ... 1K 87
(off Clarence M.)
SM6: Wall ... 6F 151
W12 ... 2E 82
(off Scott's Rd.)
W13 ... 5B 62
Raleigh Dr. KT5: Surb ... 1J 147
N20 ... 3H 15
Raleigh Gdns.
CR4: Mitc ... 3D 138
(not continuous)
SW2 ... 6K 103
Raleigh Ho. *E14 ... 2D 88*
(off Admirals Way)
SW1 ... 7C 172
(off Dolphin Sq.)
Raleigh M. *N1 ... 1B 68*
(off Packington St.)
Raleigh Rd. EN2: Enf ... 4J 7
N2 ... 2C 30
N8 ... 4A 32
SE20 ... 7K 123
TW9: Rich ... 3F 99
TW13: Felt ... 3H 113
UB2: S'hall ... 5C 78
Raleigh St. N1 ... 1B 68
Raleigh Way N14 ... 1C 16
TW13: Felt ... 5A 114
Ralph Brook Ct. *N1 ... 1F 163*
(off Chart St.)
Ralph Ct. *W2 ... 6K 65*
(off Queensway)
Ralph Perring Ct.
BR3: Beck ... 4C 142
Ralston St. SW3 ... 5D 84 (6E 170)
Ramac Ind. Est. SE7 ... 4K 89
Rama Cl. SW16 ... 7J 121
Rama Ct. HA1: Harr ... 2J 43
Ramac Way SE7 ... 4K 89
Rama La. SE19 ... 7F 123
Ramar Ho. *E1 ... 5G 69*
(off Hanbury St.)
Rambler Cl. SW16 ... 4G 121
Rame Cl. SW17 ... 5E 120
Ramilles Cl. SW2 ... 6J 103
Ramillies Pl. W1 ... 6G 67 (1A 166)
Ramillies Rd.
DA15: Sidc ... 6B 110
NW7 ... 2F 13
W4 ... 4K 81
Ramillies St.
W1 ... 6G 67 (1A 166)
Ramones Ter. CR4: Mitc ... 4J 139
Rampart St. E1 ... 6H 69
Ram Pas. KT1: King T ... 2D 134
Rampayne St.
SW1 ... 5H 85 (5C 172)
Ram Pl. E9 ... 6J 51
Rampton Cl. E4 ... 3H 19
Ramsay Ho. *NW8 ... 2C 66*
(off Townshend Est.)
Ramsay M. SW3 ... 6C 84 (7C 170)
Ramsay Pl. HA1: Harr ... 1J 43
Ramsay Rd. E7 ... 4G 53
W3 ... 3J 81
Ramscroft Cl. N9 ... 7K 7
Ramsdale Rd. SW17 ... 5E 120
Ramsden Dr. RM5: Col R ... 1G 39
Ramsden Rd. DA8: Erith ... 7K 93
N11 ... 5J 15
SW12 ... 6E 102
Ramsey Cl. NW9 ... 6B 28
UB6: G'frd ... 5H 43
Ramsey Ct. *CR0: Croy ... 2B 152*
(off Church St.)
Ramsey Ho. SW9 ... 7A 86
Ramsey Rd. CR7: Thor H ... 6K 139
Ramsey St. E2 ... 4G 69
Ramsey Wlk. *N1 ... 6D 50*
(off Handa Wlk.)
Ramsey Way N14 ... 7B 6
Ramsfort Ho. *SE16 ... 4H 87*
(off Camilla Rd.)
Ramsgate Cl. E16 ... 1K 89
Ramsgate St. E8 ... 6F 51
Ramsgill App. IG2: Ilf ... 4K 37
Ramsgill Dr. IG2: Ilf ... 5K 37
Rams Gro. RM6: Chad H ... 4E 38
Ram St. SW18 ... 5K 101
Ramulis Dr. UB4: Hayes ... 4B 60
Rancliffe Gdns. SE9 ... 4C 108
Rancliffe Rd. E6 ... 2C 72
Randall Av. NW2 ... 2A 46
Randall Cl. DA8: Erith ... 6J 93
SW11 ... 1C 102
Randall Ct. NW7 ... 7H 13
Randall Pl. SE10 ... 7E 88
Randall Rd. SE11 ... 5K 85 (4G 173)
Randall Row
SE11 ... 4K 85 (4G 173)
Randalls Rents *SE16 ... 3B 88*
(off Gulliver St.)
Randells Rd. N1 ... 1J 67
(not continuous)
Randisbourne Gdns. SE6 ... 3D 124
Randle Rd. TW10: Rich ... 4C 116
Randlesdown Rd. SE6 ... 4C 124
(not continuous)
Randolph App. E16 ... 6A 72
Randolph Av. W9 ... 2K 65 (4A 158)
Randolph Cl. DA7: Bex ... 3J 111
KT2: King T ... 5J 117
Randolph Cres. W9 ... 4A 66
Randolph Gdns. NW6 ... 2K 65
Randolph Gro.
RM6: Chad H ... 5C 38
Randolph M. W9 ... 4A 66
Randolph Rd. BR2: Short ... 1D 156
E17 ... 5D 34
UB1: S'hall ... 2D 78
W9 ... 4A 66
Randolph St. NW1 ... 7G 49
Randon Cl. HA2: Harr ... 2F 25
Ranelagh Av. SW6 ... 3H 101
SW13 ... 2C 100
Ranelagh Bri. W2 ... 5K 65
Ranelagh Cl. HA8: Edg ... 4B 12
Ranelagh Dr. HA8: Edg ... 4B 12
TW1: Twick ... 4B 98
Ranelagh Gdns. E11 ... 5A 36
IG1: Ilf ... 1D 54
SW6 ... 3G 101
(not continuous)
W4 ... 7J 81
W6 ... 4B 82
Ranelagh Gdns. Mans.
SW6 ... 3G 101
(off Ranelagh Gdns.)
Ranelagh Gro.
SW1 ... 5E 84 (5H 171)
Ranelagh Ho. *SW3 ... 5E 170*
(off Elystan Pl.)
Ranelagh M. W5 ... 2D 80
Ranelagh Pl.
KT3: N Mald ... 5A 136
Ranelagh Rd. E6 ... 1E 72
E11 ... 4G 53
E15 ... 2G 71
HA0: Wemb ... 6D 44
N17 ... 3E 32
N22 ... 1K 31
NW10 ... 2B 64
SW1 ... 5G 85 (6B 172)
UB1: S'hall ... 1B 78
W5 ... 2D 80
Ranfurly Rd. SM1: Sutt ... 2J 149
Rangbourne Ho. N7 ... 5J 49
Rangefield Rd.
BR1: Brom ... 5G 125
Rangemoor Rd. N15 ... 5F 33
Rangers House ... *1F 107*
Rangers Rd. E4 ... 1B 20
Rangers Sq. SE10 ... 1F 107
Range Way TW17: Shep ... 7C 130
Rangeworth Pl.
DA15: Sidc ... 3K 127
Rangoon St. EC3 ... 1J 169
Rankin Cl. NW9 ... 3A 28
Rankine Ho. *SE1 ... 3C 86*
(off Bath Ter.)
Ranleigh Gdns. DA7: Bex ... 7F 93
Ranmere St. SW12 ... 1F 121
Ranmoor Cl. HA1: Harr ... 4H 25
Ranmoor Gdns.
HA1: Harr ... 4H 25
Ranmore Av. CR0: Croy ... 3F 153
Ranmore Path BR5: Orp ... 4K 145
Ranmore Rd. SM2: Sutt ... 7F 149
Rannoch Cl. HA8: Edg ... 2C 12
Rannoch Rd. W6 ... 6E 82
Rannock Av. NW9 ... 7K 27
Ransomes Dock Bus. Cen.
SW11 ... 7C 84
Ransom Rd. SE7 ... 4A 90
Ranston St.
NW1 ... 5C 66 (5C 158)
Ranulf Rd. NW2 ... 4H 47
Ranwell Cl. E3 ... 1B 70
Ranworth Rd. N9 ... 2D 18
Ranyard Cl. KT9: Chess ... 3F 147
Raphael Ct. *SE16 ... 5H 87*
(off Stubbs Dr.)
Raphael Dr. KT7: T Ditt ... 7K 133
Raphael St.
SW7 ... 2D 84 (7E 164)
Rapley Ho. *E2 ... 2K 163*
(off Turin St.)
Rashleigh Ct. SW8 ... 2F 103
Rashleigh Ho. *WC1 ... 2E 160*
(off Thanet St.)
Rasper Rd. N20 ... 2F 15
Rastell Av. SW2 ... 2H 121
RATCLIFF ... 5A 70
Ratcliffe Cl. SE12 ... 7J 107
Ratcliffe Ct. *SE1 ... 7D 168*
(off Gt. Dover St.)
Ratcliffe Cross St. E1 ... 6K 69
Ratcliffe Ho. E14 ... 6A 70
Ratcliffe La. E14 ... 6A 70
Ratcliffe Orchard E1 ... 7K 69
Ratcliff Rd. E7 ... 5A 54
Rathbone Ho. *E16 ... 6H 71*
(off Rathbone St.)
NW6 ... 1J 65
Rathbone Mkt. E16 ... 5H 71
Rathbone Pl.
W1 ... 5H 67 (6C 160)
Rathbone Point *E5 ... 4G 51*
(off Nolan Way)
Rathbone Sq.
CR0: Croy ... 4C 152
Rathbone St. E16 ... 5H 71
W1 ... 5G 67 (6B 160)
Rathcoole Av. N8 ... 5K 31
Rathcoole Gdns. N8 ... 5K 31
Rathfern Rd. SE6 ... 1B 124
Rathgar Av. W13 ... 1B 80
Rathgar Cl. N3 ... 2H 29
Rathgar Rd. SW9 ... 3B 104
Rathmell Dr. SW4 ... 6H 103
Rathmore Rd. SE7 ... 5K 89
Rattray Ct. SE6 ... 2H 125
Rattray Rd. SW2 ... 4A 104
Raul Rd. SE15 ... 2G 105
Raveley St. NW5 ... 4G 49
(not continuous)
Raven Cl. NW9 ... 2A 28
Ravendale Rd.
TW16: Sun T ... 2H 131
Ravenet St. SW11 ... 1F 103
(not continuous)
Ravenfield Rd. SW17 ... 3D 120
Ravenhill Rd. E13 ... 2A 72
Raven Ho. *SE16 ... 4K 87*
(off Tawny Way)

Ravenings Pde.—Reddons Rd.

Ravenings Pde. IG3: Ilf 1A **56**
Ravenna Rd. SW15 . . . . 5F **101**
Ravenor Ct. UB6: G'frd 4F **61**
***Ravenor Farm** 3G 61*
Ravenor Pk. Rd.
UB6: G'frd 3F **61**
Raven Rd. E18 . . . . 2A **36**
Raven Row E1 . . . . 5H **69**
(not continuous)
Ravensbourne Av.
BR2: Short 7F **125**
TW19: Staines 1A 112
Ravensbourne Ct. SE6 . . . . 7C **106**
Ravensbourne Gdns.
IG5: Ilf 1E **36**
W13 . . . . 5B **62**
Ravensbourne Ho.
BR1: Brom 5F **125**
NW8 . . . . 5C 158
(off Broadley St.)
Ravensbourne Mans. *SE8 . . . . 6C 88*
(off Berthon St.)
Ravensbourne Pk. SE6 . . . . 7C **106**
Ravensbourne Pk. Cres.
SE6 . . . . 7B **106**
Ravensbourne Pl. SE13 . . . . 2D **106**
Ravensbourne Rd.
BR1: Brom 3J **143**
SE6 . . . . 7B **106**
TW1: Twick 6C **98**
Ravensbury Av.
SM4: Mord 5A **138**
Ravensbury Ct.
CR4: Mitc 4B 138
(off Ravensbury Gro.)
Ravensbury Gro.
CR4: Mitc 4B **138**
Ravensbury La.
CR4: Mitc 4B **138**
Ravensbury Path
CR4: Mitc 4B **138**
Ravensbury Rd.
BR5: Orp 3K **145**
SW18 . . . . 2J **119**
Ravensbury Ter. SW18 . . . . 2K **119**
Ravenscar *NW1 . . . . 1G 67*
(off Bayham St.)
Ravenscar Rd.
BR1: Brom 4G **125**
KT6: Surb 2F **147**
Ravens Cl. BR2: Short 2H **143**
EN1: Enf 2K **7**
KT6: Surb 6D **134**
Ravens Ct. *KT1: King T 5D 134*
(off Uxbridge Rd.)
Ravenscourt
TW16: Sun T 1H **131**
Ravenscourt Av. W6 . . . . 4C **82**
Ravenscourt Cl. HA4: Ruis 7E **22**
Ravenscourt Gdns. W6 . . . . 4C **82**
Ravenscourt Pk. EN5: Barn 4A **4**
W6 . . . . 3C **82**
Ravenscourt Pk. Mans.
W6 . . . . 3D 82
(off Paddenswick Rd.)
Ravenscourt Pl. W6 . . . . 4D **82**
Ravenscourt Rd. W6 . . . . 4D **82**
(not continuous)
Ravenscourt Sq. W6 . . . . 3C **82**
Ravenscraig Rd. N11 . . . . 4B **16**
Ravenscroft Av.
HA9: Wemb 1E **44**
NW11 . . . . 7H **29**
Ravenscroft Cl. E16 . . . . 5J **71**
Ravenscroft Cotts.
EN5: Barn 4D **4**
Ravenscroft Cres. SE9 . . . . 3D **126**
Ravenscroft Pk. EN5: Barn 3A **4**
Ravenscroft Rd.
BR3: Beck 2J **141**
E16 . . . . 5J **71**
W4 . . . . 4J **81**
Ravenscroft St.
E2 . . . . 2F **69** (1K **163**)
Ravensdale Av. N12 . . . . 4F **15**
Ravensdale Gdns. SE19 . . . . 7D **122**
Ravensdale Rd. N16 . . . . 7F **33**
TW4: Houn 3C **96**
Ravensdon St.
SE11 . . . . 5A **86** (6K **173**)
Ravensfield Cl. RM9: Dag 4D **56**
Ravensfield Gdns.
KT19: Eps 5A **148**
Ravenshaw St. NW6 . . . . 5H **47**
Ravenshill BR7: Chst 1F **145**
Ravenshurst Av. NW4 . . . . 4E **28**
Ravenside *KT1: King T 5D 134*
(off Portsmouth Rd.)
Ravenside Cl. N18 . . . . 5E **18**
Ravenside Retail Pk. N18 . . . . 5E **18**
Ravenslea Rd. SW12 . . . . 7D **102**
Ravensleigh Gdns.
BR1: Brom 5K **125**
Ravensmead Rd.
BR2: Short 7F **125**
Ravensmede Way W4 . . . . 4B **82**
Ravens M. SE12 . . . . 5J **107**
Ravenstone SE17 . . . . 5E **86**
Ravenstone Rd. N8 . . . . 3A **32**
NW9 . . . . 6B **28**
Ravenstone St. SW12 . . . . 1E **120**
Ravens Way SE12 . . . . 5J **107**
Ravenswood DA5: Bexl 1E **128**
Ravenswood Av.
BR4: W W'ck 1E **154**
KT6: Surb 2F **147**
Ravenswood Ct.
KT2: King T 6H **117**
Ravenswood Cres.
BR4: W W'ck 1E **154**
HA2: Harr 2D **42**
Ravenswood Gdns.
TW7: Isle 1J **97**
Ravenswood Ind. Est. E17 . . . . 4E **34**
Ravenswood Rd.
CR0: Croy 3B **152**
E17 . . . . 4E **34**
SW12 . . . . 7F **103**
Ravensworth Ct. *SW6 . . . . 7J 83*
(off Fulham Rd.)
Ravensworth Rd. NW10 . . . . 3D **64**
SE9 . . . . 3D **126**
Ravent Rd. SE11 . . . . 4K **85** (3H **173**)
Ravey St. EC2 . . . . 4E **68** (3G **163**)
Ravine Gro. SE18 . . . . 6J **91**
Rav Pinter Cl. N16 . . . . 7E **32**
Rawalpindi Ho. E16 . . . . 4H **71**
Rawchester Cl. SW18 . . . . 1H **119**
Rawlings Cl. BR3: Beck 5E **142**
Rawlings Cres.
HA9: Wemb 3H **45**
Rawlings St.
SW3 . . . . 4D **84** (3E **170**)
Rawlins Cl. CR2: S Croy 7A **154**
N3 . . . . 3G **29**
Rawlinson Ct. NW2 . . . . 7E **28**
Rawlinson Ho. *SE13 . . . . 4F 107*
(off Mercator Rd.)
Rawlinson Point *E16 . . . . 5H 71*
(off Fox Rd.)
Rawlinson Ter. N17 . . . . 3F **33**
Rawnsley Av. CR4: Mitc 5B **138**
Rawreth Wlk. *N1 . . . . 1C 68*
(off Basire St.)
Rawson St. SW11 . . . . 1E **102**
(not continuous)
Rawsthorne Cl. E16 . . . . 1D **90**
Rawsthorne Ct.
TW4: Houn 4D **96**
Rawstone Wlk. E13 . . . . 2J **71**
Rawstorne Pl.
EC1 . . . . 3B **68** (1A **162**)
Rawstorne St.
EC1 . . . . 3B **68** (1A **162**)
Raybell Ct. TW7: Isle 2K **97**
Rayburne Ct. IG9: Buck H 1F **21**
W14 . . . . 3G **83**
Ray Cl. KT9: Chess 6C **146**
Raydean Rd. EN5: Barn 5E **4**
Raydons Gdns. RM9: Dag 4E **56**
Raydons Rd. RM9: Dag 5E **56**
Raydon St. N19 . . . . 2F **49**
Rayfield Cl. BR2: Short 6C **144**
Rayford Av. SE12 . . . . 7H **107**
Ray Gdns. HA7: Stan 5G **11**
IG11: Bark 2A **74**
Ray Gunter Ho. *SE17 . . . . 5B 86*
(off Marsland Cl.)
Ray Ho. *N1 . . . . 1E 68*
(off Colville Est.)
Rayleas Cl. SE18 . . . . 1F **109**
Rayleigh Av. TW11: Tedd 6J **115**
Rayleigh Cl. N13 . . . . 3J **17**
Rayleigh Ct. KT1: King T 2G **135**
N22 . . . . 1C **32**
Rayleigh Ho. *BR1: Brom 1J 143*
(off Hammelton Rd.)
Rayleigh Ri. CR2: S Croy 6E **152**
Rayleigh Rd. E16 . . . . 1K **89**
IG8: Wfd G 6F **21**
N13 . . . . 3H **17**
SW19 . . . . 1H **137**
Ray Lodge Rd. IG8: Wfd G 6F **21**
Ray Massey Way *E6 . . . . 1C 72*
(off High St. Nth.)
Raymead Av.
CR7: Thor H 5A **140**
Raymede Towers *W10 . . . . 5F 65*
(off Treverton St.)
Raymere Gdns. SE18 . . . . 7H **91**
Raymond Av. E18 . . . . 3H **35**
W13 . . . . 3A **80**
Raymond Bldgs.
WC1 . . . . 5K **67** (5H **161**)
Raymond Cl. SE26 . . . . 5J **123**
Raymond Ct. N10 . . . . 7A **16**
SM2: Sutt 6K **149**
Raymond Postgate Ct.
SE28 . . . . 7B **74**
Raymond Revuebar 2C 166
(off Walkers Ct.)
Raymond Rd. BR3: Beck 4A **142**
E13 . . . . 1A **72**
IG2: Ilf 7H **37**
SW19 . . . . 6G **119**
Raymond Way KT10: Esh 6A **146**
Raymouth Ho. *SE16 . . . . 4J 87*
(off Raymouth Rd.)
Raymouth Rd. SE16 . . . . 4H **87**
Raynald Ho. SW16 . . . . 3J **121**
Rayne Ct. E18 . . . . 4H **35**
Rayne Ho. *W9 . . . . 4K 65*
(off Delaware Rd.)
Rayner Ct. *W12 . . . . 2E 82*
(off Bamborough Gdns.)
Rayners Cl. HA0: Wemb 5D **44**
Rayners Cres. UB5: N'olt 3K **59**
Rayners Gdns.
UB5: N'olt 2K **59**
RAYNERS LANE 1D 42
Rayners La. HA2: Harr 5D **24**
HA5: Harr, Pinn 5D **24**
Rayners Rd. SW15 . . . . 5G **101**
Rayner Towers *E10 . . . . 7C 34*
(off Albany Rd.)
Raynes Av. E11 . . . . 7A **36**
RAYNES PARK 4E 136
Raynes Pk. Bri. SW20 . . . . 2E **136**
Raynham *W2 . . . . 7D 158*
(off Norfolk Cres.)
Raynham Av. N18 . . . . 6B **18**
Raynham Ho. *E1 . . . . 4K 69*
(off Harpley Sq.)
Raynham Rd. N18 . . . . 5B **18**
W6 . . . . 4D **82**
Raynham Ter. N18 . . . . 5B **18**
Raynor Cl. UB1: S'hall 1D **78**
Raynor Pl. N1 . . . . 7C **50**
Raynton Cl. HA2: Harr 1C **42**
UB4: Hayes 4H **59**
Raynton Dr. UB4: Hayes 4H **59**
Ray Rd. KT8: W Mole 5F **133**
Rays Av. N18 . . . . 4D **18**
Rays Rd. BR4: W W'ck 7E **142**
N18 . . . . 4D **18**
Ray St. EC1 . . . . 4A **68** (4K **161**)
Ray St. Bri. EC1 . . . . 4K **161**
Ray Wlk. N7 . . . . 2K **49**
Raywood Cl.
UB3: Hayes 7E **76**
Reachview Cl. NW1 . . . . 7G **49**
Read Cl. KT7: T Ditt 7A **134**
Read Ct. E17 . . . . 6C **34**
Reade Ct. *W3 . . . . 3J 81*
(off Stanley Rd.)
Reade Ho. *SE10 . . . . 6F 89*
(off Trafalgar Gro.)
Reade Wlk. NW10 . . . . 7A **46**
Read Ho. SE11 . . . . 7J **173**
Reading Ho. *SE15 . . . . 6G 87*
(off Friary Est.)
W2 . . . . 6A 66
(off Hallfield Est.)
Reading La. E8 . . . . 6H **51**
Reading Rd. SM1: Sutt 5A **150**
UB5: N'olt 5F **43**
Reading Way NW7 . . . . 5A **14**
Reads Cl. IG1: Ilf 3F **55**
Reapers Cl. NW1 . . . . 1H **67**
Reapers Way TW7: Isle 5H **97**
Reardon Ct. N21 . . . . 2G **17**
Reardon Ho. *E1 . . . . 1H 87*
(off Reardon St.)
Reardon Path E1 . . . . 1H **87**
(not continuous)
Reardon St. E1 . . . . 1H **87**
Reaston St. SE14 . . . . 7K **87**
Rebecca Ct. DA14: Sidc 4B **128**
Reckitt Rd. W4 . . . . 5A **82**
Record St. SE15 . . . . 6J **87**
Recovery St. SW17 . . . . 5C **120**
Recreation Av.
RM7: Rom 5J **39**
Recreation Rd.
BR2: Short 2H **143**
DA15: Sidc 3J **127**
SE26 . . . . 4K **123**
UB2: S'hall 4C **78**
Recreation Way
CR4: Mitc 3H **139**
Rector St. N1 . . . . 1C **68**
Rectory Bus. Cen.
DA14: Sidc 4B **128**
Rectory Cl. DA14: Sidc 4B **128**
E4 . . . . 3H **19**
HA7: Stan 5G **11**
KT6: Surb 1C **146**
N3 . . . . 1H **29**
SW20 . . . . 3E **136**
TW17: Shep 3C **130**
Rectory Ct. E18 . . . . 1H **35**
SM6: Wall 4G **151**
TW13: Felt 4A **114**
Rectory Cres. E11 . . . . 6A **36**
(not continuous)
Rectory Farm Rd.
EN2: Enf 1E **6**
Rectory Fld. Cres. SE7 . . . . 7A **90**
Rectory Gdns.
BR3: Beck 1C 142
(off Rectory Rd.)
N8 . . . . 4J **31**
SW4 . . . . 3G **103**
UB5: N'olt 1D **60**
Rectory Grn. BR3: Beck 1B **142**
Rectory Gro. CR0: Croy 2B **152**
SW4 . . . . 3G **103**
TW12: Hamp 4D **114**
Rectory La. DA14: Sidc 4B **128**
HA7: Stan 5G **11**
HA8: Edg 6B **12**
KT6: Surb 1B **146**
SM6: Wall 4G **151**
SW17 . . . . 6E **120**
Rectory Orchard SW19 . . . . 4G **119**
Rectory Pk. Av. UB5: N'olt 3D **60**
Rectory Pl. SE18 . . . . 4E **90**
Rectory Rd. BR2: Kes 7B **156**
BR3: Beck 2C **142**
E8 . . . . 4G **51**
E12 . . . . 5D **54**
E17 . . . . 4D **34**
N16 . . . . 2F **51**
RM10: Dag 6H **57**
SM1: Sutt 3J **149**
SW13 . . . . 2C **100**
TW4: Houn 2A **96**
UB2: S'hall 3D **78**
UB3: Hayes 6J **59**
W3 . . . . 1H **81**
Rectory Sq. E1 . . . . 5K **69**
Rectory Way UB10: Uxb 2D **40**
Reculver Ho. *SE15 . . . . 6J 87*
(off Lovelinch Cl.)
Reculver M. N18 . . . . 4B **18**
Reculver Rd. SE16 . . . . 5K **87**
Red Anchor Cl. SW3 . . . . 6B **84**
Redan Pl. W2 . . . . 6K **65**
Redan St. W14 . . . . 3F **83**
Redan Ter. SE5 . . . . 2B **104**
Red Barracks Rd. SE18 . . . . 4D **90**
Redberry Gro. SE26 . . . . 3J **123**
Redbourne Av. N3 . . . . 1J **29**
Redbourne Dr. SE28 . . . . 6D **74**
(not continuous)
Redbourne Ho. *E14 . . . . 6B 70*
(off Norbiton Rd.)
Redbourn Ho. *W10 . . . . 4E 64*
(off Sutton Way)
REDBRIDGE 6C 36
Redbridge Ent. Cen.
IG1: Ilf 2G **55**
Redbridge Foyer *IG1: Ilf 2G 55*
(off Sylvan Rd.)
Redbridge Gdns. SE5 . . . . 7E **86**
Redbridge La. E. IG4: Ilf 6B **36**
Redbridge La. W. E11 . . . . 6K **35**
REDBRIDGE RDBT. 6B 36
Redburn St. SW3 . . . . 6D **84** (7E **170**)
Redburn Trad. Est. EN3: Enf 6E **8**
Redcar Cl. UB5: N'olt 5F **43**
Redcar St. SE5 . . . . 7C **86**
Redcastle Cl. E1 . . . . 7J **69**
Red Cedars Rd. BR6: Orp 7J **145**
Redchurch St. E2 . . . . 4F **69** (3J **163**)
Redcliffe Cl. *SW5 . . . . 5K 83*
(off Old Brompton Rd.)
Redcliffe Ct. *E5 . . . . 3H 51*
(off Napoleon Rd.)
Redcliffe Gdns. IG1: Ilf 1E **54**
SW10 . . . . 5K **83**
W4 . . . . 7H **81**
Redcliffe M. SW10 . . . . 5K **83**
Redcliffe Pl. SW10 . . . . 6A **84**
Redcliffe Rd. SW10 . . . . 5A **84**
Redcliffe Sq. SW10 . . . . 5K **83**
Redcliffe St. SW10 . . . . 6K **83**
Redclose Av. SM4: Mord 5J **137**
Redclyffe Rd. E6 . . . . 1A **72**
Redclyf Ho. *E1 . . . . 4J 69*
(off Cephas St.)
Redcourt CR0: Croy 3E **152**
Redcroft Rd. UB1: S'hall 7G **61**
Redcross Way
SE1 . . . . 2C **86** (6D **168**)
Redding Ho. SE18 . . . . 3C **90**
Reddings Cl. NW7 . . . . 4G **13**
Reddings, The NW7 . . . . 3G **13**
Reddins Rd. SE15 . . . . 6G **87**
Reddons Rd. BR3: Beck 7A **124**

Redenham Ho.—Repton Rd.

Redenham Ho. *SW15* *7C 100*
(off Ellisfield Dr.)
Rede Pl. W2 . . . . 6J 65
Redesdale Gdns.
TW7: Isle 7A 80
Redesdale St.
SW3 . . . . 6C 84 (7D 170)
Redfern Av. TW4: Houn 7E 96
Redfern Ho. *E15* *1H 71*
(off Redriffe Rd.)
Redfern Rd. NW10 . . . . 7A 46
SE6 . . . . 7E 106
Redfield La. SW5 . . . . 4J 83
Redfield M. SW5 . . . . 4K 83
Redford Av.
CR7: Thor H 4K 139
SM6: Wall 6J 151
Redford Cl. TW13: Felt 2H 113
Redford Ho. *W10* *3H 65*
(off Dowland St.)
Redford Wlk. *N1* *1C 68*
(off Popham St.)
Redgate Dr. BR2: Short 2K 155
Redgate Ter. SW15 . . . . 6F 101
Redgrave Cl. CR0: Croy 6F 141
Redgrave Rd. SW15 . . . . 3F 101
Redgrave Ter. *E2* *3G 69*
(off Derbyshire St.)
Red Hill BR7: Chst 5F 127
Redhill Ct. SW2 . . . . 2A 122
Redhill Dr. HA8: Edg 2H 27
Redhill St. NW1 . . . . 2F 67 (1K 159)
Red House ***4E 110***
Red Ho. La. DA6: Bex 4D 110
Redhouse Rd.
CR0: Croy 6H 139
Red Ho. Sq. N1 . . . . 6C 50
Redif Ho. RM10: Dag 4H 57
Redington Gdns. NW3 . . . . . . 4K 47
Redington Ho. *N1* *2K 67*
(off Priory Grn. Est.)
Redington Rd. NW3 . . . . 3K 47
Redland Gdns.
KT8: W Mole 4D 132
Redlands N15 . . . . 4D 32
TW11: Tedd 6A 116
Redlands Ct. BR1: Brom . . . 7H 125
Redlands Rd. EN3: Enf 1F 9
Redlands, The
BR3: Beck 2D 142
Redlands Way SW2 . . . . 7K 103
Red La. KT10: Esh 6A 146
Redleaf Cl. DA17: Belv 6G 93
Redleaves Av.
TW15: Ashf 6D 112
Redlees Cl. TW7: Isle 4A 98
Red Leys UB8: Uxb 7A 40
Red Lion Bus. Pk.
KT6: Surb 3F 147
Red Lion Cl. *SE17* *6D 86*
(off Red Lion Row)
Red Lion Ct. EC4 . . . 6A 68 (1K 167)
SE1 . . . . 1C 86 (4D 168)
Red Lion Hill N2 . . . . 2B 30
Red Lion La. SE18 . . . . 7E 90
Red Lion Pde. HA5: Pinn 3C 24
Red Lion Pl. SE18 . . . . 1E 108
Red Lion Rd. KT6: Surb 2F 147
Red Lion Row SE17 . . . . 6C 86
Red Lion Sq. SW18 . . . . 5J 101
WC1 . . . . 5K 67 (6G 161)
Red Lion St. TW9: Rich 5D 98
WC1 . . . . 5K 67 (5G 161)
Red Lion Yd. W1 . . . . 4H 165
Red Lodge
BR4: W W'ck 1E 154
Red Lodge Cres.
DA5: Bexl 3K 129
Red Lodge Rd.
BR4: W W'ck 1E 154
DA5: Bexl 3K 129
Redman Cl. UB5: N'olt 2A 60
Redman Ho. *EC1* *5J 161*
(off Bourne Est.)
SE1 . . . . *7D 168*
(off Borough High St.)
Redmans Rd. E1 . . . . 5J 69
Redmead La. E1 . . . . 1G 87
Redmead Rd. UB3: Hayes . . . 4G 77
Redmill Ho. *E1* *4H 69*
(off Headlam St.)
Redmond Ho. *N1* *1K 67*
(off Barnsbury Est.)
Redmore Rd. W6 . . . . 4D 82
Redo Ho. *E12* *5E 54*
(off Dore Av.)
Red Path E9 . . . . 6A 52
Red Pl. W1 . . . . . . 7E 66 (2G 165)
Redpoll Way DA18: Erith 3D 92
Red Post Hill SE21 . . . . 4D 104
SE24 . . . . 4D 104
Red Post Ho. E6 . . . . 7B 54
Redriffe Rd. E13 . . . . 1H 71
Redriff Est. SE16 . . . . 3B 88
Redriff Rd. RM7: Mawney . . . 2H 39
SE16 . . . . 4K 87
Redroofs Cl. BR3: Beck 1D 142
Redrose Trad. Cen.
EN4: Barn 5G 5
Red Rover **4C 100**
Redrup Ho. *SE14* *6K 87*
(off John Williams Cl.)
Redruth Cl. N22 . . . . 7E 16
Redruth Ho. SM2: Sutt 7K 149
Redruth Rd. E9 . . . . 1J 69
Red Sq. N16 . . . . 3D 50
Redstart Cl. E6 . . . . 5C 72
SE14 . . . . 7A 88
Redston Rd. N8 . . . . 4H 31
Redvers Rd. N22 . . . . 2A 32
Redvers St. E2 . . . . 3E 68
N1 . . . . 3E 68 (1H 163)
Redwald Rd. E5 . . . . 4K 51
Redway Dr. TW2: Twick 7G 97
Redwing Path SE28 . . . . 2H 91
Redwing Rd. SM6: Wall 7J 151
Redwood Cl. DA15: Sidc . . . 1A 128
IG9: Buck H 2E 20
N14 . . . . 7C 6
SE16 . . . . 1A 88
UB10: Uxb 2D 58
Redwood Ct. KT6: Surb 7D 134
N19 . . . . 7H 31
NW6 . . . . 7G 47
UB5: N'olt 3C 60
Redwood Est. TW5: Houn . . . 6K 77
Redwood Gdns. E4 . . . . 6J 9
Redwood Mans. *W8* *3K 83*
(off Chantry Sq.)
Redwood M. SW4 . . . . 3F 103
Redwoods SW15 . . . . 1C 118
Redwood Wlk. KT6: Surb . . . 1D 146
Redwood Way EN5: Barn 5A 4
Reece M. SW7 . . . . 4B 84 (3A 170)
Reed Cl. E16 . . . . 5J 71
SE12 . . . . 5J 107
Reede Gdns. RM10: Dag 5H 57
Reede Rd. RM10: Dag 6G 57
Reede Way RM10: Dag 6H 57
Reedham Cl. N17 . . . . 4H 33
Reedham St. SE15 . . . . 2G 105
Reedholm Vs. N16 . . . . 4D 50
Reed Rd. N17 . . . . 2F 33
Reedsfield Cl.
TW15: Ashf 4D 112
Reedsfield Rd.
TW15: Ashf 4D 112
Reeds Pl. NW1 . . . . 7G 49
Reedworth St.
SE11 . . . . . . 4A 86 (4K 173)
Reef Ho. *E14* *3E 88*
(off Manchester St.)
Reenglass Rd. HA7: Stan 4J 11
Rees Dr. HA7: Stan 4K 11
Rees Gdns. CR0: Croy 6F 141
Reesland Cl. E12 . . . . 6E 54
Rees St. N1 . . . . 1C 68
Reets Farm Cl. NW9 . . . . 6A 28
Reeves Av. NW9 . . . . 7K 27
Reeves Cnr. CR0: Croy 2B 152
Reeves Ho. *SE1* *7J 167*
(off Baylis Rd.)
Reeves M. W1 . . . . 7E 66 (3G 165)
Reeves Path UB3: Hayes 4H 77
Reeves Rd. E3 . . . . 4D 70
SE18 . . . . 6F 91
Reflection, The *E16* *2F 91*
(off Woolwich Mnr. Way)
Reform Row N17 . . . . 2F 33
Reform St. SW11 . . . . 2D 102
Regal Cl. E1 . . . . 5G 69
W5 . . . . 5D 62
Regal Ct. N18 . . . . 5A 18
Regal Cres. SM6: Wall 3F 151
Regal Dr. N11 . . . . 5A 16
Regal La. NW1 . . . . 1E 66
Regal Pl. E3 . . . . 3B 70
SW6 . . . . 7K 83
Regal Row SE15 . . . . 1J 105
Regal Way HA3: Harr 6E 26
Regan Ho. N18 . . . . 6A 18
Regan Way N1 . . . . 2E 68 (1G 163)
Regatta Ho. TW11: Tedd . . . 4A 116
Regatta Point TW8: Bford 6F 81
Regency Cl.
TW12: Hamp 5D 114
W5 . . . . 6E 62
Regency Ct. EN1: Enf 5J 7
SM1: Sutt 4K 149
TW11: Tedd 6B 116
Regency Cres. NW4 . . . . 2F 29
Regency Dr. HA4: Ruis 1G 41
Regency Gdns.
KT12: Walt T 7A 132
Regency Ho. *E16* *7J 71*
(off Pepys Cres.)
NW1 . . . . *3K 159*
(off Osnaburgh St.)
Regency Lawn NW5 . . . . 3F 49
Regency Lodge
IG9: Buck H 2G 21
NW3 . . . . *7B 48*
(off Adelaide Rd.)
Regency M. BR3: Beck 7E 124
NW10 . . . . 6C 46
SW9 . . . . 7B 86
TW7: Isle 5J 97
Regency Pl.
SW1 . . . . . . 4H 85 (3D 172)
Regency St. NW10 . . . . 4A 64
SW1 . . . . . . 4H 85 (3D 172)
Regency Ter. *SW7* *5A 170*
(off Fulham Rd.)
Regency Wlk. CR0: Croy . . . 6B 142
TW10: Rich *5E 98*
(off Grosvenor Av.)
Regency Way DA6: Bex 3D 110
Regent Av. UB10: Uxb 7D 40
Regent Bus. Cen.
UB3: Hayes 2K 77
Regent Cl. HA3: Harr 6E 26
N12 . . . . 5F 15
TW4: Houn 1K 95
Regent Ct. N3 . . . . 7E 14
N20 . . . . 2F 15
NW8 . . . . 2C 158
Regent Gdns. IG3: Ilf 7A 38
Regent Ho. *W14* *4G 83*
(off Windsor Way)
Regent Pl. CR0: Croy 1F 153
SW19 . . . . 5A 120
W1 . . . . 7G 67 (2B 166)
Regent Rd. KT5: Surb 5F 135
SE24 . . . . 6B 104
Regents Av. N13 . . . . 5F 17
Regents Bri. Gdns. SW8 . . . . 7J 85
Regents Canal Ho. *E14* *6A 70*
(off Commercial Rd.)
Regents Cl.
CR2: S Croy 6E 152
HA8: Edg 4K 11
UB4: Hayes 5H 59
Regent's College
. . . . ***4D 66 (3G 159)***
Regents Ct. BR1: Brom 7H 125
E8 . . . . *1F 69*
(off Pownall Rd.)
HA5: Pinn 2B 24
KT2: King T *1E 134*
(off Sopwith Way)
Regents Dr. BR2: Kes 5B 156
IG8: Wfd G 6K 21
Regents Ga. Ho. *E14* *7A 70*
(off Horseferry Rd.)
Regents M. NW8 . . . . 2A 66
REGENTS PARK . . . **2F 67 (2K 159)**
Regent's Pk. . . . . . ***3D 66 (1F 159)***
Regents Pk. Est. NW1 . . . . . 1A 160
Regents Pk. Gdns. M.
NW1 . . . . 1D 66
Regents Pk. Ho. *NW1* *2D 158*
(off Park Rd.)
Regent's Pk. Open Air Theatre
. . . . ***3E 66 (2G 159)***
Regents Pk. Rd. N3 . . . . 3H 29
NW1 . . . . 7D 48
(not continuous)
Regents Pk. Ter. NW1 . . . . . . 1F 67
Regents Pl. SE3 . . . . 2J 107
Regents Plaza *NW6* *2K 65*
(off Kilburn High Rd.)
Regent Sq. DA17: Belv 4H 93
E3 . . . . 3D 70
WC1 . . . . 3J 67 (2F 161)
Regents Row E8 . . . . 1G 69
Regent St. NW10 . . . . 3F 65
SW1 . . . . . . 7H 67 (3C 166)
W1 . . . . 6F 67 (7K 159)
W4 . . . . 5G 81
Regents Wharf *E8* *1H 69*
(off Wharf Pl.)
N1 . . . . 2K 67
Regina Cl. EN5: Barn 3A 4
Regina Ho. SE20 . . . . 1K 141
Reginald Pl. *SE8* *7C 88*
(off Deptford High St.)
Reginald Rd. E7 . . . . 7J 53
HA6: Nwood 1H 23
SE8 . . . . 7C 88
Reginald Sorenson Ho.
E11 . . . . 7F 35
Reginald Sq. SE8 . . . . 7C 88
Regina Point SE16 . . . . 3J 87
Regina Rd. N4 . . . . 1K 49
SE25 . . . . 3G 141
UB2: S'hall 4C 78
W13 . . . . 1A 80
Regina Ter. W13 . . . . 1B 80
Regis Ct. N8 . . . . 4K 31
NW1 . . . . *5E 158*
(off Melcombe Pl.)
Regis Ho. *W1* *5H 159*
(off Beaumont St.)
Regis Pl. SW2 . . . . 4K 103
Regis Rd. NW5 . . . . 5F 49
Regnart Bldgs. NW1 . . . . . . 3B 160
Reid Cl. HA5: Pinn 4J 23
Reidhaven Rd. SE18 . . . . 4J 91
Reigate Av. SM1: Sutt 1J 149
Reigate Rd. BR1: Brom 3H 125
IG3: Ilf 2K 55
Reigate Way SM6: Wall 5J 151
Reighton Rd. E5 . . . . 3G 51
Reinickendorf Av. SE9 . . . . . 6G 109
Reizel Cl. N16 . . . . 1F 51
Relay Rd. W12 . . . . 1E 82
Relf Rd. SE15 . . . . 3G 105
Reliance Arc. SW9 . . . . 4A 104
Reliance Sq.
EC2 . . . . 4E 68 (3H 163)
Relko Gdns. SM1: Sutt 5B 150
Relton M. SW7 . . . 3C 84 (1D 170)
Rembold Ho. *SE10* *1E 106*
(off Blissett St.)
Rembrandt Cl. E14 . . . . 3F 89
SW1 . . . . 4G 171
Rembrandt Ct. KT19: Eps . . . 6B 148
SE16 . . . . *5H 87*
(off Stubbs Dr.)
Rembrandt Rd. HA8: Edg 2G 27
SE13 . . . . 4G 107
Remembrance Rd. E7 . . . . . . 4B 54
Remington Rd. E6 . . . . 6C 72
N15 . . . . 6D 32
Remington St.
N1 . . . . 2B 68 (1B 162)
Remnant St.
WC2 . . . . 6K 67 (7G 161)
Remsted Ho. *NW6* *1K 65*
(off Mortimer Cres.)
Remus Bldg., The *EC1* *2K 161*
(off Hardwick St.)
Remus Rd. E3 . . . . 7C 52
Renaissance Wlk. *SE10* *3H 89*
(off Teal St.)
Rendle Cl. CR0: Croy 5F 141
Rendlesham Rd. E5 . . . . 4G 51
EN2: Enf 1G 7
Renforth St. SE16 . . . . 3J 87
Renfree Way
TW17: Shep 7C 130
Renfrew Cl. E6 . . . . 7E 72
Renfrew Ct. TW4: Houn 2C 96
Renfrew Ho. E17 . . . . 2B 34
Renfrew Rd. KT2: King T . . . 7H 117
SE11 . . . . . . 4B 86 (3K 173)
TW4: Houn 2B 96
Renmuir St. SW17 . . . . 6D 120
Rennell St. SE13 . . . . 3E 106
Rennels Way TW7: Isle 2J 97
Renness Rd. E17 . . . . 3A 34
Rennets Cl. SE9 . . . . 5J 109
Rennets Wood Rd. SE9 . . . . 5H 109
Rennie Cotts. *E1* *4J 69*
(off Pemell Cl.)
Rennie Ct. SE1 . . . . 4A 168
Rennie Est. SE16 . . . . 4H 87
Rennie Ho. *SE1* *3C 86*
(off Bath Ter.)
Rennie St. SE1 . . . . 1B 86 (4A 168)
(not continuous)
Renoir Ct. *SE16* *5H 87*
(off Stubbs Dr.)
Renovation, The *E16* *2F 91*
(off Woolwich Mnr. Way)
Renown Cl. CR0: Croy 1B 152
RM7: Mawney 1G 39
Rensburg Rd. E17 . . . . 5K 33
Renshaw Cl. DA17: Belv 6F 93
Renters Av. NW4 . . . . 6E 28
Renton Cl. SW2 . . . . 6K 103
Renwick Ind. Est.
IG11: Bark 2B 74
Renwick Rd. IG11: Bark 4B 74
Repens Way UB4: Hayes 4B 60
Rephidim St. SE1 . . . . 3E 86
Replingham Rd. SW18 . . . . 1H 119
Reporton Rd. SW6 . . . . 7G 83
Repository Rd. SE18 . . . . 6D 90
Repton Av. HA0: Wemb 4C 44
UB3: Hayes 4F 77
Repton Cl. SM5: Cars 5C 150
Repton Ct. BR3: Beck 1D 142
IG5: Ilf 1D 36
Repton Gro. IG5: Ilf 1D 36
Repton Ho. *E14* *6A 70*
(off Repton St.)
SW1 . . . . *4B 172*
(off Charlwood St.)
Repton Rd. HA3: Harr 4F 27

Repton St.—Rigeley Rd.

Repton St. E14 6A 70
Repulse Cl. RM5: Col R 1G 39
Reservoir Cl.
CR7: Thor H 3D 140
Reservoir Rd. HA4: Ruis 4F 23
N14 5B 6
SE4 2A 106
Reservoir Studios E1 6K 69
(off Cable St.)
Resolution Wlk. SE18 3D 90
Restell Cl. SE3 6G 89
Restmor Way SM6: Wall 2E 150
Reston Pl. SW7 2A 84
Restons Cres. SE9 6H 109
Restoration Sq. SW11 1B 102
Restormel Cl.
TW3: Houn 5E 96
Restormel Ho. SE11 4J 173
Retcar Cl. N19 2F 49
Retcar Pl. N19 2F 49
(off Retcar Cl.)
Retford St. E2 2E 68
N1 2E 68 (1H 163)
Retingham Way E4 2J 19
Retles Ct. HA1: Harr 7J 25
Retreat Cl. HA3: Harr 5C 26
Retreat Ho. E9 6J 51
Retreat Pl. E9 6J 51
Retreat Rd. TW9: Rich 5D 98
Retreat, The
CR7: Thor H 4D 140
HA2: Harr 7E 24
KT4: Wor Pk 2D 148
KT5: Surb 6F 135
NW9 5K 27
SW14 3A 100
Reubens Ct. W4 5H 81
(off Chaseley Dr.)
Reunion Row E1 7H 69
Reveley Sq. SE16 2A 88
Revell Ri. SE18 6K 91
Revell Rd. KT1: King T 2H 135
SM1: Sutt 6H 149
Revelon Rd. SE4 4A 106
Revelstoke Rd. SW18 2H 119
Reventlow Rd. SE9 1G 127
Reverdy Rd. SE1 4G 87
Reverend Cl. HA2: Harr 3F 43
Revesby Rd. SM5: Cars 6B 138
Review Rd. NW2 2B 46
RM10: Dag 1H 75
Rewell St. SW6 7A 84
Rewley Rd. SM5: Cars 6B 138
Rex Av. TW15: Ashf 6C 112
Rex Cl. RM5: Col R 1H 39
Rex Pl. W1 7E 66 (3H 165)
Reydon Av. E11 5A 36
Reynard Cl. BR1: Brom 3E 144
SE4 3A 106
Reynard Dr. SE19 7F 123
Reynard Mills Trad. Est.
TW8: Bford 5C 80
Reynard Pl. SE14 6A 88
Reynardson Rd. N17 7H 17
Reynolah Gdns. SE7 5K 89
Reynolds Av. E12 5E 54
KT9: Chess 7E 146
RM6: Chad H 7C 38
Reynolds Cl. NW11 7K 29
SM5: Cars 1D 150
SW19 1B 138
Reynolds Ct.
RM6: Chad H 3D 38
Reynolds Dr. HA8: Edg 3F 27
Reynolds Ho. E2 2J 69
(off Approach Rd.)
NW8 2B 66
(off Wellington Rd.)
SW1 4D 172
(off Erasmus St.)
Reynolds Pl. SE3 7K 89
TW10: Rich 6F 99
Reynolds Rd.
KT3: N Mald 7K 135
SE15 4J 105
UB4: Hayes 4A 60
W4 3J 81
Reynolds Way CR0: Croy 4E 152
Rheidol M. N1 2C 68
Rheidol Ter. N1 1C 68
Rheingold Way
SM6: Wall 7J 151
Rhein Ho. N8 3J 31
(off Campsfield Rd.)
Rheola Cl. N17 1F 33
Rhoda St. E2 4F 69 (3K 163)
Rhodes Av. N22 1G 31
Rhodes Ho. N1 1E 162
(off Fairbank Est.)
W12 1D 82
Rhodesia Rd. E11 2F 53
SW9 2J 103
Rhodesmoor Ho. Ct.
SM4: Mord 6J 137
Rhodes St. N7 5K 49
Rhodeswell Rd. E14 5A 70
Rhodrons Av. KT9: Chess 5E 146
Rhondda Gro. E3 3A 70
Rhyl Rd. UB6: G'frd 2K 61
Rhyl St. NW5 6E 48
Rhys Av. N11 7C 16
Rialto Rd. CR4: Mitc 2E 138
Ribble Cl. IG8: Wfd G 6F 21
Ribblesdale Av. N11 6K 15
UB5: N'olt 6F 43
Ribblesdale Ho. NW6 1J 65
(off Kilburn Va.)
Ribblesdale Rd. N8 4K 31
SW16 6F 121
Ribbon Ct. N11 6K 15
(off Ribblesdale Av.)
Ribbon Dance M. SE5 1D 104
Ribchester Av. UB6: G'frd 3K 61
Ribston Cl. BR2: Short 1D 156
Ricardo Path SE28 1C 92
Ricardo St. E14 6D 70
Ricards Rd. SW19 5H 119
Riccall Ct. NW9 1A 28
(off Pageant Av.)
Rice Pde. BR5: Orp 5H 145
Riceyman Ho. WC1 2J 161
(off Lloyd Baker St.)
Richard Anderson Ct.
SE14 7K 87
(off Monson Rd.)
Richard Burbidge Mans.
SW13 6E 82
(off Brasenose Dr.)
Richard Burton Ct.
IG9: Buck H 2F 21
(off Palmerston Rd.)
Richard Cl. SE18 4C 90
Richard Fell Ho. E12 4E 54
(off Walton Rd.)
Richard Ho. SE16 4J 87
(off Silwood St.)
Richard Ho. Dr. E16 6B 72
Richard Neale Ho. E1 7H 69
(off Cornwall St.)
Richard Neve Ho. SE18 4J 91
(off Plumstead High St.)
Richards Av. RM7: Rom 6J 39
Richards Cl. HA1: Harr 5A 26
UB3: Hayes 6F 77
UB10: Uxb 1C 58
WD23: Bush 1C 10
Richards Fld. KT19: Eps 7K 147
Richard Sharples Ct.
SM2: Sutt 7A 150
Richardson Cl. E8 1F 69
Richardson Ct. SW4 2J 103
(off Studley Rd.)
Richardson Gdns.
RM10: Dag 6H 57
Richardson Rd. E15 2G 71
Richardsons M. W1 4A 160
Richards Pl. E17 3C 34
SW3 4C 84 (3D 170)
Richard St. E1 6H 69
Richbell Pl.
WC1 5K 67 (5G 161)
Richborne Ter. SW8 7K 85
Richborough Ho.
SE15 6J 87
(off Sharratt St.)
Richborough Rd. NW2 4G 47
Richens Cl. TW3: Houn 2H 97
Riches Rd. IG1: Ilf 2G 55
Richfield Rd.
WD23: Bush 1B 10
Richford Ga. W6 3E 82
Richford Rd. E15 1H 71
Richford St. W6 2E 82
Rich Ind. Est. SE15 6H 87
Richlands Av.
KT17: Eps 4C 148
Rich La. SW5 5K 83
Richman Ho. SE8 5B 88
(off Grove St.)
RICHMOND 5D 98
Richmond Av. E4 5A 20
N1 1K 67
NW10 6E 46
SW20 1G 137
TW14: Felt 6G 95
UB10: Uxb 6D 40
Richmond Bri.
TW1: Twick 6D 98
Richmond Bldgs.
W1 6H 67 (1C 166)
RICHMOND CIRCUS 4E 98
Richmond Cl. E17 6B 34
Richmond Cotts. W14 4G 83
(off Hammersmith Rd.)
Richmond Ct. CR4: Mitc 3B 138
E8 7H 51
(off Mare St.)
HA9: Wemb 3F 45
NW6 7F 47
(off Willesden La.)
SW1 7F 165
(off Sloane St.)
Richmond Cres. E4 5A 20
N1 1K 67
N9 1B 18
Richmond Dr. IG8: Ilf 7K 21
TW17: Shep 6F 131
Richmond Gdns.
HA3: Harr 7E 10
NW4 5C 28
Richmond Grn.
CR0: Croy 3J 151
Richmond Gro.
KT5: Surb 6F 135
N1 7B 50
(not continuous)
Richmond Hill TW10: Rich 6E 98
Richmond Hill Ct.
TW10: Rich 6E 98
Richmond Ho. NW1 1K 159
(off Pk. Village E.)
SE17 5D 86
(off Portland St.)
Richmond Mans.
TW1: Twick 6D 98
Richmond M.
TW11: Tedd 5K 115
W1 6H 67 (1C 166)
Richmond Pde.
TW1: Twick 6C 98
(off Richmond Rd.)
Richmond Pk. 1G 117
Richmond Pk. Rd.
KT2: King T 1E 134
SW14 5J 99
Richmond Pl. SE18 4G 91
Richmond Rd.
CR0: Croy 3J 151
CR7: Thor H 3B 140
E4 1A 20
E7 5K 53
E8 7F 51
E11 2F 53
EN5: Barn 5E 4
IG1: Ilf 3G 55
KT2: King T 4D 116
N2 2A 30
N11 6D 16
N15 6E 32
SW20 1D 136
TW1: Twick 7B 98
TW7: Isle 3A 98
W5 2E 80
Richmond St. E13 2J 71
Richmond Ter.
SW1 2J 85 (6E 166)
Richmond Way E11 2J 53
W12 2F 83
W14 2F 83
Richmount Gdns. SE3 3J 107
Rich St. E14 7B 70
Rickard Cl. NW4 4D 28
SW2 1A 122
Rickards Cl. KT6: Surb 2E 146
Rickett St. SW6 6J 83
Rickman Ho. E1 3J 69
(off Rickman St.)
Rickman St. E1 4J 69
Rickmansworth Rd.
HA5: Pinn 2K 23
HA6: Nwood 1F 23
Rick Roberts Way E15 1E 70
Rickthorne Rd. N19 2J 49
Rickyard Path SE9 4C 108
Riddell Ct. SE5 5F 87
(off Albany Rd.)
Ridding La. UB6: G'frd 5K 43
(not continuous)
Riddons Rd. SE12 3A 126
Rideout St. SE18 4D 90
Rider Cl. DA15: Sidc 6J 109
Ride, The EN3: Enf 3D 8
TW8: Bford 5B 80
Ridgdale St. E3 2D 70
Ridge Av. N21 7H 7
Ridgebrook Rd. SE3 3B 108
Ridge Cl. NW4 2F 29
NW9 4K 27
SE28 2H 91
Ridge Ct. SE22 7G 105
Ridge Crest EN2: Enf 1E 6
Ridgecroft Cl. DA5: Bexl 1J 129
Ridge Hill NW11 1G 47
Ridgemead Cl. N14 2D 16
Ridgemont Gdns.
HA8: Edg 4D 12
Ridgemount EN2: Enf 2G 7
Ridgemount Av.
CR0: Croy 1K 153
Ridgemount Cl. SE20 7H 123
Ridgemount Gdns.
EN2: Enf 3G 7
Ridge Rd. CR4: Mitc 7F 121
N8 6K 31
N21 1H 17
NW2 3H 47
SM3: Sutt 1G 149
Ridges Yd. CR0: Croy 3B 152
Ridge, The DA5: Bexl 7F 111
EN5: Barn 5C 4
KT5: Surb 5G 135
TW2: Twick 7H 97
Ridgeview Cl.
EN5: Barn 6A 4
Ridgeview Rd. N20 3E 14
Ridge Way IG8: Wfd G 4F 21
SE19 6E 122
TW13: Felt 3C 114
Ridgeway BR2: Short 2J 155
TW10: Rich 6E 98
Ridgeway Av. EN4: Barn 6J 5
Ridgeway Dr. BR1: Brom 4K 125
Ridgeway E. DA15: Sidc 5K 109
Ridgeway Gdns. IG4: Ilf 5C 36
N6 7H 31
Ridgeway Rd. TW7: Isle 7J 79
Ridgeway Rd. Nth.
TW7: Isle 7J 79
Ridgeway, The
CR0: Croy 3K 151
E4 2J 19
EN2: Enf 1E 6
HA2: Harr 5D 24
(not continuous)
HA3: Harr 6C 26
HA4: Ruis 7J 23
HA7: Stan 6H 11
KT12: Walt T 7H 131
N3 7E 14
N11 4J 15
N14 2D 16
NW7 3H 13
NW9 4K 27
NW11 7G 29
W3 3G 81
Ridgeway Wlk. UB5: N'olt 6C 42
(off Cowings Mead)
Ridgeway W. DA15: Sidc 5J 109
Ridgewell Cl. N1 1C 68
RM10: Dag 1H 75
SE26 4B 124
Ridgmount Gdns.
WC1 5H 67 (5C 160)
Ridgmount Pl.
WC1 5H 67 (5C 160)
Ridgmount Rd. SW18 5K 101
Ridgmount St.
WC1 5H 67 (5C 160)
Ridgway SW19 7E 118
Ridgway Ct. SW19 6F 119
Ridgway Gdns. SW19 7F 119
Ridgway Pl. SW19 6G 119
Ridgway Rd. SW9 3B 104
Ridgway, The SM2: Sutt 7B 150
Ridgwell Rd. E16 5A 72
Riding Ho. St.
W1 5F 67 (6K 159)
Ridings Av. N21 5H 7
Ridings Cl. N6 7G 31
Ridings, The E11 5J 35
EN4: Barn 7G 5
KT5: Surb 5G 135
KT17: Eps 7B 148
TW16: Sun T 1J 131
W5 4F 63
Riding, The NW11 7H 29
Ridler Rd. EN1: Enf 1K 7
Ridley Av. W13 3B 80
Ridley Cl. IG11: Bark 7K 55
Ridley Ct. SW16 6J 121
Ridley Rd. BR2: Short 3H 143
DA16: Well 1B 110
E7 4A 54
E8 5F 51
NW10 2C 64
SW19 7K 119
Ridsdale Rd. SE20 1H 141
Riefield Rd. SE9 4G 109
Riesco Dr. CR0: Croy 6J 153
Riffel Rd. NW2 5E 46
Rifle Ct. SE11 6A 86 (7K 173)
Rifle St. E14 5D 70
Riga Ho. E1 5K 69
(off Shandy St.)
Rigault Rd. SW6 2G 101
Rigby Cl. CR0: Croy 3A 152
Rigby La. UB3: Hayes 2E 76
Rigby M. IG1: Ilf 2E 54
Rigden St. E14 6D 70
Rigeley Rd. NW10 3C 64

Rigg App.—Robin Hood Grn.

Rigg App. E10 1K 51
Rigge Pl. SW4 4H 103
Riggindale Rd. SW16 5H 121
Riley Ho. SW10 7B 84 (off Ann La.)
Riley Rd. EN3: Enf 1D 8
SE1 3F 87 (7H 169)
Riley St. SW10 6B 84
Rill Ho. SE5 7D 86 (off Harris St.)
Rinaldo Rd. SW12 7F 103
Ring Cl. BR1: Brom 7K 125
Ringcroft St. N7 5A 50
Ringers Ct. BR1: Brom 3J 143 (off Ringers Rd.)
Ringers Rd. BR1: Brom 3J 143
Ringford Rd. SW18 5H 101
Ring Ho. E1 7J 69 (off Sage St.)
Ringles Ct. E6 1D 72
Ringlet Cl. E16 5K 71
Ringlewell Cl. EN1: Enf 2C 8
Ringmer Av. SW6 1G 101
Ringmer Gdns. N19 2J 49
Ringmer Pl. N21 5J 7
Ringmer Way BR1: Brom 5C 144
Ringmore Ri. SE23 7H 105
Ring Rd. W12 1E 82
Ringsfield Ho. SE17 5C 86 (off Bronti Cl.)
Ringslade Rd. N22 2K 31
Ringstead Rd. SE6 7D 106
SM1: Sutt 4B 150
Ring, The W2 7B 66 (2C 164) (not continuous)
Ring Way N11 6B 16
Ringway UB2: S'hall 5B 78
Ringwold Cl. BR3: Beck 7A 124
Ringwood Av.
CR0: Croy 7J 139
N2 2D 30
Ringwood Cl. HA5: Pinn 3A 24
Ringwood Gdns. E14 4C 88
SW15 1C 118
Ringwood Rd. E17 6B 34
Ringwood Way N21 1G 17
TW12: Hamp 4E 114
Ripley Cl. BR1: Brom 5D 144
CR0: Croy 6E 154
Ripley Ct. CR4: Mitc 2B 138
Ripley Gdns. SM1: Sutt 4A 150 (not continuous)
SW14 3K 99
Ripley Ho. SW1 7A 172 (off Churchill Gdns.)
Ripley M. E11 6G 35
Ripley Rd. DA17: Belv 4G 93
E16 6A 72
EN2: Enf 1H 7
IG3: Ilf 2K 55
TW12: Hamp 7E 114
Ripley Vs. W13 6C 62
Ripon Cl. UB5: N'olt 5E 42
Ripon Gdns. IG1: Ilf 6C 36
KT9: Chess 5D 146
Ripon Rd. N9 7C 8
N17 3D 32
SE18 6F 91
Rippersley Rd.
DA16: Well 1A 110
Ripple Rd. IG11: Bark 7G 55
IG11: Bark, Dag 1B 74
RM9: Dag 1B 74
RIPPLE ROAD JUNCTION 1A 74
RIPPLESIDE 1B 74
Rippleside Commercial Est.
IG11: Bark 2C 74
Ripplevale Gro. N1 7K 49
Rippolson Rd. SE18 5K 91
Ripston Rd. TW15: Ashf 5F 113
Risboro' Cl. N10 3F 31
Risborough SE17 4C 86
Risborough Dr.
KT4: Wor Pk 7C 136
Risborough Ho. NW8 3D 158 (off Mallory St.)
Risborough St.
SE1 2B 86 (6B 168)
Risdon Ho. SE16 2J 87 (off Risdon St.)
Risdon St. SE16 3J 87
Risedale Rd.
DA7: Bex 3J 111
Riseholme Ct. E9 6B 52
Riseldine Rd. SE23 6A 106
RISE PARK 2K 39
Rise Pk. Pde.
RM1: Rom 2K 39
Rise, The DA5: Bexl 7C 110
E11 5J 35
HA8: Edg 5C 12
IG9: Buck H 1G 21
N13 4F 17
NW7 6G 13
NW10 4K 45
UB6: G'frd 5A 44
UB10: Uxb 2B 58
Risinghill St. N1 2K 67
Risingholme Cl. HA3: Harr 1J 25
WD23: Bush 1A 10
Risingholme Rd.
HA3: Harr 2J 25
Risings, The E17 4F 35
Rising Sun Ct. EC1 5B 162
Risley Av. N17 1C 32
Rita Rd. SW8 6J 85
Ritches Rd. N15 5C 32
Ritchie Ho. E14 6F 71 (off Blair St.)
N19 1H 49
SE16 3J 87 (off Howland Est.)
Ritchie Rd. CR0: Croy 6H 141
Ritchie St. N1 2A 68
Ritchings Av. E17 4A 34
Ritherdon Rd. SW17 2E 120
Ritson Ho. N1 1K 67 (off Barnsbury Est.)
Ritson Rd. E8 6G 51
Ritter St. SE18 6E 90
Ritz Pde. W5 4F 63
Rivaz Pl. E9 6J 51
Riven Ct. W2 6K 65 (off Inverness Ter.)
Rivenhall Gdns. E18 4H 35
RIVER ASH ESTATE 7H 131
River Av. KT7: T Ditt 7A 134
N13 3G 17
River Av. Ind. Est. N13 5F 17
River Bank KT7: T Ditt 5K 133
KT8: E Mos 3J 133
N21 7H 7
TW12: Hamp 3E 132
Riverbank Rd.
BR1: Brom 3J 125
Riverbank Way
TW8: Bford 6C 80
River Barge Cl. E14 2E 88
River Brent Bus. Pk. W7 3J 79
River Cl. E11 6A 36
HA4: Ruis 6H 23
UB2: S'hall 2G 79
River Ct. KT6: Surb 5D 134 (off Portsmouth Rd.)
SE1 7B 68 (3A 168)
Rivercourt Rd. W6 4D 82
River Crane Way
TW13: Felt 2D 114 (off Watermill Way)
Riverdale SE13 4E 106
Riverdale Ct. N21 5J 7
Riverdale Dr. SW18 1K 119
Riverdale Gdns.
TW1: Twick 6C 98
Riverdale Rd. DA5: Bexl 7F 111
DA8: Erith 5H 93
SE18 5K 91
TW1: Twick 6C 98
TW13: Felt 4C 114
Riverdale Shop. Cen.
SE13 3E 106
Riverdene HA8: Edg 3D 12
Riverdene Rd. IG1: Ilf 3E 54
Riverfleet WC1 1F 161 (off Birkenhead St.)
River Front EN1: Enf 3K 7
River Gdns. SM5: Cars 2E 150
TW14: Felt 5K 95
River Gdns. Bus. Cen.
TW14: Felt 5K 95
River Gro. Pk.
BR3: Beck 1B 142
Riverhead Cl. E17 2K 33
Riverhill KT4: Wor Pk 2K 147
Riverholme Dr.
KT19: Eps 7K 147
Riverhope Mans. SE18 3C 90
River Ho. SE26 3H 123
River La. TW10: Rich 7D 98
Riverleigh Ct. E4 5G 19
Rivermead KT1: King T 5D 134
KT8: W Mole 3G 133
Rivermead Cl.
TW11: Tedd 5B 116
Rivermead Ct. SW6 3H 101
Rivermead Ho. E9 5A 52
Rivermead Rd. N18 6E 18
River Meads Av.
TW2: Twick 3E 114
River Mt. KT12: Walt T 7H 131
Rivernook Cl.
KT12: Walt T 5A 132
River Pk. Gdns.
BR2: Short 7F 125
River Pk. Rd. N22 2K 31
River Pk. Trad. Est. E14 3B 88
River Pl. N1 7C 50
River Reach
TW11: Tedd 5C 116
River Rd. IG9: Buck H 1H 21
IG11: Bark 2J 73
River Rd. Bus. Pk.
IG11: Bark 3K 73
Riversdale Rd.
KT7: T Ditt 5A 134
N5 3B 50
RM5: Col R 1H 39
Riversfield Rd. EN1: Enf 3K 7
Rivers Ho. W4 5G 81 (off Chiswick High Rd.)
Riverside NW4 7D 28
SE7 3K 89 (not continuous)
TW1: Twick 1B 116
TW9: Rich 5D 98
TW16: Sun T 2B 132
TW17: Shep 7G 131
WC1 1F 161 (off Birkenhead St.)
Riverside Apartments
N13 5E 16
Riverside Av.
KT8: E Mos 5H 133
Riverside Bus. Cen.
SW18 1K 119
Riverside Cl. E5 1J 51
KT1: King T 4D 134
SM6: Wall 3F 151
W7 4J 61
Riverside Cotts.
IG11: Bark 2H 73
Riverside Ct. SE3 4H 107
SW8 6H 85 (7D 172)
TW7: Isle 2K 97 (off Woodlands Rd.)
TW14: Felt 7G 95
Riverside Dr. CR4: Mitc 5C 138
NW11 6G 29
TW10: Rich 3B 116
W4 7K 81
Riverside Gdns. EN2: Enf 2H 7
HA0: Wemb 2E 62
N3 3G 29
W6 5D 82
Riverside Ho. N1 7C 50 (off Canonbury St.)
Riverside Ind. Est. EN3: Enf 6F 9
IG11: Bark 3A 74
Riverside Mans. E1 1J 87 (off Milk Yd.)
Riverside M. CR0: Croy 3J 151
Riverside Pl. N11 3B 16
TW19: Staines 6A 94
Riverside Rd. DA14: Sidc 3E 128
E15 2E 70
N15 6G 33
SW17 4K 119
TW19: Staines 5A 94 (not continuous)
Riverside, The
KT8: E Mos 3H 133
Riverside Wlk.
BR4: W W'ck 1D 154
EN5: Barn 6A 4 (not continuous)
KT1: King T 3D 134
N12 3E 14 (not continuous)
SE10 3G 89 (Morden Wharf Rd.)
SE10 2F 89 (Tunnel Av.)
SW6 3G 101
TW7: Isle 3J 97
W4 6B 82 (off Chiswick Wharf)
Riverside Works
IG11: Bark 7F 55
Riverside Workshops
SE1 4D 168 (off Park St.)
Riverstone Ct.
KT2: King T 1F 135
River St. EC1 3A 68 (1J 161)
River Ter. W6 5E 82
WC2 3G 167
Riverton Cl. W9 3H 65
River Vw. EN2: Enf 3H 7
River Vw. Gdns.
TW1: Twick 2K 115
Riverview Gdns. SW13 6D 82
Riverview Gro. W4 6H 81
Riverview Hgts. SE16 2G 87 (off Bermondsey Wall W.)
Riverview Pk. SE6 2C 124
Riverview Rd. KT19: Eps 4J 147
W4 7H 81
River Wlk. KT12: Walt T 6J 131
W6 7E 82
River Way KT19: Eps 5K 147
SE10 3H 89
TW2: Twick 2F 115
Riverway N13 5F 17
River Wharf Bus. Pk.
DA17: Belv 1K 93
Riverwood La. BR7: Chst 1H 145
Rivet Ho. SE1 5F 87 (off Coopers Rd.)
Rivington Av. IG8: Wfd G 2B 36
Rivington Bldgs.
EC2 3E 68 (2G 163)
Rivington Ct. NW10 1C 64
Rivington Cres. NW7 7G 13
Rivington Pl.
EC2 3E 68 (2H 163)
Rivington St.
EC2 3E 68 (2G 163)
Rivington Wlk. E8 1G 69
Rivulet Rd. N17 7H 17
Rixon Ho. SE18 6F 91
Rixon St. N7 3A 50
Rixsen Rd. E12 5C 54
Roach Rd. E3 7C 52
Roads Pl. N19 2J 49
Roan St. SE10 6E 88
Robarts Cl. HA5: Pinn 6K 23
Robb Rd. HA7: Stan 6F 11
Robert Adam St.
W1 6E 66 (7G 159)
Roberta St. E2 3G 69
Robert Bell Ho. SE16 4G 87 (off Rouel Rd.)
Robert Burns M. SE24 5B 104
Robert Cl. W9 4A 66 (4A 158)
Robert Dashwood Way
SE17 4C 86
Robert Gentry Ho. W14 5G 83 (off Gledstanes Rd.)
Robert Jones Ho. SE16 4G 87 (off Rouel Rd.)
Robert Keen Cl. SE15 1G 105
Robert Lowe Cl. SE14 7K 87
Roberton Dr.
BR1: Brom 1A 144
Robert Owen Ho. N22 1A 32 (off Progress Way)
SW6 1F 101
Robert Runcie Ct. SW9 4K 103
Roberts All. W5 2D 80
Robertsbridge Rd.
SM5: Cars 1A 150
Roberts Cl. CR7: Thor H 3D 140
SE9 1H 127
SE16 2K 87
SM3: Sutt 7F 149
UB7: W Dray 1A 76
Roberts Ct. N1 1B 68 (off Essex Rd.)
NW10 6A 46
SE20 1J 141 (off Maple Rd.)
Roberts M. SW1 3E 84 (1G 171)
Robertson Rd. E15 1E 70
Robertson St. SW8 3F 103
Roberts Pl. EC1 4A 68 (3K 161)
Roberts Rd. DA17: Belv 5G 93
E17 1D 34
NW7 6B 14
Robert St. CR0: Croy 3C 152
E16 1F 91
NW1 3F 67 (2K 159)
SE18 5H 91 (not continuous)
WC2 7J 67 (3F 167)
Robert Sutton Ho. E1 6J 69 (off Tarling St.)
Robeson St. E3 5B 70
Robina Cl. DA6: Bex 4D 110
HA6: Nwood 1H 23
SE20 1G 141 (off Sycamore Gro.)
Robin Cl. NW7 3F 13
RM5: Col R 1K 39
TW12: Hamp 5C 114
Robin Ct. E14 2E 88
SE16 4G 87
Robin Cres. E6 5B 72
Robin Gro. HA3: Harr 6F 27
N6 2E 48
TW8: Bford 6C 80
Robin Hill Dr.
BR7: Chst 6C 126
ROBIN HOOD 3A 118
Robinhood Cl. CR4: Mitc 3G 139
Robin Hood Dr.
HA3: Harr 7E 10
Robin Hood Gdns. E14 7E 70 (off Woolmore St., not continuous)
Robin Hood Grn.
BR5: Orp 5K 145

Ronaldstone Rd.—Ross Rd.

Ronaldstone Rd.
DA15: Sidc ... 6J **109**
Ronald St. E1 ... 6J **69**
Rona Rd. NW3 ... 4E **48**
Ronart St. HA3: Harr ... 3K **25**
Rona Wlk. *N1 ... 6D 50*
(off Ramsey Wlk.)
Rondel Ct. DA5: Bexl ... 6E **110**
Rondu Rd. NW2 ... 5G **47**
Ronelean Rd. KT6: Surb ... 2F **147**
Ron Grn. Ct. DA8: Erith ... 6K **93**
Ron Leighton Way E6 ... 1C **72**
Ronnie La. E12 ... 4E **54**
Ronver Rd. SE12 ... 1H **125**
Rood La. EC3 ... 7E **68** (2G **169**)
Roof Ter. Apartments, The
EC1 ... 4B 162
(off Gt. Sutton St.)
Rookby Ct. N21 ... 2G **17**
Rook Cl. HA9: Wemb ... 3H **45**
Rookeries Cl. TW13: Felt ... 3K **113**
Rookery Cl. NW9 ... 5B **28**
Rookery Cres. RM10: Dag ... 7H **57**
Rookery Dr. BR7: Chst ... 1E **144**
Rookery La. BR2: Short ... 6B **144**
Rookery Rd. SW4 ... 4G **103**
Rookery Way NW9 ... 5B **28**
Rooke Way SE10 ... 5H **89**
Rookfield Av. N10 ... 4G **31**
Rookfield Cl. N10 ... 4G **31**
Rooksmead Rd.
TW16: Sun T ... 2H **131**
Rooks Ter. UB7: W Dray ... 2A **76**
Rookstone Rd. SW17 ... 5D **120**
Rook Wlk. E6 ... 6B **72**
Rookwood Av.
KT3: N Mald ... 4C **136**
SM6: Wall ... 4H **151**
Rookwood Gdns. E4 ... 2C **20**
Rookwood Ho. IG11: Bark ... 2H **73**
Rookwood Rd. N16 ... 7F **33**
Roosevelt Memorial
... 7E 66 (2H 165)
Roosevelt Way
RM10: Dag ... 6K **57**
Rootes Dr. W10 ... 5F **65**
Ropemaker Rd. SE16 ... 2A **88**
Ropemakers Flds. E14 ... 7B **70**
Ropemaker St.
EC2 ... 5D **68** (5E **162**)
Roper La. SE1 ... 2E **86** (7H **169**)
Ropers Av. E4 ... 5J **19**
Ropers Orchard *SW3 ... 6C 84*
(off Danvers St.)
Roper St. SE9 ... 5D **108**
Ropers Wlk. SW2 ... 7A **104**
Roper Way CR4: Mitc ... 2E **138**
Ropery Bus. Pk. SE7 ... 4A **90**
Ropery St. E3 ... 4B **70**
Rope St. SE16 ... 4A **88**
Rope Wlk. TW16: Sun T ... 3A **132**
Rope Wlk. Gdns. E1 ... 6G **69**
Ropewalk M. *E8 ... 7G 51*
(off Middleton Rd.)
Rope Yd. Rails SE18 ... 3F **91**
Ropley St. E2 ... 2G **69**
Rosa Alba M. N5 ... 4C **50**
Rosa Av. TW15: Ashf ... 4C **112**
Rosalind Ct. *IG11: Bark ... 7A 56*
(off Meadow Rd.)
Rosalind Ho. *N1 ... 2E 68*
(off Arden Ho.)
Rosaline Rd. SW6 ... 7G **83**
Rosaline Ter. *SW6 ... 7G 83*
(off Rosaline Rd.)
Rosamond St. SE26 ... 3H **123**
Rosamund Cl.
CR2: S Croy ... 4D **152**
Rosamun St. UB2: S'hall ... 4C **78**
Rosary Cl. TW3: Houn ... 2C **96**
Rosary Gdns. SW7 ... 4A **84**
TW15: Ashf ... 4D **112**
Rosaville Rd. SW6 ... 7H **83**
Roscoe St. EC1 ... 4C **68** (4D **162**)
(not continuous)
Roscoe St. Est.
EC1 ... 4C **68** (4D **162**)
Roscoff Cl. HA8: Edg ... 1J **27**
Roseacre Cl.
TW17: Shep ... 5C **130**
W13 ... 5B **62**
Roseacre Rd. DA16: Well ... 3B **110**
Rose All. *EC2 ... 6H 163*
(off Bishopsgate)
SE1 ... 1C **86** (4D **168**)
Rose & Crown Ct. EC2 ... 7D **162**
Rose & Crown Pas.
TW7: Isle ... 1A **98**
Rose & Crown Yd.
SW1 ... 1G **85** (4B **166**)
Rose Av. CR4: Mitc ... 1D **138**
E18 ... 2K **35**
SM4: Mord ... 5A **138**
Rosebank SE20 ... 7H **123**
SW6 ... 7E **82**
W3 ... 6K **63**
Rosebank Av. HA0: Wemb ... 4K **43**
Rose Bank Cl. N12 ... 5H **15**
Rosebank Cl.
TW11: Tedd ... 6A **116**
Rosebank Gdns. E3 ... 2B **70**
W3 ... 6K **63**
Rosebank Gro. E17 ... 3B **34**
Rosebank Rd. E17 ... 6D **34**
W7 ... 2J **79**
Rosebank Vs. E17 ... 4C **34**
Rosebank Wlk. NW1 ... 7H **49**
SE18 ... 4C **90**
Rosebank Way W3 ... 6K **63**
Rose Bates Dr. NW9 ... 4G **27**
Roseberry Av.
CR7: Thor H ... 2C **140**
Roseberry Gdns. N4 ... 6B **32**
Roseberry Pl. E8 ... 6F **51**
Roseberry St. SE1 ... 4H **87**
Rosebery Av. DA15: Sidc ... 7J **109**
E12 ... 6C **54**
EC1 ... 4A **68** (4J **161**)
HA2: Harr ... 4C **42**
KT3: N Mald ... 2B **136**
N17 ... 2G **33**
Rosebery Cl. SM4: Mord ... 6F **137**
Rosebery Ct. *EC1 ... 4J 161*
(off Rosebery Av.)
Rosebery Gdns. N8 ... 5J **31**
SM1: Sutt ... 4K **149**
W13 ... 6A **62**
Rosebery Ho. *E2 ... 2J 69*
(off Sewardstone Rd.)
Rosebery Ind. Est. N17 ... 2H **33**
Rosebery Ind. Pk. N17 ... 2H **33**
Rosebery M. N10 ... 2G **31**
Rosebery Rd.
KT1: King T ... 2H **135**
N9 ... 3B **18**
N10 ... 2G **31**
SM1: Sutt ... 6H **149**
SW2 ... 6J **103**
TW3: Houn ... 5G **97**
WD23: Bush ... 1A **10**
Rosebery Sq. EC1 ... 4J **161**
KT1: King T ... 2H **135**
Rosebine Av. TW2: Twick ... 7H **97**
Rosebury Rd. SW6 ... 2K **101**
Rosebury Sq. IG8: Ilf ... 7K **21**
Rosebury Va. HA4: Ruis ... 2J **41**
Rose Bush Ct. NW3 ... 5D **48**
Rose Ct. E1 ... 6K **163**
E8 ... 7F 51
(off Richmond Rd.)
HA0: Wemb ... 2E 62
(off Vicars Bri. Cl.)
HA2: Harr ... 2G **43**
SE8 ... 4K **87**
Rosecourt Rd. CR0: Croy ... 6K **139**
Rosecroft N14 ... 2D **16**
Rosecroft Av. NW3 ... 3J **47**
Rosecroft Gdns. NW2 ... 3C **46**
TW2: Twick ... 1H **115**
Rosecroft Rd. UB1: S'hall ... 4E **60**
Rosecroft Wlk.
HA0: Wemb ... 5D **44**
HA5: Pinn ... 5B **24**
Rosedale Av. UB3: Hayes ... 5F **59**
Rosedale Cl. HA7: Stan ... 6G **11**
SE2 ... 3B **92**
W7 ... 2K **79**
Rosedale Ct. HA1: Harr ... 4K **43**
N5 ... 4B **50**
Rosedale Gdns. RM9: Dag ... 7B **56**
Rosedale Ho. N16 ... 1D **50**
Rosedale Pl. CR0: Croy ... 7K **141**
Rosedale Rd. E7 ... 5A **54**
KT17: Eps ... 5C **148**
RM1: Col R ... 2J **39**
RM9: Dag ... 7B **56**
TW9: Rich ... 3E **98**
Rosedale Ter. *W6 ... 3D 82*
(off Dalling Rd.)
Rosedene NW6 ... 1F **65**
(not continuous)
Rosedene Av. CR0: Croy ... 7J **139**
SM4: Mord ... 5J **137**
SW16 ... 3K **121**
UB6: G'frd ... 3E **60**
Rosedene Ct. HA4: Ruis ... 1G **41**
Rosedene Gdns. IG2: Ilf ... 4E **36**
Rosedene Ter. E10 ... 2D **52**
Rosedew Rd. W6 ... 6F **83**
Rose End KT4: Wor Pk ... 1F **149**
Rosefield Cl. SM5: Cars ... 5C **150**
Rosefield Gdns. E14 ... 7C **70**
Roseford Ct. *W12 ... 2F 83*
(off Shepherd's Bush Grn.)
Rose Gdn. Cl. HA8: Edg ... 6K **11**
Rose Gdns. TW13: Felt ... 2J **113**
UB1: S'hall ... 4E **60**
W5 ... 3D **80**
Rose Glen NW9 ... 4K **27**
RM7: Rush G ... 1K **57**
Rosehart M. W11 ... 6J **65**
Rose Hatch Av.
RM6: Chad H ... 3D **38**
Roseheath Rd.
TW4: Houn ... 5D **96**
ROSEHILL ... **7A 138**
Rosehill KT10: Esh ... 6A **146**
SM1: Sutt ... 2K **149**
TW12: Hamp ... 1E **132**
Rosehill Av. SM1: Sutt ... 1A **150**
Rosehill Ct. *SM4: Mord ... 7A 138*
(off St Helier Av.)
Rosehill Ct. Pde.
SM4: Mord ... 7A 138
(off St Helier Av.)
Rosehill Gdns. SM1: Sutt ... 2K **149**
UB6: G'frd ... 5K **43**
Rosehill Pk. W.
SM1: Sutt ... 1A **150**
Rosehill Rd. SW18 ... 6A **102**
Rose Hill Rdbt. ... **7A 138**
Roseland Cl. N17 ... 7J **17**
Rose La. RM6: Chad H ... 3D **38**
Rose Lawn WD23: Bush ... 1B **10**
Roseleigh Av. N5 ... 4B **50**
Roseleigh Cl. TW1: Twick ... 6D **98**
Rosemary Av. EN2: Enf ... 1K **7**
KT8: W Mole ... 3E **132**
N2 ... 4K **29**
N3 ... 2K **29**
N9 ... 1C **18**
TW4: Houn ... 2B **96**
Rosemary Cl. CR0: Croy ... 6J **139**
UB8: Uxb ... 5C **58**
Rosemary Ct. *SE8 ... 6B 88*
(off Dorking Cl.)
Rosemary Dr. E14 ... 6F **71**
IG4: Ilf ... 5B **36**
Rosemary Gdns.
KT9: Chess ... 4E **146**
RM8: Dag ... 1F **57**
SW14 ... 3J **99**
Rosemary Ho. *N1 ... 1D 68*
(off Branch Pl.)
Rosemary La. SW14 ... 3J **99**
Rosemary Rd.
DA16: Well ... 1K **109**
SE15 ... 7F **87**
SW17 ... 3A **120**
Rosemary St. N1 ... 1D **68**
Rosemead NW9 ... 7B **28**
Rosemead Av. CR4: Mitc ... 3G **139**
HA9: Wemb ... 5E **44**
TW13: Felt ... 2H **113**
Rose M. N18 ... 4C **18**
Rosemont Av. N12 ... 6F **15**
Rosemont Rd.
KT3: N Mald ... 3J **135**
NW3 ... 6A **48**
TW10: Rich ... 6E **98**
W3 ... 7H **63**
Rosemoor St.
SW3 ... 4D **84** (4E **170**)
Rosemount Cl. IG8: Wfd G ... 6J **21**
Rosemount Dr.
BR1: Brom ... 4D **144**
Rosemount Point SE23 ... 3K **123**
Rosemount Rd. W13 ... 6A **62**
Rosenau Cres. SW11 ... 1D **102**
Rosenau Rd. SW11 ... 1C **102**
Rosendale Rd. SE24 ... 7C **104**
Roseneath Av. N21 ... 1G **17**
Roseneath Rd. SW11 ... 6E **102**
Roseneath Wlk. EN1: Enf ... 4K **7**
Rosens Wlk. HA8: Edg ... 3C **12**
Rosenthal Rd. SE6 ... 6D **106**
Rosenthorpe Rd. SE15 ... 5K **105**
Rose Pk. Cl. UB4: Hayes ... 5A **60**
Rosepark Ct. IG5: Ilf ... 2D **36**
Roserton St. E14 ... 2E **88**
Rosery, The CR0: Croy ... 6K **141**
Rose Sq. SW7 ... 5B **84** (5B **170**)
Roses, The IG8: Wfd G ... 7C **20**
Rose St. EC4 ... 6B **68** (7B **162**)
WC2 ... 7J **67** (2E **166**)
(not continuous)
Rosethorn Cl. SW12 ... 7H **103**
Rose Tree M. IG8: Wfd G ... 6H **21**
Rosetta Cl. *SW8 ... 7J 85*
(off Kenchester Cl.)
Rosetti Ter. *RM8: Dag ... 4B 56*
(off Marlborough Rd.)
Roseveare Rd. SE12 ... 4A **126**
Roseville Av. TW3: Houn ... 5E **96**
Roseville Rd. UB3: Hayes ... 5J **77**
Rosevine Rd. SW20 ... 1E **136**
Rose Wlk. BR4: W W'ck ... 2E **154**
KT5: Surb ... 5H **135**
Rose Way HA8: Edg ... 4D **12**
SE12 ... 5J **107**
Roseway SE21 ... 6D **104**
Rosewell Cl. SE20 ... 7H **123**
Rosewood KT7: T Ditt ... 2A **146**
Rosewood Av. UB6: G'frd ... 5A **44**
Rosewood Cl.
DA14: Sidc ... 3C **128**
Rosewood Ct. BR1: Brom ... 1A **144**
E11 ... 4F **53**
RM6: Chad H ... 5C **38**
Rosewood Dr.
TW17: Shep ... 5B **130**
Rosewood Gdns. SE13 ... 2E **106**
Rosewood Gro.
SM1: Sutt ... 2A **150**
Rosewood Ho. SW8 ... 6K **85**
Rosewood Sq. W12 ... 6C **64**
Rosher Cl. E15 ... 7F **53**
Roshni Ho. SW17 ... 6C **120**
Rosina St. E9 ... 6K **51**
Roskell Rd. SW15 ... 3F **101**
Roslin Ho. *E1 ... 7K 69*
(off Brodlove La.)
Roslin Rd. W3 ... 3H **81**
Roslin Way BR1: Brom ... 5J **125**
Roslyn Cl. CR4: Mitc ... 2B **138**
Roslyn Rd. N15 ... 5D **32**
Rosmead Rd. W11 ... 7G **65**
Rosoman Pl.
EC1 ... 4A **68** (3K **161**)
Rosoman St.
EC1 ... 3A **68** (2K **161**)
Rossall Cres. NW10 ... 3F **63**
Ross Av. NW7 ... 5B **14**
RM8: Dag ... 2F **57**
Ross Cl. HA3: Harr ... 7B **10**
UB3: Hayes ... 4F **77**
UB5: N'olt ... 4H **43**
Ross Ct. *E5 ... 4H 51*
(off Napoleon Rd.)
NW9 ... 3A **28**
W13 ... 5B 62
(off Cleveland Rd.)
Rosscourt Mans. *SW1 ... 1A 172*
(off Buckingham Pal. Rd.)
Rossdale SM1: Sutt ... 5C **150**
Rossdale Dr. N9 ... 6D **8**
NW9 ... 1J **45**
Rossdale Rd. SW15 ... 4E **100**
Rosse M. SE3 ... 1K **107**
Rossendale St. E5 ... 2H **51**
Rossendale Way NW1 ... 1G **67**
Rossetti Ct. *WC1 ... 5C 160*
(off Ridgmount Pl.)
Rossetti Ho. *SW1 ... 4D 172*
(off Erasmus St.)
Rossetti M. NW8 ... 1B **66**
Rossetti Rd. SE16 ... 5H **87**
Rosshaven Pl.
HA6: Nwood ... 1H **23**
Ross Ho. *E1 ... 1H 87*
(off Prusom St.)
Rossignol Gdns.
SM5: Cars ... 2E **150**
Rossindel Rd. TW3: Houn ... 5E **96**
Rossington Cl. EN1: Enf ... 1C **8**
Rossington St. E5 ... 2G **51**
Rossiter Flds. EN5: Barn ... 6B **4**
Rossiter Rd. SW12 ... 1F **121**
Rossland Cl. DA6: Bex ... 5H **111**
Rosslyn Av. E4 ... 2C **20**
EN4: Barn ... 6H **5**
RM8: Dag ... 7F **39**
SW13 ... 3A **100**
TW14: Felt ... 6J **95**
Rosslyn Cl. BR4: W W'ck ... 3H **155**
TW16: Sun T ... 6G **113**
UB3: Hayes ... 5F **59**
Rosslyn Cres. HA1: Harr ... 4K **25**
HA9: Wemb ... 4E **44**
Rosslyn Gdns.
HA9: Wemb ... 3E 44
(off Rosslyn Cres.)
Rosslyn Hill NW3 ... 4B **48**
Rosslyn Mans. *NW6 ... 7A 48*
(off Goldhurst Ter.)
Rosslyn M. NW3 ... 4B **48**
Rosslyn Pk. M. NW3 ... 5B **48**
Rosslyn Rd. E17 ... 4E **34**
IG11: Bark ... 7H **55**
TW1: Twick ... 6C **98**
Rossmore Cl. *NW1 ... 4D 158*
(off Rossmore Rd.)
Rossmore Ct.
NW1 ... 4D **66** (3E **158**)
Rossmore Rd.
NW1 ... 4C **66** (4D **158**)
Ross Pde. SM6: Wall ... 6F **151**
Ross Rd. SE25 ... 3D **140**
SM6: Wall ... 5G **151**
TW2: Twick ... 1F **115**

Roydon Cl.—Rutland Ct.

Roydon Cl. IG10: Lough 1H 21
SW11 . . . . 2D 102
(off Battersea Pk. Rd.)
Roy Gdns. IG2: Ilf 4J 37
Roy Gro. TW12: Hamp 6F 115
Royle Bldg. N1 . . . . 2C 68
(off Wenlock Rd.)
Royle Cres. W13 . . . . 4A 62
Roymount Ct. TW2: Twick . . . 3J 115
Roy Rd. HA6: Nwood 1H 23
Roy Sq. E14 . . . . 7A 70
Royston Av. E4 . . . . 5H 19
SM1: Sutt 3B 150
SM6: Wall 4H 151
Royston Cl. KT12: Walt T . . . 7J 131
TW5: Houn 1K 95
Royston Ct. E13 . . . . 1J 71
(off Stopford Rd.)
SE24 . . . . 6C 104
TW9: Rich 1F 99
Royston Gdns. IG1: Ilf 6B 36
Royston Ho. N11 . . . . 4J 15
SE15 . . . . 6H 87
(off Friary Est.)
Royston Pde. IG1: Ilf 6B 36
Royston Pk. Rd.
HA5: Pinn 5A 10
Royston Rd. SE20 . . . . 1K 141
TW10: Rich 5E 98
Roystons, The KT5: Surb . . . 5H 135
Royston St. E2 . . . . 2J 69
Rozel Ct. N1 . . . . 1E 68
Rozel Rd. SW4 . . . . 3G 103
Rozel Ter. CR0: Croy 2C 152
(off Church Rd.)
Rubastic Rd. UB2: S'hall 3A 78
Rubens Pl. SW4 . . . . 4J 103
Rubens Rd. UB5: N'olt 2A 60
Rubens St. SE6 . . . . 2B 124
Ruby Rd. E17 . . . . 3C 34
Ruby St. NW10 . . . . 7K 45
SE15 . . . . 6H 87
Ruby Triangle SE15 . . . . 6H 87
Ruckholt Cl. E10 . . . . 3D 52
Ruckholt Rd. E9 . . . . 4C 52
E10 . . . . 4C 52
Rucklidge Av. NW10 . . . . 2B 64
Rucklidge Pas. NW10 . . . . . . 2B 64
(off Rucklidge Av.)
Rudall Cres. NW3 . . . . 4B 48
Rudbeck Ho. SE15 . . . . 7G 87
(off Peckham Pk. Rd.)
Ruddington Cl. E5 . . . . 4A 52
Ruddock Cl. HA8: Edg 7D 12
Ruddstreet Cl. SE18 . . . . 4F 91
Ruddy Way NW7 . . . . 6G 13
Rudge Ho. SE16 . . . . 3G 87
(off Jamaica Rd.)
Rudgwick Ct. SE18 . . . . 4C 90
(off Woodville St., not continuous)
Rudgwick Ter. NW8 . . . . 1C 66
Rudland Rd. DA7: Bex 3H 111
Rudloe Rd. SW12 . . . . 7G 103
Rudolf Pl. SW8 . . . . 6J 85 (7F 173)
Rudolph Rd. E13 . . . . 2H 71
NW6 . . . . 2J 65
Rudyard Gro. HA8: Edg 6D 12
NW7 . . . . 6D 12
Ruegg Ho. SE18 . . . . 6E 90
(off Woolwich Comn.)
Ruffetts Cl. CR2: S Croy 7H 153
Ruffetts, The
CR2: S Croy 7H 153
Ruffle Cl. UB7: W Dray 2A 76
Rufford Cl. HA3: Harr 6A 26
Rufford St. N1 . . . . 1J 67
Rufford Twr. W3 . . . . 1H 81
Rufforth Ct. NW9 . . . . 1A 28
(off Pageant Av.)
Rufus Cl. HA4: Ruis 3C 42
Rufus Ho. SE1 . . . . 7K 169
(off Abbey St.)
Rufus St. N1 . . . . . . 3E 68 (2G 163)
Rugby Av. HA0: Wemb 5B 44
N9 . . . . 1A 18
UB6: G'frd 6H 43
Rugby Cl. HA1: Harr 4J 25
Rugby Gdns. RM9: Dag 6C 56
Rugby Mans. W14 . . . . 4G 83
(off Bishop King's Rd.)
Rugby Rd. NW9 . . . . 4H 27
RM9: Dag 6B 56
TW1: Twick 5J 97
W4 . . . . 2A 82
Rugby St. WC1 . . . . 4K 67 (4G 161)
Rugg St. E14 . . . . 7C 70
Rugless Ho. E14 . . . . 2E 88
(off E. Ferry Rd.)
Rugmere NW1 . . . . 7E 48
(off Ferdinand St.)
RUISLIP 1G 41
Ruislip Cl. UB6: G'frd 4F 61
RUISLIP COMMON 4E 22
Ruislip Ct. HA4: Ruis 2H 41
RUISLIP GARDENS 3J 41
Ruislip Lido Railway 4F 23
RUISLIP MANOR 2J 41
Ruislip Rd. UB1: S'hall 2B 60
UB5: N'olt 1A 60
UB6: G'frd 3E 60
Ruislip Rd. E. UB6: G'frd 4H 61
W7 . . . . 4J 61
W13 . . . . 4H 61
Ruislip St. SW17 . . . . 4D 120
Ruislip Woodlands Cen. 4F 23
Rumball Ho. SE5 . . . . 7E 86
(off Harris St.)
Rumbold Rd. SW6 . . . . 7K 83
Rum Cl. E1 . . . . 7J 69
Rumford Ho. SE1 . . . . 3C 86
(off Tiverton St.)
Rumney Ct. UB5: N'olt 2B 60
(off Parkfield Dr.)
Rumsey Cl. TW12: Hamp . . . 6D 114
Rumsey M. N4 . . . . 3B 50
Rumsey Rd. SW9 . . . . 3K 103
Runacres Ct. SE17 . . . . 5C 86
Runbury Circ. NW9 . . . . 2K 45
Runcorn Cl. N17 . . . . 4H 33
Runcorn Pl. W11 . . . . 7G 65
Rundell Cres. NW4 . . . . 5D 28
Rundell Twr. SW8 . . . . 1K 103
Runes Cl. CR4: Mitc 4B 138
Runnel Fld. HA1: Harr 3J 43
Running Horse Yd.
TW8: Bford 6E 80
Runnymede SW19 . . . . 1A 138
Runnymede Cl.
TW2: Twick 6F 97
Runnymede Ct. SW15 . . . . . 1C 118
Runnymede Cres.
SW16 . . . . 1H 139
Runnymede Gdns.
TW3: Houn 6F 97
UB6: G'frd 2J 61
Runnymede Ho. E9 . . . . 4A 52
Runnymede Rd.
TW2: Twick 6F 97
Runway, The HA4: Ruis 5K 41
Rupack St. SE16 . . . . 2J 87
Rupert Av. HA9: Wemb 5E 44
Rupert Ct. KT8: W Mole 4E 132
(off St Peters Rd.)
W1 . . . . 7H 67 (2C 166)
Rupert Gdns. SW9 . . . . 2B 104
Rupert Ho. SE11 . . . 4A 86 (4K 173)
Rupert Rd. N19 . . . . 3H 49
(not continuous)
NW6 . . . . 2H 65
W4 . . . . 3A 82
Rupert St. W1 . . . . . 7H 67 (2C 166)
Rural Way SW16 . . . . 7F 121
Rusbridge Cl. E8 . . . . 5G 51
Ruscoe Rd. E16 . . . . 6H 71
Ruscombe Way
TW14: Felt 7H 95
Rusham Rd. SW12 . . . . 6D 102
Rushbrook Cres. E17 . . . . 1B 34
Rushbrook Rd. SE9 . . . . 2G 127
Rushbury Ct.
TW12: Hamp 1E 132
Rush Common M. SW2 . . . . 7K 103
Rushcroft Rd. E4 . . . . 7J 19
SW2 . . . . 4A 104
Rushcutters Ct. SE16 . . . . 4A 88
(off Boat Lifter Way)
Rushden Cl. SE19 . . . . 7D 122
Rushdene SE2 . . . . 3D 92
(not continuous)
Rushdene Av. EN4: Barn 7H 5
Rushdene Cl. UB5: N'olt 2A 60
Rushdene Cres.
UB5: N'olt 2K 59
Rushdene Rd. HA5: Pinn 6B 24
Rushden Gdns. IG5: Ilf 2E 36
NW7 . . . . 6K 13
Rushen Wlk. SM5: Cars 1B 150
Rushett Cl. KT7: T Ditt 1B 146
Rushett Rd. KT7: T Ditt 7B 134
Rushey Cl. KT3: N Mald 4K 135
Rushey Grn. SE6 . . . . 7D 106
Rushey Hill EN2: Enf 4E 6
Rushey Mead SE4 . . . . 5C 106
Rushford Rd. SE4 . . . . 6B 106
RUSH GREEN 1K 57
Rush Grn. Gdns.
RM7: Rush G 1J 57
Rush Grn. Rd.
RM7: Rush G 1H 57
Rushgrove Av. NW9 . . . . 5A 28
Rushgrove Pde. NW9 . . . . 5A 28
Rushgrove St. SE18 . . . . 4D 90
Rush Hill M. SW11 . . . . 3E 102
(off Rush Hill Rd.)
Rush Hill Rd. SW11 . . . . 3E 102
Rushley Cl. BR2: Kes 4B 156
Rushmead E2 . . . . 3H 69
TW10: Rich 3B 116
Rushmead Cl. CR0: Croy . . . 4F 153
HA8: Edg 2C 12
Rushmere Ct.
KT4: Wor Pk 2C 148
Rushmere Pl. SW19 . . . . 5F 119
Rushmon Pl. SM3: Sutt 6G 149
Rushmon Vs.
KT3: N Mald 4B 136
Rushmoor Cl. HA5: Pinn 4K 23
Rushmore Cl. BR1: Brom . . . 3C 144
Rushmore Cres. E5 . . . . 4K 51
Rushmore Ho. W14 . . . . 3G 83
(off Russell Rd.)
Rushmore Rd. E5 . . . . 4J 51
(not continuous)
Rusholme Av. RM10: Dag . . . 3G 57
Rusholme Gro. SE19 . . . . . . 5E 122
Rusholme Rd. SW15 . . . . . . 6F 101
Rushout Av. HA3: Harr 6B 26
Rush, The SW19 . . . . 1H 137
(off Kingston Rd.)
Rushton Ho. SW8 . . . . 2H 103
Rushton St. N1 . . . . 2D 68
Rushworth Av. NW4 . . . . 3C 28
Rushworth Gdns. NW4 . . . . . . 3C 28
Rushworth St.
SE1 . . . . 2B 86 (6B 168)
Rushy Mdw. La.
SM5: Cars 3C 150
Ruskin Av. DA16: Well 2A 110
E12 . . . . 6C 54
TW9: Rich 7G 81
(not continuous)
TW14: Felt 6H 95
Ruskin Cl. NW11 . . . . 6K 29
Ruskin Ct. N21 . . . . 7E 6
SE5 . . . . 3D 104
(off Champion Hill)
Ruskin Dr. DA16: Well 3A 110
KT4: Wor Pk 2D 148
Ruskin Gdns. HA3: Harr 5F 27
W5 . . . . 4D 62
Ruskin Gro. DA16: Well 2A 110
Ruskin Ho. CR2: S Croy 5D 152
(off Selsdon Rd.)
SW1 . . . . 4D 172
(off Herrick St.)
Ruskin Mans. W14 . . . . 6G 83
(off Queen's Club Gdns.)
Ruskin Pde.
CR2: S Croy 5D 152
(off Selsdon Rd.)
Ruskin Pk. Ho. SE5 . . . . 3D 104
Ruskin Rd. CR0: Croy 2B 152
DA17: Belv 4G 93
N17 . . . . 1F 33
SM5: Cars 5D 150
TW7: Isle 3K 97
UB1: S'hall 7C 60
Ruskin Wlk. BR2: Short 6D 144
N9 . . . . 2B 18
SE24 . . . . 5C 104
Ruskin Way SW19 . . . . 1B 138
Rusland Hgts. HA1: Harr 4J 25
Rusland Pk. Rd.
HA1: Harr 4J 25
Rusper Cl. HA7: Stan 4H 11
NW2 . . . . 3E 46
Rusper Ct. SW9 . . . . 2J 103
(off Clapham Rd.)
Rusper Rd. N22 . . . . 2B 32
RM9: Dag 6C 56
Russell Av. N22 . . . . 2A 32
Russell Cl. BR3: Beck 3D 142
DA7: Bex 4G 111
HA4: Ruis 2A 42
NW10 . . . . 7J 45
SE7 . . . . 7A 90
W4 . . . . 6B 82
Russell Ct. E10 . . . . 7D 34
EN5: Barn 4F 5
N14 . . . . 6C 6
SE15 . . . . 2H 105
(off Heaton Rd.)
SM6: Wall 5G 151
(off Ross Rd.)
SW1 . . . . 5B 166
SW16 . . . . 5K 121
WC1 . . . . 4E 160
Russell Flint Ho. E16 . . . . 7K 71
(off Pankhurst Av.)
Russell Gdns. IG2: Ilf 7H 37
N20 . . . . 2H 15
NW11 . . . . 6G 29
TW10: Rich 2C 116
UB7: W Dray 5C 76
W14 . . . . 3G 83
Russell Gdns. M. W14 . . . . . . 2G 83
Russell Gro. NW7 . . . . 5F 13
SW9 . . . . 7A 86
Russell Ho. E14 . . . . 6C 70
(off Saracen St.)
SW1 . . . . 5A 172
(off Cambridge St.)
Russell Kerr Cl. W4 . . . . 7J 81
Russell La. N20 . . . . 2H 15
Russell Lodge E4 . . . . 2K 19
SE1 . . . . 3D 86
(off Spurgeon St.)
Russell Mead HA3: Harr 1K 25
Russell Pde. NW11 . . . . 6G 29
(off Golders Grn. Rd.)
Russell Pl. NW3 . . . . 5C 48
SE16 . . . . 3A 88
SM2: Sutt 7K 149
Russell Rd. CR4: Mitc 3C 138
E4 . . . . 4G 19
E10 . . . . 6D 34
E16 . . . . 6J 71
E17 . . . . 3B 34
Russell Rd. EN1: Enf 1A 8
IG9: Buck H 1E 20
KT12: Walt T 6J 131
N8 . . . . 6H 31
N13 . . . . 6E 16
N15 . . . . 5E 32
N20 . . . . 2H 15
NW9 . . . . 6B 28
SW19 . . . . 7J 119
TW2: Twick 6K 97
TW17: Shep 7E 130
UB5: N'olt 5G 43
W14 . . . . 3G 83
Russells Footpath SW16 . . . 5J 121
Russell Sq. WC1 . . . 5J 67 (4E 160)
Russell St. WC2 . . . . 7J 67 (2F 167)
Russell Wlk. TW10: Rich 6F 99
Russell Way SM1: Sutt 5K 149
Russell Yd. SW15 . . . . 4G 101
Russet Av. TW17: Shep 3G 131
Russet Cl. UB10: Uxb 4E 58
Russet Cres. N7 . . . . 5K 49
Russet Dr. CR0: Croy 1A 154
Russets Cl. E4 . . . . 4A 20
Russett Way SE13 . . . . 2D 106
Russia Ct. EC2 . . . . 7D 162
Russia Dock Rd. SE16 . . . . . . 1A 88
Russia La. E2 . . . . 2J 69
Russia Row EC2 . . . 6C 68 (1D 168)
Russia Wlk. SE16 . . . . 2A 88
Russington Rd.
TW17: Shep 6F 131
Rusthall Av. W4 . . . . 4K 81
Rusthall Cl. CR0: Croy 6J 141
Rustic Av. SW16 . . . . 7F 121
Rustic Pl. HA0: Wemb 4D 44
Rustic Wlk. E16 . . . . 6K 71
(off Lambert Rd.)
Rustington Wlk.
SM4: Mord 7H 137
Ruston Av. KT5: Surb 7H 135
Ruston Gdns. N14 . . . . 6K 5
Ruston M. W11 . . . . 6G 65
Ruston Rd. SE18 . . . . 3C 90
Ruston St. E3 . . . . 1B 70
Rust Sq. SE5 . . . . 7D 86
Rutford Rd. SW16 . . . . 5J 121
Ruth Cl. HA7: Stan 4F 27
Ruth Ct. E3 . . . . 2A 70
Rutherford Cl. SM2: Sutt . . . 6B 150
UB8: Uxb 4B 58
Rutherford Ho. E1 . . . . 4H 69
(off Brady St.)
HA9: Wemb 3J 45
(off Barnhill Rd.)
Rutherford St.
SW1 . . . . . . 4H 85 (3C 172)
Rutherford Twr. UB1: S'hall . . 6F 61
Rutherford Way
HA9: Wemb 4G 45
WD23: Bush 1C 10
Rutherglen Rd. SE2 . . . . 6A 92
Rutherwyke Cl.
KT17: Eps 6C 148
Ruth Ho. W10 . . . . 4G 65
(off Kensal Rd.)
Ruthin Cl. NW9 . . . . 6A 28
Ruthin Rd. SE3 . . . . 6J 89
Ruthven St. E9 . . . . 1K 69
Rutland Av. DA15: Sidc 7A 110
Rutland Cl. DA5: Bexl 2D 128
KT9: Chess 6F 147
SW14 . . . . 3H 99
SW19 . . . . 7C 120
Rutland Ct. BR7: Chst 1E 144
EN3: Enf 5C 8
KT1: King T 4D 134
(off Palace Rd.)
SE5 . . . . 4D 104
SE9 . . . . 2G 127
SW7 . . . . 7D 164
W3 . . . . 6G 63

Rutland Dr.—St Barnabas Rd.

Rutland Dr. SM4: Mord 6H **137**
TW10: Rich 1D **116**
Rutland Gdns.
CR0: Croy 4E **152**
N4 ....6B **32**
RM8: Dag 5C **56**
SW7 ....2C **84** (7D **164**)
W13 ....5A **62**
Rutland Gdns. M.
SW7 ....2C **84** (7D **164**)
Rutland Ga. BR2: Short 4H **143**
DA17: Belv 5H **93**
SW7 ....2C **84** (7D **164**)
Rutland Ga. M. SW7 ......7C **164**
Rutland Gro. W6 ....5D **82**
Rutland Ho. *UB5: N'olt 6E 42*
(off Farmlands, The)
W8 ....3K 83
(off Marloes Rd.)
Rutland M. NW8 ....1K **65**
Rutland M. E. SW7 ....1C **170**
Rutland M. Sth. SW7 ......1C **170**
Rutland M. W. SW7 ....1C **170**
Rutland Pk. NW2 ....6E **46**
SE6 ....2B **124**
Rutland Pk. Gdns. *NW2 .....6E 46*
(off Rutland Pk.)
Rutland Pk. Mans. NW2 ......6E **46**
Rutland Pl. EC1 ....4B **68** (5B **162**)
WD23: Bush 1C **10**
Rutland Rd. E7 ....7B **54**
E9 ....1K **69**
E11 ....5K **35**
E17 ....6C **34**
HA1: Harr 6G **25**
IG1: Ilf 3F **55**
SW19 ....7C **120**
TW2: Twick 2H **115**
UB1: S'hall 5E **60**
UB3: Hayes 4F **77**
Rutland St. SW7 ...3C **84** (1D **170**)
Rutland Wlk. SE6 ....2B **124**
Rutley Cl. SE17 ....6B **86**
Rutlish Rd. SW19 ....1J **137**
Rutter Gdns. CR4: Mitc 4A **138**
Rutters Cl. UB7: W Dray 2C **76**
Rutts Ter. SE14 ....1K **105**
Rutts, The WD23: Bush 1C **10**
Ruvigny Gdns. SW15 ......3F **101**
RUXLEY **7E 128**
Ruxley Cl. DA14: Sidc 6D **128**
KT19: Eps 5H **147**
Ruxley Cnr. Ind. Est.
DA14: Sidc 6D **128**
Ruxley Ct. KT19: Eps 5J **147**
Ruxley Cres. KT10: Esh 6B **146**
Ruxley La. KT19: Eps 6H **147**
Ruxley M. KT19: Eps 5H **147**
Ruxley Ridge KT10: Esh 7A **146**
Ruxley Towers KT10: Esh ...7A **146**
Ryalls Ct. N20 ....3J **15**
Ryan Cl. HA4: Ruis 1K **41**
SE3 ....4K **107**
Ryan Ct. SW16 ....7J **121**
Ryan Dr. TW8: Bford 6A **80**
Rycott Path SE22 ....7G **105**
Rycroft Way N17 ....3F **33**
Ryculff Sq. SE3 ....2H **107**
Rydal Cl. NW4 ....1G **29**
Rydal Ct. HA8: Edg 5A **12**
HA9: Wemb 7F **27**
Rydal Cres. UB6: G'frd 3B **62**
Rydal Dr. BR4: W W'ck 2G **155**
DA7: Bex 1G **111**
Rydal Gdns. HA9: Wemb 1C **44**
NW9 ....5A **28**
SW15 ....5A **118**
TW3: Houn 6F **97**
Rydal Mt. BR2: Short 4H **143**
Rydal Rd. SW16 ....4H **121**
Rydal Water
NW1 ....3G **67** (2A **160**)
Rydal Way EN3: Enf 6D **8**
HA4: Ruis 4A **42**
Rydens Ho. *SE9 ....3A 126*
(off Gro. Park Rd.)
Rydens Rd. KT12: Walt T ...7C **132**
Ryde Pl. TW1: Twick 6D **98**
Ryder Cl. BR1: Brom 5K **125**
Ryder Ct. E10 ....2D **52**
SW1 ....4B **166**
Ryder Dr. SE16 ....5H **87**
Ryder Ho. *E1 ....4J 69*
(off Colebert Av.)
Ryder M. E9 ....5J **51**
Ryders Ter. NW8 ....2A **66**
Ryder St. SW1 ....1G **85** (4B **166**)
Ryder Yd. SW1 ....1G **85** (4B **166**)
Ryde Va. Rd. SW12 ....2G **121**
Rydon M. SW19 ....7E **118**
Rydons Cl. SE9 ....3C **108**
Rydon St. N1 ....1C **68**
Rydston Cl. N7 ....7J **49**
Rye Cl. DA5: Bexl 6H **111**
Ryecotes Mead SE21 ......1E **122**
Ryecroft Av. IG5: Ilf 2F **37**
TW2: Twick 7F **97**
Ryecroft Lodge SW16 .....6B **122**
Ryecroft Rd. BR5: Orp 6H **145**
SE13 ....5E **106**
SW16 ....6A **122**
Ryecroft St. SW6 ....1K **101**
Ryedale SE22 ....6H **105**
Ryefield Av. UB10: Uxb 7D **40**
Ryefield Ct. HA6: Nwood 2J **23**
Ryefield Cres.
HA6: Nwood 2J **23**
Ryefield Path SW15 ....1C **118**
Ryefield Pde *HA6: Nwood ...2J 23*
(off Joel St.)
Ryefield Rd. SE19 ....6C **122**
Rye Hill Pk. SE15 ....4J **105**
Rye Ho. *SE16 ....2J 87*
(off Swan Rd.)
SW1 ....5J 171
(off Ebury Bri. Rd.)
Ryeland Cl. UB7: W Dray 6A **58**
Ryelands Cres. SE12 ......6A **108**
Rye La. SE15 ....1G **105**
Rye Pas. SE15 ....3G **105**
Rye Rd. SE15 ....4K **105**
Rye, The N14 ....7C **6**
Rye Wlk. SW15 ....5F **101**
Rye Way HA8: Edg 6A **12**
Ryfold Rd. SW19 ....3J **119**
Ryhope Rd. N11 ....4A **16**
Ryland Cl. TW13: Felt 4H **113**
Rylandes Rd. NW2 ....3C **46**
Ryland Rd. NW5 ....6F **49**
Rylett Cres. W12 ....2B **82**
Rylett Rd. W12 ....2B **82**
Rylston Rd. N13 ....3J **17**
SW6 ....6H **83**
Rymer Rd. CR0: Croy 7E **140**
Rymer St. SE24 ....6B **104**
Rymill St. E16 ....1E **90**
Rysbrack St.
SW3 ....3D **84** (1E **170**)
Rythe Ct. KT7: T Ditt 7A **134**

S

Sabah Ct. TW15: Ashf 4C **112**
Sabbarton St. E16 ....6H **71**
Sabella Ct. E3 ....2B **70**
Sabine Rd. SW11 ....3D **102**
Sable Cl. TW4: Houn 3A **96**
Sable St. N1 ....7B **50**
Sach Rd. E5 ....2H **51**
Sackville Av. BR2: Short 1J **155**
Sackville Cl. HA2: Harr 3H **43**
Sackville Gdns. IG1: Ilf 1D **54**
Sackville Ho. SW16 ....3J **121**
Sackville Rd. SM2: Sutt 7J **149**
Sackville St. W1 ...7G **67** (3B **166**)
Saddlebrook Pk.
TW16: Sun T 7G **113**
Saddlers Cl. HA5: Pinn 6A **10**
Saddlers M. HA0: Wemb 4K **43**
KT1: King T 1C **134**
SW8 ....1J **103**
Saddlescombe Way N12 ....5D **14**
Saddle Yd. W1 .....1F **85** (4J **165**)
Sadler Cl. CR4: Mitc 2D **138**
Sadler Ho. *EC1 ....1K 161*
(off Spa Grn. Est.)
Sadlers Ride
KT8: W Mole 2G **133**
Sadler's Wells Theatre
.........3A 68 (1K 161)
Saffron Av. E14 ....7F **71**
Saffron Cl. CR0: Croy 6J **139**
NW11 ....6H **29**
Saffron Ct. *E15 ....5G 53*
(off Maryland Pk.)
TW14: Felt 7E **94**
Saffron Hill EC1 ....5A **68** (5K **161**)
Saffron Rd. RM5: Col R 2K **39**
Saffron St. EC1 .....5A **68** (5K **161**)
Saffron Way KT6: Surb 1D **146**
Saffron Wharf *SE1 ....6K 169*
(off Shad Thames)
Sage Cl. E6 ....5D **72**
Sage St. E1 ....7J **69**
Sage Way WC1 ....2G **161**
Sahara Ct. UB1: S'hall 7C **60**
Saigasso Cl. E16 ....6B **72**
Sail Ct. *E14 ....7F 71*
(off Newport Av.)
Sailmakers Ct. SW6 ....2A **102**
Sail St. SE11 ......4K **85** (3H **173**)
Saimel *NW9 ....7G 13*
(off Satchell Mead)
Sainfoin Rd. SW17 ....2E **120**
Sainsbury Rd. SE19 ....5E **122**
St Agathas Dr.
KT2: King T 6F **117**
St Agathas Gro.
SM5: Cars 1D **150**
St Agnes Cl. E9 ....1J **69**
St Agnes Pl.
SE11 ....6A **86** (7K **173**)
St Agnes Well EC1 ....3F **163**
St Aidans Ct. IG11: Bark 2B **74**
St Aidans Rd. SE22 ....6H **105**
W13 ....2B **80**
St Albans Av. E6 ....3D **72**
TW13: Felt 5B **114**
W4 ....4K **81**
St Albans Cl. NW11 ....1J **47**
St Albans Ct. EC2 ....6D **162**
St Albans Cres.
IG8: Wfd G 7D **20**
N22 ....1A **32**
St Albans Gdns.
TW11: Tedd 5A **116**
St Albans Gro.
SM5: Cars 7C **138**
W8 ....3K **83**
St Albans La. NW11 ....1J **47**
St Albans Mans. *W8 ....3K 83*
(off Kensington Ct. Pl.)
St Albans Pl. N1 ....1B **68**
St Albans Rd. EN5: Barn 1A **4**
IG3: Ilf 1K **55**
IG8: Wfd G 7D **20**
KT2: King T 6E **116**
NW5 ....3E **48**
NW10 ....1A **64**
SM1: Sutt 4H **149**
St Albans St.
SW1 ....7H **67** (3C **166**)
(not continuous)
St Albans Ter. W6 ....6G **83**
St Albans Vs. NW5 ....3E **48**
St Alfege Pas. SE10 ....6E **88**
St Alfege Rd. SE7 ....6B **90**
St Alphage Gdn.
EC2 ....5C **68** (6D **162**)
(not continuous)
St Alphage Highwalk
EC2 ....6D **162**
St Alphage Ho. EC2 ....6E **162**
St Alphage Wlk. HA8: Edg ...2J **27**
St Alphege Rd. N9 ....7D **8**
St Alphonsus Rd. SW4 .....4G **103**
St Amunds Cl. SE6 ....4C **124**
St Andrews Av.
HA0: Wemb 4A **44**
St Andrews Chambers
W1 ....6B 160
(off Wells St.)
St Andrews Cl. HA4: Ruis 2B **42**
HA7: Stan 2C **26**
N12 ....4F **15**
NW2 ....3D **46**
SE16 ....5H **87**
SE28 ....6D **74**
TW7: Isle 1J **97**
TW17: Shep 4F **131**
St Andrews Ct. E17 ....2A **34**
SM1: Sutt 3C **150**
St Andrews Ct. SW18 ......2A **120**
St Andrews Dr. HA7: Stan ...1C **26**
St Andrews Gro. N16 ....1D **50**
St Andrews Hill
EC4 ....7B **68** (2B **168**)
(not continuous)
St Andrews Mans. *W1 .....6G 159*
(off Dorset St.)
W14 ....6G 83
(off St Andrews Rd.)
St Andrews M. N16 ....1E **50**
SE3 ....7J **89**
SW12 ....1H **121**
St Andrews Pl.
NW1 ......4F **67** (3K **159**)
St Andrews Rd.
CR0: Croy 4C **152**
DA14: Sidc 3D **128**
E11 ....6G **35**
E12 ....2C **54**
E13 ....3K **71**
E17 ....2K **33**
EN1: Enf 3J **7**
IG1: Ilf 7D **36**
KT6: Surb 6D **134**
N9 ....7D **8**
NW9 ....1K **45**
NW10 ....6D **46**
NW11 ....6H **29**
RM7: Rom 6K **39**
SM5: Cars 3C **150**
UB10: Uxb 1A **58**
W3 ....7A **64**
W7 ....2J **79**
W14 ....6G **83**
St Andrews Sq.
KT6: Surb 6D **134**
W11 ....6G **65**
St Andrews Twr.
UB1: S'hall 7G 61
(off Baird Av.)
St Andrew St.
EC1 ....5A **68** (6K **161**)
St Andrews Way E3 ....4D **70**
St Andrews Wharf SE1 ......2F **87**
St Anna Rd. EN5: Barn 5A **4**
St Annes Cl. N6 ....3E **48**
St Annes Ct.
BR4: W W'ck 4G **155**
NW6 ....1G **65**
W1 ....6H **67** (1C **166**)
St Annes Flats *NW1 ....1C 160*
(off Doric Way)
St Annes Gdns. NW10 ......3F **63**
St Annes Pas. E14 ....6B **70**
St Annes Rd. E11 ....2F **53**
HA0: Wemb 5D **44**
St Annes Row E14 ....6B **70**
St Annes Trad. Est. *E14 .....6B 70*
(off St Anne's Row)
St Anne St. E14 ....6B **70**
St Anns IG11: Bark 1G **73**
St Anns Ct. NW4 ....3D **28**
St Anns Cres. SW18 ....6K **101**
St Anns Gdns. NW5 ....6E **48**
St Anns Hill SW18 ....5K **101**
St Anns Ho. *WC1 ....2J 161*
(off Margery St.)
St Anns La.
SW1 ....3H **85** (2D **172**)
St Anns Pk. Rd. SW18 .....6A **102**
St Anns Pas. SW13 ....3A **100**
St Anns Rd. HA1: Harr 6J **25**
IG11: Bark 1G **73**
N9 ....2A **18**
N15 ....5B **32**
SW13 ....2B **100**
W11 ....7F **65**
St Anns Shop. Cen.
HA1: Harr 6J **25**
St Anns St.
SW1 ....3H **85** (1D **172**)
St Anns Ter. NW8 ....2B **66**
St Anns Vs. W11 ....1F **83**
St Anns Way
CR2: S Croy 6B **152**
St Anselms Pl.
W1 ....7F **67** (2J **165**)
St Anselms Rd.
UB3: Hayes 2H **77**
St Anthonys Av.
IG8: Wfd G 6F **21**
St Anthonys Cl. E1 ....1G **87**
SW17 ....2C **120**
St Anthonys Flats *NW1 ....1C 160*
(off Aldenham St.)
St Anthonys Way
TW14: Felt 4H **95**
St Antonys Rd. E7 ....7K **53**
St Arvans Cl. CR0: Croy 3E **152**
St Asaph Rd. SE4 ....3K **105**
St Aubins Ct. N1 ....1D **68**
St Aubyns Av. SW19 ....5H **119**
TW3: Houn 5E **96**
St Aubyns Rd. SE19 ....6F **123**
St Audrey Av. DA7: Bex 2G **111**
St Augustines Av.
BR2: Short 5C **144**
CR2: S Croy 6C **152**
HA9: Wemb 3E **44**
W5 ....2E **62**
St Augustines Ho. *NW1 ....1C 160*
(off Werrington St.)
St Augustines Mans.
SW1 ....4B 172
(off Bloomburg St.)
St Augustines Path N5 ......4C **50**
St Augustines Rd.
DA17: Belv 4F **93**
NW1 ....7H **49**
St Austell Cl. HA8: Edg 2F **27**
St Austell Rd. SE13 ....2E **106**
St Awdrys Rd. IG11: Bark 7H **55**
St Awdrys Wlk.
IG11: Bark 7G **55**
St Barnabas Cl.
BR3: Beck 2E **142**
SE22 ....5E **104**
St Barnabas Ct.
HA3: Harr 1G **25**
St Barnabas Gdns.
KT8: W Mole 5E **132**
St Barnabas Rd.
CR4: Mitc 7E **120**
E17 ....6C **34**
IG8: Wfd G 1K **35**
SM1: Sutt 5B **150**

St Barnabas St.—St James's Palace

St Barnabas St. SW1 . . . . . 5E 84 (5H 171)
St Barnabas Ter. E9 . . . . . 5K 51
St Barnabas Vs. SW8 . . . . . 1J 103
St Bartholomews Cl. SE26 . . . . . 4H 123
St Bartholomews Ct. *E6* . . . . . *2C 72* (*off St Bartholomew's Rd.*)
St Bartholomew's Hospital Mus. *6B 162*
St Bartholomews Rd. E6 . . . . . 2D 72
St Benedicts Cl. SW17 . . . . . 5E 120
St Benets Cl. SW17 . . . . . 2C 120
St Benets Gro. SM5: Cars 7A 138
St Benets Pl. EC3 . . . . . 7D 68 (2F 169)
St Bernards CR0: Croy 3E 152
St Bernards Cl. SE27 . . . . . 4D 122
St Bernards Ho. *E14* . . . . . *3E 88* (*off Galbraith St.*)
St Bernards Rd. E6 . . . . . 1B 72
St Blaise Av. BR1: Brom 2K 143
St Botolph Row EC3 . . . . . 6F 69 (1J 169)
St Botolph St. EC3 . . . . . 6F 69 (7J 163)
St Brelades Ct. N1 . . . . . 1E 68
St Brides Av. EC4 . . . . . 1A 168
HA8: Edg 1F 27
St Bride's Church . . . . . *6B 68 (1A 168)*
St Brides Cl. DA18: Erith 2D 92
St Bride's Crypt Mus. . . . . . *1A 168* (*off St Bride's Church*)
St Brides Pas. EC4 . . . . . 1A 168
St Bride St. EC4 . . . . . 6B 68 (7A 162)
St Catherines Cl. KT9: Chess 6D 146
SW17 . . . . . 2C 120
St Catherines Ct. TW13: Felt 1J 113
W4 . . . . . 3A 82
St Catherines Dr. SE14 . . . . . 2K 105
St Catherines Farm Ct. HA4: Ruis 6E 22
St Catherines M. SW3 . . . . . 4D 84 (3E 170)
St Catherines Rd. E4 . . . . . 2H 19
HA4: Ruis 6F 23
St Catherines Twr. E10 . . . . . 7D 34
St Cecilias Cl. SM3: Sutt 1G 149
St Chads Cl. KT6: Surb 7C 134
St Chads Gdns. RM6: Chad H 7E 38
St Chads Pl. WC1 . . . . . 3J 67 (1F 161)
St Chads Rd. RM6: Chad H 7E 38
St Chads St. WC1 . . . . . 3J 67 (1F 161) (not continuous)
St Charles Pl. W10 . . . . . 5G 65
St Charles Sq. W10 . . . . . 5F 65
St Christopher Rd. UB8: Uxb 6A 58
St Christophers Cl. TW7: Isle 1J 97
St Christophers Dr. UB3: Hayes 7K 59
St Christophers Gdns. CR7: Thor H 3A 140
St Christophers Ho. *NW1* . . . . . *2G 67* (*off Bridgeway St.*)
St Christophers M. SM6: Wall 5G 151
St Christophers Pl. W1 . . . . . 6E 66 (7H 159)
St Clair Cl. IG5: Ilf 2D 36
St Clair Dr. KT4: Wor Pk 3D 148
St Clair Rd. E13 . . . . . 2K 71
St Clairs Rd. CR0: Croy 2E 152
St Clare Bus. Pk. TW12: Hamp 6G 115
St Clare St. EC3 . . . . . 6F 69 (1J 169)
St Clements Ct. EC4 . . . . . 2F 169
N7 . . . . . 6K 49
SE14 . . . . . *6K 87* (*off Myers La.*)
W11 . . . . . *7F 65* (*off Stoneleigh St.*)
St Clements Hgts. SE26 . . . . . 3G 123
St Clements Ho. *E1* . . . . . *6J 163* (*off Leyden St.*)
St Clements La. WC2 . . . . . 6K 67 (1H 167)
St Clements Mans. *SW6* . . . . . *6F 83* (*off Lillie Rd.*)
St Clements St. N7 . . . . . 6A 50
St Clements Yd. SE22 . . . . . 4F 105
St Cloud Rd. SE27 . . . . . 4C 122
St Columbas Ho. E17 . . . . . 4D 34
St Crispins Cl. NW3 . . . . . 4C 48
UB1: S'hall 6D 60
St Cross St. EC1 . . . . . 5A 68 (5K 161)
St Cuthberts Rd. NW2 . . . . . 6H 47
St Cyprians St. SW17 . . . . . 4D 120
St Daniel Ct. *BR3: Beck* . . . . . *7C 124* (*off Brackley Rd.*)
St Davids Cl. BR4: W W'ck 7D 142
HA9: Wemb 3J 45
SE16 . . . . . *5H 87* (*off Masters Dr.*)
St Davids Ct. E17 . . . . . 3E 34
St Davids Dr. HA8: Edg 1F 27
St Davids M. *E3* . . . . . *3A 70* (*off Morgan St.*)
St Davids Pl. NW4 . . . . . 7D 28
St Davids Sq. E14 . . . . . 5D 88
St Denis Rd. SE27 . . . . . 4D 122
St Dionis Rd. E12 . . . . . 3C 54
SW6 . . . . . 2H 101
St Domingo Ho. *SE18* . . . . . *3D 90* (*off Leda Rd.*)
St Donatts Rd. SE14 . . . . . 1B 106
ST DUNSTAN'S 6H 149
St Dunstans All. EC3 . . . . . 2G 169
St Dunstans Av. W3 . . . . . 7K 63
St Dunstans Cl. UB3: Hayes 5H 77
St Dunstans Ct. EC4 . . . . . 6A 68 (1K 167)
St Dunstans Gdns. W3 . . . . . 7K 63
St Dunstans Hill EC3 . . . . . 7E 68 (3G 169)
SM1: Sutt 4G 149
St Dunstans La. BR3: Beck 6E 142
EC3 . . . . . 7E 68 (3G 169)
St Dunstans Rd. E7 . . . . . 6K 53
SE25 . . . . . 4F 141
TW4: Houn . . . . . 2K 95 (not continuous)
TW13: Felt 3H 113
W6 . . . . . 5F 83
W7 . . . . . 2J 79
St Edmunds Av. HA4: Ruis 6F 23
St Edmunds Cl. DA18: Erith 2D 92
NW8 . . . . . 1D 66
SW17 . . . . . 2C 120
St Edmunds Ct. *NW8* . . . . . *1D 66* (*off St Edmund's Ter.*)
St Edmunds Dr. HA7: Stan 1A 26
St Edmunds La. TW2: Twick 7F 97
St Edmunds Rd. IG1: Ilf 6D 36
N9 . . . . . 7B 8
St Edmunds Sq. SW13 . . . . . 6E 82
St Edmunds Ter. NW8 . . . . . 1C 66
St Edwards Cl. NW11 . . . . . 6J 29
St Edwards Ct. E10 . . . . . 7D 34
NW11 . . . . . 6J 29
St Edwards Way RM1: Rom 5K 39
St Egberts Way E4 . . . . . 1K 19
St Elizabeth Ct. E10 . . . . . 7D 34
St Elmo Rd. W12 . . . . . 1B 82 (not continuous)
St Elmos Rd. SE16 . . . . . 2A 88
St Erkenwald M. IG11: Bark 1H 73
St Erkenwald Rd. IG11: Bark 1H 73
St Ermins Hill SW1 . . . . . 1C 172
St Ervans Rd. W10 . . . . . 5H 65
St Eugene Ct. *NW6* . . . . . *1G 65* (*off Salusbury Rd.*)
St Fabian Twr. E4 . . . . . 6G 19
St Faiths Cl. EN2: Enf 1H 7
St Faiths Rd. SE21 . . . . . 1B 122
St Fidelis Rd. DA8: Erith 4K 93
St Fillans Rd. SE6 . . . . . 1E 124
St Francis Cl. BR5: Orp 6J 145
St Francis Ho. *NW1* . . . . . *2H 67* (*off Bridgeway St.*)
St Francis Rd. DA8: Erith 4K 93
SE22 . . . . . 4E 104
St Francis Twr. *E4* . . . . . *6G 19* (*off Burnside Av.*)
St Francis Way IG1: Ilf 4H 55
St Frideswides M. E14 . . . . . 6E 70
St Gabriels Cl. E11 . . . . . 2K 53
St Gabriels Mnr. *SE5* . . . . . *1B 104* (*off Cormont Rd.*)
St Gabriels Rd. NW2 . . . . . 5F 47
St Georges Av. E7 . . . . . 7K 53
N7 . . . . . 4H 49
NW9 . . . . . 4K 27
UB1: S'hall 7D 60
W5 . . . . . 2D 80
St Georges Bldgs. *SE1* . . . . . *3B 86* (*off St George's Rd.*)
St Georges Cir. SE1 . . . . . 3B 86 (7A 168)
St Georges Cl. HA0: Wemb 3A 44
NW11 . . . . . 6H 29
SE28 . . . . . 6D 74
SW8 . . . . . 1G 103
St Georges Ct. E6 . . . . . 4D 72
E17 . . . . . 5F 35
EC4 . . . . . 6B 68 (7A 162)
HA3: Harr . . . . . *6A 26* (*off Kenton Rd.*)
SW15 . . . . . 4H 101
St Georges Dr. SW1 . . . . . 4F 85 (4K 171)
UB10: Uxb 3B 40
ST GEORGES FIELD 7C 66
St Georges Flds. W2 . . . . . 6C 66 (1D 164)
St Georges Gdns. KT6: Surb 2H 147
St Georges Gro. SW17 . . . . . 3B 120
St Georges Ho. *NW1* . . . . . *2H 67* (*off Bridgeway St.*)
St Georges Ind. Est. KT2: King T 5D 116
N17 . . . . . 7G 17
St Georges La. EC3 . . . . . 2F 169
St Georges Mans. *SW1* . . . . . *5D 172* (*off Causton St.*)
St Georges M. NW1 . . . . . 7D 48
SE1 . . . . . 1K 173
St Georges Pde. SE6 . . . . . 2B 124
St Georges Path *SE4* . . . . . *4C 106* (*off Adelaide Av.*)
St Georges Pl. TW1: Twick 1A 116
St Georges Rd. BR1: Brom 2D 144
BR3: Beck 1D 142
St Georges Rd. BR5: Orp 6H 145
CR4: Mitc 3F 139
DA14: Sidc 6D 128
E7 . . . . . 7K 53
E10 . . . . . 3E 52
EN1: Enf 1A 8
IG1: Ilf 7D 36
KT2: King T 7G 117
N9 . . . . . 3B 18
N13 . . . . . 3E 16
NW11 . . . . . 6H 29
RM9: Dag 5E 56
SE1 . . . . . 3A 86 (1K 173)
SM6: Wall 5F 151
SW19 . . . . . 7H 119 (not continuous)
TW1: Twick 5B 98
TW9: Rich 3F 99
TW13: Felt 4B 114
W4 . . . . . 2K 81
W7 . . . . . 1K 79
St Georges Rd. W. BR1: Brom 2C 144
St Georges Shop. & Leisure Cen. HA1: Harr 6J 25
St Georges Sq. E7 . . . . . 7K 53
E14 . . . . . 7A 70
St Georges Sq. KT3: N Mald 3A 136
SE8 . . . . . 4B 88
SW1 . . . . . 5H 85 (5C 172)
St Georges Sq. M. SW1 . . . . . 5H 85 (6C 172)
St Georges Ter. NW1 . . . . . 7D 48
St George St. W1 . . . . . 7F 67 (1K 165)
St Georges Wlk. CR0: Croy 3C 152
St Georges Way SE15 . . . . . 6E 86
St Georges Wharf *SE1* . . . . . *6K 169* (*off Shad Thames*)
St George Wharf SW8 . . . . . 6J 85 (7E 172)
St Gerards Cl. SW4 . . . . . 5G 103
St Germans Pl. SE3 . . . . . 1J 107
St Germans Rd. SE23 . . . . . 1A 124
St Giles Av. RM10: Dag 7H 57
UB10: Uxb 4E 40
St Giles Cir. W1 . . . . . 6H 67 (7D 160)
St Giles Cl. RM10: Dag 7H 57
St Giles Ct. WC2 . . . . . 7E 160
St Giles High St. WC2 . . . . . 6H 67 (7D 160)
St Giles Ho. EN5: Barn 4F 5
St Giles Pas. WC2 . . . . . 1D 166
St Giles Rd. SE5 . . . . . 7E 86
St Giles Ter. *EC2* . . . . . *6D 162* (*off Beech St.*)
St Giles Twr. *SE5* . . . . . *1E 104* (*off Gables Cl.*)
St Gilles Ho. *E2* . . . . . *2K 69* (*off Mace St.*)
St Gothard Rd. SE27 . . . . . 4D 122 (not continuous)
St Gregory Cl. HA4: Ruis 4A 42
St Helena Ho. *WC1* . . . . . *2J 161* (*off Margery St.*)
St Helena Rd. SE16 . . . . . 4K 87
St Helena St. WC1 . . . . . 3A 68 (2J 161)
St Helens KT7: T Ditt 7K 133
St Helens Cres. SW16 . . . . . 1K 139
St Helens Gdns. W10 . . . . . 5F 65
St Helens Pl. EC2 . . . . . 6E 68 (7G 163)
St Helens Rd. DA18: Erith 2D 92
IG1: Ilf 6D 36
SW16 . . . . . 1K 139
W13 . . . . . 1B 80
ST HELIER 7C 138
St Helier Av. SM4: Mord 7A 138
St Helier Ct. *N1* . . . . . *1E 68* (*off De Beauvoir Est.*)
SE16 . . . . . *2K 87* (*off Poolmans St.*)
St Heliers Av. TW3: Houn 5E 96
St Heliers Rd. E10 . . . . . 6E 34
St Hildas Av. TW15: Ashf 5A 112
St Hildas Cl. NW6 . . . . . 7F 47
SW17 . . . . . 2C 120
St Hildas Rd. SW13 . . . . . 6D 82
St Hildas Wharf *E1* . . . . . *1J 87* (*off Wapping High St.*)
St Huberts Ho. *E14* . . . . . *3C 88* (*off Janet St.*)
St Hughes Cl. SW17 . . . . . 2C 120
St Hughs Rd. SE20 . . . . . 1H 141
St James Apartments *E17* . . . . . *5A 34* (*off High St.*)
St James App. EC2 . . . . . 4E 68 (4G 163)
St James Av. N20 . . . . . 3H 15
SM1: Sutt 5J 149
W13 . . . . . 1A 80
St James Cl. EN4: Barn 4G 5
HA4: Ruis 2A 42
KT3: N Mald 5B 136
N20 . . . . . 3H 15
SE18 . . . . . 5G 91
St James Ct. *E2* . . . . . *3G 69* (*off Bethnal Grn. Rd.*)
E12 . . . . . 2A 54
SE3 . . . . . 1K 107
SW1 . . . . . 3G 85 (1B 172)
St James Gdns. HA0: Wemb 7D 44
IG2: Ilf 4B 38
St James Ga. IG9: Buck H 1F 21
St James Gro. SW11 . . . . . 2D 102
St James' Mans. *NW6* . . . . . *7J 47* (*off W. End La.*)
St James M. E14 . . . . . 3E 88
E17 . . . . . *5A 34* (*off St James's St.*)
St James Pl. CR2: S Croy 6E 152
St James Residences *W1* . . . . . *2C 166* (*off Brewer St.*)
St James Rd. CR4: Mitc 7E 120
E15 . . . . . 5H 53
KT6: Surb 6D 134
N9 . . . . . 2C 18
SM1: Sutt 5J 149
SM5: Cars 3C 150
ST JAMES'S 1H 85 (4C 166)
St James's SE14 . . . . . 1A 106
SW1 . . . . . 1G 85 (4B 166)
St James's Av. BR3: Beck 3A 142
E2 . . . . . 2J 69
TW12: Hamp 5G 115
St James's Chambers *SW1* . . . . . *4B 166* (*off Jermyn St.*)
St James's Cl. *NW8* . . . . . *1D 66* (*off St James's Ter M.*)
SW17 . . . . . 2D 120
St James's Cotts. TW9: Rich 5D 98
St James's Ct. HA1: Harr 6A 26
KT1: King T 3E 134
N18 . . . . . *6A 18* (*off Fore St.*)
St James's Cres. SW9 . . . . . 3A 104
St James's Dr. SW17 . . . . . 1D 120
St James's Gdns. W11 . . . . . 1G 83 (not continuous)
St James's La. N10 . . . . . 4F 31
St James's Mkt. SW1 . . . . . 7H 67 (3C 166)
St James's Palace . . . . . *2G 85 (5B 166)*

St Mary's Mans.—St Winifred's Rd.

St Mary's Mans.
W2 ... 5B 66 (5A 158)
St Marys M. NW6 ... 7K 47
(not continuous)
TW10: Rich ... 2C 116
St Mary's Path *E1* ... *6G 69*
(off Adler St.)
N1 ... 1B 68
St Mary's Pl. SE9 ... 6D 108
W5 ... 2D 80
W8 ... 3K 83
St Marys Rd. DA5: Bexl ... 1J 129
E10 ... 3E 52
E13 ... 2K 71
EN4: Barn ... 7J 5
IG1: Ilf ... 2G 55
KT4: Wor Pk ... 2A 148
KT6: Surb ... 7C 134
(St Chads Cl.)
KT6: Surb ... 6D 134
(Victoria Rd.)
KT8: E Mos ... 5H 133
N8 ... 4J 31
N9 ... 1C 18
NW10 ... 1A 64
NW11 ... 7G 29
SE15 ... 1J 105
SE25 ... 3E 140
SW19 ... 5G 119
UB3: Hayes ... 7H 59
W5 ... 2D 80
St Mary's Sq.
W2 ... 5B 66 (5A 158)
W5 ... 2D 80
St Mary's Ter.
W2 ... 5B 66 (5A 158)
St Mary's Twr. *EC1* ... *4D 162*
(off Fortune St.)
St Mary St. SE18 ... 4D 90
St Mary's Vw.
HA3: Harr ... 5C 26
St Mary's Wlk.
SE11 ... 4A 86 (3K 173)
UB3: Hayes ... 7H 59
St Mary's Way IG7: Chig ... 5K 21
St Matthew Cl. UB8: Uxb ... 6A 58
St Matthew's Av.
KT6: Surb ... 1E 146
St Matthews Ct. E10 ... 7D 34
N10 ... 2E 30
SE1 ... *3C 86*
(off Meadow Row)
St Matthew's Dr.
BR1: Brom ... 3D 144
St Matthews Ho. *SE17* ... *6D 86*
(off Phelp St.)
St Matthew's Lodge
NW1 ... *2G 67*
(off Oakley Sq.)
St Matthew's Rd. SW2 ... 4K 103
W5 ... 1E 80
St Matthew's Row E2 ... 3G 69
St Matthew St.
SW1 ... 3H 85 (2C 172)
St Matthias Cl. NW9 ... 5B 28
St Maur Rd. SW6 ... 1H 101
St Mellion Cl. SE28 ... 6D 74
St Merryn Cl. SE18 ... 7H 91
St Merryn Ct.
BR3: Beck ... 7C 124
St Michael's All.
EC3 ... 6D 68 (1F 169)
St Michael's Av.
HA9: Wemb ... 6G 45
N9 ... 7D 8
St Michaels Cl.
BR1: Brom ... 3C 144
DA18: Erith ... 2D 92
E16 ... 5B 72
KT4: Wor Pk ... 2B 148
N3 ... 2H 29
N12 ... 5H 15
St Michaels Ct. *E14* ... *5E 70*
(off St Leonards Rd.)
SE1 ... *7D 168*
(off Trinity St.)
St Michael's Cres.
HA5: Pinn ... 6C 24
St Michael's Flats *NW1* ... *1C 160*
(off Aldenham St.)
St Michael's Gdns. W10 ... 5G 65
St Michaels M.
SW1 ... 4E 84 (4G 171)
St Michael's Ri.
DA16: Well ... 1B 110
St Michael's Rd.
CR0: Croy ... 1C 152
DA16: Well ... 3B 110
NW2 ... 4E 46
SM6: Wall ... 6G 151
SW9 ... 2K 103
TW15: Ashf ... 5C 112
St Michael's St.
W2 ... 6B 66 (7B 158)
St Michaels Ter. *N6* ... *1E 48*
(off South Gro.)
N22 ... 1J 31
St Mildred's Ct.
EC2 ... 6D 68 (1E 168)
St Mildreds Rd. SE6 ... 7G 107
SE12 ... 7H 107
St Mirren Ct. EN5: Barn ... 5F 5
St Nicholas Cen.
SM1: Sutt ... 5K 149
St Nicholas Cl. UB8: Uxb ... 6A 58
St Nicholas Ct.
KT1: King T ... *4E 134*
(off Surbiton Rd.)
St Nicholas Dr.
TW17: Shep ... 7C 130
St Nicholas' Flats *NW1* ... *1C 160*
(off Werrington St.)
St Nicholas Glebe
SW17 ... 5E 120
St Nicholas Ho. *SE8* ... *6C 88*
(off Deptford Grn.)
SE18 ... *7C 90*
(off Shrapnel Cl.)
St Nicholas Rd.
KT7: T Ditt ... 6K 133
SE18 ... 5K 91
SM1: Sutt ... 5K 149
St Nicholas St. SE8 ... 1B 106
St Nicholas Way
SM1: Sutt ... 4K 149
St Nicolas La.
BR7: Chst ... 1C 144
St Ninian's Ct. N20 ... 3J 15
St Norbert Grn. SE4 ... 4A 106
St Norbert Rd. SE4 ... 5K 105
St Olaf Ho. SE1 ... 4F 169
St Olaf's Rd. SW6 ... 7G 83
St Olaf Stairs SE1 ... 4F 169
St Olave's Ct.
EC2 ... 6D 68 (1E 168)
St Olave's Est.
SE1 ... 2E 86 (6H 169)
St Olave's Gdns.
SE11 ... 4A 86 (3J 173)
St Olave's Mans. SE11 ... 3J 173
St Olave's Rd. E6 ... 1E 72
St Olave's Ter. SE1 ... 6H 169
St Olaves Wlk. SW16 ... 2G 139
St Olav's Sq. SE16 ... 2J 87
St Onge Pde. *EN1: Enf* ... *3J 7*
(off Southbury Rd.)
St Oswald's Pl.
SE11 ... 5K 85 (6G 173)
St Oswald's Rd. SW16 ... 1B 140
St Oswulf St.
SW1 ... 4H 85 (4D 172)
St Owen Ho. *SE1* ... *3E 86*
(off Fendall St.)
ST PANCRAS ... 4K 67 (2F 161)
St Pancras Commercial Cen.
NW1 ... *1G 67*
(off Pratt St.)
St Pancras Ct. N2 ... 2B 30
St Pancras Way NW1 ... 7G 49
St Patrick's Ct.
IG8: Wfd G ... 7B 20
St Paul Cl. UB8: Uxb ... 5A 58
St Paul's All. *EC4* ... *1B 168*
(off St Paul's Chyd.)
St Paul's Arts Cen. ... *4C 88*
(off Westferry Rd.)
St Paul's Av.
HA3: Harr ... 4F 27
NW2 ... 6D 46
SE16 ... 1K 87
St Paul's Bldgs. *EC1* ... *3B 162*
(off Dallington St.)
St Paul's Cathedral
... *6C 68 (1C 168)*
St Paul's Chyd.
EC4 ... 6B 68 (1B 168)
(not continuous)
St Pauls Cl.
KT9: Chess ... 4D 146
SE7 ... 5B 90
SM5: Cars ... 1C 150
TW3: Houn ... 2C 96
TW15: Ashf ... 5E 112
UB3: Hayes ... 5F 77
W5 ... 2F 81
St Pauls Ct. SW4 ... 5H 103
TW4: Houn ... 3C 96
St Pauls Courtyard *SE8* ... *7C 88*
(off Crossfield St.)
St Paul's Cray Rd.
BR7: Chst ... 1H 145
St Paul's Cres. NW1 ... 7H 49
(not continuous)
St Paul's Dr. E15 ... 5F 53
St Paul's M. NW1 ... 7H 49
St Paul's Pl. N1 ... 6D 50
St Paul's Ri. N13 ... 6G 17
St Paul's Rd.
CR7: Thor H ... 3C 140
DA8: Erith ... 7J 93
IG11: Bark ... 1G 73
N1 ... 6B 50
N17 ... 7B 18
TW8: Bford ... 6D 80
TW9: Rich ... 3F 99
St Paul's Shrubbery N1 ... 6D 50
St Paul's Sq.
BR2: Short ... 2H 143
St Paul's Studios *W14* ... *5G 83*
(off Talgarth Rd.)
St Pauls Ter. SE17 ... 6B 86
St Pauls Twr. *E10* ... *7D 34*
(off Beaumont Rd.)
St Paul St. N1 ... 1C 68
(not continuous)
St Pauls Vw. Apartments
EC1 ... *2J 161*
(off Amwell St.)
St Paul's Wlk.
KT2: King T ... 7G 117
St Pauls Way E3 ... 5B 70
N3 ... 7E 14
St Paul's Wood Hill
BR5: Orp ... 2J 145
St Peter's All. *EC3* ... *1F 169*
(off Cornhill)
St Peters Av. E2 ... 2G 69
E17 ... 4G 35
N2 ... 7H 15
N18 ... 4B 18
St Petersburgh M. W2 ... 7K 65
St Petersburgh Pl. W2 ... 7K 65
St Peter's Cen. *E1* ... *1H 87*
(off Reardon St.)
St Peter's Chu. Ct. *N1* ... *1B 68*
(off St Peter's St.)
St Peters Cl. BR7: Chst ... 7H 127
E2 ... 2G 69
HA4: Ruis ... 2B 42
IG2: Ilf ... 4J 37
SW17 ... 2C 120
WD23: Bush ... 1C 10
St Peters Ct.
KT8: W Mole ... 4E 132
NW4 ... 5E 28
SE12 ... 5H 107
St Peter's Gdns. SE27 ... 3A 122
St Peter's Gro. W6 ... 4C 82
St Peters Ho. SE17 ... 6D 86
WC1 ... *2F 161*
(off Regent Sq.)
St Peter's Path E17 ... 3G 35
St Peters Pl. W9 ... 4K 65
St Peter's Residence ... *7G 173*
St Peters Rd. CR0: Croy ... 4D 152
KT1: King T ... 2G 135
KT8: W Mole ... 4E 132
N9 ... 1C 18
TW1: Twick ... 5B 98
UB1: S'hall ... 5E 60
UB8: Uxb ... 5A 58
W6 ... 5C 82
St Peter's Sq. E2 ... 2G 69
W6 ... 4B 82
St Peter's St.
CR2: S Croy ... 5D 152
N1 ... 1B 68
St Peter's St. M. *N1* ... *2B 68*
(off St Peters St.)
St Peter's Ter. SW6 ... 7H 83
St Peter's Vs. W6 ... 4C 82
St Peters Way N1 ... 7E 50
UB3: Hayes ... 5F 77
W5 ... 5D 62
St Peter's Wharf W4 ... 5C 82
St Philip Ho. *WC1* ... *2J 161*
(off Lloyd Baker St.)
St Philips Av.
KT4: Wor Pk ... 2D 148
N2 ... 7H 15
St Philip's Ga.
KT4: Wor Pk ... 2D 148
St Philip Sq. SW8 ... 2F 103
St Philips Rd. E8 ... 6G 51
KT6: Surb ... 6D 134
St Philip St. SW8 ... 2F 103
St Philip's Way N1 ... 1C 68
St Quentin Rd.
DA16: Well ... 3K 109
St Quintin Av. W10 ... 5E 64
St Quintin Gdns. W10 ... 5E 64
St Quintin Rd. E13 ... 3K 71
St Raphael's Way NW10 ... 5J 45
St Regis Cl. N10 ... 2F 31
St Regis Hgts. NW3 ... 3K 47
St Richard's Ho. *NW1* ... *1C 160*
(off Eversholt St.)
St Ronan's Cl. EN4: Barn ... 1G 5
St Ronan's Cres.
IG8: Wfd G ... 7D 20
St Rule St. SW8 ... 2G 103
St Saviour's Coll. SE27 ... 4D 122
St Saviours Ct. HA1: Harr ... 5J 25
N10 ... *2F 31*
(off Alexandra Pk. Rd.)
St Saviour's Est.
SE1 ... 2F 87 (7J 169)
St Saviour's Rd.
CR0: Croy ... 6B 140
SW2 ... 5K 103
St Saviour's Wharf
SE1 ... *6K 169*
(off Shad Thames)
Saints Cl. SE27 ... 4B 122
Saints Dr. E7 ... 5B 54
St Silas Pl. NW5 ... 6E 48
St Simon's Av. SW15 ... 5E 100
Saints M. CR4: Mitc ... 3C 138
St Stephen's Av. E17 ... 5E 34
W12 ... 1D 82
(not continuous)
W13 ... 6B 62
St Stephen's Cl. E17 ... 5D 34
NW8 ... 1C 66
UB1: S'hall ... 5E 60
St Stephens Ct. *EN1: Enf* ... *6K 7*
(off Park Av.)
N8 ... 6K 31
W13 ... 6B 62
St Stephen's Cres.
CR7: Thor H ... 3A 140
W2 ... 6J 65
St Stephen's Gdns.
SW15 ... 5H 101
TW1: Twick ... 6C 98
W2 ... 6J 65
(not continuous)
St Stephens Gro. SE13 ... 3E 106
St Stephens Ho. *SE17* ... *6D 86*
(off Lytham St.)
St Stephens M. W2 ... 5J 65
St Stephens Pde. E7 ... 7A 54
St Stephen's Pas.
TW1: Twick ... 6C 98
St Stephen's Rd. E3 ... 1A 70
E6 ... 7A 54
E17 ... 5D 34
EN5: Barn ... 5A 4
TW3: Houn ... 6E 96
UB7: W Dray ... 1A 76
W13 ... 6B 62
St Stephen's Row EC4 ... 1E 168
St Stephen's Ter. SW8 ... 7K 85
St Stephen's Wlk. *SW7* ... *4A 84*
(off Southwell Gdns.)
St Swithins La.
EC4 ... 7D 68 (2E 168)
St Swithun's Rd. SE13 ... 6F 107
St Theresa's Rd.
TW14: Felt ... 4H 95
St Thomas Cl. KT6: Surb ... 1F 147
St Thomas Ct. DA5: Bexl ... 7G 111
E10 ... *7D 34*
(off Beaumont Rd.)
HA5: Pinn ... 1C 24
St Thomas Dr. BR5: Orp ... 7G 145
HA5: Pinn ... 1C 24
St Thomas Gdns. IG1: Ilf ... 6G 55
St Thomas Ho. *E1* ... *6K 69*
(off W. Arbour St.)
St Thomas Rd. DA17: Belv ... 2J 93
E16 ... 6J 71
N14 ... 7C 6
W4 ... 6J 81
St Thomas's Gdns. NW5 ... 6E 48
St Thomas's Pl. E9 ... 7J 51
St Thomas's Rd. N4 ... 2A 50
NW10 ... 1A 64
St Thomas's Sq. E9 ... 7J 51
St Thomas St.
SE1 ... 1D 86 (5F 169)
St Thomas's Way SW6 ... 7H 83
St Timothys M.
BR1: Brom ... 1K 143
St Ursula Gro. HA5: Pinn ... 5B 24
St Ursula Rd. UB1: S'hall ... 6E 60
St Vincent Cl. SE27 ... 5B 122
St Vincent De Paul Ho. *E1* ... *5J 69*
(off Jubilee St.)
St Vincent Ho. *SE1* ... *3F 87*
(off Fendall St.)
St Vincent Rd. TW2: Twick ... 6G 97
St Vincent's La. NW7 ... 4K 13
St Vincent St.
W1 ... 5E 66 (6H 159)
St Wilfrid's Cl. EN4: Barn ... 5H 5
St Wilfrid's Rd. EN4: Barn ... 5H 5
St Winefride's Av. E12 ... 5D 54
St Winifred's Rd.
TW11: Tedd ... 6B 116

Sandtoft Rd. SE7 ....6K 89
Sandwell Cres. NW6 ......6J 47
Sandwich Ho. SE16 ....2J 87
　　　　(off Swan Rd.)
　WC1 ....2E 160
　　　　(off Sandwich St.)
Sandwich St.
　WC1 ....3J 67 (2E 160)
Sandwick Cl. NW7 ....7H 13
Sandycombe Rd.
　TW9: Rich 3F 99
　TW14: Felt 1J 113
Sandycoombe Rd.
　TW1: Twick 6C 98
Sandycroft SE2 ....6A 92
Sandy Dr. TW14: Felt 1G 113
Sandy Hill Av. SE18 ......5F 91
Sandy Hill Rd. SE18 ......4F 91
　SM6: Wall 7G 151
Sandyhill Rd. IG1: Ilf 4F 55
Sandy La. BR5: Orp 7D 128
　BR6: Orp 7K 145
　CR4: Mitc 1E 138
　　　(not continuous)
　DA14: Sidc 7D 128
　HA3: Harr 6F 27
　KT12: Walt T 6K 131
　SM2: Sutt 7G 149
　TW10: Rich 2C 116
　TW11: Tedd 7A 116
Sandy La. Nth.
　SM6: Wall 5H 151
Sandy La. Sth.
　SM6: Wall 7G 151
Sandymount Av.
　HA7: Stan 5H 11
Sandy Ridge BR7: Chst ...6E 126
Sandy Rd. NW3 ....2K 47
　　　(not continuous)
Sandys Row E1 ....5E 68 (6H 163)
Sandy Way CR0: Croy 3B 154
　KT12: Walt T 7H 131
Sanford La. N16 ....3F 51
Sanford St. SE14 ....6A 88
Sanford Ter. N16 ....3F 51
Sanford Wlk. N16 ....2F 51
　SE14 ....6A 88
Sanger Av. KT9: Chess ...5E 146
Sangley Rd. SE6 ....7D 106
　SE25 ....4E 140
Sangora Rd. SW11 ......4B 102
Sankey Ho. E2 ....2J 69
　　　(off St James's Av.)
Sansom Rd. E11 ....2H 53
Sansom St. SE5 ....1D 104
Sans Wlk. EC1 ....4A 68 (3K 161)
Santley Ho.
　SE1 ....2A 86 (7K 167)
Santley St. SW4 ....4K 103
Santos Rd. SW18 ....5J 101
Santway, The HA7: Stan ...5D 10
Sapcote Trad. Cen. NW10 ..6B 46
Saperton Wlk. SE11 ......3H 173
Sapperton Ct. EC1 ....3C 162
Sapphire Cl. E6 ....6E 72
　RM8: Dag 1C 56
Sapphire Ct. E1 ....7G 69
　　　　(off Cable St.)
Sapphire Rd. SE8 ....4A 88
Saracen Cl. CR0: Croy ...6D 140
Saracens Head Yd. EC3 ..1J 169
Saracen St. E14 ....6C 70
Sarah Cl. UB5: N'olt 1D 60
Sarah Ho. E1 ....6H 69
　　　(off Commercial Rd.)
Sarah St. N1 ......3E 68 (1H 163)
Sarah Swift Ho. SE1 ......6F 169
　　　　(off Kipling St.)
Sara La. Ct. N1 ....2E 68
　　　　(off Stanway St.)
Saratoga Rd. E5 ....4J 51
Sara Turnbull Ho. SE18 ...4D 90

Sardinia St.
　WC2 ....6K 67 (1G 167)
Sarita Cl. HA3: Harr 2H 25
Sarjant Path SW19 ....2F 119
　　　　(off Blincoe Cl.)
Sarjeant Ct. BR4: W W'ck ..2F 155
　　　　(off Bencurtis Pk.)
Sark Cl. TW5: Houn 7E 78
Sark Ho. EN3: Enf 1E 8
Sark Twr. SE28 ....2G 92
　　　　(off Erebus Dr.)
Sark Wlk. E16 ....6K 71
Sarnes Ct. N11 ....4A 16
　　　(off Oakleigh Rd. Sth.)
Sarnesfield Ho. SE15 .....6H 87
　　　(off Pencraig Way)
Sarnesfield Rd. EN2: Enf ...4J 7
Sarratt Ho. W10 ....5E 64
　　　(off Sutton Way)
Sarre Rd. NW2 ....5H 47
Sarsen Av. TW3: Houn 2E 96
Sarsfeld Rd. SW12 ......1D 120
Sarsfield Rd. UB6: G'frd ..2B 62
Sartor Rd. SE15 ....4K 105
Sarum Ter. E3 ....4B 70
Sassoon NW9 ....1B 28
Satanita Cl. E16 ....6B 72
Satchell Mead NW9 ......1B 28
Satchwell Rd.
　E2 ....3G 69 (2K 163)
Satchwell St. E2 ...3G 69 (2K 163)
Sattar M. N16 ....3D 50
　　　　(off Clissold Rd.)
Saul Cl. SE15 ....6F 87
Sauls Grn. E11 ....3G 53
Saunders Cl. E14 ....7B 70
　　　(off Limehouse C'way.)
Saunders Ho. SE16 ......2K 87
　　　　(off Quebec Way)
　W11 ....1F 83
Saunders Ness Rd. E14 ...5E 88
Saunders Rd. SE18 ......5K 91
　UB10: Uxb 7B 40
Saunders St.
　SE11 ....4A 86 (3J 173)
Saunders Way SE28 ......7B 74
Saunderton Rd.
　HA0: Wemb 5B 44
Saunton Av. UB3: Hayes ..7H 77
Saunton Ct. UB1: S'hall ...7G 61
　　　　(off Haldane Rd.)
Savage Gdns. E6 ....6D 72
　EC3 ....7E 68 (2H 169)
　　　(not continuous)
Savannah Cl. SE15 ....7F 87
Savernake Ct. HA7: Stan ...6G 11
Savernake Ho. N4 ....7C 32
Savernake Rd. N9 ....6B 8
　NW3 ....4D 48
Savery Dr. KT6: Surb 7C 134
Savile Cl. KT3: N Mald 5A 136
　KT7: T Ditt 7K 133
Savile Gdns. CR0: Croy ...2F 153
Savile Row W1 ....7G 67 (2A 166)
Saville Cres. TW15: Ashf ...6F 113
Saville Rd. E16 ....1C 90
　RM6: Chad H 6F 39
　TW1: Twick 1K 115
　W4 ....3K 81
Saville Row BR2: Short ...1H 155
　EN3: Enf 2E 8
Savill Gdns. SW20 ......3C 136
Savill Ho. E16 ....1F 91
　　　(off Robert St.)
　SW4 ....6H 103
Savill Row IG8: Wfd G 6C 20
Savin Lodge SM2: Sutt 7A 150
　　　　(off Walnut M.)
Savona Cl. SW19 ....7F 119
Savona Ho. SW8 ....7G 85
　　　　(off Savona St.)
Savona St. SW8 ....7G 85

Savoy Av. UB3: Hayes 5G 77
Savoy Bldgs. WC2 ....3G 167
Savoy Circus 7B 64
Savoy Cl. E15 ....1G 71
　HA8: Edg 5B 12
Savoy Ct. NW3 ....3A 48
　WC2 ....7K 67 (3F 167)
Savoy Hill WC2 ....7K 67 (3G 167)
Savoy Pde. EN1: Enf 3K 7
Savoy Pl. WC2 ....7J 67 (3F 167)
Savoy Row WC2 ....2G 167
Savoy Steps WC2 ....3G 167
Savoy St. WC2 ....7K 67 (3G 167)
Savoy Theatre 3F 167
　　　　(off Strand)
Savoy Way WC2 ....3G 167
Sawbill Cl. UB4: Hayes ...5B 60
Sawkins Cl. SW19 ......2G 119
Sawley Rd. W12 ....1B 82
Sawmill Yd. E3 ....1A 70
Sawtry Cl. SM5: Cars 7C 138
Sawyer Cl. N9 ....2B 18
Sawyer Ct. NW10 ....7K 45
Sawyers Cl. RM10: Dag ...6J 57
Sawyer's Hill TW10: Rich ...7F 99
Sawyers Lawn W13 ......6A 62
Sawyer St. SE1 ....2C 86 (6C 168)
Saxby Rd. SW2 ....7J 103
Saxham Rd. IG11: Bark ...2J 73
Saxlingham Rd. E4 ....3A 20
Saxon Av. TW13: Felt 2C 114
Saxonbury Av.
　TW16: Sun T 3K 131
Saxonbury Cl.
　CR4: Mitc 3B 138
Saxonbury Ct. N7 ....5J 49
Saxonbury Gdns.
　KT6: Surb 1C 146
Saxon Bus. Cen. SW19 ...2A 138
Saxon Cl. E17 ....7C 34
　KT6: Surb 6D 134
　UB8: Uxb 5B 58
Saxon Dr. W3 ....6G 63
Saxonfield Cl. SW2 .....1K 121
Saxon Gdns. UB1: S'hall ...7C 60
Saxon Ho. TW13: Felt 2D 114
Saxon Lea Ct. E10 ....1A 52
　　　(off Wellington Rd.)
Saxon Lodge CR0: Croy ...1C 152
　　　　(off Tavistock Rd.)
Saxon Rd. BR1: Brom 7H 125
　E3 ....2B 70
　E6 ....4D 72
　HA9: Wemb 3J 45
　IG1: Ilf 6F 55
　KT2: King T 1E 134
　N22 ....1B 32
　SE25 ....5D 140
　TW15: Ashf 6F 113
　UB1: S'hall 7C 60
Saxon Wlk. DA14: Sidc ...6C 128
Saxon Way N14 ....6C 6
Saxony Pde. UB3: Hayes ...5E 58
Saxton Cl. SE13 ....3F 107
Sayers Ho. N2 ....2B 30
　　　(off Grange, The)
Sayer's Wlk. TW10: Rich ...7F 99
Sayesbury La. N18 ....5B 18
Sayes Cl. SE8 ....6B 88
Sayes Ct. St. SE8 ....6B 88
Scads Hill Cl.
　BR6: Orp 6K 145
Scafell NW1 ....1A 160
　　　(off Stanhope St.)
Scala St. W1 .....5G 67 (5B 160)
Scales Rd. N17 ....3F 33
Scampston M. W10 ......6F 65
Scampton Rd.
　TW6: Houn 6B 94
Scandrett St. E1 ....1H 87
Scarba Wlk. N1 ....6D 50
　　　(off Marquess Rd.)

Scarborough Rd. E11 .....1F 53
　N4 ....1A 50
　N9 ....7D 8
　TW6: Houn 6E 94
Scarborough St.
　E1 ....6F 69 (1K 169)
Scarbrook Rd. CR0: Croy ...3C 152
Scarle Rd. HA0: Wemb 6D 44
Scarlet Rd. SE6 ....3G 125
Scarlette Mnr. Way SW2 ...7A 104
Scarsbrook Rd. SE3 ......3B 108
Scarsdale Pl. W8 ....3K 83
Scarsdale Rd. HA2: Harr ...3G 43
Scarsdale Vs. W8 ....3J 83
Scarth Rd. SW13 ....3B 100
Scawen Cl. SM5: Cars 4E 150
Scawen Rd. SE8 ....5A 88
Scawfell St. E2 ....2F 69
Sceaux Gdns. SE5 ....1E 104
Sceptre Ct. E1 ....3K 169
　　　　(off Tower Hill)
Sceptre Ho. E1 ....4J 69
　　　(off Malcolm Rd.)
Sceptre Rd. E2 ....3J 69
Sceynes Link N12 ....4D 14
Schafer Ho.
　NW1 ....3G 67 (2A 160)
Schiller International University
　........5J 167
　　　(off Stamford St.)
Schofield Wlk. SE3 ......7K 89
Scholars Rd. E4 ....1A 20
　SW12 ....1G 121
Scholefield Rd. N19 .....1H 49
Scholey Ho. SW11 ......3C 102
Schomberg Ho. SW1 .....3D 172
　　　　(off Page St.)
Schonfeld Sq. N16 ......2D 50
School All. TW1: Twick 1A 116
School App. E2 ...3E 68 (1H 163)
Schoolbank Rd. SE10 ....3H 89
Schoolbell M. E3 ....2A 70
School Ho. SE1 ....4E 86
　　　　(off Page's Wlk.)
School Ho. La. E1 ....7K 69
　TW11: Tedd 7B 116
School La. DA16: Well 3B 110
　HA5: Pinn 4C 24
　KT1: King T 1C 134
　KT6: Surb 1G 147
　TW17: Shep 6D 130
　WD23: Bush 1A 10
School of Advanced Study
　...........5H 67 (5D 160)
School of Hygiene &
　Tropical Medicine ...5D 160
School of Oriental &
　African Studies 4D 160
School of Pharmacy, The
　..................3F 161
　　　(off Brunswick Sq.)
School of Slavonic &
　East European Studies
　...........5H 67 (5D 160)
School Pas. KT1: King T ...2F 135
　UB1: S'hall 7D 60
School Rd. BR7: Chst 1G 145
　E12 ....4D 54
　KT1: King T 1C 134
　KT8: E Mos 4H 133
　NW10 ....4K 63
　RM10: Dag 1G 75
　TW3: Houn 3G 97
　TW12: Hamp 6G 115
　TW15: Ashf 6D 112
School Rd. Av.
　TW12: Hamp 6G 115
SCHOOL ROAD JUNCTION
　.................7D 112
School Sq. SE10 ....3H 89
School Wlk.
　TW16: Sun T 4H 131

School Way N12 ....6G 15
　RM8: Dag 3C 56
　　　(not continuous)
Schooner Cl. E14 ....3F 89
　IG11: Bark 3B 74
　SE16 ....2K 87
Schubert Rd. SW15 ......5H 101
Science Mus. 3B 84 (2B 170)
Sclater St. E1 ....4F 69 (3J 163)
Scoble Pl. N16 ....4F 51
Scoles Cres. SW2 ......1A 122
Scope Way KT1: King T ...4E 134
Scoresby St. SE1 ...1B 86 (5A 168)
Scorton Av. UB6: G'frd ...2A 62
Scorton Ho. N1 ....2E 68
　　　(off Whitmore Est.)
Scotch Comn. W13 ......5A 62
SCOTCH HOUSE 2D 84 (7E 164)
Scoter Cl. IG8: Wfd G 7E 20
Scoter Ct. SE8 ....6B 88
　　　(off Abinger Gro.)
Scot Gro. HA5: Pinn 1B 24
Scotia Bldg. E1 ....7K 69
　　　(off Jardine Rd.)
Scotia Ct. SE16 ....2J 87
　　　(off Canada Est.)
Scotia Rd. SW2 ....7A 104
Scotland Grn. N17 ....2F 33
Scotland Grn. Rd. EN3: Enf ..5E 8
Scotland Grn. Rd. Nth.
　EN3: Enf 4E 8
Scotland Pl. SW1 ...1J 85 (5E 166)
Scotland Rd. IG9: Buck H ...1F 21
Scotney Cl. BR6: Orp 4E 156
Scotney Ho. E9 ....6J 51
Scots Cl. TW19: Staines ...1A 112
Scotsdale Cl. BR5: Orp ...4J 145
　SM3: Sutt 7G 149
Scotsdale Rd. SE12 .....5K 107
Scotson Ho. SE11 ......4J 173
Scotswood St.
　EC1 ....4A 68 (3K 161)
Scotswood Wlk. N17 .....7B 18
Scott Cl. KT19: Eps 5J 147
　SW16 ....1K 139
　UB7: W Dray 4B 76
Scott Ct. W3 ....2K 81
Scott Cres. HA2: Harr ...1F 43
Scott Ellis Gdns.
　NW8 ....3B 66 (2A 158)
Scottes La. RM8: Dag 1D 56
Scott Farm Cl.
　KT7: T Ditt 1B 146
Scott Gdns. TW5: Houn ...7B 78
Scott Ho. DA17: Belv 5F 93
　E13 ....2J 71
　　　(off Queens Rd. W.)
　E14 ....2D 88
　　　(off Admirals Way)
　N1 ....1D 68
　　　(off Sherborne St.)
　N7 ....6K 49
　　　(off Caledonian Rd.)
　NW1 ....4C 158
　　　(off Ashmill St.)
　NW10 ....7K 45
　　　(off Kingthorpe Rd.)
Scott Lidgett Cres. SE16 ...2G 87
Scott Russell Pl. E14 .....5D 88
Scotts Av. BR2: Short 2F 143
　TW16: Sun T 7G 113
Scotts Ct. W12 ....2E 82
　　　　(off Scott's Rd.)
Scotts Dr. TW12: Hamp ...7F 115
Scotts Farm Rd.
　KT19: Eps 6J 147
Scott's La. BR2: Short 3F 143
Scotts Pas. SE18 ....4F 91
Scotts Rd. BR1: Brom 7J 125
　E10 ....1E 52
　UB2: S'hall 3A 78
　W12 ....2D 82

Scott's Sufferance Wharf—Sexton Ct.

Scott's Sufferance Wharf
SE1 ....7K **169**
Scott St. E1 ....4H **69**
Scotts Way
TW16: Sun T 7G **113**
Scott's Yd. EC4 ....7D **68** (2E **168**)
Scott Trimmer Way
TW3: Houn 2C **96**
Scottwell Dr. NW9 ....5B **28**
Scoulding Ho. *E14* *3C 88*
(off Mellish St.)
Scoulding Rd. E16 ....6J **71**
Scouler St. E14 ....7E **70**
Scout App. NW10 ....4A **46**
Scout La. SW4 ....3G **103**
Scout Way NW7 ....4E **12**
Scovell Cres. SE1 ....7C **168**
Scovell Rd. SE1 ....2C **86** (7C **168**)
Scrattons Ter. IG11: Bark 2D **74**
Scriven Ct. E8 ....1F **69**
Scriven St. E8 ....1F **69**
Scrooby St. SE6 ....6D **106**
Scrope Ho. *EC1* *5J 161*
(off Bourne Est.)
Scrubs La. NW10 ....3C **64**
Scrutton Cl. SW12 ....7H **103**
Scrutton St. EC2 ....4E **68** (4G **163**)
Scudamore La. NW9 ....4J **27**
Scutari Rd. SE22 ....5J **105**
Scylla Cres. TW6: Houn 6D **94**
Scylla Rd. SE15 ....3G **105**
(not continuous)
TW6: Houn 6D **94**
Seabright St. E2 ....3H **69**
Seabrook Dr.
BR4: W W'ck 2G **155**
Seabrook Gdns.
RM7: Rush G 7G **39**
Seabrook Rd. RM8: Dag 3D **56**
Seaburn Cl. RM13: Rain 2K **75**
Seacole Cl. W3 ....6K **63**
Seacon Twr. E14 ....2B **88**
Seacourt Rd. SE2 ....2D **92**
Seafield Rd. N11 ....4C **16**
Seaford Cl. HA4: Ruis 1F **41**
Seaford Ho. *SE16* *2J 87*
(off Swan Rd.)
Seaford Rd. E17 ....3D **34**
EN1: Enf 4K **7**
N15 ....5D **32**
TW6: Houn 5A **94**
W13 ....1B **80**
Seaford St. WC1 ....3K **67** (2F **161**)
Seaforth Av. KT3: N Mald 5D **136**
Seaforth Cres. N5 ....5C **50**
Seaforth Gdns.
IG8: Wfd G 5F **21**
KT19: Eps 4B **148**
N21 ....7E **6**
Seaforth Pl. SW1 ....1B **172**
Seagar Bldgs. SE8 ....1C **106**
Seagar Pl. E3 ....5B **70**
Seagrave Cl. E1 ....5K **69**
Seagrave Lodge *SW6* *6J 83*
(off Seagrave Rd.)
Seagrave Rd. SW6 ....6J **83**
Seagry Rd. E11 ....7J **35**
Seagull Cl. IG11: Bark 3A **74**
Sealand Rd. TW6: Houn 6C **94**
Sealand Wlk. UB5: N'olt 3B **60**
Seal Ho. *SE1* *7F 169*
(off Pardoner St.)
Seal St. E8 ....4F **51**
Searle Pl. N4 ....1K **49**
Searles Cl. SW11 ....7C **84**
Searles Dr. E6 ....5F **73**
Searles Rd. SE1 ....4D **86**
Searson Ho. *SE17* *4B 86*
(off Canterbury Pl.)
Sears St. SE5 ....7D **86**
Seasprite Cl. UB5: N'olt 3B **60**
Seaton Av. IG3: Ilf 5K **55**
Seaton Cl. E13 ....4J **71**
SE11 ....5A **86** (5K **173**)
SW15 ....1D **118**
TW2: Twick 6H **97**
Seaton Dr. TW15: Ashf 2A **112**
Seaton Gdns. HA4: Ruis 3H **41**
Seaton Point *E5* *4G 51*
(off Nolan Way)
Seaton Rd. CR4: Mitc 2C **138**
DA16: Well 7C **92**
HA0: Wemb 2E **62**
TW2: Twick 6G **97**
UB3: Hayes 4F **77**
Seaton Sq. NW7 ....7A **14**
Seaton St. N18 ....5B **18**
Sebastian Ct. IG11: Bark 1K **73**
Sebastian Ho. *N1* *1G 163*
(off Hoxton St.)
Sebastian St.
EC1 ....3B **68** (2B **162**)
Sebastopol Rd. N9 ....4B **18**
Sebbon St. N1 ....7B **50**
Sebergham Gro. NW7 ....7H **13**
Sebert Rd. E7 ....5K **53**
Sebright Ho. *E2* *2G 69*
(off Coate St.)
Sebright Pas. E2 ....2G **69**
Sebright Rd. EN5: Barn 2A **4**
Secker Cres. HA3: Harr 1G **25**
Secker Ho. *SW9* *2B 104*
(off Loughborough Est.)
Secker St. SE1 ....1A **86** (5J **167**)
Secombe Theatre
Sutton* *5K 149
Second Av. E12 ....4C **54**
E13 ....3J **71**
E17 ....5C **34**
EN1: Enf 5A **8**
HA9: Wemb 2D **44**
KT12: Walt T 6K **131**
N18 ....4D **18**
NW4 ....4F **29**
RM6: Chad H 5C **38**
RM10: Dag 1H **75**
SW14 ....3A **100**
UB3: Hayes 1H **77**
W3 ....1B **82**
W10 ....4G **65**
Second Cl. KT8: W Mole 4G **133**
Second Cross Rd.
TW2: Twick 2J **115**
Second Way HA9: Wemb 4H **45**
Sedan Way SE17 ....5E **86**
Sedcombe Cl.
DA14: Sidc 4B **128**
Sedcote Rd. EN3: Enf 5D **8**
Sedding St. SW1 ....4E **84** (3G **171**)
Sedding Studios *SW1* *3G 171*
(off Sedding St.)
Seddon Highwalk *EC2* *5C 162*
(off Seddon Ho.)
Seddon Ho. EC2 ....5C **162**
Seddon Rd. SM4: Mord 5B **138**
Seddon St. WC1 ....3K **67** (2H **161**)
Sedgebrook Rd. SE3 ....2B **108**
Sedgecombe Av.
HA3: Harr 5C **26**
Sedgefield Ct. *UB5: N'olt* *5F 43*
(off Newmarket Av.)
Sedgeford Rd. W12 ....1B **82**
Sedgehill Rd. SE6 ....4C **124**
Sedgemere Av. N2 ....3A **30**
Sedgemere Rd. SE2 ....3C **92**
Sedgemoor Dr.
RM10: Dag 4G **57**
Sedge Rd. N17 ....7D **18**
Sedgeway SE6 ....1H **125**
Sedgewick Av.
UB10: Uxb 7D **40**
Sedgewood Cl.
BR2: Short 7H **143**
Sedgmoor Pl. SE5 ....7E **86**
Sedgwick Ho. *E3* *5C 70*
(off Gale St.)
Sedgwick Rd. E10 ....2E **52**
Sedgwick St. E9 ....5K **51**
Sedleigh Rd. SW18 ....6H **101**
Sedlescombe Rd. SW6 ....6J **83**
Sedley Cl. EN1: Enf 1C **8**
Sedley Ct. SE26 ....2H **123**
Sedley Ho. *SE11* *5H 173*
(off Newburn St.)
Sedley Pl. W1 ....6F **67** (1J **165**)
Sedum Cl. NW9 ....5H **27**
Seeley Dr. SE21 ....4E **122**
Seelig Av. NW9 ....7C **28**
Seely Rd. SW17 ....6E **120**
Seething La.
EC3 ....7E **68** (2H **169**)
SEETHING WELLS **6C 134**
Seething Wells La.
KT6: Surb 6C **134**
Sefton Av. HA3: Harr 2H **25**
NW7 ....5E **12**
Sefton Cl. BR5: Orp 4K **145**
Sefton Ct. EN2: Enf 2G **7**
(not continuous)
TW3: Houn 1F **97**
Sefton Rd. BR5: Orp 4K **145**
CR0: Croy 1G **153**
Sefton St. SW15 ....3E **100**
Segal Cl. SE23 ....7A **106**
Sekforde St. EC1 ....4B **68** (4A **162**)
Sekhon Ter. TW13: Felt 3E **114**
Selan Gdns. UB4: Hayes 5K **59**
Selbie Av. NW10 ....5B **46**
Selborne Av. DA5: Bexl 1E **128**
E12 ....4E **54**
Selborne Gdns. NW4 ....4C **28**
UB6: G'frd 1A **62**
Selborne Rd. CR0: Croy 3E **152**
DA14: Sidc 4B **128**
E17 ....5B **34**
IG1: Ilf 2E **54**
KT3: N Mald 2A **136**
N14 ....3D **16**
SE5 ....2D **104**
Selborne Wlk. E17 ....5B **34**
Selborne Wlk. Shop. Cen.
E17 ....4B **34**
Selbourne Av. KT6: Surb 2F **147**
Selbourne Ho. SE1 ....7E **168**
Selbourne Rd. N22 ....1K **31**
Selby Chase HA4: Ruis 2K **41**
Selby Cl. BR7: Chst 6E **126**
E6 ....5C **72**
KT9: Chess 7E **146**
Selby Gdns. UB1: S'hall 4E **60**
Selby Grn. SM5: Cars 7C **138**
Selby Ho. *W10* *3G 65*
(off Beethoven St.)
Selby Rd. E11 ....3G **53**
E13 ....5K **71**
N17 ....7K **17**
SE20 ....2G **141**
SM5: Cars 7C **138**
TW15: Ashf 6E **112**
W5 ....4B **62**
Selby St. E1 ....4G **69**
Selcroft Ho. *SE10* *5H 89*
(off Glenister Rd.)
Selden Ho. *SE15* *2J 105*
(off Selden Rd.)
Selden Rd. SE15 ....2J **105**
Selden Wlk. N7 ....2K **49**
Seldon Ho. *SW1* *6A 172*
(off Churchill Gdns.)
SW8 ....*7G 85*
(off Stewart's Rd.)
Selfridges* *1H 165
(off Oxford St.)
SELHURST **6D 140**
Selhurst Cl. SW19 ....1F **119**
Selhurst New Rd. SE25 ....6E **140**
Selhurst Pk.* *4E 140
Selhurst Pl. SE25 ....6E **140**
Selhurst Rd. N9 ....3J **17**
SE25 ....6E **140**
Selina Ho. *NW8* *3B 158*
(off Frampton St.)
Selinas La. RM8: Dag 7E **38**
Selkirk Rd. SW17 ....4C **120**
TW2: Twick 2G **115**
Sellers Hall Cl. N3 ....7D **14**
Sellincourt Rd. SW17 ....5C **120**
Sellindge Cl. BR3: Beck 7B **124**
Sellons Av. NW10 ....1B **64**
Selma Ho. *W12* *6D 64*
(off Du Cane Rd.)
Selman Ho. E9 ....6A **52**
Selsdon Av. CR2: S Croy 6D **152**
Selsdon Cl. KT6: Surb 5E **134**
RM5: Col R 1J **39**
Selsdon Ct. *UB1: S'hall* *6F 61*
(off Dormers Ri.)
Selsdon Pk. Rd.
CR2: S Croy 7K **153**
Selsdon Rd. CR2: S Croy 5D **152**
E11 ....7J **35**
E13 ....1A **72**
NW2 ....2B **46**
SE27 ....3A **122**
Selsdon Way E14 ....3D **88**
Selsea Pl. N16 ....5E **50**
Selsey Cres. DA16: Well 1D **110**
Selsey St. E14 ....5C **70**
Selvage La. NW7 ....5E **12**
Selway Cl. HA5: Pinn 4K **23**
Selway Ho. *SW8* *1J 103*
(off Sth. Lambeth Rd.)
Selwood Dr. EN5: Barn 5A **4**
Selwood Pl.
SW7 ....5B **84** (5A **170**)
Selwood Rd. CR0: Croy 2H **153**
KT9: Chess 4D **146**
SM3: Sutt 1H **149**
Selwoods SW2 ....7A **104**
Selwood Ter.
SW7 ....5B **84** (5A **170**)
Selworthy Cl. E11 ....5J **35**
Selworthy Rd. SE6 ....3B **124**
Selwyn Av. E4 ....6K **19**
IG3: Ilf 6K **37**
TW9: Rich 3E **98**
Selwyn Cl. TW4: Houn 4C **96**
Selwyn Ct. *E17* *5C 34*
(off Yunus Khan Cl.)
HA8: Edg 7C **12**
HA9: Wemb 3J **45**
SE3 ....3H **107**
Selwyn Cres. DA16: Well 3B **110**
Selwyn Rd. E3 ....2B **70**
E13 ....1K **71**
KT3: N Mald 5K **135**
NW10 ....7K **45**
Semley Ga. E9 ....6B **52**
Semley Ho. *SW1* *4J 171*
(off Semley Pl.)
Semley Pl. SW1 ....4E **84** (4H **171**)
Semley Rd. SW16 ....2J **139**
Senate St. SE15 ....2J **105**
Senators Lodge *E3* *2A 70*
(off Roman Rd.)
Senator Wlk. SE28 ....3H **91**
Seneca Rd. CR7: Thor H 4C **140**
Sener Ct. CR2: S Croy 6C **152**
Senga Rd. SM6: Wall 1E **150**
Senhouse Rd.
SM3: Sutt 3F **149**
Senior St. W2 ....5K **65**
Senlac Rd. SE12 ....1K **125**
Sennen Rd. EN1: Enf 7A **8**
Sennen Wlk. SE9 ....3C **126**
Senrab St. E1 ....6K **69**
Sentinel Cl. UB5: N'olt 4C **60**
Sentinel Sq. NW4 ....4E **28**
September Ct. *UB1: S'hall* *1F 79*
(off Dormer's Wells La.)
UB8: Uxb 2A **58**
September Way
HA7: Stan 6G **11**
Septimus Pl. EN1: Enf 5B **8**
Sequoia Cl. WD23: Bush 1C **10**
Sequoia Gdns. BR6: Orp 7K **145**
Sequoia Pk. HA5: Pinn 6A **10**
Seraph Ct. *EC1* *1C 162*
(off Moreland St.)
Serbin Cl. E10 ....7E **34**
Serenaders Rd. SW9 ....2A **104**
Sergeant Ind. Est. SW18 ....6K **101**
Serica Ct. SE10 ....7E **88**
Serjeants Inn
EC4 ....6A **68** (1K **167**)
Serle St. WC2 ....6K **67** (7H **161**)
Sermon La. EC4 ....1C **168**
Serpentine Gallery
****....2B 84 (6A 164)****
Serpentine Rd.
W2 ....1C **84** (5C **164**)
Serviden Dr. BR1: Brom 1B **144**
Servite Ho. BR3: Beck 1B **142**
KT4: Wor Pk *2B 148*
(off Avenue, The)
Servius Ct. TW8: Bford 7D **80**
Setchell Rd. SE1 ....4F **87**
Setchell Way SE1 ....4F **87**
Seth St. SE16 ....2J **87**
Seton Gdns. RM9: Dag 7C **56**
Settle Point *E13* *2J 71*
(off London Rd.)
Settle Rd. E13 ....2J **71**
Settles St. E1 ....5G **69**
Settrington Rd. SW6 ....2K **101**
Seven Acres SM5: Cars 2C **150**
Seven Dials WC2 ....6J **67** (1E **166**)
Seven Dials Ct. *WC2* *1E 166*
(off Shorts Gdns.)
Sevenex Pde. HA9: Wemb 5E **44**
SEVEN KINGS **1J 55**
Seven Kings Rd. IG3: Ilf 1J **55**
Seven Kings Way
KT2: King T 1E **134**
Sevenoaks Cl. DA7: Bex 4H **111**
Sevenoaks Ct.
HA6: Nwood 1E **22**
Sevenoaks Rd. SE4 ....6A **106**
Sevenoaks Way
BR5: Orp 7C **128**
DA14: Sidc 7C **128**
Seven Sisters **5F 33**
Seven Sisters Rd. N7 ....3K **49**
N15 ....7C **32**
Seven Stars Cnr. W6 ....3C **82**
Seven Stars Yd. E1 ....5K **163**
Seventh Av. E12 ....4D **54**
UB3: Hayes 1J **77**
Severnake Cl. E14 ....4C **88**
Severn Ct. KT2: King T 1D **134**
Severn Dr. KT10: Esh 2A **146**
Severn Way NW10 ....5B **46**
Severus Rd. SW11 ....4C **102**
Seville M. N1 ....7E **50**
Seville St. SW1 ....2D **84** (7F **165**)
Sevington Rd. NW4 ....6D **28**
Sevington St. W9 ....4K **65**
Seward Rd. BR3: Beck 2K **141**
W7 ....2A **80**
SEWARDSTONE **1K 9**
Sewardstone Gdns. E4 ....5J **9**
Sewardstone Rd. E2 ....2J **69**
E4 ....7J **9**
Seward St. EC1 ....3B **68** (3B **162**)
Sewdley St. E5 ....3K **51**
Sewell Rd. SE2 ....3A **92**
Sewell St. E13 ....3J **71**
Sextant Av. E14 ....4F **89**
Sexton Ct. *E14* *7F 71*
(off Newport Av.)

338 A-Z London

Sextons Ho.—Shene Ho.

Sextons Ho. SE10 . . . . .6E 88
(off Bardsley La.)
Seymer Rd. RM1: Rom 3K 39
Seymour Av. KT17: Eps 7E 148
N17 . . . . .2G 33
SM4: Mord 7F 137
Seymour Cl. HA5: Pinn 1D 24
KT8: E Mos 5G 133
Seymour Ct. E4 . . . . .2C 20
N10 . . . . .2E 30
N21 . . . . .6E 6
NW2 . . . . .2D 46
Seymour Dr. BR2: Short 1D 156
Seymour Gdns. HA4: Ruis . . .1B 42
IG1: Ilf 1D 54
KT5: Surb 5F 135
SE4 . . . . .3A 106
TW1: Twick 7B 98
TW13: Felt 4A 114
Seymour Ho. E16 . . . . .7J 71
(off De Quincey M.)
NW1 . . . . .1D 160
(off Churchway)
SM2: Sutt 6K 149
(off Mulgrave Rd.)
WC1 . . . . .3E 160
(off Tavistock Pl.)
Seymour M. W1 . . .6E 66 (7G 159)
Seymour Pl. SE25 . . . . .4H 141
W1 . . . . .5D 66 (6E 158)
Seymour Rd. CR4: Mitc 7E 138
E4 . . . . .1J 19
E6 . . . . .2B 72
E10 . . . . .1B 52
KT1: King T 1D 134
KT8: W Mole 5G 133
N3 . . . . .7E 14
N8 . . . . .5A 32
N9 . . . . .2C 18
SM5: Cars 5E 150
SW18 . . . . .7H 101
SW19 . . . . .3F 119
TW12: Hamp 5G 115
W4 . . . . .4J 81
Seymour St. SE18 . . . . .3G 91
W1 . . . . .6D 66 (1E 164)
W2 . . . . .6D 66 (1E 164)
Seymour Ter. SE20 . . . . .1H 141
Seymour Vs. SE20 . . . . .1H 141
Seymour Wlk. SW10 . . . . . . .6A 84
Seymour Way
TW16: Sun T 7H 113
Seyssel St. E14 . . . . .4E 88
Shaa Rd. W3 . . . . .7K 63
Shacklegate La.
TW11: Tedd 4J 115
Shackleton Cl. SE23 . . . . . .2H 123
Shackleton Ct. E14 . . . . .5C 88
(off Maritime Quay)
W12 . . . . .2D 82
Shackleton Ho. E1 . . . . .1J 87
(off Prusom St.)
NW10 . . . . .7K 45
Shackleton Rd.
UB1: S'hall 7D 60
SHACKLEWELL 4F 51
Shacklewell Grn. E8 . . . . .4F 51
Shacklewell Ho. E8 . . . . .4F 51
Shacklewell Rd. N16 . . . . . . .4F 51
Shacklewell Row E8 . . . . .4F 51
Shacklewell St.
E2 . . . . .3F 69 (2K 163)
Shackwell La. E8 . . . . .5F 51
Shadbolt Cl.
KT4: Wor Pk 2B 148
Shad Thames
SE1 . . . . .1F 87 (5J 169)
SHADWELL 7H 69
Shadwell Ct. UB5: N'olt 2D 60
Shadwell Dr. UB5: N'olt 3D 60
Shadwell Gdns. E1 . . . . .7J 69
Shadwell Pierhead E1 . . . . . .7J 69
Shadwell Pl. E1 . . . . .7J 69
(off Shadwell Gdns.)
Shadybush Cl.
WD23: Bush 1B 10
Shaef Way TW11: Tedd 7A 116
Shafter Rd. RM10: Dag 6J 57
Shaftesbury Av. EN3: Enf 2E 8
EN5: Barn 4F 5
HA2: Harr 1F 43
HA3: Harr 5D 26
TW14: Felt 6J 95
UB2: S'hall 4E 78
W1 . . . . .7H 67 (3C 166)
WC2 . . . . . . .6J 67 (7E 160)
Shaftesbury Cen. W10 . . . . . .4F 65
(off Barlby Rd.)
Shaftesbury Circ.
HA2: Harr 1G 43
Shaftesbury Ct. E6 . . . . .6E 72
(off Sapphire Cl.)
N1 . . . . .2D 68
(off Shaftesbury St.)
SW6 . . . . .1K 101
(off Maltings Pl.)
SW16 . . . . .3H 121
Shaftesbury Cres.
TW18: Staines 7A 112
Shaftesbury Gdns. NW10 . . . .4A 64
Shaftesbury Lodge E14 . . . . .6D 70
(off Up. North St.)
Shaftesbury M. SE1 . . . . .3D 86
(off Falmouth Rd.)
SW4 . . . . .5G 103
W8 . . . . .3J 83
(off Stratford Rd.)
Shaftesbury Pde.
HA2: Harr 1G 43
Shaftesbury Pl. EC2 . . . . . . .6C 162
(off London Wall)
W14 . . . . .4H 83
(off Warwick Rd.)
Shaftesbury Point E13 . . . . . .2J 71
(off High St.)
Shaftesbury Rd.
BR3: Beck 2B 142
E4 . . . . .1A 20
E7 . . . . .7A 54
E10 . . . . .1C 52
E17 . . . . .6D 34
N18 . . . . .6K 17
N19 . . . . .1J 49
SM5: Cars 7B 138
TW9: Rich 3E 98
Shaftesburys, The
IG11: Bark 2G 73
Shaftesbury St. N1 . . . . .2C 68
Shaftesbury Theatre 7E 160
(off Shaftesbury Av.)
Shaftesbury Way
TW2: Twick 3H 115
Shaftesbury Waye
UB4: Hayes 5A 60
Shafto M. SW1 . . . .3D 84 (2F 171)
Shafton M. E9 . . . . .1K 69
Shafton Rd. E9 . . . . .1K 69
Shaftsbury Ct. SE5 . . . . .4D 104
Shafts Ct. EC3 . . . . .6E 68 (1G 169)
Shahjalal Ho. E2 . . . . .2G 69
(off Pritchards Rd.)
Shakespeare Av. N11 . . . . . . .5B 16
NW10 . . . . .1K 63
TW14: Felt 6J 95
UB4: Hayes 6J 59
(not continuous)
Shakespeare Cl.
HA3: Harr 6G 27
Shakespeare Ct. EN5: Barn . . .3E 4
HA3: Harr 7G 27
Shakespeare Cres. E12 . . . . .6D 54
NW10 . . . . .1K 63
Shakespeare Dr.
HA3: Harr 6F 27
Shakespeare Gdns. N2 . . . . .4D 30
Shakespeare Ho. E9 . . . . .7J 51
(off Lyme Gro.)
N14 . . . . .2C 16
Shakespeare Rd.
DA7: Bex 1E 110
E17 . . . . .2K 33
N3 . . . . .1J 29
NW7 . . . . .4G 13
SE24 . . . . .5B 104
W3 . . . . .1J 81
W7 . . . . .7K 61
Shakespeare's Globe Theatre &
Exhibition . .1C 86 (3C 168)
Shakespeare Twr. EC2 . . . . .5D 162
Shakespeare Way
TW13: Felt 4A 114
Shakspeare M. N16 . . . . .4E 50
Shakspeare Wlk. N16 . . . . . . .4E 50
Shalbourne Sq. E9 . . . . .6B 52
Shalcomb St. SW10 . . . . .6A 84
Shalden Ho. SW15 . . . . .6B 100
Shaldon Dr. HA4: Ruis 3A 42
SM4: Mord 5G 137
Shaldon Rd. HA8: Edg 2F 27
Shalfleet Dr. W10 . . . . .7F 65
Shalford Ct. N1 . . . . .2B 68
(off Charlton Pl.)
Shalford Ho. SE1 . . . . .3D 86
Shalimar Gdns. W3 . . . . .7J 63
Shalimar Rd. W3 . . . . .7J 63
Shallons Rd. SE9 . . . . .4F 127
Shalstone Rd. SW14 . . . . . . .3H 99
Shalston Vs. KT6: Surb 6F 135
Shamrock Rd. CR0: Croy . . .6K 139
Shamrock St. SW4 . . . . .3H 103
Shamrock Way N14 . . . . .1A 16
Shandon Rd. SW4 . . . . .6G 103
Shand St. SE1 . . . . .2E 86 (6H 169)
Shandy St. E1 . . . . .5K 69
Shanklin Ho. E17 . . . . .2B 34
Shanklin Rd. N8 . . . . .5H 31
Shannon Cl. NW2 . . . . .3F 47
UB2: S'hall 5B 78
SHANNON CORNER 4C 136
Shannon Cnr. Retail Pk.
KT3: N Mald 4C 136
Shannon Ct. CR0: Croy 1C 152
(off Tavistock Rd.)
N16 . . . . .3E 50
Shannon Gro. SW9 . . . . .4K 103
Shannon Pl. NW8 . . . . .2C 66
Shannon Way BR3: Beck . . .6D 124
Shanti Ct. SW18 . . . . .1J 119
Shap Cres. SM5: Cars 1D 150
Shapland Way N13 . . . . .5E 16
Shap St. E2 . . . . .2F 69
Shapwick Cl. N11 . . . . .5J 15
Shardcroft Av. SE24 . . . . . . .5B 104
Shardeloes Rd. SE14 . . . . . .2B 106
Shard's Sq. SE15 . . . . .6G 87
Sharland Cl. CR7: Thor H . . .6A 140
Sharman Ct. DA14: Sidc 4A 128
(off Carlton Rd.)
Sharnbrooke Cl.
DA16: Well 3C 110
Sharnbrook Ho. W14 . . . . . . .6J 83
Sharon Cl. KT6: Surb 1C 146
Sharon Ct. CR2: S Croy 5C 152
(off Warham Rd.)
Sharon Gdns. E9 . . . . .1J 69
Sharon Rd. EN3: Enf 2F 9
W4 . . . . .5K 81
Sharpe Cl. W7 . . . . .5K 61
Sharp Ho. SW8 . . . . .3F 103
TW1: Twick 6D 98
Sharpleshall St. NW1 . . . . . . .7D 48
Sharpness Cl. UB4: Hayes . . .5C 60
Sharpness Ct. SE15 . . . . .7F 87
(off Longhope Cl.)
Sharp's La. HA4: Ruis 7F 23
Sharratt St. SE15 . . . . .6J 87
Sharsted St.
SE17 . . . . . . .5B 86 (6K 173)
Sharvel La. UB5: N'olt 1K 59
Sharwood WC1 . . . . .1H 161
(off Penton Ri.)
Shaver's Pl. SW1 . . . . .3C 166
Shaw Av. IG11: Bark 2E 74
Shawbrooke Rd. SE9 . . . . . .5A 108
Shawbury Rd. SE22 . . . . . . .5F 105
Shaw Cl. SE28 . . . . .1B 92
WD23: Bush 2D 10
Shaw Ct. W3 . . . . .3J 81
(off All Saints Rd.)
Shaw Dr. KT12: Walt T 7A 132
Shawfield Ct.
UB7: W Dray 3A 76
Shawfield Pk. BR1: Brom . . .2B 144
Shawfield St.
SW3 . . . . . . .5C 84 (6D 170)
Shawford Ct. SW15 . . . . . . .7C 100
Shawford Rd. KT19: Eps . . .6K 147
Shaw Gdns. IG11: Bark 2E 74
Shaw Ho. DA17: Belv 5F 93
E16 . . . . .1E 90
(off Claremont St.)
Shaw Path BR1: Brom 3H 125
Shaw Rd. BR1: Brom 3H 125
EN3: Enf 1E 8
SE22 . . . . .4E 104
Shaws Cotts. SE23 . . . . .3A 124
Shaws Path KT1: King T 1C 134
(off Bennett Cl.)
Shaw Sq. E17 . . . . .1A 34
Shaw Way SM6: Wall 7J 151
Shearing Dr. SM5: Cars 7A 138
Shearling Way N7 . . . . .6J 49
Shearman Rd. SE3 . . . . .4H 107
Shears Ct. TW16: Sun T 7G 113
SHEARS, THE 7G 113
Shearwater Cl. IG11: Bark . . .3A 74
Shearwater Ct. SE8 . . . . .6B 88
(off Abinger Gro.)
Shearwater Rd.
SM1: Sutt 5H 149
Shearwater Way
UB4: Hayes 6B 60
Sheaveshill Av. NW9 . . . . . . .4A 28
Sheaveshill Ct. NW9 . . . . . . .4K 27
Sheaveshill Pde. NW9 . . . . . .4A 28
(off Sheaveshill Av.)
Sheba Ct. N17 . . . . .6B 18
(off Altair Cl.)
Sheen Comn. Dr.
TW10: Rich 4G 99
Sheen Ct. TW10: Rich 4G 99
Sheen Ct. Rd. TW10: Rich . . .4G 99
Sheendale Rd. TW9: Rich 4F 99
Sheenewood SE26 . . . . .4H 123
Sheen Ga. Gdns. SW14 . . . . .4J 99
Sheengate Mans. SW14 . . . .4K 99
Sheen Gro. N1 . . . . .1A 68
Sheen La. SW14 . . . . .5J 99
Sheen Pk. TW9: Rich 4F 99
Sheen Rd. BR5: Orp 4K 145
TW9: Rich 5E 98
TW10: Rich 5E 98
Sheen Way SM6: Wall 5K 151
Sheen Wood SW14 . . . . .5J 99
Sheepcote Cl. TW5: Houn . . .7J 77
Sheepcote La. SW11 . . . . . .2D 102
Sheepcote Rd. HA1: Harr 6K 25
Sheepcotes Rd.
RM6: Chad H 4E 38
Sheephouse Way
KT3: N Mald 1K 147
Sheep La. E8 . . . . .1H 69
Sheep Wlk. TW17: Shep 5C 130
Sheep Wlk. M. SW19 . . . . . .6F 119
Sheep Wlk., The
TW17: Shep 7B 130
Sheerness M. E16 . . . . .2F 91
Sheerwater Rd. E16 . . . . .5B 72
Sheffield Rd. TW6: Houn 6E 94
Sheffield Sq. E3 . . . . .3B 70
Sheffield St.
WC2 . . . . . .6K 67 (1G 167)
Sheffield Ter. W8 . . . . .1J 83
Sheffield Way TW14: Felt 5F 95
Shelbourne Cl.
HA5: Pinn 3D 24
Shelbourne Pl.
BR3: Beck 7B 124
Shelbourne Rd. N17 . . . . .2H 33
Shelburne Dr. TW4: Houn . . .6E 96
Shelburne Rd. N7 . . . . .4K 49
Shelbury Cl. DA14: Sidc 3A 128
Shelbury Rd. SE22 . . . . .5H 105
Sheldon Av. IG5: Ilf 2F 37
N6 . . . . .7C 30
Sheldon Cl. SE12 . . . . .5K 107
SE20 . . . . .1H 141
Sheldon Ct. EN5: Barn 4E 4
SW8 . . . . .1J 103
(off Lansdowne Grn.)
Sheldon Rd. DA7: Bex 1F 111
N18 . . . . .4K 17
NW2 . . . . .4F 47
RM9: Dag 7E 56
Sheldon St. CR0: Croy 3C 152
Sheldrake Cl. E16 . . . . .1D 90
Sheldrake Ct. E6 . . . . .2C 72
(off St Bartholomew's Rd.)
Sheldrake Ho. SE16 . . . . .4K 87
(off Tawny Way)
Sheldrake Pl. W8 . . . . .2J 83
Sheldrick Cl. SW19 . . . . . . .2B 138
Shelduck Cl. E7 . . . . .5H 53
Shelduck Ct. SE8 . . . . .6B 88
(off Pilot Cl.)
Sheldwich Ter.
BR2: Short 6C 144
Shelford Pl. N16 . . . . .3D 50
Shelford Ri. SE19 . . . . .7F 123
Shelford Rd. EN5: Barn 6A 4
Shelgate Rd. SW11 . . . . . . .5C 102
Shell Cl. BR2: Short 6C 144
Shellduck Cl. NW9 . . . . .2A 28
Shelley N8 . . . . .3J 31
(off Boyton Rd.)
Shelley Av. E12 . . . . .6C 54
UB6: G'frd 3H 61
Shelley Cl. HA8: Edg 4B 12
SE15 . . . . .2H 105
UB4: Hayes 5J 59
UB6: G'frd 3H 61
Shelley Ct. E10 . . . . .7D 34
(off Skelton's La.)
E11 . . . . .4K 35
(off Makepeace Rd.)
N19 . . . . .1K 49
SW3 . . . . .7F 171
(off Tite St.)
Shelley Cres. TW5: Houn 1B 96
UB1: S'hall 6D 60
Shelley Dr. DA16: Well 1J 109
Shelley Gdns. HA0: Wemb . . .2C 44
Shelley Ho. E2 . . . . .3J 69
(off Cornwall Av.)
SE17 . . . . .5C 86
(off Browning St.)
SW1 . . . . .7B 172
(off Churchill Gdns.)
Shelley Rd. NW10 . . . . .1K 63
Shelley Way SW19 . . . . .6B 120
Shellness Rd. E5 . . . . .5H 51
Shell Rd. SE13 . . . . .3D 106
Shellwood Rd. SW11 . . . . . .2D 102
Shelmerdine Cl. E3 . . . . .5C 70
Shelson Av. TW13: Felt 3H 113
Shelton Rd. SW19 . . . . .1J 137
Shelton St. WC2 . . .6J 67 (1E 166)
(not continuous)
Shene Ho. EC1 . . . . .5J 161
(off Bourne Est.)

A-Z London 339

Shenfield Ho.—Short Path

Shenfield Ho. *SE18* *1B 108*
(*off Portway Gdns.*)
Shenfield Rd. IG8: Wfd G 7E 20
Shenfield St. N1 . . . 2E 68 (1H 163)
(not continuous)
Shenley Av. HA4: Ruis 2H 41
Shenley Rd. SE5 . . . . 1E 104
TW5: Houn 1C 96
Shenstone W5 . . . . 1C 80
Shenstone Cl. DA1: Cray . . . 4K 111
Shepherd Cl. TW13: Felt . . . 4C 114
W1 . . . . *2G 165*
(*off Lees Pl.*)
Shepherdess Pl.
N1 . . . . 3C 68 (1D 162)
Shepherdess Wlk.
N1 . . . . 2C 68 (1D 162)
Shepherd Ho. *E14* *6D 70*
(*off Annabel Cl.*)
Shepherd Mkt.
W1 . . . . 1F 85 (4J 165)
SHEPHERD'S BUSH **2E 82**
Shepherd's Bush Grn.
W12 . . . . 2E 82
Shepherd's Bush Mkt.
W12 . . . . 2E 82
(not continuous)
Shepherd's Bush Pl. W12 . . . . 2F 83
Shepherd's Bush Rd. W6 . . . . 4E 82
Shepherds Cl. HA7: Stan 5G 11
N6 . . . . 6F 31
RM6: Chad H 5D 38
TW17: Shep 6D 130
Shepherds Ct. *W12* *2F 83*
(*off Shepherd's Bush Grn.*)
Shepherds Grn.
BR7: Chst 7H 127
Shepherd's Hill N6 . . . . 6F 31
Shepherds La. E9 . . . . 6K 51
Shepherds Leas SE9 . . . . . 4G 109
Shepherds Ley SE28 . . . . 1J 91
Shepherds Path *NW3* *5B 48*
(*off Lyndhurst Rd.*)
UB5: N'olt *6C 42*
(*off Arnold Rd.*)
Shepherds Pl.
W1 . . . . 7E 66 (2G 165)
Shepherd St. W1 . . . 1F 85 (5J 165)
Shepherds Wlk. NW2 . . . . 2C 46
NW3 . . . . 5B 48
(not continuous)
WD23: Bush 2C 10
Shepherds Way
CR2: S Croy 7K 153
Shepiston La. UB3: Hayes . . . 4D 76
Shepley Cl. SM5: Cars 3E 150
Sheppard Cl. EN1: Enf 1C 8
KT1: King T 4E 134
Sheppard Dr. SE16 . . . . 5H 87
Sheppard Ho. *E2* *2G 69*
(*off Warner Pl.*)
SW2 . . . . 1A 122
Sheppards Coll.
BR1: Brom *1J 143*
(*off London Rd.*)
Sheppard St. E16 . . . . 4H 71
SHEPPERTON **6E 130**
Shepperton Bus. Pk.
TW17: Shep 5E 130
Shepperton Ct.
TW17: Shep 6D 130
Shepperton Ct. Dr.
TW17: Shep 5D 130
Shepperton Film Studios
. . . . ***3B 130***
SHEPPERTON GREEN **4C 130**
Shepperton Rd.
BR5: Orp 6G 145
N1 . . . . 1C 68
TW18: Staines 4A 130
Sheppey Gdns. RM9: Dag . . . 7C 56
Sheppey Rd. RM9: Dag 7B 56
Sheppey Wlk. *N1* *7C 50*
(*off Church Rd.*)
Shepton Ho's. *E2* *3J 69*
(*off Welwyn St.*)
Sherard Ct. N7 . . . . 3J 49
Sherard Ho. *E9* *7J 51*
(*off Frampton Pk. Rd.*)
Sherard Rd. SE9 . . . . 5C 108
Sheraton Bus. Cen.
UB6: G'frd 2C 62
Sheraton Ho. *SW1* *7K 171*
(*off Churchill Gdns.*)
Sheraton St. W1 . . . 6H 67 (1C 166)
Sherborne Av. EN3: Enf 2D 8
UB2: S'hall 4E 78
Sherborne Cl. UB4: Hayes . . . 6A 60
Sherborne Cres.
SM5: Cars 7C 138
Sherborne Gdns. NW9 . . . . . . 3G 27
TW17: Shep 7G 131
W13 . . . . 5B 62
Sherborne Ho. SW1 . . . . 5F 85
SW8 . . . . *7K 85*
(*off Bolney St.*)
Sherborne La.
EC4 . . . . 7D 68 (2E 168)
Sherborne Rd. BR5: Orp . . . 4K 145
KT9: Chess 5E 146
SM3: Sutt 2J 149
TW14: Felt 1F 113
(not continuous)
Sherborne St. N1 . . . . 1D 68
Sherboro Rd. N15 . . . . 6F 33
Sherbourne Ct.
SM2: Sutt 6A 150
Sherbourne Pl. HA7: Stan 6F 11
Sherbrooke Cl. DA6: Bex . . . 4G 111
Sherbrooke Ho. *E2* *2J 69*
(*off Bonner Rd.*)
Sherbrooke Rd. SW6 . . . . 7G 83
Sherbrook Gdns. N21 . . . . 7G 7
Shere Cl. KT9: Chess 5D 146
Sheredan Rd. E4 . . . . 5A 20
Shere Ho. SE1 . . . . 7E 168
Shere Rd. IG2: Ilf 5E 36
Sherfield Cl.
KT3: N Mald 4H 135
Sherfield Gdns. SW15 . . . . . 6B 100
Sheridan Bldgs. *WC2* *1F 167*
(*off Martlett Ct.*)
Sheridan Cl. UB10: Uxb 4E 58
Sheridan Ct. *CR0: Croy* *4E 152*
(*off Coombe Rd.*)
HA1: Harr 6H 25
NW6 . . . . *7A 48*
(*off Belsize Rd.*)
TW4: Houn 5C 96
UB5: N'olt 5F 43
W7 . . . . *7K 61*
(*off Milton Rd.*)
Sheridan Cres. BR7: Chst . . . 2F 145
Sheridan Gdns. HA3: Harr . . . 6D 26
Sheridan Ho. *E1* *6J 69*
(*off Tarling St.*)
SE11 . . . . *4K 173*
(*off Wincott St.*)
Sheridan Lodge
BR2: Short *4A 144*
(*off Homesdale Rd.*)
Sheridan M. E11 . . . . 6K 35
Sheridan Pl. SW13 . . . . 3B 100
TW12: Hamp 1F 133
Sheridan Rd. DA7: Bex 3E 110
DA17: Belv 4G 93
E7 . . . . 3H 53
E12 . . . . 5C 54
SW19 . . . . 1H 137
TW10: Rich 3C 116
Sheridan St. E1 . . . . 6H 69
Sheridan Ter. UB5: N'olt 5F 43
Sheridan Wlk. NW11 . . . . 6J 29
SM5: Cars 5D 150
Sheridan Way BR3: Beck . . . 1B 142
Sheriden Pl. HA1: Harr 7J 25
Sheringham NW8 . . . . 1B 66
Sheringham Av. E12 . . . . 4D 54
N14 . . . . 5C 6
RM7: Rom 6J 39
TW2: Twick 1D 114
TW13: Felt 3J 113
Sheringham Ct. EN2: Enf 3G 7
TW13: Felt *3J 113*
(*off Sheringham Av.*)
Sheringham Dr.
IG11: Bark 5K 55
Sheringham Ho. NW1 . . . . . 5C 158
Sheringham Rd. N7 . . . . 6K 49
SE20 . . . . 3J 141
Sheringham Twr.
UB1: S'hall 7F 61
Sherington Av. HA5: Pinn 7A 10
Sherington Rd. SE7 . . . . 6K 89
Sherland Rd. TW1: Twick . . . 1K 115
Sherlock Ct. *NW8* *1B 66*
(*off Dorman Way*)
Sherlock Holmes Mus. ***4F 159***
Sherlock M. W1 . . . 5E 66 (5G 159)
Sherman Gdns.
RM6: Chad H 6C 38
Sherman Rd. BR1: Brom . . . 1J 143
Shernhall St. E17 . . . . 3E 34
Sherrard Rd. E7 . . . . 6A 54
E12 . . . . 6A 54
Sherrards Way EN5: Barn 5D 4
Sherren Ho. E1 . . . . 4J 69
Sherrick Grn. Rd. NW10 . . . . 5D 46
Sherriff Rd. NW6 . . . . 6J 47
Sherringham Av. N17 . . . . . . 2G 33
Sherrin Rd. E10 . . . . 4D 52
Sherrock Gdns. NW4 . . . . 4C 28
Sherry M. IG11: Bark 7H 55
Sherston Ct. *SE17* *4B 86*
(*off Newington Butts*)
WC1 . . . . 2J 161
Sherwin Ho. SE11 . . . . 7J 173
Sherwin Rd. SE14 . . . . 1K 105
Sherwood NW6 . . . . 7G 47
Sherwood Av. E18 . . . . 3K 35
HA4: Ruis 6G 23
SW16 . . . . 7H 121
UB4: Hayes 4K 59
UB6: G'frd 6J 43
Sherwood Cl. DA5: Bexl 6C 110
E17 . . . . 2B 34
SW13 . . . . 3D 100
W13 . . . . 1B 80
Sherwood Ct.
CR2: S Croy *5C 152*
(*off Nottingham Rd.*)
HA2: Harr 2F 43
SW11 . . . . 3A 102
W1 . . . . *6E 158*
(*off Bryanston Pl.*)
Sherwood Gdns. E14 . . . . 4C 88
IG11: Bark 7H 55
SE16 . . . . 5G 87
Sherwood Pk. Av.
DA15: Sidc 7A 110
Sherwood Pk. Rd.
CR4: Mitc 4G 139
SM1: Sutt 5J 149
Sherwood Rd. CR0: Croy . . . 7H 141
DA16: Well 2J 109
HA2: Harr 2G 43
IG6: Ilf 4H 37
NW4 . . . . 3E 28
SW19 . . . . 7H 119
TW12: Hamp 5G 115
Sherwood St. N20 . . . . 3G 15
W1 . . . . 7G 67 (2B 166)
Sherwood Ter. N20 . . . . 3G 15
Sherwood Way
BR4: W W'ck 2E 154
Shetland Rd. E3 . . . . 2B 70
Shield Dr. TW8: Bford 6A 80
Shieldhall St. SE2 . . . . 4C 92
Shield Rd. TW15: Ashf 4E 112
Shifford Path SE23 . . . . 3K 123
Shillaker Ct. W3 . . . . 1B 82
Shillibeer Pl. W1 . . . . 6D 158
Shillingford St. N1 . . . . 7B 50
Shilling Pl. W7 . . . . 2A 80
Shillingstone Ho. *W14* *3G 83*
(*off Russell Rd.*)
Shinfield St. W12 . . . . 6E 64
Shingle End TW8: Bford 7C 80
Shinglewell Rd.
DA8: Erith 7G 93
Shinners Cl. SE25 . . . . 5G 141
Ship All. W4 . . . . 6G 81
Ship & Mermaid Row
SE1 . . . . 2D 86 (6F 169)
Shipka Rd. SW12 . . . . 1F 121
Shiplake Ho. *E2* *2J 163*
(*off Arnold Cir.*)
Ship La. SW14 . . . . 3J 99
Shipman Rd. E16 . . . . 6K 71
SE23 . . . . 2K 123
Ship St. SE8 . . . . 1C 106
Ship Tavern Pas.
EC3 . . . . 7E 68 (2G 169)
Shipton Cl. RM8: Dag 3D 56
Shipton Ho. *E2* *1K 163*
(*off Shipton St.*)
Shipton Rd. UB10: Uxb 4B 40
Shipton St. E2 . . . . . 2F 69 (1K 163)
Shipway Ter. N16 . . . . 3F 51
Shipwright Rd. SE16 . . . . 2A 88
Shipwright Yd.
SE1 . . . . 1E 86 (5G 169)
Ship Yd. E14 . . . . 5D 88
Shirburn Cl. SE23 . . . . 7J 105
Shirebrook Rd. SE3 . . . . 3B 108
Shire Ct. DA18: Erith 3D 92
KT17: Eps 7B 148
Shirehall Cl. NW4 . . . . 6F 29
Shirehall Gdns. NW4 . . . . 6F 29
Shirehall La. NW4 . . . . 6F 29
Shirehall Pk. NW4 . . . . 5F 29
Shire Horse Way TW7: Isle . . 3K 97
Shire La. BR2: Kes 7C 156
BR6: Orp 7C 156
(not continuous)
Shire M. TW2: Twick 6G 97
Shire Pl. SW18 . . . . 7A 102
TW8: Bford 7C 80
Shires, The TW10: Rich 4E 116
Shirland M. W9 . . . . 3H 65
Shirland Rd. W9 . . . . 3H 65
Shirlbutt St. E14 . . . . 7D 70
SHIRLEY **2J 153**
Shirley Av. CR0: Croy 1J 153
DA5: Bexl 7D 110
SM1: Sutt 4B 150
Shirley Chu. Rd.
CR0: Croy 3J 153
Shirley Cl. TW3: Houn 5G 97
Shirley Ct. SW16 . . . . 7J 121
Shirley Cres. BR3: Beck 4A 142
Shirley Dr. TW3: Houn 5G 97
Shirley Gdns. IG11: Bark 6J 55
W7 . . . . 1K 79
Shirley Gro. N9 . . . . 7D 8
SW11 . . . . 3E 102
Shirley Hgts. SM6: Wall 7G 151
Shirley Hills Rd.
CR0: Croy 5J 153
Shirley Ho. *SE5* *7D 86*
(*off Picton St.*)
Shirley Ho. Dr. SE7 . . . . 7A 90
SHIRLEY OAKS **1K 153**
Shirley Oaks Rd.
CR0: Croy 1K 153
Shirley Pk. CR0: Croy 2J 153
Shirley Pk. Rd.
CR0: Croy 1H 153
Shirley Rd. CR0: Croy 7H 141
DA15: Sidc 3J 127
E15 . . . . 7G 53
EN2: Enf 3H 7
SM6: Wall 7G 151
W4 . . . . 2K 81
Shirleys Cl. E17 . . . . 5D 34
Shirley St. E16 . . . . 6H 71
Shirley Way CR0: Croy 3A 154
Shirley Windmill ***3J 153***
Shirlock Rd. NW3 . . . . 4D 48
Shobden Rd. N17 . . . . 1D 32
Shobroke Cl. NW2 . . . . 3E 46
Shoebury Rd. E6 . . . . 7D 54
Shoelands Ct. NW9 . . . . 3K 27
Shoe La. EC4 . . . . . . 6A 68 (7K 161)
Shooters Av. HA3: Harr 4C 26
SHOOTERS HILL **1E 108**
Shooters Hill DA16: Well . . . 1D 108
SE18: Well 1D 108
Shooters Hill Rd. SE3 . . . . . . 1F 107
SE10 . . . . 1F 107
SE18 . . . . 7A 90
Shooters Rd. EN2: Enf 1G 7
Shoot Up Hill NW2 . . . . 5G 47
Shop. Hall, The E6 . . . . 1C 72
Shore Bus. Cen. E9 . . . . 7J 51
Shore Cl. TW12: Hamp 6C 114
TW14: Felt 7J 95
Shorediche Cl. UB10: Uxb . . . 3B 40
SHOREDITCH . . . . . **3E 68 (1G 163)**
Shoreditch Ct. *E8* *7F 51*
(*off Queensbridge Rd.*)
Shoreditch High St.
E1 . . . . 4E 68 (4H 163)
Shore Gro. TW13: Felt 2D 114
Shoreham Cl. CR0: Croy 6J 141
DA5: Bexl 1D 128
SW18 . . . . 5K 101
Shoreham Rd. E.
TW6: Houn 5A 94
Shoreham Rd. W.
TW6: Houn 5A 94
Shoreham Way
BR2: Short 6J 143
Shore Ho. SW8 . . . . 3F 103
Shore M. *E9* *7J 51*
(*off Shore Rd.*)
Shore Pl. E9 . . . . 7J 51
Shore Rd. E9 . . . . 7J 51
Shorncliffe Rd. SE1 . . . . 5F 87
Shorndean St. SE6 . . . . 1E 124
Shorne Cl. DA15: Sidc 6B 110
Shornefield Cl.
BR1: Brom 3E 144
Shornells Way SE2 . . . . 4C 92
Shorrold's Rd. SW6 . . . . 7H 83
Shortcroft Mead Ct.
NW10 . . . . *5C 46*
(*off Cooper Rd.*)
Shortcroft Rd. KT17: Eps . . . 7B 148
Shortcrofts Rd. RM9: Dag 6F 57
Shorter St. EC3 . . . . 7F 69 (2K 169)
Short Ga. N12 . . . . 4C 14
Short Hedges TW3: Houn 1E 96
Short Hill HA1: Harr 1J 43
SHORTLANDS **2G 143**
Shortlands UB3: Hayes 6F 77
W6 . . . . 4F 83
Shortlands Cl.
DA17: Belv 3F 93
N18 . . . . 3J 17
Shortlands Gdns.
BR2: Short 2G 143
Shortlands Gro.
BR2: Short 3F 143
Shortlands Rd.
BR2: Short 3F 143
E10 . . . . 7D 34
KT2: King T 7F 117
Short La. TW19: Staines 7B 94
Short Path SE18 . . . . 6F 91

340 A-Z London

Siviter Way—South Beddington

Siviter Way RM10: Dag 7H **57**
Siward Rd. BR2: Short 3K **143**
N17 . . . . 1D **32**
SW17 . . . . 3A **120**
Six Acres Est. N4 . . . . 2K **49**
Six Bridges Ind. Est. SE1 . . . . 5G **87**
Sixth Av. E12 . . . . 4D **54**
UB3: Hayes 1H **77**
W10 . . . . 3G **65**
Sixth Cross Rd.
TW2: Twick 3G **115**
Skardu Rd. NW2 . . . . 5G **47**
Skeena Hill SW18 . . . . 7G **101**
Skeffington Rd. E6 . . . . 1D **72**
Skeffington St. SE18 . . . . 3G **91**
Skeggs Ho. *E14 . . . . 3E **88***
(off Glengall St.)
Skegness Ho. *N7 . . . . 7K **49***
(off Sutterton St.)
Skelbrook St. SW18 . . . . 2A **120**
Skelgill Rd. SW15 . . . . 4H **101**
Skelley Rd. E15 . . . . 7H **53**
Skelton Cl. E8 . . . . 6F **51**
Skelton Rd. E7 . . . . 6J **53**
Skelton's La. E10 . . . . 7D **34**
Skelwith Rd. W6 . . . . 6E **82**
Skenfrith Ho. *SE15 . . . . 6H **87***
(off Commercial Way)
Skerne Rd. KT2: King T 1D **134**
Skerne Wlk. *KT2: King T 1D **134***
(off Skerne Rd.)
Sketchley Gdns. SE16 . . . . 5K **87**
Sketty Rd. EN1: Enf 3A **8**
Skiers St. E15 . . . . 1G **71**
Skiffington Cl. SW2 . . . . 1A **122**
Skillen Lodge HA5: Pinn 1B **24**
Skinner Pl. SW1 . . . . 4G **171**
Skinners La.
EC4 . . . . 7C **68** (2D **168**)
TW5: Houn 1F **97**
Skinner's Row SE10 . . . . 1D **106**
Skinner St. EC1 . . . . 3A **68** (2A **162**)
Skip La. UB9: Uxb 1A **40**
Skipper Ct. IG11: Bark 1G **73**
Skipsey Av. E6 . . . . 3D **72**
Skipton Cl. N11 . . . . 6K **15**
Skipton Dr. UB3: Hayes 3E **76**
Skipton Ho. SE4 . . . . 4A **106**
Skipwith Ho. *EC1 . . . . 5J **161***
(off Bourne Est.)
Skipworth Rd. E9 . . . . 1J **69**
Skua Ct. *SE8 . . . . 6B **88***
(off Dorking Cl.)
Skyline Ct. *CR0: Croy 3D **152***
(off Park La.)
Skyline Plaza Bldg. *E1 . . . . 6G **69***
(off Commercial Rd.)
Skylines E14 . . . . 2E **88**
Sky Peals Rd. IG8: Wfd G 7A **20**
Skyview Apartments
*CR0: Croy 2C **152***
(off Park St.)
Sladebrook Rd. SE3 . . . . 3B **108**
Slade Ct. EN5: Barn 3E **4**
Sladedale Rd. SE18 . . . . 5J **91**
Slade Ho. TW4: Houn 6D **96**
Sladen Pl. E5 . . . . 4H **51**
Slades Cl. EN2: Enf 3F **7**
Slades Gdns. EN2: Enf 2F **7**
Slades Hill EN2: Enf 3F **7**
Slades Ri. EN2: Enf 3F **7**
Slade, The SE18 . . . . 6J **91**
Slade Twr. *E10 . . . . 2C **52***
(off Leyton Grange Est.)
Slade Wlk. SE17 . . . . 6B **86**
Slagrove Pl. SE4 . . . . 5C **106**
Slaidburn St. SW10 . . . . 6A **84**
Slaithwaite Rd. SE13 . . . . 4E **106**
Slaney Ct. NW10 . . . . 7E **46**
Slaney Pl. N7 . . . . 5A **50**
Slater Cl. SE18 . . . . 5E **90**
Slatter NW9 . . . . 7G **13**
Slattery Rd. TW13: Felt 1B **114**
Sleaford Ind. Est. SW8 . . . . 7G **85**
Sleaford St. SW8 . . . . 7G **85**
Sledmere Ct. TW14: Felt 1G **113**
Sleigh Ho. *E2 . . . . 3J **69***
(off Bacton St.)
Slievemore Cl. SW4 . . . . 3H **103**
Sligo Ho. *E1 . . . . 4K **69***
(off Beaumont Gro.)
Slindon Ct. N16 . . . . 3F **51**
Slingsby Pl. WC2 . . . . 7J **67** (2E **166**)
Slippers Pl. SE16 . . . . 3H **87**
Slipway Ho. *E14 . . . . 5D **88***
(off Burrells Wharf Sq.)
Sloane Av. SW3 . . . . 4C **84** (4D **170**)
Sloane Ct. E.
SW3 . . . . 5E **84** (5G **171**)
Sloane Ct. W.
SW3 . . . . 5E **84** (5G **171**)
Sloane Gdns.
SW1 . . . . 4E **84** (4G **171**)
Sloane Ho. *E9 . . . . 7J **51***
(off Loddiges Rd.)
Sloane Sq. SW1 . . . . 4D **84** (4G **171**)
Sloane St. SW1 . . . . 2D **84** (7F **165**)
Sloane Ter. SW1 . . . . 4E **84** (3G **171**)
Sloane Ter. Mans. SW1 . . . . 4E **84**
Sloane Wlk. CR0: Croy 6B **142**
Slocum Cl. SE28 . . . . 7C **74**
Sloman Ho. *W10 . . . . 3G **65***
(off Beethoven St.)
Slough La. NW9 . . . . 5J **27**
Sly St. E1 . . . . 6H **69**
Smaldon Cl. UB7: W Dray 3C **76**
Smallberry Av. TW7: Isle 2K **97**
Smallbrook M.
W2 . . . . 6B **66** (1A **164**)
Smalley Cl. N16 . . . . 3F **51**
Smalley Rd. Est. *N16 . . . . 3F **51***
(off Smalley Cl.)
Smallwood Rd. SW17 . . . . 4B **120**
Smarden Cl. DA17: Belv 5G **93**
Smarden Gro. SE9 . . . . 4D **126**
Smart's Pl. N18 . . . . 5B **18**
WC2 . . . . 6J **67** (7F **161**)
Smart St. E2 . . . . 3K **69**
Smeaton Cl. KT9: Chess 6D **146**
Smeaton Ct. SE1 . . . . 3C **86**
Smeaton Rd. IG8: Wfd G 5J **21**
SW18 . . . . 7J **101**
Smeaton St. E1 . . . . 1H **87**
Smedley St. SW8 . . . . 2H **103**
Smeed Rd. E3 . . . . 7C **52**
Smiles Pl. SE13 . . . . 2E **106**
Smith Cl. SE16 . . . . 1K **87**
Smithfield St.
EC1 . . . . 5B **68** (6A **162**)
Smith Hill TW8: Bford 6E **80**
Smithies Ct. E15 . . . . 5E **52**
Smithies Rd. SE2 . . . . 4B **92**
Smith's Ct. W1 . . . . 2B **166**
Smithson Rd. N17 . . . . 1D **32**
Smiths Point *E13 . . . . 1J **71***
(off Brooks Rd.)
Smith Sq. SW1 . . . . 3J **85** (2E **172**)
Smith St. KT5: Surb 6F **135**
SW3 . . . . 5D **84** (5E **170**)
Smiths Yd. *CR0: Croy 3C **152***
(off St George's Wlk.)
SW18 . . . . 2A **120**
Smith Ter. SW3 . . . . 5D **84** (6C **170**)
Smithwood Cl. SW19 . . . . 1G **119**
Smithy St. E1 . . . . 5J **69**
Smock Wlk. CR0: Croy 6C **140**
Smokehouse Yd. *EC1 . . . . 5B **162***
(off St John St.)
Smoothfield TW3: Houn 4E **96**
Smugglers Way SW18 . . . . 4K **101**
Smyrk's Rd. SE17 . . . . 5E **86**
Smyrna Rd. NW6 . . . . 7J **47**
Smythe St. E14 . . . . 7D **70**
Snakes La. EN4: Barn 3A **6**
Snakes La. E.
IG8: Buck H, Wfd G 6F **21**
Snakes La. W. IG8: Wfd G 5D **20**
SNARESBROOK **5J 35**
Snaresbrook Dr. HA7: Stan 4J **11**
Snaresbrook Hall E18 . . . . 4J **35**
Snaresbrook Rd. E11 . . . . 4G **35**
Snarsgate St. W10 . . . . 5E **64**
Sneath Av. NW11 . . . . 7H **29**
Snells Pk. N18 . . . . 6A **18**
Sneyd Rd. NW2 . . . . 5E **46**
Snowberry Cl. E15 . . . . 4F **53**
Snowbury Rd. SW6 . . . . 2K **101**
Snowden Av. UB10: Uxb 2D **58**
Snowden Dr. NW9 . . . . 6A **28**
Snowden St. EC2 . . . . 4E **68** (4G **163**)
Snowdon Cres.
UB3: Hayes 3E **76**
Snowdon Rd. TW6: Houn 6E **94**
Snowdown Cl. SE20 . . . . 1J **141**
Snowdrop Cl.
TW12: Hamp 6E **114**
Snow Hill EC1 . . . . 5B **68** (6A **162**)
Snow Hill Ct.
EC1 . . . . 6B **68** (7B **162**)
(not continuous)
Snowman Ho. NW6 . . . . 1K **65**
Snowsfields SE1 . . . . 2D **86** (6F **169**)
Snowshill Rd. E12 . . . . 5C **54**
Snowy Fielder Waye
TW7: Isle 2B **98**
Soames St. SE15 . . . . 3F **105**
Soames Wlk.
KT3: N Mald 1A **136**
Soane Cl. W5 . . . . 2D **80**
Soane Ct. *NW1 . . . . 7G **49***
(off St Pancras Way)
Sobraon Ho. *KT2: King T 7F **117***
(off Elm Rd.)
Socket La. BR2: Short 6K **143**
SOHO . . . . **6G 67 (1C 166)**
Soho Sq. W1 . . . . 6H **67** (7C **160**)
Soho St. W1 . . . . 6H **67** (7C **160**)
Soho Theatre & Writers Cen.
*. . . . **1C 166***
(off Dean St.)
Sojourner Truth Cl. E8 . . . . 6H **51**
Solander Gdns. E1 . . . . 7J **69**
Solar Ct. N3 . . . . 7E **14**
Solar Ho. E6 . . . . 5E **72**
Solarium Ct. *SE1 . . . . 4F **87***
(off Alscot Rd.)
Soldene Ct. *N7 . . . . 5K **49***
(off George's Rd.)
Solebay St. E1 . . . . 4A **70**
Solent Ho. *E1 . . . . 5A **70***
(off Ben Jonson Rd.)
Solent Ri. E13 . . . . 3J **71**
Solent Rd. NW6 . . . . 5J **47**
TW6: Houn 6B **94**
Soley M. WC1 . . . . 3A **68** (1J **161**)
Solna Av. SW15 . . . . 5E **100**
Solna Rd. N21 . . . . 1J **17**
Solomon Av. N9 . . . . 4B **18**
Solomon's Pas. SE15 . . . . 4H **105**
Solon New Rd. SW4 . . . . 4J **103**
Solon New Rd. Est. SW4 . . . . 4J **103**
Solon Rd. SW2 . . . . 4J **103**
Solway Cl. *E8 . . . . 6F **51***
(off Queensbridge Rd.)
TW4: Houn 3C **96**
Solway Ho. *E1 . . . . 4K **69***
(off Ernest St.)
Solway Rd. N22 . . . . 1B **32**
SE22 . . . . 4G **105**
Somaford Gro. EN4: Barn 6G **5**
Somali Rd. NW2 . . . . 5H **47**
Somerby Rd. IG11: Bark 7H **55**
Somercoates Cl. EN4: Barn 3H **5**
Somer Ct. *SW6 . . . . 6J **83***
(off Anselm Rd.)
Somerfield Ho. SE16 . . . . 5K **87**
Somerfield Rd. N4 . . . . 2B **50**
(not continuous)
Somerford Cl. HA5: Pinn 4J **23**
Somerford Gro. N16 . . . . 4F **51**
N17 . . . . 7B **18**
(not continuous)
Somerford Gro. Est. N16 . . . . 4F **51**
Somerford St. E1 . . . . 4H **69**
Somerford Way SE16 . . . . 2A **88**
Somerhill Av. DA15: Sidc 7B **110**
Somerhill Rd.
DA16: Well 2B **110**
Somerleyton Pas. SW9 . . . . 4B **104**
Somerleyton Rd. SW9 . . . . 4A **104**
Somersby Gdns. IG4: Ilf 5D **36**
Somers Cl. NW1 . . . . 2H **67**
Somers Cres.
W2 . . . . 6C **66** (1C **164**)
Somerset Av. DA16: Well 5K **109**
KT9: Chess 4D **146**
SW20 . . . . 2D **136**
Somerset Cl. IG8: Wfd G 1J **35**
KT3: N Mald 6A **136**
N17 . . . . 2D **32**
Somerset Ct. IG9: Buck H 2F **21**
*W7 . . . . 6K **61***
(off Copley Cl.)
Somerset Est. SW11 . . . . 1B **102**
Somerset Gdns. N6 . . . . 7E **30**
N17 . . . . 7K **17**
SE13 . . . . 2D **106**
SW16 . . . . 3K **139**
TW11: Tedd 5J **115**
Somerset Hall N17 . . . . 7K **17**
Somerset House . . . 7K 67 (2G 167)
Somerset Lodge
TW8: Bford 6D **80**
Somerset Rd. E17 . . . . 5C **34**
EN5: Barn 5E **4**
HA1: Harr 5G **25**
KT1: King T 2F **135**
N17 . . . . 3F **33**
N18 . . . . 5A **18**
NW4 . . . . 4E **28**
SW19 . . . . 3F **119**
TW8: Bford 6C **80**
TW11: Tedd 5J **115**
UB1: S'hall 5D **60**
W4 . . . . 3K **81**
W13 . . . . 1B **80**
Somerset Sq. W14 . . . . 2G **83**
Somerset Waye
TW5: Houn 6C **78**
Somersham Rd.
DA7: Bex 2E **110**
Somers Pl. SW2 . . . . 7K **103**
Somers Rd. E17 . . . . 4B **34**
SW2 . . . . 6K **103**
SOMERS TOWN . . . 3H 67 (1C 160)
Somerton Av. TW9: Rich 3H **99**
Somerton Rd. NW2 . . . . 3G **47**
SE15 . . . . 4H **105**
Somertrees Av. SE12 . . . . 2K **125**
Somervell Rd. HA2: Harr 5D **42**
Somerville Av. SW13 . . . . 6D **82**
Somerville Point SE16 . . . . 2B **88**
Somerville Rd.
RM6: Chad H 6C **38**
SE20 . . . . 7K **123**
Sonderburg Rd. N7 . . . . 2K **49**
Sondes St. SE17 . . . . 6D **86**
Sonia Cl. HA1: Harr 6K **25**
HA8: Edg 7A **12**
Sonia Gdns. N12 . . . . 4F **15**
NW10 . . . . 4B **46**
TW5: Houn 7E **78**
Sonning Gdns.
TW12: Hamp 6C **114**
Sonning Ho. *E2 . . . . 2J **163***
(off Swanfield St.)
Sonning Rd. SE25 . . . . 6G **141**
Sontan Ct. TW2: Twick 1H **115**
Soper Cl. E4 . . . . 5G **19**
SE23 . . . . 1K **123**
Soper M. EN3: Enf 1H **9**
Sophia Cl. N7 . . . . 6K **49**
Sophia Ho. *W6 . . . . 5E **82***
(off Queen Caroline St.)
Sophia Rd. E10 . . . . 1D **52**
E16 . . . . 6K **71**
Sophia Sq. *SE16 . . . . 7A **70***
(off Sovereign Cres.)
Sopwith NW9 . . . . 7G **13**
Sopwith Av. KT9: Chess 5E **146**
Sopwith Cl. KT2: King T 5F **117**
Sopwith Rd. TW5: Houn 7A **78**
Sopwith Way KT2: King T 1E **134**
SW8 . . . . 7F **85**
Sorensen Ct. *E10 . . . . 2D **52***
(off Leyton Grange Est.)
Sorrel Cl. SE28 . . . . 1A **92**
Sorrel Gdns. E6 . . . . 5C **72**
Sorrel La. E14 . . . . 6F **71**
Sorrell Cl. SE14 . . . . 7A **88**
SW9 . . . . 2A **104**
Sorrento Rd. SM1: Sutt 3J **149**
Sotheby Rd. N5 . . . . 3B **50**
Sotheran Cl. E8 . . . . 1G **69**
Sotherby Lodge *E2 . . . . 2J **69***
(off Sewardstone Rd.)
Sotheron Rd. SW6 . . . . 7K **83**
Soudan Rd. SW11 . . . . 1D **102**
Souldern Rd. W14 . . . . 3F **83**
Sth. Access Rd. E17 . . . . 7A **34**
Southacre *W2 . . . . 1C **164***
(off Hyde Pk. Cres.)
Southacre Way HA5: Pinn 1A **24**
SOUTH ACTON **2J 81**
Sth. Africa Rd. W12 . . . . 1D **82**
SOUTHALL **1D 78**
Southall Ct. UB1: S'hall 7D **60**
Southall Ent. Cen.
UB2: S'hall 2E **78**
SOUTHALL GREEN **3C 78**
Southall La. TW5: Houn 6K **77**
UB2: S'hall 6K **77**
Southall Pl. SE1 . . . . 2D **86** (7E **168**)
Southampton Bldgs.
WC2 . . . . 5A **68** (6J **161**)
Southampton Gdns.
CR4: Mitc 5J **139**
Southampton M. E16 . . . . 1K **89**
Southampton Pl.
WC1 . . . . 5J **67** (6F **161**)
Southampton Rd. NW5 . . . . 5D **48**
TW6: Houn 6A **94**
Southampton Row
WC1 . . . . 5J **67** (5F **161**)
Southampton St.
WC2 . . . . 7J **67** (2F **167**)
Southampton Way SE5 . . . . 7D **86**
TW6: Houn 6A **94**
Southam St. W10 . . . . 4G **65**
Sth. Audley St.
W1 . . . . 7E **66** (3H **165**)
South Av. E4 . . . . 7J **9**
N2 . . . . 4K **29**
NW10 . . . . 4E **64**
SM5: Cars 7E **150**
TW9: Rich 2G **99**
UB1: S'hall 7D **60**
South Av. Gdns.
UB1: S'hall 7D **60**
South Bank KT6: Surb 6E **134**
Southbank KT7: T Ditt 7B **134**
Sth. Bank Bus. Cen.
SW8 . . . . 6H **85** (7D **172**)
South Bank Cen.
*. . . . **1K 85 (4H 167)***
Sth. Bank Ter. KT6: Surb 6E **134**
South Bank University
*. . . . **3B 86 (7B 168)***
SOUTH BARNET **1K 15**
SOUTH BEDDINGTON **6H 151**

Sth. Western Rd.—Spring Grove

Sth. Western Rd.
TW1: Twick 6A **98**
Sth. W. India Dock Entrance
E14 . . . . .2E **88**
South West Middlesex Crematorium
TW13: Felt 1C **114**
Southwest Rd. E11 . . . . .1F **53**
Sth. Wharf Rd.
W2 . . . . .6B **66** (7A **158**)
Southwick M.
W2 . . . . .6B **66** (7B **158**)
Southwick Pl.
W2 . . . . .6C **66** (1C **164**)
Southwick St.
W2 . . . . .6C **66** (7C **158**)
Southwick Yd. W2 . . . . .1C **164**
SOUTH WIMBLEDON **6K 119**
Southwold Dr. IG11: Bark 5A **56**
Southwold Mans. *W9* *3J 65*
(off Widley Rd.)
Southwold Rd. DA5: Bexl . . .6H **111**
E5 . . . . .2H **51**
Southwood Av.
KT2: King T 1J **135**
N6 . . . . .7F **31**
Southwood Cl.
BR1: Brom 4D **144**
KT4: Wor Pk 1F **149**
Southwood Ct. *EC1* *2A 162*
(off Wynyatt St.)
NW11 . . . . .5K **29**
Southwood Dr. KT5: Surb . . .7J **135**
SOUTH WOODFORD **2J 35**
Sth. Woodford to Barking Relief Rd.
E12 . . . . .4E **54**
IG4: Ilf 5B **36**
Southwood Gdns. IG2: Ilf 4F **37**
KT10: Esh 3A **146**
Southwood Hall N6 . . . . .6F **31**
Southwood Hgts. N6 . . . . .7F **31**
Southwood Ho. *W11* *7G 65*
(off Avondale Pk. Rd.)
Southwood La. N6 . . . . .1E **48**
Southwood Lawn Rd. N6 . . . .7E **30**
Southwood Mans. *N6* *6E 30*
(off Southwood La.)
Southwood Pk. N6 . . . . .7E **30**
Southwood Rd. SE9 . . . . . . .2F **127**
SE28 . . . . .1B **92**
Southwood Smith Ho. *E2* *3H 69*
(off Florida St.)
Southwood Smith St. N1 . . . .1B **68**
Sth. Worple Av. SW14 . . . . .3A **100**
Sth. Worple Way SW14 . . . . .3K **99**
Southwyck Ho. SW9 . . . . . . .4B **104**
Sovereign Bus. Cen.
EN3: Enf 3G **9**
Sovereign Cl. E1 . . . . .7H **69**
HA4: Ruis 1G **41**
W5 . . . . .5C **62**
Sovereign Ct.
CR2: S Croy *5C 152*
(off Warham Rd.)
HA6: Nwood 1J **23**
KT8: W Mole 4D **132**
TW3: Houn 3E **96**
Sovereign Cres. SE16 . . . . . .7A **70**
Sovereign Gro.
HA0: Wemb 3D **44**
Sovereign Ho. *E1* *4H 69*
(off Cambridge Heath Rd.)
SE18 . . . .*3D 90*
(off Leda Rd.)
Sovereign M. E2 . . . . .2F **69**
EN4: Barn 3J **5**
Sovereign Pk. NW10 . . . . . . .4H **63**
Sovereign Pk. Trad. Est.
NW10 . . . . .4H **63**
Sovereign Pl. HA1: Harr 5K **25**
Sovereign Rd. IG11: Bark 3C **74**
Sowerby Cl. SE9 . . . . .5C **108**
Space Waye TW14: Felt 5J **95**
Spa Cl. SE25 . . . . .1E **140**
Spa Ct. SW16 . . . . .4K **121**
Spafield St. EC1 . . .4A **68** (3J **161**)
Spa Grn. Est.
EC1 . . . . .3B **68** (1K **161**)
Spa Hill SE19 . . . . .1D **140**
Spalding Cl. NW7 . . . . .7F **13**
Spalding Ho. SE4 . . . . .4A **106**
Spalding Rd. NW4 . . . . .7E **28**
SW17 . . . . .5F **121**
Spanby Rd. E3 . . . . .4C **70**
Spaniards Cl. NW11 . . . . .1B **48**
Spaniards End NW3 . . . . .1A **48**
Spaniards Rd. NW3 . . . . .2A **48**
Spanish Pl. W1 . . . .6E **66** (7H **159**)
Spanish Rd. SW18 . . . . .5A **102**
Spanswick Lodge N15 . . . . . .4B **32**
Sparkbridge Rd. HA1: Harr . . .4J **25**
Sparke Ter. *E16* *6H 71*
(off Clarkson Rd.)
Sparkford Gdns. N11 . . . . . . .5K **15**
Sparks Cl. RM8: Dag 2D **56**
TW12: Hamp 6C **114**
W3 . . . . .6K **63**
Spa Rd. SE16 . . . . .3F **87**
Sparrick's Row
SE1 . . . . .2D **86** (6F **169**)
Sparrow Cl. TW12: Hamp . . .6C **114**
Sparrow Dr. BR5: Orp 7G **145**
Sparrow Farm Dr.
TW14: Felt 7A **96**
Sparrow Farm Rd.
KT17: Eps 4C **148**
Sparrow Grn. RM10: Dag 3H **57**
Sparrow Ho. *E1* *4J 69*
(off Cephas Av.)
Sparrows Herne
WD23: Bush 1A **10**
Sparrows La. SE9 . . . . .7G **109**
Sparrows Way
WD23: Bush 1B **10**
Sparsholt Cl. *IG11: Bark* *1J 73*
(off St John's Rd.)
Sparsholt Rd. IG11: Bark 1J **73**
N19 . . . . .1K **49**
Sparta St. SE10 . . . . .1E **106**
Speaker's Corner . . . .***7D 66 (2F 165)***
Speakers Ct. CR0: Croy 1D **152**
Speakman Ho. *SE4* *3A 106*
(off Arica Rd.)
Spearman Ho. *E14* *6C 70*
(off Up. North St.)
Spearman St. SE18 . . . . .6E **90**
Spear M. SW5 . . . . .4J **83**
Spearpoint Gdns. IG2: Ilf 5K **37**
Spears Rd. N19 . . . . .1J **49**
Speart La. TW5: Houn 7C **78**
Spectacle Works E13 . . . . . . .3A **72**
Spectrum Twr. *IG1: Ilf* *2G 55*
(off Hainault St.)
Spedan Cl. NW3 . . . . .3A **48**
Speechly M. E8 . . . . .5F **51**
Speed Highwalk *EC2* *5D 162*
(off Silk St.)
Speed Ho. EC2 . . . . .5D **162**
Speedway Ind. Est.
UB3: Hayes 2F **77**
Speedwell Ho. N12 . . . . .4E **14**
Speedwell St. SE8 . . . . .7C **88**
Speedy Pl. WC1 . . . . .2E **160**
Speer Rd. KT7: T Ditt 6K **133**
Speirs Cl. KT3: N Mald 6B **136**
Speke Hill SE9 . . . . .3D **126**
Speke Rd. CR7: Thor H 2D **140**
Speke's Monument . . . .***1A 84 (4A 164)***
Speldhurst Cl.
BR2: Short 5H **143**
Speldhurst Rd. E9 . . . . .7K **51**
W4 . . . . .3K **81**
Spellbrook Wlk. N1 . . . . .1C **68**
Spelman Ho. *E1* *6K 163*
(off Spelman St.)
Spelman St. E1 . . . .5G **69** (5K **163**)
(not continuous)
Spelthorne Gro.
TW16: Sun T 7H **113**
Spelthorne La.
TW15: Ashf 1E **130**
Spence Cl. SE16 . . . . .2B **88**
Spencer Av. N13 . . . . .6E **16**
UB4: Hayes 5J **59**
Spencer Cl. IG8: Wfd G 5F **21**
N3 . . . . .2J **29**
NW10 . . . . .3F **63**
Spencer Dr. N2 . . . . .6A **30**
Spencer Gdns. SE9 . . . . . . .5D **108**
SW14 . . . . .5J **99**
Spencer Hill SW19 . . . . .6G **119**
Spencer Hill Rd. SW19 . . . .7G **119**
Spencer Ho. ***5A 166***
Spencer Ho. NW4 . . . . .5D **28**
Spencer Mans. *W14* *6G 83*
(off Queen's Club Gdns.)
Spencer M. *SW9* *1K 103*
(off Sth. Lambeth Rd.)
W6 . . . . .6G **83**
SPENCER PARK **5B 102**
Spencer Pk. KT8: E Mos . . .5G **133**
SW18 . . . . .5B **102**
Spencer Pl. CR0: Croy 7D **140**
N1 . . . . .7B **50**
Spencer Ri. NW5 . . . . .4F **49**
Spencer Rd. BR1: Brom 7H **125**
CR2: S Croy 5E **152**
CR4: Mitc 3E **138**
(Commonside E.)
CR4: Mitc 7E **138**
(Wood St.)
E6 . . . . .1B **72**
E17 . . . . .2E **34**
HA0: Wemb 2C **44**
HA3: Harr 2J **25**
IG3: Ilf 1K **55**
KT8: E Mos 4G **133**
N8 . . . . .5K **31**
(not continuous)
N11 . . . . .4A **16**
N17 . . . . .1G **33**
RM13: Rain 3K **75**
SW18 . . . . .4B **102**
SW20 . . . . .1D **136**
TW2: Twick 3J **115**
TW7: Isle 1G **97**
W3 . . . . .1J **81**
W4 . . . . .7J **81**
Spencer St. EC1 . . .3B **68** (2A **162**)
UB2: S'hall 2B **78**
Spencer Wlk. *NW3* *4A 48*
(off Perrin's Ct.)
NW3 . . . . .4B **48**
(Hampstead High St.)
SW15 . . . . .4F **101**
Spenlow Ho. *SE16* *3G 87*
(off Jamaica Rd.)
Spenser Gro. N16 . . . . .5E **50**
Spenser M. SE21 . . . . .2D **122**
Spenser Rd. SE24 . . . . .5B **104**
Spenser St. SW1 . . .3G **85** (1B **172**)
Spensley Wlk. N16 . . . . .3D **50**
Speranza Rd. SE18 . . . . .5K **91**
Sperling Rd. N17 . . . . .2E **32**
Spert St. E14 . . . . .7A **70**
Speyside N14 . . . . .6B **6**
Spey St. E14 . . . . .5E **70**
Spey Way RM1: Rom 1K **39**
Spezia Rd. NW10 . . . . .2C **64**
Spice Ct. E1 . . . . .7G **69**
Spice Quay Hgts.
SE1 . . . . .1F **87** (5K **169**)
Spicer Cl. KT12: Walt T 6A **132**
SW9 . . . . .2B **104**
Spicer Ct. EN1: Enf 3K **7**
Spice's Yd. CR0: Croy 4C **152**
Spigurnell Rd. N17 . . . . .1D **32**
Spikes Bri. Rd.
UB1: S'hall 6C **60**
Spilsby Cl. NW9 . . . . .1A **28**
Spindle Cl. SE18 . . . . .3C **90**
Spindlewood Gdns.
CR0: Croy 4E **152**
Spindrift Av. E14 . . . . .4C **88**
Spinel Cl. SE18 . . . . .5K **91**
Spinnaker Cl. IG11: Bark 3B **74**
Spinnaker Ct.
KT1: King T *1D 134*
(off Becketts Pl.)
Spinnaker Ho. *E14* *2C 88*
(off Byng St.)
Spinnells Rd. HA2: Harr 1D **42**
Spinney Cl. BR3: Beck 4D **142**
KT3: N Mald 5A **136**
KT4: Wor Pk 2B **148**
UB7: W Dray 7A **58**
Spinney Dr. TW14: Felt 7E **94**
Spinney Gdns. RM9: Dag 5E **56**
SE19 . . . . .5F **123**
Spinney Oak BR1: Brom 2C **144**
Spinneys, The
BR1: Brom 2D **144**
Spinney, The DA14: Sidc . . .5E **128**
EN5: Barn 2E **4**
HA0: Wemb 3A **44**
HA7: Stan 4K **11**
N21 . . . . .7F **7**
SM3: Sutt 4E **148**
SW13 . . . . .7D **82**
SW16 . . . . .3G **121**
TW16: Sun T 1J **131**
Spire Ho. *W2* *7A 66*
(off Lancaster Ga.)
Spires Shop. Cen., The
EN5: Barn 3B **4**
Spirit Quay E1 . . . . .1G **87**
SPITALFIELDS . . . .**5F 69 (5J 163)**
Spital Sq. E1 . . . . .5E **68** (5H **163**)
Spital St. E1 . . . . . .5G **69** (5K **163**)
Spital Yd. E1 . . . . . .5E **68** (5H **163**)
Spitfire Est., The
TW5: Houn 5A **78**
Spitfire Rd. SM6: Wall 7J **151**
TW6: Houn 6E **94**
Spitfire Way TW5: Houn 5A **78**
Splendour Wlk. *SE16* *5J 87*
(off Verney Rd.)
Spode Ho. SE11 . . . . .2J **173**
Spode Wlk. NW6 . . . . .5K **47**
Spondon Rd. N15 . . . . .4G **33**
Spoonbill Way UB4: Hayes . . .5B **60**
Spooner Ho. TW5: Houn 6E **78**
Spooners M. W3 . . . . .1K **81**
Spooner Wlk. SM6: Wall 5J **151**
Sportsbank St. SE6 . . . . .7E **106**
Spottons Gro. N17 . . . . .1C **32**
Spout Hill CR0: Croy 5C **154**
Spratt Hall Rd. E11 . . . . .6J **35**
Spray La. TW2: Twick 6J **97**
Spray St. SE18 . . . . .4F **91**
Spreighton Rd.
KT8: W Mole 4F **133**
Spriggs Ho. *N1* *7B 50*
(off Canonbury Rd.)
Sprimont Pl.
SW3 . . . . . . .5D **84** (5E **170**)
Springall St. SE15 . . . . .7H **87**
Springalls Wharf *SE16* *2G 87*
(off Bermondsey Wall W.)
Spring Bank N21 . . . . .6E **6**
Springbank Rd. SE13 . . . . . .6F **107**
Springbank Wlk. NW1 . . . . . .7H **49**
Springbourne Ct.
BR3: Beck 1E **142**
(not continuous)
Spring Bri. M. W5 . . . . .7D **62**
Springbridge Rd. W5 . . . . . . .7D **62**
Spring Cl. EN5: Barn 5A **4**
RM8: Dag 1D **56**
Spring Cl. La.
SM3: Sutt 6G **149**
Spring Cnr. TW13: Felt 3J **113**
Spring Cotts. KT6: Surb 5D **134**
Spring Ct. KT17: Eps 7B **148**
NW6 . . . . .6H **47**
W7 . . . . .7H **61**
Spring Ct. Rd. EN2: Enf 1F **7**
Springcroft Av. N2 . . . . .4D **30**
Springdale M. N16 . . . . .4D **50**
Springdale Rd. N16 . . . . .4D **50**
Spring Dr. HA5: Pinn 6J **23**
Springfield E5 . . . . .1H **51**
WD23: Bush 1C **10**
Springfield Av. N10 . . . . .3G **31**
SW20 . . . . .3H **137**
TW12: Hamp 6F **115**
Springfield Cl. HA7: Stan 3F **11**
N12 . . . . .5E **14**
Springfield Ct. IG1: Ilf 5F **55**
KT1: King T *3E 134*
(off Springfield Rd.)
NW3 . . . .*7C 48*
(off Eton Av.)
SM6: Wall 5F **151**
Springfield Dr. IG2: Ilf 5G **37**
Springfield Gdns.
BR1: Brom 4D **144**
BR4: W W'ck 2D **154**
E5 . . . . .1H **51**
HA4: Ruis 1K **41**
IG8: Wfd G 7F **21**
NW9 . . . . .5K **27**
Springfield Gro. SE7 . . . . . . .6A **90**
TW16: Sun T 1H **131**
Springfield La. NW6 . . . . . . .1K **65**
Springfield Mt. NW9 . . . . . . .5A **28**
Springfield Pde. M. N13 . . . .4F **17**
Springfield Pl.
KT3: N Mald 4J **135**
Springfield Ri. SE26 . . . . . .3H **123**
(not continuous)
Springfield Rd.
BR1: Brom 4D **144**
CR7: Thor H 1C **140**
DA7: Bex 4H **111**
DA16: Well 3B **110**
E4 . . . . .1B **20**
E6 . . . . .7D **54**
E15 . . . . .3G **71**
E17 . . . . .6B **34**
HA1: Harr 6J **25**
KT1: King T 3E **134**
N11 . . . . .5A **16**
N15 . . . . .4G **33**
NW8 . . . . .1A **66**
SE26 . . . . .5H **123**
SM6: Wall 5F **151**
SW19 . . . . .5H **119**
TW2: Twick 1E **114**
TW11: Tedd 5A **116**
TW15: Ashf 5B **112**
UB4: Hayes 1A **78**
W7 . . . . .1J **79**
Springfields *EN5: Barn* *5E 4*
(off Somerset Rd.)
Springfield Wlk.
BR6: Orp *7H 145*
(off Place Farm Av.)
NW6 . . . . .1K **65**
Spring Gdns.
IG8: Wfd G 7F **21**
KT8: W Mole 5F **133**
N5 . . . . .5C **50**
RM7: Rom 5J **39**
SM6: Wall 5G **151**
SW1 . . . . . . .1H **85** (4D **166**)
(not continuous)
SPRING GROVE **1J 97**

344 A-Z London

Stanley Pk. Dr.—Stave Yd. Rd.

Stanley Pk. Dr.
HA0: Wemb ... 1F 63
Stanley Pk. Rd.
SM5: Cars ... 7D 150
Stanley Pas. NW1 ... 2J 67
Stanley Rd. BR2: Short ... 4K 143
BR6: Orp ... 7K 145
CR0: Croy ... 7A 140
CR4: Mitc ... 7E 120
DA14: Sidc ... 3A 128
E4 ... 1A 20
E10 ... 6D 34
E12 ... 5C 54
E15 ... 1F 71
E18 ... 1H 35
EN1: Enf ... 3K 7
HA2: Harr ... 2G 43
HA6: Nwood ... 1J 23
HA9: Wemb ... 6F 45
IG1: Ilf ... 2H 55
N2 ... 3B 30
N9 ... 1A 18
N10 ... 7A 16
N11 ... 6C 16
N15 ... 4B 32
NW9 ... 7C 28
SM2: Sutt ... 6K 149
SM4: Mord ... 4J 137
SM5: Cars ... 7E 150
SW14 ... 4H 99
SW19 ... 6J 119
TW2: Twick ... 3H 115
TW3: Houn ... 4G 97
TW11: Tedd ... 4J 115
TW15: Ashf ... 5A 112
UB1: S'hall ... 7C 60
W3 ... 3J 81
Stanley Sq. SM5: Cars ... 7D 150
Stanley St. SE8 ... 7B 88
Stanley Ter. DA6: Bex ... 4G 111
N19 ... 2J 49
Stanmer St. SW11 ... 1C 102
STANMORE ... 5G 11
Stanmore Gdns.
SM1: Sutt ... 3A 150
TW9: Rich ... 3F 99
Stanmore Hill HA7: Stan ... 3F 11
Stanmore Lodge
HA7: Stan ... 4G 11
Stanmore Pl. NW1 ... 1F 67
Stanmore Rd. DA17: Belv ... 4J 93
E11 ... 1H 53
N15 ... 4B 32
TW9: Rich ... 3F 99
Stanmore St. N1 ... 1K 67
Stanmore Ter. BR3: Beck ... 2C 142
Stannard Cotts. *E1 ... 4J 69*
(off Fox Cl.)
Stannard M. *E8 ... 6G 51*
(off Stannard Rd.)
Stannard Rd. E8 ... 6G 51
Stannary Pl.
SE11 ... 5A 86 (6K 173)
Stannary St.
SE11 ... 6A 86 (7K 173)
Stannet Way SM6: Wall ... 4G 151
Stansbury Ho. *W10 ... 3G 65*
(off Beethoven St.)
Stansfeld Rd. E6 ... 5B 72
Stansfield Ho. *SE1 ... 4F 87*
(off Balaclava Rd.)
Stansfield Rd. SW9 ... 3K 103
TW4: Houn ... 2K 95
Stansgate Rd. RM10: Dag ... 2G 57
Stanstead Cl. BR2: Short ... 5H 143
Stanstead Gro. SE6 ... 1B 124
Stanstead Mnr.
SM1: Sutt ... 6J 149
Stanstead Rd. E11 ... 5K 35
SE6 ... 1K 123
SE23 ... 1K 123
TW6: Houn ... 6B 94
Stansted Cres.
DA5: Bexl ... 1D 128
Stanswood Gdns. SE5 ... 7E 86
Stanthorpe Cl. SW16 ... 5J 121
Stanthorpe Rd. SW16 ... 5J 121
Stanton Av. TW11: Tedd ... 6J 115
Stanton Cl. KT4: Wor Pk ... 1F 149
KT19: Eps ... 5H 147
Stanton Ct. *CR2: S Croy ... 5E 152*
(off Birdhurst Ri.)
Stanton Ho. *SE10 ... 6E 88*
(off Thames St.)
SE16 ... 2B 88
(off Rotherhithe St.)
Stanton Rd. CR0: Croy ... 7C 140
SE26 ... 4B 124
SW13 ... 2B 100
SW20 ... 1F 137
Stanton Sq. SE26 ... 4B 124
Stanton Way SE26 ... 4B 124
Stanway Ct. N1 ... 2E 68
Stanway Gdns. HA8: Edg ... 5D 12
W3 ... 1G 81
Stanway St. N1 ... 2E 68
STANWELL ... 7A 94
Stanwell Cl.
TW19: Staines ... 6A 94
Stanwell Rd. TW14: Felt ... 7D 94
TW15: Ashf ... 2A 112
Stanwick Rd. W14 ... 4H 83
Stanworth Ct. TW5: Houn ... 7D 78
Stanworth St.
SE1 ... 3F 87 (7J 169)
Stanyhurst SE23 ... 1A 124
Stapenhill Rd.
HA0: Wemb ... 3B 44
Staple Cl. DA5: Bexl ... 3K 129
Staplefield Cl. SW2 ... 1J 121
Stapleford *N17 ... 2E 32*
(off Willan Rd.)
Stapleford Av. IG2: Ilf ... 5J 37
Stapleford Cl. E4 ... 3K 19
KT1: King T ... 2G 135
SW19 ... 7G 101
Stapleford Rd.
HA0: Wemb ... 7D 44
Stapleford Way IG11: Bark ... 3B 74
Staplehurst Rd. SE13 ... 5F 107
SM5: Cars ... 7C 150
Staple Inn WC1 ... 6J 161
Staple Inn Bldgs.
WC1 ... 5A 68 (6J 161)
Staples Cl. SE16 ... 1A 88
STAPLES CORNER ... 1D 46
Staples Cnr. Bus. Pk.
NW2 ... 1D 46
Staples Ho. *E6 ... 6E 72*
(off Savage Gdns.)
Staple St. SE1 ... 2D 86 (7F 169)
Stapleton Gdns.
CR0: Croy ... 5A 152
Stapleton Hall Rd. N4 ... 1K 49
Stapleton Ho. *E2 ... 3H 69*
(off Ellsworth St.)
Stapleton Rd. DA7: Bex ... 7F 93
SW17 ... 3E 120
Stapley Rd. DA17: Belv ... 5G 93
Stapylton Rd. EN5: Barn ... 3B 4
Star All. *EC3 ... 2H 169*
(off Fenchurch St.)
Star & Garter Hill
TW10: Rich ... 1E 116
Starboard Way E14 ... 3C 88
Star Bus. Cen.
RM13: Rain ... 5K 75
Starch Ho. La. IG6: Ilf ... 2H 37
Star Cl. EN3: Enf ... 6D 8
Starcross St.
NW1 ... 3G 67 (2B 160)
Starfield Rd. W12 ... 2C 82
Star Hill DA1: Cray ... 5K 111
Star La. E16 ... 4G 71
Starling Cl. HA5: Pinn ... 3A 24
IG9: Buck H ... 1D 20
Starling Ho. *NW8 ... 2C 66*
(off Barrow Hill Est.)
Starling Wlk.
TW12: Hamp ... 5C 114
Starmans Cl. RM9: Dag ... 1E 74
Star Path *UB5: N'olt ... 2E 60*
(off Brabazon Rd.)
Star Pl. E1 ... 7G 69 (3K 169)
Star Rd. TW7: Isle ... 2H 97
UB10: Uxb ... 4E 58
W14 ... 6H 83
Star St. W2 ... 6C 66 (7B 158)
Starts Cl. BR6: Orp ... 3E 156
Starts Hill Rd.
BR6: Orp ... 3E 156
Starveall Cl.
UB7: W Dray ... 3B 76
Star Yd. WC2 ... 6A 68 (7J 161)
Staten Gdns.
TW1: Twick ... 1K 115
Statham Gro. N16 ... 4D 50
N18 ... 5K 17
Statham Ho. *SW8 ... 1G 103*
(off Wadhurst Rd.)
Station App. *BR1: Brom ... 3J 143*
(off High St.)
BR2: Short ... 1J 155
BR3: Beck ... 1C 142
BR4: W W'ck ... 7E 142
BR7: Chst ... 1E 144
(Chislehurst Station)
BR7: Chst ... 6C 126
(Elmstead Woods Station)
CR2: S Croy ... 7D 152
DA5: Bexl ... 1G 129
DA7: Bex ... 2J 111
(Barnehurst Rd.)
DA7: Bex ... 2E 110
(Pickford La.)
DA16: Well ... 2A 110
(not continuous)
E4 ... 6A 20
E7 ... 4K 53
E11 ... 5J 35
E17 ... 5C 34
(not continuous)
E18 ... 2K 35
EN5: Barn ... 4F 5
HA0: Wemb ... 6B 44
HA1: Harr ... 7J 25
HA4: Ruis ... 1G 41
(Ruislip Station)
HA4: Ruis ... 5K 41
(South Ruislip Station)
HA5: Pinn ... 3C 24
IG9: Buck H ... 4G 21
KT1: King T ... 1G 135
KT4: Wor Pk ... 1C 148
KT17: Eps ... 7B 148
(Ewell West Station)
KT19: Eps ... 5C 148
(Stoneleigh Station)
N11 ... 5A 16
N12 ... 4E 14
NW10 ... 3B 64
SE3 ... 3K 107
SE9 ... 1D 126
(Mottingham Station)
SE9 ... 2G 127
(New Eltham Station)
SE12 ... 6J 107
(off Burnt Ash Hill)
SE26 ... 5B 124
(Lower Sydenham Station)
SE26 ... 4J 123
(Sydenham Station)
SM2: Sutt ... 7G 149
SM5: Cars ... 4D 150
SW6 ... 3G 101
SW14 ... 3J 99
Station App. SW16 ... 6H 121
(Streatham Common Station)
SW16 ... 5H 121
(Streatham Station)
TW8: Bford ... 6C 80
(off Sidney Gdns.)
TW9: Rich ... 1G 99
TW12: Hamp ... 1E 132
TW15: Ashf ... 4B 112
TW16: Sun T ... 1J 131
TW17: Shep ... 5E 130
UB3: Hayes ... 3H 77
UB6: G'frd ... 7G 43
UB7: W Dray ... 1A 76
W7 ... 1J 79
Station App. Nth.
DA15: Sidc ... 2A 128
Station App. Rd.
SE1 ... 2A 86 (7H 167)
W4 ... 7J 81
Station Av. KT3: N Mald ... 3A 136
KT19: Eps ... 7A 148
SW9 ... 3B 104
TW9: Rich ... 1G 99
Station Bldgs.
KT1: King T ... 2E 134
(off Fife Rd.)
Station Cl. N3 ... 1J 29
N12 ... 4E 14
TW12: Hamp ... 1F 133
Station Cres.
HA0: Wemb ... 6B 44
N15 ... 4D 32
SE3 ... 5J 89
TW15: Ashf ... 3A 112
Stationer's Hall Ct.
EC4 ... 6B 68 (1B 168)
Station Est.
BR3: Beck ... 3K 141
E18 ... 2K 35
Station Est. Rd.
TW14: Felt ... 1K 113
Station Garage M.
SW16 ... 6H 121
Station Gdns. W4 ... 7J 81
Station Gro.
HA0: Wemb ... 6E 44
Station Hill BR2: Short ... 2J 155
Station Ho. M. N9 ... 4B 18
Station Pde. *DA7: Bex ... 2E 110*
(off Pickford La.)
DA14: Sidc ... 2A 128
E11 ... 5J 35
EN4: Barn ... 4K 5
HA2: Harr ... 4F 43
HA3: Harr ... 2A 26
HA8: Edg ... 7K 11
IG9: Buck H ... 4G 21
IG11: Bark ... 7G 55
N14 ... 1C 16
NW2 ... 6E 46
RM9: Dag ... 6G 57
SM1: Sutt ... 6A 150
(off High St.)
SW12 ... 1E 120
TW9: Rich ... 1G 99
TW14: Felt ... 1K 113
TW15: Ashf ... 4B 112
UB5: N'olt ... 7E 42
(Court Farm Rd.)
UB5: N'olt ... 4F 43
(Halsbury Rd. W.)
W3 ... 6G 63
W4 ... 7J 81
W5 ... 1F 81
Station Pas. E18 ... 2K 35
SE15 ... 1J 105
Station Path *E8 ... 6H 51*
(off Graham Rd.)
SW6 ... 3H 101
Station Pl. N4 ... 2A 50
Station Ri. SE27 ... 2B 122
Station Rd. BR1: Brom ... 1J 143
BR2: Short ... 2G 143
BR4: W W'ck ... 1E 154
CR0: Croy ... 1C 152
DA7: Bex ... 3E 110
DA15: Sidc ... 2A 128
DA17: Belv ... 3G 93
E4 ... 1A 20
E7 ... 4J 53
E12 ... 4C 54
E17 ... 6A 34
EN5: Barn ... 5E 4
HA1: Harr ... 4K 25
HA2: Harr ... 5F 25
HA8: Edg ... 6B 12
IG1: Ilf ... 3F 55
IG6: Ilf ... 3H 37
KT1: King T ... 1C 134
KT2: King T ... 1G 135
KT3: N Mald ... 5D 136
KT7: T Ditt ... 7K 133
KT9: Chess ... 5E 146
N3 ... 1J 29
N11 ... 5A 16
N17 ... 3G 33
N19 ... 3G 49
N21 ... 1G 17
N22 ... 2J 31
NW4 ... 6C 28
NW7 ... 6F 13
NW10 ... 2B 64
RM6: Chad H ... 7D 38
SE13 ... 3E 106
SE20 ... 6J 123
SE25 ... 4F 141
SM5: Cars ... 4D 150
SW13 ... 2B 100
SW19 ... 1A 138
TW1: Twick ... 1K 115
TW3: Houn ... 4F 97
TW11: Tedd ... 6A 116
TW12: Hamp ... 1E 132
TW15: Ashf ... 4B 112
TW16: Sun T ... 7J 113
TW17: Shep ... 5E 130
UB3: Hayes ... 4G 77
(not continuous)
UB7: W Dray ... 2A 76
W5 ... 6F 63
W7 ... 1J 79
Station Rd. Nth.
DA17: Belv ... 3H 93
Station Sq. BR5: Orp ... 5G 145
Station St. E16 ... 1F 91
Station Ter. NW10 ... 2F 65
SE5 ... 1C 104
Station Ter. M. SE3 ... 5J 89
Station Vw. UB6: G'frd ... 1H 61
Station Wlk. *IG1: Ilf ... 2F 55*
(in Exchange, The)
Station Way IG9: Buck H ... 4F 21
SE15 ... 2G 105
SM3: Sutt ... 6G 149
Station Yd. TW1: Twick ... 7A 98
Staton Ct. *E10 ... 7D 34*
(off Kings Cl.)
Staunton Ho. *SE17 ... 4E 86*
(off Tatum St.)
Staunton Rd. KT2: King T ... 6E 116
Staunton St. SE8 ... 6B 88
Staveley *NW1 ... 1A 160*
(off Varndell St.)
Staveley Cl. E9 ... 5J 51
N7 ... 4J 49
SE15 ... 1H 105
Staveley Ct. E11 ... 5J 35
Staveley Gdns. W4 ... 1K 99
Staveley Rd.
TW15: Ashf ... 6F 113
W4 ... 6J 81
Staverton Rd. NW2 ... 7E 46
Stave Yd. Rd. SE16 ... 1A 88

Sudbury Cres.—Surrey Sq.

Sudbury Cres. BR1: Brom . . .6J **125**
HA0: Wemb 5B **44**
Sudbury Cft. HA0: Wemb 4K **43**
Sudbury Gdns.
CR0: Croy 4E **152**
Sudbury Hgts. Av.
UB6: G'frd 5K **43**
Sudbury Hill HA1: Harr 2J **43**
Sudbury Hill Cl.
HA0: Wemb 4K **43**
Sudbury Ho. SW18 . . . . .5K **101**
Sudbury Rd. IG11: Bark 5K **55**
Sudeley St. N1 . . . . .2B **68**
Sudlow Rd. SW18 . . . . .5J **101**
Sudrey St. SE1 . . . .2C **86** (7C **168**)
Suez Av. UB6: G'frd 2K **61**
Suez Rd. EN3: Enf 4F **9**
SUFFIELD HATCH **4K 19**
Suffield Ho. *SE17* *5B 86*
(off Berryfield Rd.)
Suffield Rd. E4 . . . . .3J **19**
N15 . . . . .5F **33**
SE20 . . . . .2J **141**
Suffolk Ct. E10 . . . . .7C **34**
IG3: Ilf 6J **37**
Suffolk Ho. *CR0: Croy* *2D 152*
(off George St.)
SE20 . . . .*1K 141*
(off Croydon Rd.)
Suffolk La. EC4 . . . .7D **68** (2E **168**)
Suffolk Pk. Rd. E17 . . . . .4A **34**
Suffolk Pl. SW1 . . .1H **85** (4D **166**)
Suffolk Rd. DA14: Sidc 6C **128**
E13 . . . . .3J **71**
EN3: Enf 5C **8**
HA2: Harr 6D **24**
IG3: Ilf 6J **37**
IG11: Bark 7H **55**
KT4: Wor Pk 2B **148**
N15 . . . . .5D **32**
NW10 . . . . .7A **46**
RM10: Dag 5J **57**
SE25 . . . . .4F **141**
SW13 . . . . .7B **82**
Suffolk St. E7 . . . . .4J **53**
SW1 . . . . . . .7H **67** (3D **166**)
Sugar Bakers Ct. EC3 . . . . . .1H **169**
Sugar Ho. La. E15 . . . . .2E **70**
Sugar Loaf Wlk. E2 . . . . .3J **69**
Sugar Quay EC3 . . . . .3H **169**
Sugar Quay Wlk.
EC3 . . . . .7E **68** (3H **169**)
Sugden Rd. KT7: T Ditt 1B **146**
SW11 . . . . .3E **102**
Sugden St. *SE5* *6D 86*
(off Depot St.)
Sugden Way IG11: Bark 2K **73**
Sulby Ho. *SE4* *4A 106*
(off Turnham Rd.)
Sulgrave Gdns. W6 . . . . .2E **82**
Sulgrave Rd. W6 . . . . .3E **82**
Sulina Rd. SW2 . . . . .7J **103**
Sulivan Ct. SW6 . . . . .2J **101**
Sulivan Ent. Cen. SW6 . . . . .3K **101**
Sulivan Rd. SW6 . . . . .3J **101**
Sulkin Ho. *E2* *3K 69*
(off Knottisford St.)
Sullivan Av. E16 . . . . .5B **72**
Sullivan Cl. KT8: W Mole . . .3F **133**
SW11 . . . . .3C **102**
UB4: Hayes 5A **60**
Sullivan Ct. N16 . . . . .7F **33**
Sullivan Cres. UB9: Uxb 2A **22**
Sullivan Ho. *SE11* *4H 173*
(off Vauxhall St.)
SW1 . . . .*7K 171*
(off Churchill Gdns.)
Sullivan Rd.
SE11 . . . . . . .4A **86** (3K **173**)
Sullivans Reach
KT12: Walt T 7H **131**
Sultan Rd. E11 . . . . .4K **35**
Sultan St. BR3: Beck 2K **141**
SE5 . . . . .7C **86**
Sultan Ter. N22 . . . . .2A **32**
Sumatra Rd. NW6 . . . . .5J **47**
Sumburgh Rd. SW12 . . . . . . .6E **102**
Summer Av. KT8: E Mos 5J **133**
Summercourt Rd. E1 . . . . .6J **69**
Summerene Cl. SW16 . . . . . .7G **121**
Summerfield Av. NW6 . . . . . .2G **65**
Summerfield La.
KT6: Surb 2D **146**
Summerfield Rd. W5 . . . . . . .4B **62**
Summerfields
BR1: Brom *1K 143*
(off Freelands Rd.)
Summerfields Av. N12 . . . . . .6H **15**
Summerfield St. SE12 . . . . .7H **107**
Summer Gdns.
KT8: E Mos 5J **133**
Summer Hill BR7: Chst 2E **144**
Summerhill Gro. EN1: Enf 6K **7**
Summerhill Rd. N15 . . . . .4D **32**
Summerhill Vs.
BR7: Chst *1E 144*
(off Susan Wood)
Summerhill Way
CR4: Mitc 1E **138**
Summerhouse Av.
TW5: Houn 1C **96**
Summerhouse Dr.
DA2: Dart 4K **129**
DA5: Bexl, Dart 4K **129**
Summerhouse Rd. N16 . . . . .2E **50**
Summerland Gdns. N10 . . . . .3F **31**
Summerland Grange N10 . . . .3F **31**
Summerlands Av. W3 . . . . . . .7J **63**
Summerlands Lodge
BR6: Orp 4E **156**
Summerlee Av. N2 . . . . .4D **30**
Summerlee Gdns. N2 . . . . . . .4D **30**
Summerley St. SW18 . . . . . .2K **119**
Summer Rd. KT7: T Ditt 5K **133**
KT8: E Mos, T Ditt . . .5J **133**
Summersby Rd. N6 . . . . .6F **31**
Summers Cl. HA9: Wemb . . .1H **45**
SM2: Sutt 7J **149**
Summerskill Cl. SE15 . . . . .3H **105**
Summerskille Cl. N9 . . . . . . .3C **18**
Summers La. N12 . . . . .7G **15**
Summers Row N12 . . . . .6H **15**
Summers St.
EC1 . . . . .4A **68** (4J **161**)
SUMMERSTOWN **3A 120**
Summerstown SW17 . . . . . .3A **120**
Summerton Way SE28 . . . . . .6D **74**
Summer Trees
TW16: Sun T 1K **131**
Summerville Gdns.
SM1: Sutt 6H **149**
Summerwood Rd.
TW7: Isle 5K **97**
Summit Av. NW9 . . . . .5K **27**
Summit Bus. Pk.
TW16: Sun T 7J **113**
Summit Cl. HA8: Edg 7B **12**
N14 . . . . .2B **16**
NW2 . . . . .5G **47**
NW9 . . . . .4K **27**
Summit Dr. IG8: Wfd G 2B **36**
Summit Est. N16 . . . . .7G **33**
Summit Rd. E17 . . . . .4D **34**
UB5: N'olt 7E **42**
Summit Way N14 . . . . .2A **16**
SE19 . . . . .7E **122**
Sumner Av. SE15 . . . . .1F **105**
Sumner Bldgs. SE1 . . . . . . .4C **168**
Sumner Ct. SW8 . . . . .7J **85**
Sumner Est. SE15 . . . . .7F **87**
Sumner Gdns. CR0: Croy . . .1A **152**
Sumner Ho. *E3* *5D 70*
(off Watts Gro.)
Sumner Pl. SW7 . . .4B **84** (4B **170**)
Sumner Pl. M.
SW7 . . . . . . .4B **84** (4B **170**)
Sumner Rd. CR0: Croy 1A **152**
HA1: Harr 7G **25**
SE15 . . . . .6F **87**
(not continuous)
Sumner Rd. Sth.
CR0: Croy 1A **152**
Sumner St. SE1 . . . .1B **86** (4B **168**)
Sumpter Cl. NW3 . . . . .6A **48**
Sun All. TW9: Rich 4E **98**
Sunbeam Cres. W10 . . . . . . .4E **64**
Sunbeam Rd. NW10 . . . . .4J **63**
SUNBURY **3A 132**
Sunbury Av. NW7 . . . . .5E **12**
SW14 . . . . .4K **99**
Sunbury Av. Pas. SW14 . . . .4A **100**
Sunbury Cl. KT12: Walt T . . .6J **131**
SUNBURY COMMON **7H 113**
Sunbury Ct. EN5: Barn 4B **4**
Sunbury Ct. Island
TW16: Sun T 3B **132**
Sunbury Ct. M.
TW16: Sun T 2B **132**
Sunbury Ct. Rd.
TW16: Sun T 2A **132**
Sunbury Cres.
TW13: Felt 4H **113**
SUNBURY CROSS **7J 113**
Sunbury Cross Shop. Cen.
TW16: Sun T 7H **113**
Sunbury Gdns. NW7 . . . . . . .5E **12**
Sunbury Ho. *E2* *2J 163*
(off Swanfield St.)
SE14 . . . .*6K 87*
(off Myers La.)
Sunbury La. KT12: Walt T . .6J **131**
SW11 . . . . .1B **102**
(not continuous)
Sunburylock Ait
TW16: Sun T 4K **131**
Sunbury Pk. Walled Garden
. . . .***3K 131***
Sunbury Rd. SM3: Sutt 3F **149**
TW13: Felt 3H **113**
Sunbury St. SE18 . . . . .3D **90**
Sunbury Way TW13: Felt . . .5A **114**
Sunbury Workshops *E2* *2J 163*
(off Swanfield St.)
Sun Ct. EC3 . . . . .1F **169**
Suncroft Pl. SE26 . . . . .3J **123**
Sunderland Ct. SE22 . . . . . .7G **105**
TW19: Staines 6A **94**
Sunderland Mt. SE23 . . . . . .2K **123**
Sunderland Rd. SE23 . . . . . .1K **123**
TW6: Houn 6A **94**
W5 . . . . .3D **80**
Sunderland Ter. W2 . . . . .6K **65**
Sunderland Way E12 . . . . . . .2B **54**
Sundew Av. W12 . . . . .7C **64**
Sundew Cl. W12 . . . . .7C **64**
Sundew Ct. *HA0: Wemb* *2E 62*
(off Elmore Cl.)
Sundial Av. SE25 . . . . .3F **141**
Sundorne Rd. SE7 . . . . .5A **90**
Sundown Rd. TW15: Ashf . . .5E **112**
Sundra Wlk. E1 . . . . .4K **69**
SUNDRIDGE **6K 125**
Sundridge Av.
BR1: Brom 1B **144**
BR7: Chst 7C **126**
DA16: Well 2H **109**
Sundridge Ho. *E9* *7K 51*
(off Church Cres.)
Sundridge Pde.
BR1: Brom 7K **125**
SUNDRIDGE PARK **7K 125**
Sundridge Pl. CR0: Croy . . .1G **153**
Sundridge Rd. CR0: Croy . . .7F **141**
Sunfields Pl. SE3 . . . . .7K **89**
Sungate Cotts. RM5: Col R . . .1F **39**
SUN-IN-THE-SANDS **7K 89**
Sunken Rd. CR0: Croy 5J **153**
Sunkist Way SM6: Wall 7J **151**
Sunland Av. DA6: Bex 4E **110**
Sun La. SE3 . . . . .7K **89**
Sunleigh Rd. HA0: Wemb 1E **62**
Sunley Gdns. UB6: G'frd 1A **62**
Sunlight Cl. SW19 . . . . .6A **120**
Sunlight Sq. E2 . . . . .3H **69**
Sunmead Rd.
TW16: Sun T 3J **131**
Sunna Gdns.
TW16: Sun T 2K **131**
Sunniholme Ct.
CR2: S Croy *5C 152*
(off Warham Rd.)
Sunningdale N14 . . . . .5C **16**
W13 . . . .*5B 62*
(off Hardwick Grn.)
Sunningdale Av.
HA4: Ruis 1A **42**
IG11: Bark 1H **73**
TW13: Felt 2C **114**
W3 . . . . .7A **64**
Sunningdale Cl. E6 . . . . .3D **72**
HA7: Stan 6F **11**
KT6: Surb 2E **146**
SE16 . . . . .5H **87**
SE28 . . . . .6E **74**
Sunningdale Ct.
TW7: Isle *6H 97*
(off Whitton Dene)
UB1: S'hall *6G 61*
(off Fleming Rd.)
Sunningdale Gdns. NW9 . . . .5J **27**
W8 . . . .*3J 83*
(off Stratford Rd.)
Sunningdale Lodge
HA1: Harr *7J 25*
(off Grove Hill)
HA8: Edg *5A 12*
(off Stonegrove)
Sunningdale Rd.
BR1: Brom 4C **144**
SM1: Sutt 3H **149**
Sunningfields Cres. NW4 . . .2D **28**
Sunningfields Rd. NW4 . . . . .3D **28**
Sunninghill Ct. W3 . . . . .2J **81**
Sunninghill Rd. SE13 . . . . . .2D **106**
Sunny Bank SE25 . . . . .3G **141**
Sunny Cres. NW10 . . . . .7J **45**
Sunnycroft Rd. SE25 . . . . . .3G **141**
TW3: Houn 2F **97**
UB1: S'hall 5E **60**
Sunnydale BR6: Orp 2E **156**
Sunnydale Gdns. NW7 . . . . . .6E **12**
Sunnydale Rd. SE12 . . . . . .5K **107**
Sunnydene Av. E4 . . . . .5A **20**
HA4: Ruis 1J **41**
Sunnydene Gdns.
HA0: Wemb 6C **44**
Sunnydene St. SE26 . . . . . . .4A **124**
Sunnyfield NW7 . . . . .4G **13**
Sunnyfield Rd. BR7: Chst . . .3K **145**
Sunny Gdns. Pde. NW4 . . . . .2D **28**
Sunny Gdns. Rd. NW4 . . . . . .2D **28**
Sunny Hill NW4 . . . . .3D **28**
Sunnyhill Cl. E5 . . . . .4A **52**
Sunny Hill Pk. ***2D 28***
Sunnyhill Rd. SW16 . . . . . . .4J **121**
Sunnyhurst Cl.
SM1: Sutt 3J **149**
Sunnymead Av.
CR4: Mitc 3H **139**
Sunnymead Rd. NW9 . . . . . . .7K **27**
SW15 . . . . .5D **100**
Sunnymede Av.
KT19: Eps 7A **148**
Sunnymede Dr. IG2: Ilf 5F **37**
IG6: Ilf 4F **37**
Sunny Nook Gdns.
CR2: S Croy 6D **152**
Sunny Rd., The EN3: Enf 1E **8**
Sunnyside KT12: Walt T 5A **132**
NW2 . . . . .3H **47**
SW19 . . . . .6G **119**
Sunnyside Dr. E4 . . . . .7K **9**
Sunnyside Ho's. *NW2* *3H 47*
(off Sunnyside)
Sunnyside Pas. SW19 . . . . . .6G **119**
Sunnyside Rd. E10 . . . . .1C **52**
IG1: Ilf 3G **55**
N19 . . . . .7H **31**
TW11: Tedd 4H **115**
W5 . . . . .1D **80**
Sunnyside Rd. E. N9 . . . . . . .3B **18**
Sunnyside Rd. Nth. N9 . . . . .3A **18**
Sunnyside Rd. Sth. N9 . . . . . .3A **18**
Sunnyside Ter. NW9 . . . . .3K **27**
Sunny Vw. NW9 . . . . .5K **27**
Sunny Way N12 . . . . .7H **15**
Sun Pas. *SE16* *3G 87*
(off Old Jamaica Rd.)
Sunray Av. BR2: Short 6C **144**
KT5: Surb 2H **147**
SE24 . . . . .4D **104**
Sunrise Cl. TW13: Felt 3D **114**
Sunrise Vw. NW7 . . . . .6G **13**
Sun Rd. W14 . . . . .5H **83**
Sunset Av. E4 . . . . .1J **19**
IG8: Wfd G 4C **20**
Sunset Ct. IG8: Wfd G 7F **21**
Sunset Gdns. SE25 . . . . .2F **141**
Sunset Rd. SE5 . . . . .4C **104**
SE28 . . . . .1A **92**
Sunset Vw. EN5: Barn 2B **4**
Sunshine Way
CR4: Mitc 2D **138**
Sun St. EC2 . . . . . . .5D **68** (5F **163**)
(not continuous)
Sun St. Pas. EC2 . . .5E **68** (6G **163**)
Sun Wlk. E1 . . . . . . .7F **69** (3K **169**)
Sunwell Cl. SE15 . . . . .1H **105**
Sun Wharf *SE8* *7D 88*
(off Creekside)
SURBITON **6D 134**
Surbiton Ct. KT6: Surb 6C **134**
Surbiton Cres.
KT1: King T 4E **134**
Surbiton Hall Cl.
KT1: King T 4E **134**
Surbiton Hill Pk.
KT5: Surb 5F **135**
Surbiton Hill Rd.
KT6: Surb 4E **134**
Surbiton Pde. KT6: Surb 6E **134**
Surbiton Rd. KT1: King T . . .4D **134**
Surlingham Cl. SE28 . . . . . . .7D **74**
Surma Cl. E1 . . . . .4H **69**
Surmans Cl. RM9: Dag 1C **74**
Surrendale Pl. W9 . . . . .4J **65**
Surrey Canal Rd. SE15 . . . . . .6J **87**
Surrey County Cricket Club
(Oval Cricket Ground) . . .***6K 85***
Surrey Ct. N3 . . . . .2G **29**
Surrey Cres. W4 . . . . .5G **81**
Surrey Gdns. N4 . . . . .6C **32**
Surrey Gro. SE17 . . . . .5E **86**
SM1: Sutt 3B **150**
Surrey Ho. *SE16* *1K 87*
(off Rotherhithe St.)
Surrey La. SW11 . . . . .1C **102**
Surrey La. Est. SW11 . . . . . .1C **102**
Surrey M. SE27 . . . . .4E **122**
Surrey Mt. SE23 . . . . .1H **123**
Surrey Quays Rd. SE16 . . . . .3J **87**
Surrey Quays Shop. Cen.
SE16 . . . . .3K **87**
Surrey Rd. BR4: W W'ck . . .1D **154**
HA1: Harr 5G **25**
IG11: Bark 7J **55**
RM10: Dag 5H **57**
SE15 . . . . .5K **105**
Surrey Row SE1 . . .2B **86** (6A **168**)
Surrey Sq. SE17 . . . . .5E **86**

Taunton Av.—Terrace Rd.

Taunton Av. SW20 ... 2D **136**
TW3: Houn ... 2G **97**
Taunton Cl. DA7: Bex ... 2K **111**
SM3: Sutt ... 1J **149**
Taunton Dr. EN2: Enf ... 3F **7**
N2 ... 2A **30**
Taunton Ho. *W2* ... *6A 66*
(off Hallfield Est.)
Taunton M.
NW1 ... 4D **66** (4E **158**)
Taunton Pl.
NW1 ... 4D **66** (3E **158**)
Taunton Rd. SE12 ... 5G **107**
UB6: G'frd ... 1F **61**
Taunton Way HA7: Stan ... 2E **26**
Tavern Cl. SM5: Cars ... 7C **138**
Taverners Cl. W11 ... 1G **83**
Taverners Ct. *E3* ... *3A 70*
(off Grove Rd.)
Taverner Sq. N5 ... 4C **50**
Taverners Way E4 ... 1B **20**
Tavern La. SW9 ... 2A **104**
Tavern Quay SE16 ... 4A **88**
Tavistock Av. E17 ... 3K **33**
NW7 ... 7A **14**
UB6: G'frd ... 2A **62**
Tavistock Cl. N16 ... 5E **50**
TW18: Staines ... 7A **112**
Tavistock Ct. *CR0: Croy* ... *1D 152*
(off Tavistock Rd.)
WC1 ... *3D 160*
(off Tavistock Sq.)
Tavistock Cres. CR4: Mitc ... 4J **139**
W11 ... 5H **65**
(not continuous)
Tavistock Gdns. IG3: Ilf ... 4J **55**
Tavistock Ga. CR0: Croy ... 1D **152**
Tavistock Gro. CR0: Croy ... 7D **140**
Tavistock Ho. IG8: Wfd G ... 6K **21**
WC1 ... 4H **67** (3D **160**)
Tavistock M. W11 ... 6H **65**
Tavistock Pl. N14 ... 7A **6**
WC1 ... 4J **67** (3E **160**)
Tavistock Rd. BR2: Short ... 4H **143**
CR0: Croy ... 1D **152**
DA16: Well ... 1C **110**
E7 ... 4H **53**
E15 ... 6H **53**
E18 ... 3J **35**
HA8: Edg ... 1G **27**
N4 ... 6D **32**
NW10 ... 2B **64**
SM5: Cars ... 1B **150**
UB7: W Dray ... 1A **76**
UB10: Uxb ... 5F **41**
W11 ... 6H **65**
(not continuous)
Tavistock Sq.
WC1 ... 4H **67** (3D **160**)
Tavistock St.
WC2 ... 7J **67** (2F **167**)
(not continuous)
Tavistock Ter. N19 ... 3H **49**
Tavistock Twr. SE16 ... 3A **88**
Tavistock Wlk.
SM5: Cars ... 1B **150**
Taviton St.
WC1 ... 4H **67** (3C **160**)
Tavy Bri. SE2 ... 2C **92**
Tavy Cl. SE11 ... 5K **173**
(not continuous)
Tawney Rd. SE28 ... 7B **74**
Tawny Cl. TW13: Felt ... 3J **113**
W13 ... 1B **80**
Tawny Way SE16 ... 4K **87**
Tayben Av. TW2: Twick ... 6J **97**
Taybridge Rd. SW11 ... 3E **102**
Tay Bldgs. SE1 ... 7G **169**
Tayburn Cl. E14 ... 6E **70**
Tayfield Cl. UB10: Uxb ... 3E **40**
Tayler Ct. NW8 ... 1B **66**
Taylor Av. TW9: Rich ... 2H **99**
Taylor Cl. N17 ... 7B **18**
SE8 ... 6B **88**
TW3: Houn ... 1G **97**
TW12: Hamp ... 5G **115**
Taylor Ct. E15 ... 5E **52**
SE20 ... *2J 141*
(off Elmers End Rd.)
Taylor Rd. CR4: Mitc ... 7C **120**
SM6: Wall ... 5F **151**
Taylors Bldgs. SE18 ... 4F **91**
Taylors Cl. DA14: Sidc ... 3K **127**
Taylors Ct. TW13: Felt ... 2J **113**
Taylors Grn. W3 ... 6A **64**
Taylors La. EN5: Barn ... 1C **4**
NW10 ... 7A **46**
SE26 ... 4H **123**
Taylorsmead NW7 ... 5H **13**
Taymount Grange SE23 ... 2J **123**
Taymount Ri. SE23 ... 2J **123**
Tayport Cl. N1 ... 7J **49**
Tayside Ct. SE5 ... 4D **104**
Tayside Dr. HA8: Edg ... 3C **12**
Taywood Rd. UB5: N'olt ... 3D **60**
Teak Cl. SE16 ... 1A **88**
Tealby Ct. *N7* ... *5K 49*
(off George's Rd.)
Teal Cl. E16 ... 5B **72**
Teal Ct. NW10 ... 6K **45**
SE8 ... *6B 88*
(off Abinger Gro.)
Teal Dr. HA6: Nwood ... 1E **22**
Teale St. E2 ... 2G **69**
Tealing Dr. KT19: Eps ... 4K **147**
Teal Pl. SM1: Sutt ... 5H **149**
Teal St. SE10 ... 3H **89**
Teasel Cl. CR0: Croy ... 1K **153**
Teasel Cres. SE28 ... 1J **91**
Teasel Way E15 ... 3G **71**
Tea Trade Wharf *SE1* ... *6K 169*
(off Shad Thames)
Tebworth Rd. N17 ... 7A **18**
Technology Pk. NW9 ... 3A **28**
Teck Cl. TW7: Isle ... 2A **98**
Tedder Cl. HA4: Ruis ... 5J **41**
KT9: Chess ... 5C **146**
UB10: Uxb ... 7B **40**
Tedder Rd. CR2: S Croy ... 7J **153**
TEDDINGTON ... **5A 116**
Teddington Bus. Pk.
TW11: Tedd ... *6K 115*
(off Station Rd.)
Teddington Pk.
TW11: Tedd ... 5K **115**
Teddington Pk. Rd.
TW11: Tedd ... 4K **115**
Ted Hennem Ho.
RM10: Dag ... 3H **57**
Ted Roberts Ho. *E2* ... *2H 69*
(off Parmiter St.)
Tedworth Gdns.
SW3 ... 5D **84** (6E **170**)
Tedworth Sq.
SW3 ... 5D **84** (6E **170**)
Tees Av. UB6: G'frd ... 2J **61**
Tees Ct. *W7* ... *6H 61*
(off Hanway Rd.)
Teesdale Av. TW7: Isle ... 1A **98**
Teesdale Cl. E2 ... 2G **69**
Teesdale Gdns. SE25 ... 2E **140**
TW7: Isle ... 1A **98**
Teesdale Rd. E11 ... 6H **35**
Teesdale St. E2 ... 2H **69**
Teesdale Yd. *E2* ... *2H 69*
(off Teesdale St.)
Teeswater Ct. DA18: Erith ... 3D **92**
Tee, The W3 ... 6A **64**
Teevan Cl. CR0: Croy ... 7G **141**
Teevan Rd. CR0: Croy ... 1G **153**
Teignmouth Cl. HA8: Edg ... 2F **27**
SW4 ... 4H **103**
Teignmouth Gdns.
UB6: G'frd ... 2A **62**
Teignmouth Pde.
UB6: G'frd ... 2A **62**
Teignmouth Rd.
DA16: Well ... 2C **110**
NW2 ... 5F **47**
Telcote Way HA4: Ruis ... 7A **24**
Telecom Tower, The
... ***5G 67 (5A 160)***
Telegraph Hill NW3 ... 3K **47**
Telegraph La.
KT10: Esh ... 5A **146**
Telegraph M. IG3: Ilf ... 1A **56**
Telegraph Pas. SW2 ... 7J **103**
Telegraph Path BR7: Chst ... 5F **127**
Telegraph Pl. E14 ... 4D **88**
Telegraph Quarters *SE10* ... *5F 89*
(off Park Row)
Telegraph Rd. SW15 ... 7D **100**
Telegraph St.
EC2 ... 6D **68** (7E **162**)
Telemann Sq. SE3 ... 4K **107**
Telephone Pl. SW6 ... 6H **83**
Telfer Cl. W3 ... 2J **81**
Telfer Ho. EC1 ... 2B **162**
Telferscot Rd. SW12 ... 1H **121**
Telford Av. SW2 ... 1H **121**
Telford Cl. E17 ... 7A **34**
SE19 ... 6F **123**
Telford Dr. KT12: Walt T ... 7A **132**
Telford Ho. *SE1* ... *3C 86*
(off Tiverton St.)
Telford Rd. N11 ... 5B **16**
NW9 ... 6C **28**
SE9 ... 2H **127**
TW2: Twick ... 7E **96**
UB1: S'hall ... 7F **61**
W10 ... 5G **65**
Telfords Yd. E1 ... 7G **69**
Telford Ter. SW1 ... 6G **85** (7A **172**)
Telford Way UB4: Hayes ... 5C **60**
W3 ... 5A **64**
Telham Rd. E6 ... 2E **72**
Tell Gro. SE22 ... 4F **105**
Tellson Av. SE18 ... 1B **108**
Temair Ho. *SE10* ... *7D 88*
(off Tarves Way)
Temeraire St. SE16 ... 2J **87**
Tempelhof Av. NW4 ... 7E **28**
Temperley Rd. SW12 ... 7E **102**
Templar Ct. NW8 ... 2A **158**
Templar Dr. SE28 ... 6D **74**
Templar Ho. NW2 ... 6H **47**
RM13: Rain ... 2K **75**
Templar Pl. TW12: Hamp ... 7E **114**
Templars Av. NW11 ... 6H **29**
Templars Cres. N3 ... 2J **29**
Templars Dr. HA3: Harr ... 6C **10**
Templars Ho. E15 ... 5D **52**
Templar St. SE5 ... 2B **104**
Temple EC4 ... 2J **167**
Temple Av. CR0: Croy ... 2B **154**
EC4 ... 7A **68** (2K **167**)
N20 ... 7G **5**
RM8: Dag ... 1G **57**
Temple Bar ... ***1J 167***
Temple Chambers EC4 ... 2K **167**
Temple Cl. E11 ... 7G **35**
N3 ... 2H **29**
SE28 ... 3G **91**
Templecombe Rd. E9 ... 1J **69**
Templecombe Way
SM4: Mord ... 5G **137**
Temple Ct. *E1* ... *5K 69*
(off Rectory Sq.)
SW8 ... *7J 85*
(off Thorncroft St.)
Templecroft TW15: Ashf ... 6F **113**
Temple Dwellings *E2* ... *2H 69*
(off Temple St.)
TEMPLE FORTUNE ... **5H 29**
Temple Fortune Hill NW11 ... 5J **29**
Temple Fortune La. NW11 ... 6H **29**
Temple Fortune Pde.
NW11 ... 5H **29**
Temple Gdns. *EC4* ... *2J 167*
(off Middle Temple La.)
N21 ... 2G **17**
NW11 ... 6H **29**
RM8: Dag ... 3D **56**
Temple Gro. EN2: Enf ... 2G **7**
NW11 ... 6J **29**
Temple Hall Ct. E4 ... 2A **20**
Temple La. EC4 ... 6A **68** (1K **167**)
Templeman Rd. W7 ... 5K **61**
Temple Mead Cl.
HA7: Stan ... 6G **11**
Templemead Cl. W3 ... 6A **64**
Templemead Ho. E9 ... 4A **52**
Temple Mill La. E10 ... 4D **52**
(not continuous)
E15 ... 4E **52**
TEMPLE MILLS ... **4D 52**
Temple Mills E10 ... 3E **52**
Temple of Mithras (remains)
... ***1E 168***
(off Queen Victoria St.)
Temple Pde. *EN5: Barn* ... *7G 5*
(off Netherlands Rd.)
Temple Pk. UB8: Uxb ... 3C **58**
Temple Pl. WC2 ... 7K **67** (2H **167**)
Temple Rd. CR0: Croy ... 4D **152**
E6 ... 1C **72**
N8 ... 4K **31**
NW2 ... 4E **46**
TW3: Houn ... 4F **97**
TW9: Rich ... 2F **99**
W4 ... 3J **81**
W5 ... 3D **80**
Temple Sheen SW14 ... 4J **99**
Temple Sheen Rd. SW14 ... 4H **99**
Temple St. E2 ... 2H **69**
Templeton Av. E4 ... 4H **19**
Templeton Cl. N15 ... 6D **32**
N16 ... 5E **50**
SE19 ... 1D **140**
Templeton Pl. SW5 ... 4J **83**
Templeton Rd. N15 ... 6D **32**
Temple Way SM1: Sutt ... 3B **150**
Temple W. M. *SE11* ... *3B 86*
(off West Sq.)
Templewood W13 ... 5B **62**
Templewood Av. NW3 ... 3K **47**
Templewood Gdns. NW3 ... 3K **47**
Templewood Point *NW2* ... *2H 47*
(off Granville Rd.)
Tempo Ho. UB5: N'olt ... 3B **60**
Tempsford Cl. EN2: Enf ... 3H **7**
Tempsford Ct. HA1: Harr ... 6K **25**
Temsford Cl. HA2: Harr ... 2G **25**
Tenbury Cl. E7 ... 5B **54**
Tenbury Ct. SW12 ... 1H **121**
Tenby Av. HA3: Harr ... 2B **26**
Tenby Cl. N15 ... 4F **33**
RM6: Chad H ... 6E **38**
Tenby Ct. E17 ... 5A **34**
Tenby Gdns. UB5: N'olt ... 6E **42**
Tenby Ho. UB3: Hayes ... 3E **76**
W2 ... *6A 66*
(off Hallfield Est.)
Tenby Mans. *W1* ... *5H 159*
(off Nottingham St.)
Tenby Rd. DA16: Well ... 1D **110**
E17 ... 5A **34**
EN3: Enf ... 4D **8**
HA8: Edg ... 1F **27**
RM6: Chad H ... 6E **38**
Tench St. E1 ... 1H **87**
Tenda Rd. SE16 ... 4H **87**
Tendring Way
RM6: Chad H ... 5C **38**
Tenham Av. SW2 ... 1H **121**
Tenison Ct. W1 ... 7G **67** (2A **166**)
Tenison Way
SE1 ... 1K **85** (5H **167**)
Tenniel Cl. W2 ... 7A **66**
Tennis Ct. La.
KT8: E Mos ... 3K **133**
Tennison Rd. SE25 ... 4F **141**
Tennis St. SE1 ... 2D **86** (6E **168**)
Tenniswood Rd. EN1: Enf ... 1K **7**
Tennyson *N8* ... *3J 31*
(off Boyton Cl.)
Tennyson Av. E11 ... 7J **35**
E12 ... 7C **54**
KT3: N Mald ... 5D **136**
NW9 ... 3J **27**
TW1: Twick ... 1K **115**
Tennyson Cl. DA16: Well ... 1J **109**
EN3: Enf ... 5E **8**
TW14: Felt ... 6H **95**
Tennyson Ct. *SW6* ... *1A 102*
(off Imperial Rd.)
Tennyson Ho. DA17: Belv ... 5F **93**
SE17 ... *5C 86*
(off Browning St.)
Tennyson Mans. *W14* ... *6H 83*
(off Queen's Club Gdns.)
Tennyson Rd. E10 ... 1D **52**
E15 ... 7G **53**
E17 ... 6B **34**
NW6 ... 1H **65**
(not continuous)
NW7 ... 5H **13**
SE20 ... 7K **123**
SW19 ... 6A **120**
TW3: Houn ... 2G **97**
TW15: Ashf ... 5A **112**
W7 ... 7K **61**
Tennyson St. SW8 ... 2F **103**
Tensing Rd. UB2: S'hall ... 3E **78**
Tentelow La. UB2: S'hall ... 5E **78**
Tenterden Cl. NW4 ... 3F **29**
SE9 ... 4D **126**
Tenterden Dr. NW4 ... 3F **29**
Tenterden Gdns.
CR0: Croy ... 7G **141**
NW4 ... 3F **29**
Tenterden Gro. NW4 ... 3F **29**
Tenterden Ho. *SE17* ... *5E 86*
(off Surrey Gro.)
Tenterden Rd. CR0: Croy ... 7G **141**
N17 ... 7A **18**
RM8: Dag ... 2F **57**
Tenterden St.
W1 ... 6F **67** (1K **165**)
Tenter Ground E1 ... 5F **69** (6J **163**)
Tenter Pas. *E1* ... *1K 169*
(off Nth. Tenter St.)
Tent Peg La. BR5: Orp ... 5G **145**
Tent St. E1 ... 4H **69**
Terborch Way SE22 ... 5E **104**
Teredo St. SE16 ... 3K **87**
Terence Ct. *DA17: Belv* ... *6F 93*
(off Stream Way)
Terence Messenger Twr.
E10 ... *2D 52*
(off Alpine Rd.)
Teresa M. E17 ... 4C **34**
Teresa Wlk. N10 ... 5F **31**
Terling Cl. E11 ... 3H **53**
Terling Ho. *W10* ... *5E 64*
(off Sutton Way)
Terling Rd. RM8: Dag ... 2G **57**
Terling Wlk. *N1* ... *1C 68*
(off Popham St.)
Terminal Ho. HA7: Stan ... 5J **11**
Terminus Pl.
SW1 ... 3F **85** (2K **171**)
Terrace Av. NW10 ... 4E **64**
Terrace Gdns. SW13 ... 2B **100**
Terrace Hill *CR0: Croy* ... *3B 152*
(off Hanover St.)
Terrace La. TW10: Rich ... 6E **98**
Terrace Rd. E9 ... 7J **51**
E13 ... 2J **71**
KT12: Walt T ... 7J **131**

Tiltwood, The—Tours Pas.

Tiltwood, The W3 ....7J 63
Tilt Yd. App. SE9 ....6D 108
Timber Cl. BR7: Chst 2E 144
Timbercroft KT19: Eps 4A 148
Timbercroft La. SE18 ....6J 91
Timberdene NW4 ....2F 29
Timberdene Av. IG6: Ilf 1G 37
Timberland Cl. SE15 ....7G 87
Timberland Rd. E1 ....6H 69
Timber Mill Way SW4 ....3H 103
Timber Pond Rd. SE16 ....1K 87
Timberslip Dr. SM6: Wall 7H 151
Timbers, The SM3: Sutt 6G 149
Timber St. EC1 ....4C 68 (3C 162)
Timberwharf Rd. N16 ....6G 33
Timber Wharves Est.
E14 ....4C 88
(off Copeland Dr.)
Timbrell Pl. SE16 ....1B 88
Time Sq. E8 ....5F 51
Times Sq. SM1: Sutt 5K 149
Timor Ho. E1 ....4A 70
(off Duckett St.)
Timothy Cl. DA6: Bex 5E 110
SW4 ....5G 103
Timothy Ho. DA18: Erith 2E 92
(off Kale Rd.)
Timothy Rd. E3 ....5B 70
Timsbury Wlk. SW15 ....1C 118
Tindal St. SW9 ....1B 104
Tinderbox All. SW14 ....3K 99
Tinniswood Cl. N5 ....5A 50
Tinsley Rd. E1 ....5J 69
Tintagel Cres. SE22 ....4F 105
Tintagel Dr. HA7: Stan 4J 11
Tintagel Gdns. SE22 ....4F 105
Tintern Av. NW9 ....3H 27
Tintern Cl. SW15 ....5G 101
SW19 ....6A 120
Tintern Ct. W13 ....7A 62
Tintern Gdns. N14 ....7D 6
Tintern Ho. NW1 ....1K 159
(off Augustus St.)
SW1 ....4J 171
(off Abbots Mnr.)
Tintern Path NW9 ....6A 28
(off Fryent Gro.)
Tintern Rd. N22 ....1C 32
SM5: Cars 1B 150
Tintern St. SW4 ....4J 103
Tintern Way HA2: Harr 1F 43
Tinto Rd. E16 ....4J 71
Tinworth St. SE1 ....5J 85
SE11 ....5J 85 (5F 173)
Tippett Ct. E6 ....2D 72
Tippetts Cl. EN2: Enf 1H 7
Tipthorpe Rd. SW11 ....3E 102
Tipton Dr. CR0: Croy 4E 152
Tiptree NW1 ....7F 49
(off Castlehaven Rd.)
Tiptree Cl. E4 ....3K 19
Tiptree Cres. IG5: Ilf 2E 36
Tiptree Dr. EN2: Enf 4J 7
Tiptree Rd. HA4: Ruis 4K 41
Tirlemont Rd.
CR2: S Croy 7C 152
Tirrell Rd. CR0: Croy 6C 140
Tisbury Ct. W1 ....2C 166
Tisbury Rd. SW16 ....2J 139
Tisdall Pl. SE17 ....4D 86
Tissington Ct. SE16 ....4J 87
Titan Bus. Est. SE8 ....7C 88
(off Ffinch St.)
Titan Ct. TW8: Bford 5F 81
Titchborne Row
W2 ....6C 66 (1D 164)
Titchfield Rd. NW8 ....1C 66
SM5: Cars 1B 150
Titchfield Wlk.
SM5: Cars 7B 138
Titchwell Rd. SW18 ....1B 120
Tite St. SW3 ....5D 84 (6E 170)
Tithe Barn Cl.
KT2: King T 1F 135
Tithe Barn Way UB5: N'olt 2K 59
Tithe Cl. KT12: Walt T 6K 131
NW7 ....1C 28
UB4: Hayes 5H 59
Tithe Farm Av. HA2: Harr 3E 42
Tithe Farm Cl. HA2: Harr 3E 42
Tithe Wlk. NW7 ....1C 28
Titian Av. WD23: Bush 1D 10
Titley Cl. E4 ....5H 19
Titmus Cl. UB8: Uxb 6E 58
Titmuss Av. SE28 ....7B 74
Titmuss St. W12 ....2E 82
Tivendale N8 ....3J 31
Tiverton Av. IG5: Ilf 3E 36
Tiverton Cl. CR0: Croy 7F 141
Tiverton Dr. SE9 ....1G 127
Tiverton M. TW3: Houn 2G 97
Tiverton Rd. CR7: Thor H 5A 140
HA0: Wemb 2E 62
HA4: Ruis 3J 41
HA8: Edg 2F 27
N15 ....6D 32
N18 ....5K 17
NW10 ....1F 65
TW3: Houn 2G 97
Tiverton St. SE1 ....3C 86
Tiverton Way KT9: Chess 5D 146
NW7 ....7A 14
Tivoli Ct. SE16 ....1B 88
Tivoli Gdns. SE18 ....4C 90
(not continuous)
Tivoli Rd. N8 ....5H 31
SE27 ....5C 122
TW4: Houn 4C 96
Toad La. TW4: Houn 4D 96
Tobacco Dock E1 ....7H 69
Tobacco Quay E1 ....7H 69
Tobago St. E14 ....2C 88
Tobin Cl. NW3 ....7C 48
Toby Ct. N9 ....7D 8
(off Tramway Av.)
Toby La. E1 ....4A 70
Toby Way KT6: Surb 2H 147
Todd Ho. N2 ....2B 30
(off Grange, The)
Todds Wlk. N7 ....2K 49
Todhunter Ter. EN5: Barn 4D 4
Tokenhouse Yd.
EC2 ....6D 68 (7E 162)
Token Yd. SW15 ....4G 101
TOKYNGTON 6H 45
Tokyngton Av. HA9: Wemb 6G 45
Toland Sq. SW15 ....5C 100
Tolcairn Ct. DA17: Belv 5G 93
Tolcarne Dr. HA5: Pinn 2J 23
Tolchurch W11 ....6H 65
(off Dartmouth Cl.)
Toley Av. HA9: Wemb 7E 26
Tolford Rd. E5 ....5H 51
Toll Bar Ct. SM2: Sutt 7K 149
Tollbridge Cl. W10 ....4G 65
Tollesbury Gdns. IG6: Ilf 3H 37
Tollet St. E1 ....4K 69
Tollgate Dr. SE21 ....2E 122
UB4: Hayes 7B 60
Tollgate Gdns. NW6 ....2K 65
Tollgate Ho. NW6 ....2K 65
(off Tollgate Gdns.)
Tollgate Rd. E6 ....5B 72
E16 ....5A 72
Tollgate Sq. E6 ....5D 72
Tollhouse Way N19 ....2G 49
Tollington Pk. N4 ....2K 49
Tollington Pl. N4 ....2K 49
Tollington Rd. N7 ....4K 49
Tollington Way N7 ....3J 49
Tolmers Sq.
NW1 ....4G 67 (3B 160)
(not continuous)
Tolpaide Ho. SE11 ....4J 173
Tolpuddle Av. E13 ....1A 72
(off Queens Rd.)
Tolpuddle St. N1 ....2A 68
Tolson Rd. TW7: Isle 3A 98
Tolverne Rd. SW20 ....1E 136
TOLWORTH 2H 147
Tolworth B'way.
KT6: Surb 1H 147
Tolworth Cl. KT6: Surb 1H 147
Tolworth Gdns.
RM6: Chad H 5D 38
TOLWORTH JUNCTION (TOBY JUG)
....2H 147
Tolworth Pde.
RM6: Chad H 5E 38
Tolworth Pk. Rd.
KT6: Surb 2F 147
Tolworth Ri. Nth.
KT5: Surb 1H 147
Tolworth Ri. Sth.
KT5: Surb 2H 147
Tolworth Rd. KT6: Surb 2E 146
Tolworth Twr. KT6: Surb 2H 147
Tomahawk Gdns.
UB5: N'olt 3B 60
Tom Allen Arts Cen. 6F 53
Tom Coombs Cl. SE9 ....4C 108
Tom Cribb Rd. SE28 ....3G 91
Tom Groves Cl. E15 ....5F 53
Tom Hood Cl. E15 ....5F 53
Tom Jenkinson Rd. E16 ....1J 89
Tomkyns Ho. SE11 ....3J 173
Tomlins All. TW1: Twick 1A 116
Tomlin's Gro. E3 ....3C 70
Tomlinson Cl. E2 ....3F 69 (2K 163)
W4 ....5H 81
Tomlins Orchard
IG11: Bark 1G 73
Tomlins Ter. E14 ....6A 70
Tomlins Wlk. N7 ....2K 49
Tom Mann Cl. IG11: Bark 1J 73
Tom Nolan Cl. E15 ....2G 71
Tom Oakman Cen. E4 ....2A 20
Tompion Ho. EC1 ....3B 162
(off Percival St.)
Tompion St. EC1 ....3B 68 (2A 162)
(not continuous)
Tom Smith Cl. SE10 ....6G 89
Tomson Ho. SE1 ....7J 169
(off Riley Rd.)
Tomswood Ct. IG6: Ilf 1G 37
Tomswood Hill IG6: Ilf 1F 37
Tomswood Rd. IG7: Chig 6K 21
Tom Williams Ho. SW6 ....6H 83
(off Clem Attlee Ct.)
Tonbridge Cres. HA3: Harr 4E 26
Tonbridge Ho's. WC1 ....2E 160
(off Tonbridge St.)
Tonbridge Rd.
KT8: W Mole 4D 132
Tonbridge St.
WC1 ....3J 67 (1E 160)
Tonbridge Wlk. WC1 ....1E 160
Toneborough NW8 ....1K 65
(off Abbey Rd.)
Tonfield Rd. SM3: Sutt 1H 149
Tonge Cl. BR3: Beck 5C 142
Tonsley Hill SW18 ....5K 101
Tonsley Pl. SW18 ....5K 101
Tonsley Rd. SW18 ....5K 101
Tonsley St. SW18 ....5K 101
Tonstall Rd. CR4: Mitc 2E 138
Tony Cannell M. E3 ....3B 70
Tony Law Ho. SE20 ....1H 141
Tooke Cl. HA5: Pinn 1C 24
Tookey Cl. HA3: Harr 7F 27
Took's Ct. WC2 ....6A 68 (7J 161)
Tooley St. SE1 ....1D 86 (4F 169)
Toomy Cen. E16 ....7K 71
(off Evelyn Rd.)
Toorack Rd. HA3: Harr 2H 25
TOOTING 5C 120
TOOTING BEC 3D 120
Tooting Bec Gdns.
SW16 ....4H 121
(not continuous)
Tooting Bec Rd. SW16 ....4F 121
SW17 ....3E 120
Tooting B'way. SW17 ....5C 120
TOOTING GRAVENEY 6D 120
Tooting Gro. SW17 ....5C 120
Tooting High St. SW17 ....6C 120
Tooting Mkt. SW17 ....4D 120
Tootswood Rd.
BR2: Short 5G 143
Topaz Wlk. NW2 ....7F 29
Topham Ho. SE10 ....7E 88
(off Prior St.)
Topham Sq. N17 ....1C 32
Topham St. EC1 ....4A 68 (3J 161)
Top Ho. Ri. E4 ....7K 9
Topiary Sq. TW9: Rich 3F 99
Topley St. SE9 ....4A 108
Topmast Point E14 ....2C 88
Top Pk. BR3: Beck 5G 143
Topp Wlk. NW2 ....2E 46
Topsfield Cl. N8 ....5H 31
Topsfield Pde. N8 ....5J 31
(off Tottenham La.)
Topsfield Rd. N8 ....5J 31
Topsham Rd. SW17 ....3D 120
Tora Ct. IG9: Buck H 2F 21
Torbay Ct. NW1 ....7F 49
Torbay Mans. NW6 ....1H 65
(off Willesden La.)
Torbay Rd. HA2: Harr 2C 42
NW6 ....7H 47
Torbay St. NW1 ....7F 49
Torbitt Way IG2: Ilf 5K 37
Torbridge Cl. HA8: Edg 7K 11
Torbrook Cl. DA5: Bexl 6E 110
Tor Ct. W8 ....2J 83
Torcross Dr. SE23 ....2J 123
Torcross Rd. HA4: Ruis 3K 41
Tor Gdns. W8 ....2J 83
Tor Gro. SE28 ....1J 91
Tor Ho. N6 ....6F 31
Tormead Cl. SM1: Sutt 6J 149
Tormount Rd. SE18 ....6J 91
Tornay Ho. N1 ....2K 67
(off Priory Grn. Est.)
Torney Ho. E9 ....7J 51
Toronto Av. E12 ....4D 54
Toronto Rd. IG1: Ilf 1F 55
Torquay Gdns. IG4: Ilf 4B 36
Torquay St. W2 ....5K 65
Torrance Cl. SE7 ....6B 90
Torrens Ct. SE5 ....3D 104
Torrens Rd. E15 ....6H 53
SW2 ....5K 103
Torrens Sq. E15 ....6H 53
Torrens St. EC1 ....2A 68
Torres Sq. E14 ....5C 88
Torre Wlk. SM5: Cars 1C 150
Torrey Dr. SW9 ....2A 104
Torriano Av. NW5 ....5H 49
Torriano Cotts. NW5 ....5G 49
Torriano M. NW5 ....5G 49
Torridge Gdns. SE15 ....4J 105
Torridge Rd. CR7: Thor H 5B 140
Torridon Ho. NW6 ....2K 65
(off Randolph Gdns.)
Torridon Rd. SE6 ....7F 107
Torrington Av. N12 ....5G 15
Torrington Cl. N12 ....4G 15
Torrington Ct. SE26 ....5G 123
(off Crystal Pal. Pk. Rd.)
Torrington Dr. HA2: Harr 4F 43
Torrington Gdns. N11 ....6B 16
UB6: G'frd 1C 62
Torrington Gro. N12 ....5H 15
Torrington Pk. N12 ....5F 15
Torrington Pl. E1 ....1G 87
WC1 ....5H 67 (5C 160)
Torrington Rd. E18 ....3J 35
HA4: Ruis 3J 41
RM8: Dag 1F 57
UB6: G'frd 1C 62
Torrington Sq. CR0: Croy 7D 140
WC1 ....4H 67 (4D 160)
Torrington Way
SM4: Mord 6J 137
Tor Rd. DA16: Well 1C 110
Torr Rd. SE20 ....7K 123
Tortington Ho. SE15 ....7G 87
(off Friary Est.)
Torver Rd. HA1: Harr 4J 25
Torwood Rd. SW15 ....5C 100
Tothill Ho. SW1 ....3D 172
(off Page St.)
Tothill St. SW1 ....2H 85 (7D 166)
Totnes Rd. DA16: Well 7B 92
Totnes Vs. N11 ....5B 16
(off Telford Rd.)
Totnes Wlk. N2 ....4B 30
Tottan Ter. E1 ....6K 69
Tottenhall NW1 ....7E 48
(off Ferdinand St.)
Tottenhall Rd. N13 ....6F 17
TOTTENHAM 2F 33
Tottenham Ct. Rd.
W1 ....4G 67 (4B 160)
Tottenham Grn. E. N15 ....4F 33
TOTTENHAM HALE 2G 33
TOTTENHAM HALE GYRATORY
....4G 33
Tottenham Hale Retail Pk.
N15 ....4G 33
Tottenham Hotspur F.C.
(White Hart Lane) 7B 18
Tottenham La. N8 ....6J 31
Tottenham M.
W1 ....5G 67 (5B 160)
Tottenham Rd. N1 ....6E 50
Tottenham St.
W1 ....5G 67 (6B 160)
Totterdown St. SW17 ....4D 120
TOTTERIDGE 1C 14
Totteridge Comn. N20 ....2H 13
Totteridge Grn. N20 ....2D 14
Totteridge La. N20 ....2D 14
Totteridge Village N20 ....1B 14
Totternhoe Cl. HA3: Harr 5C 26
Totton Rd. CR7: Thor H 3A 140
Toulmin St. SE1 ....2C 86 (7C 168)
Toulon St. SE5 ....7C 86
Toulouse Ct. SE16 ....5H 87
(off Rossetti Rd.)
Tourist Info. Cen.
Bexley 6J 111
Bexleyheath 4G 111
City of London
....6C 68 (1C 168)
Croydon 3C 152
Greenwich 6E 88
Hackney 6H 51
Harrow 4J 25
Heathrow Terminals 1, 2 & 3
....3D 94
Heathrow Terminals
1,2 & 3 Station 3D 94
Hounslow 3F 97
Ilford 3F 55
Kingston 2D 134
Kingston Upon Thames
....2D 134
Lewisham 4E 106
Richmond upon Thames
....5D 98
Southwark 4F 169
(off Tooley St.)
Twickenham 1B 116
Waterloo International
Terminal 2K 85 (6H 167)
Tournay Rd. SW6 ....7H 83
Tours Pas. SW11 ....4A 102

A-Z London 355

Triangle, The—Turpentine La.

Triangle, The *DA15: Sidc ...7A 110*
(off Burnt Oak La.)
E8 ...1H 69
EC1 ...4B 68 (3B 162)
IG11: Bark ...6G 55
KT1: King T ...2H 135
N13 ...4E 16
Trickett Ho. SM2: Sutt ...7K 149
Tricycle Theatre ...7H 47
(off Kilburn High Rd.)
Trident Bus. Cen. SW17 ...5D 120
Trident Gdns. UB5: N'olt ...3B 60
Trident Ho. *E14 ...6E 70*
(off Blair St.)
Trident St. SE16 ...4K 87
Trident Way UB2: S'hall ...3K 77
Trig La. EC4 ...7C 68 (2C 168)
Trigon Rd. SW8 ...7K 85
Trilby Rd. SE23 ...2K 123
Trillo Ct. IG2: Ilf ...7J 37
Trimdon NW1 ...1G 67
Trimmer Wlk. TW8: Bford ...6E 80
Trim St. SE14 ...6B 88
Trinder Gdns. N19 ...1J 49
Trinder M. TW11: Tedd ...5A 116
Trinder Rd. EN5: Barn ...5A 4
N19 ...1J 49
Tring Av. HA9: Wemb ...6G 45
UB1: S'hall ...6D 60
W5 ...1F 81
Tring Cl. IG2: Ilf ...5H 37
Tring Ct. TW1: Twick ...4A 116
Trinidad Gdns. RM10: Dag ...7K 57
Trinidad Ho. *E14 ...7B 70*
(off Gill St.)
Trinidad St. E14 ...7B 70
Trinity Av. EN1: Enf ...6A 8
N2 ...3B 30
Trinity Buoy Wharf *E14 ...7G 71*
(off Orchard Pl.)
Trinity Bus. Pk. E4 ...6G 19
Trinity Chu. Pas. SW13 ...6D 82
Trinity Chu. Rd. SW13 ...6D 82
Trinity Chu. Sq.
SE1 ...3C 86 (7D 168)
Trinity Cl. BR2: Short ...1C 156
CR2: S Croy ...7E 152
E8 ...6F 51
E11 ...2G 53
NW3 ...4B 48
SE13 ...4F 107
SW4 ...4G 103
TW4: Houn ...4C 96
Trinity Cotts. TW9: Rich ...3F 99
Trinity Ct. CR0: Croy ...2C 152
EN2: Enf ...2H 7
N1 ...1E 68
(off Downham Rd.)
NW2 ...5E 46
SE1 ...7D 168
(off Brockham St.)
SE7 ...4B 90
SE25 ...6E 140
SE26 ...3J 123
W2 ...6A 66
(off Gloucester Ter.)
WC1 ...3G 161
Trinity Cres. SW17 ...2D 120
Trinity Dr. UB8: Uxb ...5E 58
Trinity Gdns. E16 ...5H 71
SW9 ...4K 103
Trinity Grn. E1 ...4J 69
Trinity Gro. SE10 ...1E 106
Trinity Hospital (Almshouses)
SE10 ...5F 89
Trinity Ho. *SE1 ...3C 86*
(off Bath Ter.)
Trinity M. *E1 ...5J 69*
(off Redman's Rd.)
SE20 ...1H 141
W10 ...6F 65
Trinity Path SE23 ...3J 123
Trinity Pl. DA6: Bex ...4F 111
EC3 ...7F 69 (2J 169)
Trinity Ri. SW2 ...1A 122
Trinity Rd. IG6: Ilf ...3G 37
N2 ...3B 30
N22 ...7D 16
(not continuous)
SW17 ...1C 120
SW18 ...4A 102
SW19 ...6J 119
TW9: Rich ...3F 99
UB1: S'hall ...1C 78
Trinity Sq. EC3 ...7E 68 (2H 169)
Trinity St. E16 ...5H 71
EN2: Enf ...2H 7
SE1 ...2C 86 (7D 168)
(not continuous)
Trinity Twr. *E1 ...7G 69*
(off Vaughan Way)
Trinity Wlk. NW3 ...6A 48
Trinity Way E4 ...6G 19
W3 ...7A 64
Trio Pl. SE1 ...2C 86 (7D 168)
Tristan Ct. *SE8 ...6B 88*
(off Dorking Cl.)
Tristan Sq. SE3 ...3G 107
Tristram Cl. E17 ...3F 35
Tristram Rd. BR1: Brom ...4H 125
Triton Ho. *E14 ...4D 88*
(off Cahir St.)
Triton Sq. NW1 ...4G 67 (3A 160)
Tritton Av. CR0: Croy ...4J 151
Tritton Rd. SE21 ...3D 122
Triumph Cl. UB3: Hayes ...1E 94
Triumph Ho. IG11: Bark ...3A 74
Triumph Rd. E6 ...6D 72
Triumph Trad. Est. N17 ...6B 18
Trocadero Cen. ...7H 67 (3C 166)
Trocette Mans. *SE1 ...3E 86*
(off Bermondsey St.)
Trojan Ct. NW6 ...7G 47
Trojan Ind. Est. NW10 ...6B 46
Trojan Way CR0: Croy ...3K 151
Troon Cl. SE16 ...5H 87
SE28 ...6D 74
Troon Ho. *E1 ...6A 70*
(off White Horse Rd.)
Troon St. E1 ...6A 70
Tropical Ct. *W10 ...3F 65*
(off Kilburn La.)
Trosley Rd. DA17: Belv ...6G 93
Trossachs Rd. SE22 ...5E 104
Trothy Rd. SE1 ...4G 87
Trotman Ho. *SE14 ...1J 105*
(off Pomeroy St.)
Trott Rd. N10 ...7J 15
Trott St. SW11 ...1C 102
Troughton Rd. SE7 ...5K 89
Troutbeck NW1 ...2K 159
Troutbeck Rd. SE14 ...1A 106
Trout Rd. UB7: W Dray ...7A 58
Trouville Rd. SW4 ...6G 103
Trowbridge Rd. E9 ...6B 52
Trowlock Av. TW11: Tedd ...6C 116
Trowlock Way
TW11: Tedd ...6D 116
Troy Ct. SE18 ...4F 91
W8 ...3J 83
(off Kensington High St.)
Troy Ind. Est. HA1: Harr ...5K 25
Troy Rd. SE19 ...6D 122
Troy Town SE15 ...3G 105
Trubshaw Rd. UB2: S'hall ...3F 79
Truesdale Rd. E6 ...6D 72
Trulock Ct. N17 ...7B 18
Trulock Rd. N17 ...7B 18
Truman Cl. HA8: Edg ...7C 12
Trumans Rd. N16 ...5F 51
Trumble Gdns.
CR7: Thor H ...4B 140
Trumpers Way W7 ...3J 79
Trumpington Rd. E7 ...4H 53
Trump St. EC2 ...6C 68 (1D 168)
Trundlers Way
WD23: Bush ...1D 10
Trundle St. SE1 ...2C 86 (6C 168)
Trundleys Rd. SE8 ...5K 87
Trundley's Ter. SE8 ...4K 87
Truro Gdns. IG1: Ilf ...7C 36
Truro Ho. HA5: Pinn ...1D 24
Truro Rd. E17 ...4B 34
N22 ...7D 16
Truro St. NW5 ...6E 48
Truro Way UB4: Hayes ...3G 59
Truslove Rd. SE27 ...5A 122
Trussley Rd. W6 ...3E 82
Trust Wlk. SE21 ...1B 122
Tryfan Cl. IG4: Ilf ...5B 36
Tryon Cres. E9 ...1J 69
Tryon St. SW3 ...5D 84 (5E 170)
Trystings Cl. KT10: Esh ...6A 146
Tuam Rd. SE18 ...6H 91
Tubbs Rd. NW10 ...2B 64
Tucklow Wlk. SW15 ...7B 100
Tudor Av. KT4: Wor Pk ...3D 148
TW12: Hamp ...6E 114
Tudor Barn Theatre, The
...4C 108
Tudor Cl. BR7: Chst ...1D 144
HA5: Pinn ...5J 23
IG7: Chig ...4K 21
IG8: Wfd G ...5E 20
KT9: Chess ...5E 146
N6 ...7G 31
NW3 ...5C 48
NW7 ...6H 13
NW9 ...2J 45
SM3: Sutt ...5F 149
SM6: Wall ...7G 151
SW2 ...6K 103
TW12: Hamp ...5G 115
TW15: Ashf ...4A 112
Tudor Ct. DA14: Sidc ...3A 128
E17 ...7B 34
N1 ...6E 50
N22 ...7D 16
SE9 ...4C 108
SE16 ...1K 87
(off Princes Riverside Rd.)
TW11: Tedd ...6K 115
TW13: Felt ...4A 114
TW19: Staines ...6A 94
W3 ...2G 81
Tudor Ct. Nth.
HA9: Wemb ...5G 45
Tudor Ct. Sth.
HA9: Wemb ...5G 45
Tudor Cres. EN2: Enf ...1H 7
Tudor Dr. KT2: King T ...5D 116
SM4: Mord ...6F 137
Tudor Ent. Pk. HA1: Harr ...3K 43
HA3: Harr ...3H 25
Tudor Est. NW10 ...2H 63
Tudor Gdns.
BR4: W W'ck ...3E 154
(not continuous)
HA3: Harr ...2H 25
NW9 ...2J 45
SW13 ...3A 100
TW1: Twick ...1K 115
W3 ...5G 63
Tudor Gro. E9 ...7J 51
Tudor Ho. E9 ...7J 51
E16 ...7K 71
(off Wesley Av.)
HA5: Pinn ...2A 24
(off Pinner Hill Rd.)
W14 ...4F 83
(off Windsor Way)
Tudor M. E17 ...4B 34
Tudor Pde. RM6: Chad H ...7D 38
SE9 ...4C 108
Tudor Pl. CR4: Mitc ...7C 120
SE19 ...7F 123
Tudor Rd. BR3: Beck ...3E 142
E4 ...6J 19
E6 ...1A 72
E9 ...1H 69
EN5: Barn ...3D 4
HA3: Harr ...2H 25
HA5: Pinn ...2A 24
IG11: Bark ...1K 73
KT2: King T ...7G 117
N9 ...7C 8
SE19 ...7F 123
SE25 ...5H 141
TW3: Houn ...4H 97
TW12: Hamp ...7E 114
TW15: Ashf ...6F 113
UB1: S'hall ...7C 60
UB3: Hayes ...6F 59
Tudor Sq. UB3: Hayes ...5F 59
Tudor Stacks SE24 ...4C 104
Tudor St. EC4 ...7A 68 (2K 167)
Tudor Wlk. DA5: Bexl ...6E 110
Tudor Way BR5: Orp ...6H 145
N14 ...1C 16
UB10: Uxb ...6C 40
W3 ...2G 81
Tudor Well Cl. HA7: Stan ...5G 11
Tudor Works UB4: Hayes ...1B 78
Tudway Rd. SE3 ...3K 107
TUFNELL PARK ...4G 49
Tufnell Pk. Rd. N19 ...4G 49
Tufton Ct. *SW1 ...2E 172*
(off Tufton St.)
Tufton Gdns.
KT8: W Mole ...2F 133
Tufton Rd. E4 ...4H 19
Tufton St. SW1 ...3J 85 (1E 172)
Tugboat St. SE28 ...2J 91
Tugela Rd. CR0: Croy ...6D 140
Tugela St. SE6 ...2B 124
Tulip Cl. CR0: Croy ...1K 153
E6 ...5D 72
TW12: Hamp ...6D 114
UB2: S'hall ...2G 79
Tulip Gdns. E4 ...3A 20
IG1: Ilf ...6F 55
Tullis Ho. *E9 ...7J 51*
(off Frampton Pk. Rd.)
Tull St. CR4: Mitc ...7D 138
Tulse Cl. BR3: Beck ...3E 142
TULSE HILL ...1B 122
Tulse Hill SW2 ...6A 104
Tulse Hill Est. SW2 ...6A 104
Tulse Ho. SW2 ...6A 104
Tulsemere Rd. SE27 ...2C 122
Tumbling Bay
KT12: Walt T ...6J 131
Tummons Gdns. SE25 ...2E 140
Tunbridge Ho. EC1 ...1K 161
Tuncombe Rd. N18 ...4K 17
Tunis Rd. W12 ...1E 82
Tunley Grn. E14 ...5B 70
Tunley Rd. NW10 ...1A 64
SW17 ...1E 120
Tunmarsh La. E13 ...3K 71
Tunnanleys E6 ...6E 72
Tunnel App. E14 ...7A 70
SE10 ...2G 89
SE16 ...2J 87
Tunnel Av. SE10 ...2F 89
(not continuous)
Tunnel Av. Trad. Est. SE10 ...2F 89
Tunnel Gdns. N11 ...7B 16
Tunnel Link Rd.
TW6: Houn ...5C 94
Tunnel Rd. SE16 ...2J 87
Tunnel Rd. E. TW6: Houn ...1D 94
Tunnel Rd. W. TW6: Houn ...1C 94
Tunstall Rd. CR0: Croy ...1E 152
SW9 ...4K 103
Tunstall Wlk. TW8: Bford ...6E 80
Tunstock Way DA17: Belv ...3E 92
Tunworth Cl. NW9 ...6J 27
Tunworth Cres. SW15 ...6B 100
Tun Yd. *SW8 ...2F 103*
(off Silverthorne Rd.)
Tupelo Rd. E10 ...2D 52
Tupman Ho. *SE16 ...2G 87*
(off Scott Lidgett Cres.)
Tuppy St. SE28 ...2G 91
Turenne Cl. SW18 ...4A 102
Turin Rd. N9 ...7D 8
Turin St. E2 ...3G 69 (2K 163)
Turkey Oak Cl. SE19 ...1E 140
Turks Cl. UB8: Uxb ...3C 58
Turk's Head Yd.
EC1 ...5B 68 (5A 162)
Turk's Row SW3 ...5D 84 (5F 171)
Turle Rd. N4 ...2K 49
SW16 ...2J 139
SW16 ...2J 139
Turlewray Cl. N4 ...1K 49
Turley Cl. E15 ...1G 71
Turnagain La. EC4 ...7A 162
Turnage Rd. RM8: Dag ...1E 56
Turnberry Cl. NW4 ...2F 29
SE16 ...5H 87
Turnberry Quay E14 ...3D 88
Turnberry Way BR6: Orp ...7H 145
Turnbull Ho. N1 ...1B 68
Turnbury Cl. SE28 ...6D 74
Turnchapel M. SW4 ...3F 103
Turner Av. CR4: Mitc ...1D 138
N15 ...4E 32
TW2: Twick ...3G 115
Turner Cl. HA0: Wemb ...6D 44
NW11 ...6K 29
SE5 ...7B 86
UB4: Hayes ...2E 58
Turner Ct. *SE16 ...2J 87*
(off Albion St.)
Turner Dr. NW11 ...6K 29
Turner Ho. *NW8 ...2C 66*
(off Townshend Est.)
SW1 ...4D 172
(off Herrick St.)
TW1: Twick ...6D 98
(off Clevedon Rd.)
Turner Pl. SW11 ...5C 102
Turner Rd. E17 ...3E 34
HA8: Edg ...2E 26
KT3: N Mald ...7K 135
Turner's All. EC3 ...7E 68 (2G 169)
Turners Mdw. Way
BR3: Beck ...1B 142
Turners Rd. E3 ...5B 70
Turner St. E1 ...5H 69
E16 ...6H 71
Turner's Way CR0: Croy ...2A 152
Turners Wood NW11 ...7A 30
Turneville Rd. W14 ...6H 83
Turney Rd. SE21 ...7C 104
TURNHAM GREEN ...4A 82
Turnham Grn. Ter. W4 ...4A 82
Turnham Grn. Ter. M. W4 ...4A 82
Turnham Rd. SE4 ...5A 106
Turnmill St. EC1 ...4B 68 (4A 162)
Turnour Ho. *E1 ...6H 69*
(off Walburgh St.)
Turnpike Cl. SE8 ...7B 88
Turnpike Ct. DA6: Bex ...4D 110
Turnpike Ho. EC1 ...3B 68 (2B 162)
Turnpike La. N8 ...4K 31
SM1: Sutt ...5A 150
UB10: Uxb ...3A 58
Turnpike Link CR0: Croy ...2E 152
Turnpike Pde. *N8 ...3B 32*
(off Green Lanes)
Turnpike Way TW7: Isle ...1A 98
Turnpin La. SE10 ...6E 88
Turnstone Cl. E13 ...3J 71
NW9 ...2A 28
UB10: Uxb ...5D 40
Turpentine La.
SW1 ...5F 85 (5K 171)

Turpin Cl.—Upland Rd.

Turpin Cl. E1 . . . . 7K **69**
Turpington Cl. BR2: Short 6C **144**
Turpington La. BR2: Short 7C **144**
Turpin Ho. SW11 . . . . . . 1F **103**
Turpin Rd. TW14: Felt 6H **95**
Turpin's La. IG8: Wfd G 5J **21**
Turpin Way N19 . . . . . . 2H **49**
(not continuous)
SM6: Wall 7F **151**
Turquand St. SE17 . . . . . . 4C **86**
Turret Gro. SW4 . . . . . . 3G **103**
Turton Rd. HA0: Wemb 5E **44**
Turville Ho. *NW8* *3C 158*
(off Grendon St.)
Turville St. E2 . . . . 4F **69** (3J **163**)
Tuscan Ho. *E2* *3J 69*
(off Knottisford St.)
Tuscan Rd. SE18 . . . . . . 5H **91**
Tuscany Ho. E17 . . . . . . 2B **34**
Tuskar St. SE10 . . . . . . 6G **89**
Tustin Est. SE15 . . . . . . 6J **87**
Tuttlebee La. IG9: Buck H . . 2D **20**
Tuttle Ho. *SW1* *6C 172*
(off Aylesford St.)
Tweedale Ct. E15 . . . . . . 5E **52**
Tweed Ct. *W7* *6J 61*
(off Hanway Rd.)
Tweeddale Gro. UB10: Uxb 3E **40**
Tweeddale Rd. SM5: Cars 1B **150**
Tweed Glen RM1: Rom 1K **39**
Tweed Grn. RM1: Rom 1K **39**
Tweed Ho. *E14* *2E 70*
(off Teviot St.)
Tweedmouth Rd. E13 . . . . 2K **71**
Tweed Way RM1: Rom 1K **39**
Tweedy Cl. EN1: Enf 5A **8**
Tweedy Rd. BR1: Brom 1J **143**
Tweezer's All. WC2 . . . . . . 2J **167**
Twelvetrees Cres. E3 . . . . 4E **70**
(not continuous)
E16 . . . . . . 4F **71**
Twentyman Cl. IG8: Wfd G . . 5D **20**
TWICKENHAM **1A 116**
Twickenham Bri. TW1: Twick 5C **98**
Twickenham Cl. CR0: Croy 3K **151**
Twickenham Gdns.
HA3: Harr 7D **10**
UB6: G'frd 5A **44**
Twickenham Rd. E11 . . . . 2E **52**
TW7: Isle 5A **98**
TW9: Rich 4C **98**
TW11: Tedd 4A **116**
(not continuous)
TW13: Felt 3D **114**
Twickenham Rugby Union Football Ground *6J 97*
Twickenham Stadium Tours *6J 97*
(Twickenham Rugby Union Football Ground)
Twickenham Trad. Est. TW1: Twick 6K **97**
Twig Folly Cl. E2 . . . . . . 2K **69**
Twigg Cl. DA8: Erith 7K **93**
Twilley St. SW18 . . . . . . 7K **101**
Twin Bridges Bus. Pk. CR2: S Croy 6D **152**
Twine Cl. IG11: Bark 3B **74**
Twine Ct. E1 . . . . . . 7J **69**
Twineham Grn. N12 . . . . . . 4D **14**
Twine Ter. *E3* *4B 70*
(off Ropery St.)
Twining Av. TW2: Twick 3G **115**
Twinn Rd. NW7 . . . . . . 6B **14**
Twin Tumps Way SE28 . . . . 7A **74**
Twisden Rd. NW5 . . . . . . 4F **49**
Twybridge Way NW10 . . . . . . 7J **45**
Twycross M. SE10 . . . . . . 5G **89**
Twyford Abbey Rd. NW10 . . . . 3F **63**
Twyford Av. N2 . . . . . . 3D **30**
W3 . . . . . . 7G **63**
Twyford Ct. *HA0: Wemb* *2E 62*
(off Vicars Bri. Cl.)
N10 . . . . . . 3E **30**
Twyford Cres. W3 . . . . . . 1G **81**
Twyford Ho. N5 . . . . . . 3B **50**
N15 . . . . . . *6E 32*
(off Chisley Rd.)
Twyford Pl. WC2 . . . 6K **67** (7G **161**)
Twyford Rd. HA2: Harr 1F **43**
IG1: Ilf 5G **55**
SM5: Cars 1B **150**
Twyford St. N1 . . . . . . 1K **67**
Tyas Rd. E16 . . . . . . 4H **71**
Tybenham Rd. SW19 . . . . 3J **137**
Tyberry Rd. EN3: Enf 3C **8**
Tyburn La. HA1: Harr 7K **25**
Tyburn Way W1 . . . 7D **66** (2F **165**)
Tyers Est. SE1 . . . . . . 6G **169**
Tyers Ga. SE1 . . . . 2E **86** (7G **169**)
Tyers St. SE11 . . . . 5K **85** (6G **173**)
Tyers Ter. SE11 . . . 5K **85** (6G **173**)
Tyeshurst Cl. SE2 . . . . . . 5E **92**
Tylecroft Rd. SW16 . . . . . . 2J **139**
Tylehurst Gdns. IG1: Ilf 5G **55**
Tyler Cl. E2 . . . . . . 2F **69**
Tyler Rd. UB2: S'hall 3F **79**
Tylers Ct. *E17* *4C 34*
(off Westbury Rd.)
HA0: Wemb 2E **62**
W1 . . . . . . 1C **166**
Tylers Ga. HA3: Harr 6E **26**
Tylers Path SM5: Cars 4D **150**
Tyler St. SE10 . . . . . . 5G **89**
(not continuous)
Tylney Av. SE19 . . . . . . 5F **123**
(not continuous)
Tylney Ho. *E1* *6H 69*
(off Nelson St.)
Tylney Rd. BR1: Brom 2B **144**
E7 . . . . . . 4A **54**
Tynamara *KT1: King T* *4D 134*
(off Portsmouth Rd.)
Tynan Cl. TW14: Felt 1J **113**
Tyndale Ct. *E14* *5D 88*
(off Transom Sq.)
Tyndale La. N1 . . . . . . 7B **50**
Tyndale Mans. *N1* *7B 50*
(off Upper St.)
Tyndale Ter. N1 . . . . . . 7B **50**
Tyndall Gdns. E10 . . . . . . 2E **52**
Tyndall Rd. DA16: Well . . . 3K **109**
E10 . . . . . . 2E **52**
Tyne Ct. *W7* *6J 61*
(off Hanway Rd.)
Tyneham Cl. SW11 . . . . . . 3E **102**
Tyneham Rd. SW11 . . . . . . 2E **102**
Tyne Ho. KT1: King T 1D **134**
Tynemouth Cl. E6 . . . . . . 6F **73**
Tynemouth Dr. EN1: Enf 1B **8**
Tynemouth Rd. CR4: Mitc . . 7E **120**
N15 . . . . . . 4F **33**
SE18 . . . . . . 5J **91**
Tynemouth St. SW6 . . . . 2A **102**
Tyne St. E1 . . . . 6F **69** (7K **163**)
Tynsdale Cl. NW10 . . . . . . 6A **46**
Tynwald Ho. SE26 . . . . . . 3G **123**
Type St. E2 . . . . . . 2K **69**
Tyrawley Rd. SW6 . . . . . . 1K **101**
Tyre La. NW9 . . . . . . 4A **28**
Tyrell Cl. HA1: Harr 4J **43**
Tyrell Ct. SM5: Cars 4D **150**
Tyrell Ho. *BR3: Beck* *5D 124*
(off Beckenham Hill Rd.)
Tyrols Rd. SE23 . . . . . . 1K **123**
Tyrone Rd. E6 . . . . . . 2D **72**
Tyron Way DA14: Sidc 4J **127**
Tyrrell Av. DA16: Well 5A **110**
Tyrrell Ho. *SW1* *7B 172*
(off Churchill Gdns.)
Tyrrell Rd. SE22 . . . . . . 4G **105**
Tyrrell Sq. CR4: Mitc 1C **138**
Tyrrel Way NW9 . . . . . . 7B **28**
Tyrwhitt Rd. SE4 . . . . . . 3C **106**
Tysoe St. EC1 . . . . 3A **68** (2K **161**)
Tyson Gdns. SE23 . . . . . . 7J **105**
Tyson Rd. SE23 . . . . . . 7J **105**
Tyssen Pas. E8 . . . . . . 6F **51**
Tyssen Rd. N16 . . . . . . 3F **51**
Tyssen St. E8 . . . . . . 6F **51**
N1 . . . . . . 2E **68**
Tytherton *E2* *2J 69*
(off Cyprus St.)
Tytherton Rd. N19 . . . . . . 3H **49**

U

Uamvar St. E14 . . . . . . 5D **70**
Uckfield Gro. CR4: Mitc 7E **120**
Udall St. SW1 . . . . 4G **85** (4B **172**)
Udimore Ho. *W10* *5E 64*
(off Sutton Way)
Udney Pk. Rd. TW11: Tedd 6A **116**
Uffington Rd. NW10 . . . . . . 1C **64**
SE27 . . . . . . 4A **122**
Ufford Cl. HA3: Harr 7A **10**
Ufford Rd. HA3: Harr 7A **10**
Ufford St. SE1 . . . . . . 2A **86** (6K **167**)
Ufton Ct. UB5: N'olt 3B **60**
Ufton Gro. N1 . . . . . . 7D **50**
Ufton Rd. N1 . . . . . . 7D **50**
(not continuous)
Uhura Sq. N16 . . . . . . 3E **50**
Ujima Ct. SW16 . . . . . . 4J **121**
Ullathorne Rd. SW16 . . . . 4G **121**
Ulleswater Rd. N14 . . . . . . 3D **16**
Ullin St. E14 . . . . . . 5E **70**
Ullswater E18 . . . . . . 2J **35**
Ullswater Cl.
BR1: Brom 7G **125**
SW15 . . . . . . 4K **117**
UB4: Hayes 2G **59**
Ullswater Ct. HA2: Harr 7E **24**
Ullswater Cres. SW15 . . . . . . 4K **117**
Ullswater Ho. *SE15* *6J 87*
(off Hillbeck Cl.)
Ullswater Rd. SE27 . . . . . . 2B **122**
SW13 . . . . . . 7C **82**
Ulster Gdns. N13 . . . . . . 4H **17**
Ulster Pl. NW1 . . . . 4F **67** (4J **159**)
Ulster Ter. NW1 . . . . . . 3H **159**
Ulundi Rd. SE3 . . . . . . 6G **89**
Ulva Rd. SW15 . . . . . . 5F **101**
Ulverscroft Rd. SE22 . . . . 5F **105**
Ulverstone Rd. SE27 . . . . 2B **122**
Ulverston Rd. E17 . . . . . . 2F **35**
Ulysses Rd. NW6 . . . . . . 5H **47**
Umberston St. E1 . . . . . . 6G **69**
Umbria St. SW15 . . . . . . 6C **100**
Umfreville Rd. N4 . . . . . . 6B **32**
Undercliff Rd. SE13 . . . . . . 3C **106**
UNDERHILL **5D 4**
Underhill EN5: Barn 5D **4**
Underhill Ct. EN5: Barn 5D **4**
Underhill Ho. *E14* *5C 70*
(off Burgess St.)
Underhill Pas. *NW1* *1F 67*
(off Camden High St.)
Underhill Rd. SE22 . . . . . . 5G **105**
Underhill Stadium *5D 4*
Underhill St. NW1 . . . . . . 1F **67**
Underne Av. N14 . . . . . . 2A **16**
Undershaft EC3 . . . . . . 6E **68** (1G **169**)
Undershaw Rd. BR1: Brom 3H **125**
Underwood CR0: Croy 5E **154**
Underwood Ct. *E10* *1D 52*
(off Leyton Grange Est.)
Underwood Ho. *W6* *3D 82*
(off Sycamore Gdns.)
Underwood Rd. E1 . . . . . . 4G **69**
E4 . . . . . . 5J **19**
IG8: Wfd G 7F **21**
Underwood Row N1 . . . . . . 3C **68** (1D **162**)
Underwood St. N1 . . . . . . 3C **68** (1D **162**)
Underwood, The SE9 . . . . 2D **126**
Undine Rd. E14 . . . . . . 4D **88**
Undine St. SW17 . . . . . . 5D **120**
Uneeda Dr. UB6: G'frd 1H **61**
Unicorn Bldg. *E1* *7K 69*
(off Jardine Rd.)
Union Cl. E11 . . . . . . 4F **53**
Union Cotts. E15 . . . . . . 7G **53**
Union Ct. EC2 . . . . . . 7G **163**
SW4 . . . . . . 2J **103**
TW9: Rich 5E **98**
W9 . . . . . . *5J 65*
(off Elmfield Way)
Union Dr. E1 . . . . . . 4A **70**
Union Gro. SW8 . . . . . . 2H **103**
Union M. SW4 . . . . . . 2J **103**
Union Rd. BR2: Short 5B **144**
CR0: Croy 7C **140**
HA0: Wemb 6E **44**
N11 . . . . . . 6C **16**
SW8 . . . . . . 2H **103**
UB5: N'olt 2E **60**
Union Sq. N1 . . . . . . 1C **68**
Union St. E15 . . . . . . 1F **71**
EN5: Barn 3B **4**
KT1: King T 2D **134**
SE1 . . . . . . 1B **86** (5A **168**)
Union Theatre *5B 168*
Union Wlk. E2 . . . . 3E **68** (1H **163**)
Union Wharf N1 . . . . . . 1C **68**
Union Yd. W1 . . . . 6F **67** (1K **165**)
Unitair Cen. TW6: Houn 6E **94**
Unit Workshops *E1* *6G 69*
(off Adler St.)
Unity Cl. CR0: Croy 7D **154**
NW10 . . . . . . 6C **46**
SE19 . . . . . . 5C **122**
Unity M. NW1 . . . . . . 2H **67**
Unity Trad. Est. IG8: Wfd G 2B **36**
Unity Way SE7 . . . . . . 3B **90**
Unity Wharf *SE1* *6K 169*
(off Mill St.)
University Cl. NW7 . . . . . . 7G **13**
University College . . . . . . *4H 67 (4C 160)*
University College Department of Geological Science *4C 160*
University College London *2D 160*
(off Cartwright Gdns.)
Campbell House *4H 67*
Chemistry Building . . . . . . *4H 67 (3C 160)*
University Gdns. DA5: Bexl 7F **111**
University of Central London
Gordon St. *4G 67*
Taviton St. *4G 67*
University of East London
Annexe *2H 71*
Docklands Campus . . . *7E 72*
Maryland Ho. *6G 53*
(off Manbey Pk. Rd.)
Stratford Campus . . . *6G 53*
(off Water La.)
University of Greenwich *6E 88*
Avery Hill Campus . . *6G 109*
Old Royal Naval College Campus *6F 89*
Woolwich Campus . . . *3E 90*
(Beresford St.)
Woolwich Campus . . . *4E 90*
(Wellington St.)
University of London
College Hall . . . . . . *5H 67 (4C 160)*
Commonwealth Hall *3J 67*
Connaught Hall . . . *3D 160*
(off Tavistock Sq.)
Hughes Parry Hall . . *3J 67*
Institute of Advanced Legal Studies *4D 160*
Observatory *6G 13*
Senate House . . . . . . *5H 67 (5D 160)*
Union . . . . *4H 67 (4D 160)*
Warburg Institute . . . . . . *4H 67 (4D 160)*
University of North London
Highbury Cres. *6A 50*
Highbury Gro. *5C 50*
University of Westminster
Cavendish Campus . . . . . . *5F 67 (5K 159)*
(Bolsover St.)
Cavendish Campus . . . . . . *5G 67 (5A 160)*
(Hanson St.)
Euston Cen. . . . . . . *4G 67 (3A 160)*
Harrow Campus *7A 26*
Library . . . *5G 67 (6A 160)*
Marylebone Campus . . . . . . *5E 66 (5G 159)*
Regent Campus . . . *6A 160*
(Lit. Titchfield St.)
Regent Campus . . . . . . *6F 67 (7K 159)*
(Regent St.)
Regent Campus . . . *7B 160*
(Wells St.)
School of Languages . . . . . . *4G 67 (3A 160)*
University Pl. DA8: Erith 7J **93**
University Rd. SW19 . . . . 6B **120**
University St. WC1 . . . . . . 4G **67** (4B **160**)
University Way E16 . . . . . . 7E **72**
Unwin Av. TW14: Felt 5F **95**
Unwin Cl. SE15 . . . . . . 6G **87**
Unwin Mans. *W14* *6H 83*
(off Queen's Club Gdns.)
Unwin Rd. SW7 . . . 3B **84** (1A **170**)
TW7: Isle 3J **97**
Upbrook M. W2 . . . 6A **66** (1A **164**)
Upcerne Rd. SW10 . . . . . . 7A **84**
Upchurch Cl. SE20 . . . . . . 7H **123**
Upcott Ho. *E9* *7J 51*
(off Frampton Pk. Rd.)
Upcroft Av. HA8: Edg 5D **12**
Updale Rd. DA14: Sidc 4K **127**
Upfield CR0: Croy 3H **153**
Upfield Rd. W7 . . . . . . 5K **61**
Upgrove Mnr. Way SE24 . . 7A **104**
Uphall Rd. IG1: Ilf 5F **55**
Upham Pk. Rd. W4 . . . . . . 4A **82**
Uphill Dr. NW7 . . . . . . 5F **13**
NW9 . . . . . . 5J **27**
Uphill Gro. NW7 . . . . . . 4F **13**
Uphill Rd. NW7 . . . . . . 4F **13**
Upland M. SE22 . . . . . . 5G **105**
Upland Rd. CR2: S Croy 5D **152**
DA7: Bex 3F **111**
E13 . . . . . . 4J **71**
SE22 . . . . . . 5G **105**
SM2: Sutt 7B **150**

358 A-Z London

Uplands—Vanbrugh Ter.

Uplands BR3: Beck 2C 142
Uplands Av. E17 ....2K 33
Uplands Bus. Pk. E17 ......3K 33
Uplands Cl. SW14 ....5H 99
Uplands Ct. *N21* *7F 7*
(off Green, The)
Uplands End IG8: Wfd G 7H 21
Uplands Pk. Rd. EN2: Enf 2F 7
Uplands Rd. EN4: Barn 1K 15
IG8: Wfd G 7H 21
N8 ....5K 31
RM6: Chad H 3D 38
Uplands, The HA4: Ruis 1J 41
Uplands Way N21 ....5F 7
Upnall Ho. SE15 ....6J 87
Upney La. IG11: Bark 6J 55
Upnor Way SE17 ....5E 86
Uppark Dr. IG2: Ilf 6G 37
Up. Abbey Rd. DA17: Belv ...4F 93
Up. Addison Gdns. W14 ....2G 83
Up. Bardsey Wlk. *N1* *6C 50*
(off Douglas Rd. Nth.)
Up. Belgrave St.
SW1 ......3E 84 (1H 171)
Up. Berenger Wlk. *SW10* *7B 84*
(off Berenger Wlk.)
Up. Berkeley St.
W2 ....6D 66 (1E 164)
Up. Beulah Hill SE19 ......1E 140
Up. Blantyre Wlk. *SW10* *7B 84*
(off Blantyre Wlk.)
Up. Brighton Rd.
KT6: Surb 6D 134
Up. Brockley Rd. SE4 ......3B 106
(not continuous)
Up. Brook St.
W1 ....7E 66 (2G 165)
Up. Butts TW8: Bford 6C 80
Up. Caldy Wlk. *N1* *7C 50*
(off Arran Wlk.)
Up. Camelford Wlk. *W11* *6G 65*
(off St Mark's Rd.)
Up. Cavendish Av. N3 ....3J 29
Up. Cheyne Row SW3 .....7C 170
UPPER CLAPTON **2H 51**
Up. Clapton Rd. E5 ....2H 51
Up. Clarendon Wlk. *W11* *6G 65*
(off Clarendon Rd.)
Up. Dartrey Wlk. *SW10* *7A 84*
(off Whistler Wlk.)
Up. Dengie Wlk. *N1* *1C 68*
(off Baddow Wlk.)
UPPER EDMONTON **5B 18**
UPPER ELMERS END **5B 142**
Up. Elmers End Rd.
BR3: Beck 4A 142
Up. Farm Rd.
KT8: W Mole 4D 132
Upper Feilde *W1* *2G 165*
(off Park St.)
Up. Fosters *NW4* *4E 28*
(off New Brent St.)
Up. Green E. CR4: Mitc 3D 138
Up. Green W. CR4: Mitc 2D 138
(not continuous)
Up. Grosvenor St.
W1 ....7E 66 (3G 165)
Up. Grotto Rd.
TW1: Twick 2K 115
Upper Ground
SE1 ....1A 86 (4J 167)
Upper Gro. SE25 ....4E 140
Up. Grove Rd. DA17: Belv ...6F 93
Up. Gulland Wlk. *N1* *6C 50*
(off Church Rd.)
UPPER HALLIFORD **4G 131**
Up. Halliford By-Pass
TW17: Shep 5G 131
Up. Halliford Grn.
TW17: Shep 4G 131
Up. Halliford Rd.
TW17: Shep 3G 131
Up. Hampstead Wlk. NW3 ...4A 48
Up. Ham Rd. TW10: Rich ...4D 116
Up. Handa Wlk. *N1* *6D 50*
(off Handa Wlk.)
Up. Hawkwell Wlk. *N1* *1C 68*
(off Maldon Cl.)
Up. Hilldrop Est. N7 ....5H 49
UPPER HOLLOWAY **2G 49**
Up. Holly Hill Rd.
DA17: Belv 5H 93
Up. James St. W1 ..7G 67 (2B 166)
Up. John St. W1 ...7G 67 (2B 166)
Up. Lismore Wlk. *N1* *6D 50*
(off Clephane Rd.)
Upper Mall W6 ....5C 82
(not continuous)
Upper Marsh
SE1 ....3K 85 (1H 173)
Up. Montagu St.
W1 ....5D 66 (5E 158)
Up. Mulgrave Rd.
SM2: Sutt 7G 149
Up. North St. E14 ....5C 70
UPPER NORWOOD **1E 140**
Up. Palace Rd.
KT8: E Mos 3G 133
Up. Park Rd. BR1: Brom ...1K 143
DA17: Belv 4H 93
KT2: King T 6G 117
N11 ....5A 16
NW3 ....5D 48
Up. Phillimore Gdns. W8 ....2J 83
Up. Ramsey Wlk. *N1* *6D 50*
(off Ramsey Wlk.)
Up. Rawreth Wlk. *N1* *1C 68*
(off Basire St.)
Up. Richmond Rd. SW15 ...4B 100
Up. Richmond Rd. W.
TW10: Rich 4G 99
Upper Rd. E13 ....3J 71
SM6: Wall 5H 151
UPPER RUXLEY **7G 129**
Up. St Martin's La.
WC2 ....7J 67 (2E 166)
Up. Selsdon Rd.
CR2: S Croy 7F 153
Up. Sheridan Rd.
DA17: Belv 4G 93
UPPER SHIRLEY **4K 153**
Up. Shirley Rd.
CR0: Croy 2J 153
Upper Sq. TW7: Isle 3A 98
Upper St. N1 ....2A 68
Up. Sunbury Rd.
TW12: Hamp 1C 132
Up. Sutton La. TW5: Houn ...7E 78
UPPER SYDENHAM **3H 123**
Up. Tachbrook St.
SW1 ....4G 85 (3B 172)
Up. Talbot Wlk. *W11* *6G 65*
(off Talbot Wlk.)
Up. Teddington Rd.
KT1: King T 7C 116
Upper Ter. NW3 ....3A 48
Up. Thames St.
EC4 ....7B 68 (2B 168)
Up. Tollington Pk. N4 ....1A 50
(not continuous)
Upperton Rd. DA14: Sidc ...5K 127
Upperton Rd. E. E13 ....3A 72
Upperton Rd. W. E13 ....3A 72
UPPER TOOTING **4D 120**
Up. Tooting Pk. SW17 .....2D 120
Up. Tooting Rd. SW17 .....4D 120
Up. Town Rd. UB6: G'frd 4F 61
Up. Tulse Hill SW2 ....7K 103
Up. Vernon Rd.
SM1: Sutt 5B 150
UPPER WALTHAMSTOW **4F 35**
Up. Walthamstow Rd. E17 ...4E 34
Up. Whistler Wlk. *SW10* *7A 84*
(off Worlds End Est.)
Up. Wickham La.
DA16: Well 7B 92
Up. Wimpole St.
W1 ....5E 66 (5H 159)
Up. Woburn Pl.
WC1 ....3H 67 (2D 160)
Uppingham Av.
HA7: Stan 1B 26
Upsdell Av. N13 ....6F 17
Upshire Ho. E17 ....2B 34
Upstall St. SE5 ....1B 104
UPTON
BEXLEYHEATH **5D 110**
WEST HAM **7J 53**
Upton Av. E7 ....7J 53
Upton Cl. DA5: Bexl 6F 111
NW2 ....3G 47
Upton Ct. *SE20* *7J 123*
(off Blean Gro.)
Upton Dene SM2: Sutt 7K 149
Upton Gdns. HA3: Harr 5B 26
Upton La. E7 ....7J 53
Upton Lodge E7 ....6J 53
Upton Lodge Cl.
WD23: Bush 1B 10
UPTON PARK **1B 72**
Upton Pk. Rd. E7 ....7K 53
Upton Park Stadium ***2A 72***
Upton Rd.
CR7: Thor H 2D 140
DA6: Bex 4E 110
N18 ....5B 18
SE18 ....6G 91
TW3: Houn 3E 96
Upton Rd. Sth.
DA5: Bexl 6F 111
Upton Vs. DA6: Bex 4E 110
Upway N12 ....6H 15
Upwey Ho. N1 ....1E 68
Upwood Rd. SE12 ....6J 107
SW16 ....1J 139
Urlwin St. SE5 ....6C 86
Urlwin Wlk. SW9 ....1A 104
Urmston Dr. SW19 ....1G 119
Urmston Ho. *E14* *4E 88*
(off Seyssel St.)
Urquhart Ct.
BR3: Beck 7B 124
Ursula Lodges
DA14: Sidc 5B 128
Ursula M. N4 ....1C 50
Ursula St. SW11 ....1C 102
Urswick Gdns.
RM9: Dag 7E 56
Urswick Rd. E9 ....5J 51
RM9: Dag 7D 56
Usborne M. SW8 ....7K 85
Usher Rd. E3 ....1B 70
Usk Rd. SW11 ....4A 102
Usk St. E2 ....3K 69
Utopia Village NW1 ....7E 48
Uvedale Rd. EN2: Enf 5J 7
RM10: Dag 3G 57
Uverdale Rd. SW10 ....7A 84
UXBRIDGE **7A 40**
Uxbridge Ct.
KT1: King T *5D 134*
(off Uxbridge Rd.)
Uxbridge Rd. HA3: Harr 7B 10
HA5: Pinn 2A 24
KT1: King T 4D 134
TW13: Felt 4E 114
(Hampton Rd. E.)
TW13: Felt 2A 114
(Harlington Rd. E.)
UB1: S'hall 1E 78
UB10: Uxb 3C 58
W3 ....7E 62
W5 ....7E 62
W7 ....1K 79
W12 ....1B 82
W13 ....1B 80
Uxbridge St. W8 ....1J 83
Uxendon Cres.
HA9: Wemb 1E 44
Uxendon Hill
HA9: Wemb 1F 45

V

Vaine Ho. E9 ....6A 52
Vaizeys Wharf *SE7* *3K 89*
(off Riverside)
Valance Av. E4 ....1B 20
Valan Leas BR2: Short 3G 143
Vale Cl. BR6: Orp 4E 156
N2 ....3D 30
TW1: Twick 3A 116
W9 ....3A 66
Vale Cotts. SW15 ....3A 118
Vale Ct. EN5: Barn 4E 4
W3 ....1B 82
W9 ....3A 66
Vale Cres. SW15 ....4A 118
Vale Cft. HA5: Pinn 5C 24
Vale Dr. EN5: Barn 4C 4
Vale End SE22 ....4F 105
Vale Est., The W3 ....1A 82
Vale Gro. N4 ....7C 32
W3 ....2K 81
Vale La. W3 ....5G 63
Vale Lodge SE23 ....2J 123
Valence Av. RM8: Dag 1D 56
Valence Cir. RM8: Dag 3D 56
Valence House Mus. & Gallery
................***3E 56***
Valence Rd. DA8: Erith 7K 93
Valence Wood Rd.
RM8: Dag 3D 56
Valencia Rd. HA7: Stan 4H 11
Valentia Pl. SW9 ....4A 104
Valentine Av.
DA5: Bexl 2E 128
Valentine Ct. SE23 ....2K 123
(not continuous)
Valentine M. N19 ....2H 49
Valentine Pl.
SE1 ....2B 86 (6A 168)
Valentine Rd. E9 ....6K 51
HA2: Harr 3F 43
Valentine Row
SE1 ....2B 86 (7A 168)
Valentines Rd. IG1: Ilf 1F 55
Valentine's Way
RM7: Rush G 2K 57
VALE OF HEALTH **3A 48**
Vale of Health NW3 ....3B 48
Vale Pde. SW15 ....3A 118
Valerian Way E15 ....3G 71
Valerie Ct. SM2: Sutt 7K 149
Vale Ri. NW11 ....1H 47
Vale Rd. BR1: Brom 1E 144
CR4: Mitc 3H 139
E7 ....6K 53
KT4: Wor Pk 3B 148
KT19: Eps 4B 148
N4 ....7C 32
SM1: Sutt 4K 149
Vale Rd. Nth.
KT6: Surb 2E 146
Vale Rd. Sth.
KT6: Surb 2E 146
Vale Row N5 ....3B 50
Vale Royal N7 ....7J 49
Vale Royal Ho. *WC2* *2D 166*
(off Charing Cross Rd.)
Valery Pl.
TW12: Hamp 7E 114
Valeside Ct. EN5: Barn 4E 4
Vale St. SE27 ....3D 122
Valeswood Rd.
BR1: Brom 5H 125
Vale Ter. N4 ....6C 32
Vale, The CR0: Croy 2K 153
HA4: Ruis 4A 42
IG8: Wfd G 7D 20
N10 ....1E 30
N14 ....7C 6
NW11 ....3F 47
SW3 ......6B 84 (7A 170)
TW5: Houn 6C 78
TW14: Felt 6K 95
TW16: Sun T 6J 113
W3 ....1K 81
Valetta Gro. E13 ....2J 71
Valetta Rd. W3 ....2A 82
Valette Ct. *N10* *4F 31*
(off St James's La.)
Valette Ho. E9 ....6J 51
Valette St. E9 ....6J 51
Valiant Cl. RM7: Mawney ...2H 39
UB5: N'olt 3B 60
Valiant Ho. *E14* *2E 88*
(off Plevna St.)
SE7 ....5A 90
Valiant Path NW9 ....1A 28
Valiant Way E6 ....5D 72
Vallance Rd. E2 ....3G 69
N22 ....2G 31
Vallentin Rd. E17 ....4E 34
Valley Av. N12 ....4G 15
Valley Cl. HA5: Pinn 2K 23
Valley Dr. NW9 ....6G 27
Valleyfield Rd. SW16 ......5K 121
Valley Flds. Cres. EN2: Enf ...2F 7
Valley Gdns. HA0: Wemb 7F 45
SW19 ....7B 120
Valley Gro. SE7 ....5A 90
Valley Leisure Pk.
CR0: Croy 1J 151
Valleylink Est. EN3: Enf 6F 9
Valley M. TW1: Twick 2K 115
Valley Rd. BR2: Short 2G 143
BR5: Orp 7B 128
DA8: Erith 4J 93
DA17: Belv 4H 93
SW16 ....5K 121
UB10: Uxb 2A 58
Valley Side E4 ....2H 19
SE7 ....5B 90
Valley Side Pde. E4 ....2H 19
Valley, The ***5A 90***
Valley Vw. EN5: Barn 6B 4
Valley Wlk. CR0: Croy 2J 153
Valliere Rd. NW10 ....3C 64
Valliers Wood Rd.
DA15: Sidc 1J 127
Vallis Way KT9: Chess 4D 146
W13 ....5A 62
Valmar Rd. SE5 ....1C 104
Valmar Trad. Est. SE5 .....1C 104
Val McKenzie Av. N7 ....3A 50
Valnay St. SW17 ....5D 120
Valognes Av. E17 ....1A 34
Valois Ho. *SE1* *3F 87*
(off Grange, The)
Valonia Gdns. SW18 ......6H 101
Vambery Rd. SE18 ....6G 91
Vanbrough Cres.
UB5: N'olt 1A 60
Vanbrugh Castle *SE3* *6G 89*
(off Maze Hill)
Vanbrugh Cl. E16 ....5B 72
Vanbrugh Ct. SE11 ....4K 173
Vanbrugh Dr.
KT12: Walt T 7A 132
Vanbrugh Flds. SE3 ....6H 89
Vanbrugh Hill SE10 ....5H 89
Vanbrugh Ho. *E9* *7J 51*
(off Loddiges Rd.)
Vanbrugh Pk. SE3 ....7H 89
Vanbrugh Pk. Rd. SE3 ......7H 89
Vanbrugh Pk. Rd. W. SE3 ...7H 89
Vanbrugh Rd. W4 ....3K 81
Vanbrugh Ter. SE3 ....1H 107

Vanburgh Cl.—Victoria Ct.

Vanburgh Cl. BR6: Orp . . . 7J 145
Vanburgh Ho. E1 . . . 5J 163
(off Folgate St.)
Vancouver Ho. E1 . . . 1H 87
(off Reardon Path)
Vancouver Mans.
HA8: Edg . . . 1H 27
Vancouver Rd.
HA8: Edg . . . 1H 27
SE23 . . . 2A 124
TW10: Rich . . . 4C 116
UB4: Hayes . . . 4K 59
Vanderbilt Rd. SW18 . . . 1K 119
Vanderville Gdns. N2 . . . 2A 30
Vandome Cl. E16 . . . 6K 71
Vandon Ct. SW1 . . . 1B 172
(off Petty France)
Vandon Pas.
SW1 . . . 3G 85 (1B 172)
Vandon St.
SW1 . . . 3G 85 (1B 172)
Van Dyck Av.
KT3: N Mald . . . 7K 135
Vandyke Cl. SW15 . . . 7F 101
Vandyke Cross SE9 . . . 5C 108
Vandy St. EC2 . . . 4E 68 (4G 163)
Vane Cl. HA3: Harr . . . 6F 27
NW3 . . . 5B 48
Vanessa Cl. DA17: Belv . . . 5G 93
Vanessa Way DA5: Bexl . . . 3K 129
Vane St. SW1 . . . 4G 85 (3B 172)
Vangaurd NW9 . . . 7F 13
Vange Ho. W10 . . . 5E 64
(off Sutton Way)
Van Gogh Cl. TW7: Isle . . . 3A 98
Van Gogh Ct. E14 . . . 3F 89
Vanguard Bldg. E14 . . . 2B 88
Vanguard Cl. CR0: Croy . . . 1B 152
E16 . . . 5J 71
RM7: Mawney . . . 2G 39
Vanguard Ct. SE5 . . . 1E 104
Vanguard St. SE8 . . . 1C 106
Vanguard Trad. Est. E15 . . . 1E 70
Vanguard Way SM6: Wall . . . 7J 151
TW6: Houn . . . 2G 95
Vanneck Sq. SW15 . . . 5C 100
Vanoc Gdns. BR1: Brom . . . 4J 125
Vansittart Rd. E7 . . . 4H 53
Vansittart St. SE14 . . . 7A 88
Vanston Pl. SW6 . . . 7J 83
Vantage M. E14 . . . 1E 88
(off Preston's Rd.)
Vantage Pl. W8 . . . 3J 83
Vantage W. W3 . . . 4F 81
Vantrey Ho. SE11 . . . 4J 173
Vant Rd. SW17 . . . 5D 120
Varcoe Rd. SE16 . . . 5H 87
Vardens Rd. SW11 . . . 4B 102
Varden St. E1 . . . 6H 69
Vardon Cl. W3 . . . 6K 63
Vardon Ho. SE10 . . . 1E 106
Varley Ho. NW6 . . . 1J 65
Varley Pde. NW9 . . . 4A 28
Varley Rd. E16 . . . 6K 71
Varley Way CR4: Mitc . . . 2B 138
Varna Rd. SW6 . . . 7G 83
TW12: Hamp . . . 1F 133
Varndell St.
NW1 . . . 3G 67 (1A 160)
Varsity Dr. TW1: Twick . . . 5J 97
Varsity Row SW14 . . . 2J 99
Vartry Rd. N15 . . . 6D 32
Vassall Ho. E3 . . . 3A 70
(off Antill Rd.)
Vassall Rd. SW9 . . . 7A 86
Vat Ho. SW8 . . . 7J 85
(off Rita Rd.)
Vauban Est. SE1 . . . 3F 87
Vauban St. SE16 . . . 3F 87
Vaudeville Ct. N4 . . . 2A 50
Vaudeville Theatre . . . 3F 167
(off Strand)
Vaughan Almshouses
TW15: Ashf . . . 5D 112
(off Feltham Hill Rd.)
Vaughan Av. NW4 . . . 5C 28
W6 . . . 4B 82
Vaughan Cl.
TW12: Hamp . . . 6C 114
Vaughan Est. E2 . . . 1J 163
Vaughan Gdns. IG1: Ilf . . . 7D 36
Vaughan Ho. SE1 . . . 6A 168
(off Blackfriars Rd.)
SW4 . . . 7G 103
Vaughan Rd. DA16: Well . . . 2K 109
E15 . . . 6H 53
HA1: Harr . . . 7G 25
KT7: T Ditt . . . 7B 134
SE5 . . . 2C 104
Vaughan St. SE16 . . . 2B 88
Vaughan Way E1 . . . 7G 69
Vaughan Williams Cl. SE8 . . . 7C 88
VAUXHALL . . . 5J 85 (5H 173)
Vauxhall Bri.
SW1 . . . 5J 85 (6E 172)
Vauxhall Bri. Rd.
SW1 . . . 3G 85 (2A 172)
VAUXHALL CROSS
. . . 5J 85 (6F 173)
Vauxhall Cross
SE1 . . . 5J 85 (6F 173)
Vauxhall Distribution Pk.
SW8 . . . 7C 172
Vauxhall Gdns.
CR2: S Croy . . . 6C 152
Vauxhall Gro.
SW8 . . . 6K 85 (7G 173)
Vauxhall St.
SE11 . . . 5K 85 (5H 173)
Vauxhall Wlk.
SE11 . . . 5K 85 (5G 173)
Vawdrey Cl. E1 . . . 4J 69
Veals Mead CR4: Mitc . . . 1C 138
Vectis Gdns. SW17 . . . 6F 121
Vectis Rd. SW17 . . . 6F 121
Veda Rd. SE13 . . . 4C 106
Vega Rd. WD23: Bush . . . 1B 10
Veitch Cl. TW14: Felt . . . 7H 95
Veldene Way HA2: Harr . . . 3D 42
Velde Way SE22 . . . 5E 104
Velletri Ho. E2 . . . 2K 69
(off Mace St.)
Vellum Dr. SM5: Cars . . . 3E 150
Venables Cl. RM10: Dag . . . 4H 57
Venables St.
NW8 . . . 4B 66 (5B 158)
Vencourt Pl. W6 . . . 4C 82
Venetian Rd. SE5 . . . 2C 104
Venetia Rd. N4 . . . 6B 32
W5 . . . 2D 80
Venice Ct. NW8 . . . 3B 158
(off Fisherton St.)
SE5 . . . 7C 86
(off Bowyer St.)
Venner Rd. SE26 . . . 6J 123
Venners Cl. DA7: Bex . . . 2K 111
Venn Ho. N1 . . . 1K 67
(off Barnsbury Est.)
Venn St. SW4 . . . 4G 103
Ventnor Av. HA7: Stan . . . 1B 26
Ventnor Dr. N20 . . . 3E 14
Ventnor Gdns. IG11: Bark . . . 6J 55
Ventnor Rd. SE14 . . . 7K 87
SM2: Sutt . . . 7K 149
Venture Cl. DA5: Bexl . . . 7E 110
Venture Ct. SE12 . . . 7J 107
Venture Ho. W10 . . . 6F 65
(off Bridge Cl.)
Venue St. E14 . . . 5E 70
Venus Ho. E14 . . . 4C 88
(off Westferry Rd.)
Venus Rd. SE18 . . . 3D 90
Vera Av. N21 . . . 5F 7
Vera Lynn Cl. E7 . . . 4J 53
Vera Rd. SW6 . . . 1G 101
Verbena Cl. E16 . . . 4H 71
Verbena Gdns. W6 . . . 5C 82
Verdant Ct. SE6 . . . 7G 107
(off Verdant La.)
Verdant La. SE6 . . . 7G 107
Verdayne Av. CR0: Croy . . . 1K 153
Verdi Ho. W10 . . . 2G 65
(off Herries St.)
Verdun Rd. SE18 . . . 6A 92
SW13 . . . 6C 82
Vereker Dr.
TW16: Sun T . . . 3J 131
Vereker Rd. W14 . . . 5G 83
Vere St. W1 . . . 6F 67 (1J 165)
Veritas Ho. DA15: Sidc . . . 2A 128
(off Station Rd.)
Verity Cl. W11 . . . 7G 65
Vermeer Ct. E14 . . . 3F 89
Vermeer Gdns. SE15 . . . 4J 105
Vermont Cl. EN2: Enf . . . 4G 7
Vermont Ho. E17 . . . 2B 34
Vermont Rd. SE19 . . . 6D 122
SM1: Sutt . . . 3K 149
SW18 . . . 6K 101
Verne Ct. W3 . . . 3J 81
(off Vincent Rd.)
Verney Gdns. RM9: Dag . . . 4E 56
Verney Ho. NW8 . . . 3B 158
Verney Rd. RM9: Dag . . . 4E 56
(not continuous)
SE16 . . . 6G 87
Verney St. NW10 . . . 3K 45
Verney Way SE16 . . . 5H 87
Vernham Rd. SE18 . . . 6G 91
Vernon Av. E12 . . . 4D 54
IG8: Wfd G . . . 7E 20
SW20 . . . 2F 137
Vernon Cl. KT19: Eps . . . 6J 147
Vernon Ct. HA7: Stan . . . 1B 26
NW2 . . . 3H 47
W5 . . . 7C 62
Vernon Cres. EN4: Barn . . . 6K 5
Vernon Dr. HA7: Stan . . . 1A 26
Vernon Ho. SE11 . . . 6H 173
WC1 . . . 6F 161
(off Vernon Pl.)
Vernon M. E17 . . . 5B 34
W14 . . . 4G 83
Vernon Pl. WC1 . . . 5J 67 (6F 161)
Vernon Ri. UB6: G'frd . . . 5H 43
WC1 . . . 3K 67 (1H 161)
Vernon Rd. E3 . . . 2B 70
E11 . . . 1G 53
E15 . . . 7G 53
E17 . . . 5B 34
IG3: Ilf . . . 1K 55
N8 . . . 3A 32
SM1: Sutt . . . 5A 150
SW14 . . . 3K 99
TW13: Felt . . . 2H 113
Vernon Sq.
WC1 . . . 3K 67 (1H 161)
Vernon St. W14 . . . 4G 83
Vernon Yd. W11 . . . 7H 65
Veroan Rd. DA7: Bex . . . 2E 110
Verona Ct. SE14 . . . 6K 87
(off Myers La.)
TW15: Ashf . . . 4D 112
Verona Dr. KT6: Surb . . . 2E 146
Verona Rd. E7 . . . 7J 53
Veronica Gdns. SW16 . . . 1G 139
Veronica Ho. SE4 . . . 3B 106
Veronica Rd. SW17 . . . 2F 121
Veronique Gdns. IG6: Ilf . . . 5G 37
Verran Rd. SW12 . . . 7F 103
Versailles Rd. SE20 . . . 7G 123
Verulam Av. E17 . . . 6B 34
Verulam Bldgs. WC1 . . . 5H 161
Verulam Ct. NW9 . . . 7C 28
UB1: S'hall . . . 6G 61
(off Haldane Rd.)
Verulam Ho. W6 . . . 2E 82
(off Hammersmith Gro.)
Verulam Rd. UB6: G'frd . . . 4E 60
Verulam St.
WC1 . . . 5A 68 (5J 161)
Verwood Dr. EN4: Barn . . . 3J 5
Verwood Ho. SW8 . . . 7K 85
(off Cobbett St.)
Verwood Lodge E14 . . . 3F 89
(off Manchester Rd.)
Verwood Rd.
HA2: Harr . . . 2G 25
Veryan Ct. N8 . . . 5H 31
Vesage Ct. EC1 . . . 6K 161
(off Leather La.)
Vesey Path E14 . . . 6D 70
Vespan Rd. W12 . . . 2C 82
Vesta Rd. SE4 . . . 2A 106
Vestris Rd. SE23 . . . 2K 123
Vestry Ct. SW1 . . . 2D 172
(off Monck St.)
Vestry House Mus. . . . 4D 34
Vestry M. SE5 . . . 1E 104
Vestry Rd. E17 . . . 4D 34
SE5 . . . 1E 104
Vestry St. N1 . . . 3D 68 (1E 162)
Vevey St. SE6 . . . 2B 124
Veysey Gdns.
RM10: Dag . . . 3G 57
Viaduct Bldgs.
EC1 . . . 5A 68 (6K 161)
Viaduct Pl. E2 . . . 3H 69
Viaduct Rd. N2 . . . 2B 30
Viaduct St. E2 . . . 3H 69
Viaduct, The E18 . . . 2J 35
HA0: Wemb . . . 1E 62
Vian St. SE13 . . . 3D 106
Viant Ho. NW10 . . . 7K 45
(off Fawood Av.)
Vibart Gdns. SW2 . . . 7K 103
Vibart Wlk. N1 . . . 1J 67
(off Outram Pl.)
Vibia Cl. TW19: Staines . . . 7A 94
Vicarage Av. SE3 . . . 7J 89
Vicarage Cl. DA8: Erith . . . 6J 93
HA4: Ruis . . . 7F 23
KT4: Wor Pk . . . 1A 148
UB5: N'olt . . . 7D 42
Vicarage Ct. BR3: Beck . . . 3A 142
IG1: Ilf . . . 5F 55
TW14: Felt . . . 7E 94
W8 . . . 2K 83
Vicarage Cres. SW11 . . . 1B 102
Vicarage Dr. BR3: Beck . . . 1C 142
IG11: Bark . . . 7G 55
SW14 . . . 5K 99
Vicarage Farm Ct.
TW5: Houn . . . 7D 78
Vicarage Farm Rd.
TW3: Houn . . . 2C 96
Vicarage Flds.
KT12: Walt T . . . 6A 132
Vicarage Fld. Shop. Cen.
IG11: Bark . . . 7G 55
Vicarage Gdns.
CR4: Mitc . . . 3C 138
SW14 . . . 5J 99
W8 . . . 1J 83
Vicarage Ga. W8 . . . 1K 83
Vicarage Gro. SE5 . . . 1D 104
Vicarage Ho.
KT1: King T . . . 2F 135
(off Cambridge Rd.)
Vicarage La. E6 . . . 3D 72
E15 . . . 7G 53
IG1: Ilf . . . 1H 55
KT17: Eps . . . 7C 148
(not continuous)
Vicarage M. NW9 . . . 2K 45
Vicarage Pde. N15 . . . 4C 32
Vicarage Pk. SE18 . . . 5G 91
Vicarage Path N8 . . . 7J 31
Vicarage Rd. CR0: Croy . . . 3A 152
DA5: Bexl . . . 1H 129
E10 . . . 7C 34
E15 . . . 7H 53
IG8: Wfd G . . . 7H 21
KT1: King T . . . 1C 134
(Cedars Rd.)
KT1: King T . . . 2D 134
(Thames Side)
N17 . . . 1G 33
NW4 . . . 6C 28
RM10: Dag . . . 7H 57
SE18 . . . 5G 91
(not continuous)
SM1: Sutt . . . 4K 149
SW14 . . . 5J 99
TW2: Twick . . . 6G 97
(Kneller Rd.)
TW2: Twick . . . 2J 115
(Popes Av.)
TW11: Tedd . . . 5A 116
TW16: Sun T . . . 5H 113
Vicarage Wlk.
KT12: Walt T . . . 7J 131
SW11 . . . 1B 102
Vicarage Way HA2: Harr . . . 7E 24
NW10 . . . 3K 45
Vicars Bri. Cl. HA0: Wemb . . . 2E 62
Vicars Cl. E9 . . . 1J 69
E15 . . . 1J 71
EN1: Enf . . . 2K 7
Vicar's Hill SE13 . . . 4D 106
Vicars Moor La. N21 . . . 7F 7
Vicars Oak Rd. SE19 . . . 6E 122
Vicar's Rd. NW5 . . . 5E 48
Vicars Wlk. RM8: Dag . . . 3B 56
Viceroy Cl. N2 . . . 4C 30
Viceroy Ct. CR0: Croy . . . 1D 152
NW8 . . . 2C 66
(off Prince Albert Rd.)
Viceroy Pde. N2 . . . 4C 30
(off High Rd.)
Viceroy Rd. SW8 . . . 1J 103
Vickers Cl. SM6: Wall . . . 7K 151
Vickers Rd. DA8: Erith . . . 5K 93
Vickers Way TW4: Houn . . . 5C 96
Vickery Ct. EC1 . . . 3D 162
(off Mitchell St.)
Victor Cazalet Ho. N1 . . . 1B 68
(off Gaskin St.)
Victor Gro. HA0: Wemb . . . 7E 44
Victoria & Albert Mus.
. . . 3B 84 (2B 170)
Victoria Arc. SW1 . . . 2K 171
(off Victoria St.)
Victoria Av. E6 . . . 1B 72
EC2 . . . 5E 68 (6H 163)
EN4: Barn . . . 4G 5
HA9: Wemb . . . 6H 45
KT6: Surb . . . 6D 134
KT8: W Mole . . . 3F 133
N3 . . . 1H 29
SM6: Wall . . . 3E 150
TW3: Houn . . . 5E 96
UB10: Uxb . . . 6D 40
Victoria Bldgs. E8 . . . 1H 69
(off Mare St.)
Victoria Cl. EN4: Barn . . . 4G 5
HA1: Harr . . . 6K 25
KT8: W Mole . . . 3E 132
UB3: Hayes . . . 6F 59
Victoria Colonnade
WC1 . . . 6F 161
(off Southampton Row)
Victoria Cotts. E1 . . . 5G 69
(off Deal St.)
N10 . . . 2E 30
TW9: Rich . . . 1F 99
Victoria Ct. E18 . . . 3K 35
HA9: Wemb . . . 6G 45
SE26 . . . 6J 123
W3 . . . 2G 81

Victoria Cres.—Voss St.

Victoria Cres. N15 .....5E 32
SE19 .....6E 122
SW19 .....7H 119
Victoria Dock Rd. E16 .....6H 71
Victoria Dr. SW19 .....7F 101
Victoria Emb.
EC4 .....7A 68 (6F 167)
SW1 .....2J 85 (6F 167)
WC2 .....1J 85 (6F 167)
Victoria Gdns.
TW5: Houn 1C 96
W11 .....1J 83
Victoria Gro. N12 .....5G 15
W8 .....3A 84
Victoria Gro. M. W2 .....7J 65
Victoria Hall *E16* *1J 89*
(off Wesley Av., not continuous)
Victoria Ho. E6 .....6E 72
HA8: Edg 6C 12
SW1 .....*3B 172*
(off Francis St.)
SW1 .....*5J 171*
(off Ebury Bri. Rd.)
SW8 .....*7J 85*
(off Sth. Lambeth Rd.)
Victoria Ind. Est. W3 .....5A 64
Victoria La. EN5: Barn 4C 4
UB3: Hayes 5E 76
Victoria Mans. NW10 .....7D 46
SW8 .....*7J 85*
(off Sth. Lambeth Rd.)
Victoria M. E8 .....6G 51
NW6 .....1J 65
SW4 .....4F 103
SW18 .....1A 120
Victorian Gro. N16 .....4E 50
Victorian Rd. N16 .....3E 50
Victoria Palace Theatre ***2A 172***
(off Victoria St.)
Victoria Pde. *TW9: Rich* *1G 99*
(off Sandycombe Rd.)
Victoria Pk. Ct. *E9* *7J 51*
(off Well St.)
Victoria Pk. Ind. Cen. *E9* *7C 52*
(off Rothbury Rd.)
Victoria Pk. Rd. E9 .....1J 69
Victoria Pk. Sq. E2 .....3J 69
Victoria Pas. NW8 .....3B 158
Victoria Pl. TW9: Rich 5D 98
Victoria Pl. Shop. Cen.
SW1 .....3K 171
Victoria Point *E13* *2J 71*
(off Victoria Rd.)
Victoria Retail Pk.
HA4: Ruis 5B 42
Victoria Ri. SW4 .....3F 103
Victoria Rd. BR2: Short 5B 144
BR7: Chst 5E 126
CR4: Mitc 7C 120
DA6: Bex 4G 111
DA8: Erith 6K 93
(not continuous)
DA15: Sidc 3K 127
E4 .....1B 20
E11 .....4G 53
E13 .....2J 71
E17 .....2E 34
E18 .....2K 35
EN4: Barn 4G 5
HA4: Ruis 1J 41
IG9: Buck H 2G 21
IG11: Bark 6F 55
KT1: King T 2F 135
KT6: Surb 6D 134
N4 .....7K 31
N9 .....4A 18
N15 .....4G 33
N18 .....4A 18
N22 .....1G 31
NW4 .....4E 28
NW6 .....2H 65
NW7 .....5G 13
Victoria Rd. NW10 .....5K 63
RM10: Dag 5H 57
SM1: Sutt 5B 150
SW14 .....3K 99
TW1: Twick 7B 98
TW11: Tedd 6A 116
TW13: Felt 1K 113
UB2: S'hall 3D 78
W3 .....5K 63
W5 .....5B 62
W8 .....3A 84
WD23: Bush 1A 10
Victoria Sq. SW1 .....3F 85 (1K 171)
Victoria St. DA17: Belv 5F 93
E15 .....7G 53
SW1 .....3G 85 (2K 171)
Victoria Ter. HA1: Harr 1J 43
N4 .....1A 50
NW10 .....4B 64
SW8 .....2F 103
W5 .....1D 80
Victoria Vs. TW9: Rich 3F 99
Victoria Way HA4: Ruis 5B 42
SE7 .....5K 89
Victoria Wharf *E2* *2K 69*
(off Palmers Rd.)
E14 .....7A 70
SE8 .....*5B 88*
(off Dragoon Rd.)
Victoria Works NW2 .....2D 46
Victoria Yd. E1 .....6G 69
Victor Rd. HA2: Harr 3G 25
NW10 .....3D 64
SE20 .....7K 123
TW11: Tedd 4J 115
Victors Dr. TW12: Hamp 6C 114
Victors Way EN5: Barn 3C 4
Victor Vs. N9 .....3J 17
Victor Wlk. *NW9* *2A 28*
(off Booth Rd.)
Victory Av. SM4: Mord 5A 138
Victory Bus. Cen.
TW7: Isle 4K 97
Victory Ct. *W9* *4J 65*
(off Hermes Cl.)
Victory Pk. HA9: Wemb 3D 44
Victory Pl. E14 .....7A 70
SE17 .....4D 86
SE19 .....7E 122
Victory Rd. E11 .....4J 35
SW19 .....7A 120
Victory Rd. M. SW19 .....7A 120
Victory Wlk. SE8 .....1C 106
Victory Way
RM7: Mawney 2H 39
SE16 .....2A 88
TW5: Houn 5A 78
Vidler Cl. KT9: Chess 6C 146
Vienna Cl. IG5: Ilf 2B 36
View Cl. HA1: Harr 4H 25
N6 .....7D 30
View Ct. SE12 .....3A 126
View Cres. N8 .....5H 31
Viewfield Cl. HA3: Harr 7E 26
Viewfield Rd. DA5: Bexl 1C 128
SW18 .....6H 101
Viewland Rd. SE18 .....5K 91
View Rd. N6 .....7D 30
View, The SE2 .....5E 92
Viga Rd. N21 .....6F 7
Vigilant Cl. SE26 .....4G 123
Vignoles Rd.
RM7: Rush G 7G 39
Vigo St. W1 .....7G 67 (3A 166)
Viking Bus. Cen.
RM7: Rush G 7J 39
Viking Cl. E3 .....2A 70
Viking Ct. SW6 .....6J 83
Viking Gdns. E6 .....4C 72
Viking Ho. *SE5* *2C 104*
(off Denmark Rd.)
Viking Pl. E10 .....1B 52
Viking Rd. UB1: S'hall 7C 60
Viking Way DA8: Erith 3J 93
Villacourt Rd. SE18 .....7A 92
Village Arc. E4 .....1A 20
Village Cl. E4 .....5K 19
NW3 .....*5B 48*
(off Belsize La.)
Village Ct. *E17* *5D 34*
(off Eden Rd.)
SE3 .....*3G 107*
(off Hurren Cl.)
Village Hgts. IG8: Wfd G 5C 20
Village M. NW9 .....2K 45
Village Pk. Cl. EN1: Enf 6K 7
Village Rd. EN1: Enf 5K 7
N3 .....2G 29
Village Row SM2: Sutt 7J 149
Village, The NW3 .....2A 48
SE7 .....6A 90
Village Way BR3: Beck 2C 142
HA5: Pinn 7C 24
NW10 .....4K 45
SE24 .....6D 104
TW15: Ashf 4B 112
Village Way E. HA2: Harr 7E 24
Villa Rd. SW9 .....3A 104
Villas on the Heath NW3 .....3A 48
Villas Rd. SE18 .....5G 91
(not continuous)
Villa St. SE17 .....5D 86
Villa Wlk. *SE17* *5D 86*
(off Inville Rd.)
Villiers Av. KT5: Surb 5F 135
TW2: Twick 1D 114
Villiers Cl. E10 .....2C 52
KT5: Surb 4F 135
Villiers Gro. SM2: Sutt 7F 149
Villiers M. NW2 .....6C 46
Villiers Path KT6: Surb 5E 134
Villiers Rd. BR3: Beck 2K 141
KT1: King T 4F 135
NW2 .....6C 46
TW7: Isle 2J 97
UB1: S'hall 1D 78
Villiers St. WC2 .....1J 85 (3E 166)
Vincam Cl. TW2: Twick 7E 96
Vincennes Est. SE27 .....4D 122
Vincent Av. KT5: Surb 2J 147
Vincent Cl. BR2: Short 4K 143
DA15: Sidc 1J 127
EN5: Barn 3E 4
SE16 .....2A 88
UB7: W Dray 6C 76
Vincent Ct. HA6: Nwood 1H 23
N4 .....1J 49
NW4 .....4F 29
SW9 .....1K 103
W1 .....*7E 158*
(off Seymour Pl.)
Vincent Dr. TW17: Shep 3G 131
UB10: Uxb 1B 58
Vincent Gdns. NW2 .....3B 46
Vincent Ho. *SW1* *4C 172*
(off Vincent Sq.)
Vincent M. E3 .....2C 70
Vincent Rd. CR0: Croy 7E 140
E4 .....6A 20
HA0: Wemb 7F 45
KT1: King T 3G 135
N15 .....4C 32
N22 .....2A 32
RM9: Dag 7E 56
SE18 .....4F 91
TW4: Houn 2B 96
TW7: Isle 1H 97
W3 .....3J 81
Vincent Row
TW12: Hamp 6G 115
Vincents Path *UB5: N'olt* *6C 42*
(off Arnold Rd.)
Vincent Sq. N22 .....2A 32
SW1 .....4H 85 (3C 172)
Vincent Sq. Mans. *SW1* *3B 172*
(off Walcott St.)
Vincent St. E16 .....5H 71
SW1 .....4H 85 (3C 172)
Vincent Ter. N1 .....2B 68
Vince St. EC1 .....3D 68 (2F 163)
Vine Cl. KT5: Surb 6F 135
SM1: Sutt 3A 150
UB7: W Dray 4C 76
Vine Cotts. *E1* *6J 69*
(off Sidney Sq.)
Vine Ct. E1 .....5G 69
HA3: Harr 6E 26
Vinegar All. E17 .....4D 34
Vine Gdns. IG1: Ilf 5G 55
Vinegar St. E1 .....1H 87
Vinegar Yd. SE1 .....2E 86 (6G 169)
Vine Gro. UB10: Uxb 7C 40
Vine Hill EC1 .....4A 68 (4J 161)
Vine La. SE1 .....1E 86 (5H 169)
UB10: Uxb 1B 58
Vine Pl. TW3: Houn 4F 97
W5 .....*1E 80*
(off St Mark's Rd.)
Viner Cl. KT12: Walt T 6A 132
Vineries Bank NW7 .....5J 13
Vineries Cl. RM9: Dag 6F 57
UB7: W Dray 6C 76
Vineries, The EN1: Enf 3K 7
N14 .....6B 6
SE6 .....1C 124
Vine Rd. E15 .....7H 53
KT8: E Mos 4G 133
SW13 .....3B 100
Vinery Way W6 .....3D 82
Vines Av. N3 .....1K 29
Vine Sq. *W14* *5H 83*
(off Star Rd.)
Vine St. EC3 .....6F 69 (1J 169)
RM7: Rom 4J 39
W1 .....7G 67 (3B 166)
Vine St. Bri. EC1 .....4A 68 (4K 161)
Vine Yd. SE1 .....6D 168
Vineyard Av. NW7 .....7B 14
Vineyard Cl.
KT1: King T 3F 135
SE6 .....1C 124
Vineyard Gro. N3 .....1K 29
Vineyard Hill Rd. SW19 .....4H 119
Vineyard M. EC1 .....3K 161
TW10: Rich 5E 98
Vineyard Pas.
TW10: Rich 5E 98
Vineyard Path SW14 .....3K 99
Vineyard Rd. TW13: Felt 3J 113
Vineyard Row
KT1: King T 1C 134
Vineyards, The
TW13: Felt *3J 113*
(off High St.)
TW16: Sun T 3J 131
Vineyard, The
TW10: Rich 5E 98
Vineyard Wlk.
EC1 .....4A 68 (3J 161)
Viney Bank CR0: Croy 7B 154
Viney Rd. SE13 .....3D 106
Vining St. SW9 .....4A 104
Vinlake Av. UB10: Uxb 3B 40
Vinopolis, City of Wine
.....***1D 86 (4E 168)***
Vinson Cl. BR6: Orp 7K 145
Vintners Ct.
EC4 .....7C 68 (3D 168)
Vintners Hall ***2D 168***
(off Up. Thames St.)
Vintner's Pl. EC4 .....7C 68
Vintry M. E17 .....4C 34
Viola Av. SE2 .....4B 92
TW14: Felt 6A 96
TW19: Staines 1A 112
Viola Sq. W12 .....7B 64
Violet Av. EN2: Enf 1J 7
UB8: Uxb 5B 58
Violet Cl. E16 .....4G 71
SE8 .....6B 88
SM3: Sutt 1G 149
SM6: Wall 1E 150
Violet Gdns. CR0: Croy 5B 152
Violet Hill NW8 .....2A 66
Violet Hill Ho. *NW8* *2A 66*
(off Violet Hill, not continuous)
Violet La. CR0: Croy 6B 152
Violet Rd. E3 .....4D 70
E17 .....6C 34
E18 .....2K 35
Violet St. E2 .....4H 69
V.I.P. Trading Est. SE7 .....4A 90
Virgil Pl. W1 .....5D 66 (6E 158)
Virgil St. SE1 .....3K 85 (1H 173)
Virginia Cl. KT3: N Mald 4J 135
RM5: Col R 1J 39
Virginia Ct. *SE16* *2K 87*
(off Eleanor Cl.)
WC1 .....*3D 160*
(off Burton St.)
Virginia Gdns. IG6: Ilf 2G 37
Virginia Ho. *E14* *7E 70*
(off Newby Pl.)
Virginia Rd.
CR7: Thor H 1B 140
E2 .....3F 69 (2J 163)
Virginia St. E1 .....7G 69
Virginia Wlk. SW2 .....6K 103
Viscount Cl. N11 .....6A 16
Viscount Ct. *W2* *6J 65*
(off Pembridge Vs.)
Viscount Dr. E6 .....5D 72
Viscount Gro. UB5: N'olt 3B 60
Viscount Rd.
TW19: Staines 1A 112
Viscount St. EC1 .....4C 68 (4C 162)
Viscount Way TW6: Houn 4G 95
(not continuous)
Vista Av. EN3: Enf 2E 8
Vista Dr. IG4: Ilf 5B 36
Vista, The DA14: Sidc 5K 127
SE9 .....6B 108
Vista Way HA3: Harr 6E 26
Vittoria Ho. *N1* *1K 67*
(off High Rd.)
Viveash Cl. UB3: Hayes 3H 77
Vivian Av. HA9: Wemb 5G 45
NW4 .....5D 28
Vivian Comma Cl. N4 .....3B 50
Vivian Ct. N12 .....5E 14
Vivian Gdns. HA9: Wemb 5G 45
Vivian Mans. *NW4* *5D 28*
(off Vivian Av.)
Vivian Rd. E3 .....2A 70
Vivian Sq. SE15 .....3H 105
Vivian Way N2 .....5B 30
Vivien Cl. KT9: Chess 7E 146
Vivienne Cl. TW1: Twick 6D 98
Vixen M. *E8* *7F 51*
(off Haggerston Rd.)
Voce Rd. SE18 .....7H 91
Voewood Cl.
KT3: N Mald 6B 136
Vogans Mill SE1 .....2F 87 (6K 169)
Vogler Ho. *E1* *7J 69*
(off Cable St.)
Vogue Ct. BR1: Brom 1K 143
Vollasky Ho. *E1* *5K 163*
(off Daplyn St.)
Volta Cl. N9 .....3D 18
Voltaire Rd. SW4 .....3H 103
Voltaire Way UB3: Hayes 7G 59
Volt Av. NW10 .....3A 64
Volta Way CR0: Croy 1K 151
Voluntary Pl. E11 .....6J 35
Vorley Rd. N19 .....2G 49
Voss Ct. SW16 .....6J 121
Voss St. E2 .....3G 69

Walston Ho.—Warsaw Cl.

Walston Ho. *SW1* ... *5C 172* *(off Aylesford St.)*
Walter Besant Ho. *E1* ... *3K 69* *(off Bancroft Rd.)*
Walter Ct. *W3* ... *6J 63* *(off Lynton Ter.)*
Walter Grn. Ho. *SE14* ... *1J 105* *(off Lausanne Rd.)*
Walter Hurford Pde. *E12* ... *4E 54* *(off Walton Rd.)*
Walter Langley Ct. *SE16* ... *2J 87* *(off Brunel Rd.)*
Walter Rodney Cl. E6 ... 6D **54**
Walter Savil Twr. *E17* ... *6C 34* *(off Colchester Rd.)*
Walters Cl. *SE17* ... *4D 86* *(off Brandon St.)*
UB3: Hayes ... 2H **77**
Walters Ho. *SE11* ... *6B 86* *(off Otto St.)*
Walters Rd. EN3: Enf ... 4D **8**
SE25 ... 4E **140**
Walter St. E2 ... 3K **69**
KT2: King T ... 1E **134**
Walters Way SE23 ... 6K **105**
Walters Yd. BR1: Brom ... 2J **143**
Walter Ter. E1 ... 6K **69**
Walterton Rd. W9 ... 4H **65**
Walter Wlk. HA8: Edg ... 6D **12**
Waltham Av. NW9 ... 6G **27**
UB3: Hayes ... 3E **76**
Waltham Dr. HA8: Edg ... 2G **27**
Waltham Ho. NW8 ... 1A **66**
Waltham Pk. Way E17 ... 1C **34**
Waltham Rd. IG8: Wfd G ... 6H **21**
SM5: Cars ... 7B **138**
UB2: S'hall ... 3C **78**
WALTHAMSTOW ... **3C 34**
Walthamstow Av. E4 ... 6G **19**
Walthamstow Bus. Cen. E17 ... 2E **34**
Walthamstow Stadium (Greyhound) ... ***7J 19***
Waltham Way E4 ... 3G **19**
Waltheof Av. N17 ... 1D **32**
Waltheof Gdns. N17 ... 1D **32**
Walton Av. HA2: Harr ... 5D **42**
HA9: Wemb ... 3H **45**
KT3: N Mald ... 4B **136**
SM3: Sutt ... 3H **149**
Walton Bri. TW17: Shep ... 7G **131**
Walton Bri. Rd. TW17: Shep ... 7G **131**
Walton Cl. E5 ... 3K **51**
HA1: Harr ... 4H **25**
NW2 ... 2D **46**
SW8 ... 7J **85**
Walton Ct. *CR2: S Croy* ... *5C 152* *(off Warham Rd.)*
EN5: Barn ... 5F **5**
Walton Cft. HA1: Harr ... 4J **43**
Walton Dr. HA1: Harr ... 4H **25**
NW10 ... 6K **45**
Walton Gdns. HA9: Wemb ... 2E **44**
TW13: Felt ... 4H **113**
W3 ... 5H **63**
Walton Grn. CR0: Croy ... 7D **154**
Walton Ho. E2 ... 4F **69**
E4 ... *5H 19* *(off Chingford Mt. Rd.)*
E17 ... *3D 34* *(off Drive, The)*
Walton La. KT13: Weyb ... 7F **131**
TW17: Shep ... 7F **131**
WALTON-ON-THAMES ... **7J 131**
Walton Pl. SW3 ... 3D **84** (1E **170**)
Walton Rd. DA14: Sidc ... 2C **128**
E12 ... 4E **54** (not continuous)
E13 ... 2A **72**
HA1: Harr ... 4H **25**
KT8: E Mos, W Mole ... 4D **132**
KT12: Walt T ... 5A **132**
N15 ... 4F **33**
RM5: Col R ... 1F **39**
Walton St. EN2: Enf ... 1J **7**
SW3 ... 4C **84** (3D **170**)
Walton Way CR4: Mitc ... 4G **139**
W3 ... 5H **63**
Walt Whitman Cl. SE24 ... 4B **104**
WALWORTH ... **5C 86**
Walworth Pl. SE17 ... 5C **86**
Walworth Rd. SE17 ... 4C **86**
Walwyn Av. BR1: Brom ... 3B **144**
Wanborough Dr. SW15 ... 1D **118**
Wanderer Dr. IG11: Bark ... 3C **74**
Wandle Bank CR0: Croy ... 3J **151**
SW19 ... 7B **120**
Wandle Ct. CR0: Croy ... 3J **151**
KT19: Eps ... 4J **147**
Wandle Ct. Gdns. CR0: Croy ... 3J **151**
Wandle Ho. BR1: Brom ... 5F **125**
NW8 ... *5C 158* *(off Penfold St.)*
Wandle Pk. Trad. Est., The CR0: Croy ... 1B **152**
Wandle Rd. CR0: Croy ... 3C **152** (Pump Pail Sth.)
CR0: Croy ... 3J **151** (Richmond Rd.)
SM4: Mord ... 4A **138**
SM6: Wall ... 3F **151**
SW17 ... 2C **120**
Wandle Side CR0: Croy ... 3K **151**
SM6: Wall ... 3F **151**
Wandle Way CR4: Mitc ... 5D **138**
SW18 ... 1K **119**
Wandon Rd. SW6 ... 7K **83** (not continuous)
WANDSWORTH ... **5K 101**
Wandsworth Bri. SW6 ... 3K **101**
SW18 ... 3K **101**
Wandsworth Bri. Rd. SW6 ... 1K **101**
WANDSWORTH COMMON ... **1D 120**
Wandsworth Comn. W. Side SW18 ... 5A **102**
Wandsworth Gyratory ... **5K 101**
Wandsworth High St. SW18 ... 5J **101**
Wandsworth Plain SW18 ... 5K **101**
Wandsworth Rd. SW8 ... 3F **103** (7E **172**)
Wandsworth Shop. Cen. SW18 ... 6K **101**
Wangey Rd. RM6: Chad H ... 7D **38**
Wangford Ho. *SW9* ... *4B 104* *(off Loughborough Pk.)*
Wanless Rd. SE24 ... 3C **104**
Wanley Rd. SE5 ... 4D **104**
Wanlip Rd. E13 ... 4K **71**
Wannock Gdns. IG6: Ilf ... 1F **37**
Wansbeck Ct. *EN2: Enf* ... *3G 7* *(off Waverley Rd.)*
Wansbeck Rd. E3 ... 7B **52**
E9 ... 7B **52**
Wansey St. SE17 ... 4C **86**
Wansford Rd. IG8: Wfd G ... 1A **36**
WANSTEAD ... **6K 35**
Wanstead Cl. BR1: Brom ... 2A **144**
Wanstead Gdns. IG4: Ilf ... 6B **36**
Wanstead La. IG1: Ilf ... 6B **36**
Wanstead Pk. Av. E12 ... 1B **54**
Wanstead Pk. Rd. IG1: Ilf ... 6B **36**
Wanstead Pl. E11 ... 6J **35**
Wanstead Rd. BR1: Brom ... 2A **144**
Wansunt Rd. DA5: Bexl ... 1J **129**
Wantage Rd. SE12 ... 5H **107**
Wantz Rd. RM10: Dag ... 4H **57**
WAPPING ... **1H 87**
Wapping Dock St. E1 ... 1H **87**
Wapping High St. E1 ... 1G **87**
Wapping La. E1 ... 7H **69**
Wapping Wall E1 ... 1J **87**
Warbank La. KT2: King T ... 7B **118**
Warberry Rd. N22 ... 2K **31**
Warboys App. KT2: King T ... 6H **117**
Warboys Cres. E4 ... 5K **19**
Warboys Rd. KT2: King T ... 6H **117**
Warbreck Rd. W12 ... 1D **82**
Warburton Cl. HA3: Harr ... 6C **10**
N1 ... *6E 50* *(off Culford Rd.)*
Warburton Ct. HA4: Ruis ... 2J **41**
Warburton Ho. *E8* ... *1H 69* *(off Warburton St.)*
Warburton Rd. E8 ... 1H **69**
TW2: Twick ... 1F **115**
Warburton St. E8 ... 1H **69**
Warburton Ter. E17 ... 2D **34**
Wardalls Gro. SE14 ... 7J **87**
Wardalls Ho. *SE8* ... *6B 88* *(off Staunton St.)*
Ward Cl. CR2: S Croy ... 6E **152**
DA8: Erith ... 6K **93**
Wardell Cl. NW7 ... 7F **13**
Wardell Fld. NW9 ... 1A **28**
Wardell Ho. *SE10* ... *6E 88* *(off Welland St.)*
Warden Av. HA2: Harr ... 1D **42**
Warden Rd. NW5 ... 6E **48**
Wardens Gro. SE1 ... 1C **86** (5C **168**)
Wardle St. E9 ... 5K **51**
Wardley St. SW18 ... 7K **101**
Wardo Av. SW6 ... 1G **101**
Wardour M. W1 ... 1B **166**
Wardour St. W1 ... 6G **67** (7B **160**)
Ward Point SE11 ... 4A **86** (4J **173**)
Ward Rd. E15 ... 1F **71**
N19 ... 3G **49**
SW19 ... 1A **138**
Wardrobe Pl. EC4 ... 1B **168**
Wardrobe Ter. EC4 ... 2B **168**
Wardrobe, The *TW9: Rich* ... *5D 98* *(off Old Pal. Yd.)*
Wards Rd. IG2: Ilf ... 7H **37**
Ware Ct. SM1: Sutt ... 4H **149**
Wareham Cl. TW3: Houn ... 4F **97**
Wareham Ct. *N1* ... *7E 50* *(off Hertford Rd.)*
Wareham Ho. SW8 ... 7K **85**
Warehouse Theatre ... ***2D 152***
Waremead Rd. IG2: Ilf ... 5F **37**
Warepoint Dr. SE28 ... 2H **91**
Warfield Rd. NW10 ... 3F **65**
TW12: Hamp ... 1F **133**
TW14: Felt ... 7G **95**
Warfield Yd. *NW10* ... *3F 65* *(off Warfield Rd.)*
Wargrave Av. N15 ... 6F **33**
Wargrave Ho. *E2* ... *2J 163* *(off Navarre St.)*
Wargrave Rd. HA2: Harr ... 3G **43**
Warham Rd. CR2: S Croy ... 5B **152**
HA3: Harr ... 2K **25**
N4 ... 5A **32**
Warham St. SE5 ... 7B **86**
Waring & Gillow Est. W3 ... 4G **63**
Waring Rd. DA14: Sidc ... 6C **128**
Waring St. SE27 ... 4C **122**
Warkworth Gdns. TW7: Isle ... 7A **80**
Warkworth Rd. N17 ... 7J **17**
Warland Rd. SE18 ... 7H **91**
Warley Av. RM8: Dag ... 7F **39**
UB4: Hayes ... 6J **59**
Warley Cl. E10 ... 1B **52**
Warley Rd. IG5: Ilf ... 1E **36**
IG8: Wfd G ... 7E **20**
N9 ... 2D **18**
UB4: Hayes ... 6J **59**
Warley St. E2 ... 3K **69**
Warlingham Rd. CR7: Thor H ... 4B **140**
Warlock Rd. W9 ... 4H **65**
Warlters Cl. N7 ... 4J **49**
Warlters Rd. N7 ... 4J **49**
Warltersville Mans. N19 ... 7J **31**
Warltersville Rd. N19 ... 7J **31**
Warmington Cl. E5 ... 3K **51**
Warmington Rd. SE24 ... 6C **104**
Warmington St. E13 ... 4J **71**
Warmington Twr. SE14 ... 1A **106**
Warminster Gdns. SE25 ... 2G **141**
Warminster Rd. SE25 ... 2F **141**
Warminster Sq. SE25 ... 2G **141**
Warminster Way CR4: Mitc ... 1F **139**
Warmley Ct. *SE15* ... *6E 86* *(off Watling St.)*
Warmsworth *NW1* ... *1G 67* *(off Pratt St.)*
Warndon St. SE16 ... 4K **87**
Warneford Rd. HA3: Harr ... 3D **26**
Warneford St. E9 ... 1H **69**
Warne Pl. DA15: Sidc ... 6B **110**
Warner Av. SM3: Sutt ... 2G **149**
Warner Cl. E15 ... 5G **53**
NW9 ... 7B **28**
TW12: Hamp ... 5D **114**
UB3: Hayes ... 7F **77**
Warner Ho. NW8 ... 3A **66**
SE13 ... *2D 106* *(off Russett Way)*
Warner Pde. UB3: Hayes ... 7F **77**
Warner Pl. E2 ... 2G **69**
Warner Rd. BR1: Brom ... 7H **125**
E17 ... 4A **34**
N8 ... 4H **31**
SE5 ... 1C **104**
Warners Cl. IG8: Wfd G ... 5D **20**
Warners La. KT2: King T ... 4D **116**
Warners Path IG8: Wfd G ... 5D **20**
Warner St. EC1 ... 4A **68** (4J **161**)
Warner Ter. *E14* ... *5D 70* *(off Broomfield St.)*
Warner Yd. EC1 ... 4J **161**
Warnford Ho. *SW15* ... *6A 100* *(off Tunworth Cres.)*
Warnford Ind. Est. UB3: Hayes ... 2G **77**
Warnham *WC1* ... *2G 161* *(off Sidmouth St.)*
Warnham Ct. Rd. SM5: Cars ... 7D **150**
Warnham Ho. *SW2* ... *7K 103* *(off Up. Tulse Hill)*
Warnham Rd. N12 ... 5H **15**
Warpiner Dr. N9 ... 3B **18**
Warple M. W3 ... 2A **82**
Warple Way W3 ... 1A **82** (not continuous)
Warren Av. BR1: Brom ... 7G **125**
CR2: S Croy ... 7K **153**
E10 ... 3E **52**
TW10: Rich ... 4H **99**
Warren Cl. DA6: Bex ... 5G **111**
HA9: Wemb ... 2D **44**
N9 ... 7E **8**
SE21 ... 7C **104**
UB4: Hayes ... 5A **60**
Warren Ct. BR3: Beck ... 7C **124**
CR0: Croy ... 1E **152**
N17 ... *3G 33* *(off High Cross Rd.)*
NW1 ... *3B 160* *(off Warren St.)*
W5 ... 5C **62**
Warren Cres. N9 ... 7A **8**
Warren Cutting KT2: King T ... 7K **117**
Warrender Rd. N19 ... 3G **49**
Warrender Way HA4: Ruis ... 7J **23**
Warren Dr. HA4: Ruis ... 7B **24**
UB6: G'frd ... 4F **61**
Warren Dr. Nth. KT5: Surb ... 1H **147**
Warren Dr. Sth. KT5: Surb ... 1J **147**
Warren Dr., The E11 ... 7A **36**
Warren Farm Cotts. RM6: Chad H ... 4F **39**
Warren Flds. HA7: Stan ... 4H **11**
Warren Footpath TW1: Twick ... 1C **116**
Warren Gdns. E15 ... 5F **53**
Warren Ho. *W14* ... *4H 83* *(off Beckford Cl.)*
Warren La. HA7: Stan ... 2F **11**
SE18 ... 3F **91**
Warren La. Ga. SE18 ... 3F **91**
Warren M. W1 ... 4G **67** (4A **160**)
Warren Pk. KT2: King T ... 6J **117**
Warren Pk. Rd. SM1: Sutt ... 6B **150**
Warren Pl. *E1* ... *6K 69* *(off Caroline St.)*
Warren Pond Rd. E4 ... 1C **20** (not continuous)
Warren Ri. KT3: N Mald ... 1K **135**
Warren Rd. BR2: Short ... 2J **155**
CR0: Croy ... 1E **152**
DA6: Bex ... 5G **111**
DA14: Sidc ... 3C **128**
E4 ... 2K **19**
E10 ... 3E **52**
E11 ... 6A **36** (not continuous)
IG6: Ilf ... 5H **37**
KT2: King T ... 6J **117**
NW2 ... 2B **46**
SW19 ... 6C **120**
TW2: Twick ... 6G **97**
TW15: Ashf ... 7G **113**
UB10: Uxb ... 4A **40**
WD23: Bush ... 1B **10**
Warrens Shawe La. HA8: Edg ... 2C **12**
Warren St. W1 ... 4G **67** (4A **160**)
Warren Ter. RM6: Chad H ... 4D **38**
Warren, The E12 ... 4C **54**
KT4: Wor Pk ... 4K **147**
TW5: Houn ... 7D **78**
UB4: Hayes ... 6J **59**
Warren Wlk. SE7 ... 6A **90**
Warren Way NW7 ... 6B **14**
Warren Wood Cl. BR2: Short ... 2H **155**
Warriner Gdns. SW11 ... 1D **102**
Warrington Ct. *CR0: Croy* ... *3B 152* *(off Warrington Rd.)*
Warrington Cres. W9 ... 4A **66**
Warrington Gdns. W9 ... 4A **66**
Warrington Pl. *E14* ... *1E 88* *(off Yabsley St.)*
Warrington Rd. CR0: Croy ... 3B **152**
HA1: Harr ... 5J **25**
RM8: Dag ... 2D **56**
TW10: Rich ... 5D **98**
Warrington Sq. RM8: Dag ... 2D **56**
Warrior Sq. E12 ... 4E **54**
Warsaw Cl. HA4: Ruis ... 6K **41**

Waverley Vs.—Wellington St.

Waverley Vs. N17 ..... 2F 33
Waverley Way
SM5: Cars 6C 150
Waverton Ho. E3 ..... 1B 70
Waverton Rd. SW18 ..... 7A 102
Waverton St.
W1 ..... 1E 84 (4J 165)
Wavertree Ct. SW2 ..... 1J 121
Wavertree Rd. E18 ..... 2J 35
SW2 ..... 1K 121
Waxlow Cres.
UB1: S'hall 6E 60
Waxlow Ho. UB4: Hayes 5B 60
Waxlow Rd. NW10 ..... 2J 63
Waxwell Cl. HA5: Pinn 2B 24
Waxwell Farm Ho.
HA5: Pinn 2B 24
Waxwell La. HA5: Pinn 2B 24
Wayborne Gro.
HA4: Ruis 6E 22
Waye Av. TW5: Houn 1J 95
Wayfarer Rd. UB5: N'olt 3B 60
Wayfield Link SE9 ..... 6H 109
Wayford St. SW11 ..... 2C 102
Wayland Av. E8 ..... 5G 51
Wayland Cl. E8 ..... 5G 51
Wayland Ho. SW9 ..... 2A 104
(off Robsart St.)
Waylands UB3: Hayes 5F 59
Waylands Mead
BR3: Beck 1D 142
Waylett Ho. SE11 ..... 6J 173
Waylett Pl. HA0: Wemb 4D 44
SE27 ..... 3B 122
Wayman Ct. E8 ..... 6H 51
Wayne Kirkum Way NW6 ..... 5H 47
Waynflete Av.
CR0: Croy 3B 152
Waynflete Sq. W10 ..... 7F 65
Waynflete St. SW18 ..... 2A 120
Wayside CR0: Croy 6D 154
NW11 ..... 1G 47
SW14 ..... 5J 99
Wayside Cl. N14 ..... 6B 6
Wayside Commercial Cen.
IG11: Bark 1K 73
Wayside Ct. HA9: Wemb 3G 45
TW1: Twick 6C 98
Wayside Gdns.
RM10: Dag 5G 57
Wayside Gro. SE9 ..... 4D 126
Wayside M. IG2: Ilf 5E 36
Weald Cl. BR2: Short 2C 156
SE16 ..... 5H 87
Weald La. HA3: Harr 2H 25
Weald Ri. HA3: Harr 7E 10
Weald Rd. UB10: Uxb 2C 58
Weald Sq. E5 ..... 2G 51
WEALDSTONE 3J 25
Wealdstone Rd.
SM3: Sutt 2H 149
Weald, The BR7: Chst 6D 126
Weald Way RM7: Rom 6H 39
UB4: Hayes 3G 59
Wealdwood Gdns.
HA5: Pinn 6A 10
Weale Rd. E4 ..... 3A 20
Weall Ct. HA5: Pinn 4C 24
Weardale Gdns. EN2: Enf 1J 7
Weardale Rd. SE13 ..... 4F 107
Wearmouth Ho. E3 ..... 5B 70
(off Joseph St.)
Wear Pl. E2 ..... 3H 69
(not continuous)
Wearside Rd. SE13 ..... 4D 106
Weatherbury W2 ..... 6J 65
(off Talbot Rd.)
Weatherbury Ho. N19 ..... 3H 49
(off Wedmore St.)
Weatherley Cl. E3 ..... 5B 70
Weaver Cl. CR0: Croy 4F 153
E6 ..... 7F 73
Weavers Almshouses
E11 ..... 6H 35
(off Cambridge Rd.)
Weavers Cl. TW7: Isle 4J 97
Weavers Ho. E11 ..... 6J 35
(off New Wanstead)
Weavers La.
SE1 ..... 1E 86 (5H 169)
Weavers Ter. SW6 ..... 6J 83
(off Micklethwaite Rd.)
Weaver St. E1 ..... 4G 69
Weavers Way NW1 ..... 1H 67
Weaver Wlk. SE27 ..... 4C 122
Webb Cl. W10 ..... 4E 64
Webb Ct. SE28 ..... 7B 74
(off Attlee Rd.)
Webber Row SE1 ..... 1K 173
(Gerridge St.)
SE1 ..... 2B 86
(Valentine Row)
Webber St. SE1 ..... 2A 86 (6K 167)
Webb Est. E5 ..... 7G 33
Webb Gdns. E13 ..... 4J 71
Webb Ho. RM10: Dag 3G 57
(off Kershaw Rd.)
SW8 ..... 7H 85
TW13: Felt 3C 114
Webb Pl. NW10 ..... 3B 64
Webb Rd. SE3 ..... 6H 89
Webbscroft Rd.
RM10: Dag 4H 57
Webbs Rd. SW11 ..... 4D 102
UB4: Hayes 3K 59
Webb St. SE1 ..... 3E 86
Webheath NW6 ..... 7H 47
Webster Gdns. W5 ..... 1D 80
Webster Rd. E11 ..... 3E 52
SE16 ..... 3G 87
Weddell Ho. E1 ..... 4K 69
(off Duckett St.)
Wedderburn Rd.
IG11: Bark 1J 73
NW3 ..... 5B 48
Wedgewood Ct.
BR2: Short 3H 143
(off Cumberland Rd.)
DA5: Bexl 7F 111
Wedgewood Ho. SW1 ..... 6K 171
(off Churchill Gdns.)
Wedgewood M.
W1 ..... 6H 67 (1D 166)
Wedgwood Ho. E2 ..... 3K 69
(off Warley St.)
SE11 ..... 2J 173
Wedgwood Wlk. NW6 ..... 5K 47
(off Dresden Cl.)
Wedgwood Way SE19 ..... 7C 122
Wedlake St. W10 ..... 4G 65
Wedmore Av. IG5: Ilf 1E 36
Wedmore Ct. N19 ..... 2H 49
Wedmore Gdns. N19 ..... 2H 49
Wedmore M. N19 ..... 3H 49
Wedmore Rd.
UB6: G'frd 3H 61
Wedmore St. N19 ..... 3H 49
Weech Rd. NW6 ..... 4J 47
Weedington Rd. NW5 ..... 5E 48
Weedon Ho. W12 ..... 6C 64
Weekley Sq. SW11 ..... 3B 102
Weigall Rd. SE12 ..... 5J 107
Weighhouse St.
W1 ..... 6E 66 (1H 165)
Weighton M. SE20 ..... 2H 141
Weighton Rd.
HA3: Harr 1H 25
SE20 ..... 2H 141
Weihurst Ct. SM1: Sutt 5C 150
Weihurst Gdns.
SM1: Sutt 5B 150
Weimar St. SW15 ..... 3G 101
Weirdale Av. N20 ..... 2J 15
Weir Hall Av. N18 ..... 6J 17
Weir Hall Gdns. N18 ..... 5J 17
Weir Hall Rd. N17 ..... 5J 17
N18 ..... 5J 17
Weir Rd. DA5: Bexl 7H 111
KT12: Walt T 6J 131
SW12 ..... 7G 103
SW19 ..... 3K 119
Weir's Pas.
NW1 ..... 3H 67 (1D 160)
Weiss Rd. SW15 ..... 3F 101
Welbeck Av. BR1: Brom 4J 125
DA15: Sidc 1A 128
UB4: Hayes 4K 59
Welbeck Cl.
KT3: N Mald 5B 136
KT17: Eps 7C 148
N12 ..... 5G 15
Welbeck Ct. W14 ..... 4H 83
(off Addison Bri. Pl.)
Welbeck Ho. W1 ..... 7J 159
(off Welbeck St.)
Welbeck Rd. E6 ..... 3B 72
EN4: Barn 6H 5
HA2: Harr 1F 43
SM1: Cars, Sutt 2B 150
SM5: Cars 2B 150
Welbeck St. W1 ..... 5E 66 (6H 159)
Welbeck Vs. N21 ..... 2H 17
Welbeck Wlk.
SM5: Cars 1B 150
Welbeck Way
W1 ..... 6F 67 (7J 159)
Welbourne Rd. N17 ..... 3F 33
Welby Ho. N19 ..... 7H 31
Welby St. SE5 ..... 1B 104
Welch Pl. HA5: Pinn 1A 24
Welcome Ct. E17 ..... 7C 34
(off Boundary Rd.)
Weldon Cl. HA4: Ruis 6K 41
Weldon Ct. N21 ..... 5E 6
Weldon Dr.
KT8: W Mole 4D 132
Weld Pl. N11 ..... 5A 16
(not continuous)
Welfare Rd. E15 ..... 7G 53
Welford Cl. E5 ..... 3K 51
Welford Ct. NW1 ..... 7F 49
(off Castlehaven Rd.)
SW8 ..... 2G 103
W9 ..... 5J 65
(off Elmfield Way)
Welford Pl. SW19 ..... 4G 119
Welham Rd. SW17 ..... 5E 120
Welhouse Rd.
SM5: Cars 1C 150
Wellacre Rd. HA3: Harr 6B 26
Wellan Cl. DA15: Sidc 5B 110
Welland Ct. SE6 ..... 2B 124
(off Oakham Cl.)
Welland Gdns.
UB6: G'frd 2K 61
Welland Ho. SE15 ..... 4J 105
Welland M. E1 ..... 1G 87
Wellands Cl.
BR1: Brom 2D 144
Welland St. SE10 ..... 6E 88
Well App. EN5: Barn 5A 4
Wellbrook Rd.
BR6: Orp 4E 156
Wellby Cl. N9 ..... 1B 18
Wellby Ct. E13 ..... 1A 72
Well Cl. HA4: Ruis 3C 42
SW16 ..... 4K 121
Wellclose Sq. E1 ..... 7G 69
Wellclose St. E1 ..... 7G 69
E3 ..... 2A 70
(off Driffield Rd)
Wellcome Cen. for
Medical Science 3C 160
Wellcome Mus. 7H 161
(off Portugal St.)
Well Cott. Cl. E11 ..... 6A 36
Well Ct. EC4 ..... 6C 68 (1D 168)
(not continuous)
Welldon Ct. HA1: Harr 5J 25
Welldon Cres. HA1: Harr 5J 25
Weller Ho. SE16 ..... 2G 87
(off George Row)
Wellers Ct. N1 ..... 2J 67 (1E 160)
Weller St. SE1 ..... 2C 86 (6C 168)
Welles Ct. E14 ..... 7C 70
(off Premiere Pl.)
Wellesley Av. W6 ..... 3D 82
Wellesley Cl. SE7 ..... 5A 90
Wellesley Ct. NW2 ..... 2C 46
SM3: Sutt 1G 149
W9 ..... 3A 66
(off Maida Va.)
Wellesley Ct. Rd.
CR0: Croy 2D 152
Wellesley Cres.
TW2: Twick 2J 115
Wellesley Gro.
CR0: Croy 2D 152
Wellesley Ho. NW1 ..... 2D 160
(off Wellesley Pl.)
SW1 ..... 5J 171
(off Ebury Bri. Rd.)
Wellesley Lodge
SM2: Sutt 7J 149
(off Worcester Rd.)
Wellesley Mans. W14 ..... 5H 83
(off Edith Vs.)
Wellesley Pde.
TW2: Twick 3J 115
Wellesley Pk. M.
EN2: Enf 2G 7
Wellesley Pas.
CR0: Croy 2C 152
Wellesley Pl.
NW1 ..... 3H 67 (2C 160)
NW5 ..... 5E 48
Wellesley Rd.
CR0: Croy 1C 152
E11 ..... 5J 35
E17 ..... 6C 34
HA1: Harr 5J 25
IG1: Ilf 2F 55
N22 ..... 2A 32
NW5 ..... 5E 48
SM2: Sutt 6A 150
TW2: Twick 3H 115
W4 ..... 5G 81
Wellesley St. E1 ..... 5K 69
Wellesley Ter.
N1 ..... 3C 68 (1D 162)
Wellfield Av. N10 ..... 3F 31
Wellfield Rd. SW16 ..... 4J 121
Wellfield Wlk. SW16 ..... 5K 121
(not continuous)
Wellfit St. SE24 ..... 3B 104
Wellgarth UB6: G'frd 6B 44
Wellgarth Rd. NW11 ..... 1K 47
Well Gro. N20 ..... 1F 15
Well Hall Pde. SE9 ..... 4D 108
Well Hall Rd. SE9 ..... 3C 108
WELL HALL RDBT. 4C 108
Wellhouse La.
EN5: Barn 4A 4
Wellhouse Rd.
BR3: Beck 4C 142
WELLING 3B 110
Welling High St.
DA16: Well 3B 110
Wellington N8 ..... 4J 31
(not continuous)
Wellington Arch 6H 165
Wellington Av.
DA15: Sidc 6A 110
E4 ..... 2H 19
HA5: Pinn 1D 24
KT4: Wor Pk 3E 148
N9 ..... 3C 18
N15 ..... 6F 33
Wellington Av.
TW3: Houn 5E 96
Wellington Bldgs.
SW1 ..... 5E 84 (6H 171)
Wellington Cl.
KT12: Walt T 7H 131
RM10: Dag 7J 57
SE14 ..... 1K 105
W11 ..... 6J 65
Wellington Ct.
HA5: Pinn 1D 24
(off Wellington Rd.)
NW8 ..... 2B 66
(off Wellington Rd.)
SW1 ..... 7E 164
(off Knightsbridge)
SW6 ..... 1K 101
(off Maltings Pl.)
TW11: Tedd 5H 115
TW19: Staines 7A 94
Wellington Cres.
KT3: N Mald 3J 135
Wellington Dr.
RM10: Dag 7J 57
Wellington Est. E2 ..... 2J 69
Wellington Gdns. SE7 ..... 6A 90
TW2: Twick 4H 115
Wellington Gro. SE10 ..... 7F 89
Wellington Ho. E16 ..... 7J 71
(off Pepys Cres.)
NW3 ..... 6D 48
(off Eton Rd.)
UB5: N'olt 7E 42
(off Farmlands, The)
W5 ..... 3E 62
Wellington Mans. E10 ..... 1C 52
Wellington M. N7 ..... 6K 49
(off Roman Way)
SE7 ..... 6A 90
SE22 ..... 4G 105
SW16 ..... 3H 121
Wellington Monument 6H 165
Wellington Mus.
..... 2E 84 (6H 165)
Wellington Pde.
DA15: Sidc 5A 110
Wellington Pk. Est.
NW2 ..... 1C 46
Wellington Pas. E11 ..... 5J 35
(off Wellington Rd.)
Wellington Pl. N2 ..... 5C 30
NW8 ..... 3B 66 (1B 158)
Wellington Rd.
BR2: Short 4A 144
CR0: Croy 7B 140
DA5: Bexl 5D 110
DA17: Belv 5F 93
E6 ..... 1D 72
E7 ..... 4H 53
E10 ..... 1A 52
E11 ..... 5J 35
E17 ..... 4A 34
EN1: Enf 5K 7
HA3: Harr 3J 25
HA5: Pinn 1D 24
NW8 ..... 2B 66 (1B 158)
NW10 ..... 3F 65
SW19 ..... 2J 119
TW12: Hamp 5H 115
TW14: Felt 5G 95
TW15: Ashf 5A 112
W5 ..... 3C 80
Wellington Rd. Nth.
TW4: Houn 3D 96
Wellington Rd. Sth.
TW4: Houn 4D 96
Wellington Row
E2 ..... 3F 69 (1K 163)
Wellington Sq.
SW3 ..... 5D 84 (5E 170)
Wellington St.
IG11: Bark 1G 73

Wellington St. SE18 . . . 4E 90
WC2 . . . 7K 67 (2G 167)
Wellington Ter. E1 . . . 1H 87
HA1: Harr . . . 1H 43
N8 . . . 3A 32
(off Turnpike La.)
W11 . . . 7J 65
Wellington Way E3 . . . 3C 70
Welling Way
DA16: Well . . . 3J 109
SE9 . . . 3G 109
Well La. SW14 . . . 5J 99
Wellmeadow Rd.
SE13 . . . 6G 107
(not continuous)
W7 . . . 4A 80
Wellow Wlk.
SM5: Cars . . . 1B 150
Well Pl. NW3 . . . 3B 48
Well Rd. EN5: Barn . . . 5A 4
NW3 . . . 3B 48
Wells Cl. CR2: S Croy . . . 5E 152
UB5: N'olt . . . 3A 60
Wells Ct. *NW6 . . . 2J 65*
(off Cambridge Av.)
Wells Dr. NW9 . . . 1K 45
Wells Gdns. IG1: Ilf . . . 7C 36
RM10: Dag . . . 5H 57
Wells Ho. *BR1: Brom . . . 5K 125*
(off Pike Cl.)
EC1 . . . 1K 161
(off Spa Grn. Est.)
IG11: Bark . . . 7A 56
(off Margaret Bondfield Av.)
SE16 . . . 3J 87
(off Howland Est.)
W5 . . . 1D 80
(off Grove Rd.)
Wells Ho. Rd. NW10 . . . 5A 64
Wellside Cl. EN5: Barn . . . 4A 4
Wellside Gdns. SW14 . . . 4J 99
Wells M. W1 . . . 5G 67 (6B 160)
Wellsmoor Gdns.
BR1: Brom . . . 3E 144
Wells Pk. Rd. SE26 . . . 3G 123
Wells Path UB4: Hayes . . . 3G 59
Wells Pl. SW18 . . . 7A 102
Wells Ri. NW8 . . . 1D 66
Wells Rd. BR1: Brom . . . 2D 144
W12 . . . 2E 82
Wells Sq. WC1 . . . 3K 67 (2G 161)
Wells St. W1 . . . 5G 67 (6A 160)
Wellstead Av. N9 . . . 7E 8
Wellstead Rd. E6 . . . 2E 72
Wells Ter. N4 . . . 2A 50
Wells, The N14 . . . 7C 6
Well St. E9 . . . 7J 51
E15 . . . 6G 53
Wells Way SE5 . . . 6D 86
SW7 . . . 3B 84 (1A 170)
Wells Yd. N7 . . . 5A 50
Well Wlk. NW3 . . . 4B 48
Wellwood Rd. IG3: Ilf . . . 1A 56
Welsby Ct. W5 . . . 5C 62
Welsford St. SE1 . . . 4G 87
(not continuous)
Welsh Cl. E13 . . . 3J 71
Welsh Ho. *E1 . . . 1H 87*
(off Wapping La.)
Welshpool Ho. *E8 . . . 1G 69*
(off Welshpool St.)
Welshpool St. E8 . . . 1G 69
Welshside *NW9 . . . 6A 28*
(off Ruthin Cl.)
Welshside Wlk. NW9 . . . 6A 28
Welstead Ho. *E1 . . . 6H 69*
(off Cannon St. Rd.)
Welstead Way W4 . . . 4B 82
Weltje Rd. W6 . . . 4C 82
Welton Ct. SE5 . . . 1E 104
Welton Ho. *E1 . . . 5K 69*
(off Stepney Way)

Welton Rd. SE18 . . . 7J 91
Welwyn Av. TW14: Felt . . . 6H 95
Welwyn St. E2 . . . 3J 69
Welwyn Way UB4: Hayes . . . 4G 59
WEMBLEY . . . 5E 44
Wembley Arena . . . 4G 45
Wembley Commercial Cen.
HA9: Wemb . . . 2D 44
Wembley Conference Cen.
. . . 4G 45
Wembley Hill Rd.
HA9: Wemb . . . 3F 45
WEMBLEY PARK . . . 3G 45
Wembley Pk. Bus. Cen.
HA9: Wemb . . . 4H 45
Wembley Pk. Dr.
HA9: Wemb . . . 4F 45
Wembley Retail Pk.
HA9: Wemb . . . 4H 45
Wembley Rd.
TW12: Hamp . . . 1E 132
Wembley Stadium . . . 4G 45
Wembley Stadium Ind. Est.
HA9: Wemb . . . 4H 45
Wembley Way
HA9: Wemb . . . 6H 45
Wemborough Rd.
HA7: Stan . . . 1B 26
Wembury M. N6 . . . 7G 31
Wembury Rd. N6 . . . 7F 31
Wemyss Rd. SE3 . . . 2H 107
Wendela Ct. HA1: Harr . . . 2J 43
Wendell Rd. W12 . . . 3B 82
Wenderholme
CR2: S Croy . . . 5D 152
(off Sth. Park Hill Rd.)
Wendle Ct. SW8 . . . 6J 85 (7E 172)
Wendling Rd.
SM1: Sutt . . . 1B 150
Wendon St. E3 . . . 1B 70
Wendover SE17 . . . 5E 86
(not continuous)
Wendover Cl.
UB4: Hayes . . . 4C 60
Wendover Ct.
BR2: Short . . . 3K 143
(off Wendover Rd.)
NW2 . . . 3J 47
NW10 . . . 4H 63
W1 . . . 6G 159
(off Chiltern St.)
Wendover Dr.
KT3: N Mald . . . 6B 136
Wendover Ho. *W1 . . . 6G 159*
(off Chiltern St.)
Wendover Rd.
BR2: Short . . . 4K 143
NW10 . . . 2B 64
SE9 . . . 3B 108
Wendover Way
DA16: Well . . . 5A 110
Wendy Cl. EN1: Enf . . . 6A 8
Wendy Way HA0: Wemb . . . 1E 62
Wenham Ho. SW8 . . . 7G 85
Wenlake Ho. *EC1 . . . 3C 162*
(off Old St.)
Wenlock Barn Est. *N1 . . . 2D 68*
(off Wenlock St.)
Wenlock Ct. N1 . . . 2D 68 (1F 163)
Wenlock Gdns. NW4 . . . 4D 28
Wenlock Rd. HA8: Edg . . . 7C 12
N1 . . . 2C 68 (1D 162)
Wenlock St.
N1 . . . 2C 68 (1D 162)
Wennington Rd. E3 . . . 2K 69
Wensdale Ho. E5 . . . 2G 51
Wensley Av. IG8: Wfd G . . . 7C 20
Wensley Cl. N11 . . . 6K 15
SE9 . . . 6D 108
Wensleydale Av. IG5: Ilf . . . 2C 36
Wensleydale Gdns.
TW12: Hamp . . . 7F 115

Wensleydale Pas.
TW12: Hamp . . . 1E 132
Wensleydale Rd.
TW12: Hamp . . . 6E 114
Wensley Rd. N18 . . . 6C 18
Wentland Cl. SE6 . . . 2F 125
Wentland Rd. SE6 . . . 2F 125
Wentway Ct. *W13 . . . 4K 61*
(off Ruislip Rd. E.)
Wentworth Av. N3 . . . 7D 14
Wentworth Cl.
BR2: Short . . . 2J 155
KT6: Surb . . . 2D 146
N3 . . . 7E 14
SE28 . . . 6D 74
SM4: Mord . . . 7J 137
TW15: Ashf . . . 4D 112
Wentworth Ct.
TW2: Twick . . . 3J 115
W6 . . . 6G 83
(off Paynes Wlk.)
Wentworth Cres. SE15 . . . 7G 87
UB3: Hayes . . . 3F 77
Wentworth Dr. HA5: Pinn . . . 5J 23
Wentworth Dwellings
E1 . . . 7J 163
(off Wentworth St.)
Wentworth Flds.
UB4: Hayes . . . 2F 59
Wentworth Gdns. N13 . . . 3G 17
Wentworth Hill
HA9: Wemb . . . 1F 45
Wentworth M. E3 . . . 4A 70
Wentworth Pk. N3 . . . 7D 14
Wentworth Pl. HA7: Stan . . . 6G 11
Wentworth Rd.
CR0: Croy . . . 7A 140
E12 . . . 4B 54
EN5: Barn . . . 3A 4
NW11 . . . 6H 29
UB2: S'hall . . . 4A 78
Wentworth St.
E1 . . . 6F 69 (7J 163)
Wentworth Way
HA5: Pinn . . . 4C 24
Wenvoe Av. DA7: Bex . . . 2H 111
Wepham Cl. UB4: Hayes . . . 5B 60
Wernbrook St. SE18 . . . 6G 91
Werndee Rd. SE25 . . . 4G 141
Werneth Hall Rd. IG5: Ilf . . . 3D 36
Werrington St.
NW1 . . . 2G 67 (1B 160)
Werter Rd. SW15 . . . 4G 101
Wesleyan Pl. NW5 . . . 4F 49
Wesley Av. E16 . . . 1J 89
NW10 . . . 3K 63
TW3: Houn . . . 2C 96
Wesley Cl. HA2: Harr . . . 2G 43
N7 . . . 2K 49
SE17 . . . 4B 86
Wesley Ct. SE16 . . . 3H 87
Wesley Rd. E10 . . . 7E 34
N2 . . . 1C 30
NW10 . . . 1J 63
UB3: Hayes . . . 7J 59
Wesley's House, Chapel &
Mus. of Methodism
. . . 4D 68 (3F 163)
Wesley Sq. W11 . . . 6G 65
Wesley St. W1 . . . 5E 66 (6H 159)
Wessex Av. SW19 . . . 3J 137
Wessex Cl. IG3: Ilf . . . 6J 37
KT1: King T . . . 1H 135
Wessex Ct. BR3: Beck . . . 1A 142
EN5: Barn . . . 4A 4
TW19: Staines . . . 6A 94
Wessex Dr. HA5: Pinn . . . 1C 24
Wessex Gdns. NW11 . . . 1G 47
Wessex Ho. SE1 . . . 5F 87
Wessex La. UB6: G'frd . . . 3H 61
Wessex Rd. TW6: Houn . . . 2A 94
Wessex St. E2 . . . 3J 69

Wessex Wlk. DA5: Bexl . . . 2K 129
Wessex Way NW11 . . . 1G 47
Westacott UB4: Hayes . . . 5G 59
Westacott Cl. N19 . . . 1H 49
WEST ACTON . . . 6G 63
West App. BR5: Orp . . . 5G 145
W. Arbour St. E1 . . . 6K 69
West Av. E17 . . . 4D 34
HA5: Pinn . . . 6D 24
N2 . . . 3K 29
N3 . . . 6D 14
NW4 . . . 5F 29
SM6: Wall . . . 5J 151
UB1: S'hall . . . 7D 60
UB3: Hayes . . . 7H 59
W. Avenue Rd. E17 . . . 4C 34
West Bank EN2: Enf . . . 2H 7
IG11: Bark . . . 1F 73
N16 . . . 7E 32
Westbank Rd.
TW12: Hamp . . . 6G 115
WEST BARNES . . . 4D 136
W. Barnes La.
KT3: N Mald . . . 5C 136
(not continuous)
WEST BECKTON . . . 6B 72
WEST BEDFONT . . . 6B 94
Westbeech Rd. N22 . . . 3A 32
Westbere Dr. HA7: Stan . . . 5J 11
Westbere Rd. NW2 . . . 4G 47
West Block *SE1 . . . 7H 167*
(off Addington St.)
Westbourne Av.
SM3: Sutt . . . 2G 149
W3 . . . 6K 63
Westbourne Bri. W2 . . . 5A 66
Westbourne Cl.
UB4: Hayes . . . 4A 60
Westbourne Cres.
W2 . . . 7B 66 (2A 164)
Westbourne Cres. M.
W2 . . . 2A 164
Westbourne Dr. SE23 . . . 2K 123
Westbourne Gdns. W2 . . . 6K 65
WESTBOURNE GREEN . . . 6H 65
Westbourne Gro. W11 . . . 7H 65
Westbourne Gro. M. W11 . . . 6J 65
Westbourne Gro. Ter.
W2 . . . 6K 65
Westbourne Ho. *SW1 . . . 5J 171*
(off Ebury Bri. Rd.)
TW5: Houn . . . 6E 78
Westbourne Pde.
UB10: Uxb . . . 4D 58
Westbourne Pk. Pas. W2 . . . 5J 65
(not continuous)
Westbourne Pk. Rd.
W11 . . . 6G 65
Westbourne Pk. Vs. W2 . . . 5J 65
Westbourne Pl. N9 . . . 3C 18
Westbourne Rd.
CR0: Croy . . . 6F 141
DA7: Bex . . . 7D 92
N7 . . . 6K 49
SE26 . . . 6K 123
TW13: Felt . . . 3H 113
UB10: Uxb . . . 4D 58
Westbourne St.
W2 . . . 7B 66 (2A 164)
Westbourne Ter. *SE23 . . . 2K 123*
(off Westbourne Dr.)
W2 . . . 6A 66 (1A 164)
Westbourne Ter. M. W2 . . . 6A 66
Westbourne Ter. Rd. W2 . . . 5K 65
Westbourne Ter. Rd. Bri.
W2 . . . 5A 66
(off Westbourne Ter. Rd.)
Westbridge Cl. W12 . . . 2C 82
Westbridge Rd. SW11 . . . 1B 102
WEST BROMPTON . . . 6A 84
Westbrook Av.
TW12: Hamp . . . 7D 114

Westbrook Cl. EN4: Barn . . . 3G 5
Westbrook Cres.
EN4: Barn . . . 3G 5
Westbrooke Cres.
DA16: Well . . . 3C 110
Westbrooke Rd.
DA15: Sidc . . . 2H 127
DA16: Well . . . 3B 110
Westbrook Ho. *E2 . . . 3J 69*
(off Victoria Pk. Sq.)
Westbrook Rd.
CR7: Thor H . . . 1D 140
SE3 . . . 1K 107
TW5: Houn . . . 7D 78
Westbrook Sq. EN4: Barn . . . 3G 5
Westbury Av.
HA0: Wemb . . . 7E 44
N22 . . . 3B 32
UB1: S'hall . . . 4E 60
Westbury Cl. HA4: Ruis . . . 7J 23
TW17: Shep . . . 6D 130
Westbury Ct. *IG11: Bark . . . 1H 73*
(off Westbury Rd.)
Westbury Gro. N12 . . . 6D 14
Westbury Ho. E17 . . . 4B 34
Westbury La.
IG9: Buck H . . . 2E 20
Westbury Lodge Cl.
HA5: Pinn . . . 3B 24
Westbury Pl. TW8: Bford . . . 6D 80
Westbury Rd.
BR1: Brom . . . 1B 144
BR3: Beck . . . 3A 142
CR0: Croy . . . 6D 140
E7 . . . 6K 53
E17 . . . 4B 34
HA0: Wemb . . . 7E 44
Westbury Rd. IG1: Ilf . . . 2E 54
IG9: Buck H . . . 2F 21
IG11: Bark . . . 1H 73
KT3: N Mald . . . 4K 135
N11 . . . 6D 16
N12 . . . 6D 14
SE20 . . . 1K 141
TW13: Felt . . . 1B 114
W5 . . . 6E 62
Westbury St. *SW8 . . . 2G 103*
(off Portslade Rd.)
Westbury Ter. E7 . . . 6K 53
W. Carriage Dr.
W2 . . . 7C 66 (3C 164)
(not continuous)
W. Central St.
WC1 . . . 6J 67 (7E 160)
W. Centre Av. NW10 . . . 4D 64
West Chantry HA3: Harr . . . 1F 25
Westchester Dr. NW4 . . . 3F 29
West Cl. EN4: Barn . . . 4K 5
HA9: Wemb . . . 1F 45
N9 . . . 3A 18
TW12: Hamp . . . 6C 114
TW15: Ashf . . . 4A 112
UB6: G'frd . . . 2G 61
Westcombe Av.
CR0: Croy . . . 7J 139
Westcombe Ct. SE3 . . . 7H 89
Westcombe Dr. EN5: Barn . . . 5D 4
Westcombe Hill SE3 . . . 7J 89
Westcombe Lodge Dr.
UB4: Hayes . . . 5G 59
Westcombe Pk. Rd. SE3 . . . 6G 89
West Comn. Rd.
BR2: Short . . . 1J 155
UB8: Uxb . . . 5A 40
Westcoombe Av. SW20 . . . 1B 136
Westcote Ri. HA4: Ruis . . . 7E 22
Westcote Rd. SW16 . . . 5G 121
West Cotts. NW6 . . . 5J 47
Westcott Cl. BR1: Brom . . . 5D 144
CR0: Croy . . . 7D 154
N15 . . . 6F 33
Westcott Cres. W7 . . . 6J 61

Westcott Ho. E14 ......7C 70
Westcott Rd. SE17 ......6B 86
West Ct. E17 ....4C 34
  HA0: Wemb 2C 44
  TW7: Isle 7G 79
Westcroft Cl. EN3: Enf 1D 8
  NW2 ....4G 47
Westcroft Gdns.
  SM4: Mord 3H 137
Westcroft Rd.
  SM5: Cars, Wall 4E 150
  SM6: Wall 4E 150
Westcroft Sq. W6 ......4C 82
Westcroft Way NW2 ......4G 47
W. Cromwell Rd. W14 ....5H 83
W. Cross Cen.
  TW8: Bford 6A 80
W. Cross Route W10 ......7F 65
W. Cross Way
  TW8: Bford 6B 80
Westdale Pas. SE18 ......6F 91
Westdale Rd. SE18 ......6F 91
Westdean Av. SE12 ......1K 125
W. Dean Cl. SW18 ......6K 101
West Dene SM3: Sutt 6G 149
Westdown Rd. E15 ......4E 52
  SE6 ....7C 106
WEST DRAYTON 2A 76
W. Drayton Pk. Av.
  UB7: W Dray 3A 76
W. Drayton Rd.
  UB8: Uxb 6D 58
West Dr. HA3: Harr 6C 10
  SM2: Sutt 7F 149
  SW16 ....4G 121
West Dr. Gdns.
  HA3: Harr 6C 10
WEST DULWICH 2D 122
WEST EALING 1B 80
W. Ealing Bus. Cen. W13 ...7A 62
W. Eaton Pl.
  SW1 ......4E 84 (3G 171)
W. Eaton Pl. M. SW1 ....2G 171
W. Ella Rd. NW10 ......7A 46
WEST END 2B 60
W. End Av. E10 ....5F 35
  HA5: Pinn 4B 24
Westend Cl. NW10 ......7J 45
W. End Cl. HA5: Pinn 4B 24
  NW6 ....7K 47
W. End Gdns.
  UB5: N'olt 2A 60
W. End La. EN5: Barn 4A 4
  HA5: Pinn 3B 24
  NW6 ....5J 47
  (not continuous)
  UB3: Hayes 7E 76
W. End Rd.
  HA4: N'olt, Ruis ...2G 41
  UB1: S'hall 1C 78
  UB5: N'olt 7A 42
Westerdale Rd. SE10 ....5J 89
Westerfield Rd. N15 ....5F 33
Westergate W5 ....5E 62
Westergate Ho.
  KT1: King T 4D 134
  (off Portsmouth Rd.)
Westergate Rd. SE2 ....6E 92
Westerham NW1 ....1G 67
  (off Bayham St.)
Westerham Av. N9 ......3J 17
Westerham Dr.
  DA15: Sidc 6B 110
Westerham Ho. SE1 .....3D 86
  (off Law St.)
Westerham Lodge
  BR3: Beck 7C 124
  (off Park Rd.)
Westerham Rd.
  BR2: Kes 6B 156
  E10 ....7D 34
Westerley Cres. SE26 ...5B 124

Western Av. HA4: Ruis 6E 40
  NW11 ....6F 29
  RM10: Dag 6J 57
  UB5: N'olt 7A 42
  UB6: G'frd 2H 61
  UB10: Ruis, Uxb ...6E 40
  UB10: Uxb 5A 40
  W3 ....4G 63
  W5 ....4F 63
Western Av. Bus. Pk. W3 ...4H 63
Western Beach Apartments
  E16 ....7J 71
Western Ct. N3 ....6D 14
  W3 ....6K 63
  W9 ....2H 65
Western Dr.
  TW17: Shep 6F 131
Western Gdns. W5 ......7G 63
Western Intl. Mkt.
  UB2: S'hall 4K 77
Western La. SW12 ......7E 102
Western Mans. EN5: Barn ...5E 4
  (off Gt. North Rd.)
Western M. W9 ....4H 65
Western Pde. EN5: Barn 5D 4
Western Pl. SE16 ......2J 87
Western Rd. CR4: Mitc ...1B 138
  E13 ....2A 72
  E17 ....5E 34
  N2 ....4D 30
  N22 ....2K 31
  NW10 ....4J 63
  SM1: Sutt 5J 149
  SW9 ....3A 104
  SW19 ....1B 154
  UB2: S'hall 4A 78
  W5 ....7D 62
Western Ter. W6 ....5C 82
  (off Chiswick Mall)
Western Vw. UB3: Hayes 2H 77
Westerville Gdns.
  IG2: Ilf 7G 37
Western Way EN5: Barn 6D 4
  SE28 ....3H 91
WEST EWELL 7K 147
Westferry Cir. E14 ......1B 88
Westferry Rd. E14 ......7B 70
Westfield Cl. EN3: Enf 3F 9
  NW9 ....3J 27
  SM1: Sutt 4H 149
  SW10 ....7A 84
Westfield Ct. KT6: Surb ...5D 134
  (off Portsmouth Rd.)
  NW10 ....3F 65
  (off Chamberlayne Rd.)
Westfield Dr. HA3: Harr ...4D 26
Westfield Gdns.
  HA3: Harr 4D 26
  RM6: Chad H 6C 38
Westfield Ho. SE16 .....4K 87
  (off Rotherhithe New Rd.)
  SW18 ....1K 119
Westfield La. HA3: Harr 5D 26
  (not continuous)
Westfield Pk. HA5: Pinn ...1D 24
Westfield Pk. Dr.
  IG8: Wfd G 6H 21
Westfield Rd.
  BR3: Beck 2B 142
  CR0: Croy 2B 152
  CR4: Mitc 2C 138
  DA7: Bex 3J 111
  KT6: Surb 5D 134
  KT12: Walt T 7C 132
  NW7 ....3E 12
  RM9: Dag 4E 56
  SM1: Sutt 4H 149
  W13 ....1A 80
Westfields SW13 ......3B 100
Westfields Av. SW13 ....3A 100
Westfields Rd. W3 ......5H 63
Westfield St. SE18 ......3B 90

Westfield Way E1 ......3A 70
  HA4: Ruis 3G 41
W. Garden Pl.
  W2 ......6C 66 (1D 164)
West Gdns. E1 ....7H 69
  SW17 ....6C 120
Westgate W5 ....3E 62
Westgate Cen., The E8 ....1H 68
  (off Bocking St.)
Westgate Ct. SE12 ......1J 125
  (off Burnt Ash Hill)
  SW9 ....3A 104
  (off Canterbury Cres.)
Westgate M. W10 ......4G 65
  (off West Row)
Westgate Rd.
  BR3: Beck 1E 142
  SE25 ....4H 141
Westgate St. E8 ......1H 69
Westgate Ter. SW10 ....5K 83
Westglade Cl. HA3: Harr ...5D 26
WEST GREEN 4B 32
W. Green Pl. UB6: G'frd 1H 61
W. Green Rd. N8 ......4B 32
West Gro. IG8: Wfd G 6F 21
  SE10 ....1E 106
Westgrove La. SE10 ....1E 106
W. Halkin St.
  SW1 ......3E 84 (1G 171)
West Hallowes SE9 ....1B 126
W. Hall Rd. TW9: Rich 1H 99
WEST HAM 1H 71
W. Ham La. E15 ......7F 53
WEST HAMPSTEAD 6K 47
W. Hampstead M. NW6 ...6K 47
West Ham United F.C.
  (Upton Park) 2A 72
W. Harding St.
  EC4 ......6A 68 (7K 161)
WEST HARROW 7G 25
W. Hatch Mnr. HA4: Ruis ...1H 41
Westhay Gdns. SW14 ...5H 99
WEST HEATH 6D 92
W. Heath Av. NW11 ....1J 47
W. Heath Cl. NW3 ......3J 47
W. Heath Ct. NW11 ....1J 47
W. Heath Dr. NW11 ....1J 47
W. Heath Gdns. NW3 ...2J 47
W. Heath Rd. NW3 .....2J 47
  SE2 ....6C 92
WEST HENDON 7C 28
WEST HILL 6H 101
West Hill CR2: S Croy ...7E 152
  HA2: Harr 2J 43
  HA9: Wemb 1F 45
  SW15 ....7F 101
W. Hill Ct. N6 ....3E 48
Westhill Pk. N6 ......2D 48
  (not continuous)
Westholm NW11 ....4K 29
West Holme DA8: Erith ...1J 111
Westholme BR6: Orp 7J 145
Westholme Gdns.
  HA4: Ruis 1J 41
Westhope Ho. E2 ......4G 69
  (off Derbyshire St.)
Westhorne Av. SE9 .....6A 108
  SE12 ....7J 107
Westhorpe Gdns. NW4 ...3E 28
Westhorpe Rd. SW15 ...3E 100
West Ho. Cl. SW19 .....1G 119
West Ho. Cotts.
  HA5: Pinn 4B 24
Westhurst Dr. BR7: Chst ...5F 127
W. India Av. E14 ......1C 88
W. India Dock Rd. E14 ...7B 70
  (not continuous)
W. India Ho. E14 ......7C 70
  (off W. India Dock Rd.)
WEST KENSINGTON 4H 83

W. Kensington Ct. W14 ...5H 83
  (off Edith Vs.)
W. Kensington Mans.
  W14 ....5H 83
  (off Beaumont Cres.)
WEST KILBURN 3H 65
Westlake SE16 ....4J 87
  (off Rotherhithe New Rd.)
Westlake Cl. N13 ......3F 17
  UB4: Hayes 4C 60
Westlake Rd.
  HA9: Wemb 2D 44
Westland Cl.
  TW19: Staines 6A 94
Westland Ct. UB5: N'olt ...3B 60
  (off Seasprite Cl.)
Westland Dr.
  BR2: Short 2H 155
Westland Ho. E16 ......1E 90
  (off Rymill St.)
Westland Pl. N1 ...3D 68 (1E 162)
Westlands Cl.
  UB3: Hayes 4J 77
Westlands Ter. SW12 ...6G 103
West La. SE16 ....2H 87
Westlea Rd. W7 ....3A 80
Westleigh Av. SW15 ....5D 100
Westleigh Cl.
  CR2: S Croy 4E 152
  (off Birdhurst Rd.)
  E11 ....5J 35
Westleigh Dr.
  BR1: Brom 1C 144
Westleigh Gdns.
  HA8: Edg 1G 27
Westlington Cl. NW7 ....6C 14
West Lodge E16 ....7J 71
  (off Britannia Ga.)
W. Lodge Av. W3 ......1G 81
W. Lodge Ct. W3 ......1G 81
West London Crematorium
  NW10 ....4D 64
Westmacott Dr.
  TW14: Felt 1H 113
Westmacott Ho. NW8 ....4B 158
  (off Hatton St.)
West Mall W8 ....1J 83
  (off Palace Gdns. Ter.)
West Mead
  HA4: Ruis 4A 42
  KT19: Eps 6A 148
Westmead SW15 ......6D 100
Westmead Av.
  SM5: Cars 4C 150
Westmead Rd.
  SM1: Sutt 4B 150
Westmere Dr. NW7 .....3E 12
W. Mersea Cl. E16 .....1K 89
West M. N17 ....7C 18
  SW1 ....4A 172
Westmill Ct. N4 ....2C 50
  (off Brownswood Rd.)
WESTMINSTER ...2J 85 (7E 166)
Westminster Abbey
  ....3J 85 (1E 172)
Westminster Abbey Chapter House
  ....1E 172
  (in Westminster Abbey)
Westminster Abbey Mus.
  ....1E 172
  (in Westminster Abbey)
Westminster Abbey Pyx Chamber
  ....1E 172
  (in Westminster Abbey)
Westminster Av.
  CR7: Thor H 2B 140
Westminster Bri.
  SW1 ......2J 85 (7F 167)
Westminster Bri. Rd.
  SE1 ......2K 85 (7G 167)
Westminster Bus. Sq.
  SE11 ......5K 85 (6G 173)

Westminster Cl. IG6: Ilf ...2H 37
  TW11: Tedd 5A 116
  TW14: Felt 1J 113
Westminster Ct. E11 ....6J 35
  (off Cambridge Pk.)
  SE16 ....1K 87
  (off King & Queen Wharf)
Westminster Dr. N13 ....5G 16
Westminster Gdns. E4 ...1B 20
  IG6: Ilf 2G 37
  IG11: Bark 2J 73
  SW1 ....3E 172
  (off Marsham St.)
Westminster Hall 7E 166
Westminster Ho.
  HA3: Harr 7E 10
Westminster Ind. Est.
  SE18 ....3B 90
Westminster Mans.
  SW1 ....3H 85
Westminster Pal. Gdns.
  SW1 ....2C 172
Westminster R.C. Cathedral
  ....3G 85 (2A 172)
Westminster Rd. N9 ....1C 18
  SM1: Sutt 2B 150
  W7 ....1J 79
Westminster Theatre 1A 172
  (off Palace St.)
Westmoat Cl.
  BR3: Beck 7E 124
WEST MOLESEY 4E 132
Westmoor Gdns. EN3: Enf ...2E 8
Westmoor Rd. EN3: Enf 2E 8
Westmoor St. SE7 ......3A 90
Westmoreland Av.
  DA16: Well 3J 109
Westmoreland Bldgs.
  SM2: Sutt 7K 149
Westmoreland Ho. E16 ...7J 71
  (off Gatcombe Rd.)
Westmoreland Pl.
  BR1: Brom 3J 143
  SW1 ......5F 85 (6K 171)
  W5 ....5D 62
Westmoreland Rd.
  BR2: Short 5G 143
  NW9 ....3F 27
  SE17 ....6D 86
  (not continuous)
  SW13 ....1B 100
Westmoreland St.
  W1 ......5E 66 (6H 159)
Westmoreland Ter.
  SW1 ......5F 85 (6K 171)
Westmoreland Wlk.
  SE17 ....6D 86
  (not continuous)
Westmorland Cl. E12 ....2B 54
  TW1: Twick 6B 98
Westmorland Ct.
  KT6: Surb 7D 134
Westmorland Rd. E17 ...6C 34
  HA1: Harr 5F 25
Westmorland Sq.
  CR4: Mitc 5J 139
  (off Westmorland Way)
Westmorland Ter.
  SE20 ....7H 123
Westmorland Way
  CR4: Mitc 4H 139
Westmount Cl. W5 .....6F 63
Westmount Rd. SE9 ....2D 108
WEST NORWOOD 4C 122
West Norwood Crematorium
  SE27 ....3C 122
West Oak BR3: Beck 1F 143
Westoe Rd. N9 ....2C 18
Weston Av. KT7: T Ditt ...7J 133
  KT8: W Mole 3C 132
Westonbirt Ct. SE15 ....6F 87
  (off Ebley Cl.)

Weston Ct.—Whitchurch Cl.

Weston Ct. KT1: King T ...3E 134
(off Grove Cres.)
N4 ...3C 50
Weston Dr. HA7: Stan ...1B 26
West One Ho. W1 ...6A 160
(off Wells St.)
Westone Mans.
IG11: Bark ...7K 55
(off Upney La.)
Weston Gdns. TW7: Isle ...1J 97
WESTON GREEN ...7J 133
Weston Grn. RM9: Dag ...4F 57
Weston Gro. BR1: Brom ...1H 143
Weston Ho. E9 ...1J 69
(off King Edward's Rd.)
NW6 ...7G 47
Weston Pk. KT1: King T ...2E 134
KT7: T Ditt ...7J 133
N8 ...6J 31
Weston Ri.
WC1 ...3K 67 (1H 161)
Weston Rd. BR1: Brom ...7H 125
EN2: Enf ...2J 7
RM9: Dag ...4E 56
W4 ...3J 81
Weston St. SE1 ...2E 86 (7F 169)
(not continuous)
Weston Wlk. E8 ...7H 51
Westover Hill NW3 ...2J 47
Westover Rd. SW18 ...7A 102
Westow Hill SE19 ...6E 122
Westow St. SE19 ...6E 122
West Pk. SE9 ...2C 126
W. Park Av. TW9: Rich ...1G 99
W. Park Cl. RM6: Chad H ...5D 38
TW5: Houn ...6D 78
W. Park Rd. TW9: Rich ...1G 99
UB2: S'hall ...1G 79
West Parkside SE10 ...2G 89
West Pl. SW19 ...5E 118
West Point E14 ...7B 70
(off Grenade St.)
SE1 ...5G 87
Westpoint Trad. Est. W3 ...5H 63
Westpole Av. EN4: Barn ...4K 5
Westport Ct. UB4: Hayes ...4A 60
Westport Rd. E13 ...4K 71
Westport St. E1 ...6K 69
W. Poultry Av.
EC1 ...5B 68 (6A 162)
West Quarters W12 ...6C 64
West Quay SW10 ...1A 102
W. Quay Dr. UB4: Hayes ...5C 60
West Ramp TW6: Houn ...1C 94
W. Ridge Gdns.
UB6: G'frd ...2G 61
West Ri. W2 ...2D 164
West Rd. E15 ...1H 71
EN4: Barn ...1K 15
KT2: King T ...1J 135
N2 ...2B 30
N17 ...6C 18
RM6: Chad H ...6D 38
RM7: Rush G ...7K 39
SE1 ...2K 85 (6H 167)
SW3 ...5D 84 (6F 171)
SW4 ...5H 103
TW14: Felt ...6F 95
UB7: W Dray ...3B 76
W5 ...5E 62
West Row W10 ...4G 65
Westrow SW15 ...6E 100
Westrow Dr. IG11: Bark ...5A 56
Westrow Gdns. IG3: Ilf ...2K 55
WEST RUISLIP ...2E 40
W. Ruislip Ct.
HA4: Ruis ...2F 41
(off Ickenham Rd.)
W. Sheen Va.
TW9: Rich ...4F 99
West Side NW4 ...2D 28
Westside N2 ...3D 30
W. Side Comn. SW19 ...5E 118
Westside Ct. W9 ...4J 65
(off Elgin Av.)
West Smithfield
EC1 ...5B 68 (6A 162)
West Sq. SE11 ...3B 86 (2K 173)
West St. BR1: Brom ...1J 143
CR0: Croy ...4C 152
DA7: Bex ...3F 111
DA8: Erith ...4K 93
E2 ...2H 69
E11 ...3G 53
E17 ...5D 34
HA1: Harr ...1H 43
SM1: Sutt ...5K 149
SM5: Cars ...3D 150
TW8: Bford ...6C 80
WC2 ...6H 67 (1D 166)
West St. La.
SM5: Cars ...4D 150
(not continuous)
W. Street Pl. CR0: Croy ...4C 152
(off West St.)
W. Temple Sheen SW14 ...5H 99
W. Tenter St. E1 ...6F 69 (1K 169)
West Ter. DA15: Sidc ...1J 127
West Towers HA5: Pinn ...6B 24
Westvale M. W3 ...2A 82
West Vw. NW4 ...4E 28
TW14: Felt ...7E 94
Westview W7 ...6J 61
W. View Cl. NW10 ...5B 46
Westview Cl. W10 ...6E 64
Westview Ct. N20 ...1F 15
Westview Cres. N9 ...7K 7
Westview Dr. IG8: Wfd G ...2B 36
Westville Rd.
KT7: T Ditt ...1A 146
W12 ...2C 82
West Wlk. EN4: Barn ...7K 5
UB3: Hayes ...1J 77
W5 ...5E 62
Westward Rd. E4 ...5G 19
(not continuous)
Westward Way HA3: Harr ...6E 26
W. Warwick Pl.
SW1 ...4G 85 (4A 172)
West Way
BR4: W W'ck ...6F 143
CR0: Croy ...2A 154
HA4: Ruis ...1H 41
HA5: Pinn ...4B 24
HA8: Edg ...6C 12
NW10 ...3K 45
TW5: Houn ...1D 96
TW17: Shep ...6F 131
Westway BR5: Orp ...5H 145
N18 ...4J 17
SW20 ...3D 136
W2 ...5B 66 (6A 158)
W10 ...5H 65
W12 ...7B 64
Westway Cl. SW20 ...3D 136
Westway Ct. UB5: N'olt ...1E 60
Westway Cross Retail Pk.
UB6: G'frd ...1J 61
W. Way Gdns. CR0: Croy ...2K 153
West Ways HA6: Nwood ...2J 23
Westways KT19: Eps ...4B 148
Westwell M. SW16 ...6J 121
Westwell Rd. SW16 ...6J 121
Westwell Rd. App.
SW16 ...6J 121
Westwick KT1: King T ...2G 135
(off Chesterton Ter.)
Westwick Gdns.
TW4: Houn ...2K 95
W14 ...2F 83
WEST WICKHAM ...1E 154
Westwood Av.
HA2: Harr ...4F 43
SE19 ...1C 140
Westwood Bus. Cen.
NW10 ...4A 64
Westwood Cl.
BR1: Brom ...2B 144
HA4: Ruis ...6D 22
Westwood Ct.
HA0: Wemb ...4B 44
UB6: G'frd ...5H 43
Westwood Gdns. SW13 ...3B 100
Westwood Hill SE26 ...5G 123
Westwood Ho. W12 ...1E 82
(off Wood La.)
Westwood La.
DA15: Sidc ...5A 110
DA16: Well ...3K 109
Westwood Pk. SE23 ...7H 105
Westwood Pk. Trad. Est.
W3 ...5H 63
Westwood Pl. SE26 ...4G 123
Westwood Rd. E16 ...1K 89
IG3: Ilf ...1K 55
SW13 ...3B 100
West Woodside
DA5: Bexl ...7E 110
Wetheral Dr. HA7: Stan ...1B 26
Wetherby Cl. UB5: N'olt ...6F 43
Wetherby Gdns. SW5 ...4A 84
Wetherby Mans. SW5 ...5K 83
(off Earls Ct. Sq.)
Wetherby M. SW5 ...5K 83
Wetherby Pl. SW7 ...4A 84
Wetherby Rd. EN2: Enf ...1H 7
Wetherby Way
KT9: Chess ...7E 146
Wetherden St. E17 ...7B 34
Wetherell Rd. E9 ...1K 69
Wetherill Rd. N10 ...1E 30
Wevco Wharf SE16 ...6H 87
Wevell Ho. N6 ...7E 30
(off Hillcrest)
Wexford Ho. E1 ...5J 69
(off Sidney St.)
Wexford Rd. SW12 ...7D 102
Weybourne St. SW18 ...2A 120
Weybridge Ct. SE16 ...5H 87
(off Argyle Way)
Weybridge Point SW11 ...2D 102
Weybridge Rd.
CR7: Thor H ...4A 140
Wey Ct. KT19: Eps ...4J 147
Weydown Cl. SW19 ...1G 119
Weyhill Rd. E1 ...6G 69
Weylands Cl.
KT12: Walt T ...7D 132
Weylond Rd. RM8: Dag ...3F 57
Weyman Rd. SE3 ...1A 108
Weymarks, The N17 ...6J 17
Weymouth Av. NW7 ...5F 13
W5 ...3C 80
Weymouth Cl. E6 ...6F 73
Weymouth Ct. E2 ...2F 69
(off Weymouth Ter.)
SM2: Sutt ...7J 149
Weymouth Ho.
BR2: Short ...2H 143
(off Beckenham La.)
SW8 ...7K 85
(off Bolney St.)
Weymouth M.
W1 ...5F 67 (5J 159)
Weymouth Rd.
UB4: Hayes ...3G 59
Weymouth St.
W1 ...5E 66 (6H 159)
Weymouth Ter.
E2 ...2F 69 (1K 163)
Weymouth Wlk.
HA7: Stan ...6F 11
Whadcoat St. N4 ...2A 50
Whalebone Av.
RM6: Chad H ...6F 39
Whalebone Ct. EC2 ...7E 162
Whalebone Gro.
RM6: Chad H ...6F 39
Whalebone La. E15 ...7G 53
Whalebone La. Nth.
RM6: Chad H, Col R ...1E 38
Whalebone La. Sth.
RM6: Chad H, Dag ...7F 39
RM8: Dag ...7F 39
Whales Yd. E15 ...7G 53
(off W. Ham La.)
Wharfdale Cl. N11 ...6K 15
Wharfdale Rd. N1 ...2J 67
Wharfedale Ct. E5 ...4K 51
Wharfedale Gdns.
CR7: Thor H ...4K 139
Wharfedale Ho. NW6 ...1K 65
(off Kilburn Va.)
Wharfedale St. SW10 ...5K 83
Wharf La. TW1: Twick ...1A 116
Wharf Pl. E2 ...1H 69
Wharf Rd. E15 ...1F 71
EN3: Enf ...6F 9
N1 ...2C 68 (1C 162)
(Angel)
N1 ...2J 67
(King's Cross)
NW1 ...1H 67
Wharf Rd. Ind. Est.
EN3: Enf ...6F 9
Wharfside Rd. E16 ...5G 71
Wharf St. E16 ...5G 71
Wharf, The EC3 ...1F 87 (4H 169)
Wharf Vw. Ct. E14 ...6E 70
(off Athol Sq.)
Wharncliffe Dr.
UB1: S'hall ...1H 79
Wharncliffe Gdns. SE25 ...2E 140
Wharncliffe Rd. SE25 ...2E 140
Wharton Cl. NW10 ...6A 46
Wharton Cotts.
WC1 ...3A 68 (2J 161)
Wharton Ho. SE1 ...7J 169
(off Maltby St.)
Wharton Rd. BR1: Brom ...1K 143
Wharton St.
WC1 ...3K 67 (2H 161)
Whateley Rd. SE20 ...7K 123
SE22 ...5F 105
Whatley Av. SW20 ...3F 137
Whatman Ho. E14 ...6B 70
(off Wallwood St.)
Whatman Rd. SE23 ...7K 105
Wheatfields E6 ...6F 73
EN3: Enf ...1F 9
Wheatfield Way
KT1: King T ...2E 134
Wheathill Ho. SE20 ...2H 141
(off Croydon Rd.)
Wheathill Rd. SE20 ...3H 141
Wheatland Ho. SE22 ...3E 104
Wheatlands
TW5: Houn ...6E 78
Wheatlands Rd. SW17 ...3E 120
Wheatley Cl. NW4 ...2C 28
Wheatley Cres.
UB3: Hayes ...7J 59
Wheatley Gdns. N9 ...2K 17
Wheatley Ho. SW15 ...7C 100
(off Ellisfield Dr)
Wheatley Mans.
IG11: Bark ...7A 56
(off Bevan Av.)
Wheatley Rd. TW7: Isle ...3K 97
Wheatley St.
W1 ...5E 66 (6H 159)
Wheat Sheaf Cl. E14 ...4D 88
Wheatsheaf Cl.
UB5: N'olt ...5C 42
Wheatsheaf La. SW6 ...7E 82
SW8 ...7J 85
(not continuous)
Wheatsheaf Ter. SW6 ...7H 83
Wheatstone Cl.
CR4: Mitc ...1C 138
Wheatstone Rd.
DA8: Erith ...5K 93
W10 ...5G 65
Wheeler Cl. IG8: Wfd G ...6J 21
Wheeler Gdns. N1 ...1J 67
(off Outram Pl.)
Wheelers Cross
IG11: Bark ...2H 73
Wheelers Dr. HA4: Ruis ...6E 22
Wheel Farm Dr.
RM10: Dag ...3J 57
Wheel Ho. E14 ...5D 88
(off Burrells Wharf Sq.)
Wheelock Cl. DA8: Erith ...7H 93
Wheelwright St. N7 ...7K 49
Whelan Way SM6: Wall ...3H 151
Wheler Ho. E1 ...4J 163
(off Quaker St.)
Wheler St. E1 ...4F 69 (4J 163)
Whellock Rd. W4 ...3A 82
Whenman Av. DA5: Bexl ...2J 129
Whernside Cl. SE28 ...7C 74
WHETSTONE ...2F 15
Whetstone Cl. N20 ...2G 15
Whetstone Pk.
WC2 ...6K 67 (7G 161)
Whetstone Rd. SE3 ...2A 108
Whewell Rd. N19 ...2J 49
Whidborne Bldgs. WC1 ...2F 161
(off Whidborne St.)
Whidborne Cl. SE8 ...2C 106
Whidborne St.
WC1 ...3J 67 (2F 161)
(not continuous)
Whimbrel Cl. SE28 ...7C 74
Whimbrel Way
UB4: Hayes ...5B 60
Whinchat Rd. SE28 ...3H 91
Whinfell Cl. SW16 ...5H 121
Whinyates Rd. SE9 ...3C 108
Whipps Cross E17 ...5F 35
Whipps Cross Ho. E17 ...5F 35
(off Wood St.)
Whipps Cross Rd. E11 ...5F 35
(not continuous)
Whiskin St. EC1 ...3B 68 (2A 162)
Whisperwood Cl.
HA3: Harr ...1J 25
Whistler Gdns. HA8: Edg ...2F 27
Whistler M. RM8: Dag ...5B 56
(off Fitzstephen Rd.)
SE15 ...7F 87
Whistlers Av. SW11 ...7B 84
Whistler St. N5 ...5B 50
Whistler Twr. SW10 ...7A 84
(off Worlds End Est.)
Whistler Wlk. SW10 ...7B 84
Whiston Ho. N1 ...7B 50
(off Richmond Gro.)
Whiston Rd. E2 ...2F 69
Whitbread Cl. N17 ...1G 33
Whitbread Rd. SE4 ...4A 106
Whitburn Rd. SE13 ...4D 106
Whitby Av. NW10 ...3H 63
Whitby Ct. N7 ...4J 49
Whitby Gdns. NW9 ...3G 27
SM1: Sutt ...2B 150
Whitby Ho. NW8 ...1A 66
(off Boundary Rd.)
Whitby Pde. HA4: Ruis ...2A 42
Whitby Rd. HA2: Harr ...3G 43
HA4: Ruis ...3K 41
SE18 ...4D 90
SM1: Sutt ...2B 150
Whitby St. E1 ...4F 69 (3J 163)
(not continuous)
Whitcher Cl. SE14 ...6A 88
Whitcher Pl. NW1 ...6G 49
Whitchurch Av. HA8: Edg ...7A 12
Whitchurch Cl. HA8: Edg ...6A 12

Whitchurch Gdns.
HA8: Edg 6A 12
Whitchurch Ho. W10 ....6F 65
(off Kingsdown Cl.)
Whitchurch La. HA8: Edg ...7J 11
Whitchurch Pde.
HA8: Edg 7B 12
Whitchurch Rd. W11 ...7F 65
Whitcomb Ct. SW1 .....3D 166
Whitcombe M. TW9: Rich ...1H 99
Whitcomb St.
WC2 ....7H 67 (3D 166)
Whiteadder Way E14 ....4D 88
Whitear Wlk. E15 ....6F 53
Whitebarn La.
RM10: Dag 1G 75
Whitebeam Av.
BR2: Short 7E 144
Whitebeam Cl. SW9 ......7K 85
White Bear Pl. NW3 .....4B 48
White Bear Yd. EC1 ....4J 161
(off Clerkenwell Rd.)
White Bri. Av.
CR4: Mitc 3B 138
Whitebridge Cl.
TW14: Felt 6H 95
White Butts Rd.
HA4: Ruis 3B 42
WHITECHAPEL 5G 69
Whitechapel Art Gallery
.................7K 163
(off Whitechapel High St.)
Whitechapel High St.
E1 ....6F 69 (7K 163)
Whitechapel Rd.
E1 ....5G 69 (7K 163)
White Chu. La.
E1 ....6G 69 (7K 163)
White Chu. Pas. E1 ......7K 163
(off White Chu. La.)
WHITE CITY 7D 64
WHITE CITY 6E 64
White City Cl. W12 ......7E 64
White City Est. W12 .....7D 64
White City Rd. W12 .....7E 64
White Conduit St. N1 ....2A 68
Whitecote Rd.
UB1: S'hall 6G 61
Whitecroft Cl.
BR3: Beck 4F 143
Whitecroft Way
BR3: Beck 5E 142
Whitecross Pl.
EC2 ....5D 68 (5F 163)
Whitecross St.
EC1 ....4C 68 (3D 162)
Whitefield Av. NW2 ......1E 46
Whitefield Cl. SW18 .....6G 101
Whitefoot La.
BR1: Brom 4E 124
Whitefoot Ter.
BR1: Brom 3G 125
Whitefriars Av. HA3: Harr ...2J 25
Whitefriars Ct. N12 .....5G 15
Whitefriars Dr. HA3: Harr ...2H 25
Whitefriars St.
EC4 ....6A 68 (1K 167)
Whitefriars Trad. Est.
HA3: Harr 3H 25
White Gdns. RM10: Dag ...6G 57
Whitegate Gdns.
HA3: Harr 7E 10
Whitehall 6G 149
Whitehall SW1 ...1J 85 (5E 166)
Whitehall Ct.
SW1 ....1J 85 (5E 166)
(not continuous)
Whitehall Cres.
KT9: Chess 5D 146
Whitehall Gdns. E4 ....1B 20
SW1 ....5E 166
W3 ....1G 81

Whitehall Gdns. W4 ......6H 81
Whitehall La.
IG9: Buck H 2D 20
Whitehall Lodge N10 ....3E 30
Whitehall Pk. N19 ....1G 49
Whitehall Pk. Rd. W4 ...6H 81
Whitehall Pl. E7 ....5J 53
SM6: Wall 4F 151
SW1 ....1J 85 (5E 166)
Whitehall Rd.
BR2: Short 5B 144
CR7: Thor H 5A 140
E4 ....2B 20
HA1: Harr 7J 25
IG8: Wfd G 2B 20
W7 ....2A 80
Whitehall St. N17 ....7A 18
Whitehall Theatre 4E 166
(off Whitehall)
White Hart Cl.
UB3: Hayes 6F 77
White Hart Ct. EC2 ......6G 163
White Hart La. N22 .....1K 31
NW10 ....6B 46
RM7: Col R, Mawney
.................1G 39
SW13 ....3A 100
White Hart Lane Stadium
.................7B 18
White Hart Rd. SE18 ....4J 91
White Hart Rdbt.
UB5: N'olt 2B 60
White Hart Slip
BR1: Brom 2J 143
White Hart St.
EC4 ....6B 68 (1B 168)
SE11 ....5A 86 (5K 173)
White Hart Yd.
SE1 ....1D 86 (5E 168)
Whitehaven Cl.
BR2: Short 4J 143
Whitehaven St.
NW8 ....4C 66 (4C 158)
Whitehead Cl. N18 ......5J 17
SW18 ....7A 102
Whiteheads Gro.
SW3 ....4C 84 (4D 170)
White Heart Av.
UB8: Uxb 5E 58
Whiteheath Av.
HA4: Ruis 7E 22
White Heather Ho. WC1 ...2F 161
(off Cromer St.)
White Heron M.
TW11: Tedd 6K 115
White Horse All. EC1 ....5A 162
White Horse Hill
BR7: Chst 4E 126
White Horse La. E1 .....4K 69
Whitehorse La. SE25 ....4D 140
Whitehorse M.
SE1 ....3A 86 (1K 173)
White Horse Rd. E1 ......5A 70
(not continuous)
E6 ....3D 72
Whitehorse Rd.
CR0: Croy 7C 140
CR7: Thor H 7C 140
White Horse St.
W1 ....1F 85 (5K 165)
White Horse Yd.
EC2 ....6D 68 (7E 162)
White Ho. SW4 ....7H 103
(off Clapham Pk. Est.)
SW11 ....1B 102
White Ho. Ct. N14 ....2D 16
White Ho. Dr. HA7: Stan ...4H 11
IG8: Wfd G 6C 20
Whitehouse Est. E10 ....6E 34
White Ho. La. EN2: Enf ...1H 7
White Ho., The NW1 ...3K 159
Whitehouse Way N14 ....2A 16

Whitehurst Dr. N18 ......5E 18
White Kennett St.
E1 ....6E 68 (7H 163)
Whitelands Ho. SW3 ....5F 171
(off Cheltenham Ter.)
Whiteledges W13 ....6C 62
Whitelegg Rd. E13 ......2H 71
Whiteley Rd. SE19 ......5D 122
Whiteleys Cen. W2 ......6K 65
Whiteley's Cotts. W14 ...4H 83
Whiteleys Pde. UB8: Uxb ...4D 58
Whiteley's Way
TW13: Felt 3E 114
White Lion Cl. EC3 ......1G 169
SE15 ....6J 87
TW7: Isle 3B 98
White Lion Hill
EC4 ....7B 68 (2B 168)
White Lion St. N1 ....2A 68
White Lodge SE19 ....7B 122
W5 ....5C 62
White Lodge Cl. N2 .....6B 30
SM2: Sutt 7A 150
TW7: Isle 2A 98
White Lyon Ct. EC2 .....5C 162
Whiteoak Cl. BR7: Chst ...6E 126
White Oak Dr.
BR3: Beck 2E 142
White Oak Gdns.
DA15: Sidc 7K 109
Whiteoaks La.
UB6: G'frd 3H 61
White Orchards
HA7: Stan 5F 11
N20 ....7C 4
White Post La. E9 ....7B 52
White Post St. SE15 .....7J 87
White Rd. E15 ....7G 53
White Rose Trad. Est.
EN4: Barn 5G 5
(off Margaret Rd.)
Whites Av. IG2: Ilf 6J 37
White's Grounds
SE1 ....2E 86 (7H 169)
White's Grounds Est.
SE1 ....6H 169
White's Mdw.
BR1: Brom 4E 144
White's Row
E1 ....5F 69 (6J 163)
Whites Sq. SW4 ....4H 103
Whitestile Rd.
TW8: Bford 5C 80
Whitestone La. NW3 .....3A 48
Whitestone Wlk. NW3 ...3A 48
White St. UB1: S'hall 2B 78
Whiteswan M. W4 ......5A 82
Whitethorn Av.
CR0: Croy 2H 153
EN2: Enf 5J 7
Whitethorn Gdns.
CR0: Croy 2H 153
EN2: Enf 5J 7
Whitethorn Ho. E1 ......1J 87
(off Prusom St.)
Whitethorn Pas. E3 .....4C 70
(off Whitethorn St.)
Whitethorn Pl.
UB7: W Dray 1B 76
Whitethorn St. E3 ....5C 70
White Tower, The 7F 69
(in Tower of London, The)
Whitewebbs Way
BR5: Orp 1K 145
Whitfield Ct. IG1: Ilf 1D 36
Whitfield Ho. NW1 ......4C 158
(off Salisbury St.)
Whitfield Pl. W1 ....4A 160
Whitfield Rd. DA7: Bex ...7F 93
E6 ....7A 54
SE3 ....1F 107
Whitfield St.
W1 ....4G 67 (4A 160)

Whitford Gdns.
CR4: Mitc 3D 138
Whitgift Av.
CR2: S Croy 5B 152
Whitgift Cen. CR0: Croy ...2C 152
Whitgift Ct. CR2: S Croy ...5C 152
(off Nottingham Rd.)
Whitgift Ho.
SE11 ....4K 85 (3G 173)
Whitgift Sq. CR0: Croy ...2C 152
Whitgift St. CR0: Croy ...3C 152
SE11 ....4K 85 (3G 173)
Whiting Av. IG11: Bark ...7F 55
Whitings IG2: Ilf 5J 37
Whitings Rd. EN5: Barn ...5A 4
Whitings Way E6 ....5E 72
Whitland Rd. SM5: Cars ...1B 150
Whitley Cl.
TW19: Staines 6A 94
Whitley Ho. SW1 ....7B 172
(off Churchill Gdns.)
Whitley Rd. N17 ....2E 32
Whitlock Dr. SW19 .....7G 101
Whitman Ho. E2 ....3J 69
(off Cornwall Av.)
Whitman Rd. E3 ....4A 70
Whitmead Cl.
CR2: S Croy 6E 152
Whitmore Cl. N11 ....5A 16
Whitmore Est. N1 ....1E 68
Whitmore Gdns. NW10 ...2E 64
Whitmore Ho. N1 ....1E 68
(off Whitmore Est.)
Whitmore Rd.
BR3: Beck 3B 142
HA1: Harr 7G 25
N1 ....1E 68
Whitnell Way SW15 .....5E 100
Whitney Av. IG4: Ilf 4B 36
Whitney Rd. E10 ....7D 34
Whitney Wlk.
DA14: Sidc 6E 128
Whitstable Cl.
BR3: Beck 1B 142
HA4: Ruis 2G 41
Whitstable Ho. W10 ....6F 65
(off Silchester Rd.)
Whitstable Pl.
CR0: Croy 4C 152
Whitstone La.
BR3: Beck 5D 142
Whittaker Av. TW9: Rich ...5D 98
Whittaker Pl. TW9: Rich ...5D 98
(off Whittaker Av.)
Whittaker Rd. E6 ....7A 54
SM3: Sutt 3H 149
Whittaker St.
SW1 ....4E 84 (4G 171)
Whittaker Way SE1 .....4G 87
Whittaker St.
BR3: Beck 2D 142
Whitta Rd. E12 ....4B 54
Whittell Gdns. SE26 .....3J 123
Whittingham N17 ....7C 18
Whittingham Ct. W4 .....7A 82
Whittingstall Rd. SW6 ...1H 101
Whittington Av.
EC3 ....6E 68 (1G 169)
UB4: Hayes 5H 59
Whittington Ct. N2 .....5D 30
Whittington M. N12 .....4F 15
(off Fredericks Pl.)
Whittington Rd. N22 ....7D 16
Whittington Way
HA5: Pinn 5C 24
Whittlebury Cl.
SM5: Cars 7D 150
Whittle Cl. E17 ....6A 34
UB1: S'hall 6F 61
Whittle Rd. TW5: Houn ...7A 78
UB2: S'hall 2F 79
Whittlesea Cl. HA3: Harr ...7B 10
Whittlesea Path
HA3: Harr 1G 25

Whittlesea Rd. HA3: Harr ...7B 10
Whittlesey St.
SE1 ....1A 86 (5J 167)
WHITTON 7G 97
Whitton Av. E. UB6: G'frd ...5J 43
Whitton Av. W. UB5: N'olt ...5F 43
UB6: G'frd 5F 43
Whitton Cl. UB6: G'frd ...6B 44
Whitton Dene
TW3: Houn 5G 97
Whitton Dr. UB6: G'frd ...6A 44
Whitton Mnr. Rd.
TW7: Isle 6G 97
Whitton Rd. TW2: Twick ...6J 97
TW3: Houn 4F 97
WHITTON ROAD RDBT. ...6K 97
Whitton Wlk. E3 ....3C 70
Whitton Waye
TW3: Houn 6E 96
Whitwell Rd. E13 ....3J 71
Whitworth Ho. SE1 ......3C 86
Whitworth Rd. SE18 .....7E 90
SE25 ....3E 140
Whitworth St. SE10 .....5G 89
Whorlton Rd. SE15 ......3H 105
Whymark Av. N22 ......3A 32
Whytecroft TW5: Houn ...7B 78
Whyteville Rd. E7 ....6K 53
Whytlaw Ho. E3 ....5B 70
(off Baythorne St.)
Wickersley Rd. SW11 ....2E 102
Wickers Oake SE19 .....4F 123
Wicker St. E1 ....6H 69
Wicket Rd. UB6: G'frd ...3A 62
Wickets, The
TW15: Ashf 4A 112
Wicket, The CR0: Croy ...5C 154
Wickfield Ho. SE16 .....2H 87
(off Wilson Gro.)
Wickford Ho. E1 ....4J 69
(off Wickford St.)
Wickford St. E1 ....4J 69
Wickford Way E17 ......4K 33
Wickham Av. CR0: Croy ...2A 154
SM3: Sutt 5E 148
Wickham Chase
BR4: W W'ck 1F 155
Wickham Cl. E1 ....5J 69
EN3: Enf 3C 8
KT3: N Mald 6B 136
Wickham Ct. KT5: Surb ...5F 135
(off Cranes Pk.)
Wickham Ct. Rd.
BR4: W W'ck 2E 154
Wickham Cres.
BR4: W W'ck 2E 154
Wickham Gdns. SE4 .....3B 106
Wickham La. SE2 ....5A 92
Wickham M. SE4 ....2B 106
Wickham Rd.
BR3: Beck 2D 142
CR0: Croy 2J 153
E4 ....7K 19
HA3: Harr 2H 25
SE4 ....4B 106
Wickham St. DA16: Well ...2J 109
SE11 ....5K 85 (5G 173)
Wickham Way
BR3: Beck 4E 142
Wick Ho. KT1: King T 1D 134
(off Station Rd.)
Wick La. E3 ....1C 70
Wickliffe Av. N3 ....2G 29
Wickliffe Gdns.
HA9: Wemb 2H 45
Wicklow Ho. N16 ....1F 51
Wicklow St.
WC1 ....3K 67 (1G 161)
Wick M. E9 ....6A 52
Wick Rd. E9 ....6K 51
TW11: Tedd 7B 116
Wicks Cl. SE9 ....4B 126

Willow Lodge—Windmill Dr.

Willow Lodge SW6 . . . . .1F 101
Willowmead Cl. W5 . . . . .5D 62
Willow Mt. CR0: Croy 3E 152
Willow Pl.
SW1 . . . . . . .4G 85 (3B 172)
Willow Rd. E12 . . . . .3D 54
EN1: Enf 3K 7
KT3: N Mald 4J 135
NW3 . . . . .4B 48
RM6: Chad H 6E 38
SM6: Wall 7F 151
W5 . . . . .2E 80
Willows Av. SM4: Mord 5K 137
Willows Cl. HA5: Pinn 2A 24
Willowside Ct. EN2: Enf 3G 7
Willows Ter. NW10 . . . . .2B 64
(off Rucklidge Av.)
Willows, The
BR3: Beck 1C 142
E6 . . . . .7D 54
Willow St. E4 . . . . .1A 20
EC2 . . . . .4E 68 (3G 163)
RM7: Rom 4J 39
Willow Tree Cl. E3 . . . . .1A 70
SW18 . . . . .1K 119
UB4: Hayes 4A 60
Willowtree Cl.
UB10: Uxb 3E 40
Willow Tree Ct.
DA14: Sidc 5A 128
HA0: Wemb 5D 44
Willow Tree La.
UB4: Hayes 4A 60
Willow Tree Wlk.
BR1: Brom 1K 143
Willowtree Way
CR7: Thor H 1A 140
Willow Va. BR7: Chst 6F 127
W12 . . . . .1C 82
Willow Vw. SW19 . . . . .1B 138
Willow Wlk. E17 . . . . .5B 34
IG1: Ilf 2F 55
N2 . . . . .2B 30
N15 . . . . .4B 32
N21 . . . . .6E 6
SE1 . . . . .3E 86
SM3: Sutt 3H 149
Willow Way HA0: Wemb 3A 44
KT19: Eps 6K 147
N3 . . . . .7E 14
SE26 . . . . .3J 123
TW2: Twick 2F 115
TW16: Sun T 4J 131
W11 . . . . .7F 65
Willow Wood Cres.
SE25 . . . . .6E 140
Willow Wren Wharf
UB2: S'hall 4K 77
Willrose Cres. SE2 . . . . .5B 92
Willsbridge Ct. SE15 . . . . . . .6E 86
Wills Cres. TW3: Houn 6F 97
Wills Gro. NW7 . . . . .5H 13
(not continuous)
Wilman Gro. E8 . . . . .7G 51
Wilmar Cl. UB4: Hayes 4F 59
Wilmar Gdns.
BR4: W W'ck 1D 154
Wilmcote Ho. W2 . . . . .5K 65
(off Woodchester Sq.)
Wilment Ct. NW2 . . . . .3E 46
Wilmer Cl. KT2: King T 5F 117
Wilmer Cres.
KT2: King T 5F 117
Wilmer Gdns. N1 . . . . .1E 68
(not continuous)
Wilmer Lea Cl. E15 . . . . .7E 52
Wilmer Pl. N16 . . . . .2F 51
Wilmers Ct. NW10 . . . . .1K 63
(off Stracey Rd.)
Wilmer Way N14 . . . . .5C 16
Wilmington Av. W4 . . . . .7K 81
Wilmington Ct. SW16 . . . . . .7J 121
Wilmington Gdns.
IG11: Bark 6H 55
Wilmington Sq.
WC1 . . . . . . .3A 68 (2J 161)
(not continuous)
Wilmington St.
WC1 . . . . . . .3A 68 (2J 161)
Wilmot Cl. N2 . . . . .2A 30
SE15 . . . . .7G 87
Wilmot Pl. W7 . . . . .1J 79
Wilmot Rd. E10 . . . . .2D 52
N17 . . . . .3D 32
SM5: Cars 5D 150
Wilmot St. E2 . . . . .4H 69
NW1 . . . . .7G 49
Wilmount St. SE18 . . . . .4F 91
Wilna Rd. SW18 . . . . .7A 102
Wilsham St. W11 . . . . .1F 83
Wilshaw Ct. NW4 . . . . .3C 28
Wilshaw Ho. SE8 . . . . .7C 88
Wilshaw St. SE14 . . . . .1C 106
Wilsmere Dr. HA3: Harr 7D 10
UB5: N'olt 5C 42
Wilson Av. CR4: Mitc 1C 138
(not continuous)
Wilson Cl. CR2: S Croy 5D 152
HA9: Wemb 7F 27
Wilson Dr. HA9: Wemb 7F 27
Wilson Gdns. HA1: Harr 7G 25
Wilson Gro. SE16 . . . . .2H 87
Wilson Rd. E6 . . . . .3B 72
IG1: Ilf 7D 36
KT9: Chess 6F 147
SE5 . . . . .1E 104
Wilson's Av. N17 . . . . .2F 33
Wilson's Pl. E14 . . . . .6B 70
Wilson's Rd. W6 . . . . .5F 83
Wilson St. E17 . . . . .5E 34
EC2 . . . . .5D 68 (5F 163)
N21 . . . . .7F 7
Wilson Wlk. W6 . . . . .4B 82
(off Prebend Gdns.)
Wilstone Cl. UB4: Hayes 4C 60
Wiltern Ct. NW2 . . . . .6G 47
Wilthorne Gdns.
RM10: Dag 7H 57
Wilton Av. W4 . . . . .5A 82
Wilton Cl. UB7: W Dray 6A 76
Wilton Ct. E1 . . . . .6H 69
(off Cavell St.)
Wilton Cres.
SW1 . . . . . . .2E 84 (7G 165)
SW19 . . . . .7H 119
Wilton Dr. RM5: Col R 1J 39
Wilton Est. E8 . . . . .6G 51
Wilton Gdns.
KT8: W Mole 3E 132
Wilton Gro.
KT3: N Mald 6B 136
SW19 . . . . .1H 137
Wilton Ho. CR2: S Croy 5C 152
(off Nottingham Rd.)
Wilton M. SW1 . . . .3E 84 (1H 171)
Wilton Pde. TW13: Felt 1K 113
Wilton Pl. HA1: Harr 6K 25
SW1 . . . . . . .2E 84 (7G 165)
Wilton Rd. EN4: Barn 4J 5
N10 . . . . .2E 30
SE2 . . . . .4C 92
SW1 . . . . . . .3F 85 (2A 172)
SW19 . . . . .7C 120
TW4: Houn 3B 96
Wilton Row
SW1 . . . . . . .2E 84 (7G 165)
Wilton Sq. N1 . . . . .1D 68
Wilton St.
SW1 . . . . . . .3F 85 (1J 171)
Wilton Ter.
SW1 . . . . . . .3E 84 (1G 171)
Wilton Vs. N1 . . . . .1D 68
(off Wilton Sq.)
Wilton Way E8 . . . . .6G 51
Wiltshire Cl. NW7 . . . . .5G 13
SW3 . . . . . . .4D 84 (3E 170)
Wiltshire Ct.
CR2: S Croy 5C 152
IG1: Ilf 6G 55
N4 . . . . .1K 49
(off Marquis Rd.)
Wiltshire Gdns. N4 . . . . .6C 32
TW2: Twick 1G 115
Wiltshire La. HA5: Pinn 3H 23
Wiltshire Rd. BR6: Orp 7K 145
CR7: Thor H 3A 140
SW9 . . . . .3A 104
Wiltshire Row N1 . . . . .1D 68
Wilverley Cres.
KT3: N Mald 6A 136
Wimbart Rd. SW2 . . . . .7K 103
WIMBLEDON 6H 119
Wimbledon
(All England Lawn
Tennis & Croquet Club)
. . . . .4G 119
Wimbledon Bri. SW19 . . . . .6H 119
Wimbledon Cl. SW20 . . . . . .7F 119
Wimbledon Common 4C 118
Wimbledon Common Postmill &
Mus. 2D 118
Wimbledon Greyhound Stadium
. . . . .4A 120
Wimbledon Hill Rd:
SW19 . . . . .6G 119
Wimbledon Lawn Tennis Mus.
. . . . .4G 119
Wimbledon Mus. of Local History
. . . . .6G 119
WIMBLEDON PARK 3J 119
Wimbledon Pk. Rd.
SW19 . . . . .2G 119
Wimbledon Pk. Side
SW19 . . . . .3F 119
Wimbledon Rd. SW17 . . . . .4A 120
Wimbledon Stadium Bus. Cen.
SW17 . . . . .3K 119
Wimbolt St. E2 . . . . .3G 69
Wimborne Av. BR5: Orp 4K 145
BR7: Chst 3K 145
UB2: S'hall 4E 78
UB4: Hayes 6K 59
Wimborne Cl.
IG9: Buck H 2E 20
KT4: Wor Pk 1E 148
SE12 . . . . .5H 107
Wimborne Ct. SW12 . . . . . .3G 121
UB5: N'olt 6E 42
Wimborne Dr. HA5: Pinn 7B 24
NW9 . . . . .3G 27
Wimborne Gdns. W13 . . . . . .5B 62
Wimborne Ho. E16 . . . . .7H 71
(off Victoria Dock Rd.)
NW1 . . . . .4D 158
(off Harewood Av.)
SW8 . . . . .7K 85
(off Dorset Rd.)
Wimborne Rd. N9 . . . . .2B 18
N17 . . . . .2E 32
Wimborne Way
BR3: Beck 3K 141
Wimbourne Ct. N1 . . . . .2D 68
(off Wimbourne St.)
Wimbourne St. N1 . . . . .2D 68
Wimpole Cl.
BR2: Short 4A 144
KT1: King T 2F 135
Wimpole M. W1 . . . .5F 67 (5J 159)
Wimpole Rd.
UB7: W Dray 1A 76
Wimpole St. W1 . . . .5F 67 (6J 159)
Wimshurst Cl.
CR0: Croy 1J 151
Winans Wlk. SW9 . . . . .2A 104
Winant Ho. E14 . . . . .7D 70
(off Simpson's Rd.)
Wincanton Ct. N11 . . . . .6K 15
(off Martock Gdns.)
Wincanton Cres.
UB5: N'olt 5E 42
Wincanton Gdns. IG6: Ilf 3F 37
Wincanton Rd. SW18 . . . . . .7H 101
Winchcombe Bus. Cen.
SE15 . . . . .6E 86
Winchcombe Ct. SE15 . . . . . .6E 86
(off Longhope Cl.)
Winchcombe Rd.
SM5: Cars 7B 138
Winchcomb Gdns. SE9 . . . . .3B 108
Winchelsea Av. DA7: Bex 7F 93
Winchelsea Cl. SW15 . . . . . .5F 101
Winchelsea Cres.
KT8: W Mole 2G 133
Winchelsea Ho. SE16 . . . . . . .2J 87
(off Swan Rd.)
Winchelsea Rd. E7 . . . . .3J 53
N17 . . . . .3E 32
NW10 . . . . .1K 63
Winchelsey Ri.
CR2: S Croy 6F 153
Winchendon Rd. SW6 . . . . .1H 101
TW11: Tedd 4H 115
Winchester Av. NW6 . . . . . . .1G 65
NW9 . . . . .3G 27
TW5: Houn 6D 78
Winchester Cl.
BR2: Short 3H 143
E6 . . . . .6D 72
EN1: Enf 5K 7
KT2: King T 7H 117
SE17 . . . . .4B 86
Winchester Ct. W8 . . . . .2J 83
(off Vicarage Ga.)
Winchester Dr. HA5: Pinn . . .5B 24
Winchester Ho. IG11: Bark . . .7A 56
(off Keir Hardie Way)
SE18 . . . . .7B 90
(off Portway Gdns.)
SW3 . . . . .7B 170
SW9 . . . . .7A 86
W2 . . . . .6A 66
(off Hallfield Est.)
Winchester Pk.
BR2: Short 3H 143
Winchester Pl. E8 . . . . .5F 51
N6 . . . . .1F 49
Winchester Rd.
BR2: Short 3H 143
DA7: Bex 2D 110
E4 . . . . .7K 19
HA3: Harr 4E 26
HA6: Nwood 2H 23
IG1: Ilf 3H 55
KT12: Walt T 7J 131
N6 . . . . .7F 31
N9 . . . . .1A 18
NW3 . . . . .7B 48
TW1: Twick 6B 98
TW13: Felt 3D 114
UB3: Hayes 7G 77
Winchester Sq. SE1 . . . . . . .4E 168
Winchester St.
SW1 . . . . . . .5F 85 (5K 171)
W3 . . . . .1J 81
Winchester Wlk.
SE1 . . . . .1D 86 (4E 168)
Winchet Wlk. CR0: Croy 6J 141
Winchfield Cl.
HA3: Harr 6C 26
Winchfield Ho. SW15 . . . . . .6B 100
Winchfield Rd. SE26 . . . . . .5A 124
Winch Ho. E14 . . . . .3D 88
(off Tiller Rd.)
SW10 . . . . .7A 84
(off King's Rd.)
Winchilsea Ho. NW8 . . . . . .2B 158
(off St John's Wood Rd.)
WINCHMORE HILL 7F 7
Winchmore Hill Rd. N14 . . . .1C 16
N21 . . . . .1C 16
Winchmore Vs. N21 . . . . .7E 6
(off Winchmore Hill Rd.)
Winchstone Cl.
TW17: Shep 4B 130
Winckley Cl. HA3: Harr 5F 27
Wincott St.
SE11 . . . . . . .4A 86 (4K 173)
Wincrofts Dr. SE9 . . . . .4H 109
Windall Cl. SE19 . . . . .1G 141
Windborough Rd.
SM5: Cars 7E 150
Windermere NW1 . . . . .2K 159
(off Albany St.)
Windermere Av.
HA4: Ruis 7A 24
HA9: Harr, Wemb 7C 26
N3 . . . . .3J 29
NW6 . . . . .1G 65
SW19 . . . . .3K 137
Windermere Cl.
TW14: Felt 1H 113
TW19: Staines 1A 112
Windermere Ct.
HA9: Wemb 7C 26
SM5: Cars 3E 150
SW13 . . . . .6B 82
Windermere Gdns.
IG4: Ilf 5C 36
Windermere Gro.
HA9: Wemb 1C 44
Windermere Hall
HA8: Edg 5A 12
Windermere Ho. E3 . . . . .4B 70
EN5: Barn 4E 4
Windermere Point SE15 . . . . .7J 87
(off Old Kent Rd.)
Windermere Rd.
BR4: W W'ck 2G 155
CR0: Croy 1F 153
DA7: Bex 2J 111
N10 . . . . .1F 31
N19 . . . . .2G 49
SW15 . . . . .4A 118
SW16 . . . . .1G 139
UB1: S'hall 5D 60
W5 . . . . .3C 80
Windermere Way
UB7: W Dray 1A 76
Winders Rd. SW11 . . . . .2C 102
(not continuous)
Windfield Cl. SE26 . . . . . . .4K 123
Windham Rd. TW9: Rich 3F 99
Winding Way HA1: Harr 4J 43
RM8: Dag 3C 56
Windlass Pl. SE8 . . . . .4A 88
Windlesham Gro.
SW19 . . . . .1F 119
Windley Cl. SE23 . . . . .2J 123
Windmill WC1 . . . . .5G 161
(off New Nth. St.)
Windmill Av. UB2: S'hall 1G 79
Windmill Bridge Ho.
CR0: Croy 1E 152
(off Freemasons Rd.)
Windmill Bus. Cen.
UB2: S'hall 1G 79
Windmill Bus. Village
TW16: Sun T 1G 131
Windmill Cl.
KT6: Surb 1C 146
SE1 . . . . .4G 87
(off Beatrice Rd.)
SE13 . . . . .2E 106
TW16: Sun T 7G 113
Windmill Ct. NW2 . . . . .6G 47
W5 . . . . .4C 80
(off Windmill Rd.)
Windmill Dr. BR2: Kes 4A 156
NW2 . . . . .3G 47
SW4 . . . . .5F 103

Windmill Gdns.—Woburn Wlk.

Windmill Gdns. EN2: Enf 3F 7
Windmill Grn.
TW17: Shep *7G 131*
(off Walton La.)
Windmill Gro. CR0: Croy ...6C 140
Windmill Hill EN2: Enf 3G 7
HA4: Ruis 7H 23
NW3 ....3A 48
Windmill Ho. E14 ....4C 88
Windmill La. E15 ....6F 53
KT6: Surb 6B 134
UB2: Isle, S'hall 1G 79
UB6: G'frd 4G 61
WD23: Bush 1D 10
Windmill M. W4 ....4A 82
Windmill Pas. W4 ....4A 82
Windmill Ri.
KT2: King T 7H 117
Windmill Rd. CR0: Croy 7C 140
CR4: Mitc 5G 139
N18 ....4J 17
SW18 ....6B 102
SW19 ....2D 118
TW12: Hamp 5F 115
TW16: Sun T 1G 131
W4 ....4A 82
W5 ....4C 80
Windmill Rd. W.
TW16: Sun T 2G 131
Windmill Row
SE11 ....5A 86 (6J 173)
Windmill St.
W1 ....5H 67 (6C 160)
(not continuous)
WD23: Bush 1D 10
Windmill Ter.
TW17: Shep 7G 131
Windmill Wlk.
SE1 ....1A 86 (5K 167)
Windmill Way HA4: Ruis 1H 41
Windmore Cl.
HA0: Wemb 5A 44
Windover Av. NW9 ....4K 27
Windrose Cl. SE16 ....2K 87
Windrush KT3: N Mald 4H 135
SE28 ....1B 92
Windrush Cl. N17 ....1E 32
SW11 ....4B 102
UB10: Uxb 4B 40
W4 ....1J 99
Windrush La. SE23 ....3K 123
Windrush Rd. NW10 ....1K 63
Windsock Cl. SE16 ....4B 88
Windsor Av. E17 ....2A 34
HA8: Edg 4C 12
KT3: N Mald 5J 135
KT8: W Mole 3E 132
SM3: Sutt 3G 149
SW19 ....1A 138
UB10: Uxb 1D 58
Windsor Cen., The *N1* *1B 68*
(off Windsor St.)
Windsor Cl. BR7: Chst 5F 127
HA2: Harr 3E 42
HA6: Nwood 2J 23
N3 ....2G 29
SE27 ....4C 122
TW8: Bford 6B 80
Windsor Cotts. *SE14* *7B 88*
(off Amersham Gro.)
Windsor Ct. HA5: Pinn 3B 24
KT1: King T *4D 134*
(off Palace Rd.)
N12 ....5J 15
N14 ....7B 6
NW2 ....*6G 47*
(off Chatsworth Rd.)
NW3 ....4J 47
NW11 ....*6G 29*
(off Golders Grn. Rd.)
SE16 ....*7K 69*
(off King & Queen Wharf)
Windsor Ct. *SW3* *5D 170*
(off Jubilee Pl.)
SW11 ....2B 102
TW16: Sun T 7J 113
W2 ....*7K 65*
(off Moscow Rd.)
W10 ....*6F 65*
(off Bramley Rd.)
Windsor Cres. HA2: Harr 3E 42
HA9: Wemb 3H 45
Windsor Dr. EN4: Barn 6J 5
Windsor Gdns.
CR0: Croy 3J 151
UB3: Hayes 3F 77
W9 ....5J 65
Windsor Gro. SE27 ....4C 122
Windsor Hall *E16* *1K 89*
(off Wesley Av.)
Windsor Ho. *E2* *3K 69*
(off Knottisford St.)
N1 ....2C 68
NW1 ....1K 159
UB5: N'olt *6E 42*
(off Farmlands, The)
Windsor M. SE6 ....1E 124
SE23 ....1A 124
SW18 ....*7A 102*
(off Wilna Rd.)
Windsor Pk. Rd.
UB3: Hayes 7H 77
Windsor Pl.
SW1 ....3G 85 (3B 172)
Windsor Rd.
CR7: Thor H 2B 140
DA6: Bex 4E 110
E4 ....4J 19
E7 ....5K 53
E10 ....2D 52
E11 ....1J 53
EN5: Barn 6A 4
HA3: Harr 1G 25
IG1: Ilf 4F 55
KT2: King T 7E 116
KT4: Wor Pk 2C 148
N3 ....2G 29
N7 ....3J 49
N13 ....3F 17
N17 ....2G 33
NW2 ....6D 46
RM8: Dag 3E 56
TW4: Houn 2K 95
TW9: Rich 2F 99
TW11: Tedd 5H 115
Windsor Rd.
TW16: Sun T 6J 113
UB2: S'hall 3D 78
W5 ....7E 62
(not continuous)
Windsors, The
IG9: Buck H 2H 21
Windsor St. N1 ....1B 68
Windsor Ter.
N1 ....3C 68 (1D 162)
Windsor Wlk. SE5 ....2D 104
Windsor Way W14 ....4F 83
Windsor Wharf E9 ....6C 52
Windspoint Dr. SE15 ....6H 87
Windus Rd. N16 ....1F 51
Windus Wlk. N16 ....1F 51
Windy Ridge
BR1: Brom 1C 144
Windy Ridge Cl. SW19 .....5F 119
Wine Cl. E1 ....7J 69
(not continuous)
Wine Office Ct. EC4 ....6A 68
Winery La. KT1: King T 3F 135
Winford Ct. SE15 ....1H 105
Winford Ho. E3 ....7B 52
Winford Pde. *UB1: S'hall* *6F 61*
(off Marconi Way)
Winforton St. SE10 ....1E 106
Winfrith Rd. SW18 ....7A 102
Wingate Cres.
CR0: Croy 6J 139
Wingate Rd. DA14: Sidc 6C 128
IG1: Ilf 5F 55
W6 ....3D 82
Wingate Trad. Est. N17 .....7B 18
Wingfield Ct. DA15: Sidc ...2K 127
E14 ....*7F 71*
(off John Smith M.)
Wingfield Ho. *E2* *2J 163*
(off Virginia Rd.)
NW6 ....*2K 65*
(off Tollgate Gdns.)
Wingfield M. SE15 ....3G 105
Wingfield Rd. E15 ....4G 53
E17 ....5D 34
KT2: King T 6F 117
Wingfield St. SE15 ....3G 105
Wingfield Way HA4: Ruis 6K 41
Wingford Rd. SW2 ....6J 103
Wingmore Rd. SE24 ....3C 104
Wingrad Ho. *E1* *5J 69*
(off Jubilee St.)
Wingrave SE17 ....4D 86
(not continuous)
Wingrave Rd. W6 ....6E 82
Wingreen *NW8* *1K 65*
(off Abbey Rd.)
Wingrove E4 ....7H 9
Wingrove Ct. RM7: Rom 5J 39
Wingrove Rd. SE6 ....2G 125
Wings Cl. SM1: Sutt 4J 149
Winicotte Ho. *W2* *5B 158*
(off Paddington Grn.)
Winifred Pl. N12 ....5F 15
Winifred Rd. DA8: Erith 5K 93
RM8: Dag 2E 56
SW19 ....1J 137
TW12: Hamp 4E 114
Winifred St. E16 ....1D 90
Winifred Ter. EN1: Enf 7A 8
Winkfield Rd. E13 ....2K 71
N22 ....1A 32
Winkley Ct. HA2: Harr 3E 42
N10 ....*4F 31*
(off St James's La.)
Winkley St. E2 ....2H 69
Winkworth Cotts. *E1* *4J 69*
(off Cephas St.)
Winlaton Rd.
BR1: Brom 4F 125
Winmill Rd. RM8: Dag 3F 57
Winnett St. W1 ....7H 67 (2C 166)
Winningales Ct. IG5: Ilf 2C 36
Winnings Wlk. UB5: N'olt 6C 42
Winnington Cl. N2 ....6B 30
Winnington Ho. *SE5* *7C 86*
(off Wyndham Est.)
Winnington Rd. N2 ....6B 30
Winnock Rd.
UB7: W Dray 1A 76
Winn Rd. SE12 ....1J 125
Winns Av. E17 ....3B 34
Winns Comn. Rd. SE18 .....6J 91
Winns M. N15 ....4E 32
Winns Ter. E17 ....3C 34
Winsbeach E17 ....2F 35
Winscombe Cres. W5 ......4D 62
Winscombe St. N19 ....2F 49
Winscombe Way
HA7: Stan 5F 11
Winsford Rd. SE6 ....3B 124
Winsford Ter. N18 ....5J 17
Winsham Gro. SW11 ......5E 102
Winsham Ho. *NW1* *1D 160*
(off Churchway)
Winslade Rd. SW2 ....5J 103
Winslade Way SE6 ....7D 106
Winsland M.
W2 ....6B 66 (7A 158)
Winsland St.
W2 ....6B 66 (7A 158)
Winsley St. W1 ....6G 67 (7B 160)
Winslow SE17 ....5E 86
Winslow Cl. HA5: Pinn 6K 23
NW10 ....3A 46
Winslow Gro. E4 ....2B 20
Winslow Rd. W6 ....6E 82
Winslow Way
TW13: Felt 3B 114
Winsmoor Ct. EN2: Enf 3G 7
WINSOR PARK 5F 73
Winsor Ter. E6 ....5E 72
Winstanley Est. SW11 .....3B 102
Winstanley Rd. SW11 .....3B 102
(not continuous)
Winstead Gdns.
RM10: Dag 5J 57
Winston Av. NW9 ....7A 28
Winston Churchill's Britain at War Experience *5G 169*
Winston Cl. HA3: Harr 6E 10
RM7: Mawney 4H 39
Winston Ct. *BR1: Brom* *1K 143*
(off Widmore Rd.)
HA3: Harr 7A 10
Winston Ho. *N1* *2D 68*
(off Cranston Est.)
W13 ....*2A 80*
(off Balfour Rd.)
WC1 ....3D 160
Winston Rd. N16 ....4D 50
Winston Wlk. W4 ....3K 81
Winston Way IG1: Ilf 3F 55
Winter Av. E6 ....1C 72
Winterbourne Ho. *W11* *7G 65*
(off Portland Rd.)
Winterbourne Rd.
CR7: Thor H 4A 140
RM8: Dag 2C 56
SE6 ....1B 124
Winter Box Wlk.
TW10: Rich 5F 99
Winterbrook Rd. SE24 .....6C 104
Winterburn Cl. N11 ....6K 15
Winterfold Cl. SW19 ....2G 119
Wintergreen Cl. E6 ....5C 72
Winterleys *NW6* *2H 65*
(off Denmark Rd.)
Winter Lodge *SE16* *5G 87*
(off Fern Wlk.)
Winter's Ct. E4 ....3J 19
Winterslow Ho. *SE5* *2C 104*
(off Flaxman Rd.)
Winters Rd. KT7: T Ditt 7B 134
Winterstoke Gdns. NW7 ....5H 13
Winterstoke Rd. SE6 ......1B 124
Winterton Ct.
KT1: King T *1D 134*
(off Lwr. Teddington Rd.)
SE20 ....2G 141
Winterton Ho. *E1* *6J 69*
(off Deancross St.)
Winterton Pl.
SW10 ......6A 84 (7A 170)
Winterwell Rd. SW2 ....5J 103
Winthorpe Rd. SW15 ......4G 101
Winthrop Ho. *W12* *7D 64*
(off White City Est.)
Winthrop St. E1 ....5H 69
Winthrop Wlk.
HA9: Wemb 3E 44
Winton Av. N11 ....7B 16
Winton Cl. N9 ....7E 8
Winton Gdns. HA8: Edg 7A 12
Winton Way SW16 ....5A 122
Wirrall Ho. SE26 ....3G 123
Wirral Wood Cl.
BR7: Chst 6E 126
Wisbeach Rd. CR0: Croy ...5D 140
Wisbech *N4* *1K 49*
(off Lorne Rd.)
Wisborough Rd.
CR2: S Croy 7F 153
Wisden Ho. SW8 ...6K 85 (7H 173)
Wisdom Ct. *TW7: Isle* *3A 98*
(off South St.)
Wisdons Cl. RM10: Dag 1H 57
Wise La. NW7 ....5H 13
UB7: W Dray 4A 76
Wiseman Rd. E10 ....2C 52
Wise Rd. E15 ....1F 71
Wiseton Rd. SW17 ....1C 120
Wisham Wlk. N13 ....6D 16
Wishart Rd. SE3 ....2B 108
Wisley Ho. *SW1* *5C 172*
(off Rampayne St.)
Wisley Rd. BR5: Orp 7A 128
SW11 ....5E 102
Wisteria Cl. IG1: Ilf 5F 55
NW7 ....6G 13
Wisteria Gdns.
IG8: Wfd G 5D 20
Wisteria Rd. SE13 ....4F 107
Witanhurst La. N6 ....1E 48
Witan St. E2 ....3H 69
Witham Ct. E10 ....3D 52
SW17 ....3D 120
Witham Rd. RM10: Dag 5G 57
SE20 ....3J 141
TW7: Isle 1H 97
W13 ....1A 80
Witherby Cl. CR0: Croy 5E 152
Witherington Rd. N5 ....5A 50
Withers Cl. KT9: Chess 6C 146
Withers Mead NW9 ....1B 28
Withers Pl. EC1 ....4C 68 (3D 162)
Witherston Way SE9 ....2E 126
Withycombe Rd. SW19 ....7F 101
Withy Ho. *E1* *4K 69*
(off Globe Rd.)
Withy La. HA4: Ruis 5E 22
Withy Mead E4 ....3A 20
Witley Ct. WC1 ....4E 160
Witley Cres. CR0: Croy 6E 154
Witley Gdns. UB2: S'hall 4D 78
Witley Ho. SW2 ....7J 103
Witley Ind. Est.
UB2: S'hall 4D 78
Witley Rd. N19 ....2G 49
Witney Cl. UB10: Uxb 4B 40
Witney Path SE23 ....3K 123
Wittenham Way E4 ....3A 20
Wittering Cl.
KT2: King T 5D 116
Wittersham Rd.
BR1: Brom 5H 125
Witts Ho. *KT1: King T* *3F 135*
(off Winery La.)
Wivenhoe Cl. SE15 ....3H 105
Wivenhoe Ct. TW3: Houn 4D 96
Wivenhoe Rd. IG11: Bark 2A 74
Wiverton Rd. SE26 ....6J 123
Wixom Ho. SE3 ....4A 108
Wix Rd. RM9: Dag 1D 74
Wix's La. SW4 ....3F 103
Woburn *W13* *5B 62*
(off Clivedon Ct.)
Woburn Cl. SE28 ....6D 74
SW19 ....6A 120
Woburn Ct. CR0: Croy 1C 152
E18 ....2J 35
SE16 ....*5H 87*
(off Masters Dr.)
Woburn M.
WC1 ....4H 67 (4D 160)
Woburn Pl.
WC1 ....4J 67 (4E 160)
Woburn Rd. CR0: Croy 1C 152
SM5: Cars 1C 150
Woburn Sq.
WC1 ....4H 67 (4D 160)
Woburn Twr. *UB5: N'olt* *3B 60*
(off Broomcroft Av.)
Woburn Wlk.
WC1 ....3H 67 (2D 160)

Wodehouse Av.—Woodlands Rd.

Wodehouse Av. SE5 . . . 1F 105
Wodehouse Ct. W3 . . . 3J 81
(off Vincent Rd.)
Woffington Cl.
KT1: King T . . . 1C 134
Woking Cl. SW15 . . . 4B 100
Wolcot Ho. NW1 . . . 1B 160
(off Aldenham St.)
Woldham Pl.
BR2: Short . . . 4A 144
Woldham Rd.
BR2: Short . . . 4A 144
Wolds Dr. BR6: Orp . . . 4E 156
Wolfe Cl. BR2: Short . . . 6J 143
UB4: Hayes . . . 3K 59
Wolfe Cres. SE7 . . . 5B 90
SE16 . . . 2K 87
Wolfe Ho. W12 . . . 7D 64
(off White City Est.)
Wolferton Rd. E12 . . . 4D 54
Wolffe Gdns. E15 . . . 6H 53
Wolfington Rd. SE27 . . . 4B 122
Wolfram Cl. SE13 . . . 5G 107
Wolftencroft Cl. SW11 . . . 3C 102
Wollaston Cl. SE1 . . . 4C 86
Wollett Ct. NW1 . . . 7G 49
(off St Pancras Way)
Wolmer Cl. HA8: Edg . . . 4B 12
Wolmer Gdns. HA8: Edg . . . 3B 12
Wolseley Av. SW19 . . . 2J 119
Wolseley Gdns. W4 . . . 6H 81
Wolseley Rd. CR4: Mitc . . . 7E 138
E7 . . . 7K 53
HA3: Harr . . . 3J 25
N8 . . . 6H 31
N22 . . . 1K 31
RM7: Rush G . . . 7K 39
W4 . . . 4J 81
Wolseley St.
SE1 . . . 2G 87 (7K 169)
Wolsey Av. E6 . . . 3E 72
E17 . . . 3B 34
KT7: T Ditt . . . 5K 133
Wolsey Cl. KT2: King T . . . 1H 135
KT4: Wor Pk . . . 4C 148
SW20 . . . 7D 118
TW3: Houn . . . 4G 97
UB2: S'hall . . . 3G 79
Wolsey Ct. NW6 . . . 7A 48
SW11 . . . 1C 102
(off Westbridge Rd.)
Wolsey Cres. CR0: Croy . . . 7E 154
SM4: Mord . . . 7G 137
Wolsey Dr. KT2: King T . . . 5E 116
KT12: Walt T . . . 7B 132
Wolsey Gro. HA8: Edg . . . 7E 12
Wolsey M. NW5 . . . 6G 49
Wolsey Rd. EN1: Enf . . . 2C 8
KT8: E Mos . . . 4H 133
N1 . . . 5D 50
TW12: Hamp . . . 6F 115
TW15: Ashf . . . 4A 112
TW16: Sun T . . . 7H 113
Wolsey Spring
KT2: King T . . . 7J 117
Wolsey St. E1 . . . 5J 69
Wolsey Way
KT9: Chess . . . 5G 147
Wolsley Cl. DA1: Cray . . . 5K 111
Wolstonbury N12 . . . 5D 14
Wolvercote Rd. SE2 . . . 2D 92
Wolverley St. E2 . . . 3H 69
Wolverton SE17 . . . 5E 86
(not continuous)
Wolverton Av.
KT2: King T . . . 1G 135
Wolverton Gdns. W5 . . . 7F 63
W6 . . . 4F 83
Wolverton Rd. HA7: Stan . . . 6G 11
Wolverton Way N14 . . . 5B 6
Wolves La. N22 . . . 7F 17
Womersley Rd. N8 . . . 6K 31
Wonersh Way
SM2: Sutt . . . 7F 149
Wonford Cl. KT2: King T . . . 1A 136
Wontner Cl. N1 . . . 7C 50
Wontner Rd. SW17 . . . 2D 120
Wooburn Cl. UB8: Uxb . . . 4D 58
Woodall Cl. E14 . . . 7D 70
KT9: Chess . . . 6D 146
Woodall Ho. N22 . . . 1A 32
Woodall Rd. EN3: Enf . . . 6E 8
Woodbank Rd.
BR1: Brom . . . 3H 125
Woodbastwick Rd.
SE26 . . . 5K 123
Woodberry Av. HA2: Harr . . . 4F 25
N21 . . . 2F 17
Woodberry Cl. NW7 . . . 7A 14
TW16: Sun T . . . 6J 113
Woodberry Cres. N10 . . . 3F 31
Woodberry Down N4 . . . 7C 32
Woodberry Down Est. N4 . . . 1C 50
(Woodberry Down)
N4 . . . 7C 32
(Woodberry Gro.)
Woodberry Gdns. N12 . . . 6F 15
Woodberry Gro.
DA5: Bexl . . . 3K 129
N4 . . . 7C 32
N12 . . . 6F 15
Woodberry Way E4 . . . 7K 9
N12 . . . 6F 15
Woodbine Cl.
TW2: Twick . . . 2H 115
Woodbine Gro. EN2: Enf . . . 1J 7
SE20 . . . 7H 123
Woodbine La.
KT4: Wor Pk . . . 3D 148
Woodbine Pl. E11 . . . 6J 35
Woodbine Rd.
DA15: Sidc . . . 1J 127
Woodbines Av.
KT1: King T . . . 3D 134
Woodbine Ter. E9 . . . 6J 51
Woodborough Rd.
SW15 . . . 4D 100
Woodbourne Av. SW16 . . . 3H 121
Woodbourne Cl. SW16 . . . 3J 121
Woodbourne Gdns.
SM6: Wall . . . 7F 151
Woodbridge Cl. N7 . . . 2K 49
NW2 . . . 3C 46
Woodbridge Ct.
IG8: Wfd G . . . 7H 21
Woodbridge Ho. E11 . . . 1H 53
Woodbridge Rd.
IG11: Bark . . . 5K 55
Woodbridge St.
EC1 . . . 4B 68 (3A 162)
(not continuous)
Woodbrook Rd. SE2 . . . 6A 92
Woodburn Cl. NW4 . . . 5F 29
Woodbury Cl. CR0: Croy . . . 2F 153
E11 . . . 4K 35
Woodbury Ho. SE26 . . . 3G 123
Woodbury Pk. Rd. W13 . . . 4B 62
Woodbury Rd. E17 . . . 4D 34
Woodbury St. SW17 . . . 5C 120
Woodchester Sq. W2 . . . 5K 65
Woodchurch Cl.
DA14: Sidc . . . 3H 127
Woodchurch Dr.
BR1: Brom . . . 7B 126
Woodchurch Rd. NW6 . . . 7J 47
Wood Cl. E2 . . . 4G 69
HA1: Harr . . . 7H 25
NW9 . . . 7K 27
Woodclyffe Dr.
BR7: Chst . . . 2E 144
Woodcock Ct. HA3: Harr . . . 7E 26
Woodcock Dell Av.
HA3: Harr . . . 7D 26
Woodcock Hill HA3: Harr . . . 5C 26
Woodcock Ho. E14 . . . 5C 70
(off Burgess St.)
Woodcocks E16 . . . 5A 72
Woodcombe Cres. SE23 . . . 1J 123
Woodcote Av.
CR7: Thor H . . . 4B 140
NW7 . . . 6K 13
SM6: Wall . . . 7F 151
Woodcote Cl. EN3: Enf . . . 6D 8
KT2: King T . . . 5F 117
Woodcote Ct. SM2: Sutt . . . 6J 149
Woodcote Dr. BR6: Orp . . . 7H 145
Woodcote Grn.
SM6: Wall . . . 7G 151
Woodcote Ho. SE8 . . . 6B 88
(off Prince St.)
Woodcote M.
SM6: Wall . . . 6F 151
Woodcote Pl. SE27 . . . 5B 122
Woodcote Rd. E11 . . . 7J 35
SM6: Wall . . . 6F 151
Woodcote Vs. SE27 . . . 5C 122
(off Woodcote Pl.)
Wood Crest SM2: Sutt . . . 7A 150
(off Christchurch Pk.)
Woodcroft N21 . . . 1F 17
SE9 . . . 3D 126
UB6: G'frd . . . 6A 44
Woodcroft Av. HA7: Stan . . . 1A 26
NW7 . . . 6F 13
Woodcroft Cres.
UB10: Uxb . . . 1D 58
Woodcroft M. SE8 . . . 4A 88
Woodcroft Rd.
CR7: Thor H . . . 5B 140
Wood Dene SE15 . . . 1H 105
(off Queen's Rd.)
Wood Dr. BR7: Chst . . . 6C 126
Woodedge Cl. E4 . . . 1C 20
WOOD END
HAYES . . . 5H 59
NORTHOLT . . . 5G 43
Wood End UB3: Hayes . . . 6G 59
Woodend SE19 . . . 6C 122
SM1: Sutt . . . 2A 150
Wood End Av. HA2: Harr . . . 4F 43
Wood End Cl. UB5: N'olt . . . 5H 43
Wood End Gdns.
UB5: N'olt . . . 5G 43
Woodend Gdns. EN2: Enf . . . 4D 6
WOOD END GREEN . . . 5G 59
Wood End Grn. Rd.
UB3: Hayes . . . 5F 59
Wood End La. UB5: N'olt . . . 6F 43
(not continuous)
Wood End Rd. HA1: Harr . . . 4H 43
Woodend Rd. E17 . . . 2E 34
Woodend, The
SM6: Wall . . . 7F 151
Wood End Way
UB5: N'olt . . . 5G 43
Wooder Gdns. E7 . . . 4J 53
Wooderson Cl. SE25 . . . 4E 140
Woodfall Av. EN5: Barn . . . 5C 4
Woodfall Rd. N4 . . . 2A 50
Woodfall St.
SW3 . . . 5D 84 (6E 170)
Woodfarrs SE5 . . . 4D 104
Wood Fld. NW3 . . . 5D 48
Woodfield Av.
HA0: Wemb . . . 3C 44
NW9 . . . 4A 28
SM5: Cars . . . 6E 150
SW16 . . . 3H 121
W5 . . . 4C 62
Woodfield Cl. EN1: Enf . . . 4K 7
SE19 . . . 7C 122
Woodfield Cres. W5 . . . 4C 62
Woodfield Dr. EN4: Barn . . . 1K 15
Woodfield Gdns.
KT3: N Mald . . . 5B 136
Woodfield Gro. SW16 . . . 3H 121
Woodfield Ho. SE23 . . . 3K 123
(off Dacres Rd.)
Woodfield La. SW16 . . . 3H 121
Woodfield Pl. W9 . . . 4H 65
Woodfield Ri.
WD23: Bush . . . 1C 10
Woodfield Rd.
TW4: Houn . . . 2K 95
W5 . . . 4C 62
W9 . . . 5H 65
Woodfield Way N11 . . . 7C 16
WOODFORD . . . 6F 21
Woodford Av. IG2: Ilf . . . 5D 36
IG4: Ilf, Wfd G . . . 3B 36
WOODFORD BRIDGE . . . 6H 21
Woodford Bri. Rd.
IG4: Ilf . . . 3B 36
Woodford Ct. W14 . . . 2F 83
(off Shepherd's Bush Grn.)
Woodford Cres.
HA5: Pinn . . . 2K 23
Woodforde Ct. UB3: Hayes . . . 5F 77
WOODFORD GREEN . . . 6D 20
Woodford Hall Path E18 . . . 1H 35
Woodford Ho. E18 . . . 4J 35
Woodford New Rd. E17 . . . 4G 35
IG8: Wfd G . . . 1G 35
Woodford Pl.
HA9: Wemb . . . 1E 44
Woodford Rd. E7 . . . 3K 53
E18 . . . 4J 35
WOODFORD SIDE . . . 5C 20
Woodford Trad. Est.
IG8: Wfd G . . . 2B 36
WOODFORD WELLS . . . 3E 20
Woodgate Av.
KT9: Chess . . . 5D 146
Woodgate Dr. SW16 . . . 7H 121
Woodger Rd. W12 . . . 2E 82
Woodget Cl. E6 . . . 6C 72
Woodgrange Av. EN1: Enf . . . 6B 8
HA3: Harr . . . 5C 26
N12 . . . 6G 15
W5 . . . 1G 81
Woodgrange Cl.
HA3: Harr . . . 5D 26
Woodgrange Gdns.
EN1: Enf . . . 6B 8
Woodgrange Mans.
HA3: Harr . . . 5D 26
Woodgrange Rd. E7 . . . 5K 53
Woodgrange Ter. EN1: Enf . . . 6B 8
WOOD GREEN . . . 2K 31
Wood Green Shop. City
N22 . . . 2A 32
Woodhall NW1 . . . 2A 160
(off Robert St.)
Woodhall Av. HA5: Pinn . . . 1C 24
SE21 . . . 3F 123
Woodhall Cl. UB8: Uxb . . . 5A 40
Woodhall Dr. HA5: Pinn . . . 1B 24
SE21 . . . 3F 123
Woodhall Ga.
HA5: Pinn . . . 1B 24
Woodham Ct. E18 . . . 4H 35
Woodham Rd. SE6 . . . 3E 124
Woodhatch Cl. E6 . . . 5C 72
Woodhaven Gdns.
IG6: Ilf . . . 4G 37
Woodhayes Rd. SW19 . . . 7E 118
Woodheyes Rd. NW10 . . . 5K 45
Woodhill SE18 . . . 4C 90
Woodhill Cres.
HA3: Harr . . . 6D 26
Woodhouse Av.
UB6: G'frd . . . 2K 61
Woodhouse Cl.
UB3: Hayes . . . 3G 77
UB6: G'frd . . . 1K 61
Woodhouse Gro. E12 . . . 6C 54
Woodhouse Rd. E11 . . . 3H 53
N12 . . . 6G 15
Woodhurst Av.
BR5: Orp . . . 6G 145
Woodhurst Rd. SE2 . . . 5A 92
W3 . . . 7J 63
Woodington Cl. SE9 . . . 6E 108
Woodknoll Dr.
BR7: Chst . . . 1D 144
Woodland App.
UB6: G'frd . . . 6A 44
Woodland Av. E12 . . . 3C 54
Woodland Cl.
IG8: Wfd G . . . 3E 20
KT19: Eps . . . 6A 148
NW9 . . . 6J 27
SE19 . . . 6E 122
UB10: Uxb . . . 2D 40
Woodland Ct. E11 . . . 6J 35
(off New Wanstead)
Woodland Cres. SE10 . . . 6G 89
SE16 . . . 2K 87
Woodland Gdns. N10 . . . 5F 31
TW7: Isle . . . 3J 97
Woodland Hill SE19 . . . 6E 122
Woodland M. SW16 . . . 3J 121
Woodland Ri. N10 . . . 4F 31
UB6: G'frd . . . 6A 44
Woodland Rd.
CR7: Thor H . . . 4A 140
E4 . . . 1K 19
N11 . . . 5A 16
SE19 . . . 5E 122
WOODLANDS . . . 2J 97
Woodlands BR2: Short . . . 4H 143
DA6: Bex . . . 5H 111
HA2: Harr . . . 4E 24
NW11 . . . 5G 29
SW20 . . . 4E 136
Woodlands Art Gallery . . . 6J 89
Woodlands Av.
DA15: Sidc . . . 1J 127
E11 . . . 1K 53
HA4: Ruis . . . 7A 24
KT3: N Mald . . . 1J 135
KT4: Wor Pk . . . 2B 148
N3 . . . 7F 15
RM6: Chad H . . . 6E 38
W3 . . . 1H 81
Woodlands Cl.
BR1: Brom . . . 2D 144
KT10: Esh . . . 7A 146
NW11 . . . 5G 29
Woodlands Ct.
BR1: Brom . . . 1H 143
HA1: Harr . . . 5K 25
NW10 . . . 1F 65
(off Wrentham Av.)
SE23 . . . 7H 105
Woodlands Dr. HA7: Stan . . . 6E 10
TW16: Sun T . . . 2A 132
Woodlands Gdns. E17 . . . 4G 35
Woodlands Ga. SW15 . . . 5H 101
Woodlands Gro. SE10 . . . 5G 89
TW7: Isle . . . 2J 97
Woodlands Ho. NW6 . . . 7G 47
Woodlands Pde.
TW15: Ashf . . . 6E 112
Woodlands Pk.
DA5: Bexl . . . 4K 129
Woodlands Pk. Rd. N15 . . . 5B 32
SE10 . . . 6G 89
(not continuous)
Woodlands Rd.
BR1: Brom . . . 2C 144
DA7: Bex . . . 3E 110
E11 . . . 2G 53
E17 . . . 3E 34
EN2: Enf . . . 1J 7
HA1: Harr . . . 5K 25
IG1: Ilf . . . 3G 55
KT6: Surb . . . 7D 134
N9 . . . 1D 18
SW13 . . . 3B 100

Wordsworth Ho.—Yeading Ct.

Wordsworth Ho. *NW6* *3J* ***65***
(off Stafford Rd.)
SE18 .... *6E* ***90***
(off Woolwich Comn.)
Wordsworth Pde. N15 ...... 4B **32**
Wordsworth Pl. NW3 .... 5D **48**
Wordsworth Rd.
DA16: Well 1J **109**
N16 .... 4E **50**
SE1 .... 4F **87**
SE20 .... 7K **123**
SM6: Wall 6G **151**
TW12: Hamp 4D **114**
Wordsworth Wlk. NW11 ..... 4J **29**
Wordsworth Way
UB7: W Dray 4A **76**
Worfield St. SW11 .... 7C **84**
Worgan St.
SE11 .... 5K **85** (5G **173**)
SE16 .... 4K **87**
Worland Rd. E15 .... 7G **53**
World Bus. Cen.
TW6: Houn 1E **94**
WORLD'S END **3E 6**
Worlds End Est. SW10 ...... 7B **84**
World's End La. N21: Enf 5E **6**
World's End Pas. *SW10* *7B* ***84***
(off Worlds End Est.)
World's End Pl. *SW10* *7B* ***84***
(off Worlds End Est.)
Worlidge St. W6 .... 5E **82**
Worlingham Rd. SE22 ..... 4F **105**
Wormholt Rd. W12 .... 7C **64**
Wormwood St.
EC2 .... 6E **68** (7G **163**)
(not continuous)
Wornington Rd. W10 .... 4G **65**
(not continuous)
Wornum Ho. *W10* *2G* ***65***
(off Kilburn La.)
Woronzow Rd. NW8 .... 1B **66**
Worple Av. SW19 .... 7F **119**
TW7: Isle 5A **98**
Worple Cl. HA2: Harr 1D **42**
Worple Rd. SW20 .... 2E **136**
TW7: Isle 4A **98**
Worple Rd. M. SW19 ...... 6H **119**
Worple St. SW14 .... 3K **99**
Worple Way HA2: Harr 1D **42**
TW10: Rich 5E **98**
Worship St.
EC2 .... 4D **68** (4F **163**)
Worslade Rd. SW17 .... 4B **120**
Worsley Bri. Rd.
BR3: Beck 6C **124**
SE26 .... 4B **124**
Worsley Grange
BR7: Chst 6G **127**
Worsley Gro. E5 .... 4G **51**
Worsley Ho. SE23 .... 2J **123**
Worsley Rd. E11 .... 4G **53**
Worsopp Dr. SW4 .... 5G **103**
Worthfield Cl.
KT19: Eps 7K **147**
Worth Gro. SE17 .... 5D **86**
Worthing Cl. E15 .... 1G **71**
Worthing Rd.
TW5: Houn 6D **78**
Worthington Cl.
CR4: Mitc 4F **139**
Worthington Ho. *EC1* *1K* ***161***
(off Myddelton Pas.)
Worthington Rd.
KT6: Surb 1F **147**
Wortley Rd. CR0: Croy 7A **140**
E6 .... 7B **54**
Worton Ct. TW7: Isle 4J **97**
Worton Gdns. TW7: Isle 2H **97**
Worton Hall Ind. Est.
TW7: Isle 4J **97**
Worton Rd. TW7: Isle 4H **97**
Worton Way TW7: Isle 2H **97**
Wotton Ct. *E14* *7F* ***71***
(off Jamestown Way)
Wotton Rd. NW2 .... 3E **46**
SE8 .... 6B **88**
Wouldham Rd. E16 .... 6H **71**
Wragby Rd. E11 .... 3G **53**
Wrampling Pl. N9 .... 1B **18**
Wrangthorn Wlk.
CR0: Croy 4A **152**
Wray Av. IG5: Ilf 3E **36**
Wrayburn Ho. *SE16* *2G* ***87***
(off Llewellyn St.)
Wray Cres. N4 .... 2J **49**
Wrayfield Rd. SM3: Sutt 3F **149**
Wray Rd. SM2: Sutt 7H **149**
Wraysbury Cl.
TW4: Houn 5C **96**
Wrays Way UB4: Hayes 4G **59**
Wrekin Rd. SE18 .... 7G **91**
Wren Av. NW2 .... 5E **46**
UB2: S'hall 4D **78**
Wren Cl. E16 .... 6H **71**
N9 .... 1E **18**
Wren Ct. *CR0: Croy* *4D* ***152***
(off Coombe Rd.)
Wren Cres. WD23: Bush 1B **10**
Wren Gdns. RM9: Dag 5D **56**
Wren Ho. *E3* *2A* ***70***
(off Gernon Rd.)
KT1: King T *2D* ***134***
(off High St.)
SW1 .... *6C* ***172***
(off Aylesford St.)
Wren Landing E14 .... 1C **88**
Wrenn Ho. SW13 .... 6E **82**
Wren Path SE28 .... 3H **91**
Wren Rd. DA14: Sidc 4C **128**
RM9: Dag 5D **56**
SE5 .... 1D **104**
Wren's Av. TW15: Ashf 4E **112**
Wren's Pk. Ho. E5 .... 2H **51**
Wren St. WC1 ..... 4K **67** (3H **161**)
Wrentham Av. NW10 .... 2F **65**
Wrenthorpe Rd.
BR1: Brom 4G **125**
Wrenwood Way
HA5: Pinn 4K **23**
Wrestlers Ct. EC3 .... 7G **163**
Wrexham Rd. E3 .... 2C **70**
Wricklemarsh Rd. SE3 ..... 2K **107**
(not continuous)
Wrigglesworth St. SE14 ..... 7K **87**
Wright Cl. SE13 .... 4F **107**
Wright Gdns.
TW17: Shep 5C **130**
Wright Rd. N1 .... 6E **50**
TW5: Houn 7A **78**
Wrights All. SW19 .... 6E **118**
Wrights Cl. RM10: Dag 4H **57**
Wrights Grn. SW4 .... 4H **103**
Wright's La. W8 .... 3K **83**
Wrights Pl. NW10 .... 6J **45**
Wrights Rd. E3 .... 2B **70**
(not continuous)
SE25 .... 3E **140**
Wrights Row SM6: Wall 4F **151**
Wrights Wlk. SW14 .... 3K **99**
Wrigley Cl. E4 .... 5A **20**
Writtle Ho. NW9 .... 2B **28**
Wrotham Ho. *BR3: Beck* *7B* ***124***
(off Sellindge Cl.)
SE1 .... *3D* ***86***
(off Law St.)
Wrotham Rd.
DA16: Well 1C **110**
EN5: Barn 2B **4**
NW1 .... 7G **49**
W13 .... 1C **80**
Wrottesley Rd. NW10 ...... 2C **64**
SE18 .... 6G **91**
Wroughton Rd. SW11 ..... 5D **102**
Wroughton Ter. NW4 .... 4D **28**
Wroxall Rd. RM9: Dag 6C **56**
Wroxham Gdns. N11 .... 7C **16**
Wroxham Rd. SE28 .... 7D **74**
Wroxham Way IG6: Ilf 1F **37**
Wroxton Rd. SE15 .... 2J **105**
Wrythe Grn. SM5: Cars 3D **150**
Wrythe Grn. Rd.
SM5: Cars 3D **150**
Wrythe La. SM5: Cars 1A **150**
WRYTHE, THE **3D 150**
Wulfstan St. W12 .... 5B **64**
(not continuous)
Wyatt Cl. SE16 .... 2B **88**
TW13: Felt 1B **114**
UB4: Hayes 5J **59**
WD23: Bush 1C **10**
Wyatt Ct. HA0: Wemb 7E **44**
Wyatt Dr. SW13 .... 6D **82**
Wyatt Ho. *NW8* *4B* ***158***
(off Frampton St.)
SE3 .... 2H **107**
TW1: Twick 6D **98**
Wyatt Pk. Rd. SW2 .... 2J **121**
Wyatt Point *SE28* *2G* ***91***
(off Erebus Dr.)
Wyatt Rd. E7 .... 6J **53**
N5 .... 3C **50**
Wyatts La. E17 .... 3E **34**
Wybert St.
NW1 .... 4G **67** (3A **160**)
Wyborne Ho. NW10 .... 7J **45**
Wyborne Way NW10 .... 7J **45**
Wyburn Av. EN5: Barn 3C **4**
Wyche Gro.
CR2: S Croy 7D **152**
Wych Elm Lodge
BR1: Brom 7H **125**
Wych Elm Pas.
KT2: King T 7F **117**
Wycherley Cl. SE3 .... 7H **89**
Wycherley Cres.
EN5: Barn 6E **4**
Wychombe Studios NW3 .... 6D **48**
Wychwood Av.
CR7: Thor H 3C **140**
HA8: Edg 6J **11**
Wychwood Cl. HA8: Edg 6J **11**
TW16: Sun T 6J **113**
Wychwood End N6 .... 7G **31**
Wychwood Gdns. IG5: Ilf 4D **36**
Wychwood Way SE19 ...... 6D **122**
Wyclif Ct. *EC1* *2A* ***162***
(off Wyclif St.)
Wycliffe Cl. DA16: Well 1K **109**
Wycliffe Rd. SW11 .... 2E **102**
SW19 .... 6K **119**
Wyclif St. EC1 ..... 3B **68** (2A **162**)
Wycombe Gdns. NW11 ...... 2J **47**
Wycombe Ho. *NW8* *3C* ***158***
(off Grendon St.)
Wycombe Pl. SW18 .... 6A **102**
Wycombe Rd.
HA0: Wemb 1G **63**
IG2: Ilf 5D **36**
N17 .... 1G **33**
Wycombe Sq. W8 .... 1H **83**
Wydehurst Rd.
CR0: Croy 7G **141**
Wydell Cl. SM4: Mord 6F **137**
Wydeville Mnr. Rd.
SE12 .... 4K **125**
Wye Cl. BR6: Orp 7K **145**
HA4: Ruis 6E **22**
TW15: Ashf 4D **112**
Wye Ct. *W13* *5B* ***62***
(off Malvern Way)
Wyemead Cres. E4 .... 2B **20**
Wye St. SW11 .... 2B **102**
Wyevale Cl. HA5: Pinn 3J **23**
Wyfields IG5: Ilf 1F **37**
Wyfold Ho. *SE2* *2D* ***92***
(off Wolvercote Rd.)
Wyfold Rd. SW6 .... 7G **83**
Wyhill Wlk. RM10: Dag 6J **57**
Wyke Cl. TW7: Isle 6K **79**
Wyke Gdns. W7 .... 3A **80**
Wykeham Av. RM9: Dag 6C **56**
Wykeham Cl.
UB7: W Dray 5C **76**
Wykeham Ct. *N11* *2K* ***15***
(off Wykeham Rd.)
NW4 .... *5E* ***28***
(off Wykeham Rd.)
Wykeham Grn. RM9: Dag 6C **56**
Wykeham Hill
HA9: Wemb 1F **45**
Wykeham Ri. N20 .... 1B **14**
Wykeham Rd. HA3: Harr 4B **26**
NW4 .... 4E **28**
Wyke Rd. E3 .... 7C **52**
SW20 .... 2E **136**
Wylchin Cl. HA5: Pinn 3H **23**
Wyldes Cl. NW11 .... 1A **48**
Wyldfield Gdns. N9 .... 2A **18**
Wyld Way HA9: Wemb 6H **45**
Wyleu St. SE23 .... 7A **106**
Wylie Rd. UB2: S'hall 3E **78**
Wyllen Cl. E1 .... 4J **69**
Wymans Way E7 .... 4A **54**
Wymering Mans. *W9* *3J* ***65***
(off Wymering Rd., not continuous)
Wymering Rd. W9 .... 3J **65**
Wymond St. SW15 .... 3E **100**
Wynan Rd. E14 .... 5D **88**
Wynash Gdns.
SM5: Cars 5C **150**
Wynaud Ct. N22 .... 6E **16**
Wyncham Av.
DA15: Sidc 1J **127**
Wyncham Ho.
DA15: Sidc *2A* ***128***
(off Longlands Rd.)
Wynchgate HA3: Harr 7D **10**
N14 .... 1C **16**
N21 .... 1C **16**
UB5: N'olt 5D **42**
Wyncroft Cl. BR1: Brom 3D **144**
Wyndale Av. NW9 .... 6G **27**
Wyndcliff Rd. SE7 .... 6K **89**
Wyndcroft Cl. EN2: Enf 3G **7**
Wyndham Cl. SM2: Sutt 7J **149**
Wyndham Ct. W7 .... 4A **80**
Wyndham Cres. N19 .... 3G **49**
TW4: Houn 6E **96**
Wyndham Deedes Ho.
E2 .... *2G* ***69***
(off Hackney Rd.)
Wyndham Est. SE5 .... 7C **86**
Wyndham Ho. *E14* *2D* ***88***
(off Marsh Wall)
Wyndham M.
W1 .... 5D **66** (6E **158**)
Wyndham Pl.
W1 .... 5D **66** (6E **158**)
Wyndham Rd. E6 .... 7B **54**
EN4: Barn 1J **15**
KT2: King T 7F **117**
(not continuous)
SE5 .... 7C **86**
W13 .... 3B **80**
Wyndhams Ct. *E8* *7F* ***51***
(off Celandine Dr.)
Wyndhams Theatre ***2E 166***
(off St Martin's La.)
Wyndham St.
W1 .... 5D **66** (5E **158**)
Wyndham Yd.
W1 .... 5D **66** (6E **158**)
Wyneham Rd. SE24 .... 5D **104**
Wynell Rd. SE23 .... 3K **123**
Wynford Ho. *N1* *2K* ***67***
(off Wynford Rd.)
Wynford Pl. DA17: Belv 6G **93**
Wynford Rd. N1 .... 2K **67**
Wynford Way SE9 .... 3D **126**
Wynlie Gdns. HA5: Pinn 2K **23**
Wynn Bri. Cl. IG8: Wfd G 1B **36**
Wynndale Rd. E18 .... 1K **35**
Wynne Ho. SE14 .... 1K **105**
Wynne Rd. SW9 .... 2A **104**
Wynn's Av. DA15: Sidc 5K **109**
Wynnstay Gdns. W8 .... 3J **83**
Wynter St. SW11 .... 4A **102**
Wynton Gdns. SE25 .... 5F **141**
Wynton Pl. W3 .... 6H **63**
Wynyard Ho. SE11 .... 5H **173**
Wynyard Ter.
SE11 .... 5K **85** (5H **173**)
Wynyatt St.
EC1 .... 3B **68** (2A **162**)
Wyre Gro. HA8: Edg 3C **12**
UB3: Hayes 4J **77**
Wyresdale Cres.
UB6: G'frd 3K **61**
Wyteleaf Cl. HA4: Ruis 6E **22**
Wythburn Ct. *W1* *7E* ***158***
(off Wythburn Pl.)
Wythburn Pl.
W1 .... 6D **66** (1E **164**)
Wythenshawe Rd.
RM10: Dag 3G **57**
Wythens Wlk. SE9 .... 6F **109**
Wythes Cl. BR1: Brom 2D **144**
Wythes Rd. E16 .... 1C **90**
Wythfield Rd. SE9 .... 6D **108**
Wyvenhoe Rd. HA2: Harr 4G **43**
Wyvern Est.
KT3: N Mald 4C **136**
Wyvil Rd. SW8 .... 7J **85**
Wyvis St. E14 .... 5D **70**

X

Xylon Ho. KT4: Wor Pk 2D **148**

Y

Yabsley St. E14 .... 1E **88**
Yalding Rd. SE16 .... 3G **87**
Yale Cl. TW4: Houn 5D **96**
Yale Ct. NW6 .... 5K **47**
Yaohan Plaza NW9 .... 3K **27**
Yarborough Rd. SW19 ..... 1B **138**
Yardley Cl. E4 .... 5J **9**
Yardley Ct. SM3: Sutt 4E **148**
Yardley La. E4 .... 5J **9**
Yardley St. WC1 ... 3A **68** (2J **161**)
(not continuous)
Yard, The *N1* *1F* ***161***
(off Caledonian Rd.)
Yarlington Ct. *N11* *5K* ***15***
(off Sparkford Gdns.)
Yarmouth Cres. N17 .... 5H **33**
Yarmouth Pl.
W1 .... 1F **85** (5J **165**)
Yarnfield Sq. SE15 .... 1G **105**
Yarnton Way
DA18: Belv, Erith 3F **93**
SE2 .... 2C **92**
Yarrow Cres. E6 .... 5C **72**
Yarrow Ho. *E14* *3E* ***88***
(off Stewart St.)
W10 .... *5E* ***64***
(off Sutton Way)
Yateley St. SE18 .... 3B **90**
Yates Ct. *NW2* *6F* ***47***
(off Willesden La.)
Yates Ho. *E2* *3G* ***69***
(off Roberta St.)
Yatton Ho. *W10* *5E* ***64***
(off Sutton Way)
YEADING **4A 60**
Yeading Av. HA2: Harr 2C **42**
Yeading Ct. UB4: Hayes 4A **60**

HOSPITALS and HOSPICES
covered by this atlas
with their map square reference

N.B. Where Hospitals and Hospices are not named on the map, the reference given is for the road in which they are situated.

ASHFORD HOSPITAL 2A **112**
London Road
ASHFORD
TW15 3AA
Tel: 01784 884488

ATHLONE HOUSE 1D **48**
Hampstead Lane
LONDON
N6 4RX
Tel: 020 83485231

ATKINSON MORLEY'S HOSPITAL 7D **118**
31 Copse Hill
LONDON
SW20 0NE
Tel: 020 89467711

BARKING HOSPITAL 7K **55**
Upney Lane
BARKING
IG11 9LX
Tel: 0208 9838000

BARNES HOSPITAL 3A **100**
South Worple Way
LONDON
SW14 8SU
Tel: 020 88784981

BARNET HOSPITAL 4A **4**
Wellhouse Lane
BARNET
EN5 3DJ
Tel: 020 82164000

BECKENHAM HOSPITAL 2B **142**
379 Croydon Road
BECKENHAM
BR3 3QL
Tel: 01689 863000

BECONTREE DAY HOSPITAL 2E **56**
508 Becontree Avenue
DAGENHAM
RM8 3HR
Tel: 0208 2767288

BELVEDERE DAY HOSPITAL 1C **64**
341 Harlesden Road
LONDON
NW10 3RX
Tel: 020 84593562

BELVEDERE PRIVATE CLINIC 5C **92**
Knee Hill
LONDON
SE2 0AT
Tel: 020 83114464

BETHLEM ROYAL HOSPITAL, THE 7C **142**
Monks Orchard Road
BECKENHAM
BR3 3BX
Tel: 020 87776611

BLACKHEATH BMI HOSPITAL, THE 3H **107**
40-42 Lee Terrace
LONDON
SE3 9UD
Tel: 020 83187722

BOLINGBROKE HOSPITAL 5C **102**
Bolingbroke Grove
LONDON
SW11 6HN
Tel: 020 72237411

BRITISH HOME & HOSPITAL FOR INCURABLES ...5B **122**
Crown Lane
LONDON
SW16 3JB
Tel: 020 86708261

BUSHEY BUPA HOSPITAL 1E **10**
Heathbourne Road,
Bushey Heath
BUSHEY
WD23 1RD
Tel: 020 89509090

CAMDEN MEWS DAY HOSPITAL 7G **49**
1-5 Camden Mews
LONDON
NW1 9DB
Tel: 020 75304780

CARSHALTON WAR MEMORIAL HOSPITAL 6D **150**
The Park
CARSHALTON
SM5 3DB
Tel: 020 86475534

CASSEL HOSPITAL, THE 4D **116**
1 Ham Common
RICHMOND
TW10 7JF
Tel: 020 89408181

CENTRAL MIDDLESEX HOSPITAL 3J **63**
Acton Lane
LONDON
NW10 7NS
Tel: 020 89655733

CHARING CROSS HOSPITAL 6F **83**
Fulham Palace Road
LONDON
W6 8RF
Tel: 020 88461234

CHASE FARM HOSPITAL 1F **7**
127 The Ridgeway
ENFIELD
EN2 8JL
Tel: 020 83666600

CHELSEA & WESTMINSTER HOSPITAL 6A **84**
369 Fulham Road
LONDON
SW10 9NH
Tel: 020 87468000

CHILDREN'S HOSPITAL, THE (LEWISHAM)
....5D **106**
Lewisham University Hospital
Lewisham High Street
LONDON
SE13 6LH
Tel: 020 83333000

CLAYPONDS HOSPITAL 4E **80**
Sterling Place
LONDON
W5 4RN
Tel: 020 85604011

CLEMENTINE CHURCHILL BMI HOSPITAL, THE
....3K **43**
Sudbury Hill
HARROW
HA1 3RX
Tel: 020 88723872

COLINDALE HOSPITAL 2A **28**
Colindale Avenue
LONDON
NW9 5HG
Tel: 020 89522381

CROMWELL HOSPITAL, THE 4K **83**
162-174 Cromwell Road
LONDON
SW5 0TU
Tel: 020 74602000

EALING HOSPITAL 1H **79**
Uxbridge Road
SOUTHALL
UB1 3HW
Tel: 020 89675000

EASTMAN DENTAL HOSPITAL & DENTAL INSTITUTE, THE
....4K **67** (3G **161**)
256 Gray's Inn Road
LONDON
WC1X 8LD
Tel: 020 79151000

EDENHALL MARIE CURIE CENTRE 5B **48**
11 Lyndhurst Gardens
LONDON
NW3 5NS
Tel: 020 78533400

EDGWARE COMMUNITY HOSPITAL 7C **12**
Burnt Oak Broadway
EDGWARE
HA8 0AD
Tel: 020 89522381

ELIZABETH GARRETT ANDERSON & OBSTETRIC
HOSPITAL, THE 4G **67** (4B **160**)
Huntley Street
LONDON
WC1E 6DH
Tel: 020 73803501

Hospitals & Hospices

ERITH & DISTRICT HOSPITAL 6K **93**
Park Crescent
ERITH
DA8 3EE
Tel: 020 83083131

FINCHLEY MEMORIAL HOSPITAL 7F **15**
Granville Road
LONDON
N12 0JE
Tel: 020 83493121

FLORENCE NIGHTINGALE DAY HOSPITAL
.................5C **66** (5D **158**)
1B Harewood Row
LONDON
NW1 6SE
Tel: 020 77259940

FLORENCE NIGHTINGALE HOSPITAL
.................5C **66** (5D **158**)
11-19 Lisson Grove
LONDON
NW1 6SH
Tel: 020 75357700

GAINSBOROUGH CLINIC, THE
.................3A **86** (1K **173**)
22 Barkham Terrace
LONDON
SE1 7PW
Tel: 020 79285633

GARDEN BMI HOSPITAL, THE 3E **28**
46-50 Sunny Gardens Road
LONDON
NW4 1RP
Tel: 020 84574500

GOODMAYES HOSPITAL 5A **38**
Barley Lane
ILFORD
IG3 8XJ
Tel: 020 89838000

GORDON HOSPITAL 4H **85** (4C **172**)
Bloomburg Street
LONDON
SW1V 2RH
Tel: 020 87468733

GREAT ORMOND STREET HOSPITAL FOR CHILDREN
.................4J **67** (4F **161**)
Great Ormond Street
LONDON
WC1N 3JH
Tel: 020 74059200

GREENWICH & BEXLEY COTTAGE HOSPICE
.................5C **92**
185 Bostall Hill
LONDON
SE2 0QX
Tel: 020 83122244

GUY'S HOSPITAL 1D **86** (5E **168**)
St Thomas Street
LONDON
SE1 9RT
Tel: 020 79555000

GUY'S NUFFIELD HOUSE 2D **86** (6E **168**)
Newcomen Street
LONDON
SE1 1YR
Tel: 020 79554257

HAMMERSMITH HOSPITAL 6C **64**
Du Cane Road
LONDON
W12 0HS
Tel: 020 83831000

HARLEY STREET CLINIC, THE
.................5F **67** (5J **159**)
35 Weymouth Street
LONDON
W1G 8BJ
Tel: 020 79357700

HAYES GROVE PRIORY HOSPITAL 2J **155**
Prestons Road
BROMLEY
BR2 7AS
Tel: 020 84627722

HEART HOSPITAL, THE 5E **66** (6H **159**)
16-18 Westmoreland Street
LONDON
W1D 8PH
Tel: 020 75738888

HEATHVIEW DAY CENTRE 6C **92**
Lodge Hill
LONDON
SE2 0AY
Tel: 020 83197100

HIGHGATE PRIVATE HOSPITAL 6D **30**
17 View Road
LONDON
N6 4DJ
Tel: 020 83414182

HILLINGDON HOSPITAL 5B **58**
Pield Heath Road
UXBRIDGE
UB8 3NN
Tel: 01895 238282

HOLLY HOUSE HOSPITAL 2E **20**
High Road
BUCKHURST HILL
IG9 5HX
Tel: 0208 5053311

HOMERTON UNIVERSITY HOSPITAL
.................5K **51**
Homerton Row
LONDON
E9 6SR
Tel: 020 85105555

HORNSEY CENTRAL HOSPITAL 5H **31**
Park Road
LONDON
N8 8JL
Tel: 020 82191700

HOSPITAL FOR TROPICAL DISEASES
.................4G **67** (4B **160**)
Mortimer Market
Capper Street
LONDON
WC1E 6AU
Tel: 020 73879300

HOSPITAL OF ST JOHN & ST ELIZABETH
.................2B **66**
60 Grove End Road
LONDON
NW8 9NH
Tel: 020 78064000

KING EDWARD VII'S HOSPITAL SISTER AGNES
.................5E **66** (5H **159**)
5-10 Beaumont Street
LONDON
W1G 6AA
Tel: 020 74864411

KING GEORGE HOSPITAL 5A **38**
Barley Lane
ILFORD
IG3 8YB
Tel: 020 89838000

KING'S COLLEGE HOSPITAL 2D **104**
Denmark Hill
LONDON
SE5 9RS
Tel: 020 77374000

KING'S COLLEGE HOSPITAL, DULWICH 4E **104**
East Dulwich Grove
LONDON
SE22 8PT
Tel: 020 77374000

KING'S OAK BMI HOSPITAL, THE 1F **7**
The Ridgeway
ENFIELD
EN2 8SD
Tel: 020 83709500

KINGSBURY COMMUNITY HOSPITAL 4G **27**
Honeypot Lane
LONDON
NW9 9QY
Tel: 020 89031323

KINGSTON HOSPITAL 1H **135**
Galsworthy Road
KINGSTON UPON THAMES
KT2 7QB
Tel: 020 85467711

LAMBETH HOSPITAL 3J **103**
108 Landor Road
LONDON
SW9 9NT
Tel: 020 74116100

LATIMER DAY HOSPITAL 5G **67** (5A **160**)
40 Hanson Street
LONDON
W1W 6UL
Tel: 020 73809187

LEWISHAM UNIVERSITY HOSPITAL 5D **106**
Lewisham High Street
LONDON
SE13 6LH
Tel: 020 83333000

LISTER HOSPITAL, THE 5F **85** (6J **171**)
Chelsea Bridge Road
LONDON
SW1W 8RH
Tel: 020 77303417

LONDON BRIDGE HOSPITAL 1D **86** (4F **169**)
27 Tooley Street
LONDON
SE1 2PR
Tel: 020 74073100

LONDON CHEST HOSPITAL 2J **69**
Bonner Road
LONDON
E2 9JX
Tel: 020 73777000

LONDON CLINIC, THE 4E **66** (4H **159**)
20 Devonshire Place
LONDON
W1G 6BW
Tel: 020 79354444

LONDON FOOT HOSPITAL 4G **67** (4A **160**)
33 & 40 Fitzroy Square
LONDON
W1P 6AY
Tel: 020 75304500

LONDON INDEPENDENT BMI HOSPITAL, THE
.... .5K **69**
1 Beaumont Square
LONDON
E1 4NL
Tel: 020 77802400

LONDON LIGHTHOUSE 6G **65**
111-117 Lancaster Road
LONDON
W11 1QT
Tel: 020 77921200

LONDON WELBECK HOSPITAL
.... .5E **66** (6H **159**)
27 Welbeck Street
LONDON
W1G 8EN
Tel: 020 72242242

MAUDSLEY HOSPITAL, THE 2D **104**
Denmark Hill
LONDON
SE5 8AZ
Tel: 020 87776611

MAYDAY UNIVERSITY HOSPITAL 6B **140**
Mayday Road
THORNTON HEATH
CR7 7YE
Tel: 020 84013000

MEADOW HOUSE HOSPICE 2H **79**
Ealing Hospital
Uxbridge Road
SOUTHALL
UB1 3HW
Tel: 020 8967 5179

MEMORIAL HOSPITAL 2E **108**
Shooters Hill
LONDON
SE18 3RZ
Tel: 020 88366000

MIDDLESEX HOSPITAL, THE
.... .5G **67** (6B **160**)
Mortimer Street
LONDON
W1T 3AA
Tel: 020 76368333

MILDMAY MISSION HOSPITAL
.... .3F **69** (2J **163**)
Hackney Road
LONDON
E2 7NA
Tel: 020 76136300

MILE END HOSPITAL 4K **69**
Bancroft Road
LONDON
E1 4DG
Tel: 020 73777000

MOLESEY HOSPITAL 5E **132**
High Street
WEST MOLESEY
KT8 2LU
Tel: 020 89414481

MOORFIELDS EYE HOSPITAL
.... .3D **68** (2E **162**)
162 City Road
LONDON
EC1V 2PD
Tel: 020 72533411

MORLAND ROAD DAY HOSPITAL
.... .7G **57**
Morland Road
DAGENHAM
RM10 9HU
Tel: 0208 2767933

NATIONAL HOSPITAL FOR NEUROLOGY &
NEUROSURGERY, THE 4J **67** (4F **161**)
Queen Square
LONDON
WC1N 3BG
Tel: 020 78373611

NELSON HOSPITAL 2H **137**
Kingston Road
LONDON
SW20 8DB
Tel: 020 82962000

NEW VICTORIA HOSPITAL 1A **136**
184 Coombe Lane West
KINGSTON UPON THAMES
KT2 7EG
Tel: 020 89499000

NEWHAM GENERAL HOSPITAL 4A **72**
Glen Road
LONDON
E13 8SL
Tel: 020 74764000

NORTH LONDON HOSPICE 3F **15**
47 Woodside Avenue
LONDON
N12 8TT
Tel: 020 83438841

NORTH LONDON NUFFIELD HOSPITAL, THE
.... .2F **7**
Cavell Drive
ENFIELD
EN2 7PR
Tel: 020 83662122

NORTH LONDON PRIORY HOSPITAL 1D **16**
The Bourne
LONDON
N14 6RA
Tel: 020 88828191

NORTH MIDDLESEX HOSPITAL, THE
.... .5K **17**
Sterling Way
LONDON
N18 1QX
Tel: 020 88872000

NORTHWICK PARK HOSPITAL 7A **26**
Watford Road
HARROW
HA1 3UJ
Tel: 020 88643232

NORTHWOOD & PINNER COMMUNITY HOSPITAL
.... .1J **23**
Pinner Road
NORTHWOOD
HA6 1DE
Tel: 01923 824182

OLDCHURCH HOSPITAL 6K **39**
Oldchurch Road
ROMFORD
RM7 0BE
Tel: 01708 345533

PARKSIDE HOSPITAL 3F **119**
53 Parkside
LONDON
SW19 5NX
Tel: 020 89718000

PENNY SANGHAM DAY HOSPITAL 3D **78**
Osterley Park Road
SOUTHALL
UB2 4EU
Tel: 020 85719676

PLAISTOW HOSPITAL 2A **72**
Samson Street
LONDON
E13 9EH
Tel: 020 85866200

PORTLAND HOSPITAL FOR WOMEN & CHILDREN, THE
.... .4F **67** (4K **159**)
209 Great Portland Street
LONDON
W1N 6AH
Tel: 020 75804400

PRINCESS GRACE HOSPITAL 4E **66** (4G **159**)
42-52 Nottingham Place
LONDON
W1U 5NY
Tel: 020 74861234

PRINCESS GRACE HOSPITAL ANNEXE
.... .5E **66** (5H **159**)
29-31 Devonshire Street
LONDON
W1G 6PU
Tel: 020 74861234

PRINCESS LOUISE HOSPITAL 5F **65**
St Quintin Avenue
LONDON
W10 6DL
Tel: 020 89690133

PRINCESS ROYAL UNIVERSITY HOSPITAL
.... .3E **156**
Farnborough Common
ORPINGTON
BR6 8ND
Tel: 01689 814100

QUEEN CHARLOTTE'S & CHELSEA HOSPITAL
.... .6C **64**
Du Cane Road
LONDON
W12 0HS
Tel: 020 83831111

QUEEN ELIZABETH HOSPITAL 7C **90**
Stadium Road
LONDON
SE18 4QH
Tel: 020 88366000

Hospitals & Hospices

QUEEN MARY'S HOSPITAL 5A **128**
Frognal Avenue
SIDCUP
DA14 6LT
Tel: 020 83022678

QUEEN MARY'S HOSPITAL FOR CHILDREN 1A **150**
Wrythe Lane
CARSHALTON
SM5 1AA
Tel: 020 82962000

QUEEN MARY'S HOUSE 3A **48**
23 East Heath Road
LONDON
NW3 1DU
Tel: 020 74314111

QUEEN MARY'S UNIVERSITY HOSPITAL 6C **100**
Roehampton Lane
LONDON
SW15 5PN
Tel: 020 87896611

RAVENSCOURT PARK HOSPITAL 4C **82**
Ravenscourt Park
LONDON
W6 0NT
Tel: 020 88467777

REDFORD LODGE PSYCHIATRIC HOSPITAL 2B **18**
15 Church Street
LONDON
N9 9DY
Tel: 020 89561234

RICHARD HOUSE CHILDREN'S HOSPICE 7B **72**
Richard House Drive
LONDON
E16 3RG
Tel: 020 75110222

RICHMOND ROYAL HOSPITAL 3E **98**
Kew Foot Road
RICHMOND
TW9 2TE
Tel: 020 89403331

RODING BUPA HOSPITAL 3B **36**
Roding Lane South
ILFORD
IG4 5PZ
Tel: 020 85511100

ROEHAMPTON PRIORY HOSPITAL 4B **100**
Priory Lane
LONDON
SW15 5JJ
Tel: 020 88768261

ROYAL BROMPTON HOSPITAL 5C **84** (5C **170**)
Sydney Street
LONDON
SW3 6NP
Tel: 020 73528121

ROYAL BROMPTON HOSPITAL (ANNEXE) ..5B **84** (5B **170**)
Fulham Road
LONDON
SW3 6HP
Tel: 020 73528121

ROYAL FREE HOSPITAL, THE 5C **48**
Pond Street
LONDON
NW3 2QG
Tel: 020 77940500

ROYAL HOSPITAL FOR NEURO-DISABILITY 6G **101**
West Hill
LONDON
SW15 3SW
Tel: 020 87804500

ROYAL LONDON HOMOEOPATHIC HOSPITAL, THE
.................5J **67** (5F **161**)
Great Ormond Street
LONDON
WC1N 3HR
Tel: 020 78378833

ROYAL LONDON HOSPITAL 5H **69**
Whitechapel Road
LONDON
E1 1BB
Tel: 020 73777000

ROYAL MARSDEN HOSPITAL (FULHAM), THE
.................5B **84** (5B **170**)
Fulham Road
LONDON
SW3 6JJ
Tel: 020 73528171

ROYAL NATIONAL ORTHOPAEDIC HOSPITAL 2G **11**
Brockley Hill
STANMORE
HA7 4LP
Tel: 020 89542300

ROYAL NATIONAL ORTHOPAEDIC HOSPITAL
(OUTPATIENTS) 4F **67** (4K **159**)
45-51 Bolsover Street
LONDON
W1W 5AQ
Tel: 020 73875070

ROYAL NATIONAL THROAT, NOSE & EAR HOSPITAL
.................3K **67** (1G **161**)
330 Gray's Inn Road
LONDON
WC1X 8DA
Tel: 020 79151300

ROYAL NATIONAL THROAT, NOSE & EAR HOSPITAL -
SPEECH & LANGUAGE UNIT 5C **62**
10 Castlebar Hill
LONDON
W5 1TD
Tel: 020 89978480

ST ANDREW'S AT HARROW 2J **43**
Bowden House Clinic
London Road
HARROW
HA1 3JL
Tel: 020 89667000

ST ANDREW'S HOSPITAL 4D **70**
Devas Street
LONDON
E3 3NT
Tel: 020 74764000

ST ANN'S HOSPITAL 5C **32**
St Ann's Road
LONDON
N15 3TH
Tel: 020 84426000

ST ANTHONY'S HOSPITAL 2F **149**
London Road
LONDON
SM3 9DW
Tel: 020 83376691

ST BARTHOLOMEW'S HOSPITAL
.................5B **68** (6B **162**)
West Smithfield
LONDON
EC1A 7BE
Tel: 020 73777000

ST BERNARD'S HOSPITAL 2H **79**
Uxbridge Road
SOUTHALL
UB1 3EU
Tel: 020 89675000

ST CHARLES HOSPITAL 5F **65**
Exmoor Street
LONDON
W10 6DZ
Tel: 020 89692488

ST CHRISTOPHER'S HOSPICE 5J **123**
51-59 Lawrie Park Road
LONDON
SE26 6DZ
Tel: 020 87789252

ST CLEMENT'S HOSPITAL 3B **70**
2A Bow Road
LONDON
E3 4LL
Tel: 020 73777000

ST GEORGE'S HOSPITAL (TOOTING)
.................5B **120**
Blackshaw Road
LONDON
SW17 0QT
Tel: 020 86721255

ST HELIER HOSPITAL 1A **150**
Wrythe Lane
CARSHALTON
SM5 1AA
Tel: 020 82962000

ST JOHN'S AND AMYAND HOUSE 7A **98**
Strafford Road
TWICKENHAM
TW1 3AD
Tel: 020 87449943

ST JOHN'S HOSPICE 2B **66** (1A **158**)
Hospital of St John & St Elizabeth
60 Grove End Road
LONDON
NW8 9NH
Tel: 020 78064040

ST JOSEPH'S HOSPICE 1H **69**
Mare Street
LONDON
E8 4SA
Tel: 020 85256000

ST LUKE'S HOSPITAL FOR THE CLERGY
.................4G **67** (4A **160**)
14 Fitzroy Square
LONDON
W1T 6AH
Tel: 020 73884954

ST LUKE'S KENTON GRANGE HOSPICE 5D **26**
Kenton Grange
Kenton Road
HARROW
HA3 0YG
Tel: 020 83828000

ST LUKE'S WOODSIDE HOSPITAL 4E **30**
Woodside Avenue
LONDON
N10 3HU
Tel: 020 82191800

ST MARK'S HOSPITAL 7B **26**
Watford Road
HARROW
HA1 3UJ
Tel: 020 88643232

ST MARY'S HOSPITAL 6B **66** (7B **158**)
Praed Street
LONDON
W2 1NY
Tel: 020 77256666

ST PANCRAS HOSPITAL 1H **67**
4 St Pancras Way
LONDON
NW1 0PE
Tel: 020 75303500

ST RAPHAEL'S HOSPICE 1F **149**
St Anthony's Hospital
London Road
SUTTON
SM3 9DW
Tel: 020 83354575

ST THOMAS' HOSPITAL 3K **85** (1G **173**)
Lambeth Palace Road
LONDON
SE1 7EH
Tel: 020 79289292

SHIRLEY OAKS BMI HOSPITAL
....7J **141**
Poppy Lane
CROYDON
CR9 8AB
Tel: 020 86555500

SLOANE BMI HOSPITAL, THE 1F **143**
125-133 Albemarle Road
BECKENHAM
BR3 5HS
Tel: 020 84666911

SPRINGFIELD UNIVERSITY HOSPITAL
....3C **120**
61 Glenburnie Road
LONDON
SW17 7DJ
Tel: 020 86826000

SURBITON HOSPITAL 6E **134**
Ewell Road
SURBITON
KT6 6EZ
Tel: 020 83997111

TEDDINGTON MEMORIAL HOSPITAL
....6J **115**
Hampton Road
TEDDINGTON
TW11 0JL
Tel: 020 84088210

THORPE COOMBE HOSPITAL 3E **34**
714 Forest Road
LONDON
E17 3HP
Tel: 0208 5395522

TOLWORTH HOSPITAL 2G **147**
Red Lion Road
SURBITON
KT6 7QU
Tel: 020 83900102

TRINITY HOSPICE 4F **103**
30 Clapham Common North Side
LONDON
SW4 0RN
Tel: 020 77871000

UNIVERSITY COLLEGE HOSPITAL 4G **67** (4B **160**)
Gower Street
LONDON
WC1E 6AU
Tel: 020 73879300

UPTON CENTRE 4E **110**
14 Upton Road
BEXLEYHEATH
DA6 8LQ
Tel: 020 83017900

WELLINGTON HOSPITAL, THE 3B **66** (1B **158**)
8a Wellington Place
LONDON
NW8 9LE
Tel: 020 75865959

WEMBLEY (MATS) HOSPITAL 6D **44**
116 Chapin Road
WEMBLEY
HA0 4UX
Tel: 020 89031323

WESTERN OPHTHALMIC HOSPITAL
....5D **66** (5E **158**)
153 Marylebone Road
LONDON
NW1 5QH
Tel: 020 78866666

WEST MIDDLESEX UNIVERSITY HOSPITAL
....2A **98**
Twickenham Road
ISLEWORTH
TW7 6AF
Tel: 020 85602121

WHIPPS CROSS UNIVERSITY HOSPITAL
....6F **35**
Whipps Cross Road
LONDON
E11 1NR
Tel: 020 85395522

WHITTINGTON HOSPITAL 2G **49**
Highgate Hill
LONDON
N19 5NF
Tel: 020 72723070

WILLESDEN COMMUNITY HOSPITAL 7C **46**
Harlesden Road
LONDON
NW10 3RY
Tel: 020 84518017

RAIL, CROYDON TRAMLINK, DOCKLANDS LIGHT RAILWAY AND LONDON UNDERGROUND STATIONS

with their map square reference

A

Abbey Wood (Rail) 3C 92
Acton Central (Rail) 1K 81
Acton Main Line (Rail) 6J 63
Acton Town (Tube) 2G 81
Addington Village (CT) 6C 154
Addiscombe (CT) 1G 153
Albany Park (Rail) 2D 128
Aldgate (Tube) 6F 69 (1J 169)
Aldgate East (Tube) 6F 69 (7K 163)
Alexandra Palace (Rail) 2J 31
All Saints (DLR) 7D 70
Alperton (Tube) 1D 62
Ampere Way (CT) 1K 151
Anerley (Rail) 1H 141
Angel (Tube) 2A 68
Angel Road (Rail) 5D 18
Archway (Tube) 2G 49
Arena (CT) 5J 141
Arnos Grove (Tube) 5B 16
Arsenal (Tube) 3A 50
Ashford (Rail) 4B 112
Avenue Road (CT) 2K 141

B

Baker Street (Tube) 4D 66 (4F 159)
Balham (Rail & Tube) 1F 121
Bank (DLR & Tube) 6D 68 (1E 168)
Barbican (Rail & Tube) 5C 68 (5C 162)
Barking (Rail & Tube) 7G 55
Barkingside (Tube) 3H 37
Barnehurst (Rail) 2J 111
Barnes (Rail) 3C 100
Barnes Bridge (Rail) 2B 100
Barons Court (Tube) 5G 83
Battersea Park (Rail) 7F 85
Bayswater (Tube) 7K 65
Beckenham Hill (Rail) 5E 124
Beckenham Junction (Rail & CT) 1C 142
Beckenham Road (CT) 1A 142
Beckton (DLR) 5E 72
Beckton Park (DLR) 7D 72
Becontree (Tube) 6D 56
Beddington Lane (CT) 6G 139
Belgrave Walk (CT) 4B 138
Bellingham (Rail) 3D 124
Belsize Park (Tube) 5C 48
Belvedere (Rail) 3H 93
Bermondsey (Tube) 3G 87
Berrylands (Rail) 4H 135
Bethnal Green (Rail) 4H 69
Bethnal Green (Tube) 3J 69
Bexley (Rail) 1G 129
Bexleyheath (Rail) 2E 110
Bickley (Rail) 3C 144
Birkbeck (Rail) 3J 141
Blackfriars (Rail & Tube) 7B 68 (2A 168)
Blackheath (Rail) 3H 107
Blackhorse Lane (CT) 7G 141
Blackhorse Road (Rail & Tube) 4K 33
Blackwall (DLR) 7E 70
Bond Street (Tube) 6F 67 (1J 165)
Borough (Tube) 2C 86 (7D 168)
Boston Manor (Tube) 4A 80
Bounds Green (Tube) 6C 16

Bow Church (DLR) 3C 70
Bowes Park (Rail) 7D 16
Bow Road (Tube) 3C 70
Brent Cross (Tube) 7F 29
Brentford (Rail) 6C 80
Brimsdown (Rail) 3F 9
Brixton (Rail & Tube) 4A 104
Brockley (Rail) 3A 106
Bromley-by-Bow (Tube) 3D 70
Bromley North (Rail) 1J 143
Bromley South (Rail) 3J 143
Brondesbury (Rail) 7H 47
Brondesbury Park (Rail) 1G 65
Bruce Grove (Rail) 2F 33
Buckhurst Hill (Tube) 2G 21
Burnt Oak (Tube) 1J 27
Bush Hill Park (Rail) 6A 8

C

Caledonian Road (Tube) 6K 49
Caledonian Road & Barnsbury (Rail) 7K 49
Cambridge Heath (Rail) 2H 69
Camden Road (Rail) 7G 49
Camden Town (Tube) 1F 67
Canada Water (Tube) 2J 87
Canary Wharf (DLR) 1C 88
Canary Wharf (Tube) 1D 88
Canning Town (Rail, DLR & Tube) 6G 71
Cannon Street (Rail & Tube) 7D 68 (2E 168)
Canonbury (Rail) 5C 50
Canons Park (Tube) 7K 11
Carshalton (Rail) 4D 150
Carshalton Beeches (Rail) 6D 150
Castle Bar Park (Rail) 5K 61
Catford (Rail) 7C 106
Catford Bridge (Rail) 7C 106
Chadwell Heath (Rail) 7D 38
Chalk Farm (Tube) 7E 48
Chancery Lane (Tube) 5A 68 (6J 161)
Charing Cross (Rail & Tube) 1J 85 (4E 166)
Charlton (Rail) 5A 90
Cheam (Rail) 7G 149
Chessington North (Rail) 5E 146
Chessington South (Rail) 7D 146
Chigwell (Tube) 3K 21
Chingford (Rail) 1B 20
Chislehurst (Rail) 2E 144
Chiswick (Rail) 7J 81
Chiswick Park (Tube) 4J 81
Church Street (CT) 2C 152
City Thameslink (Rail) 6B 68 (7A 162)
Clapham Common (Tube) 4G 103
Clapham High Street (Rail) 3H 103
Clapham Junction (Rail) 3C 102
Clapham North (Tube) 3J 103
Clapham South (Tube) 6F 103
Clapton (Rail) 2H 51
Clock House (Rail) 1A 142
Cockfosters (Tube) 4K 5
Colindale (Tube) 3A 28
Colliers Wood (Tube) 7B 120
Coombe Lane (CT) 5J 153
Covent Garden (Tube) 7J 67 (2F 167)
Cricklewood (Rail) 4F 47
Crofton Park (Rail) 5B 106
Crossharbour & London Arena (DLR)
....3D 88

Crouch Hill (Rail) 7K 31
Crystal Palace (Rail) 6G 123
Custom House for ExCel (Rail & DLR) 7K 71
Cutty Sark for Maritime Greenwich (DLR) ...6E 88
Cyprus (DLR) 7E 72

D

Dagenham Dock (Rail) 2F 75
Dagenham East (Tube) 5J 57
Dagenham Heathway (Tube) 6F 57
Dalston Kingsland (Rail) 5E 50
Denmark Hill (Rail) 2D 104
Deptford (Rail) 7C 88
Deptford Bridge (DLR) 1C 106
Devons Road (DLR) 4D 70
Dollis Hill (Tube) 5C 46
Drayton Green (Rail) 6K 61
Drayton Park (Rail) 4A 50
Dundonald Road (CT) 7H 119

E

Ealing Broadway (Rail & Tube) 7D 62
Ealing Common (Tube) 1F 81
Earl's Court (Tube) 4K 83
Earlsfield (Rail) 1A 120
East Acton (Tube) 6B 64
Eastcote (Tube) 7A 24
East Croydon (Rail & CT) 2D 152
East Dulwich (Rail) 4E 104
East Finchley (Tube) 4C 30
East Ham (Rail) 7C 54
East India (DLR) 7F 71
East Putney (Tube) 5G 101
Eden Park (Rail) 5C 142
Edgware (Tube) 6C 12
Edgware Road (Tube) 5C 66 (6C 158)
Edmonton Green (Rail) 2B 18
Elephant & Castle (Rail & Tube) 4C 86
Elmers End (Rail & CT) 4K 141
Elmstead Woods (Rail) 6C 126
Eltham (Rail) 5D 108
Elverson Road (DLR) 2D 106
Embankment (Tube) 1J 85 (4F 167)
Enfield Chase (Rail) 3H 7
Enfield Town (Rail) 3K 7
Erith (Rail) 5K 93
Essex Road (Rail) 7C 50
Euston (Rail & Tube) 3H 67 (2C 160)
Euston Square (Tube) 4G 67 (3B 160)
Ewell West (Rail) 7A 148

F

Fairlop (Tube) 1H 37
Falconwood (Rail) 4H 109
Farringdon (Rail & Tube) 5B 68 (5A 162)
Feltham (Rail) 1K 113
Fenchurch Street (Rail) 7F 69 (2J 169)
Fieldway (CT) 7D 154
Finchley Central (Tube) 1J 29
Finchley Road (Tube) 6A 48
Finchley Road & Frognal (Rail) 5A 48
Finsbury Park (Rail & Tube) 2A 50
Forest Gate (Rail) 5J 53

Rail, Croydon Tramlink, Docklands Light Railway & London Underground Stations

Forest Hill (Rail) 2J 123
Fulham Broadway (Tube) 7J 83
Fulwell (Rail) 4H 115

G

Gallions Reach (DLR) 7F 73
Gants Hill (Tube) 6E 36
George Street (CT) 2C 152
Gipsy Hill (Rail) 5E 122
Gloucester Road (Tube) 4A 84
Golders Green (Tube) 1J 47
Goldhawk Road (Tube) 2E 82
Goodge Street (Tube) 5H 67 (5C 160)
Goodmayes (Rail) 1A 56
Gordon Hill (Rail) 1G 7
Gospel Oak (Rail) 4E 48
Grange Park (Rail) 5G 7
Gravel Hill (CT) 6A 154
Great Portland Street (Tube) 4F 67
Greenford (Rail & Tube) 1H 61
Green Park (Tube) 1G 85 (4K 165)
Greenwich (Rail & DLR) 7D 88
Grove Park (Rail) 3K 125
Gunnersbury (Rail & Tube) 5H 81

H

Hackbridge (Rail) 2F 151
Hackney Central (Rail) 6H 51
Hackney Downs (Rail) 5H 51
Hackney Wick (Rail) 6C 52
Hadley Wood (Rail) 1F 5
Hammersmith (Tube) 4E 82
Hampstead Heath (Rail) 4C 48
Hampstead (Tube) 4A 48
Hampton (Rail) 1E 132
Hampton Court (Rail) 4J 133
Hampton Wick (Rail) 1C 134
Hanger Lane (Tube) 3E 62
Hanwell (Rail) 7J 61
Harlesden (Rail & Tube) 2K 63
Harringay (Rail) 6A 32
Harringay Green Lanes (Rail) 6B 32
Harrington Road (CT) 3J 141
Harrow & Wealdstone (Rail & Tube) 4J 25
Harrow-on-the-Hill (Rail & Tube) 6J 25
Hatton Cross (Tube) 4H 95
Haydons Road (Rail) 5A 120
Hayes (Rail) 1J 155
Hayes & Harlington (Rail) 3H 77
Headstone Lane (Rail) 1F 25
Heathrow Central (Rail) 3C 94
Heathrow Terminals 1, 2 & 3 (Tube) 3D 94
Heathrow Terminal 4 (Rail & Tube) 5E 94
Hendon (Rail) 6C 28
Hendon Central (Tube) 5D 28
Herne Hill (Rail) 6B 104
Heron Quays (DLR) 1C 88
Highams Park (Rail) 6A 20
High Barnet (Tube) 4D 4
Highbury & Islington (Rail & Tube) 6B 50
Highgate (Tube) 6F 31
High Street Kensington (Tube) 2K 83
Hillingdon (Tube) 5D 40
Hither Green (Rail) 6K 67 (6G 161)
Holborn (Tube) 6K 67 (6G 161)
Holland Park (Tube) 1H 83
Holloway Road (Tube) 5K 49
Homerton (Rail) 6K 51
Honor Oak Park (Rail) 6K 105
Hornsey (Rail) 4K 31
Hounslow (Rail) 5F 97
Hounslow Central (Tube) 3F 97
Hounslow East (Tube) 2G 97
Hounslow West (Tube) 2C 96
Hyde Park Corner (Tube) 2E 84 (6H 165)

I

Ickenham (Tube) 4E 40
Ilford (Rail) 3E 54
Island Gardens (DLR) 4E 88
Isleworth (Rail) 2K 97

K

Kennington (Tube) 5B 86
Kensal Green (Rail & Tube) 3E 64
Kensal Rise (Rail) 2F 65
Kensington Olympia (Rail & Tube) 3G 83
Kent House (Rail) 1A 142
Kentish Town (Rail & Tube) 5G 49
Kentish Town West (Rail) 6F 49
Kenton (Rail & Tube) 6B 26
Kew Bridge (Rail) 5F 81
Kew Gardens (Rail & Tube) 1G 99
Kidbrooke (Rail) 3K 107
Kilburn (Tube) 6H 47
Kilburn High Road (Rail) 1K 65
Kilburn Park (Tube) 2J 65
Kingsbury (Tube) 5G 27
King's Cross (Rail) 2J 67 (1F 161)
King's Cross St Pancras (Tube) 3J 67 (1E 160)
King's Cross Thameslink (Rail) 3J 67 (1F 161)
Kingston (Rail) 1E 134
Knightsbridge (Tube) 2D 84 (7F 165)

L

Ladbroke Grove (Tube) 6G 65
Ladywell (Rail) 5D 106
Lambeth North (Tube) 3A 86 (1J 173)
Lancaster Gate (Tube) 7B 66 (2A 164)
Latimer Road (Tube) 7F 65
Lebanon Road (CT) 2E 152
Lee (Rail) 6J 107
Leicester Square (Tube) 7J 67 (2D 166)
Lewisham (Rail & DLR) 3E 106
Leyton (Tube) 3E 52
Leyton Midland Road (Rail) 1E 52
Leytonstone (Tube) 1G 53
Leytonstone High Road (Rail) 2G 53
Limehouse (DLR) 6A 70
Limehouse (Rail) 6A 70
Liverpool Street (Rail & Tube) 5E 68 (6G 163)
Lloyd Park (CT) 4F 153
London Bridge (Rail & Tube) 1D 86 (5F 169)
London Fields (Rail) 7H 51
Loughborough Junction (Rail) 3B 104
Lower Sydenham (Rail) 5B 124

M

Maida Vale (Tube) 3K 65
Maiden Manor (Rail) 7A 136
Manor Park (Rail) 4B 54
Mansion House (Tube) 7C 68 (2D 168)
Marble Arch (Tube) 6D 66 (1F 165)
Maryland (Rail) 6G 53
Marylebone (Rail & Tube) 4D 66 (4E 158)
Maze Hill (Rail) 6G 89
Merton Park (CT) 1J 137
Mile End (Tube) 4B 70
Mill Hill Broadway (Rail) 6F 13
Mill Hill East (Tube) 7B 14
Mitcham (CT) 4C 138
Mitcham Junction (Rail & CT) 5E 138
Monument (Tube) 7D 68 (2F 169)
Moorgate (Rail & Tube) 5D 68 (6E 162)
Morden (Tube) 3K 137
Morden Road (CT) 2K 137
Morden South (Rail) 5J 137

Mornington Crescent (Tube) 2G 67
Mortlake (Rail) 3J 99
Motspur Park (Rail) 5D 136
Mottingham (Rail) 1D 126
Mudchute (DLR) 4D 88

N

Neasden (Tube) 5A 46
New Barnet (Rail) 5G 5
New Beckenham (Rail) 7B 124
Newbury Park (Tube) 6H 37
New Cross (Rail & Tube) 7B 88
New Cross Gate (Rail & Tube) 1A 106
New Eltham (Rail) 1F 127
New Malden (Rail) 3A 136
New Southgate (Rail) 5A 16
Norbiton (Rail) 1G 135
Norbury (Rail) 1K 139
North Acton (Tube) 5K 63
North Dulwich (Rail) 5D 104
North Ealing (Tube) 6F 63
Northfields (Tube) 3C 80
North Greenwich (Tube) 2G 89
North Harrow (Tube) 5F 25
Northolt (Tube) 6E 42
Northolt Park (Rail) 4F 43
North Sheen (Rail) 4G 99
Northumberland Park (Rail) 7C 18
North Wembley (Rail & Tube) 3D 44
Northwick Park (Tube) 7B 26
Northwood Hills (Tube) 2J 23
North Woolwich (Rail) 2E 90
Norwood Junction (Rail) 4G 141
Notting Hill Gate (Tube) 1J 83
Nunhead (Rail) 2J 105

O

Oakleigh Park (Rail) 7G 5
Oakwood (Tube) 5B 6
Old Street (Rail & Tube) 4D 68 (2F 163)
Osterley (Tube) 7H 79
Oval (Tube) 6A 86
Oxford Circus (Tube) 6G 67 (1A 166)

P

Paddington (Rail & Tube) 6B 66 (1A 164)
Palmers Green (Rail) 4E 16
Park Royal (Tube) 4G 63
Parsons Green (Tube) 1J 101
Peckham Rye (Rail) 2G 105
Penge East (Rail) 6J 123
Penge West (Rail) 6H 123
Perivale (Tube) 2A 62
Petts Wood (Rail) 5G 145
Phipps Bridge (CT) 3B 138
Piccadilly Circus (Tube) 7H 67 (3C 166)
Pimlico (Tube) 5H 85 (5C 172)
Pinner (Tube) 4C 24
Plumstead (Rail) 4H 91
Ponders End (Rail) 5F 9
Poplar (DLR) 7D 70
Preston Road (Tube) 1E 44
Prince Regent (Rail) 7A 72
Pudding Mill Lane (DLR) 1D 70
Putney (Rail) 4G 101
Putney Bridge (Tube) 3H 101

Q

Queensbury (Tube) 3F 27
Queen's Park (Rail & Tube) 2H 65
Queen's Road (Peckham), (Rail) 1J 105

Rail, Croydon Tramlink, Docklands Light Railway & London Underground Stations

Queenstown Road (Battersea) (Rail) 1F 103
Queensway (Tube) 7K 65

Ravensbourne (Rail) 7F 125
Ravenscourt Park (Tube) 4D 82
Rayners Lane (Tube) 7D 24
Raynes Park (Rail) 2E 136
Rectory Road (Rail) 3F 51
Redbridge (Tube) 6B 36
Reeves Corner (CT) 2B 152
Regent's Park (Tube) 4F 67 (4J 159)
Richmond (Rail & Tube) 4E 98
Roding Valley (Tube) 4G 21
Rotherhithe (Tube) 2J 87
Royal Albert (DLR) 7C 72
Royal Oak (Tube) 5K 65
Royal Victoria (DLR) 7J 71
Ruislip (Tube) 1G 41
Ruislip Gardens (Tube) 4J 41
Ruislip Manor (Tube) 1J 41
Russell Square (Tube) 4J 67 (4E 160)

St Helier (Rail) 6J 137
St James's Park (Tube) 2H 85 (1C 172)
St James Street Walthamstow (Rail) 5A 34
St Johns (Rail) 2C 106
St John's Wood (Tube) 2B 66
St Margarets (Rail) 6B 98
St Pancras (Rail) 3J 67 (1E 160)
St Paul's (Tube) 6C 68 (7C 162)
Sanderstead (Rail) 7D 152
Sandilands (CT) 2F 153
Selhurst (Rail) 5E 140
Seven Kings (Rail) 1J 55
Seven Sisters (Rail & Tube) 5E 32
Shadwell (Tube & DLR) 7H 69
Shepherd's Bush (Tube)
  Central Line 2F 83
  Hammersmith & City Line 1E 82
Shepperton (Rail) 5E 130
Shoreditch (Tube) 4F 69 (4K 163)
Shortlands (Rail) 2G 143
Sidcup (Rail) 2A 128
Silver Street (Rail) 4A 18
Silvertown (Rail) 1B 90
Sloane Square (Tube) 4E 84 (4G 171)
Snaresbrook (Tube) 5J 35
South Acton (Rail) 3J 81
Southall (Rail) 2D 78
South Bermondsey (Rail) 5J 87
Southbury (Rail) 4C 8
South Croydon (Rail) 5D 152
South Ealing (Tube) 3D 80
Southfields (Tube) 1H 119
Southgate (Tube) 1C 16
South Greenford (Rail) 3J 61
South Hampstead (Rail) 7A 48
South Harrow (Tube) 3G 43
South Kensington (Tube) 4B 84 (3B 170)
South Kenton (Rail) 1C 44
South Merton (Rail) 3H 137
South Quay (DLR) 2D 88
South Ruislip (Rail & Tube) 5A 42

South Tottenham (Rail) 5F 33
Southwark (Tube) 1B 86 (5A 168)
South Wimbledon (Tube) 7K 119
South Woodford (Tube) 2K 35
Stamford Brook (Tube) 4B 82
Stanmore (Tube) 4J 11
Stepney Green (Tube) 4K 69
Stockwell (Tube) 2J 103
Stoke Newington (Rail) 2F 51
Stonebridge Park (Rail & Tube) 7H 45
Stoneleigh (Rail) 5C 148
Stratford (Low Level) (Rail, Tube & DLR)
  ....7F 53
Stratford (Rail) 6F 53
Strawberry Hill (Rail) 3K 115
Streatham (Rail) 5H 121
Streatham Common (Rail) 7H 121
Streatham Hill (Rail) 2J 121
Sudbury & Harrow Road (Rail) 5B 44
Sudbury Hill (Tube) 4J 43
Sudbury Hill Harrow (Rail) 4J 43
Sudbury Town (Tube) 6B 44
Sunbury (Rail) 1J 131
Sundridge Park (Rail) 7K 125
Surbiton (Rail) 6E 134
Surrey Quays (Tube) 4K 87
Sutton (Rail) 6A 150
Sutton Common (Rail) 2K 149
Swiss Cottage (Tube) 7B 48
Sydenham (Rail) 4J 123
Sydenham Hill (Rail) 3F 123
Syon Lane (Rail) 7A 80

Teddington (Rail) 6A 116
Temple (Tube) 7K 67 (2J 167)
Thames Ditton (Rail) 7K 133
Therapia Lane (CT) 7J 139
Thornton Heath (Rail) 4C 140
Tolworth (Rail) 2H 147
Tooting (Rail) 6D 120
Tooting Bec (Tube) 3E 120
Tooting Broadway (Tube) 5C 120
Tottenham Court Road (Tube) 6H 67 (7D 160)
Tottenham Hale (Rail & Tube) 3H 33
Totteridge & Whetstone (Tube) 2F 15
Tower Gateway (DLR) 7F 69 (2J 169)
Tower Hill (Tube) 7F 69 (2J 169)
Tulse Hill (Rail) 2B 122
Turnham Green (Tube) 4A 82
Turnpike Lane (Tube) 3B 32
Twickenham (Rail) 7A 98

Upney (Tube) 7K 55
Upper Halliford (Rail) 2G 131
Upper Holloway (Rail) 2H 49
Upton Park (Tube) 1A 72

Vauxhall (Rail & Tube) 6J 85 (6F 173)
Victoria (Rail & Tube) 3F 85 (3K 171)
Victoria Coach (Bus) 4F 85 (4K 171)

Waddon (Rail) 4A 152
Waddon Marsh (CT) 2A 152
Wallington (Rail) 6F 151
Walthamstow Central (Rail & Tube)
  ....5C 34
Walthamstow Queens Road (Rail) 5C 34
Wandle Park (CT) 2A 152
Wandsworth Common (Rail) 1D 120
Wandsworth Road (Rail) 2G 103
Wandsworth Town (Rail) 4K 101
Wanstead (Tube) 6K 35
Wanstead Park (Rail) 4K 53
Wapping (Tube) 1J 87
Warren Street (Tube) 4G 67 (3A 160)
Warwick Avenue (Tube) 4A 66
Waterloo (Rail & Tube) 2A 86 (6J 167)
Waterloo East (Rail) 1A 86 (5K 167)
Waterloo International (Rail) 2K 85
Wellesley Road (CT) 2D 152
Welling (Rail) 2A 110
Wembley Central (Rail & Tube) 5E 44
Wembley Park (Tube) 3G 45
Wembley Stadium (Rail) 5F 45
West Acton (Tube) 6G 63
Westbourne Park (Tube) 5H 65
West Brompton (Rail & Tube) 6J 83
Westcombe Park (Rail) 5J 89
West Croydon (Rail & CT) 1C 152
West Drayton (Rail) 1A 76
West Dulwich (Rail) 2D 122
West Ealing (Rail) 7B 62
Westferry (DLR) 7B 70
West Finchley (Tube) 6E 14
West Ham (Rail & Tube) 3G 71
West Hampstead (Rail) 6J 47
West Hampstead (Tube) 6K 47
West Hampstead Thameslink (Rail) 6J 47
West Harrow (Tube) 6G 25
West India Quay (DLR) 7C 70
West Kensington (Tube) 5H 83
Westminster (Tube) 2J 85 (7E 166)
West Norwood (Rail) 4B 122
West Ruislip (Rail & Tube) 2E 40
West Sutton (Rail) 4J 149
West Wickham (Rail) 7E 142
Whitechapel (Tube) 5H 69
White City (Tube) 7E 64
White Hart Lane (Rail) 7A 18
Whitton (Rail) 7G 97
Willesden Green (Tube) 6E 46
Willesden Junction (Rail & Tube) 3B 64
Wimbledon (Rail, CT & Tube) 6H 119
Wimbledon Chase (Rail) 2G 137
Wimbledon Park (Tube) 3J 119
Winchmore Hill (Rail) 7G 7
Woodford (Tube) 6E 20
Woodgrange Park (Rail) 5B 54
Wood Green (Tube) 2A 32
Woodside (CT) 6H 141
Woodside Park (Tube) 4E 14
Wood Street Walthamstow (Rail) 4F 35
Woolwich Arsenal (Rail) 4F 91
Woolwich Dockyard (Rail) 4D 90
Worcester Park (Rail) 1C 148

The representation on the maps of a road, track or footpath is no evidence of the existence of a right of way.

The Grid on this map is the National Grid taken from Ordnance Survey mapping with the permission of the Controller of Her Majesty's Stationery Office.

Copyright of Geographers' A-Z Map Co. Ltd.

No reproduction by any method whatsoever of any part of this publication is permitted without the prior consent of the copyright owners.